*Frommer's*

# Greece

## 4th Edition

by John S. Bowman & Sherry Marker

*with cruise coverage by Heidi Sarna*

Here's what the critics say about Frommer's:

"Amazingly easy to use. Very portable, very complete."
—*Booklist*

"Detailed, accurate, and easy-to-read information for all price ranges."
—*Glamour Magazine*

"Hotel information is close to encyclopedic."
—*Des Moines Sunday Register*

"Frommer's Guides have a way of giving you a real feel for a place."
—*Knight Ridder Newspapers*

WILEY

Wiley Publishing, Inc.

Published by:

**Wiley Publishing, Inc.**

111 River St.

Hoboken, NJ 07030

Editor: Amy Lyons

Production Editor: Donna Wright

Cartographers: Roberta Stockwell and Nicholas Trotter

Photo Editor: Richard Fox

Production by Wiley Indianapolis Composition Services

Front cover photo: Roussanou Monastery, The Meteora.

Back cover photo: The Parthenon, Athens.

For information on our other products and services or to obtain technical support, please contact our Customer Care Department within the U.S. at 800-762-2974, outside the U.S. at 317-572-3993 or fax 317-572-4002.

Wiley also publishes its books in a variety of electronic formats. Some content that appears in print may not be available in electronic formats.

Manufactured in the United States of America

ISBN 0-7645-2456-9

ISSN 1089-6007

5 4 3

# Contents

# List of Maps

## An Invitation to the Reader

In researching this book, we discovered many wonderful places—hotels, restaurants, shops, and more. We're sure you'll find others. Please tell us about them, so we can share the information with your fellow travelers in upcoming editions. If you were disappointed with a recommendation, we'd love to know that, too. Please write to:

*Frommer's Greece*, 4th Edition
Wiley Publishing, Inc. • 111 River St. • Hoboken, NJ 07030

## An Additional Note

Please be advised that travel information is subject to change at any time—and this is especially true of prices. We therefore suggest that you write or call ahead for confirmation when making your travel plans. The authors, editors, and publisher cannot be held responsible for the experiences of readers while traveling. Your safety is important to us, however, so we encourage you to stay alert and be aware of your surroundings. Keep a close eye on cameras, purses, and wallets, all favorite targets of thieves and pickpockets.

## About the Authors

**John S. Bowman** has been a freelance writer and editor for more than 35 years. He specializes in nonfiction ranging from archaeology to zoology, baseball to biography. He first visited Greece in 1956 and has traveled and lived there over the years. He is the author of numerous guides to various regions of Greece. He currently resides in Northampton, Massachusetts.

**Sherry Marker** majored in classical Greek at Harvard, studied archaeology at the American School of Classical Studies in Athens, and did graduate work in ancient history at the University of California at Berkeley. The author of a number of guides to Greece, she has also written for the *New York Times*, *Travel & Leisure*, and *Hampshire Life*. When not in Greece she lives in Massachusetts.

**Heidi Sarna** has cruised on more than 75 ships of all shapes and sizes, and she loves them all (well, OK, some more than others). Heidi's a contributing editor to *Travel Holiday* magazine, and her work has appeared in numerous magazines, major guidebooks, websites, and newspapers including the *New York Times*, *Star Ledger*, and *Boston Herald*. When she's not off cruising somewhere, she lives in the Big Apple with her husband, Arun, and their baby boys.

---

## Other Great Guides for Your Trip:

*Frommer's Greek Islands*

*Frommer's Europe*

*Frommer's Europe from $70 a Day*

*Frommer's European Cruises & Ports of Call*

*Frommer's Gay & Lesbian Europe*

## Frommer's Star Ratings, Icons & Abbreviations

Every hotel, restaurant, and attraction listing in this guide has been ranked for quality, value, service, amenities, and special features using a **star-rating system**. In country, state, and regional guides, we also rate towns and regions to help you narrow down your choices and budget your time accordingly. Hotels and restaurants are rated on a scale of zero (recommended) to three stars (exceptional). Attractions, shopping, nightlife, towns, and regions are rated according to the following scale: zero stars (recommended), one star (highly recommended), two stars (very highly recommended), and three stars (must-see).

In addition to the star-rating system, we also use **eight feature icons** that point you to the great deals, in-the-know advice, and unique experiences that separate travelers from tourists. Throughout the book, look for:

| | |
|---|---|
| *Finds* | Special finds—those places only insiders know about |
| *Fun Fact* | Fun facts—details that make travelers more informed and their trips more fun |
| *Kids* | Best bets for kids and advice for the whole family |
| *Moments* | Special moments—those experiences that memories are made of |
| *Overrated* | Places or experiences not worth your time or money |
| *Tips* | Insider tips—great ways to save time and money |
| *Value* | Great values—where to get the best deals |
| *Warning* | Warning—traveler's advisories are usually in effect |

The following **abbreviations** are used for credit cards:

| | | | | | |
|---|---|---|---|---|---|
| AE | American Express | DISC | Discover | V | Visa |
| DC | Diners Club | MC | MasterCard | | |

## Frommers.com

Now that you have the guidebook to a great trip, visit our website at **www.frommers.com** for travel information on more than 3,000 destinations. With features updated regularly, we give you instant access to the most current trip-planning information available. At Frommers.com, you'll also find the best prices on airfares, accommodations, and car rentals—and you can even book travel online through our travel booking partners. At Frommers.com, you'll also find the following:

- Online updates to our most popular guidebooks
- Vacation sweepstakes and contest giveaways
- Newsletter highlighting the hottest travel trends
- Online travel message boards with featured travel discussions

# What's New in Greece

**PLANNING YOUR TRIP** Perhaps the major development for all travelers since the last edition is the heightened **concern for security.** Greece has proven to be about as safe as any other place—and indeed it is probably far safer than many places. During the Olympics year of 2004, Greece will be even more security conscious than ever. The price one pays for this, of course, involves a few concessions: arriving at airports well in advance of flight departures, protecting unexposed film from the more powerful x-ray machines that process checked baggage.

Speaking of the **Olympics 2004,** if you are only now thinking of making plans to attend events, it is probably getting a bit late to obtain tickets—at least for the more popular events. Those with a special interest in some of the less popular events might find tickets, but even these are now most likely part of "package deals" sold by travel agencies. (See chapter 3 for Olympics information) Hotels in and around Athens, in fact, are also pretty much booked up by these same travel agencies. In any case, prices for hotels are to be raised extremely high—in all fairness, as happens in all Olympic cities. (Hotel prices in this guide were accurate at press time but hikes of 50% to 300% for hotels in and around Athens are said to be planned for the period surrounding the games, while increases of 20% or more for hotels throughout Greece are rumored as hoteliers anticipate increased traffic

from the August Olympics.) We would advise people not intent on seeing the 2004 Olympics to avoid Athens while the games are in session, August 13 though 29, and instead travel elsewhere in Greece, visiting Athens before or after. You might figure, too, that many of the thousands of people who will converge on Athens from all over the world will be traveling in the days immediately before and after the games.

Since the last edition, Greece has converted to the **euro €.** As the €/US$ exchange rate has fluctuated considerably, we give prices only in euros; we advise everyone to check the rate when on the scene.

Another change in Greece is in their **phone numbers:** all now have a 2 before the area/city code and a 0 at the end of the same. The net effect is that every number dialed in Greece now must have 10 digits.

Greek hotels are only beginning to offer **smoke-free** hotel rooms and to provide access to the **handicapped.** We try to single out such, but Greece has a long way to go before it gets gold stars for either. Also, since November 2002, smoking has been banned in many public areas and restaurants are supposed to offer smoke-free areas, but the law is loosely enforced. If it matters, ask before sitting down in a restaurant.

Another major development is the use of **online sites** for making travel plans and reservations. All very well, but read the small print about cancellation policies: they can be pretty unforgiving! A site such as **http://frommers.travelocity.com** offers discounts as well as reservations.

Still another new development is the desire by travelers to maintain **access to the Internet**—at last for e-mail. Increasing numbers of hotels are claiming internet access, but most travelers are probably better off leaving their laptops at home and going into one of the many **Internet cafes** now found throughout Greece: just make sure you are signed on with some service that allows you to get into your e-mail from a third party.

Oh yes, that other accoutrement of the modern traveler—**cellphones.** Again, make sure your phone has the hardware and service that will work in Greece; otherwise it might be best to rent a phone in Greece. See chapter 2.

**Visitor Information** Since 2001, the Greek National Tourist Organization (GNTO, or EOT in its Greek-language acronym) has drastically cut back its operations. In North America, for instance, only the offices in New York City and Toronto remain open. The office in Athens remains open (2 Amerikis, ☎ 210/331-0562) but all other offices in Greece have been turned over to regional tourism "directorates." In most instances, these retain the same offices and phone numbers as the former GNTO; it remains to be seen whether these offices have the budgets for the services formerly provide by the GNTO.

**Travel Within Greece** In recent years there have been numerous attempts to start airlines that could compete with Olympic with domestic flight. Most have fallen by the way, but one seems to be surviving—**Aegean Airlines,** often referred to simply as Aegean Air. It offers a limited number of flights between major destinations and offers some choice when you are on the scene. Its main office in Athens is at 572 Leoforos Vouliagmenis (☎ **210/998-8300).**

Several of the major Greek national tourist sites have taken to selling "combination tickets" that may represent some small discount over those bought separately. Such combinations include the Acropolis, agora, National Archaeological Museum, theaters, etc. of ancient Athens; Knossos and the Iraklion Archaeological Museum; Delphi site and museum. Visitors are advised to inquire about the possibilities.

## SETTLING INTO ATHENS

**Where to Stay** By the time that you visit Athens, The Grande Bretagne Hotel, Syntagma Square (☎ **210/ 333-0000)** and the Hilton Hotel, 46 Leoforos Vas. Sofias (☎ **210/728- 1000)** will both have reopened after complete renovations and redecoration. At press time, precise details on changes were not available, but the Grande Bretagne, formerly with no pool, now boasts two pools—while the Hilton has improved its outdoor pool.

**Where to Dine** If you haven't been to Athens for a few years, you'll be pleased to discover that Aigli (☎ **210/ 336-9363),** the long-time favorite just off Syntagma Square in the National Gardens, is back beside the Zappion Building, serving gourmet meals and snacks. Aigli offers some compensation for the closing of another long-time Athenian favorite just off Syntagma Square: Zonar's, for decades the city's best known café. See chapter 5.

**EXPLORING ATHENS** Exploring Athens is easier than ever thanks to the new Metro system—and pleasanter than ever thanks to the pedestrianized walks linking the major archaeological sites. If you stop in at the main Metro station in Syntagma Square, you can get a map of the system. The Greek National Tourist Office (EOT) at 2

Amerikis promises to have maps of the "Archaeological Park," which stretches from Hadrian's Gate past the Acropolis and Ancient Agora to the Kerameikos. As you explore Athens, on foot and by Metro, be sure to take in the two new museums in the Acropolis and Syntagma Metro stations, with displays of antiquities found during the Metro excavations. See chapter 6.

## THE SARONIC GULF ISLANDS

At press time, both Minoan Flying Dolphins and Ceres Flying Dolphins had been absorbed by Hellas Flying Dolphins, which serves the Saronic Gulf Islands. There may be—there almost certainly will be—changes in nomenclature and service by the time you arrive, so do double-check all island boat information before you travel. And, it is a good idea to keep in mind that the recent proliferation of high speed flying dolphin service to these islands has made it increasingly imperative to have both transportation and hotel reservations in summer. A couple of websites are www.saronicnet.com and www.magicaljourneys.com. See chapter 7.

## THE PELOPONNESE

By the time that you visit Greece, the new Rio-Antirio bridge, scheduled to be completed by the end of 2004, may be open. The bridge will replace the ferry service across the Gulf of Corinth and cut as much as an hour off traveler's journeys between Central Greece and the Peloponnese. You can follow progress on the bridge at www.gefyra.gr.

**Where to Stay** Patras, the largest port in the Peloponnese, has a new hotel, the first "boutique" hotel in that city. The 14-unit Primarolia Art Hotel, 33 Othonos and Amalias (© **2610/624-900**) has already made it into *Odyssey* magazine's list of the best hotels in Greece for its elegant rooms and the art on display throughout the hotel. See chapter 8.

There's another very welcome new hotel in the Peloponnese: For years, Andritsena, the delightful village near the Temple of Bassae, has been years served by only one desultory hotel. Now the 5-unit Epikourias Apollon, the Plateia (© **26260/22-840**), under efficient and caring family management, makes it a pleasure to spend the night in this perfect mountain village. See chapter 8.

**What to See & Do** Theater buffs will want to take in the new Epidaurus Festival Museum, near the entrance to the site, usually open on performance days. There are displays of costumes, masks, theatrical memorabilia, and entrance is free. See chapter 8.

**CRETE Where to Stay** Greek hotels are constantly renovating and updating but one of the more impressive makeovers within the last couple of years is that of the **Lato Hotel** in Iraklion, 15 Epimenidou (© **2810/228-103**). The lobby and dining room have not changed that much, but the decor and furniture of bedrooms are now strikingly stylish, bathrooms are state of the art, and several suites are quite grand. See chapter 9.

**THE CYCLADES What to See & Do** The Museum of Prehistoric Thera, Fira (© **22860/22-217**) opened in 2000 and has several frescoes from the Minoan site of Akrotiri, as well as elegantly decorated pottery found there. See chapter 10.

The world-class restaurant Selene, Fira (© **22860/22-249**) now offers cooking classes where you can learn about local delicacies, learn to make local dishes, and then get to eat the results! See chapter 10.

It's long been possible to explore Santorini's huge caldera, the bay left when the island's volcano exploded around 1450 B.C. on small boats. Now it is possible to explore what's under the surface, on a "Touristic Submarine." See chapter 10.

**THE DODECANESE Where to Stay** Patmos is one of the better secrets of those in the know about Greek islands—a place that offers both a restful retreat and stylish diversions. One of the nicer places that has recently upgraded itself is the **Petra Hotel and Apartments** at Grikos on the southern coast (© **22470/31-035**). In particular, it now offers meals that make this family-operated hotel more memorable than ever. See chapter 11.

**CENTRAL GREECE What to See & Do** Kalambaka, the stopping-off point for visiting the Monasteries of the Meteora, has a new museum: the Center of Contemporary Art, 38 Patriarchou Dimitriou (© **24320/22-346**), which houses the extensive private collection of Leonidas Belsios. The contrast with the art work of the monasteries could hardly be greater, and travelers may enjoy the museum for just that reason. See chapter 12.

In Ambelakia, the enchanting mountain-top village facing Mount Olympus, the Schwarz House (no phone), an 18th century mansion, has been undergoing restoration, making its elegant woodwork and frescoes even more handsome. See chapter 12.

**THE SPORADES Shopping** On Skopelos, not a new shop but a new find for us is **Ploumisti** (midway along the Paralia, © **24240/22-059**, kalaphskp@skt.forthnet.gr); it sells beautiful Greek rugs, blankets, jewelry, pottery and crafts, and its friendly proprietors, Voula and Kostas Kalafatis, are full of helpful information for visitors, especially about the rembetiko music scene. See chapter 13.

**THE IONIAN ISLANDS Where to Stay** At the very crossroads of Corfu Town, the totally renovated—virtually rebuilt—**Arcadion Hotel**

is now reopened at 44 Kapodistriou (© **26610/30-104**). It should appeal to all who prefer to stay at the heart of an historic city and also appreciate up-to-date facilities (including computer dataports in each bedroom). See chapter 15.

**What to See & Do** Perhaps not high on everyone's list of things to do while in Greece, a day excursion to Albania might appeal to someone who's "been there, done that." The **Petrakis Line**, 9 Venizelou, Corfutown, © **26610/31-649**, offers several 1-day excursions a week in high season. See chapter 15.

**HIGHLIGHTS OF NORTHERN GREECE Where to Stay** There are two new boutique hotels in Thessaloniki: the 44-unit Andromeda, 5 Kommninion (© **2310/373-700**) just off Aristotle Square, is every bit as luxurious and welcoming as one would expect of the owners of the Andromeda in Athens. The 16-unit Capsis Bristol, 2 Oplopiou & Katouni (© **2310/506-500**) in the Ladadika district, is decorated with antiques and paintings. See chapter 16.

**What to See & Do** Displays at the new **Jewish Museum of Thessaloniki**, 13 Ayios Mina (© **2310/250-406**) tell the story of what was for centuries one of the city's most influential groups. Of the 60,000 Jews living here when World War II began, only 1,800 survived deportation and the death camps. See chapter 16.

First Athens had one and now Thessaloniki does: the city's **Concert Hall** (Megaron Mousikis, 25 Martiou & Paralia (© **2310/895-800**) opened in 2001 and has a full program of concerts. See chapter 16.

**THE NORTHEASTERN AEGEAN ISLANDS Where to Stay** Completely renovated since 2000, the Chios Chandris Hotel (© **22710/44-401**) at the far end of the waterfront of Chios Town, offers many of the amenities of a resort hotel—including a pool—with the convenience of walking-distance to the town's attractions. See chapter 17.

**Where to Dine**   Meanwhile, a new recommendation at Molivos, on the northeastern coast of Lesvos (Mitilini), is the **Octopus** (© **2330/71-332**); actually one of the oldest restaurants along the harbor, it offers a no-nonsense ambience with an authentic island menu. See chapter 17.

# 1

# The Best of Greece

Greece is, of course, the land of ancient sites and architectural treasures—the Acropolis in Athens, the amphitheater of Epidaurus, and the reconstructed palace at Knossos being among the best known. But Greece is much more: it offers age-old spectacular natural sights, for instance—from Santorini's caldera to the gray pinnacles of rock of the Meteora—and modern diversions ranging from elegant museums vying for your attention. It can be bewildering to plan your trip with so many options vying for your attention. Take us along and we'll do the work for you. We've traveled the country extensively and chosen the very best that Greece has to offer. We've explored the archaeological sites, visited the museums, inspected the hotels, reviewed the tavernas and ouzeries, and scoped out the beaches. Here's what we consider to be the best of the best.

- **Making Haste Slowly:** Give yourself time to sit in a seaside taverna and watch the fishing boats come and go. If you're visiting Greece in the spring, take the time to smell the flowers: the fields are covered with poppies and daisies. Even in Athens, you'll see hardy species growing through the cracks in concrete sidewalks—or better yet, visit Athens's ancient agora, which will be carpeted in a dazzling variety of wildflowers. See chapter 6.

- **Island-Hopping in the Cyclades:** Though the Cyclades are bound by unmistakable family resemblance, each island has its own unique personality. Distances between islands are small, making travel by ferry pleasant and logistically straightforward (at least in principle). If you are traveling off season, when you do not need to have hotel reservations, your vacation will be much less stressful if you don't plan too much in advance and allow yourself to "go with the flow"—a tactful way of suggesting that you be prepared

for the unexpected in island boat schedules! See chapter 10.

- **Leaving the Beaten Path:** Persist against your body's and mind's signals that "this may be pushing too far," leave the main routes and major attractions behind, and make your own discoveries of landscape, villages, or activities. For instance, seek out some obscure church or monastery such as Moni Ayios Nikolaos outside Metsovo—to be rewarded by a moving encounter with the church and its caretaker.

- **Exploring the Naturalists' Greece:** There is a Greece beyond the columns and cafes—a land of rugged terrain and wildflowers and birds and other natural forms and phenomena. Sign up to join a special tour (see chapter 2) or go it alone with one of the several beautifully illustrated handbooks available, such as Oleg Polunin's *Flowers of Greece and the Balkans* (Oxford Univ. Press) or *Birds of Europe* (McGraw-Hill), by Bertel Bruun and Arthur Singer. And don't forget your binoculars!

- **Sunrise, Sunset:** Get up a little earlier than usual and see the sun rise (preferably out of the Aegean, illuminating the islands) and then watch it sink over the mountains (anywhere in Greece, but try not to miss the sunsets that make the Ionian Sea change from the deepest blue to a fiery red.)

## 2 The Best of Ancient Greece

- **The Acropolis** (Athens): No matter how many photographs you've seen, nothing can prepare you for watching the light turn the marble of the buildings, still standing after thousands of years, from honey to rose to deep red to stark white. If the crowds get you down, remember how crowded the Acropolis was during religious festivals in antiquity. See p. 176.

- **Nemea** (Peloponnese): This gem of a site has it all: a beautifully restored stadium, a handsome museum, and picnic tables with a view of the romantic Doric temple with its three long-standing columns—and several newly restored and re-erected ones. If you're lucky, you may see Nemea's archaeologists at work lovingly reconstructing and re-erecting more columns from the temple's north facade in their ambitious restoration project. See p. 261.

- **Olympia** (Peloponnese) **and Delphi** (Central Greece): Try to visit both Olympia, where the Olympic Games began, and Delphi, home of the Delphic Oracle. That's the only way you'll be able to decide whether you think Olympia, with its massive temples and shady groves of trees, or Delphi, perched on mountain slopes overlooking olive trees and the sea, is the most beautiful ancient site in Greece. See chapters 8 and 12.

- **Palace of Knossos** (Crete): A seemingly unending maze of rooms and levels and stairways and corridors and frescoed walls—the Minoan Palace of Knossos. It can be packed at peak hours, but it still exerts its power if you enter into the spirit of the labyrinth, where King Minos ruled over the richest and most powerful of Minoan cities and, according to legend, his daughter Ariadne helped Theseus kill the Minotaur and escape. See p. 300.

- **Delos** (Cyclades): This tiny isle just 3.2km (2 miles) offshore of Mykonos, was considered by the ancient Greeks to be both the geographical and spiritual center of the Cyclades; many considered this the holiest sanctuary in all Greece. The extensive remains here testify to the island's former splendor. From Mount Kinthos (really just a hill, but the island's highest point), you can see many of the Cyclades most days and the whole archipelago on a very clear day. The 3 hours allotted by excursion boats from Mykonos or Tinos are hardly sufficient to explore this vast archaeological treasure. See chapter 10.

- **Vergina** (Northern Greece): In the brilliantly designed museum here, you can peek into what may have been the tomb of Alexander the Great's father, Philip of Macedon; nearby there are more than 300 burial mounds that stretch for miles across the Macedonian plain. See chapter 16.

- **Messene** (Peloponnese): This sprawling 4th century B.C. site has the best-preserved ancient fortification walls in Greece, an enormous Sanctuary of Asklepios and a stadium—and views of almost all Messene and Laconia from the summit of Mount Ithomi. See p. 282.

# Greece

Adriatic Sea

ALBANIA

FORMER YUGOSLAV REPUBLIC OF MACEDONIA

Tirana

Ionian Sea

Corfu

Igoumenitsou

Paxos

Preveza

EPIRUS

Ioannina

Lake Pamvotis

Metsovo

Kalpaki

ZAGORI

Kastoria

Edessa

Pella

Gianitsa

Kilkis

Serres

Thessaloniki

MACEDONIA

Vergina

Dion

Mt. Olympus

Trikkala

Meteora (Kalambaka)

Karditsa

Elassona

Larisa

THESSALY

Kozani

Stratoni

Lefkada

Kefalonia

Ithaka

Astakos

Vonitsa

Arta

Agrinio

Karpenissi

Messolongi

CENTRAL GREECE

Lamia

Volos

Pelion Peninsula

Skiathos

Skopelos

IONIAN ISLANDS

Zakinthos

Kyllini

Pirgos

Olympia

Andritsena

Megalopolis

Tripoli

PELOPONNESE

Mycenae

Argos

Corinth

Livadia

Loutra Edipsou

Delphi

Mt. Parnassus

Megara

Thebes

SARONIC GULF ISLANDS

Piraeus

Athens

Nafplion

Epidaurus

Patras

Mistra

Sparta

Kalamata

Githio

Areopolis

Pilos

Monemvassia

Kythira

Mediterranean Sea

Sea of Crete

Mediterranean Sea

CRETE

To Crete (approx. 60 miles from mainland)

Chania

Rethymnon

Ayia Galini

Iraklion

Ayios Nikolaos

Ierapetra

Mediterranean Sea

Aegean Sea

Greece

Athens

CRETE

N

0    25 km
0    25 mi

Black Sea

Sea of Marmara

EUROPE

GREECE

TURKEY

TURKEY

Izmir

NORTHEASTERN
AEGEAN ISLANDS

BULGARIA

THRACE

Komotini
Xanthi
Alexandroupolis

Drama
Kavala

Samothraki

Thasos

Limnos

Mt. Athos

Skyros

Alonissos

SPORADES

Aegean Sea

Lesvos
(Mitilini)

Hios

Ikaria

Samos

Patmos

Kalimnos

Kos

Simi

Rhodes

DODECANESE

Karpathos

Amorgos

Donoussa

Anafi

Naxos

Mykonos

Tinos

Andros

Delos

Paros

Antiparos

Ios

Santorini

Folegandros

CYCLADES

Siros

Karystos

Kea

Sifnos

Serifos

Milos

Sounion

Kimi

EVVIA

Mountain

## 3 The Best of Byzantine & Medieval Greece

- **Mistra** (Peloponnese): This Byzantine ghost town has streets lined with the remains of homes both humble and palatial, as well as some of the most beautiful churches in all Greece. If you have the energy, climb to the top of the defense walls for the superb view over the plain of Sparta. Try to visit in the spring, when Mistra is carpeted with wildflowers. See chapter 8.

- **The Churches of Thessaloniki** (Northern Greece): Thessaloniki's Byzantine churches are the finest not just in Greece, but in the entire world. From the tiny Osios David to the towering Ayios Dimitrios, these churches boast mosaics and frescoes that give you an astonishing glimpse of the artistic grandeur of the mighty Byzantine empire. See chapter 16.

- **Nea Moni** (Hios, Northeastern Aegean): Once home to 1,000 monks, this 12th-century monastery high in the interior mountains of Hios is now quietly inhabited by one elderly but sprightly nun and two friendly monks—try to catch one of the excellent tours sometimes offered by the monks. The mosaics in the cathedral dome are works of extraordinary power and beauty; even in the half-obscurity of the nave they radiate a brilliant gold. Check out the small museum, and take some time to explore the extensive monastery grounds. See chapter 17.

- **Monemvassia** (Peloponnese): Long-called "The Gibralter of Greece," this rocky promontory crowned by a medieval citadel and church has only one real street (just wide enough for two donkeys to pass each other), no cars, cobbled lanes, beautifully restored stone houses (some of which are now hotels), and views that stretch forever over the sea. See chapter 8.

- **A Profusion of Byzantine Churches in the Cyclades:** The fertile countryside of the island of Naxos is dotted with well-preserved Byzantine chapels, Parikia, the capital of Paros, has the Byzantine era cathedral of Panaya Ekatondapiliani, and Santorini boasts the 11th/12th century church of the Panagia in the hamlet of Gonias Episkopi. See chapter 10.

## 4 The Best Beaches

- **Nafplion** (Peloponnese): After a vigorous and tiring day of sightseeing, this small municipal beach can seem like the best in Greece. Handy changing rooms and showers make this a great place for a quick break between exploring the ruins at Mycenae and heading off to take in a play at Epidaurus. See chapter 8.

- **Plaka** (Naxos, Cyclades): Naxos has the longest stretches of sea sand in the Cyclades, and Plaka is the most beautiful and pristine beach on the island. A 4.8km (3-mile) stretch of mostly undeveloped shoreline, you could easily imagine yourself here as Robinson Crusoe in his island isolation (bending the plot somewhat to include a few sunbathing Fridays). If you need abundant amenities and a more active social scene, you can always head north to Ayia Anna or Ayios Prokopios. See chapter 10.

- **Paradise** (Mykonos, Cyclades): Paradise is the quintessential party beach, known for wild revelry that continues through the night. An extensive complex built on the beach includes a bar, taverna, changing rooms, and souvenir shops. This is a place to see and be seen, a place to show off muscles laboriously acquired during the long winter months. See chapter 10.

- **Grammata** (Siros, Cyclades): The small beach is enclosed by a lush oasis of palm trees at the outlet of a natural spring, sheltered and hidden by a rocky promontory extending into the bay. The beach is only accessible on foot or by boat, so it's rarely crowded. See chapter 10.

- **Lalaria Beach** (Skiathos, Sporades): This gleaming white pebble beach boasts vivid aquamarine water and white limestone cliffs, with natural arches cut into them by the elements. Lalaria is not nearly as popular nor accessible as Skiathos's famous Koukounaries,

which is one of the reasons why it's still gorgeous and pristine. See chapter 13.

- **Megalo Seitani** (Samos, Northeastern Aegean): Megalo Seitani and its neighbor, Micro Seitani, are situated on the mountainous and remote northwest coast of Samos. There aren't any roads to this part of the island, so the only way to reach the beaches is a short boat ride or a rather long (and beautiful) hike. You won't regret taking the trouble, since both beaches are superb: Micro Seitani's crescent of pebbles in a rocky cove, and Megalo Seitani's expanse of pristine sand. See chapter 17.

- **Vroulidia** (Hios, Northeastern Aegean): White sand, a cliff-rimmed cove, and a remote location at the southern tip of the island of Hios combine to make this one of the most exquisite small beaches in the Northeastern Aegean. The rocky coast conceals many cove beaches similar to this one, and it's rare for them to become crowded. See chapter 17.

- **Finikounda** (Peloponnese): This long stretch of sand is one of the best beaches in the Peloponnese. The little fishing village is now a resort town, with lots of places to stay and to eat. See chapter 8.

- **Monemvassia and Nafplion** (Peloponnese): Everyone says it, and for once, everyone is right: Nafplion is the loveliest town in the Peloponnese, and Monemvassia is the region's most spectacular village. Thanks to the speedy hydrofoils (Flying Dolphins), you

can visit both spots and decide for yourself which has the best cafes, castles, and sunsets. See chapter 8.

- **Chania** (Crete): Radiating from its handsome harbor and backdropped by the White Mountains, Chania has managed to hold on to much of its Venetian-Renaissance and later

Turkish heritage. This allows you to wander the old town's narrow lanes, filled with a heady mix of colorful local culture, yet still enjoy its charming hotels, excellent restaurants, interesting shops, and swinging nightspots. See chapter 9.

- **Hora** (Folegandros, Cyclades): In this town huddled at the edge of a cliff, one square spills into the next, its green and blue paving slates outlined in brilliant white. On a steep hill overlooking the town is the looming form of Panayia, the church that holds an icon of the Virgin which is paraded through the streets of Hora with great ceremony and revelry each Easter Sunday. Mercifully free of vehicular traffic, Hora is one of the most beautiful and least spoiled villages in the Cyclades. See chapter 10.

- **Yialos** (Simi, Dodecanese): The entirety of Yialos, the main port of the tiny, rugged island of Simi, has been declared a protected architectural treasure, and for good reason. This pristine port with its extraordinary array of neoclassical mansions is a large part of why Simi is known as "the jewel of the Dodecanese." See chapter 11.

- **Skopelos Town** (Skopelos, Sporades): The amazingly well preserved Skopelos, a traditional whitewashed island port town, is adorned everywhere with pots of flowering plants. It offers some fairly sophisticated diversions, several excellent restaurants, some good hotels, and lots of shopping. See chapter 13.

- **Metsovo** (Western Greece): Steep slopes, ever-green conifers, stone houses with slate and slanted roofs, stolid villagers in traditional clothing speaking a Latin-based language—if this is Thursday, you must be in Switzerland. But no, it's Metsovo, in Epirus. Occasionally jammed with excursionists, this mountain town still comes through as an authentic locale, refreshing in the summer and invigorating in the winter ski season. See chapter 14.

- **Corfu Town** (Corfu, Ionian Islands): With its Esplanade framed by a 19th-century palace and the arcaded Liston, its old town a Venice-like warren of structures practically untouched for several centuries, its massive Venetian fortresses, and all this enclosing a lively population and constant visitors, here is urban Greece at its most appealing. See chapter 15.

- **Piryi and Mesta** (Hios, Northeastern Aegean): These two small towns, in the pastoral southern hills of Hios, are marvelous creations of the medieval imagination. Connected by their physical proximity and a shared history, each is quirkily unique and a delight to explore. In Piryi, every available surface is covered with elaborate geometric black-and-white decorations known as *Ksisti*, a technique that reaches extraordinary levels of virtuosity in the town square. Mesta has preserved its medieval urban fabric, and conceals two fine churches within its maze of narrow streets. See chapter 17.

## 6 The Best Islands

- **Hydra** (Saronic Gulf Islands): Old-timers keep waiting for Hydra, with its handsome stone mansions overlooking a picture-postcard harbor, to be "spoiled." After all, even before Mykonos and Santorini, Hydra was one of the first Greek islands to be "discovered." So far, so good: donkeys still outnumber motorcycles, and the day-trippers who blitz the appealing harborside shops leave at twilight. That means you can almost always find the table you want at one of Hydra's pleasant small restaurants. See chapter 7.

- **Crete:** Whether for its rugged mountains or its countless beaches, its ancient remains or its ultramodern hotels, its layered history or its intense people, Crete cannot be denied. It is not just a distinctive Greek island—it is a world unto itself. See chapter 9.

- **Santorini** (Cyclades): This is undoubtedly one of the most spectacular islands in the world. The streets of Fira and Ia are carved into the face of a high cliff, overlooking the circular caldera left by an ancient volcanic eruption and now filled with the deep blue waters of the Aegean. The site of Akrotiri offers a unique glimpse into life in a Minoan city, frozen in time by the eruption 3,600 years ago. Add to this the Fira nightlife scene, and you'll see why this is one of the most popular (and overcrowded) summer vacation spots in the Aegean. See chapter 10.

- **Siros** (Cyclades): This tiny island has it all: a vivacious, cosmopolitan capital town; thriving beach resorts; and a starkly beautiful region of farming communities, archaeological remains, and remote beaches to

the north. Siros is also one of the centers of *rembetika*, a form of Greek traditional music with roots in Asia Minor; the *Fragosiriani*, a classic known throughout Greece, was composed by the Siriot Markos Vamvakaris, and you're sure to hear its simple and infectious rhythms many times during your stay here. See chapter 10.

- **Rhodes** (Dodecanese): The island of Rhodes has everything a visitor could want—dazzling ancient and medieval ruins, great food, spectacular beaches, and the hottest nightlife outside of Athens—the one drawback being that everyone knows it. See chapter 11.

- **Skyros** (Sporades): Winding roads and remote beaches, one main town and a few minor villages, some ancient legends and 20th-century tales: Skyros's charms remain perhaps the most elusive of the four Northern Sporades. But though the island remains a bit difficult to access and still not overstocked with touristy amenities, Skyros also offers both a living local culture and some natural wildness. See chapter 13.

- **Corfu** (Ionian Islands): Lush vegetation, some still undeveloped interior and unspoiled coast, ancient sites and a 19th-century presence, a dash of Italy and a dose of the cosmopolitan, Corfu is a Greek island like no other. Tourism may be rampant, but Corfu's attractions have survived worse. See chapter 15.

- **Hios** (Northeastern Aegean): You'd think that an island with such gorgeous beaches, exquisite medieval towns, and remarkable scenery wouldn't remain a secret for long. Despite the qualities that attract a small group of devotees year after year, Hios remains surprisingly quiet. If you like the idea of getting away from the tour buses, being alone on a beach to rival any in the Cyclades, and exploring towns that preserve the contours of medieval life, Hios is for you. Another benefit: the local hospitality hasn't worn thin here, as it has on many of the more heavily toured islands. See chapter 17.

• **Sifnos** (Cyclades): Sifnos is a green island of ravines, mountaintops, and pristine beaches. Despite its small size (a hardy walker can explore the entire island on foot), Sifnos has numerous attractive small towns which can be used as bases for your explorations. Apollonia, in the central hills, offers elegant small-town civility, with the added benefit of being the hub of an excellent public transportation system. Kastro, on its seaside rock, is the medieval locus of the island, while Platis Yialos is a quiet beach resort. Don't visit in August, when the island is mobbed with vacationing Athenians. See chapter 10.

## 7 The Best Places to Get Away from It All

• **National Garden** (Athens): It's all too easy to overlook this oasis of calm and cool in the heart of Athens. If you explore, you'll discover shady benches, a small café, and lots of opportunities to enjoy watching Greek families out for a stroll. See chapter 6.

• **Folegandros** (Cyclades): Many visitors have passed the formidable Folegandros cliffs from the Santorini-Paros ferry, and glimpsed whitewashed Kastro walls perched 300m (984 ft.) above the sea. The austere beauty of Hora, the fine beaches, and the great walking trails are no longer a secret, but if you arrive off season, Folegandros still offers a restful retreat. Completely free from the commercialism that has engulfed so many Aegean isles, the only shopping here seems to involve milk, bread, and eggs. There's still no bank; a recent addition is a taxi that travels up and down the island's only paved road. See chapter 10.

• **Mount Lycabettus** (Athens): Walk up Lycabettus at dawn and enjoy the sunrise over the hills that surround Athens. Come back for sunset, and you may encounter others strolling here, but the sounds (and smells!) of Athens's ferocious traffic will be pleasantly distant here. See chapter 6.

## 8 The Best Museums

• **National Archaeological Museum** (Athens): This stunning collection has it all: superb red and black figured vases, bronze statues, Mycenaean gold, marble reliefs of gods and goddesses, and the hauntingly beautiful frescoes from Akrotiri, the Minoan site on the island of Santorini. See p. 184.

• **Museum of Greek Popular Musical Instruments** (Athens): Life-size photos of musicians beside their actual instruments and recordings of traditional

Greek music make this one of the country's most charming museums to visit. On our last visit, an elderly Greek gentleman listened to some music, transcribed it, stepped out into the courtyard, and played it on his own violin! See p. 186.

- **Archaeological Museum of Iraklion** (Crete): Few museums in the world can boast of holding virtually all the important remains of a major culture. This museum's Minoan collection is just that, including superb frescoes from Knossos, elegant bronze and stone figurines, and exquisite gold jewelry. The museum also contains Neolithic, Archaic Greek, and Roman finds from throughout Crete. See p. 299.

- **Archaeological Museum of Chania** (Crete): Let's hear it for a truly engaging provincial museum, not one full of masterworks but rather

of representative works from thousands of years, a collection that lets us see how most people probably experienced their worlds. All this in a former Italian-Renaissance church that makes you feel you're in a special place. See p. 310.

- **Archaeological Museum of Thessaloniki** (Northern Greece): This is the place to go to see the gold star of Vergina, a profusion of delicate gold wreaths, and the gold box that may have held the bones of Philip of Macedon, father of Alexander the Great—all found in the royal tombs at and around Vergina. These Macedonian treasures tend to draw the crowds, so you may find that you have the rest of the collection—including fascinating exhibits on the early history of Thessaloniki—almost to yourself. Just next door is the superb **Museum of Byzantine Culture.** See p. 562.

## 9 The Best of Greece's Religious Treasures

- **Panayia Evanyelistria** (Tinos, Cyclades): The most revered religious shrine in Greece. See chapter 10.

- **Patmos** (Dodecanese): For 2 millennia, this small island of more than 300 churches has been hallowed ground, a place of pilgrimage. The Monastery of St. John the Divine and the Cave of the Apocalypse, where St. John is said to have dictated the Book of Revelation, are among the most revered and wondrous Byzantine treasures in the world. See chapter 11.

- **The Monasteries of the Meteora** (Central Greece): Even from a distance, the monasteries perched atop the weird rock formations and mini-mountains of the Meteora are one of the most awesome sights in Greece. Inside, the monasteries are equally impressive,

with fine collections of manuscripts, frescoed chapels, shy monks, and chatty nuns. See chapter 12.

- **The Aslan Pasha Mosque and Cami at Ioannina** (Western Greece): Little of Greece's Turkish-Muslim phase has survived beyond the odd minaret, but here on the promontory of the walled quarter of Ioannina are the still-solid fine old mosque (now a museum), minaret, and school. Picturesque from afar, they speak up close of Ioannina's—and Greece's—diverse past. See chapter 14.

- **Mount Athos** (Northern Greece): Only men can visit the Holy Mountain, where monks still live in isolation in some of the most isolated—and beautiful—monasteries in all Greece. If you can't go to Athos itself, take heart; the boats from Ouranopolis that cruise around the penin-sula offer excellent views of the

rugged, pine-clad promontory and some of the monasteries. See chapter 16.

## 10 The Best Resorts & Hotels

- **Andromeda Hotel** (Athens; © 210/643-7302): The city's only real "boutique" hotel, located on a wonderfully quiet side street, the classy Andromeda offers charm, comfort, and a reassur-ingly helpful staff. See p. 157.

- **Malvasia** (Monemvassia, Pelo-ponnese; © 27320/62-223): Each room in the Malvasia is dif-ferent, with some of the nicest overlooking the sea; all are taste-fully furnished with hand-loomed rugs and antiques. A visit here gives the illusion of staying in the home of wealthy Greek friends of enormous taste—who just happen to be away, but have left the staff behind to tend to your needs. See p. 274.

- **Atlantis Hotel** (Iraklion, Crete; © 2810/229-103): There are many more luxurious hotels in Greece, but few can beat the Atlantis's urban attractions: a cen-tral location, modern facilities, and views over a busy harbor. You can swim in the pool, work out in the fitness center, send e-mail via your laptop, and then within minutes be enjoying a fine meal or visiting a museum. See p. 302.

- **Doma** (Chania, Crete; © 28210/51-772): A former neoclassical mansion east of downtown, the Doma has been converted into a comfortable and charming hotel, furnished with the proprietor's family heirlooms. Although not for those seeking the most luxuri-ous amenities, its atmosphere appeals to many. See p. 313.

- **Astra Apartments** (Santorini, Cyclades; © 22860/23-641): This small hotel with handsomely appointed apartments looks like a miniature whitewashed village—and has spectacular views over Santorini's famous caldera. The sunsets here are not to be believed, the staff is incredibly helpful, and the village of Imerovigli itself offers an escape from the touristic madness that overwhelms the island each summer. If you decide to get married here, you have but to speak to the manager, George Karayiannis (before you arrive, unless you want to tie the knot on a return visit). See p. 346.

- **Anemomilos Apartments** (Fole-gandros, Cyclades; © 22860/41-309) and **Castro Hotel** (Fole-gandros, Cyclades; © 22860/41-230): The small island of Fole-gandros has two of the nicest hotels in the Cyclades. Both have terrific cliff-top locations. Anemomilos has all the creature comforts, tradi-tional decor, and is just out of town, with a delicious pool and sea views that stretch forever. Castro built into the walls of the 12th-century Venetian castle that encircles the village, has lots of character, and the necessary mod-ern comforts. See p. 355.

- **Rodos Palace** (Rhodes, Dode-canese; © 22410/25-222): The largest five-star hotel in Greece and possibly in the entire Mediterranean, this is truly a famed palace, decorated, in fact, by the famed designer of *Ben Hur* and *Quo Vadis*. Located in Ixsia, just outside Rhodes city, it offers all the amenities imaginable—the latest addition is a new family cen-ter, a resort within a resort designed to provide the ultimate holiday for families with children. See p. 428.

- **Hotel Nireus** (Simi, Dodecanese; © **22410/72-400**): Perfect island, perfect location, unpretentious, and tasteful. The views from the sea-facing rooms, framed by the fluid swirls of the wrought-iron balcony, define the spell of this little gem of an island. You'll never regret one more night on Simi, and here's the place to spend it. See p. 442.

- **Petra Hotel and Apartments** (Grikos, Patmos; © **22470/ 31-035**): This charming small hotel on the south coast of Patmos has upgraded itself in recent years and now offers a delightful combination of comfortable accommodations, a restful environment, family-owned hospitality, fine meals, and sophisticated ambience—and internet connections! See p. 462.

- **White Rocks Hotel & Bungalows** (Kefalonia, Ionian Islands; © **26710/28-332**): For those who appreciate understated elegance, a shady retreat from all that sunshine, a private beach, and quiet but attentive service, this hotel, located a couple of miles outside Argostoli, can be paradise. See p. 543.

- **Mediterranean Palace Hotel** (Thessaloniki; © **2310/521-321**). This hotel has it all: location (overlooking the harbor, in the trendy Ladadika district) and luxury. The lobby is, as one might expect, seriously glitzy—but the really pleasant surprise here is how comfortable and elegant the guestrooms are. The service here is usually excellent and the two restaurants are good enough to tempt you to stay in at least one night rather than exploring the hot spots of Ladadika. See p. 576.

See p. 428.

## 11 The Best Restaurants

- **Daphne's** (Athens; © **210/ 322-7971**): There are Pompeian-style frescoes on the walls, one of the nicest gardens in Athens, and consistently delicious food that makes you wonder why other Greek restaurants can't make supposedly simple dishes like eggplant salad or yogurt with quince taste this distinctive—and delicious. Not only that, but there are strolling musicians—and the owners and staff are so delightful that you hate to leave, even when you can't eat another prawn with toasted almonds. See p. 164.

- **Vlassis** (Athens; © **210/646-3060**): This small restaurant with a very loyal following, ranging from prominent ambassadors to struggling artists, serves traditional (*paradisiako*) Greek cooking at its very best. A tempting choice if you have only one night in Athens—but be sure to make a reservation. See p. 172.

- **Varoulko** (Piraeus; © **201/411-2043**): Everything here is seafood, and everything here is so good that many Athenians believe chef/owner Lefteris Lazarou has created not just the finest restaurant serving only seafood, but the finest restaurant in the greater Athens area. See p. 171.

- **Nykterida** (Chania, Crete; ☎ 28210/64-215): We're not denying that the location may influence your taste buds here, but the spectacular views from this restaurant high above Chania and Soudha Bay can definitely make you feel you're eating a meal like few others in Greece. See p. 314.

- **Selene** (Santorini, Cyclades; ☎ 22860/22-249): The best restaurant on an island with lots of good places to eat, Selene is one of the finest restaurants in all Greece. The reason: Owners George and Evelyn Hatzyiannakis are constantly experimenting with local produce to turn out their own innovative versions of traditional dishes. Inside, the dining room is elegant, and the terrace has a wonderful view over the caldera. See p. 349.

- **To Koutouki Tou Liberi** (Siros, Cyclades; ☎ 22810/85-580): Open only 2 days a week and devilishly difficult to find (even the local taxi drivers have a hard time), this restaurant is so popular that you may need to book a table

several days in advance. Amazingly, it's worth the trouble—the food is excellent, the view is stunning, and you might even catch an impromptu traditional music session if you're willing to stay around until the early hours of the morning. See p. 414.

- **Petrino** (Kos, Dodecanese; ☎ 22420/27-251): When royalty come to Kos, this is where they dine. Housed in an exquisitely restored, two-story, century-old stone (*petrino*) private residence, this is hands-down the most elegant taverna in Kos, with cuisine to match. This is what Greek home cooking would be if your mother were part divine. See p. 451.

- **Venetian Well** (Corfu, Ionian Islands; ☎ 26610/44-761): A bit severe in its setting at the edge of a small enclosed square in Corfu town, with no attempt at the picturesque, this restaurant gets by on its more esoteric, international, and delicate menu. It's for those seeking a break from the standard Greek scene. See p. 535.

## 12 The Best Nightlife

- **Theater Under the Stars** (Athens and Epidaurus, Peloponnese): If you can, take in a performance of whatever is on at the Herodes Atticus Theater in Athens, the theater at Epidaurus, or the theater at Dodona. You'll be sitting where people have sat for thousands of years to enjoy a play under Greece's magical night sky. See chapters 6 and 8.

- **Mykonos** (Cyclades): Mykonos isn't the only island town in Greece with nightlife that continues through the morning, but it was the first and still offers the

most abundant, varied scene in the Aegean. Year-round, the town's narrow, labyrinthine streets play host to a remarkably diverse crowd—Mykonos's unlimited ability to reinvent itself has assured it of continuous popularity. The spring and fall tend to be more sober and sophisticated, while the 3 months of summer are reserved for unrestrained revelry. See chapter 10.

- **Rhodes** (Dodecanese): From cafes to casinos, Rhodes has not only the reputation, but also the stuff to back it up. A good nightlife scene is ultimately a matter of who shows up—and this, too, is where Rhodes stands out. It's the place to be seen, and, if nobody seems to be looking, you can always watch. See chapter 11.

- **Skiathos** (Sporades): With as many as 50,000 foreigners packing this tiny island during the high season, the many nightspots in Skiathos town are often jammed with the mostly younger set. If you don't like the music at

one club, just move across the street. See chapter 13.

- **Corfu** (Ionian Islands): If often-raucous nightspots are what you look for on a holiday, Corfu offers probably the largest concentration in all Greece. Most of these are at beach resorts frequented by young foreigners. Corfu town, however, also offers more sedate locales. Put simply, Corfu hosts a variety of music and dancing and "socializing" opportunities. See chapter 15.

## 13 The Best Natural Wonders

- **The Caves of Dirou** (Peloponnese): No one knows just how far these caves run into the seaside cliffs of Dirou in the Peloponnese's Mani peninsula. You can get some idea of how vast they are by taking a tour on one of the boats that explore this underground labyrinth. See chapter 8.

- **Samaria Gorge** (Crete): At 18km (11 miles) long, the Samaria is the longest gorge in Europe. But although its walls reach up to 500m (1,640 ft.) and at one point are only 2m (6½ ft.) apart, it's not the physical dimensions that attract thousands each year. For that, you can credit the wildflowers, the cold stream, and the whole experience of making your way from the heart of Crete to its coast. See chapter 9.

- **The Santorini Caldera** (Cyclades): As you approach Santorini by ferry, the whitewashed clifftop villages of Ia and Fira resemble at first a new dusting of mountain snow. Then the ferry enters the caldera, the cliff walls rise steeply on either side, and you're suddenly enclosed in a fantastic bowl whose sides are formed of red, yellow, and ochre rock, and whose surface is the shimmering blue Aegean. Some 3,600 years ago, the center of the island was blown away in a colossal volcanic eruption, leaving behind a roughly circular depression in the sea floor and the crescent-shaped sliver of rock known as Santorini. The best places to view the caldera are the walking path between Fira and Ia, or the clifftop streets in either of these two towns. See chapter 10.

## 14 The Best Shopping

- **Traditional Arts and Crafts:** So many places in Greece pride themselves on their needlework that it is hard to single out even a few, but among those few would be Crete, Rhodes, and Skyros.

Two places in Athens deserve mention: The Center of Hellenic Tradition (59 Mitropoleos and 36 Pandrossou) and the National Welfare Organization (6 Ipatias and Apollonos). The Center of

Hellenic Tradition has ceramics, woodcarvings, prints—and one of the finest views of the Acropolis in Athens. The National Welfare Organization has hand-loomed rugs and silk embroidery done by village women, and excellent copper and ceramics.

- **Leatherwork:** Both Rhodes and Crete feature local leatherwork, from sandals to handbags, from belts to jackets. Pay attention to quality and prices.

- **Furs:** Kastoria, in northwestern Greece, is the center of the fur trade and fur products are everywhere. Athens, of course, has expensive fur coats. Rhodes also features fur coats. As we would say wherever furs are sold, be sure you know what you are buying.

- **Jewelry:** It now seems that half of Greece's retail stores are selling jewelry, so shop around. Much of it is really no different from what can be found in cities allover the world, but Athens does have some major internationally known jewelers, such as Lalaounis and Zolotas. Chania, Crete, has some sophisticated local artisans' work. Islands such as Santorini, Skiathos, and Rhodes have scores of stores appealing to the tourist trade.

- **Ceramics:** As with needlework, pots and ceramics of all kinds are to be found throughout Greece. Some of the more traditional may be found on Chios, Crete, Mitilini, Sifnos, and Skopelos.

- **Rugs/Weavings:** Crete probably offers the largest variety of rugs and weavings. Metsovo has some distinctive textiles. If you like rag rugs, keep an eye out for *kourouloudes* on sale at small shops as you travel the Peloponnese.

- **Wood:** Corfu seems to be the center of olive wood products—carvings boards, bowls, utensils,

Rethymnon, Crete, also has a selection. In the Peloponnese, woodcarvings and utensils are often found in the villages of Arcadia. Chios and Mitilini also boast wood-carving traditions.

- **Icons and Ecclesiastical Books and Items:** The streets around the Greek Orthodox Cathedral (Metropolitan) in Athens have many shops where votive offerings, candles, and reproductions of icons are sold. In Thessaloniki, the Apostolic Diakonta Bookstore (© 2310/275-126) has a wide selection of religious items. Most of the most important religious shrines, such as the Panagia Evangelistria on Tinos, and many convents and monasteries, including most of the Monasteries of the Meteora, sell reproductions of icons and other religious items. On Crete, the Petrakis couple in Elounda paint traditional icons that are sought internationally.

- **Museum Reproductions:** officially approved and fine replicas of many famous museum pieces—may be purchased at the Archaeological Museum, Byzantine, Benaki, Goulandris, and Lalaounis museums in Athens; at the Archaeological and Byzantine museums in Thessaloniki; and at official archaeological service stores in Rhodes Old Town, and at Rethymnon, Crete.

- **Books:** Whether looking for books about Greece or for **holiday reading**, in Athens the places to go are **Eleftheroudakis** (© 210/331-4480), Compendium (© 210/322-1248), **Reymondos** (© 210/364-8189), **Folia tou Bibliou** (© 210/323-1703), **Patakis** (© 210/381-1850) and **Panatelides** (© 210/362-9763). In Thessaloniki, the superb **Molhos** (© 2310/275-271) is the place to go.

- **Natural Products:** In the last few years, Greece has begun to produce superb organic and natural products, including olive oil, honey, jams, and cosmetics. Keep an eye out for food products with the Peloponnese, Gaea, Milelia, Nefeli, Yiam, and Stater labels in groceries and delis. Good places to look in Athens include most specialty food shops in Kolonaki and the Mesogaia delicatessen in the Plaka section of Athens. The Green Farm store (*C* **210/361-4001**) in Kolonaki sells only organic produce. Korres Natural Products (**www.korres.com**), including a wide range of herbal shampoos and lotions, and Apivita's Aromatherapy Essential Oils (**www.apivita.gr**) are now carried in many Greek pharmacies and cosmetics stores (such as the widespread Hondos Centers) throughout Greece.

# 2

# Planning Your Trip to Greece

*by John S. Bowman*

**B**efore any trip, most of us like to do a bit of advance planning. When should I go? What is this trip going to cost me? Will there be a special holiday when I visit? What special bits of practical advice might I appreciate? We'll answer these and other questions for you in this chapter.

## 1 The Regions in Brief

Greece is a land of sea and mountains. Over a fifth of the Greek land mass is comprised of islands, numbering several thousand if you count every floating crag—and nowhere in Greece will you find yourself more than 96km (60 miles) from the sea. It should come as no surprise that the sea molds the Greek imagination, as well as its history.

Mainland Greece, meanwhile, is a great vertebrate, with the Pindos range reaching from north to south, and continuing, like a tail, through the Peloponnese. The highest of its peaks is Mount Olympus, the seat of the gods, nearly 3,000m (10,000 ft.) above sea level. Eighty percent of the Greek mainland is mountainous, which you will rapidly discover whether you make your way on foot or on wheels.

**ATHENS**  Whether you're arriving by sea or air, chances are you'll be debarking in Athens. The city is not always pleasant and is sometimes exhausting, yet it's simply invaluable. Its **archaeological sites** and its **museums** alone warrant a couple of days of exploration. Between visits to the sites, a stroll in the **National Garden** will prove reviving. Then, after dark as the city cools, the old streets of the **Plaka**

district at the foot of the Acropolis, offer chances to stroll, shop, and have dinner with an Acropolis view. The central square, pedestrianized side streets and residential streets of **Kolonaki** are where fashionable Athenians head to see and be seen—and for some serious shopping. **Piraeus,** as in antiquity, serves as the port of Athens and the jumping-off point to most of the islands.

Athens is also a great base for day trips and overnight excursions, whether to the temple of Poseidon at **Cape Sounion,** the forested slopes of **Mount Hymettus (Imittos),** the monastery of **Kaisariani (Kessariani),** the sanctuary of Artemis at **Brauron (Vravrona),** the Byzantine monastery of **Daphni,** the legendary plains of **Marathon,** or the ruins of **Eleusis,** place of ancient mysteries.

**THE SARONIC GULF ISLANDS** Cupped between Attica and the Peloponnese, in the sheltering Saronic Gulf, these islands offer both proximity and retreat for the nearly four million Athenians who, like their visitors, long for calming waters and cooler breezes. The accessibility of these islands, on any given day, especially on any given weekend, in high season, can be their downfall. Choose carefully your day and island, or you may be part of the crowd you're trying to avoid.

**Aegina,** so near to Athens as to be a daily commute, is the most besieged and yet possesses its own character and charm. The main port town of Aegina is picturesque and pleasant, while across the island to the east, set atop a pine-crested hill, stands the remarkably preserved temple of Aphaia, a Doric gem. **Poros,** next in line proceeding south, is convenient both to Athens and to the Peloponnese. Its beaches and lively port are a real draw, and there's an ancient temple thrown in, scenically situated on a shady hill, but now mostly picturesque rubble.

Still further to the south lies car-less **Hydra,** remarkable for its natural beauty and the handsome stone mansions of sea captains. The port of Hydra has a lot to offer and knows it, all of which is reflected in the prices. It's a great place for pleasant strolls, views, and a swim off the rocks. **Spetses,** the furthest of these islands from Athens, has glades of pine trees and fine beaches—and a great many hotels catering to package holiday tours from Europe.

**THE PELOPONNESE** Crossing the narrow isthmus—less than 6.5km (4 miles) across at its narrowest point—into the southern peninsula of Greece is a move you will never regret. The Peloponnese retains a sense of remove from the north and from the rest of Greece. Its often barren landscape is virtually forested with stunning archaeological remains, each with a richly evocative past: **Mycenae,** the mountain citadel of Agamemnon; **Olympia,** birthplace of the Olympic Games; **Sparta,** home of Helen and Menelaus; the palace of Nestor at **Pylos;** the magnificent and still-used theater of **Epidaurus;** the temple and stadium at **Nemea;** and the Bema at **Corinth,** where Paul addressed the Corinthians. The small but stately

port of **Nafplion** provides a comfortable, convenient base from which to explore the surrounding sites.

The mountain and seaside roads of the Peloponnese are unrivalled in Greece. Here are some suggestions on several particularly spectacular routes. Try to take in the vertiginous route from Sparta to Kalamata past the Byzantine ghost town of Mistra and on through the twists and turns of Langada pass, one of Greece's most beautiful mountain passes. Follow the excellent road from Tripolis to Olympia that cuts through some of the most beautiful mountain scenery in Arcadia, with some of the region's loveliest traditional villages. And allow yourself a day or two to head to the Mani, the southernmost region of the Peloponnese, where tower villages dot the hillsides and the coastal roads wind high above the sea.

**CRETE** The largest of the Greek islands, birthplace of the painter El Greco, possesses a landscape so diverse, concentrated, and enchanting that no description is likely to do it justice. Especially if you rent a car and do your own exploring, a week will pass like a day. More or less circling the island on the national highway (don't imagine an interstate) will take you to a ring of inviting ports like **Iraklion,** the capital, **Ayios Nikolaos, Ierapetra, Rethymnon,** and **Chania.**

Venturing into the heartland of Crete—not far, since Crete's width ranges from 12km to 56km (7½ miles–35 miles)—you'll find the legendary palaces of the Minoans just as they once were, with a little imagination: **Knossos, Phaestos,** and **Ayia Triadha,** to mention only a few. This is not to say that Crete is without classical sites, Byzantine monasteries, Venetian structures, and Turkish remains. It's Greece, after all. For the energetic, the **Gorge of Samaria** calls out, as does the sea.

When night falls, remember that Crete has been known for thousands of years for its wines, which complement nicely the fresh goat cheese and olives, all local and all part of Crete's spell.

**THE CYCLADES** In antiquity, the "Cyclades"—the "encirclers" or "circling islands"—had at their center the small island of Delos, where mythology tells us that Apollo and his sister Artemis were born. Declared a sanctuary, where both birth and death were prohibited, Delos was an important spiritual, cultural, and commercial hub of the Aegean. Today, its extensive remains remind visitors of its former importance. It's easy to make a day trip here from **Mykonos,** whose white, cube-like houses, and narrow, twisting streets began to attract first a trickle and then a flood of visitors in the 1960s. Today, almost every cruise ship puts into Mykonos for at least a few hours, so that visitors can take in the proliferation of cafes, restaurants, and shops. Those who spend a few days here can stay in boutique hotels, sip martinis in sophisticated bars—or head inland to visit the island's less-visited villages.

**Paros** (sometimes called "the poor man's Mykonos"), is the transport hub of the Cyclades, with a gentle landscape, appealing villages, good beaches and opportunities for windsurfing. From here you can get to **Tinos,** home to perhaps the most revered of all Greek Orthodox churches; **Naxos,** whose fertile valleys and high mountains lure hikers and campers; **Folegandros,** much of whose capital Hora is built within the walls of a medieval *kastro* (castle); and **Santorini,** which some believe to be the lost Atlantis. Santorini has a black lava beach, the impressive remains of the Minoan settlement at Akrotiri, chic restaurants, and the most spectacular sunsets in all Greece.

**CENTRAL GREECE** Central Greece, for our purposes, stretches from the Corinth Canal to Mount Olympus. Its landscape is vastly diverse, from the fertile Boetian plains to the snowy peaks of **Parnassus** and **Olympus.** Also here are the legendary battlegrounds of **Thermopylae** (where the Spartans under Leonidas delayed the Persian invasion in 480 B.C.) and **Chaironeia** (where Philip of Macedon defeated the Greeks in 338 B.C.).

**THE DODECANESE** This string of islands, named "the 12" despite the fact that they number more than that, nearly embrace the Turkish shoreline. Except for Rhodes and Kos, all of the Dodecanese are deforested, bare bones exposed to sun and sea. But what bones! Far to the north lies **Patmos,** already in the 5th century nicknamed "the Jerusalem of the Aegean," a holy island where the Book of Revelation is said to have been penned and where the Monastery of St. John still dominates the island. Far to the south basks **Rhodes,** "the city of the Sun," with more than 300 days of sunshine per year. It's the most touristed of the islands, and for obvious reasons, Rhodes has it all: history and hysteria, ruins and resorts, knights and nightlife. There's even peace and quiet—we'll tell you where to find it.

Between these two lie an array of possibilities: from the uncompromised traditional charm of tiny **Simi** to the ruins and well-known beaches of **Kos.** The truth is that part of the popularity of the southern Dodecanese comes from its proximity to Rhodes—a simple matter of overflow for those who can't fit on or afford the most popular package-tour destination in Greece. Note that "proximity" often doesn't mean quick links when planning a holiday. *One other tip:* With Turkey so near, you may want to consider a side trip, quite easy to arrange.

## Greece on the Web

Anyone with access to the World Wide Web can obtain a fair amount of information about Greece. Remember that these sources cannot necessarily be counted on for the most up-to-date, definitive, or complete information. We advise that you use all such computer searches as *supplements only*, and then check out specific "facts" if you are going to base your travel plans on the information. Sites are constantly being changed and added, but among the most useful for broad-based searches are:

- www.frommers.com
- www.greekembassy.org
- www.greektravel.com
- www.gtp.gr
- www.phantis.com
- www.perseus.tufts.edu

Central Greece's best known site is the sanctuary of **Delphi,** whose imposing ruins and spectacular mountainside location dazzle visitors. Further north, in Thessaly, the monasteries on the lofty otherworldly heights of **Meteora,** give a glimpse into the Byzantine and modern Greek world of the Orthodox church. If you have a less austere retreat in mind, the traditional villages on the lush, gentle slopes of **Pelion,** once roamed by centaurs, are an ideal place to relax under the chestnut trees and read up on all that you've seen—and all that you plan to see—in Greece.

**THE SPORADES** Whether by air, ferry, or hydrofoil, the Sporades, strewn north and east of the island of Evvia (Euboea), are readily accessible from the mainland and offer verdant forest landscapes, golden-sand beaches, and crystalline waters. That's the good news. The bad news is that they are no secret. **Skiathos** is the most in demand with all that that implies. **Skopelos,** whose lovely port is one of the most striking in Greece, is more rugged and remote than Skiathos, with more trails and fewer

nightclubs. Relatively far-off **Skyros** is well worth a visit, offering underwater fishing and diving, sandy beaches, and luminously clear waters.

**WESTERN GREECE** Northwestern Greece, or **Epirus,** is predominantly mountainous and mostly cut off by those mountains from the sea. You won't likely encounter many tourists here. Much of its appeal is to nature lovers and trekkers, for whom the **Vikos Gorge** and mountainous **Zagori** region pose engaging challenges. Epirus is not, however, without its amenities and attractions.

**Ioannina,** on the shores of Lake Pamvotis, is the largest and most appealing city in the region; it is one of the few places in Greece where the long Muslim occupation is still manifestly visible. The traditional mountain village of **Metsovo,** perched several thousand feet up in the Pindos mountains, offers a number of local attractions and vista-providing hiking.

Only 32km (20 miles) from Ioannina lie the ruins of one of the most famous of ancient shrines, the Oracle of Zeus at **Dodona,** where the voice of the great lord of Olympus was

## Security in Greece: Red Alert

Inevitably and understandably, there might be some concern about the threat of terrorists in Greece. Those who have been following the news since 2002 will have read that Greek authorities have finally cracked down on the notorious November 17 band of homegrown terrorists. Admittedly, they were strongly anti-American and anti-British, but they did not attack tourists (with perhaps one exception). In any case, that group seems to have been put out of operation. As for Al-Qaeda or Islamic militants, there has never been any indication that they have a presence in Greece. For one thing, Greece is pro-Palestinian, and militant Muslims have no desire to offend. This is not to say that there might not be some angry and anti-American Middle Easterners in Greece. In fact, many Greeks oppose U.S. foreign policies. But in all locales where tourists are apt to be, they will find at least formal politeness. To conclude: the potential threat from terrorists in Greece is no greater than in any place in the world today.

believed to speak through the rustling leaves of a sacred oak tree, though not the one currently planted there.

**THE IONIAN ISLANDS** Across centuries, these islands have been the apple of more than one empire's eye. Lush, temperate, blessed with ample rain and sun, and tended like an architectural garden, they are quite splendid. **Corfu**, the most noted and ornamented, is a gem, and is sought after accordingly. **Ithaka** is as yet somewhat out of the tourist loop, but needs no introduction for readers of the *Odyssey*. With certain adjustments for the nearly three millennia that have elapsed, Homer's descriptions of the island still hold their own. If you can do without name recognition, **Kefalonia**, still relatively inconspicuous and unspoiled, has a lot to offer: picturesque traditional villages, steep rocks plunging into the sea, fine beaches, and excellent local wine.

**THESSALONIKI & NORTHERN GREECE** Just as it once was the urban understudy of Constantinople, **Thessaloniki** is modern Greece's second city. With less than 20% of Athens's population, however, it is not a close second. Even so, among Greece's major cities, it may be second to none in visual appeal and international flair. Among the city's many attractions are the legendary White Tower and its archaeological and Byzantine museums. As a home base, it offers comfortable proximity to many of Macedonia's major sites.

**Macedonia** is Greece's largest geographical region—rich in natural beauty, soaked in history, and mostly removed from the epicenters of the tourist explosion that, in places, has almost leveled the diverse traditions and cultures of Greece. Besides Thessaloniki, Macedon is also home to three major archaeological sites associated with Alexander and his father—**Pella, Vergina,** and **Dion**—as well as to the independent religious state of **Mount Athos.** This mountaintop theocracy, off-limits to women since the year 1060, may be viewed from cruise ships (departing from Thessaloniki) or visited with special permission—but only by men.

**THE NORTHEASTERN AEGEAN ISLANDS** The four major islands comprising this group form Europe's traditional sea border with the east. Beyond their strategic and thus richly historic location, they offer a taste of Greece that is less compromised by tourism and more deeply influenced by nearby Asia Minor and modern Turkey. **Samos,** unique among the islands in the extent to which it is covered with trees, also produces some excellent local wine. Its important archaeological sites and opportunities for outdoor activities make it a congenial and interesting destination, and it is an ideal point from which to enter and explore the northwestern Turkish coast. **Hios** is unspoiled and welcoming, offering isolated and quite spectacular beaches, as well as the stunning monastery of Nea Moni, and some of Greece's most striking village architecture. The remaining islands of **Lesvos** and **Limnos,** for various reasons not major tourist destinations, each have their ways of inviting and rewarding those who explore them.

## 2 Visitor Information

The **Greek National Tourism Organization** (GNTO, or EOT in Greece—and increasingly referred to as the Hellenic Tourism Organization) has offices throughout the world that can provide you with information concerning all aspects of travel to and in Greece. Look for them at **www.gnto.gr** or contact one of the following GNTO offices:

**UNITED STATES** Olympic Tower, 645 Fifth Ave., 5th Floor, New York, NY 10022 (© **212/421-5777;** fax 212/826-6940).

**AUSTRALIA & NEW ZEALAND** 51 Pitt St., Sydney, NSW 2000 (© 02/ **241-1663;** fax 02/235-2174).

**CANADA** 1300 Bay St., Toronto, ON M5R 3K8 (© **416/968-2220;** fax 416/968-6533); 1170 Place du Frères André, Montreal, H3B 3C6 (© **514/871-1535;** fax 514/871-1498).

**UNITED KINGDOM & IRELAND** 4 Conduit St., London W1S 2DJ (© **0207/734-5997;** fax 0207/287-1369).

For the latest information about security issues, health risks, and such issues in the U.S., you can call, fax, or send a self-addressed, stamped envelope to the **Overseas Citizens Emergency Center,** Department of State, Room 4811, Washington, DC 20520 (© **202/647-5225;** www.travel.state. gov) and ask for Consular Information Sheets. You can also get the latest information by contacting any U.S. embassy, consulate, or passport office.

## 3 Entry Requirements & Customs

### ENTRY REQUIREMENTS

For information on how to get a passport, go to the Fast Facts section of this chapter—the websites listed provide downloadable passport applications as well as the current fees for processing passport applications. For an up-to-date country-by-country listing of passport requirements around the world, go the "Foreign Entry Requirement" web page of the U.S. State Department at **http://travel.state.gov/foreignentry reqs.html.**

For entry into Greece, citizens of Australia, Canada, New Zealand, South Africa, the United States, and almost all other non-EU countries are required to have a **valid passport,** which is stamped upon entry and exit, for stays up to 90 days. All U.S. citizens, even infants, must have a valid passport, but Canadian children under 16 may travel without a passport if accompanied by either parent. Longer stays must be arranged with the **Bureau of Aliens,** Leoforos

Alexandras 173, 11522 Athens (© 210/770-5711).

Citizens of the United Kingdom and other members of the European Union are required to have only a valid passport for entry into Greece, and it is no longer stamped upon entry; they may stay an unlimited period (although they should inquire at a Greek consulate or their embassy in Greece if they intend to stay for an extended period). Children under 16 from EU countries may travel without a passport if accompanied by either parent. But all EU citizens should check to see what requirements are for non-EU countries they may be traveling through to get to Greece!

## CUSTOMS
### WHAT YOU CAN BRING INTO GREECE

Passengers from North America arriving in Athens aboard international flights are generally not searched, and if they have nothing to declare, continue through a green lane. (Because of the continuing threat of terrorism, baggage is X-rayed before boarding domestic flights.) But citizens of the United States, Canada, Australia, New Zealand and other non-EU countries do face a few commonsensical restrictions on what they can bring into Greece. Clearly, no narcotics; Greece is VERY tough on drug users! No explosives or weapons—although sportsmen might upon application be able to bring in a legitimate hunting weapon. Medicines except for amounts properly prescribed for your own use are prohibited, as are plants with soil. Dogs and cats can be brought in, but they must have proof of recent rabies and other health shots. But no parrots are allowed. You are allowed to bring into Greece duty-free personal belongings including clothes, camping gear, and most sports equipment. (Certain watersports equipment, such as windsurfers, can be brought in only if a Greek citizen residing in Greece guarantees they will be re-exported.) Anyone traveling with their own SCUBA tank must have it sealed on entry and it will be unsealed at the recognized SCUBA locales. Visitors from outside the European Union are allowed up to 10 kilos of food and beverage, 200 cigarettes, 50 cigars, 250 grams of tobacco, 50 distilled alcohol or 2 liters of wine, 1 liter of grams of perfume, 500 grams of coffee, and 100 grams of tea.

You may bring two cameras with 10 rolls of film each, a movie or video camera, a portable radio, a phonograph or tape recorder, a typewriter, and a laptop computer. Probably these won't even be inspected, but in some cases it could be written into your passport and you better have it when you leave. In fact, it is unlikely that you will even be stopped at entry but if you were and they learn that you are carrying much over US $1,000, they might write this in your passport and then expect to see receipts if

## Tips   Passport Savvy

Allow plenty of time before your trip to apply for a passport; in the United States at least, processing normally takes 3 weeks but can take longer during busy periods (especially spring). And keep in mind that if you need a passport in a hurry, you'll pay a higher processing fee. When traveling, safeguard your passport in an inconspicuous, inaccessible place like a money belt and keep a copy of the critical pages with your passport number in a separate place. If you lose your passport, visit the nearest consulate of your native country as soon as possible for a replacement.

you intend to leave without it. Entering with your own car or other motor vehicle requires a fair amount of paperwork: check with Greek embassy or consular authorities before setting out.

There are presently no restrictions on the amount of traveler's checks either arriving or departing, though amounts over $1,000 should technically be declared. If you plan to leave the country with more than $1,000 in bank notes (or its equivalent in other currency), technically you must declare at least that sum on entry. No Greek money more than 1,000€ per traveler may be imported or exported.

U.K. citizens and those of other EU nations are relatively free from most of these restrictions, but even they must comply with some, such as those pertaining to drugs, firearms, certain plants, some animals, and SCUBA tanks. There are also restrictions on young people importing alcohol and tobacco. Even large sums of currency or unusual amounts of electronic equipment might warrant some notice. Basically, you are allowed to bring in what is reasonable for personal use but not to engage in a business.

## WHAT YOU TAKE HOME FROM GREECE

Greek antiquities are strictly protected by law, and no genuine antiquities may be taken out of Greece without prior special permission from the **Archaeological Service,** 3 Polignotou, Athens. Also, you should expect to explain how you acquired any genuinely old objects—in particular, icons or religious articles. A dealer or shopkeeper must provide you with an export certificate for any object dating from before 1830.

Remember to keep receipts for at least all major purchases for clearing Customs on your return home.

Returning **U.S. citizens** who have been away for at least 48 hours are allowed to bring back, once every 30 days, $800 worth of merchandise duty-free. You'll be charged a flat rate of 4% duty on the next $1,000 worth of purchases. Be sure to have your receipts handy. On mailed gifts, the duty-free limit is $200. You cannot bring fresh fruits, vegetables, or animal products from Greece into the United States. For specifics on what you can bring back, download the invaluable free pamphlet *Know Before You Go* online at **www.customs.gov.** (Click on KNOW BEFORE YOU GO.) Or contact the **U.S. Customs Service,** 1300 Pennsylvania Ave, NW, Washington, DC 20229 (© **202/927-1770)**, and request the pamphlet.

For a clear summary of **Canadian** rules, write for the booklet *I Declare,* issued by the **Canada Customs and Revenue Agency** (© **800/461-9999** in Canada, or 204/983-3500; www.ccra-adrc.gc.ca). Canada allows its citizens a C$750 exemption, and you're allowed to bring back duty-free one carton of cigarettes, 1 can of tobacco, 40 imperial ounces of liquor, and 50 cigars. In addition, you're allowed to mail gifts to Canada valued at less than C$60 a day, provided they're unsolicited and don't contain alcohol or tobacco (write on the package "Unsolicited gift, under $60 value").

All valuables should be declared on the Y-38 form before departure from Canada, including serial numbers of valuables you already own, such as expensive foreign cameras. *Note:* The C$750 exemption can only be used once a year and only after an absence of 7 days.

**Citizens of the U.K.** who are **returning directly from Greece or another European Union (EU) country** will go through a separate Customs Exit (called the "Blue Exit") especially for EU travelers. In essence, there is no limit on what you can bring back from an EU country, as long as the items are for personal use (this includes gifts), and you have already paid the necessary duty and tax. However, customs law sets out guidance levels. If you bring in more than these levels, you may be asked to prove that the goods are for your own use. Guidance levels on goods bought in the EU for your own use are 800 cigarettes, 200 cigars, 1kg smoking tobacco, 10 liters of spirits, 90 liters of wine (of this not more than 60 liters can be sparkling wine), and 110 liters of beer.

The duty-free allowance in **Australia** is A$400 or, for those under 18, A$200. Citizens can bring in 250 cigarettes or 250 grams of loose tobacco, and 1,125 milliliters of alcohol. If you're returning with valuables you already own, such as foreign-made cameras, you should file form B263. A helpful brochure available from Australian consulates or Customs offices is *Know Before You Go.* For more information, call the **Australian Customs**

Service at © **1300/363-263,** or log on to www.customs.gov.au.

The duty-free allowance for **New Zealand** is NZ$700. Citizens over 17 can bring in 200 cigarettes, 50 cigars, or 250 grams of tobacco (or a mixture of all 3 if their combined weight doesn't exceed 250g); plus 4.5 liters of wine and beer, or 1.125 liters of liquor. New Zealand currency does not carry import or export restrictions. Fill out a certificate of export, listing the valuables you are taking out of the country; that way, you can bring them back without paying duty. Most questions are answered in a free pamphlet available at New Zealand consulates and Customs offices: *New Zealand Customs Guide for Travellers, Notice no. 4.* For more information, contact **New Zealand Customs,** The Customhouse, 17–21 Whitmore St., Box 2218, Wellington (© **04/473-6099** or 0800/ 428-786; www.customs.govt.nz).

## 4 Money

Greece is no longer quite the bargain country it once was, although it is still considerably cheaper than many major nations with advanced economies. Certainly for most visitors, the hotels and restaurants will be cheaper than in major cities such as New York or London. That said, you will be spending money day in and day out, so it is important to understand the ins and outs of how to handle your money.

### CURRENCY

The currency in Greece is the **euro** (pronounced *euro* in Greek), abbreviated "Eu" and symbolized by €.

(Anyone possessing the old Drachma currency can exchange it in branches of the National Bank of Greece.) The exchange rate with the U.S. Dollar, British Pound, and other non-EU currencies varies—often from day to day—but we have chosen here to go with a rate of 1€ per U.S. dollar and €.67 per British Pound.

The euro € comes in 7 paper notes and 8 coins. The notes are in different sizes and colors. They are in the following denominations: 5, 10, 20, 50, 100, 200, and 500. (Considering that each euro is worth about $1, those last bills are quite pricey!) Six of the coins

## Regarding the Euro

Since the euro's inception, the U.S. dollar and the euro have traded almost on par (i.e., $1 approximately equal 1€); therefore, all prices in this book are given in euros. But as this book went to press, 1€ was worth approximately $1.15 and gaining in strength, so your dollars might not go as far as you'd expect. For up-to-the-minute exchange rates between the euro and the dollar, check the currency converter website www.xe.com/ucc.

are officially "cents"—but in Greece they have become referred to as *lepta*, the old Greek name for sums smaller than the Drachma. They come in different sizes and their value is: 1, 2, 5, 10, 20, 50. There are also 1€ and 2€ coins.

Although one side of the coins differs in each of the member EU nations, all coins and bills are legal tender in all countries of the euro area.

It's a good idea to exchange at least some money—just enough to cover airport incidentals and transportation to your hotel—before you leave home, so you can avoid lines at airport ATMs (automated teller machines). You can exchange money at your local American Express or Thomas Cook office or your bank. If you're far away from a bank with currency-exchange services, American Express offers traveler's checks and foreign currency, though with a $15 order fee and additional shipping costs, at www.american express.com or 800/807-6233.

## ATMS

The easiest and best way to get cash away from home is from an ATM. The **Cirrus** (© 800/424-7787; www.mastercard.com) and **PLUS** (© 800/843-7587; www.visa.com) networks span the globe; look at the back of your bank card to see which network you're on, then call or check online for ATM locations at your destination. If your bank, credit, or debit card is affiliated with one of the major international credit cards (such as **MasterCard** or **Visa**), you should not

have any trouble getting money in Greece; if in doubt, ask your bank or credit-card company if your card will be acceptable in Greece.

In commercial centers, airports, all cities and larger towns, and most tourist centers, you will find at least a couple of machines accepting a wide range of cards; smaller towns will often have only one ATM—and it may not accept your card. The **Commercial Bank** (Emboriki Trapeza) services PLUS and Visa, **Credit Bank** (Trapeza Pisteos) accepts Visa and American Express, **National Bank** (Ethiniki Trapeza) takes Cirrus and MasterCard/Access. To check if your destination has ATMs for Visa holders, use the ATM locator function at www.visa.com; for MasterCard, go to www.mastercard.com.

**Transaction fees** are usually built into the exchange rate you get; in any case, exchange rates are usually based on the wholesale rates of the major banks, so you may actually save money by withdrawing larger sums and paying your bills in cash. However, just as at home, there is usually some limit on how much you can withdraw in 1 day. Note, too, that the sums withdrawn are designated on the ATM screen in euros—not other currencies. Also keep in mind that many banks impose a fee every time a card is used at a different bank's ATM, and that fee can be higher for international transactions (up to $5 or more) than for domestic ones (where they're rarely more than $2). On top of this, the bank from which you withdraw cash may charge its own fee. To compare banks' ATM fees within the U.S., use www.bankrate.com. For international withdrawal fees, ask your bank.

## CURRENCY-EXCHANGE OFFICES

Private and commercial foreign-exchange offices are found in major cities, larger towns, and centers of tourism throughout Greece. They are generally competitive, but their rates vary, so shop around if you must use one.

## TRAVELER'S CHECKS

Traveler's checks are something of an anachronism from the days before the ATM made cash accessible at any time. Traveler's checks used to be the only sound alternative to traveling with dangerously large amounts of cash. They were as reliable as currency, but, unlike cash, could be replaced if lost or stolen.

These days, traveler's checks are less necessary because most cities have 24-hour ATMs that allow you to withdraw small amounts of cash as needed. However, keep in mind that you will likely be charged an ATM withdrawal fee if the bank is not your own, so if you're withdrawing money every day, you might be better off with traveler's checks—provided that you don't mind showing identification every time you want to cash one.

It should also be said that although in Greece today most hotels and shops still accept traveler's checks, many no longer do and in any case they usually charge a small commission or give a poor exchange rate. Do not expect any Greek operations to cash your traveler's checks, however, unless you are paying for their services or goods.

You can get traveler's checks at almost any bank. **American Express** offers denominations of $20, $50, $100, $500, and (for cardholders only) $1,000. You'll pay a service charge ranging from 1% to 4%. If your bank charges more, you can call the check issuers about more competitive rates. Some organizations sell traveler's checks at reduced rates; the Automobile Association of America, for example, sells American Express checks in several currencies without commission. You can also get American Express traveler's checks over the phone by calling ☎ **800/221-7282;** Amex gold and platinum cardholders who use this number are exempt from the 1% fee. AAA members can obtain checks without a fee at most AAA offices.

**Visa** offers traveler's checks at Citibank locations nationwide, as well as at several other banks. The service charge ranges between 1.5% and 2%; checks come in denominations of $20, $50, $100, $500, and $1,000. In the U.S. or Canada, call **Visa/Interpayment Services** ☎ **800/732-1322** for information (☎ **800/453-4284** from most other countries), which also sells Visa checks issued by Barclays Bank and Bank of America. **MasterCard** also offers traveler's checks. Call ☎ **800/223-9920** for a location near you. When abroad, contact the local operator and ask to place a collect call to 33/318-550 in the U.K. or 609/987-7300 in the U.S. **Citicorp** (☎ **800/645-6556** in the U.S. and Canada; elsewhere, contact the local operator and ask to place a collect call to 813/623-1709 in the U.S.) also issues traveler's checks. Most British banks can issue their account holders a **Eurocheque** card and checkbook, which can be used at most cash machines and at Greek banks for an annual fee and a 2% charge.

**Foreign currency traveler's checks** are useful if you're traveling to one country, or to the euro zone; they're accepted at locations such as bed & breakfasts where dollar checks may not be, and they minimize the amount

## (Tips) Credit Cards in Greece

Credit cards are effectively required for renting a car these days. In Greece, they are accepted in the better hotels and most shops. *But note:* Even many of the better restaurants in major cities do *not* accept credit cards, and certainly most restaurants and smaller hotels in Greece still do not accept them. Also, some hotels that require credit cards when making advance reservations will demand payment in cash; inquire beforehand if this might be a problem.

of math you have to do at your destination. **American Express** offers checks in Australian dollars, Canadian dollars, British pounds, euros and Japanese yen. **Visa** checks come in Australian, Canadian, British, and euro versions; **MasterCard** offers those four plus yen and South African rands.

If you choose to carry traveler's checks, be sure to keep a record of their serial numbers separate from your checks in the event that they are stolen or lost. You'll get a refund faster if you know the numbers.

## CREDIT/CHARGE/DEBIT CARDS

Visa is the most widely accepted, and MasterCard is usually accepted where you see signs for Access or Eurocard. Diners Club is also increasingly recognized. American Express is less frequently accepted because it charges a higher commission and is more protective of the cardholder in disagreements.

Even when credit cards are accepted, most smaller restaurants and shops are reluctant to accept payment in plastic unless the bill is above a certain amount. Many small establishments will accept them only if you agree to pay their commission (usually about 6%); this seems fair enough, especially in some of the more out-of-the-way destinations where negotiating and receiving payment remains

difficult and time-consuming for the proprietors.

Credit cards are a safe way to carry money, they provide a convenient record of all your expenses, and they generally offer good exchange rates. You can also withdraw cash advances from your credit cards at banks or ATMs, provided you know your PIN. If you've forgotten yours, or didn't even know you had one, call the number on the back of your credit card and ask the bank to send it to you. It usually takes 5 to 7 business days, though some banks will provide the number over the phone if you tell them your mother's maiden name or some other personal information. Your credit card company will likely charge a commission (1% or 2%) on every foreign purchase you make, but you may be getting a good deal with credit cards when you factor in things like ATM fees and higher traveler's check exchange rates.

Keep in mind that credit card companies try to protect themselves from theft by limiting the funds someone can withdraw outside their home country, so call your credit card company before you leave home. And remember: If you use your charge card to obtain cash, you are borrowing money and presumably going to pay very high interest. It might be better to use your bank's card as a debit card, which means you are simply taking cash out of your bank account.

**Tips  Dear Visa: I'm Off to Mykonos!**

Increasingly there are reports of American travelers abroad who discover that their credit cards are invalidated after their first purchase: an automated security system "kicks in" to protect you on the assumption that your card has been stolen. To be sure this won't happen, call your credit card company or the bank that issued it and inform them of your impending trip. Even if you don't call your credit card company in advance, you can always call the card's toll-free emergency number (see "Fast Facts," later in this chapter) if a charge is refused—a good reason to carry the phone number with you. But perhaps the most important lesson is to carry more than one card on your trip; if one card doesn't work for any number of reasons, you'll have a backup card just in case.

For tips and telephone numbers to call if your wallet is stolen or lost, go to "Lost and Found" in the Fast Facts section later in this chapter.

**EMERGENCY CASH**  In an emergency, you can arrange to send money from home to a Greek bank. Telex transfers from the United Kingdom usually take at least 3 days and sometimes up to a week, with a charge of about 3%. Bank drafts are more expensive but potentially faster if you are in Athens. From Canada and the United States, money can be wired by **Western Union** (✆ **800/325-6000**)

or **MoneyGram** (✆ **800/543-4080**). In Greece, call Western Union in the United States (✆ **001-314/298-2313**) to learn the location of an office. For MoneyGram, call the head office in Athens (✆ **01/322-0005**). For a fee (usually 4%–10%, depending on the sum involved) money can be available in minutes at an agent for Western Union or Moneygram. And, of course, you can always borrow cash on your credit card from an ATM (so long as you're prepared to pay the high interest rate).

## 5 When to Go

**WEATHER**  Greece has a generally mild climate, though in the mountainous northern interior the winters are rather harsh and summers brief. Southern Greece enjoys a relatively mild winter, with temperatures averaging around 55°F to 60°F (13°C–16°C) in Athens. Summers are generally hot and dry, with daytime temperatures rising to 85°F to 95°F (30°C–35°C), usually cooled by prevailing north winds (the *meltemi*), especially on the islands, which often cool appreciably in the evenings. And at some point in most summers, usually July, the temperature will rise to over 100°F (38°C).

The best time to visit is **late April to mid-June**, when the wildflowers are blooming and before summer arrives in force with hordes of tourists, higher prices, overbooked facilities, and strained services. **Orthodox Easter**—close to but usually not exactly concurrent with Western Easter—is a particularly delightful time to visit, though reservations are necessary and service is not the best, as so many Greeks living abroad return for the holiday. After Easter, most of the island resorts crank up for the season.

**Average Monthly Temperature & Precipitation**

| Month | Athens | | | Crete | | |
|---|---|---|---|---|---|---|
| | ADT | | RF | ADT | | RF |
| | F° | C° | Inches | F° | C° | Inches |
| January | 52 | 12 | 2.4 | 54 | 13 | 3.7 |
| February | 54 | 13 | 2.0 | 54 | 13 | 3.0 |
| March | 58 | 15 | 1.3 | 57 | 14 | 1.6 |
| April | 65 | 19 | 0.9 | 62 | 17 | 0.9 |
| May | 74 | 24 | 0.8 | 68 | 20 | 0.7 |
| June | 86 | 30 | 0.2 | 74 | 24 | 0.1 |
| July | 92 | 33 | 0.1 | 78 | 26 | 0.0 |
| August | 92 | 33 | 0.2 | 78 | 26 | 0.1 |
| September | 82 | 28 | 1.1 | 75 | 24 | 0.7 |
| October | 72 | 23 | 2.0 | 69 | 21 | 1.7 |
| November | 63 | 18 | 2.9 | 63 | 18 | 2.7 |
| December | 56 | 14 | 4.1 | 58 | 15 | 4.0 |

*ADT = Average Daytime Temperature, RF = Rainfall*

If you possibly can, avoid traveling in **July and August** (and especially on or around Aug 15)—the crowds from Europe overwhelm southern Greece and the islands. In overcrowded southern Greece and the islands, midday temperatures are too high for much except beach and water activities. We strongly recommend you not go unless you have firm reservations and enjoy close encounters with masses of fellow tourists and footloose students. Of course, the higher elevations remain cooler and less crowded, a plus for hikers, bikers, and those who don't demand sophisticated pleasures.

By **mid-September,** temperatures begin to fall and crowds thin, but it can still be hot. The weather remains generally calm and balmy well into October. If you can't get to Greece in the spring, and beaches are not your primary goal, this is a fine time to visit.

By **late October,** ferry service and flights are cutting back and most facilities on the islands begin to close for the winter, but the cooler fall atmosphere makes Athens and the mainland all the more pleasant. If you have the time, visit the islands first, then return for a tour of the mainland archaeological sites.

**Winter** (say, Nov–Mar) is no time for fun in the sun, unless you want to join the Greeks for skiing and winter sports in the mountains—but some hotels and many good tavernas are open still, prices are at their lowest, and the southern mainland and Crete remain inviting, especially for those interested in archaeology and authentic local culture.

**HOLIDAYS** The legal national holidays of Greece are: **New Year's Day,** January 1; **Epiphany** (Baptism of Christ), January 6; **Clean Monday** (Kathari Deftera), day before Shrove Tuesday, 41 days before Easter (which in Greece may come in late March to late April; every few years it coincides with Easter Sunday in Western Christian lands); **Independence Day,** March 25; **Good Friday to Easter,** including the Monday after Easter Sunday; **May Day** (Labor Day), May 1; **Whitmonday** (Holy Spirit Monday), day after Whitsunday (Pentecost), the 7th Sunday after Easter; **Assumption of the Virgin,** August 15; **Ochi Day,** October 28; **Christmas,** December 25 and 26.

On these holidays, government offices, banks, post offices, most stores, and many restaurants are closed; a few museums and attractions may remain open on several of the lesser holidays. Meanwhile, visitors are often included in the celebration. Consult the "Greece Calendar of Events," below, if you are in the planning stage. If you are already in Greece, ask at your hotel or find one of the current English-language publications, such as the *Athens News,* the *Kathimerini* insert in the *International Herald Tribune,* the weekly brochure *Athens Today,* or the *Athenscope* section of the weekly *Hellenic Times.*

# GREECE CALENDAR OF EVENTS

## January

**Feast of St. Basil** (Ayios Vassilios). St. Basil is the Greek equivalent of Santa Claus. The holiday is marked by the exchange of gifts and a special cake, *vassilopita,* made with a coin in it; the person who gets the piece with the coin will have good luck. January 1.

**Epiphany** (Baptism of Christ) is celebrated with the blessing of baptismal fonts and water. A priest may throw a cross into the harbor and young men will try to recover it; the finder wins a special blessing. Children, who have been kept good during Christmas with threats of the *kalikantzari* (goblins), are allowed on the 12th day to help chase them away, January 6.

**Gynecocracy** (Gynaikokratia, Rule of Women). Some villages in Thrace celebrate with the women taking over the cafes while the men stay home and do the housework. January 8.

## February

**Carnival (Karnavali)** is celebrated with parades, marching bands, costumes, drinking, dancing, and more or less loosening of inhibition, depending on the locale. Some scholars say the name comes from the Latin for "farewell meat," while others hold that it comes from "car naval," the chariots celebrating the ancient sea god Poseidon (Saturn, to the Romans). The city of Patras shows its support of the latter theory with its famous chariot parade and wild Saturnalia, private parties and public celebrations. Masked revels are also widely held in Macedonia. On the island of Skyros, the pagan "Goat Dance" is performed, reminding us of the primitive Dionysiac nature of the festivities. Crete has its own colorful versions, while in the Ionian islands, festivities are more Italian. In Athens, people bop each other on the head with plastic hammers. Celebrations last the 3 weeks before the beginning of Lent.

## March

**Independence Day and the Feast of the Annunciation** are celebrated simultaneously with military parades, especially in Athens. The religious celebration is particularly important on the islands of Tinos

## Holy Week Celebrations

Orthodox Easter, a time of extraordinary festivities in Greece, usually falls one or more weeks after Easter in the West—inquire ahead! The Good Friday exodus from Athens is truly amazing, and you can remain and enjoy the deserted city or, if you're fortunate—and have made reservations, because Greeks take up most travel facilities—you can be among the celebrants in any town or village. Holy Week is usually marked by impressive solemn services and processions; serious feasting on roasted lamb, the traditional margaritsa soup, and homemade wine; and dancing, often in traditional costumes. One unique celebration occurs on Patmos, where the Last Supper is reenacted at the monastery of St. John the Divine. **Tip:** Tourists should remember to dress appropriately, especially at this Easter time (shorts, miniskirts, and sleeveless shirts will all cause offense).

and Hydra and in churches or monasteries named *Evanyelismos* (Bringer of Good News) or *Evanyelistria* (the feminine form of the name). March 25.

### April

**Sound-and-light performances** begin on the Acropolis in Athens and the Old Town on Rhodes. Nightly to October.

**Procession of St. Spyridon (Ayios Spyridon)** is held in Corfu town on Palm Sunday. (St. Spyridon's remains are also paraded through the streets of Corfu town on Holy Sat, Aug 1, and the first Sun in Nov.)

**Feast of St. George** (Ayios Yioryios), the patron saint of shepherds, is an important rural celebration with dancing and feasting. Arachova, near Delphi, is famous for its festivities. The island of Skyros also gives its patron saint a big party. April 23. (If the 23rd comes before Easter, the celebration is postponed until the Mon after Easter.)

### May

**May Day.** On this important urban holiday, families have picnics in the country and pick wildflowers, which are woven into wreaths and hung from balconies and over doorways. May Day is still celebrated by

Greek Communists and socialists as a working-class holiday. May 1.

**Folk-dance performances** begin in the amphitheater on Filopappos Hill in Athens and continue to September. Among the most regular and popular groups is the Dora Stratou Dance Troupe.

**Hippocratic Oath.** Ritual recitations of the oath by the citizens of Kos honor their favorite son Hippocrates. Young girls in ancient dress, playing flutes, accompany a young boy in procession until he stands and recites in Greek the timeless oath of physicians everywhere. May through September.

**Sound-and-light shows** begin in Corfu town and continue to the end of September.

**Feast of St. Constantine** (Ayios Konstandinos), the first Orthodox emperor, and his mother, **St. Helen** (Ayia Eleni), is celebrated, most interestingly, by fire-walking rituals (*anastenaria*) in four villages in Macedonian Greece: Ayia Eleni, Ayios Petros, Langada, and Meliki. It's a big party night for everyone named Costa and Eleni. (Namedays, rather than birthdays, are celebrated in Greece.) The anniversary of the Ionian reunion with Greece is also celebrated, mainly in Corfu. May 21.

## June

**Athens Festival** features superb productions of ancient drama, opera, orchestra performances, ballet, modern dance, and popular entertainers in the handsome Odeum of Herodes Atticus, on the southwest side of the Acropolis. June to early October.

**Folk-dance performances** are given in the theater in the Old Town of Rhodes.

**Wine Festival** is held annually at Daphni, about 10km (7 miles) west of Athens; other wine festivals are held on Rhodes and elsewhere.

The **Simi Festival** is a 4-month feast of concerts, theater, storytelling, and dance, featuring acclaimed Greek and international artists. With its epicenter on the tiny island of Simi, the events spill over into seven other neighboring islands: Astypalea, Halki, Kastellorizo, Karpathos, Kassos, Nissiros, and Tilos. June through September.

**Lycabettus Theater** presents a variety of performances at the amphitheater on Mount Likavitos (Lycabettus) overlooking Athens, from mid-June to late August.

The **Miaoulia**, celebrated on a mid-June weekend on Hydra, honors Hydriot Admiral Miaoulis, who set much of the Turkish fleet on fire by ramming them with explosives-filled fireboats.

**Aegean Festival** on Skiathos presents ancient drama, modern dance, folk music and dance, concerts, and art exhibits in the Bourtzi Cultural Center in the harbor of Skiathos town. June through September.

**International Classical Musical Festival** is held annually for one week in June or July at Nafplion, in the Peloponnese.

**Midsummer Eve** (June 23–24) is celebrated by burning the dry wreaths picked on May Day to drive away witches, a remnant of pagan ceremonies now associated with the birth of John the Baptist on Midsummer Day, June 24.

**The Feast of the Holy Apostles** (Ayii Apostoli, Petros, and Pavlos) is another important name-day. June 29.

**Navy Week** is celebrated throughout Greece. In Volos, the voyage of the Argonauts is reenacted. On Hydra, the exploits of Adm. Andreas Miaoulis, naval hero of the War of Independence, are celebrated. Fishermen at Plomari on Lesvos stage a festival. End of June and beginning of July.

## July

Hydra's annual **puppet festival** has drawn puppeteers from countries as far away as Togo and Brazil. Early July.

**Dodoni Festival** presents classical dramas at the ancient theater of Dodoni, south of Ioannina. For information, call © **26510/20-090.** July through September.

**Epidaurus Festival** of classical Greek drama begins in the famous amphitheater and continues to early September. For information, contact the **Greek Festival Office,** 4 Stadiou (© **210/322-1459** or 210/322-3111 to 3119, ext. 137).

**International Folklore Festival** at Naoussa, in northern Greece, features both amateur and professional dance companies from all over the world. For information, call © **23320/20211** or e-mail cioff@nao.forthnet.gr.

The **Northern Greece National Theater** performs classical drama in the amphitheaters in Phillipi and on the island of Thasos. Here's a way to see these productions free of the hassles of Athens. For information, call © **2510/223-504.** July and August.

**Hippokrateia Festival** brings art, music, and theater to the medieval castle of the Knights of St. John, in the main harbor of Kos. July and August.

**Kalamata International Dance Festival** is held each summer in Kalamata, in the southern Peloponnesos, with performances by prestigious dance companies from all over the world.

**Dionysia Wine Festival** is held on the island of Naxos. Not a major event, but fun if you're there. For information, call © **22850/22-923.** Mid-July.

**Wine Festival** at Rethymnon, Crete, continues through the middle weeks of July. Rethymnon also hosts a **Renaissance Festival** starting in July and running into early September. There are now wine festivals and arts festivals all over Greece, but among the more engaging are those held in Rethymnon. Sample the wines, then sample something of the Renaissance theatrical and musical performances.

**Feast of Ayia Marina,** protector of crops, is widely celebrated in rural areas. July 17.

**Feast of the Prophet Elijah** (Profitis Elias) is celebrated in the hilltop shrines formerly sacred to the sun god Helios, the most famous of which is on Mount Taygetos, near Sparta. July 18 to 20.

**Feast of Ayia Paraskevi** continues the succession of Saint Days celebrated at the height of summer, when agricultural work is put on hold. July 26.

**August**

**Feast of the Transfiguration** (Metamorphosi) is celebrated in the

numerous churches and monasteries of that name, though it isn't much for name-day parties. August 6.

**Aeschylia festival** of ancient drama stages classical dramas at the archaeological site of Eleusis, home of the ancient Mysteries and birthplace of Aeschylus, west of Athens. August to mid-September.

**Feast of the Assumption of the Virgin** (Apokimisis tis Panayias) is an important day of religious pilgrimage. Many take the opportunity to go home for a visit, so rooms are particularly hard to find. The holiday reaches monumental proportions in Tinos; thousands of people descend on the small port town to participate in an all-night vigil at the cathedral of Panayia Evanyelistria, in the procession of the town's miraculous icon, and in the requiem for the soldiers who died aboard the Greek battleship *Elli* on this day in 1940. August 15.

**Epirotika Festival** in Ioannina presents theatrical performances, concerts, and exhibitions. August to early September.

**Olympus Festival** presents cultural events in the Frankish Castle of Platamonas, near Mount Olympus.

**Santorini festival of classical music** features international musicians and singers in outdoor performances for 2 weeks beginning at the end of the month.

**September**

**Feast of the Birth of the Virgin** (Yenisis tis Panayias) is another major festival, especially on Spetses, where the anniversary of the Battle of the Straits of Spetses is celebrated with a re-enactment in the harbor, fireworks, and an all-night bash. September 8.

**Feast of the Exaltation of the Cross** (Ipsosi to Stavrou) marks the end of the summer stretch of feasts, and even Stavros has had enough for a while. September 14.

**Thessaloniki International Trade Fair.** This is one of the world's major trade fairs. Rooms are scarce in the city, so if the fair's not your destination, try to come to Thessaloniki at another time. For information, call ☎ **2310/271-888.** Mid-September.

**Thessaloniki Film Festival and Festival of Popular Song.** That lively and sophisticated city continues to live it up. End of September.

## October

**Feast of St. Demetrius** (Ayios Dimitrios) is particularly important in Thessaloniki, where he is the patron saint, and the Demetrius Festival features music, opera, and ballet. New wine is traditionally untapped. October 26.

**Ochi Day,** when General Metaxa's negative reply (*ochi* is Greek for "no") to Mussolini's demands in 1940 gives a convenient excuse for continuing the party with patriotic outpourings, including parades,

folk music and dancing, and general festivity. October 28.

## November

**Feast of the Archangels Gabriel and Michael** (Gavriel and Mihail), with ceremonies in the many churches named for them. November 8.

**Feast of St. Andrew** (Ayios Andreas), patron saint of Patras, is another excuse for a party in that swinging city. November 30.

## December

**Feast of St. Nikolaos** (Ayios Nikolaos). This St. Nick is the patron saint of sailors. Numerous processions head down to the sea and the many chapels dedicated to him. December 6.

**Christmas.** The day after Christmas Mass honors the Gathering Around the Holy Family (Synaksis tis Panayias). December 25 and 26.

**New Year's Eve,** when children go out singing Christmas carols (*kalanda*) while their elders play cards, talk, smoke, eat, and imbibe. December 31.

---

## 6 Travel Insurance

Greece presents no special problems when it comes to insurable "incidents," although it should be noted that most Greeks do not carry very much insurance so you would not be able to collect much if you were in an accident. So check your existing homeowner's, medical, automobile insurance policies and credit-card coverage before you buy travel insurance. You may already be covered for lost luggage, cancelled tickets or medical expenses. If you are prepaying for your trip or taking a flight that has cancellation penalties, consider cancellation insurance. The cost of travel insurance varies widely, depending on the cost and length of your trip, your age, health, and the type of trip you're taking.

**TRIP-CANCELLATION INSUR-ANCE** Trip-cancellation insurance helps you get your money back if you have to back out of a trip, if you have to go home early, or if your travel supplier goes bankrupt. Allowed reasons for cancellation can range from sickness to natural disasters to the State Department declaring your destination unsafe for travel (since you booked). (Insurers usually won't cover vague fears, though, as many travelers discovered who tried to cancel their trips in October 2001 because they were wary of flying.) In this unstable world, trip-cancellation insurance is a good buy if you're getting tickets well in advance—who knows what the state of the world, or of your airline, will be in 9 months? Insurance policy details vary, so read the fine print—and especially make sure that your airline or cruise line is on the list of carriers covered in case of bankruptcy. For information, contact one of the following insurers: **Access America** (© 800/284-8300; www.access america.com); **Travel Guard International** (© 800/826-1300; www.travel guard.com); **Travel Insured International** (© 800/243-3174; www.travel insured.com); and **Travelex Insurance Services** (© 800/228-9792; www.travelex-insurance.com).

**MEDICAL INSURANCE** Citizens of the U.K. and other EU-nations will know of their rights when traveling in other EU countries; if in doubt, check with the appropriate authorities. For non-EU nationals, most health insurance policies cover you if you get sick away from home—but check, particularly if you're insured by an HMO. With the exception of certain HMOs and Medicare/Medicaid, your medical insurance should cover medical treatment—even hospital care—overseas. However, most out-of-country hospitals make you pay your bills up front, and send you a refund after you've returned home and filed the necessary paperwork. And in a worst-case scenario, there's the high cost of emergency evacuation. If you require additional medical insurance, try **MEDEX International** (© 800/527-0218; outside the U.S. and Canada, call 410/453-6300; www.medexassist.com) or **Travel Assistance International** (© 800/821-2828; www.travelassistance.com; for general information on services, call the company's **Worldwide Assistance**

**Services, Inc,** at © 800/777-8710). Other companies that can provide insurance and further information are: **Travel Guard International** (© 800/782-5151); **Travel Insured International** (© 800/243-3174); **International Medical Group** (© 800/628-4664; insurance@imglobal.com); **Fortis Health** (© 800/989-2345; www.buyinternationaltravel.com); **Wallach and Co.,** (© **800/237-6615;** www.wallach.com).

**LOST-LUGGAGE INSURANCE** On domestic flights, checked baggage is covered up to $2,500 per ticketed passenger. On international flights (including US portions of international trips), baggage is limited to approximately $9.07 per pound, up to approximately $635 per checked bag. If you plan to check items more valuable than the standard liability, see if your valuables are covered by your homeowner's policy, get baggage insurance as part of your comprehensive travel-insurance package or buy Travel Guard's "Bag-Trak" product. Don't buy insurance at the airport, as it's usually overpriced. Be sure to take any valuables or irreplaceable items with you in your carry-on luggage, as many valuables (including books, money and electronics) aren't covered by airline policies.

If your luggage is lost, immediately file a lost-luggage claim at the airport, detailing the luggage contents. For most airlines, you must report delayed, damaged, or lost baggage within 4 hours of arrival. The airlines are required to deliver luggage, once found, directly to your house or destination free of charge.

---

**⌒Tips  Quick ID**

Tie a colorful ribbon or piece of yarn around your luggage handle, or slap a distinctive sticker on the side of your bag. This makes it less likely that someone will mistakenly appropriate it. And if your luggage gets lost, it will be easier to find.

## GENERAL AVAILABILITY OF HEALTH CARE

There are no immunization requirements for getting into Greece, though it's always a good idea to have polio, tetanus, and typhoid covered when traveling anywhere. In Greece itself, modern hospitals, clinics, and pharmacies are to be found everywhere, and personnel, equipment, and supplies ensure excellent treatment. Virtually all doctors in Greece can speak English or some other European language. You should bring along a sufficient quantity of any prescription medication you are taking and keep it in your carry-on luggage. Just in case, ask your doctor to write you new prescriptions, using the generic—not the brand—name. Dental care is also widely available.

For serious medical problems that arise while in Greece, your embassy or consulate or hotel can recommend an English-speaking doctor. In an emergency, call a **first-aid center** (© 166), the nearest **hospital** (© 106), or the **tourist police** (© 171).

### COMMON AILMENTS

Diarrhea is no more of a problem in Greece than it might be anytime one changes diet and water supplies, but yes, occasionally visitors do experience it. Common over-the-counter preventatives and cures are available in Greek pharmacies, but if you are concerned, bring your own. (Cola soft drinks are said to be helpful for those having digestive difficulties stemming from too much olive oil in their food.) If you expect to be taking sea trips and are inclined to get seasick, bring some preventative. Allergy sufferers should carry along some antihistamines, especially in the spring.

**SUN** Between mid-June and September, too much exposure to the sun during the midday could lead to sunstroke or heatstroke. Sunscreen and a hat are strongly advised.

### DIETARY RED FLAGS

There is nothing in the Greek diet requiring any special warning. Greece's natural water is excellent, although these days you will usually be served—and charged for—bottled water. Milk is pasteurized, though refrigeration is sometimes not the best, especially in out-of-the-way places. Vegetarians should find the Greek menu especially congenial as there are so many vegetables, grains, and fruits available; all except vegans will also enjoy the seafood and yogurt. Greece, however, is not geared for serving kosher meals.

### BUGS, BITES & OTHER WILDLIFE CONCERNS

There is no particular risk of poisonous bites, although mosquitoes can certainly be a nuisance: You might well travel with some "bug-off" substance. Dogs, by the way, should not present a danger of rabies, but you are strongly advised not to reach out and touch the dogs that roam around Greece.

### WHAT TO DO IF YOU GET SICK AWAY FROM HOME

Those with chronic illnesses should discuss their travel plans with their physician before departure. Those with epilepsy, diabetes, or significant cardiovascular disease should wear a Medic Alert identification tag or bracelet, which will alert a health-care provider to the condition and provide the telephone number of the 24-hour hot line from which your medical record can be obtained. Before setting off, contact the **Medic Alert Foundation** (© 800/432-5378). If you have special concerns, before heading abroad you might check out the United States Centers for Disease Control and Prevention (© 800/311-3435; **www.cdc.gov/travel**) or **www.istm.org** for advice on health and medical situations in foreign lands.

Pack **prescription medications** in your carry-on luggage, and carry prescription medications in their original containers, with pharmacy labels—otherwise they won't make it through airport security. Also bring along copies of your prescriptions in case you lose your pills or run out. Don't forget an extra pair of contact lenses or prescription glasses. Carry the generic name of prescription medicines, in case a local pharmacist is unfamiliar with the brand name.

One of the best sources for travelers with medical problems is the **International Association for Medical Assistance for Travelers (IAMAT)**. It not only has a list of English-speaking doctors (who agree to reasonable fees) in some 120 cities abroad, but also puts out specialized publications on diseases such as malaria. It can be reached in the United States at 417 Center St., Lewiston, NY 14092 (© 716/754-4883), and in Canada at 40 Regal Rd., Guelph, ON N1K 1B5 (© 519/836-0102); you can also write the office at 57 Voirets, 1212 Grand-Lancy, Geneva, Switzerland, or browse **www.iamat.org**.

And **Travelmed** claims it can provide everything from accessible transportation and wheelchairs to oxygen and dressings to almost any point in Greece with enough warning (© **800/878-3627** in the U.S; 702/454-6628 from abroad; www.travelmedintl.com).

You can also try the emergency room at a local hospital; many have walk-in clinics for emergency cases that are not life-threatening. You may not get immediate attention, but you won't pay the high price of an emergency room visit. Emergency treatment is usually given free of charge in state hospitals, but be warned that only basic needs are met. The care in outpatient clinics, which are usually open in the mornings (from 8am to noon), is often somewhat better; you can find them next to most major hospitals, on some islands, and occasionally in rural areas, usually indicated by prominent signs.

Citizens of EU nations should inquire before leaving, but their policies will probably cover treatment in Greece. In most cases, your existing health plan will provide the coverage you need. But double-check; you may want to buy **travel medical insurance** instead. (See the section on insurance, above.) Bring your insurance ID card with you when you travel. Greeks have a national medical insurance and although you would receive emergency care with no questions make sure you have coverage at home.

## STAYING SAFE

Greece is undeniably exposed to earthquakes, but there are few known instances of tourists ever being injured or killed in one of these. Far more of a potential danger might be automobile accidents: Greece has one of the worst vehicle accident rates in Europe. All that can be said is that great caution should be exercised when driving over unfamiliar, often winding, and often poorly maintained roads. This holds especially when driving at night. As for those who insist on renting motorbikes or similar vehicles, at the very least wear a helmet.

Crime directed at tourists was traditionally unheard of in Greece but in more recent years there are occasional reports of cars broken into, pickpockets, purse-snatchers, and such. (Perhaps you should ask yourself whether it is necessary to be traveling with irreplaceable valuables like jewelry.) Normal precautions are called for. For instance, never turn hand luggage containing truly expensive items, whether jewelry or cameras, to an individual unless you are absolutely sure it is safe. Tourists who report crimes to the local police would probably feel that they are not being taken all that seriously, but it is more likely that the Greek police have realized there is little they can do without solid identification of the culprits. As for the other side of the coin—police being exceptionally hard on foreigners—say, when enforcing traffic violations—although there is the rare reported incident, it does not seem to be a widespread practice.

## DEALING WITH DISCRIMINATION

There is no denying that many Greeks are opposed to American foreign policies in recent years but they almost never direct this at individual travelers.

That said, if you were to get to speaking with Greeks who dislike American policies, they will not be bashful about expressing their opinion and challenging yours. The special issues raised by the recent emergence of terrorism have been discussed above.

African Americans and other people of Color should not experience any different treatment in Greece than anyone else unless it is curiosity from people not accustomed to seeing such people—in particular, they may be stared at.

## 8 Specialized Travel Resources

## TRAVELERS WITH DISABILITIES

Most disabilities shouldn't stop anyone from traveling. There are more options and resources out there than ever before. That said, few concessions exist for the disabled in Greece. Steep steps, uneven pavement, almost no cuts at curbstones, narrow walks, slick stone, and traffic congestion can cause problems. Archaeological sites by their very nature are usually difficult to navigate, and crowded public transportation can be all but impossible. (The Greeks have announced plans to make the Acropolis handicapped accessible by the Olympics of 2004 but it is not clear just what will be in place.) More modern and private facilities are only now beginning to provide ramps, but little else has been done. (That said, foreigners in wheelchairs—accompanied by companions—are becoming a more common sight in Greece, and we have read a first-person account of a wheelchair-using individual who found a cruise ship well designed to service her needs.)

Many travel agencies offer customized tours and itineraries for travelers with disabilities, but few as yet offer such services for Greece. Perhaps the best on-line source for free travel information for the disabled is **Access-Able Travel Source** (www.access-able.com).

Organizations that offer assistance to disabled travelers include Philadelphia's **Moss Rehab Hospital** (www.mossresourcenet.org), which provides a library of accessible-travel resources online; the **Society for Accessible Travel and Hospitality** (© 212/447-7284; www.sath.org; annual membership fees: $45 adults, $30 seniors and students), which offers a wealth of travel resources for all types of disabilities and informed recommendations on destinations, access guides, travel agents, tour operators, vehicle rentals, and companion services; and the **American Foundation for the Blind** (© 800/232-5463; www.afb.org), which provides information on traveling with Seeing Eye dogs.

For more information specifically targeted to travelers with disabilities, the community website **iCan** (www.icanonline.net/channels/travel/index.cfm) has destination guides and several regular columns on accessible travel. Also check out the quarterly magazine *Emerging Horizons* ($15 per year, $20 outside the U.S.; www.emerginghorizons.com); **Twin Peaks Press** (© 360/694-2462;

**New Directions** (© 805/967-2841; www.newdirectionstravel.com) will discuss the possibilities of arranging tours for people with developmental disabilities.

http://disabilitybookshop.virtualave. net/blist84.htm), offering travel-related books for travelers with special needs; and *Open World* magazine, published by the Society for Accessible Travel and Hospitality (see above; subscription: $18/year, $35 outside the U.S.).

## GAY & LESBIAN TRAVELERS

Greece—or at least parts of Greece—has a long tradition of being tolerant of homosexual men and in recent years these locales, at least, have extended this tolerance to lesbians. But it should be said: Although Greeks in Athens, Piraeus and perhaps a few other major cities may not care one way or the other, Greeks in small towns and villages—indeed, most Greeks—do not appreciate flagrant displays of dress or behavior. Among the best known hangouts for gays and lesbians are Mykonos and Chania, Crete, but in fact increasing numbers of gays and lesbians simply travel all over Greece like everyone else.

The **International Gay & Lesbian Travel Association (IGLTA)** (© **800/ 448-8550** or 954/776-2626; www. iglta.org) is the trade association for the gay and lesbian travel industry, and offers an online directory of gay and lesbian-friendly travel businesses; go to their website and click on "Members".

Many agencies offer tours and travel itineraries specifically for gay and lesbian travelers. **Above and Beyond Tours** (© **800/397-2681;** www.abovebeyondtours.com) is one such. **Now, Voyager** (© **800/255-6951;** www.nowvoyager.com) is a well-known San Francisco–based gay-owned and operated travel service. **Olivia Cruises & Resorts** (© **800/ 631-6277** or 510/655-0364; www. olivia.com) charters entire resorts and ships for exclusive lesbian vacations and offers smaller group experiences for both gay and lesbian travelers.

The following travel guides are available at most travel bookstores and

gay and lesbian bookstores, or you can order them from **Giovanni's Room** bookstore, 345 South 12th St., Philadelphia, PA 19107 (© **215/923-2960;** www.giovannisroom.com): *Frommer's Gay & Lesbian Europe,* an excellent travel resource; **Out & About** (© **800/929-2268** or 415/ 644-8044; www.outandabout.com), which offers guidebooks and a newsletter 10 times a year packed with solid information on the global gay and lesbian scene; *Spartacus International Gay Guide* and *Odysseus,* both good, annual English-language guidebooks focused on gay men; the *Damron* guides, with separate, annual books for gay men and lesbians; and *Gay Travel A to Z: The World of Gay & Lesbian Travel Options at Your Fingertips,* by Marianne Ferrari (Ferrari Publications; Box 35575, Phoenix, AZ 85069), a very good gay and lesbian guidebook series.

Another helpful source is *Our World,* a magazine designed specifically for gay and lesbian travelers (10 issues a year, $12); at 1104 N. Nova Rd., Suite 251, Daytona Beach, FL 32117 (© **904/441-5367;** www.our worldmagazine.com); it not only is full of ads for travel agencies and facilities that accommodate gays and lesbians, but also carries firsthand accounts of visits to locales all around the world.

In Athens, information about the **Hellenic Homosexual Liberation Movement (EOK)** can be found at 31 Apostolou Pavlou, Thisio/Athens (© **2940/771-9291**). The *Greek Gay Guide,* published by Kraximo Press, P.O. Box 4228, 10210 Athens (© **210/ 362-5249**), can be purchased at some kiosks.

## SENIOR TRAVEL

There are not that many "senior-citizen discounts" available in Greece. Some museums and archaeological sites offer discounts for those 60 and over, but the practice seems unpredictable and in general these are restricted to citizens of an EU nation. For general information before you go, visit the U.S. Department of State website at http://travel.state.gov/olderamericans.html for information specifically for older Americans.

Try mentioning the fact that you're a senior citizen when you make your travel reservations. Although almost all major US airlines have cancelled their senior discount and coupon book programs, many hotels still offer discounts for seniors.

Members of **AARP** (formerly known as the American Association of Retired Persons), 601 E St. NW, Washington, DC 20049 (© 800/424-3410; www.aarp.org), get discounts on hotels, airfares, and car rentals. AARP offers members a wide range of benefits, including *Modern Maturity* magazine and a monthly newsletter. Anyone over 50 can join.

Many reliable agencies and organizations target the 50-plus market. **Elderhostel** (© 877/426-8056; www.elderhostel.org) arranges study programs for those aged 55 and over (and a spouse or companion of any age) in the U.S. and in more than 80 countries around the world. Most courses last 5 to 7 days in the U.S. (2–4 weeks abroad), and many include airfare, accommodations in university dormitories or modest inns, meals, and tuition. **Interhostel,** University of New Hampshire, 6 Garrison Ave., Durham, NH 03824 (© 800/733-9753; www.learn.unh.edu/interhostel), offers 2-week programs in more than three dozen countries for people over 50. In Greece, groups typically settle in one area for a week or so, with excursions that focus on getting to know the history and culture. **ElderTreks** (© 800/741-7956; www.eldertreks.com) offers small-group tours to off-the-beaten-path or adventure-travel locations, restricted to travelers 50 and older.

Recommended publications offering travel resources and discounts for seniors include: the quarterly magazine *Travel 50 & Beyond* (www.travel50andbeyond.com); *Travel Unlimited: Uncommon Adventures for the Mature Traveler* (Avalon); *101 Tips for Mature Travelers,* available from Grand Circle Travel (© 800/248-3737; www.gct.com), which specializes in travel for seniors. One of the better guides for older travelers is *Unbelievably Good Deals and Great Adventures That You Absolutely Can't Get Unless You're Over 50* (McGraw Hill).

**Vantage Travel** (© 800/322-6677; www.vantagetravel.com), which also arranges for tours for seniors, offers a free booklet, *99 Travel Tips for Mature Travelers.* The monthly newsletter *The Mature Traveler* is available for $30 a year by contacting P.O. Box 50400, Reno, NV 89513 (© 800/460-6676; www.thematuretraveler.com). **Saga International Holidays,** 222 Berkeley St., Boston, MA 02116 (© 800/343-0273; www.sagaholidays.com), specializes in all-inclusive tours in Greece for those ages 50 and older.

## FAMILY TRAVEL

If you have enough trouble getting your kids out of the house in the morning, dragging them thousands of miles away may seem like an insurmountable challenge. But family travel can be immensely rewarding, giving you new ways of seeing the world through smaller pairs of eyes. *How to Take Great Trips with Your Kids* (The Harvard Common Press) is full of good general advice that can apply to travel anywhere.

Individual families will have to know what their goals in Greece are to be and whether their children are of an age to appreciate them. Clearly, if you are simply heading for the beaches, children of all ages can enjoy these; at the other extreme, if it is to all museums/archaeological sites, think twice. Traveling with infants and very young children—say up to about age 5—can work; most children get restless with historical sites between about 6 and 16; if you're lucky, your children may tune into history at some point in their teens.

There are the occasional "kid-friendly" distractions in Greece: playgrounds all over; some waterparks here and there; zoos. Greeks boys now play pickup basketball in even small towns—if your kids go for that, it's a great way to quickly be accepted. The kid friendly icon throughout the book indicates any places we feel might appeal to young people.

Most hotels allow children under 6 a free bed or cot in the room, and reduced prices for children under about 12. Some museums have children's prices but by and large, Greece is not set up to offer reductions at every turn.

As for passport requirements for children, see "Entry Requirements," earlier in this chapter.

**Familyhostel (© 800/733-9753;** www.learn.unh.edu/familyhostel) takes the whole family, including kids ages 8 to 15, on moderately priced domestic and international learning vacations. Lectures, field trips, and sightseeing are guided by a team of academics.

You can find good family-oriented vacation advice on the Internet from sites like **Traveling Internationally with Your Kids** (www.travelwith yourkids.com), a comprehensive site offering sound advice for long-distance and international travel with children; and **Family Travel Files** (www.thefamilytravelfiles.com), which offers an online magazine and a directory of off-the-beaten-path tours and tour operators for families.

## WOMEN TRAVELERS

Women traveling in Greece should not run into any particularly different situations from men. That said, young women—especially singles or small groups—may well find Greek males "coming on" to them, especially at beaches and clubs and such tourist locales. But our informants tell us that, unlike in certain countries that may go nameless, Greek males (a) do not attempt any physical contact and (b) they respect "No." One "tactic" said to work is to say, "I'm a Greek-American." The other advice is simply not to leave well-attended locales with someone you don't really know. Women should also be aware that there are still some cafes and even restaurants that are effectively male-only haunts; the males will not appreciate attempts by foreign women to integrate these places.

**Women Welcome Women World Wide (5W)** (www.womenwelcome women.org.uk) works to foster international friendships by enabling women of different countries to visit one another (men can come along on the trips; they just can't join the club). It's a big, active organization, with more than 3,500 members from all walks of life in some 70 countries.

You might also look into *Safety and Security for Women Who Travel,* by Sheila Swan Laufer and Peter Laufer (Travelers' Tales, Inc.), offering commonsense advice and tips on safe travel.

## STUDENT TRAVEL

**Hanging Out in Greece** (www.frommers.com/hangingout), published by Frommer's, is the top student travel series for today's students, covering everything from adrenaline sports to the hottest club and music scenes.

In Greece, students with proper identification (ISIC and IYC cards) are given reduced entrance fees to archaeological sites and museums, as well as discounts on admission to most artistic events, theatrical performances, and festivals. So you'd be wise to arm yourself with an International Student Identity Card (ISIC), which offers substantial savings on rail passes, plane tickets, and entrance fees. It also provides you with basic health and life insurance and a 24-hour help line The ISIC card, which costs $22, can also gain students various reductions in phone calls, e-mail, and related services; contact the International Student Travel Confederation (www.istc.org). The card is also available from STA Travel (© 800/781-4040, and if you're not in North America there's probably a local number in your country; www.statravel.co.uk the biggest student travel agency in the world. (Note: In 2002, STA Travel bought competitor Council Travel, but Council Travel still maintains its own website, www.counciltravel.com.)

If you're no longer a student but are still under 26, you can get an International Youth Travel Card (IYTC) for the same price from the same people, which entitles you to some discounts (but not on museum admissions). You can also purchase this card through the website, www.isic.org. Travel CUTS (© 800/667-2887; www.travelcuts.com) offers similar services for both Canadians and US residents.

In the United States, one of the major organizations for arranging overseas study for college-age students is the Council on International Education Exchange, or CIEE (© 800/407-8839; www.ciee.org).

A Hostelling International membership can save students money in some 5,000 hostels in 70 countries, where sex-segregated, dormitory-style sleeping quarters cost about $15 to $35 a night. In the United States, membership is available through Hostelling International–American Youth Hostels, 8401 Colesville Rd., Silver Spring MD 20910 (© 301/494-1240; www.hiayh.org). One-year membership is free for ages 17 and under; $28; for ages 18 to 54; $18 for ages 55 and over.

In Greece, an International Guest Card can be obtained at the Greek Association of Youth Hostels (OESE), in Athens at 11 Botassi near Kaningos Square, behind Omonia (© 210/330-2340).

## SINGLE TRAVELERS

Many people prefer traveling alone, and for independent travelers, solo journeys offer infinite opportunities to make friends and meet locals. Unfortunately, if you like resorts, tours or cruises, you're likely to get hit with a "single supplement" to the base price. Single travelers can avoid these supplements, of course, by agreeing to room with other single travelers on the trip. An even better idea is to find a compatible roommate before you go from one of the many roommate locator agencies.

Travel Companion Exchange (TCE) (© 631/454-0880; www.travelcompanions.com) is one of the nation's oldest roommate finders for single travelers. Register with them and find a travel mate who will split the cost of the room with you and be around as little, or as often, as you like during the day. Travel Buddies Singles Travel Club (© 800/998-9099; www.travelbuddiesworldwide.com), based in Canada, runs small, intimate, single-friendly group trips and will match you with a roommate free of charge and save you the cost of single supplements. TravelChums (© 212/787-2621; www.travelchums.com) is an Internet-only travel-companion matching service with elements of an online personals-type site, hosted by the respected New York–based Shaw Guides travel service. The Single

## Frommers.com: The Complete Travel Resource

For an excellent travel-planning resource, we highly recommend Frommers.com (www.frommers.com). We're a little biased, of course, but we guarantee that you'll find the travel tips, reviews, monthly vacation giveaways, and online-booking capabilities indispensable. Among the special features are our popular **Message Boards**, where Frommer's readers post queries and share advice (sometimes we authors even show up to answer questions); **Frommers.com Newsletter**, for the latest travel bargains and insider travel secrets; and **Frommer's Destinations Section**, where you'll get expert travel tips, hotel and dining recommendations, and advice on the sights to see for more than 3,000 destinations around the globe. When your research is done, the **Online Reservations System** (www.frommers.com/book_a_trip) takes you to Frommer's preferred online partners for booking your vacation at affordable prices.

**Gourmet Club** (© 617/497-0444; www.singlegourmet.com/chapters.html) is an international social, dining, and travel club for singles of all ages, with offices in a dozen cities in the U.S. and Canada. Membership costs $375 for the first year; $175 to renew. Many reputable tour companies offer singles-only trips. **Singles Travel International** (© 877/765-6874; www.singlestravelintl.com) offers singles-only trips to places like London, Fiji and the Greek Islands.

For more information, check out Eleanor Berman's *Traveling Solo: Advice and Ideas for More Than 250 Great Vacations* (Globe Pequot), a guide with advice on traveling alone, whether on your own or on a group tour. Or turn to the **Travel Alone and Love It** website (www.travelaloneandloveit.com), designed by former flight attendant Sharon Wingler, the author of the book of the same name. Her site is full of tips for single travelers.

## 9 Getting There

### BY PLANE

The vast majority of travelers reach Greece by plane and most of them arrive at the new Athens airport—officially the Eleftherios Venizelos International Airport, and sometimes referred to by its new location, the Spata airport.

#### FROM NORTH AMERICA

**UNITED STATES** At press time, only two regularly scheduled airlines offer direct, nonstop flights from the States to Athens—Olympic and Delta. Some travelers find the planes a bit shabby, the personnel inattentive, and the occasional delays aggravating, but **Olympic Airways** (© 800/223-1226; www.olympic-airways.gr) has long offered nonstop service daily from New York, twice weekly from Boston, and twice weekly from Chicago via New York. **Delta Air Lines** (© 800/241-4141; www.delta.com) offers satisfactory service from throughout the United States, with all flights connecting to their nonstop Athens flights at JFK in New York (and in Atlanta during the summer).

All the other airlines make stops at some major European airport, where they usually require a change of planes. **Alitalia** (☏ 800/223-5730; www.alitalia.com) offers flights from JFK that go to Greece via Rome. **British Airways** (☏ 800/247-9297; www.british-airways.com) has service to Athens from a number of major U.S. cities, all stopping in London (most at Heathrow, but some at Gatwick). **Lufthansa** (☏ 800/645-3880; www.lufthansa.com) provides superior service to Athens, Thessaloniki, and Crete from 10 U.S. cities, via Frankfurt. **Northwest/KLM Royal Dutch Airlines** (☏ 800/374-7747; www.klm.nl) has superior service from 10 major cities in the United States to Athens, with all flights stopping in Amsterdam. **Swissair International Airlines** (☏ 877/359-7947; www.swissair.com) offers excellent service from Boston as well as New York, with all flights connecting to Athens at Zurich. **Virgin Atlantic Airways** (☏ 800/862-8621; www.virgin-atlantic.com) offers flights via London, with daily flights from Los Angeles and the New York area, and less frequent service from several other cities.

**CANADA** In addition to the various airlines flying out of the United States, Canadians have a number of other choices. **Olympic Airways** (☏ 800/223-1226; www.olympicairways.gr) offers the only direct flights from Canada to Athens—two flights a week from Montreal and Toronto. **Air Canada** (☏ 888/247-2262; www.aircanada.ca) flies from Calgary, Montreal, Toronto, and Vancouver to various airports in Europe, with connections on Olympic to Athens. **Air France** (☏ 800/237-2747; www.airfrance.com), **British Airways** (☏ 800/247-9297; www.british-airways.com), **CSA Czech Airlines** (☏ 800/223-2365; www.csa.cz), **Iberia** (☏ 800/772-4642; www.iberia.com), **KLM Royal Dutch Airlines** (☏ 800/361-5073; www.klm.nl), **Lufthansa** (☏ 800/645-3880; www.lufthansa.com), **Swissair** (☏ 877/359-7947; www.swissair.com), and **TAP Air Portugal** (☏ 800/221-7370; www.tap-airportugal.pt) all have at least one flight per week from Calgary, Montreal, Toronto, or Vancouver via other European cities to Athens.

## FROM EUROPE

**IRELAND** Aer Lingus (☏ 01/844-4777 in Dublin; www.aerlingus.ie) and **British Airways** (☏ 0345/222-111 in Belfast; www.british-airways.com) both fly to Athens via London's Heathrow. Less-expensive charters operate in the summer from Belfast and Dublin to Athens, less frequently to Corfu, Crete, Mykonos, and Rhodes. Contact any major travel agency for details. Students should contact USIT, at Aston Quay, O'Connell Bridge, Dublin 2 (☏ 01/679-8833), or at Fountain Centre, College Street, Belfast (☏ 1232/324-073).

**UNITED KINGDOM** British Airways (☏ 0845/773-3377; www.ba.com), **Olympic Airways** (☏ 0870/606-0460), and **Virgin Atlantic** (☏ 01293/450-150; www.virgin-atlantic.com) have several flights daily from London's Heathrow Airport. For the smaller companies that offer no-frill flights, contact **EasyJet** (☏ 0870/600-0000; www.easyjet.com). Or consider the US$99 "pass" sold by **Europebyair** (in North America, ☏ 888/387-2749; www.europebyair.com), which allows flights all over Europe. Several of the Eastern European airlines, such as **CSA Czech Airlines** (☏ 0870/4443-747; www.czechairlines.co.uk, have offered cheaper alternatives, but in recent years the status of some has been in doubt; make inquiries at the time you are prepared to book. There are also connecting flights to Athens and to Thessaloniki with various airlines from Aberdeen, Belfast, Birmingham, Bristol, Edinburgh, Glasgow, Leeds, Liverpool, Newcastle, and Southampton; as well as flights to Athens and the major islands from Birmingham, Cardiff, Gatwick, Glasgow, Luton, and Manchester.

## FROM AUSTRALIA & NEW ZEALAND

**AUSTRALIA**  Service to Athens is offered daily from Perth and Sydney and several times weekly from Brisbane and Melbourne by **Alitalia** (© 02/247-1308 in Sydney; www.alitalia.com), via Bangkok and Rome; **KLM Royal Dutch Airlines** (© 800/505-747 throughout Australia; www.klm.nl), via Singapore and Amsterdam; **Lufthansa** (© 02/367-3800 in Sydney; www.lufthansa.com), via Frankfurt; and **Olympic Airways** (© 02/251-2204 in Sydney; www.olympic-airways.gr), via Bangkok.

Generally, the lowest fares are offered by **Aeroflot** (© 02/233-7148 in Sydney; www.aeroflot.org), which provides weekly service from Sydney via Moscow; and by **Thai Airways** (© 02/844-0900 in Sydney; www.thaiair.com), which flies from Brisbane, Melbourne, Perth, and Sydney to Greece, via Bangkok. **British Airways** (© 02/258-3000 in Sydney; www.british-airways.com) and **Qantas Airways** (© 02/957-0111 in Sydney; www.qantas.com) have regular service to London; the "Global Explorer Pass" allows you to make up to six stopovers wherever the two airlines fly, except to South America.

**NEW ZEALAND**  The cheapest fares at press time were offered by **Singapore Airlines** (© 09/303-2506 in Auckland; www.singaporeair.com) with service via Singapore, and **Thai Airways** (© 09/377-3886 in Auckland; www.thaiair.com), with service via Bangkok. **Air New Zealand** (© 09/309-6171 in Auckland; www.airnz.co.nz) and **Qantas Airways**

(© 09/303-3209 in Auckland; www.qantas.com) offer connections through **Lufthansa** (© 09/303-1529 in Auckland) to Athens. **British Airways** (© 09/367-7500 in Auckland; www.british-airways.com) and **Qantas** can get you to Europe; ask about the "Global Explorer Pass," with up to six stopovers. **Alitalia** (© 09/379-4457; www.alitalia.com) also flies to Athens, via Rome.

## FROM SOUTH AFRICA

**Olympic Airways** (© 11/880-1614; www.olympic-airways.gr) offers the only direct flights from Johannesburg to Athens—about three times a week, each way. **Air France** (© 01/880-8040; www.airfrance.com), **Alitalia** (© 01/880-9254; www.alitalia.com), **British Airways** (© 01/975-3931; www.british-airways.com), and **Ethiopian Airlines** (© 01/616-7624; www.ethiopianairlines.com) also offer occasional flights to and from Johannesburg, with connections via other foreign cities.

## GETTING THROUGH THE AIRPORT

Citizens of the USA, UK and other nations should be well briefed on their own nation's security policies and practices before setting out for Greece. Along with almost all countries, Greece has upgraded its security at airports but it is relatively uncomplicated compared to security at U.S. airports. Still, you should plan to arrive at the airport at least **1 hour** before a domestic flight and at least **2 hours** before an international flight; if you show up late, tell an airline employee and she'll probably whisk you to the front of the line.

As a foreign traveler in Greece you will have a passport but just in case you might also want to bring a **current, government-issued photo ID** such as a driver's license. If you've got an e-ticket, print out the **official**

## Tips  Don't Stow It—Ship It

If ease of travel is your main concern and money is no object, you can ship your luggage with one of the growing number of luggage-service companies that pick up, track, and deliver your luggage (often through couriers such as Federal Express) with minimum hassle for you. Traveling luggage-free may be ultra-convenient, but it's not cheap: One-way overnight shipping can cost from $100 to $200, depending on what you're sending. Still, for some people, especially the elderly or the infirm, it's a sensible solution to lugging heavy baggage. Specialists in door-to-door luggage delivery are **Virtual Bellhop** (www.virtualbellhop.com), **SkyCap International** (www.skycapinternational.com), and **Luggage Express** (www.usxpluggageexpress.com).

**confirmation page;** you'll need to show your confirmation at the security checkpoint, and your ID at the ticket counter or the gate. (Non-EU children need passports even for domestic flights.)

Speed up security by **not wearing metal objects** such as big belt buckles or clunky earrings. If you've got metallic body parts, a note from your doctor can prevent a long chat with the security screeners. Keep in mind that only **ticketed passengers** are allowed past security, except for folks escorting disabled passengers or children.

The new security regulations have stabilized **what you can carry on** and **what you can't.** The general rule is that sharp objects are out, nail clippers are okay. Bring food in your carry-on rather than checking it, as explosive-detection machines used on checked luggage have been known to mistake food (especially chocolate, for some reason) for bombs. Travelers in Greece are allowed one carry-on bag, plus a "personal item" such as a purse, briefcase, or laptop bag. Carry-on hoarders can stuff all sorts of things into a laptop bag; as long as it has a laptop in it, it's still considered a personal item. In general, though, Greek domestic flights have lower limits on the weight of free luggage allowed so you might on occasion be expected to pay a

surcharge if you are checking in unusual quantities.

At press time, in the U.S. the TSA is also recommending that you **not lock your checked luggage** so screeners can search it by hand if necessary. The agency says to use plastic "zip ties" instead, which can be bought at hardware stores and can be easily cut off.

## GETTING THERE BY SHIP

Most people who travel by ship to Greece from foreign ports come from Italy, although there is occasional service from Cyprus, Egypt, Israel, and Turkey. Brindisi to Patras is the most common ferry crossing, about a 10-hour voyage, with as many as seven departures a day in summer. There is also regular service, twice a day in summer, from Ancona and Bari, once daily from Otranto, and two or three times a week from Trieste or Venice. Most ferries stop at Corfu or Igoumenitsou, often at both; in summer, occasionally a ship will also stop at Kefalonia.

If you want to learn more about the various ferry services between Greece and foreign ports, try the London-based agency **Viamare Travel,** Graphic House, 2 Sumatra Rd., London NW6 1PU (© **0870/4160-040;** www.viamare.com; ferries@viamare.com). There is also the new **Superfast Ferries Line,** Leoforos Alkyonidon

157, 16673 Athens (© 210/969-1100; www.superfast.com), which offers service between Ancona and Patras (17 hr.) or Ancona and Igoumenitsa (15 hr.); also between Bari and Patras (12 hr.) or Bari and Igoumenitsa (8 hr.). Not all these so-called superfast ferries actually save that much time if you take into consideration the time required to board and disembark from any ship, and they cost almost twice as much as regular ferries.

On the regular ferries, one-way fares during high season from Brindisi to Patras at press time cost from about 50€ for a tourist-class deck chair to about 150€ for an inside double cabin. Vehicles cost at least another 75 to 150€. (*Note:* The lines usually offer considerable discounts on round-trip/return tickets.) Fares to Igoumenitsou are considerably cheaper, but by no means a better value unless your destination is nearby. Because of the number of shipping lines involved and the variations in schedules, we're not able to provide more concrete details. Consult a travel agent about the possibilities, book well ahead of time in summer, and reconfirm with the shipping line on the day of departure.

## GETTING THERE BY CAR

It is unlikely that anyone would find it worth while to bring their own car all the way from North America just to drive around Greece, but many Europeans do drive down into Greece—and perhaps some North Americans bring their rented cars in. Many of these drivers would be coming from Italy via ferry, usually disembarking at Patras, from which the drive to Athens is some 209km (130 miles). Others would almost certainly be entering from the Former Yugoslavian Republic of Macedonia (FYROM). (The road from Albania, although passable, is probably not going to attract many.) There are no particular problems or delays at the border crossings providing all papers are in order.

Assuming you were coming through Skopje, FYROM, the road via Titov Veles to the southeast leads to the border where it picks up an expressway down to the edge of Thessaloniki (242km/150 miles). Over to the west, there is a decent enough road via Vitola, FYROM, that leads to Florina, Greece, (290km/180 miles) and then east to Thessaloniki (another 161km/100 miles) or south to Kosani (another 89km/55 miles). Any of those would be a long day's drive!

In any case, arm yourself with a good up-to-date map such as the ones published by Baedeker, Hallwag, Michelin, or Freytag & Berndt.

## DRIVING YOUR OWN VEHICLE

To bring your own vehicle into Greece, valid registration papers, an

## Street Names

The Greek word for "street" is *odos* and the word for "avenue" is *leoforos*, often abbreviated *Leof.*, usually applied to major thoroughfares. In practice, Greeks seldom employ either of those words—they just use the name. Also, Greeks customarily write the numbers after rather than before the street name. But in the interest of simplifying things, we provide the numbers before the names and drop the word "Odos" (as Greeks do). *Leoforos*, however, we retain as an indication of a major throughfare. By the way, *plateia*—think "place" or "plaza"—is Greek for square, and usually means a large public square, such as Syntagma (Constitution) Square in Athens, although sometimes a *plateia* may be little more than a wide area where important streets meet.

international third-party insurance certificate, and a driver's license are required. Valid American and EU licenses are accepted in Greece. A free entry card allows you to keep your car in the country up to 4 months, after which another 8 months can be arranged without having to pay import duty. Check with your own car insurance company to make sure you are fully covered.

**CAR FERRIES** Car ferry service is available on most larger ferries, and there's regular service from Piraeus to Aegina and Poros in the Saronic Gulf, most of the Cyclades, Chania and Iraklion on Crete, Hios, Kos, Lesvos, Rhodes, and Samos. For the Cyclades, crossing is shorter and less expensive from Rafina, an hour east of Athens. From Patras, there's daily service to Corfu, Ithaka, and Kefalonia. In the summer, there are four car ferries daily from Kyllini to Zakinthos. The Sporades have service from Ayios Konstandinos, Kimi, and Volos (and then among the several islands). The short car ferry across the Gulf of Corinth from Rio to Antirio can save a lot of driving for those traveling between the

northwest and the Peloponnese or Athens. There's also service between many of the islands, even between Crete and Rhodes, as well as car crossing to and from Turkey between Hios and Çesme, Lesvos and Dikeli, and Samos and Kusadasi. (If you intend to continue on with your vehicle into either country coming from the other, you better inquire long before setting off for either country and make sure that you have all the necessary paperwork.)

## GETTING THERE BY TRAIN

In the late 1990s, train service from Western Europe was disrupted by the trouble in the Balkans. Even when running, the trains tend to be slow, and uncomfortable in the summer. But a Eurail Pass is valid for connections all the way to Athens or Istanbul and includes the ferry service from Italy. There are endless types of passes now offered—long stays, short stays, combinations with airlines etc. Note that North Americans must purchase their Eurail Passes before arriving in Europe. For information, see **www.raileurope.com**, or in the U.S. call ② **800/438-7245.**

## 10 Escorted General-Interest Tours

Escorted tours are structured group tours, with a group leader. The price usually includes everything from airfare to hotels, meals, tours, admission costs, and local transportation. Two of the major organizers of such tours in Greece are **Homeric Tours** (② **800/223-5570;** www.homerictours.com) and **Tourlite International** (② **800/272-7600,** www.tourlite.com). All fall into the "moderate" category in terms of pricing and accommodations, and both carry the risk of all such charter flights—that is, delays. Both offer some variety—often these tours simply provide local guides and often they include short cruises as part of the entire stay.

Many people derive a certain ease and security from escorted trips. Escorted tours—whether by bus, motor coach, train, or boat—let travelers sit back and enjoy their trip without having to spend lots of time behind the wheel. All the little details are taken care of; you know your costs up front; and there are few surprises. Escorted tours can take you to the maximum number of sights in the minimum amount of time with the least amount of hassle—you don't have to sweat over the plotting and planning of a vacation schedule. Escorted tours are particularly convenient for people with limited mobility.

On the downside, an escorted tour often requires a big deposit up front, and lodging and dining choices are predetermined. As part of a cloud of tourists, you'll get little opportunity for serendipitous interactions with locals. The tours can be jam-packed with activities, leaving little room for individual sightseeing, whim, or adventure—plus they also often focus only on the heavily touristed sites, so you miss out on the lesser-known gems.

Before you invest in an escorted tour, ask about the **cancellation policy:** Is a deposit required? Can they cancel the trip if they don't get enough people? Do you get a refund if they cancel? If *you* cancel? How late can you cancel if you are unable to go? When do you pay in full? *Note:* If you choose an escorted tour, think strongly about purchasing trip-cancellation insurance, especially if the tour operator asks you to pay up front. See the section on "Travel Insurance," earlier in this chapter.

You'll also want to get a complete **schedule** of the trip to find out how much sightseeing is planned each day and whether enough time has been allotted for relaxing or wandering solo. The **size** of the group is also important to know up front. Generally, the smaller the group, the more flexible the itinerary, and the less time you'll spend waiting for people to get on and off the bus. Find out the **demographics of the group** as well. What is the age range? What is the gender breakdown? Is this mostly a trip for couples or singles?

Discuss what is included in the **price**. You may have to pay for transportation to and from the airport. A box lunch may be included in an excursion, but drinks might cost extra. Tips may not be included. Find out if you will be charged if you decide to opt out of certain activities or meals.

Before you invest in a package tour, get some answers. Ask about the **accommodation choices** and prices for each. Then look up the hotels' reviews in a Frommer's guide and check their rates for your specific dates of travel online. You'll also want to find out what **type of room** you get. If you need a certain type of room, ask for it; don't take whatever is thrown your way. Request a nonsmoking room, a quiet room, a room with a view, or whatever you fancy.

Finally, if you plan to travel alone, you'll need to know if a **single supplement** will be charged and if the company can match you up with a roommate.

## 11 Special-Interest Trips

### ACTIVE TRAVELERS

Increasing numbers of travelers of all ages are seeking more active ways to experience Greece. This is to be encouraged, but we advise everyone to investigate closely just what is involved—the level of difficulty, that is.

**BICYCLING** Increasing numbers of foreigners are choosing to travel in Greece by bicycle, and those interested in the possibility can get more information from the **Greek Cycling Federation**, the National Velodrome, Marousi (ⓒ **210/689-3403**).

**Trekking Hellas**, 7 Filellinon, 10557 Athens (ⓒ **210/331-0323;** fax 210/323-4548; www.trekking.gr), can also assist you in arranging mountain-biking trips. But Greece is not the place to start learning how to tour on a bicycle; Greek drivers have little experience in accommodating bicyclists, road shoulders in Greece are often nonexistent and even at best are not generous, and roads are not especially well maintained.

In the United States, **Classic Adventures**, Box 143, Hamlin, NY 14464 (ⓒ **800/777-8090;** www.classicadventures.com) has been around since 1979 and has a fine reputation for its bicycle tours, such as a 11-day excursion that follows the coast and includes Corinth, Epidaurus, Mycenae, Olympia, and the island of Zakinthos, or a 12-day tour of Crete.

**Mountain bikes** are better suited for Greek terrain, and you can even bring your own along by train (for a small fee) or plane (free, though not easy). You can take them along on Greek ferries and trains usually at no extra cost. You should also bring along spare parts, as they are rarely available outside the major cities.

If you insist on trying a bicycle in Greece, you can rent an old bike for very little in most major resorts, and good mountain bikes are increasingly available. On Crete, mountain bikes are available for rent in Iraklion at **Creta Travel Bureau,** 20–22 Epimenidou (© **2810/227-002**), which also has offices in Rethymnon and Ayios Nikolaos. In Chania, try **Athanasakis Tours,** 25 Halidon (© **28210/24-965**). On Paros, the **Mountain Bike Club,** near the post office in Parikia (© and fax **22840/23-778**), rents good mountain bikes. On Rhodes, they are available at **Mike's Motor Club,** 23 Kazouli (© **22410/37-420**). Kos is also well suited to cycling, and bicycles are widely available for rent there.

**CAMPING**  Greece offers a wide variety of camping facilities throughout the country. Rough or freelance camping—setting up your camp on some apparently unoccupied land—is forbidden by law but may be overlooked by some local authorities. The **Greek National Tourism Organization** should have further information on its many licensed facilities, as well as a very informative booklet, *Camping in Greece,* published by the **Greek Camping Association,** 102 Solonos, 10680 Athens (© **210/362-1560;** fax 210/346-5262).

**DIVING**  Scuba diving is currently restricted throughout most of Greece because of potential harm to sunken antiquities and the environment. That said, there are now many locales where diving is allowed under supervision by accredited "schools." On the mainland, these may be found along the coast of Attica, off the Peloponnese peninsula, and off Halkidiki and a few other places in the north. There is also limited diving off the islands of Corfu, Crete, Hydra, Kalimnos, Kefalonia, Mykonos, Paros, Rhodes, Santorini, Skiathos, and Zakinthos.

Just to single out a few at the more popular locales, on Corfu there is **Calypso Scuba Divers,** Ayios Gordis (© **26610/53-101;** fax 26610/34-319); on Rhodes, the **Dive Med Center,** 5 Dragoumi Rhodes town (© **22410/33-654**); on Crete, the **Paradise Dive Center,** 51 Giamboudaki, Rethymnon (© and fax **28310/53-258**); and on Mykonos, **Lucky Scuba Divers,** Ornos Beach (© **22890/22-813;** fax 22890/23-764). Even if you are qualified, you must dive under supervision. And above all, you are forbidden to even photograph, let alone remove, anything that might possibly be regarded as an antiquity.

For more information, contact the **Organization of Underwater Activities** (© **210/982-3840**) or the **Union of Greek Diving Centers** (© **220/922-9532**). If you're a serious underwater explorer, contact the **Department of Underwater Archaeology,** 4 Al Soutsou, 10671 Athens (© **210/360-3662**).

**Snorkeling,** however, is permitted, and the unusually clear water makes it a special pleasure. Simple equipment is widely available for rent or sale.

**FISHING**  Opportunities for fishing abound. Contact the **Amateur Anglers and Maritime Sports Club,** Akti Moutsopoulou, 18537 Piraeus (© **210/451-5731**).

**GOLF**  There are relatively few golf courses in Greece, although several more are in the planning stages. Those now in existence are in Glifada (along the coast outside of Athens), Halkidiki, Corfu, Crete (Elounda), and Rhodes. Any travel agent can supply the details.

**HIKING** Greece offers endless opportunities for hiking, trekking, and walking. Greeks themselves are now showing interest in walking for pleasure, and there are a number of well-mapped and even signed routes.

Probably the best and most up-to-date source for information on nature-oriented tours or groups are the ads in magazines geared toward people with these interests—*Audubon Magazine*, for instance, for birders. But it is important to realize that one need not sign up for special (and expensive) tours to enjoy the wildlife of Greece. Bring your own binoculars, and buy one of the many illustrated handbooks such as *Wildflowers of Greece*, by George Sfikas (Efstathiadis Books, Athens), or *Birds of Europe*, by Bertel Brun (McGraw-Hill).

In Greece, we recommend **Trekking Hellas,** in Athens at 7 Filellinon 7 (© **210/331-0323;** fax 210/323-4548), and in Thessaloniki at 71 Tsimiski (© **2310/222-128;** fax 2310/222-129), for both guided tours and help in planning your own private trek. Other Greek travel agencies specializing in nature tours include: **Adrenaline Team,** 2 Kornarou and 28 Hermou, 10563 Athens (© **210/331-1777;** fax 210/331-1778); **Athenogenes,** Plateia Kolonaki 18, 10673 Athens (© **210/361-4829);** and **Ey-Zhn,** Leoforos Syngrou 132, 17671 Athens (© **210/921-6285).** In the Sporades, try **Ikos Travel,** Patitiri, 37005 Alonissos (© **24240/65-320).** In the United States, the **Appalachian Mountain Club,** 5 Joy St, Boston, MA 02108 (© **617/523-0636;** www.outdoors.com), often organizes hiking tours in Greece.

**Classic Adventures,** Box 143, Hamlin, NY 14464 (© **800/777-8090;** www.classicadventures.com), offers hiking tours of Crete and the Zagori region of Epirus. **Mountain Travel-Sobek,** 6420 Fairmount Ave., El Cerrito, CA 94530 (© **800/227-2384;** www.mtsobek.com), sometimes conducts summer hikes and kayaking trips in the Greek mountains. **Country Walkers,** P.O. Box 180, Waterbury VT 05676 (© **800/464-9255;** www.countrywalkers.com), is another company that conducts occasional walking tours through regions of Greece.

Birders and nature lovers should contact the **Hellenic Ornithological Society,** Vassiliou Irakleiou 24, 10682 Athens (© **210/822-7937). Questers Worldwide Nature Tours,** 381 Park Ave. S., Suite 1201, New York, NY 10016 (© **800/468-8668;** www.questers.com), sometimes offers nature tours in Greece. Also specializing in walking tours is **Alternative Travel Group,** 69–71 Banbury Rd., Oxford, OX2 6PE England (© **44/1865-315678,** or 800/527-5997 in the U.S.).

**HORSEBACK RIDING** There are a fair number of opportunities for horseback riding in Greece. Near Athens you'll find the **Athletic Riding Club** of Ekali (© **210/813-5576),** the **Hellenic Riding Club** in Maroussi (© **210/682-6128),** and the **Riding Club of Parnitha** (© **210/240-2413);** call for directions and reservations. Good facilities are also located near Thessaloniki and on the islands of Corfu, Crete, Rhodes, and Skiathos, with smaller stables elsewhere (inquire at local travel agencies).

In the United States, **Equitour,** Box 807, Dubois, WY 82513 (© **800/545-0019** or 307/455-3363), offers an 8-day riding tour of the beautiful Mount Pelion coast.

**MOUNTAINEERING** Those interested in more strenuous trekking and mountain climbing should contact the **Hellenic Federation of Mountaineering & Climbing,** 5 Milloni, 10673 Athens (© 210/364-5904; fax 210/364-4687).

**SKIING** There are a number of attractive skiing centers in Greece. They can't compare to those further north in deep snow and posh facilities, but they don't approach them in steep prices either, and there is much charm in their little hotels and lively après-ski life. The season generally begins after Christmas and continues until the end of April, depending on the weather.

The best developed is the **Parnassos Ski Center,** near Arachova, on Mount Parnassus (© 22340/22-694; fax 22340/22-596), with 20 runs, chairlifts, tow bars, classes, equipment rental, snack bars and restaurants, and even child care. There is also skiing on the gentler slopes of Mount Pelion and at charming Metsovo, in Epirus northeast of Ioannina, where the season is somewhat shorter. Other centers are found on the Peloponnese at Helmos, near Kalavrita; in central Greece at Velouhi, near Karpenissi; and in Macedonia, at Pisoderi, near Florina, and Vermion, near Naoussa. For more information, contact the **Greek Skiers Organization,** P.O. Box 8037, Athens 10010 (© 210/524-0057; fax 210/524-8821).

**SPELUNKING** If you don't know what the word refers to, then you won't be wanting to do it. It refers to cave exploring, and there are numerous caves in Greece and numerous individuals who are skilled in exploring them. For details, contact the **Hellenic Speleological Society,** Sina Cave 32, Athens (© 210/361-7824).

**WATERSPORTS** Watersports of various kinds are available at most major resort areas, and we mention the more important facilities in the relevant chapters that follow. Parasailing is possible at the larger resorts in summer. Although some of these facilities are limited to patrons of the hotels and resorts, in many places they are available to anyone willing to pay.

River rafting and kayaking are definite possibilities, especially in Epirus, with more limited opportunities on the Peloponnese peninsula. Contact the **Alpine Club,** Plateia Kapnikarea 2, 11743 Athens (© 210/321-2355). One quite special opportunity is the kayaking trip occasionally conducted by the American agency **Mountain Travel-Sobek,** 6420 Fairmount Ave., El Cerrito, CA 94530 (© 800/227-2384 or 510/527-8105).

Waterskiing facilities are widely available; there are several schools at Vouliagmeni, south of Athens, and usually at least one on each of the major islands. Contact the **Hellenic Water-Ski Federation,** Leoforos Poseidonos, 16777 Glyfada (© 210/894-7413).

Windsurfing has become increasingly popular in Greece, and boards are widely available for rent. The many coves and small bays along Greece's convoluted coastline are ideal for beginners, and instruction is usually available at reasonable prices. The best conditions and facilities are found on the islands of Corfu, Crete, Lefkada, Lesvos, Naxos, Paros, Samos, and Zakinthos. There are a number of excellent schools. Contact the **Hellenic Wind-Surfing Association,** 7 Filellinon, 10557 Athens (© 210/323-0068), for details.

## EXTENDING THE MIND

**ARCHAEOLOGICAL DIGS** The **American School of Classical Studies at Athens,** 6–8 Chariton St., Princeton, NJ 08540 (© 609/683-0800; www.ascsa.org), often sponsors tours in Greece and adjacent Mediterranean lands guided by archaeologists and historians. **Archaeological Tours,**

271 Madison Avenue, Suite 904, New York, NY 10016 (© **212/986-3054;** www.archaeologicaltrs.com), offers tours led by expert guides; typical tours might be to classical Greek sites or to Cyprus/Crete/Santorini. **Free-Gate Tourism,** 585 Stewart Ave., Suite 310, Garden City, NY 11530 (© **800/223-0304;** www.freegate tours.com), also specializes in guided trips in Greece.

**ART International Study Tours,** 120 Sylvan Ave., Englewood Cliffs NJ 07632 (© **800/833-2111**) offers studies in the architecture, art, and culture of Greece, led by professionals. Especially attractive are the **Aegean Workshops** run by Harry Danos, a Greek-American architect and water-colorist; in the spring and autumn, he leads groups to various regions of Greece, where he provides instruction in drawing and watercolors (and also ends up teaching some of the language). To learn more, call (© **860/739-0378** from mid-May through October, or © **239/455-2623** from November to mid-May.

The **Athens Center for the Creative Arts,** 48 Archimidou, Pangrati, 11636 Athens (© **210/701-2268**), offers summer programs. The **Hellas Art Club** on the island of Hydra, at the Leto Hotel, 18040 Hydra (© **22980/53-385;** fax 210/361-2223 in Athens), offers classes in painting, ceramics, music, theater,

photography, Greek dancing, and cooking.

**MODERN GREEK** There are numerous courses offered at both formal educational institutions and private language institutes throughout the English-speaking world; there are also several quite decent courses on tape for self-study. Just be sure that it is modern Greek that you want to study—and not classical Greek! If you are already in Greece, the **Athens Center for the Creative Arts,** 48 Archimidou, Pangrati, 11636 Athens (© **210/701-2268**), is highly recommended. The **School of Modern Greek Language of Aristotle University in Thessaloniki** also offers summer courses.

**PERSONAL GROWTH** The **Skyros Center,** which can be contacted in the United Kingdom at 92 Prince of Wales Rd., London NW5 3NE (© **020/7267-4424;** www.skyros. com), offers "personal growth" vacations on the island of Skyros, with courses in fitness, holistic health, creative writing, and handicrafts.

**COOKING** Rosemary Barron, an American food expert based in San Francisco, has for many years run a cooking school, Kandra Kitchen—usually on Crete or Santorini—in which participants learn how to prepare Greek foods. For more information, try her website, **www.rosemary barronsgreece.com.**

## 12 Getting Around Greece

### BY PLANE

Compared to the cheaper classes on ships and ferries, air travel within Greece can be expensive, but we recommend it for those pressed for time and/or heading for the more distant destinations (even if the planes don't always hold strictly to schedule). Until the late 1990s, **Olympic Airways** (© **210/966-6666;** www.olympic-airways.gr) maintained a monopoly

on domestic air travel and thus had little incentive to improve service; in fact, it effectively became bankrupt and was placed under new management, which has been steadily improving service. Better computerized booking has reduced the possibility of finding out at the last minute that you don't actually have a seat, but delayed flights are still common; although the quality of the service is criticized by some, Olympic actually has one of the best safety records of any major airline. (Their domestic flight attendants tend to be more pleasant than their international counterparts.) Book as far ahead of time as possible (especially in the summer), reconfirm your booking before leaving for the airport, and try to arrive at the airport at least an hour before departure; the scene at a check-in counter can become quite hectic.

Olympic Airways has a number of offices in Athens, though most travel agents sell tickets as well. It offers service on the **mainland** to Akraion Preveza, Alexandroupolis, Ioannina, Kalamata, Kavala, Kastoria, Kozani, and Thessaloniki; and for **islands**, to Astipalea, Corfu (Kerkira), Crete (Iraklion, Chania, Sitia), Chios, Ikaria, Karpathos, Kassos, Kastellorizo, Kefalonia, Kos, Kithira, Leros, Limnos, Milos, Mykonos, Mitilini (Lesvos), Naxos, Paros, Rhodes, Samos, Santorini (Thira), Skiathos, Skyros, Siros, Sitia, and Zakinthos. All of Olympic's domestic flights leave from the new international airport at Spata. Most flights are to or from Athens, though there is some interisland service. The baggage allowance is 15 kilos (33 lb.) per passenger, except with a connecting international flight; even the domestic flights generally ignore the weight limit unless you are way over. Smoking is prohibited on all domestic flights.

Round-trip tickets cost simply double the one-way fare. Some sample one-way fares (including taxes) at this writing are: Athens to Corfu, Rhodes, Thessaloniki, 135€; Athens to Iraklion, Chania, 115€; Athens to Ioannina, Santorini, 110€; Athens to Mykonos, Samos, 100€; Athens to Skiathos, Syros, 92€. As you can see, the shorter trips, such as to Mykonos or Santorini, are not especially cheap, but there's no denying that for those with limited time, air travel is the best way to go. Ask about Olympic's new offer of reduced fares for trips between Monday and Thursday and trips that include a Saturday-night stay.

In recent years, however, a major competitor with Olympic has the emerged in Greece, **Aegean Airlines** (©210/998-8300, www.aegeanair.com). Although it only flies to fourteen cities in Greece (Athens, Thessaloniki, Heraklion, Chania, Rhodes, Kos, Chios, Myrilini, Mykonos, Santorini, Kavala, Alexandroupolis, Corfu, Ioannina) and to Rome, Milan, Frankfurt, Munich, Stuttgart, Dusseldorf, and Larnaca, Cyprus, Aegean's domestic service covers the destinations most popular with tourists. All of Aegean's planes are jets and passengers describe them as generally more comfortable than many of Olympic's older planes; Aegean also offers more in-flight amenities (drinks, hand wipers) on more of its flights; generally, too, Aegean personnel seem more "upbeat" than Olympic's. Now that Aegean offers electronic ticketing on its website, as well as English-speaking clerks on its reservations phoneline (above), those planning to fly to within Greece should definitely consider Aegean's service; travel agencies everywhere should now also be able to book flights on Aegean. As neither Aegean nor Olympic offer discounts for roundtrips, a combination of the two airlines flights may well offer the most convenient arrangements.

*Note:* Most of these Greek domestic tickets are nonrefundable, and changing your flight can cost you up to 30% within 24 hours of departure and 50% within 12 hours.

## BY BOAT

**BY FERRY**  Ferries are the most common, cheapest, and generally the most "authentic" way to visit the islands, though the slow roll of a ferry can be authentically stomach-churning. A wide variety of vessels sail Greek waters—some huge, sleek, and new, with comfortable TV lounges, discos, and good restaurants; some old and illkept, but pleasant enough if you stay

## Greece by Plane

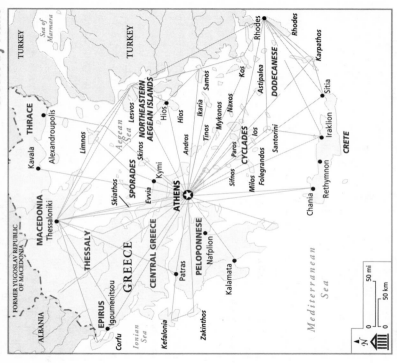

outside. Now, too, there are the "flying dolphins," or hydrofoils, that service all the major islands. These are undoubtedly faster, but they cost almost twice as much as regular ferries and their schedules are often interrupted by weather conditions. (Never rely on a tight connection between a hydrofoil and, say, an airplane flight.) Ferries, too, often don't hold exactly to their schedules, but they can be fun if you enjoy opportunities to meet people. Drinks and snacks are almost always sold, but the prices and selection are never that good, so you may want to bring along your own.

The map of Greece offered by the Greek Tourist Organization (EOT), which has the common routes indicated, is very useful in planning your sea travels. Once you've learned what is possible, you can turn your attention

to what is available. Remember that the summer schedule is the fullest, spring and fall have reduced service, and winter schedules are skeletal.

There are dozens of shipping companies, each with its own schedule—which, by the way, are regulated by the government. Your travel agent might have a copy of *Hellenic Travelling* (www.travelling.gr), a monthly travel guide published by GNTO, or another similar summary of schedules. *Greek Travel Pages* (www.gtp.gr). But it's best to go straight to an official information office, a travel agency, or the port authority as soon as you arrive at the place that you intend to leave via ferry.

Photos can give you some idea of the ships, but remember any photo displayed was probably taken when the ship was new, no matter when it was reproduced, and it is unlikely that anyone will be able (or willing) to tell you its actual age. The bigger ferries offer greater stability during rough weather. Except in the summer, you can usually depend on getting aboard a ferry by showing up about an hour before scheduled departure—inter-island boats sometimes depart before their scheduled time—and purchasing a ticket from a dockside agent or aboard the ship itself, though this is often more expensive.

Your best bet is to buy a ticket from an agent ahead of time. In Athens, we recommend **Galaxy Travel** (F **210/322-5960;** www.galaxytravel.gr), near Syntagma Square. **Alkyon Travel,** 97 Akademias, near Kanigos Square (F **210/383-2545;** fax 210/383-0394). During the high season, both keep long hours from Monday through Saturday. **But be aware:** Different travel agencies sell tickets to different lines—this is usually the policy of the line itself—and one agent might not know or bother to find out what else is being offered (although we believe that if you press reputable agencies like those above, they will at least tell you of the other possibilities). The port authority is the most reliable source of information, and the shipping company itself or its agents usually offer better prices and may have tickets when other agents have exhausted their allotment. It often pays to shop around a little to compare vessels and prices.

First class usually has roomy air-conditioned cabins and its own lounge and on some routes costs almost as much as flying; but consider that on longer overnight hauls, you're essen-tially on a comfortable floating hotel and thus save that cost. Second class has smaller cabins (which you will probably have to share with strangers) and its own lounge. The tourist-class fare entitles you to a seat on the deck or in a lounge. (Tourists usually head for the deck, while the Greeks stay inside, watch TV, and smoke copi-ously.) Hold on to your ticket; crews usually conduct ticket-control sweeps.

**Note:** Those taking a ferry to Turkey from one of the Dodecanese islands must submit their passport and payment to an agent the day before departure.

We include more details on service and schedules in the relevant chapters that follow, as well as suggested travel agencies and sources of local informa-tion. But just to give some sense of the fares, here are examples for first-class travel from Piraeus at press time: to Crete (Iraklion), 80€; Kos, 110€; Mitilini (Lesvos), 80€; Mykonos, 60€; Naxos, 65€; Rhodes, 130€; Santorini, 65€. A small embarkation tax may also be added.

**BY HYDROFOIL** Hydrofoils (often referred to by the principal line's trade name, **Flying Dolphins,** or by Greeks as *to flying*) are nearly twice as fast as ferries, and have com-fortable airline-style seats. Their stops are much shorter, and they are less likely to cause seasickness. Although they cost nearly twice as much as fer-ries, are frequently fully booked in summer, can be quite bumpy during rough weather, and give little or no view of the passing scenery, they're the best choice for those with limited time, and everyone should try one of these sleek little craft at least once.

## Early-Season Ferries

In the early weeks of the tourist season, from April to early May, the boat services are altogether unpredictable. Boat schedules, at the best of times, are tentative—but during this time, they are wish lists, nothing more. Our best advice is to wait until you get to Greece, and then go to a major travel agency and ask for help.

# Greek Ferry Routes

There is presently regular hydrofoil service to nearly all the major islands, with new service appearing every year. Longer trips over open sea, such as between Santorini and Iraklion, Crete, may make them well worth the extra expense. (Smoking is prohibited, and actually less likely to be indulged in, possibly because the cabins seem so much like those of an aircraft.) The forward compartment offers better views but is also bumpy.

The Flying Dolphins are now operated by **Hellas Flying Dolphins**, Akti Kondyli & 2 Aitolikou, 18545 Piraeus (© **210/419-9100;** www.dolphins.gr). The service from Zea Marina in Piraeus to the Saronic Gulf islands and the Peloponnese is especially good. (The fare to Spetses is about 35€ as compared to about 18€ for tourist-class ferry service.) Flying Dolphin service in the Sporades is also recommended for its speed and regularity. There is also service from Rafina, on the east coast of Attika, to several of the Cyclades islands.

**BY SAILBOAT & YACHT** Increasing numbers of people are choosing to explore Greece by sailboat or yacht. Sailing and yachting require such specialized skills and equipment that it is unlikely that anyone wanting to undertake either of these activities in Greece will depend on a general guide such as this. But clearly there are numerous facilities and possibilities for both. Experienced sailors interested in renting a boat in Greece can contact the **Hellenic Professional**

Yacht Owners' Association, Zea Marina, 18536 Piraeus (℃ 210/452-6335). One possibility is to sign up for one of the flotillas—a group of around 12 or more sailboats that sail about as a group led by a boat crewed by experienced sailors; the largest of such organizations is **Sunsail**, 980 Awald Rd., Annapolis, MD 21403 (℃ 800/327-2276), but travel agencies should be able to put you in touch with one of these organizations.

At the other extreme, those who want to charter a yacht with anything from a basic skipper to a full crew should probably first contact the **Hellenic Professional Yacht Owners' Association** (listed above) or **Ghiolman Yachts**, 7 Filellinon, 10557 Athens (℃ 210/323-0330; fax 210/322-3251; www.ghiolman.com). If you feel competent to make your own arrangements, contact **Valef Yachts Ltd.**, P.O. Box 391, Ambler, PA 19002 (℃ 215/641-1624; www.valefyachts.com). In Greece, you can either contact one of these associations or a private agency such as **Alpha Yachting**, Leoforos Vasileos Yioryios 67, 16674 Glyfada (℃ 210/968-0486); **Aris Drivas Yachting**, 147 Neorion, Piraeus (℃ 210/411-3194); or **Thalassa Charter and Yacht Brokers**, 72 Grypari, Kallithea, Athens (℃ 210/956-6866).

## BY CAR

Driving in Greece is a bit of an adventure but it's the best way to see the country at your own pace. Greece has one of the highest accident rates in Europe, probably due somewhat to treacherous roads, mountain terrain, and poor maintenance of older cars as much as to reckless driving—although Greeks are certainly aggressive drivers. Athens is a particularly intimidating place to drive in at first, and parking spaces are practically nonexistent in the center of town. (Main routes in and out of cities are sometimes signed by white arrows on blue markers.) Several of the major cities are linked by modern expressways with tolls; Athens to Thessaloniki, for instance, is expected to go up to 30€. Accidents must be reported to the police for insurance claims.

The **Greek Automobile Touring Club (ELPA)**, 2 Mesoyion Athens (℃ 210/606-800), with offices in most cities, can help you with all matters relating to **your car, issue international driver's licenses, and provide maps and information** (℃ 174, 24 hr. daily). The emergency road service number is ℃ 104, and the service provided by the able ELPA mechanics is free for light repairs, but you should definitely give a generous tip.

Gasoline is very expensive: .90€ a liter, which works out to about $3.75 for an American gallon—but there is no shortage of gasoline stations in all cities and good-sized town and major touristic centers. But if you are setting off for an excursion into one of the more remote mountain areas or an isolated beach, yes, fill up on gas before setting out.

**CAR RENTALS** There is an abundance of rental cars, with considerable variation in prices. However, many cars have a standard shift; if you must have an automatic, you are strongly advised to make your reservation before leaving home and well in advance. Always ask if the quoted price includes insurance; many credit cards make the collision-damage waiver unnecessary, but you will find that most rental agencies simply include this in their rates. You can sometimes save by booking at home before you leave, and this is especially advisable in summer. When shopping around for a bargain, be sure to carry along and display a number of brochures from competitors.

Most companies require that the renter be at least 21 years old (25 for some models, and sometimes no older than 70 to 75: Inquire!); possess a valid Australian, Canadian, EU-nation, U.S., or international driver's license; and have a major credit card or be prepared to leave a large cash deposit.

The major rental companies in Athens are **Avis** (℃ **210/322-4951**), **Budget** (℃ **210/921-4771**), **Hertz** (℃ **210/922-0102**), and **National** (℃ **210/459-6381**), all with additional offices in major cities, at most airports, and on most islands. Smaller local companies usually have lower rates, but their vehicles are often older and not as well maintained. If you prefer to combine your car rental with your other travel arrangements, we recommend **Galaxy Travel**, 35 Voulis, near Syntagma Square (℃ **210/322-5960**; www.galaxytravel.gr). It's open Monday through Saturday during the tourist season.

Rental rates vary widely—definitely inquire around. In high season, the cheaper daily rates would be about 50€ for a compact and 125€ for a fullsize; weekly rates would be about 250€ for a compact and 450€ for a full size. In low season, rates are often negotiable when you are there in Greece. And be prepared to have about 18% in VAT taxes plus 2% in municipal taxes added to the quoted price! (There's often a surcharge for pickup and drop-off at airports.)

**Note:** You must have written permission from the car-rental agency to take your car on a ferry or into a foreign country.

**DRIVING RULES** You drive on the right in Greece, pass on the left, and yield right-of-way to vehicles approaching from the right except where otherwise posted. Greece has adopted international road signs, though many Greeks apparently haven't learned what they mean yet. The maximum speed limit is 100km per hour (65 mph) on open roads, and 50km per hour (30 mph) in town, unless otherwise posted. Seat belts are required. The police have become increasingly strict in recent years, especially with foreigners in rental cars; alcohol tests can be given and fines imposed on the spot. (If you feel you have been stopped or treated unfairly, get the officer's name and report him at the nearest tourist police station.) Honking is illegal in Athens, but you can hear that law broken by tarrying at a traffic signal.

**PARKING** Parking a car has become a serious challenge in the cities and towns of Greece. The better hotels probably provide parking, either on their premises or by some arrangement with a nearby lot. There are few parking garages or lots in Greece. Follow the blue signs with their white "P" and you may be lucky enough to find an available space. Most Greek city streets have restricted parking of one kind or another. But in some cities, signs—usually yellow, and with the directions in English as well as Greek—will indicate that you can park along the street but must purchase a ticket from the nearest kiosk. Otherwise, be prepared to park fairly far from your base or destination. If you lock your car and remove all obvious valuables from sight, you should not have to worry about it being broken into.

## BY TRAIN

Greek trains are generally slow, but inexpensive and fairly pleasant. The **Hellenic State Railway (OSE)** also operates some bus service from stations adjacent to major terminals. (Bus service is faster, but second-class train fare is nearly 50% cheaper, and trains offer a more comfortable and scenic ride.) If you are interested in some of the special arrangements involving rail passes for Greece (sometimes in combination with Olympic flights within Greece), check out www.raileurope.com or call ⓒ 888/ 382-7245 (in the U.S. only).

For information and tickets in Athens, visit the **OSE office** at 1–3 Karolou (ⓒ **210/522-4563**), or 6 Sina (ⓒ **210/362-4402**), both near Omonia Square.

Purchase your ticket and reserve a seat ahead of time, as a 50% surcharge is added to tickets purchased on the train and some lines are packed, especially in summer. A first-class ticket may be worth the extra cost, as seats are more comfortable and less crowded. There is sleeper service (costly, but a good value if you can sleep on a train; also, you must be prepared to share a compartment with three to five others) on the Athens–Thessaloniki run, and express service (6 hr.) twice a day, at 7am and 1pm.

**Trains to northern Greece** (Alexandroupolis, Florina, Kalambaka, Lamia, Larissa, Thessaloniki, Volos, etc.) leave from the Larissa Station (Stathmos Larissis). **Trains to the Peloponnese** (Argos, Corinth, Patras) leave from the nearby Peloponnese Station (Stathmos Peloponnisou). Take trolley no. 1 or 5 from Syntagma Square to both stations.

The Peloponnese circuit from Corinth to Patras, Pirgos (near Olympia), Tripolis, and Argos is one way to experience this scenic region, though the Athens–Patras stretch is often crowded. The spectacular spur between Diakofto and Kalavrita is particularly recommended for train enthusiasts.

## BY BUS

Public buses are inexpensive but often overcrowded. Local buses vary from place to place, but on most islands the bus stop is usually fairly central with a posted schedule; destinations are (usually—so ask!) displayed in front of the bus. Fare is collected after departure by a conductor.

But note that in Athens and other large cities, a ticket MUST be purchased before boarding—kiosks usually offer them, as well as schedule information—and validated after boarding. Tickets cost 45€.

*Note:* Save your ticket in case an "inspector" comes aboard! Without a ticket, the fine can be 18€!

Greece has an extensive **long-distance bus service (KTEL),** an association of regional operators with green-and-yellow buses that usually leave from convenient central stations. For information about the long-distance offices, contact the KTEL office in Athens (ⓒ **210/512-4910**).

In Athens, **most buses heading to destinations within Attica** leave from the Mavromate terminal, north of the National Archaeological Museum; **most buses to central Greece** leave from 60 Liossion, 5km (3 miles) north of Omonia Square (take local bus no. 024 from Leoforos Amalias in front of the entrance to the National Garden and tell the driver your destination); **most buses to the Peloponnese, Western, and Northern Greece leave** from the terminal at 100 Kifissou, 4km (2½ miles) northeast of Omonia Square (take local bus No. 051 from 2 blocks west of Omonia, near the big church of Ayios Konstandinos, at Zinonos and Menandrou).

**Express buses** between major cities, usually air-conditioned, can be booked through travel agencies. Make sure you're pronouncing your destination properly, or at least are being understood—you wouldn't be the first to see a bit more of Greece than bargained for—and determine the bus's schedule and comforts before purchasing your ticket. Many buses are not air-conditioned, take torturous routes, and make frequent stops. (NO SMOKING signs are generally disregarded by drivers and conductors, as well as by many older male passengers.)

Organized and guided **bus tours** are widely available; some of them will pick you up at your hotel. Ask at your hotel or almost any travel agent in Athens. One that is especially recommended is **CHAT Tours**, (www.chatours.com) the oldest and probably most experienced in providing a wide selection of bus tours led by highly articulate guides. Almost any travel agent can book its tours, but if you want to deal with the organization directly, contact its office at 214 Bedford Rd, Toronto, Ontario M5R 2K9 (© **800/268-1180**). In Athens, the CHAT office is at 9 Xenofontos, 10557 Athens (© **210/323-0827**). Then there is the longtime favorite, **American Express**, with offices all over North America and Europe; the Athens office is located prominently on Syntagma Square. *Note:* Readers have complained that some bus groups are so large that they feel removed from the leader; inquire about group size if this concerns you.

## BY TAXI

Taxis are one of the most convenient means of getting about in Greece. They can also be the most exasperating, although there have been improvements in recent years. For instance, you no longer have to fight for a cab at most airports; just find the line. Cabs are considerably less expensive in Athens than they are in London, New York, or Toronto. There are probably no greater percentage of cheats among the drivers than in all major cities around the world—and many Greek taxi drivers are good-natured, helpful, and informative. Language and cultural difficulties, however, can make it easier for them to gouge you, and some drivers take advantage of the opportunity. The converse, though, is sometimes true: Language gaps often lead to genuine misunderstandings. There are some legitimate surcharges—for heavy luggage, from midnight to 6am (almost

twice the regular rate!), on holidays, from and to airports, etc. Ask to see the official rate sheet that the driver is required to carry.

Get your hotel desk to help you in hailing or booking a taxi. Radio cabs cost 2.05€ extra, but you'll have some leverage. Restaurants and businesses can also help in calling or hailing a cab, negotiating a fare, and making sure your destination is understood. Take a card from your hotel, have your destination written down, or learn to pronounce it at least semi-correctly. Be willing to share a cab with other passengers picked up on the way, especially during rush hour; think of it as your contribution to better efficiency and less pollution (and you are not supposed to pay more than your proportion of the shared fare). Always have some vague idea of where you're going on the map, so you don't end up going to Plaka from Syntagma by way of Kolonaki. (There are, however, several ways of getting to Plaka from Syntagma.) Don't be bothered by bullying or bluster; try to find it amusing and counter with your own bluff, showing your superiority by keeping your cool. See also "Taxi Tips," below.

## BY MOPED, MOTORBIKE & MOTORCYCLE

There seems to be no end to the number of mopeds, motorbikes, motorcycles, and related vehicles available for rent in Greece. They can be an inexpensive way to get around, especially in the islands, but they are not recommended for everyone: Greek hospitals admit scores of tourists injured on mopeds or motorbikes every summer, and there are a number of fatalities. Roads are often poorly paved and without shoulders; loose gravel or stones are another common problem. Meanwhile, as of 2000, Greek law requires that all renters of mopeds and motorcycles be licensed to operate such vehicles; it remains to be seen

## Taxi Tips

- Taxi rates are in constant (upwards!) flux, so all we can do is provide the rates as we go to press. First, though, check to see that the little window next to the euro display on the meter will be set on "2" for midnight-to-6am or outside-the-city-limits rates (which are about double the regular rate). If that's not the case, reach over and indicate that you notice.

- Then check that the meter starts at no more than 1.17€ as you set off—that is the maximum starting rate. Drivers have been known either to start with a much higher number already registered or by leaving the meter off, then trying to extort a much larger fare from you. Even if you don't speak a word of Greek besides "taxi," point at the meter and say "meter." The rate per kilometer then has been about .24€ within the city and about double that outside city limits. The minimum for any trip is 1.50€.

- With a group of tourists, a driver may insist that each person pay the full metered fare. Pay one fare only if you are going to the same destination. (In pairs or groups, have a designated arguer; the others can write down names and numbers, stick with the luggage, or look for help—from a policeman, maître d', or desk clerk.)

- Late at night, especially at airports, ferry stops, and bus and railroad stations, a driver may refuse to use his meter and demand an exorbitant fare. Smile, shake your head, and look for another cab; if none are available, begin to write down the license number of the first driver and he will probably relent.

- Legal surcharges include: .90€ from and to airports; .45€ pickup at port, bus, or train terminal; .30€ per piece of luggage over 10 kilos (22 lbs). (Toll roads are also charged to the passengers—1€ in case of new road from airport to Athens.)

- A driver may say that your hotel is full, but he knows a better and cheaper one. Laugh, and insist you'll take your chances at your hotel.

- A driver may want to let you off where it's most convenient for him. Be cooperative if it's easier and quicker for you to cross a busy avenue than for him to get you to the other side, but you don't have to get out of the cab until you're ready.

If things are obviously not going well for you, conspicuously write down the driver's name and number and by all means report him to the **tourist police** (℡ 171) if he has the nerve to call your bluff. One of the best counteractics is to simply reach for the door latch and open the door slightly; he won't want to risk damaging it. (Two of you can each open a door.)

Our final advice: Don't sweat the small change. So the driver is charging you 13€ for a ride you have been told should be about 10€; are you prepared to go to court for 3€? Any difference above 5€ probably should be questioned—but it may have to do with traffic delays when the meter ticks at the rate of 6.75€ per hour). Most cabbies are honest—we don't want to make you paranoid, just aware of the possibilities. And please be sure to reward good service with a tip.

## ⓘ Warning  Renting a Moped

Although mopeds are the vehicle of choice in Greece, especially on the islands, be aware that there is a Greek law (prompted by a huge number of accidents) requiring a motorcycle license for anyone driving a moped. Agencies offering moped rentals rarely tell tourists this because very few tourists have motorcycle licenses. This makes for a whirlwind of troubles if an accident occurs and the rider is found to not have been licensed. The rider will not be covered by insurance and will have broken the law. Better check with your own driver's and/or medical insurance plan to see if you are covered for such an eventuality.

how this will be enforced. In any case, make sure you have insurance and that the machine is in good working condition before you take it. Helmets are required by law and strongly recommended, although you will rarely see Greeks wearing them.

Some might wish the larger motorbikes and motorcycles were forbidden on all the islands, as Greek youths seem to delight in punching holes in the muffler and tearing around all hours of the day and night. (Some islands are wisely banning them from certain areas and restricting the hours of use, as they are the single most common cause of complaint from tourists and residents alike.) The motorcycles rented to

tourists are usually a bit quieter, but they are more expensive and at least as dangerous; strictly speaking, a special license is required to rent one.

## BY BICYCLE

Bicycles are not nearly as common in Greece as they are throughout most of Europe, as they are not well suited to Greek terrain or temperament and would be downright dangerous in traffic. In less hectic towns and countryside, however, a bicycle might be a fine way to get about short distances. Older bikes are usually available for rent at modest prices in most resort areas, and good mountain bikes are increasingly available. (See "Active Travelers," above, for more information.)

## 13 Tips on Accommodations

Greece now offers a full spectrum of accommodations, ranging from the extravagant deluxe to basic camping facilities. Within a given locale, of course, not all options are available, but most users of this guide will find the kinds of places that appeal. All the hotels that we list and recommend would have the basic amenities that our readers would expect, and where there is something missing (e.g. an elevator, phone in the room) we note that.

The Greek government used to impose a grading system that hotels had to publicize. There are still Classes with limits placed on prices depending on facilities (e.g. public areas, pools,

in-room amenities, etc.), but basically it is a market economy: Hotels know better than to ask for too much because competitors will undercut them. Again, our own rating system of stars and icons for special features takes care of all such differences.

There are a few of the major chains that international travelers are familiar with—the Hilton, Best Western—and there are also a number of Greek chains—Louis, Chandris, and such. These latter tend to be fairly upscale hotels. But most Greek hotels are still independent and usually run by hands-on owners.

## Tips Booking a Room

Try to make reservations by fax so that you have a written record of what room and price were agreed upon. Also, a double room in Greece usually does not mean a room with a double bed, but a room with two twin beds. Double beds in Greece are called "matrimonial beds," and rooms with such beds are often designated "honeymoon rooms." This can lead to misunderstandings.

Note that in a few instances—usually at the most expensive hotels—the prices quoted are per person. Note, too, that room prices, no matter what people say officially, are often negotiable, especially at the edges of the season. Because of Greek law and EOT regulations, hotel keepers are often reluctant to provide rates far in advance and often quote prices higher than their actual rates. When you bargain, don't cite our prices, which may be too high, but ask instead for the best current rate. Actual off-season prices may be as much as 25% lower than the lowest rate given to us for the book.

## SAVING ON YOUR HOTEL ROOM

The **rack rate** is the maximum rate that a hotel charges for a room. Hardly anybody pays this price, however. To lower the cost of your room:

• **Ask about special rates or other discounts.** Always ask whether a room less expensive than the first one quoted is available, or whether any special rates apply to you. You may qualify for corporate, student, military, senior, or other discounts. Mention membership in AAA, AARP, frequent-flier programs, or trade unions, which may entitle you to special deals as well. Find out the hotel policy on children—do kids stay free in the room or is there a special rate?

• **Dial direct.** When booking a room in a chain hotel, you'll often get a better deal by calling the individual hotel's reservation desk than at the chain's main number.

• **Book online.** Many hotels offer Internet-only discounts, or supply rooms to Priceline, Hotwire or Expedia at rates much lower than

the ones you can get through the hotel itself.

• **Remember the law of supply and demand.** Resort hotels are most crowded and therefore most expensive on weekends, so discounts are usually available for midweek stays. Business hotels in downtown locations are busiest during the week, so you can expect big discounts over the weekend. Many hotels have high-season and low-season prices, and booking the day after 'high season' ends can mean big discounts.

• **Look into group or long-stay discounts.** If you come as part of a large group, you should be able to negotiate a bargain rate, since the hotel can then guarantee occupancy in a number of rooms. Likewise, if you're planning a long stay (at least 5 days), you might qualify for a discount. As a general rule, expect one night free after a seven-night stay.

• **Avoid excess charges and hidden costs.** When you book a room, ask whether the hotel charges for parking. Use your own cellphone, pay phones, or prepaid phone cards instead of dialing direct from hotel phones, which usually have exorbitant rates. And don't be tempted by the room's minibar offerings: Most hotels charge through the nose for water, soda, and snacks. Finally, ask about local taxes and service charges, which can increase the cost of a room by 15% or more. If a hotel insists upon tacking on a surprise "energy surcharge" that wasn't mentioned at check-in or a "resort fee" for amenities you didn't use, you can often make a case for getting it removed.

• Consider the pros and cons of **all-inclusive** resorts and hotels. The term "all-inclusive" means different things at different hotels. Many all-inclusive hotels will include 3 meals daily, sports equipment, spa entry, and other amenities; others may include all or most drinks. In general, you'll save money going the "all-inclusive" way—as long as you use the facilities provided. The down side is that your choices are limited and you're stuck eating and playing in one place for the duration of your vacation.

• Carefully consider your hotel's meal plan. If you enjoy eating out and sampling the local cuisine, it makes sense to choose a **Continental Plan (CP),** which includes breakfast only, or a **European**

Plan **(EP),** which doesn't include any meals and allows you maximum flexibility. If you're more interested in saving money, opt for a **Modified American Plan (MAP),** which includes breakfast and one meal, or the **American Plan (AP),** which includes three meals. If you must choose a MAP, see if you can get a free lunch at your hotel if you decide to do dinner out.

• **Book an efficiency.** A room with a kitchenette allows you to shop for groceries and cook your own meals. This is a big money saver, especially for families on long stays.

## LANDING THE BEST ROOM

Somebody has to get the best room in the house. It might as well be you. Although it is unlikely that the average visitor to Greece will be staying at a hotel with a "frequent-guest" program, inquire if you think it might be a possibility. Always ask about a corner room. They're often larger and quieter, with more windows and light, and they often cost the same as standard rooms. When you make your reservation, ask if the hotel is renovating; if it is, request a room away from the construction. Ask about nonsmoking rooms, rooms with views, rooms with twin, queen- or king-size beds. If you're a light sleeper, request a quiet room away from vending machines, elevators, restaurants,

_Tips_ **Hotel Bathrooms**

The bathrooms in all the newer and higher-grade Greek hotels are now practically "state of the art," but there are a few things travelers might appreciate knowing in advance. Few hotels ever provide washcloths, and the soap is often the old-fashioned minibar—and increasingly gel from a dispenser! Many hotels still don't offer generous-sized towels, and even many midpriced hotels provide only cramped showers. As it happens, the one thing the Greeks are generous with is slippery marble: Be very careful getting in and out of tubs or showers.

bars, and discos. Ask for one of the rooms that have been most recently renovated or redecorated.

If you aren't happy with your room when you arrive, say so. If another room is available, most lodgings will be willing to accommodate you.

In resort areas, particularly in warm climates, ask the following questions before you book a room:

- **What's the view like?** Cost-conscious travelers may be willing to pay less for a back room facing the parking lot, especially if they don't plan to spend much time in their room.

- **Does the room have air-conditioning or ceiling fans? Do the windows open?**

  If they do, and the nighttime entertainment takes place alfresco, you may want to find out when show time is over.

- **What's included in the price?** Your room may be moderately priced, but if you're charged for beach chairs, towels, sports equipment, and other amenities, you could end up spending more than you bargained for.

- **How far is the room from the** beach and other amenities? If it's far, is there transportation to and from the beach?

### Rentals (Apartments & Houses)

An increasingly popular way to experience Greece is to rent an apartment or house; the advantages include freedom from the formalities of a hotel, often a more desirable location, and a kitchen that allows you to avoid the costs and occasional crush of restaurants. Such rentals do not come cheap, but if you calculate what two or more people

might pay for a decent hotel, not to mention all the meals eaten out, it can turn out to be a good deal. (Costs per person per day in really nice apartments might run about 100€; the fancier villas might cost about 200€ a day for two bedrooms.) Any full-service travel agency in your home country or in Greece should be able to put you in touch with an agency specializing in such rentals.

The fact is that the British dominate this field in Greece, both in terms of experience and sheer numbers of offerings. So via the internet, anyone can now see what's offered and contact such outfits as **Abercrombie & Kent** (Sloan Square House, London SW1W 8NS (© **0845/0700-618**; www.villa-rentals.com); **Simply Travel Ltd.**, 598–608 Chiswick High Rd., London W4 5XY (© **020/8541-2203**; www.simplytravel.co.uk), or **Pure Crete**, 79 George St., Croydon, Surrey CRO 1LD (© **020/8760-0879**; www.pure-crete.com). Among those in the United States are **Villas International**, 4830 Redwood Highway, San Rafael, CA 94903 (© **800/221-2260**; www.villasintl.com). In Canada, try **Grecian Holidays,** 75 The Donaway West, Don Mills, Ontario M3C 2E9 (© **800/268-6786**; © 416/510-8811; fax 416/510-1509). For those interested in investigating further possibilities on the Web, try **www.crete.tournet.gr, www.vacationhomes.com,** or **www.villavacations.com.**

Another possibility is to rent a traditional house in one of about 12 relatively rural or remote villages or settlements throughout Greece. These small traditional houses have been

**Tips** **Dial E for Easy**

For quick directions on how to call Greece, see the "Telephone" listing in the "Fast Facts" section at the end of this chapter or check out the "Telephone Tips" on the inside front cover of the book.

restored by the Greek National Tourist Organization (GNTO); to learn more about this possibility, contact the GNTO office nearest you. (See "Visitor Information," earlier in this chapter, or go to **www.gnto.gr**.)

## 14 Tips on Dining

Most everything that might be said about dining in Greece is in the section at the back of the book, "A Taste of Greece." One thing not stated there is that a distinctive aspect of restaurants in Greece is that you can get as little or as much as you want from the menu—and at almost any hour of the day. Not in every little village and not in every restaurant, but many will start serving the elements of a meal by late morning and on through to late at night. And you can assemble a meal from any items of the menu—all appetizers, if you wish—and Greeks won't object.

Most hotels now include satisfying buffet breakfasts with their room price, but if you come down too late, there is usually at least one cafe that can come up with some basics. Don't expect fresh orange juice everywhere though! And if you have definite preferences

for tea—especially herbal—you might consider carrying your own teabags.

You can expect lunch to be served from 11am on through 2:30pm. Greeks themselves eat their evening meal quite late but restaurants are now prepared to accommodate foreigners who like to sit down by as early as 5:30pm.

Most restaurants now have a "cover charge" that includes the table setting and a small basket of bread. It used to be that Greek waiters brought ice cold pitchers of fresh water to each table without even being asked to, but this custom has pretty much vanished. If you request "natural" water, they may bring it to your table, but just asking for water means that you will be brought a plastic bottle of water—and charged for it. (Under Greek law, they are supposed to open the sealed top in your presence.)

## FAST FACTS: Greece

**American Express** Long the most prominent and favorite of travelers to Greece as elsewhere, it maintains an extensive network of offices and agents throughout Greece. The Athens office is located prominently overlooking Syntagma Square. We indicate these offices and agencies throughout the guide, just as we indicate the various travel arrangements and financial services American Express offers.

**Appropriate Attire** Dress—or undress!—codes have greatly relaxed at Greek beach resorts in recent years, but Greeks still are uncomfortable with beachwear or even slovenly garb in villages or cities. And women are still expected to have coverings for their arms and upper legs to enter monasteries and churches. Some priests and monks are stricter than others and may flatly bar men as well as women if they feel they are not dressed suitably.

**ATMs** See "Money," earlier in this chapter.

**Avoiding Offense** Do not direct the open-hand wave at Greeks—this is regarded as giving the "evil eye." Either wave sideways or in a little circle, but always with the palm turned away. Aside from monasteries and churches enforcing the dress code referred to above, Greeks in general do not appreciate beachwear off the beach. And in a reverse instance of offending, Greeks do not put a priority on punctuality, so do not be offended if they do not show up until well after the appointed time.

**Banks** Banks are open to the public Monday through Thursday from 8am to 2pm, Friday from 8am to 1:30pm. Some banks have additional hours for foreign currency exchange. All banks are closed on the long list of Greek holidays (see "When to Go," earlier in this chapter).

**Business Hours** Greek business and office hours take some getting used to, especially in the afternoon, when most English-speaking people are accustomed to getting things done in high gear. Compounding the problem is that it is virtually impossible to pin down the precise hours of opening. We can start by saying that almost all stores and services are still closed on Sunday—except, of course, tourist-oriented shops and services. On Monday, Wednesday, and Saturday, hours are usually 9am to 3pm; Tuesday, Thursday, and Friday, 9am to 2pm and 5 to 7pm. The afternoon siesta is still generally observed from 3 to 5pm, though many tourist-oriented businesses have a minimal crew during nap time and may keep extended hours, often from 8am to 10pm. (In fact, in tourist centers, shops may be open at all kinds of hours.) Most government offices are open Monday through Friday only, from 8am to 3pm. We suggest you call ahead to check the hours of businesses you *must* deal with and that you not disturb Greek friends during siesta hours. **Final advice:** Anything you really need to accomplish in a government office, business, or store should be done on weekdays between about 9am and 1pm.

**Car Rentals** See "Getting Around," earlier in this chapter.

**Climate** See "When to Go," earlier in this chapter.

**Climate Control** Almost all Greek hotels in the categories patronized by most users of this guide now promise air-conditioning in the hot season and heating in the colder months. The equipment is indeed there, but you should be aware that—except in the most expensive hotels—neither will necessarily be as adequate as you might like.

**Crime** Crimes against tourists are not a significant concern in Greece. Athens is probably the safest capital in Europe. Pocket-picking and purse-snatching may be slightly on the rise, especially in heavily touristed areas, but breaking into cars remains rare. Tourists, however, are conspicuous and much more likely to be carrying valuables, so take normal precautions—lock the car, don't leave cameras and such gear visible, etc. Young women should observe the obvious precautions in dealing with males in isolated locales.

**Currency** See "Money," earlier in this chapter.

**Customs** See "Entry Requirements & Customs" earlier in this chapter.

**Dentists & Doctors** Ask your embassy or consulate in a major city or your hotel's management to direct you to a dentist or doctor who speaks either English or some other common European language.

**Driving Rules** See "Getting Around By Car" earlier in this chapter.

**Drugs** Greek authorities and laws are extremely tough when it comes to finding foreigners with drugs—starting with marijuana. Do not attempt to bring any illicit drugs into or out of Greece.

**Drugstores** These are called Pharmikon in Greek; aside from the obvious indications in windows and interiors, they are identified by a green cross. For minor medical problems, go first to the nearest **pharmacy.** Pharmacists usually speak English and many medications can be dispensed without prescription. In the larger cities, if it is closed, there should be a sign in the window directing you to the nearest open one. Newspapers also list the pharmacies that are open late or all night.

**Electricity** Electric current in Greece is 220 volts AC, alternating at 50 cycles. (Some larger hotels have 110-volt low-wattage outlets for electric shavers, but they aren't good for hair dryers and most other appliances.) Electrical outlets require Continental-type plugs with two round prongs. U.S. travelers will need an adapter plug *and* a transformer/converter, unless their appliances are dual-voltage. (Such transformers can be bought in stores like Radio Shack.) Laptop-computer users will want to check their requirements; a transformer may be necessary, and surge protectors are recommended.

**Embassies & Consulates** See "Fast Facts: Athens" in chapter 5 for a list of embassies and consulates. United Kingdom citizens can get emergency aid by calling ⓒ **210/723-6211** during the day; at night, try ⓒ **210/723-7727** or 210/724-1331. United States citizens can get emergency aid by calling ⓒ **210/721-2951** during the day; at night, try ⓒ **210/729-4301** or 210/729-4444.

**Emergencies** These numbers can be used throughout Greece. For the regular **police,** dial ⓒ **100;** for **tourist police,** dial ⓒ **171.** For **fire,** dial ⓒ **199.** For **medical emergencies** and/or first aid and/or an ambulance, dial ⓒ **166.** For **hospitals,** dial ⓒ **106.** For **automobile emergencies,** put out a triangular danger sign and telephone ⓒ **104** or **174. Embassies, consulates, and many hotels** can recommend an English-speaking doctor.

**Gestures** Upon being introduced to a Greek for the first time, the handshake is normal. When you get to know Greeks fairly well, the kiss on both cheeks is the accepted greeting. By the way, when Greeks meet small children, they tend to pinch them on the cheeks or pat them.

**Gifts** If invited to a Greek's home for a meal or social event, flowers or chocolates would be an appropriate gift.

**Haggling** Greek merchants resent foreigners who try to haggle over prices. In general, the marked price is it. That said, there are some "games" that can be played. Hesitate, consult with your companions with the appropriate expressions of regret, set the object down—with thanks!—and head for the exit. You may well be offered a lower price. But that is the merchant's prerogative and all depends on the manner in which this is conducted. If you have come across as demanding, or disapproving, you can forget any further negotiating.

*Faxes* Almost all hotels in the higher categories, many telephone offices, some post offices, and some travel agencies will send and receive faxes locally and internationally for you at set fees. But don't forget: Sending a fax is the equivalent of making a phone call, so you must be prepared to pay for that plus the extra service of the fax machine.

*Guides* Some individuals may prefer to employ local guides to take them and/or a small circle of fellow travelers to visit sites or cities. Professional guides in Greece are thoroughly trained, and the fees they charge are well regulated. Most reputable travel agencies can arrange for such guides. You can also contact the **Union of Official Guides,** 9A Apollonos 10557 Athens (ⓒ **210/322-9705;** fax 210/323-9200). We might only caution that as good as these official guides are, they are trained to produce a stream of facts, not make small talk.

*Holidays* See "When to Go," earlier in this chapter.

*Information* See "Visitor Information," earlier in this chapter.

*Language* Language is usually not a problem for English speakers in Greece, as so much of the population has lived abroad, where English is the primary language; meanwhile, young people learn it in school, from Anglo-American-dominated pop culture, and in special classes meant to prepare them for the contemporary world of business. Many television programs are also broadcast in their original language, and American prime-time soaps are very popular, nearly inescapable. Even advertisements have an increasingly high English content.

Don't let all this keep you from trying to pick up at least a few words of Greek; your effort will be rewarded by your hosts, who realize how difficult their language is for foreigners and will patiently help you improve your pronunciation and usage. There are various taped programs, including **Berlitz's Greek for Travelers** and **Passport's Conversational Greek in 7 Days,** which can be very helpful.

Appendix A, "The Greek Language," will teach you the basics.

*Laptops* Increasing numbers of travelers are choosing to take their laptops along, whether to keep up with work assignments, write personal notes, or stay in touch with the outside world via the Internet. Since Greece operates on 220 volts, you must make sure that your computer has a built-in capacity to handle this voltage or else travel with a transformer and probably a surge protector (See "Electricity," above). That will take care of the computer for all non-modem functions, but if you want to use it to gain access to the Internet, considerably more is involved.

*Laundry & Dry Cleaning* All cities and towns of any size will have both laundry and dry-cleaning establishments. Many travelers will prefer to make arrangements through their hotel desks; this is fine, but be prepared to pay heavily for even the smallest bundle. (Then again, everything including socks will have been ironed!) If you are more ambitious (or frugal), you can seek out one of the laundries that we try to mention in later chapters wherever available. In most instances, these are attended; you can leave your laundry to be picked up later (be sure you are in agreement as to the time it will be ready, especially if you must leave town!). A medium-size bag of laundry may cost about 15€, washed, dried, and neatly folded.

*Legal Aid* If you were to have need of legal assistance, the best advice is to contact your own or another English-speaking embassy or consulate.

*Liquor Laws* The minimum age for being served alcohol in public locales is 18. Wine and beer are generally available in eating places but not in all coffeehouses or dessert cafes. Alcoholic beverages are sold in foodstores as well as liquor stores. Although a certain amount of high spirits is appreciated, Greeks do NOT appreciate public drunkenness. The resort centers where mobs of young foreigners party every night are tolerated as necessary for the tourist trade but the behavior wins no respect for foreigners.

*Lost & Found* Be sure to tell all of your credit card companies the minute you discover your wallet has been lost or stolen and file a report at the nearest police precinct. Your credit card company or insurer may require a police report number or record of the loss. Most credit card companies have an emergency toll-free number to call if your card is lost or stolen; they may be able to wire you a cash advance immediately or deliver an emergency credit card in a day or two. Visa's U.S. emergency number is Ⓒ 800/847-2911 or 410/581-9994. American Express cardholders and traveler's check holders should call Ⓒ 800/221-7282. MasterCard holders should call Ⓒ 800/307-7309 or 636/722-7111. For other credit cards, call the toll-free number directory at Ⓒ 800/555-1212.

If you need emergency cash over the weekend when all banks and American Express offices are closed, you can have money wired to you via Western Union (Ⓒ 800/325-6000; www.westernunion.com).

Identity theft or fraud are potential complications of losing your wallet, especially if you've lost your driver's license along with your cash and credit cards. Notify the major credit-reporting bureaus immediately; placing a fraud alert on your records may protect you against liability for criminal activity. The three major U.S. credit-reporting agencies are Equifax (Ⓒ 800/766-0008; www.equifax.com), Experian (Ⓒ 888/397-3742; www.experian.com), and TransUnion (Ⓒ 800/680-7289; www.transunion.com). Finally, if you've lost all forms of photo ID call your airline and explain the situation; they might allow you to board the plane if you have a copy of your passport or birth certificate and a copy of the police report you've filed.

*Mail* The mail service of Greece is reliable—but slow. (Postcards usually arrive weeks after you have arrived home.) You can receive mail addressed to you c/o Poste Restante, General Post Office, City (or Town), Island (or Province), Greece. You will need your passport to collect this mail. Many hotels will accept, hold, and even forward mail for you also; ask first. American Express clients can receive mail at any Amex office in Athens, Corfu, Iraklion, Mykonos, Patras, Rhodes, Santorini, Skiathos, and Thessaloniki, for a nominal fee and with proper identification. If you are in a particular hurry, try FedEx or one of the other of the major international private carriers; travel agencies will be able to direct you to these.

Postage rates have been going up in Greece as elsewhere. But as of this writing, a postcard and a letter under 20 grams (about .7 oz) cost .65€ to North America and Europe; 20 to 50 grams (up to 1.75 oz), 1.15€; 50 to 100 grams (3.5 oz) 1.6€. Rates for packages depend on size as well as weight so are impossible to list but they are reasonable; but do not wrap or seal any package—you must be prepared to show the contents to a postal clerk.

**Maps** See "Getting Around By Car," above.

**Newspapers & Magazines** All cities, large towns, and major tourist centers now have at least one shop or kiosk that carries a selection of foreign-language publications; most of these are flown or shipped in on the very day of publication. English-language readers have a wide selection, including most of the British papers (*Daily Telegraph, Financial Times, Guardian, Independent, Times*), the *International Herald Tribune* (with its inserted English-language version of the well-known Athens newspaper, *Kathimerini*), and *USA Today*. A decent (and cheaper!) alternative is the English-language paper published in Athens, *Athens News,* widely available throughout Greece.

**Passports  For Residents of the United States:** Whether you're applying in person or by mail, you can download passport applications from the U.S. State Department website at **http://travel.state.gov.** For general information, call the **National Passport Agency** (© **202/647-0518**). To find your regional passport office, either check the U.S. State Department website or call the **National Passport Information Center** (© **900/225-5674**); the fee is 55¢ per minute for automated information and $1.50 per minute for operator-assisted calls.

**For Residents of Canada:** Passport applications are available at travel agencies throughout Canada or from the central **Passport Office,** Department of Foreign Affairs and International Trade, Ottawa, ON K1A 0G3 (© **800/567-6868;** www.dfait-maeci.gc.ca/passport).

**For Residents of the United Kingdom:** To pick up an application for a standard 10-year passport (5-year passport for children under 16), visit your nearest passport office, major post office, or travel agency or contact the **United Kingdom Passport Service** at © **0870/521-0410** or search its website at www.ukpa.gov.uk.

**For Residents of Ireland:** You can apply for a 10-year passport at the **Passport Office,** Setanta Centre, Molesworth Street, Dublin 2 (© **01/671-1633;** www.irlgov.ie/iveagh). Those under age 18 and over 65 must apply for a 12€3-year passport. You can also apply at 1A South Mall, Cork (© **021/272-525**) or at most main post offices.

**For Residents of Australia:** You can pick up an application from your local post office or any branch of Passports Australia, but you must schedule an interview at the passport office to present your application materials. Call the **Australian Passport Information Service** at © **131-232.** or visit the government website at www.passports.gov.au.

**For Residents of New Zealand:** You can pick up a passport application at any New Zealand Passports Office or download it from their website. Contact the **Passports Office** at © **0800/225-050** in New Zealand or 04/474-8100, or log on to www.passports.govt.nz.

**Pets** See "Entry Requirements & Customs," above.

**Pharmacies** See "Drugstores" above.

**Photocopying** In most Greek cities, the bookstores offer commercial photocopying services.

*Photography* In several locales around Greece, photographing military or police installations is forbidden. These locales are posted and you are expected to observe the law. Cameras, film, accessories, and photo developing (including express service) are widely available, though slightly more expensive, in Greece.

*Police* To report a crime or medical emergency, or for information or other assistance, first contact the local tourist police (telephone numbers will be found under "Essentials" in the particular destination chapters that follow), where an English-speaking officer is more likely to be found. If there is no tourist police officer available (© 171), contact the local police. The telephone number for emergencies throughout Greece is © 100.

*Radio & Television* The Greek ERT 1 radio station has weather and news in English at 7:40am. The BBC World Service can be picked up on shortwave frequencies, often at 9.140, 15.07, and 12.09 Mhz; on FM it is usually at 107.1. Antenna TV, CNN, Eurochannel, and other cable networks are widely available. Many better hotels offer cable television.

*Reservations* Only the rare expensive restaurant in Athens and a few resorts would expect advance reservations. If your schedule is tight and you have very determined goals, you are advised to make travel arrangements well in advance. But at the height of the tourist season, hotels, airlines, ship lines, and the major festival performances require reservations. Anyone with a tight schedule for getting to and from islands is definitely advised to secure a reservation.

*Restrooms* Public restrooms are generally available in any good-sized Greek town, and though they are sometimes rather crude, they usually do work. (Old-fashioned stand-up/squat facilities are still found.) Carry some type of tissue or toilet paper with you at all times. In some places—even quite modern restaurants and hotels—you are still told not to flush it down the toilet; use the receptacles provided. In an emergency, you can ask to use the facilities of a restaurant or shop, though near major attractions they have to be denied to all but customers because the traffic is simply too heavy. If you use any such facilities, respect its sponsor and leave at least a small tip to any attendant.

*Safety* See "Health & Safety," earlier in this chapter.

*Smoking* Greeks continue to be among the most persistent smokers. Smoking is prohibited on all domestic flights, in certain areas or types of ships, and in some public buildings (e.g. post offices), but except on airplanes, many Greeks—and some foreigners—feel free to puff away at will. (The airport in Athens is virtually a cancer culture lab.) Hotels are only beginning to claim that they have set aside rooms or even floors for nonsmokers, so ask if it matters to you. If you are really bothered by smoke while eating, about all you can do is position yourself as best as possible—and then be prepared to move if it gets really bad.

*Taxes & Service Charges* Unless otherwise noted, all hotel prices include a service charge, usually 12%, a 6% value-added tax (VAT), and a 4½% community tax. In most restaurants, a 13% service charge, an 8% VAT, and some kind of municipal tax (in Athens it is 5%) are also included in the prices and final bill. (By the way, don't confuse any of these charges with a standard "cover charge" that may be .50 to 1€ per setting. Also see "Tipping," below.) A VAT of 18% is added to rental-car rates.

All purchases also include a VAT tax of anywhere from 4% to 18%. If you have purchased an item that costs 100€ or more and are a citizen of a non-European Union nation, you can get at least most of this refunded (provided you are exporting it within 90 days of time of purchase). The easiest thing to do is to shop at stores that display the sign TAX-FREE FOR TOURISTS. But any store should be able to provide you with a Tax-Free Check Form, which you complete in the store. (It is also usually the case when you use your charge card, the receipt will list the VAT tax separately from the cost of the item.) As you are leaving the country, you present a copy of this to the refund desk (usually with the Customs office); be prepared to show both the goods and the receipt as proof of purchase, and be prepared to wait a fair amount of time before you get the refund. (In fact, the process at the airport seems designed to discourage you from ever obtaining the refund.)

*Telephone* In the old days, most foreigners went to the offices of the **Telecommunications Organization of Greece** (*Organismos Tilepikinonion tis Ellados*) **OTE**—pronounced *oh-tay*—to place most of their phone calls, especially overseas calls. But because phone cards are now so widespread throughout Greece, this is no longer necessary, once you get the hang of using them. You must first purchase a phone card at an OTE office or at most kiosks. (If you expect to make any phone calls while in Greece, you should buy one at the OTE office at the airport on first arriving.) These come in various denominations, from 3€ to 25€ the more costly the card, the cheaper the units.

A local call of up to 3 minutes to a fixed phone costs about .09€ or three units off a phone card; for each minute beyond that, it costs another .06€ or two units off the card (so that a 10-min. local call costs 17 units or 51€).

By the way, all calls, including to next door, cost Greeks something, so if you ever get to use someone's telephone even for a local call, do offer to pay the charges.

In larger cities and larger towns, some kiosks have telephones from which you can make local calls for .10€ for 3 minutes. (In remote areas, they will let you make long-distance calls from these phones.) A few of the older public telephones that required coins are still to be found but you will really do better to buy a phone card. If you must use one, deposit the required coin and listen for a dial tone, an irregular beep. A regular beep indicates the line is busy.

*Note:* As of November 2002, ALL phone numbers in Greece require dialing 10 digits. All (except for mobile phones—see below) also precede the city/area code with a 2 and end that with a 0; Athens then has a 6-digit number, but all other numbers in Greece are 5 digits. In all cases, even if you are calling someone in the same building, you must dial all 10 digits.

**Calling a mobile (cell) phone** in Greece requires substituting a 6 for the 2 that preceded the area code.

**Long-distance calls,** both domestic and international, can be quite expensive in Greece, especially at hotels, which may add a surcharge up to 100%, unless you have a telephone credit card from a major long-distance provider such as AT&T, MCI, or Sprint.

If you still prefer to make your call from an OTE office, these are usually centrally and conveniently located. (Local offices are given under "Essentials" for the destinations in the chapters that follow.) At OTE offices, you first go to one of the clerks, who will assign you a booth with a metered phone. You can make collect calls, but this can take much longer, so it's easier to pay cash, unless you have a phone card or intend to use your own international credit card.

To call Greece from the United States or Canada:

1. Dial the international access code: 011
2. Dial the country code 30
3. Dial the city/area code which now always begins with 2 and ends with a 0, and then the number. So the whole number you'd dial would be 011-30-area code-number

If you are calling Greece from other countries:
Dial one of the following international access codes:
From the United Kingdom, Ireland, and New Zealand, **00;** from Australia, **0011.** After that, everything is as described above for calls from North America.

To make international calls from Greece;
The easiest and cheapest way is to make use of your long-distance service provider; call your company before leaving home to determine the access number that you must dial in Greece. The principal access codes in Greece are: **AT&T,** ✆ **00800-1311; MCI,** ✆ **00800-1211;** and **Sprint,** ✆ **00800-1411.** Most companies also offer a recorded-message service in case the number you're calling at home is busy or doesn't answer.

If you must use the Greek phone system, to make a direct call abroad—whether placing the call from an OTE office, a card phone, or a coin phone—dial the country code plus the area code (omitting the initial zero if any), then the number. Some country codes are: **Australia, 0061; Canada,** 001; **Ireland,** 00353; **New Zealand, 0064; United Kingdom, 0044;** and **United States,** 001. Note that if you are going to put all the charges on your phone card (that is, not on your long-distance provider), you will be charged at quite a high rate per minute (at least 3 € to North America), so you should not start a call unless your phone card has a fair number of euros still valid.

**For operator assistance:** If you need operator assistance in making a call within Greece, dial ✆ **131.** If you're trying to make an international call, dial ✆ **139.**

**Toll-free numbers:** Numbers beginning with 080 within Greece are toll-free, but calling a 1-800 number in the States from Greece will probably not be accepted; if it is, it will costs the same as an overseas call.

*Time* The European system of a 24-hour clock is used officially, and on schedules you'll usually see noon written as 1200, 3:30pm as 1530, and 11pm as 2300. In informal conversation, however, Greeks express time much as we do—though noon may mean anywhere from noon to 3pm, afternoon is 3 to 7pm, and evening is 7pm to midnight.

*Time Zone* Greece is 2 hours ahead of Greenwich Mean Time. With reference to North American time zones, it's 7 hours ahead of Eastern Standard Time, 8 hours ahead of Central Standard Time, 9 hours ahead of Mountain Standard Time, and 10 hours ahead of Pacific Standard Time. Note that Greece does observe daylight savings time, although it may not start and stop on the exact days as in North America.

*Tipping* A 10% to 15% service charge is included in virtually all restaurant bills. (It is no longer shown in a 2nd column of prices next to the menu item.) Nevertheless, it's customary to leave an additional 5% to 10% for the waiter, especially if there has been some special service. Certainly round off on larger bills; even on small bills, change up to the nearest 1€ is left. Good taxi service merits a tip of 10% or so. (Greeks rarely tip taxi drivers, but tourists are expected to.) Hotel chambermaids should be left about 2€ per night per couple. Bellhops and doormen should be tipped 1€ to 5€, depending on the services provided.

*Useful Phone Numbers* U.S. Dept. of State Travel Advisory ✆ **202/647-5225** (manned 24 hr.)

U.S. Passport Agency ✆ **202/647-0518.**

U.S. Centers for Disease Control International Traveler's Hotline: ✆ **404/332-4559.**

*Water* The public drinking water in Greece is safe to drink, although it can be slightly brackish in some locales near the sea. For that reason, many people prefer the bottled water commonly available at restaurants, hotels, cafes, food stores, and kiosks, but don't expect all brands to be especially "lively." The days when Greek restaurants automatically served glasses of cold fresh water are gone; you are now usually made to feel that you must order bottled water, at which point you will have to choose between natural or carbonated *(metalliko)*, and domestic or imported. Cafes, however, still tend to provide a glass of natural water.

# 3

# Olympics 2004: The Summer Games in Athens

*by John S. Bowman & Sherry Marker*

*The information provided here was correct at the time this book went to press, and the general conditions will most likely be as described. Individuals intent on seeing only specific events should check carefully with travel agents and the media before making their final plans and once in Athens should check immediately at the official Olympics visitors kiosks as to the schedules and venues for these events.*

The ancient Olympics were revived in 1896 with a relatively modest set of events in Athens and it has taken over a century for the Olympics to return to the land of its origins. Athens has changed greatly since then, and finally, in 2004, the XXVIII Olympiad is being held in Athens—and in fact in several other cities in Greece as well as around Athens—between August 13 and 29. (Preliminary football [soccer] games will actually start on August 11.) For a nation of only about 11 million people, providing the necessary facilities has proven to be an incredible effort, but although there have been some touch-and-go moments, it appears that Greece will meet the challenge. As with every city or country that hosts the Olympics, there has had to be a great deal of construction—not only of facilities for the games themselves but also of infrastructure to support the expected crowds. Some of these latter projects were "in the works" independent of the Olympics—the new airport, its expressway link to Athens, a new subway system in Athens, several other expressways to relieve traffic congestion in and around Athens. Then, in addition to constructing an entire new "village" (some 2,290 units!) to house 17,300 athletes, there

have been a number of new or thoroughly-renovated buildings—including major hotels and museum—much landscaping, and a general "sprucing up" of Athens.

It is traditional for the Olympics year to start with the lighting of a torch by the sun's rays at the site of ancient Olympia, in western Greece; the flame is then passed from torch to torch carried by runners (who must occasionally take to the air or ship to cover major "gaps") to the site of that year's games. Because Olympia is only some 322km (200 miles) from downtown Athens, the organizers came up with a dramatic way to make something more of this tradition. Thirty-five days before the formal Opening Ceremony, the first runner will set out, and then the flame will be passed from torch to torch as runners go to all five continents and pass through every city around the world that has ever hosted a Summer Olympic Games, plus Beijing, host of the 2008 games, plus Cairo, Cape Town, Rio de Janeiro, New York City, Lausanne, and Nicosia (Cyprus). (Other cities may be added to the route, and the final route in Greece was not determined at press time.)

The Games will be formally opened with the Opening Ceremony in the

## Tips Security & Crime

Security has become a major concern of all recent Olympics, and the games in Athens in 2004 will undeniably heighten such concern. Greek authorities, working closely with international security experts and other national police forces, plan to install advanced security technology and to have a specially trained security force of 45,000 personnel working round the clock. Greece's homegrown November 17 terrorist organization, once potentially threatening, has apparently been stamped out, and Greece, which has been consistently supportive of Arab states in the Middle East, is not expected to be subjected to acts that would weaken that support. The world has learned that no place can be 100% absolutely secure, but the 2004 Olympics should be as safe as possible. For those who remain concerned, it should be noted that Cartan Tours, one of the two companies officially selling tickets to events to U.S. residents (See "Getting Tickets," below), has included a provision in all its travel/ticket packages that allows for cancellation in the event of terrorist acts.

Visitors, especially during the Olympics, are advised to exercise all safety precautions including being aware of petty criminals such as pickpockets.

Olympic Stadium, also to be the site of the Closing Ceremony on August 29. Between those two events there will be some 1,800 separate competitions (including preliminaries) with 301 medal events in 28 separate sports. Approximately 20,000 athletes from some 200 countries will vie for the coveted gold, silver, and bronze, and it can be assumed that both competitors and spectators will be feeling a special frisson when these medals are awarded in the land that gave birth to these games.

## 1 Sources of Information

The official—and very thorough—website of the Athens Organizing Committee for the 2004 Olympics is the best place to start for general information: **www.athens2004.com**. Most participating nations' Olympic committees maintain websites with information specific to its citizens. For a list of the various national Olympic Committees and links to their website, go to **www.olympic.org/uk/organisation/index_uk.asp**.

Up-to-date information on events in the Cultural Olympiad festivities is expected to be available from **www.cultural-olympiad.gr**.

For Athens itself, the Olympics Organizing Committee in May 2003 announced plans to have kiosks—easily identified by the Olympics colors and logo—at various locales in central Athens and at all major venues. Open from early morning through the early evening, 7 days a week, these kiosks' staffs should be able to answer visitors' questions about transportation to the venues, schedules, ticket availability, special events, etc. Desk clerks at major hotels should also be able to at least direct visitors to the best transportation to the venues.

Also in Greece, for the most up-to-date news on possible changes in scheduling and sites, check out the Athens Daily News or the English-language edition of the Kathimerini insert in the International Herald Tribune.

## 2  Venues & Events

The 37 venues for events will be somewhat scattered—not only in and around Athens but in a number of more distant points—but most events will be held at one of three or four locales. The map shows where these venues are located and the grid chart indicates where each event is to be held. Not shown are the several cities elsewhere in Greece where certain preliminary events will be held: Thessaloniki; Patras, Volos, and Iraklion, Crete.

## 3  Getting Tickets

Tickets are divided into two Types—I and II—indicative of the popularity and demand of the event, and many ticketing arrangements require you to purchase at least one Type II for each Type I. Then tickets are priced by three categories, with Category A seats offering the best views, Category B offer moderately good viewing, while category C seats are further back form the action. Each day's events will be split up into two sessions, with the finals taking place mostly in the afternoon sessions.

### GETTING TICKETS IN ADVANCE

Of the 5.3 million tickets available for the Olympics, 2.3 million were distributed by early 2003 to the international Olympic Committee, national Olympic Committees, sponsors, broadcaster, the Greek government, and Athens 2004 Organizing Committee officials. Some of these may show up for sale to the public in various countries but most will be given or sold to selected few. That left 3 million tickets to be sold to the general public, and Greeks were given the first crack at these between May 12 to June 12, 2003. People in countries belonging to the European Union and European Economic Area were able to start applying at the same time by calling a number in Athens—**210/373-000** or via the internet: **www.athens2004.com/tickets**. All these tickets will presumably have long been sold by the time this book is published.

All other peoples of the world must seek tickets through the procedures and outlets established by their respective national Olympic committees. For a list of the various national Olympic Committees and links to their website, go to www.olympic.org/uk/organisation/index_uk.asp.

## SARS & Health Concerns

At the time this book went to press, SARS did not seem to be a problem in Greece nor did it seem that SARS would be a threat at the Olympics or in the transportation to and from Greece. By August 2004, however, a great deal might have happened with SARS and presumably everyone will be well aware of that situation. Aside from SARS, the Greek Olympic organizers have committed all kinds of resources to providing first-response medical service for spectators as well as athletes. Medical personnel and ambulances will be in attendance at all events, and there are plans for speedy transfer to hospitals.

By the way, the Greeks have declared that all venues be smoking free, if that is a concern (and if that is possible to enforce in a country like Greece . . .).

In the United States, Caravan Tours is the Official Ticket Agent for the exclusive sale of tickets to the general public. To request information, call ☎ **800/ 360-2004** or visit the website **www.caravan.com**. Caravan's home office is 1334 Parkview Avenue, Manhattan Beach, CA 90266 (sales@caravan.com).

Here are the official agents for Olympics tickets in the following countries:

- **Australia:** Sportsworld PLC, 73 Walker Street, North Sydney, NSW 2060 (☎ **02-9492/9100**; fax 02-9518/5224; **www.sportsworld-athens2004.com**).
- **Canada:** CoSport, (☎ **877/457-4647**; fax 908/766-2033; **www.cosport.com**).
- **New Zealand:** Sportsworld International, 155 The Strand, Parnell, Auckland. (☎ **0011-649/307-0770**; fax 0011-649/309-6191; **www.sportsworld-athens2004.com**).
- **United Kingdom:** Sportsworld Travel, New Abbey Court, Stert Street, Abingdon, Oxfordshire OX14 3JZ (☎ **01235/554-844**; fax 01235/554-8441; **www.sportsworld-athens2004.com**).

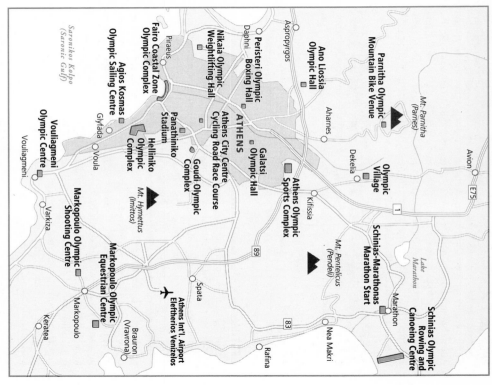

## Athens 2004 Olympic Games Competition Schedule

Please note that these dates are subject to change.

| Sports | Wed 11 | Thurs 12 | Fri 13 | Sat 14 | Sun 15 | Mon 16 | Tues 17 | Wed 18 | Thurs 19 | Fri 20 | Sat 21 | Sun 22 | Mon 23 | Tues 24 | Wed 25 | Thurs 26 | Fri 27 | Sat 28 | Sun 29 |
|---|---|---|---|---|---|---|---|---|---|---|---|---|---|---|---|---|---|---|---|
| Archery | | | | • | • | • | • | • | • | • | • | | | | | | | | |
| Athletics | | | | | | | | | | • | • | • | • | • | • | • | • | • | • |
| Badminton | | | | • | • | • | • | • | • | • | • | | | | | | | | |
| Baseball | | | | | • | • | | • | | • | • | | • | • | | | | | |
| Basketball | | | | • | • | • | • | • | • | • | • | • | • | • | • | • | • | • | |
| Beach Volleyball | | | | • | • | • | | • | • | • | • | • | • | • | | | | | |
| Boxing | | | | • | • | • | • | • | • | • | • | • | • | • | • | • | • | • | |
| Canoe/Kayak Flatwater Racing | | | | | | | | | | | | | | | • | • | • | • | |
| Canoe/Kayak Slalom Racing | | | | | | | • | • | • | • | | | • | • | | | | | |
| Cycling Mountain Bike | | | | | | | | | | | | | | | | | | • | |
| Cycling Road | | | | • | • | | | • | | | | | | | | | | | |
| Cycling Track | | | | | | | | | | • | • | • | • | • | | | | | |
| Diving | | | | • | • | • | | • | • | • | • | • | • | • | • | • | • | • | |
| Equestrian | | | | • | • | • | • | • | • | • | • | | • | • | | • | | | |
| Fencing | | | | • | • | • | • | • | • | • | • | | | | | | | | |
| Football | • | | | | | • | • | • | | | • | • | • | | | | | • | |
| Gymnastics Artistic | | | | • | • | | | • | | | | • | Gala | | | | | | |
| Gymnastics Rhythmic | | | | | | | | | | | | | | | | | | | |
| Gymnastics Trampoline | | | | | | | | | | | | | | | | | | | |
| Handball | | • | | • | • | • | • | • | • | • | • | • | • | • | • | • | • | • | |
| Hockey | | • | | • | • | • | • | • | • | • | • | • | • | • | • | • | • | • | |
| Judo | | | | | | | | • | • | • | • | | | | | | | | |
| Modern Pentathlon | | | | | | | | | | | | | | | | | | | |
| Rowing | | | | | • | • | • | • | • | • | • | • | | | | | | | |
| Sailing | | | | • | • | • | • | • | • | • | • | • | • | • | • | • | | | |
| Shooting | | | | • | • | • | • | • | • | • | • | • | | • | • | | | | |
| Softball | | | | • | • | • | • | • | • | • | • | • | • | | | | | | |
| Swimming | | | | • | • | • | • | • | • | • | | | | | | | | | |
| Synchronised Swimming | | | | | | | | | | | | | | • | • | • | • | | |
| Table Tennis | | | | | | | | | | | • | • | • | • | • | • | • | | |
| Taekwondo | | | | | | | | | | | | | | | | • | • | • | |
| Tennis | | | | | • | • | • | • | • | • | • | | | • | • | • | • | | |
| Triathlon | | | | | | | | | | | | | | | • | • | | | |
| Volleyball | | | | • | • | • | • | • | • | • | • | • | • | • | • | • | • | • | • |
| Water Polo | | | | • | • | • | • | • | • | • | • | • | • | • | • | • | • | • | • |
| Weightlifting | | | | • | • | • | • | • | • | • | | | • | • | • | • | • | • | |
| Wrestling | | | | | | | | | | | • | • | • | • | • | • | • | • | • |
| Ceremonies | | • | | | | | | | | | | | | • | • | | | | • |

> **Fun Fact** **Olympics Mascot**
>
> Olympics' mascots have become little more than a marketing "tool"—above all, a way for commercial vendors to increase sales. For the 2004 Olympics, the Greeks came up with two mascots, Phevos and Athena. Phevos is the Greek name for Apollo, god of light and music; his sister, Athena, is of course the goddess of wisdom and patron deity of the city of Athens. The mascots themselves are two rather clumpy figures, based on ancient Greek dolls from the 7th century B.C. If not conventionally "cute," they are intended to be childlike and joyful, so let's not be spoilsports. By the way, they are owned and copyrighted by the Greek organizing committee, so some share of all money spent on goods bearing the symbol of the mascot as well as the official Olympics symbol does go to support the Olympics. Visitors are therefore urged to buy such products sold only in the souvenir shops displaying the official Olympics logo.

It should be noted that people outside Greece will most likely have to buy a "package" that includes travel arrangements and accommodation as well as tickets. CoSport, one of the official sponsors of the 2004 U.S. Olympic Team and Athens 2004 Games, offers such packages. They can be contacted by calling toll free **877/457-4647** or by going into their website, **www.cosport.com.** Cartan Tours, mentioned above as a source for tickets, can also arrange for package tours.

Although these packages may be fairly reasonable, if you have your heart set on seeing particular events—especially the finals—you must check carefully to see what tickets are included in your package deal. You might decide to try to buy your tickets independently—not that easy to do at this late date but if you succeed, then you must decide how to make your travel and accommodation arrangements separately. If you do not work through a travel agency, see "Accommodations During the Games," below for tips on finding lodging. And if you do reserve accommodations on your own, be sure to get written confirmation of your reservation and the quoted room rates.

## TICKET PRICES

Ninety percent of all tickets for the Games will cost US$35 or less, with many costing as little as US$14 per session. For example, for US$14 you can see qualification rounds of such sports as soccer, volleyball, baseball, and softball. Tickets for the qualification rounds of such events as track and field or swimming are more in demand but if you don't mind sitting in the back rows, you can get these for as little as US$42.

When it comes to the final events, ticket pries rise dramatically, with ringside seats for the track and field events costing as much as $410. And for a ticket to the Opening Ceremony, the best seats cost US$1,700, the cheapest US$468; the Closing Ceremony is somewhat cheaper—US$936 for the best, US$140 for the cheapest.

## GETTING TICKETS AT THE LAST MINUTE

Although you will read that there is no guarantee that tickets will be available just before or during the Games, the fact is that not all events of the Olympics sell out. For every session, it's likely that at least some tickets will be on sale at the door or from scalpers. This is especially true for such low-demand events as baseball (remember, this is in Europe), handball, wrestling, judo, taekwando, rowing, and kayaking. In the 1996 Olympics Games in Barcelona, Spain, a country with almost four times the population of Greece, some 1.76 million tickets were reserved for the Spanish, and they weren't close to selling out. Meanwhile, hundreds of thousands of tickets are sold in advance to the sponsors and national Olympic committees of the 200 countries that send athletes to the Games. These groups are forced to buy packages that include the most popular events as well as the less popular ones. This means that the sponsors and national committees usually arrive at the Olympics with many tickets they couldn't unload. They will most likely sell these tickets to ticket brokers in Athens, who will then sell them at the best prices they can get. Even tickets to premium events may sell at the last minute for less than the face value.

**To sum up:** If you are intent on seeing only some particular event, you had better buy your ticket well in advance—and be prepared to pay a premium price and a package deal. But if all you want is to be able to say you saw some Olympic events in the land of their origin, you may be able to buy some tickets on the scene.

## 4 Accommodations During the Games

Virtually all the better hotels in and around Athens, as well as some in Olympia itself, have long ago been completely booked for the entire period of the Games. (In case you're wondering who these "insiders" are, most of these rooms were taken over by the Greek National Organizing Committee for officials, visiting dignitaries, and other national committees, and by corporate sponsors for their own promotional use.)

Prices are expected to vary considerably. Hotels are going to exploit the law of supply and demand to the utmost and are said to be charging 2 to 4 times their regular rates. Thus, a basic hotel that might be expected to charge some 100€ for

 **Handicapped Accessibility**

Athens has not hitherto been known for being especially accessible to the physically handicapped. This was due largely to the fact that the city's infrastructure—sidewalks, crossings, stairways, public transport, and so on—was put into place long before the physically handicapped expected to be able to move about a large city. Also, the very nature of the archaeological sites that have always been the city's main attractions did not seem to allow for any such accommodations. But in preparation of the 2004 Olympics, efforts were being made to at least make all Olympic venues accessible to the handicapped—specifically, for those confined to wheelchairs. Central Athens and its hotels and restaurants have much to do before they can be called "handicapped accessible," but, increasingly, people in wheelchairs do get around with the help of others, whether personal companions or strangers.

a double will probably charge 250€ or more for the same during the Olympics. There is nothing illegal about this—and it goes on during all Olympics. No one ever said you can't combine free enterprise with the Olympic spirit!

In addition to exploring the options listed below, international visitors should contact their country's National Olympic committee for the name of the officially appointed tour operator(s) responsible for ticket sales and package tours to the Games (See "Getting Tickets," above). The authorized travel agency for the U.S. Olympic Committee for the 2004 Olympics, for instance, is Cartan Tours, Inc. (© **800/360-2004;** www.cartan.com) and they can provide accommodations as well as other transportation services (as well as insurance for cancellation as a result of terrorism).

The Greeks confronted a challenge of a drastic surge in visitors requiring accommodations. The existing Greek hotel operators protested that if a lot of new hotels were built—especially with any form of government subsidies—they would lose their chance to make a bit of extra money; meanwhile, it was recognized that if they built all these new hotels, there would be a glut of rooms immediately following the Olympics and everyone would suffer with the collapse in prices. Being a relatively small country, hotels in cities outside Athens also have taken up a share of the trade: many popular tourist destinations lie within a 2 hour drive of Athens. But that still seemed to leave a shortage of rooms during the peak days.

To take some of the pressure off the hotels and prices, the Greeks have come up with two solutions. One is used by many if not all host cities: many Greeks in Athens are renting their apartments or homes. This program is being operated by two organizations in Athens: Alpha Philoxenia 2004 (© **210/326-6156;** fax 210/326-6148; cpallis@alphaastikaakinita.gr) and Elliniki Philoxenia (© **210/684-9222,** fax 210/684-9221; gmanzavinatos@eurobank.gr). These apartments and houses are scheduled to be inspected by the organizers and all should offer minimum standards for amenities (bathroom, kitchen, and so on). Prices range from about 100€ to 200€ per night *per person* (depending on the quality of the accommodations and the distance from venues and public transportation) and must be rented for minimum periods—what the agents refer to as "waves," usually 6 or 7 nights. (Cleaning service will be provided about every 3 days.) There may also be a "black market" in apartments and homes for rent, but we cannot advise you on how to deal with this.

The other solution to the housing shortage is what might be called "Odyssean"—that is, a canny Greek nautical one: seven large luxury cruise ships have been leased to berth at the port of Piraeus, some 8km (5 miles) from the heart of Athens. Cabins at various price levels are available, and in addition to providing meals (for extra charge) and free public transportation to the venues, the ships will be opening all their facilities (including swimming pools, exercise rooms, and so on). Cabins range from 450€ to 1,410€ *per person* (double occupancy) per night—but minimum 4 nights stay is required. To learn more about these ships, contact one or more of the three lines offering these accommodations: info@cma-greece.gr; sportius@otenet.gr; sales@roc.gr. In addition, the brand new *Queen Mary 2* is scheduled to berth at Piraeus and make its magnificent new facilities available; its status was still somewhat uncertain at the time this book went to press and there was no specific contact point. Travel agents will know of this possibility, and you can be sure it will be very expensive.

*Tips* **Dining During the Games**

The massive influx of people from not only foreign lands but from Greece itself will put a tremendous burden on even the many restaurants that Athens maintains for the tourist trade. Many of the better ones in the center of the city, furthermore, will have been totally reserved by the Greek Organizing Committee and corporate sponsors. Even many of the second-tier restaurants will be booked in advance by package groups. So if you are an independent traveler in Athens during these days, you have to adopt some tactics. If you are staying in a hotel that serves meals, it may be easiest (if not the most adventurous dining) to see if you can get meal reservations, too. If you cannot make your own reservations at a hotel or restaurant, then plan to eat your meals outside regular hours—which really means quite early, because Greeks usually eat quite late compared to many people. Try to establish some good relationship with a waiter or proprietor by showing up regularly—they may find a way to accommodate you no matter how crowded they seem. Plan to eat some meals "on the run"—from street vendors and such. Athens has a fair number of souvlaki stands—where the meat is roasted and sliced from a vertical slab and wrapped in pita bread (often quite tasty). Athens also has a great many small grocery stores and supermarkets where visitors can buy sandwiches, yogurt, and more than enough provisions for picnic and snack meals. (You might consider traveling with a small eating-utensil kit.)

## 5 Transportation During the Games

Don't even think about driving a car in Athens during the Games. The traffic is bad enough during normal times, and it will be a nightmare during the Games. (Not to mention the strict control of parking that will be in effect in the central city.) Even renting a car to travel to events outside greater Athens is not advised: take one of the public conveyances that will be available to take people to and from all venues. The Greeks have been working overtime to add to and upgrade their various transport systems—the new light rail, or trams, scheduled to go direct to the sea at Faliro; the electric railway; the metro (subway); and the extensive network of surface buses. There will be frequent service to all venues from and to the center of Athens.

As for just getting around the central city during this period, plan on doing a lot of walking because even the buses and metro (subway) will be packed. Taxis will probably be close to impossible to "hail." And for travel elsewhere in Greece—independent of the Games, that is—you must make reservations well in advance for internal flights and ferries. Likewise many ferry sailings. Realize that many of those attending the Games will be taking a once-in-a-lifetime advantage of their visit to Greece to see its traditional attractions. And since most attendees of the Games will spend only about a week at the Games themselves, this means that on any given day in August many of the hundreds of thousands who attend will be on the road throughout Greece.

## 6 The Cultural Olympiad/Olympic Arts Festival

As has become traditional, the athletic competitions of the Athens Olympic Games will be complemented by a **Cultural Olympiad** featuring various museum shows, concerts, dance performances, theater, and other special events. In May of 2003, for example, Christos Lambrakis, president of the Athens Concert Hall (the Megaron), announced that it would be the site of many special events in conjunction with the Olympics, including the staging of *La Traviata* in May of 2004. In the case of Athens, and Greece in general, there are already so many unique and notable cultural events during the summer months that no one interested in this aspect of Greece will feel disappointed. Many cultural institutions are planning to present special shows that will reflect some aspect of the Olympics.

Athens' museums alone have some of the world's single-most outstanding collections: the newly renovated National Museum (with its comprehensive collection of unique objects from the ancient Greek world) is scheduled to reopen in time for the Olympics; the brand new Acropolis Museum will probably not be completed in time for the Olympics (and in any case was unable to persuade the British to loan them any of the Elgin marbles) but the existent Acropolis Museum is still a treat; the Goulandris Museum of Cycladic Art; the Benaki and Byzantine Museums (both with world-class collections of Byzantine and medieval art), and the Museum of Greek Folk Art. Full details about all these museums may be found in chapter 5.) The Museum of the Olympic Games and the Archaeological Museum at Olympia are, of course, of particular interest to Olympics visitors (see chapter 8). And of course museums elsewhere in Greece have other distinctive collections—just to single out one, the Archaeological Museum in Iraklion, Crete, has the world's major collection of Minoan art (see chapter 9).

Beyond museums, there will be a constant series of theatrical and dance performances as well as concerts for all kinds of music by world-class groups or individuals. In Athens itself, these will be part of the annual Athens Festival—with most performances at the Odeon of Herodes Atticus at the foot of the Acropolis (see chapter 5). There are also the annual Sound and Light performances that focus on the Acropolis (see chapter 6). Within a same-day return visit from Athens is the Epidaurus Festival, with performances of classical Greek dramas in one of the world's greatest ancient amphitheaters (see chapter 8). Elsewhere throughout Greece, there are several other regularly scheduled cultural events: the summer-long arts festival of Iraklion, Crete (See chapter 9); an International Music Festival on Santorini (see chapter 10); dramas at the ancient amphitheater at Dodona, in northwest Greece (see chapter 12); the Sound and Light and Traditional Folk Dance performances on Rhodes (see chapter 11).

For the most up-to-date information, check out **www.cultural-olympiad.gr,** which is the umbrella organization handling cultural events during the build up to and for the 2004 Olympics.

## 7 The Paralympic Games

The Paralympic movement will be observing its 44th anniversary at the 2004 Games in Athens by holding its competitions for the physically handicapped. (The 1st Paralympic Games were held in Rome in 1960.) Some 4,000 athletes from 130 countries are expected to compete at the Games of the XII Paralympiad, to be held in Athens from September 17 to 28. Although not drawing anywhere near the crowds as those attending the Olympics in August, there will be a significant demand placed on accommodations in Athens during this event.

Athletes will compete in 19 major sports at the Athens 2004 Paralympic Games, 15 of which are also part of the regular 2004 Olympics. The full medal sports at the Paralympics are: archery, athletics (track, throwing, jumping, pentathlon, marathon), basketball (wheelchair), boccia (the Italian bowling game played by athletes with cerebral palsy because the object is to roll balls along a earthen "alley" and place the balls closest to a white target ball), cycling, equestrian, fencing (wheelchair), football (soccer), goalball (played by blind competitors who try to throw balls equipped with bells into the opponents' goal), judo, lawn bowls (like boccia except played on open grass field), powerlifting, rugby (wheelchair), sailing, shooting, swimming, table tennis, tennis (wheelchair), and volleyball. The Paralympic Games include some 700 medal events—more than twice the number of Olympic events because Paralympic athletes compete according to degree of disability and functional level, creating additional categories. Events will utilize most of the Olympic venues as well as some other locations around Athens.

For further information about the Paralympics, check out **www. paralympic.org**.

# Cruising the Greek Islands

*by Heidi Sarna*

The dramatic approach into the beautiful bowl-shaped harbor of Santorini, a partially submerged crater of an ancient volcano whose steep parched slopes are crowned by a whitewashed village, is what cruising the Greek Islands is all about. Dropdead gorgeous scenery. Plus, of course, ancient historic sites and lots of local culture, all without the hassle of deciphering ferry schedules and changing hotel rooms. You get on the ship, you unpack once, and the ship goes with you as your floating hotel. It's your familiar retreat after a long day of touring or a place to just kick back and bask in the Greek sun.

Among the most beautiful regions to cruise in all the world, the seas are

relatively calm and the islands are individual in character, offering travelers a satisfying mix of local culture, stunning scenery, and ancient and medieval ruins to explore.

Most Greek island itineraries highlight the region's history with optional guided **shore excursions** that take in the major sights, spicing up the vacation brew with other, less historyminded excursions such as visits to beaches, meals at local restaurants, and fishing or sailing excursions.

Of course, you can also choose to get off the ship at each port of call and head off on your own to explore the sights, hit the beach, or check out the local color at the nearest taverna. Solo is often the best way to go.

## 1 Choosing the Right Cruise for You

In choosing your cruise, you need to think about what you want to see and in what level of comfort you want to see it.

We recommend you first decide **what you want to see.** Are you looking to visit the most popular islands—Mykonos, Santorini, and Rhodes—or are you interested in places off the beaten path? Whichever it is, you'll want to make sure the itinerary you choose allows enough time for you to experience the place or places that really take your fancy. Some ships visit a port and spend the full day, while others visit two ports in 1 day, which limits your sightseeing time in each.

In the past, Greek law was designed so that only Greek-flagged ships could cruise between Greek ports, meaning that foreign-flagged vessels had to visit en route between other European ports, usually in Italy or Turkey. This law officially changed in 1999, but many Greek islands cruises still maintain a similar routing, either beginning or ending their itineraries elsewhere. You'll have to consider embarkation and disembarkation points in making your decision. Do you mind flying to Venice or Istanbul to catch your ship?

Greece is also visited by ships as part of European itineraries where Greece is not the sole focus, but only one of several countries visited. If you're looking for a trip that includes several countries, that's fine. But if you're looking to spend most of your time in Greece, make sure you choose an appropriate itinerary.

Next, consider **how long you want to spend cruising the islands**—3 days, a week, 2 weeks? If you have the time, you may want to consider a **cruisetour,** which combines a cruise to the islands with a guided tour of important sights on the mainland. This is made easy in Greece by the fact that some lines offer cruises of only 3 or 4 days, which you can combine with a land tour into a 1-week vacation, and 1-week cruises you can combine with a land tour to make a 2-week vacation.

Also consider **when you want to cruise.** While Greece has traditionally been a summer destination, the season has been stretched in recent years, and some lines now offer cruises here virtually year-round. While most of the action on the islands still takes place in the warmer months, from late April through October, traveling at other times has its own special charms, including the fact that it allows you to avoid the tourist crush (although some visitor facilities may be closed in the off-season) and the months of highest temperatures (in July and August, temperatures can reach 38°C/100°F). For the record, August is the month the islands are most crowded with European vacationers (expect beaches, bars, and discos to be packed) and April and November are the rainiest months. May and October are relatively problem-free, making them particularly nice times to sail in Greece.

You'll also want to think about **what you want out of the cruise experience.** Is the purpose of your cruise to see as much as you can of the islands, or to relax by the ship's pool? And what level of comfort, entertainment, onboard activities, and so forth do you require? Some ships spend a day or more at sea, meaning they don't visit a port at all that day, and while some experienced cruisers enjoy those days the most, treasuring the opportunity they offer for real relaxation, they won't do you much good if your goal is seeing as much of Greece as you can.

## CHOOSING YOUR SHIP

Ships cruising the Greek islands range from small yacht-type vessels carrying fewer than 50 passengers to traditional midsize ships to resort-like, 2,000 passenger megaships. Which you choose has a lot to do with your personality and vacation goals.

**MEGASHIPS & LARGE SHIPS**    Cruises aboard these vessels focus as much on onboard activities as they do on the destination they're visiting. The ships are floating resorts—some of the glitzy variety—offering American-style luxury and amenities and attentive service. In a recent brochure, Holland America Line unabashedly said that "When asked which European city he liked best, one guest replied 'My Holland America ship—that was my favorite city.'" We think that kind of says it all.

These ships, which tend to be newer, feature Las Vegas–style shows, lavish casinos, big spas and gyms, plenty of bars, extravagant meals, lots of daytime activities (such as games, contests, cooking lessons, wine tastings, and sport tournaments), and generally few ethnic Greek offerings.

**CLASSIC & MIDSIZE SHIPS**    Ships in this category include older, classic vessels as well as some newer ships. Destination is more a focus than on the bigger ships, and itineraries may be very busy, with the ship visiting an island a day, or sometimes two. This leaves little time for onboard daytime activities, although some will be offered. In the Greek market, some of these ships feature Greek crews and cuisine, and service tends to be a big area of focus. Because these ships are popular with Europeans, you'll likely hear many languages spoken on board. The ships offer a variety of bars and lounges, at least one swimming pool and a small casino, a spa and gym, and plenty of open deck space, and have entertainment generally in a main show lounge, with some also having cinemas that show recent-release films. Like the megaships, these ships' cabins are comfortable and often roomy, but not opulent.

**SMALL SHIPS & YACHTS**   Small ships and yachts tend to offer more of a relaxed pace and may seek itineraries that focus on smaller size and shallow draft (the amount of ship that rides beneath the waterline). They may offer a "soft adventure" cruise experience, with nature- and outdoor-oriented activities as a big focus, or they may offer more of a luxury yacht experience. Some of the ships feature Greek crews and Greek cuisine. There will typically be more interaction with fellow passengers than on larger ships—partially because there will be less entertainment, and there may or may not be a swimming pool, casino, spa, or gym. Both cabins and public rooms range from small and serviceable to large and luxurious, depending on which ship you choose. Some are fully engine-powered while others are sailing vessels (though even on these the sails are typically more for show than for power).

## 2 Calculating the Cost

Cruises in the Greek islands range from 3 nights to 2 weeks, with prices per day ranging from around 100€ to over 1,000€, double occupancy. These days, the lowest prices are usually offered a month or two before sailing and they're almost always substantially less than **brochure prices** (which are the prices we quote in this chapter). Like new-car sticker prices, brochure rates are notoriously inflated, and in fact, inside sources tell me some lines are considering not printing them up at all in the near future. Travel agencies and web-based cruise-only agencies offer the best and "real" prices (see "Booking Your Cruise," below, for a list of recommended sources). Depending on demand, you may snag a two-for-one deal or free airfare or free hotel stays.

At press time, in the spring of 2003, with tensions in the Middle East high along with travelers apprehensions to plan vacations in Europe, many lines were offering enticing prices, while others were moving most of their ships from the Mediterranean to other parts of the world, including the Caribbean, and Northern Europe and the Baltic. Since 2004 rates won't be available until after press time, we feature actual prices for the summer 2003 season.

No matter what price you wind up paying, rates include three meals a day (with a couple of exceptions, which we've noted in the ship reviews below), accommodations, onboard activities and entertainment, and, if you book your airfare through the cruise line, a transfer from the airport to the ship. Some rates even include airfare (the inclusion of airfare is more common on European cruises than Caribbean cruises), and in rare cases the fare may also include tips, shore excursions, and/or pre- and/or post-cruise hotel stays. Some cruises are packaged as cruisetours, meaning they include both hotel stays and land tours. Rarely included in the price are alcoholic beverages or spa and beauty treatments. Port charges, taxes, and other fees are usually, but not always, included in the cruise fare. We've noted exceptions below.

Cruise prices are based on two people sharing a cabin. Most lines have special **single supplement** prices for solo passengers wishing to have a cabin to themselves, usually ranging from 150% to 200% of the per-person rate. The "supplement," in this case, goes to the cruise line as their compensation for not getting two passenger fares for the cabin. At the opposite end, most lines offer highly discounted rates for a third or fourth person sharing a cabin with two full-fare passengers.

**Senior citizens** may be able to get extra savings on their cruise. Some lines will take 5% off the top for those 55 and over, and the senior rate applies even if the second person in the cabin is younger. Membership in groups such as AARP is not required, but such membership may bring additional savings.

Some of the more upscale lines will reward customers willing to pay their full fare in advance (thus giving the cruise line cash in hand), with savings of as much as 10%.

If your package does not include **airfare,** you should consider booking air transportation through the cruise line. While the rates offered by the lines may or may not be as low as you could find on your own, booking through the line allows the cruise company to keep track of you if, for instance, your flight is delayed. In this case, the ship may be able to wait for you. The cruise lines also negotiate special deals with hotels at port cities if you want to come in a few days before your flight or stay after.

## 3 Booking Your Cruise

Today, practically everybody has a website, and the difference between so-called **web-based cruise sellers** and more **traditional travel agencies** is that the former rely on their sites for most of their actual bookings, while the latter use theirs as glorified advertising space to promote their offerings, doing most of their actual business in person or over the phone. As far as cruise prices go, there's no absolutely quantifiable difference between the real live travel agents and Internet-based cruise sellers. Sometimes you'll get the best price on the Web and sometimes you'll get it through an agent—especially in the current market, where prices offered to agents and sites tend to be very similar across the board. Some agencies, online or off, get better prices from certain cruise lines because they sell a high volume of that line's product.

In deciding how to book your cruise, consider your level of experience as a cruiser and as an Internet user. Most websites give you only a menu of ships and itineraries to select from, plus a basic search capability that takes into account only destination, price, length of trip, and date, without consideration of the type of cruise experience each line offers. If you've cruised before and know exactly what you want, no problem. If, on the other hand, you have limited experience with cruising and with booking on the web, it may be better to go through a traditional agent, who can help you wade through the choices and answer your questions, from which cabins have their views obstructed by lifeboats to information on dining and tuxedo rentals. No matter which way you wind up booking your cruise, you may want to first check out the cruise line websites and www.cruisemates.com and AOL's www.cruisecritic.com for ship reviews, virtual tours, chats and industry news.

To find an agent, rely on referrals from trusted friends and colleagues. Some agents really know the business—they travel themselves to sample what they sell—others are not much more than order-takers. We also recommend these agencies below, which specialize in selling cruises with mainstream lines such as Princess, Celebrity, and Holland America. While all have websites to promote current deals, the agencies listed primarily operate from a combination of walk-in business and toll-free telephone-based business.

- **Cruise Brothers,** 950 Wellington Ave., Cranston, RI 02910 (© **800/827-7779** or 401/941-3999; www.cruisebrothers.com)
- **The Cruise Company,** 10760 Q St., Omaha, NE 68127 (© **800/289-5505** or 402/339-6800; www.thecruisecompany.com)
- **Cruises By Brennco,** 508 E. 112th St., Kansas City, MO 64131 (© **800/955-1909** or 816/942-1000; www.brennco.com)
- **Cruises Only,** 220 Congress Park Dr., Delray Beach, FL 33445 (© **800/278-4737;** www.cruisesonly.com) is part of the My Travel family of cruise companies, which also include CruiseOne and Cruises Inc.
- **Cruise Value Center,** 6 Edgeboro Rd., Ste. 400, East Brunswick, NJ 08816 (© **800/231-7447;** www.cruisevalue.com)
- **Just Cruisin' Plus,** 5640 Nolensville Rd., Nashville, TN 37211 (© **800/888-0922** or 615/833-0922; www.justcruisinplus.com)

This sampling of reputable agencies, both cruise-only and full-service who also work mostly by phone, specializes in selling ultraluxury cruises such as Cunard, Seabourn, Crystal and Windstar.

- **Altair Travel,** 2025 S. Brentwood Blvd., St. Louis, MO 63144 (© **800/844-5598** or 314/968-9600; www.altairtravelinc.com)
- **Golden Bear Travel/Mariner Club,** 16 Digital Dr., Novado, CA 94949 (© **800/551-1000** or 415/382-8900; www.goldenbeartravel.com)
- **Jean Rose Travel,** 140 Intracoastal Pointe Dr., Jupiter FL 33477 (© **800/441-4846** or 561/575-2901)
- **Largay Travel,** 5 F Village St., Southbury, CT 06488 (© **800/955-6872** or 203/264-6581; www.largaytravel.com)
- **Pisa Brothers,** 630 Fifth Ave., New York, NY 10111 (© **800/729-7472** or 212/265-8420; www.pisabrothers.com)

The following sites are reputable web-based cruise specialists, though they all can be reached via phone as well. All allow searches by destination, date of travel, and other variables. In most cases, when booking on line you'll have to wait up to 24 hours for a confirmation via e-mail, fax, or phone call.

- **Cruise.com** (www.cruise.com; © **800/800-9552** or 888/333-3116)
- **Cruise411.com** (www.cruise411.com; © **800/553-7090**)
- **11th Hour Vacations** (www.11thhourvacations.com; © **864/331-1140**)
- **Expedia.com** (www.Expedia.com; © **800/397-3342**)
- **Icruise.com** (www.icruise.com; © **888/909-6242** or 212/929-6046)
- **Travelocity** (www.travelocity.com; © **877/815-5446**).

## CHOOSING A CABIN

One of your biggest decisions once you choose the ship you want to sail on is what type of cabin you need. Will you be happy with a slightly cramped space without a window (the most budget-minded choice) or do you require a suite with a private veranda?

Obviously, price will be a determinant here. If you aren't planning to spend time in your cabin except to sleep, shower, and change clothes, an **inside cabin** (that is, one without a porthole or window) might do just fine. If you get claustrophobic, however, or insist on sunshine first thing in the morning, or intend to hole up in your cabin for extended periods, pay a bit more and take an **outside cabin** (one with a window and sometimes a private balcony too).

When you book your cabin, you generally will not be choosing a specific cabin number but rather a cabin category, within which all units have the same amenities. With this in mind, one concern if you do go the window route is **obstructed views.** Check to make sure none of the cabins in the category you've selected have windows that directly face lifeboats or other objects that may stand between you and your view of the clear blue sea. You can determine this by looking at a diagram of the ship (included in the cruise brochure) or consulting with your travel agent.

Most ships offer cabins for two with private bathrooms and showers (bathtubs are considered a luxury on most ships, and are usually offered only in the most expensive cabins) and twin beds that may be convertible to a queen. There are other variations, of course. For instance, a number of ships have some cabins with bunk beds (referred to in the brochures as "upper and lower berths"), many ships have cabins designed for three or four people, and some have connecting cabins for families.

**Cabin amenities** vary by line, and often include TVs (with a closed system of programmed movies and features), VCRs, hair dryers, safes, and minirefrigerators. If any of these are must-haves, let your agent know.

Usually the higher on the ship the cabin is located, the more expensive it is. But upper decks also tend to be rockier in rough seas than the middle or lower parts of the ship, a factor to consider if you're prone to seasickness.

**Size of cabin** is determined in terms of square feet, and keep in mind ship cabins are generally smaller than the equivalent hotel rooms you'd find on land. As a rough guide, 120 square feet is low-end and cramped, 180 square feet is midrange and fairly roomy, and 250 square feet and larger is suite-sized and very comfortable.

If noise bothers you, try to pick a cabin far from the engine room and nowhere near the disco.

## CHOOSING A MEALTIME

Because most ship dining rooms are not large enough to accommodate all passengers at one dinner seating (exceptions include Seabourn and SeaDream Yacht Club), times and tables are assigned. When you book your trip, you will have to indicate your preferred mealtime for most ships. Early, or "main," seating is usually 6 or 6:30pm, late seating at 8 or 8:30pm. Lines catering to a majority of European clientele may offer seatings an hour or so later than these.

There are advantages to both times. **Early seating** is usually less crowded, and the preferred time for families and older passengers who want to get to bed early. Food items are fresher (they don't have to sit in warmers), but the waiters know that the second wave is coming in a couple hours, and so may be rushed. Early diners get first dibs on nighttime entertainment venues, and might be hungry enough in a few hours to take advantage of the midnight buffet. **Late seating** allows time for a nap or late spa appointment before dinner. Service is slower paced, and you can linger with after-dinner drinks, then catch the late show at 10pm.

When choosing a mealtime, you also need to consider **table size** (on most ships, you can request to be at a table for 2, 4, 8, 10, or 12) and whether you want to sit at a **smoking or nonsmoking table**—a particularly important factor in Europe, where smoking is still quite popular (though, many dining rooms are completely non-smoking). It's usually tough to snag a table for two since they're usually in great demand.

On most ships, **breakfast** and **lunch** are open seating, but you may be requested to eat at an assigned time. (Early means breakfast at 7 or 8am, lunch at noon; late, breakfast at 8:30 or 9am, lunch at 1:30pm.) On ships with buffet restaurants, you can also choose to have both meals there, at any time during their open hours.

You should inform the cruise line at the time you make your reservations if you have any **special dietary requests.** Some lines offer kosher menus; all will have vegetarian, low-fat, low-salt, and sugar-free options available.

## DEPOSITS, CANCELLATIONS & EXTRAS

After you've made your decision as to which ship you will vacation on, you will be required to put down a deposit if you're booking 2 or more months in advance (with the remaining fare usually paid no later than 2 months in advance of your departure date) or pay the entire fare if booking within 60 or 70 days of your sailing date.

Cruise lines have varying policies regarding cancellations, and it's important to look at the fine print in the line's brochure to make sure you understand the policy. Traditionally, most lines allow you to cancel for a full refund on your deposit and payment any time up to about 70 days before the sailing, after which you have to pay a penalty. If you cancel at the last minute, you would traditionally lose the entire fare paid. However, the volatile state of world events at press time in spring of 2003, especially in the Middle East, prompted many lines to temporarily offer enhanced cancellation and optional insurance policies to encourage bookings. Lines including SeaDream Yacht Club, for instance, were allowing you to cancel for any reason (whether you bought travel insurance or not) up until the day before departure and get full credit for a future cruise for what you paid. Many optional insurance policies sold by the cruise lines were also offering cash refunds and/or cruise credits for 90% to 100% of fare paid for cancellations for any reason up until one to three days before departure, including Seabourn, Oceania Cruises, First European, Radisson Seven Seas and Costa. As many of these new policies, at press time, were only being promoted through 2003, before booking your cruise ask your agent or cruise line for an update.

An agent will discuss with you optional **airfare programs** offered by the lines, **transfers** from the airport to the pier, and any pre- or post-cruise **hotel or tour programs** (this kind of information is not always as easy to assess on a website without talking to a live agent). Some lines also let you purchase **shore excursions** in advance (for more on shore excursions, see below). And there may also be packages of onboard spa services available for prebooking.

If you are not booking airfare through the cruise line, make sure to allow several hours between the plane's arrival and when you need to get on the ship. It may be best, in terms of reducing anxiety, to come in a day before and spend the night in a hotel.

## 4 Cruise Preparation Practicalities

About 1 month before your cruise and no later than 1 week before, you should receive your **cruise documents,** including your airline tickets (if you purchased them from the cruise line), a boarding document with your cabin number and sometimes dining choices on it, boarding forms to fill out, luggage tags, and your prearranged bus transfer vouchers and hotel vouchers (if applicable).

There will also be information about **shore excursions** and additional material detailing things you need to know before you sail. Most lines also list excursions on their websites and in some cases, allow you to book shore excursions in advance of your sailing (on line or via fax), which will give you first dibs at popular offerings that may sell out later.

Read all of this pre-trip information carefully. Make sure your cabin category and dining preferences are as you requested and that your airline flight and arrival times are what you were told. If there are problems, call your agent immediately. Make sure there is enough time so you can arrive at the port no later than an hour before departure time.

You will be required to have a passport for your trip (see chapter 2 for more on this). If you are flying into Istanbul, you will also be required to have a Turkish visa, which can be obtained at Istanbul airport once you arrive.

We recommend you confirm your flight 3 days before departure. Also, before you leave for the airport, tie the tags provided by the cruise line onto your luggage and fill in your boarding cards. This will save you time when you arrive at the ship.

## CASH MATTERS

You already paid the lion's share of your vacation when you paid for your cruise, but you will need a credit card or traveler's checks to handle your **onboard expenses** (such as bar drinks, dry cleaning and laundry, emailing, massage and other spa services, beauty-parlor services, photos taken by the ship's photographer, babysitting, wine at dinner, and souvenirs) as well as **shore excursions** and **tips** (see below for tips on tipping). Expect to spend anywhere from 250€ to 800€ per person for the "extras" on a weeklong cruise, depending on how much you drink, shop and so on.

Some ships (but not all) will take a personal check for onboard expenses. If you want to pay in cash or by traveler's check, you will be asked to leave a deposit, usually 250€ for a 1-week sailing. Some ships have ATMs if you need to get cash while aboard, and some (but not all) offer currency-exchange services.

We suggest you keep careful track of your onboard expenses to avoid an unpleasant surprise at the end of your cruise. Some ships make this particularly easy by offering interactive TVs in cabins: by pushing the right buttons, you can check your account from the comfort of your own stateroom. On other ships, you can get this information at the purser's office or guest-relations desk.

You will want to have some cash in hand when going ashore for expenses such as taxis, snacks or meals, drinks, small purchases, and tips for guides.

## PACKING

Generally, ships describe their **daily recommended attire** as casual, informal, and formal, prompting many people to think they'll have to bring a steamer trunk full of clothes just to get through their trip. Not true; you can probably get along with about half of what you think you need. Also, almost all ships offer laundry and dry-cleaning services, and some have coin-operated self-serve laundries aboard, so you have the option of packing less and just having your clothes cleaned midway through your trip.

During the day, the onboard style is casual, but keep in mind some ships do not allow swimsuits or tank tops in the dining room. For dinner, there are usually two formal nights and two informal nights during a 5- to 7-day cruise, with the rest casual. There will usually be proportionally more formal nights on longer cruises.

The daily bulletin delivered to your cabin each day will advise you of the proper dress code for the evening. **Formal** means a tux or dark suit with tie for men and a nice cocktail dress, long dress, long dress, gown, or dressy pantsuit for women. **Informal** is a jacket, tie, and dress slacks or a light suit for men (jeans are frowned upon) and a dress, skirt and blouse, or pants outfit for women. **Casual** means different things to different people. Typically it means a sports shirt or open dress shirt with slacks for men; women can wear skirts, dresses, or pants outfits. Though jeans and shorts are usually frowned upon, many people do wear them to dinner on casual nights.

Check your cruise documents to determine the number of formal nights (if any) during your cruise. Men who don't own a tuxedo might be able to rent one in advance through the cruise line's preferred supplier (who delivers the tux right to the ship). Information on this service often is sent with your cruise documents. Also, some cruises offer **theme nights**, so you may want to check your cruise documents to see if there are any you'll want to bring special clothes for. (For instance, Greek night means everyone wears blue and white—the Greek national colors.)

If you want to bring the crown jewels, be careful. If you're not wearing them, leave them either in your in-room safe (if there is one) or with the purser.

In general, for Greece you're best off packing loose and comfortable cotton or other lightweight fabrics. You'll also want to pack a swimsuit, a sun hat, sunglasses, and plenty of sunscreen—the Greek sun can be intense. Obviously, you should adjust your wardrobe depending on when you plan to travel (summer is hotter than spring and fall). Even if you're traveling in August, though, you should bring a sweater, as you'll be in and out of air-conditioning. And don't forget an umbrella.

**For shore excursions,** comfortable walking shoes are a must, as some involve walking on stone or marble. Also, some tours may visit religious sites that have a "no shorts or bare shoulders" policy, so it's best to bring something to cover up with. (If you're taking the tour through the cruise line, you'll be advised of this before you go.)

If you plan on bringing your own hair dryer, electric razor, curling iron, or other electrical device, you will want to check out the electric current available on the ship in advance. An adapter may be required.

## 5 Embarkation

Check-in is usually 2 to 3 hours before sailing. You will not be able to board the ship before the scheduled embarkation time. You have up until a half-hour (on some ships it's 1 hour) before departure to board.

At check-in, your boarding documents will be checked and your passport will likely be taken for immigration processing. You will get it back sometime during the cruise (you might want to carry a photocopy as backup). Depending on the cruise line, you may establish your **onboard credit account** at this point by presenting a major credit card or making a deposit in cash or traveler's checks (usually 250€). On other ships you need to go to the purser's office on board to establish your account.

You may be given your **dining-room table assignment** in advance of your sailing (on your tickets) or as you check in, or find a card with your table number waiting for you in your stateroom. If you do not receive a card with your table assignment by the time you get to your stateroom, you will be directed to a maître d's desk.

## Tips  Dealing with Seasickness

If you suffer from seasickness, plan on packing some **Bonine** or **Dramamine** in case your ship encounters rough seas. Keep in mind that with both these medications it is recommended you not drink alcohol; Dramamine in particular can make you drowsy. Both can be bought over the counter, and ships also stock supplies onboard, available at either the purser's office or the medical center (in both cases it's usually free).

Another option is the **Transderm patch**, available by prescription only, which goes behind your ear and time-releases medication. The patch can be worn for up to 3 days, but comes with all sorts of side-effect warnings. Some people have also had success in curbing seasickness with **ginger capsules** available at health-food stores. If you prefer not to ingest anything, you might try the **acupressure wristbands** available at most pharmacies. When set in the proper spot on the wrist, they effectively ease seasickness, although if the seas are particularly rough they may have to be supplemented with some medication.

This is also the place to go to make any changes if your assignment does not meet with your approval.

Once aboard you'll be shown to your cabin by a crewmember, who will probably offer to help carry your hand luggage. No tip is required for this service; though feel free to slip the steward a few bucks if you're feeling generous.

In your cabin you will find a **daily program** detailing the day's events, mealtimes, and so forth, as well as important information on the ship's **safety procedures** and possibly a **deck plan** of the ship. There are also deck plans and directional signs posted around the ship, generally at main stairways and elevators.

If you are planning to use the ship's **spa services,** it's best to stop by as soon as you board the ship to make appointments so you can get your preferred times (the best times go fast, and some popular treatments sell out).

Note the ship's casino and shops are always closed when the ship is in port, and the swimming pool(s) will also likely be tarped. They will be filled with either fresh or saltwater after the ship sets sail.

Some lines offer **escorted tours** of the public rooms to get you acquainted with the ship. Check the daily program in your cabin for details.

## LIFEBOAT/SAFETY DRILL

Ships are required by law to conduct safety drills the first day out. Most do this either right before the ship sails or shortly thereafter. If you try and hide out in your cabin to avoid the drill, you'll likely get a knock my cabin steward reminding you to please join the others. A notice on the back of your cabin door will list the procedures and advise as to your assigned **muster station** and how to get there. You will also find directions to the muster station in the hallway. You will be alerted as to the time in both the daily program and in repeated public announcements (and probably by your cabin steward as well).

At the start of the drill, the ship will broadcast its emergency signal. At this time, you will be required to return to your cabin, grab your **life jacket** (which you're shown as soon as you arrive in your cabin), and report to your assigned muster station—usually in a lounge, the casino, or other public room. If you're traveling with children, make sure your cabin is equipped with special children's life jackets. If not, alert your steward.

## 6 End-of-Cruise Procedures

Your shipboard account will close in the wee hours before departure, but prior to that time you will receive a preliminary bill in your cabin. If you are setting your account with your credit card, you don't have to do anything but make sure all the charges are correct. If there is a problem, you will have to report to the purser's office.

If you are paying by cash or traveler's check, you will be asked to settle your account either during the day or night before you leave the ship. This will require you to report to the purser's office. A final invoice will be delivered to your room before departure.

### TIPS

You will typically find tipping suggestions in your cabin on the last day of your cruise. These are only suggestions, but, since service personnel make most (or all) of their salaries through tips, we don't recommend tipping less—unless, of course, bad service warrants it. (A few lines operate on a **no-tipping-required** basis, but the staff will still accept a tip if it's offered. On some very upscale lines, acceptance of tips is strictly forbidden.)

Each passenger should usually tip his or her cabin steward and waiter about 3.50€ per day each, and the bus boy about 2€ (the cruise line will provide suggested minimums). That totals up to a minimum of 63€ for a 7-night cruise (you do not have to include disembarkation day). You are, of course, free to tip more. On some European ships, the suggested minimums are even less. The reason: Europeans aren't as used to tipping as Americans. On some ships you are also encouraged to tip the maitre d' and head waiter (don't feel you have to give either more than 7€ per person, unless they have given you particularly great service). You may also encounter cases where tips are pooled: you hand over a suggested amount and it's up to the crew to divide it among themselves. Some luxury lines, including Radisson and Silversea, include tips in the cruise fare.

You may have to pay tips in cash (U.S. dollars are okay), although some lines let you put the tips on your charge account.

Bar bills often automatically include a 15% tip, but if the wine steward, for instance, has served you exceptionally well, you can slip him or her a bill, too. If you have spa or beauty treatments, you can tip that person at the time of the service (you can even do it on your shipboard charge account).

Don't tip the captain or other officers. They're professional, salaried employees.

The porters who carry your bags at the pier will likely expect a tip.

### PACKING UP

Because of the number of bags being handled, big ships require guests to pack the night before departure and leave their bags in the hallway, usually by midnight. (Be sure they're tagged with the cruise line's luggage tags, which are color-coded to indicate deck number and disembarkation order.) The bags will be picked up overnight and removed from the ship before passengers are allowed to disembark (don't pack bottles or other breakables; luggage is often thrown from bin to bin as it's being off-loaded). You'll see them again in the cruise terminal, where they'll most likely be arranged by deck number.

Pack all the purchases you made during the trip in one suitcase. This way you can easily retrieve them if you're stopped at customs.

## 7 The Cruise Lines & Their Ships

In this section, we describe the ships offering Greek islands cruises. Later in the chapter, we describe ships that visit Greece as part of longer itineraries.

The lines are listed alphabetically. Rates are 2003 **brochure prices.** As stated earlier, brochure rates are just about always inflated, count on getting some kind of discounted rate (easily half off of the brochure rate), whether for booking last minute, or taking advantage of a two-for-one promotion and so on. Most lines also offer special savings for third and fourth passengers sharing a cabin, and some have special rates for children (as noted below). Prices given are per-person, per day, based on double occupancy. To get an estimate of the per-person cruise price, you can multiply the listed **per diem rate** by the number of nights you'll be on the ship.

The **itineraries** we list are also for the 2003 season. Both prices and itineraries are subject to change.

We've listed the **sizes of ships** in two ways: **passenger capacity** and **gross registered tons (GRTs).** Rather than describing actual tonnage, the latter is a measure of interior space used to produce revenue on a vessel. One GRT = 100 cubic feet of enclosed, revenue-generating space.

Please also note that Piraeus, mentioned frequently below as an embarkation and disembarkation point, is the port city for Athens.

## COSTA CRUISE LINES

World Trade Center, 80 SW 8th St., Miami, FL 33130-3097. © **800/462-6782.** www.costacruises.com.

This Italian line traces its origins back to 1860 and the Italian olive-oil business. Today, Carnival Corporation, parent of Carnival Cruise Lines, is the owner. Onboard, Italy shows through in nearly everything Costa offers, from the food (which can be disappointing) to the Italian design of the vessels to the Italian-speaking crew (although they are not all from Italy) to the mostly Italian entertainers. The Italian experience is presented in a casual, warm and humorous manner. You'll feel like you're a part of one big Italian family.

The line's ships represent one of the newest fleets in the industry, sporting blue-and-yellow smokestacks emblazoned with a huge letter C. They are popular in the U.S./Caribbean market but are not designed strictly for a North American audience, and therein lies their charm. In Europe, the ships attract a good share of Italian and French passengers.

Entertainment includes puppet and marionette shows, mimes, and acrobats. Opera singers sometimes come aboard to entertain. The line also offers an activities program for kids and teens.

The **CostaClassica** (built in 1991; 1,300 passengers, 54,000 GRTs) offers spacious public rooms done up in contemporary Italian design, with Italian marble and original artwork, including sculptures, paintings, murals, wall hangings, and handcrafted furnishings. The ship's 446 cabins average almost 200 square feet each (that's big by industry standards). There are also 10 spacious suites with verandas.

The **CostaAtlantica** (built in 2000; 2,112-passengers, 84,000 GRTs) is the line's new flagship, and boasts a large number of cabins with private verandas (nearly 65% of the ship's outside cabins have them). Other neat features include Caffè Florian, a replica of the landmark 18th-century cafe of the same name in Venice.

## ITINERARIES & RATES

**COSTA ATLANTICA** 7-night Venice-to-Istanbul itinerary calls at Bari (Italy), Katakolon, Piraeus, and Kusadasi (Turkey). May 4 through Nov. 2, 2003. **Per diem rates: 143€ to 577€ outside. 5-night Venice-to-Genoa** cruise visits Bari (Italy), Corfu, Malta, and Naples (Italy). June to November, 2003. **Per diem rates: 128€ to 422€ outside.**

**COSTA CLASSICA** 7-day round-trip from Venice visits Bari, Katakolon, Santorini, Mykonos, Rhodes, Dubrovnik (Croatia). April 14 to early November, 2003. **Per diem rates start at: 125€. 7-night Venice-to-Istanbul** itinerary visits Bari (Italy), Katakolon, Piraeus, and Kusadasi (Turkey). April through early November **Per diem rates: 143€ to 577€ outside. 11-night departure out of Genoa** features a range of ports in Italy and Turkey, including the Greek ports of Corfu, Piraeus, Heraklion Crete, and Katakolon. **Per diem rates: 133€ to 507€ outside.**

## FAR & WIDE

120 Sylvan Avenue, Englewood Cliffs, NJ 07632. ☎ 800/447-5667. www.zeustours.com.

This 50-plus-year-old firm represents several lines, including the yacht cruises known as Zeus Cruises, Galileo Cruises, Harmony Cruises and the large ocean liners of Royal Olympic Cruises, First European Cruises, Orient Lines and the sailing ships of Star Clippers.

The yachts, the *Zeus I* and *Zeus II* (built in 1995; 40 passengers), offer a casual, reasonably priced, soft-adventure cruise experience with an international group of passengers, visiting both popular and out-of-the-way ports. The *Zeus I* has sails, although it is also motor-powered. The *Zeus II* is a motorized yacht. The company chooses which ship you will sail aboard. Both ships feature outside cabins that are small but comfortable and fitted with picture windows. Some have upper and lower beds. There's also a dining room, bar, and lounge.

Two meals are served each day, breakfast and either lunch or dinner (passengers are in port for the 3rd meal). Local wine, beer, *ouzo*, and soft drinks are free. The crew is Greek and adds much to the ambience. An English-speaking cruise leader is also aboard each yacht. Each cruise features a Beach BBQ, a Greek day with Greek dancing, and a Captain's Dinner.

The *Galileo Sun* (built in 1994; 34 passengers, GRT's unavailable), provides a more comfortable yacht experience. Cabins are all outside; some have double beds. A special emphasis is put on cuisine, which is served in a wood-paneled dining room. Public rooms also include a bar/lounge. Again, the crew is Greek, with an English-speaking cruise leader.

The *Harmony G* (built in 2002; 50 passengers, GRT's unavailable), on the other hand, provides a luxurious, upscale yacht experience. Cabins are all outside; some have double beds. A special emphasis is put on white-glove service. Public rooms also include a bar and lounge. Again, the crew is Greek, with an English-speaking cruise leader.

## ITINERARIES & RATES

Zeus Tours offers 7-day cruises on the *Zeus, Galileo, and Harmony* ships that can be purchased as cruise-only or with a 3-day hotel stay in Athens.

**HARMONY G** 7-day round-trip from Piraeus visits Kea, Delos, Mykonos, Santorini, Crete, Kithira, Monemvasia, Nauplion and Hydra. April through August. **Per diem rates: 275€ to 325€ outside suite. Port charges are an additional 90€.**

**GALILEO SUN   7-day round-trip from Piraeus** visits Santorini, Amorgos, Patmos, Samos, Delos, Rhinia, Mykonos, and Cape Sounion, plus Kusadasi (Turkey). May through October. **Per diem rates:** 253€ to 313€ outside (no inside cabins or suite). Port charges are an additional 80€.

**ZEUS I/ZEUS II   7-day round-trip from Piraeus** visits Santorini, Ios, Paros, Delos, Mykonos, Tinos, Kea, and Cape Sounion (on the mainland). April through October. **7-day round-trip from Corfu** visits Paxi, Lefkada, Kefalonia, Ithaka, Zakinthos, and Parga (on the mainland). May through September. **7-day round-trip from Rhodes** visits Kalimnos, Kos, Patmos, Lipsi, Leros, and Simi, plus Marmaris (Turkey). May through October. **Per diem rates:** 151€ to 220€ outside (no inside cabins or suites). Port charges of 30€ to 50€ are extra.

## FIRST EUROPEAN CRUISES

95 Madison Ave, Suite 1203, New York, NY 10016. © **888/983-8767** or 212/779-7168. www.first-european.com.

First European is the name adopted by European line Festival Cruises for U.S. marketing purposes. The company was established in 1992 in Athens by Greek entrepreneur George Poulides, who has ambitious growth plans.

Two of its vessels, *Azur* and *European Vision*, will sail in Greek waters in 2003 and 2004. The vessels cater to a diverse European audience, with Americans making up about 15% of the passenger complement.

*Azur* (built in 1971; 750-passengers, 15,000 GRTs) is an oldie but a goodie. It offers small-ship intimacy, but not at the cost of public areas. The ship has a casino, disco, swimming pools, and fitness center.

Sister ship *European Vision* (built in 2001; 1,500 passengers, 58,600 GRTs) is a larger vessel and was built at the same shipyard in France. It debuts this year. The ship has 132 suites with balconies, and also adds a golf simulator and climbing wall, as well as an Internet cafe.

**AZUR   10-day round-trip from Venice** visits Dubrovnik, Bari, Corfu, Santorini, Rhodes, Piraeus, Corinth Canal. March 3 to December 28, 2003, and January 7 to December 23, 2004. **Per diem rates:** 185€. Port charges of 90€ are extra. Children 2 through 17 pay 500€ to 680€ per cruise, plus port taxes of 80€. Book 120 days or more prior to departure and save 15% per person. **Per diem rates:** 109€ inside, 129€ outside. Port charges are an additional 110€.

**EUROPEAN VISION   7-day round-trip from Venice** visits Dubrovnik, Bari, Corfu, Santorini, Rhodes, Piraeus through November 16, 2003. From May 9 to November 7, 2004, the ship will sail on 7-day roundtrips from Venice calling at Bari, Corfu, Santorini, Piraeus, Katakolon and Dubrovnik. **Per diem rates:** 170€ inside, 185€ outside, 278€ to 357€ suite. Port charges are an additional 90€.

## ITALIAN MSC CRUISES

420 Fifth Ave, New York, NY 10018-2702. © **800/666-9333** or 212/764-4800. www.mscruise.com.

This Swiss/Italian line offers "classic Italian cruising" on older ships that aren't the fanciest afloat, but do offer good value for the money. The vessels are mid-sized and have been updated with modern decor that's more comfortable than plush. Most passengers are European. Itineraries are port-intensive, and the onboard experience friendly and fun.

The *Rhapsody* (built in 1974; 768 passengers, 16,852 GRTs) was once operated by Cunard as the *Cunard Princess* and still shows some signs of elegance, although the onboard atmosphere today is informal. Cabins are small, but the ship's public rooms are big, and there's a good deal of open deck space. It will spend 5 months on Mediterranean sailings that include Greek ports in 2003.

In addition to these itineraries, the line's brand-new *Lirica* (built in 2003; 1,550 passengers, 58,600 GRTs) will ply European waters on a series of 7-night itineraries out of Genoa that include Italian ports, Tunisia, the Balearic Islands, Spain and France. A series of 11-night itineraries will include port calls in Greece, Egypt, Cyprus, Turkey, and Malta.

### ITINERARY & RATES

**RHAPSODY** 7-day round-trip from Genoa, Naples (Italy), Malta, Tunis, Ibiza (Spain), and St. Tropez (France). Late May through September. **Per diem rates:** 178€ to 257€ inside, 228€ to 314€ outside, 278€ to 357€ suite. Port charges are an additional 99€.

## OCEANIA CRUISES

8120 NW 53rd Street, Miami, FL 33166. ✆ 800/531-5658. www.OceaniaCruises.com.

The new Oceania Cruises was founded by two well known cruise executives: Joe Watters, the former president of luxury operator Crystal Cruises, and Frank Del Rio, an executive from the now-defunct Renaissance Cruises. After extensive refits to two of the larger Renaissance ships, renamed the Insignia (built in 1998, 680-passengers, 30,277 GRTs) and Regatta (built in 1998, 680 passengers, 30,277 GRTs). Although both ships will offer Europe itineraries, only the Insignia will operate on itineraries that include Greek ports.

**INSIGNIA** 14-day roundtrip from Barcelona cruise visits Monte Carlo, Florence, and Rome and Naples, Rome and Taormina (Italy), Santorini, Mykonos, Rhodes, and Malta. October 4, 2003 **Per diem rates:** 249€ to 499€ for owner's suites. **12-day Barcelona-to-Rome** itinerary calls at Malta, Corfu and Dubrovnik (Croatia), Venice, Ancona, Messina, Sorrento (Italy). Oct. 18, 2003. **Per diem rates:** 208€ to 508€ for owner's suites.

## ORIENT LINES

7665 Corporate Center Drive, Miami, FL 33126. ✆ 800/333-7300. www.orientlines.com.

Orient is a two-ship line that was owned by a British entrepreneur until he decided to sell to Norwegian Cruise Line in 1998. The line offers a good value on cruisetours, which combine a cruise and a land tour to create a more in-depth travel experience.

The **Crown Odyssey** (built in 1988; 1,050 passengers, 34,272 GRTs) which Norwegian Cruise Line will transfer back to its fleet in late 2003 and rename the *Norwegian Crown*, is a larger and newer vessel that boasts a good range of public rooms done up with marble and glass. Cabins are larger than on the *Marco Polo*, and many have bathtubs. The top suite offer verandas, and some cabins have bay windows.

The line's original ship, the **Marco Polo** (built in 1965, refitted in 1993; formerly the *Alexandr Pushkin*; 800 passengers, 22,080 GRTs), built in East Germany in 1965 and completely refitted in 1993, offers classic style and is comfortable and slightly upscale, with Art-Deco interiors featuring Oriental art and antiques. Though often deployed in the Aegean, the ship did not offer Greece itineraries in 2003.

Cuisine aboard both ships is Continental/American, and the passengers—who tend to be older, American, and experienced travelers—tend to dress up at night. The line's goal is to offer an enriching travel experience, and to that end puts a special emphasis on shore excursions and hires expert lecturers to join the sailings. Local entertainers are brought aboard at various ports of call to add to the experience of your destination.

## ITINERARIES & RATES

**CROWN ODYSSEY 18-night Barcelona-to-Venice** cruisetour includes 2 days on land (with hotel stays and tours in Barcelona) and cruise stops in Monte Carlo, Rome, Sorrento, Malta, Santorini, Piraeus, Kusadasi, Istanbul (Turkey), Mykonos, and Dubrovnik (Croatia). **Per diem rates:** 221€ inside to 291€ outside.

Pre- and post-cruise hotel stays, transfers, and sightseeing included. May 5, 31, June 26, July 22, 2003. **11-day Venice-to-Rome** cruisetour includes two post-cruise days in Rome, with cruise stops at Korcula (Croatia), Corfu, Malta and Italy's Taormina, Sorrento and Rome. May 21, June 16, July 12, August 7. **Per diem rates:** 208€ inside to 263€ outside. Pre-and post-cruise hotel stays, transfers and sightseeing included. **10-day Piraeus-to-Rome** cruisetour includes two post-cruise stays in Athens and two pre-cruise stays in Rome, with calls at Mykonos, Taormina and Sorrento. Pre- and post-cruise hotel stays, transfers and sightseeing. August 24. 225€ inside to 280€ outside. **11-day Venice-Rome** visits Korcula (Croatia), Corfu, Malta; and Taormina and Sorrento (Italy). May 21, June 16 and July 12 and August 7, 2003. Guests embark in Venice and after an overnight shipboard stay visit and Rome. The CruiseTour include a 2-day post-cruise deluxe hotel stay in Rome. **Per diem rates:** 208€ inside to 263€ outside.

## RADISSON SEVEN SEAS CRUISES

600 Corporate Dr., Suite 410, Fort Lauderdale, FL 33334. Ⓒ **800/477-7500.** www.rssc.com.

In 1992, Radisson Hotels Worldwide decided to translate its hospitality experience to the cruise industry, offering to manage and market upscale ships for their international owners (though the "Radisson" is gradually being phased out in favor of just "Seven Seas Cruises"). The ships all offer itineraries geared towards affluent travelers, plus excellent cuisine, service, and amenities. A no-tipping policy is employed aboard all their ships, as is a no-tie-required policy.

The line assumes most of its passengers want to entertain themselves, so organized activities are limited, though they do include lectures by well-known authors, producers, and oceanographers, among others. There are also card and board games, shuffleboard, and dance lessons.

The **Radisson Diamond** (built in 1992; 350 passengers, 20,295 GRTs) is to the cruise industry what the DeLorean was to the car industry, sporting an unusual design concept: two side-by-side hulls, with the main passenger areas perched above and across them, creating a ship that is in essence a giant, very wide catamaran—only 126m (420 ft.) long, she is nonetheless only .5m (2 ft.) narrower (at 31m/102 ft.) than the QE2, which is more than twice as long at 289m (963 ft.).

Thanks to her design, the *Diamond* is quite roomy. The ship's cabins are all large and luxurious suites, and there are two VIP master suites that are even bigger and more luxurious. All the suites are outside, 121 offering balconies and 53 offering bay windows.

The smaller **Song of Flower** (built in 1986; 172 passengers, 8,292 GRTs) offers good-size cabins, all with outside views, bathtub or shower, TV/VCR, radio, phone, hair dryer, refrigerator, and fully stocked complimentary minibar. Some cabins offer sitting areas. There are also 20 suites, 10 with private verandas.

Both ships have a pool, gym, spa, and casino. The *Diamond* also has a free-floating retractable marina that provides easy access to watersports including sailing, windsurfing, and waterskiing.

The new *Seven Seas Voyager* (built in 2003; 700 passengers, 50,000 GRTs) is an all-suite, all-balcony luxury vessel. It's both larger and faster than the earlier Radisson ships.

## ITINERARIES & RATES

**RADISSON DIAMOND** **7-night Piraeus-to-Istanbul and Istanbul-to-Piraeus** cruises visit Santorini, Rhodes, Patmos, Samos, and Mykonos, plus Kusadasi and Dikili (Turkey). September through October, 2003. **Per diem rates:** 514€ to 1,070€ suites (no standard cabins). Port charges are an additional 175€.

**SEVEN SEAS VOYAGER** **7-night Venice-to-Istanbul** calls at Dubrovnik (Croatia), Kusadasi (Turkey) Rhodes, and Mykonos. September 17 and September 24. **7-night Venice-to-Rome** itinerary calls at Dubrovnik (Croatia), Corfu, Malta, Taormina, and Sorrento (Italy). October 1. **7-night Venice-to-Istanbul** calls at Dubrovnik (Croatia), Corfu, Piraeus, Rhodes, and Kusadasi (Turkey). October 15 **Per diem rates:** 556€ to 1,542€ suites (no standard cabins). Port charges are an additional 175€.

**SONG OF FLOWER** **7-night Venice-to-Istanbul** visits Split (Croatia), Itea, Mykonos, Kusadasi (Turkey), and Lesbos. October 1. **7-night Istanbul-to-Piraeus** visits Lesbos, Kusadasi (Turkey), Mykonos, Rhodes, Santorini, and Itea. October 8 and 15. **9-night Istanbul-to-Barcelona** calls at Lesbos, Kusadasi (Turkey), Heraklion, Taormina, Sorrento, and Civitavecchia (Italy). **Per diem rates:** 595€ to 842€ outside, 1,056€ to 1,085€ suites (no inside cabins). In May 2004, *Song of Flower* is scheduled to return to the region on a series of 7-night itineraries that sail between Civitavecchia and Istanbul, Piraeus and Istanbul, Istanbul and Venice. The Itineraries will call on a host of Greek ports, including Rhodes, Santorini, Mykonos, Nauplion, Gythion, Corfu, and Dikili.

## ROYAL CARIBBEAN INTERNATIONAL

1050 Caribbean Way, Miami, FL 33132. © 800/ALL-HERE. www.rcl.com.

Royal Caribbean International is one of the most successful cruise companies in the world, selling a big-ship, American-style experience that's reasonably priced and designed to please everyone—except, perhaps, those turned off by crowds. The line's ships are well-run and offer a consistent product, overseen by a veritable army of service employees.

The line is known for offering a wealth of onboard activities, although in Europe the ports are more the focus than in, say, the Caribbean. Entertainment is varied and top-notch.

The company's vessel in Greece, the *Brilliance of the Seas* (built in 2002; 2,100 passengers, 90,090 GRTs), is, by Royal Caribbean International standards, on the diminutive side. The line's Voyager-class ships, for instance, are 138,000 GRTs and hold a staggering 3,114 passengers. For their part, *Brilliance of the Seas*, and her slightly older sister ship, *Radiance of the Seas*, come with a whole set of cruise industry firsts: General Electric gas turbine engines, which protect the environment; a pair of self-leveling pool tables in the Bombay Billiards Club, and the extensive use of glass—nearly three acres of exterior glass, in fact. More than 70% of the ships outside staterooms have balconies.

**BRILLIANCE OF THE SEAS   12-night roundtrip from Barcelona** visits Villefranche (France), Florence and Rome (Italy), Santorini, Kusadasi, Piraeus, Mykonos, and Naples (Italy). May 24, June 17, July 11, August 4 and 28, October 15, 2003. **Per diem rates:** 316€ inside to 383€ outside. **12-night roundtrip from Barcelona** visits Villefranche (France), Florence and Naples (Italy), Dubrovnik (Croatia), Corfu, and Rome. May 12, June 5 and 29, July 23, August 16, September 9, October 3, 2003. **Per diem rates:** 316€ inside to 383€ outside.

## ROYAL OLYMPIA CRUISES

805 Third Ave, New York, NY 10022. ℂ **800/872-6400.** www.royalolympiccruises.com.

Royal Olympic is to Greece what Carnival Cruise Lines is to the Caribbean: the dominant market giant. The line was formed in 1995 by the merger of top Greek lines Sun Line and Epirotiki, and in 2001 will have seven ships sailing the Greek islands, including some that also visit Egypt and Israel. The fleet includes two brand-new ships and a variety of older, classic vessels.

The Royal Olympic ships focus on destination as much as the shipboard experience (the line makes more onboard revenue on its shore excursions than on selling drinks) and passengers usually have a goal of seeing as much of the islands as is possible in 3, 4, or 7 days. Some of the itineraries are consequently quite loaded, visiting as many as two ports a day. The line offers special shore-excursion rates for kids, and packages all its excursions so you can book several and save.

The onboard atmosphere is relaxed. Passengers tend to go to bed pretty early, exhausted from busy days of sightseeing (although the ships do offer late-night discos for those who want to stay up late).

The Royal Olympic experience includes a friendly and accommodating Greek crew who offer a talent show complete with Greek music and Zorba-style dancing at least once during each cruise. Food on the ships is continental but with Greek specialties. On these ships, you won't forget you're in Greece.

The cruises are affordably priced and attract about 60% Americans, with the other 40% predominantly Europeans. Most tend to be seasoned travelers, but these ships, with their intimate atmosphere, are also suitable for first-timers and families. Children's and teens' activities are offered based on need—if there are enough kids booked, the line will put a youth counselor on board.

The *Olympic Voyager* and *Olympic Explorer* (built in 2000/2001; 840 passengers, 25,000 GRTs) are the new ships in the fleet, mid-sized sister vessels built in Germany, and among the fastest cruise ships afloat, able to cruise comfortably at upwards of 27 knots. Their speed allows them to do interesting itineraries like a Three Continents cruise that starts in Piraeus and includes port calls in Greece, Turkey, Israel, and Egypt, all in 1 week. The new vessels are fancier than their older peers, boasting modern and well-designed public rooms and a good number of suites, a few with verandas.

The other ships vary in style and design. The *Stella Solaris* (built in 1953; 620 passengers, 18,000 GRTs) is the fanciest of the older vessels; the *Olympia Countess* (built in 1976, 814 passengers, 18,000 GRTs) was formerly one of Cunard's lesser vessels. Along with the *Triton* (built in 1971; 620 passengers, 14,000 GRTs), *World Renaissance* (built in 1966; 400 passengers, 12,000 GRTS) and *Odysseus* (built in 1962, 400 passengers, 12,000 GRTs) all the older ROC ships have classic features like teak decking, brass fittings, and expansive decks, and the line has been busy lately renovating and upgrading. Cabins are comfortably furnished but can be a bit cramped (they're bigger on the *Stella*

*Solaris* than on the other old ships). Most cabins, except for some suites, do not come with TVs, though they do have radios. All the ships offer at least a few suites. Public rooms are comfortable, and there are plenty of quiet nooks to get away from it all.

## ITINERARIES & RATES

**WORLD RENAISSANCE.** 3- and 4-day round-trip Piraeus sailings call at Mykonos, Rhodes, Kusadasi (Turkey), and Patmos on 3-day trips and add the ports of Heraklion and Santorini on the 4-day itineraries. March to September 2003. **Per diem rates:** 212€ to 280€ inside, 252€ to 349€ outside, 359€ to 549€ suite. **7-day round-trip Piraeus** itinerary visits Thessaloniki, Istanbul (Turkey), Mykonos, Kusadasi (Turkey) Patmos, Rhodes, Heraklion, and Santorini. April to October. **Per diem rates:** 321€ to 379€ inside, 397€ to 455€ outside, 550€ to 777€ suite.

**ODYSSEUS** 7-day round-trip from Piraeus visits Thessaloniki, Istanbul (Turkey), Mykonos, Kusadasi (Turkey), Patmos, Rhodes, Heraklion, and Santorini. April to October. **Per diem rates:** 321€ to 379€ inside, 397€ to 455€ outside, 550€ to 777€ suite.

**OLYMPIC VOYAGER** 7-day round-trip from Piraeus visits Villefranche (France), Civitavecchia and Taormina (Italy) Kusadasi (Turkey) Samos, Rhodes, Kos, and Piraeus. May through October. **Per diem rates:** 321€ to 379€ inside, 550€ to 455€ outside, 550€ to 777€ suite.

**OLYMPIC EXPLORER** 7-day round-trip from Venice visits Dubrovnik (Croatia), Katakolon, Istanbul (Turkey), Mykonos, Santorini, Piraeus, and Corfu. April to October. **Per diem rates:** inside, 397€ to 455€ outside, 550€ to 777€ suite.

**STELLA SOLARIS** 7-day round-trip from Piraeus visits Kos (Turkey), Alexandria and Port Said (Egypt), Cyprus, Antalya (Turkey), and Mykonos. October 10. **Per diem rates:** 261€ to 299€ inside, 320€ to 367€ outside, 460€ to 585€ suite. **7-day round-trip Piraeus** calls at Volos, Istanbul and Kusadasi (Turkey), Rhodes, Heraklion, and Santorini. **Per diem rates:** 261€ to 299€ inside, 320€ to 367€ outside, 460€ to 585€ suite. **4-day round-trip from Piraeus** visits Mykonos, Heraklion, Santorini, Rhodes, Kusadasi (Turkey) and Patmos. September and October. **Per diem rates:** 212€ to 280€ inside, 252€ to349€ outside, 359€ to349€ suite.

**TRITON** 7-day round-trip from Piraeus visits Thessaloniki, Istanbul (Turkey), Mykonos, Kusadasi (Turkey), Patmos, Rhodes, Heraklion, and Santorini. March through November. **Per diem rates:** 261€ to 299€ inside, 320€ to 367€ outside, 460€ to 585€ suite. 3- and 4-day sailings round-trip from Piraeus visit Mykonos, Rhodes, Kusadasi, and Patmos. 4-day cruise adds Heraklion and Santorini. **Per diem rates:** 212€ to 280€ inside, 252€ to 349€ outside, 359€ to 549€ suite. **10-day round-trip from Venice** visits Thessaloniki, Kavala, Crete, and Piraeus, transits the Corinth Canal twice, and also visits Istanbul and Kusadasi (Turkey). October and November. **11-day Holy Lands cruise from Venice** includes port calls in Piraeus, Itea, Patmos, and Corfu, plus Kusadasi (Turkey), a Corinth Canal transit, and port calls in Israel, Egypt, and Croatia. Late October. **Per diem rates:** 229€ to 264€ inside, 282€ to 324€ outside, 408€ to 465€ suite.

**SEABOURN CRUISE LINE**

6100 Blue Lagoon Dr., Suite 400, Miami, Fl 33126 ℗ 800/929-9391. www.seabourn.com.

Seabourn excels in many areas, including food, service, itineraries, and its refined environment. That said, the Seabourn cruise experience is not for everyone. These cruises are very pricey, and the customers who can afford them are often very discriminating, though the atmosphere is probably a tad more laid-back and casual than it used to be. Still, these ships aren't for the Carnival crowd, that's for sure!

Discretion is key on these ships, and the discreet environment and decor prove it. Like the passengers, the staff and crew are well mannered.

In Greece, **Seabourn Spirit** (built in 1989; 204 passengers, 10,000 GRTs) is currently the only ship scheduled to stop in Athens. Although the ambience aboard the ships can be casual during the day, it becomes decidedly more formal in the evenings. Men wear dinner jackets and everyone dresses up for formal nights.

The line enhances its cruises with guest lecturers, past examples of which have included celebrities like Walter Cronkite and Art Linkletter. Nighttime entertainment is on the low-key side, though cabaret nights with themes like 1950s rock 'n' roll can get the audience going.

All the cabins on the *Seabourn Spirit* and *Seabourn Pride* are outside suites, and each has a 5-foot-wide picture window and comes with a fully stocked complimentary bar. Owner's suites are very plush and offer private verandas; 36 cabins recently received the added feature of French balconies with doors you can open to let in the ocean breezes (but which are too narrow to sit on).

The ships come equipped with a floating marina that, when lowered, provides a teak-decked platform for watersports (Sunfish, kayaks, snorkeling gear, high-speed banana boats, and water skis are available for passenger use). There's also a mesh net that becomes a saltwater swimming pool.

## ITINERARIES & RATES

**SEABOURN SPIRIT**   The ship will ply Mediterranean waters from April to November 2003, and again from May to October 2004. A number of 7-day itineraries visit smaller ports and some popular ones, too. Many can be combined to create 14-day itineraries. Some sample 2003 itineraries include **7-day Istanbul-to-Venice** calls at Volos, Itea, Corfu, and Korcula (Croatia). **Per diem rates for all 2003 7-day itineraries:** 554€ to 1,467€ suite (no standard cabins). All rates include tops, in-suite bar setup and wine at lunch and dinner. 7-day Piraeus-to-Istanbul will visit Capri and Taormina (Italy), Katakolon, Galaxhidi, and Navplion. Another 7-day **Piraeus-to-Istanbul** cruise will make stops at Monemvasia, Amorgoros, Mykonos, and Bodrum and Kusadasi (Turkey). 7-day Venice-to-Rome sailing will call at Dubrovnik (Croatia), Cephalina, and Messina, Amalfi, and Sorrento (Italy). **7-day Istanbul-to-Piraeus** will call at Navplion, Santorini, Rhodes, and Kusadasi (Turkey). A 12-day Istanbul-to-Alexandria sailing will call at Kusadasi (Turkey), Mykonos, Navplion, Monemvasia, Aghios Nikolaos, Rhodes, Antalya and Alanya (Turkey), and Cyprus. **Per diem rates:** 476€ to 1,387€ suite. For all intents and purposes, the same series of itineraries will be offered in 2004. **Rates for 2004 7-day sailings range from 612€ to 1,641€.**

**SEABOURN PRIDE   16-day Barcelona-to-Istanbul** in 2004 cruise will call at Monte Carlo, Sorrento and Taormina (Italy), Dubrovnik (Croatia), Venice (Italy), Corfu, and Piraeus. April 21. **Per diem rate:** 465€ to 1,347€.

## SEADREAM YACHT CLUB

2601 South Bayshore Dr., Penthouse 1B, Coconut Grove, FL 33133. ℂ 800/707-4911. www.seadream yachtclub.com.

SeaDream Yacht Club was founded in 2001 by Seabourn Cruise Line founder Atle Brynestad and former Seabourn president, Larry Pimentel. The two men plan to carry on the Seabourn tradition of luxury and elegance, albeit on a smaller, more yacht-like scale. SeaDream purchased the 116-passenger *Sea Goddess I* and *Sea Goddess II* from Seabourn, and after renovations renamed them *SeaDream I* and *SeaDream II.* In fact, the company defines itself not as a cruise line but an ultra-luxury yacht company whose vessels journey to smaller, less chartered destinations. The experience is designed to provide guests with an unstructured, casually elegant vacation with no shortage of fun diversions. Toys carried aboard include ski jets, mountain bikes and a Segway Human Transporter (two-wheeled scooter gizmo), plus on deck guests love the bed-sized loungers, binoculars, and MP3 players.

### ITINERARIES & RATES

**SEADREAM 1** **7-night Rome-to-Piraeus** sailings visit Capri, Sorrento and Taormina (Italy), Katakolon, and Galaxidhi on August 16. **7-night Piraeus-to-Istanbul** cruise, departing August 23, calls at Monemvasia, Santorini, Mykonos, and Kusadasi (Turkey). **7-night Piraeus-to-Rome** September 13 departure calls at Hydra, Itea, Cephalonia and Taormina and Sorrento (Italy). In 2004, the ship will operate on eight 7-day itineraries that incorporate Greek ports. **7-night Venice-to-Piraeus** sailing calls at Lossinj and Dubrovnik (Croatia), Corfu, Cephalonia, Itea, and Hydra. **7-night Istanbul-Nafplion** itinerary departing August 14 will visit Volos, Skiathos, Samos, Rhodes, and Bodrum. **7-night Nafplion-to-Venice** sailing on August 21 will make calls at Hydra, Itea, Cephalonia, Corfu, and Dubrovnik and Hvar (Croatia). **7-night Venice-to-Piraeus** cruise on August 29 will make calls at Dubrovnik (Croatia), Corfu, Cephalonia, Itea, and Hydra. **7-night Piraeus-to-Istanbul** trip on September 4 will visit Nafplion, Monemvasia, Santorini, Mykonos, and Kusadasi (Turkey). **7-night Istanbul-to-Piraeus** cruise on September 11 will call at Volos, Skiathos, Samos, Rhodes, and Bodrum (Turkey). On September 18, the ship will operate on a **7-night Piraeus-to-Venice** itinerary with calls at Hydra, Itea, Cephalonia, Corfu and Dubrovnik and Hvar (Croatia). 7-day Venice-to-Civitavechhia sailing on September 25 will feature calls at Lossinj, Hvar and Dubrovnik (Croatia), Corfu, and Taormina and Sorrento (Italy). **Per diem rate:** 385€

## SILVERSEA CRUISES

110 E. Broward Blvd., Fort Lauderdale, FL 33301. ℂ 800/722-9055. www.silversea.com.

The luxurious sister ships *Silver Cloud* and *Silver Wind* (both built in 1994; 296 passengers, 16,800 GRTs) and new *Silver Shadow* (built in 2000; 388 passengers, 28,258 GRTs) carry their guests in true splendor, in an atmosphere that's elegant but low-key, and in a milieu that's sociable rather than stuffy. Passengers are generally experienced cruisers, not necessarily American, and certainly are well traveled. Most are in the over-50 group. These ships are not for kids.

On the *Silver Cloud* and *Silver Wind,* all accommodations are outside suites with picture windows, writing tables, sofas, walk-in closets, marble bathrooms, and all the amenities you'd expect of a top-of-the-line ship. Throughout, both vessels allot more space to each passenger than most other ships. There's also more crew, with the large staff at your service, ready to cater to your every desire on a 24-hour basis.

The newer *Silver Shadow* and *Silver Wind* carry on the fine tradition in a slightly larger format The all-suite vessels also features suites with verandas, poolside dining venues, a larger spa facility, a computer center, a cigar lounge designed by noted cigar purveyor Davidoff, and a wine and champagne bar designed by Moët & Chandon.

The fine accouterments that complement the luxurious experience aboard all three ships include Limoges china, Christofle silverware, and soft down pillows. Activities offerings include bridge and other games, aerobics, dance lessons, wine tastings, and lectures (including a *National Geographic Traveler* series), as well as such cruise staples as bingo and quiz shows. Nighttime entertainment venues include showrooms for resident musicians and local talent, a piano bar, a small casino, and rooms for dancing.

The ships offer five-star cuisine served in a single seating, with guests able to dine when, where, and with whom they choose.

## ITINERARIES & RATES

**SILVER CLOUD    8-day Barcelona-to-Piraeus** visits Ibiza (Spain), Porto Empedocle (Italy), Malta, Rhodes, and Bodrum (Turkey). May 22, 2003. **Per diem rates:** 715€ to 898€ suite (no standard cabins). Rates include tips, a shoreside cultural event (such as a local folk performance), airfare, hotel accommodations, transfers, wines and spirits, champagne, and more. **10-day Piraeus-to-Malta** itinerary calls at Istanbul and Kusadasi (Turkey), Santorini, Scorpio Island, and Dubrovnik (Croatia). September 2. **Per diem rates:** 598€ to 751€ suite. All rates for all ships and itineraries include tips, a shoreside cultural event (such as a local folk performance), airfare, hotel accommodations, transfers, wines and spirits, champagne, and more.

**SILVER SHADOW    12-day Malta-to-Istanbul** on June 10, 2003, visits Nafplion, Santorini, Crete, Antalya and Kas (Turkey), Rhodes, Paros, and Kusadasi (Turkey). **Per diem rates:** 647€ to 812€. **9-day Istanbul-to-Marseille** cruise calls at Kusadasi (Turkey), Santorini and Sorrento, Livorno, and Portofino (Italy). July 2. **Per diem rates:** 662 to 832€. **7-day Rome-to-Athens** visits Naples (Italy), Messina (Italy), Aghios Nikolaos, and Nafplion. September 29. **Per diem rates:** 575€ to 713€ suite. In 2004, the ship will embark on a **14-day journey from Piraeus-to-Portugal** with calls at Kusadasi (Turkey), Mykonos, Santorini, Messina and Sorrento (Italy), Barcelona, Palma de Mallorca, Málaga, and Cadiz (Spain). May 3. **Per diem rates:** 617€ to 767€ suite. **7-day Rome-to-Athens** voyage will call at Naples, Messina and Siracusa (Italy), and Aghios Nikolaos and Nafplion. September 29. **Per diem rates:** 576€ to 712€ suite.

**SILVER WHISPER    9-day Barcelona-to-Piraeus** visits Marseille (France), Malta, Taormina (Italy), Katakolon, Mykonos, and Patmos. **Per diem rates:** 632€ to 788€ suite (no standard cabins). June 7, 2004. **124-day Istanbul-to-Venice** cruise calls at Kusadasi and Marmaris (Turkey), Rhodes, Santorini, Corfu, Dubrovnik and Korcula (Croatia), and Ancona (Italy). July 1. **Per diem rates:** 647€ to 767€ suite. 8-day round-trip Venice calls at Split and Dubrovnik (Croatia), Corfu, Katakolon, and Ravenna. July 13. **Per diem rates:** 539€ to 672€ suite. Other itineraries that include Greek ports are an 11-day **Athens to Venice** sailing on August 30, a 10-day **Venice-to-Rome** cruise on September 10, a 5-day **Rome-to-Athens** sailing on October 14 and a 17-day **Athens-to-Dubai** voyage on October 19.

**SILVER WIND 7-day Nice-to-Athens** sailing visits Portofino, Livorno, Rome, Sorrento (Italy), and Katakolon, June 8, 2003. **Per diem rates:** 600€ to 700€ suite (no standard cabins). **8-day Piraeus-to-Monte Carlo** cruise visits Mykonos, Crete, Taormina, Sorrento, Amalfi, Elba (Italy). **Per diem rates:** 600€ to 700€ suite (no standard cabins).

## STAR CLIPPERS

4101 Salzedo St., Coral Gables, Fl 33146. © **800/442-0551.** www.starclippers.com.

The **Star Flyer** (built in 1991; 170 passengers, 3,025 GRTs), the vessel this three-ship sailing line operates in Greece, is a replica of the big 19th-century clipper sailing ships (or barkentines) that once circled the globe. Its tall square rigs carry enormous sails and are glorious to look at, and a particular thrill for history buffs.

And on this ship, the sails are more than just window dressing. The *Star Flyer* was constructed using original drawings and the specifications of a leading 19th-century naval architect, but updated with modern touches so that today it is among the tallest and fastest clipper ships ever built—it has reached speeds of more than 19 knots.

The atmosphere onboard is akin to being on a private yacht rather than a mainstream cruise ship. It's casual in an L.L. Bean sort of way, and friendly. Passengers generally fall into the 30-to-60 age range.

Cabins are pleasant, and decorated with wood accents. There is one owner's suite. The public rooms include a writing room, an open-seating dining room, and an Edwardian-style library with a Belle-Epoque fireplace and walls lined with bookshelves. There are two swimming pools.

Local entertainment is sometimes brought aboard, and there's also a resident pianist and a makeshift disco in the Tropical Bar. Movies are piped into passenger cabins.

Activities on the ship tend toward the nautical, such as visiting the bridge, observing the crew handle the sails, and participating in knot-tying classes.

It should be noted that despite stabilizers, movement on this vessel may be troublesome to those who get seasick.

### ITINERARIES & RATES

**STAR FLYER 7-day Northern Cyclades itinerary round-trip from Piraeus** visits Delos/Mykonos, Patmos, and Kea, as well as Kusadasi and Gulluk (Turkey). **7-day Southern Cyclades itinerary round-trip from Piraeus** visits Rhodes, Santorini, and Hydra, as well as Bodrum and Dalyan River (Turkey). Both itineraries include a full day at sea. May through September. **Per diem rates:** 239€ inside, 268€ to 399€ outside, 542€ suite. Port charges are an extra 175€.

## SWAN HELLENIC

631 Commack Road, Comack, NY 11725. © **877/219-4239.** www.swanhellenic.com.

This British firm is owned by Peninsular and Orient Steam Navigation Company (P&O), the firm that owned U.S.-based Princess Cruises before it was acquired by Carnival Corp in early 2003. (Carnival Corp, the leading cruise firm in the U.S., owns Carnival Cruise Lines, Costa, Cunard, Holland America Line, Windstar, and Seabourn).

The line's sole ship, *Minerva* (built in 1996; 300 passengers, 12,000 GRTs), was replaced by the *Minerva II* (built in 2001, 684 passengers, 30,277 GRTs). Swan Hellenic offers a small-ship experience that is both high-quality and enriching, visiting ports off the beaten path. All the itineraries feature acclaimed guest lecturers who are authorities in their fields, and the passengers—a mix of British and Americans—tend to be experienced, inquisitive travelers.

## ITINERARIES & RATES

**MINERVA II** In 2004, the ship visits a number of Greek ports on 14-day itineraries, which, on occasion, can be split into 7-day itineraries. The sailings are available from late April to late October. **7-day Istanbul-to-Piraeus** cruise will call at Dikili, Kusadasi (Turkey), and Delos. June 5. 7-day Piraeus-to-Istanbul will visit Delos, Mykonos, Santorini, and Canakkale (Turkey). **Per diem rates:** 300€ average. Rates include shore excursions, tips, transfers, and airfare from London. Special half-price rates are available on some sailings for those up to the age 26 when traveling with a full-fare adult passenger.

## TRAVEL DYNAMICS INTERNATIONAL

132 E. 70th St., New York, NY 10021. ✆ 800/257-5767. www.traveldynamicsinternational.com.

This operator of small yachts offers a number of interesting itineraries that include Greek ports. The journeys, which are available in late summer and fall of 2003 and 2004, are tailored to be unique, visiting some of the smaller and less known ports, and are complemented by high-quality onboard educational programs.

The Corinthian (built in 2002; 92 passengers, 3,000 GRTs) features 37 staterooms, all of which have ocean views, televisions, minibars and double beds that convert to queens. The ship's nine suites come equipped with balconies. Public areas include a restaurant with single seating dining, a lounge and deck bar, fitness center and a marina with swimming platform at the ship's stern.

## ITINERARIES & RATES

**CORINTHIAN** **11-night round-trip from Athens** cruisetour visits Delphi, Katakolon, Gytheion, Heraklion, Santorini, Rhodes, Kusadasi (Turkey), and Mykonos. October 28, 2003. **Per diem rates:** 881€ to 635€ outside (no inside or suite). Rates include hotel stays and shore excursion. **11-night Athens-to-Rome** sailing calls at Dikili, Kusadasi, Santorini, Delos, Itea, Syracuse, Palermo, and Naples. November 7, 2003. **Per diem rates:** 881€ to 635€ outside. **11-night cruisetour from Rome to Athens** calls at Sorrento and Messina (Italy), Katakolon, Heraklion, Rhodes, Santorini, and Nafplion. **Per diem rates:** 881€ to 635€ outside. July and August 2004. 13-night Athens-to-Rome sailing calls at Odunluk (Turkey), Kavalla, Mykonos, Heraklion, Strophades Islands, Preveza, Saranda (Albania), Taormina (Italy), Tunisias, Trapani, and Naples (Italy). August 29. **Per diem rates:** 881€ to 635€ outside. **11-night Venice-to-Lavrion** itinerary call at Split and Dubrovnik (Croatia), Saranda (Albania, Nkopolis, Taormina (Italy) Syracuse, Athens, Kusadasi (Turkey), Odulunk. September 21 and October 15, 2004. Per diem rates: 881€ to 635€. 13-night roundtrip Piraeus itinerary will visit Odunluk, Nafplion, Pylos, Malta, Trapani, Sorrento, Lipari Island, Taormina (Italy), Corfu, and Ithica. October 2, 2004. **Per diem rates:** 881€ to 635€ outside.

## WINDSTAR

300 Elliott Ave W., Seattle, WA 98119. ✆ 800/258-7245. www.windstarcruises.com.

Although they look like sailing ships of yore, the *Wind Spirit* (built in 1988; 144 passengers, 5,350 GRTs) and her sisters *Wind Song* (built 1987, 144 passengers, 5,350 GRTs), *Wind Star* built in 1987, 144 passengers, 5,350 GRTs) and *Wind Surf* (built in 2000, 308 passengers, 30,745 GRTs, 308 passengers) are more like luxury floating resorts with the flair of sailing ships. These vessels feature top-notch service and extraordinary cuisine. Million-dollar computers operate the sails, and stabilizers allow for a smooth ride.

Casual, low-key elegance is the watchword on these vessels. There's no set regime, unless you consider pampering a regime. Most of the passengers are well heeled and range in age from 30 to 70.

Cabins are all outside and roomy (through not suite-sized) and boast teak-decked bathrooms and large portholes. The top-level owner's cabins are slightly bigger. Amenities include VCRs and CD players.

A watersports platform at the stern allows for a variety of activities when the ships are docked. Daytime entertainment is low-key and sometimes includes local entertainers brought aboard at ports of call. The ships also have small casinos. Passengers can visit the bridge whenever they want.

The line is owned by Carnival Corp, which is also the parent of Carnival, Holland America Line, Costa, Seabourn, and Cunard, and in 2003 also acquired Princess Cruises.

## ITINERARIES & RATES

**WIND SPIRIT** 11-day **Venice-to-Piraeus** sailing on August 5, 2003 will call at Havar and Dubrovnik (Croatia), Katakolon, 11-day **Piraeus-to-Venice** cruise on August 16 visits Mykonos, Kusadasi (Turkey), Patmos, Santorini, Kythira, Katakolon, and Dubrovnik and Korkula (Croatia). Kythira, Santorini, Patmos, Kusadasi (Turkey), and Mykonos. 7-day **Rome-to-Athens** on September 6 visits Capri and Messina (Italy), Gython, Navplion, and Ermoupolis. The 7-day **Piraeus-to-Istanbul and Istanbul-to-Piraeus** itineraries on September 13 and 20, and October 18 and 25 visit Mykonos, Santorini, Rhodes, and Bodrum and Kusadasi (Turkey). **Per diem rates: 552€ to 940€** outside. 7-day Piraeus-to-Rome cruise calls at Syros, Navplion, and Messina and Capri (Italy). **Per diem rates: 413€** for outside cabins and **546€** for owner's suite.

## 8 Ships Visiting Greece on Longer Mediterranean Itineraries

The following lines and ships visit Greece as part of longer itineraries.

**Celebrity Cruises**   Celebrity, a decently priced yet upscale U.S. operator, offers 14 itineraries, that, for the most part, operate in the Mediterranean aboard new *Millennium* (built in 2000; 1,950 passengers, 91,000 GRTs). The 12-night itineraries begin or end in Venice or Barcelona. From Barcelona, the ship calls at Nice (France), Florence, Civitavecchia and Naples (Italy), Piraeus, Santorini, and Dubrovnik (Croatia). The itinerary features a lengthy stay in Santorini. May through early October.

1050 Caribbean Way, Miami, FL 33132. ℰ 800/327-6700. www.celebrity-cruises.com.

**Crystal Cruises**   This luxury operator offers Greece on the *Crystal Symphony* (built in 1997; 940 passengers, 51,004 GRTs) and new *Crystal Serenity* (built in 2003; 1,080 passengers, 68,000 GRTs) and as part of 12-day cruises in August and September. Departures are from Rome, Venice, or Piraeus, with the itinerary including Italy and Croatia or Italy, France, and Malta. Greek stops are either Santorini and Mykonos, Corfu, or Mykonos and Rhodes, and three of the four itineraries also stop at Kusadasi (Turkey).

2049 Century Park E, Suite 1400, Los Angeles, CA 90067. ℰ 310/785-9300. www.crystalcruises.com.

**Fred Olsen Cruise Lines**   On its fleet of intimate small- to mid-sized ships, Fred Olsen offers several itineraries that call on Greek islands on the *Black*

Travel Tip: He who finds the best hotel deal has more to spend on facials involving knobbly vegetables.

Hello, the Roaming Gnome here. I've been nabbed from the garden and taken round the world. The people who took me are so terribly clever. They find the best offerings on Travelocity. For very little cha-ching. And that means I get to be pampered and exfoliated till I'm pink as a bunny's doodah.

*Watch* (built in 1972; 761-passengers, 28,492 GRTs), which is doing a 20-night cruise in October (2003) with calls to Corfu and Katakalon; *Braemar* (built in 1966; 727-passengers, 11,209 GRTs), a small, upscale, European-style ship, that's doing a 14-night cruise in April (2004) that visits Piraeus and Rhodes; and *Black Prince* (built in 1992; 727-passengers, 19,089 GRTs), which is doing a 21-night cruise in April (2004) that includes calls to Katakolon, Piraeus, and Mykonos.

P.O. Box 342, New York, NY 10014. © 888/875-5880. www.fredolsencruises.co.uk.

**Holland America Line**   Holland America offers Greece on 12-day itineraries aboard the line's newest ship, the *Oosterdam* (built in 2003; 1,848 passengers, 85,000 GRTs), and the line's oldest ship, the *Noordam* (built in 1984; 1,214 passengers, 33,930 GRTs). On October 26, the Oosterdam will operate a 12-day itinerary between Rome and Venice, with calls at Monte Carlo, Marseille (France), Barcelona and Palma de Mallorca (Spain), Malta, Loutraki, Corfu, and Dubrovnik (Croatia). Fares start at 2,289€. On May 8, September 23 and October 23, the Noordam will sail between Rome and Barcelona on itineraries that include the port calls in Dubrovnik, Corfu, Malta, Mahon (Spain), and St. Tropez and Sete (France).

300 Elliott Ave. W., Seattle, WA 98119. © 800/426-0327. www.hollandamerica.com.

**Lindblad Expeditions**   Soft adventure operator Lindblad Expeditions (formerly Special Expeditions) is offering four 16-day itineraries—two in 2003 and another two in 2004—that incorporate Greek ports aboard the expedition ship *Endeavour* (built in 1966 and refitted in 200; 110 passengers, 3,905 GRTs). The 16-day itineraries will sail between Seville and Venice on September 17 and October 1, and again in 2004 on September 21 and October 5. Port Calls will include Granada and Manorca (Spain), Cagliari and Arigento (Italy), Malta, Katakolon, and Dubrovnik and Korcula (Croatia).

720 Fifth Ave, New York, NY 10019. © 800/397-3348. www.lindbladexpeditions.com.

**P&O Cruises**   British operator P&O visits Greece on several sailings in late 2003, most round-trip from Southampton (U.K.) aboard its newest ships, the *Adonia* (built in 1998; 2,016 passengers, 77,000 GRTs), *Oceana* (built in 2000, 1,870 passengers, 77,000 GRTs) and *Aurora*, (1,870 passengers, 76,000 GRTs). The Aurora will sail on a 16-day round-trip Southhampton itinerary that departs on August 1 and features calls at Málaga (Spain), Piraeus, Dikili, Istanbul (Turkey), Myrilene, Palermo (Italy), and Gibraltar. The *Oceana* will depart Southampton on August 16 for round-trip itinerary that will call at Palma, Rhodes, Ephesus, Piraeus, Zakinthos, Messina, and Málaga. The *Adonia* will depart on an 18-day itinerary on September 9 a 18-day sailing on September 9 round-trip from Southampton that calls at Palma (Spain), Rhodes, Marmaris (Turkey), Piraeus, Cephalonia, Dubrovnik (Croatia), and Gibraltar.

77 New Oxford St., London, WC1A 1PP England. © 44-171-800-2345. In the U.S., contact Princess Tours, 2815 Second Ave, Ste. 400, Seattle, WA 98121-1299. © 800/340-7074. www.pocruises.com.

**Peter Deilmann EuropAmerica Cruises**   This German company, which operates river ships in Europe as well as two oceangoing vessels, offers Eastern Mediterranean sailings from April to May 2004 on its elegant oceangoing flagship *Deutschland* (built in 1998; 505 passengers, 22,400 GRTs). An 18-day sailing departing Bombay to Piraeus on March 27 will call at Rhodes. On April 14, the ship will sail roundtrip from Piraeus on a 6-day cruise with calls at Samos, Skiathos, Athos, and Istanbul (Turkey). On April 20, another roundtrip Piraeus itinerary, this one is 8 days in length, will call at Mykonos, Santorini, and Heraklion. A 10-day itinerary that departs April 28 form Piraeus to Civitavecchia (Italy) will call at Italian and Greek ports, including Chios, Kos, and Kythira.

1800 Diagonal Rd., Suite 170, Alexandria, VA 22314. © **800/348-8287.** www.dellmann-cruises.com.

**Princess Cruises** Premium U.S. operator Princess, which at presstime was expected to merge with Carnival Corp., which owns Carnival Cruise Lines, Costa, Cunard Holland America Line and Windstar, will operate its brand-new *Star Princess* (built in 2003; 2,600 passengers, 109,000 GRTs) 10 Europe itineraries in 2004. A 12-day Grand Mediterranean sailing, departing between May 16 and September 1, will include overnights in Barcelona and Venice, and port calls at Monte Carlo, Florence (Italy), Piraeus, Kusadasi, and Istanbul (Turkey.) The ship will also sail on five new itineraries, include three highlighting the Greek Isles and another, "Mediterranean Mosaic," that will included a transatlantic crossing. A 12-day Greek Isle sailing, which will operate between Venice and Rome on April 10 and September 25, will make calls at Santorini, Rhodes, Mykonos, Corfu, Piraeus, Kusadasi, Dubrovnik (Croatia), and Naples (Italy). On May 4, the ship will depart Venice and sail on a 12-day Venice-to-Barcelona itinerary with calls at Corfu, Katakolon, Piraeus, Mykonos, Kusadasi (Turkey), Santorini, Civitavecchia (Italy), and Cannes (France). Another "Mediterranean Mosaic" 12-day itinerary, from Barcelona-to-Rome, will operate on September 13. On November 15, 3002, the Royal Princess (built 1984, refurbished 2001; 1,200 passengers, 45,000 GRTs) will sail on a 1-day Civitavecchia (Italy)-to-Athens sailing that will call at Naples, Taormina and Venice (Italy), Katakolon, Santorini, and Kusadasi (Turkey).

1000 Santa Monica Blvd., Suite 1800, Los Angeles, CA 90067. © **800/421-0522.** www.princess cruises.com.

## 9 Best Shore Excursions in the Ports of Call: Greece

Shore excursions are designed to help you make the most of your limited time in port, taking you by various transport to sites of historical or cultural value or natural or artistic beauty. The tours are usually booked on the first day of your cruise, are sold on a first-come, first-served basis, and are nonrefundable. Some lines allow bookings in advance, and some include shore excursions in their cruise fares.

Generally, shore excursions that take you well beyond the port area are the ones most worth taking—you'll get professional commentary and avoid having to hassle with local transportation. In ports whose attractions are all within walking distance of the pier, however, you may be best off touring on your own. In some cases, it may also be more enjoyable to take a taxi to an attraction and skip the crowded bus tours (for instance, in Rhodes).

Keep in mind that shore excursions are a revenue-generating area for the cruise lines, and the tours may be heavily promoted aboard the ship. They aren't always offered at bargain prices.

When touring in Greece, remember to wear comfortable walking shoes and bring a hat, sunscreen, and bottled water to ward off the effects of the hot sun. Most lines make bottled water available as you disembark, usually for a fee.

Remember, in some places such as churches and other religious sites, modest attire may be required, meaning shoulders and knees should be covered.

Below we highlight a selection of shore-excursion offerings at the major cruise ports. Keep in mind that not all the tours will be offered by every line and prices will vary. For more information on many of these ports, consult the relevant chapters in this book.

## CORFU (KERKIRA)

See chapter 15 for complete sightseeing information.

**ACHILLEION PALACE & PALEOKASTRITSA** (4 hr., 42€): Visit Achilleion Palace and see the statues of Achilles. Continue on to Paleokastritsa to visit the 13th-century Monastery of the Virgin Mary. There's usually free time and an opportunity to swim in Paleokastritsa. Stop in Corfu town and visit St. Spyridon Church, named for the patron saint of Corfu, or stroll the narrow streets.

## IRAKLION & AYIOS NIKOLAOS (CRETE)

See chapter 9 for complete sightseeing information.

**THE PALACE OF KNOSSOS** (3 hr., 47€): Travel by motor coach from Iraklion to Knossos, once the capital of the prehistoric Minoan civilization, and thought to be the basis for the original mythological Minotaur's labyrinth. Visit the excavation of the palace of King Minos. Return to Iraklion for a museum tour or free time. Similar tours are offered from Rethymnon (5 hr., 53€) and from Ayios Nikolaos, including lunch (7 hr., 136€).

**EXPLORING CRETE** (4 hr., 47€): Ride by bus to Ayios Nikolaos, stopping for photos outside the archaeological site of Mallia, home of King Radamanthys. Travel to the Greek Orthodox monastery of St. George Selinaris. Take photos at scenic Elounda Bay. Free time in Ayios Nikolaos.

## ITEA (DELPHI)

See chapter 12 for complete sightseeing information.

**DELPHI EXCURSION** (4 hr., 55€): Delphi is located on the slope of Mount Parnassus. Visit the Sanctuary of Apollo to see the Temple of Apollo, the theater, the treasury buildings, and the Sacred Way. Visit the Archaeological Museum. There's usually a short stop at Castalian Spring.

## KATAKOLON (OLYMPIA)

See chapter 8 for complete sightseeing information.

**EXCURSION TO OLYMPIA** (4 hr., 52€–72€): Visit the site of the original Olympic Games, held from 776 B.C. to A.D. 393. See the Temple of Hera, in front of which burns the Olympic Flame; the Temple of Zeus, which once housed the gold-and-ivory statue of Zeus that was one of the Seven Wonders of the Ancient World; and the original stadium and bouleuterion, where Olympic competitors swore an oath to conform to the rules of the games. Visit the famous Archaeological Museum of Olympia to see the marble statue of the Temple of Zeus and the statue of Hermes. Also included is a short stop in the town of Olympia.

## MYKONOS (& DELOS)

See chapter 10 for complete sightseeing information.

**DELOS APOLLO SANCTUARY** (3–4½ hr., 37€–63€): Travel by small boat from Mykonos harbor to Delos for a 2-hour guided walking tour of the tiny island that was once the religious and commercial hub of the Aegean, but now is home only to ancient ruins and their caretakers. View the Agora; the Sacred Way, which leads to the Sanctuary of Apollo; and the Terrace of the Lions, where marble beasts from the 7th century B.C. guard the now-dry Sacred Lake. View the remains of the Maritime Quarter with its harbors, water houses, and villas (including the House of Cleopatra) and the renowned mosaic floors in the House of the Masks and the House of Dionysos. Also visit the Archaeological Museum (if it's open).

## NAFPLION

See chapter 8 for complete sightseeing information.

**PALAMIDI CASTLE & MYCENAE** (4 hr, 59€–72€): Visit the area ruled by Agamemnon. Visit the Palamidi Castle, which was built by Venetians and seized by the Turks. The path up consists of nearly a thousand steps (motor coaches can drive up to the gate). At Mycenae, you walk through the Lion Gate to view the ruins, which will remind you of Homer's *Iliad*.

**EPIDAURUS & PALAMIDI CASTLE** (4 hr, 56€): See the countryside as you travel to Epidaurus, the town dedicated to Asklepios, god of healing. Visit the 4th-century B.C. theater with its remarkable acoustics. On the way back, stop by Palamidi Castle, located on a hill above Nafplion.

**COMBO TOUR OF EPIDAURUS & MYCENAE** (5–7 hr, 76€–89€): Includes lunch at a traditional restaurant.

**ANCIENT CORINTH** (4 hr, 49€): Visit the ancient city where the most impressive relic is the 6th-century B.C. Doric temple of Apollo. You can also view the canal from 60m (200 ft.) up on the bridge that straddles the waterway.

## PATMOS

See chapter 11 for complete sightseeing information.

**THE MONASTERY OF ST. JOHN & CAVE OF THE APOCALYPSE** (2½–4 hr, 32€–68€): Depart the Port of Skala and travel by bus to the village of Hora and the 900-year-old Monastery of St. John. Visit the main church and view the ecclesiastical treasures in the museum. Continue on by bus to the nearby Cave of the Apocalypse to see the silver niches in the wall that mark the pillow and ledge used as a desk by the author of the Book of Revelation and the crack made by the Voice of God. Longer tours may include a visit to the 300-year-old Simandris House, which boasts a rich collection on antiques, and a stop for a wine tasting at a local taverna.

**EXPLORATION OF HORA** (3½ hr, 42€): Depart the port of Skala by bus to visit the Cave of the Apocalypse (see above). Walk uphill to Hora, where you will visit Plateia Xanthos, which houses the City Hall and the bust of Emmanuel Xanthos, one of the Greek independence leaders of 1821. Also visit Symantiri House, a typical Parmian Mansion, and the historical chapel and museum of the Monastery of St. John. The trip includes a visit to a local tavern to sample *mezedes* (Greek hors d'oeuvres) and *ouzo*, and to be entertained by local musicians.

**AFTERNOON AT THE BEACH** (2 hr, 15€): Depart the ship on tenders to Kambos beach, where you'll have 2 hours to swim and tan. Changing facilities are available and sun beds and umbrellas will be provided, along with soft drinks.

## PIRAEUS/ATHENS

See chapter 6 for complete sightseeing information.

**ATHENS CITY TOUR** (3½–4 hr, 38€–42€): Includes a guided tour of the Acropolis, Athens's most prominent historical and architectural site; a drive past other Athens highlights, including Constitution Square, the Parliament, the Temple of Zeus, Hadrian's Arch, and Olympic Stadium; and time for souvenir shopping in the Plaka. A full-day city tour (8½–9 hr, 90€–92€) also includes a visit to the National Archeological Museum and sometimes a stop at the Temple of Poseidon, located high on a cliff overlooking the Aegean Sea.

**ATHENS, THE ACROPOLIS & THE CORINTH CANAL** (9 hr, 91€): Visit the Acropolis and, by bus, tour past other sights in Athens, then take the highway from Athens to the Corinth Canal (about 96km/60 miles) for views of the canal and to visit Ancient Corinth, once a grand city with a forum larger than that of Rome. Also visit the Corinth Museum.

**A DAY TOUR OF DELPHI** (9–10 hr, 89€–109€): If you've been to Athens before or just aren't into big cities and crowds, you may want to try this full-day trip to one of the great sights of antiquity. The tour visits the ruins of the Temple of Apollo, located in a stunning setting on the slope of Mount Parnassus. Lunch is included.

## RHODES

See chapter 11 for complete sightseeing information.

**RHODES & LINDOS COMBINED** (4–4½ hr, 40€–56€): Travel by bus through the scenic countryside to Lindos, an important city in ancient times. At Lindos, view the medieval walls, which were constructed by the Knights of St. John in the 14th century. Walk or take a donkey up to the ancient Acropolis, where there are ruins and great views—and, of course, souvenir shops on the way (unfortunately), this site can get extremely crowded, especially during July and August). The trip may include a walking tour of Old Town Rhodes (see description below), a stop at a workshop selling Rhodian ceramics, and/or a visit to Mount Smith to view the ruins of ancient Rhodes, the Temple of Apollo, and Diagoras Stadium.

**LINDOS WITH LUNCH BY THE BEACH** (7½–8 hr, 65€–87€): Drive to Lindos and explore the city (see above). Enjoy lunch at a beachfront restaurant or other scenic location. Return to Rhodes, driving along the walls of the medieval city and stopping at Port d'Amboise for a walk through Old Town. View the Palace of the Knights and the medieval houses, as well as the Hospital of the Knights of St. John. The tour may stop at a ceramics workshop to see how Rhodian ceramics are made.

## SANTORINI (THIRA)

See chapter 9 for complete sightseeing information.

**AKROTIRI EXCAVATIONS & FIRA TOWN** (3 hr, 48€–57€): Visit Akrotiri, an excavation site that dates back to the 2nd millennium B.C. See pottery, two- and three-story houses, and a variety of rooms, all 3,600 years old. Visit Fira, perched on the caldera rim, and take a stroll through town. Take a cable car ride or mule back down the slope to your ship.

## VOLOS

See chapter 12 for complete sightseeing information.

THE MONASTERIES OF THE METEORA (9 hr., 99€): Visit the Meteora, where incredible granite rocks soaring hundreds of feet in the air served as a refuge for medieval monks. Originally, the only way to get to the site was via net baskets operated by rope pulley, but now a road leads close to the base of the site, and many steps have been cut into the stone, leading to the top. You'll visit monastic buildings that contain Byzantine artifacts, icons, and wall paintings, and enjoy sweeping views of the low plains and neighboring monasteries. Shopping time is offered in Kalambaka, and lunch at a local hotel is included.

VOLOS & MAKRINITSA VILLAGE (3½ hr., 36€–53€): Visit the Volos Archaeological Museum, which houses a collection of ancient treasures. Also visit Makrinitsa village, located on the slopes of Mount Pelion. The narrow cobblestone streets are filled with small shops selling candied fruit, herbs, spices, and the like. The village square offers a stunning view of the surrounding countryside. Free time to shop is also included. In addition, some tours visit Portoria, a resort village located high above sea level, and offering stunning views of the Aegean below.

## 10 Best Shore Excursions in the Ports of Call: Turkey

The following Turkish ports of call are commonly visited on Greek itineraries.

### ISTANBUL

HIGHLIGHTS OF ISTANBUL (7–9 hr., 79€–97€): Includes the Hippodrome, once the largest chariot race grounds of the Byzantine Empire; Sultan Ahmet Mosque, also known as the Blue Mosque for its 21,000 blue Iznik tiles; the famous St. Sophia, once the largest church of the Christian world; and Topkapi Palace, the official residence of the Ottoman Sultans and home to treasures that include Spoonmaker's Diamond, one of the biggest diamonds in the world. Also visit the Grand Bazaar, with its 4,000 shops. Some tours bring you back to the ship for lunch, while others include lunch in a first-class restaurant. Shorter tours are also available that include some, but not all, of the above.

BYZANTINE UNDERGROUND CISTERN & GRAND BAZAAR (3 hr., 22€): Visit the underground cistern (also known as "The Underground Palace"), which dates from the 6th century and is supported by 336 Corinthian columns. You reach the water-filled cavern by traveling with a guide down steep steps and along a raised walkway. Also visit the Grand Bazaar and view the outside of St. Sophia.

BEYLERBEYI PALACE (2½ hr., 34€): Visit Istanbul's grandest seaside mansion, built by Sultan Abdulaziz on the Asian side of the Bosporos in 1865. The tour includes the palace's harem, men's quarters, and grand central hall.

ISTANBUL NIGHTLIFE WITH DINNER (4 hr., 55€): Enjoy traditional Turkish cuisine and belly dancing in a city nightclub.

DOLMABAHCE PALACE & CHORA MUSEUM (8 hr., 75€): Visit the 285-room 19th-century palace, the principal imperial residence of the late years of the Ottoman Empire. Drive across the Bosporos Bridge to enjoy a panoramic view of Istanbul from the Asian side. Drive past gardens, old mansions, fortresses, and fishermen's villages. Return to the European side via Fatih Bridge, arriving at the suburb of Tarabya for a Turkish seafood lunch. After lunch, drive to the modern part of Istanbul and across the Golden Horn to visit the Chora Museum and a Byzantine church that dates back to the 11th century. The tour ends at the Grand Bazaar. Some lines also offer a tour of Dolmabahçe Palace as a half-day excursion (4 hr, 46€).

# KUSADASI

**EPHESUS** (3–4 hr, 30€–46€): *Visit one of the best-preserved ancient cities in the world. Your guide will take you down the city's actual marble streets to the baths, theater, and incredible library building, and along the way you'll pass columns, mosaics, monuments, and ruins. The tour may include a stop at a shop for a presentation of Turkish carpets (with an emphasis on getting you to buy).*

**EPHESUS & THE HOUSE OF THE VIRGIN MARY** (3½–4½ hr, 47€–52€): This tour combines a visit to Ephesus with the House of the Virgin Mary, a humble chapel located in the valley of Bulbuldagi. Located here is the site where the Virgin Mary is believed to have spent her last days. The site was officially sanctioned for pilgrimage in 1892.

**EPHESUS, ST. JOHN'S BASILICA & THE HOUSE OF THE VIRGIN MARY** (4½ hr, 52€): This tour combines the above two with a visit to St. John's Basilica, another holy pilgrimage site. It is believed to be the site where St. John wrote the fourth book of the New Testament. A church at the site, which is now in ruins, was built by Justinian over a 2nd-century tomb believed to contain St. John the Apostle. This tour may also be offered as a full-day excursion, including lunch at a local restaurant and a visit to the museum of Ephesus (6½–7½ hr, 75€–89€).

**THREE ANCIENT CITIES** (6–7 hr, 69€–85€): This tour takes in the ruins that surround the region of Ephesus, including Priene, known for its Athena Temple bankrolled by Alexander the Great; Didyma, known for the Temple of Apollo; and Miletus, which includes a stadium built by the Greeks and expanded by the Romans to hold 15,000 spectators. A light lunch at a restaurant in Didyma is included.

**EPHESUS, PRIENE & DIDYMA** (7½ hr, 75€): Includes the above plus Ephesus and a buffet lunch at a five-star hotel.

# 5

# Settling into Athens

*by Sherry Marker*

Athens is the city that Greeks love to hate, complaining that it's too expensive, too crowded, too polluted. Some 40% of the country lives here, making the city burst at the seams with five million inhabitants, a rumored 15,000 taxis—but try to find one that's empty—and streets so congested that you'll suspect that each of the five million Athenians has a car. The new Metro (subway) opened its first station in Syntagma Square in January 2000 and hopes continue that the entire new line will be finished in time for the summer 2004 Olympics. Greeks are getting ready to welcome visitors from around the world to the first home of the Olympic games for the 2004 Olympics, to be held in and around Athens from August 13 to 29, 2004. Anticipation for the Olympic Games in Greece has been matched only by the considerable anxiety that not everything (the road and Metro from the airport into Athens, the Olympics venues, and facilities to house both contestants and the spectators) will be finished in time. It's too soon to say what will happen when the dust settles, but it's fair to say that most Athenians will be very glad to see the last of the dust settle and an end to almost a decade of construction. (See chapter 3 for coverage of the 2004 Olympic Games.)

In short, Athens, as usual, is busy reinventing itself. Newly pedestrianized Dionissiou Areopayitou Street links what is being called an "Archaeological Park," stretching from Hadrian's Gate past the Acropolis and Ancient Agora to the Kerameikos. The legendary Grande Bretagne Hotel in Syntagma Square and the Hilton on Vassilis Sophia Boulevard have been entirely remodeled in honor of visitors in the Olympic year and beyond. The Metro has significantly diminished Athens's endemic gridlock and *nefos* (smog). Still, traffic in central Athens can be fierce. Visitors may be forgiven for sometimes wondering, if Athens, with all its fabled glories, is the ideal holiday destination. Don't despair: Quite soon, you'll almost certainly develop your own love-hate relationship with Athens, snarling at the traffic and gasping in wonder at the Acropolis, fuming at the taxi driver who tries to overcharge you—and marveling at the stranger who realizes that you're lost and walks several blocks out of his way to take you where you're going.

Even though you've probably come here to see the "glory that was Greece," perhaps best symbolized by the Parthenon and the superb statues and vases in the National Archaeological Museum, allow some time to make haste slowly in Athens. Your best moments may come sitting at a small cafe, sipping a tiny cup of the sweet sludge that the Greeks call coffee, or getting hopelessly lost in the Plaka—only to find yourself in the shady courtyard of an old church, or suddenly face to face with an ancient monument you never knew existed. With only a little advance planning, you can find a good hotel here, eat well in convivial restaurants, enjoy local customs such as the refreshing afternoon siesta and the leisurely evening *volta* (promenade or stroll)—and leave Athens planning to return, as the Greeks say, *tou chronou* (next year).

And if you do get caught in an Athenian gridlock, just remember what it was like when the Parthenon was built: Teams of mules dragged carts laden with 12-ton blocks of marble from Mount Pendeli along today's Queen Sophia Avenue to the Acropolis. If an axle broke, traffic stopped for several days until the damage was repaired.

If you take a look at "Suggested Itineraries for First-Time Visitors" in the beginning of chapter 6, you'll get some good ideas on how to approach the city. As far as when to go, from mid-March through May it's almost always pleasant and mild in Athens, although Greeks rightly say that the March wind has "teeth." Between June and August, the temperature usually rises steadily, making August a good month to emulate Athenian practice and try to avoid the city. If you do come here in August, you'll find that Athens, like Paris, belongs to the tourists: some 60% of all Athenians take their summer holiday between the first and fifteenth of August. September is usually balmy, with occasional light rain, although it's not unknown for August heat to spill over well into September. October usually offers beautiful summer/autumn weather, with rain and some high winds likely, and might be intermittently chilly. Most rain falls between November and February, when Athens can be colder and windier than you might expect. Average daytime temperatures range from 11°C (52°F) in January to 33°C (92°F) in August. Stretches when it's well over 38°C (100°F) are not uncommon in August, when anyone with health problems such as asthma should be wary of Athens's *nefos*. The city can be very hot and exhausting—be sure to give yourself time off for a coffee or a cold drink in a cafe. After all, you're on vacation!

# 1 Orientation

## ARRIVING
## BY PLANE

The new Athens International Airport Eleftherios Venizelos (© 210/353-0000; www.aia.gr), 27km (17 miles) northeast of Athens at Spata, opened in 2001. The airport is also popularly known simply as "Spata," from its nearest town. Time will tell whether Spata, with its two runways, will meet its goal of handling 50 million passengers annually and become the leading airport in Southeastern Europe—the first big test will come in 2004, when Athens hosts the summer Olympics. The good news about the new airport is that in contrast to the old Hellenikon airport, Venizelos airport is certainly a large, modern, facility, with ample restrooms, interesting shops, and acceptable restaurants. The bad news is that it is a serious slog from Athens; no longer do you have the option of heading back into Athens for a few extra hours of sightseeing if your flight is delayed.

Throughout the airport, there are stands with free brochures on the airport facilities, however, neither these publications nor the airport's website can always be relied on for accurate up-to-date information. Here is a basic introduction to Athens' airport, based on information that was up-to-date at press time.

**ARRIVALS**  Most flights arrive at the Main Terminal, which has both an "A" and "B" area, but some flights—including most charter flights—arrive and depart from Spata's first of a projected cluster of satellite terminals. In addition, you may deplane down a steep flight of stairs onto the tarmac, where a bus will take you to the terminal. When planning your carry-on luggage, you may want to keep in mind that you may have quite a trek from your arrival point to the luggage area and customs hall.

The luggage arrivals area has ATMs, telephones, toilets, and luggage carts. Luggage carts cost 1€; there is often an attendant beside the carts who can make change for you if you do not have a 1€ coin. There are also several free telephones in the luggage arrival area from which you can telephone for a porter. When we passed through the airport in March of 2003, porters' fees were highly negotiable.

If your luggage does not greet you in the luggage arrivals area, proceed to one of the desks marked "Baggage Tracing."

Signs in the luggage arrival area indicate which route to use for Customs (Citizens of Common Market countries [EEC] do not need to go through passport control; citizens of non-EEC countries, such as the U.S., do go through passport control.)

If you are being met, you may want to rendezvous at the clearly marked Meeting Point (across from the Greek National Tourist Organization desk) between exits 2 and 3 in the Main Terminal Arrivals Hall.

The Pacific baggage storage (left luggage) facility is in the Main Arrivals Terminal; this service is officially open 24 hours a day and charges 2€ per piece per day.

Exits from the Main Arrivals Terminal are signposted for taxi and bus connections into Athens.

## GETTING INTO ATHENS   Getting to Athens

**Since** buses run on erratic schedules, the easiest way into town is to take a **taxi** from immediately outside the terminal. This is not as simple as it sounds: Greeks regard waiting in line with amusement, and getting a cab is usually a fiercely competitive sport. A cab into the center (*kentro*) of town usually costs 15€ to 25€, and more between midnight and 5am. Depending on traffic, the cab ride can take under 30 minutes or well over an hour—something to remember when you return to the airport. This includes a 2€ airport surcharge and a charge of 1€ per suitcase. The toll on the pay road from the airport into Athens (currently 1.60€) will be added to your tab. If you ask for the air-conditioning to be turned on, you'll pay another 2€; if the driver has it on, you pay nothing extra. As always, be sure that the meter is turned on to 1 (6am–midnight) or to 2 (midnight–6am).

If you want to take a **bus** from the airport into central Athens, be prepared for what may be a substantial wait and a slow journey. **Bus service** from the airport to Syntagma Square or to Piraeus costs 4€. Do *not* assume that the destination indicated on the front of the bus, or on the sign at the bus stop, is the actual destination of the bus. Ask the driver where the bus is going. In theory, bus no. 019 (and, confusingly, sometimes bus no. 091) runs to Syntagma and Omonia squares before continuing to Piraeus every half-hour from 7am to 10pm (1€), and then every hour from about 10:15pm to 6:30am (3€). The official bus schedules are as follows:

**Spata–Syntagma (E95):** every 16 minutes from 6am to 8:30pm and every 30 minutes from 8:30pm to midnight, with NO service from midnight to 6am.

**Spata–Ethniki Amina (E94):** Every 25 minutes from 6am to midnight and every 35 minutes from midnight to 6am. As the Ethniki Amina Metro stop

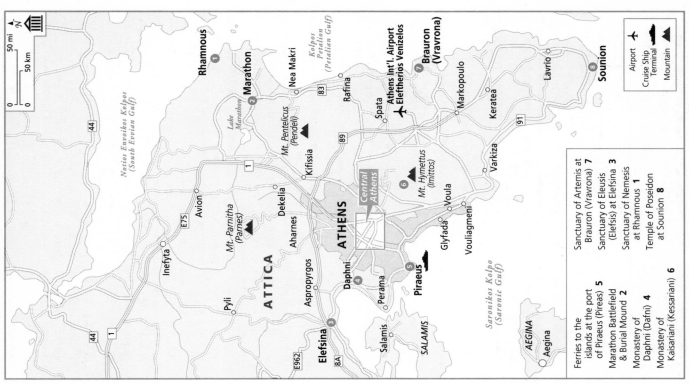

## Athens & Environs

**N**

50 mi

50 km

Rhamnous **1**

Marathon **2**

Nea Makri

*Kolpos Petalion (Petalian Gulf)*

*Lake Marathon*

Rafina

83

*Notios Evvoikos Kolpos (South Evvian Gulf)*

Mt. Pentelicus (Pendeli)

Kifissia

Spata

Athens Int'l. Airport Eleftherios Venizelos

Brauron (Vravrona) **7**

Sounion **8**

Lavrio

Markopoulo

Keratea

89

Mt. Hymettus (Imittos) **6**

Varkiza

91

44

1

E75

Avion

Dekelia

Aharnes

Mt. Parnitha (Parnes)

**Central Athens**

**ATHENS**

Voula

Vouliagmeni

Glyfada

Varkiza

Inefyta

Pyli

Asropyrgos

Daphni **4**

Perama

**Piraeus 5**

*Saronikos Kolpo (Saronic Gulf)*

44

1

E962

8A

**Elefsina 3**

Salamis

*SALAMIS*

*AEGINA*

Aegina

*ATTICA*

| | |
|---|---|
| Airport | ✈ |
| Cruise Ship Terminal | ◣ |
| Mountain | ▲ |

Ferries to the islands at the port of Piraeus (Pireas) **5**

Marathon Battlefield & Burial Mound **2**

Monastery of Daphni (Dafni) **4**

Monastery of Kaisariani (Kessariani) **6**

Sanctuary of Artemis at Brauron (Vravrona) **7**

Sanctuary of Eleusis (Elefsis) at Elefsina **3**

Sanctuary of Nemesis at Rhamnous **1**

Temple of Poseidon at Sounion **8**

(confusingly also known as Pentagono) is outside central Athens, this service is not likely to be of use to most travelers.

If you chose to drive yourself into Athens, remember that although the direct six-lane link road to Athens is now officially complete, not all exits, entrances, and feeder-roads have been completed, nor are they accurately signposted.

At press time, signs were not promising that the **Metro** link into Athens would be completed in time for the summer Olympics in 2004.

However you head into Athens, you'll be passing through the region known as "Mesogeia" (the "inland"). Until the new airport was built, this was one of the loveliest sections of Greece, with vineyards stretching for miles, sleepy country villages, and handsome chapels. Much of the area constituted the protected "Attic Park"; now, the once-protected wetlands and vineyards are busily being turned into new towns, sub-developments, malls—and yet more roads.

**DEPARTURES** If you are taking a taxi to the airport, try to have the desk clerk at your hotel order it for you well in advance of your departure. Many taxis refuse to go to the airport, fearing that they will have a long wait before they get a return fare. Allow a minimum of an hour for the ride and 2 hours to check-in for an international flight.

For information on taxi fares to the airport, see above under "Arrivals."

For information on bus service to the airport from Syntagma, Ethniki Amyna, and Piraeus see above under "Arrivals." For precise details on where to catch the airport bus from Athens to the airport, check with your hotel, the Greek National Tourist Office or—if you are very well organized and not too tired—at an information desk when you arrive at the airport.

The flight information screens should indicate where you check in and what your departure gate is. Make sure that the information on your boarding pass agrees with the information on the flight information screen.

There have been frequent complaints that adequate information on arrivals, departures, cancellations, delays, and gate changes is not always posted on the flight information screens. Nonetheless, it is important to check these screens, and at the information desks, as there are NO flight announcements.

Last minute changes in the departure gate are not unknown; arrive at your gate as early as possible, as your best chance of learning of a change is at the original gate.

**CONNECTING FLIGHTS** The airport authority advises allowing a minimum of 45 minutes to make a flight connection; this should be adequate if you arrive and depart from the Main Terminal and do NOT have to clear Customs. Allow at least an hour (an hour and a half is better) if you have to clear Customs or if you arrive or depart from the Satellite Terminal. At present, many charter flights arrive at and depart from the Satellite terminal.

**AIRPORT FACILITIES** The airport has some 35 shops ranging from Bulgari and Hermès boutiques to twelve Travel Value and Duty Free Shops. There are

## Tips Taking a Taxi

If you decide to take a taxi from the airport into Athens, ask an airline official or a policeman what the fare should be, and let the taxi driver know you've been told the official rate before you begin your journey. If you're taking a taxi to the airport, try to have the desk clerk at your hotel order it for you well in advance of your departure. Many taxis refuse to go to the airport, fearing that they'll have a long wait before they get a return fare.

ten restaurants and cafes, including a Food Village with seven food "hubs" in the Main Departure Lounge; a McDonalds overlooking the runways perches on the upper level of the Main Terminal Building. As with airports around the world, both food and goods are overpriced, although books, newspapers, and magazines are reasonably priced.

Duty-free shops have different regulations for Intra-Schengen and Extra-Schengen passengers. In short, Intra-Schengen refers to flights within the Common Market (EEC); Extra-Schengen refers to flights outside the EEC. If you are flying from Athens to a country outside the EEC, you may find it worth while to check out the duty free prices on perfumes and spirits.

The Greek National Tourism Organization (abbreviated GNTO in English-speaking countries and EOT in Greece) has an information desk in the arrivals terminal.

Hertz, Avis, and Alamo, rental cars are available at the airport. **Warning:** All these companies levy a steep surcharge (at least 10%) if you collect your car at the airport rather than at their in-town offices.

There is both short- (3€ per hour) and long- (12€ per day) term parking at the airport; much of the long-term parking is a serious walk from the Main Terminal.

Useful telephone numbers at Athens International Airport include: Information: ℂ **210/353-0000;** Customs: ℂ **210/353-2014;** Police: ℂ **210/663-5140;** First Aid: ℂ **166** (from airport courtesy phones and information desks) and ℂ **210/353-9408** from pay phones.

**GETTING BETWEEN THE AIRPORT & PIRAEUS (PIREAS)** A taxi from the airport to Piraeus should cost 15€ to 25€. It's important to know that island boats leave from several **different** Piraeus harbors. Most ferryboats and hydrofoils (Flying Dolphins) for Aegina leave from the **Main Harbor.** Hydrofoils for other islands leave from **Marina Zea,** a vigorous half-hour walk from the Main Harbor. All this makes Piraeus a good place to take a taxi to and from the airport. If you do not know which harbor your boat is leaving from, tell your taxi driver your final destination and he can probably find out the harbor and even the pier you are leaving from.

In theory, there is bus service from the airport to Piraeus every hour (4€). The bus usually leaves passengers in Karaiskaki Square, several blocks from the harbor. The official schedule is as follows:

**Spata–Piraeus (E96):** Every 20 minutes from 5am to 7pm; every 30 minutes from 7pm to 8:30pm; every 40 minutes from 8:30pm to 5am.

**AIRLINE OFFICES** Most international carriers have ticket offices in or near Syntagma Square. Try to find out the location of your airline's Athens office

*Tips* **New Museum**

If you find yourself with 2 or more hours to kill at the new Eleftherios Venezelos Airport at Spata (and called Spata by most Greeks), consider taking a taxi (12€) to the nearby Attica Zoological Park in Spata, which opened in 2001. Unlike the grim zoo in Athens's National Gardens, this zoo (with 2,000 birds from more than 300 species) is a delight; open daily from 10am to 5pm October through April and 9am to 7:30pm May through September. Admission is 8€.

before you leave home, as these offices can move without warning. The **Air Canada** office is at 10 Othonos (© 210/322-3206). The **American Airlines** office is located at 15 Panepistimiou (© 210/331-1045 or 210/331-1046). The **British Airways** office is at 1 Themistokleous, at 130 Leoforos Vouliagmenis, Glyfada (© 210/890-6666). The **Delta Air Lines** office is at 4 Othonos (© 210/331-1660-8). The **Lufthansa Airlines** office is at 11 Leoforos Vas. Sofias (© 210/617-5200). The **Qantas Airways** office is at 2 Nikodimou (© 210/323-9063). The **Swissair** office is at 4 Othonos (© 210/323-5811). The **Turkish Airlines** office is at 19 Filellinon (© 210/324-6024).

**Olympic,** the national carrier, offers both international and domestic service and has offices just off Syntagma Square at 15 Filellinon (© 210/926-7555), at 6 Othonos (© 210/926-7444), and at 96 Leoforos Syngrou (© 210/926-7251 to 7254). The main reservations and information numbers are (© **210/966-6666** or 210/936-9111; www.olympic-airways.gr) At press time, it seemed that when the Hilton Hotel, 46 Leoforos Vas. Sofias, reopened, it would again have an **Olympic Office** (phone not available). If so, this office is usually less crowded and easier to use than the main offices.

## BY CAR

If you arrive by car **from Corinth** (to the southwest), the signs into Athens will direct you fairly clearly into Omonia Square, which you will enter from the west along Ayiou Konstantinou. In Omonia, signs *should* direct you on towards Syntagma Square and other points in central Athens (signs in Omonia disappear mysteriously). If you arrive **from Thessaloniki** (to the north), the signs point-ing you into central Athens are few and far between. It is not a good idea to attempt this for the first time after dark, as you may well miss the turn for Omonia Square. If this happens, your best bet is to try to spot the Acropolis and head toward it until you pick up signs for Omonia Square or Syntagma Square.

## BY BUS

Before you start out on any bus trip, check with the **Tourist Police** (© 210/171) or the **Greek National Tourism Organization (EOT)** office (© **210/327-1300** or 210/331-0562) for current schedules and fares. As the new Metro continues to open stations, bus routes and fares will change. It's best to double-check all routes and to be prepared for fare increases. If possible, get someone to write down the name and address of your bus station in Greek; this will be a great help to you when you take a taxi or bus to the station. Keep in mind that many buses run both with and without a "0" prefix: as 024 and 24, for example.

There are two principal stations for **KTEL,** the national bus company. **Terminal A,** 100 Kifissou (© **210/512-9233**), off the road out of Athens toward Corinth, handles buses **to and from the Peloponnese and parts of**

**Northern Greece.** A taxi here from Syntagma Square should cost 4€ to 6€; if traffic is light, the journey is less than 20 minutes, but it can take an hour. If you don't have much to carry, take public bus no. 051 to the terminal (.50€). It leaves from the corner of Zinonos and Menandrou, several blocks off Omonia Square; you can catch the same bus at the terminal for the trip into town.

**Terminal B** (℘ **210/831-7096**), handles buses **to and from Central Greece** (including Delphi, Thebes, Evvia, and Meteora) and some destinations **to the north and east of Athens.** The GNTO, for reasons known best to itself, lists the address for Terminal B as 260 Liossion; no; this is where the bus for the terminal stops. When you get off the bus, turn right into Yousiou and you will see the terminal at the end of the street. Bus no. 024, which stops at Leoforos Amalias in front of the entrance to the National Garden (a block south of Syntagma Square), will take you to and from the terminal for .50€. If you take this bus, tell the driver you want to get off at the bus terminal and then head right onto Yousiou to reach the terminal. The **Mavromateon terminal** at Patission and Alexandras, a few hundred meters north of the Archaeological Museum, handles buses for most **destinations in Attica.**

## BY TRAIN

Trains **from the south and west,** including Eurail connections via Patras, arrive at the **Peloponnese Station** (Stathmos Peloponnisou; ℘ **210/513-1601**), about a mile northwest of Omonia Square on Sidirodromeon. Trains **from the north** arrive at **Larissa Station** (Stathmos Larissis; ℘ **210/529-8837**), just across the tracks from the Peloponnese Station on Deligianni. The Larissa Station has both an exchange office, usually open daily from 8am to 9:15pm, and luggage storage, usually open from 6:30am to 9pm.

To get to the train stations, you can take the **Metro** (subway) to Larissa (line 2), close to both stations. A taxi from the center of town should cost no more than 3€. The Metro runs from Omonia, Syntagma, and Koukaki to the Larissa Station by the train stations. The most central place from which to catch the Metro is the stop in front of the Parliament Building in Syntagma Square.

You can purchase train tickets just before your journey at the station (running the risk that all seats may be sold); at the Omonia Square ticket office, 1 Karolou (℘ **210/524-0647**); at 17 Filellinon, off Syntagma Square (℘ **210/323-6747**); or at most travel agents. Information (in theory in English) on timetables is available by dialing ℘ **145** or **147.**

(Tips) **Hotels Near the Airport**

If you have an early flight out of Spata, you might consider spending the night at the Hotel Avra (℘ **22940/22-780**) on the waterfront in the nearby port of Rafina. This is an old hotel, with minimal charm, but you can take a swim, eat at a harborside restaurant—and get to the airport in less than half an hour by taxi. Prices are currently from 70€, but may rise, due to renovations. If you want to be at the airport itself, with considerable creature comforts, the charmless but convenient and efficient 345-room Sofitel Athens Airport Hotel (℘ **210/681-0882**), with its own restaurants, fitness club, and swimming pool is the logical place to stay if you have a very early flight, or get in very late. Prices are from 220€ double.

**Tips** **Trying to Catch a Connection**

A word about making air connections after an island trip: it is unwise—even foolhardy—to allow anything less than 24 hours between your return to Piraeus by island boat and your departure by air, as rough seas can make for significant delays.

## BY BOAT

**Piraeus,** the main harbor of Athens's main seaport, 11km (7 miles) southwest of central Athens, is a 15-minute Metro ride from Monastiraki and Omonia squares. The subway runs from about 5am to midnight and costs 1 €. The far slower bus no. 040 runs from Piraeus to central Athens (with a stop at Fililli-non, off Syntagma Square) every 15 minutes between 5am and 1am and hourly from 1am to 5am for .70€.

You may prefer to take a **taxi** to avoid what can be a long hike from your boat to the bus stop or subway terminal. Be prepared for some serious bargaining. The normal fare on the meter from Piraeus to Syntagma should be about 6€–10€, but many drivers simply offer a flat fare, which can easily be as much as 20€. Pay it if you're desperate, or walk to a nearby street, hail another taxi, and insist that the meter be turned on.

If you arrive at Piraeus by hydrofoil (Flying Dolphin), you'll probably arrive at the **Zea Marina** harbor, about a dozen blocks south across the peninsula from the main harbor. Even our Greek friends admit that getting a taxi from Zea Marina into Athens can involve a wait of an hour or more—and that drivers usually drive a hard (and exorbitant) bargain. To avoid both the wait and big fare, you can walk up the hill from the hydrofoil station and catch bus no. 905 for .70€, which connects Zea to the Piraeus subway station, where you can complete your journey into Athens. You must buy a ticket at the small stand near the bus stop or at a newsstand before boarding the bus. **Warning:** If you arrive late at night, you may not be able to do this, as both the newsstand and the ticket stand may be closed.

If you've landed at the port of **Rafina** (about an hour's bus ride east of Athens), you'll see a bus stop up the hill from the ferryboat pier. Inquire about the bus to Athens; it runs often and will return you within the hour to the **Areos Park Terminal,** 29 Mavromateon, near the junction of Leoforos Alexandras and Patission (about 25 min. by trolley from Syntagma Square or 1 block from the Victoria Square Metro stop). From the terminal, there are buses to Rafina every half-hour.

In August 2000, the Greek government announced plans to expand the port of **Lavrion,** 52km (32 miles) southeast of Athens, by summer 2001. By the spring of 2003 little had happened. Should this project go forward, the hope is that this will take pressure off the very crowded ports of Piraeus and Rafina. You may want to check with the GNTO to see if Lavrion has been expanded and is operational when you visit Greece.

## VISITOR INFORMATION

In 2003, the **Greek National Tourist Office (GNTO),** also known as the Hellenic Tourism Organization (EOT), closed its main office just off Syntagma Square at 2 Amerikis. The new main office is at 7 Tsochas St., Ambelokipi

© **210/870-000;** www.gnto.gr) well out of central Athens. The office is open Monday through Friday 8am to 3pm and is closed weekends.

Information about Athens, free city maps, transportation schedules, hotel lists, and other booklets on many regions of Greece are available in Greek, English, French, and German—although whenever we stop by, many publications we ask for are described as "all gone"—even when we can see them on display just out of reach. The staff members often appear bored with their jobs and irritated by any questions; be persistent.

Information on Greece is also available on the Internet; see chapter 2 for details.

Available 24 hours a day, the **Tourist Police** (© **210/171**) speak English, as well as other languages, and will help with problems or emergencies.

## CITY LAYOUT

As you begin to explore Athens, you may find it helpful to look up to the **Acropolis,** west of Syntagma Square, and **Mount Likavitos** (Lycabettus), to the northeast. You can see both Acropolis and Likavitos, whose marble lower slopes give way to pine trees and a summit crowned with a small white church, from most parts of the city.

Think of central Athens as an almost perfect equilateral triangle, with its points at **Syntagma (Constitution) Square, Omonia (Harmony) Square,** and **Monastiraki (Little Monastery) Square,** near the **Acropolis.** In government jargon, the area bounded by Syntagma, Omonia, and Monastiraki squares is defined as the commercial center, from which cars are banned (in theory, if not in practice) except for several cross streets. Most Greeks think of **Omonia Square**—Athens's commercial hub—as the city center, but most visitors take their bearings from **Syntagma Square,** site of the House of Parliament. The two squares are connected by the parallel **Stadiou** and **Panepistimiou.** (Panepistimiou is also known as Eleftheriou Venizelou.) Flanking the Parliament Building is Athens's largest park, the **National Garden.** West of Syntagma Square, **Ermou** and **Mitropoleos** lead slightly downhill to **Monastiraki Square,** home of the city's famous flea market. From Monastiraki Square, **Athinas** leads north back to Omonia past the modern Central Market. The old warehouse district of **Psirri**—now the home of many chic galleries, cafes, and restaurants—is between Athinas and Ermou.

If you stand in Monastiraki Square and look south, you'll see the Acropolis. At its foot are the **Ancient Agora** (Market) and the **Plaka,** Athens's oldest neighborhood, many of whose street names honor Greek heroes from either classical antiquity or the Greek War of Independence. The twisting labyrinth of streets in the Plaka can challenge even the best navigators. Don't panic: The Plaka is small enough that you can't go far astray, and its side streets with small houses and neighborhood churches are so charming that you won't mind being lost. One excellent map may help: the Greek Archaeological Service's **Historical Map of Athens,** which has maps of the Plaka and of the city center showing the major archaeological sites. The map costs about 4€ and is sold at many bookstores, museums, ancient sites, and newspaper kiosks. And remember: Many Athenians speak some English, and almost all are helpful to direction-seeking strangers—unless you happen to be the tenth person in as many minutes to ask where the Acropolis is when it is clearly visible!

**FINDING AN ADDRESS**   If possible, have the address you want to find written out in Greek so that you can show it to your taxi driver or ask for help

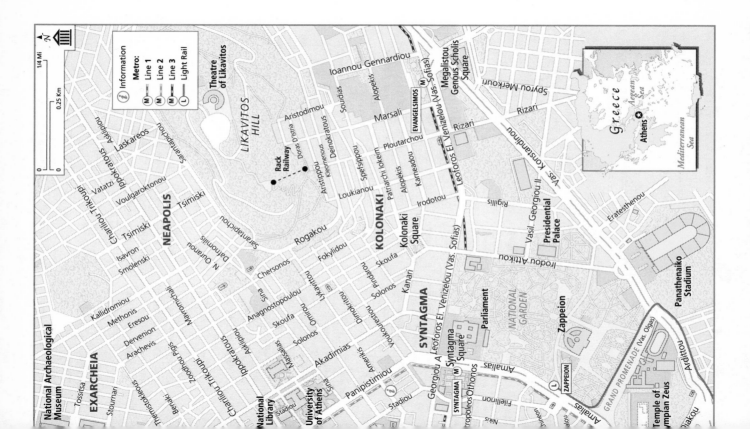

138 **CHAPTER 5** · SETTLING INTO ATHENS

from pedestrians. Most street signs are given both in Greek and a transliteration, which is a great help. Most taxi drivers carry a good Athens street guide in their glove compartment, and can usually find any destination, although, increasingly, a certain number of Athenian cabbies are newcomers to the capital, and may have trouble with out-of-the-way addresses.

**STREET MAPS**   As already mentioned, you can get a free map of central Athens from the **Greek National Tourism Office** at 2 Amerikis, off Syntagma Square. With its small print and poor-quality paper, this is not a great map, and you may prefer to stop at a newspaper kiosk or bookstore to pick up a copy of the *Historical Map of Athens* or another congenial city map (see "Books" under "Shopping A to Z," in chapter 6).

## NEIGHBORHOODS IN BRIEF

It's not easy to see that this sprawling city is divided into distinct districts and neighborhoods, each with its own character and associations, each with its favorite cafe and bakery. If you have the time to explore Athens, here are some of the neighborhoods that await you. Unless you have a specific goal and limited time, why not just stroll, get lost—and be pleasantly surprised when you discover that you're on a street where almost all the shops sell only icons or sugared almonds (an essential gift for guests at weddings and baptisms), or find a little park where you can sit on a bench and study your map. And don't forget to take in the new "Archaeological Park," pedestrianized walkways stretch from Hadrian's Gate past the Acropolis on pedestrianized Dionissiou Areopayitou to the Ancient Agora and on to the Kerameikos.

### Central Athens

**The Commercial Center**   The commercial center (as you might suspect, a bureaucratic name no one uses, and that appears on no map) lies between **Omonia, Syntagma,** and **Monastiraki** squares, and includes the **Plaka** and **Psiri** districts. In theory, vehicles are mostly forbidden here; in practice, they're endemic. Nonetheless, certain streets are pedestrian, which makes parts of the area quite pleasant. Keep in mind that many motorists and virtually all motorcycle riders assume that pedestrian-only regulations do not apply to them.

**Omonia Square** is the heart of the working city of Athens, a tumultuous square around a circular fountain that's currently but a memory, thanks to the ongoing Metro construction. You'll probably pass through Omonia when you walk to the National Archaeological Museum or head out of Athens by car or bus. Take a look at the few remaining 19th-century building facades around Omonia. Once, many housed some of Athens nicest hotels, now abandoned or desultory at best. One thing that hasn't changed much: **Athinas,** between Omonia and Monastiraki squares. This is where you'll find Athens's **Central Market,** where you can browse the fish and meat halls, buy vegetables and fruits from all over Greece, sample cheeses from distant islands—or buy a pair of shoes or sunglasses from a street vendor. By day, this is the best street in town to get a sense of Athens's nonstop bustle. By night, most of the Omonia area has something of the tacky ambience of New York's Times Square in the mid-1980s, although the area has been considerably smartened up in the last few years. Still, if you are going to be approached with offers of cheap sex or drugs, it may well be in or around Omonia. You may also encounter refugees from Albania and Eastern Europe, who will try to sell you pirated CDs, leather jackets, and, sometimes, themselves.

**Syntagma (Constitution) Square** is, for most visitors, the heart of Athens. This is where you'll find the major banks, travel agencies, American Express and Thomas Cook, and several fine hotels, including the **Grande Bretagne,** the grand old lady of Greek hotels. The Grande Bretagne underwent an extensive face-lift in 2002/3 and is now more splendid than ever—if you are not staying here, take a discreet peek at the magnificent beaux-arts lobby. The **central post office** is at the corner of Mitropoleos. For years, the sidewalk cafes here were popular places to watch the world go by, but with the proliferation of the fast-food joints that attract teeny bopper Athenians and bands of student travelers, you may not want to linger.

Syntagma is the home of much of governmental Athens: The handsome neoclassical building at the head of the square is the **Greek Parliament building,** formerly the Royal Palace. That's where you'll see the changing of the guard several times a day and may hear a band playing on Sundays around 11am. The soldiers who march in front of the parliament building and the **Tomb of the Unknown Soldier** often wear the *evzone* uniforms (frilly white skirts and pom-pommed red shoes) of their ancestors who fought to gain Greece's freedom during the War of Independence (1821–28). Most foreigners find the evzones' uniforms rather droll; Greeks do not, something to remember when you watch

the changing of the guard. Laughing at this ceremony is equivalent to snickering when taps is played at the Tomb of the Unknowns at Arlington Cemetery in the United States.

South of Syntagma Square, **Monastiraki Square** and the **Plaka** area are Athens's two main tourist destinations. Monastiraki's flea markets are open every day, but are usually best—and most crowded—on Sundays. In the Plaka, wall-to-wall shops and restaurants have displaced many of the area's elegant 19th-century homes, especially along Adrianou (Hadrian) and Filellinon.

**Psirri** is the district between Athinas and Ermou which until only a few years ago would not have merited any mention. Now, it's where you'll find some of Athens's newest and most popular restaurants, cafes, and galleries. The district is being reclaimed by young entrepreneurs drawn here by relatively low rents. The area can still be rather deserted at night, but is usually perfectly safe—although it's not a great idea for a woman to walk here alone in the wee hours, as Athinas has a vigorous drug and prostitution trade. Near Psirri, two more districts are being revitalized: **Gazi,** formerly known only for its once noxious gasworks, but now the home of the Athens Municipal Technopolis Center gallery; and **Rouf,** site of the fruit and vegetable market—and, increasingly, of cafes, galleries, and restaurants.

**Kolonaki** This is the posh area in town, on the slopes of **Mount Likavitos** (Lycabettus), a few blocks northwest of Syntagma Square, spreading out around a central square. The **square** is officially named Plateia Filikis Eterias (Square of the Friendly Society), but is usually called Kolonaki, after the fragmentary marble column in the square.

Although many Athenians have fled the city's smog and congestion for northern suburbs, Kolonaki remains one of *the* places to live—or at least see and be seen—in Athens. If you're here on a Friday, try to take in the **street market** snaking along Xenokratous. You may be surprised at how many Asian women you see shopping here: Most of these young women, usually from the Philippines, work as maids and nannies in the homes of the Kolonaki elite.

If you're in Kolonaki on a Saturday, you can't miss seeing the beautiful people and the wannabes promenading up and down the streets, thronging in front of favorite boutiques to ogle the latest fashions before collapsing into street cafes to revive their spirits with cool drinks. There are more shoe stores per inch in Kolonaki than almost anywhere else in Greece, a nation that takes its footwear very seriously.

If you tire of window-shopping, you may want to take the funicular railway up Mount Likavitos to enjoy the panoramic view (smog permitting) of the entire metropolitan area and the sea and mountains beyond. If you walk down, you'll end up passing through some of central Athens's nicest and greenest streets, that wind around Likavitos's lower slopes.

**The University Area** Kolonaki gradually merges to the northwest with the university area, spread loosely between the 19th-century university buildings on Panepistimiou and the Polytechnic some 10 blocks to the northwest. Lots of publishers have their offices in this area, and bibliophiles may enjoy the window displays of everything from children's books on Hercules to mathematical texts. A few blocks from the Polytechnic, **Exarchia Square**, with its many sandwich shops, cafes, and bars, is usually full of students. When there are demonstrations at any of Athens's institutions of higher learning, Exarchia Square is often where speeches are made.

**Koukaki & Makriyanni Koukaki,** once the working-class counterpart to Kolonaki, has been increasingly gentrified and is one of Athens's most desirable neighborhoods. The district lies at the base of **Filopappos Hill** (Lofos Filopappou), also known as the Hill of the Muses (Lofos Mousseon). There are a number of pleasant paths leading from streets at the base of Filopappos up through its pine-clad slopes, some ending at the Dora Stratou Theater or the Observatory. The main road through Koukaki is Veikou, along which buses and trolleys run, and where there are some unpretentious cafes and restaurants as well as reasonably priced hotels. This is a nice area to stay in if you want to be out of tourist Athens, enjoy shopping in neighborhood groceries and shops—and don't mind the 15 to 20 minute walk back into tourist Athens.

**Makriyanni,** the neighborhood just north of Koukaki, at the southern base of the Acropolis, has more office buildings, shops, and hotels than apartments. There are some quite luxurious hotels here, as well as some middle-of-the-road places and several good restaurants, including the popular **Symbosio, Strofi, and Socrates's Prison** (also known as the Samaria). This is a good area to stay in if you want to be almost as centrally located as you would be in the Plaka or Syntagma, but a bit out of the tourist maelstrom.

## Tips    Plaka Tram Rides

In spring 1998, a tram service leaving from and returning to Palia Agora Square in the Plaka was initiated. The tram does a loop through the Plaka, out onto Dionissiou Areopayitou, past the Acropolis, and back into the Plaka. The ride lasts 30 to 40 minutes, costs 5€, and is offered from 10am to 10pm in summer and sometimes on weekends the rest of the year.

Something to keep in mind if you're thinking of staying in Koukaki or Makriyanni: The pedestrianization of Dionissiou Areopayitou has brought an unwelcome incursion of traffic into both areas. If you did not know the area before Dionissiou Areopayitou was pedestrianized, this probably will not bother you, as Koukaia and Makriyanni remain quieter than much of the rest of the city.

**Pangrati & Mets** Surrounding the reconstructed Athens Stadium known to the Greeks as **Kallimarmaro** (Beautiful Marble), **Pangrati** is popular with those who can't afford Kolonaki, and seems to have a high percentage of foreigners, including academics attached to various schools of archaeology in Athens. If you enjoy baroque funerary monuments, don't miss the sprawling **First Cemetery,** where luminaries such as the late Prime Minister Andreas Papandreou are buried. If you prefer your green spaces without tombs, explore Pangrati's lovely green **park**, almost a miniforest in the heart of Athens. There are lots of neighborhood restaurants and tavernas scattered in Pangrati, so you won't go hungry here.

**Mets** is southeast of Pangrati, on the other side of the Stadium, between the temple of Zeus and the First Cemetery. There are still some elegant private homes here, although most of Mets has Athens's typical low, concrete apartment buildings. Mets takes its name from a popular 19th-century café, the Metz, that once flourished here. Appropriately, the district still has some elegant bars and good restaurants—including the long-time favorite Manesis.

**The Embassy District** Leoforos Vas. Sofias (Queen Sophia Boulevard) runs from Syntagma Square toward Athens's fashionable northeastern suburb of Kifissia. If you walk along Vas. Sofias and explore the side streets that run uphill from it into Kolonaki, you'll notice the national flags of many countries on elegant office buildings and town houses. This is the Embassy District, which stretches as far as the Hilton, where many embassy workers head for lunch or a drink after work.

### The Northeast Suburbs

Athens is growing every-which-way, but much of its expansion is to the northeast, in the valley between the mountains of Penteli to the east and Parnitha to the west. Two major roads—the **National Road** to the west and **Leoforos Kifissias** to the east—run north from Athens through wall-to-wall bedroom suburbs before reaching Kifissia, some 12km (8 miles) from the center of Athens.

Cooler than Athens, thanks to its elevation, **Kifissia** was fashionable enough for the Royal Family to have a villa here. Until recently, many wealthy Athenian mothers and children decamped to the elegant hotels in Kifissia for the summer, leaving the men behind to work (and, some said, play) in Athens. Now, Kifissia has a distinctly suburban feel, with large supermarkets and incipient malls, although its spreading plane trees still give many streets a rural feel. There are some good restaurants, and several fine hotels, but there's no reason to trek out here until you've spent a lot of time in central Athens.

### Piraeus (Pireas)

The main port of Athens, Piraeus is a city very much in its own right—although even locals have trouble telling precisely where Athens ends and Piraeus begins. Piraeus prides itself on being rough and tough—a stronghold of communism, the home of *rembetika* (street-slang songs of political protest), and the workplace of a profusion of prostitutes. Probably none of this will be particularly obvious when you come here to catch a boat to the islands from the **Main Harbor**, or **Megas Limani** (Great Harbor), or **Zea Marina**, also called Pasalimani. What will be obvious if you go to any of the many fish tavernas in the little harbor of **Mikrolimani**

(Little Harbor), which is also still called by its former name of Turkolimani (Turkish Harbor), is the prices, which range from exorbitant to extortionate.

### The Southern Suburbs

Heading southeast out of Athens along the coast are a string of once-pleasant suburbs, now virtually entirely absorbed by Athens. This used to be a good place for a swim, but now there are frequent pollution alerts for these, and virtually no other, beaches in Greece.

**Paleo Faliro**, a once-lovely coastal suburb, has become almost a city by the sea, full of apartment buildings. South of the large yacht harbor of Kalamaki along Leoforos Poseidonos, the coast road, there's a big, busy public beach at **Ayios Kosmas**. Farther south, **Glyfada**, Attica's largest resort, with a yacht harbor, has lots of restaurants, bars, discos, food and clothing stores—and an almost always crowded, but decent, public beach.

**Voula**, farther southeast, has another public beach. The major resort area of **Vouliagmeni**, 23km (14 miles) south of Athens, has two good public beaches and several hotels, notably the luxury Astir Palace.

## BY PUBLIC TRANSPORTATION

### BY METRO

The first station on the new Metro (subway), opened at Syntagma Square in January 2000. When the entire system is completed (a "when" no one can put an accurate time to!), there will be easy public transportation available in much of central Athens and beyond. You may want to stop at the Syntagma station, or at the GNTO, to see what stations have opened by the time of your visit. To travel on the Metro, buy your ticket at the station, validate it in the machines as you enter, and hang on to your ticket until you get off. At present, tickets on the old line cost 0.60€; tickets on the new line cost 0.75€; day pass 3 €—but don't be surprised if these prices have gone up by the time you arrive in Athens. Validate your ticket in the machine as you enter the waiting platform or risk a fine. Metro and bus tickets aren't interchangeable.

## Athens's Metro Finally Gets Moving

In January 2000, the long-awaited new branch of the Athens Metro opened after 8 years of construction and the expenditure of at least 700 billion drachmas. The new Metro, which adds 13 stations, is an extension of the existing 130-year-old Athens subway, which already carried 350,000 passengers a day. Try to pick up a map at the new hub at Syntagma Square.

At present, the Metro usually runs at least every 10 minutes from 5am to midnight from the Defense Ministry (known as the Pentagon) to Sepolia (individual tickets cost .75€; from mid-July to early September, when Athenians leave town, service may stop at 10pm. Press releases trumpeted that pollution was cut by 70 metric tons on the first day that the new Metro ran, when 100,000 fewer vehicles entered central Athens. As this reduction in atmospheric pollution continues day by day, Athens's infamous nefos (smog) should diminish considerably. In addition, city buses now have a fighting chance of running on schedule, with fewer cars clogging the roads. (Keep in mind that the new Metro and on-going Metro construction leave many bus routes in a state of flux).

Plans (perhaps over-optimistic) call for the entire 21-station Metro system, carrying 450,000 additional passengers a day, to be up and running by 2004 when the Olympics are held in and around Athens. Now, if only someone could figure out how to build adequate parking lots near the new Metro stops so that commuters wouldn't leave their cars on every available inch of sidewalk!

Try to allow a little extra time when you catch the Metro in central Athens: two stations—Syntagma Square and Acropolis—handsomely display finds from the subway excavations in what amounts to Athens's newest small museums. You can get advance information on the Athens Metro at **www.ametro.gr.**

Even if you do not use the Metro to get around Athens, you may take it from Omonia or Monastiraki to Piraeus to catch a boat to the islands. (Don't miss the spectacular view of the Acropolis as the subway comes above ground by the Agora.) If you're not carrying much luggage, the harbor in Piraeus is a 5-minute walk (head left) from the station.

## BY BUS & TROLLEY BUS

The public transportation system is cheap—and, if you use it, you may think deservedly so. Although you can get almost everywhere you want to in central Athens and the suburbs by bus or trolley, you would need more time than you will probably have to figure out which bus to take. This is especially so at present, when many bus routes are changing as new Metro stations open. Even if you know which bus to take, you will usually have to wait a long time until the bus appears—usually stuffed with passengers. The bus service does have an information number (© **210/185**), but it's usually busy.

If you find none of this daunting, tickets cost .50€ each and can be bought from the kiosks (*periptera*) scattered throughout the city. The tickets are sold individually and in packets of 10. Tickets are good for a ride anywhere on the system. Be certain to validate yours when you get on. **Hold onto it:** Uniformed and plainclothes inspectors periodically check tickets and can levy a basic fine of 5€, or a more punitive fine of 20€ on the spot.

If you're heading out of town and take a blue A-line bus for transferring to another blue A-line bus, your ticket will still be valid on the transfer bus. In central Athens, the minibuses numbered 60 and 150 serve the commercial area free of charge.

Buses heading out to farther points of Attica leave from **Mavromateon** on the western edge of the Pedion tou Areos park at the western end of Leoforos Alexandras.

## BY TAXI

It's rumored that there are more than 15,000 taxis in Athens, but finding one empty is almost never easy. Especially if you have travel connections to make, it's a good idea to reserve a radio taxi (see below). Fortunately, taxis are inexpensive in Athens, and most drivers are honest men trying to wrest a living by maneuvering through the city's endemic gridlock. However, some drivers, notably those working Piraeus, the airports, and popular tourist destinations, can't resist trying to overcharge obvious foreigners. When you get into a taxi, check to see that the meter is turned on and set on "1" rather than "2"; the meter should be set on "2" (double fare) only between midnight and 5am, or if you take a taxi outside the city limits (if you plan to do this, try to negotiate a flat rate in advance). When the driver turns on the meter, it will register 1€, the cheapest fare. Unless your cab is caught in very heavy traffic, a trip to the center of town from the airport between 5am and midnight should not cost more than 15€–25€. Don't be surprised if your driver picks up other passengers en route; the driver will work out everyone's fair share of the fare.

Keep in mind that your driver may have difficulty understanding your pronunciation of your destination: If you are taking a taxi from your hotel, a staff member can assist you by telling the driver your destination or writing down the address for you to show to the driver. If you carry a business card from your hotel with you, you can show it to the taxi driver for your return.

If you suspect that you have been overcharged, before you pay the fare, ask for help at your hotel or other destination.

At press time, the minimum fare is 2€, and the "1" meter rate is .30€ per kilometer, with a surcharge of 1€ for service from a port or rail or bus station, or airport; luggage costs .50€ per 10 (22 lb.). These prices will almost certainly be higher by the time you visit Greece, as increases were scheduled to go into effect at press time.

There are about 15 **radio taxi** companies in Athens; as their phone numbers often change, it's worth checking the daily listing in "Your Guide" in the *Athens News*. Some established companies include **Athina** (© **210/921-7942**), **Express** (© **210/993-4812**), **Parthenon** (© **210/532-3300**), and **Piraeus** (© **210/418-2333**). If you're trying to make travel connections or traveling during rush hour, a radio taxi is well worth the 2€ surcharge. Your hotel can make the call for you and make sure that the driver knows where you want to go. Most restaurants will call a taxi for you without charge.

The GNTO's pamphlet *Helpful Hints for Taxi Users* has information on taxi fares as well as a complaint form, which you can send to the **Ministry of**

**Transport and Communication,** Xenophondos 13, 10191 Athens. Replies to complaints should be forwarded to the *Guinness Book of Records.* See also the "Taxi Tips" feature in chapter 2 of this book.

## BY CAR

In Athens, a car is more trouble than convenience. The traffic is heavy and finding a parking place is so difficult that once, in desperation, we drove to the airport, left the car in the long-term parking lot there, and took a cab back into town.

If you want to drive outside Athens, there are plenty of rental agencies south of Syntagma Square. Some of the better agencies include: **Athens Cars,** 10 Filellinon (© 210/323-3783 or 210/324-8870); **Autorental,** 11 Leoforos Syngrou (© 210/923-2514); **Avis,** 46–48 Leoforos Amalias (© 210/322-4951 to 4957); **Budget Rent a Car,** 8 Leoforos Syngrou (© 210/921-4771 to 4773); 29 **Eurodollar Rent a Car,** Leoforos Syngrou (© 210/922-9672 or 210/923-0548); **Hellascars,** 148 Leoforos Syngrou (© 210/923-5353 to 5359); **Hertz,** 12 Leoforos Syngrou (© 210/922-0102 to 0104) and 71 Leoforos Vas. Sofias (© 210/724-7071 or 210/722-7391); **Interrent-Europcar/Batek SA,** 4 Leoforos Syngrou 4 (© 210/921-5789 or 210/921-5789); and **Thrifty Hellas Rent a Car,** 24 Leoforos Syngrou (© 210/922-1211 to 1213). Prices for rentals range from about 50€ to 100€ per day. *Warning:* Be sure to take full insurance and ask if the price you are quoted includes everything—taxes, drop-off fee, gasoline charges, etc.

## ON FOOT

Since most of what you want to see and do in Athens is in the city center, it's easy to do most of your sightseeing on foot. Fortunately, Athens has created pedestrian zones in sections of the **Commercial Triangle** (the area bounded by Omonia, Syntagma, and Monastiraki squares), the **Plaka,** and **Kolonaki,** making strolling, window-shopping, and sightseeing infinitely more pleasant. Dionissiou Areopayitou, at the southern foot of the Acropolis, is also pedestrianized, with links to pedestrian walks past the ancient agora and Kerameikos. Still, don't relax completely even on pedestrian streets: The multitude of kamikaze motorcyclists in Athens seldom respects the rules, and you should remember that here, as in many large cities, a red traffic light or stop sign is no guarantee that cars will stop for pedestrians.

Wheelchair users will find Athens a major challenge, although curbs on some streets are being redesigned. The government announced plans in 1998 to make the Acropolis more easily accessible for those in wheelchairs before the 2004 Olympics.

### FAST FACTS: Athens

*American Express* The office at 2 Ermou, near the southwest corner of Syntagma Square (© **210/324-4975**), is open Monday through Friday from 8:30am to 4pm and Saturday from 8:30am to 1:30pm; it often closes earlier in winter. For lost or stolen credit cards and checks, you can call collect during off-hours to the American Express office in London (© **0044/273/675-975**).

*ATMs* Automatic teller machines are increasingly common at banks throughout Athens, and the **National Bank of Greece** operates a 24-hour ATM in Syntagma Square.

*Banks* Banks are generally open Monday through Thursday from 8am to 2pm and Friday from 8am to 1:30pm. In summer, the **National Bank of Greece**, in Syntagma Square (② **210/334-0015**) usually has an exchange office open Monday through Thursday from 3:30 to 6:30pm, Friday from 3 to 6:30pm, Saturday from 9am to 3pm, and Sunday from 9am to 1pm. Other centrally located banks include **Citibank**, in Syntagma Square (② **210/322-7471**); **Bank of America**, 39 Panepistimiou (② **210/324-4975**); and **Barclays Bank**, 15 Voukourestiou (② **210/364-4311**). All banks are closed on the long list of Greek holidays (See "When to Go," in chapter 2). Most banks exchange currency at the rate set daily by the government. This rate is usually more favorable than that offered at unofficial exchange bureaus. Still, it's worth doing a little comparison shopping. Some hotels offer better-than-official rates, usually only for cash, as do some stores, usually only when you are making an expensive purchase.

*Business Hours* Even Greeks get confused by their complicated and changeable business hours. In winter, Athens's shops are generally open Monday and Wednesday from 9am to 5pm; Tuesday, Thursday, and Friday from 10am to 7pm; and Saturday from 8:30am to 3:30pm. In summer, shops are generally open Monday, Wednesday, and Saturday from 8am to 3pm; and Tuesday, Thursday, and Friday from 8am to 2pm and 5:30 to 10pm.

Most food stores are open Monday and Wednesday from 9am to 4:30pm, Tuesday from 9am to 6pm, Thursday from 9:30am to 6:30pm, Friday from 9:30am to 7pm, and Saturday from 8:30am to 4:30pm.

Many shops geared to tourists stay open late into the night—but often only if the shop owner thinks that business will be good. In other words, the shop that was open late yesterday may close early today.

*Dentists & Doctors* Embassies (see below) usually have a list of dentists and doctors; some English-speaking physicians advertise in the daily *Athens News.*

*Drugstores* See "Pharmacies," below.

*Embassies & Consulates* **Australia**, 37 Leoforos Dimitriou Soutsou (② 210/645-0404-5); **Canada**, 4 Ioannou Yenadiou (② 210/727-3400 or 210/725-4011); **Ireland**, 7 Vas. Konstantinou (② 210/723-2771); **New Zealand**, Xenias 24, Ambelokipi (② 210/771-0112); **South Africa**, 60 Kifissias, Maroussi (② 210/680-6645); **United Kingdom**, Ploutarchou 1 (② 210/723-6211); **United States**, 91 Leoforos Vas. Sofias (② 210/721-2951; emergency number 210/729-4301). Be sure to phone ahead before you go to any embassy; most keep limited hours and are usually closed on their own as well as Greek holidays.

*Emergencies* In an emergency, dial ② **100** for the **police** and ② **171** for the **tourist police**. Dial ② **199** to report a **fire** and ② **166** for an **ambulance** and the **hospital**. If you need an English-speaking doctor or dentist, call your embassy for advice or try **SOS Doctor** ② **210/331-0310** or 210/331-0311). There are two medical hot line numbers for foreigners: ② **210/721-2951** (day) and 210/729-4301 (night) for U.S. citizens and ② **210/723-6211** (day) and 210/723-7727 (night) for British subjects. The English-language daily *Athens News* (published on Fri.) lists some American- and British-trained doctors and hospitals offering emergency services. Most of the larger hotels have doctors whom they can call for you in an emergency, and embassies will sometimes recommend local doctors.

**KAT**, the emergency hospital in Kifissia (② 210/801-4411 to 4419), and **Asklepion Voulas**, the emergency hospital in Voula (② 210/895-3416 to 3418), both have emergency rooms open 24 hours a day. **Evangelismos**, a respected centrally located hospital below the Kolonaki district on 9 Vas. Sophias (② 210/722-0101), usually has English-speaking staff on duty. If you need medical attention fast, don't waste time trying to call these hospitals: Just go. Their doors are open and they will see to you as soon as possible once you arrive.

In addition, one of the major hospitals takes turns each day being on emergency duty. A recorded message in Greek at ② 210/106 tells which hospital is open for emergency services and gives the telephone number.

*Eyeglasses* If anything happens to your glasses, **Artemiadis**, which has two branches, (4 Hermou, Syntagma ② 210/323-8555; and 3 Stadiou [in the Kalliga Arcade], Syntagma, ② 210/324-7043; info@ARTEMIADIS.GR), offers next day (sometimes even same day) replacement service as does **Optical**, 2 Patriarchou Ioakim, Kolonaki (② 210/724-3564). Both also sell sunglasses and have English-speaking staff.

*Hospitals* Except for emergencies, hospital admittance is gained through a physician. See "Dentists & Doctors," above.

*Information* See "Visitor Information," earlier in this chapter.

*Internet Access* Internet cafes, where you can check and send e-mail, are proliferating almost as fast as cellular telephones in Athens. For a current list of Athenian cybercafes, check out **www.netcafeguide.com**.

As a general rule, most cybercafes charge about 5€ an hour. The very efficient **Sofokleous.com Internet C@fe**, 5 Stadiou, a block off Syntagma Square (②) and fax 210/324-8105; sofos1@ath.forthnet.gr or sofos1@telehouse.gr), is open daily from 10am to 10pm. The **Astor Internet Cafés**, 17 Patission, a block off Omonia Square (② 210/523-8546), is open Monday through Saturday from 10am to 10pm and Sunday from 10am to 4pm. Across from the National Archaeological Museum is the **Central Music Coffee Shop**, 28 Octobriou, also called Patission (② 210/883-3418), open daily from 9am to 11pm. In Plaka, **Plaka Internet World** (② 210/331-6056; plakaworld@internet.gr), 29 Pandrossou, offers air-conditioned chat rooms and an Acropolis view!

*Laundry & Dry Cleaning* The **self-service launderette** at 10 Angelou Yeronda, in Filomouson Square, off Kidathineon, Plaka, is open daily from 8:30am to 7pm; it charges 7€ per load, including wash, dry, and soap. The **National Dry Cleaners and Laundry Service**, 17 Apollonos (② 210/323-2226), next to the Hermes Hotel, is open Monday and Wednesday from 7am to 4pm and Tuesday, Thursday, and Friday from 7am to 8pm; laundry costs 5€ per kilo (2.2 lb.). Hotel chambermaids will often do laundry as well. Dry cleaning in Athens is reasonable, about 3€ for a pair of slacks, and next-day service is usually possible.

*Lost & Found* If you lose something on the street or on public transport, it is probably gone for good, just as it would be in any large American city. If you wish, contact the **police lost and found**, 173 Leoforos Alexandras (© **210/642-1616**), open Monday through Saturday from 9am to 3pm. Lost passports and other documents may be returned by the police to the appropriate embassy, so check there as well. It's an excellent idea to travel with a photocopy of all important documents, including your passport, prescriptions, tickets, and important phone numbers and addresses.

*Luggage Storage/Lockers* If you're coming back to stay, many hotels will store excess luggage while you travel. Just southwest of Syntagma Square, **Pacific Ltd.**, 26 Nikis (© **210/324-1007** or 210/322-3213), has a per-piece charge of 1€ per day, 3€ per week, 10€ per month; open Monday through Saturday from 8am to 8pm. **Bellair Travel and Tourism Inc.**, 15 Nikis (© **210/323-9261** or 210/321-6136), is open Monday through Friday from 9am to 5pm and has similar charges. Although both Pacific and Bellair keep regular hours, you may want to phone ahead to make sure they are open before you lug your luggage over. There are storage facilities at the Metro station in Piraeus, at both train stations, and across from the entrance at the East Air Terminal.

*Newspapers & Magazines* The *Athens News* is published every Friday in English, with a weekend section listing events of interest; it's available at kiosks everywhere. Most central Athens newsstands also carry the *International Herald Tribune*, which has an English-language insert of highlights from the Greek daily *Kathimerini*, and *USA Today*. Local weeklies include the *Hellenic Times*, with its entertainment listings, and *Athinorama* (in Greek), which has comprehensive listings of events. *Athens Best Of* (monthly) and *Now in Athens*, published every other month, have information on restaurants, shopping, museums and galleries, and are usually available free in major hotels and sometimes from the Greek National Tourism Organization.

*Pharmacies* *Pharmakia*, identified by green crosses, are scattered throughout Athens. Hours are usually Monday through Friday from 8am to 2pm. In the evening and on weekends most are closed, but usually post a notice listing the names and addresses of pharmacies that are open or will open in an emergency. Newspapers such as the *Athens News* list the pharmacies open outside regular hours.

*Police* In an **emergency,** dial © **100.** For help dealing with a troublesome taxi driver, hotel, restaurant, or shop owner, stand your ground and call the **tourist police** at © **171.**

*Post Offices* The main post offices in central Athens are at 100 Eolou, just south of Omonia Square, and in Syntagma Square at the corner of Mitropoleos. These are open Monday through Friday from 7:30am to 8pm, Saturday from 7:30am to 2pm, and Sunday from 9am to 1pm.

All the post offices can accept parcels, but the **parcel post office** is at 4 Stadiou inside the arcade (© **210/322-8940**), open Monday through Friday from 7:30am to 8pm. It usually sells twine and cardboard shipping boxes in four sizes. Parcels must be open for inspection before you seal them at the post office.

You can receive correspondence in Athens in care of **American Express,** 2 Ermou, 10225 Athens, Greece (© **210/324-4975**), near the southwest corner of Syntagma Square, open Monday through Friday from 8:30am to 4pm and Saturday from 8:30am to 1:30pm. If you have an American Express card or traveler's checks, the service is free; otherwise, each article costs 2€.

*Radio & Television* Generally, English-language radio—BBC and Voice of America—is available only via shortwave radio. CNN and various European channels such as STAR are available on cable TV. Most foreign-language films shown on Greek TV are not dubbed, but have the original soundtracks with Greek subtitles. All current-release foreign-language films shown in Greek cinemas have the original soundtracks with Greek subtitles.

*Restrooms* There are public restrooms in the underground station beneath Omonia and Syntagma Squares and beneath Kolonaki Square, but you'll probably prefer a hotel or restaurant restroom. (Toilet paper is often not available, so carry some tissue with you. Do not flush paper down the commode; use the receptacle provided.)

*Safety* **Pickpocketing** is common, especially in the Plaka and the Omonia Square area, on the Metro and buses, and even on the Acropolis. Alas, it is a good idea to be wary of gypsy children. Visitors, especially during the Olympics, are advised to exercise all the usual precautions. As always, leave your passport and valuables in a security box at the hotel. Carry a photocopy of your passport, not the original.

*Taxes* A VAT (value-added tax) of between 4% and 18% is added onto everything you buy. Some shops will attempt to cheat you by quoting you one price and then, when you hand over your credit card, adding on a hefty VAT charge. Be wary. In theory, if you are not a member of a Common Market/EU country, you can get a refund on major purchases at Hellenikon airport when you leave Greece. In practice, you would virtually have to arrive at the airport a day before your flight to get to the head of the line, do the paperwork, get a refund, and catch your flight.

*Telephone/Telegrams/Faxes* Many of the city's public phones now accept only phone cards, available at newsstands and **Telecommunications Organization of Greece (OTE)** offices in several denominations, currently starting at 3€. Some kiosks still have metered phones; you pay what the meter records. At present, local phone calls cost .20€. North Americans can phone home directly by contacting **AT&T** (© **00/800-1311**), **MCI** (© **00/800-1211**), or **Sprint** (© **00/800-1411**); calls can be collect or billed to your phone charge card. You can send a telegram or fax from OTE offices. The OTE office at 15 Stadiou, near Syntagma, is open 24 hours a day. The Omonia Square OTE, at 50 Athinas, and the Victoria Square OTE, at 85 Patission, are open Monday through Friday from 7am to 9pm, Saturday from 9am to 3pm, and Sunday from 9am to 2pm. Outside Athens, most OTEs are closed on weekends.

*Tipping* Athenian restaurants include a service charge in the bill, but many visitors add a 10% tip. Most Greeks do not give a percentage tip to taxi drivers, but often round out the fare to 3€ for example, on a fare of 2.90€.

**Tips** **A Warning About ATMs**

It is not a good idea to rely on using ATMs exclusively in Athens, since the machines here are often out of service when you need them most: on holidays or during bank strikes.

If your PIN includes letters, be sure that you know their numerical equivalent, as Greek ATMs do not have letters.

## 3 Where to Stay

Virtually all Greek hotels are clean and comfortable; few are charming, elegant, or memorable. Most, in fact, are monotonous, with one bedroom a bit larger, another a bit smaller—but very few with any individual touch to warm the traveler's heart. We do our best to give you an idea of the individual virtues of the hotels we recommend, but do urge you to keep in mind that, in the absence of truly distinguishing characteristics, often location is the most important factor in choosing your hotel. When a hotel is truly distinctive, we are sure to draw it to your attention.

A few suggestions: In summer, we strongly advise that you reserve ahead of time. If shower and tub facilities are important to you, be sure to have a look at the bathroom: Many Greek tubs are tiny, and the showers are hand held. Don't assume that just because a hotel says it has air-conditioning, the air-conditioning is working, and be sure to check to see if there's adequately functioning central heating in the winter. And keep in mind that decent reading lamps are virtually unknown—consider using one of the little traveler's night-lights that clip onto your book.

Although many guide books do, we do not recommend staying in any of the luxury hotels on Syngrou Avenue. Although the Metropolitan, the Leda Marriot, and the Athenaem-Intercontinental have all the creature comforts, Syngrou Avenue is ugly, noisy, and away from everything that you want to see in Athens. In short, the Syngrou hotels are just fine for the business people here for conferences who never leave their hotels—but not for visitors to Athens.

The **Syntagma Square** area and the **Plaka/Monastiraki** district are the most convenient locations for sightseeing. If you have only a few days in Athens, you should seriously consider staying here. There are also good choices in **Makriyanni** and the **Embassy District**, as well as some good budget choices near the National Archaeological Museum. We've enjoyed staying in **Kolonaki**, the upscale Athenian neighborhood on the slopes of Mount Likavitos, although there were times we didn't look forward to the uphill walk back to the hotel. We have friends who always stay in the **Koukaki** district, near Filopappos Hill and off the non-Acropolis side of Dionissiou Areopayitou. They love the quiet residential streets and the bonus of being out of the heart of tourist Athens in a real Greek neighborhood. If you do stay there, you'll be doing extra walking to get to almost everything you want to do. Sadly, the neighborhoods are not as quiet as they were before Dionysiou Areopayitou was pedestrianized in January 2000, forcing motorists to find new routes on the south side of the Acropolis.

## THE PLAKA
### EXPENSIVE

**Electra Palace** ★★   The Electra, just a few blocks southwest of Syntagma Square on a relatively quiet side street, is the most modern and stylish Plaka hotel. The rooms on the 5th, 6th, and 7th floors are smaller than those on lower floors, but the top-floor rooms are where you want to be, both for the view of the Acropolis and to escape traffic noise. (Ask for a top-floor unit when you make your reservation. Your request will be honored "subject to availability.") Guest rooms here are hardly drop-dead elegant, but they are pleasant, decorated in soft pastels. Don't miss the rooftop pool with a terrific view of the Acropolis. If you're too tired to go out for dinner, the hotel restaurant is quite decent

18 Nikodimou, Plaka, 105 57 Athens. ⓒ 210/324-1401 or 210/324-1407. Fax 210/324-1975. 106 units. 200€–250€ double. Rates include breakfast buffet. AE, DC, MC, V. The Electra is about 2 blocks down on the left as you walk along Ermou with Syntagma Sq. behind you. **Amenities:** Restaurant; bar; rooftop pool. *In room:* A/C, TV, minibar, hair dryer.

## MODERATE

**Acropolis House Hotel** ✷    This small hotel in a handsomely restored 150-year-old villa retains many of its original classical architectural details. It offers a central location—just off Kidathineon in the heart of the Plaka, a 5-minute walk from Syntagma Square—and the charm of being on a quiet pedestrian side street. Rooms 401 and 402 have good views and can be requested (but not guaranteed) when making a reservation. The newer wing, only 60 years old, isn't architecturally special; each unit's spartan bathroom is across the hall. There's a book-swap spot and a washing machine, free after a 4-day stay.

If the Acropolis House is full, try the **Adonis Hotel**, on the same street at Kodrou 3 (ⓒ **210/324-9737;** fax 210/323-1602); it's architecturally undistinguished, and somewhat haphazard, but does have an appealing location and a rooftop garden cafe with a view of the Acropolis. A few steps away, the **Kouros Hotel**, Kodrou 11 (ⓒ **210/322-7431**), is very basic and can be noisy.

6–8 Kodrou, 105 58 Athens. ⓒ **210/322-2344.** Fax 210/324-4143. 25 units, 15 with bathroom. 60€ double without bathroom; 75€ double with bathroom. 10€ surcharge for A/C. Rates include continental breakfast. V. Walk 2 blocks out of Syntagma Sq. on Mitropoleos and turn left on Voulis, which becomes pedestrianized Kodrou. **Amenities:** Washing machine (for a small fee; free after a 4-day stay). *In room:* A/C.

**Byron Hotel**    Every year we come close to eliminating the Byron, where the indifferent-at-best service is a real draw-back. Still, there's one real plus here: the relatively quiet central Plaka location just off recently pedestrianized Dionysiou Areopayitou Street. The price is fair (and often negotiable). That said, if you don't remember the dingy Byron before its remodeling 3 years ago, the new decor, which lacks charm, might not impress you. I've also had reports that the air-conditioning is temperamental at best. Alas, the same can be said for the service, which is usually haphazard and often curt.

19 Vyronos, 105 58 Athens. ⓒ **210/325-3554.** Fax 210/323-0327. 20 units. 80€ double. Rates include breakfast. V. From Syntagma Sq., walk south on Amalias Ave. past Hadrian's Arch, stay right, and turn right on Dionysiou Areopayitou; Vyronos ("Byron" in Greek) is the 2nd street on the right, and hotel (with a portrait of Lord Byron by the door) is on the right. **Amenities:** Bar. *In room:* A/C.

**Hotel Plaka** ✷✷    This hotel is popular with Greeks, who prefer its modern conveniences to the old-fashioned charms of most other hotels in the Plaka area.

---

*Tips* **Beware of Price Gouging During the Olympics**

Hotel prices were accurate at press time, but price increases of 20% and more are rumored as hoteliers throughout Greece gear up for the August 2004 Olympics in and around Athens. Horrific price hikes of between 50% and an unbelievable 300% are rumored for the period leading up to, during, and after the games.

# Athens Accommodations

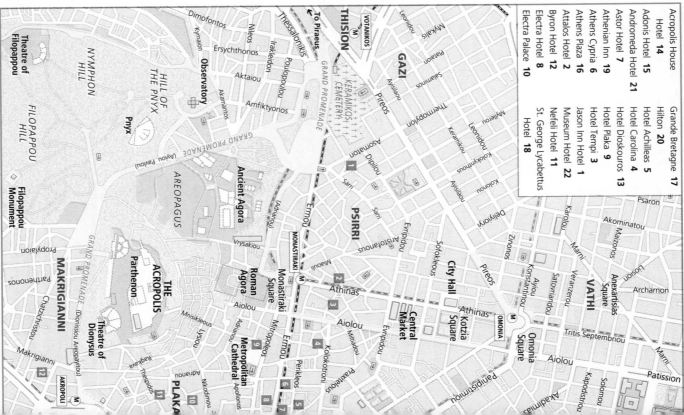

Acropolis House Hotel **14**
Adonis Hotel **15**
Andromeda Hotel **21**
Astor Hotel **7**
Athenian Inn **19**
Athens Cypria **6**
Athens Plaza **16**
Attalos Hotel **2**
Byron Hotel **12**
Electra Hotel **8**
Electra Palace **10**

Grande Bretagne **17**
Hilton **20**
Hotel Achilleas **5**
Hotel Carolina **4**
Hotel Dioskouros **13**
Hotel Plaka **9**
Hotel Tempi **3**
Jason Inn Hotel **1**
Museum Hotel **22**
Nefeli Hotel **11**
St. George Lycabettus Hotel **18**

National Archaeological Museum

**EXARCHEIA**

22

Tositsa

Stournari

Thermokastroolou

Bakari

Zoodohou Pigis

Charilaou Trikoupi

Mavromichali

Methonis

Kallidromiou

Eresou

Dervenion

Arachevis

Asklipiou

Ippokratous

Massalias

Solonos

Akadimias

Panipistimiou

National Library

University of Athens

Georgiou A'

16 17

**SYNTAGMA**

Syntagma Square

M SYNTAGMA

Stadiou

Amalias

Filellinon

Nikis

Mitropoleos Othonos

15

4

13

Athinon

**Temple of Olympian Zeus**

Ardittou

Panatheniako Stadium

Eratesthenou

**NEAPOLIS**

Asklipiou

Laskareos

Ippokratous

Vatatzi

Voulgaroktonou

Tsimiski

Tsimiski

Tsimiski

Sarandapichou

Isavron

Smolenski

Charilaou Trikoupi

N. Ourani

Bathomiis

Sina

Anagnostopoulou

Skoufa

Solonos

Dimokritou

Lykavitou

Voukourestiou

Amerikis

Kanari

Skoufa

Solonos

Omirou

Fokylidou

Chersonos

Rogakou

Sarandapichou

Loukianou

**LIKAVITOS HILL**

**Theatre of Likavitos**

Rack Railway

Doras D'Istria

Aristodimou

Kleomenous

Deinokratous

Aristippou

19

18

Souidias

Marsali

Alopekis

Ploutarchou

Patriarchi Iokeim

Alopekis

Karneadou

Spefsippou

Irodotou

**KOLONAKI**

Kolonaki Square

**Ioannou Gennadiou**

**Megalistou Genous Scholis Square**

M EVANGELISMOS

EVANGELISMOS (Vas. Sofias)

Rizari

Rizari

Spyrou Merkouri

Vas. Konstandinou

Leoforos El. Venizelou (Vas. Sofias)

Rigillis

Vasil. Georgiou II

**Presidential Palace**

Irodou Attikou

Leoforos El. Venizelou (Vas. Sofias)

**Parliament**

**NATIONAL GARDEN**

**Zappeion**

M

Syntagma

Amalias

**ZAPPEION**

L ZAPPEION

GRAND PROMENADE (Vas. Olgas)

21

20

Information

Metro:
M Line 1
M Line 2
M Line 3
L Light Rail

1/4 mi

0.25 km

N

It has a terrific location just off Syntagma Square. Most guest rooms have balconies; those on the fifth and sixth floors in the rear (where it's usually quieter) have views of the Plaka and the Acropolis, also visible from the roof-garden snack bar. Friends who stayed here recently were not charmed by the service, but enjoyed the location, the roof-top bar, and the blue and white color scheme.

*Mitropoleos and 7 Kapnikareas, 105 56 Athens.* ② **210/322-2096.** Fax 210/322-2412. plaka@tourhotel.gr. 67 units (38 with shower only). 100€–125€ double. Rates include breakfast. AE, MC, V. Follow Mitropoleos out of Syntagma Sq, past cathedral and turn left onto Kapnikareas. **Amenities:** Bar; roof garden. *In room:* A/C, TV, minibar, hair dryer.

**Nefeli Hotel** ✦ The charming little Nefeli (Cloud) was completely redecorated in 1999; the rooms—most with air-conditioning—are small (as are the bathrooms) and pleasantly spare, with real character, unlike so many Athenian hotels. We also found the breakfast room congenial and the staff, particularly manager Tasos Kanellopoulos, courteous and helpful. We've had some recent reports from guests of considerable nighttime street noise from the pedestrianized Angelikes Hatzimihali beside this once-quiet hotel. Evidently, the authorities are turning a blind eye to motorcyclists and revelers. We look forward to hearing from off-season visitors and hope to learn that the Nefeli is still quiet then.

*16 Iperidou, 10558 Athens.* ② **210/322-8044.** Fax 210/322-5800. 18 units (13 with shower only). 80€ double. Rates include continental breakfast. AE, V. **Amenities:** Breakfast room. *In room:* A/C, TV.

## INEXPENSIVE

**Hotel Dioskouros (also known as the Dioskouros Guest House)** This is as good a deal as you'll get in the Plaka. Student friends who have stayed here found the staff very helpful, enjoyed the small garden, and didn't mind the cramped rooms, the Plaka noise, or the lack of air-conditioning and ceiling fans. Ah, to be young again!

*6 Pittakou, Plaka, 10558 Athens.* ② **210/324-8165.** Fax 210/321-0907. 12 units, none with bathroom. 25€–30€. No credit cards.

## MONASTIRAKI
### MODERATE

**Attalos Hotel** ✦ *Value* The six-story Attalos is well-situated for those wanting to take in the frenzied daytime street life of the nearby Central Market and the exuberant nighttime scene at the cafes and restaurants of the Psirri district. The rooms here are plain, but pleasant; 40 have balconies and 12 have Acropolis views; unusually in Greece (especially in moderately priced hotels), no-smoking rooms are available, and all rooms have lock boxes. The roof garden offers fine views of the city and the Acropolis. The Attalos (whose staff is usually very helpful) often gives a 10% discount to Frommer's readers. **One caution:** drug dealing and prostitution is not unknown on Athinas Street.

*29 Athinas, 105 54 Athens.* ② **210/321-2801.** Fax 210/324-3124. atthot@hol.gr. 80 units. 80€–100€ double. Rates include buffet breakfast. AE, MC, V. From Monastiraki Sq, walk about 1½ blocks north on Athinas. **Amenities:** Luggage storage. *In room:* A/C, TV, hair dryer (most rooms).

**Jason Inn Hotel** ✦ *Value* This newly renovated hotel (admittedly on a dull street, but just a few blocks from the Agora and the Plaka and the newly fashionable Psirri district) offers attractive, comfortable rooms with double-paned windows for extra quiet. If you don't mind walking a few extra blocks to Syntagma, this is currently one of the best values in Athens, with an eager-to-help staff.

If the Jason Inn is full, the staff may be able to find you a room in one of their other hotels: the similarly priced **Adrian Hotel**, on busy Hadrian in the Plaka, or the slightly less expensive **King Jason** or **Jason Hotels**, both a few blocks from Omonia Square.

12 Ayion Assomaton, 10553 Athens. © **210/325-1106.** Fax 210/523-4786. douros@otenet.gr. 57 units. 90€–120€ double. Rates include American buffet breakfast. AE, MC, V. From Monastiraki Sq., head west on Ermou, turn right at Thisio Metro station, pass small below-ground church and bear left. **Amenities:** Breakfast room; bar. *In room:* A/C, TV, minibar.

## INEXPENSIVE

**Hotel Tempi** ✹    If you believe that location is all for a hotel, consider the three-story Tempi, which faces the flower market by the church of Ayia Irini on a basically pedestrian-only street. The Tempi has very simply furnished rooms (bed, table, chair), the mattresses are overdue for replacement, and plumbing here can be a problem—hot water is intermittent, and the toilets have been known to smell. But 10 rooms have balconies from which (if you lean) you can see the Acropolis. This hotel is very popular with students and other spartan travelers able to ignore the Tempi's drawbacks and focus on its location, price, and handy communal kitchen facilities.

29 Eolou, 10551 Athens. © **210/321-3175.** Fax 210/325-4179. 24 units, 8 with bathroom. 55€ double without bathroom, 60€ double with bathroom. AE, MC, V. From Syntagma Sq., take Ermou to Eolou.

# SYNTAGMA
## VERY EXPENSIVE

**Athens Plaza** ✹✹    The Athens Plaza, managed by the Grecotel group, reopened its glitzy doors in March 1998 after a complete remodeling, and we were pretty excited to stay here shortly thereafter. There are acres of marble in the lobby, and almost as much in some bathrooms, which have their own phones and hair dryers. Many of the bedrooms are larger than most living rooms, and many have balconies overlooking Syntagma Square. That said, the service, although perfectly professional, lacks any personal touch.

Syntagma Sq., 10564 Athens. © **210/323-5301.** Fax 210/323-5856. 207 units. 325€–400€ double. AE, DC, MC, V. **Amenities:** 2 restaurants; 2 bars; health club and spa with Jacuzzi; concierge; tour desk; car-rental desk; courtesy car or airport pickup arranged; business center; 24-hr. room service; same-day laundry/dry cleaning services; nonsmoking rooms; partially handicapped accessible. *In room:* A/C, TV, dataport. minibar, hair dryer, iron, safe.

**Grande Bretagne** ✹✹✹    The legendary Grande Bretagne, one of Athens' most distinguished 19th century buildings, is back after a year and a half $70 million renovation. The exquisite beaux-arts lobby has been preserved, the chic GB Corner Restaurant is back, a swimming pool has been added, and the rooms are once again very grand, indeed. If you decide to stay at the hotel where everyone from Winston Churchill to Sting has been a guest, be sure to insist on a room with a balcony overlooking Syntagma Square, the Parliament building, and Acropolis. The Grande Bretagne prides itself on its service, and this is one hotel where you are unlikely to be disappointed.

Syntagma Sq., 105 64 Athens. © **210/333-000.** Fax 210/333-0160. Info@GrandeBretagne-ath.gr. 290 units, 38 suites. 350€–800€ double. AE, DC, MC, V. **Amenities:** 2 restaurants; 2 bars; 2 pools (indoors and outdoors); health club and spa with Jacuzzi; concierge; tour desk; car-rental desk; courtesy car or airport pickup arranged; business center; 24-hr. room service; same-day laundry/dry cleaning services; nonsmoking rooms; partially handicapped accessible. *In room:* A/C, TV, dataport. minibar, hair dryer, iron, safe.

## EXPENSIVE

**Electra Hotel** ★ *Value* If Ermou remains pedestrian—as promised through the 2004 Olympics—the Electra has a location that is both central (steps from Syntagma Square) and quiet. Most of the guest rooms have comfortable armchairs, large windows, and modern bathrooms with hair dryers. Be sure to have a look at your room before you accept it: Although most are large, some are quite tiny. The front desk is sometimes understaffed, but the service is generally acceptable, although it can be brusque when groups are checking in and out.

5 Ermou, 10563 Athens. ② **210/322-3223.** Fax 210/322-0310. electrahotels@ath.forthnet.gr. 110 units. 150€–200€ double. Rates include buffet breakfast. AE, DC, MC, V. The Electra is about 2 blocks down on the left as you walk along Ermou with Syntagma Sq. behind you. **Amenities:** Restaurant; bar. *In room:* A/C, TV, minibar, hair dryer.

## MODERATE

**Astor Hotel** We've never been very impressed with this hotel, which does a heavy business in tour groups, and has service that is impersonal at best. That said, a well-traveled journalist tells me that he always stays here when in Athens because of the central location (Karayioryi Servias runs into Syntagma Square), bright rooms (some with Acropolis views), and efficient (if not pleasant) front desk staff. The journalist also says that he sometimes succeeds in bargaining down the room price.

16 Karayioryi Servias 16, 10562 Athens. ② **210/335-1000.** Fax 210/325-5115. www.astorhotel.gr. 131 units. 100€–150€ double. Rates include buffet breakfast. AE, V. **Amenities:** Restaurant; bar. *In room:* A/C, TV.

**Athens Cypria** ★★ After extensive renovations, the former Diomia Hotel has been reborn as the spanking new Athens Cypria. Gone are the Diomia's gloomy lobby and bedrooms, but the convenient central location on a street with (usually) no traffic and the splendid Acropolis views from units 603 to 607 remain. The halls and rooms throughout have been painted bright white, the units have cheerful floral bedspreads and curtains, and the bathrooms (with hair dryers) are freshly tiled with all new fixtures. The breakfast buffet offers hot and cold dishes from 7 to 10am. In short, the Athens Cypria promises to be an excellent addition to the city's moderately priced hotels.

5 Diomias, 10562 Athens. ② **210/323-8034.** Fax 210/324-8792. 71 units. 125€–135€. Reductions possible off season. Rates include buffet breakfast. AE, MC, V. Take Karayioryi Servias out of Syntagma Sq; Diomias is on the left, after Lekka. **Amenities:** Breakfast room; bar; snack bar; luggage storage. *In room:* A/C, TV, minibar, hair dryer.

**Hotel Achilleas** The Achilleas (Achilles), on a relatively quiet side street, steps from Syntagma Square, had a total renovation in 2001. The good-sized bedrooms are now bright and cheerful and the beds have new mattresses; some rear rooms have small balconies; several on the fifth floor can be used as interconnecting family suites. The very central location of the Hotel Achilleas and its fair prices make it a good choice. If you want a room with a safe, or to borrow a hair dryer, ask at the main desk upon check-in.

21 Lekka, 10562 Athens. ② **210/323-3197.** Fax 210/322-2412. www.achilleashotel.gr. 34 units. 150€ double. Rates include breakfast. AE, DC, MC, V. Take Karayioryi Servias out of Syntagma Sq. for 2 blocks and turn right onto Lekka. **Amenities:** Breakfast room; snack bar. *In room:* A/C, TV, minibar.

## INEXPENSIVE

**Hotel Carolina** ★★ The friendly family owned and operated Carolina, on the outskirts of Plaka, a brisk 5 minute walk from Syntagma, has always been popular with students. In the last few years, the Carolina has undertaken extensive remodeling and now attracts a wide range of frugal travelers. Bedrooms have double glazed windows and air-conditioning; many, like rooms 407 and 308, have large balconies. Several rooms, such as 308, have 4 or 5 beds and are popular with families and students.

55 Kolokotroni, 105 60 Athens. © **210/324-3551.** Fax 210/324-3350. hotelcarolina@galaxynet.gr. 31 units. 75€–100€ double; breakfast 5€. MC, V. Take Stadiou out of Syntagma Sq. to Kolokotroni St (on left). **Amenities:** Breakfast room; bar. *In room:* A/C, TV.

## KOLONAKI
### VERY EXPENSIVE

**St. George Lycabettus Hotel ★★**    Kolonaki is a fashionable residential and shopping neighborhood northeast of Syntagma at the foot of Mount Likavitos. As yet, the Saint George Lycabettus does not get many tour groups, which contributes to the tranquil tone here. The rooftop pool is a real plus, as are the two excellent restaurants, and the hotel is just steps from the chic Kolonaki restaurants and shops—but keep in mind that when you head back to the hotel, those steps are steeply uphill. Most of the distinctively appointed rooms (different floors have different decorative motifs, from baroque to Italian modern) look toward Mount Likavitos or a small park; a few have interior views. Some have views of both Likavitos and the Acropolis; in short, a distinctive and classy hotel (much-used by wealthy Greeks for private events), although the surrounding street traffic keeps this from being an absolute oasis of calm.

2 Kleomenous, 106 75 Athens. © **210/729-0711.** Fax 210/721-0439. Info@sglycabettus.gr. www. sglycabettus.gr. 167 units. 225€–300€ double. Breakfast 20€. AE, DC, MC, V. From Kolonaki Sq., take Patriarchou Ioachim to Loukianou; follow Loukianou uphill to Kleomenous; turn left on Kleomenous; the hotel overlooks Dexamini Park. **Amenities:** 2 restaurants; 2 bars; pool; concierge; business center; 24-hr. room service; same-day laundry/dry cleaning services; nonsmoking rooms. *In room:* A/C, TV, minibar, hair dryer.

## MODERATE

**Athenian Inn ★**    The Athenian Inn's quiet location 3 blocks from Kolonaki Square is a blessing, as Hellenophile Lawrence Durrell indicated in the guest book: "At last the ideal Athens hotel, good and modest in scale but perfect in service and goodwill." Some of the balconies look out on Mount Likavitos. Breakfast is served in a small lounge with a fireplace, piano, and TV. Keep in mind that if you stay here, you will be doing a good deal of walking (some of it fairly steeply uphill) to get to and from the central attractions. Neighborhood doves coo vigorously at night, a sound you will probably find either soothing, or infuriating. Between stays, we tend to forget how small the rooms are, which suggests that the staff is doing a good job of making guests feel comfortable and at home.

22 Haritos, Kolonaki, 10675 Athens. © **210/723-8097.** Fax 210/724-2268. 28 units. 125€ double. Rates include breakfast. AE, DC, V. From Syntagma Sq., go east on Vas. Sofias Ave. to Loukianou; turn left on Loukianou and take it 6 blocks uphill to Haritos. **Amenities:** Breakfast room. *In room:* A/C.

## EMBASSY DISTRICT
### VERY EXPENSIVE

**Andromeda Hotel ★★★**    The city's only boutique hotel is easily the most charming in Athens, with a staff that makes you feel like this is your home away from home. Rooms are large and elegantly decorated, with furniture and paintings you'd be happy to live with. This very quiet hotel overlooks the garden of the American ambassador's home, and serves marvelous breakfasts and snacks (at present there is no on-site restaurant). The only drawbacks: It's a serious hike (20–30 min.) or 10-minute taxi ride to Syntagma, and there are few restaurants in this residential neighborhood, although the superb Vlassis is just around the corner. If you're planning a long stay in Athens, check out the Andromeda's new (and very lovely) service apartments just across the street.

22 Timoleontos Vassou (off Plateia Mavili), 11521 Athens. ⓒ 210/643-7302. Fax 210/646-6361. www.andromedahotels.gr. 42 units. 435€–580€ double. Breakfast included. Special rates sometimes available. AE, DC, MC, V. **Amenities:** Restaurant; breakfast room; bar. *In room:* A/C, TV, minibar, hair dryer, wall safe; all rooms fully wired for Internet.

**Hilton** ★★★     When the Hilton opened in 1963, it was the tallest building on the horizon—and the most modern hotel in town. In 2001, it closed for a long-overdue renovation and, 3 years and 96 million euros later, it reopened. Everything that was tired in furnishings is now spanking new and fresh—and more than a dozen new conference rooms have been added. As before, small shops, a salon, and cafes and restaurants surround the glitzy lobby. The guest rooms (looking toward either the hills outside Athens or the Acropolis) have large marble bathrooms and are decorated in the generic (but comfortable) international Hilton style, with some Greek touches. The Plaza Executive floor of rooms and suites offers a separate business center and higher level of service. Facilities include a large outdoor pool—and a handy ATM in the lobby. The Hilton often runs promotions, so ask about special rates before booking.

46 Leoforos Vas. Sofias, 11528 Athens. ⓒ **800/445-8667** in the U.S., 210/728-1000. Fax 210/728-1111. www.hilton.com. 506 units. 325€–600€ double. AE, DC, MC, V. **Amenities:** 4 restaurants; 3 bars; outdoor freshwater pool; health club and spa with Jacuzzi; game room; concierge; tour desk; car-rental desk; airport pickup arranged; business center; secretarial services; shopping arcade; salon; 24-hr. room service; babysitting; same-day laundry/dry-cleaning services; nonsmoking rooms; partly handicapped accessible. *In room:* A/C, TV, dataport, minibar, hair dryer, safe.

## KOUKAKI & MAKRIYANNI (NEAR THE ACROPOLIS)

Keep in mind that with all the Makriyanni/Koukaki hotels, you'll be doing some extra walking to get to most places you want to visit.

### VERY EXPENSIVE

**Divani-Palace Acropolis** ★★     Just 3 blocks south of the Acropolis, in a quiet residential neighborhood (there's a handy SPAR supermarket a block away at Parthenos 4, as well as a shop at Parthenos 7 that sells American and English newspapers), the Divani Palace Acropolis does a brisk tour business, but is welcoming to independent travelers. The blandly decorated bedrooms are large and comfortable and some of the large bathrooms even have two wash basins. The cavernous marble-and-glass lobby contains copies of classical sculpture and a section of Athens's 5th century B.C. defense wall is preserved behind glass in the basement, by the gift shop. The same hotel group operates the **Divani Caravel Hotel,** near the National Art Gallery and the Hilton at Leoforos Vas. Alexandrou 2 (ⓒ **210/725-3725;** fax 210/725-3770).

19–25 Parthenonos, Makriyanni, 11742 Athens. ⓒ 210/922-2945. Fax 210/921-4993. divanis@acropolis.gr. 253 units. 200€–350€ double. AE, DC, MC, V. From Syntagma Sq. take Amalias Ave. to pedestrianized Dionysiou Areopagitou; turn left into Parthenos; the hotel is on your left after about 3 blocks. **Amenities:** Restaurant; 2 bars; pool; concierge; business center; 24-hr. room service. *In room:* A/C, TV, dataport, minibar, hair dryer, safe.

### MODERATE

**Acropolis View Hotel** ⊙     This nicely maintained hotel is on a pleasant residential side street off Rovertou Galli, not far from the Herodes Atticus theater. The usually quiet neighborhood, at the base of Filopappos Hill (itself a pleasant area to explore) is a 10- to 15-minute walk from the heart of the Plaka. The

**ACCOMMODATIONS** ■

Acropolis View Hotel **3**
Art Gallery Hotel **10**
Austria Hotel **9**
Byron Hotel **1**
Divani-Palace Acropolis **7**
Herodion Hotel **5**
Hotel Hera **11**
Hotel Philippos **8**
Marble House Pension **13**
Parthenon Hotel **2**
Tony's Hotel **12**

**DINING** ◆

Socrates's Prison **6**
Strofi Tavern **4**

---

guest rooms (most freshly painted each year) are small but pleasant, with good bathrooms; 16 units have balconies. Some, like room 405, overlook Filopappos Hill, while others, like room 407, face the Acropolis. There's a congenial breakfast room and a bar in the lobby.

Rovertou Galli and 10 Webster, 117 42 Athens. (C) **210/921-7303.** Fax 210/923-0705. 32 units. 125€ double. Rates include buffet breakfast. Substantial reductions Nov–Apr 1. AE, MC, V. From Syntagma Sq. take Amalias Ave. to Dion. Areopagitou; head west past Herodes Atticus theater to Rovertou Galli Webster (Gouemster on some maps) is the little street intersecting Rovertou Galli between Propilion and Garabaldi. **Amenities:** Breakfast room; bar. *In room:* A/C, TV, minibar.

**Art Gallery Hotel**   As you might expect, this small hotel—in a half-century-old house that has been home to several artists—has an artistic flair (and a nice old-fashioned cage elevator). Rooms are small and plain, but comfortable, many with polished hardwood floors and ceiling fans. There's a nice Victorian-style breakfast room on the fourth floor, with heavy marble-topped tables and old velvet-covered chairs.

5 Erechthiou, Koukaki, 117 42 Athens. (C) **210/923-8376.** Fax 210/923-3025. ecote@otenet.gr. 22 units. 50€–80€ double. Rates include generous breakfast. Hotel sometimes closed Nov–Mar; when open, prices reduced. AE, MC, V. *In room:* A/C, TV.

**Austria Hotel**   ★   This very well-maintained hotel at the base of wooded Philopappos Hill is operated by a Greek-Austrian family, who can point you to local sites (including a convenient neighborhood laundry!) The Austria's rooms and bathrooms are rather spartan (the linoleum floors aren't enchanting) but more than acceptable—and the very efficient staff is a real plus here. There's a great view over Athens and out to sea (I could see the island of Aegina) from the rooftop, where you can sun or sit under an awning.

7 Mousson, Filopappou, 117 42 Athens. ℡ 210/923-5151. Fax 210/924-7350. Austria@austriahotel.com. 36 units (11 with shower only). 120€ double. Rates include breakfast. AE, DC, MC, V. Follow Dionysiou Areopagitou around south side of Acropolis to where it meets Roverto Galli; take Garibaldi around base of Filopappou Hill until reaching Mousson. Amenities: Breakfast room; rooftop terrace. In room: A/C, TV.

Herodion Hotel  An archaeologist friend who always stays at this attractive hotel a block south of the Acropolis, near the Herodes Atticus theater, reports that there's considerably more traffic noise on Rovertou Galli since Dionyssiou Areopayitou was pedestrianized. Still, the rooms here are good-sized, many with balconies. The lobby leads to a lounge and patio garden where you can have drinks and snacks under the trees. The same owners run the nearby Hotel Philippos, Mitseon 3, Makriyanni (℡ 210/922-3611; fax 210/922-3615).

4 Roverrou Gall, Makriyanni, 11742 Athens. ℡ 210/923-6832 or 210/923-6836. Fax 210/921-6150. herodion@otenet.gr. 90 units. 150€ double. Rates include breakfast. AE, DC, MC, V. Amenities: Breakfast room; bar. In room: A/C, TV.

Hotel Hera  The Hera boasts a garden behind its breakfast room and great views of the Acropolis from the rooftop garden. That's a lot of greenery in Athens, and since the bland bedrooms have balconies with hanging plants and are perfectly comfortable, you may find that the location out of the heart of tourist Athens is just what you want. If you have a car, you'll appreciate the garage here.

9 Falirou, Makriyani, 11742 Athens. ℡ 210/923-6682. Fax 210/924-7334. hhera@hol.gr. 49 units. 120€. Rates include breakfast. AE, MC, V. Amenities: Breakfast room; bar. In room: A/C, TV.

Parthenon  This modern, recently redecorated hotel has an excellent location just steps from the Plaka and the Acropolis. The carpeted bedrooms have bright, cheerful bedspreads and decent-sized bathrooms. There's also a very welcome small garden. The Parthenon is one of a group of four hotels; if it's full, the management will try to get you a room at the Christina, a few blocks away, or at the Riva or Alexandros, near the Megaron (the Athens Concert Hall). One warning: On occasion we have found the desk staff at the Parthenon less than helpful and infuriatingly vague about room prices.

6 Makri, 11527 Athens. ℡ 210/923-4594. Fax 210/644-1084. 79 units. 100€–120€ double. MC, V. Amenities: Restaurant; bar. In room: A/C, TV.

## INEXPENSIVE

Travelers planning a long stay in Athens should consider Tony's Hotel, Zacharitsa 26, Koukaki (℡ 210/923-6370 or 210/923-5761), which is popular with students and frugal travelers. Located between Filopappou Hill and Leoforos Syngrou, Tony's Hotel (also known as Tony's Pension) has communal lounges and kitchens and a roof garden with a barbecue. In addition to the 10 rooms, there are also 11 studio apartments; prices range from 50€ to 70€.

Marble House Pension  Named for its marble facade, usually covered by bougainvillea, this small hotel, whose front rooms offer balconies overlooking quiet Zinni Street, is famous among budget travelers (including many teachers) for its friendly staff. Over the last several years, the pension has been remodeled and redecorated, gaining all new bathrooms and bedroom furniture (including small fridges); there are two easy-access ground floor bedrooms, two rooms with kitchenettes, nine rooms with A/C. If you're spending more than a few days in Athens and don't mind being out of the center (and a partly up-hill 25-min. walk to get there), this is a homey base.

35 A. Zinni, Koukaki, 11741 Athens. © **210/923-4058.** Fax 210/922-6461. 16 units; 12 with bathroom. 45€ double without bathroom, 55€ double with bathroom; 9€ supplement for A/C. Monthly rates available off-season. No credit cards. From Syntagma Sq. take Amalias Ave. to Syngrou Ave; turn right into Zinni; the hotel is in the cul de sac beside the small church. *In room:* A/C, TV, minibar

## 4 Where to Dine

Greek restaurants are required to display a menu with prices either in the window or another prominent place. Most restaurants have menus in Greek and English, but many don't keep their printed (or handwritten) menus up-to-date. If the menu is not in English, there's almost always someone working at the restaurant who will either translate or rattle off suggestions for you in English. Consequently, you may be offered some fairly repetitive suggestions, as restaurant staff tend to suggest what most tourists request. In Athens, that means *moussaka* (baked eggplant casserole, usually with ground meat), *souvlaki* (chunks of beef, chicken, pork, or lamb grilled on a skewer), *pastitsio* (baked pasta, usually with ground meat and a béchamel sauce), or *dolmadakia* (grape leaves stuffed usually with rice and ground meat). Although these dishes can be delicious—you may have eaten them outside of Greece and looked forward to enjoying the real thing here—you may end up cherishing your memories and regretting your meal. All too often, restaurants catering to tourists tend to serve profoundly dull moussaka and unpleasantly chewy *souvlaki.* We hope that the places we're suggesting do better.

In the last few years, a number of Athenian restaurants have begun to experiment with a "nouvelle Greek" cuisine. Usually, this involves aspects of *paradisiako* (traditional) cooking, but with a lighter hand on the olive oil and an adventurous combination of familiar ingredients. In our reviews, we draw attention to these restaurants.

Since November 2002, restaurants have been required by law to offer non-smoking seating. You may or may not find this law enforced.

### THE PLAKA

Some of the most charming old restaurants in Athens are in the Plaka—as are some of the worst tourist traps. Here are a few things to keep in mind when you head off for a meal in the Plaka.

Some Plaka restaurants station waiters outside who don't just urge you to come in and sit down, but virtually pursue you down the street with an unrelenting sales pitch. The hard sell is almost always a giveaway that the place caters to tourists. (That said, remember that announcing what's for sale is not invariably a ploy reserved for tourists. If you visit the Central Market, you'll see and hear stall owners calling out the attractions of their meat, fish, and produce to passersby—and even waving particularly tempting fish and fowl in front of potential customers.)

In general, it's a good idea to avoid places with floor shows; many charge outrageous amounts (and levy surcharges not always openly stated on menus) for drinks and food. If you get burned, stand your ground, phone the **Tourist Police** (© 171), and pay nothing before they arrive. Often the mere threat of calling the Tourist Police has the miraculous effect of causing a bill to be lowered.

Abyssinia Cafe **1**
Aigli **34**
Aprooto **31**
Athinaikon **5**
Bajazzo **35**
Damigos (Bakaliarakia) **15**
Daphne's **13**
Dimokritos **21**
Diporto **8**
Eden Vegetarian
Restaurant **12**
GB Corner **28**
Gerofinikas **29**
Ideal **7**
Kalliste **20**
Kostoyannis **19**
Kouklis Ouzeri
(To Yerani) **14**
Manesis **37**
Myrtia **36**

Neon (Kolonaki) **27**
Neon (Omonia) **6**
Neon (Syntagma) **30**
Papandreou **8**
Platanos Taverna **11**
Rhodia **26**
Socrate's Prison **17**
Strofi Tavern **16**
Symbosio **18**
Taki 13 **3**
Taverna Sigalas **19**
Taverna Xinos **32**
Taygetos **4**
Thanasis **10**
To Kafenio **23**
To Ouzadiko **24**
To Prytaneion **22**
To Tristato **33**
Vlasis **25**
Zeidoron **2**

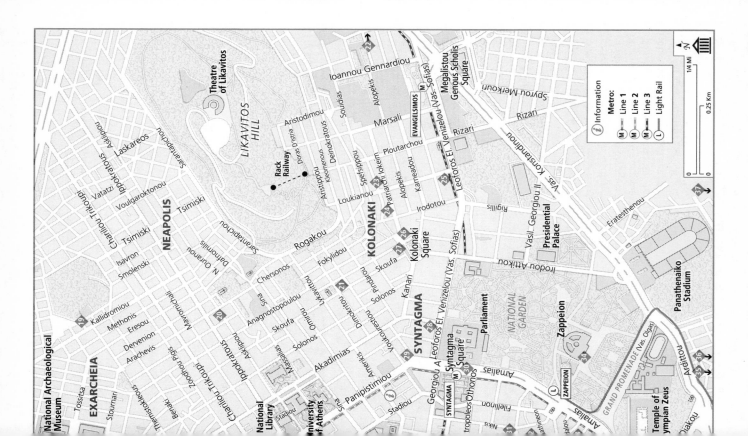

National Archaeological Museum

EXARCHEIA

NEAPOLIS

LIKAVITOS HILL

Theatre of Likavitos

Ioannou Gennardiou

Rack Railway

KOLONAKI

Kolonaki Square

EVANGELISMOS

Megalistou Genous Scholis Square

Spyrou Merkouri

Rizari

Presidential Palace

Panathenaiko Stadium

SYNTAGMA

Syntagma Square

Parliament

NATIONAL GARDEN

Zappeion

ZAPPEION

Temple of Olympian Zeus

GRAND PROMENADE (Vas. Olgas)

National Library

University of Athens

Information

Metro:
Line 1
Line 2
Line 3
Light Rail

1/4 Mi
0.25 Km

**Tips** **A Note on Credit Cards**

One of my most humiliating travel moments happened a number of years ago when I was taking Athenian friends out to dinner—and planning to pay with a credit card. The restaurant took only cash, and my friends ended up having to take me to dinner. Much has changed in Athens since then, but one thing that has not changed is that many Athenian restaurants still do not accept credit cards. Consider yourself warned.

## EXPENSIVE

**Daphne's** ★★★ ELEGANT GREEK/NOUVELLE There are frescoes on the walls of this neo-classical 1830s former home, a shady garden courtyard with bits of ancient marble found here when the restaurant was built, and sophisticated Athenians at many tables. The outside garden courtyard makes Daphne's a real oasis in Athens, especially when summer nights are hot. The cuisine here (recommended in the *New York Times* and *Travel and Leisure*—and just about everywhere else!) gives you all the old favorites with new distinction (try the zesty "eggplant salad), and combines familiar ingredients in innovative ways (delicious hot pepper and feta cheese dip). We could cheerfully just eat the hors d'oeuvres all night, but have also enjoyed the *stifado* (stew) of rabbit in *mavrodaphne* (sweet wine) sauce and the tasty prawns with toasted almonds. Most nights, there's a pair of strolling musicians, whose repertoire ranges from Greek favorites to "My Darling Clementine." The staff is attentive, encouraging, endearing, and beyond excellent.

4 Lysikratous. ☏ and fax 210/322-7971. Main courses 16€–25€, with some fish priced by the kilo. AE, DC, MC, V. Daily 7pm–1am. Closed Dec 20–Jan 15.

## MODERATE

**Aprooto** GREEK/MEZEDES This is a good place near Syntagma to make a meal of familiar Greek mezedes like tzatziki and taramosalata (or that American and British standby, the baked potato). Main courses include grills and a nice pork stew with mushrooms (the mushrooms, a somewhat unusual touch in Greece). The ambience is cozy, the food good—and the place is not yet overwhelmed by tourists. The same is true of **Palea Athina**, at 46 Nikis, and **Delfi,** at 13 Nikis.

48 Nikis. ☏ 210/322-0521. Main courses 6€–15€ No credit cards. Mon–Sat about 11am–2pm and about 7pm–midnight.

**Eden Vegetarian Restaurant** ✿ VEGETARIAN You can find vegetarian dishes at almost every Greek restaurant, but if you want to experience organically grown products, soy (rather than eggplant) moussaka, mushroom pie with a whole-wheat crust, freshly squeezed juices, and salads with bean sprouts, join the young Athenians and Europeans who patronize the Eden. The prices are reasonable, if not cheap, and the decor is engaging, with 1920s-style prints and mirrors and wrought-iron lamps.

12 Lissiou ☏ and fax 210/324-8858. Main courses 6€–15€. AE, MC, V. Daily noon–midnight. Closed Tues and usually closed Aug. From Syntagma Sq., head south on Filellinon or Nikis to Kidathineon, which intersects Adrianou; turn right on Adrianou and take Mnissikleos up 2 blocks toward Acropolis to Lissiou.

**Platanos Taverna** ★★ TRADITIONAL GREEK This taverna on a quiet pedestrian square has tables outdoors in good weather beneath a spreading plane tree ("Platanos" means plane tree). Inside, where locals usually congregate to escape the summer sun at midday and the tourists in the evening, you can enjoy looking at the old paintings and photos on the walls. The Platanos has been serving good *spitiko fageto* (home cooking) since 1932 and has managed to keep steady customers happy while enchanting visitors. If artichokes or spinach with lamb are on the menu, you're in luck: They're delicious. The house wine is tasty, and there's a wide choice of bottled wines from many regions of Greece. If possible, plan to come here and relax, not rush, through a meal.

4 Dioyenous. ⓒ 210/322-0666. Fax 210/322-8624. Main courses 6€–12€. No credit cards. Mon–Sat noon–4:30pm and 8pm–midnight; Sun in Mar, Apr, May, Sept, and Oct noon–4:30pm. From Syntagma Sq., head south on Filellinon or Nikis to Kidathineon; turn right on Adrianou, and take Mnissikleos up 1 block toward the Acropolis and turn right on Dioyenous.

**Taverna Xinos** ★ TRADITIONAL GREEK    Despite the forgivable spelling lapse, Xinos's business card says it best: "In the heart of old Athens there is still a flace [sic] where the traditional Greek way of cooking is upheld." In summer, there are tables in the courtyard; in winter, you can warm yourself by the coal-burning stove and admire the wall frescoes. While the strolling musicians may not be as good as the Three Tenors, they do sing wonderful Greek golden oldies, accompanying themselves on the guitar and bouzouki. (If you're serenaded, you may want to give the musicians a tip. If you want to hear the theme from Never on Sunday, ask for "Ena Zorbas.") Most evenings, tourists predominate until after 10pm, when locals begin to arrive—as they have since Xinos opened in 1935.

4 Geronta. ⓒ 210/322-1065. Main courses 6€–15€. No credit cards. Daily 8pm–anywhere from 11pm–1am; sometimes closed Sun, usually closed part of July and Aug. From Syntagma Sq., head south on Filellinon or Nikis to Kidathineon; turn right on Geronta and look for the sign for Xinos in the cul de sac.

## INEXPENSIVE

**Damigos** (The Bakaliarakia) ★★★ GREEK/CODFISH    This basement taverna, with enormous wine barrels in the back room and an ancient column supporting the roof in the front room, has been serving delicious deep-fried codfish and eggplant, as well as chops and stews, since 1865. The wine comes from the family vineyards, and there are few pleasures greater than sipping retsina—if you wish, you can buy a bottle to take away—while you watch the cook turn out unending meals in his absurdly small kitchen. Don't miss the delicious *skordalia* (garlic sauce), equally good with cod, eggplant, bread—well, you get the idea.

41 Kidathineon. ⓒ 210/322-5084. Main courses 4€–10€. No credit cards. Daily 7pm–anywhere from 11pm–1am. Usually closed June–Sept. From Syntagma Sq., head south on Filellinon or Nikis to Kidathineon; Damigos is downstairs on left just before Adrianou.

**Kouklis Ouzeri** (To Yerani) ★ GREEK/MEZEDES    Besides Kouklis Ouzeri and To Yerani, Greeks call this popular old favorite with its winding staircase to the second floor the "Skolario" because of the nearby school. Sit down at one of the small tables and a waiter will present a large tray with about a dozen plates of mezedes—appetizer portions of fried fish, beans, grilled eggplant, taramosalata, cucumber-and-tomato salad, olives, fried cheese, sausages, and other seasonal specialties. Accept the ones that appeal. If you don't order all 12, you can enjoy a tasty and inexpensive meal, washed down with the house *krasi* (wine). No prices are posted, but the waiter will tell you what everything costs if you ask. Now if only the staff could be just a bit more patient when foreigners are trying to decide what to order.

14 Tripodon. ⓒ 210/324-7605. Appetizers 2€–17€. No credit cards. Daily 11am–2am. From Syntagma Sq., head south on Filellinon or Nikis to Kidathineon; take Kidathineon across Adrianou to Thespidos and climb toward Acropolis; Tripodon is 1st street on right after Adrianou.

## MONASTIRAKI

### INEXPENSIVE

**Abyssinia Cafe** ★ GREEK  This small café in a ramshackle building has a nicely restored interior featuring lots of gleaming dark wood and polished copper. It faces lopsided Abyssinia Square off Ifaistou, where furniture restorers ply their trade and antiques shops sell everything from gramophones to hubcaps. You can sit indoors or out and have just a coffee, but it's tempting to snack on Cheese Abyssinia (feta scrambled with spices and garlic), mussels and rice pilaf, or *keftedes* (meatballs).

Plateia Abyssinia, Monastiraki. (°) 210/321-7047. Appetizers and main courses 4€–15€. No credit cards. Tues–Sun 10:30am–2pm (often open evenings as well). Usually closed for a week at Christmas and Easter; sometimes closed part of Jan and Feb and mid-July to mid-Aug Abyssinia Sq. is just off Ifaistou (Hephaistos) across from entrance to Ancient Agora on Adrianou.

**Diporto** GREEK  This little place, sandwiched between olive shops, serves up salads, stews, and delicious *revithia* (chickpeas), a Greek winter dish popular among stall owners, shoppers, and Athenians who make their way to the market for cheap and delicious food.

Central Market, Athinas. No phone. Main courses 3€–8€. No credit cards. Mon–Sat 6am–6pm.

**Papandreou** GREEK  The butcher, the baker, and the office worker duck past the sides of beef hanging in the Meat Hall and head to this hole-in-the-wall for zesty tripe dishes. Don't like tripe? Don't worry: There's usually something on the menu that doesn't involve it. Papandreou has a virtually all-male clientele, but a woman alone need not hesitate to eat here.

Central Market, Athinas. (°) 210/321-4970. Main courses 5€–8€. No credit cards. Mon–Sat from about 8am–5pm.

**Taverna Sigalas** GREEK  This longtime Plaka taverna, housed in a vintage 1879 commercial building with a newer courtyard pavilion, boasts that it is open 365 days a year. Its lively interior has huge old retsina kegs in the back and dozens of black-and-white photos of Greek movie stars on the walls. After 8pm nightly, there's Greek Muzak. At all hours, both Greeks and tourists wolf down large portions of stews, moussaka, grilled meatballs, baked tomatoes, gyros, and other hearty dishes, washed down with the house red and white retsinas.

2 Plateia Monastiraki. (°) 210/321-3036. Main courses 5€–15€. No credit cards. Daily 7am–2am. Sigalas is across Monastiraki Sq. from the Metro station.

**Thanasis** ★ GREEK/SOUVLAKI  Thanasis serves terrific souvlaki and pita—and exceptionally good french fries—both to go and at its outdoor and indoor tables; as always, prices are higher if you sit down to eat. On weekends, it often takes the strength and determination of an Olympic athlete to get through the door and place an order here. It's worth the effort: This is both a great budget choice and a great place to take in the local scene, which often includes a fair sprinkling of gypsies.

69 Mitropoleos. (Just off the northeast corner of Monastiraki Sq.) (°) 210/324-4705. Main courses 2€–8€. No credit cards. Daily 9am–2am.

## SYNTAGMA

### EXPENSIVE

**Aigli** ★★ INTERNATIONAL  For years, the bistro in the Zappeion gardens was a popular meeting spot and when it closed in the 1970s, it was sorely missed. Now it is back, along with a cinema and fine restaurant. Once more,

## Quick Bites in Syntagma

In general, Syntagma Square is not known for good food, but there are a number of places in the area to get a snack. The **Apollonion Bakery**, 10 Nikis, and the **Elleniki Gonia**, 10 Karayioryi Servias, make sandwiches to order and sell croissants, both stuffed and plain. **Ariston** is a small chain of *zaharoplastia* (confectioners) with a branch at the corner of Karayioryi Servias and Voulis (just off Syntagma Square) selling snacks as well as pastries. **Floca** is another excellent pastry-shop chain; look in the arcade on Panepistimiou near Syntagma Square. As always, you pay extra to be served at one of the tables.

For the quintessentially Greek, *loukoumades* (round donut-center–like pastries that are deep-fried, then drenched with honey and topped with powdered sugar and cinnamon), nothing beats **Doris**, 30 Praxitelous, a continuation of Lekka, a few blocks from Syntagma Square. If you're still hungry, Doris serves hearty stews and pasta dishes for absurdly low prices Monday through Saturday until 3:30pm. **Everest** is another chain worth trying; there's one a block north of Kolonaki Square at Tsakalof and Iraklitou. Also in Kolonaki Square, **To Kotopolo** serves succulent grilled chicken to take out or eat in. In the Plaka, the **K. Kotsolis Pastry Shop**, 112 Adrianou, serving excellent coffee and sweets, is an oasis of old-fashioned charm in the midst of the souvenir shops. The **Oraia Ellada** (Beautiful Greece) cafe at the Center of Hellenic Tradition, opening onto both 36 Pandrossou and 59 Mitropoleos near the flea market, has a spectacular view of the Acropolis. You can revive yourself here with a cappuccino and a few pastries.

chic Athenian families head here, in the cool of the Zappeion Gardens, for the foie gras, oysters, Chinese ravioli, rich profiteroles and delicious yogurt crème brûlée. There are tables indoors or outdoors by the trees, where you can relax with a morning cup of coffee and watch the balloon sellers tempting families with their wares. In the evening, you can take in a movie at the open-air cinema here before dinner, or have a drink and snack at one of several cafes. In short, a wonderful spot to wile away an afternoon or evening.

Zappeion Gardens (adjacent to the National Gardens fronting Vas. Amalias Blvd.) © 210/336-9363. Main courses 16€–25€. Reservations recommended. Daily 10am–12am. Sometimes closed in August.

## MODERATE

**Gerofinikas** GREEK/INTERNATIONAL   For years, this was *the* place to go for a special lunch or dinner. The food is still very good—which is why tour groups have, alas, discovered it. Still, it's always pleasant to walk down the passageway into Gerofinikas (the old palm tree), look at the long display cases of tempting dishes and try to decide between the shrimp with feta cheese, the rabbit stew with onions, and the tasty eggplant dishes—all the while saving room for one of Gerofinikas's rich desserts. The fixed-price menu is good value—but this is a place where choosing what to order is half the fun.

10 Pindar. © 210/363-6710. Reservations strongly recommended. Main courses 8€–20€. Fixed-price menu 25€, not including beverage. AE, DC, MC, V. Daily usually noon–2pm and 7pm–midnight.

## INEXPENSIVE

**Neon** ★ Value GREEK/INTERNATIONAL If you're tired of practicing your restaurant Greek, the Neon restaurants are a good place to eat, since most things are self-service. This centrally located member of the chain is very convenient, although not as pleasant as the original on Omonia Square. There is also a very handy Neon a block north of Kolonaki Square at Tsakalof and Iraklitou. You're sure to find something to your taste—maybe a Mexican omelet, spaghetti Bolognese, the salad bar, or sweets ranging from Black Forest cake to tiramisu.

3 Mitropoleos (on the southwest corner of Syntagma Sq.). ⓒ 210/322-8155. Snacks 2€–6€; sandwiches 3€–6€; main courses 4€–20€. No credit cards. Daily 9am–midnight.

## KOLONAKI
## MODERATE

**Filipou** ★ TRADITIONAL GREEK This long-time Athenian favorite almost never disappoints. The traditional dishes such as stuffed cabbage, stuffed vine leaves, vegetable stews and fresh salads are consistently good. In the heart of Kolonaki, near the very fashionable George Lykabettus Hotel, this is a place to head for when you want good "spitiko" (home) cooking in the company of the Greeks and resident expatriates who prize the food here.

19 Xenokratous. ⓒ 210/721-6390. Main courses 6€–20€. No credit cards. Main courses 7€–15€. Mon–Fri 830pm–midnight Sat lunch. Closed Sun. From Kolonaki Sq., take Patriarch Ioakim to Ploutarchou, turn left on Ploutarchou and then right on Xenokratous.

**To Kafeneio** ★★ GREEK/INTERNATIONAL This is hardly a typical kafeneio (coffee shop/cafe). If you relax, you can easily run up a substantial tab (50€ for lunch or dinner for two is easy), but you can also eat more modestly and equally elegantly. If you have something light, like the artichokes a la polita, leeks in crème fraîche, or onion pie (one, not all three!), washed down with draft beer or the house wine, you can finish with profiteroles and not put too big a dent in your budget. I've always found this an especially congenial spot when I'm eating alone (perhaps because I love people-watching and profiteroles).

26 Loukianou. ⓒ 210/722-9056. Reservations recommended. Main courses 6.€–25€. No credit cards. Mon–Sat 11am–midnight or later. Closed Sun and most of Aug. From Kolonaki Sq., follow Patriarkou Ioakim several blocks uphill to Loukianou and turn right on Loukianou.

**To Ouzadiko** ★★ GREEK/MEZEDES This ouzo bar has at least 40 kinds of ouzo and as many mezedes, including fluffy keftedes (meatballs) that make all others taste leaden. To Ouzadiko is very popular with Athenians young and old who come to see and be seen while having a snack or a full meal, often after concerts and plays. A serious foodie friend of mine goes here especially for the wide variety of horta (greens), which she says are the best she's ever tasted. If you see someone at a nearby table eating something you want and aren't sure which of the bean or eggplant dishes it is, ask your waiter, and it will appear for you—sometimes after a bit of a wait, as the staff here is often seriously overworked.

25–29 Karneadou (in the Lemos International Shopping Center), Kolonaki. ⓒ 210/729/5484. Reservations recommended. Mezedes and main courses 7€–18€. No credit cards. Tues–Sat 1pm–12:30am. From Kolonaki Sq. take Kapsali across Irodotou into Karneadou. The Lemos Center is the mini-skyscraper on your left.

**To Prytaneion** ★ GREEK/INTERNATIONAL The trendy bare stone walls here are decorated with movie posters and illuminated by baby spotlights. Waiters with cellphones serve customers with cellphones tempting plates of some of Athens's most expensive and eclectic mezedes, including beef carpaccio, smoked salmon, bruschetta, and shrimp in fresh cream, as well as Greek olives and that international favorite, the hamburger. This place is so drop-dead chic that it comes as a pleasant surprise to learn that it functioned as a neighborhood hangout during the earthquake of 1999 and the snowstorm that shut down Athens in 2001.

7 Milioni, Kolonaki. © **210/364-3353** or 210/364-3354. www.prytaneion.gr. Prytaniou@otenet.gr. Reservations recommended. Mezedes and snacks 7€–25€. No credit cards. Mon–Sat 10am–3am. From Kolonaki Sq., head downhill a (pedestrianized) block or 2 until you hit Milioni on your right. To Prytaneion is on your left.

**Rhodia** ✸ TRADITIONAL GREEK   This respected taverna in a handsome old Kolonaki house has tables in its small garden in good weather—although the interior, with its tile floor and old prints, is so charming that you might be tempted to eat indoors. The Rhodia is a favorite of visiting archaeologists from the nearby British and American Schools of Classical Studies, as well as of Kolonaki residents. It may not sound like just what you'd always hoped to have for dinner, but the octopus in mustard sauce is terrific, as are the veal and *dolmades* (stuffed grape leaves) in egg-lemon sauce. The house wine is excellent, as is the halva, which manages to be both creamy and crunchy.

44 Aristippou. © **210/722-9883.** Main courses 7€–15€. No credit cards. Mon–Sat 8pm–2am. From Kolonaki Sq., take Patriarkou Ioakim uphill to Loukianou; turn left on Loukianou, climb steeply uphill to Aristippou, and turn right.

## INEXPENSIVE

**Neon** GREEK/INTERNATIONAL   The Kolonaki Neon serves the same food as the Syntagma and Omonia branches, but the reasonable prices are especially welcome in this pricey neighborhood. Tsakalof is a shady pedestrian arcade, and the Neon has tables inside and outdoors.

Tsakalof 6, Kolonaki Sq. © **210/364-6873.** Snacks 2€–6€; sandwiches 3€–6€; main courses 4€–20€. No credit cards. Daily 9am–midnight.

# OMONIA SQUARE & UNIVERSITY AREA (NEAR EXARCHIA SQUARE/ARCHAEOLOGICAL MUSEUM)

## MODERATE

**Athinaikon** ✸✸ GREEK/OUZERIE   Not many tourists come to this favorite haunt of lawyers and businesspeople working in the Omonia Square area. You can have just some appetizers (technically, this is an ouzeri) or a full meal. Obviously, the way to have a reasonably priced snack is to stick to the appetizers, including delicious *loukanika* (sausages) and *keftedes* (meatballs) and pass on the more pricey grilled shrimp or seafood paella. Whatever you have, you'll enjoy taking in the old photos on the walls, the handsome tiled floor, the marble-topped tables and bentwood chairs, and the regular customers, who combine serious eating with animated conversation.

2 Themistokleous. © **210/383-8485.** Appetizers and main courses 4€–16€. No credit cards. Mon–Sat 11am–midnight. Closed Sun and usually in Aug. From Omonia Sq., take Panepistimiou a block to Themistokleous; the Athinaikon is almost immediately on your right.

**Ideal** ✸ GREEK TRADITIONAL   The oldest restaurant in the heart of Athens, today's Ideal has an Art Deco decor and lots of old favorites, from egg-lemon soup to stuffed peppers, pork with celery and lamb with spinach. This is a favorite of businessmen, and the service is usually brisk, especially at lunch time. Not the place for a quiet rendezvous, but definitely the place for good, hearty Greek cooking.

46 Panepistimiou. © **210/330-3000.** Reservations recommended. Main courses 8€–15€. AE, DC, MC, V. Mon–Sat noon–midnight. From Omonia or Syntagma take Panepistimiou (the Ideal is just outside Omonia Sq.).

## INEXPENSIVE

**Neon** *Value* GREEK/INTERNATIONAL   In a handsome 1920s building, the Neon serves up cafeteria-style food, including cooked-to-order pasta, omelets, and grills, as well as salads and sweets. Equally good for a meal or a snack, the Neon proves that fast food doesn't have to be junk food.

1 Dorou, Omonia Sq. (ℂ) **210/522-9939.** Snacks 1€–3€; sandwiches 3€–6€; main courses 4€–20€. No credit cards. Daily 9am–midnight.

**Taygetos** ★ *Value* GREEK/SOUVLAKI   This is a great place to stop for a quick meal on your way to/from the National Archaeological Museum. The service is swift, and the souvlaki and fried potatoes are excellent, as are the chicken and the grilled lamb. The menu sometimes also includes delicious *koko-retsi* (grilled entrails). The Elliniikon Restaurant next door is also a good value.

4 Satovriandou. (ℂ) **210/523-5352.** Main courses 5€–9€; grilled lamb priced by the kilo. No credit cards. Mon–Sat 9am–1am. From Omonia Sq. take Patrision (28 Oktovriou) toward National Museum; Satovriandou is 3rd major turning on your left.

## METS

### MODERATE

**Manesis** GREEK   This longtime favorite, with a pleasant garden and wide range of delicious mezedes, continues to be popular with locals, and increasingly attracts visitors (including the occasional tour group). The swordfish souvlaki here is usually excellent, the *loukanika* (sausage) tasty, and the stews nicely seasoned with dill and lemon. The basic menu hasn't changed in years, although more nonmeat dishes have been added, including an excellent, creamy hummus.

3 Markou Mouzourou. (ℂ) **210/922-7684.** Main courses 8€–15€. No credit cards. Daily about 7pm–midnight.

## KOUKAKI & MAKRIYANNI (NEAR THE ACROPOLIS)

See the "Accommodations & Dining South of the Acropolis" map on p. 159 to locate these restaurants.

### MODERATE

**Socrates' Prison/Samaria** ★ GREEK/CONTINENTAL   This long-time visitors' favorite has moved around the corner to a new location (and a new name that not everyone uses), where it remains an excellent place to head when you want good food near the Plaka, but want to avoid the frenzy of the central Plaka. The new place has a roof garden with an Acropolis view, a real plus for summer evenings. Greeks, as well as American and European expats living in Athens, love this place, with its tables outdoors in good weather and in the pleasant indoor rooms year-round. In addition to the usual Greek meat dishes, the menu includes tasty veggie croquettes, salade Niçoise and—for those who can't decide between veggies and meat—vegetable-stuffed pork roll. The retsina is excellent, and there's a wide choice of bottled wines and beers.

17 Robertou Galli. (ℂ) **210/922-3434.** Main courses 10€–15€. AE, DC, MC, V. Mon–Sat 11am–4pm and 7pm–1am. Closed Aug. From Syntagma Sq., take Amalias Ave. to pedestrianized Dionysiou Areopagitou, walk away from Temple of Zeus on the side of Dionysiou Areopagitou across from Acropolis, and turn left onto Mitseon and right onto Robertou Galli.

**Strofi Tavern** GREEK   The Strofi serves standard Greek taverna fare (although the *mezedes* are especially good here), but the view of the Acropolis is so terrific that everything tastes particularly good. Keep this place in mind if you're staying south of the Acropolis, an area that is not packed with restaurants.

Strofi is popular with the after-theater crowd that pours out of the nearby Herodes Atticus theater during the Athens Festival.

25 Rovertou Galli, Makriyianni. © **210/921-4130.** Reservations recommended. Main courses 8€–18€. DC, MC, V. Mon–Sat 8pm–2am. Located 2 blocks south of Acropolis.

**Symbosio** ★★ ELEGANT GREEK/CONTINENTAL   This is a very pretty place to eat: a lovingly cared for 1920s Makriyianni town house with its own garden. Initially, we thought that the food here, although delicious, could be too fussy, with a bit too much lily gilding and use of sauces. On the last few times we have been here, we were swept away by the mezedes, the quality of the fish, the delicate seasonings used in meat dishes, the fresh veggies, and the excellent wine list. Did we mention the amazing mushrooms? The wild boar? All that and more is here.

46 Erechthiou. © **210/922-5321.** Fax 210/923-2780. Main courses 12€–28€; fish priced by the kilo. AE, MC, V. Mon–Sat about 8pm–midnight. Usually closed 2nd half of Aug; sometimes closed in Jan.

## WORTH THE JOURNEY

**AristeraDexia** ★ GREEK/INTERNATIONAL   Gazi, the district best known as the home of Athens's gasworks, is following in Psirri's fashionable footsteps. Certainly, AristeraDexia was all the rage in 2002, with its glass catwalk over the wine cellar, open kitchen, and endless small tables packed with hipsters with cellphones. As for the food, it draws on traditional Greek flavors and ingredients, but combines them in unusual ways. The menu is always changing, but has recently included crayfish dressed with lavender, sweet moschato wine, and squid in egg lemon sauce.

3 Andronkou, Gazi. © **210/342-2380.** Reservations recommended. Main courses 12€–25€; fish priced by the kilo. AE, V. Mon–Sat 9pm–1am.

**Kalliste** ★★ ELEGANT GREEK   In a beautifully restored 19th-century house with polished wooden floors and ornamental plaster ceilings, Kalliste manages to be both cozy and elegant. The constantly changing menu usually includes traditional dishes with a distinctive flair, such as lentil soup with pomegranate, and chicken with hazelnuts and celery purée. Even that old standby crème caramel is enlivened by the addition of rose liqueur. It would be difficult to improve on this lovely refuge from the bustle of Athens.

137 Asklepiou, off Akadimias above the University of Athens. © **210/645-3179.** Reservations recommended. Main courses 10€–25€. No credit cards. Mon–Sat about noon–2pm and 8pm–midnight.

**Spondi** ★★★   *Athinorama*, the weekly review of the Athenian scene, has chosen Spondi several years running as the best place in town. There are light dishes on the menu—the fresh fish, especially the salmon, is superb—as well as a number of dishes that you will either find delightful, or a bit cloying (roast pork with myzithra cheese and a fig and yogurt sauce). The setting (a handsome 19th-century town house, with a lovely courtyard) is lovely, the wine list is extensive, the service is excellent, the desserts are divine. You'll probably want to take a cab here: Pyrronos runs between Empedokleous and Dikearchou, behind the Olympic Stadium.

5 Pyrronos, Pangrati. © **210/752-0658.** Reservations recommended. Main courses 20€–28€. No credit cards. Mon–Sat 8pm–1am.

**Varoulko** ★★★   In an unlikely location on a side street in Piraeus, chef-owner Lefteris Lazarou has created what many consider not just the finest seafood restaurant, but the finest restaurant in the greater Athens area. I had one of the best meals in my life here—smoked eel; artichokes with fish roe; crayfish with sun-dried tomatoes; monkfish livers with soy sauce, honey, and balsamic vinegar—and the best sea bass and monkfish I have ever eaten. The barebrick walls of the restaurant are softened with art work and the food is beautifully presented—and absolutely delicious.

14 Deligeorgi, Piraeus. © 210/411-2043. Fax 210/422-1283. Reservations necessary (arrange several days in advance). Dinner for 2 from about 120€; fish priced by the kilo. No credit cards. Mon–Sat about 8pm–midnight. Closed Sun and most of June–Sept, when it often relocates outdoors at the Peace and Friendship Stadium. We recommend taking a taxi to this restaurant, which is hard to find and not in central Piraeus.

**Vlassis ★★★ TRADITIONAL GREEK** Greeks call this kind of food paradisiako-traditional, but paradisiacal is just as good a description. This very reasonably priced food is fit for the gods: delicious fluffy vegetable croquettes, eggplant salad that tastes like no other, hauntingly tender lamb in egg-lemon sauce. It's a sign of Vlassis's popularity with Athenians—each time I eat here, I seem to be the only obvious foreigner—that there's not even a discreet sign announcing its presence in a small apartment building on hard-to-find Paster. Figure the price of a taxi (no more than 10€) into your meal tab; you may feel so giddy with delight after eating you won't mind the half-hour walk back to Syntagma.

8 Paster (off Plateia Mavili). © 210/646-3060. 7€–20€. Reservations recommended. No credit cards. Mon–Sat 8pm–1am. Closed much of June–Sept. From Syntagma Sq., take Vasilissis Sophias Ave. to Plateia Mavili, and follow D. Tsoustou out of Plateia Mavili to Chatzikosta; Paster is the cul de sac on the left after you turn right into Chatzikosta.

# 6

# Exploring Athens

*by Sherry Marker*

It's quite likely that you'll arrive in Athens in the late afternoon, groggy and disoriented after a seriously long flight. The ride into town from the airport is unlikely to help your spirits: You'll whiz along an efficient, but anonymous, highway that could be anywhere, before being fed into Athens's ferocious traffic. Somewhere, you know, not far away, must be the blue Aegean and the lofty Acropolis. But where? Surrounded by cars that are either stuck in gridlock or maniacally jockeying for position with no apparent respect for lanes, deafened by the explosions of hordes of mufflerless kamikaze motorcycles, you'll almost certainly be debating asking your cab driver to make a U-turn and take you back to the airport.

Don't despair. When you get to your hotel, jump in the shower, take a nap, and then set off for an evening stroll through **Syntagma (Constitution Square** past the House of Parliament (now with its own website, www. parliament.gr). Take a few minutes to explore Syntagma's handsome new

marble **Metro** station, with its display of finds from the excavations here. If it's warm out, escape into the shade of the **National Garden**, and join the Athenians feeding pigeons. Then head into the **Plaka**, the old neighborhood on the slopes of the Acropolis that has more restaurants, cafes, and souvenir shops than private homes. If you get off the Plaka's main drag, Kidathineon and Adrianou, and follow one of the streets such as Thespidos that runs up the slope of the Acropolis, you'll find yourself in **Anafiotika**. This Plaka district, built in the 19th century by immigrants from the Cycladic island of Anafi, retains much of its old village character. From time to time as you stroll, look up: You're bound to see the Acropolis, perhaps floodlit, and the best possible reminder of why you came.

After you have your first Greek meal, perhaps washed down with some astringent retsina wine, head back to your hotel and get a good night's sleep so that you'll be ready for your first real day in Athens.

## An Important Warning

**Strikes** that close museums and archaeological sites can occur without warning. Decide what you most want to see, and go there as soon as possible after your arrival. The fact that something is open today says nothing about tomorrow. If you're visiting in the off season, check with the **Greek National Tourism Organization** at 2 Amerikis (☎ **210/327-1300;** 210/331-0562; www.gnto.gr) for the abbreviated **winter hours** of sites and museums. Keep in mind that the opening hours posted at sites and those listed at the tourist office often vary considerably. Alas, no information is utterly reliable.

# Athens Attractions

Academy of Arts & Letters 18
Acropolis Museum 11
Athens Cathedral 20
Ayios Yióryios 19
Benaki Museum 22
Byzantine Museum 24
Goulandris Museum of Cycladic Art 23
Greek Folk Art Museum 25
Hadrian's Arch 28
Hadrian's Library 6
Ilias Lalaounis Jewelry Museum 13
Kerameikos Cemetery 1
Monastiraki Church 5
National Archaeological Museum 14

National Historical Museum 15
National Library 16
National Picture Gallery 27
Numismatic Museum 21
Odeum of Herodes Atticus 9
Parthenon 10
Presidential Palace 26
Roman Agora 7
Stoa of Attalos 4
Temple of Olympian Zeus 3
Theater of Dionysos 29
Theseion (Temple of Hephaistos) 2
Tower of Winds (Aerides) 8
University 17

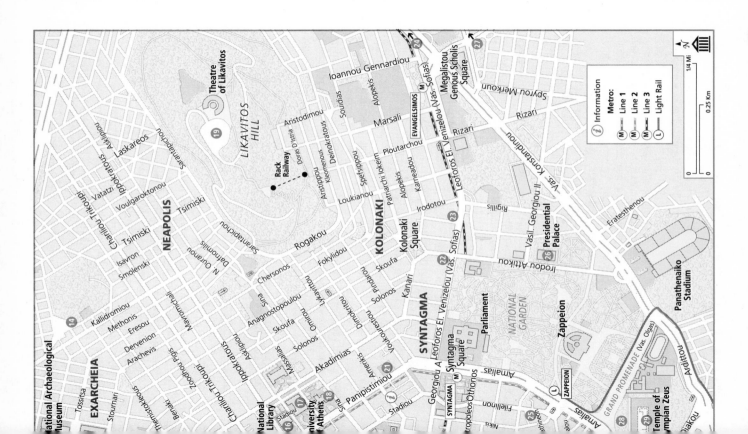

**Tips** **A National Archaeological Museum Update**

The National Archaeological Museum closed for renovations in 2002; it is slated to reopen in May of 2004 in time for the August 2004 Summer Olympics. The second floor of the National Archaeological Museum, where most of the extensive collection of Greek vases was housed, had already been closed since an earthquake shook Athens in 1999. At press time, it was not clear whether the restored 3500 B.C. Thira frescoes (displayed on the 2nd floor before the earthquake) would remain in the museum when it reopens or be sent back to the island of Thira (Santorini). In addition, it was not known at press time where objects would be displayed; therefore, for now, we can give you an idea of the museum's main attractions, but not of where they will be displayed.

## 1 The Top Attractions

At press time, ticket prices for many monuments and museums were in flux. Our prices are based on the prices available at press time and "guesstimates" offered by some museums. As if that were not sufficiently confusing, keep in mind that virtually all the major attractions plan to raise their admissions fees in 2004. As there is—surprise!—no fixed policy on cheaper tickets for students and seniors, be sure to ask about a discounted ticket if you are a senior or a student. Often these discounts apply only to members of Common Market countries.

**The Acropolis** ★★★     The Acropolis is one of a handful of places in the world that are so well known it's hard not to be nervous when you finally get here. Will it be as beautiful as its photographs? Will it be, ever so slightly, a disappointment? Rest assured: The Acropolis does not disappoint—but it usually is infuriatingly crowded. What you want here is some time—time to watch as the columns of the Parthenon appear first beige, then golden, then rose, then stark white in changing light; time to stand on the Belvedere and take in the view over Athens (and listen for the muted sounds of conversations floating up from the Plaka); time to think of all those who have been here before you.

When you climb up the Acropolis—the heights above the city—you know that you're on your way to see Greece's most famous temple, the **Parthenon.** What you may not know is that people lived on the Acropolis as early as 5,000 B.C. The Acropolis's sheer sides made a superb natural defense, just the place to avoid enemies and be able to see any invaders coming across the sea or the plains of Attica. And, of course, it helped that in antiquity there was a spring here.

In classical times, when Athens's population had grown to around 250,000, people moved down from the Acropolis, which had become the city's most important religious center. The city's **civic and business center**—the **Agora**—and its **cultural center**, with several theaters and concert halls, bracketed the Acropolis. When you peer over the sides of the Acropolis at the houses in the Plaka, and the remains of the ancient Agora and the theater of Dionysos, you'll see the layout of the ancient city. Syntagma and Omonia squares, the heart of today's Athens, were well out of the ancient city center.

Even the Acropolis's superb heights couldn't protect it from the Persian invasion of 480 B.C., when most of its monuments were burned and destroyed. You

# The Acropolis & Monastiraki

**1** Flea Market

**4** Greek Orthodox Cathedral (Metropolis)

**5** Panayia Gorgoepikoos (Little Metropolis)

**2** Roman Agora

**6** Temple of Athena Nike

**7** Propylaia

**3** Tower of the Winds

## ⚠ Warning Renovations at the Acropolis

At press time, the monuments of the Acropolis were undergoing extensive renovation. The temple of Nike had been entirely dismantled for restoration. The Propylaia and Parthenon were encased in scaffolding. We are attempting to describe what you should see when the renovations are completed.

may notice some immense column drums built into the Acropolis's walls. When the great Athenian statesman Pericles ordered the monuments of the Acropolis rebuilt, he had these drums from the destroyed Parthenon built into the walls lest Athenians forget what had happened—and so they would remember that they had rebuilt what they had lost. Pericles's rebuilding program began about 448 B.C.; the new Parthenon was dedicated 10 years later, but work on other monuments continued for a century.

As you enter the Acropolis, you'll first go through the **Beulé Gate**, built by the Romans, and named for the French archaeologist who discovered it in 1852. After that, you'll pass through the **Propylaia**, the monumental 5th-century B.C. entranceway. It's characteristic of the Roman mania for building that they found it necessary to build an entranceway to an entranceway!

Just above the Propylaia is the little temple of **Athena Nike** (Athena of Victory); this beautifully proportioned Ionic temple was built in 424 B.C. and heavily restored in the 1930s. To the left of the Parthenon is the **Erechtheion**, which the Athenians honored as the tomb of Erechtheus, a legendary king of Athens. A hole in the ceiling and floor of the northern porch indicates the spot where Poseidon's trident struck to make a spring gush forth during his contest with Athena to have the city named in his honor. Athena countered with an olive tree; the olive tree planted beside the Erechtheion reminds visitors of her victory—as, of course, does Athens's name.

Give yourself a little time to enjoy the delicate carving on the Erechtheion, and be sure to see the original **Caryatids** in the Acropolis Museum. The Caryatids presently holding up the porch of the Erechtheion are the casts put there when the originals were moved to prevent further erosion by Athens's acid *nefos* (smog).

However charmed you are by these elegant little temples, you're probably still heading resolutely toward the **Parthenon**, dedicated to Athena Parthenos (Athena the Virgin), patron goddess of Athens, and, of course, the most important religious shrine here. You may be disappointed to realize that visitors are not allowed inside, both to protect the monument and to allow restoration work to proceed safely. If you find this frustrating, keep in mind that in antiquity only priests and honored visitors were allowed in to see the monumental—some 11m (36 ft.) tall—statue of Athena designed by the great Phidias, who supervised Pericles's building program. Nothing of the huge gold-and-ivory statue remains, but there's a small Roman copy in the National Archaeological Museum—and horrific renditions on souvenirs ranging from T-shirts to ouzo bottles. Admittedly, the gold-and-ivory statue was not understood; the 2nd-century A.D. traveler Pausanias, one of the first guidebook writers, recorded that the statue stood "upright in an ankle-length tunic with a head of Medusa carved in ivory on her breast. She has a Victory about 2.5m (8 ft.) high, and a spear in her hand and a shield at her feet, with a snake beside the shield, possibly representing Erechtheus."

If you look over the edge of the Acropolis toward the **Temple of Hephaistos** (now called the **Theseion**) in the ancient Agora, and then at the Parthenon, you can't help but be struck by how much lighter and more graceful the Parthenon is. Scholars tell us that this is because Ictinus, the architect of the Parthenon, was something of a magician of optical illusions. The columns and stairs—the very floor—of the Parthenon all appear straight because all are minutely curved. The exterior columns are slightly thicker in the middle (a device known as *entasis*), which makes the entire column appear straight. That's why the Parthenon, with 17 columns on each side and eight at each end (creating an exterior colonnade of 46 relatively slender columns), looks so graceful, while the Temple of Hephaistos, with only six columns at each end and 13 along each side, seems so squat and stolid.

Of course, one reason the Parthenon looks so airy is that it is, quite literally, open to the air. The Parthenon's entire roof and much of its interior were blown to smithereens in 1687, when the Venetians attempted to capture the Acropolis from the Turks. A shell fired from nearby Mouseion Hill struck the Parthenon—where the Turks were storing gunpowder and munitions—and caused appalling damage to the building and its sculptures. Most of the remaining sculptures were carted off to London by Lord Elgin in the early 19th century. Those surviving sculptures—known as the **Elgin Marbles**—are on display in the British Museum, causing ongoing pain to generations of Greeks, who continue to press for their return. Things heated up again in the summer of 1988, when English historian William St. Clair's book *Lord Elgin and the Marbles* received a lot of publicity. According to St. Clair, the British Museum "over-cleaned" the marbles in the 1930s, removing not only the outer patina, but also many sculptural details. The museum countered by saying that the damage wasn't all that bad—and that the marbles would remain in London.

The Parthenon originally had sculpture on both of its pediments, as well as a frieze running around the entire temple. The frieze was made up of alternating **triglyphs** (panels with three incised grooves) and **metopes** (sculptured panels). The east pediment showed scenes from the birth of Athena, while the west pediment showed Athena and Poseidon's contest for possession of Athens. The long frieze showed the battle of the Athenians against the Amazons, scenes from the Trojan war, and the struggles of the Olympian gods against giants and centaurs. The message of most of this sculpture was the triumph of knowledge and civilization—that is, Athens—over the forces of darkness and barbarians. An interior frieze showed scenes from the Panathenaic Festival each August, when citizens processed through the streets, bringing a new tunic for the statue of Athena. Only a few fragments of any of these sculptures remain in place, and visitors will have to decide for themselves whether it's a good or a bad thing that Lord Elgin removed so much before the smog became endemic in Athens and ate away much of what he left here.

*Tips*  **The August Full Moon**

For the past couple of years, 55 ancient sites throughout Greece—including, of course, the Acropolis—were open to the public on the night of the August full moon. The Culture Ministry plans to do this every August—and even stage free concerts at some of the moonlit sites.

If you're lucky enough to visit the Acropolis on a smog-free and sunny day, you'll see the gold and cream tones of the Parthenon's handsome Pentelic marble at their most subtle. It may come as something of a shock to realize that in antiquity, the Parthenon—like most other monuments here—was painted in gay colors that have since faded, revealing the natural marble. If it's a clear day, you'll also get a superb view of Athens from the Belvedere at the east end of the Acropolis.

Near the Belvedere, the **Acropolis Archaeological Museum** hugs the ground to detract as little as possible from the ancient monuments. Inside, you'll see the four original Caryatids from the Erechtheion still in Athens (one disappeared during the Ottoman occupation and one is in the British Museum). Other delights include statues of smiling *korai* (maidens) and *kouroi* (young men). You'll have to decide whether you find their smiles insufferably smug or becomingly modest. While you're deciding, don't miss the graceful 5th-century relief called the **Mourning Athena**, the athletic **Calfbearer**, and the three-headed figure of the **Tryphon**, whose tripartite body ends in a snaky tail. You can see clear traces of the ancient paint that decorated much ancient sculpture on the Tryphon.

As you leave the Acropolis, you'll probably feel that you've seen a great many monuments. In fact, almost all of what you've seen comes from Athens's heyday in the mid-5th-century B.C., when Pericles rebuilt what the Persians destroyed. In the following centuries, every invader who came built monuments, most of which were resolutely destroyed by the next wave of invaders. If you had been here a century ago, you could have seen the remains of mosques and churches, plus a Frankish bell tower. The great archaeologist Schliemann, the discoverer of Troy and excavator of Mycenae, was so offended by the bell tower that he paid to have it torn down.

If you'd like to know more about the Acropolis and its history, as well as the Elgin Marbles controversy, you can check to see whether the **Center for Acropolis Studies**, on Makriyanni just southeast of the Acropolis (© **210/923-9381**), is open (usually 9am–2:30pm; admission is free). The center has been shut intermittently since excavations in 1998 for the adjacent new **museum** unearthed important Byzantine (and earlier) antiquities. The center houses artifacts, reconstructions, photographs, drawings, and plaster casts of the Elgin Marbles.

If you find the Acropolis too crowded, you can usually get a peaceful view of its monuments from one of three nearby hills (all signposted from the Acropolis): the **Hill of the Pnyx**, where the Athenian assembly met; the **Hill of the Areopagus**, where the Athenian upper house met; and the **Hill of Filopappos** (also known as the Hill of the Muses), named after the 2nd-century A.D. philhellene Filopappos, whose funeral monument tops the hill.

**Ancient Agora** ★★   The Agora was Athens's commercial and civic center. Its buildings were used for a wide range of political, educational, philosophical, theatrical, and athletic purposes—which may be why it now seems such a jumble

Dionysiou Areopayitou. © 210/321-0219. Admission 12€ adults. Free Sun. This ticket, which is valid for 1 week, includes admission to the Acropolis, Acropolis Museum, Ancient Agora, Theater of Dionysos, Karameikos Cemetery, Roman Forum, Tower of the Winds, and Temple of Olympian Zeus. It is still possible to buy individual tickets at the other sites. The Acropolis is usually open Summer daily 8am–7pm; winter daily 8:30am–2:30pm. The Acropolis Museum usually closes at least half an hour earlier than the Acropolis. From ticket booth, along with a small post office and a snack bar, are slightly below the Acropolis entrance. From Syntagma Sq., take Amalias Ave. into pedestrianized Dionysiou Areopayitou, and follow marble path up to the Acropolis. Metro: Acropolis.

of ancient buildings, inscriptions, and fragments of sculpture. This is a nice place to wander, to enjoy the views up toward the Acropolis, and to take in the herb garden and flowers planted around the 5th-century B.C. Temple of Hephaistos and Athena (the Theseion).

Find a shady spot by the temple, sit a while, and imagine the Agora teeming with merchants, legislators, and philosophers—but very few women, who didn't often go into public places. Athens's best-known philosopher, **Socrates,** often strolled here with his disciples, including **Plato,** in the shade of the Stoa of Zeus Eleutherios, asking questions that alternately infuriated and delighted his friends. In 399 B.C., Socrates was accused of "introducing strange gods and corrupting youth," and sentenced to death. He drank his cup of hemlock in a prison in the southwest corner of the Agora—where excavators centuries later found small, clay cups, just the right size for a fatal drink. Another figure who spoke in the Agora and irritated most Athenians was **St. Paul,** who rebuked them as superstitious when he saw an inscription here to the "Unknown God."

The one monument you can't miss in the Agora is the 2nd-century B.C. **Stoa of Attalos,** built by King Attalos of Pergamon, in Asia Minor, and totally reconstructed by American archaeologists in the 1950s. (You may be grateful that they chose to include an excellent modern toilet in the stoa.) The museum in the stoa's ground floor has finds from 5,000 years of Athenian history, including sculpture and pottery, a voting machine, and a child's potty seat, all with labels in English. The stoa is open Tuesday through Sunday from 8:30am to 2:45pm.

As you leave the stoa, take a moment to look at the charming little 11th-century Byzantine **Church of the Holy Apostles,** also restored by the Americans. The church is almost always closed, but its delicate proportions come as a relief after the somewhat heartless facade of the Stoa of Attalos.

Below the Acropolis on the edge of Monastiraki (entrance on Adrianou, near Ayiou Philippou Sq., east of Monastiraki Sq. and on Ay. Apostoli, the road leading down into Plaka from the Acropolis). © 210/321-0185. Admission (includes museum) 4€. Metro: Monastiraki.

**Hadrian's Arch** ★  The Roman emperor Hadrian built a number of monuments in Athens, including this enormous triumphal arch with its robust, highly ornamental Corinthian columns. Although Hadrian was a philhellene, he didn't hesitate to use his arch to let the Athenians know who was boss: An inscription facing the Acropolis side reads THIS IS ATHENS, THE ANCIENT CITY OF THESEUS. On the other side it states THIS IS THE CITY OF HADRIAN, NOT OF THESEUS. Ironically, much more of ancient Athens is visible today than of Hadrian's Athens, and much of Roman Athens lies unexcavated under modern Athens.

Hadrian's Arch is still a symbolic entrance to Athens: A number of times when demonstrations blocked traffic from the airport into central Athens, our taxi driver told us that he could get us as far as Hadrian's Gate, and that we'd have to walk into town from there.

On Leoforos Amalias, near the Temple of Olympian Zeus, and easily seen from the street. Free. Metro: Syntagma or Acropolis.

**The Kerameikos** ★  You may not immediately think that you'd want to visit ancient Athens's most famous ancient cemetery, located just outside the city walls—but this is a lovely spot. Many handsome monuments from the 4th century B.C. and later are still lined up along the Street of the Tombs, and relatively few visitors come here. This can be a nice place to sit and imagine **Pericles** putting the final touches on his **Funeral Oration** for the Athenian soldiers killed during the first year's fighting in the Peloponnesian War. Athens, Pericles said, was the "school of Hellas" and a "pattern to others rather than an imitator of any." Offering comfort to the families of the fallen, he urged the widows to remember that the greatest glory belonged to the woman who was "least talked of among men either for good or for bad"—which must have caused a few snickers in the audience, since Pericles's own mistress, Aspasia, was the subject of considerable gossip.

Very often ancient Greek words turn out to hide familiar English words, and that's true of the Kerameikos. The name honors the hero Keramos, who was something of a patron saint of potters, giving his name both to the ceramics made here and to the district itself. The Kerameikos was a major crossroads in antiquity, rather like today's Omonia Square, where major roads from outside Athens converged before continuing into the city. You can see remains of the massive **Dipylon Gate,** where most roads converged, and the **Sacred Gate,** where marchers in the Panathenaic Festival gathered before marching through the ancient Agora and climbing up to the Parthenon. What you can't see is the remains of **Plato's Academy,** which was in this district, but has thus far eluded archaeologists.

The **Oberlaender Museum,** with a collection of terra-cotta figures and finds from the Kerameikos, is usually open when the site is. If you like cemeteries, ancient and modern, be sure to visit Athens's enormous **First Cemetery,** near the Athens Stadium, which has acres of monuments, many at least as elaborate as anything you'll see at the Kerameikos.

148 Ermou. ☎ 210/346-3553. Admission 2€. Tues–Sun 8:30am–3pm. Walk west from Monastiraki Sq. on Ermou past Thisío Metro station; cemetery is on the right. Metro: Monastiraki or Thesíon.

**The Roman Agora (Forum)** ★ One of the nicest things about the Roman Agora is that, if you don't want to inspect it closely, you can take it in from one of the Plaka cafes and restaurants on its periphery.

In addition to building a number of monuments on the Acropolis and in the ancient Agora, Roman leaders, beginning with Julius Caesar, built their own agora, or forum, an extension of the Greek agora. If the area between the Greek agora and the Roman forum were to be excavated, we'd have lots more of both. That's just what some archaeologists want, and precisely what Plaka merchants and fans of the district do not want. At present, the Roman Agora is a pleasant mélange of monuments from different eras, including a mosque built here after the Byzantine Empire was conquered by Mehmet II in 1453.

The Roman Agora's most endearing monument is the octagonal **Tower of the Winds,** with its relief sculptures of eight gods of the winds, including Boreas blowing on a shell. Like so many monuments in Athens—the Parthenon itself had a church inside it for centuries—the Tower of the Winds has had a varied history. Built by a 1st-century B.C. astronomer as a combination sundial and water-powered clock, it became a home for whirling dervishes in the 18th century. When Lord Byron visited Athens, he lodged near the tower, spending much of his time writing lovesick poetry to the beautiful "Maid of Athens."

You can usually find the remains of the Roman latrine near the Tower of the Winds by following the sound of giggles and seeing people taking pictures of each other in the seated position. The less-well-preserved remains of the enormous and once-famous **library of Emperor Hadrian** go largely unnoticed. Draw your own conclusions.

Enter from corner of Pelopida and Eolou. Admission 2€. Tues–Sun 8:30am–2:45pm. Metro: Acropolis.

**The Theater of Dionysos and The Odeum (Odeion; also known as the Irodio) of Herodes Atticus** ★    This theater of Dionysos was built in the 4th century B.C. to replace and enlarge the earlier theater in which the plays of the great Athenian dramatists were first performed. The new theater seated some 17,000 spectators in 64 rows of seats, 20 of which survive. Most spectators sat on limestone seats—and probably envied the 67 grandees who got to sit in the handsome Pentelic marble thronelike seats in the front row. The most elegant throne belonged to the priest of Dionysos, the god of wine, revels, and theater; appropriately, carved satyrs and bunches of grapes ornament the priest's throne.

The Odeum (Music Hall) was one of an astonishing number of monuments built in Greece by the wealthy 2nd-century A.D. philhellene Herodes Atticus. If you think it looks suspiciously well preserved, you're right: It was reconstructed in the 19th century. Although your 2€ entrance ticket for the Theater of Dionysos in theory allows you entrance to the Odeum, this is misleading, as the Odeum is usually closed, and open only for performances—when, obviously, you can not wander around. The best way to see the Odeum is either looking down from the Acropolis or, better yet, by attending one of the performances staged here during the Athens Festival each summer. If you come to an event here, bring a cushion: marble seats are as hard as you'd expect, and the cushions provided are lousy.

Dionissiou Areopayitou, on the south slope of the Acropolis. ℂ 210/322-4625. Admission 2€ (for both monuments). Theater of Dionysos daily 8:30am–3pm; Odeum during performances and sometimes on the day of performances. Metro: Acropolis.

**The Temple of Olympian Zeus (the Olympieion, also known as the Kolonnes [the columns])** ★★    Hadrian also built this massive temple—or, rather, he finished the construction that had begun in the 6th century B.C. and continued on and off (more of than on) for 700 years. At 108m long and 43m wide (360 ft. by 143 ft.), this was one of the largest temples in the ancient world. The thirteen 17m- (56-ft.-) high Pentelic marble columns that remain standing, as well as the one sprawled on the ground, give a good idea of how impressive this forest of columns must have been—although we have a sneaking suspicion that it may be more appealing as a ruin than it ever was as a contender for the title "mother of all temples." Inside, side by side, were statues of Zeus and of Hadrian.

At Leoforos Vas. Olgas and Amalias and easily seen from the street. ℂ 210/922-6330. Admission 2€. Tues–Sun 8:30am–3pm. Metro: Syntagma or Acropolis.

## TOP MUSEUMS

**Benaki Museum** ★★    This stunning private collection includes treasures from the Neolithic era to the 20th century. The folk art collection (including magnificent costumes and icons) is superb, as are the two entire rooms from 18th-century northern Greek mansions, the ancient Greek bronzes, gold cups, Fayum portraits, and rare early Christian textiles. A new wing doubles the exhibition space of the original 20th-century neoclassical town house that belonged to the wealthy Benaki family. The museum shop is excellent, the café (which offers a 25€ buffet dinner Thurs evenings) has a spectacular view over Athens, and new galleries will house special exhibitions. A very pleasant place to spend several hours.

1 Koumbari (at Leoforos Vasilisis Sofias, Kolonaki; 5 blocks east of Syntagma Sq.). ℂ 210/367-1000. www. benaki.gr. Admission 6€; free Thurs. Mon, Wed, Fri, Sat 9am–5pm; Thurs 9am–midnight; Sun 9am–3pm; closed Tues. Metro: Syntagma.

**Byzantine Museum** ✪✪  If you love icons (paintings, usually of saints, usually on wood) or want to find out about them, this is the place to go. As its name makes clear, this museum, in a 19th-century Florentine-style villa, is devoted to the art and history of the Byzantine era (roughly A.D. 4th–15th centuries), and is devoted to the art and history of the Byzantine era (roughly A.D. 4th–15th centuries). Selections from Greece's most important collection of icons and religious art-along with sculptures, altars, mosaics, religious vestments, Bibles, and a small-scale reconstruction of an early Christian basilica-are exhibited on several floors around a courtyard. Allow at least an hour for your visit; two is better; if there is a special exhibit, try to allow 3 hours or more.

22 Vasilissis Sofias Ave. ☎ 210/723-1570 or 210/721-1027. Admission 4€. Tues–Sun 8:30am–3pm. From Syntagma Sq., walk along Queen Sophias Ave. for about 15 min. The museum is on your right. If you come to the Hilton Hotel, you have gone too far.

**Greek Folk Art Museum** ✪✪  This endearing small museum has dazzling embroideries and costumes from all over the country, and a small room with zany frescoes of gods and heroes done by the eccentric artist Theofilos Hadjimichael, who painted in the early part of the 20th century. We stop by here every time we're in Athens, always finding something new, always looking forward to our next visit—and always glad we weren't born Greek women 100 years ago, when we would have spent endless hours embroidering, crocheting, and weaving. Much of what is on display was made by young women for their *proikas* (dowries) in the days when a bride was supposed to arrive at the altar with enough embroidered linen, rugs, and blankets to last a lifetime.

17 Kidathineon, Plaka. ☎ 210/322-9031. Admission 2€. Tues–Sun 10am–2pm. Metro: Syntagma or Acropolis.

**National Archaeological Museum** ✪✪✪  This is an enormous and enormously popular museum; try to be at the door when it opens so that you can see the exhibits, and not just the backs of other visitors. Early arrival, except in high summer, should give you at least an hour before most tour groups arrive; alternatively, get here an hour before closing or at lunchtime, when the tour groups may not be as dense. If possible, come more than once, so that your experience here is a pleasure rather than an endurance contest.

Unfortunately, at press time, the museum was closed and there had been no announcement of how the collection would be reinstalled when the museum reopened in May of 2004. Therefore, we are giving you a sense of what some of the treasures here are, although we can not tell you where they will be. You may want to e-mail the museum for additional information before your visit at protocol@eam.culture.gr. or check out the Ministry of Culture's website (www.culture.gr).

The **Mycenaean Collection** includes gold masks, cups, dishes, and jewelry unearthed from the site of Mycenae by Heinrich Schliemann in 1876. Many of these objects are small and delicate, and very hard to see when the museum is crowded. Don't miss the stunning **burial mask** that Schliemann misnamed the "Mask of Agamemnon." Alas, Schliemann was wrong: Spoilsport archaeologists are sure that the mask is not Agamemnon's, but belonged to an earlier, unknown monarch. Also not to be missed are the stunning **Vaphio cups,** showing mighty bulls, unearthed in a tomb at a seemingly insignificant site in the Peloponnese. If little Vaphio could produce these riches, what else remains to be found in future excavations?

The museum also has a stunning collection of **Cycladic figurines,** named after the island chain. Although these figurines are among the earliest known Greek sculpture (about 2,000 B.C.), almost everyone is struck by how modern they look, often comparing the idols' faces to those wrought by Modigliani. One figure, a musician with a lyre, seems to be concentrating on his music, cheerfully oblivious to his onlookers. If you are fond of these Cycladic sculptures, be sure to take in the superb collection at the N.P. Goulandris Foundation Museum of Cycladic Art (see below).

The museum has a staggeringly large sculpture collection. You may want to simply wander along, stopping when something catches your fancy. Almost everyone's fancy is captured by the **bronzes,** from the tiny jockey to the monumental figure variously identified as Zeus or Poseidon. Much ink has been spilt trying to prove that the god was holding either a thunderbolt (which would make him Zeus) or a trident (which would mean that he was Poseidon). And who could resist the bronze figures of the staggeringly handsome young men, perhaps athletes, seemingly about to step forward and sprint away through the crowds?

In the past, the museum's second floor has housed its vast collection—not surprisingly, the finest in the world—collection of Greek vases. This is also where the **frescoes** from the site of Akrotiri on the island of Santorini (Thira) were displayed. Check to see if the magnificent vases and splendid frescoes are once more on display here. Around 1450 B.C., the volcanic island exploded, destroying not just most of the island itself but also, some say, the Minoan civilization of Crete. Could Santorini's virtual disappearance have given rise to the legend of the lost civilization of Atlantis? Perhaps. Fortunately, these beautiful frescoes survived and were brought to Athens for safekeeping and display. Just as Athens wants the Elgin Marbles back, the present-day inhabitants of Santorini want their frescoes back, hoping that the crowds who come to see them in Athens will come instead to Santorini. There are as many theories on what these frescoes show as there are tourists in the museum on any given day. Who were the boxing boys? Were there monkeys on Santorini, or does the scene show another land? Are the ships sailing off to war, or returning home? No one knows, but it's impossible to see these lilting frescoes and not envy the people of Akrotiri who looked at such beauty every day.

44 Patission. C **210/821-7724.** Fax 210/821-3573. Admission 6€ or 12€ with admission to the Acropolis. Anticipated hours Mon 12:30–5pm; Tues–Fri 8am–5pm; Sat–Sun and holidays 8:30am–3pm. (The museum is sometimes open to 7pm, but you cannot count on this.) The museum is a 3rd of a mile (10 min. on foot) north of Omonia Sq. on the road named Leoforos 28 Octobriou but usually called Patission. Metro: Omonia.

**N. P. Goulandris Foundation Museum of Cycladic Art** ★★★ This handsome museum opened its doors in 1986 and houses the astonishing collection of Nicolas and Aikaterini Goulandris, the largest collection of Cycladic art outside the National Archaeological Museum. There are some 230 stone and pottery vessels and figurines from the 3rd millennium B.C. on view, and if you didn't make up your mind at the National Museum that the faces of the idols remind you of the work of Modigliani, here's your chance. Despite the impressive number of displays, this museum is as congenial as the National Museum is overwhelming. It helps that the Goulandris does not usually get the same huge crowds, and it also helps that the galleries here are small and well lit, with labels throughout in Greek and English. The collection of Greek vases is both small and exquisite—the ideal place to find out if you prefer black or red figure vases. The museum's elegant little shop, which takes most major credit cards, has reproductions of a number of items from the collection, including a pert Cycladic pig.

When you've seen all you want to here (and perhaps refreshed yourself with something in the basement snack bar), be sure to walk through the courtyard into the museum's newest acquisition: the elegant 19th-century **Stathatos Mansion**, with some of the original furnishings, providing a glimpse of how wealthy Athenians lived a hundred years ago.

4 Neophytou Douka. © 210/722-8321. www.cycladic-m.gr. Admission 4€. Mon and Wed–Fri 10am–4pm; Sat 10am–3pm. Metro: Syntagma.

**Museum of Greek Popular Musical Instruments** ★★   Photographs show the musicians, while recordings let you listen to the tambourines, Cretan lyres, lutes, pottery drums, and clarinets on display. Not only that, but this museum is steps from the excellent Platanos taverna, so you can alternate the pleasures of food, drink, and music. Once when we were here, an elderly Greek gentleman listened to some music, transcribed it, stepped out into the courtyard, and played it on his own violin! The shop has a wide selection of CDs and cassettes.

1–3 Diogenous (around the corner from the Tower of the Winds). © 01-325-0198. Free admission. Tues and Thurs–Sun 10am–2pm; Wed noon–6pm. Diogenous 1–3 (around the corner from the Tower of the Winds). © 01-325-0198. Free admission. Tues and Thurs–Sun 10am–2pm; Wed noon–6pm. Metro: Acropolis or Monastiraki.

## 2 More Museums & Galleries

### MORE MUSEUMS

**The Athens City Museum**   This handsomely restored 19th-century Athenian town house is where modern Greece's first king, young King Otho, and his bride, Amalia, lived while a more spacious royal palace (now the Parliament) was built. Poor Otho (a Bavarian princelet) attempted to ingratiate himself with his Greek subjects by wearing the *foustanella* (short pleated skirt); most thought him listened to some music, transcribed it, stepped out into the courtyard, and dotry. He and Amalia were sent packing in 1862 and Greece imported a new king, George I, from Denmark.

The museum has a wonderful collection of watercolors of 19th-century Athens, including many by the English painter—and author of *The Owl and the Pussy-Cat*—Edward Lear. Amalia's piano is still here, along with some nice portraits of the royal couple. There's even a mini–throne room where the royal couple received important visitors—and a wonderful model of the amazingly small town of Athens in 1842.

7 Paparigopoulou (Klathmonos Sq., off Stadiou). © 210/323-0168. Fax 210/322-0765. www.athenscitymuseum.gr. Admission 2€. Mon, Wed, and Fri–Sat 9am–1:30pm. Possible Sun openings. Metro: Syntagma.

**Hellenic Cosmos** *Kids*   This high-tech museum, housed in a former factory, has interactive displays showing the history of Greece from ancient to modern times, a cafe, an Internet cafe, and museum shop. There's usually an English-speaking guide on duty, but if you call ahead, you can make sure that one is available (and that there are not lots of school groups visiting when you want to come).

254 Pireos, Tavros (near Kallithea metro station). © 210/483-5300. http://hellenic-cosmos.gr. Admission 4€. Mon–Fri 9am–4pm, Sun 11am–3pm. Metro: Kallithea.

**Ilias Lalaounis Jewelry Museum** ★   The 3,000 pieces of jewelry on display here are so spectacular that even those with no special interest in baubles will enjoy this glitzy new museum, founded by one of Greece's most successful jewelry designers. The first floor contains a boutique and small workshop. The second and third floors display pieces honoring ancient, Byzantine, and Cycladic designs, as well as plants, animals, and insects. The shop carries copies of some of the displays, and jewelers in the museum's workshop take orders, in case you want your own gold necklace inspired by insect vertebrae.

12 Kalisperi (at Karyatidon). © **210/922-1044.** Fax 210/923-7358. www.lalaounis-jewelrymuseum.gr. jewelrymuseum@ath.forthnet.gr. Admission 4€. Mon and Thurs–Sat 9am–4pm, Wed 9am–9pm (free after 3pm), Sun 10am–4pm. Walk 1 block south of the Acropolis between the Theater of Dionysos and the Odeum of Herodes Atticus. Metro: Acropolis.

**The Jewish Museum** ★ Greece's Jewish community, a strong presence throughout the country, and a dominant force in Thessaloniki, was essentially obliterated in the Holocaust. Heartrending exhibits here include the wedding photograph of Yosef Levy and Dona Habif, who married in April 1944 and a month later were sent to Auschwitz, where they were killed. Articles of daily life and religious ceremony include children's toys and special Passover china. Perhaps the most impressive exhibit is the handsome reconstruction of the Patras synagogue. Most exhibits have English labels. If you contact museum curator Zanet Battinou in advance of your visit, she will try to have a staff member take you through the collection.

39 Nikis (on the left side of Nikis as you walk away from Syntagma Sq.). © **210/322-5582.** Fax 210/323-1577. www.jewishmuseum.gr. jmg@otenet.gr. Admission 3€. Mon–Fri 9am–2:30pm; Sun 10am–2pm. Metro: Syntagma.

**The Kanellopoulos Museum** The Kanellopoulos, in a former private home with a wonderful position high on the slopes of the Acropolis, is another nice place to visit when you've had your fill of big museums. This private collection has some superb red and black figure vases, stunning Byzantine and post-Byzantine icons, and even some Mycenaean pottery baby bottles. The house itself, with some fine painted ceilings, is a delight.

Theorias and Panos, Plaka. © **210/321-2313.** Admission 2€. Tues–Sun 8:30am–3pm.

**The National Gallery** The core collection here is small, and of that, little is on display. Still, it's well worth finding out if there's a special exhibit on: The El Greco exhibit in 1999 and 2000 was a blockbuster.

50 Vasileos Konstantinou. © **210/723-5857.** Admission 6€. Mon and Wed–Sat 9am–3pm; Sun 10am–2pm. Sometimes open Mon and Wed 6–9pm during special exhibits. Metro: Evangelismos.

**The Numismatic Museum** Many Greek coins were works of art, and it's nice to see them handsomely displayed in the magnificent 19th-century town house of the great archaeologist Henrich Schliemann. Until this museum opened in 1999, visitors could only imagine the decor behind the ornate arcaded facade of Schliemann's mansion. Lest anyone forget that he had discovered Troy, Schliemann emblazoned the inscription *Iliou Melathron* (Palace of Troy) across the facade. The interior is equally impressive, as are the more than 60,000 ancient bronze, silver, and gold coins on view (many displayed with helpful magnifying lenses).

12 Panepistimiou. © **210/364-3774.** Admission 3€; free Sun. Tues–Sun 8am–2:30pm. Metro: Syntagma.

## GALLERIES

One of the great pleasures of visiting Athens is browsing in its small art galleries. This is a wonderful way to get a sense of the contemporary Greek art scene—and possibly buy something to take home. Openings are usually open to the public, so if you see a notice of one, feel free to stop by. A good way to check on what's on is to pick up a free copy of the quarterlies **Art and the City** or **The**

**Athens Contemporary Art Map.** Both are free, bilingual in Greek and English, and usually available in hotels and galleries. In case you don't immediately find a copy, here are some galleries to keep an eye out for.

In trendy Psiri, the **Epistrofi Gallery,** Taki 6–8 (☎ 210/321-8640; www. epistrofi.gr), has occasional concerts as well as shows. The **Epikentro Gallery,** Armodiou 10 (☎ 210/331-2187), stages frequent exhibits in its improbable location in the Athens Central Market, while not far away is one of the city's best known galleries, the **Rebecca Kamhi Gallery,** Sophokleous 23 (☎ 210/321-0448), open by appointment only in August. **Bernier/Eliades Gallery,** Eptachalkou 11, Thession (☎ 210/341-3935), stages group exhibitions, as does **Kappatos,** Agias Irenes 6 (☎ 210/321-7931). There are also frequent shows at the **Melina Mercouri Cultural Center,** Iraklidon and Thessalonikis 66 (☎ 210/345-2150), near the Thession, and at the **Melina Mercouri Foundation,** Polygnotou 9–11 (☎ 210/331-5601), in Plaka.

The fashionable Kolonaki district is chock-a-block with galleries; The **Athens Art Center,** Glyconos 4, Dexameni (☎ 210/721-3938), **Photohoros,** Tsakalof 44 (☎ 210/321-0448), and **Medussa,** Xenokratous 7 (☎ 210/724-4552), are three to look for. The **Athens Arts and Technology School** (☎ 210/381-3700) usually stages shows around town in July and August, when many galleries close or move out of town. One just-out-of-town suburban gallery that's open year-round and well worth a visit (in part for its great cafe and shop) is the **Deste Foundation for Contemporary Art★,** Omirou 8, Nea Psychico (☎ 210/672-9460; www.deste.gr) a 20-minute cab ride from Syntagma.

One small, graceful monument that you might easily miss is the 4th-century B.C. **Choregic Monument of Lysikrates,** on Lysikratous in the Plaka, handily located just a few steps from the excellent **Daphne's** restaurant (p. 164). This circular monument with Corinthian columns and a domed roof bears an inscription stating that Lysikrates erected it when he won the award in 334 B.C. for the best musical performance with a "chorus of boys." There's a lovely frieze showing Dionysos busily trying to turn evil pirates into friendly dolphins.

Three hills near the Acropolis deserve at least a respectful glance: the **Areopagus,** the **Pnyx,** and **Filopappos.** The **Areopagus** is the bald marble hill across from the entrance to the Acropolis; it is so slippery, despite its marble steps, that it is never an easy climb, and is positively treacherous in the rain. This makes it hard to imagine the distinguished Athenians who served on the Council and Court making their way up here to try homicide cases. Still harder to imagine is St. Paul thundering our criticisms of the Athenians for their superstitious devotion to the Unknown God from this slippery perch.

From the Areopagus and Acropolis, you can see two nearby wooded hills. The one with the monument visible on its summit is **Filopappos** (also known as the Hill of the Muses), and the monument is the funeral stele of the Roman consul after whom the hill is named. There are some nice walks on the wooded slopes of this hill; one nice Byzantine church, **Ayios Demetrios,** and the **Dora Stratou Theater,** where folk dances take place (p. 201). If you climb to the summit (don't try this, or any wanderings here or on the Pnyx, alone at night) and face the Acropolis, you can imagine the wretched moment in 1687 when the Venetian commander Morosini shouted "Fire!"—and his cannon shells struck the Parthenon.

The **Pnyx**, crowned by the Athens Observatory, is where Athens's citizen assembly met. The Pnyx, as much as any spot in Athens—which is to say, any place in the world—is the "birthplace of democracy." Here, for the first time in history, every citizen could vote on every matter of common importance. True, citizens did not include women, and there were far more slaves than citizens in Athens—but that was the case in most of the world for a very long time after democracy was born in Athens.

## 4 Historic Buildings

Athens was a small village well into the mid-19th century, and did not begin to grow until it became capital of Independent Greece in 1834. It's hard to believe in today's traffic-clogged Athens, but the **Byzantine Museum**, at 22 Vas. Sofias, occupies the Renaissance-style villa that the Duchess of Plaisance built—imagine this, in today's Athens—as her country retreat in the 1840s. Several other buildings from the same period, including the **Parliament House** (the former royal palace), the **Grande Bretagne Hotel** (a former mansion), and Schliemann's house, the **Iliou Melathron** (see the Numismatic Museum, above) are still standing in Syntagma Square. Unfortunately, all too many of the neoclassical buildings built in the 19th century were torn down in Athens's rapid expansion after World War II. Here are a few suggestions of some buildings you may pass on your explorations of central Athens.

In the Plaka, several 19th-century buildings have survived, tucked between the T-shirt shops and restaurants on busy Adrianou (Hadrian) and Kidathineon. **96 Adrianou** is thought to be one of the oldest surviving prevolutionary houses in Athens, dating from the Turkish occupation, and the nearby 19th-century **Demotic School** has a pleasant neoclassical facade. Over on Kidathineon is the house in which mad **King Ludwig** of Bavaria stayed when he visited Athens in 1835 (there's no number on the house, but a small plaque identifies it), and several other buildings here are former houses from the same period.

Finally, if you climb up through the Plaka to the **Anafiotika district** on the slopes of the Acropolis, you'll find yourself in a delightful neighborhood with many small 19th-century homes. This district is often compared to an island village, and small wonder: Most of the homes were built by stonemasons from the Cycladic island of Anafi, who came to Athens to work on the buildings of the new capital of independent Greece.

## 5 Churches & Synagogues

As you stroll through Athens, you'll discover scores of charming churches. Many date from the Byzantine era of A.D. 330 to A.D. 1453—although virtually nothing survives from the early centuries of that Christian empire. Alas, vandals and thieves have forced many churches to lock their doors, so you may not be able to go inside unless a caretaker is present. If you do go inside, **remember to dress suitably:** Shorts, miniskirts, and sleeveless shirts cause offense. If you wish, you can leave a donation in the collection boxes. Below we list a few churches to keep an eye out for.

Athens's 19th-century **Greek Orthodox Cathedral (Metropolis)** on Mitropoleos gets almost universally bad press: too big, too new, too . . . well, ugly. It also suffers terribly in comparison with the adjacent 12th-century **Little Metropolis**, with the wonderful name of the **Panayia Gorgoepikoos** (the Virgin Who Answers Prayers Quickly). The little church has a number of fragments of classical masonry, including inscriptions, built into its walls that create a delightful crazy-quilt effect.

The square in front of the cathedral is a great place to people-watch on summer weekends, when nonstop weddings often take place, usually in the evening. As one bride leaves the church, the next one (and her flowers, attendants, and guests) are poised to enter. It's a very Greek assembly line, with limousines pulling up, horns blaring, and everyone having a fantastic time.

Also on Mitropoleos, crouched on the sidewalk below an ugly modern building, is the minuscule chapel of **Ayia Dynamis**, a good place for women to light a candle if they want to become pregnant.

If you walk from Syntagma to Monastiraki Square, you can take in a few more churches. A few blocks from Syntagma Square, on Skouleniou, the little 11th-century **Church of St. Theodore** is also below street level, another reminder of how the ground level has risen over the centuries. Over on Hrissopileotissis, the small **Church of the Virgin** is a good place to stop and buy some incense from one of the street vendors usually here. At the **Square of St. Irene**, off Eolou, there's a very nice flower market in front of the church, and on Monastiraki Square, the **Church of the Pantanassa** is all that remains of a convent on this spot. A short walk away on busy Ermou, the 11th-century **Kapnikarea Church** sits right in the middle of the road.

If you like spying (from a respectful distance) on weddings and baptisms, continue on to the 12th-century **Church of Ayia Aikaterini**, in the little square off Frinihou. The church sits well below ground level, an indication of just how Athens has grown over the centuries. You'll notice some ancient columns strewn around the courtyard, and may even decide to sit on one while you watch the comings and goings.

If you're walking along busy Leoforos Vas. Sofias, you may want to sit for a bit and rest in the courtyard of the **Church of Ayios Nikolaos**. A few blocks further along on Gennadius, the 12th-century **Church of the Taxachi** is set in a small park.

**Beth Shalom**, the Athens synagogue, on Melidoni, stands in what was, before World War II, a vibrant Jewish neighborhood. Across the street from Beth Shalom is the old synagogue, which Beth Shalom, with its marble facade, replaced. You can get information on visiting the synagogue and on services from the **Jewish Museum**, 39 Nikis (© **210/322-5582;** fax 210/323-1577).

## 6 Parks & Gardens

In addition to the parks and gardens listed here, see "Especially for Kids," below.

The **National Garden**, between Leoforos Amalias and Irodou Attikou, south of Vas. Sofias, was once the royal family's palace garden. Now a public park, the area combines a park, a garden, and a small, rather sad zoo with shady trees, benches, and small lakes and ponds with ducks, swans, and a few peacocks. There are several cafes tucked away in the garden, and you can also picnic here. In summer 2000, the elegant **Aigli** café/restaurant reopened—after being closed for more than a decade—and staged a number of musical evenings. The large neoclassical exhibition/reception hall in the garden was built by the brothers Zappas and so is known as the **Zappion**. The garden is open daily from 7am to 10pm. *Note:* This is not a good place to loiter alone at night.

**Mount Likavitos** (Lycabettus), which dominates the northeast of the city, is a favorite retreat for Athenians and a great place to get a bird's-eye view of Athens and its environs—if the *nefos* (smog) isn't too bad. Even when the nefos

191

Panathenaiko Stadium

Diakou

Ardittou

Temple of Olympian Zeus

Grand Promenade (Vas. Olgas)

AKROPOLI Ⓜ

Finihou

MAKRIGIANNI

Makrigianni

Grand Promenade (Dionissiou Areopagitou)

Parthenonos

Frinihou

Lisikratous

Gouria

Thalou

Herefondos

Vironas

Stratonos

ZAPPEION Ⓛ

Amalias

Dedalou

Thespidos

Rangava

Zappeion

Presidential Palace

Irodou Attikou

Kidathineon

Kekropos iperidou

Adrianou

Scholiou

Flessa

Mnisikleous

Epimenidou

Klepsidras

Lysiou

Kirriston

Eretheos

NATIONAL GARDEN

Filellinon

Nikodimou

Nikodimou

A. Filotheis

Diogenous

Kirriston

Adrianou

Parliament

Amalias

Xenofondos

Voulis

Niks

Apollonos

Aiolou

Leoforos El. Venizelou

Othonos

Mitropoleos

Mitropoleos

Kolonaki Square

Kanari

Syntagma Square

SYNTAGMA

SYNTAGMA Ⓜ

Georgiou A.

Ermou

Monastiraki Square

Perikleos

MONASTIRAKI Ⓜ

0    100 meters
0    1/10 mile

N

Ⅲ

Metro:
Ⓜ Line 1
Ⓜ Line 2
Ⓜ Line 3
Ⓛ Light Rail

is bad, sunsets can be spectacular here. On top, there's a small **Chapel of Ayios Yioryios** (St. George), whose name-day is celebrated on April 23. Each summer, there are performances at the Lykavitos Theater here. You can take the funicular (which leaves every 20 min. in summer) from the top of Ploutarchou (2€), or walk up from Dexameni Square, which is the route preferred by young lovers, the energetic—and all too many who come here to dump kittens and garbage, and to use drugs.

If you find yourself heading along Leoforos Vas. Sofias, check to see whether the planned expansion of **Eleftherias Park**, beside Athens's handsome concert hall (the Megaron), has been completed. If so, this will be another very welcome addition to the much-needed "green lungs" of central Athens.

## 7 Especially for Kids

The **National Garden** off Syntagma Square has a small **zoo**, several duck ponds, a playground, and lots of room to run around. There's also a **Children's Library** with books in English and some toys and coloring materials (adults are usually not allowed to stay with their children). The library is usually open Tuesday through Saturday from 8:30am to 3pm, and is closed in August. The National Garden is open from sunrise to well after sunset.

There are other small parks and gardens scattered throughout Athens, but the National Garden is the best for children. That said, if you're staying in Kolonaki, try **Dexamini Square**, which has a small playground and several cafes and is below the St. George Lycabettos hotel off Kleomenous.

The very impressively privately operated **Attica Zoological Park** ★★ (© **210/ 663-4724;** atticapark@internet.gr), Spata, is home to more than 2,000 birds from some 320 species, a butterfly garden, and a small farm; the zoo, which plans to add more exhibits, is open daily from 10am to 7pm and charges 8€ admission (4€ for children). The zoo is not far from the new airport at Spata; given the state of most airports in the summer, the zoo might seem an oasis of tranquility.

The ride up **Mount Likavitos** on the cable-car railway (*teleferique*) is often a hit with kids. It usually operates every 20 minutes in summer (2€). There's a cafe on top that sells ice cream, and children can let off steam by running along any number of paths downhill.

A good place to check to see if there are any special activities going on is the **Museum of Greek Children's Art,** 9 Kodrou, Plaka (© **210/331-2621),** where admission is 2€. It's open Tuesday through Saturday from 10am to 2pm and Sunday from 11am to 2pm; closed in August. This small museum has changing displays of children's art from throughout Greece, and your children may enjoy seeing what Greek kids like to draw. Workshops for children are offered (and conducted in Greek). There are also workshops at the **Children's Museum,** around the corner at 14 Kidathineon. There are also **Karaghiozis Puppet Shows** (shadow theater) a few doors away at the **Greek Folk Art Museum,** 17 Kidathineon. You don't need to understand Greek to appreciate the slapstick comedy of Karaghiozis.

The multimedia center **Hellenic Cosmos** was founded in 1998 by the **Foundation for the Hellenic World,** 254 Pireos, Tavros (© **210/342-2292** or 210/483-5300; fax 210/342-2272; www.hellenic-cosmos.gr). It's open Monday, Tuesday, and Thursday from 9am to 6pm, Wednesday and Friday from 9am to 9pm, and Saturday and Sunday from 11am to 3pm; at press time, admission was free, with rumors of a fee in the offing. The interactive exhibits focus on Greek history and culture through the ages and draw lots of children. You can visit ancient Miletus on a virtual reality tour, browse the Web in the Internet cafe, and, more traditionally, see a collection of Greek costumes. Kalithea is the nearest Metro stop (a 10-min. walk away), but if you're bringing small children, you might want to take a taxi to avoid the walk.

There are usually lots of new-release American **movies** showing in central Athens, and a couple of hours in an air-conditioned theater is not a bad way to pass a hot afternoon. Check the English-language daily *Athens News* (www.athensnews.gr) or the daily *Kathimerini* insert in the *International Herald Tribune* for listings.

The "Scope" section in the weekly *Hellenic Times* lists activities of interest to children in Athens, including Girl Scout meetings, hiking excursions, and day camps, in its "Kids Corner."

## 8 Organized Tours

Many independent travelers (ourselves included) tend to turn up their noses at organized tours. Nonetheless, this can be an efficient and easy way to get an overview of an unfamiliar city. We're impressed by how many people we know who have confessed that they were very glad they had taken one of these tours, which helped them orient themselves and find out what they wanted to go back and see thoroughly. Almost all the tour guides have passed stiff tests to get their licenses.

The best-known Athens-based tour groups are **CHAT Tours,** 4 Stadiou (© **210/322-3137** or 210/322-3886); **GO Tours,** Voulis 31–33 (© **210/322-5951**); and **Key Tours,** 4 Kalirois (© **210/923-3166**). Each offers half- and full-day tours of the city, Athens by Night tours, and day excursions from Athens. Expect to pay about 50€ for a half-day tour, 80€ for a full-day tour, and around 100€ for Athens by Night (including dinner, and sometimes a folk-dance performance at the Dora Stratou Theater). With all these tours, you must book, and usually pay, in advance. At that time, you will be told when you will be picked up at your hotel, or where you should meet the tour.

Each company also offers excursions from Athens. A visit to the very popular **Temple of Poseidon at Sounion** costs about 50€ for a half-day trip, including swimming and a meal. A trip to **Delphi** usually costs about 100€ for a full day, which often includes a stop at the Monastery of Osios Loukas and the village of Arachova. If you want to spend the night in Delphi (hotel, site and museum admissions, dinner, breakfast, and sometimes lunch included), the price goes up about 50€ to 150€. (We've heard high praise for the GO excursion to Delphi.) Rates for excursions to the **Peloponnese,** taking in Corinth, Mycenae, and Epidaurus, are similar to those for Delphi. If your time in Greece is limited, you may find one of these day trips considerably less stressful than renting a car for the day and driving yourself.

Other companies include **Educational Tours & Cruises,** 1 Artemidos, Glyfada (© **210/898-1741**), which can arrange tours in Athens and throughout Greece, including individual tours; and **Amphitriton Holidays,** 2 Karayioryi Servias (© **210/322-8884**), which places an emphasis on history and education. If you want to hire a private guide, you can speak to the concierge at your hotel or contact the **Association of Guides,** 91 Apollonas (© **210/322-9705**). Expect to pay from 100€ for a 5-hour tour.

## 9 Spectator Sports

The Greeks are passionately devoted to soccer and basketball, and betting (legal and nationwide) on sports events is heavy. All sports events are listed in the Greek press and sometimes in the English-language daily *Athens News*. You can also try to get information by stopping by the office of the **Greek National Tourism Organization,** 2 Amerikis, and asking if anyone is playing (unless you speak Greek, do not try this by phone). The best-known soccer teams are the fierce rivals **Olympiakos** (Piraeus) and **Panathanaikos** (Athens).

The Greek national basketball team endeared itself to the nation when it won the European Championship by defeating Russia in 1987. Celebrations went on all night. (We should know: We were among the few people in Greece trying to sleep that night.) The championships take place in July or August at different venues in Europe. You may also be able to catch a game between Greek teams in Athens.

If you're in Greece when major international sports events in the world of soccer or basketball take place, you probably will be able to see them on Greek television or CNN. If you're in Greece during Wimbledon and not staying in a hotel with CNN or STAR cable service, you may have to settle for listening to the live radio coverage on the BBC.

## 10 Shopping

### THE SHOPPING SCENE

You may find a copy of the monthly magazines *Athens Today* and *Now in Athens,* both of which have a shopping section, in your hotel room; sometimes copies are also available at the **Greek National Tourism Organization,** 2 Amerikis. Keep in mind that most of the restaurants and shops featured pay for the privilege.

You're in luck shopping in Athens, because almost everything you'll probably want to buy can be found in the central city, bounded by Omonia, Syntagma, and Monastiraki squares. This is where you'll find most of the shops frequented by Athenians, including a number of large **department stores.**

**Monastiraki** has its famous **flea market,** which is especially lively on Sundays. Although there's a vast amount of ticky-tacky stuff for sale here, there are still some real finds, including retro clothes and old copper. Many Athenians furnishing new homes head here to try to pick up old treasures.

The **Plaka** has pretty much cornered the market on souvenir shops, with enough T-shirts, reproductions of antiquities (including obscene playing cards, drink coasters, bottle openers, and more), fishermen's sweaters (increasingly made in the Far East), and jewelry (often not real gold) to circle the globe.

In the Plaka-Monastiraki area, several shops worth seeking out amidst the endlessly repetitive souvenir shops include **Stavros Melissinos,** the Poet-Sandalmaker of Athens, 89 Pandrossou (☎ 210/321-9247); **Iphanta,** the weaving workshop, 6 Selleu (☎ 210/322-3628); **Emanuel Masmanidis' Gold Rose Jewelry Shop,** 85 Pandrossou (☎ 210/321-5662); the **Center of Hellenic Tradition,** 59 Mitropoleos and 36 Pandrossou (☎ 210/321-3023), which sells arts and crafts; and the **National Welfare Organization,** 6 Ipatias and Apollonos, Plaka (☎ 210/325-0524), where a portion of the proceeds from everything sold (including handsome woven and embroidered carpets) goes to the National Welfare Organization, which encourages traditional crafts. Two shops in Monastiraki have impressive selections of traditional Greek musical instruments, including bouzoukis, tambourines, and lyres; **Vasilios Kevorkian**, 6 Ifestou (☎ **210/321-0024**), and **Xannis Samouelian's Musical Instruments**, 36 Ifestou (☎ **210/321-2433**).

**Kolonaki**, up on the slopes of Mount Likavitos, is boutique heaven—but a better place to window-shop than to buy, since much of what you see here is imported and heavily taxed. If you're here during the January or August sales, you may find some bargains. If not, it's still a lot of fun to work your way up pedestrian Voukourestiou, along Tsakalof and Anagnostopoulou (with perhaps the most expensive boutiques in Athens), before collapsing at a cafe by one of the pedestrian shopping streets in Kolonaki Square—perhaps the very fashionable Milioni. Then you can engage in the other really serious business of Kolonaki: people watching. Give yourself about 15 minutes to figure out the season's must-have accessory.

## SHOPPING A TO Z

### ANTIQUES

*Warning:* If you're hoping to take home an antique—perhaps an icon or a wood carving—keep in mind that not everything sold as an antique is genuine, and that it's illegal to take antiquities and icons more than 100 years old out of Greece without a hard-to-obtain export license.

If you're looking for first editions, prints showing 19th-century Athens, a silver sword, or amber worry beads, try **Antiqua**, 2–4 Leoforos Vas. Sofias, off Syntagma Square (☎ **210/323-2220**). This is one of Athens's oldest antiques stores, and perhaps the best, with handsome ancient coins and old icons—but take heed of the warning above.

Also near Syntagma Square, **Giannoukos**, 4 Vas. Amalias (☎ **210/324-1700**), has a sound reputation, and the small but tempting **Mati**, 20 Voukourestiou (☎ **210/362-6238**), has some antiques as well as icons, plus a range of items in blue glass to ward off the evil eye. If you're near Syntagma and looking for antiquarian books, maps, and prints, try **Salaminia**, with branches at 47 Panepistimiou (☎ **210/321-8155**), and 22 Stadiou (☎ **210/331-3944**).

Over in Monastiraki on Pandrossou, there are any number of pseudo-antiques shops, and one or two good ones. **Martinos**, 50 Pandrossou (☎ **210/321-3110**), has Venetian and ancient glass, embroidery and kilims, swords and side tables. **Anita Patrikiadon**, 58 Pandrossou (☎ **210/324-6325**), also has a good selection of weavings and wood carvings. If you're more interested in reproductions than the real thing, **Orpheus**, 28B Pandrossou (☎ **210/324-5034**), has museum copies of classical and Byzantine art.

Up in Kolonaki, the eponymous proprietor of **Argyriadis**, 42 Patriarchou Ioakim (☎ **210/725-1727**), specializes in 18th-century furniture and also has a variety of more transportable bibelots. **Mihalarias Art**, 1–3 Alopekis (☎ **210/721-3079**), in a gorgeous neoclassical Kolonaki mansion, has museum-quality furniture, paintings, and just about anything else you can imagine.

### BOOKS

**Eleftheroudakis** ★, with its old quarters still open at 4 Nikis (☎ **210/322-2255**), has a new eight-story headquarters at 17 Leoforos Panepistimiou (☎ **210/331-4480**), with Athens's widest selection of English-language books and a good range of CDs, including much Greek music. There's also a cafe (with some free newspapers and journals to read) and clean restrooms. The staff seems amazingly tolerant of tourists who stop by to read, but not buy, the wide selection of books on Greece. Check the bulletin board by the cafe to see if there are any readings by local authors (sometimes in English) or upcoming concerts.

**Compendium**, 28 Nikis (© 210/322-1248), on the edge of the Plaka near Syntagma Square, is a small but fine English-language bookstore, selling both new and used fiction and nonfiction, plus magazines and maps. Local writers sometimes hold readings here. Just off Panepistimiou and steps from Syntagma Square, **Reymondos**, 18 Voukourestiou (© 210/364-8189), has a good selection in English (including some dazzling photography books on Greece), stocks English-language magazines and newspapers, and is often open after usual shop hours. In the stoa, one floor up, **Folia tou Bibliou** (The Book Nest), 25–29 Panepistimiou (© 210/323-1703), has lots of English fiction and a wide selection of maps and books on Greece, as does **Pantelis**, 11 Amerikis, up from Panepistimiou (© 210/362-3673).

In Kolonaki, try **Rombos**, 6 Kapsali, off Kolonaki Square (© 210/724-2082), for English-language books, including books on Greece.

## CRAFTS

There are lots of mass-produced so-called "crafts" for sale in Athens, which is why it's good to know about some shops that have quality work. The **Center of Hellenic Tradition**, 3 Mitropoleos and 36 Pandrossou in the Plaka (© 210/321-3023), is a wonderful place for quality traditional Greek art, including icons, pottery, wood carvings, embroideries, and prints. Best of all, you can take a break from shopping and look at the Acropolis while you have coffee and a snack at the café here. While you are on and around Mitropoleos, named after Athens's Metropolitan cathedral, keep an eye out for the shops where craftsmen are still turning out decent reproductions of icons for the faithful.

Also in the Plaka, **Anoyi**, 1 Sotiros (© 210/322-6487), is an absolute delight, with old prints, furniture, reproduced icons, and fabrics. On the fringes of the Plaka, the **National Welfare Organization** (Ethnikos Organismos Pronias), 6 Ypatias and Apollonos, just east of the Cathedral (© 210/325-0524), has gorgeous embroideries, rugs, pottery, icons, and, usually, very bored and unhelpful salespeople. The **Greek Women's Institution**, 3 Kolokotroni (© 210/325-0524), specializes in embroidery from the islands and copies of embroideries from the Benaki Museum.

## DEPARTMENT STORES

Head toward Omonia Square to see the city's best-known department stores: **Lambropoulos**, 99 Eolou (© 210/324-5811); **Minion**, 17 Veranzerou at Patission (© 210/523-8901); and **British Home Stores (BHS)** and **Klaudatos**, 3–5 Kratinou at Athinas (© 210/324-1915). BHS occupies the first two floors including mezzanine, Klaudatos all the upper floors. The building faces north on Kotzia Square 3 blocks south of Omonia on Athinas, and isn't easy to see until you're right at one of the two entrances. The self-service restaurant on the eighth floor is just a bit lower than the Acropolis and treats the startling view casually.

### Tips  Insider Tip

Serious shoppers should keep an eye out for the "Best of Athens" issue of the English language magazine *Odyssey*. The issue, usually published in July or August, and available at many book stores and kiosks, is filled with shopping tips—as well as lots of scoops on what's in and what's out in Athens.

## FASHION

If you do any window-shopping in Athens, you'll soon see how expensive most things are, except during the January and August sales. Not surprisingly, Athens's poshest clothing stores are in **Kolonaki**. Much of what you'll see is American or European and carries a hefty import duty; most of the rest is Greek designer wear. Good streets to browse include Voukourestiou, Kanari, Milioni, Tsakalof, Patriarchou Ioakim, and perhaps the most expensive street in town, Anagnostopoulou—where Versace, Ferre, Lagerfeld, and Guy Laroche have boutiques, as do well-known Athenian designers such as Aslanis, Nikos, Filemon, and Sofos. If shoes are your thing, head for Tsakalof, with a heavy concentration of the shoe stores that most Athenians find irresistible.

Here are a few individual shops near Kolonaki Square: **Artisti Italiani,** 5 Kanari (© 210/363-9085), has Italian-designed clothes for men and women. The well-known French firm **Lacoste** has men's and women's sportswear at 5 Solonos (© 210/361-8030). **Jade,** 3 Anagnostopoulou (© 210/364-5922), **Ritsi,** 13 Tsakalof (© 210/363-8677), and **Sofos,** 5 Anagnostopoulou (© 210/361-8713), all sell designer women's clothing. **Elina Lembessi,** 13 Irakleitou (© 210/363-1731), has elegantly casual tops, bottoms, and accessories. **Desmina,** 5 Koubare (© 210/364-1010), offers sportier women's clothing, with lots of pantsuits and casual wear. **New Man,** 25 Solonos at Voukourestiou (© 210/360-8876), has casual men's clothes, while nearby **Berto Lucci,** 8 Solonos (© 210/360-3775), has more trendy attire. See also "Shoes" and "Sweaters," below.

## JEWELRY

All that glitters most definitely is not gold in Athens's myriad jewelry shops. Unless you know your gold very well, you'll want to exercise caution in shopping here, especially in the Plaka and Monastiraki stores that cater to tourists.

Greece's best-known jewelry stores are **Zolotas,** 10 Panepistimiou (© 210/361-3782), and **Lalaounis,** 6 Panepistimiou 6 (© 210/362-1371), both at the foot of pedestrian Voukourestiou. Both shops have gorgeous reproductions of ancient and Byzantine jewelry, as well as their own designs. You can see more of the Lalaounis designs at the Lalaounis museum (see "More Museums" and "Galleries," earlier in this chapter).

Up on Voukourestiou, there are at least five excellent jewelers, of which we prefer **Mati,** Voukourestiou 20 (see "Antiques," above). A bit further along, **Ioannidis,** 9 Valaoritou (© 210/361-0677), is the place to head if you want a Faberge egg or Piaget watch.

One of the best shops for silver is **Nisiotis,** 23 Lekka, just off Syntagma Square (© 210/324-4183). Off Syntagma, but toward Plaka, **Pantelis Mountis,** 27 Apollonos (© and fax 210/324-4574), has reproductions of Byzantine icons and religious medals.

We've been pleased with the quality and prices at Emanuel Masmanidis's small **Gold Rose Jewelry shop,** 85 Pandrossou (© 210/321-5662). Others report satisfaction in dealings with **Stathis,** 2 Pa. Venizelou, Mitropoleos Square (© 210/322-4691).

## MARKETS & GROCERIES

The **Central Market ★** (fish, meat, vegetables, and more) on Athinas is open Monday through Saturday from about 8am to 6pm. You may not want to take advantage of all of the bargain prices (two sheeps' heads for the price of one is our all-time favorite), but this is a great place to buy Greek spices and herbs, cheeses, and sweets—and to see how Athens is fed.

Every Friday from about 8am until 2pm, **Xenokratous** in Kolonaki turns into a street market selling flowers, fruits, and vegetables. This is a very different scene from the rowdy turmoil of the Central Market, although it's lively enough. Many Kolonaki matrons come here with their Filipino servants, then let the servants lug their purchases home while they head off for some shopping and light lunch (perhaps at the fashionable **To Kafenio**). Every neighborhood has a weekly market and if you want to take in a number of them, ask for pointers at your hotel.

## MUSIC

You won't have trouble finding **Metropolis**, 66 Panepistimiou and 15 Tsakalof (C 210/361-1463). Athens's largest music store: Just follow the booming vibrations. At **Slammin'**, 22 Asklepiou (C 210/361-3611), you can buy CDs and clothes. The excellent bookstore **Eleftheroudakis** (see above) has a wide selection of CDs, as does the **Virgin Megastore**, 7 Stadiou (C 210/361-8080).

## SHOES

If you walk along Tsakalof or Patriarchou Ioakim in Kolonaki, or almost any street in central Athens, you'll begin to get an idea of how serious Greeks are about their footwear. Sometimes the biggest crowds in town on a Saturday night are the window-shoppers eyeing the shoes on Ermou off Syntagma Square. Some good-quality stores include **Kaloyirou**, at 12 Pandrossou, Plaka (C 210/331-0727), and 4 Patriarchou Ioakim, Kolonaki (C 210/722-8804); **Mouriadis**, 4 Stadiou (C 210/322-1229); and **Moschoutis**, 12 Voulis at Ermou (C 210/324-6504).

## SWEATERS

Several travelers recommend **Nick's Corner**, 48 Pandrossou, Monastiraki (C 210/321-2990), for the heavy-knit sweaters that are usually bargains in Greece. Look downstairs. You'll see many more sweaters along Adrianou in the Plaka and, if you don't mind that many of these "authentic" Greek sweaters are made by machines and imported from third-world countries, you can find decent prices almost everywhere.

## SWEETS

You'll have no problem satisfying your sweet tooth in Athens. If anything, you'll come up gasping for air as you eat the seriously sweet sweets that most Greeks adore.

The long-established **Aristokratikon**, 9 Karayioryi Servias, just off Syntagma Square (C 210/322-0546), has excellent chocolates, glazed pistachio nuts, and *loukoumia* (Turkish delight). Beware—even chocoholics may find the truffles coated with white chocolate too sweet. Next, head over to **Karavan**, the hole-in-the-wall at Voukourestiou 11 (no phone), with the best Levantine delights in town. Serving excellent coffee and sweets, **K. Kotsolis Pastry Shop**, 112 Adrianou, is an oasis of old-fashioned charm in the midst of the Plaka souvenir shops.

*Loukoumades* are the Greek donut with a difference—they are about the size of an American donut hole, served hot, drenched in honey, and covered with cinnamon. Delicious. If you're near Syntagma Square, try **Doris**, 30 Praxitelous (C 210/323-2671), and if you're nearer Omonia Square, try **Aigina**, 46 Panepistimiou (C 210/381-4621). Better yet, try both.

## 11 Athens After Dark

Greeks enjoy their nightlife so much that they take an afternoon nap to rest up for it. The evening often begins with a leisurely *volta* (stroll); you'll see this in most neighborhoods, including the main drags through the Plaka and Kolonaki Square. Most Greeks don't think of dinner until at least 9pm in winter, 10pm in summer. Around midnight, the party may move on to a club for music and dancing.

Check the daily *Athens News* or the daily *Kathimerini* insert in the *International Herald Tribune* for current cultural and entertainment events, including films, lectures, theater, music, and dance. The weekly *Hellenic Times* and monthly *Now in Athens* list nightspots, restaurants, movies, theater, and much more.

## FESTIVALS

New festivals spring up every year in Athens and throughout Greece. You may want to check with the Greek National Tourism Organization to see what's new where you're going.

**THE ATHENS FESTIVAL**    From early June through September, the Athens Festival (also known as the **Greek** or **Hellenic Festival**) features famous Greek and foreign artists from Elton John to Placido Domingo performing on the slopes of the Acropolis. You may catch an opera, concert, drama, or ballet here—and, usually, see the Acropolis illuminated over your shoulder at the same time. To enjoy the performance to the fullest, bring some kind of cushion to sit on (the cushions available are often minimal). Schedules are usually available at the **Hellenic Festival Office,** 39 Panepistimiou (in the arcade); © **210/322-1459.** The office is usually open Monday through Saturday from 8:30am to 2pm and 5 to 7pm, Sunday from 10am to 1pm; you will have better luck coming here in

## Tips Ticket Information for the Athens, Lycabettus & Epidaurus Festivals

Tickets for the Athens, Lycabettus, and Epidaurus Festivals are available at the Hellenic Festival Box Office, 39, Panepistimiou (in the arcade); © **210/322-1459;** Monday through Friday 8:30 to 4pm, Saturday 9am to 2:30pm. Advance booking for the Athens and Epidaurus Festivals starts 3 weeks before each performance; 10 days before each event for the Lycabettus Festival. Ticket reservation and telephone booking (as above) is also possible by credit card (MasterCard or Visa), with the exact date and performance, number and category of tickets, and the number and expiration date of the credit card. Tickets (if available) also on sale at the box offices at each theater 2 hours before each performance.

Additional information on the Hellenic Festival, including the Athens, Epidaurus, and Lycabettus Festivals is available at www. hellenicfestival.gr, www.cultureguide.gr, and www.greektourism.com. Many of these events, and others, are sponsored by the Cultural Olympiad (www.cultural-olympiad.gr), which is part of the build-up to the 2004 Olympics.

person than trying to reach the office by phone. If available—and that's a big if—tickets can also be purchased at the office by phone. If available—and that's a big **Odeon of Herodes Atticus** (© 210/323-2771 or 210/323-5582) several hours before the performance. Again, you will probably have better luck going to the ticket office than phoning there, although if your hotel has a concierge, you may be able to arrange for tickets over the phone. Shows usually begin at 9pm.

**THE LYCABETTUS (LIKAVITOS) FESTIVAL** There are usually pop-music concerts (the Pet Shop Boys and the Buena Vista Social Club have made appearances here) and other special events at the outdoor amphitheater near the top of Likavitos during the summer. For information, check with the **Hellenic Festival Office** (see above) or the **Likavitos Theater** (© 210/722-7209). Tick-ets are sometimes also available at the **Ticket House**, Panepistimiou 42 (© 210/618-9300 or 210/360-8366).

**THE EPIDAURUS FESTIVAL** From late June to late August, performances of ancient Greek tragedies and comedies (usually given in modern Greek trans-lations) take place at Epidaurus, in Greece's most beautiful ancient theater. This makes for a long evening, but a memorable one. If you take advantage of the bus service that you can purchase with your ticket (about 2 hr. each way), the evening doesn't have to be exhausting. You may also want to inquire at the Greek National Tourist Office or at the Hellenic Festival Office as to whether the bus/boat excursion from Piraeus to Epidaurus that was offered in 2002 has been reinstituted. For information, check with the **Hellenic Festival Office** (see above) or the **Rex Theater** box office (© 210/330-1881), on Panepistimiou just outside Spiromilios Arcade. You can also sometimes get tickets at Epidaurus (© 0753/22-026) just before a performance.

**THE ROCKWAVE FESTIVAL** What started as a one-time event in 1996 has taken place every summer since then, with concerts at various venues in and around Athens. Groups performing in 2002 included Oasis and Supergrass, although a number of last-minute cancellations disappointed fans. For informa-tion on what's taking place during your visit, check with the Greek National Tourism Organization or Ticket House (see above).

## THE PERFORMING ARTS

The acoustically marvelous new **Megaron Mousikis Concert Hall**, 89 Leoforos Vas. Sofias (© **210/729-0391** or 210/728-2333), hosts a wide range of classi-cal-music programs that include quartets, operas in concert, symphonies, and recitals. On performance nights, the box office is open Monday through Friday from 10am to 6pm, Saturday from 10am to 2pm, and Sunday from 6 to 10:30pm. Tickets are also sold Monday through Friday from 10am to 5pm in the Megaron's convenient downtown kiosk in the Spiromilios Arcade, Stadiou 4. Ticket prices run from 5€ to as much as 100€, depending on the perform-ance. The Megaron has a limited summer season, but is in full swing the rest of the year.

The **Greek National Opera** performs at the **Olympia Theater**, 59 Akadimias, at Mavromihali (© **210/361-2461**). The summer months are usually off-season.

The **Pallas Theater**, 1 Voukourestiou (© **210/322-8275**), hosts many jazz and rock concerts, as well as some classical performances. Prices vary from performance to performance, but you can usually get a cheap ticket from about 10€.

The **Hellenic American Union**, 22 Massalias between Kolonaki and Omonia squares (© **210/362-9886**), often hosts performances of English-language theater and American-style music (tickets are usually about 10€ and up). If you arrive early, check out the art shows or photo exhibitions in the adjacent gallery.

The **Athens Center**, 48 Archimidous (© **210/701-8603**), often stages free performances of ancient Greek and contemporary international plays in June and July.

Since 1953, the **Dora Stratou Folk Dance Theater** has been giving performances of traditional Greek folk dances on Filopappos Hill. At present, performances take place May through September, Tuesday through Sunday at 10:15pm, with additional performances at 8:15pm on Wednesday and Sunday. There are no performances on Monday. You can buy tickets at the **box office**, 8 Scholio, Plaka, from 8am to 2pm (© **210/924-4395**, or 210/921-4650 after 5:30pm). Prices range from 12€ to 25€. Tickets are also usually available at the theater before performances.

Seen from the Pnyx, **Sound-and-Light** shows illuminate (sorry) Athens's history by telling the story of the Acropolis. As lights pick out monuments on the Acropolis and the music swells, the narrator tells of the Persian attack, the Periclean days of glory, the invidious Turkish occupation—you get the idea. Shows are held April through October. The 45-minute performances in English are given at 9pm on Monday, Wednesday, Thursday, Saturday, and Sunday. Tickets can be purchased at the **Hellenic Festival Office**, 39 Panepistimiou (© **210/322-7944**), or at the entrance to the Sound-and-Light (© **210/922-6210**). Tickets are 10€. You'll hear the narrative best if you do not sit too close to the very loud public address system.

## THE CLUB, MUSIC & BAR SCENE

Your best bet here is to have a local friend; failing that, try asking someone at your hotel. The listings in the weekly *Athinorama* (Greek), or publications such as the English language *Athens News*, the *Kathimerini* insert in the *Herald Tribune*, and hotel hand-outs such as *Athens best of* and *Welcome to Athens* can be very helpful. If you ask a taxi driver, he's likely to take you to either his cousin George's joint or the place that gives him drinks for bringing you.

Wherever you go, you're likely to face a cover charge of at least 15€. Thereafter, each drink will probably cost—ouch!—between 10€ and 20€. Many clubs plop down a bottle on your table that's labeled as, but doesn't necessarily contain, Johnny Walker Red or Black, and then try very hard to charge you at least 100€ whether you drink it or not. It's best to go to these clubs with someone *trustworthy* who knows the scene.

**Polis**, 7 Pezmatzoglou (© **210/324-9587-8**), a short ride from Syntagma Square, is usually open from mid-morning to well after midnight, offering up everything from recorded classical to live jazz and pop (both Greek and American). Since it's open most of the day, Polis draws regulars who hang out to read the newspaper, write letters—and, of course, talk on cellphones. Polis serves coffee, drinks, and snacks, but not full meals.

Be especially wary of heading out of the city to the places that spring up each summer on the airport road; these spots are usually overpriced and often unsavory. That said, the **Asteria Club** (© **210/894-4558**) and the **Bio-Bio Club** (© **210/894-1300**) in Glyfada have been popular of late, along with **Riba's** (© **210/965-5555**) in Varkiza and **Gefira** (© **210/940-9221**) at 26–28 Posidonos, Tzitzifies. Expect to pay at least 20€ for a couple of drinks after paying a cover of at least that much, and quite possibly a good deal more at all these live-music joints.

## TRADITIONAL MUSIC

Walk the streets of the Plaka on any night and you'll find plenty of tavernas offering pseudo-traditional live music. As noted, many are serious clip joints, where if you sit down and ask for a glass of water, you'll be charged 100€ for a bottle of scotch. At most of these places, there's a cover (usually at 10€). We've had good reports on **Taverna Mostrou,** 22 Mnissikleos (© **210/324-2441**), which is large, old, and best known for traditional Greek music and dancing. Shows begin around 11pm and usually last until 2am. The cover of 30€ includes a fixed-menu supper. A la carte fare is available but expensive (as are drinks). Nearby, **Palia Taverna Kritikou,** 24 Mnissikleos (© **210/322-2809**), is another lively open-air taverna with music and dancing.

Several appealing tavernas that usually offer low-key music include fashionable **Daphne's,** 4 Lysikratous (© **210/322-7971**); **Nefeli,** 24 Panos (© **210/ 321-2475**); **Dioyenis,** 4 Sellei (Shelley) (© **210/324-7933**); **Stamatopoulou,** 26 Lissiou (© **210/322-8722**); and longtime favorite **Xinos,** 4 Agelou Geronta (© **210/322-1065**).

## POP MUSIC

For Greek pop music, try **Zoom,** 37 Kidathineon, in the heart of the Plaka (© **210/322-5920**). Performers, who are likely to have current hit albums, are showered with carnations here by adoring fans. The minimum order is 25€. Almost next door, **Brettos,** 41 Kidathineon (© **210/323-2110**) plays some pop and some traditional music in a very charming old-fashioned bar. If you want to check out the local rock and blues scene along with small doses of metal, Athenian popsters play at **Memphis,** 5 Ventiri, near the Hilton east of Syntagma Square (© **210/722-4104**); open Tuesday through Friday from 10:30pm to 2:30am.

## REMBETIKA & BOUZOUKIA

Those interested in authentic *rembetika* (music of the urban poor and dispossessed) and *bouzoukia* (traditional and pop music featuring the *bouzouki,* a kind of guitar, today almost always loudly amplified) should consult their hotel concierge, or the listings in *Athinorama,* the weekly *Hellenic Times,* or *Kathimerini,* the daily insert in the *International Herald Tribune,* to find out what's going on. Another good place to ask is at the shop of the Museum of Greek Popular Musical Instruments (see earlier in this chapter). Rembetika performances usually don't start until nearly midnight, and though there's rarely a cover, drinks can cost as much as 20€. Keep in mind that many clubs close during the summer.

One of the more central places for rembetika is the **Stoa Athanaton**, 19 Sofokleous, in the Central Meat Market (© **210/321-4362**), which serves good food and has live rembetika from 3 to 6pm and after midnight. It's closed Sunday. **Taximi**, 29 Isavron, Exarchia (© **210/363-9919**), is consistently popular. Drinks cost 12€; it's closed Sundays and the months of July and August. Open Wednesday through Monday, **Frangosyriani**, 57 Arachovis, Exarchia (© **210/360-0693**), specializes in the music of rembetika legend Markos Vamvakaris. The downscale, smoke-filled **Rebetiki Istoria**, in a neoclassical building at 181 Ippokratous (© **210/642-4967**), features old-style rembetika, played to a mixed crowd of older regulars and younger students and intellectuals. The music usually starts at 11pm, but arrive earlier to get a seat. The legendary Maryo I Thessaloniki (Maryo from Thessaloniki), sometimes described as the Bessie Smith of Greece, sometimes sings rembetika at **Perivoli t'Ouranou**, 19 Lysikratous 19 (© **210/323-5517** or 210/322-2048), in Plaka. Expect to pay at least 10€ a drink in these places, most of which have a cover of at least 25€.

## JAZZ

A number of clubs and cafes specialize in jazz, but also offer everything from Indian sitar music to rock and punk. The very popular—and very well-thought of—**Half Note Jazz Club**, 17 Trivonianou, Mets (© **210/921-3310**), has everything from medieval music to jazz nightly; performance times vary from 8 to 11pm and later. The **Café Asante**, 78 Damareos (© **210/756-0102**), in Pangrati, has music most nights from 11pm. At the **House of Art**, Sahtouri and 4 Sari (© **210/321-7678**), and **Pinakothiki**, 5 Ayias Theklas 5 (© **210/324-7741**), both in newly fashionable Psirri, you can often hear jazz from 11pm. The **Rodon Club**, 24 Marni (© **210/523-6293**), west of Omonia Square, features live jazz and pop many nights from 10pm. Expect to pay at least 10€ a drink in these places, most of which have a cover of at least 25€.

## DANCE CLUBS & DISCOS

In the newly trendy Psirri district, **Astron**, 3 Taki (© **0977/469-356**), describes itself as "freestyle" and has both canned and live music. The cover varies at this bar, which serves wicked shots of vodka and cointreau as well as a wide range of less lethal drinks. Astron practically bursts at the seams on Saturday nights. Hidden on the outskirts of the Plaka, **Booze**, 57 Kolokotroni, second floor (© **210/324-0944**), blasts danceable rock to a hip student crowd. There's art on every wall, stage lights, and two bars. If it's disco you're craving, head east to **Absolut**, 23 Filellinon (no phone), **Lava Bore**, **25 Filellinon** (© **210/324-5335**), **Q Base**, 49 Evripidou, Omonia (© **210/321-8256**), or **R-Load**, 161 Ermou (© **210/345-6187**). If you feel a bit too old there, head north to Panepistimiou, where the **Wild Rose**, in the arcade at 10 Panepistimiou (© **210/364-2160**), and **Mercedes Rex**, 48 Panepistimiou (© **210/361-4591**), usually have varied programs. If you go to a place that plays recorded music, keep an ear out for *I Learned to Live Free*, a medley sung by 12 monks from a monastery in Central Greece. It climbed to the top of the charts in the summer of 2000; the monks' second CD, *SOS*, was a hit in 2002. Expect to pay at least 5€ per drink and at least that much for the cover charge at all these places.

## GAY & LESBIAN BARS

The gay scene is fairly low-key; get-togethers are sometimes advertised in the English-language press. Information is also available from the Greek national gay and lesbian organization AKOE-AMPHI, P.O. Box 26002, 10022 Athens.

The friendliest gay bar is **Aleko's Island**, 42 Tsakalof, Kolonaki (no phone), a fun place where you can actually have a conversation. **Granazi**, 20 Lembesi (℡ **210/325-3979**), attracts a loud and lively young crowd. The disco **Lambda**, 15 Lembesi and 9 Syngrou Ave. (℡ **210/922-4202**), is hip and trendy with the young locals. In Kolonaki, **Alexander's**, 44 Anagnostopoulou, Kolonaki (℡ **210/364-6660**), is more sedate, with more variety. **Porta**, 10 Phalirou (℡ **210/924-3858**), and **Fairytale**, 25 Kolleti (℡ **210/330-1763**), are well-established lesbian bars.

There's also a lively transvestite cruising scene along Leoforos Syngrou; **Koukles** (the name means "dolls"), at the corner of Zan. Moreas & Syngrou (no phone), has nightly drag shows.

See also "For Gay & Lesbian Travelers," in chapter 2.

## MOVIES

Central Athens has lots of air-conditioned theaters showing new-release Greek, American, and European films. Listings appear in the *Athens News*, *Kathimerini* (the English language insert in the *International Herald Tribune*), and in the weekly *Hellenic Times*.

If you're in Athens in summer, keep an eye out for listings of neighborhood open-air cinemas, still a very pleasant way to pass an evening, although some old favorites have closed in recent years. Many of the open-air cinemas are family-owned and -run, and all are great places to watch Athenian families watching films—which is to say, talking to each other, pursuing toddlers who are trying to run away, munching snacks and sipping cold drinks, all the while keeping up a running commentary on the film. We're fond of the **Dexameni** (℡ **210/362-3942**), in Dexameni Square, Kolonaki, where there always seems to be a little breeze on a hot evening. The **Cine Paris** (℡ **210/322-2071**), on Kidathineon in the Plaka, is one of the oldest in town—and has great views of the Acropolis.

## 12 Piraeus: A Jumping-Off Point to the Islands

Piraeus has been the port of Athens since antiquity, and is still where you catch most island boats and cruise ships. What's confusing is that Piraeus has **three harbors:** the main harbor (**Megas Limani**), where you'll see everything from tankers to cruise ships; Zea Marina (**Zea Limani**), the port for most of the swift hydrofoils that dart to the islands; and **Mikrolimano** (Little Harbor, also called Turkolimano, or Turkish Harbor), with a yacht harbor and a number of fish restaurants. As if that weren't confusing enough, the absence of helpful signs at both the main harbor and Zea Limani and the constant hustle and bustle here mean that this is not an easy place to navigate. To be on the safe side, even if you have your tickets, try to get here an hour before your ship is scheduled to sail— and then don't be surprised if you curse this advice because your ship sails later than announced.

As in antiquity, today's Piraeus has the seamier side of a sailors' port of call and the color and bustle of an active harbor—both aspects, somewhat sanitized, were portrayed in the film that made Melina Mercouri an international star, *Never on Sunday*. Piraeus also has a sprawling street market just off the main harbor, where you can buy produce brought each day on island boats, including bread baked that morning on distant islands. There are a number of fish restaurants here, but many are overpriced and serve fish that's less fresh than the bread. You're probably not going to fall in love with Piraeus, but if you have some time to kill, here are some suggestions.

Aegean Ferries **2**
Crete Ferries **5**
Cyclades Ferries **4**
Flying Dolphins to
Poros, Hydra, Spetses **7**
International Ferries **6**
Northeast Aegean Ferries **3**
Saronic Gulf Ferries,
Flying Dolphin to Aegina **1**

*Note:*
*All departure locations*
*subject to change*

## ESSENTIALS

As always, keep in mind that these prices were accurate at press time and probably will have gone up by the time that you arrive here.

**GETTING THERE   By Metro**   The fastest and easiest way to Piraeus is to take the Metro from Omonia Square or Monastiraki to the last stop (1€), which will leave you a block from the domestic port. (This can feel like a very long block if you are carrying heavy luggage.)

**By Bus**   From Syntagma Square, take the (very slow) Green Depot bus no. 40 from the corner of Filellinon; it will leave you a block from the international port, about a 10-minute walk along the water from the domestic port. From the airport, bus no. 19 goes to Piraeus; the fare is 1€.

**By Taxi**   A taxi from Syntagma Square will cost up to 10€. A taxi from the airport to the port costs about 15€ to 25€.

**RETURNING TO ATHENS**   The easiest way is to take the Metro to central Athens, to either Monastiraki or Omonia squares. Most taxi drivers will try to overcharge tourists disembarking from the boats. They often offer a flat rate two or three times the legal fare. If you stand on the dock, you'll get no mercy. The only option is to pay up, try to get a policeman to help you, or walk to a nearby street, hail a cab, and hope for a fair rate.

**VISITOR INFORMATION**   For boat schedules, transit information, and other tourist information 24 hours a day, dial © **171**. The *Athens News* and the

## Tips For the Insider

From mid-July through the end of August, boats leaving Piraeus for the islands are heavily booked, and often overbooked. It is sometimes possible to get deck passage without a reservation, but even that can be difficult when as many as 100,000 passengers are leaving Piraeus on a summer weekend (as was common in July and 2002). Most ships will not allow passengers to board without a ticket. If possible, purchase your tickets in advance.

And since schedules depend on the weather, and sailings are often delayed or canceled, it's not a good idea to plan to return to Athens by boat less than 24 hours before your flight home. Also, as with most ports, this is not a good place to wander around in alone in the wee hours—unless you are looking for a walk on the wild side.

---

*Kathimerini* insert in the *International Herald Tribune* print major ferry schedules. The closest **Greek National Tourism Organization (EOT)** office (© 210/413-5716 or 210/413-5730) is inconveniently located on the street above Zea Marina (the hydrofoil port) on the second floor of a shopping arcade stocked with yacht supplies. It's open Monday through Friday from 9am to 2:30pm, but its limited resources probably won't warrant the 20-minute walk from the ferry piers. You'd do better to try to get a ferry schedule from the **GNTO** office in central Athens at 2 Amerikis (© **210/327-1300** or 210/331-0562). The small **tourist office** (© **210/412-1181**) in the Piraeus Metro station on Akti Posei-donos is usually open from 8am to 8pm. The number for the Harbor Police is **210/412-2501** or 210/451-1311.

**FAST FACTS** There are several **banks** along the waterfront. The **National Bank**, on Ethniki Antistaseos, has extended hours in summer. A portable **post office** opposite the Aegina ferry pier also offers currency exchange; it's open Monday through Saturday from 8am to 8pm, Sunday from 8am to 6pm. The **main post office** is on Tsamadoy; it's usually open from 8am to 4pm. There is also a sub-station in the Metro office on Akti Poseidonos. The **telephone office (OTE)** is a block away from the post office and is usually open 24 hours. There is another branch by the water, on Akti Miaouli at Merachias, open daily from 7am to 9:30pm. You'll find secure **luggage storage** in the Metro station at the **Central Travel Agency** (© **210/411-5611**); hours are usually from 6am to 8pm.

**TICKETS TO THE ISLANDS** The quay of the main harbor is lined with **ticket agents**, many concentrated in Plateia Karaiskaki; some sell tickets for one or two lines or destinations only, some for more. Usually, there's a sign in the window telling you what the agent sells. Almost every agent will give you one. Some readers have reported good luck dealing with **Explorations Unlimited**, 2 Kapodistriou (© **210/411-6395** or 210/411-1243), just off Akti Poseidonos near the Metro; open Monday through Friday from 8am to 7pm and Saturday from 9am to 2pm.

**FERRIES TO THE ISLANDS** You will be confused as to where to catch your boat; this is inevitable. Allow plenty of time. Even the person you buy your ticket from may give you a bum steer. Any information below may change at any moment. Sorry—but we thought you should know the truth!

Ferry tickets can be purchased at a ticket office up to 1 hour before departure; after that they can usually be bought on the boat. To book first-class cabins or buy advance-sale tickets, see one of the **harborside travel agents** (around Karaiskaki Square by the domestic ferries and along Akti Miaouli; opposite the Crete ferries). Most open at 6am and some will hold your baggage for the day (but without security). The **GNTO** publishes a list of weekly sailings, and the **tourist police** (© **171**) or the **Port Authority** (© **210/412-2501** or 210/451-1311) can provide you with schedule information.

Boats for the eastern Cyclades (including Mykonos and Santorini) usually leave in the morning from Akti Tzelepi across from Plateia Karaiskaki. Aegina boats usually leave from Akti Poseidonos. Boats for Rhodes usually sail in the afternoon from Akti Miaouli. Boats for the western Cyclades (including Sifnos) usually sail in the early evening from Akti Kalimassioti near Plateia Karaiskaki. Boats for Crete usually sail in the early evening from Akti Kondyli. Many additional island boats leave from the quay opposite the Metro station. Boats heading out of Greece leave from the quay on Akti Miaouli farthest away from the quays near the Metro and train stations. Boats for Aegina, Poros, Hydra, Spetses, Peloponnesian ports, and Kithira go from Zea Marina, across the Piraeus peninsula and opposite the great harbor, from which it is a good 30-minute walk.

## WHAT TO SEE & DO

If you're stuck between boats, you may not want to do anything except pass the time as quietly as possible. If so, you might simply walk inland from the harbor on Demosthenous or Vas. Georgiou to Plateia Korai and sit at a cafe. Or, if you want to be by the sea, stroll or take the no. 904 bus (.50€) from the main harbor to Akti Themistokleous, where there are also cafes.

More energetic suggestions, if you're in Piraeus in the summer, include finding out if there's an **open-air theatrical performance** at the Kastella Theater, a few blocks inland from Mikrolimano. In 2000, the first **Poseidon Festival**, with a wide range of concerts, took place in Piraeus; it seems to be on its way to being an annual event, and you might want to get details at the Piraeus Municipal Theater, Ayiou Konstantinou (© **210/419-4550**). In the winter, performances are staged indoors, at the Public Theater on the green at Leoforos King Constantine. The Sunday **flea market** on and around Alipedou and Skylitsi is an equally crowded variation on the Monastiraki flea market, with generally lower-quality goods. The daily **street market** just off the main harbor is a good place to get picnic supplies for your boat trip.

The **Maritime Museum**, Akti Themistokleous, near the pier for the hydrofoils (© **210/452-1598**), has handsome models of ancient and modern ships. Don't miss the classical warship (*trireme*); scholars are still trying to figure out just how all those oarsmen rowed in unison. Open Tuesday through Saturday from 9am to 2pm; admission is 2€. If you have time, stop by the **Archaeological Museum**, 32 Harilaou Trikoupi (© **210/452-1598**), to see three superb monumental bronzes, one depicting a youth (some say Apollo) and two goddesses (some say Athena and Artemis). Open Tuesday through Sunday from 8:30am to 3pm; admission is 2€.

## WHERE TO STAY

With Athens so close by Metro, we don't recommend an overnight stay in Piraeus, but if it makes sense in your travel plans, try one of these decent, moderately priced choices: the 74-unit **Hotel Mistral**, 105 Vassileos Pavlou, Kastella

(☎ 210/411-7150; fax 210/412-2096), with a nice roof garden; or the recently renovated 31-unit **Ideal Hotel**, 142 Notara (☎ 210/429-4050; fax 210/429-3890). If you want something a bit nicer, try the 32-unit **Hotel Castella**, 75 Vasileos Pavlou (☎ 210/411-4735) or the 74-unit **Cavo D'Oro**, 19 Vasileos Pavlou (☎ 210/411-3744; fax 210/412-2210). The Cavo D'Oro has a pool, but it also has a disco that can be very noisy. Frugal traveling friends who visit Greece every year always stay at the 56-unit **Hotel Triton**, 8 Tsamadou (☎ 210/4173-4578), which they praise for its relatively quiet location—and double glazed windows to cut out what noise there is.

## WHERE TO DINE

While there are some good restaurants in Piraeus, the places to eat along the harbor are generally mediocre at best. You'll do better if you walk in a few blocks along Demosthenous to Plateia Korai, where there are a number of small cafes and restaurants actually patronized by Greeks. If you do decide to try one of the seafood restaurants in central Piraeus or Mikrolimani, make sure you know the price before ordering; some of these places prey on the unwary. If the final tab seems out of line, insist on a receipt, phone the tourist police, and sit tight.

For the best, freshest, most inventively prepared seafood you can imagine, see p. 171 for a review of **Varoulko ★**, 14 Deligeorgi (☎ 210/411-2043; fax 210/422-1283).

**Aschimopapo (The Ugly Duckling) ★** GREEK   Ano Petralona is the neighborhood between the western edge of the Filopappos Hill and the Athens-Piraeus train line, technically in Piraeus. It's not far from the center of town, but you'll need a cab driver who either knows this taverna or has the Athens street guide to get here. The Aschimopapo is on the last stretch of Ionon before the ring road around the Filopappos Hill, and the entrance is marked only by a light. Still, the food here is very good, and if you are spending the night in Piraeus, you may want to head here. You may find the journey worth it. The menu offers such specialties as lamb cooked in a clay pot, snails, and *eksohiko* (pork baked in aluminum foil in individual servings), plus many other good dishes, tasty mezedes, and wine from the barrel.

61 Ionon, Ano Petralona. ☎ 210/346-3282. Reservations suggested. Main courses 8€–25€. No credit cards. Mon–Sat 8:30pm–1am.

**Dourambeis** SEAFOOD   This fish taverna near the Delphinario theater in Piraeus is where many locals go when they want a good fish dinner. The decor is simple, the food excellent. The crayfish soup alone is worth the trip, but the whole point of going is for the excellent grilled fish.

29 Dilaveri. ☎ 210/412-2092. Reservations suggested. Fish prices (by the kilo) change daily. No credit cards. Mon–Sat noon–5pm and 8pm–1am.

**Vassilenas ★** SEAFOOD/GREEK   Vassilenas has been serving its flat-fee menu for decades. Come here hungry, and even then you probably won't be able to eat everything in the more than 15 courses set before you. There's plenty of seafood, plus good Greek dishes. This is a great place to come with friends, so you can compare notes on favorite dishes. Since Vassilenas is a fair hike from the waterfront, you may want to take a taxi.

72 Etoliikou, Ayia Sofia. ☎ 210/461-2457. Reservations recommended Fri–Sat. Meals 25€. No credit cards. Mon–Sat 8pm–midnight. Closed Aug.

## 13 Day Trips from Athens

Although there are a number of tempting excursions from Athens, simply getting in and out of the city is so unpleasant that we suggest you visit most of these places as you head off to the Peloponnese (Daphni and Eleusis are on the way) or visit Central or Northern Greece (you could take in Marathon or Brauron). Nonetheless, there are two excursions—the Monastery at Kaisariani and the Temple of Poseidon at Sounion—that can be easily done as day trips from Athens.

All these excursions take you into Attica, today, as in antiquity, the name of the countryside around Athens. According to legend, the hero Theseus unified the 12 towns of Attica under Athens. Although by no means one of the most fertile areas of Greece, the Attic countryside provided Athens with wine grapes, olives, honey, grains, fruits, marvelous marble from **Mount Pentelicus** (Pendeli) and **Mount Hymettus** (Imittos), and silver from the mines at Laurium, near Sounion. Today the Attic *Mesogeion* (the word means "the middle of the earth" and refers to the Attic plain) is still known for its fine grapes, most often used in making white retsina.

Sadly, serious fires have raged through much of Attica every summer since 1995. Some forests on Mounts Pentelicus and Hymettus have been totally destroyed. Much farmland has been wiped out, and the museum at Marathon was almost lost. Be prepared to see the signs of these terrible fires for some years when you visit Attica. In addition, the new roads engendered by the airport at Spata—and for some Olympic events—have transformed much of a rural paradise into a spreading suburbia.

### THE TEMPLE OF POSEIDON AT SOUNION

One of the easiest and most popular day trips from Athens is to the 5th-century B.C. Temple of Poseidon on the cliffs above Cape Sounion, 70km (43 miles) east of Athens (about 2 hr. by bus). This is a very popular place at sunset for individuals, families, and tour groups—so popular that, if at all possible, you should not come on a weekend.

The easiest way to visit Sounion is on an **organized tour** run by CHAT, Key, or GO (see "Organized Tours," earlier in this chapter). If you want to go on your own for far less money, take the Sounion **bus** leaving from Mavromateon along the west side of the Pedion tou Areos park (off the eastern end of Leoforos Alexandras). Buses leave about every half-hour, take 2 hours to reach Sounion, and cost less than 5€. To verify times, ask a Greek speaker to telephone the local **ticket office** (© 210/823-0179). Once you're in Sounion, you can catch a cab or walk the

---

remaining kilometer to the temple. If you go to Sounion **by car**, heading out of Athens on Syngrou or Vouliagmenis boulevards, you'll probably fight your way through heavy traffic almost all the way, in both directions.

**The Temple of Poseidon** ★★   Cape Sounion is the southernmost point of Attica, and in antiquity, as today, sailors knew they were getting near Athens when they caught sight of the Temple of Poseidon's slender Doric columns. According to legend, it was at Sounion that the great Athenian hero Theseus's father, King Aegeus, awaited his son's return from his journey to Crete to slay the Minotaur. The king had told his son to have his ship return with white sails if he survived the encounter, with black sails if he met death in the Cretan labyrinth. In the excitement of his victory, Theseus forgot his father's words, and the ship returned with black sails. When Aegeus saw the black sails, he threw himself, heartbroken, into the sea—forever after known as the Aegean.

One of the things that makes Sounion so spectacular, other than its site, is that 15 of the temple's original 34 columns are still standing. A popular pastime here is trying to find the spot on one column where Lord Byron carved his name. After you find Byron's name, you may wish to sit in the shade of a column, enjoy the spectacular view over the sea, envy the solitude and quiet Byron found here, and recite these lines on Sounion from the poet's *Don Juan*:

> *Place me on Suniam's marbled steep,*
> *Where nothing, save the waves and I*
> *May hear our mutual murmurs sweep . . . .*

There was also a Temple of Athena here (almost entirely destroyed) and it's easy to think of Sounion as purely a religious spot in antiquity. Nothing could be more wrong: The entire sanctuary (of which little remains other than the Poseidon temple itself) was heavily fortified during the Peloponnesian War because of its strategic importance overlooking the sea routes. Much of the grain that fed Athens arrived from outside Attica in ships that had to sail past Cape Sounion. In fact, Sounion had something of an unsavory reputation as the haunt of pirates in antiquity; it would be uncharitable to think that their descendants run today's nearby souvenir shops, restaurants, and cafes. If you wish, you can take a swim in the sea below Sounion and grab a snack at one of the overpriced seaside restaurants, of which the Akrogiali (here since 1887), by the Aegeon Hotel, is the best. Or, bring a picnic to enjoy on the beach.

Cape Sounion. © 0292/39-363. Admission 4€. Daily 10am–sunset (sometimes in summer from 8am–sunset).

## THE MONASTERY OF KAISARIANI (KESSARIANI) & MOUNT HYMETTUS (IMITTOS)

The beautiful Kaisariani Monastery stands in a cool, bird-inhabited grove of pines and cypresses on the lower slopes of Mount Hymettus, famous for its beautiful marble and delicious honey. In fact, the 4th-century A.D. philosopher Synesius of Cyrene tells the story that the Sophists lured students to their lectures "not by the fame of their eloquence, but by pots of honey from Hymettus." This has long been a lovely place to escape the heat of Athens, especially after most of the bees left Hymettus and no longer vexed visitors. Alas, the forests were damaged in the fires of 1998, when four firemen died fighting the blazes. Keep in mind that the remaining pine groves here are a potential tinderbox. As always, be very careful if you smoke or use matches.

Kaisariani is 8km (5 miles) east of central Athens. The easiest way to visit is to take a **taxi** from Athens for about 15€. Then, if you wish, you can return by

Kaisariani is still an active church. Remember to dress appropriately: Shorts, miniskirts, and sleeveless or skimpy shirts will cause offense.

bus, having spotted the bus stop on your way up to Kaisariani. If you want the cab to wait while you visit the monastery, negotiate a price in advance. Every 20 minutes, **bus no. 224** leaves from Plateia Kaningos on Academias and from Panepistimiou and Vas. Sofias, northeast of Syntagma Square, for the suburb of Kaisariani. If it's not a hot day, it's a pleasant 2km (1¼-miles) walk (follow the signs) up the road to the wooded site, or you can take one of the cabs that waits for business by the bus stop.

We suggest that you do not drive unless you want to explore Mount Hymettus, which is no longer the woodsy place fabled in antiquity, but has become bleak after its recent fires. Kaisariani is poorly signposted, and you may have trouble finding it, even with a good map.

**The Kaisariani Monastery** ★  When a spot is holy in Greece, it has usually been holy for a very long time indeed. Today's monastery occupies the site of an ancient temple to Aphrodite, probably built here because of the spring, part of the headwaters of the River Ilissos, that flowed through Athens in antiquity. You'll see the water pouring forth through the open mouth of the marble goat's head at the monastery's entrance. Incredibly, this spring once supplied much of Athens with drinking water. Now, Greek brides who wish to become pregnant often journey here to drink from the spring, whose waters are believed to speed conception.

This monastery was built in the 11th century over the ruins of a 5th-century Christian church, itself built over the temple. The monks supported themselves by bee-keeping and selling the honey, much as some religious orders today sell jams and liqueurs. The monastery's kitchen and refectory, which now house some sculptural fragments, are on the west side of a paved, flower-filled courtyard. To the south, the old monks' cells and a bathhouse are being restored (exploration at your own risk is usually permitted). The well-preserved church, built like so many in Greece in the shape of a Greek cross, has a dome supported by four ancient Roman columns. Most of the frescoes are relatively late, dating from the 17th and 18th centuries; the distinctive bell tower is from the 19th century.

© 210/723-6619. Admission 4€. Tues–Sun 8:30am–3pm.

# THE SANCTUARY OF ARTEMIS AT BRAURON (VRAVRONA)

This little shrine to Artemis in the Attic hills is not much visited; more is the pity, since it's a lovely tranquil spot—in danger of losing its peace to the proliferating roads and increasing overhead noise from planes heading in and out of the new Athens International Airport at Spata. Brauron is located 38km (22 miles) east of central Athens between Porto Rafi and Loutsa, on the east coast of Attica.

Take **bus no. 304** for the Zappion to the village of Loutsa, which is about 2km (1¼ miles) from the site. **By car,** check for directions at your hotel, as new roads were under construction at press time. What follows is what was accurate at press time. From Athens, head toward Porto Rafi. In Porto Rafi, follow signs for Vravrona and Artemida. On the left about 600m (1,968 ft.) before the site are the remains of a 6th-century church. Traffic often backs up on the road between Stavrou and Markopoulo, particularly in Peania, so the trip probably will take the better part of an hour. You can also take the new highway from Athens to the airport and continue on to Rafina and ask for directions there to Brauron.

**The Sanctuary of Artemis** ★ Just when you think that you're beginning to understand the ancient Greeks a little bit, you encounter something like the cult of Artemis at Brauron. According to legend, Agamemnon's ill-fated daughter Iphigenia served as a priestess here, and was buried here after her ritual sacrifice on the eve of the expedition to Troy. That's the easy part. The hard part is understanding why Iphigenia and Artemis were honored here with a quadrennial festival in which little girls were dressed as bear cubs. According to one story, the custom began when an epidemic broke out after a youth killed a bear that had attacked his sister. An oracle suggested that a purifying ceremony take place in which young girls dressed like bears, and that this continued every 4 years throughout antiquity. As you sit on a shady slope, you may want to imagine the procession of little girls who came here in saffron-colored robes, and their bear-like antics. Just to confuse matters further, these ceremonies were believed to assist women in childbirth.

The most striking structure at Brauron is the **stoa**, restored in 1961. The stoa was built in the shape of an incomplete Greek letter "p" facing south toward the hill. Six rooms on the north of the stoa contained 11 small beds for the children, with stone tables by the beds. Four rooms on the west of the stoa may also have been used as bedrooms for the children. You can also see the foundations of the 5th-century **Temple of Artemis** here, as well as a cave, usually called the **Tomb of Iphigenia**. There's also a sacred spring and two chapels in this altogether delightful spot.

The **museum** is very charming, with a number of marble portrait heads of the little girls, plus some bear masks, handsome geometric vases from the nearby cemetery at Anavyssos, and grave markers found in the surrounding area.

ⓘ 22990/27-020. Site and museum admission 3€. Both open Tues–Sun 8:30am–3pm.

## MARATHON

In 490 B.C., the vastly outnumbered Athenians and their allies from the little Boeotian town of Plataea defeated the invading Persian army on the plain of Marathon, and saved Athens and much of Greece (and, some say, much of Europe) from Persian rule. In honor of their valor, the 192 Athenians who fell here were buried on the battlefield in an enormous burial mound. Beyond that, there's little to see at Marathon, as there is little to see at Gettysburg and Runnymede, but such sites are moving because of the battles that once tore up the ground and shaped the course of history. When Lord Byron came to Greece to fight in the War of Independence, he came to Marathon and wrote:

*The mountains look on Marathon,*
*And Marathon looks on the sea.*
*And musing there an hour alone,*
*I dreamed that Greece might still be free . . .*

Alas, before he could fight to free Greece, Byron succumbed to fever in the boggy, cholera-infested town of Mesolongi, where he died on April 19, 1824. Marathon is 42km (26 miles) northeast of Athens between the villages of Nea Makri and Marathona. **Buses** leave Athens from Mavromati along the east side of the Pedion tou Areos Park approximately every half-hour in the morning and every hour in the afternoon. The trip costs about 4€ and takes about 2½ hours. For departure times, call the **tourist police** (© 210/821-0872). **By car**, drive north from Athens along Leoforos Kifissias, the more scenic route that rounds Mount Pendeli through Dionissos to the sea at Nea Makri, or along the National Highway toward Thessaloniki, from which signs will direct you to Marathon.

**Marathon Battlefield & Burial Mound ★** By September of 490 B.C., the advancing force of Persia—then the most powerful empire in the world—reached Marathon, anchored its fleet in the bay, and made plans to attack Athens by land and by sea. The Athenians sent their swiftest runner, Pheidippides, to Sparta to ask for help, and marched their entire army of perhaps 9,000 men north to Marathon. When Pheidippides reached Sparta (some say that it took him about a day and a half—clearly the gods were on his side), the Spartans said they would be delighted to join the Athenians—as soon as an important Spartan religious festival observing the full moon was concluded. This was widely thought to be a delaying tactic, and Athens prepared to stand alone—and did, except for a small contingent of perhaps 1,000 soldiers from the little town of Plataea in Boeotia. The Persian force was at least 24,000 strong.

For some days, the two forces eyed each other, but neither attacked. Then, before dawn on September 12, the Athenians launched a surprise attack. As the Athenian right and left wings forged forward, the center gave way—but when the Persians pressed forward, the Athenian flanks surrounded them and the serious slaughter began. Many of the Persians tried to flee to the safety of their ships, anchored offshore, but were cut down in the marshy plain that lay between the battlefield and the sea. By nightfall, the victory was won, and Pheidippides was again dispatched, this time to run to Athens with news of the victory at Marathon. Pheidippides ran flat out, burst into the Athenian Agora, shouted "We have won"—and fell dead from exhaustion. Today's marathons commemorate Pheidippides's run. (If you want information on the annual rerunning of the Marathon in Nov, check out www.athensmarathon.com.)

Although the Athenians won the battle at Marathon, the Persian navy had not been harmed, and it set sail for Athens. The weary Athenian army marched post-haste back to Athens and prepared to do battle again, but the Persians, for whatever reason, after sailing up and down the coast of Attica, reversed course and returned to Asia Minor. Ten years later, they would be back—only to be defeated decisively in the Battle of Salamis.

The Athenian victory at Marathon, against such great odds, became the stuff of legend. Some said that the Athenian hero Theseus himself fought alongside his descendants. Others said that the god Pan had bewitched and confused the Persians, leading them to plunge to their deaths in the marshy swamp—leading them, in short, to panic, the word derived from the god's name. According to one legend, Pan also appeared to Pheidippides as he ran with news of the victory to Athens. Pointedly, Pan asked why the Athenians built so few shrines to him—a situation that was quickly rectified throughout Attica.

Although it was customary to bury war casualties in the Kerameikos cemetery in Athens, the 192 Athenian dead from this astonishing victory were cremated and buried together in the mound, which still stands on the battlefield. When the Athenian mound was excavated in the late 19th century, quantities of ashes and burnt bones were found.

Half a millennium after the battle, when the traveler Pausanias visited Marathon, he wrote, "Here every night you can hear the noise of whinnying horses and of men fighting." Indeed, there are those today who claim to have heard sounds of battle on moonlit nights at Marathon.

The mound where the Plataeans were buried, and the small archaeological museum with finds from the site and area, are both 2km (1¼ miles) from the battlefield in the village of Marathona. This area was one of many severely threatened in the fires that swept across Greece in the summer of 1998. At press time, construction of the Rowing and Canoeing Center at Schinas for the 2004 Olympics further threatened the area and its previously protected wetlands.

If you're not bothered by swimming near where so many Persians drowned in the marshy swamp, there are lots of opportunities to take a dip and enjoy a bite at a taverna along the coast here.

© 0294/55-155. Admission of 3€ includes both the mound and museum. Museum open Tues–Sun 8:30am–3pm.

## THE MONASTERY OF DAPHNI (DAFNI)

If you've never seen Byzantine mosaics and wonder what all the fuss is about, Daphni is the place to come. Daphni is one of the greatest masterpieces of the Byzantine empire, which was founded by the first Christian emperor, Constantine, in the 4th century A.D. and conquered by the Turks in 1453. The great art historian of Byzantine Greece, Sir David Talbot-Rice, has called Daphni "the most perfect monument" of the 11th century—and this sober scholar was not given to hyperbole.

Unfortunately, getting here is an ordeal. If possible, see Daphni on your way to or from the Peloponnese; if you're driving, you can easily stop here, or if you're traveling with a tour, most stop at Daphni. You could brave a taxi, but it's a very ugly ride—and the 9km (5½-miles) trip west of Athens can take an hour.

**By bus,** take no. 860 from Panepistimiou north of Sina (behind the university); nos. 853, 862, 873, or 880 from Eleftheria Square off Leoforos Pireos (northwest of Monastiraki); or nos. A15 or B16, marked Elefsina, from Sachtouri, southeast of Eleftheria Square (this trip can be combined with a visit to **Eleusis,** reviewed below). The trip will take about an hour, and the bus stop at Daphni is about 150m (492 ft.) from the monastery, which is behind the wall where you see trees.

If you're **driving,** follow the signs for Corinth out of Omonia Square. You will be on a very ugly and very crowded road for the entire journey of at least half an hour (an hour is not unusual). After you cross an overpass over the National Road that runs north to Thessaloniki (Salonika), the road rises steadily for 5km (3 miles) to the gentle crest of a hill. There is a traffic light just over the crest and another traffic light approximately 500 yards further on. Turn left at the second light and then right along the parallel road some 300 yards to the monastery. *Warning:* Due to the heavy traffic, turning off the National Road is not always easy, so allow yourself plenty of time to get to the left to make the turn.

---

**Tips** Daphni—Open or Closed?

Be sure to check with the Greek National Tourist Office (© 210/327-1300; 210/331-0562) to see whether Daphni, closed at press time, has reopened.

**The Monastery of Daphni** ★★    When you reach Daphni, you may want to take a few minutes in the courtyard to look at the church's lovely brickwork and think about the long history of this sacred spot. There have been shrines here since antiquity, when there was a temple to Apollo. The temple is long since gone (except for one column near the entrance), but the name "Daphni" (Greek for "laurel," Apollo's favorite plant), still honors that god.

In the 6th century, a small monastery was built here, later greatly expanded in the 11th century. The monastic buildings have been almost entirely destroyed, but the domed church dedicated to the Virgin Mary remains. This is something of a miracle: Over the centuries, Daphni has been repeatedly damaged by invaders and earthquakes, and repeatedly rebuilt. You'll see an example of that rebuilding in the twin Gothic arches in front of the church's west entrance. These were added by the Cistercian monks who turned Daphni into a Catholic monastery after the Crusaders captured Constantinople in 1204. During the long period of the Turkish occupation, there was no functioning monastery here—indeed, for a while, the buildings were used as army barracks. After the Greek War of Independence, Daphni was reclaimed by the Greek Orthodox church and restored to its former glory.

A severe earthquake in the 1980s prompted another round of restoration in which the church was strengthened and its dazzling mosaic cycle repaired. When you step inside and let your eyes become accustomed to the dark, here's some of what you'll see. The **central dome** has the commanding mosaic of Christ Pantocrator (the Almighty). This image of Christ as an awesome judge is quite different from the Western tradition of Christ as a suffering mortal. If you're familiar with the Old and New Testament, you'll be able to pick out familiar stories in the mosaics throughout the rest of the church. As is traditional in Greek Orthodox churches, the Annunciation, Nativity, Baptism, and Transfiguration are in the squinches supporting the dome, and the 16 major prophets are displayed between the windows of the dome. The Adoration of the Magi and the Resurrection are in the **barrel vault** inside the main (southern) entrance of the church, and the Entry into Jerusalem and the Crucifixion are in the **northern barrel vault.** Mosaics showing scenes from the life of the Virgin are in the **south bay** of the narthex (passage between the entrance and nave). Even if you're not familiar with the stories, and even if you find the mosaic of Christ Pantocrator grim rather than awesome, you may well be enchanted by the charming details in scenes such as the Adoration of the Magi.

Ⓒ 210/581-1558. Admission 3€. Daily (except on major holidays) 8:30am–2:45pm.

## THE SANCTUARY OF ELEUSIS (ELEFSIS)

Although Eleusis was the site of the most famous and revered of all the ancient Mysteries, the present-day site is so grim (surrounded by the horrors, and horrible smells, of the industrial city of Elefsina), that you'll need a very keen interest in either archaeology, mystery cults, or oil refineries to enjoy a visit here. That said, we must admit that we have one friend who says that Eleusis is her favorite site near Athens. This makes absolutely no sense to us, but if you come here, you can see if she has a point.

Eleusis is 23km (14 miles) west of Athens. To get here **by bus,** take no. A16, 853, or 862 from Eleftherias Square off Leoforos Pireos near Omonia. (This trip can be combined with a visit to Daphni Monastery.) Ask the driver to let you off at the Sanctuary (Heron), which is off to the left of the main road, before the center of town. If you're **driving,** take the National Road and exit at Elefsina. At press time, the signs pointing to the site had been removed; you may have to ask repeatedly for directions. You'll know you're getting close when you go through a small, pleasantly wooded square with several restaurants and catch a glimpse of the site off to the side.

**The Sanctuary of Eleusis** ★ The unknown and the famous were initiated into the sacred rites here, yet we know almost nothing about the Eleusinian Mysteries. What we do know is that the Mysteries commemorated the abduction of Demeter's daughter Persephone by the god of the underworld, Hades (Pluto). Demeter was able to strike a bargain with the god, who allowed Persephone to leave the underworld and rejoin her mother for 6 months each year. The Mysteries celebrated this—and the cycle of growth, death, and rebirth of each year's crops.

Despite its substantial remains and glorious past—this was already a religious site in Mycenaean times—the sanctuary's present surroundings make it difficult to warm to the spot. Admittedly, there are the considerable remains of a **Temple of Artemis,** a 2nd-century A.D. **Roman Propylaea** (monumental entrance), and **triumphal arches** dedicated to the Great Goddesses and to the emperor Hadrian. Hadrian's arch here, by the way, inspired the Arc de Triomphe, on the Champs-Elysées in Paris. Nearby is the **Telesterion,** the Temple of Demeter, where only initiates of the cult knew what really happened—and they kept their silence.

One poignant spot at the Sanctuary is the **Kallichoron Well,** where the goddess Demeter wept over the loss of her daughter, whom Hades (Pluto) spirited away. The dark god may have dragged Persephone with him through the cave here known as **Ploutonion,** which was believed to be an entrance to the underworld. It seems ironic that modern Elefsina itself is so ghastly that it has become something of a hell on earth.

If you're in luck, the small **museum,** which has been closed more or less continuously since the 1999 earthquake, but has been intermittently open of late, will be open. It has finds from the site, including several **figures of Demeter** and a lithe **statue of Antinous,** the beautiful boy who won the emperor Hadrian's heart.

Elefsina. ☎ 210/554-6019. Admission 3€; free Sun. Tues–Sun 8:30am–3pm.

# 7

# The Saronic Gulf Islands

*by Sherry Marker*

The islands of the Saronic Gulf, which lies between Attica and the Peloponnese, are so close to Athens that each summer they are inundated by Athenians—all of whom, of course, are seeking to avoid the crowds of Athens. These islands are especially packed on summer weekends, as well as whenever there is a serious heat wave in Athens. In addition, the Saronic Gulf islands are popular destinations for travelers whose time is limited, but who are determined not to go home without seeing at least one Greek island. Book well in advance; reservations in summer are almost invariably a necessity, especially on weekends. Keep in mind that most hotels charge a **supplementary fee of 10%** for a stay of less than three nights.

The easiest island to visit is **Aegina**, a mere 30km (17 nautical miles) from Piraeus. The main attractions here are the graceful Doric temple of **Aphaia** (one of the best-preserved Greek temples), several good beaches, and some pleasant pine and pistachio groves. That's the good news. The bad news is that Aegina is so close to the metropolitan sprawl of Athens and Piraeus that it's not easy here to get a clear idea of why the Greek islands are so beloved as refuges from urban life. Aegina has become a bedroom suburb for Athens, with many of its 10,000 inhabitants commuting to work by boat. That said, Aegina town still has its pleasures and both the Temple of Aphaia and the deserted medieval town of Paleohora are terrific.

**Poros** is hardly an island at all: only a narrow (370m/1,214 ft.) inlet separates it from the Peloponnese. There are several good beaches and landscape is wooded, gentle, and rolling, like the adjacent mainland, with the wonderful citrus groves of Limonodassos. Poros is popular both with young Athenians (in part because the Naval Cadets' Training School here means that there are lots of young men eager to party) and tour groups. On summer nights, the waterfront is either very lively or hideously crowded, depending on your point of view.

**Hydra (Idra)**, with its bare hills, superb natural harbor, and elegant stone mansions, is the most strikingly beautiful of the Saronic Gulf islands. One of the first Greek islands to be

## Insider Tip

With virtually all of the hydrofoils and ferries that serve the Saronic Gulf Islands, it is impossible to book a round trip. As soon as you arrive at your island destination, head for the ticket office and book your return ticket. If you do not do this, you may end up spending longer than you planned—or wished—on one or more of the islands. At press time, both Minoan Flying Dolphins and Ceres Flying Dolphins had been absorbed by Hellas Flying Dolphins.

**Tips** **Beware of Price Gouging During the Olympics**

Hotel prices were accurate at press time, but price increases of 20% and more are rumored as hoteliers throughout Greece gear up for the August 2004 Olympics in and around Athens. Horrific price hikes of between 50% and an unbelievable 300% are rumored for the period leading up to, during, and after the games.

---

"discovered" by artists, writers, and *bon vivants*, Hydra, like Mykonos, is not the place to go to experience traditional village life. The island has been declared a national monument and cars have been banished, which makes it blessedly quiet (although motorcycles are beginning to infiltrate the scene). One drawback: There's almost no decent beach, but lots of places to swim off the rocks. Despite the hydrofoils that link Hydra with other islands and the mainland, the island manages to maintain a certain sense of resolute individuality.

**Spetses** has always been popular with wealthy Athenians, who built handsome villas here. There are several good beaches, but most are home to the large hotels that house tour groups. If you like your islands wooded, you'll love Spetses; if you believe that an island should be bare and austere, you may find Spetses a bit too bland for your taste. Alas, in the last few years, summer forest fires have destroyed some of Spetses's pine groves.

## 1 Aegina

30km (17 nautical miles) SW of Piraeus

Triangular Aegina (Egina), the largest of the Saronic Gulf islands, continues to be the most visited island of Greece, due to its proximity to Athens. In fact, many of the 10,000 who live here commute daily to Athens. If you have only 1 day for one island, you may decide on a day trip here to see the famous Doric temple of **Aphaia**. Most ships arrive and depart from the main port and capital of **Aegina town** on the west coast, though there are a few that stop at the resort town of **Souvala** on the north coast and the port of **Ayia Marina** on the east coast. Ayia Marina is about as charmless as it's possible to be, but this port is your best choice if your principal destination here is the temple of Aphaia.

Despite massive tourism and the rapid development that is devouring much farmland, there are still almond, olive, and, especially, **pistachio** orchards here. In fact, the island has an endemic water problem simply because of watering the pistachio groves. Wherever you buy pistachios in Greece, the vendor may assure you that they are from Aegina to indicate their superior quality.

## ESSENTIALS

**GETTING THERE** **Car ferries** and **excursion boats** to Aegina usually leave from Piraeus's main harbor, confusingly, **hydrofoils** leave both from the main harbor and from Marina Zea harbor. Hydrofoil service is at least twice as fast as ferries and at least 40% more expensive (except to Aegina, for which the charge is only about 10% more expensive). The sleek little hydrofoils are outfitted like broad aircraft with airline seats, toilets, and a minimum of luggage facilities. (The fore-sections offer better views, but they're also bumpier.) The newer Super Cats are bigger, faster, and more comfortable, with food and beverage service. Reservations are

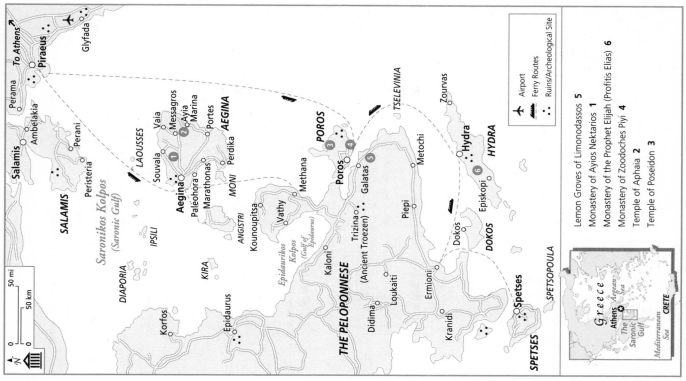

# The Saronic Gulf Islands

**To Athens →**

Piraeus

Glyfada

Perama

Ambelakia

Perani

Peristeria

**SALAMIS**

Salamis

*Saronikos Kolpos*
*(Saronic Gulf)*

*DIAPORIA*

*KIRA*

*IPSILI*

*ANGISTRI*

*LAOUSSES*

Vaia

Messagros

Ayia Marina

Portes

**1**

**2**

Souvala

Paleohora

Marathonas

**Aegina**

Perdika

*MONI*

Pedika

**AEGINA**

*SPETSOPOULA*

Korfos

Epidaurus

Kounoupitsa

Vathy

Methana

Kaloni

Trizina
(Ancient Troezen)

**THE PELOPONNESE**

Didima

Loukaiti

Kranidi

Ermioni

**SPETSES**

Spetses

*Epidavrikos*
*Kolpos*
*(Gulf of*
*Epidaurus)*

**POROS**

**3**

**4**

Poros

Galatas

**5**

Piepi

Metochi

*TSELEVINIA*

Zourvas

**Hydra**

**6**

Episkopi

**HYDRA**

Dokos

*DOKOS*

**Airport**

**∴ Ferry Routes**

**∴ Ruins/Archeological Site**

Lemon Groves of Limonodassos **5**

Monastery of Ayios Nektarios **1**

Monastery of the Prophet Elijah (Profitis Elias) **6**

Monastery of Zoodoches Piyi **4**

Temple of Aphaia **2**

Temple of Poseidon **3**

50 mi

50 km

0

**N**

*Greece*

*Aegean*
*Sea*

Athens

*The*
*Saronic*
*Gulf*

*Mediterranean*
*Sea*

**CRETE**

## Tips  Strategies for Seeing the Islands

If possible, avoid June through August—unless you have a hotel reservation and think that you'd enjoy the hustle and bustle of high season. Also, from mid-July through August, boats leaving Piraeus for the islands are heavily booked, and often overbooked. It is sometimes possible to get a deck passage without a reservation, but even that can be difficult when as many as 100,000 Athenians leave Piraeus on a summer weekend. Most ships will not allow passengers to board without a ticket.

If you go to an island on a **day trip**, remember that, unlike the more sturdy ferry boats, hydrofoils cannot travel when the sea is rough. You may find yourself an unwilling overnight island visitor, grateful to be given the still-warm bed in a private home surrendered by a family member to make some money. We speak from experience.

There are frequent **hydrofoils** from Piraeus to all these islands; you can usually visit any one for no more than 40€ round trip. Unfortunately, some hydrofoils leave from the Piraeus Main Harbor while others leave from the Marina Zea harbor—and some leave from both harbors! In addition, the schedules (and carriers) change with irritating regularity, so it's a good idea to get up-to-date information from the **Greek National Tourism Office** (© 210/327-1300 or 210/331-0562) 2 Amerikis, off Syntagma Square. (Go to the office in person to get reliable information.) At press time, **Hellas Flying Dolphins** (© 210/419-9200 or 210/419-9000; www.dolphins.gr), 2 Aetolikou & Akti Kondyli, Piraeus, served Hydra, Poros, and Spetses. **Saronic Dolphins** (© 210/422-4980), 2 Gounari, Piraeus, served Aegina and Salamis. Several cruises offer day trips to Hydra, Poros, and Aegina; for details, see chapter 4, "Cruising the Greek Islands," and below under "Essentials" for Aegina.

*Greek Island Hopping*, published annually by Thomas Cook, is by its own admission, out of date by the time it sees print. That said, it's a very useful volume for finding out where (if not when) you can travel among the Greek islands.

**By Organized Tour** A good way to see the Saronic Gulf is via a 3-island day cruise, which can be booked through a travel agent, such as **Viking Star Cruises** (© 210/898-0729 or 210/898-0829), or your hotel desk. **Epirotiki Lines** (© 210/429-1000) provides transportation to and from your hotel in Athens to Flisvos Marina, where its *Hermes* departs daily around 8:30am for **Hydra** (swimming and shopping), **Poros** (lunch and sightseeing), and **Aegina** (the Temple of Aphaia or swimming), returning to Athens about 7:30pm. Lunch is served onboard. For about 100€, you get a good tour and an introduction to travel aboard a cruise ship.

Ferry and excursion boat tickets can be purchased at the pier. For information on schedules for most Argo-Saronic ferries call © **210/412-4585** and 210/459-3123 or the **Piraeus Port Authority** (© **210/451-1456**).

recommended on weekends. Often, in order to continue to another one of the Saronic Gulf islands by hydrofoil, you must return to Piraeus and change to another hydrofoil. Some ferries go from Aegina to the other Saronic Gulf islands.

**VISITOR INFORMATION** There are a string of travel agencies on the harbor front in Aegina town, including the usually efficient **Aegina Island Holidays, 47** Demokratias (ⓒ and fax **22970/26-430**). For those wanting to pursue Aegina's history, look for Anne Yannoulis's *Aegina* (Lycabettus Press), usually on sale at **Kalezis Boatokshop**, which stocks foreign newspapers, (ⓒ **22970/25-956**) on the harbor.

**GETTING AROUND** The **bus station** is on Plateia Erhatneyersias, to the left from the ferry pier. There's good service to most of the island, with trips every hour in summer to the Temple of Aphaia and Ayia Marina (2€); tickets must be purchased before boarding. **Taxis** are available nearby; fare to the temple should cost about 12€. You can sometimes negotiate a decent rate for a round-trip with an hour's wait at the temple. **Bicycles** and **mopeds** can be rented at the opposite end of the waterfront, near the beach. *Careful!* Prices can be exorbitant. An ordinary bike should cost about 5€ a day, and mopeds should cost about 20€.

**FAST FACTS** The **National Bank of Greece** is one of four waterfront banks with currency-exchange service and ATMs; some travel agents, including **Aegina Island Holidays** (ⓒ **22970/23-333**), often exchange money both during and after normal bank hours, usually at less favorable rates. The island **clinic** (ⓒ **22970/22-251**) is on the northeast edge of town; for **first aid**, dial ⓒ **22970/22-222**. The **police** (ⓒ **22970/22-391**) and the **tourist police** (ⓒ **22970/23-333**) share a building on Leonardou Lada, about 200m (656 ft.) inland from the port. The **port authority** (ⓒ **22970/22-328**) is on the waterfront. The **post office** is in Plateia Erhatneyersias, around the corner from the hydrofoil pier. The **telephone office (OTE)** is 5 blocks inland from the port, on Aiakou. The **Nesant Internet Café**, 13 Afeas, is just off the harbor.

## WHAT TO SEE & DO
## EXPLORING AEGINA TOWN

Before you head out, try to pick up the useful pamphlet *Essential Aegina*, often available from travel agents, hotels, and the tourist police. Aegina town has a legacy of neoclassical buildings from its brief stint as the first capital of newly independent Greece (1826–28), but your primary impression of this harbor town will be of fishing boats and the small cargo vessels that ply back and forth to the mainland. Try to have a snack at one of the little restaurants in the **fish market** just off the harborfront. (Follow your nose and you'll find the fish market!) This is where the men who catch your snacks of octopus and fried sprats come to eat their catches and although tourists do come here, the food is usually much better than at the harborfront places that most tourists plop down at when they arrive. If you take a horse-drawn carriage (about 15€–20€) or wander the streets back from the port, you'll easily see the neoclassical buildings, including the restored **Markelos Tower**, where the first Greek parliament met. Fans of Nikos Kazantzakis may want to take a cab to **Livadi**, just north of town, to see the house where he lived when he wrote *Zorba the Greek*.

North of the harbor, behind the town beach, and sometimes visible from boats entering the harbor, is the lone worn Doric column that marks the site of the **Temple of Apollo**, open Tuesday through Sunday from 8:30am to 3pm; admission is 2€. The view here is nice, the ruins very ruined.

About 4.75km (3 miles) out of Aegina town, the ruins of **Paleohora**, capital of the island from the 9th to the 19th centuries, sprawl over a steep hillside. This is a wonderful spot to explore (be sure to wear sturdy shoes and a sun hat), with ruined houses and a number of carefully preserved churches. You can walk here from town, or take the bus to Ayia Marina, which makes a stop for Paleohora.

## SEEING THE TEMPLE OF APHAIA

The **Temple of Aphaia** (★★), set on a pine-covered hill 12km (7½ miles) east of Aegina town (☎ 22970/32-398), is one of the best-preserved and most handsome Greek temples. No one really knows who Aphaia was, although it seems that she was a very old, even prehistoric, goddess who eventually became associated both with the huntress goddess Artemis and with Athena, the goddess of wisdom. According to some legends, Aphaia lived on Crete, where King Minos, usually preoccupied with his labyrinth and Minotaur, fell in love with her. When she fled Crete, he pursued her, and she finally threw herself into the sea off Aegina to escape him. At some point in the late 6th or early 5th centuries B.C., the temple was built (on the site of earlier shrines) to honor Aphaia.

Thanks to the work of restorers, 25 of the original 32 Doric columns still stand. The pedimental sculpture, showing scenes from the Trojan war, was carted off in 1812 by King Ludwig of Bavaria. Whatever you think about the removal of art treasures from their original homes, Ludwig probably did us a favor by taking it to the Glyptothek in Munich: when Ludwig had the sculpture removed, locals were busily burning much of the temple to make lime and hacking up other bits to use in building their homes. Admission to the site is 4€; it's open Monday through Friday from 8:30am to 7pm, Saturday and Sunday from 8:30am to 3pm. Allow 4 hours for your visit if you come here by bus; by taxi, you might only spend 2 hours.

## WHERE TO STAY

**Eginitiko Archontiko** (Traditional Hotel) ★ This mansion, near the cathedral, only a couple of hundred feet from the harbor, was built in 1820 and renovated in 1988 with some loss of original detail, although some lovely painted ceilings remain. The guest rooms are rather small, but are traditionally furnished, comfortable, and quiet—although here, as elsewhere in Greece, motorcycles can be irritating. The pleasant downstairs lobby retains much 19th-century charm, while the garden is a very welcome sanctuary. The owners care about this handsome building (Greece's 1st president, Ioannis Kapodistrias, once stayed here) and try to make guests comfortable.

Ag. Nikolaou and 1 Eakou, 18010 Aegina. ☎ 22970/24-968. Fax 22970/24-156. 12 units, 80€ double. AE, MC, V. Closed Nov–Mar. **Amenities:** Breakfast room; communal kitchen. *In room:* A/C.

**Hotel Apollo** Ayia Marina, with lots of resort hotels, is not our cup of tea. That said, friends with small children who stayed at this glitzy beach hotel were pleased with their large bathroom and bedroom (with balcony overlooking the sea).

**Ayia Marina,** 18010 Aegina. © **2297/32-271.** Fax 22970/32-688. 107 units. 100€–150€ double. Compulsory breakfast buffet 5€; lunch or dinner 15€. AE, DC, MC, V. Closed Nov–Mar. **Amenities:** Restaurant; bar; fresh and saltwater pools; tennis. *In room:* A/C, TV, minibar, hair dryer.

**House of Peace (Spiti tis Irinis)** ★ This place is popular with young travelers, who appreciate its e-mail facilities and travel information, garden, and kitchen. The bedrooms (in double-occupancy bungalows) have high ceilings, with some overlooking the very lovely garden. Children under 12 are not accepted as guests—but everyone else is made more than welcome.

Plateia Ethatneyersias, 18010 Aegina. © **22970/28-726.** Fax 22970/28-818. the_house_of_peace @yahoo. com. 12 units, 6 with bathroom. 60€–70€ double. No credit cards. Closed Nov–Mar. **Amenities:** Breakfast room. *In room:* Some units with kitchenette.

**Moondy Bay Bungalows** *Kids* This bungalow complex, 7km (4½ miles) south of Aegina town in well-kept grounds overlooking the sea, is a good place for families. The bungalows have the usual pine furniture, and the bathrooms are decent sized. In addition to the pool and sports facilities, there is a children's playground.

Profitis Elias, Perdika, 18010 Aegina. © **22970/61-662.** Fax 22970/61-147. 90 units. 85€–100€ double. AE, V. Closed Nov–May. **Amenities:** Restaurant; bar; pool; tennis; minigolf; playground. *In room:* A/C, TV, minibar.

## WHERE TO DINE

It's a good idea to keep in mind that fish is priced by the kilo at most restaurants; the price varies from catch to catch, so it's a good idea to check the price before you order.

**Estiatorion Economou** ★ GREEK A reader suggested this portside taverna with a dark-blue canopy about midway along the waterfront, and several visits have confirmed its high quality. We recommend the lemony fish soup and grilled fish; there are also meat dishes. Grilled local lobster is sometimes available; expect to pay as much as 60€ a kilo.

Demokratias. © **22970/25-113.** Main courses 4€–12€. AE, MC, V. Daily 9am–midnight.

**Maridaki** GREEK This lively portside spot has a wide selection of fish, grilled octopus, and the usual taverna fare of souvlaki and moussaka. The mezedes here are usually very good, and you can make an entire meal of them if you wish.

Demokratias. © **22970/25-869.** Main courses 5€–12€; fish priced by the kilo. No credit cards. Daily 8am–midnight.

**Mezedopoleio To Steki** ★★ SEAFOOD Locals and Athenians head to this little place by the Fish Market for its delicious *mezedes,* including succulent grilled octopus. You can make a meal of mezedes here. If you want to eat as the Greeks do, you'll wash down what you eat here with ouzo.

45 Pan Irioti. © **22970/23-910.** Mezedes 4€–10€. No credit cards. Daily 8am–midnight.

**Taverna Vatsoulia** ★ GREEK This local favorite (but only for dinner) is about a 10-minute walk out of town on the road to the Temple of Aphaia; call ahead before you go to make sure it's open. The menu includes delectable chops, fresh vegetables (including croquettes) and a tasty rabbit stew with onions. There's sometimes live music in the flower-scented garden.

Ayii Assomati. © **22970/22-711.** Main courses 5€–12€. No credit cards. Wed and Sat-Sun 6pm–1am. Sometimes closed Thurs.

## AEGINA AFTER DARK

At sunset, the harbor scene gets livelier as everyone comes out for an evening *volta* (stroll). The **Perdikiotika,** in another one of Aegina's handsome 19th-century houses, sometimes has live music. Kanella's **Piano Restaurant** usually has live pop music (heavy on the amplified boatuzouki), while **N.O.A.**, a portside ouzeri, offers a more traditional scene, as does **Avli, Mousiki Skini** also has *traditional rembetika* music—sometimes all night! Dancers will want to find **Disco Elpianna** or the **Vareladiko** in Faros for Greek music, and the scene in Ayia Marina is sure to be lively, if a bit sordid (some holidaymakers attempt to set records for the amount of beer and retsina they consume). For more sedentary entertainment, there are two outdoor cinemas, the **Akroyiali and Olympia.**

## 2 Poros

55km (31 nautical miles) SW of Piraeus

Poros shares the gentle, rolling landscape of the adjacent Peloponnesian coastline, and has several good beaches, some decent tavernas, and a lively summer nightlife. If that sounds like lukewarm praise, we're afraid it is: Poros does not have enough of the atmosphere of an island to make us want to return often—and, in July and August, the island virtually sinks under the weight of package-tour groups.

As someone once said, "Geography is destiny": Poros (the word means "straits" or "ford") is separated from the Peloponnese by a narrow channel only 370m (1,214 ft.) wide. This makes the island so easy to reach from the mainland that weekending Athenians and many tourists flock here each summer. In fact, there's a car ferry across the straits almost every 20 minutes in summer—which means there are a *lot* of cars here.

If you wish, you can use Poros as a base for visiting the nearby attractions on the mainland, including Epidaurus, ancient Troezen (modern Tizina), and the lemon groves of Limonodasos. In a long day trip, you can visit Nafplion (Nafplio), Mycenae, and Tiryns.

## ESSENTIALS

**GETTING THERE**   Most **Hydrofoils** to Poros, Hydra, and Spetses leave from Zea Marina in Piraeus; some leave from the Piraeus Great Harbor. Most people take ferries or hydrofoils from Piraeus or the other Saronic islands, but some cross the narrow (540m/1,771 ft.) strait from Galatas by ferry, which costs 1€ and takes only a few minutes. For information, call the **Hellas Flying Dolphins** in Athens (℡ **210/419-9200** or 210/419-9000; www.dolphins.gr) or **Marinos Tours** (℡ **22980/22-297**) in Poros (the local agent for the hydrofoils). Reservations are recommended on weekends.

The other Saronic islands are all easy to reach from Poros. In addition, in summer Marinos Tours usually offers a weekly **round-trip hydrofoil excursion** to Tinos (3½ hr. each way) for 70€, and to Mykonos via Hydra (4 hr. each way) for 100€. (The one-way fare to Mykonos is 70€.)

**VISITOR INFORMATION**   The waterfront hotels are generally too noisy for all except heavy sleepers, so if you want to stay in town we suggest you check with **Marinos Tours** (℡ **22980/22-297;** fax 22980/22-980), which handles several hundred rooms and apartments, as well as many island hotels. We've also had good reports of **Saronic Gulf Travel** (℡ **22980/24-800;** fax 22980/24-802), which often has an excellent free map of the island available. To learn more about Poros, look for Niki Stavrolakes's enduring classic, *Poros* (Lycabettus Press), usually on sale on the island.

**GETTING AROUND**   You can walk anywhere in Poros town. The **island's bus** can take you to the beaches or to the **Monastery of the Zoodhochou Pigis**

and the remains of the **Temple of Poseidon;** the conductor will charge you according to your destination. The **taxi station** is near the hydrofoil dock, or you can call for one (© **22980/23-003;** the fare to or from the beach Askeli should cost about 6€. **Kostas Bikes** (© **22980/23-565**), opposite the Gal as ferry pier, rents bicycles for about 6€ a day and mopeds from about 12€ a day. (Motorcycle and moped agents are supposed to, but do not always, ask for proof that you are licensed to drive such vehicles.)

**FAST FACTS** The **National Bank of Greece** is one of a handful of waterfront banks with an ATM where you can also exchange money. The **police** (© **22980/22-256**) and **tourist police** (© **22980/22-462**) are on the paralia. The **port authority** (© **22980/22-274**) is on the harborfront. For **first aid,** call © **22980/22-600.** The **post office** and **telephone office (OTE)** are also on the waterfront; their hours are Monday through Friday from 8am to 2pm. In summer, in addition to the normal weekday hours, the OTE is usually open Sunday 8am to 1pm and 5 to 10pm. Coconuts Internet Café (© **22980/35-407**) by the harbor, charges 8€ per hour.

## WHAT TO SEE & DO
## ATTRACTIONS IN POROS TOWN

As you cross over to the island, you'll see the streets of Poros town, the capital, climbing a hill topped with a clock tower. Poros town is itself an island, joined to the rest of Poros by a causeway. (In short, the island of Poros is made up of two, linked islands). The narrow streets along the harbor are usually crowded with visitors inching their way up and down past the restaurants, cafés, and shops. At night, the adjacent hills are, indeed, alive to the sound of music; unfortunately, even the "Greek" music is usually heavily amplified pop.

Poros town has a **Naval Cadets's Training School**—which means that there are usually a lot of young men looking for company here. Anyone wishing to avoid their attention might wish to visit the small **Archaeological Museum** (© **22980/23-276**), with finds from ancient Troezen. It's usually open Monday through Sunday from 9am to 3pm; admission is free.

## EXPLORING THE ISLAND

By car or moped, it's easy to make a circuit of the island in half a day and see what there is to see. What remains of the 6th century B.C. **Temple of Poseidon** lies scattered beneath pine trees on the low plateau of Palatia, east of Poros town. The remains are scant, largely because the inhabitants of the nearby island of Hydra plundered the temple and hauled away most of the marble to build their harborside Monastery of the Virgin.

The Temple of Poseidon was the scene of a famous moment in Greek history in 322 B.C. when Demosthenes, the Athenian 4th-century orator and statesman, fled here for sanctuary from Athens's Macedonian enemies. When his enemies tracked him down, the great speech writer asked for time to write a last letter—and then bit off his pen nib, which contained poison. Even in his death agonies, Demosthenes had the presence of mind to leave the temple, lest his death defile the sanctuary. It seems fitting that Demosthenes, who lived by his pen, died by the same instrument.

Those who enjoy monasteries might want to continue on the road that winds through the interior to the 18th-century **Monastery of the Zoodhochou Pigis** (monastery of the life-giving spring), south of Poros town. There are usually no monks in residence, but the caretaker should let you in (if you wish, leave a small donation in the offerings box in the church) and there's a little taverna nearby.

Poros's beaches are not an enchantment. The beach northwest of town, **Neo-rio**, is not always unpolluted; the better beaches are found southeast of town at **Askeli** and **Kanali.**

## OFF THE ISLAND: A FESTIVAL, ANCIENT TROEZEN & LEMON GROVES

If you're in Poros in mid-June, you might want to catch the ferry across to Galatas and take in the annual **Flower Festival,** with floral displays and parades with floats and marching bands. (There are usually lots of posters up in Poros town advertising the festival.)

From Galatas you can catch a bus the 8km (5 miles) west to **Trizina** (ancient Troezen), birthplace of the great Athenian hero Theseus, and the scene of the tragedy of his wife, Phaedra, and son, Hippolytus. Phaedra, in one of the misogynistic fables beloved of the Greeks, fell in love with her stepson. When the dust settled, both she and Hippolytus were dead and Theseus was bereft. There are the remains of a temple to Asklepius here—but again, these ruins are very ruined.

About 4km (2½ miles) south of Galatas near the beach of Aliki, you'll find the olfactory wonder of **Limonodassos** (Lemon Grove), where more than 25,000 lemon trees fill the air with their fragrance each spring. Alas, many were harmed in a harsh storm in March 1998, and another storm in 2002. Some trees survived and yet others were planted. There are several tavernas nearby where you can get freshly squeezed lemonade.

## WHERE TO STAY

**Hotel Dionyssos** ✴ The Dionyssos occupies a nicely restored traditional town house across from the Galatas ferry. This makes it popular with frequent visitors to Poros, and you should book ahead of your visit. As with the Hotel Latsi (below), it can be a bit noisy here, with the comings and goings of the car ferry.

78 Papadopoulou, 18020 Poros, Trizinias. ✆ **22980/23-511.** 12 units, 80€–100€. No credit cards. Closed Nov–Mar. **Amenities:** Bar/breakfast room. *In room:* A/C, TV.

**Hotel Latsi** The Latsi is on the quieter north end of the port near the Naval School, opposite the Galatas ferry, with balconies overlooking the port and the Peloponnese. Rooms are worn, but clean and comfortable.

74 Papadopoulou, 18020 Poros, Trizinias. ✆ **22980/22-392.** 39 units, most with bathroom. 70€ without bathroom; 85€ with bathroom. No credit cards. Closed Nov–Mar. **Amenities:** Bar/breakfast room. *In room:* TV.

**Hotel Sirene** ★ **Kids** If you're talking creature comforts, and/or are traveling with children, the Sirena, on the beach east of town beyond Askeli, is the best hotel on the island. Those creature comforts mean that the Sirena is very popular with tour groups; if you want to stay here, you must make a reservation well in advance—and be prepared to be one of the few guests not with a tour group. Just about all the spacious rooms in this six-story building have excellent views. There's a saltwater pool near the private beach, and the restaurant is perfectly okay.

Monastiri, Askeli, 18020 Poros, Trizinias. ✆ **22980/22-741.** Fax 22980/22-744. 120 units, 100€–140€ double. Half-board (30€) optional. MC. Closed Nov–Mar. **Amenities:** Restaurant; bar; pool. *In room:* A/C, TV, hair dryer.

## WHERE TO DINE

If you're willing to give up your view of the harbor, head into town, a bit uphill, and try one of the restaurants near the church of Ayios Yeorgios, such as the **Platanos, Dimitris,** or **Kipos.** As is often the case, these places tend to draw a more Greek crowd than the harborside spots. It's a good idea to keep in mind that fish is priced by the kilo at most restaurants; the price varies from catch to catch, so it's a good idea to check the price before you order.

**Caravella Restaurant** GREEK   This portside taverna prides itself on serving organic home-grown vegetables and local (not frozen) fish. Specialties include traditional dishes such as snails, veal stifado, moussaka, souvlaki, and stuffed eggplant, as well as seafood and lobster.

Paralia, Poros town. ℭ **22980/23-666.** Main courses 5€–15€. AE, MC, V. Daily 11am–1am.

**Lucas Restaurant** GREEK   You'll find this small restaurant across from the private yacht marina. Fresh seafood and traditional dishes are well prepared and reasonably priced, especially for this upscale area.

Paralia, Poros town. ℭ **22980/22-145.** Main courses 5€–15€. No credit cards. Daily 11am–1am.

**Taverna Grill Oasis** ✫ GREEK   Tables indoors and outdoors, excellent fresh fish, and the usually cheerful staff make this traditional taverna not far from the post office live up to its name as a pleasant oasis for lunch or dinner.

Paralia, Poros town. ℭ **22980/22-955.** Main courses 5€–18€. No credit cards. Daily 11am–midnight.

## POROS AFTER DARK

There's plenty of evening entertainment in Poros town, especially if you're in the mood to dance. **Lithatos** and **Korali,** in town, and **Scirocco,** about a kilometer south of town, are popular discos. There's also a movie theater, the **Diana,** with films most summer nights.

## 3 Hydra (Idra)

65km (35 nautical miles) S of Piraeus

Hydra is one of a handful of places in Greece that seemingly can't be spoiled. Even in summer, when the waterfront teems with day-trippers, many side streets remain quiet. If you can, arrive here in the evening, when most of the day-trippers have left.

With the exception of a handful of municipal vehicles, there are no cars on Hydra. You'll probably run into at least one example of a popular form of local transportation: the donkey. When you see Hydra's splendid 18th- and 19th-century stone *archontika* (mansions) along the waterfront and on the steep streets above, you won't be surprised to learn that the entire island has been declared a national treasure by both the Greek government and the Council of Europe. You'll probably find Hydra town so charming that you'll forgive its one serious flaw: no beach. Do as the Hydriotes do, and swim from the rocks at Spilia, just beyond the main harbor.

Whatever you do, be sure to go out on the deck of your ship as you arrive, so you can see Hydra's bleak mountain hills suddenly reveal a perfect horseshoe harbor. This truly is a place where arrival is half the fun.

## ESSENTIALS

**GETTING THERE**   Several **ferries** and **excursion boats** make the 4-hour voyage between Piraeus and Hydra daily; there's also connecting service to several ports on the Peloponnese peninsula as well as with the other Saronic islands. **Hydrofoils** to Poros, **Hydra,** and Spetses leave from Zea Marina in Piraeus. For information, call the **Hellas Flying Dolphins** (ℭ **210/419-9200** or 210/419-9000; www.dolphins.gr), or the **Piraeus Port Authority** (ℭ **210/451-1311**) or

## Festivals in Hydra

On a mid-June weekend, Hydra celebrates the **Miaoulia**, honoring Hydriot Admiral Miaoulis, who set much of the Turkish fleet on fire by ramming them with explosives-filled fireboats. In early July, Hydra has an annual **puppet festival** that, in recent years, has drawn puppeteers from countries as far away as Togo and Brazil. As these two festivals are not on set dates, you should attempt to get additional information from the **Hydra tourist police** (© **22980/52-205**), or check out www.vacation-greece.com/argosaronicos/hydra.

**Hydra Port Authority** (© **22980/52-279**) for schedules. Reservations are recommended on weekends.

**VISITOR INFORMATION** The free publications *Holidays in Hydra* and *This Summer in Hydra* are widely available and contain much useful information, including maps and a list of rooms to rent; keep in mind that shops and restaurants pay to appear in these publications. **Saitis Tours** (© **22980/52-184**), in the middle of the harborfront, can exchange money, provide information on rooms and villas, book excursions, and help you make long-distance calls or send faxes. For those wanting to pursue Hydra's history, we recommend Catherine Vanderpool's *Hydra* (Lycabettus Press), usually on sale on the island.

**GETTING AROUND** Walking is the only means of getting around on the island itself, unless you bring or rent a donkey or bicycle. **Caïques** provide water-taxi service to the island's beaches (Molos, Avlaki, Bitsi, and Limnioniza are the best) and the little offshore islands of Dokos, Kivotos, and Petasi, as well as to secluded restaurants in the evening; rates run from about 5€ to 15€, depending on destination and time of day.

**FAST FACTS** The **National Bank of Greece** and the **Commercial Bank** are on the harbor; both have ATMs. Travel agents on the harbor will exchange money from about 9am to 8pm, usually a less favorable rate. The small health **clinic** is signposted on the harbor; cases requiring complicated treatment are taken by boat or helicopter to the mainland. The **tourist police** (© **22980/52-205**) are on the second floor at Votsi 9 (signposted in the harbor). The **port authority** (© **22980/52-184**) is on the harborside. The **post office** is just off the harborfront on Ikonomou, the street between the two banks. The **telephone office** (OTE), across from the police station on Votsi, is open Monday through Saturday from 7:30am to 10pm, Sunday from 8am to 1pm and 5 to 10pm. For **Internet access**, try HydraNet (© **22980/54-150**), signposted the OTE.

## WHAT TO SEE & DO
## ATTRACTIONS IN HYDRA TOWN

In the 18th and 19th centuries, ships from Hydra transported cargo around the world and made Hydra very rich indeed. Just as on the American island of Nantucket, ships' captains demonstrated their wealth by building the fanciest houses money could buy. The captains' lasting legacy is the handsome stone *archontika* (mansions) that give Hydra town its distinctive character.

One archontiko that you can hardly miss is the **Tombazi house**, which dominates the hill that stands directly across the harbor from the main ferry quay. This is now a branch of the School of Fine Arts, with a hostel for students, and you can usually get a peek inside. Call the **mansion** (© **22980/52-291**) or the

Athens Polytechnic (© 210/619-2119) for information about the program or exhibits.

The nearby **Ikonomou-Miriklis mansion** (sometimes called the Voulgaris) is not open to the public, nor is the hilltop **Koundouriotis mansion**, built by an Albanian family that contributed generously to the cause of independence. If you wander the side streets on this side of the harbor, you will see many more handsome houses, some of which are being restored so that they can once again be private homes, while others are being converted into stylish hotels.

Hydra's waterfront is a mixed bag, with a number of ho-hum shops selling nothing of distinction—and a handful of very nice boutiques and jewelry shops, especially in the area below the Tombazi house. **Hermes Art Shop** (© 22980/52-689) has a wide array of jewelry, some good antique reproductions, and a few interesting textiles. **Donna Needlepoint** (© 22980/52-959) has engaging needlepoint rugs and cushion covers, with Greek motifs of dolphins, birds, and flowers. **Vangelis Rafalias's Pharmacy** is a lovely place to stop in, even if you don't need anything, just to see the jars of remedies from the 19th century.

When you've finished with the waterfront, take Iconomou steeply uphill to see a number of quite interesting shops. **Meltemi** (© 22980/54-138) has original jewelry, including some drop-dead earrings, and ceramics. Although the shop is small, just about everything here is borderline irresistible—especially the winsome blue ceramic fish. The owners, Vangelis and Zoe, speak English. Across from Meltemi, **Emporium** (no phone) shows and sells works by Hydriote and other artists. If you want to take home a painting, or a wood or ceramic model of an island boat, try here.

Like many islands, Hydra boasts that it has 365 churches, one for every day of the year. The most impressive, the mid-18th-century **Monastery of the Assumption of the Virgin Mary,** is by the clock tower on the harbor front. This is the monastery built of the marble blocks that were hacked out of the (until then) well-preserved Temple of Poseidon on the nearby island of Poros. The buildings here no longer function as a monastery, and the cells are now municipal offices. The church itself has rather undistinguished 19th-century frescoes, but the elaborate 18th-century marble iconostasis (altar screen) is terrific. Like the marble from Poros, this altar screen was "borrowed" from another church and brought here. Seeing it is well worth leaving a donation, as suggested.

## EXPLORING THE ISLAND: A MONASTERY, A CONVENT & BEACHES

If you want to take a vigorous uphill walk (with no shade), head up A. Miaouli past Kala Pigadia (Good Wells), still the town's best local source of water. A walk of about an hour will bring you to the **Convent of Ayia Efpraxia** and the **Monastery of the Prophet Elijah** (Profitis Elias). Both have superb views, both are still active, and the nuns sell their hand-woven fabrics. (**Note:** Both the nuns and monks observe the midday siesta from 1 to 5pm. Dress appropriately—no shorts or tank tops.)

The only real **beach** on the island is at **Mandraki,** a 20-minute walk east of town, where a large hotel has been built. Just outside town, you can swim off the rocks at **Spilia** or **Kamini.** Farther west along a donkey trail is **Kastello,** with the small fort that gives it its name, and another rocky beach with less crowded swimming. Still farther west is the pretty pine-lined cove of **Molos.** The donkey path continues west to the cultivated plateau. **Episkopi,** from which a faint trail leads on west to **Bisti** and **Ayios Nikolaos** for more secluded swimming. (Most of these beaches are best reached by water taxi from the main harbor.)

One fairly good beach on the south coast, **Limioniza**, can be reached with strong legs, sturdy shoes, and a good map from Ayia Triada, though it's much easier to take a water taxi here and to Molos, Avlaki, and Bisti. The island of **Dokos**, northwest off the tip of Hydra, an hour's boat ride from town, has a good beach and excellent diving conditions—it was here that Jacques Cousteau found a sunken ship with cargo still aboard, believed to be 3,000 years old. You may want to take a picnic with you, as the taverna here keeps unpredictable hours.

## WHERE TO STAY

In addition to the following choices, you might also try the 19-unit **Hotel Greco**, Kouloura (☎ 22980/53-200; fax 22980/53-511), a former fishing-net factory in a quiet neighborhood; or the newly redecorated (in traditional island style) **Hotel Leto** (☎ 22980/53-385) just off the harbor.

**Hotel Angelika** This pension, in a restored traditional Hydriot home, stands on a quiet street 10 minutes away from the port and out of the usual tourist hubbub. The rooms are simple, with touches of local decor in the prints and furnishings. Most overlook the quiet garden courtyard, where breakfast is served. You can request, but will not be guaranteed, one of the rooms with a rooftop terrace (rooms 6, 8, 9, and 10).

42 Miaouli, 18040 Hydra. ☎ 22980/53-202. Fax 22980/53-542. angelicahotel@hotmail.com. 15 units. 90€ double. MC, V. Closed Nov–Mar. **Amenities:** Breakfast room. *In room:* A/C.

**Hotel Bratsera** ★ *Value* The Bratsera keeps turning up on everyone's list of the best hotels in Greece, which says a lot about the state of hotels in Greece. True, this small hotel, in a lovingly restored 1860 sponge factory a short stroll from the harbor, is one of Hydra's nicest. The rooms are all different, many with antique four-poster beds, all distinctively decorated in Hydriot style. The small pool with wisteria-covered trellises is very welcoming; meals are sometimes served poolside in fair weather. The hotel restaurant offers such slightly off-beat treats as fisherman's linguine. So, what's the problem? For one thing, we've had reports that room-service trays left in the hall after breakfast were still not collected by dinner time, and we know that messages left for guests aren't always delivered. And surely a fisherman's linguine should be topped with more than a solitary shrimp and one forlorn crayfish! We're eager to hear more from readers about their experiences here.

Tombazi, 18040 Hydra. ☎ 22980/53-971. Fax 22980/53-626. bratsera@yahoo.com. 23 units, 125€–175€ double. Rates include breakfast. AE, DC, MC, V. Closed mid-Jan to mid-Feb. **Amenities:** Restaurant, bar, pool. *In room:* A/C.

**Hotel Hydra** ★ *Value* This is one of the best bargains in town if you don't mind the steep walk up to the beautifully restored two-story, gray-stone mansion on the western cliff, to the right as you get off the ferry. The rooms are carpeted, with high ceilings, and simply furnished, many with balconies overlooking the town and harbor.

8 Voulgari, 18040 Hydra. ☎ 22980/52-102. Fax 22980/53-330. hydrahotel@aig.forthnet.gr. 12 units, 8 with bathroom. 60€ double without bathroom; 70€–80€ double with bathroom. MC, V. Open year-round. **Amenities:** Breakfast room. *In room:* TV.

**Hotel Miranda** ★ Once, when we were trapped for the night on Hydra by bad weather, we were lucky enough to get the last room at the Miranda. The room was small, with a tiny bathroom and no real view—so it's a tribute to this hotel that we have wonderful memories of that visit. Most of the rooms here are good sized, with nice views of the lovely garden courtyard and town. Throughout, this handsome 1820 captain's mansion is decorated with oriental rugs, antique cabinets, worn wooden chests, marble tables, contemporary paintings, and period naval engravings. There's even a small art gallery—in short, this is a very classy place.

Miaouli, 18040 Hydra. **©** **22980/53-230.** Fax 22980/53-510. mirhydra@hol.gr. 14 units. 90€–150€ double. Compulsory breakfast 8€. AE, V. Closed Nov–Mar. **Amenities:** Breakfast room. *In room:* A/C, TV, minibar.

**Hotel Mistral**   The three-story Mistral (named for the strong northerly winds that cool the late summer) is another small hotel near the harbor in a nicely restored, traditional Hydriot house. The furnishings here are standard hotel contemporary, with some nice watercolors of local views. One plus here: the large courtyard, where the proprietor Sophia will, time permitting, serve dinner—but only to hotel guests.

18040 Hydra. **©** **22980/52-509.** Fax 22980/53-412. 20 units. 90€ double. **Amenities:** Restaurant (for guests). *In room:* A/C.

**Hotel Orloff** (★   This recently restored mansion, just a short walk from the port, was built in the 18th century by a Russian philhellene, Count Orloff. Today it's a pleasant small hotel, distinctively decorated with antique furnishings. Each room is distinctive and comfortable, and there's a very nice basement lounge with a bar. Breakfast is excellent.

9 Rafalia, 18040 Hydra. **©** **22980/52-564.** Fax 22980/53-532. 10 units. 100€–150€. Price includes buffet breakfast. AE, MC, V. Closed Nov–Mar. **Amenities:** Bar. *In room:* A/C.

**Hydroussa**   If you don't need a swimming pool, the Hydroussa is almost as charming as the Bratsera, and less expensive; ask about the mid-week discounts here. Many of the spare but pleasant guest rooms have fine views over the town and harbor; some even have endurable reading lamps—a real plus in Greece!

18040 Hydra. **©** **22980/52-217.** Fax 22980/52-161. 40 units. 80€–120€ double. AE, V. Closed Nov–Mar. **Amenities:** Breakfast room. *In room:* A/C.

## WHERE TO DINE

The harborside eateries are predictably expensive and not very good, although the view is so nice that you may not care. There are also a number of cafes along the waterfront, including **To Roloi** (The Clock), by the clock tower. Just off the harbor, the **Ambrosia Cafe** serves vegetarian fare and good breakfasts. It's a good idea to keep in mind that fish is priced by the kilo at most restaurants; the price varies from catch to catch, so it's a good idea to check the price before you order.

**Bratsera** GREEK/INTERNATIONAL   This restaurant in the Hotel Bratsera just off the harbor gets generally favorable reviews, although we've heard complaints of terribly slow service and small portions. The indoor dining area is charmingly rustic and decorated with antique maps, however sitting outdoors under the wisteria-covered trellis beside the pool may be more enjoyable. The menu includes pastas, fresh seafood, grilled meats, and even a few Chinese specialties. (See also the Hotel Bratsera under "Where to Stay," above.)

Tombazi. **©** **22980/52-794.** Reservations recommended in summer and on weekends. Main courses 10€–25€. AE, DC, MC, V. Daily 8am–11pm.

**Marina's Taverna** (★ GREEK   Several readers report that they have enjoyed both the food and the spectacular sunset at this seaside taverna, appropriately nicknamed the Iliovasilema (Sunset). Perched on the rocks west of the swimming place at Kamini, it's a 10€ water-taxi ride from town. The menu is basic, but the food is fresh and carefully prepared by Marina; her *kleftiko* (pork pie, an island specialty) is superb.

Vlihos. **©** **22980/52-496.** Main courses 6€–14€. No credit cards. Daily noon–11pm.

**Moita** ★★ GREEK   Friends who visited Hydra kept seeing cards and flyers advertising Moita, so they headed up from the Clock Tower, turned left toward the OTE, and found the place that calls itself a "gourmet restaurant, cafe, and deli." Our friends left wanting to return, after a delicious meal of fresh grilled fish, pasta and salads, under the spreading bouganvillia. We agree—and are looking forward to Eggs Benedict for brunch (weekends only in high season, when most people head to the beach by brunch-time). There's also a delicious special menu weeknights of two courses and two glasses of wine for 30€. No wonder this place gets e-mail reservation requests from satisfied returning guests en route from London and Berlin!

Off Miaouli. © 22980/52-020. Moita@otenet.gr. Snacks and main courses 6€–20€. No credit cards. Daily from about 11am–4pm and 8pm–at least midnight in season.

**O Kipos (The Garden)** GREEK   This very popular *pisseriá* (grill) is in a tree-filled garden behind whitewashed walls. Grilled meat is, of course, the specialty, but there is also excellent swordfish souvlaki. The mezedes alone will be enough for many. The specialty is lamb wrapped in filo (thin leaves of pastry). We've always enjoyed eating here, except on one or two occasions when boisterous tour groups were in evidence.

Several blocks up from the quay side of the harbor. © 22980/52-329. Reservations recommended in the summer. Main courses 8€–16€. No credit cards. Daily 7pm–midnight.

**To Steki** GREEK   This small taverna, a few blocks up from the quay-side end of the harbor, has simple food at reasonable prices. The walls inside have framed murals showing a rather idealized traditional island life. The daily specials, such as moussaka and stuffed tomatoes, come with salad, vegetables, and dessert.

Miaouli. © 22980/53-517. Main courses 5€–18€; daily specials 8€–15€. No credit cards.

## HYDRA AFTER DARK

Hydra has a very energetic nightlife, with restaurants, bars, and discos all going full steam ahead in summer. The **Veranda** (up from the right [west] end of the harbor, near the Hotel Hydra) is a wonderful place to escape the full frenzy of the Hydra harbor scene, sip a glass of wine, watch the sunset, and plan the evening. In fact, sitting under the umbrellas on the Veranda's terrace is so seductive that you may end up lingering and having snacks or a meal (there's often a reasonable fixed-price dinner menu).

There are several discos, most of them fairly low-key and usually open from June to September. **Heaven** (© 22980/52-716), which has grand views, is up the hill on the west side of town, while **Kavos** (© 22980/52-716), west above the harbor, has a pleasant garden for a rest from the dancing. **Hydronetta** tends to play more western than Greek music—although the music at all these places is so loud that it's hard to be sure.

Portside, there are plenty of bars. **The Pirate** (© 22980/52-711), near the clock tower, is the best known, although nearby **To Roloi** is probably a quieter place for a nightcap. Friends report enjoying a drink the **Amalour**, just off the harbor, where they were surrounded by hip, black-clad 20- and 30-somethings. There are also a few local haunts left around the harbor; if you see them, you'll recognize them.

## 4 Spetses

98km (53 nautical miles) SW of Piraeus; 3km (2 nautical miles) from Ermioni

Despite a series of dreadful fires, Spetses's pine groves still make it the greenest of the Saronic Gulf islands. In fact, this island was called "Pityoussa" (pine-tree island) in antiquity. Although the architecture here is less impressive than on Hydra, there are some handsome *archontika* (mansions), built by wealthy 18th- and 19th-century sea captains, and the island has long been popular with wealthy Athenians.

Many Spetses homes have handsome pebble mosaic courtyards; if you're lucky, you'll catch a glimpse of some when garden gates are open. One real plus for visitors here: Cars are not allowed to circulate freely in Spetses town, which would make for a good deal of tranquility if motorcycles were not increasingly endemic.

In recent years, Spetses has become very popular with foreign tourists, especially the British. Some are pilgrims to see the island where John Fowles set his cult novel *The Magus*, but more are with tour groups. Consequently, there are times when you can hear as much English as Greek spoken in cafes and restaurants. As always, if you come here off season, you're bound to have a more relaxed experience and get a better sense of island life—even though some restaurants, shops, and small hotels will be closed.

## ESSENTIALS

**GETTING THERE**     Several **ferries** and **excursion boats** make the 5-hour voyage from Piraeus daily, connecting with the other Saronic islands; contact the **Piraeus Port Authority** (© 201/451-1311) for schedules. (*Note:* Cars are not allowed on the island without express permission.) Several **hydrofoils** leave Piraeus's Zea Marina daily, most connecting with the other Saronic islands; express service takes 90 minutes. Contact **Hellas Flying Dolphins** (© 210/419-9200 or 210/419-9000, 210/752-0540 in Piraeus; www.dolphins.gr) for schedules. Reservations are recommended on weekends.

There is less frequent service from Spetses to the island of Kithira and various ports on the Peloponnese; again, check with Hellas Flying Dolphins.

**VISITOR INFORMATION**     The island's main travel agencies are **Alasia Travel** (© 22980/74-098; alasia@otenet.gr) and **Spetses & Takis Travel** (© 22980/72-215). Andrew Thatomas's *Spetses* (Lycabettus Press), usually on sale on the island, is recommended to those wanting to pursue Spetses's history.

**GETTING AROUND**     The island's limited public transportation consists of two municipal **buses** and a handful of **taxis. Mopeds** can be rented everywhere, beginning about 15€. **Bikes** are also widely available, and the terrain along the road around the island makes them sufficient means of transportation; three-speed bikes cost about 6€ a day, while newer 21-speed models go for about 10€. **Horse-drawn carriages** can take you from the busy port into the quieter backstreets, where most of the island's handsome old mansions are. (Take your time choosing a driver; some are friendly and informative, others are surly. Fares are highly negotiable.)

The best way to get to the various beaches around the island, as well as to the beach Kosta, on the Peloponnese, is by **water taxi** (locally called a *venzina*, "gasoline"); these little boats hold about 8 to 10 people. A tour around the island costs about 30€; shorter trips, such as from Dapia to the Old Harbor, cost about 10€. Schedules are posted on the pier. You can also hire a water taxi to take you anywhere on the island, to another island, or to the mainland. Again, prices are highly negotiable.

**FAST FACTS**     The **National Bank of Greece** is one of several banks on the harbor with an ATM. Most travel agencies (usually open 9am–8pm) will also exchange money, usually at a less favorable rate than a bank. The **clinic** (© 22980/72-201) is inland from the east side of the port. The **police**

(© 22980/73-100) and **tourist police** (© 22980/73-744) are to the left off the Dapia pier, where the hydrofoils dock, on Boatassi. The **port authority** (© 22980/72-245) is on the harborfront. The **post office** is on Boatassi near the police station; it's open from 8am to 2pm. The **telephone office** (OTE), open daily from 7:30am to 3pm, is to the right off the Dapia pier, behind the Hotel Soleil. **Internet access** is available at Delphina Net-Café (© 22980/74-385) on the harborfront.

## WHAT TO SEE & DO
## EXPLORING SPETSES TOWN (KASTELLI)

Spetses town (also called Kastelli) meanders along the harbor and inland in a lazy fashion, with most of its neoclassical mansions partly hidden from envious eyes by high walls and greenery. Much of the town's street life takes place on the **Dapia**, the square where the ferries and hydrofoils now arrive; the old harbor, **Baltiza**, largely silted up, is just east of town, before the popular swimming spots at **Ayia Marina.**

If you sit at a café on the Dapia, you'll see pretty much everyone here coming and going. The handsome black-and-white pebble mosaic commemorates the moment during the War of Independence when the first flag with the motto "Freedom or Death" was raised. Thanks to its large fleet, Spetses played an important part in the War of Independence, routing the Turks in the Straits of Spetses on September 8, 1822. The victory is commemorated every year on the weekend closest to **September 8** with celebrations, church services, and the burning of a ship that symbolizes the defeated Turkish fleet.

As you stroll along the waterfront, you can't help noticing the monumental bronze statue of a woman, her left arm shielding her eyes as she looks out to sea. The statue commemorates one of the greatest heroes of the War of Independence, **Laskarina Bouboulina,** the daughter of a naval captain from Hydra. Bouboulina financed the warship *Agamemnon,* oversaw its construction, served as its captain, and was responsible for several naval victories. She was said to be able to drink any man under the table, and straitlaced citizens sniped that she was so ugly, the only way she could keep a lover was with a gun. You can see where Bouboulina lived when she was ashore by visiting the **Laskarina Bouboulina House** (© 22980/72-077) in Pefkakia, just off the port. It keeps somewhat flexible hours (which are usually posted at the house), but is usually open part of the morning and afternoon, with an English-speaking guide often giving a half-hour tour; admission is 3€. You can even see Bouboulina's bones, along with some archaeological finds and mementos of the War of Independence, at the **Spetses Mexis Museum,** in the handsome stone Mexis mansion (signposted on the waterfront). It's open daily from 9:30am to 2:30pm; admission is 2€.

The **Hotel Possidonion** itself figures in Spetses's history. It was built in 1911 as one of Greece's first "European-style" hotels by the island's greatest benefactor, Sotiris Anaryiros. He also built Anaryiros College, just outside town, modeled on an English public school. The college is now most famous because John Fowles taught here, and is closed most of the year except during August, when it hosts the Anaryiria festival of art exhibits.

The harborfront has the usual tourist shops, but you might have a look by the OTE, behind the Hotel Soleil, **Piryoussa** (no phone), which has a collection of decorative folk paintings, ceramics, and interesting gift items. The **Astrolavos-Spetses Gallery** (© 22980/75-228) sometimes has special events for children in the summer, as well as exhibits by well-known Greek artists.

If you head east away from the Dapia, you'll come to the picturesque **Old Harbor** (the Baltiza, or Paleo Limani), where the wealthy moor their yachts. The **Cathedral of Ayios Nikolaos** (St. Nicholas) here is the oldest church in town; it has a lovely bell tower on which the Greek flag was first raised on the island. A pebble mosaic shows the event, as do a number of similar pebble mosaics in Spetses town. While you're at the old harbor, have a look at the boat yards where you can usually see caïques (*kaïkia*) being made with tools little different from those used when Bouboulina's mighty *Agamemnon* was built here.

## BEACHES

**Ayia Marina,** signposted and about a 30-minute walk east of Spetses town, is the best town beach. There are a number of tavernas, cafes, and discos here. On the south side of the island, **Ayii Anaryiri** has one of the best sandy beaches anywhere in the Saronic Gulf, a perfect **C**-shaped cove lined with trees, bars, and several tavernas (we prefer the Taverna Tassos). The best way to get here is by water taxi. Whichever beach you pick, go early, as both are usually seriously crowded by midday.

Some prefer the beach at **Ayia Paraskevi,** which is smaller and more private because it's more closely bordered by pine trees. There's a cantina and the **Villa Yasemia,** residence of the Magus himself. West over some rocks is the island's official nudist beach. **Zogeria** is on the northwest coast, with a few places to eat and some pretty rocky coves for swimming. West of Spetses town, **Paradise Beach** is usually crowded, littered, and to be avoided.

## WHERE TO STAY

Finding a good, quiet, centrally located room in spread-out Spetses is not easy. Below are some suggestions. If you are planning a lengthy stay, check out the **Hotel Nissia** (*C*) **22980/75-000;** www.nissia.gr), which is usually open all year and consists of 31 rooms and flats in a cluster recreating "traditional residences" around a pool, a 5-minute walk from the center of Spetses town.

**Hotel Faros** (*Value*)  Though there's no *faros* (lighthouse) nearby, this older hotel shares the busy central square with a Taverna Faros, a Faros Pizzeria, and other establishments whose tables and chairs curb the flow of vehicular traffic. Try for the top floor, where the simple, comfortable, twin-bedded rooms are quietest, with balcony views of the island.

Plateia Kentriki (Central Sq.), 18050 Spetses. (*C*) **22980/72-613.** Fax 22980/74-728. 50 units. 65€ double. No credit cards. **Amenities:** Breakfast room.

**Hotel Possidonion** (★★)  The landmark Poseidon (as we would spell it) is a grand and gracious hotel that was built in 1911 and, under new management, was completely renovated in the early 1990s. This Belle-Epoque classic boasts two grand pianos in its lobby and the statue of Bouboulina guarding the plaza in front. The spacious, high-ceilinged guest rooms are sparsely but elegantly furnished; the old-fashioned bathrooms have large tubs. The view over the harbor from the tall front windows is superb.

Dapia, 18050 Spetses. (*C*) **22980/72-208** or 22980/72-006. Fax 22980/72-208. 55 units. 85€–110€ double; 120€ double with sea view. Rates include breakfast. AE, DC, MC, V. **Amenities:** Restaurant; bar. *In room:* A/C, TV.

**Spetses Hotel**  The Spetses sits on its own beach and has its own restaurant, which makes it a good choice if you don't want to hassle with the summertime crowds in other restaurants. The rooms here are furnished with the standard Greek hotel twin beds and bedside tables. If you stay for more than a week, there is usually a discount of about 10€ a night.

18050 Spetses. ℃ 22980/72-602. Fax 22980/72-494. 77 units. 120€–150€. MC, V. **Amenities:** Restaurant. *In room:* A/C, TV.

**Star Hotel** ★ *Value* This blue-shuttered, five-story hotel—the best in its price range—is flanked by a pebble mosaic, making it off-limits to vehicles. All guest rooms have balconies, the front ones with views of the harbor. Each large bathroom has a bathtub, shower, and bidet. Breakfast is available a la carte in the large lobby.

Plateia Dapia. 18050 Spetses. ℃ 22980/72-214 or 22980/72-728. Fax 22980/72-872. 37 units. 70€ double. No credit cards. **Amenities:** Breakfast room.

## WHERE TO DINE

Spetses's restaurants can be packed with Athenians on weekend evenings, and you may want to eat unfashionably early (about 9pm) to avoid the Greek crush. The island's considerable popularity with tour groups seems to have led to a decline in the quality of restaurant fare. Let us know if you find someplace that you think is particularly good. It's a good idea to keep in mind that fish is priced by the kilo at most restaurants; the price varies from catch to catch, so it's a good idea to check the price before you order.

For standard Greek taverna food, usually including a number of vegetable dishes, try the rooftop taverna **Lirakis**, Dapia, over the Lirakis supermarket (℃ **22980/72-188**), with a nice view of the harbor. **To Kafeneio**, a long-established coffeehouse and ouzo joint on the harborfront, is a good place to sit and watch the passing scene, as is **To Byzantino. Orloff**, on the road to the Old Harbor, has a wide variety of *mezedes*.

Spetses has some of the best **bakeries** in the Saronic Gulf; all serve an island specialty called *amygdalota*, small cone-shaped almond cakes flavored with rosewater and covered with powdered sugar.

**The Bakery Restaurant** GREEK/CONTINENTAL This restaurant is on the deck above one of the island's more popular patisseries. There area a few ready dishes, but most of what you order is prepared when you order. The chef obviously understands foreign palates and offers smoked trout salad, grilled steak, roasted lamb with peas, and the usual Greek dishes.

Dapia. No phone. Main courses 6€–16€. MC, V. Daily 6:30pm–midnight.

**Exedra Taverna** ★ GREEK/SEAFOOD This traditional taverna on the Old Harbor, where yachts from all over Europe moor, is also known by locals as Siora's, after the proprietor. This is a good place to try fish Spetsiota (a broiled fish-and-tomato casserole). The freshly cooked zucchini, eggplant, and other seasonal vegetables are also excellent. If you can't find a table for supper, try the nearby **Taverna Liyeri**, also known for good seafood.

Paleo Limani. ℃ 22980/73-497. Main courses 6€–16€. Fish priced by the kilo. No credit cards. Daily noon–3pm and 7pm–midnight.

**Lazaros Taverna** ★ GREEK This traditional place is decorated with ported ivy, family photos, and big kegs of homemade retsina lining the walls. It's popular with locals (always a good sign) who come here for the good, fresh, reasonably priced food. The small menu features grilled meats and daily specials, such as goat in lemon sauce.

Dapia (inland and uphill about 400m/1,312 ft. from the water). No phone. Main courses 5€–14€. No credit cards. Daily 6:30pm–midnight.

## SPETSES AFTER DARK

There's plenty of nightlife on Spetses, with bars, discos, and bouzouki clubs from the Dapia to the Old Harbor to Ayia Marina, and even the more remote beaches. For bars, try **Socrates,** in the heart of Dapia. The **Anchor** is more upscale, and there's the **Bracera Music Bar** on the yachting marina. For something a little more sedate, head to the **Halcyon** or the **Veranda,** with softer Greek music. To the west of town, in Kounoupitsa, near the popular Patralis Fish Taverna, **Zorba's** and **Kalia** are popular spots. **Bar Spetsa,** just off Plateia Agias Mamas, is another popular drinking and listening spot.

As for discos, there's **Figaro,** with a seaside patio and international funk until midnight, when the music switches to Greek and the dancing follows step—often till dawn. The **Delfina Disco** is opposite the Dapia town beach on the road to the Old Harbor. **Disco Fever,** with its flashing lights, draws the British crowd, while **Naos,** which looks more like a castle than a temple, features techno music. The **Fox** often has live Greek music and dancing; obvious tourists are usually encouraged to join in—information that may help you decide whether or not to come here, or to stay away!

# 8

# The Peloponnese

*by Sherry Marker*

**W**hat's special about the Peloponnese? It's tempting to answer, "Everything." With the exception of Athens and Delphi, just across the Gulf of Corinth, virtually every famous ancient site in Greece is in the Peloponnese—the awesome Mycenaean palaces of the Kings Agamemnon and Nestor at Mycenae and Pylos (Pilos); the mysterious thick-walled Mycenaean fortress at Tiryns; the magnificent classical temples at Corinth, Nemea, Vassaí, and Olympia; and the monumental theaters at Argos and Epidaurus, still used for performances today.

But the Peloponnese isn't just a grab bag of famous ancient sites. This peninsula, divided from the mainland by the Corinth Canal, is studded with medieval castles and monasteries, bounded by sand beaches, and dominated by two of Greece's most impressive mountain ranges: Taygetos and Parnon. Tucked away in the valleys and hanging precipitously from the mountainsides are hundreds of the villages that are among the Peloponnese's greatest treasures. An evening under the plane trees in tiny Andritsena, where the sheep bells are usually the loudest sound at night and oregano and flowering broom scent the hills, is every bit as memorable as a visit to one of the famous ancient sites. This is perhaps especially true in the mountains of Arcadia and deep in the Mani peninsula, where traditional Greek hospitality hasn't been eroded by too many busloads of visitors.

While many of the Aegean islands sag under the weight of tourists from

May until September, the Peloponnese is still relatively uncrowded, even in midsummer. That doesn't mean that if you're going to have Olympia all to yourself if you arrive at high noon in August, but it does mean that if you get to Olympia early in the morning, you may have a quiet hour under the pine trees. If you're traveling with a car and can set your own pace, you can avoid the crowds at the most popular tourist destinations of Corinth, Mycenae, Epidaurus, and Olympia by visiting early in the morning or late in the afternoon.

Still, even the most avid travelers do not live by culture alone, and one of the great delights of seeing the Peloponnese comes from the quiet hours spent in seaside cafes, watching fishermen mend their nets while Greek families settle down for a leisurely meal. *Leisurely* is the word to remember in the Peloponnese, an ideal place to make haste slowly. And what better place to watch shepherds on the hills or fishing boats on the horizon as you wait for dinner?

Peloponnesian culinary favorites include rabbit stew (*kouneli stifado*) with a surprising hint of cinnamon, or fish a la Spetsai (fish baked with tomato sauce). In summer—when it seems that every tree on the plain of Argos hangs with apricots and every vine is heavy with tomatoes—Peloponnesian food is at its freshest and best. If you're here in spring, look for delicious fresh artichokes and delicate little strawberries. The fresh lettuce grown here during the cool winter months is superb, Greek hothouses produce excellent tomatoes year-round, and there's less competition in restaurants to get the best and freshest fish. And don't forget to sample the local wines; the vineyards at Nemea, Patras and Mantinia are famous. Unfortunately, the 2002 vintage in the Peloponnese (and much of Greece) was badly affected by that autumn's bad weather. (You can find out more about Greek wines at www.greekwine.gr).

A few suggestions for your trip to the Peloponnese: Don't forget sunscreen, a broad-brimmed hat, good walking shoes, and some books to read while you're sitting in that cafe. Bookstores with a good selection of English titles are few and far between here, although you will find excellent stores in Nafplion and Olympia. Most banks have ATMs, and all banks, most hotels, and many post offices change money at competitive rates.

Speaking of competitive rates, don't hesitate to ask if there's a cheaper rate for a room than the one first quoted at hotels. This is especially true for a long stay, or off season, when many hotels are willing to be quite flexible in their prices.

You'll probably be pleasantly surprised at how very impressed locals are if you master the linguistic basics of hello (*ya-sis*) and thank you (*efcharisto*). If you have trouble pronouncing "*efcharisto*," here's a suggestion: It sounds a lot like the name "F. Harry Stowe." If you're still having trouble, try *merci* (French for "thank you"), which most Greeks use interchangeably with *efcharisto*.

And however relaxed you get on your Peloponnesian holiday, it's a good idea to remember that this is still one of the more conservative areas of Greece, and virtually the only area where some sentiment lingers to restore the monarchy and bring back the good old days. Most Peloponnesians are at best amused and at worst deeply offended by public drunkenness, elaborate displays of affection, and swimsuits or shorts and halters worn anywhere but on the beach (especially in, or in the precincts of, churches). That said, *kalo taxidi* (bon voyage) on your trip to the Peloponnese, the most beautiful and historic part of Greece.

**STRATEGIES FOR SEEING THE REGION** You can tour the region in either a clockwise or counterclockwise direction. Whichever approach you choose, at some point you'll probably head into the center of the Peloponnese, to see the Byzantine ghost town of **Mistra** outside ancient **Sparta**, or to take in some of the lovely mountain villages of Arcadia and the **temple of Apollo at Vassae.** Here's one suggested itinerary based on the assumption that you have your own car. If you're traveling by public transportation, you'd be wise to double the time allowed. Even if you do have a car, don't let yourself be deceived by the short distances between what you want to see in the Peloponnese. You'll be astonished at how long even a short drive on a winding mountain road can take—especially when you have to stop repeatedly to let flocks of goats cross that road!

In 2 days, you can see most of the important sites in the northern Peloponnese as well as the lovely harbor town of Nafplion. Head from Athens to **Corinth,** have a look at the canal, and visit the ancient site as well as **Acrocorinth,** the sugarloaf mountain that looms over the plain of Corinth. Head on to **Mycenae** before ending up for the night in **Nafplion,** where you can take a swim at the public bathing beach. In the morning, explore Nafplion and drive over to **Epidaurus,** to see the famous theater and site, before heading back along the coast to Athens.

If you have a couple of more days to spend here, you can head from Nafplion to **Tripolis** and **Olympia,** taking in some of the Arcadian mountain villages, and perhaps the **temple of Vassae,** en route. Then, you can head back to Athens along the **Gulf of Corinth,** which offers lots of chances for a swim. At this point, you still will have missed a great deal in the Peloponnese—so we hope you have at least a week to spend here.

---

### Tips   Beware of Price Gouging During the Olympics

Hotel prices were accurate at press time, but price increases of 20% and more are rumored as hoteliers throughout Greece gear up for the August 2004 Olympics in and around Athens. Horrific price hikes of between 50% and an unbelievable 300% are rumored for the period leading up to, during, and after the Olympics.

## 1 Corinth

89km (55 miles) W of Athens

Today, as in antiquity, Corinth, along with Patras, is one of the two major gateways to the Peloponnese. Still, gates are there to pass through, not to linger in. There's no reason not to stop to see the ships slipping through the impressive Corinth Canal that cuts across the isthmus; then head straight for ancient Corinth, bypassing the modern city altogether. Mycenae and Nafplion both have excellent hotels and restaurants—and are only about an hour's drive from Corinth.

In fact, the entire modern town of Corinth (pop. 24,000) has remarkably little to recommend it. The town was moved here in 1834, after an earthquake devastated the settlement at ancient Corinth; successive earthquakes in 1858, 1928, and 1981 destroyed virtually every interesting building in the new town. As a result, Corinth is now a thicket of undistinguished, flat-roofed buildings, supposedly built to withstand future quakes.

All this makes modern Corinth a far cry from ancient Corinth, which was famously splendid and lively. As one Greek proverb had it, "See Corinth and die," suggesting that there was nothing to look forward to after visiting the splendid monuments (and fleshpots) of the city that dominated trade in Greece for much of the 7th and 8th centuries B.C. and had a second golden age under the Romans in the 2nd century A.D.

**A LOOK AT THE PAST**    Historians are fond of saying that "geography is destiny," and much of Corinth's power and prosperity came from its strategic location overlooking the sea and land routes into the Peloponnese. No enemy could sneak across the isthmus without being spotted by the soldiers stationed on Corinth's towering acropolis, Acrocorinth (559m/1,863 ft.).

During the 8th and 7th centuries B.C., Corinth controlled much of the trade in the Mediterranean and founded colonies as far away as Syracuse in Sicily. This was when Corinth made and exported the distinctive red-and-black figured pottery decorated with lively animal motifs, examples of which are on display in the excavation museum. Great sailors, the Corinthians were credited with refining the design of the *trireme*, the standard warship in Greek antiquity. The only obstacle Corinth couldn't overcome was the isthmus itself: Ships had to be dragged from the port of Kenchreai on the east to the port of Lechaion on the west.

Although Corinth's greatest period of prosperity was between the 8th and 5th centuries B.C., most of the ancient remains here are from the Roman period. Razed and destroyed when the Romans conquered Greece in 146 B.C., Corinth was refounded by Julius Caesar in 44 B.C. and began a second period of wealth and prosperity. When St. Paul visited here in A.D. 52, he found Corinth all too sophisticated and chastised the Corinthians for their wanton ways.

By the 2nd century A.D., with some 300,000 citizens and 500,000 slaves, Corinth was much larger and more powerful than Athens. During the next 100 years, a series of barbarian invasions and attacks undermined Corinth's prosperity. Thereafter, although the long series of invaders—Normans, Franks, Venetians, and Turks—fought for control of the strategic citadel of Acrocorinth, Corinth itself was a provincial backwater with a glorious past.

## ESSENTIALS

**GETTING THERE**  **By Train**  There are several trains a day from Athens's Stathmos Peloponnisou (Train Station for the Peloponnese) to the Corinth station off Demokratias (© 27410/22-522 or 27410/22-523). These trains are almost invariably late, often taking 3 hours or more. For information on schedules and fares, call © 210/512-4913.

**By Bus**  There are at least 15 buses a day, taking 2 to 2½ hours from the Stathmos Leoforia Peloponnisou (Bus Station for the Peloponnese) in Athens, 100 Kifissou (© 210/513-4110 or 201/512-9233), to the Corinth station at Ermou and Koliatsou (© 27410/24-481 or 27410/25-645), where you can catch a bus (15–20 minutes) to Archaia Korinthos. For information on Athens-Corinth-Athens schedules and fares, call © 210/512-8233.

Buses for the Peloponnese leave Corinth from the station at the corner of Konstantinou and Aratou (© 27410/244-03). For most destinations beyond Tripolis, you'll find yourself changing buses at Tripolis. At press time, there were rumors of new bus stations opening in Corinth. Be sure to confirm the above information before setting out.

**By Car**  The National Highway runs from Athens to Corinth. The highway, which has been widened over the last decade, still contains some three-lane stretches that are particularly dangerous. The highway now sweeps over the Corinth Canal; if you want to stop here, look for the signs indicating the Canal Tourist Area. Shortly after the canal, you'll see signs for Corinth (the modern town and ancient site), Isthmia (site of the Isthmian Games), and Patras. Allow at least 1½ hours for the journey from Athens.

**FAST FACTS**  You can find **ATMs** and exchange currency at the **National Bank of Greece**, 7 Ethniki Antistaseos, and several banks on Leoforos Vas. Konstantinou. The **hospital** (© 27410/25-711) is clearly signposted in town. The **police** (© 100 or 27410/22-143) and the **tourist police** (© 27410/23-282)

---

## Tour Alternatives

If you don't want to travel through the Peloponnese on your own, but hate the thought of a conventional tour, you might want to contact one of the two English companies that run "green" tours to various sections of Greece, including the Peloponnese. **Filoxenia ✭**, Sourdock Hill, Barkisland, Halifax, West Yorkshire HX4 OAG (© 01422/375-999 or 01422/371-796; fax 01422/310-340; www.filoxenia.co.uk; travel@filoxenia.co.uk) offers fly-drive trips to the Peloponnese for small groups, as well as a wide range of rental villas and houses in appealing villages. **Zoe Holidays**, 34 Thornhill Rd., Surbiton, Surrey, KT6 7TL 9 (© 0810/390-7623) specializes in "alternative" Greece, arranging stays in monasteries, restored homes, and women's cooperatives in several villages. **Magicaljourneys.com**, based in Canada, also arranges visits to the Peloponnese (and throughout Greece).

are both at 51 Ermou, near the Athens bus station. The **telephone office (OTE)**, 33 Kolokotroni (open from 6am to midnight), and the **post office**, by the park on Adimantou (open Mon–Fri from 7:30am to 2pm), are both signposted.

## WHAT TO SEE & DO

The new highway rushes you over the **Corinth Canal** very quickly, and unless you're vigilant you can miss the turnoff to the **Canal Tourist Area**. Before the new road was completed in 1997, almost everyone stopped here for a coffee, a souvlaki, and a look at the Corinth Canal that separates the Peloponnese from the mainland. Now, much traffic hurtles past, and the cafes, restaurants, and shops here are hurting. There's a small post office at the canal, along with a kiosk with postcards and English-language newspapers; most of the large souvlaki places have clean toilet facilities (and very tough souvlaki). *One word of warning:* Be sure to lock your car door. This is a popular spot for thieves to prey on unwary tourists.

The French engineers who built the Corinth Canal between 1881 and 1893 used lots of dynamite, blasting through 86m (285 ft.) of sheer rock to make this 6.4km-long (4-mile), 30-yard-wide passageway. This utterly revolutionized shipping in the Mediterranean: Ships that previously had made their way laboriously around Cape Matapan at the southern tip of the Peloponnese could dart through the canal. The journey from Brindisi, Italy, to Athens was immediately shortened by more than 320km (200 miles).

Although it took modern technology to build the canal, the Roman emperors Caligula and Nero had tried, and failed, to dig a canal with slave labor. Nero was obsessed with the project, going so far as to lift the first shovelful of earth with a dainty golden trowel. That done, he headed back to Rome and left the real work to the 6,000 Jewish slaves he had brought here from Judea.

**Acrocorinth** ★  A road twists from the ancient site to the summit of Acrocorinth, the rugged limestone sugarloaf mountain that looms 566m (1,885 ft.) above the plain. On a clear day, the views from the summit are superb, although it's been a long time since the atmosphere was clear enough to spot the glistening columns of the Parthenon on the Athenian acropolis.

A superb natural acropolis, Acrocorinth was fortified first in antiquity. Everyone who came later—the Byzantines, Franks, Venetians, and Turks—simply added to the original walls. Today, there are three courses of outer walls, massive gates with towers, and a jumble of ruined houses, churches, and barracks. Before you head down, you can stop for a cold drink at the small cafe here and reflect on the fact that there was a Temple of Aphrodite on this summit in antiquity, staffed by an estimated 1,000 temple prostitutes—some of whom worked the streets in town, but others who worked here, awaiting those hardy customers who walked up from Corinth.

Old Corinth. © 27410/319-66. Free admission. Usually daily 8: 30am–7pm in summer; 9am–3pm in winter.

**Ancient Corinth** ★★  If you visit in summer, try to come here first thing in the morning or late in the afternoon: There will be fewer tourists, and the sun on this virtually shadeless site will be less fierce.

The most conspicuous—and the most handsome—surviving building at ancient Corinth is clearly the 6th-century B.C. **Temple of Apollo**, which stands on a low hill overlooking the extensive remains of the **Roman Agora** (the Roman forum, or marketplace). Only seven of the temple's 38 monolithic Doric columns are standing, the others having long since been toppled by earthquakes.

From the temple, ancient Corinth's main drag, a 12m (40-ft.) -wide marble-paved road that ran from the port of Lechaion into the heart of the marketplace, is clearly visible. Pottery from Corinth was carried down this road to the ships that took it around the world; back along the same road came the goods Corinthian merchants bought in every corner of the Mediterranean. Everything made here and brought here was for sale in countless shops, many of whose foundations are still clearly visible in the agora. Excavations continue here and since 1995, excavations southeast of the agora have unearthed a Roman town house, a small 6th-century A.D. bathhouse—and the foundations of several more recent 19th century houses.

Two spots in the agora are especially famous: the **Bema** and the **fountain of Peirene.** In the 2nd century A.D., the famous Roman traveler, philhellene, and benefactor Herodes Atticus rebuilt the original modest fountain house. Like most Romans, Herodes seemed to think that bigger was better: When he was done, the spring was encased in an elaborate two-storied building with arches and arcades and a 50-square-foot courtyard. Peirene, by the way, was a woman who wept so hard when she lost her son that she finally dissolved into the spring that still flows here. As for the Bema, this was the public platform where St. Paul had to plead his case when the Corinthians, irritated by his constant criticisms, hauled him up in front of the Roman governor Gallo in A.D. 52.

Old Corinth ℂ 27410/31-443. Admission 6€, which includes admission to the museum (see below). Summer daily 8am–8pm; winter daily 8am–3pm.

**The Archaeological Museum**   As you'd expect, this museum has a particularly fine collection of the famous Corinthian pottery that is often decorated with charming red-and-black figures of birds and animals. In addition, there are a number of statues of Roman worthies and several mosaics, including one in which Pan is shown piping away to a clutch of cows. The museum also has an extensive collection of finds from the shrine of Asklepios; as many of these are graphic representations of intimate body parts, they are kept in a room that is usually locked. If you express a scholarly interest, a guard may unlock the room. The museum courtyard is a shady spot to sit and read up on the ancient site. When you visit, be sure to see the handsome sculpture and vases stolen from the museum in 1990, found in Miami, Florida, in 1998, and officially handed over to Greece in 2001, again now on display.

Old Corinth, on the site of ancient Corinth. ℂ 27410/31-207. Admission 6€, which includes admission to the site (see above). Summer daily 8am–8pm; winter daily 8am–3pm.

## WHERE TO STAY

As noted, if at all possible, do not stay in Corinth, a noisy and unappealing town. If you must, try the 45-unit **Hotel Ephira,** Ethniki Antistaseos 52 (ℂ 27410/22-434; fax 27410/24-514), near the park. The hotel is rather charmless, but the rooms are air-conditioned and have cable TV; a double goes for about 50€. In Old Corinth, the 20-unit **Marinos Rooms** (ℂ 27410/31-209) was completely remodeled in 2000 and has clean, comfortable rooms about 300m (984 ft.) from the ancient site.

**Kalamaki Beach Hotel** ★ 👶   This sprawling beach resort, about 10km (6 miles) outside Corinth near Isthmia, is an appealing place for families with children. There's good swimming here, both in the hotel pools and in the Gulf itself—and lots of Greek families with children. The guest rooms are plainly furnished, with tile floors, decent beds, semi-comfortable reading chairs, and good-sized balconies and bathrooms. The floor-to-ceiling sliding glass doors that open on the balcony allow you to take in the view. If you're exploring the archaeological sites in the northern Peloponnese and want to stay on the water, you might consider the Kalamaki—but remember that this place gets lots of tour and conference groups, as well as families: independent travelers are very much in the minority here. The hotel offers demi and full pension, and if you're traveling with children, that might be a good choice. The food is ample, but not particularly interesting.

P.O. Box 22, 20100 Cointh. ⓒ **27410/37-653** or 210/323-5605 in Athens. Fax 27410/37-652, or 210/324-1092 in Athens. www.kalamakibeach.gr. 82 units. 100€–175€ double. Compulsory breakfast 8€. MC, V. **Amenities:** Restaurant; 2 outdoor pools (1 freshwater, 1 saltwater); tennis; parking. *In room:* A/C, TV, minibar, hair dryer.

## WHERE TO DINE

None of the cafes or restaurants along the Corinth Canal out of town or along the waterfront in town deserve to be singled out; most deserve to be avoided. Similarly, the restaurants near the ancient site tend to have high prices and mediocre food. That said, here are some suggestions if you find yourself hungry in Corinth (and can't wait until you get to Nafplion, where there are lots of good places to eat).

Locals speak well of the grandly named **Splendid** restaurant across from the site; a lunch or dinner of simple stews, chops, and salads costs around 10€. The **Ancient Corinth** on the main square offers much the same food at similar prices.

In the modern town, a light meal goes for around 10€ at any of the following three places: The **Pantheon Restaurant,** Ethniki Antistaseos (ⓒ **27410/25-780**), serves standard Greek fare such as chops, salads, moussaka, and *pastitsio* (macaroni with cream sauce). If you're tired of struggling with Greek menus, try the **Neon** (ⓒ **27410/23-337**), one of a popular cafeteria-style chain, where much of the food is on display. If you like sardines, try **Theodorakis Taverna,** on the waterfront.

## SIDE TRIPS FROM CORINTH

### ISTHMIA

Isthmia was one of the four places in Greece where Panhellenic Games were held (the others being Delphi, Olympia, and Nemea). According to legend, the games here were founded in 582 B.C. in honor of a certain Melicrtes, whose body was carried ashore by a dolphin at the very moment that the Delphic Oracle had revealed that a harsh famine would end only when the Corinthians honored someone who had died at sea. The Isthmian Games took place every 2 years at the Sanctuary of Poseidon, of which regrettably little remains. To get here from ancient Corinth, drive back toward the canal. Isthmia is signposted on your right just before you reach the canal.

The **Site and Museum of Isthmia** (ⓒ **27410/37-244**) are officially open Wednesday through Monday from 9am to 3pm. Admission is 2€ for the museum; site entrance is free. The principal **temple** in Isthmia was dedicated to Poseidon; foundations remain of the structure built in the 7th century B.C., first rebuilt after a fire in the 5th century B.C., and then rebuilt once again when the Romans refounded Corinth in 44 B.C. Speaking of the temple, even the excavator, Oscar Broneer, admitted that "the casual visitor will marvel chiefly, perhaps, at the thoroughness of its destruction." The **ancient stadium,** with its elaborate starting gate, which Broneer lovingly reconstructed, is better preserved.

Isthmia's interesting small **museum** seems to be closed unpredictably. If you do get in, you'll see exhibits on the Isthmian Games and some handsome **glass-mosaic panels** showing land- and townscapes and the figure of a philosopher, sometimes identified as Plato. These panels were found carefully packed in wooden crates, which preserved them for posterity after the ship they were on sank in the harbor of Kenchreai. Archaeologists speculate that the panels may have been intended to decorate the elegant home of one of the Roman officials who lived at Corinth.

## LOUTRAKI & PERACHORA

To get to Loutraki from Corinth, cross the Corinth Canal. Once you're on the mainland, you'll see that Loutraki is signposted on your left. For Perachora, continue through Loutraki to Perachora, 32km (20 miles) or 30 minutes away by car.

**Loutraki** is the famous Greek spa whose springs churn out a good deal of the bottled water you'll see in restaurants. If possible, avoid visiting Loutraki or Perachora on summer weekends: It's slow going getting through Loutraki, which bursts at the seams with the Athenians who stream here to enjoy the beaches and "take the waters" at the **Hydrotherapy Thermal Spa**, 26 G. Lekka (© 27440/22-215); open Monday through Saturday from 8am to 1pm.

En route to Perachora from Loutraki, you'll see signs of the severe fires that raged here during the summer of 1998. You'll also pass **Lake Vouliagmeni**, a saltwater inlet from the Gulf of Corinth. There are a number of equally good fish restaurants along the lake; make your choice depending on what's on the menu.

After sprawling Corinth, **Perachora** ✪ will seem like a miniature model of an ancient site. The site was founded in the 8th century B.C. and had several temples to Zeus's wife, Hera, several stoas, and a number of useful water cisterns. Perched at the end of the peninsula, around a tiny cove, this is an idyllic spot; there's also a picturesque lighthouse chapel here. There would be more antiquities to see if the Romans hadn't dismantled the temples and stoas and ferried the stones across the gulf to rebuild Corinth.

The **Site of Perachora** is open daily, in summer from 8am to 7pm; in winter from 8am to 3pm. Admission is free. The ancient Corinthians called this spot Perachora, which means "the land beyond," meaning the land beyond the gulf. On a clear day, you can see the land beyond just about everything: There are superb views south across the Gulf to Acrocorinth and the mountains of the Peloponnese and along the north coast to the mountains of Central Greece.

This is an ideal spot to spend a few lazy hours swimming and picnicking (but not on weekends, when too many other people have the same idea). You may prefer simply to dangle your toes in the water and not swim in the cove, although there is good snorkeling. Sharks are not unknown just outside the harbor in the gulf.

## 2 Nafplion

145km (90 miles) SW of Athens

It's easy to overlook contemporary Greece as you travel from one ancient site to another in the Peloponnese. Nafplion (pop. 10,000) brings you face to face with the beginnings of modern Greece. For several years after the Greek War of Independence (1821–28), this was Greece's first capital. Although the palace of Greece's young King Otto—a mail-order monarch from Bavaria—burned down in the 19th century, you can still see the former mosque off Plateia Syntagma (Constitution Square) where Greece's first parliament met. Another legacy of those years is the impressive number of handsome neoclassical civic buildings and private houses, as well as the generous number of commemorative statues of revolutionary heroes in Nafplion's squares and parks.

## *Tips*  Hairdressers

Women travelers might like to know that several of the staff at **AD Hair Studio** (© 27520/24-861), at the corner of Ypsilanti and Kotsonopoulou 5, speak English and do good work. There's another hairdresser nearby, so make sure that you get this one.

All this would be reason enough to visit this port on the east coast of the Gulf of Argos, but Nafplion also has two hilltop Venetian fortresses, a miniature castle on an island in the harbor, shady parks, an interesting assortment of small museums, and better-than-average hotels, restaurants, and shops.

In short, Nafplion is far and away the most charming town in the Peloponnese. You could spend several pleasant days here simply enjoying the port town itself, but you'll probably want to use Nafplion as your home base for day trips to the ancient sites at Argos, Nemea, Mycenae, Tiryns, Epidaurus, and—if you didn't see it on the way to Nafplion—Corinth. Keep in mind that *lots* of Athenians head here on weekends, when it's best not to arrive without a hotel reservation.

## ESSENTIALS

**GETTING THERE   By Car**   From Athens, head south to the Corinth Canal. If you want to stop at Mycenae and/or Nemea en route, take the winding old road to Nafplion. If you want to stop at Epidaurus en route, turn left just after the canal at the sign for Epidaurus. If you want to get to Nafplion as quickly as possible, take the new Corinth-Tripolis road as far as the Argos exit. Follow the signs first into Argos itself, about 10km (6 miles) from the exit and thence on to Nafplion. You will almost certainly get lost at least once in Argos, which has an abysmal system of directional signs. Allow at least 3 hours for the drive from Athens to Nafplion, including a brief stop at the Corinth Canal and some time thrashing around in Argos. When you reach Nafplion, leave your car—and be sure to lock it—in the large municipal **parking lot** (no charge) by the harbor.

**By Train**   Unless you are a totally dedicated train buff, it makes no sense to come here by train. That said, there are several trains a day from Athens to Corinth and Argos, where you can catch a bus to Nafplion. Information on schedules and fares is available from the Stathmos Peloponnisou (Train Station for the Peloponnese) in Athens (© **210/513-1601**).

**By Bus**   There are at least a dozen buses a day to Nafplion from the Stathmos Leoforia Peloponnisou (Bus Station for the Peloponnese) in Athens, 100 Kifissou (© **210/513-4110** or 201/512-9233). The trip is a slow one (about 4 hr.) because the bus goes into both Corinth and Argos before reaching the Nafplion station on Plateia Kapodistrias (© **27520/28-555**).

**By Boat**   Monday through Saturday, there is Flying Dolphin hydrofoil service from Marina Zea, Piraeus, to Nafplion, weather permitting. The hydrofoil makes a number of stops and takes almost as long as the bus to reach Nafplion. It usually leaves Athens for Nafplion in the late afternoon and departs Nafplion for Athens in the early morning. For information on fares and schedules, call © **27520/28-054**, 210/419-9000, or 210/453-6107.

**VISITOR INFORMATION**   The **municipal tourist office** is at 25 Martiou (© **27520/24-444**), catercorner from the bus station. It's usually open Monday through Friday from 9am to 1pm and 5 to 8pm (although it is often mysteriously closed during work hours). Ask for the useful brochure *Nafplion Day and Night*. Information and tickets for special events, such as the concerts in the **Nafplion Music Festival**, usually held during the first half of June, are sometimes available from the Town Hall (Demarkeion) in the old high-school building on Iatrou Square (© **27520/23-332**); you can also check at www.nafplionfestival.gr. There are a number of travel agencies in Nafplion, such as **Staikos Travel**, by the harbor (© **27520/27-950**), and **Yiannopoulos Travel**, on Plateia Syntagma (© **27520/28-054**), where you can get information on car rentals and day trips from Nafplion.

**FAST FACTS** The **National Bank of Greece**, on Plateia Syntagma (Constitution Square), has an ATM and currency exchange, as do most other banks in town. The **hospital** (© **27520/27-309**) is at Kolokotroni and Asklepiou streets. The **police** are in National Assembly Square (© **27520/27-776**). The **tourist police** (© **27520/21-051**) are at 25 Martiou, next to the municipal tourist information office. The **post office**, on Plateia Kapodistrias, and the **telephone office (OTE)**, on 25 Martiou flanking Plateia Kapodistrias, are both signposted from the bus station. **Internet access** is available at DADIS, 15 Asklipiou (© **27520/29-688**; dadosnik@otenet.gr) and the Diplo-Internet Café, 43 Bouboulinas (© **27520/21-280**). Both charge 6€ an hour.

## WHAT TO SEE & DO

Nafplion is a stroller's delight; one of the great pleasures here is simply wandering along the harbor, through the parks (Kolokotronis and Kapodistrias parks run into each other), and up and down the stepped side streets, discovering unexpected Turkish fountains and small churches. Don't make the mistake of ending your harborside stroll when you come to the last of the large seaside cafes by the Hotel Agamemnon: If you continue on, you can watch fishing boats putting in at the pier, explore several cliffside chapels, and wind your way past the small beach on a cliffside path under the Acronafplia. In the summer, if you walk from the center of town with the harbor on your left, you'll soon reach **Luna Park**, a seasonal amusement park with tipsy-turvy rides. And don't ignore Nafplion's lush green parks at the foot of the Palamidi: You can usually find a cool spot to sit here even at midday. Nafplion is so small that you can't get seriously lost, so have fun exploring. Below are some suggestions on how to take in the official sights after you've had your initial stroll.

## ACRONAFPLIA & PALAMIDI

Nafplion's two massive fortifications, the **Acronafplia** and the **Palamidi**, dominate the skyline. As you'll realize when you visit these fortresses, whoever held the heights here could keep a close watch on both the gulf and the plain of Argos. The Greeks began to fortify Acronafplia and Palamidi, and the Romans, Byzantines, Venetians, Franks, and Turks added a wall here and a turret there, with the results you see today. If you're here in the summer, try to visit the fortresses in the relative cool of either morning or evening; there's no charge to visit Acronafplia. If you're in Nafplion during the June **Music Festival**, check to see if any evening concerts are being held at the **Palamidi**, which is open in summer, Monday through Friday from 8am to 7pm, Saturday, and Sunday from 8am to 3pm; in winter, daily from 8am to 3pm. Admission is 3€.

If you want to walk up to the cliffs above Nafplion, known as the Acronafplia, follow signs in the lower town to the **church of St. Spyridon**; one of its walls has the mark left by one of the bullets that killed Ioannis Kapodistrias, the first governor of modern Greece. From St. Spyridon, follow signs further uphill to the Catholic **church of the Metamorphosis.** Note that this is not an easy walk, and you may prefer to take a taxi.

This church is as good a symbol as any for Nafplion's vexed history. Built by the Venetians, it was converted into a mosque by the Turks, and then reconsecrated as a church after the War of Independence. Inside, an ornamental doorway has an inscription listing philhellenes who died for Greece, including the nephews of both Lord Byron and George Washington. Greece's first king, young Otho of Bavaria, worshipped here wearing the Greek national costume, the short pleated skirt known as the *foustanella,* which he adopted to show solidarity with his new subjects. Ironically, while Otho wore his foustanella, the more fashion-conscious of his subjects here abandoned their Greek costumes and copied the Western clothes worn by the members of Otho's court.

As you continue to climb toward Acronafplia, you may see several **carvings of the winged lion** that was the symbol of St. Mark, the protector of Venice. The most important fortifications on Acronafplia were built during the first (1388–1540) and second (1686–1715) Venetian occupations. In the days before the Greek historical preservation movement dug in its tentacles, both the Xenia and the Xenia Palace Hotels were built over the fortifications, one reason that the original structures have been obscured. Unless you are a military historian, you may have to take it on faith that what you're looking at here is a Frankish castle and Venetian defense tower to the east and a Byzantine castle to the west. Nafplion retained its strategic importance well into this century: During World War II, the German occupying forces had gun emplacements here.

If you're not staying in the **Xenia Palace Hotel** (recently renamed the Nafplia Palace), whose bedrooms overlook the harbor, be sure to enjoy the view from Acronafplia of the **Bourtzi fortress** in the harbor. The Venetians built the Bourtzi to guard the entrance to the harbor in the 15th century. Since then, it's had a checkered career, serving as a home for retired executioners in the 19th century and briefly as a small hotel in this century.

From Acronafplia, you can look down at the Bourtzi and up at the Palamidi. If you're not in the mood to climb the 800-plus steps to the **summit of Palamidi,** you can take a taxi up and then walk down. The Venetians spent 3 years building the Palamidi, only to be conquered the next year by the Turks in 1715. You'll enter the fortress the way the Turkish attackers did, through the main gate to the east. Once inside, you can trace the course of the massive wall that encircled the entire summit and wander through the considerable remains of the five defense fortresses that failed to stop the Turkish attack. Kolokotronis, the hero of the Greek war of Independence who later tried to subvert the new nation and seize power for himself, was held prisoner for 20 months in **Fort Miltiades,** the structure to your right as you enter the Palamidi.

## MUSEUMS

**The Peloponnesian Folklore Foundation** ★★ Shortly after it opened in 1981, this museum—with its astonishingly rich collection of traditional Greek costumes—won the European Museum of the Year Award. The museum

---

## Take a Dip

The best place to swim is at the Arvanitia beach beneath the Palamidi. With the Bourtzi on your right, walk as far as you can along the quay until you come to the beach.

highlights "The Best of the Peloponnesian Folk Foundation." Exhibits from the collection of more than 25,000 items include coins, ceramics, furniture, and farm implements—as well as all those costumes. The museum occupies three full floors in an elegant 18th-century house, with a shady courtyard and a welcome snack bar. Throughout, labels are in English as well as Greek; a number of dioramas (our favorite shows nine elegant matrons in a 19th-century parlor) help visitors imagine life in Greece. The excellent small gift shop offers pottery, weavings, Greek music CDs, and nice children's books and toys.

1 V. Alexandros. ② 27520/28-947. Fax 27520/27-960. www.pli.gr. Admission 4€. Wed–Mon museum 9am–3pm, shop daily 9am–2pm and 6–10pm. Closed Feb.

**The Archaeological Museum** ★  **Note:** In the Summer of 2003, the museum closed for restoration work. Officials hope to reopen the museum by Summer 2004. The Archaeological Museum is housed in the handsome 18th-century Venetian arsenal that dominates Plateia Syntagma. The thick walls make this a deliciously cool place to visit on even the hottest day. Displays are from sites in the area and include pottery, jewelry, and some quite horrific Mycenaean terra-cotta idols as well as a handsome bronze Mycenaean suit of armor.

Plateia Syntagma (Constitution Sq.). ② 27520/27-502. Admission 2€. Year-round Tues–Sun 8:30am–1pm.

**The Military Museum**  If you like old prints and old photographs, not to mention muskets, you'll enjoy strolling through the exhibits here, which cover Greek wars from the War of Independence to World War II.

Leoforos Amalias. ② 27520/25-591. Free admission. Year-round Tues–Sun 9am–2pm.

**The Museum of Childhood**  An offshoot of the Folklore Museum, this museum has an eclectic collection of dolls, baby clothes, and toys. It seems to keep especially fluid hours; if you arrive and the door is locked, you can see a fair amount by peering through the windows.

Stathmos, Kolokotronis Park. Admission 2€. Year-round Mon–Fri 9am–8pm; Sat 9am–1pm. Frequent unscheduled closings.

## SHOPPING

Nafplion has not escaped the invasion of mass-produced-souvenir shops that threatens to overwhelm Greece, but there are also some genuinely fine shops here, many on or just off **Spiliadou,** the street immediately above Plateia Syntagma (Constitution Square) and **Vas. Konstantinou,** which is parallel to Spiliadou. No shop that we mention is more than a 5-minute walk from Plateia Syntagma. As in most Greek towns heavily dependent on tourism, many of these shops are closed in winter. On Saturdays, the weekly **market** occupies most of the road alongside Kolokotronis Park, from around 7am to 1pm. You can buy everything from handsaws to garlic here.

For a wide range of handsome handcrafted jewelry, try **Preludio,** 2 Vas. Constantinou, just off Plateia Syntagma (② 27520/25-277), with a very helpful staff, headed by George Gouveris. Almost everything sold here is made and designed by the owners, who travel as far away as Afghanistan and Australia to find fine gem stones. Consequently, the jewelry here is a very pleasant departure from the mass-produced trinkets sold at many shops. Just two doors away at 4 Vas. Constantinou, Cleopatra Pomoni at **Morphes** has handsome wooden chests, antique locks and keys, jewelry, and other objets d'art. **Mayamba,** 26

Vas. Konstantinou (℡ 27520/25-272), has glitzy and stylish costume jewelry, all-cotton bedspreads and throws, and a nice selection of bibelots.

You'll know that you've found **To Enotion**, Staikopoulou (no phone and no visible street number), when you see a window full of handsome museum-quality reproductions of characters from the Greek shadow theater, from country bumpkins to damsels in distress. The smallest of the colorful marionettes begin at about 20€. A few doors along, **Nafplio tou Nafpliou**, 56A Staikopoulou (no phone), paints and sells reproductions of icons showing virtually every saint in the Greek Orthodox church.

The **Komboloi Museum**, 25 Staikopoulou (℡ and fax 27520/21-618; www. cs-net.gr/komboloi), is on the second floor of a shop selling *komboloi*, usually referred to as "worry beads" (and priced from a few to many thousand euros); museum admission is 1.50€. Owner Aris Evangelinos will lovingly explain the differences between the grades of amber and wood used to make the komboloi; his book *The Komboloi and its History* is on sale for 10€. **Premier Jewellery** (sic), at 19 Vas. Constantinou (℡ 27520/22-324), also has a wide selection of *komboloi*.

**Konstantine Beselmes**, 6 Ath. Siokou (℡ 27520/25-842), has magical paintings of village scenes, sailing ships, and idyllic landscapes. Although new, the paintings are done on weathered boards, which gives them a pleasantly aged look.

The **Odyssey**, Plateia Syntagma (℡ 27520/23-4300), has a wide selection of newspapers, magazines, and books in English, as well as a startling collection of pornographic drink coasters. This is also a good place to pick up a copy of Timothy Gregory's *Nafplion* (Lycabettus Press); although printed in 1980, this remains the best guide to the city's history and monuments.

The **Wine Shop**, 5 Amalias (℡ and fax 27520/24-446), is one of the best wine shops in the Peloponnese and an excellent place to head if you want to browse and learn about Greek wines. Dimitris Karonis, the very knowledgeable owner, is often able to schedule reasonably priced wine tasting sessions. If your tastes run to honey, stop in at **Nektar and Ambrosia**, 6 Pharmakopoulou (℡ 27520/43-001), for a wide selection of delicious organic honey products and herbs.

## WHERE TO STAY

Nafplion has enough hotels that you can usually find a room here, although you may end up on the outskirts of town in high season. Be sure to make a reservation if you want a view of the harbor, or if you are going to be here when there is a performance at Epidaurus, when tour groups reserve entire hotels. If you arrive without a reservation and have trouble finding a room, try the Municipal Tourist Office, 25 Martiou, across from the bus station. They often can find rooms in small pensiones.

### EXPENSIVE

**Hotel Ilion** ★★    The elegant little Ilion, is Nafplion's latest boutique hotel. You'll have to decide whether you find the decor in this restored town house on a stepped street above Plateia Syntagma engaging or overwhelming. Virtually every ceiling is painted (often with cupids) and wall frescoes with scenes from Greek mythology alternate with borders of fruits and flowers; many walls are deep rose or gold. Windows and beds alike are draped with filmy hangings; the mattresses are excellent; French-style upholstered chairs and side tables are elegant. A friend who spent a happy week here reported that the service was excellent, the neighborhood quiet, and the breakfasts delicious.

**Hotel Nafsimedon** ★ This new boutique hotel, in a handsome mid-19th-century neoclassical house painted a warm peach color, is a welcome addition to Nafplion's lodging choices. It's set back from the street, with two ornamental palms in the front garden, and overlooks relatively quiet Kolokotronis Park. The rooms, many done in shades of apricot and peach, have handsome chandeliers, marble-topped tables, some old paintings—and good sized bathrooms and beds with firm mattresses.

9 Sidiras Merarhias (on Kolokotronis Park), 21100 Nafplion. © **27520/25-060.** Fax 27520/26-913. www.nafsimedon.gr. 13 units. Double 76€–99€. No credit cards. **Amenities:** Bar/breakfast room; courtyard. *In room:* A/C, TV.

**Nafplia Palace Hotel (formerly Xenia Palace Hotel)** ★ When it was built as the Xenia Palace Hotel in the 1970s, the disco, minibars, and in-bathroom telephones made this hotel relentlessly modern. By the 1990s, it was sadly down at the heels, and had a thorough renovation in 1999. Unfortunately, the service is lax, the room decor is bland and the lobby is monumentally gloomy; the food is exceptionally boring. Still, virtually every room in this hotel has splendid views of the harbor and Bourtzi. The Nafplia Palace does most of its business with tour groups, which means that service here really plummets when tourism to Greece sags.

Acronaflia, 21000 Nafplion. © **27520/28-981** and 27520/752-99-555. Fax 27520/28-783. helios@helios hotel.gr. 51 units, 54 bungalow units 200€ double, 170€ bungalow. Significant off-season reductions possible. Rates include breakfast. AE, DC, MC, V. **Amenities:** Restaurant; bar; pool. *In room:* A/C, TV, minibar.

## MODERATE

**Byron Hotel** ★★ The Byron was one of the first hotels here to attempt to add individual charm and creature comfort to a pleasant location, and has just finished a thorough renovation. The hotel is in a quiet, breezy location overlooking the Church of Agiou Spiridona, a short, but steep, hike up from the main platia. There're a number of nice bits of Victoriana in the sitting rooms and bedrooms, as well as modern conveniences. Word has gotten out about the Byron's charm, and it's almost impossible to stay here in July or August without a reservation, especially on weekends, when the entire hotel can be taken over by Athenians. The cheapest rooms are quite small and with no view; for another 10€, you'll get a view of Nafplion—and enough space that you won't feel the burden of togetherness with your roommate.

2 Platonos, Plateia Agiou Spiridona, Nafplion 21100. © **27520/22-351.** Fax 27520-26-338. www.byron hotel.gr. 17 units, 60€–85€ double. AE, MC, V. **Amenities:** Breakfast room; terrace. *In room:* A/C, TV, minibar; hair dryer.

**Hotel Agamemnon** ★ *(Value)* The Agamemnon is on the harbor just past the string of cafes, which means that you're bound to hear voices if you have a front room with a balcony. Still, friends who have stayed here claim they were not bothered by noise and loved the view. The guest rooms are of the generic variety found in hotels throughout Greece. They're furnished with two single beds with pine bed frames and nightstands. The Agamemnon has its own quiet good restaurant and rooftop bar with a magnificent view.

3 Akti Miaouli, 21100 Nafplion. © **27520/28-021.** Fax 27520/28-022. 40 units. 60€–80€ double. AE, MC, V. Demi-pension available for 15€. **Amenities:** Restaurant; bar. *In room:* A/C, TV.

4 Efthimiopoulou & 6 Kapoditriou Sts., 21100 Nafplion. © **27520/25-114.** Fax 27520/24-497. lilionhot@ otenetgr. 15 units (10 suites, 5 studios). Studios 78€–90€, suites 90€–150€. Breakfast 9€. **Amenities:** Bar/breakfast room. *In room:* A/C, TV, minibar.

**Hotel Leto** ★  Your effort in climbing up to the Leto, perched under Acronafplia is rewarded with fine views over Nafplion. Rooms are simply furnished, with decent-size bathrooms; ask for a room with a balcony. The staff here has been praised as helpful.

28 Zigomala. 21100 Nafplion. $\mathcal{C}$ **27520/28-098.** Fax 27520/29-588. 15 units. 60€. No credit cards. In room: A/C, TV, minibar.

**Pension Acronafplia**  The Acronafplia has rooms in 5 restored buildings, several of which have steep staircases up to the rooms and poor cross-ventilation and can be hot in summer, despite air-conditioning. That said, many rooms have attractive stone walls, old prints, brass beds, and nice views over Nafplion. If you stay here, let us know what you think: we seem to get raves or rants about this place.

34 Papanikolaou, 20 Vas. Konstantinou, 6 Agios Spiridon, 21100 Nafplion. $\mathcal{C}$ **27520/24-481.** Fax 27520/24-076. penacrop@otenet.gr. 30 units. 65€ double. Amenities: Lounge. In room: A/C, TV, minibar.

## INEXPENSIVE

**Epidaurus Hotel**  Rooms here are small but acceptable, with good, firm beds, small bathrooms, and wooden hanging cupboards large enough for a stay of at least a month. The location, on a quiet street just off the main square, is excellent and usually quiet, although adjacent nightclubs, restaurants, and bars can make things noisy on summer weekends. The staff here is neither wildly welcoming nor noticeably efficient. The Epidauros has an annex across the street, as well as nearby pension quarters at 30€ for a double.

2 Kokkinou (beside the Commercial Bank), Nafplion 21100. $\mathcal{C}$ and fax **27520/27-541.** 30 units, 25 with full bathroom. 60€ double. No credit cards. Amenities: Bar.

**King Otho** ★  This long-time favorite (we first stayed here in the early 1960s) was getting down-at-the-heels before its complete and completely successful renovation in 2000. Now, once again, this splendid old town house, with its high ceilings, wood floors, marvelous curved staircase, and marble-topped tables is a delightful place to stay. The small garden is a real plus for breakfast or a quiet hour's reading.

4 Farmakapoulou, Nafplion 21100. $\mathcal{C}$ **27520/27585.** Fax 27520/27595. 12 units. 50€–60€ double. No credit cards. Amenities: Breakfast room. In room: A/C, TV.

**Omorfi Poli Pension** ★★  What a lovely place! This small pension/hotel above the charming cafe by the same name (Beautiful City) has gone all out: The restoration of the building gives guests the sense that they are staying in a Nafplion home—but with privacy. The beds are good, the tile floors and prints on the walls are nice—there's nothing to fault here. This makes a very pleasant base for touring the area. Families will like the rooms with fridges and sleeping lofts for children as well as the breakfasts with freshly baked bread. The **Omorfi** café on the ground floor is also very charming.

5 Sofroni, 21100 Nafplion. $\mathcal{C}$ **27520/21-565.** www.greek-tourism.gr/nafplio/omorfi-poli. 9 units, all with shower only. 55€ double, 65€–75€ family suite for up to 5 persons. Rates include breakfast.

## WHERE TO DINE

Oddly enough, not all the restaurants in and just off Plateia Syntagma (Constitution Square) are the tourist traps youd expect. Furthermore, you'll see a good number of Greeks at the big harborside cafes on Akti Miaouli. In short, Nafplion has lots of good restaurants—and some excellent sweet shops, including the superb Antica Gelateria di Roma.

**Hellas Restaurant** ★ (Kids) GREEK   Children who normally squirm in restaurants will enjoy the Hellas: between courses, they can join the Greek kids kicking soccer balls and racing up and down Plateia Syntagma. Shady trees and awnings make this a cool spot to eat outdoors; there's also an indoor dining room, where locals tend to congregate year-round. Reliable dolmades with egg-lemon sauce are usually on the menu, as well as stuffed tomatoes and peppers in season. Just about everyone in town passes through Plateia Syntagma, so this is a great spot to watch the world go by.

Plateia Syntagma. ☎ 27520/27-278. Main courses 5€–10€. AE, MC, V. Daily 9am–midnight.

**Karamanlis** GREEK   This simple harborfront taverna several blocks east of the cluster of cafes tends to get fewer tourists than most of the places in town. It serves up good grills and several kinds of meatballs (keftedes, soussourakia, and yiouvarlakia). If you like the food here, you'll probably also enjoy the **Kanares Taverna** and the **Hundalos Taverna**, both also on Bouboulinas.

1 Bouboulinas. ☎ 27520/27-668. Main courses 5€–12€; fresh fish priced by the kilo. AE, MC, V. Usually daily 11am to about midnight.

**Noufara** INTERNATIONAL/ITALIAN/GREEK   Of late, the Noufara has been resting a bit too lazily on its laurels: the excellent pasta dishes here are now quite ordinary. Still, if you're not sure that you can face another stuffed tomato, you can get pasta and pizza here. You can sit under the umbrellas and have a cool drink or a full meal—or you can retreat inside to the mildly air-conditioned dining room. The **Noufara** also has a branch with the same menu (but a wider offering of fish) just outside Nafplion, on the shore in Nea Chios (☎ 27520/52-314).

Plateia Syntagma. ☎ 27520/23-648. Fax 27520/23-945. Main courses 5€–16€. MC, V. Usually daily about 8am–1am.

**Savouras Psarotaverna** ★ FISH   This restaurant has been here for more than 20 years; its fresh fish attracts Greek day-trippers from Tripolis and even Athens. What you eat depends on what was caught that day. Expect to pay at least $60 for two fish dinners, a salad, and some house wine. On summer weekends, this restaurant can be terribly crowded.

79 Leoforos Bouboulinas 79. ☎ 27520/27-704. Fish priced by the kilo according to availability. AE, MC, V. Daily about noon–11pm.

**Taverna Old Mansion (Palio Archontiko)** ★ GREEK   Sometimes when it's snowing in New England, where we spend part of the year, I think of being here on a winter evening. In summer, when I'm usually in town, tables spill out along Siokou St., but I have happy memories of some cozy winter evenings here, enjoying the good food and the local scene. The menu offers consistently good traditional Greek spitiko (home) cooking: stews, chops, and, usually, several vegetarian choices. There's sometimes live music here in the evening.

7 Siokou. ☎ 27520/22-449. Main courses 5€–12€. MC, V. Daily 7pm–midnight and 12pm–4pm summer weekends.

**Ta Phanaria** ★ GREEK   A shaded table under Ta Phanaria's enormous scarlet bougainvillea makes for one of the prettiest places in town for lunch or dinner. Ta Phanaria usually has several inventive vegetable dishes on the menu in addition to such standbys as moussaka. The stews and chops here are also good, and in winter there are usually hearty bean dishes available. Like the Hellas, Ta Phanaria continues to attract steady customers, despite doing much of its business with tourists.

13 Staikopoulo. ☎ 27520/27-141. Main courses 5€–12€. MC, V. Daily about noon–midnight.

**To Italikon** ITALIAN   If you come here for pizza, and ask to have it made with real Italian mozzarella, you'll get a very good pizza made in the wood oven. The pasta dishes are less consistently good, but usually tasty. In summer, you eat outside facing the greenery of Kolokotrones Park.

Corner of Vas. Pavlo and Vas. Konstantinou. © 27520/26-887. Main dishes 5€–15€. MC,V.

## OUZERIES, CAFES & SWEET SHOPS

**Antica Gelateria di Roma** ★★★ SWEETS/ICECREAM/COFFEES/DRINKS   What a wonderful addition to Nafplion! Marcello and Claudia Raffo make and sell delicious ice creams and ices. You can have anything from a banana split to a tiny cup with just a taste. Don't miss the hazelnut, lemon, mango, strawberry, chocolate—well, you get the idea. If you tire of ice creams, you can always have a freshly-made panini (sandwich) with tomato and mozzarella and finish off with a real espresso.

3 Pharmakopoulou & Komninou. © 27520/23-520. spyde@tri.forthnet.gr. Sweets and sandwiches from 1€–10€. Daily from about 10am–midnight.

**Sokaki** COFFEE/DRINKS/SNACKS/BREAKFAST   In the morning, tourists tuck into the full American breakfast here, while locals toy with tiny cups of Greek coffee. In the evening, young men lounge here, some eyeing the women who pass by, others eyeing the men. A nice place to take a break and watch people watching people, over a yogurt and honey in the morning or a margarita in the evening.

8 Ethniki Antistaseos. © 27520/26-032. Drinks and snacks 1.50€–12€. No credit cards. Daily about 8am–8pm (until midnight in summer).

**Stathmos Café** ★ DRINKS/SNACKS   When school is in session, this is usually a quiet spot to sit and take a break from tourist Nafplion; when school is out, high school students often hang out here. Still, a good place to take a break, perhaps after visiting the Museum of Childhood next door. The old train station is decorated with a splendid painting of a steam engine, and has elaborate wooden gingerbread trim, comfortable chairs under shady trees, and a cozy inside room for cold weather.

In the old Nafplion railroad station. No phone. Drinks and snacks 1€–5€. No credit cards. Daily about 9am–midnight.

## NIGHTLIFE

There are a number of nightclubs and discos around Nea Chios on the coast road from Nafplion to Muloi; all are serious clip-joints, charging as much as 100€ for a bottle of scotch. These places are popular with the sailors who turn up in Nafplion, with area twenty and thirty somethings who come here for a night on the town, and the scene is anything but sedate; unfortunately, all are serious clip-joints. Some of the better known places (with combo tacky/garish decor that has to be seen to be believed) include Shiva of Liquid Club, Liquid Live, and the Rusty Club. There's no point in phoning ahead: No one ever answers the phones at these places.

## 3 Mycenae

50km (31 miles) S of Corinth; 115km (71 miles) SW of Athens

According to Greek legend and the poet Homer, King Agamemnon of Mycenae was the most powerful leader in Greece at the time of the Trojan War. It was Agamemnon, Homer says, who led the Greeks from Mycenae, which he called "rich in gold," to Troy (around 1250 B.C.). There, the Greeks fought for 10 years to reclaim fair Helen, the wife of Agamemnon's brother Menelaus, from her seducer, the Trojan prince Paris.

The German archaeologist Heinrich Schliemann, who found and excavated Troy, began to excavate at Mycenae in 1874. There, the Greeks fought for 10 years prove that what Homer wrote was based on an actual event—and not myth or legend? Scholars are suspicious, although most admit that Mycenae could have been built to order from Homer's descriptions of Mycenaean palaces.

After you visit here, see if you agree with something that the English philhellene Robert Liddell once wrote: "Mycenae is one of the most ancient and fabulous places in Europe. I think it should be visited first for the lovely landscape, and thirdly for the excavations."

## ESSENTIALS

**GETTING THERE    By Car    From Corinth,** take the new national highway toll road to the Nemea exit, where you will join the old Corinth-Argos highway, which has a clearly-marked turn-off for Mycenae. If you prefer, you can take the old road from Corinth to the Mycenae turn-off. This takes longer and you may get stuck behind a bus or truck, but you will have a better sense of the countryside than on the elevated highway. Either way, Mycenae is about 90km (56 miles) south of Corinth. **From Nafplion,** take the road out of town toward Argos. When you reach the Corinth-Argos highway, turn right and then, after about 16km (10 miles) right again at the sign for Mycenae. (If you are going to Nafplion when you leave Mycenae, try the very pleasant back road that runs through villages and rich farmland. You'll see the sign for Nafplion on your left shortly after you leave Mycenae.)

**By Bus**    There is frequent bus service from the Stathmos Leoforia Peloponnisou (Bus Station for the Peloponnese), at 100 Kifissou in Athens (© **210/513-4100** or 512-9233), to Corinth, Argos, and Nafplion (allow 3–4 hr.). From any of these places you can travel on by bus to Mycenae (allow an hour). The Athens-Argos bus is usually willing to drop Mycenae-bound travelers at the turnoff at Fihtia—but don't count on finding a taxi to take you the rest of the way (about 2km, a bit more than a mile).

**FAST FACTS**    You can buy stamps and change money at the **mobile post office** at the ancient site, Monday through Friday from 8am to 2pm. This office is sometimes open on weekends and after 2pm, but don't count on it. There is a **pay phone** near the mobile post office.

## WHAT TO SEE & DO

### The Citadel and the Treasury of Atreus ★★★    As you walk uphill to Mycenae, you begin to get an idea of why people settled here as long ago as 3,000 B.C.: Mycenae straddles a low bluff between two protecting mountains and is a superb natural citadel. The site overlooks one of the richest plains in Greece, and whoever held Mycenae could control all the land between the narrow Dervenakia Pass to the north and the Gulf of Argos, some 16km (10 miles) to the south.

By about 1,400 B.C., Mycenae controlled not just the Plain of Argos, but also much of mainland Greece, as well as Crete, many of the Aegean islands, and outposts in distant Italy and Asia Minor. Then, some unknown disaster struck Mycenaean Greece; by about 1,100 B.C., the Mycenaeans were on the decline. By the time of the classical era, almost all memory of the Mycenaeans had been lost, and Greeks speculated that places like Mycenae and Tiryns had been built

## Insider Tip

If at all possible, visit Mycenae early in the morning (to avoid the mid-morning and mid-day tour groups) or in the hour or two before closing (when crowds usually thin out) and wear a hat and sturdy shoes. There's no shade at the site (except in the cistern and the beehive tombs), and the rocks are very slippery. Bring a flashlight if you plan to explore the cistern.

by the Cyclopes. Only those enormous giants, people reasoned, could have moved the enormous rocks used to build the ancient citadel's defense walls.

You'll enter Mycenae through just such a wall, passing under the massive **Lion Gate**, whose two lions probably symbolized Mycenae's strength. The door itself (missing, like the lions' heads) would have been of wood, probably covered with bronze for additional protection; cuttings for the door jambs and pivots are clearly visible in the lintel. Soldiers stationed in the **round tower** on your right would have shot arrows down at any attackers who tried to storm the citadel. Since soldiers carried their shields on their left arms, the tower's position made the attackers vulnerable to attack on their unprotected right side.

One of the most famous spots at Mycenae is immediately ahead of the Lion Gate: the so-called **Grave Circle A,** where Schliemann found the gold jewelry now on display at the National Archaeological Museum in Athens. When Schliemann opened the tombs and found some 14 kilos of gold here, including several solid-gold face masks, he concluded that he had found the grave of Agamemnon himself. At once, Schliemann fired off a telegram to the king of Greece, saying, "I have looked upon the face of Agamemnon bare." More sober scholars have concluded that Schliemann was wrong, and that the kings buried here died long before Agamemnon was born.

From the grave circle, head uphill past the low remains of a number of **houses.** Mycenae was not merely a palace, but a small village, with the palace at the crest of the hill and administrative buildings and homes on the slopes. The **palace** was considerably grander than these small houses and had several court rooms, bedrooms, a throne room, and a large megaron (ceremonial hall). You can see the imprint of the **four columns** that held up the roof in the megaron, as well as the outline of a **circular altar** on the floor.

If you're not claustrophobic, head to the northeast corner of the citadel and climb down the flight of stairs to have a look at Mycenae's enormous **cistern.** You may find someone here selling candles, but it's a good idea to bring your own flashlight. Along with Mycenae's great walls, this cistern, which held water channeled from a spring 500 meters away, helped to make Mycenae impregnable for several centuries.

If it's not too hot when you visit, try to give yourself some time to sit on the citadel and contemplate the sad history of the House of Atreus and enjoy the view of the farm fields below. On your way back down, take a look at the **little bathtub** in the palace, which Schliemann thought was the very bathtub where Agamemnon was stabbed to death by his wife, Clytemnestra.

There's one more thing to see before you leave Mycenae: the massive tomb known as the **Treasury of Atreus,** the largest of the tholos (beehive) tombs found here. You'll see signs for it on your right as you head down the modern road away from Mycenae. This treasury may have been built around 1300 B.C., at about the same time as the Lion Gate, in the last century of Mycenae's real greatness. The enormous tomb, with its 118-ton lintel, is 13m (43 ft.) high and 14m (47 ft.) wide. To build it, workers first cut the 35m (115-ft.) -long passageway into the hill and faced it with stone blocks. Then the tholos chamber itself was built, by placing slightly overlapping courses of stone one on top of the other until a capstone could close the final course. As you look up toward the ceiling, you'll see why these are called beehive tombs. Once your eyes get accustomed to the poor light in the tomb, you can make out the bronze nails that once held hundreds of bronze rosettes in place in the ceiling. This tomb was robbed even in antiquity, so we'll never know what it contained, although the contents of Grave Circle A give an idea of what riches must have been here. If this was the family vault of Atreus, it's entirely possible that Agamemnon himself was buried here—indeed, some still call this the Tomb of Agamemnon.

Admission 6€ (includes Treasury of Atreus). Summer daily 8am–7pm; winter daily 8am–5pm.

## WHERE TO STAY & DINE

Most of the restaurants in Mycenae specialize in serving up set, fixed-price meals to groups. You won't starve if you eat at one of these big, impersonal roadside restaurants, but you're likely to be served a bland, lukewarm meal. You'll have better luck trying the smaller restaurants at one of the following hotels. It's also sometimes possible to avoid tour groups at the **Achilleus**, on the main street (© 27510/76-027), where you can eat lunch or dinner from about 12€.

**La Belle Helene**    The real reason to stay here is to add your name to that of Schliemann and other luminaries in the guest book. Sentiment aside, this small hotel, one of the most famous in Greece, is usually quiet (although it does do a brisk business with tour groups in its large restaurant); the simple rooms are clean and comfortable. If you stay here, be sure to drive or walk up to the ancient site at night, especially if it's a full moon.

Mycenae, Argolis, 21200. © 27510/76-225. Fax 27510/76-179. 8 units, none with bathroom. 30€–55€ double, sometimes lower in off season. Rates include breakfast. DC, V. **Amenities:** Restaurant.

**La Petite Planete ★**    This would be a nice place to stay even without its swimming pool, which is irresistible after a hot day's trek around Mycenae. We've usually found it quieter here than at La Belle Helene, and friends who stayed here recently praised the restaurant and enjoyed the view over the hills from their window.

Mycenae, Argolis, 21200. © 27510/76-240. 30 units. 70€ double. AE, V. Usually closed Apr–Oct. **Amenities:** Restaurant; bar; outdoor freshwater pool. In room: A/C, TV.

## 4 Epidaurus

32km (20 miles) E of Nafplion; 63km (39 miles) S of Corinth

The Theater of Epidaurus is one of the most impressive sights in Greece. Probably built in the 4th century, possibly by Polykleitos, the architect of the Tholos, this theater seated—and still seats—some 14,000 spectators. Unlike so many ancient buildings, including almost everything at the Sanctuary of Asklepios, the theater was not pillaged for building blocks in antiquity. As a result, it is astonishingly well preserved; restorations have been both minimal and tactful.

The village of Palea Epidaurus, a beach resort 10km (6 miles) from Epidaurus, is sometimes signposted ANCIENT EPIDAURUS; the theater and sanctuary are usually signposted ANCIENT THEATER.

To confuse things further, Palea Epidaurus has its own small theater and festival. If you want a swim, Palea Epidaurus is the nearest beach—but it is heavily developed.

## ESSENTIALS

**GETTING THERE    By Car**    If you're coming from Athens or Corinth, turn left for Epidaurus immediately after the Corinth Canal and take the coast road to the Theatro (ancient theater), not to Nea Epidaurus or Palaia Epidaurus. From Nafplion, follow the signs for Epidaurus. If you drive to Epidaurus from Nafplion for a performance, be alert: The road will be clogged with tour buses and other travelers who are driving the road for the first time.

**By Bus**    Two buses a day run from the Stathmos Leoforia Peloponnisou (Bus Station for the Peloponnese), 100 Kifissou, Athens (© **210/513-4110** or 210/512-9233), to Epidaurus. Buses take about 3 hours. There are three buses a day from the Nafplion bus station, off Plateia Kapodistrias (© **27520/27-323**), to Epidaurus, as well as extra buses when there are performances at the Theater of Epidaurus. This bus takes about an hour.

**FAST FACTS**    The ancient site has both a **mobile post office** and a **pay phone.**

## WHAT TO SEE & DO

**The Sanctuary, Museum, and Theater at Epidaurus** ★★    Although it's pleasant to wander through the shady **Sanctuary of Asklepios,** it's not at all easy to decipher the scant remains here—visit the excavation museum first (see below). As at Olympia, the Asklepion had accommodations for visitors, several large bathhouses, civic buildings, a stadium, a gymnasium, and several temples and shrines. The remains here are so meager that you may have to take this on faith, but try to find the round **tholos** that you'll pass about halfway into the sanctuary. The famous 4th-century B.C. architect Polykleitos, who built similar round buildings at Olympia and Delphi, was the architect here. If you wonder why the inner foundations of the tholos are so convoluted and labyrinthine, you're in good company: Scholars still aren't sure what went on here, although some suspect that Asklepios's healing serpents lived in the labyrinth.

Next to the tholos are the remains of **two long stoas,** where patients slept in the hopes that Asklepios would reveal himself to them in a dream. Those who had dreams and cures dedicated the votive offerings and inscriptions now in the museum.

As you wander around the site, you'll probably notice signs of recent excavation and restoration work on the early 4th-century B.C. **altar of Apollo Maleatas.** Archaeologists think that the altar was destroyed in the 1st century B.C. by a band of Silician pirates, irritated when they couldn't find any buried treasure here. The Greek Archaeological Service hopes to finish restoring the altar soon. So far, no hidden treasure has been found.

At the entrance to the site, the **excavation museum** helps to put some flesh on the bones of the confusing remains of the sanctuary. It has an extensive collection of architectural fragments from the sanctuary, including lovely acanthus flowers from the mysterious tholos. The terra-cotta body parts are votive offerings that show precisely what part of the anatomy was cured. The display of surgical implements will send you away grateful that you didn't have to go under the knife here, although hundreds of inscriptions record the gratitude of satisfied patients.

If you climb to the top of the **ancient theater,** you can look down over the 55 rows of seats, divided into a lower section of 34 rows and an upper section with 21 rows. The upper seats were added when the original theater was enlarged in the 2nd century B.C. The theater's acoustics are famous: You'll almost certainly see someone demonstrating how a whisper can be heard all the way from the round orchestra to the topmost row of seats. Just as the stadium at Olympia brings out the sprinter in many visitors, the theater at Epidaurus tempts many to step stage center and recite poetry, declaim the opening of the Gettysburg Address, or burst into song. Still, there's almost always a respectful silence here when a performance of a classical Greek play begins, as the sun sinks behind the orchestra and the first actor steps onto the stage (see "Epidaurus After Dark," below).

If you're a theater buff, be sure to take in the new **Epidaurus Festival Museum,** near the entrance to the site, with its displays of props, costumes, programs, and memorabilia from past performances. It's usually open daily from 1 May until 30 September when the site is open (and until 9pm on performance nights); entrance free.

Combined admission 6€. Hours for all site, theater, archaeological museum: summer Mon–Fri 8am–7pm, Sat–Sun 8:30am–3:15pm; winter Mon–Fri 8am–5pm, Sat–Sun 8:30am–3:15pm.

## WHERE TO STAY & DINE

There are several kiosks selling snacks and cold drinks near the ticket booth at Epidaurus. In Nea and Palaia Epidaurus, you'll find a number of boring restaurants, most of which cater to large groups. In other words, you won't starve, but there's no place worth seeking out, with the possible exception of **Leonidas** (✆ 27530/22-115). This small restaurant on the main Epidauros road attracts a post-theater crowd that often includes actors who relax here after performances. There's a garden and the food here (excellent grills and stews) is usually much better than that served at the tourist places.

**Epidaurus Xenia Hotel**    The best place to stay overnight at Epidaurus is this hotel, at the site itself. Once everyone leaves, this is a lovely, quiet spot in a pine grove. The 26 bungalowlike units go quickly on the night of a performance, so book well in advance. The bungalows are, admittedly, absolutely undistinguished in terms of decor: Here, as so often, it's location, location, location that makes this the place to stay. The restaurant serves bland but acceptable food. Liguorio, Nafplias, 21059 Peloponnese. ✆ 0753/22-005. 26 units, 12 with bathroom. 70€ double, sometimes lower in off season. Rates include breakfast. No credit cards. **Amenities:** Restaurant; bar.

## EPIDAURUS AFTER DARK

**Classical performances** at the **ancient theater** are usually given Saturday and Sunday at around 9pm from June through September. Many productions are staged by the **National Theater of Greece,** some by foreign companies. Ticket prices at press time ranged from 10€ to 35€. For the latest ticket prices and other information, contact the **Hellenic Festival Box Office,** 39 Panepestimiou (in the arcade) (✆ 210/322-1459), or the **Epidaurus Festival Box Office** (✆ 0753/22-006). It's also possible to buy tickets at most of the travel agencies in Nafplion and at the theater itself, starting at 5pm on the day of a performance. The ancient tragedies are usually performed either in classical or modern Greek; programs (4€) usually have a full translation or synopsis of the play. The excellent Odyssey bookstore in Nafplion (see "Shopping" in section 2, earlier in this chapter) usually has English translations of the plays being performed at Epidaurus.

If you are in Epidauros in July, check out the delightful **Musical July Festival** at the **Little Theater** of Ancient Epidauros, 7km (4½ miles) from Epidaurus. Performances in the past have ranged from chamber music to flamenco. Information on ticket prices and chartered bus and excursion boat transportation from Athens is usually available from the **Athens Concert Hall** (Megaron Mousikis), 1 Kokkali and Vas, Sophias (ⓒ **210/728-2000**), the **Greek National Tourism Organization** (ⓒ **210/327-1300** or 210/331-0562) or the **Municipality of Palea Epidaurus** (ⓒ **27530/41-250**) by June.

## 5 Nemea

25km (15 miles) SE of Corinth; 35km (21 miles) N of Argos

Panhellenic Games were held every 4 years at Olympia and Delphi and every 2 years at Isthmia, near Corinth, and at Nemea, in a gentle valley in the eastern foothills of the Arcadian mountains. The first Olympic Games were held in 776 B.C. and didn't begin at Nemea until 573 B.C. By about 100 B.C., Nemea's powerful neighbor Argos moved the festival from Nemea to Argos itself, putting an end to the games here. But, thanks to the Society for the Revival of the Nemean Games, games were held here for the first time in 2,000 years on June 1, 1996, when 1,000 contestants from around the world, ranging in age from 12 to 90, raced here. The 2000 games drew an even larger crowd, and the next games are planned for July 31, 2004. So, when you visit Nemea, you won't see just the stadium where athletes once contended, but also the site of the new Nemean Games. Contestants run barefoot, as in antiquity, but wear short tunics, rather than run naked. If you want to know more about the Nemean Games, contact the **Society for the Revival of the Nemean Games** (ⓒ **510/642-5924** in the U.S.; www.nemeagames.gr).

Two excellent site guides are on sale at the museum: *Nemea* (10€) and *The Ancient Stadium of Nemea* (2€). You'll find shady spots to read them both at the site and at the stadium.

## ESSENTIALS

**GETTING THERE   By Car**   From Athens, take the National Road to Corinth and then follow signs for Argos and Tripolis. The road divides just after the sign for Ancient Corinth. The speedy new Corinth–Tripolis toll road has green signposts with a drawing of a highway. Take the Nemea turnoff and follow signs to the site. If you take the old road, you'll see signs for Nemea just after the Nemea train station, where the main road bends sharply left; continue straight toward Nemea. Allow 30 minutes from Corinth to Nemea on the new road and an hour on the old road.

**By Bus**   There are about five buses a day from the Stathmos Leoforia Peloponnisou (Bus Station for the Peloponnese) in Athens, 100 Kifissou (ⓒ **210/ 513-4110** or 210/512-9233), to Nemea, usually via Corinth. Allow about 3 hours

---

(Tips   **In Vino Veritas**

Nemea is famous for its wines, especially its red wines, many known as the "blood of Herakles." Some to look for include Nemea Reserve Parparousi, Nemea Nasiakou, Domain Papaioannou Palea Klima, Nemea Selected Tsantali.

for the trip and ask to be let off at the ancient site of Nemea (*Ta Archaia*) on the outskirts of the hamlet of Archaia Nemea, not in the village of Nea Nemea.

**By Train** It's possible to take the train from Athens to the station several kilometers from the ancient site. The train, however, is very slow; it makes better sense to take the bus.

**FAST FACTS** Nea Nemea has both a **post office** and a **telephone office**, but it's unlikely that you'll want to go there. There's a **pay phone** by the ancient site.

## WHAT TO SEE & DO

**The Museum and Ancient Site** ★★ The Nemea Museum, set on an uncharacteristically Greek green lawn, is one of the most charming small museums in Greece. You'll get an excellent sense of the history of the excavation of Nemea and the Nemean Games, as well as the early Christian village here, much of which was built from material pillaged from ancient Nemea.

A display map just inside the museum's main gallery shows all the cities in the Greek world whose coins were found at Nemea and illustrates just how far people came to see these games. There are a number of excellent photographs of the excavations as well as enlarged photos of important finds, such as the small bronze figure of the infant Opheltes, in whose honor the Nemean Games may have been founded.

According to legend, the Seven Theban Champions founded the games in memory of the infant, who—not as agile as Heracles (Hercules)—was killed by a serpent. Because they were perceived as funeral games, the judges wore black mourning robes, just as they do today at the revived Nemean Games. Another legend says that the games were established not to honor Opheltes but to honor Heracles, who killed a fierce lion that had his lair in one of the caves in Evangelistria hill, just behind the stadium. Fortunately, lions are unknown in today's Greece.

While you're in the museum, be sure to take a look out of one of the large picture windows that overlook the ancient site where the coins, vases, athletic gear, and architectural fragments on display were found. A raised stone path tactfully suggests the route from the museum to the site, passing a carefully preserved early Christian burial tomb and skirting a large Christian basilica and Roman bath before arriving at the Temple of Zeus.

This temple was built of local limestone around 330 B.C. on the site of an earlier temple, which may have burned down. When Pausanias came by here in the 2nd century A.D., he felt that the temple was worth seeing but complained that "the roof has collapsed." Sometime later, the columns followed suit, perhaps when early Christian squatters pillaged the temple for building blocks, or after one of the many earthquakes that rocked the Peloponnese. For perhaps 1,500 years, only three of the original 32 exterior Doric columns were left standing; the drums of the others lay scattered on the ground. In 1999, University of California archaeologist Stephen Miller initiated an ambitious plan to reerect a number of the fallen columns, starting with two columns at the temple's north end. It is hoped that another four columns will be re-erected before the 2004 Nemean games and that summer's Athens Olympics. For more information on the Nemean Games, contact www.nemeagames.gr.

Joint admission to site, museum and stadium 4€. Year-round Tues-Sun 8:30am–3pm.

**The Stadium** ★★ To reach the stadium, leave the site and head several hundred yards back along the road that brought you into Nemea. *The Ancient Stadium* of Nemea, on sale at the ticket booth, contains a self-guided tour of the stadium. The locker room just outside the stadium caused quite a stir when it was discovered in 1991, with few journalists able to resist cracks about what a locker room must smell like after 2,500 years.

Athletes would have stripped down in the locker room, oiled their bodies with olive oil, and then entered the stadium through the vaulted tunnel, just as football players today rush onto the playing field. Once you pass through the tunnel, you'll see where the judges sat while spectators sprawled on earthen benches carved out of the hillside itself. When they got thirsty, they could have a drink from the water carried around the racetrack in a stone channel. If you want, walk down onto the 178-meter race course and stand at the stone starting line where the athletes took their places for the footraces. Running naked and barefoot, the athletes kept their balance at the starting line by gripping the indentations in the stone with their toes.

*©* 27460/22-739. Joint Admission to site, museum, and stadium 4€. Year-round Tues–Sun 8:30am–3pm.

## WHERE TO STAY & DINE

There's no hotel here as yet. The **Pisina Restaurant,** in Nea Nemea next to the municipal swimming pool, keeps irregular hours.

48km (30 miles) S of Corinth

Argos was the most powerful city in the Peloponnese in the 7th century B.C. when it was ruled by its skillful tyrant, Pheidon, often credited with inventing coinage in Greece. There should be lots of impressive remains to visit here, but since modern Argos (pop. 20,000) is built precisely on top of the ancient city, there's little to see in town except the 4th-century theater and the excellent museum. Out of town is a different story: The fortifications on Argos's twin citadels, the Aspis and the Larissa, are very impressive.

As for the modern town itself, repeated earthquakes have left Argos with an undistinguished agglomeration of flat-roofed buildings, with only the occasional neoclassical house as a reminder of how nice this town once was. That said, the central plateia is very lively and the street market on Wednesday and Saturday mornings is one of the largest in the Peloponnese.

If your time in the Peloponnese is limited, you might consider saving Argos for a return trip. If you can spend a few hours here, give the theater a passing glance, concentrate on the museum, and try to drive up to the Larissa and Aspis citadels to take in the Venetian fortifications and the view over the plain.

## ESSENTIALS

**GETTING THERE   By Train**   There are about five trains a day from Athens to Argos. Information on schedules and fares is available from the Stathmos Peloponnisou (Railroad Station for the Peloponnese) in Athens (*©* **210/513-1601**) or at the Corinth train station (*©* **27510/27-212**). Trains take at least 3 hours. The Argos train station, on Leoforos Vas. Sofias (*©* **27510/67-212**), is about a kilometer from the central square.

**By Bus**   There are five buses a day to Argos from the Stathmos Leoforia Peloponnisou (Bus Station for the Peloponnese) in Athens, 100 Kifissou (*©* **210/513-4110** or 210/512-9233). Buses usually take just under 3 hours. Argos is also served by frequent buses from Nafplion (about 30 min.). Argos has two bus stations: the Athinon Station (buses to and from Athens), on Leoforos Vas.

## A Word of Caution

Argos's confusing system of one-way streets and potentially lethal three-way intersections make driving almost as chaotic as the night in 272 B.C. when Pyrrus of Epirus stormed the city with a large force—including two war elephants, one of which overturned and blocked the main gate into the city. In short, drive with particular care here.

Georgiou B. (© **27510/673-24**), and the Arcadia-Laconia Station (buses for Tripolis), at 24 Peithonos (© **27510/67-324**).

**By Car**  From Athens, take the National Road to Corinth, and then follow signs for Argos and Tripolis. The road divides just after the sign for Ancient Corinth. The speedy new Corinth-Tripolis toll road has green signposts with drawings of highways. Take the Argos exit and follow the exit road until it reaches an obvious main road (the old Corinth-Argos road). Turn right, cross the bridge, and you'll soon enter Argos. If you take the old road to Argos, it runs straight into the town. It's never easy to park in Argos, but you'll probably find a place on one of the side streets off the central square or by the ancient theater.

**FAST FACTS**  The **National Bank of Greece,** along with several others on the main square, Plateia Ayios Petros, all have ATMs. The **hospital** (© **27510/24-455**) is signposted on the main road into town from Athens. The **police** are at Agelou Bobou 10 (© **27510/67-222**). The **post office,** 16 Danaou, off the central square, is open Monday through Friday from 7am to 2pm. The **telephone office** (OTE), 8 Nikitara, is usually open Monday through Friday from 7am to midnight. The **Café Net** at 4 Oktaviou 28th, has Internet facilities for 4€ per hour.

## WHAT TO SEE & DO

### The Theater at Argos ★

If you've already seen the theater at Epidaurus, you'll find it hard to believe that Argos's 4th-century theater was not just larger, but probably the largest in classical Greece. Twenty thousand spectators could sit here, in 89 tiers of seats, many of which were carved from the hillside itself. The thronelike seats in the front rows were added by the Romans and reserved for visiting bigwigs, including the Roman emperor. The Romans remodeled the theater, so that the orchestra (stage) could be flooded and mock naval battles staged. Fortunately, they had a genius for building the aqueducts needed to channel enough water to create a temporary inland sea. There was enough water left over to service the baths, whose remains are next to the theater. Also near the theater are the minimal remains of the ancient agora, as yet largely unexcavated, as it lies under today's Argos.

© 27510/68-819. Admission 2€; joint admission to theater, agora, Heraion, Archaeological Museum 3€. Summer Mon–Sat 9am–6pm; Sun 10am–3pm. Often open in winter as well. Sometimes closed unexpectedly (but clearly visible from the Argos-Tripolis road).

### The Museum at Argos

This small museum has a handful of superlative pieces that you'll want to take in, including the fragment of a 7th-century B.C. clay krater (vessel) showing a determined Ulysses blinding the one-eyed Cyclops Polyphemus. Nearby are a handsome lyre made from a tortoise shell and a stunning late geometric bronze helmet and suit of body armor. Downstairs, in the Lerna room, the tiny, stout Neolithic clay figure of a woman or goddess found at Lerna is one of the oldest known sculptural representations of the human body yet found in Europe. Nearby is a handsome pitcher in the shape of a bird with its head thrown back in song—and ornamental breasts on its chest.

Outside, in the museum's shady courtyard, are some terrific Roman mosaics showing the god Dionysos and the seasons. The figures in the seasons mosaics are bundled up in cloaks and heavy leggings in the cold months and casually dressed in light tunics and filmy cloaks in the summer months.

If you visit the museum (which has a welcome icy cold water fountain and very clean toilets) on Wednesday or Saturday morning, don't miss the **street market** that runs for several blocks to your left as you leave. This is the place to get anything from water glasses, baseball caps, and farm implements to live chickens and every possible seasonal fruit and flower. If you're here on a non-market day and need supplies, there's a large **supermarket** (Pharmatetras) just off the main square. To get to it, turn right as you leave the museum and then right again in the square.

Olgas St. (No street number), off the main square, Plateia Ayiou Petrou. © 27510/68-819. Admission 2€; Joint admission to theater, agora, Heraion, Archaeological Museum 3€. Tues–Sun 8: 30am–3pm.

**The Larissa and the Aspis** Argos was famous in antiquity for its two citadels; the 905-foot-high Larissa was well fortified by the 6th century B.C. When you reach the Larissa summit, you'll be able to spot the more elegant ancient blocks that were reused in the medieval battlements. There's an inner and outer system of walls, with several towers and the ruins of a church. The view's the thing here, and you get a bird's-eye view of the plain, Argos, the Gulf of Nafplion, and the lower citadel, the Aspis (98m/328 ft. high).

The Greek word Aspis means "shield," which is what the Argives thought this hill looked like. This was the city's first acropolis, abandoned when the higher Larissa was fortified. With the exception of one tower, the summit here really is a confusing jumble of low walls and the indeterminate depressions in the earth that mark building foundations. Still, the views are tremendous.

You can wander around the Larissa or Aspis as you wish. Not many visitors come here, so be especially cautious about doing any dangerous climbing on the walls if you're alone.

You can climb up to the Larissa from Argos's ancient theater (allow at least an hour), and then hike across the ridge called the Deiras to the Aspis. If you drive, ask for directions to the Kastro, or castle, as the Larissa is called, at the theater, the Archaeological museum, or the police station, as roads in Argos are in a seemingly constant state of flux.

Free admission. Usually open from sunrise to sunset.

## WHERE TO STAY & DINE

With Nafplion just down the road, there's really no reason to stay overnight in Argos unless you prefer the bustle of this crowded Greek market town to Naf-plion's more sybaritic pleasures. If you do stay here, the 24-unit **Hotel Mycenae,** 10 Plateia Ayiou Petrou (© 27510/68-754), is probably your best bet (although with no air-conditioning, this hotel can be very hot in summer); double rooms, many with balconies, start at around 50€. Although the Hotel Mycenae is on Argos's energetic main square, the rooms are relatively quiet and you're certainly where the action is.

None of the small cafes and restaurants in Argos is worth seeking out, but the conveniently located **Retro** and **Aigle,** on the main square, have the usual chops, salads, and souvlaki, as well as pizza and veal in lemon sauce (moskari lemonato). Lunch or dinner costs from 10€ with beer or wine. If you want a sweet, try the little place directly across from the Archaeological Museum; it offers snacks and drinks, including cappuccino.

## 7 Sparta (Sparti)

248km (153 miles) SW of Athens; 58km (36 miles) S of Tripolis

Few sights in the Peloponnese are more imposing than the immense bulk of Mount Taygetos towering above Sparta. There's often snow on Taygetos until well into the summer, and when the sun sinks behind the mountain, the temperature seems to plummet instantly. The rich plain watered by the bottle-green Eurotas River that has made Sparta prosperous since antiquity stretches between the Taygetos and Parnon mountain ranges. Lush olive and citrus groves run for miles between the ranges, and there are even ornamental orange trees planted along Sparta's main avenues.

The Spartans earned their reputation for courage and military heroism in 580 B.C., when the Spartan general Leonidas and a band of only 300 soldiers faced down the invading Persian army at Thermopylae. From 431 to 404 B.C., Sparta and Athens fought the Peloponnesian War; Sparta finally won, but was exhausted by the effort. From then on, Sparta was a sleepy provincial town with a great future behind it. Greece's first king, young Otto of Bavaria, paid tribute to Sparta's past by redesigning the city with the wide boulevards and large central square that make it still charming today.

In a famously accurate prediction, the 5th-century B.C. Athenian historian Thucydides wrote that if Sparta were ever "to become desolate, and the temples and the foundations of the public buildings were left, no one in future times would believe that this had been one of the preeminent cities of Greece." The ancient remains here are so meager that only the truly dedicated will seek them out. Others will prefer to take in the small archaeological museum, enjoy the bustling town of Sparta itself, and head 8km (5 miles) down the road to the very impressive remains of the Byzantine city of Mistra.

## ESSENTIALS

**GETTING THERE** **By Bus** From Athens, seven buses a day depart from the Stathmos Leoforia Peloponnisou (Bus Station for the Peloponnese), 100 Kifissou (© 210/513-4110 or 210/512-9233), for the Sparta bus station on the east side of town on Lykourgou and Dafnou. (© 27310/26-441). There are frequent buses from Sparta to Mistra.

**By Car** From Athens, allow 5 hours; from Corinth, 3 hours; from Patras, 3 hours; from Tripolis, 2 hours. From Athens or Corinth, the new Corinth-Tripolis road is well worth taking.

**VISITOR INFORMATION** It is usually possible to get visitor information in the Town Hall, on the main square (© 27310/26-517 or 27310/24-852); hours are Monday through Friday from 8am to 3pm. Ask whether the English-language pamphlet *Laconia Traveller* is available. In recent years, there has been a **summer music and drama festival** in Sparta, sometimes called Artistic Summer Sparta (fax 27310/82-470); inquire at the Town Hall.

**FAST FACTS** Two **National Bank of Greece** offices on Paleologou exchange currency and have ATMs. The **hospital** (© 27310/28-671) is signposted in town. The **police** and **tourist police** are at 8 Hilonos (© 27310/20-492). Both the **post office**, on Kleombrotou, and the **telephone office** (OTE), at 11 Kleombrotou, are signposted. The Cosmos Club Internet Café (© 27310/21-500) charges 5€ an hour.

## WHAT TO SEE & DO

If you'd like to sign up for a guided half or full-day tour or hikes around Sparta, contact **Dimitra G. Colomvakou** (€) and fax **27310/82-804;** mobile 0932/948-119; spartanhiking@hotmail.com). The **Hellenic Alpine Club of Sparta,** 97 Gortsologou (near the central square) (€ **27310/22-574)** has information on climbing Mount Taygetos and local hikes; *Taygetos,* published by the Municipality of Sparta, is an invaluable guide (9€).

**The Acropolis and Ancient Theater** The ancient Spartans boasted that they didn't need fortifications because the Taygetos and Parnon mountains were their defense walls. In addition, as Thucydides reminds us, Spartans did not go in for much building. Consequently, there's not a lot to see on the Spartan acropolis.

The acropolis is at the north end of town, just beyond the monumental statue of Leonidas near the supposed site of his tomb. The grove of trees here makes this a pleasant place to sit and read at sunset, but you'll probably enjoy the view of Taygetos more than the scattered remains of the 2nd-century B.C. theater. Originally, this was one of the largest theaters in Greece, seating 16,000. The theater was dismantled and the blocks were carted off for reuse when the Franks built Mistra in the 13th century. The theater is sometimes used during the summer festival here.

Free admission. Usually open Tues–Sun 8: 30am to 3pm.

**The Archaeological Museum** The prize of this museum is a handsome 5th-century marble bust, believed to show Leonidas and to have stood on his tomb. The Spartans, however, were famous as soldiers, not as artists, and the museum's collection reflects Sparta's lack of a lively artistic tradition. Still, it's worth stopping here to see the statue of Leonidas, several fine Roman mosaics, and a small collection of objects found at Mycenaean sites in the countryside near Sparta. The museum's rose garden, peopled with decapitated Roman statues, is a nice spot to sit and read. *Be warned:* This museum has no rest rooms.

On the Square between Ayios Nikolaos and Paleologou Sts. € **27310/28-575.** Admission 2€ Tues–Sat 8: 30am–3pm; Sun 8: 30am–12: 30pm.

**The Menelaion** To visit the Menelaion, take the Tripolis road north out of town and turn right immediately after the bridge; the Menelaion is signposted about 5km (3 miles) down the road. The shrine, in honor of Helen of Troy's long-suffering husband, Menelaus, has three terraces of gray limestone blocks and is about a 10-minute walk uphill from the chapel, where you can park your car. Beside the shrine are the low remains of several Mycenaean houses, none of which seems remotely grand enough to have belonged to Menelaus. Again, as with the acropolis of ancient Sparta, the real reason to come here is for the view of the plain and Taygetos.

Free admission. Usually open Tues–Sun 8: 30am to 3pm.

**The Temple of Artemis Orthia** If you continue out of town on the Tripolis road, you'll see a small yellow sign for the Temple of Artemis Orthia, where little Spartan boys were whipped to learn courage and endurance. Today, the site, which dates from the 10th century B.C. but was extensively remodeled by the Romans, is often crowded with gypsy children, aggressively begging for money. Consequently, this can be an unpleasant place to visit, especially alone.

Free admission. Usually open Tues–Sun 8: 30am–3pm.

## WHERE TO STAY

**Hotel Byzantion** ★ This family-owned and operated hotel is the place to stay if you want to be poised to visit Mistra first thing in the morning. There's very little traffic on the road through Mistra at night, but whatever there is passes by here, although the double-glazed windows keep out most sounds of traffic. Rooms in the back overlook a pleasant garden with a fish pool. Bedrooms and bathrooms are on the small side but are spotless and perfectly pleasant; the staff is exceptionally helpful and the breakfast buffet is ample. There are several small tavernas in Mistra if you don't want to go to Sparta for dinner.

23100 Mistra, Laconia. ℂ **27310/83-309.** Fax 27310/20-019. Byzanthl@otenet.gr. 22 units, 55–65€ double. MC, V. Usually closed Dec–March 15. **Amenities:** Breakfast room; garden. *In room:* A/C, TV.

**Hotel Maniatis** Despite its location at the corner of Paleologou and Lycourgou, Sparta's two main streets, the Maniatis is reasonably quiet (the rooms in back are smaller but quieter). The marble-and-glass lobby is considerably grander than the bedrooms, which, if not spartan, are simple, with functional bedside tables, straight chairs, and small bathrooms. The hotel restaurant, the Dias, is decorated in pastels that should be soothing but somehow aren't. The food is okay, but the place is often filled with noisy tour groups; it's worth walking a couple blocks to the excellent Diethnes restaurant (see below).

72 Paleologou, 23100 Sparta, Laconia. ℂ **27310/22-665.** Fax 27310/29-994. 80 units, 65€–75€ double. MC, V. **Amenities:** Restaurant; bar. *In room:* A/C, TV.

**Hotel Melelaion** ★ It's good to see the handsome neoclassical Menelaion, built in 1935, looking good again. For too many years, this once-elegant hotel, with high ceilings and stylish architectural detail, let itself go. Now redone, with a very nice swimming pool in the central courtyard, the Menelaion is an appealing place to stay (although the rooms fronting Paleologou get lots of traffic noise as well as noise from the main taxi stand). Friends who stayed here recently had no complaints, although those who like extra-firm mattresses might find the beds a bit soft.

91 Paleologou, 23100 Sparta, Laconia. ℂ **27310/22-161.** Fax 27310/26-332. 48 units, 75€ double. Rates include breakfast. MC, V. **Amenities:** Restaurant; bar; pool. *In room:* A/C, TV, minibar.

**Hotel Sparta Inn** This large hotel with a roof garden has a quiet location on a side street, but is often taken over by not-so-quiet tour groups. Guest rooms are air-conditioned, with firm beds, decent reading lights, and good-size bathrooms. There's nothing charming about the Hotel Sparta, whose muted color scheme is rather gloomy, but its quiet location and two (small) pools are real pluses in Sparta, which tends to be noisy and hot in the summer. Ask for the hotel's handy English printout of area attractions.

109 Thermopilion, 23100 Sparta, Laconia. ℂ **27310/21-021,** or 416/362-4342 in Toronto. Fax 27310/24-855. info@spartainn.com. 150 units, 65€–75€ double. V. **Amenities:** Restaurant; roof garden bar; 2 pools. *In room:* A/C, TV, minibar.

**Tips Shopping in Sparta**

The weekly **market** in Sparta is on Saturday. **Lampropoulou** and **Liakos,** both on Paleologou, stock English-language guides, newspapers, magazines, and books.

## WHERE TO DINE

**Diethnes** ★ GREEK   On summer Saturdays, all of Sparta seems to eat lunch in the Diethnes's shady garden after shopping at the street market around the corner. If you're only going to eat one meal in Sparta, it should be here; in fact, unless you really don't like eating in the same place more than once, why go anywhere else? The grills (including local loukanika sausages) are excellent; the vegetables are drizzled, not drenched, in oil; the local wine is eminently drinkable; and the waiters move with the speed of light through the crowds.

105 Paleologou. ℃ 27310/28-636. Main courses 4.50€–10€. No credit cards. Daily about 8am–midnight.

**Elysse Restaurant** GREEK   If the Diethnes weren't just a few doors away, this would be a very tempting place to eat. The food is good, the staff is efficient, but in the summer, it's much more pleasant to sit in the garden at the Diethnes than in the Elysse's indoor dining room. If you're tired of Greek food by the time you reach Sparta, check to see whether any of the continental dishes listed on the Elysse's menu are actually being served: Chicken Madeira and Veal Marsala have been known to appear here.

113 Paleologou. ℃ 27310/29-896. Main courses 4.50€–9€. No credit cards. Daily about 11am–11pm.

**The Stoa Cafeteria** ★ LOUKOUMADES/SNACKS   This little hole-in-the-wall next to a florist is the place to go for a Spartan favorite: *loukoumades*, airy deep-fried puffs of pastry drenched in honey syrup.

140 Lycourgou. ℃ 27310/23-237. Coffee and loukoumades 3€. Mon–Fri 8am–evening; Sat 8am–noon.

**A LOOK AT THE PAST**   In 1204, the Frankish leader William de Villehardouin chose this site as the headquarters for his Greek empire. De Villehardouin crowned Mistra with a fortress and defense walls, built himself a palace on the slopes below, and had 10 good years here, until the Byzantine Greeks defeated him at the Battle of Pelagonia in 1259. According to legend, de Villehardouin would have escaped capture if a Greek soldier had not identified him by his famously protruding buck teeth.

Mistra's real heyday came under the Byzantine Greeks, when most of its churches and more than 2,000 houses, as well as the enormous Palace of the Despots, were built. Some 25,000 people lived in Mistra—twice the population of Sparta today. Among them were the philosophers, writers, architects, and artists who made Mistra something of an international center of culture.

Mistra was such an important city that many Byzantine emperors sent their heirs here for some on-the-job training. After Constantinople and the Byzantine empire fell to the Turks in 1453, Mistra held out; the last emperor of Byzantium was crowned in the Cathedral at Mistra, which finally fell to the Turks in 1460.

The Venetians captured Mistra from the Turks in 1687 and ruled here for a half century, during which time Mistra swelled to an enormous city of more than 40,000, largely supported by a flourishing silk industry. When the Turks regained power, Mistra began its long decline into what it is today: Greece's most picturesque ghost town.

**THE ARCHAEOLOGICAL SITE OF MISTRA**   If you start your tour of Mistra at the top, you can orient yourself by taking in the fine view over the entire site from de Villehardouin's **Castle** (the Kastro). The **Palace of the Despots,** which has been undergoing restoration for some years, stands out clearly, surrounded by the roofs of Mistra's magnificent **churches.** In 2002, two special exhibits, one of the Byzantine City and one on the Palace's kitchen, were opened in the palace and excellent information signs in Greek and English were erected by most of the monuments. As you head down from the kastro, you'll begin to pass some of the churches, most of which have elaborate brickwork decoration, a multiplicity of domes, and superb frescoes. Despite what one scholar described as Mistra's "picturesque incoherence," you should be able to find the most beautiful churches—the **Saint Sophia,** the **Pantanassa,** the **Panayia Hodegetria,** the **Peribleptos,** and the **Cathedral.**

Give your eyes time to adjust to the poor light inside the churches; once they do, you'll be able to pick out vivid scenes, such as the *Raising of Lazarus* and the *Ascension* in the 15th-century frescoes in the Pantannasa Monastery, the *Marriage of Cana* in the 14th-century Panayia Hodegetria, and the stunning *Birth of Christ* in the 14th-century Peribleptos Monastery. The frescoes that decorated Greek churches have been described as the "Books of the Illiterate"; any devout Byzantine Greek could have "read" these frescoes and identified every New and Old Testament scene, just as their descendants can today.

The site (① 27310/93-377) is open from 8am to 3pm and sometimes later in summer. Admission is 5€.

If you enjoyed Mystra's churches, try Chrysafa, a village 12 km (7 miles) from Sparta with a clutch of Byzantine churches. The churches are usually locked, but many are open on Sunday and others can be visited if you ask around in the main square to see who has the keys.

45km (27 miles) from Megalopolis to Andritsena; 24km (15 miles) from Andritsena to Vassae

Vassae is one of the most impressive 5th-century Greek temples, its gray granite columns the perfect complement to its remote mountain setting. Unfortunately, the temple, badly damaged by time and earthquakes, is now hidden under a bizarre protective tent that looks rather like the Sydney opera house. When fires threatened to engulf Vassae in August 1998, the staff here hosed the tent all day and all night and successfully protected both tent and temple from the flames. Every year, the guard here says that he hopes Vassae will be mended and the tent removed "next year," a phrase that in Greek does not carry the specificity that its English translation suggests. Hearteningly, in the summer of 2000, the Committee for the Preservation of the Temple announced government-funded plans to begin a 20-year restoration. Initially, the foundation along the temple's north end, along with 10 columns, will be restored. Of course, when this vital work begins, and while it goes on, the entire temple itself will be even less visible to visitors.

Although it's perfectly possible to visit Vassae on a day trip from Olympia, **Andritsena★,** with the scent of oregano and the sound of sheep bells everywhere, is one of the most charming of the Peloponnesian mountain villages. There's a welcome new hotel here and a number of small restaurants. The main street is punctuated by enormous plane trees, several of which have been fitted with pipes gushing forth the delicious local spring water. In the evening, villagers stroll the main street while sheep bells echo in the hills. In short, if you want to get away from it all and spend the night in a Greek mountain village, try to make it Andritsena.

## ESSENTIALS

### GETTING THERE   **By Bus**   There are several buses a day to Andritsena from Athens and from Argos, Tripolis, Olympia, and Megalopolis. The Greek National Tourism Organization office in Athens can provide information on these services.

**By Car** All the routes to Andritsena go through spectacular mountain countryside. The roads are excellent, but each winding mile takes about twice as long to drive as you might have anticipated.

**FAST FACTS** Everything you might need—the **bus station**, the **OTE**, the **post office**, the **bank**, the **police**—is clearly signposted on or just off Andritsena's main street.

## WHAT TO SEE & DO
## THE TEMPLE OF VASSAE

Coming around the last turn in the road and suddenly seeing the severe gray limestone columns of this 5th-century Doric temple to Apollo used to be one of the great sights in the Peloponnese. It seemed almost impossible that such a staggeringly impressive building should have been built in such a remote location—and designed by none other than Ictinus, the architect of the Parthenon. Evidently, the temple was built by the inhabitants of the tiny hamlet of Phigaleia, to thank Apollo for saving them from a severe plague.

If you saw the temple before it disappeared under its tent, cherish your memories and don't bother to visit now. The tent fits so snugly that the only way to get a sense of what the temple actually looks like is to buy a postcard.

If you haven't seen Vassae, you'll have to decide whether you want to see it this way, or hope that the guard will be right and that "next year" the tent will be gone. The temple is usually open daily from 8am to 7pm in summer, to 3pm in winter. Admission is 3€.

## THE VILLAGE OF ANDRITSENA

Tiny Andritsena has one of the finest libraries in Greece, the legacy of a 19th-century philhellene. If you like old books, check to see if the **library,** recently moved into a grand new building just off the main street, is opened. If not, you can console yourself at the **Club Mylos Internet Café** on the plateia.

The small **folk museum,** on the plateia below the main street, is usually locked, despite its posted hours. Admission is 1€; contributions are welcome. To see the endearing collection of local wedding costumes, rugs, farm tools, and family photographs, ask to be let in at the house nearest to the museum. If the people there don't have the keys, they'll phone Kyria Vasso at the Sigouri Restaurant (see below).

If you can, plan to be in Andritsena on Saturday, when the main street is taken over by the weekly **market,** an excellent place to buy every manner of sheep, goat, and cow bells, mountain tea, and herbs.

## WHERE TO STAY

**Epikourias Apollon Hotel** ✪ Frequent travelers to Andritsena rejoiced when this 5-room hotel on the main plateia opened in 2001. The rooms are simple, spotless, and have pleasant views over the town. Kuria Maria, who is in charge here, could not be more helpful. Since there are only 5 rooms, you probably should make a reservation, lest you be forced back on the Theoxenia, or find yourself driving on to Olympia, the nearest place with a good number of hotels.

Plateia, 27061 Andritsena, Eleia. © **26260/22-840.** 5 units. 45€ double without breakfast, 50€ double with breakfast. **Amenities:** Breakfast room. *In room:* Heating in winter.

**Theoxenia Hotel** This 1950s hotel is a casualty of the excellent Andritsena-Olympia road; now visitors who once spent the night here stop briefly to see Vassae and speed on to Olympia. Understandably (but not enjoyably), the hotel has let itself go; you can almost always show up and get a room here. The views from the front rooms overlooking the valley below Andritsena, but are surprisingly noisy, because bus and truck drivers often use the hotel parking lot to turn their vehicles around. Students of kitsch will appreciate the needlework pictures hanging on many walls—but no one will appreciate the shabby decor and borderline grubby carpets and bathrooms. Room rates are somewhat flexible, so be sure to ask if there is a cheaper room if the price seems high. Avoid the restaurant, and hold onto your room key, as there's often no one at the front desk.

27061 Andritsena, Eleia. © **26260/22-219.** 45 units. 40€–50€ double. No credit cards. **Amenities:** Restaurant.

## WHERE TO DINE

**Andritsena Kafezakeroplasteion (Coffee-Sweet Shop)** COFFEE/SWEETS
If you're staying at the Theoxenia, avoid your hotel breakfast by coming here for bread and honey, yogurt, or an omelet. In nice weather, you can sit outside under the umbrellas, looking at the elegant lace curtains in the café's six decorative fan windows.

On the main street, Andritsena. © **26260/22-004.** Full breakfast 4€. No credit cards. Daily about 7am–11pm.

**Georgitsis** GREEK   Sit under the plane trees here and dine on simple grills and vegetable dishes. If you want some water, you can fill your glass from the spring water that gushes out of a pipe in one of the trees.

On the main street, Andritsena. No phone. Lunch or dinner from 9€. No credit cards. Usually open 11am–3pm and 7–10pm or so.

**Sigouri** ★ GREEK HOME COOKING   Kyria Vasso's *briam* (vegetable stew) is excellent, as are her stuffed tomatoes and barrel wine. A meal here consists of a salad, main course, and the local wine. If you like *kourouloudes* (rag rugs), ask to see the ones she makes and sells by the meter; for about 25€, you can take home a colorful hand-loomed bedside rug. Kyria Vasso also usually has the keys to the Folk Museum. She may even have a Frommer's sticker on her window!

Sofokleos (across from the metalworker's shop above the main plateia), Andritsena. © **26260/22-197.** Lunch or dinner from 9€. No credit cards. Open most days for lunch and dinner, usually closing by 10pm.

**The Trani Brisi** GREEK   This small restaurant has tables outside under extra-large beach umbrellas, in a widening of the road between the two upper plateias (squares). The menu varies from day to day, but often features some kind of lamb stew, fresh vegetables, and the local wine. If you like the wine, you can usually buy some to take away with you.

On the main street, Andritsena. No phone. Lunch or dinner from 9€. No credit cards. Open most days for lunch and dinner, usually closing by 10pm.

## 9 Monemvassia

97km (60 miles) S of Sparta; 340km (210 miles) S of Athens

Nicknamed "the Gibraltar of Greece" because of its strategic importance during the Middle Ages, Monemvassia was a virtual ghost town by the 20th century. Today, this rocky island just off the easternmost tip of the Peloponnese has a new lease on life: For some years, wealthy foreigners and Greeks have been buying and restoring old houses here. Furthermore, word is getting out that in addition to its medieval fortress, handsome churches, and drop-dead sunsets, Monemvassia has several of the most stylish small hotels in the Peloponnese (and increasingly good restaurants.) Monemvassia draws visitors year-round; when we stopped here for lunch on a late January weekend in 2002, the restaurants were full—and so were the hotels.

Unfortunately, an increasing number of round-the-Peloponnese bus tours make a brief stop here; try to arrive in the late afternoon or evening, have a swim, relax, and do your sightseeing in the early morning before the first tour bus arrives.

Although Monemvassia is an island, it's connected to the mainland by a causeway that you can drive or stroll across. Once you step through the massive Venetian Gate that is Monemvassia's only entrance (*mone emvasis* means "one entrance" in Greek), you're in a separate world. Cars are banned here—a wise decision, since the only approximation of a street on "the rock" is barely wide enough for two donkeys (which bring in supplies) to squeeze past each other.

## ESSENTIALS

**GETTING THERE    By Bus**    There is one direct bus a day from the Stathmos Leoforia Peloponnisou (Bus Station for the Peloponnese), at 100 Kifissou in Athens, to Gefyra (on the mainland directly across the causeway from Monemvassia), and six daily buses via Sparta. Call © **210/513-4110** or 210/512-9233 for schedule information.

**By Car**    Take the National Road from Athens-Corinth-Tripolis. Head south to Monemvassia via Sparta. Allow at least 6 hours for the trip.

**By Boat**    The Hellas Flying Dolphin hydrofoil leaving from Marina Zea in Piraeus links Athens and Monemvassia for most of the year and is the fastest way to reach Monemvassia from Athens. For information, call © **210/419-9200** or 210/419-9000, or check www.dolphins.gr. Information in Monemvassia is available at the port authority (© **27320/61-113**).

**FAST FACTS**    The **National Bank of Greece** in Gefyra (on the shore across the causeway from the old town) exchanges currency and has an ATM. You'll find the **post office** and the **OTE** in Gefyra. For **first aid**, call © **27320/61-204**. The **police** are at 137 Spartis (© **27320/61-210**). The **Malvasia Travel Agency** (© **27320/61-752**; fax 27320/61-432) in Gefyra has several helpful English-speaking staff members.

## WHAT TO SEE & DO

### SHOPPING

There's no shop on "the rock" that's truly outstanding, but those along **Ritsos** have thus far avoided the infestation of T-shirts and cheap museum reproductions so common elsewhere. Shops (most with nice pottery, glass, and jewelry) seem to come and go here with some alacrity, but one that's been here a long time is just inside Monemvassia's gate: **Costas Lekakis** has a good selection of books in English, including R. Klaus and U. Steinmuller's excellent guide *Monemvassia* (6€). **Ioanna Angelatou's shop**, next to the Byzantion hotel, often has a good selection of the deep-blue glassware made in Greece and well-done reproductions of antique wood carvings and copper. The **Livieratou Anastasia Jewelry Shop** has excellent quality jewelry, much of it adaptations of ancient and Byzantine motifs. The **Kelari** has a good selection of wines and local souvenirs; Takis Papadakis at the Kelari often has information on renting rooms and small apartments locally (© **27320/61-695**).

## WHERE TO STAY

Our preference is to stay on the rock, but there are a number of new hotels on the mainland in and around Gefyra, including the **Flower of Monemvassia** (Louloudi tis Monemvasias) (© **27320/61-395**; fax 27320/61-391), with views (over buildings) of the beach and the rock. As for Monemvassia itself, there are so few rooms here that this is one place where it's essential to try to make a reservation. We say "try" because records of reservations sometimes disappear mysteriously; even after several phone calls. If at all possible, arrive here early in the day; reservations also seem to disappear toward evening, when hotels may worry about no-shows.

**Ardamis Castle** ★  This small boutique hotel had hardly opened when it started turning up on lists of the best hotels in Greece with adjectives like "romantic" and "distinctive" heaped up in reviews. Rooms are lovingly restored and furnished with appropriate antiques and period pieces—and most have sea views. If the management is as careful as it seems to be, the Ardamis is going to give the long-time favorite the Malvasia a run for the money here.

23070 Monemvassia. ⓒ **27320/61-886.** www.ardamis.gr. 6 units. 100€ double DC, MC, V. **Amenities:** Breakfast room/bar. *In room:* A/C.

**Byzantion**  There's only one problem with staying in this small hotel in a beautifully restored and furnished house with wood beams and tile floors: A number of the rooms are built flush against a hillside, do not get adequate cross-ventilation, and can be stuffy, with an odor of mildew. Ask for a bedroom with ventilation and a balcony (although you may hear street noise and sounds from the Byzantion's cafe). Some rooms are available with air-conditioning, TVs, and refrigerators.

Ritsos, 23070 Monemvassia. ⓒ **27320/61-351.** Fax 27320/61-331. 18 units 60€–80€ double or suite. DC, MC, V. **Amenities:** Breakfast room. *In room:* A/C.

**Kellia**  It is nice to be able to recommend the Kellia. This former convent was (mis)managed as a hotel by the GNTO, but has perked up greatly now that it is operated privately; Kuria Athena is very helpful and the once-neglected rooms and garden are well-tended.

By the Panayia Chrysafiotissa church. 23070 Monemvassia. ⓒ **27320/61-520.** 15 units. 60€–70€ double. DC, V. **Amenities:** Restaurant; garden. *In room:* A/C.

**Lazaretto** ★  The Lazaretto is very nice indeed, offering tastefully furnished guest rooms with beamed ceilings, hand-loomed rugs, and sea or garden views. The hotel restaurant is well above average. The only possible fly in the ointment: Although set back from the causeway, with sturdy stone walls between guests and traffic, the fact remains that the Lazaretto is on the causeway, and on weekends, there's a lot of traffic to and from Monemvassia itself. The management has plans to build a pool; check to see if they have when you visit, as that would be an enormous plus.

On the causeway, 23070 Monemvassia. ⓒ **27320/61-991.** Fax 27320/61-992. 14 units. 135€–150€ double, 200€ suite. MC, V. **Amenities:** Restaurant; bar; garden. *In room:* A/C, TV, minibar, hair dryer.

**Malvasia** ★★  This remains the finest hotel in Monemvassia and one of the most charming in Greece. Over the years, the owners have bought up a number of old houses, restored them, and furnished the rooms with old copper, hand-loomed rugs and bedspreads, and handsome wooden furniture. This would be a wonderful place to stay a week, or even a month (long-term reduced rates are available). If you can't do that, at least stay for a night and hope for a sea-view room in the Stellaki Mansion on the ramparts, or in the hotel's original building on Ritsos. If you're here in winter, ask for a room with a fireplace. Some units have phones and refrigerators; some suites have full kitchens.

Headquarters on Ritsos, 23070 Monemvassia. © **27320/61-323.** Fax 27320/61-722. 35 units. 60€–80€ double; 85€–150€ suite. MC, V. **Amenities:** Restaurant; breakfast room; gardens. *In room:* A/C, TV (in some rooms), minibar (in some rooms), hair dryer (in some rooms), kitchenette (in some rooms).

## 10 The Mani

*Githio is 301km (186 miles) S of Athens and 45km (27 miles) S of Sparta; Areopoli is 32km (20 miles) W of Githio*

The innermost of the Peloponnese's three tridentlike prongs, the Mani is still one of the least-visited areas in Greece. That's changing fast, as word gets out about the fine beaches near Githio and Kardamili and the haunting landscape of the Inner Mani (the southernmost Mani). Good new roads mean that you can now drive the circuit of the entire Mani in a day, but it's more fun to spend at least a night here, perhaps in one of the restored tower-house hotels.

The Inner Mani's barren mountains are dotted with tiny olive trees and enormous prickly pear cactuses. It's hard to believe that 100 years ago, this was a densely populated area, with almost every hillside cultivated. If you squint, you can still make out the stone walls and terraces that farmers built on the deserted hillsides.

Originally, the Maniotes chose to live in tower houses because they were easy to defend, an important consideration for these constantly feuding Peloponnesians who spent much of their time until the early 20th century lobbing cannonballs at their neighbors. Fortunately, many tower houses survived, and the towers of the virtually deserted villages of Koita and Nomia look like miniature skyscrapers from a distance.

When the Maniotes weren't trying to destroy their neighbors' homes, they seem to have atoned by building churches. The area is dotted with tiny medieval chapels tucked in the folds of the hills. Keep an eye out for the stands of cypress trees that often mark the chapels, many of which have decorative brickwork and ornately carved marble doors. If you don't want to tramp around the countryside in search of chapels, at least take a look at the **Church of the Taxiarchoi (Archangels)** in Areopoli. Don't miss the droll figures of the saints and signs of the zodiac carved on the church's facade.

After World War II, when most Maniotes moved away, to Athens or abroad, entire villages of austere gray-stone tower houses were deserted. In recent years, many of these handsome houses have been restored as vacation or retirement houses by Maniotes, other Greeks, and foreigners. Villages that were ghost towns 10 years ago are gaining a new lease on life in this austere and beautiful region.

## ESSENTIALS

**GETTING THERE** **By Car** This is a long trip, but not as tedious as the bus, which makes many stops. Take the National Road Athens-Corinth-Tripolis, and then head south to Githio and Areopoli via Sparta.

**By Bus** It's possible to travel from Athens to the Sparta bus station (© **27310/ 26-441**) and from Sparta to the Githio bus station (© **27330/22-228**) or the Areopoli bus station (© **27330/51-229**), but this is a trip that takes a full day. For schedule information, call © **210/513-4110** or 210/512-9233 or the numbers above for the bus stations in Sparta, Githio, and Areopoli.

**By Ship** Gythion is served by Hellas Flying Dolphin from Piraeus and intermediate stops (© **210/419-9200;** www.dolphins.gr. There are also sailings from Gythion to the islands of Kythera and Krete. The **Rozakis Ship Brokers & Travel Agency,** 5 Vas. Pavlou (the harbor front) (© **27330/22-650;** fax 27330/22-229; rosakigy@otenet.gr has information sailings (including the Patras-Ancona Super

Ferry service) and can make reservations and issue tickets. Rozakis also rents cars from minis to vans from 36€ to 75€ per day.

**GETTING AROUND** Longtime visitors to Greece wax nostalgic about the days when they had to hoof it around the Mani. You can get around today by local bus, but by far the most efficient method is by car.

**FAST FACTS** There are **banks** with ATMs in both Githio and Areopoli. Don't count on finding banks elsewhere in the Mani. In Areopoli, most services are on or just off the main square: the **bank** (usually open Mon–Fri from 9am–noon), the **post office**, the OTE, the **bus station**, several **restaurants**, and an excellent small **bookstore, Mani** (© 27330/53-670), where you can pick up Patrick Leigh Fermor's enduring classic, *Mani*, and Bob Barrow's helpful *The Mani*. You can also visit their website and order books at www.mani.org.gr/adoulotimani (adoulotimani@mani.org.gr). The **police** (© 27330/51-209) are signposted on the main square in Areopoli.

## WHAT TO SEE & DO

### The Caves of Dirou (Glyfada and Alepotrypa) ★★

Here's the good news: the crystal-studded stalactites (the ones hanging from the ceilings like icicles) and stalagmites (the ones rising up from the cave's floor) here are spectacular, in shades of rose, green, amber, black, blood red, and purple. The bad news:

These caves, a very popular holiday destination for Greeks, are mobbed in summer, so try to arrive as soon as they open. If you get here later in the day, buy your ticket immediately; usually visitors are taken in some kind of order. Guided tours through the Glyfada cave take about 30 minutes and as wonderful as they are, are not recommended for the claustrophobic: Although the cave's passageways through the caverns—the largest is 100 meters long—are illuminated with multicolored lights, you are well-aware that you are far, far underground. Guides pole small boats (each holding up to a dozen passengers) past the strange formations and call out the stalactite's and stalagmites's nicknames (ranging from the reverential to the obscene). The guides also delight in warning passengers not to trail their fingers in the cool subterranean waters that reach depths of 20 meters: Giant eels are rumored to live just below the surface. Visitors usually disembark from the boat for a short excursion on foot through a segment of the cave; this part of the visit would be awkward for anyone nervous about slippery surfaces.

The Pirgos Dirou Caves were discovered in 1955 by a dog that crawled through a hole into the caves and returned several days later coated in red clay. Fortunately, his owner, spelunker Anna Petroclides, was curious about the red clay and followed her dog when he next set off on explorations. What she found was a vast network of caves, of which some 5,000m (50,003 ft.) have now been explored. The caves themselves are impressive, but what has made them famous is the Paleolithic and Neolithic remains found here. In short, the Pirgos Dirou caves are one of the oldest inhabited spots in Greece, and the pottery, bone tools, and even garbage found here has shed light on Greece's earliest history.

Before you leave Pirgos Dirou, check to see if the small **Neolithic Museum** (© 27330/52-233), with displays of artifacts found in the caves, is open. Admission is 1€.

Pirgos Dirou. © 27330/52-222. Fax 27330/52-223. Admission 15€. The visiting hours for the caves vary unpredictably; in general, the caves are open 9am–5pm in summer, with shorter hours off season.

**The Demaglion Folklore Museum** This small private collection in the village of Thalames, some 20km (12 miles) north of Areopoli, has old prints, costumes,

## Tips Insider Tip

As you approach Vathia, you'll see a breathtaking cluster of Maniote towers, for some years operated as a hotel. Alas, although the towers look beautiful from outside, inside is another story. We do not recommend staying in the restored tower houses in Vathia; these were not great as the Vathia Tower Hotel, when they were (mis)managed by the Greek National Tourist Office, and they have not improved since they became the privately-operated Zenonas Vathia a few years ago. Let's hope that someday these towers get the care and attention that they deserve and that we can recommend them—and visitors can stay in this potentially charming hotel.

olive presses, farm tools, ceramic plates commemorating various Greek monarchs—and just about anything else you'd expect to find if you cleaned out a number of Maniote attics. The owner, Mr. Demaglion, is a local schoolteacher who speaks a little English and a lot of German and enjoys lecturing visitors. From time to time, Mr. Demaglion sells duplicate items from his collection; you may be able to buy an inexpensive antique wood carving or piece of embroidery. Items for sale are usually on display in front of the museum.

Thalames. Admission 3€. Usually open May 1–Sept 30, most days 9: 30am–8pm; often closed at midday.

## WHERE TO STAY

Our recommendations below are in the Mani itself, but if you want to stay on the outskirts of the Mani, here are some suggestions. In Githio, harborfront choices offering doubles under 70€ at press time included the venerable (but recently restored) **Aktaion** (℡ **27330/23-500;** fax 27330/22-294), our favorite with its seaside balconies; the **Gythion** (℡ **27330/23-452;** fax 27330/23-523), in a charming 19th century former businessmen's club; the **Pantheon** (℡ **27330/ 22-289;** fax 27330/22-284); and **Leonidas** (℡ **27330/22-389;** fax 27330/ 22-595). In Messenian Mani, at the seaside hamlet of Kardamili, the **Kalamitsi Hotel & Bungalows** (℡ **27210/73-131;** fax 27210/73-135; ponireas@ compulink.gr) has doubles in the main building for 70€; suites and bungalows are also available.

**Akroyiali Hotel** ★ For years, the family-run Akroyiali Hotel, overlooking the harbor (front-facing rooms have balconies), was a pleasantly modest 12-room hotel with an excellent restaurant that served fresh seafood. In 2000, the Akroyiali added 23 units in the Xenonas Gerolimenas, a handsome stone building built in traditional Maniote style beside their original hotel. A year later, they added 20 furnished apartments in yet another stone building, a short, stiff walk uphill from the harbor, which many rooms overlook. In short, if you stay in Gerolimenas, the Theodorakis family (many of whom have lived in Canada and speak English) is almost certain to have what you want. The original rooms are the most modest; all the new units have air-conditioning and the furnished apartments also have TV and complete kitchenettes; many units have balconies. All these rooms are very popular in summer with vacationing Greeks and Europeans; it's best to make a reservation, especially if you plan to be here on a weekend.

Gerolimenas, 23071 Lakonia, Mani. ℡ **27330/54-204.** Fax 27330/54-272. 55 units 45€–50€ double; 75€ with breakfast; 1- and 2-room apts 45€–75€. No credit cards. **Amenities:** Restaurant. *In room:* Most with A/C and TV, some with kitchenettes.

**Hotel Itilo** ✪  This beachfront family-run hotel on the Gulf of Itilo, just north of Areopoli, attracts lots of families, whose children enjoy the little beachside playground. Many of the large guest rooms overlook the sea. If you show up here for just a night or two in high season, you may be relegated to the annex, just across the road from the beach. The hotel food, with lots of fresh fish, is excellent, but, as always with fish, expensive. Children love the ice-cream sundaes served with little parasols and, sometimes, sparklers.

Neo Itilo, 23062 Lakonia, Mani. ✆ 27360/59-222. Fax 27360/29-234. 26 units, 75€ double. Rates include breakfast. AE, MC, V. **Amenities:** Restaurant; children's play area. *In room:* A/C, TV.

**Kapetanakou Tower Hotel** ✪  One of the first of the traditional settlement hotels managed by the Greek National Tourism Organization, and now privately owned, the 180-year-old Kapetanakou Tower stands in a walled garden just off the main street in Areopoli. Some of the rooms have sleeping lofts, several have balconies or little patios, and most have colorful rag rugs and locally handmade weavings. This is a wonderful place to stay to get an idea of what it was like to live in a Maniote tower. (Noisy, for one thing: When the wind blows, or other guests walk on the wooden staircase, you know it!) The hotel serves breakfast, and it's only a 5-minute stroll to Areopoli's restaurants. The television in the lobby is sometimes left on, but the manager will usually turn it down or off if you ask.

Areopoli, 26062 Laconia, Mani. ✆ 27330/51-233. 8 units (2 shared bathrooms on each floor). 50€–60€ double. AE, MC, V. **Amenities:** Breakfast room.

**Limeni Village Hotel** ✪✪  Before we stayed here, we regarded this hotel, built as a Maniote tower village, as a glaring example of bringing coals to Newcastle. But after enjoying the swimming pool each day before and after sightseeing, and taking in the sunset while sipping a gin and tonic on the balcony, we dropped our objections. The bedrooms (two units to most bungalows; some bungalows rented as suites) are outfitted with rag rugs, stone floors, and balconies overlooking the Bay of Itilo. The breakfast buffet is fine, if not inspired; the restaurant is desultory (but the superb Fish Taverna To Limeni is minutes away; see below). Most guests here seem to be Greek families visiting the Mani.

Limeni, Areopoli, 23062 Laconia, Mani. ✆ 27330/51-111. Fax 27330/51-182. 32 units, 105€; lower off season. AE, MC, V. **Amenities:** Restaurant; bar; pool. *In room:* A/C, TV, minibar.

**Londas Tower Guesthouse** ✪  Small and very nicely appointed, the Londas Guesthouse has 3 doubles and a triple in a restored 18th-century tower off Ayii Taxiarches Square. Each of the rooms has an en suite bathroom, done with more attention to detail that is customary in this part of Greece. There are views over the town from the rooms and their terraces. There's no air-conditioning (the winds here are so fierce that it is almost never needed) and, to ensure tranquility, no TVs. Owner/managers Hans Kleiner and Iakovos Xenakis speak most languages you will probably need and are most helpful.

Limeni, Areopoli, 23062 Laconia, Mani. ✆ 27330/51-360. Fax 27330/51-012. Londas@otenet.gr. 4 units. 80€ double. AE, MC, V. **Amenities:** Breakfast room/bar.

**Tsimova Guesthouse** ✪  How often do you get to stay in a private home that is also a museum? If you speak some Greek and want to find out about the Mani, this guesthouse in a 300-year-old tower with gun slits is the place to stay. Owner George Bersakos has lived all his life in the Mani and turned much of his house into a small museum (which you can visit without staying here), stuffed with Maniote memorabilia. If you don't speak Greek, Mr. Bersakos will entertain you in his distinctive English, French, or German, or call in his daughter, who does speak English. You'll be beautifully taken care of, but you'll inevitably have less privacy than you would in a hotel. Several of the rooms have TVs.

Areopoli, 26062 Laconia, Mani. ⓒ 27330/51-301. 10 units, 8 with bathroom. 50€ double. Reductions possible off season. No credit cards. **Amenities:** Breakfast room.

**Tsitsiris Castle** ★   This tower-house hotel—10km (6 miles) south of Areopoli, in the virtually deserted hamlet of Stavri—has its lobby and dining room in a 200-year-old restored tower, with most of the bedrooms in two new wings flanking a garden with roses and geraniums. The lobby and dining room have lots of exposed stone walls and woven rugs. The bedrooms are more mundane, although when we stayed here, we had our own icon shrine and wonderful views across the hills. Not many independent travelers make their way here; you may either have the place to yourself, or be surrounded by tour groups and Greek families. The restaurant is excellent when there are a good number of guests; otherwise, choice is limited and the cooking can be desultory. The hotel is now family-owned and -operated, and Kuria Antigone, who cooks and oversees the hotel, is very helpful and has useful suggestions on what to see locally.

Stavri, 23071 Laconia, Mani. ⓒ 27330/56-297. Fax 27330/56-296. 20 units. 50€–65€ double. Rates include breakfast. MC, V. **Amenities:** Restaurant; TV lounge. *In room:* A/C.

## WHERE TO DINE

In **Kardamili**, we've eaten well at **Lela's** (ⓒ **27210/73-541**) by the sea, reached by the twisting road from the main plateia. When Lela's is closed, there's usually a sign posted with directions to another family-run place.

We've eaten at most of the seaside seafood restaurants on the harbor in **Githio**—and still haven't found one that's good enough to make us come back again and again. You should get good, fresh fish at any one of these places, so you may want to make your choice based on other factors, such as atmosphere and noise level. Just off the seafront, by the minuscule traffic round-about, there are several ouzeries, including **Korali**, that serve snacks and light meals at considerably lower prices than the seaside places. En route from Githio to Areopoli, in the narrow pass dominated by the castle of Passava, 10km (6 miles) out of Githio, the family-run **Kali Kardia** (ⓒ **27330/93250**) serves good *spitiko* (homestyle) food.

The three basically interchangeable restaurants on **Areopoli's main square** serve equally good—or bad, depending on your point of view—food, featuring grilled meats and salads. Lunch or dinner at any one of these costs from about 10€.

**Barba-Petros** ★   GREEK   This little taverna on Areopoli's sinuous main street, which runs from the main square to the cathedral, has a pleasant small garden and much better food than the restaurants on the square. If someone could only persuade the youths on motorcycles not to race up and down the street, this would be a totally gratifying place to sip the local wine and enjoy the tasty fried zucchini and eggplant, as well as chops and stews.

On the main street, Areopoli. ⓒ 27330/51-205. Main courses 6€–10€. No credit cards. Usually open noon–11pm (often closed mid-afternoon).

**Fish Taverna To Limeni** ★★★   SEAFOOD   The superb fresh fish at this small restaurant in Limeni, the harbor of Areopoli, draws customers from as far away as Kalamata, so be sure to make a reservation if you want a seaside table. This is not the place to eat if you are squeamish about seeing fish cleaned a few feet away from where you are eating. On the other hand, the seafood here is so good that you may find yourself coming back meal after meal while you're in the Mani. The price per kilo for the seafood varies from day to day and is never cheap; be sure to ask the price of the fish you select unless price is no object. The lobster diavolo (lobster with spaghetti in a tangy sauce with green peppers) is memorable, and costs around 55€ for two.

Limeni, Areopoli. © 27330/51-327. Fish and lobster priced by the kilo. No credit cards. Reservations recommended weekends. Usually open noon–midnight; sometimes closed during the week in winter.

## 11 Pylos (Pilo/Navarino)

50km (31 miles) W of Kalamata; 108km (67 miles) W of Sparta, 317km (196 miles) SW of Athens

We must admit that all too often in Greece, the modern village with a famous ancient name—Argos or Corinth, for example—is a disappointment. That's not the case at Pylos (also known as Navarino), where the modern harbor town has enormous charm. The harborfront, the tree-shaded main square with its statues and cafes, the cobblestoned side streets, all make Pylos a perfect place to wander, especially in the cool of the evening, when breezes blow from the sea. Pylos is developing some sprawling suburbs, and a few of the nearby beaches are being developed with a vengeance, but the harbor and leafy main square are untouched —so pleasant that it's hard to realize that Pylos's harbor has seen some very bloody battles. The Athenians trapped a Spartan force on the offshore island of Sfaktiria in 424 B.C., and in 1827, a combined French, Russian, and British armada defeated the massed Ottoman fleet here. More than 6,000 Ottoman sailors were butchered in what proved to be one of the critical battles of the Greek War of Independence. There's a monument to the three victorious admirals in Pylos's main square, which is understandably called the Square of the Three Admirals— and has lots of cafes that stay open late for after-dinner wanderers.

Some memorabilia from the battle, as well as archaeological finds from the area, are on view in the little **Antonopouleion Museum,** just off the main square (usually open Tues–Sun 8:30am–3pm; Admission 2€).

Ancient Pylos, site of the Mycenaean palace of King Nestor, is located about 17km (10 miles) north of the town on the hill of Englianos. Homer described Pylos as "sandy Pylos, rich in cattle," and the hilltop palace still overlooks sandy beaches flanked by rich farmland. Ancient Pylos seems to be a site that people take to—or don't. For every visitor who complains about the protective plastic roof over the site, another raves about the palace's idyllic setting, with its views out over farmfields and hills. Some call the remains here "scanty," while others find this the perfect place to imagine Nestor telling his tall tales while his couriers cast surreptitious glances out over the gentle countryside.

## ESSENTIALS
### GETTING THERE

**By Bus**   There are several buses a day from the Stathmos Leoforia Peloponnisou (Bus Station for the Peloponnese) in Athens, 100 Kifissou (© 210/513-4110 or 210/512-9233), to the Pylos station (© 27230/22-230).

**By Car**   Pylos is a full day's drive from Athens and 3 to 4 hours from either Patras or Sparta. The drive from Sparta to Pylos via the **Langada pass to Kalamata** takes in one of the most beautiful mountain roads in the Peloponnese.

**FAST FACTS**   Both **banks** in the main square offer currency exchange and have ATMs. The **hospital** (© 27230/22-315) is signposted in town. The **post office,** the **telephone office (OTE),** the **police** (© 27230/22-316), and the **tourist police** (© 27230/23-733) are all signposted in the main square.

## WHAT TO SEE & DO

**Ancient Pylos (Nestor's Palace) and Museum** ★★    The palace at Pylos belonged to Nestor, the garrulous old king who told stories and gave unsolicited advice while the younger warriors fought at Troy. The palace was rediscovered in 1939 by the American archaeologist Carl Blegen, who had the unbelievable good fortune of discovering the palace archives on his first day working here. Blegen uncovered some 600 clay tablets written in a mysterious language initially called Linear B, and later shown to be an early form of Greek.

Unlike Mycenae and Tiryns, Pylos was not heavily fortified: You'll see a sentry box, but no massive walls. The royal apartments are well preserved, and include a more-than-adequate bathroom with the rub still in place. Archaeologists have suggested that the small block beside the tub was a step, installed when the elderly King Nestor had trouble stepping into his bath. The palace, with its central courtyard, was originally two stories high and richly decorated with frescoes, some of which are on display at the small archaeological museum a mile away in the village of Hora.

© **0763/31-358.** Admission to each 3€. Tues–Sat 8: 30am–3pm; Sun 9: 30am–2: 30pm. Head north out of Pylos on the main road and follow the signs for Hora.

**Neokastro** ★    The Turkish fortress above the harbor, known as Neokastro, to distinguish it from an earlier fortress, now contains a splendid small museum in a restored 19th-century barracks. The museum features the extensive collection of maps, prints, and watercolors of the French phillhellene, Rene Puaux, as well as a number of marvelously kitschy porcelain figurines of the English phillhellene, Lord Byron. Neokastro also contains a small church, clearly a former mosque, some impressive fortification walls, shady trees and beds of vibrant geraniums and roses, and fine views over the harbor.

Admission 3€. Daily 8am–7pm.

## WHERE TO STAY

**Hotel Miramare** ★    The Miramare is just above Pylos's public bathing beach and has its own small restaurant. The guest rooms are simply furnished, the bathrooms are on the small side, but most rooms have balconies overlooking the harbor; some units have minibars. This hotel is usually considerably quieter than the Karalis Hotel, but not as quiet as seaside rooms at the Karalis Beach Hotel.

Paralia, 24001 Pylos, Messenia. © **27230/22-751.** Fax 27230/22-226. 26 units, all with shower only. 60€–75€ double. AE, MC, V. **Amenities:** Restaurant; bar. In room: A/C, TV.

**Hotel Zoe** ★ **Kids**    This pleasant seaside hotel about 5km (3 miles) north of Pylos is very popular with German families. If you're traveling with children, the chance to begin and end a day of sightseeing with a swim here might be the salvation of a family holiday. The guest rooms are decent-sized, spare, and ferociously clean.

Yalova Pylou 24001, Messenia. © 27230/22-025. Fax 27230/22-026. 35 units. 45€–65€. No credit cards. **Amenities:** Restaurant. In room: TV, some units with fridge.

---

**(Tips) Taking a Boat Tour**

If you'd like to take a boat tour of the magnificent Pylos harbor and the island of Sfaktiria, look for signs advertising excursions, usually posted by the harbor. An hour trip should cost around 12€; if the water is calm, you may see some of the ships that were sunk here during the Battle of Navarino in 1827.

**Karalis Beach Hotel**  With the best location in town, at the end of the harbor below the Turkish kastro, far from most traffic, this used to be the nicest place to stay in Pylos. But for the last few years, the management has been dreadful: It takes forever to get a room cleaned and there's seldom anyone at the desk. The lobby is often filled with young friends of staff members—most of them talking on cellphones. Nor is it endearing to have TV brackets—but no TVs—in some bedrooms. In short, there's only one reason to stay here: If you can get one of the seaside rooms with a balcony. Otherwise, you'd probably be happier at the Hotel Miramare (see above).

The Karalis Beach Hotel often sends its overflow to the **Karalis Hotel**, Kalamateas 26 (© **27230/22-980**), which is under the same management. Rooms here are pleasant, but suffer from traffic noise.

Paralia, 24001 Pylos, Messenia. © **27230/23-021**. Fax 27230/22-970. 14 units, 4 with shower only. 65€ double. MC, V. Usually closed Nov–Apr. **Amenities:** Breakfast room; bar. *In room:* Some units with TV.

**Navarone Hotel/Bungalows** ★  Friends who stayed here report enjoying this new hotel and its pool, about 5km (3 miles) north of Pylos and a 5-minute walk from an excellent sand beach. Many of the rooms have seafront balconies, and most have good reading lights and handy desks. Keep in mind that the Navarone gets lots of tour groups.

Petrochori, 24001 Pilias, Messenia. © 27230/41-571. Fax 27230/41-575. navaron1@otenet.gr. 17 units, 41 bungalows. 50€–70€. DC, MC, V. **Amenities:** Restaurant; pool. *In room:* TV.

## WHERE TO DINE

**Diethnes Taverna** ★  GREEK/SEAFOOD  The Diethnes has been here forever, serving meals both indoors and at tables by the quay overlooking the harbor. As you'd expect from a restaurant on the sea and next to the government fish-inspection station, the seafood here is very fresh. Fish in Greece is never cheap, so be sure you understand how much your fish will cost before ordering. There are usually a number of chicken and meat dishes on the menu, as well as a good *briam* (vegetable stew). If you like the food here and want to try a different restaurant with a similar menu, try the **Pende Adelphia**, or the **4 Epoches**, also along the harborfront.

Paralia. © 27230/22-772. Fish priced by the kilo. No credit cards. Mid-May to mid-Sept daily noon–at least 11pm.

**Philip Restaurant**  GREEK  The Philip prides itself on "traditional home cooking," including fish soup, stews, and both octopus and eggplant salads. The menu offers good seafood as well as a wide range of other dishes, often including spicy *loukanika* (sausages).

On Pylos-Kalamata road. © 27230/22-741. Fax 0723-23-261. Main courses from 5€; fish priced by the kilo. No credit cards. Daily about 11am–midnight.

**Restaurant 1930** ★  GREEK  As you might guess from the name, the decor here is emphasized, with the dining room aiming to recreate the ambience of 1930s Pylos. The menu offers good seafood as well as a wide range of other dishes, often including spicy *loukanika* (sausages).

On Pylos-Kalamata road by the Karalis Hotel. © 27230/22-032. Main courses 6€–14€; fish priced by the kilo. No credit cards. Most evenings in high season 8pm–midnight; sometimes open for lunch.

## 12 Messene (Ithomi/Mavromati)

25km (16 miles) N of Kalamata; 60km (39 miles) E of Pylos

Between 370 and 369 B.C., the great Theban general and statesman Epaminondas built the sprawling city of Messene and its almost 9.5km (6 miles) of walls below Mount Ithomi in the hopes of checking the power of Sparta. Today, the defense wall, with its two-story towers and turreted gates, is the best preserved classical fortification in the Peloponnese. Even though Messene's walls and towers knock the socks off the remains at many better-known classical sites, not many visitors come here. All the more reason to visit.

To get here by car from Pylos, Kalamata, or Tripolis, take the main Kalamata-Pylos road to the modern town of Messini, where the road to ancient Messene is signposted. The site of ancient Messene (also called Ithomi) is in the village of Mavromati, approximately 20km (13 miles) north of Messini.

## WHAT TO SEE & DO

**Ancient Messene ★★**    The most impressive stretches of the ancient wall are outside the site, north of the village of Mavromati. As you pass through Mavromati, try to pick up a copy of the excellent site guide at the postcard shop next to the village spring (4€). Even at a distance, the sheer size of the wall, with its towers and gates, makes most visitors gasp. The **Arcadian Gate** is especially well preserved, with the grooves cut in the marble pavement by ancient chariot wheels still clearly visible. As you drive back toward Mavromati, you'll pass more of the defense wall and the site museum, which has been closed for some time and shows no signs of reopening.

The excavated ruins of Messene are clearly signposted past the museum. This is a vast, sprawling site, with a **Sanctuary of Asklepios** so large that it was originally thought to be the agora (marketplace). The partially excavated **Stadium,** with many of its marble benches well preserved, lies along the dirt road beyond the Asklepeion. To walk the entire site takes a minimum of several hours, but it's possible to see just the Asklepeion in an hour.

A rough, but adequate, road runs from the site to the summit of Mt. Ithomi (800m/2,624 ft.). The views of Messene and Lakonia are spectacular; there are remains of a Temple of Zeus and the small medieval monastery of Voulkanos. At sunset, there are few more spectacular spots in Greece. At present, the summit site is unfenced and there is no admission charge.

Admission 3€. Tues–Sun 8am–3pm.

## WHERE TO STAY & DINE

**Ithome Restaurant** GREEK    This very simple restaurant has a terrific view over the ancient site and serves souvlaki, grills, salads, french fries, and the occasional vegetable dish.

Mavromati-Ithome (across from the Klepsidra Spring). ⓒ **2724/51-498.** Fax 2724/51-298. Lunch or dinner with a beer from 10€. No credit cards.

**Pension Zeus**    This small family-run pension—which is about as far from the Greece of tour-group hotels as you can get—has several small bedrooms with balconies. The family is very helpful and pleasant, and the rooms perfectly acceptable. The only problem: You're on the one road through town, and will hear whatever traffic there is.

Mavromati-Ithome, 24200 Messenia. ⓒ **2724/51-025.** 5 units, 3 with bathroom. 55€ double. Rates include breakfast. No credit cards.

## 13 Olympia

311km (199 miles) W of Athens; 90km (55 miles) S of Patras; 21km (13 miles) E of Pirgos

With its shady groves of pine, olive, and oak trees, the considerable remains of two temples, and the stadium where the first Olympic races were run in 776 B.C., Olympia is the most beautiful major site in the Peloponnese—although the

## The Ancient Olympic Games

The 5-day Olympic festival was held every 4 years between 776 B.C. and A.D. 393 at full moon in mid-August or September, after the summer harvest. Participants came from as far away as Asia Minor and Italy, and the entire Greek world observed a truce to allow athletes and spectators to make their way to Olympia safely. During all the years that the games took place, the truce was broken only a handful of times.

By the time the games opened, literally thousands of people had poured into Olympia; much of the surrounding countryside was a tent city. Women were barred from watching or participating in the games, although they had their own games in honor of Hera, Zeus's long-suffering wife, in non-Olympic years. Any woman caught sneaking into the Olympic Games was summarily thrown to her death from a nearby mountain.

No one knows precisely what the order of events was, but the 5 days included footraces, short and long jumps, wrestling and boxing contests, chariot races, the arduous pentathlon (discus, javelin, jumping, running, and wrestling), and the vicious pankration, which combined wrestling and boxing techniques.

The 3rd-century A.D. writer Philostratos recorded that participants in the pentathlon "must have skill in various methods of strangling." The most prestigious event was the stade, or short footrace, which gave its name to the stadium. Each Olympiad was named after the winner of the stade, and athletes like the 2nd-century B.C. Leonidas of Rhodes, who won at four successive Olympics, became international heroes. In addition to the glory, each victor won a crown made of olive branches and free meals for life in his hometown.

**A LOOK AT THE PAST**    There's really no modern equivalent for ancient Olympia, which was both a religious sanctuary and an athletic complex, where the games took place every 4 years from 776 B.C. to A.D. 393. Thereafter, the sanctuary slipped into oblivion, and buildings were toppled by repeated earthquakes and covered by the flooding of the Alfios and Kladeos rivers. When the English antiquarian Richard Chandler rediscovered the site in 1766, most of Olympia lay under 3m (10 ft.) of mud and silt. The Germans began to excavate here in 1852 and are still at it today.

Reports of the rediscovery of Olympia prompted the French Baron de Coubertin to work for the reestablishment of the Olympic Games in 1896. The first modern games were held in Athens in 1896, and Greece was very sorry to lose the 1996 100th anniversary games to Atlanta. Greeks are hoping that at least one event in the 2004 Olympics in Athens can take place here, where it all began. At a minimum, the lighting of the Olympic torch will take place here, as it always does for the Olympics.

forest fires of 1998 badly damaged neighborhood groves and almost engulfed the site itself. When you realize that the archaeological museum is one of the finest in Greece, you'll see why you can easily spend a full day here.

**OLYMPIA TODAY**    The straggling modern village of Olympia (confusingly known as Ancient Olympia) is bisected by its one main street, Leoforos Kondili. The town has the usual assortment of tourist shops selling jewelry, T-shirts, and reproductions of ancient pottery and statues, as well as more than a dozen hotels and restaurants. Two things worth visiting in town: the Museum of the Olympic Games and the excellent Galerie Orphee bookstore (see below).

The ancient site of Olympia is an easily walkable 15 minutes south of the modern village, but if you have a car, you might as well drive: The road teems with tour buses and the walk is less than relaxing.

## ESSENTIALS

**GETTING THERE    By Train**    There are several trains a day from Athens to Pirgos, where you change to the train for Olympia. Information on schedules and fares is available from the Stathmos Peloponnisou (Railroad Station for the Peloponnese) in Athens (© **210/513-1601**).

**By Bus**    There are three buses a day to Olympia from the Stathmos Leoforia Peloponnisou (Bus Station for the Peloponnese) in Athens, Kifissou 100 (© **210/513-4110** or 210/512-9233). There are also frequent buses from Patras to Pirgos, with connecting service to Olympia. In Patras, KTEL buses leave from the intersection of Zaimi and Othonos (© **2610/273-694**).

**By Car**    Olympia is at least a 6-hour drive from Athens, whether you take the coast road that links Athens-Corinth-Patras and Olympia or head inland to Tripolis and Olympia on the new Corinth-Tripolis road. Heavy traffic in Patras means that the drive from Patras to Olympia can easily take 2 hours.

**VISITOR INFORMATION**    Olympia is basically a one-street town; the few things you do not find on **Praxitelous Kondili** will be just off it. The **tourist office,** on the way to the ancient site near the south end of the main street, is usually open daily, in summer from 9am to 10pm, and in winter from 11am to 6pm. Ask here for a map of the site and town and information on accommodations (© **26240/23-100** or 26240/23-125). The **tourist police** (© **26240/22-550**) are handily located behind the tourist office.

**FAST FACTS**    The **National Bank of Greece,** on Praxitelous Kondili (the main drag), exchanges currency and has an ATM. The **health clinic** (© **26240/22-222**) is signposted in town. The **police** (© **26240/22-100**) are at 6 Ethnossinelefseos. Both the **post office** (on the main street) and the **telephone office** (just off the main street) are signposted.

## WHAT TO SEE & DO

**The Archaeological Museum** ★★★    If ever a building should not be judged by its facade, this is it. From outside, the museum has all the charm of a small factory. Inside, one of the finest collections in Greece is beautifully displayed in well-lit rooms, some of which look onto an interior courtyard. In August 1998, when forest fires were less than half a kilometer from both the site and museum, it was revealed that the museum owned, but had not installed, a fire-extinguishing system. Subsequent statements from the archaeological service suggested that the only thing unusual here was that a fire-extinguishing system had actually been purchased.

Even though you'll be eager to see the ancient site, it's a good idea to first visit the museum whose collection makes clear Olympia's astonishing wealth and importance in antiquity: Every victorious city and almost every victorious athlete dedicated a bronze or marble statue here. Nothing but the best was good enough for Olympia, and many of these superb works of art are on view. Most of the exhibits are displayed in rooms to the right and left of the main entrance and follow a chronological sequence from severe Neolithic vases to baroque Roman imperial statues, neither of which will probably tempt you from heading straight ahead to see the museum's superstars.

The monumental **sculpture from the Temple of Zeus** is probably the finest surviving example of archaic Greek sculpture. The sculpture from the west pediment shows the battle of the Lapiths and Centaurs raging around the magisterial figure of Apollo, the god of reason. On the east pediment, Zeus oversees the chariot race between Oinomaos, the king of Pisa, and Pelops, the legendary figure who wooed and won Oinomaos's daughter by the unsporting expedient of loosening his opponent's chariot pins. On either end of the room, sculptured metopes show scenes from the Labors of Hercules, including the one he performed at Olympia: cleansing the foul stables of King Augeus by diverting the Alfios River.

Just beyond the sculpture from the Temple of Zeus are the 5th-century B.C. **winged victory,** done by the artist Paionios, and the 4th-century B.C. figure of Hermes and the infant Dionysos, known as the **Hermes of Praxitelous.** The Hermes has a room to itself—or would, if tourists didn't make a beeline to admire Hermes smiling with amused tolerance at his chubby half-brother Dionysos. If you want to impress your companions, mention casually that many scholars think that this is not an original work by Praxitelous, but a Roman copy.

In addition to several cases of glorious bronze heads of snarling griffins and the lovely terra cotta of a resolute Zeus carrying off the youthful Ganymede, the museum has a good deal of **athletic paraphernalia** from the ancient games: stone and bronze weights that jumpers used, bronze and stone discuses, and even an enormous stone with a boastful inscription that a weight lifter had raised it over his head with only one hand.

Before you leave the museum, have a look at the two excellent **site models** just inside the main entrance. As the models make clear, ancient Olympia was quite literally divided by a low wall into two distinct parts: the Altis, or religious sanctuary, containing temples and shrines; and the civic area, with athletic and municipal buildings.

Admission to museum and site 9€. Summer Mon noon–6pm, Tues–Sat 8am–5pm. Winter Mon noon–6pm, Tues–Sat 11am–5pm.

**The Ancient Site**    In antiquity, every 4 years during the Olympic Games, so many people thronged here that it was said by the time the games began, not even one more spectator could have wedged himself into the stadium. So, if the site is very crowded when you visit, just remember that it would have been much worse in antiquity.

Olympia's setting is magical. Pine trees shade the little valley, dominated by the conical Hill of Kronos, that lies between the Alfios and Kladeos rivers. In July 2000, archaeologists excavating beside the Kladeos discovered a Mycenaean tholos (beehive) tomb with more than 100 amphorae, and expect to find more tombs as excavations continue. The discovery was a reminder of how much is yet to be discovered here.

The handsome temples and the famous stadium that you've come to Olympia to see are not immediately apparent as you enter the site. Immediately to the left are the unimpressive low walls that are all that remain of the **Roman baths,** where athletes and spectators could enjoy hot and cold plunges. The considerably more impressive remains with the slender columns on your right mark the **gymnasium** and **palestra,** where athletes practiced their footracing and boxing skills. The enormous gymnasium had a roofed track, precisely twice the length of the stadium, where athletes could practice in bad weather. Still ahead on the right are the fairly meager remains of a number of structures, including a **swimming pool** and the large square **Leonidaion**, which served as a hotel for visiting dignitaries until a Roman governor decided it would do nicely as his villa.

The **religious sanctuary** was, and is, dominated by two temples: the good-sized temple of Hera and the massive temple of Zeus. The **Temple of Hera**, with its three standing columns, is the older of the two, built around 600 B.C. If you look closely, you'll see that the temple's column capitals and drums are not uniform. That's because this temple was originally built with wooden columns, and as each column decayed, it was replaced; inevitably, the new columns had variations. The Hermes of Praxitelous was found here, buried under the mud that covered Olympia for so long due to the repeated flooding of the Alfios and Kladeos rivers.

The **Temple of Zeus**, which once had a veritable thicket of 34 stocky Doric columns, was built around 456 B.C. The entire temple—so austere and gray today—was anything but austere in antiquity: Gold, red, and blue paint decorated it, and inside stood the enormous gold-and-ivory statue of Zeus, seated on an ivory-and-ebony throne. The statue was so ornate that it was considered one of the Seven Wonders of the Ancient World—and so large that people joked that if Zeus stood up, his head would go through the temple's roof. In fact, the antiquarian Philo of Byzantium suggested that Zeus had created elephants simply so that the sculptor Phidias would have the ivory to make the statue of Zeus.

Not only do we know that Phidias made the 13-meter-tall statue, we know where he made it: The **Workshop of Phidias** was on the site of the well-preserved brick building clearly visible west of the temple, just outside the sanctuary. How do we know that this was Phidias's workshop? Because a cup with "I belong to Phidias" written on it and artists' tools were found here.

Between the temples of Zeus and Hera you can make out the low foundations of a round building. This is all that remains of the **shrine** that Philip of Macedon, never modest, built here to pat himself on the back after conquering Greece in 338 B.C.

Beyond the two temples, built up against the Hill of Kronos itself, are the curved remains of a once-elegant **Roman fountain** and the foundations of 11 **treasuries** where Greek cities stored votive offerings and money. In front of the treasuries are the low bases of a series of bronze **statues of Zeus**, dedicated not by victorious athletes but by those caught cheating in the stadium. These statues would have been the last thing that competitors saw before they ran through the vaulted tunnel into the stadium.

Ancient tradition clearly shows that the Olympic Games began here in 776 B.C. and ended in A.D. 395, but is less clear on just why they were held every 4 years. According to one legend, Herakles (Hercules) initiated the games to celebrate the completion of his 12 labors, one of which took place nearby when the hero diverted the Alfios River to wash out the fetid Augean stables that King Augeas had neglected for more than a decade. With the stables clean, Herakles paced off the stadium and then ran its entire length of 192m (600 Olympic ft.) without having to take a single breath.

Admission to site and museum 9€. Usually open summer Mon–Fri 8: 30am–7pm, Sat–Sun 8:30am–3pm; winter Mon–Fri 8am–5pm, Sat–Sun 8: 30am–3pm.

**The Museum of the Olympic Games**    When you head back to town, try to set aside half an hour to visit the Museum of the Olympic Games. Not many tourists come here, and the guards are often glad to show visitors around. Displays include victors' medals, commemorative stamps, and photos of winning athletes, such as former King Constantine of Greece and the great African-American athlete Jesse Owens. There's also a photo of the bust of the founder of the modern Olympics, Baron de Coubertin. (The bust itself stands just off the main road east of the ancient site and marks the spot where de Coubertin's heart is buried.) Admission 2€. Mon–Sat 8am–3:30pm, Sun and holidays 9am–2:30pm.

## WHERE TO STAY

Olympia has more than 20 hotels, which means that you can almost always find a room—although if you arrive without a reservation in July or August, you may not get your first choice. As is often the case in major tourist centers, hotels here often raise and lower their rates depending on what kind of a season they're having. In winter, many hotels are closed.

**Grecotel Lakopetra Beach** ★ *Kids*    This resort hotel, with just about everything you would want at a resort after a long day's sightseeing, is set in extensive gardens a short walk from the beach. With a car, you can be at ancient Olympia in less than 30 minutes. The rooms here are large, with balconies or terraces, and the bathrooms are well appointed. And, if you are traveling with children, this could be just the spot to compensate them for all those hours looking at what my own children always called "those old things you want to see." Kato Achaia, 25200 Achaia. © **26930/51-713.** Fax 26930/51-045. 192 units. 100€–150€ double. Rates include breakfast. MC, V. **Amenities:** 2 restaurants; bar; pool; fitness center with sauna; shops. *In room:* A/C, TV, minibar, hair dryer.

**Hotel Europa** ★★    The Europa is the best hotel in town-and one of the best in the Peloponnese. Part of the Best Western chain, it's a few minutes' drive out of town on a hill overlooking both the modern village and the ancient site. Most rooms overlook a large pool and garden, and several have views of a bit of the ancient site. Rooms are large, with extra-firm mattresses and sliding glass doors opening onto generous balconies. One drawback, pointed out to us by a recent visitor on crutches: although there is an elevator, you have to use the stairs to get to the pool and the breakfast room. 270 65 Ancient Olympia, Peloponnese. © **800/528-1234** in the U.S. 26240/22-650, or 26240/22-700. Fax 26240/23-166. 80 units. 120€ double. Considerable reductions off season. Rates include breakfast. AE, DC, MC, V. **Amenities:** Restaurant; bar; pool. *In room:* A/C, TV unstocked minifridge, hair dryer.

**Hotel Neda** *Value*    With a pleasant rooftop cafe, comfortable lobby, serviceable restaurant, and distinctive red-and-white facade, the Neda offers good value. The large double rooms, many decorated in shades of pink and rose, contain colorful shaggy flokati rugs and good bedside reading lamps. Some of the rooms have double beds, but most have twin beds, so specify which you want. All units have balconies, and are usually quieter than those at hotels on the main street.

*Finds*  **A Great Book Place for Books & Music**

**Galerie Orphee**, Antonios Kosmopoulos's bookstore on the main street in Ancient Olympia (© **26240/23-555**), carries an extensive range of cassettes and CDs of Greek music, plus frequent displays of contemporary art. It's a pleasant contrast to Olympia's other shops, which have all too many T-shirts, museum reproductions, and machine-made rugs and embroideries sold as genuine handmade crafts.

**Hotel Pelops** ★ The English-speaking owner, Susanna Spiliopoulou, described by many visitors here as especially helpful, makes this one of the most welcoming hotels in Olympia. She must be doing something right: the hotel was taken over by the Olympics committee for all of 2003; after a total renovation, it will be open again to customers in 2004. At press time, the renovations had not begun, but Ms. Spiliopoulou promised to retain the best of the past (perhaps the fluffy flokati rugs on the floors, and the plants and vines shading the terrace) while improving "everything."

2 Varela, 27065 Ancient Olympia. © **26240/22-543.** hotel_pelops@hotmail.com. 25 units. Price not available at press time, but probably around 70€–80€ double. MC, V. Sometimes closed Nov–Feb. **Amenities:** Breakfast room. *In room:* A/C, TV.

**Hotel Olympia Palace** ★★ Back for a return engagement (for many years this was the Altis Hotel), the completely remodeled Olympia Palace is an excellent choice if you want to be poised on Olympia's main street to investigate the village. If you don't want to go out, the hotel itself has restaurants, shops, and a pool. Rooms in the front can be noisy, rooms in the back have views over the countryside. The bedrooms here are good sized, very tastefully decorated (with nice rugs on the floor and attractive furniture); the bathrooms are modern and good sized. This hotel avoids the pallid anonymous colors so beloved of most Greek hotels.

2 Praxiteleous Kondili, 27065 Ancient Olympia. © **26240/23-101.** Fax 26240/22-525. 58 units. 90€–120€ double. AE, MC, V. **Amenities:** 2 restaurants; bar; pool; shops. *In room:* A/C, TV, minibar, hair dryer.

**Hotel Praxitelous** ★ (Value This small, family-run hotel is the best bargain in town. It's just one street back from Olympia's main drag, and the neighborhood has a nice feel, with children often playing ball in front of the police station. The guest rooms are very small and spare, and some of the beds are showing signs of wear; the front rooms have balconies. If you want to avoid the murmurs of conversation from the Praxitelous's excellent restaurant on the sidewalk below the balconies, ask for a room at the back (and hope that the neighborhood dogs are quiet).

7 Spiliopoulou, 27065 Ancient Olympia. © **26240/225-92.** 10 units. 55€–65€ double. AE, V. **Amenities:** Restaurant.

## WHERE TO DINE

There are almost as many restaurants as hotels in Olympia. The ones on and just off the main street with large signs in English and German tend to have indifferent food and service, although it's possible to get good snacks of yogurt or *tiropites* (cheese pies) in most of the cafes.

**Taverna Ambrosia** ★ GREEK This large restaurant with a pleasant outside veranda continues to attract locals, although it does a brisk business with tour groups as well. You'll find the usual grilled chops and souvlaki, stuffed tomatoes and dolmades, but the vegetable dishes are unusually good, as is the lamb stew with lots of garlic and oregano.

Behind the train station, Ancient Olympia. © **26240/23-755.** Fax 26240/22-439. Main courses 6€–12€. AE, MC, V. Daily 8–11pm. Often closed Nov–Apr, but sometimes open then on weekends.

**Taverna Kladeos** ★★ GREEK The charming Kladeos, with the best food in town, is at the end of the little paved road that runs steeply downhill past the Ambrosia restaurant. You may not be the only foreigner, but you probably will find lots of locals here. In good weather, tables are set up under canvas awnings and roofs made of rushes. If you sit on the hillside, you'll be serenaded by the frogs that live beside the river. The menu varies according to what's in season, but often includes lamb flavored with oregano. In summer, the lightly grilled green peppers, zucchini, and eggplant are especially delicious. The house wine, a light rosé, is heavenly. If you want to buy some to take with you, give your empty water bottle to your waiter and ask him to fill it with *krasi* (wine).

Behind the train station, Ancient Olympia. ⓒ 26240/23-322. Main courses 6€–12€. MC, V. Daily 1:30–3pm and 6pm–1am. Sometimes closed Nov–Apr.

**Taverna Praxitelous ★** GREEK  The reputation of the Hotel Praxitelous's excellent and reasonably priced restaurant has spread rapidly—and it's packed almost every evening, first with foreigners, eating unfashionably early for Greece, and then with locals, who start showing up around 10pm. Although the main courses are very good, especially the rabbit stew with onions (*stifado*), you can make an entire meal out of the delicious and varied *mezedes*, which may include octopus, eggplant salad, taramosalata, fried cheese, and a handful of olives: order a *poikilia* (assortment) plate and find out just how good they are. In good weather, tables are set outside on the sidewalk, the rest of the time, meals are served in the pine-paneled dining room, where there's often a fire in the fireplace on chilly evenings.

7 Spiliopoulou, Ancient Olympia. ⓒ 26240/23-570 or 26240/22-592. Main courses 5€–12€. AE, V. Daily about 11am–3pm and about 7pm–midnight.

---

## 14 Patras (Patra)

207km (128 miles) SW of Athens

The third-largest city in Greece and far and away the largest in the Peloponnese, Patras's unappealing urban sprawl now extends for miles north and south of the city center. You'll see work going on in the city to smarten it for its role as the European City of Culture in 2006. For now, although Patras does have sights worth seeing—the Cathedral of St. Andrew, the Archaeological Museum, a Roman Odeon (music hall) on the slopes of the ancient Acropolis, and a medieval castle on the summit—there's nothing here worth lingering over unless you have to mark time waiting for the ferry to Italy. In July and August, however, the **Patras International Festival of the Arts** (ⓒ 2610/276-540 or 2610/279-008) brings performances of everything from ancient drama to popular music to the Roman Odeon and the Patras Municipal Theater (ⓒ 2610/623-730). Or you may prefer to concentrate on the **Wine Festival,** featuring tastings at the Achaia Clauss winery (ⓒ 2610/325-051); check with the tourist office for schedule information. Patras also has a vigorous **carnival** that lasts nearly a month, with parades, costumes, and floats, ending the Monday before Lent.

## ESSENTIALS

**GETTING THERE   By Train**   There are frequent trains from the Stathmos Peloponnisou (Railroad Station for the Peloponnese) in Athens (ⓒ 210/513-1601). The Patras train station, 14 Othonos Amalias (ⓒ 2610/273-694), is on the waterfront near the boat departure piers. If you're catching a ferryboat, keep in mind that Greek trains usually run late and allow extra time for your journey.

**By Bus**   There are some 15 buses to Patras daily from the Stathmos Leoforia Peloponnisou (Bus Station for the Peloponnese) in Athens, 100 Kifissou (ⓒ 210/513-4110 or 210/512-9233). The Patras bus station (ⓒ 2610/623-886) is on Amalias.

**By Car**   The drive on the National Highway from Athens to Patras takes about 6 hours. At press time, there was one gas station on the National Highway itself between Corinth and Patras. *Note:* In the Patras city center, the system of one-way streets, not always obviously marked, along with the profusion of foreign drivers who have just arrived from Europe by ferryboat, mean that you should drive with particular care.

If you're heading from Patras across the Gulf of Corinth into Central Greece, you'll take the Rio-AntiRio car ferry, which runs twice an hour from early morning until about 11pm. Keep an eye out for work on the ambitious new Rio-AntiRio bridge, scheduled to be up by the 2004 Olympics.

**VISITOR INFORMATION**   The **tourist office (EOT)** is at 1 Iroon Polytechniou, on the harbor near ferryboat gate no. 6 (© **2610/650-353**); it's usually open Monday through Friday from 7am to 9pm, Saturday and Sunday from 2 to 9pm. The **tourist police** (© **2610/220-902**) are in the same building.

**FAST FACTS**   A number of **banks** on the waterfront and on Plateia Georgiou exchange currency and have ATMs. The **post office** is signposted at the intersection of Mezonas and Zaimi. There is a **telephone office (OTE)** on the waterfront by the customs sheds. Most of the **car-rental agencies** (Avis, Hertz, Kemwell) have clearly marked offices on the waterfront. The **hospital** (© **2610/22-3812**) is signposted in town. There is also an **emergency first-aid station** (© **2610/ 277-386**) at the corner of Karolou and Ayiou Dionysion. For Internet use, try

## The Ferry to the Ionian Islands & Italy

The major ferryboat and shipping companies all have offices on the waterfront. There is usually daily ferry service from Patras to the **Ionian islands and Corfu**. There are many daily services from Patras to the Italian towns of **Brindisi and Ancona**. The fastest service to Italy is the 18-hour **Super Ferry Crossing** from Patras to Ancona, offered by **Superfast Ferries** (© **2610/622-500**, or 210/969-1100 in Athens, or 310/544-3551 in the U.S.; fax 2610/623-547, or 3210/541-0166 in the U.S.; superfaxt@superfast.com). In 2003, a deluxe cabin for two cost 300€; a bunk in a shared four-bunk cabin cost 30€.

**Nerp@rk** (© **2610/279-699**), 37 Gerokostopoulou or the **Netrino Internet Café** (© **2610/623-344**), 133 Karaisaki. Both charge 4€ per hour. Both these places are off the waterfront; it is entirely possible that by the time you visit Patras, someone will have opened an Internet cafe on the harbor. Inquire at the tourist office (see above). **Discover** (© **2610/624-916**), which also sells CDs, is a good bookshop at 58 Mezonos, near the Archaeological Museum.

### WHAT TO SEE & DO

If you find yourself with a few hours in Patras, we suggest you head inland on Gerokostopoulou to **Plateia Yioryiou** (George Square). Sit at a cafe and take in the facades of the handsome neoclassical theater and banks on the square. Patras was burnt by the Turks during the War of Independence, and has been hit repeatedly by earthquakes. These buildings are among the few that remain from the 19th century, when the city was famous for its arcaded streets and neoclassical architecture. Patras still boasts attractive squares: in addition to Plateia Yioryiou, there's Plateia Olga and Plateia 25 Martiou, all with cafes, restaurants, and shops.

Then, head down to the waterfront to the **Cathedral of St. Andrew.** Although the present rather hideous church was only built after World War II, the mosaics give a vivid picture of old Patras. Be sure to dress appropriately to visit the cathedral, a major pilgrimage shrine thanks to the presence of St. Andrew's skull in an ornate gold reliquary to the right of the altar. There are several pleasant cafes in the shaded park across from the cathedral.

If you have an attack of conscience, head for the **Archaeological Museum,** 42 Mezonos (© **2610/220-829**), open Tuesday through Sunday from 8:30am to 5pm; free admission. If you're here on the weekend and feel energetic, take in the **Patras Fortress,** a medieval castle on the ancient acropolis that's open Saturday and Sunday from about 8am to 7pm; free admission. If you drive up, be pleasantly surprised if you don't get lost. If you're taking the Rio-AntiRio ferry from the Peloponnese across to Central Greece, you can take in another fortress, the 15th-century **Fortress of Rio,** while you wait for your boat. The fortress is open daily from 8am to 7pm; admission is free.

### WHERE TO STAY

**Astir Hotel** If you arrive too late to continue your journey or have an early-morning boat to catch, this is a convenient hotel whose best feature is its roof garden with pool. The bedrooms are nothing special, and many seem to have been decorated by someone who couldn't decide on just which color to go with. Some units have harbor views, as does the rooftop terrace. For Patras, this is a quiet place to spend the night—which is to say that the street noise here is usually endurable.

16 Ayiou Andreas, 26223 Patras. © **2610/277-502.** Fax 2610/271-644. 120 units. 100€–150€ double. MC, V. **Amenities:** Restaurant; bar; pool. *In room:* A/C, TV, minibar.

**Porto Rio Hotel/Casino** *Kids*  This sprawling hotel complex on the beach, a 20-minute drive north of Patras, does a brisk business with business conventions, tour groups, and European families on holiday. The Rio has several pools, a health club (with saunas and Jacuzzi), and two tennis courts. The Casino has slot machines and various card games. The guest rooms are large, and most have either a terrace or a balcony overlooking the extensive gardens. This is a good place to stay if you have a day to kill before catching a ferry in Patras—especially if you are traveling with children. The only drawback is the unimaginative food—but there are lots of small restaurants along the beach road.

26500 Rion. © **2610/992-102.** Fax 2610/992-115. 269 units, 48 bungalows. 75€–150€ double. AE, MC, V. **Amenities:** 2 restaurants; bar; pool; tennis; playground. *In room:* A/C, TV, minibar.

**Primarolia Art Hotel** ★  This boutique hotel has its own art gallery in a former brewery, elegantly restored as a small hotel. This place is popular with business travelers on expense accounts and couples in search of a romantic spot to spend the night before boarding a ship. If you have to spend the night in Patras, and don't mind the price, this is the place to stay: the bedrooms are elegant, with art on display in each room—and also have all the mod cons you'd hope for in the bathroom.

33 Othonos & Amalias, 26223 Patras. © **2610/624-900.** Fax 2610/623-559. www.arthotel.gr. 14 units. 170€–258€ double and suites. AE, DC, V. **Amenities:** Restaurant; bar; sauna. *In room:* A/C, TV, fax, dataport, minibar, hairdryer, safe.

## WHERE TO DINE

The restaurants along the harbor near the train station serve consistently mediocre food to the hordes of tourists arriving from and departing for Italy. You won't starve at any one of these places, but you can do better. If you are pressed for time and want to eat near the train station, try **To Konaki,** across from train station, which has dependably good food. (Unfortunately, for most of the summer, To Konaki moves shop to the beach at Rio.) If you just want an ouzo before dinner or a sweet after, head for any of the cafes in the main square, Plateia Yioryiou. There are several old-fashioned tavernas along Ayiou Nikolaou, including the **Majestic** and **Nikolaras.** If you visit the Kastro, you might have a meal at **Krini,** 57 Pandokratoros, which is usually open for lunch and dinner and has its own garden.

One place we can recommend is **Trikoyia,** Amalias 46 (no phone), a hole-in-the-wall taverna that serves up excellent fresh fish and octopus. Chops and one or two other meat dishes are usually available as well. It's a 15-minute walk along the harbor from the main port.

Next door at Amalias 48 (the number is not posted on the building) is the **Pharos Fish Taverna** (© **2610/336-500),** with equally fresh fish. There are usually lots of locals eating here—always a good sign. Head inside first and choose your fish; if you arrive and sit at a table, the waiter will probably ignore you, thinking that you haven't made up your mind yet.

# 9

# Crete

*by John S. Bowman*

Few travelers need to be sold on the glories of the Minoan culture of Crete. But how many know that Crete also offers visitors cities with layers of at least 4,000 years of continuous inhabitation, including the vibrant heritage of centuries of Orthodox Christianity and the distinctive imprint left by almost 700 years of Venetian and Turkish rule? Not to mention endless beaches and magnificent mountains, intriguing caves and resonant gorges, and countless villages and sites that provide unexpected and unforgettable experiences. Per square mile, Crete must be one of the most "loaded" places in the world—loaded, that is, in the diversity of history, archaeological sites, natural attractions, tourist amenities, and more. In a world where increasing numbers of travelers have "been there, done that," Crete remains an endlessly fascinating and satisfying destination.

An elaborate service industry has grown up to please the thousands of foreigners who visit Crete each year. There are facilities now for everyone's taste, ranging from luxury resorts to guest rooms in villages that have hardly changed over several centuries. You can spend a delightful day in a remote mountain environment where you're treated to fresh goat cheese and olives; then be back at your hotel within an hour, lying on the beach and enjoying a cool drink.

Crete isn't always and everywhere a gentle Mediterranean idyll—its terrain can be raw, its sites austere, its tone brusque. But for those looking for a distinct destination, Crete will be rewarding.

## STRATEGIES FOR SEEING THE ISLAND

If possible, go in June or September, even late May or early October (unless you seek only a sun-drenched beach): Crete has become an island on overload in July and August (it's also very hot!). The overnight ferry from Piraeus is still the purists' way to go, but the hour-long flights give you more time for activities. There's enough to do to fill up a week, if not a lifetime of visits; by flying, you can actually see the major sites in 2 packed days. (By the way, you can fly into Iraklion and out of Chania, or vice versa.)

The following selection of destinations is designed to fill 5 to 7 days—allowing for a mix of activities and even time for collapsing on a beach at the end of the day. Iraklion is a must, what with its archaeological museum and nearby Knossos. An excursion to Phaestos, its associated sites, and the caves at Matala could occupy most of a 2nd day; if you don't need to see that second Minoan palace, we recommend you move on to Chania or Rethymnon—each can easily fill a day of strolling. (The old road that winds through the mountains and villages has its charms, while the coastal expressway offers some impressive vistas and a "tunnel" of flowering oleanders.) The walk through the famed Samaria Gorge requires 1 long day for the total excursion. Those seeking less strenuous activity might prefer a trip eastward to Ayios Nikolaos and its

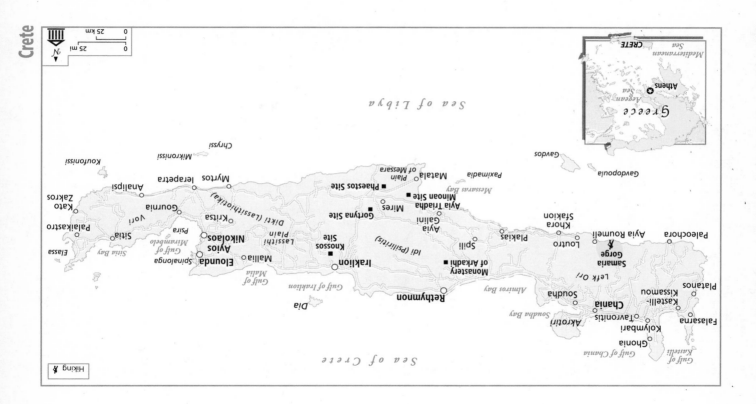

Hiking

N

0        25 mi
0        25 km

**CRETE**

Mediterranean
Sea

Aegean
Sea

*Greece*

✪ Athens

*Sea of Libya*

Koufonissi

Chryssi

Mikronissi

Gavdos

Gavdopoula

Kato
Zakros

Palaikastro

Sitia

Elassa

Sitia Bay

Vaï

Psira

Gournia

Analipsi

Ierapetra

Myrtos

Plain
of Messara

Matala

Paximadia

Messara Bay

Ayia
Triadha

Minoan Site ■

Dikti (Lassithiotika)

■ Phaestos Site

Gulf of
Mirambelo

Krit̄sa

Spinalonga

Gortyna Site ■

Mires

Ayia
Galini

Idi (Psiloritis)

Plakias

Khora
Sfakion

Paleochora

Ayia Roumeli

Samaria
Gorge

Lefk̄ Ori

Loutro

Platanos

Falasarna

Kastelli-
Kissamou

Ghonia

Kolymbari

Tavronitis

Chania

Soudha

Akrotiri

Soudha Bay

Gulf of Chania

Gulf of
Kastelli

*Sea of Crete*

Dia

Gulf of Iraklion

Gulf of
Malia

Almiros Bay

Rethymnon

Monastery
of Arkadhi ■

Knossos
Site ■

Iraklion

Malia

Elounda

Ayios
Nikolaos

Lassithi
Plain

Spili

Vori

Gournia

nearby attractions. None of these trips require a car as public transportation or tour groups are so frequent. However, you might want to rent a car (although not in the cities or towns) as this allows you to leave the overdeveloped tourist trail and gives you access to countless villages, spectacular scenery, beaches at the end of the roads, and lesser known archaeological, historical, and cultural sites.

## A LOOK AT THE PAST Crete's

diversity and distinction begin with its history; a past that has left far more remains than the Minoan sites many people first associate with the island. After being settled by humans around 6500 B.C., Crete passed through the late Neolithic and early Bronze ages, sharing the broader eastern Mediterranean culture.

Sometime around 3000 B.C., new immigrants arrived; by about 2500 B.C., there began to emerge a fairly distinctive culture that has been named Early Minoan. By about 2000 B.C., the Minoans were moving into a far more ambitious phase, the Middle Minoan—the civilization that gave rise to the palaces and superb works of art that now attract thousands of visitors to Crete every year.

Mycenaean Greeks appear to have taken over the palaces about 1500 B.C., and by about 1200 B.C., this Minoan-Mycenaean civilization had pretty much gone under. For several centuries, Crete was a relatively marginal player in the great era of Greek classical civilization.

When the Romans conquered the island in 67 B.C., they revived certain centers (including Knossos) as imperial colonies. Early converts to Christianity, the Cretans slipped into the shadows of the Byzantine world, but the island was pulled back into the light in 1204, when Venetians broke up the Byzantine Empire and took over Crete. The Venetians made the island a major colonial outpost, revived trade and agriculture, and eventually built quite elaborate structures.

By the late 1500s, the Turks were conquering the Venetians' eastern Mediterranean possessions, and in 1669 captured the last major holdout on Crete, the city of Candia—now Iraklion. Cretans suffered considerably under the Turks, and although some of Greece finally threw off the Turkish yoke in the late 1820s, Crete was left behind. A series of rebellions marked the rest of the 19th century, resulting in the Great Powers' sponsoring a sort of independent Crete in 1898.

Finally in 1913, Crete was for the first time formally joined to Greece. Crete had yet another cameo role in history when the Germans invaded it in 1941 with gliders and parachute troops; the ensuing occupation was another low point for the people of Crete. Since 1945, Crete has advanced amazingly in the economic sphere, powered by its agricultural products as well as by its tourist industry. Not all Cretans are pleased by the development, but all would agree that, for better or worse, Crete owes much to its history.

## 1 Iraklion (Iraklio)

Iraklion is home to the world's only comprehensive collection of Minoan artifacts, and is the gateway to Knossos, the major Minoan palace site. Beyond that, it has magnificent fortified walls and several other testimonies to the Venetians' time of power.

Iraklion is also big enough (Greece's 6th-largest city) and confident enough to have its own identity as a busy modern city. It often gets bad press simply because it's bustling with traffic and commerce and construction—the very things most travelers want to escape. At any rate, give Iraklion a chance. If you follow some of the advice we proffer, you just may come to like it.

Harbor Fort
(The Koules)

To
Bus Terminals

Archaeological
Museum

Xanthoudidou

**4**

**3** Epimenidou

Sea of Crete

Pediada

Democratias **10**

Knossou

Kainouriya (Gesu) Gate

Kastrinaki

**2**

25 Avgusto

**5** **6**

Dikeosinis

Hatzimihali Gianari

Evans

Police **7** **8** 1866

Averof

Evans

Neas Ionias

Nikolaou Plastira

Akadimias

Papandreou G.

Plateia
Venizelou

Theotokopoulou

Handaka

Palelogou

Sof. Venizelou

Historical
Museum of Crete

Idis

1821

Giamalaki

Odos 1878

Delimarkou

Kaloterinou

Giankou

Vikela

Giamboudi

Vikela

Ioustinianou

Skordilon

Sof. Venizelou

Valestra

Papadopoulou

Kisssamou

Makariou

Nikolaou Plastira

Kondilaki

Nikolaou Plastira

Kounali

Tomb of Nikos Kazantzakis

Georgiadi

Erofilis

Grigoraki

Thenon

Chania (Panigra) Gate

250 m

250 y

N

Church
First Aid
Information
OTE
Post Office

ACCOMMODATIONS ■

Atlantis Hotel **4**
Atrion Hotel **1**
Galaxy Hotel **10**
Lato Hotel **3**

DINING ◆

Giovanni **6**
Ionia **7**
Ippocampus **2**
Kyriakos **9**
Loukoulos **5**
Pantheon **8**

Greece

Aegean
Sea

Athens

Mediterranean
Sea

CRETE

Iraklion

CRETE

**297**

## ESSENTIALS

**GETTING THERE    By Plane**    Aside from the many who now fly from European cities directly to Crete on charter/package tour flights, most visitors will take the 40-minute flight from Athens to Iraklion or Chania on **Olympic Airways** (© **210/926-9111;** www.olympic-airways.gr), at a cost of some 115€ one-way. In summer, Olympic also offers service between Athens and Sitia (in eastern Crete); between Iraklion and Mykonos, Rhodes, Santorini, and Thessaloniki; and between Chania and Thessaloniki. Reservations are a necessity in high season.

At this writing, there is one privately owned alternative to Olympic, **Aegean Airlines,** which flies from Athens to Iraklion and Chania. Their fares are somewhat cheaper, but their schedules are also rather spotty. Ask your travel agent for information, or contact the Athens offices of Aegean Airlines (© **210/998-8300;** www.aegeanair.com).

Iraklion's airport is about 5km (3 miles) east of the city, along the coast. Major car-rental companies have desks at the airport. A taxi to Iraklion costs about 10€, and the public bus is 2€).

To get back to the airport, you have the same two choices—taxi or public bus no. 1. You can take either from Plateia Eleftheria (Liberty Square) or at other points along the way. Inquire in advance at your hotel about the closest possibility.

**By Boat**    Throughout the year, there is at least one ship (and as many as two or three in high season) a day from Piraeus to Iraklion, and other ships to Chania and Rethymnon. (All trips take about 10 hr.) Less frequent ships link Crete to Rhodes (and Karpathos, Kassos, and Khalki, the islands between the two); Santorini and some of the other Cycladic islands en route to or from Piraeus; and even to Thessaloniki and various Greek ports en route. In high season, occasional ships from Italy, Cyprus, and Israel put into Iraklion. For information on all ships, inquire at a travel agency or call the Iraklion **Port Authority** (© **2810/244-912).**

If you have arrived at Iraklion's harbor by ship, you'll probably want to take a taxi up into the town, as it's a steep climb. Depending on where you want to go, the fare may be 3€ to 10€.

**By Bus**    The third common mode of arrival in Iraklion is by public bus from one of the other Cretan cities or towns. Where you end up depends on where you've come from. Those arriving from points to the west, east, or southeast—Chania or Rethymnon, for instance, or Ayios Nikolaos or Sitia to the east—end up down along the harbor and will have a choice of three approaches to the center of town: walking, taking a taxi, or catching the public bus. The bus starts its route at the terminal where buses from the east and southeast stop; directly across the boulevard is the station for the Rethymnon-Chania buses. Those arriving from the south—Phaestos, Matala, and such—will end up at the Chania Gate on the southwest edge of town; walking will not appeal to most, but you have the choice of a public bus or a taxi.

**VISITOR INFORMATION**    The **National Tourist Office** is at 1 Xanthoudidou, opposite the Archaeological Museum (© **2810/228-225;** fax 2810/226-020). Open Monday through Friday 8am to 2:30pm. Among the most reliable travel agencies in Iraklion are **Adamis Tours,** 23 25th Avgusto (© **2810/346-202;** fax 2810/224-717; adamistours@her.forthnet.gr), **Creta Travel Bureau,** 20 Epimenidou (© **2810/227-002;** fax 2810/223-749), and **Arabatzoglou Travel,** 54 25th Avgusto (© **2810/226-697;** fax 2810/222-184). For those interested in renting an apartment or villa on Crete, see the agencies listed in chapter 2 under "Landing the Best Room."

**GETTING AROUND   By Bus**   Public buses remain a solid possibility for seeing much of Crete. They're cheap, relatively frequent, and connect to all but the most isolated locales. The downside is that the schedules are not always the most convenient for travelers with limited time. Certainly you can take them between all major points. The long-distance bus system is operated by **KTEL**, which services all of Greece. Ask your travel agent or call © **2810/221-765** to find out more about KTEL buses to Rethymnon-Chania and points west. For buses to Mallia, Ayios Nikolaos, Sitia, Ierapetra, and points east, call © **2810/245-019.** For buses to Phaestos and other points south, call © **2810/255-965.**

**By Car & Moped**   A car gives maximum flexibility in seeing the island, and there is no shortage of rental agencies in all the main centers of Crete (including the airports). In Iraklion we recommend the locally owned **Motor Club,** 18 Plateia Agglon at the bottom of 25th Avgusto, overlooking the harbor (© **2810/222-408;** www.motorclub.gr) or **Hertz,** 34 25th Avgusto (© **2810/341-734).** As for mopeds and motorcycles, be *very* sure you can control such a vehicle in chaotic urban traffic and on dangerous mountain roads (with few shoulders but many potholes and much gravel). If you want to go this route, try the aforementioned Motor Club for rentals.

**By Taxi**   Taxis are reasonable if two or three people are sharing a trip to a site; no place on Crete is more than a day's round-trip from Iraklion. Ask a travel agent to find you a driver who speaks at least rudimentary English; he can then serve as your guide as well. One we can recommend is **Antonis Gratsas,** who offers a 4-hour tour of the city for about 100€; he is best reached (while on Crete) via his mobile phone (© **69440-796237).**

**By Boat**   There are now several excursion boats that take visitors on day trips to offshore islands or isolated beaches as well as to Santorini; inquire at a travel agency.

**FAST FACTS**   The official **American Express** agency is Adamis Travel Bureau, 23 25th Avgusto (© **2810/346-202;** fax 2810/224-717). There are numerous **banks** and **ATMs** (as well as several currency-exchange machines) throughout the center of Iraklion, with many along 25th Avgusto. The **British Consul** is at 16 Papa Alexandrou, opposite the Archaeological Museum (© **2810/224-012);** there is no American consulate in Iraklion. The **Venizelou Hospital** (© **2810/237-502)** is on Knossos Road. For general **first-aid** information, call © **2810/222-222.** For **Internet access,** try the Konsova Internet Cafe, 25 Dikeossinas, (© **2880/288-143;** konsova@yahoo.com) or the Cyberpoint Café, 117 Paraskiyo-poulou (www.cyberpoint.gr). Both open by at least mid-morning and stay open till midnight.

The most convenient **laundry** is at 25 Merebellou (one street behind the Archaeological Museum); open Monday through Saturday from 9am to 9pm. You can leave **luggage** at the airport for 3€ per piece per day; most hotels will also hold luggage for brief periods. The **tourist police,** 10 Dikiosenis, the main street linking the top of 25th Avgusto to Plateia Eleftheria (© **2810/283-190),** are open daily from 7am to 11pm. The main **post office** (© **2810/289-995)** is on Plateia Daskalojiannis; open daily from 7:30am to 8pm. The **telephone office (OTE),** 10 Minotaurou (the far side of El Greco Park), is open daily from 6am to 11pm.

## WHAT TO SEE & DO ATTRACTIONS

**The Archaeological Museum** ✪✪✪   This is the world's premier collection of art and artifacts from the Minoan civilization. Although many of its most spectacular objects are from Knossos, it does have finds from other sites. The variety of objects, styles, techniques, and materials will amaze all who have not previously focused on the Minoans. Among the most prized objects are the **snake goddesses** from Knossos, the **bee pendant** from Mallia, the **carved vases** from Ayia Triadha and Kato Zakros, and various objects testifying to the famous bull-leaping. Upstairs are the **original frescoes from Knossos** and other sites, their restored sections clearly visible (the frescoes now at Knossos are copies of these). Most displays have decent labels in English, but you may want to invest in one of the guidebooks for sale in the lobby. You will need at least 1 hour for a quick walk-through. To avoid the tour groups in high season, plan to visit either very early or late in the day; also there are fewer groups on Sundays.

1 Xanthoudidou. © 2810/226-092. Admission 10€ adults, 6€ students with official ID and EU citizens 65 and over. Apr to mid-Oct Tues–Sun 8am–8pm; Mon 12:30–8pm. Mid-Oct to Mar, closes daily at 5pm. Far corner of Plateia Eleftheria. Parking in immediate area impossible.

**Harbor Fort (The Koules)** Kids You may feel you're walking through a Hollywood set—but this is the real thing! The harbor fort, built on the site of a series of earlier forts, went up between 1523 and 1540, and although greatly restored, is essentially the Venetian original. Both its exterior and interior are impressive in their dimensions, workmanship, and details: thick walls, spacious chambers, great ramparts, cannonballs, the Lion of St. Mark plaques are well worth the hour's diversion.

At mole on old harbor. © 2810/288-484. Admission 3€. Daily 9am–1pm and 4–7pm.

**Historical Museum of Crete** ★ This museum picks up where the Archaeological Museum leaves off, displaying artifacts and art from the early Christian era up to the present. You get some sense of the role the Cretans' long struggle for independence still plays in their identity. On display are traditional Cretan **folk arts**; the re-created study of **Nikos Kazantzakis**, Crete's great modern writer; and works attributed to the painter **El Greco**, another of the island's admired sons. Even if you take only an hour for this museum, it will reward you with some surprising insights on Crete.

7 Lysimakos Kalokerinou (facing coast road 450m/1,500 ft. west of harbor). © 2810/283-219. www.historical-museum.gr. Admission 3€, 2€ students. Mar–Oct Mon–Fri 9am–5pm; Sat 9am–2pm. Reduced hours in winter.

**The Palace of Knossos** ★★★ Kids Undeniably one of the great archaeological sites of the world, yet until Arthur Evans began excavating here in 1900, little was known about the ancient people who inhabited it. Using every possible clue and remnant, he rebuilt large parts of the palace—walls, floors, stairs, windows, and columns. Visitors must now stay on a walkway, but you still get a good sense of the structure's labyrinthine nature. Realize that you are seeing the remains of two major palaces plus several restorations that were made from about 2000 B.C. to 1250 B.C. Understand, too, that this was not a palace in the modern sense of a royal residence, but a combination of that and the Minoans' chief religious-ceremonial center as well as their administrative headquarters and royal workshops. This is one place where a guided tour might be worth the expense; your hotel or a travel agency can arrange this. On your own, you'll need at least 2 hours for a cursory walkthrough. The latter part of the day tends to be less crowded; Sunday is far less frequented by tour groups.

Knossos Rd., 5km (3 miles) south of Iraklion. © 2810/231-940. Admission 6€, 4€ students with official ID and EU citizens 65 or over. Apr to mid-Oct daily 8am–8pm. Mid-Oct to Mar Mon–Fri 8am–5pm; Sat–Sun 8:30am–3pm. Free parking down slope on left 90m (295 ft.) before main entrance.

**Venetian Walls and Tomb of Nikos Kazantzakis** ★   These great walls and bastions were part of the fortress-city the Venetians called Candia. Two of the great city gates have survived fairly well: the Pantocrator or Panigra Gate, better known now as the Chania Gate (dating from about 1570), at the western edge; and the Gate of Gesu, or Kainouryia Gate (about 1587), at the southern edge. You can walk around the outer perimeter of the walls and get a feel for their sheer massiveness. They were built, of course, by the forced labor of Cretans.

But one non-Venetian presence has now come to rest on one of the bastions, the Martinengo Bastion at the southern corner. Here is the grave of Nikos Kazantzakis (1883–1947), a native of Iraklion and author of *Zorba the Greek* and *The Last Temptation of Christ*. From Kazantzakis's tomb is one of the best views to the south of Mount Iouktas, which appears in profile to be the head of a man. According to one ancient myth, this is the head of the buried god Zeus. A special visit here requires an hour, two if combined with a visit to a gate and a segment of the wall.

The tomb is on the Martinengo Bastion, at the southern corner of the walls, along Plastira. Free admission. Open sunrise to sunset.

## A STROLL AROUND IRAKLION

Start your stroll at **Fountain Square** (also known as Lions Square, officially Plateia Venizelou), perhaps fortified with a plate of *bougatsa* at one of the two cafes serving this distinctive filled pastry—in fact, it's not Cretan but was introduced by Greeks from Armenia. The **fountain** ★ was installed here in 1628 by the Venetian governor of Crete, Francesco Morosini. Note the now fading but still elegant relief carvings around the basin. Across from the fountain is the **Basilica of St. Mark**, restored to its original 14th-century Italian style and used for exhibitions and concerts.

Proceeding south 50m (164 ft.) to the crossroads, you'll see the **market street** (officially 1866); now, alas, increasingly taken over by tourist shops but still a must-see with its purveyors of fresh fruits and vegetables, meats, and wines.

At the far end of the market street, you come out onto **Kornarou Square**, with its lovely Turkish fountain; beside it is the **Venetian Bembo Fountain** (1588). The modern statue at the far side of the square commemorates the hero and heroine of Vincenzo Kornarou's Renaissance epic poem *Erotokritos*, a Cretan-Greek classic.

Turning right onto Vikela, proceed (always bearing right) until you come out at the imposing, if not artistically notable, 19th-century **Cathedral of Ayios Menas**, dedicated to the patron saint of Iraklion. Below and to the left is the medieval **Church of Ayios Menas**, which boasts some old wood carvings and icons.

At the far corner of the cathedral (to the northeast) is the 15th-century **Church of St. Katherine.** During the 16th and 17th centuries, this hosted the Mount Sinai Monastery School, where Domenico Theotokopoulou is alleged to have studied before moving on to Venice, Spain, and fame as **El Greco;** it now houses a small museum of icons, frescoes, and wood carvings. It's open Monday through Saturday from 10am to 1pm, with additional hours Tuesday, Thursday, and Friday from 4 to 6pm. Admission is 5€.

Taking the narrow street (Ayii Dheka) that leads directly away from the facade of St. Katherine's, you'll come out onto **Leoforos Kalokerinou,** the main shopping street for locals. Turn right onto it and proceed up to the crossroads of the market and 25 Avgusto. Turn left and go back down past Fountain Square and, on the right, the (totally reconstructed) **Venetian Loggia,** originally dating from the early 1600s. The leading Venetians once met here to conduct affairs; it now houses offices of the city government.

A little farther down 25th Avgusto, also on the right, is the **Church of Ayios Titos**, dedicated to the patron saint of all Crete (the Titus of the Bible, who introduced Christianity to Crete). Head down to the **harbor** (with a side visit to the **Venetian fort**, or *Koules*, if you have the energy at this time; see description above), then pass, along the right, the two sets of great **Venetian arsenali**—where ships were built and repaired (the sea then came in this far). Climbing the stairs just past the arsenali, you turn left onto Bofor and curve up under the **Archaeological Museum** to **Plateia Eleftheria (Liberty Square)**—where you can take a much deserved refreshing drink at any one of the numerous cafes at the far side.

## SHOPPING

Costas Papadopoulos, the proprietor of **Daedalou Galerie**, 11 Daedalou (between Fountain Square and Plateia Eleftheria) (© 2810/346-353), has been offering his tasteful selection of traditional Cretan-Greek arts and crafts for several decades—icons, jewelry, porcelain, silverware, pistols, and more. Some of it is truly old, and he'll tell you when it isn't.

**Eleni Kastrinoyanni-Cretan Folk Art, 3** Ikarou, (opposite the Archaeological Museum) (© 2810/226-186), is the premier store in Iraklion for some of the finest in embroidery, weavings, ceramics, and jewelry; all new pieces but reflecting traditional Cretan folk methods and motifs. Get out your credit card and go for something you'll enjoy for years to come. It's closed October through February.

For one of Crete's finest selections of antique and old Cretan textiles (rugs, spreads, coverlets, and more) along with some unusual pieces of jewelry, try **Grimm's Handicrafts of Crete**, 96 25th Avgusto (opposite the Venetian Loggia; © 2810/282-547). The finest objects are not cheap, but you get exactly what you pay for here, and even when not especially old, the textiles can be stunning.

A popular type of store that has sprung up all over Crete (and for that matter, all over Greece) is one that specializes in local agricultural products such as olive oil (Crete's is rated as among the finest in the world), honey, wines and spirits, raisins, olives, herbs, and spices. They are to be seen all over town, and one is as good as the other.

## WHERE TO STAY

In recent years, the trend of mass tourism on Crete has moved toward beach hotels, but there is still a good selection of accommodations in Iraklion—and you may still need reservations in high season.

Iraklion lies annoyingly close to the flight patterns of commercial airliners and occasional jet fighters of the Greek Air Force. Not to deny the nuisance element, but the total time of the overhead noise adds up to probably less than 40 minutes every 24 hours—and the sound of scooters and motorcycles outside your hotel at night will probably be more annoying. There are plans to add a runway out into the sea to eliminate the flights over Iraklion, but it will take some years for this to happen. All we can say is that we have made the search for quiet a major criterion in our selection of hotels; in any case, air-conditioning promises the best defense.

## INSIDE THE CITY

**Atlantis Hotel** ★★ *Value*    The Atlantis is probably the best value for the money if you want to feel like you're in the center of things. There are more luxurious hotels in Greece, but few can beat the Atlantis's urban attractions: a central location, modern facilities, and views over a busy harbor. This superior Class A hotel is in the heart of Iraklion, yet just enough removed from the noise of the city (especially if you use the air-conditioning). The staff is friendly and helpful, and although the Atlantis is especially popular with conference groups—it has major conference facilities—individuals will still get individual attention. Bedrooms are not plush nor especially large but are certainly comfortable. You can swim in the pool, send e-mail via your laptop, and then within minutes be enjoying a fine meal or visiting a museum.

2 Iyias (behind the Archaeological Museum), 71202 Iraklion. © **2810/229-103**. www.greece-athens-hotels. com/heraklion-hotels/atlantis. 162 units. High season 115€–130€ double; low season 90€–110€ double. Rates include breakfast. Reduction possible for longer stays. Special rates for business travelers and half-board (breakfast and dinner). AE, DC, MC, V. Private parking arranged. **Amenities:** Restaurant; 2 bars; small indoor pool; rooftop garden; tennis court across street; Jacuzzi; bike rental; children's playground (across the street); video rentals; concierge; tour desk; car-rental desk; pickup at airport by arrangement; secretarial service; salon; 24-hr. room service; massage; babysitting; laundry/dry-cleaning service; nonsmoking rooms. *In room:* A/C, TV, minibar, fridge, hair dryer, safe.

**Atrion Hotel** Nothing spectacular here, but we have long liked this hotel for its location and now we can add to that its recently completed (2003) renovation. It's in a quiet, seemingly remote corner yet in fact only a 10-minute walk to the center of town, and an even shorter walk to the coast road and the harbor. True, the adjacent streets are not that attractive but they are perfectly safe, and once inside you can enjoy your oasis of comfort and peace. This hotel has well-appointed public areas—a lounge, a refreshing patio garden—and pleasant, good-size guest rooms.

9 Chronaki (behind the Historical Museum). 71202 Iraklion. © **2810/ 229-225**. Fax 2810/223-292. www. atrion.gr. 74 units, some with tub only, some with shower only. High season 95€–110€ double; low season 85€–105€ double. Rates include buffet breakfast. Reductions for children. AE, MC, V. Parking on street. Public bus within 200m (656 ft.). **Amenities:** Cafeteria; bar/restaurant; babysitting; laundry service; nonsmoking rooms. *In room:* A/C, TV, minibar.

**Galaxy Hotel** ★ This has a reputation as one of the fancier hotels on Crete, and it is classy—once you get past its rather forbidding exterior. The public areas are striking, and the Galaxy boasts (for now at least) the largest indoor swimming pool in Iraklion. Guest rooms are stylish but don't expect American-style size; ask for an interior unit since you lose nothing in a view and gain in quietness. They also offer several expensive suites. Although one reader once reported a less than gracious tone from desk staff, we have always found them courteous in handling all the usual requests for services. Perhaps it will appeal most to those who prefer a familiar international ambience to folksiness. By the way, although its restaurant serves the standard Greek/international menu, the pastry shop and ice-cream parlor attract locals, who consider the fare delicious.

67 Leoforos Demokratias (about a ½ mile out main road to Knossos), 71306 Iraklion. © **2810/238-812**. Fax 2810/211-211. www.galaxy-hotel.gr. 137 units, some with shower only, some with tub only. High season 125€–150€ double; low season 100€–125€ double. AE, DC, MC, V. Parking on street. Frequent bus to center within yards of entrance. **Amenities:** Restaurant; pastry shop; bar; indoor pool; sauna; concierge; 24-hr. room service; same day laundry/dry cleaning service; executive-level rooms; nonsmoking rooms. *In room:* A/C, TV, minibar, hair dryer.

**Lato Hotel** ★ (*Value* Long one of our favorites in all of Greece, the Lato has now jumped to the head of the line when it comes to providing not only value for the money but also a discreetly stylish environment and warm hospitality. Nothing pretentious, but its latest renovations have enlarged the hotel, redone the public areas, and completely transformed the rooms' decor and furnishings (not to mention installing fire and smoke detectors and high security door locks). A few rooms are a bit small, five are (more expensive) handsome suites, but all are perfectly adequate—and all have state of the art bathrooms. The buffet breakfast continues to be both tasty and satisfying. Also a major plus is its location: convenient to the town's center and with most rooms offering a view of the harbor. (Airplanes overhead—heard throughout Iraklion, in fact—can be drowned out by closed windows and the air-conditioning.) Parking can be a problem but the accommodating staff will take over, just as they are always ready to help you make the most of your stay in Iraklion.

15 Epimenidou, 71102 Iraklion. © **2810/228-103**. Fax 2810/240-350. www.iato.gr. 58 units (some with shower only). High season 130€–175€ double; low season 120€–165€ double. Rates include buffet breakfast. 10% discount for Internet reservations. 50% discount for children 6–12. AE, DC, MC, V. Parking on street. **Amenities:** Breakfast room; bar; concierge; fax and Internet facilities; room service 8am–11pm; car-rental service; laundry/dry cleaning service; non-smoking rooms. *In room:* A/C, TV, minibar, hair dryer, safe.

**Poseidon** *(Value* We include the Poseidon because it's a longtime favorite of Frommer's loyalists, and for good reason. Its owner/host, John Polychronides, and the desk staff (fluent in English) provide useful support and show genuine concern for your stay on Crete. Yes, it's on a not especially attractive street—but that's true of most of Iraklion's hotels, and few can match the fresh breezes and the view over the port. Yes, it gets the airplane noise—but so do virtually all the other hotels in Iraklion, and this one's new sound-insulating windows cut out most of the noise. It is a budget hotel—no elevator (but only three floors), small rooms, basic showers—but everything is clean and functional. Frequent buses and cheap taxi fares let you come and go into Iraklion center, a 20-minute walk away.

54 Poseidonos, Poros, 71102 Iraklion. (about 2.5km/1½ miles from Plateia Eleftheria, off the main road to the east). © **2810/222-545**, poseidonhotel@hotmail.com. 26 units, all with shower only. High season 70€ double; low season 60€. Rates include continental breakfast. Ask about a 10% reduction for Frommer's users who make reservations and pay cash. AE, V. Parking all around and frequent public buses 180m (590 ft.) at top of street. *In room:* A/C available for 8€ daily surcharge.

## OUTSIDE THE CITY

One solution to avoiding the city noise is to stay on the coast. We're assuming that you want to be fairly close to Iraklion—if you just want a remote beach on Crete, such accommodations are described elsewhere. Although the hotels below can be reached by public bus, a car or taxi will save you some valuable time.

**Candia Maris ★** The grandest of the resort hotels on the western edge of Iraklion is the deluxe-class Candia Maris, which offers just about everything from special "Cretan nights" with traditional music and dancing to a squash court. Although the beach on the west coast is not always as pleasant as that on the east, it's perfectly clean. And although you have to pass through a rather dreary edge of Iraklion to get here, this area has the advantage of being really close to town. It was also one of the first hotels in Greece to be handicapped accessible. The exterior and layout are a bit severe, but the rooms are good-sized and cheerful, the bathrooms up to date. (If it looks like a brick-factory owner's idea of a hotel, it's because the owner is just that.) Considering that you won't be spending much time looking at the outside of the building, this shouldn't deter you from trying this first-class resort hotel.

Amoudara, Gazi (on beach about 6km/4 miles west of Iraklion center), 71303 Iraklion. © **2810/377-000**. Fax 2810/250-669. www.maris.gr. 258 units. High season 85€–100€ double in hotel; 105€–125€ seafront bungalow. Low season 45€–58€ double in hotel; 58€–68€ bungalow. All rates are per person per day, buffet breakfast included. Reductions for extra person in room and for children; half-board plan (including breakfast and dinner) available for additional 24€. AE, DC, MC, V. Public bus every half-hour to Iraklion. **Amenities:** 4 restaurants; 4 bars; 6 pools (2 outdoor, 4 indoor) plus children's pool; tennis courts; squash court; minigolf; volleyball; basketball; bowling; billiards; health club and spa; watersports; bike rental; children's program;

game room; concierge; tour arrangements; car-rental desk; airport transport arrangements; conference facilities; salon; room service 7am–12pm; babysitting; laundry/dry cleaning service; Internet access. *In room:* A/C, TV, minibar, fridge, hair dryer.

**Minoa Palace** ★  Here's your chance to visit the Minoans while living in a palace of greater comfort than anything they ever knew. Everything here is first class, but the atmosphere is informal. The weekly "Cretan night" with traditional music and dancing is especially lively here. What also makes the Minoa Palace appealing is its location: east of the airport's noise yet only 11km (7 miles) from the center of Iraklion. The rooms are good-size and well appointed, and most have views of the sea—definitely insist on this! The beach is beautifully maintained, and there are as many activities as you care to engage in. With your own vehicle, you're only a couple of hours from any point of interest on the whole island.

Amnisos Beach (about 10km/6 miles east of Iraklion), 71110 Iraklion. © **2810/380-404.** Fax 2810/380-422. www.ellada.net/minoapal. 127 units. 4 suites. High season 105€ double; low season 85€ double. Rates include buffet breakfast. Half-board plan (including breakfast and dinner) may be arranged for 15€ extra. AE, DC, MC, V. Closed Nov–Mar. Public bus every half-hour to Iraklion or points east. **Amenities:** 2 restaurants; bar; 2 pools plus children's pool; tennis court (lit at night); exercise room; aerobic program; watersports; children's program; video room; concierge; tour and car-rental arrangements; airport transport arranged; conference facilities; shopping arcade; salon; room service 7am–midnight; babysitting; laundry and dry cleaning service; volleyball; billiards; table tennis; horseback-riding arranged. *In room:* A/C, TV, minibar, hair dryer.

**Xenia-Helios** ★  We single out the Xenia-Helios because you can save a bit of money and feel you're contributing to the future of young Greeks. It's one of three such hotels run by the Greek Ministry of Tourism to train young people for careers in the hotel world (one is outside Athens, the other outside Thessaloniki). The physical accommodations may not be quite as glitzy as some of the other beach resorts, but they're certainly first class and the service is especially friendly. The beach here is especially lovely.

Kokkini Hani (about 13km/8 miles east of Iraklion), 71500 Iraklion. © **2810/761-502.** Fax 2810/418-363. 108 units. High season 70€ double; low season 58€ double. Rates include half-board plan. AE, MC, V. Closed Oct–May. Buses every half-hour to Iraklion or points east. **Amenities:** Restaurant; bar; pool; tennis courts; conference facilities; watersports equipment; salon. *In room:* A/C.

## WHERE TO DINE

Avoid eating a meal on either Fountain Square or Liberty Square (Plateia Eleftheria) unless you simply want to have the experience—the food at those establishments is, to put it mildly, nothing special. Save these squares for a coffee or beer break.

## EXPENSIVE

**Kyriakos** ★  GREEK  In recent years, this restaurant has gained the reputation of offering the most style as well some of the finest cooking in Iraklion. The menu is essentially traditional Greek, but it offers several specialties such as artichokes with potatoes and lettuce, lamb fricassee, and aubergines stuffed with feta. Snails are another specialty, and if that doesn't tempt you, come back at Christmas for the turkey. The wine choices are appropriately fine (and expensive). A couple should expect to drop between 50€ and 75€ for the full works here, but think what you'd pay at home for such a meal. What might disappoint some visitors is that it is located at the edge of town on a busy boulevard and so seems to lack any special Cretan "atmosphere." For those serious about what's on their plate, then, rather than the ambience, it's a restaurant that makes an occasion.

53 Leoforos Demokratias (about a ½ mile from center on the road to Knossos). © **2810/224-649.** Reservations recommended for dinner in high season. Appetizers 3€–6€; main courses 6€–25€. AE, DC, MC, V. Daily noon–5pm and 7pm–1am. Closed Sun from about June 2–July 10. Frequent public bus service to the restaurant.

**Loukoulos** ★ ITALIAN/GREEK   Another restaurant that has gained a stylish reputation, but with a setting almost the opposite of the Kyriakos (see above). It's in the very heart of the city, cramped into a tiny patio on a back street and featuring fanciful umbrellas over the tables. But the chairs are comfortable, the table settings lovely, and the selection of pasta dishes, such as a delicious rigatoni with a broccoli-and-Roquefort-cream sauce. Treat yourself just once to Iraklion's "in" place.

5 Korai (1 street behind Daedalou). ⓒ 2810/224-435. Reservations recommended for dinner in high season. Main courses 6€–18€; fixed-price lunch about 15€. AE, DC, V. Mon–Sat noon–1am; Sun 6:30pm–midnight.

## MODERATE

**Giovanni** GREEK   A taverna with some pretensions to chic, this appeals to a slightly younger and more informal set than its neighbor, Loukoulos (described above). For some reason, it, instead of Loukoulos, has the Italian name while its fare is traditional Greek. House specialties include shrimp in tomato sauce with cheese, baked eggplant with tomato sauce, and kokhoretsi (a sort of oversize sausage made from the innards of lamb; much better than it may sound)—all quite tasty.

12 Korai (1 street behind Daedalou). ⓒ 2810/246-338. Main courses 6€–18€. AE, MC, V. Mon–Sat 12:30pm–2am; Sun 5pm–1:30am.

**Pantheon** Moments GREEK   Anyone who spends more than a few days in Iraklion should take at least one meal in "Dirty Alley," and this one is a long-time favorite. Although it long ago lost its rough-hewn atmosphere, Dirty Alley still provides a sense of being in a foreign locale. The menu here (much the same as at the several "Dirty Alley" locales) offers taverna standards—stews of various meats, chunks of meat or chicken or fish in tasty sauces, vegetables such as okra or zucchini or stuffed tomatoes. These places are not especially cheap—the proprietors know enough to charge for the atmosphere—but the food's all tasty. And if you sit in the Pantheon, on the corner of the market street, you'll get a choice view of the passing scene.

2 Theodosaki ("Dirty Alley," connecting the market street and Evans). ⓒ 2810/241-652. Main courses 5€–12€. No credit cards. Mon–Sat 11am–11pm.

## INEXPENSIVE

**Ionia** GREEK   Undistinguished as it now appears, this is in some respects the Nestor of Iraklion's restaurants. Founded in 1923, Ionia has served generations of Cretans as well as all the early archaeologists. Although it's greatly reduced in size, the food is as good as ever, and the staff encourages foreigners to step over to the kitchen area and select from the warming pans. You may find more refined food and fancier service elsewhere on Crete, but you won't taste heartier dishes than the Ionia's green beans or lamb joints in sauce. We recommend a visit to what is clearly a fading tradition.

3 Evans (just to the left of the market street). ⓒ 2810/28-313. Main courses 3.50€–9€. MC, V. Mon–Fri 8am–10:30pm; Sat 8am–4pm.

**Ippocampus** SEAFOOD/GREEK   This is something of an institution among locals, who line up for a typical Cretan meal of nothing but little appetizers. The zucchini slices, dipped in batter and deep-fried, are fabulous. A plate of tomatoes and cukes, another of sliced fried potatoes, some small fish, perhaps the fried squid—that's it. You can assemble a whole meal for as little as 12€—but go early.

3 Mitsotaki 3 (off to left of traffic circle as you come down 25 Avgusto). ⓒ 2810/282-081. Main courses 2.50€–7€. No credit cards. Mon–Fri 1–3:30pm and 7pm–midnight.

## IRAKLION AFTER DARK

To spend an evening the way most Iraklians themselves do, stroll about (the famous Mediterranean **volta**), then sit in a cafe and watch others stroll by. The prime locations for the latter have been Plateia Eleftheria (Liberty Square) or Fountain Square, but the packed-in atmosphere of these places—and the overly aggressive solicitation of your presence by some waiters—has considerably reduced their charm.

For far more atmosphere, go down to the old harbor and the **Marina Cafe** (directly across from the restored Venetian arsenals). For as little as 1.50€ for a coffee or as much as 6€ for an alcoholic drink, you can enjoy the breeze as you contemplate the illuminated Venetian fort, looking much like a stage set.

Another alternative is the **Four Lions Roof-Garden Cafe** (© **2810/222-333**), entered by an interior staircase in the shopping arcade on Fountain Square. It attracts a younger set of Iraklians, but adult foreigners are welcome. The background music is usually Greek. You get to sit above the crowded crossroads, and with no cover or minimum, enjoy anything from a coffee (2€) or ice cream (from 3€) to an alcoholic drink (from 3€).

There is no end to the number of **bars** and **discos** featuring rock 'n' roll and/or Greek popular music, although they come and go from year to year to reflect the latest fads. **Disco Athina**, 9 Ikarou, just outside the wall on the way to the airport, is an old favorite with the young set; newer favorites include the **Veneto Bar** and the **Club Itan**, both on Epimenidou.

For those seeking **traditional** **Cretan music** and **dancing**—and by the way, almost every Class A hotel now has a **Cretan night**, when performers come to the hotel—there are a couple of clubs: **Aposperides**, out on the road toward Knossos, and **Sordina**, about 5km (3 miles) to the southwest of town, are well regarded; take a taxi to either.

For many years now, Iraklion has hosted an **arts festival** that, although hardly competitive with the major festivals of Europe, provides some interesting possibilities for those spending a few nights in town. The schedule usually begins in late June and ends about mid-September. Some of the performers have world-class reputations—ballet troupes, pianists, and such—but most come from the Greek realm and perform ancient and medieval-Renaissance dramas, dances based on Greek themes, and Greek music both traditional and modern. Most performances take place outdoors in one of three venues: on the roof of the **Koules** (the Venetian fort in the harbor), the **Kazantzakis Garden Theater,** or the **Hadzidakis Theater.** Ticket prices vary from year to year and for individual events, but are well below what you'd pay at such cultural events elsewhere. Maybe you didn't come to Crete expecting to hear Vivaldi, but why not enjoy it while you're here?

## SIDE TRIPS FROM IRAKLION

Travel agencies arrange excursions setting out from Iraklion to virtually every point of interest on Crete, such as the **Samaria Gorge** in the far southwest (p. 317). In that sense, Iraklion can be used as the home base for all your touring on Crete. If you have only 1 extra day on Crete, we recommend the following trip.

### GORTYNA, PHAESTOS, AYIA TRIADHA & MATALA ★★

If you have an interest in history and archaeology, this is probably the trip to make if you have only one other day after visiting Knossos and Iraklion's museum. The distance isn't that great—a round-trip of some 165km (100 miles)—but it would be a full day indeed to take it all in. If you don't have your own car, a taxi or guided tour is advisable as bus schedules won't allow you to fit in all the stops. (You can, of course, stay at one of the hotels down at the south coast, but they're usually booked up in high season.)

The road south takes you right up and across the **mountainous spine** of central Crete, and at about the 25th mile you get the experience of leaving the **Sea of Crete** (to the north) behind and seeing the **Libyan Sea** to the south. You then descend onto the **Messara**, the largest plain on Crete (some 32km/20 miles by 5km/3 miles), long a major agricultural center. At about 45km (28 miles), you'll see on your right the **remains of Gortyna;** many more lie scattered in the fields off to the left. Gortyna (or Gortyn or Gortys) first emerged as a center of the Dorian Greeks who moved to Crete after the end of the Minoan civilization. By 500 B.C., it was advanced enough to have a law code that was inscribed in stone. The inscribed stones were found in the late 19th century and reassembled here, where you can see this unique—and to scholars, invaluable—document testifying to the legal and social arrangements of this society.

Then, after the Romans took over Crete (after 67 B.C.), Gortyna enjoyed yet another period of glory: It was the capital of Roman Crete and Cyrenaica (Libya), and as such was endowed with the full selection of Roman structures—temples, a stadium, and so on. These are situated in the fields to the left. On the right (Admission 4€; open daily 8am–7pm high season; reduced hours off season), along with the **Code of Gortyna,** ★ you'll see a small **Hellenistic Odeon,** or theater, as well as the remains of the **Basilica of Ayios Titos**—dedicated to the Titus commissioned by Paul to head the first Christians on Crete; the church was begun in the 6th century but was later greatly enlarged.

Proceeding down the road another 15km (10 miles), turn left at the sign and ascend to the ridge where the **palace of Phaestos** ★★ sits in all its splendor. (Admission 5€; daily 8am–7pm high season; reduced hours off season.) Regarded by scholars as the second most powerful Minoan center, it is also considered the most attractive by many visitors because of its setting—on a prow of land that seems to float between the plain and the sky. Italians began to excavate Phaestos soon after Evans began at Knossos, but they made the decision to leave the remains pretty much as they found them. The **ceremonial staircase** is as awesome as it must have been to the ancients, while the **great court** remains one of the most resonant public spaces anywhere.

Leaving Phaestos, continue down the main road 4km (2½ miles) and turn left onto a side road. Park here and make your way to at least pay your respects to another Minoan site, a mini-palace complex known as **Ayia Triadha.** To this day, scholars cannot be certain exactly what it was—something between a satellite of Phaestos and a semi-independent palace. Several of the most impressive artifacts now in the Iraklion Museum were found here, including the painted sarcophagus (on the second floor).

Back on the road, follow the signs to **Kamilari** and then **Pitsidia.** And now you've earned your rest and swim, and at no ordinary place: the nearby **beach at Matala** ★. It's a small cove enclosed by bluffs of age-old packed earth in which humans—possibly beginning under the Romans but most likely no earlier than A.D. 500—once dug **chambers,** some complete with bunk beds. Cretans long used them as summer homes, the German soldiers used them as storerooms during World War II, and hippies took them over in the late 1960s. They are now off limits except for looking at during the day. Matala has become one more overcrowded beach in peak season, so after a dip and a bit of refreshment, you'll be glad to depart and make your way back to Iraklion (going straight up via **Mires,** avoiding the turnoff back to Ayia Triadha and Phaestos).

# 2 Chania (Hania/Xania/Canea)

150km (95 miles) W of Iraklion

Until the 1980s, Chania was one of the best-kept secrets of the Mediterranean: a delightful town nestled between mountains and sea, a labyrinth of atmospheric streets and structures from its Venetian-Turkish era. Since then, tourists have flocked here, and there's hardly a square inch of the Old Town, which fans back from the harbor, that's not dedicated to satisfying them. Chania was heavily bombed during World War II; ironically, some of its atmosphere is due to still-unreconstructed buildings that are now used as shops and restaurants.

What's amazing is how much of Chania's charm has persisted since the Venetians and Turks effectively stamped the old town in their own image between 1210 and 1898. Try to visit any time except July and August, but whenever you come, dare to strike out on your own and see the old Chania.

## ESSENTIALS

**GETTING THERE    By Plane    Olympic Airways** offers at least three flights daily to and from Athens in high season. (Flight time is about 40 min.) Olympic also has one flight weekly to and from Thessaloniki. **Aegean Airlines** also offers a few flights weekly to and from Athens. See section 1, "Getting There" in this chapter, for contact information. The airport is located 15km (10 miles) out of town on the Akrotiri. Public buses meet all flights except for the last one at night, but almost everyone takes a taxi (about 10€).

**By Boat**    One ship sails daily between Piraeus and Chania, usually leaving early in the evening (10 hr.). This ship arrives at and departs from Soudha, a 20-minute bus ride from the stop outside the Municipal Market. Many travel agents around town sell tickets. In high season, those with cars should make reservations in advance.

**By Bus**    There are almost hourly buses from early in the morning until about 10:30pm (depending on the season), connecting Chania to Rethymnon and Iraklion. There are less frequent (and often inconvenient) buses between destinations in western Crete. The main **bus station** (to points all over Crete) is at 25 Kidonias (⟨ℂ⟩ **28210/93-306**).

**VISITOR INFORMATION**    The locally sponsored **Tourist Information** office (⟨ℂ⟩ **28210/20-369;** skel@chania-cci.gr) is on Akti Tombazi, at the back of the Mosque of Djamissis, the domed building at the east side of the harbor. Hours at this time are unpredictable and although the staff tries, at best they cannot provide much detailed information. Of the many travel agencies, we recommend **Lissos Travel,** Plateia 1866 (⟨ℂ⟩ **28210/93-917;** fax 28210/95-930) and **Plimakis-Kriti Agency,** 10 Xiotaki (⟨ℂ⟩ **28210/55-655**). A useful source of insider's information is **The Bazaar,** 46 Daskaloyiannis, the main street down to the new harbor (to the right of the Municipal Market). This shop sells used foreign-language books and assorted "stuff." Owned and staffed by non-Greeks, it maintains a listing of all kinds of helpful services.

---

## A Taxi Tip

To get a taxi driver accustomed to dealing with English speakers, call **Andreas** at ⟨ℂ⟩ **28210/50-821,** or try him on his mobile phone at ⟨ℂ⟩ **69450/365-799.**

**GETTING AROUND** Almost any place you will want to visit in Chania itself is best reached by foot. There are public buses to both nearby points and all the main destinations in western Crete. If you want to explore the countryside or one or more remote points in western Crete, we recommend renting a car to make the best use of your time.

**FAST FACTS** **Banks** in the new city have ATMs. For the **tourist police**, dial ⓒ **171.** The **hospital** (ⓒ **28210/27-231**) is on Venizelou in the Halepa Quarter. **Internet cafes** include the Café Santé, on a second floor at the far (west) corner of the old harbor; Hotel Manos at 24 Zambeliou; Club Electric, 16 Apokoronou; and the one at Theotokopouli 53. The **Speedy Laundry,** Kordiki 17, on the corner of Koroneou, a block west of Plateia 1866 (ⓒ **28210/88-411**), promises wash and dry in 90 minutes and will pick up and deliver for free. For **luggage storage,** try the KTEL bus station on Kidonias. The **post office** is on Tzanakaki (leading away from the Municipal Market); open Monday through Friday from 8am to 8pm, Saturday from 8am to noon. Beside it is the **telephone office (OTE),** open daily from 7:30am to 11:30pm.

## WHAT TO SEE & DO

In summer, there are now several small **excursion ships** that offer 3- to 5-hour trips to the waters and islets off Chania. These trips depart from the old and new harbors and include stops for swimming at one or another of the islets; some provide free snorkeling gear. The glass-bottomed *Evangelos* features views of underwater life. The cost tends to run about 20€, with children under 12 going along for free.

**Archaeological Museum** ★ Even short-term visitors should stop in here, if only for a half-hour's walk-through. The museum is housed in the 16th-century Venetian Catholic Church of St. Francis (carefully restored in the early 1980s), and gives a fascinating glimpse of the different cultures that have played out on Crete, from the Neolithic through the Minoan, on to the Romans and early Christians. You'll come away with a sense of how typical people of these periods lived, as opposed to the various elites featured in so many museums.
30 Halidon. ⓒ **28210/90-334.** www.culture.gr. Admission 5€ Mon 12:30–7pm, Tues–Sat 8am–7pm, Sun 8am–2:30pm. No parking.

## SHOPPING

Jewelers, leather-goods shops, and souvenir stores are everywhere—but it's hard to find that very special item that's both tasteful and distinctively Cretan. Our choices below offer authentic Cretan objects—or at least items you will not find anyplace else. Unless otherwise noted, the following shops are open daily.

**Carmela,** at 7 Anghelou, the narrow street across from the entrance to the Naval Museum (ⓒ **28210/90-487**), has some of the finest ceramics, jewelry, and works of art in all of Crete—all original, but inspired by ancient works of art and even employing some of the old techniques.

To step into **Cretan Rugs and Blankets,** 3 Anghelou (ⓒ **28210/98-571**), is to enter a realm probably not to be experienced anywhere else on Crete. It's an old Venetian structure filled with gorgeously colored rugs, blankets, and kilims. Prices range from 100€ to 2,000€. Or visit **Roka Carpets,** 61 Zambeliou (ⓒ **28210/74-736**), even if only to see a traditional weaver at his trade. There are patterns and colors and sizes for every taste, with prices from 15€ and up. These are not artsy textiles, but traditional Cretan weaving.

# Chania

**ATTRACTIONS**
Archaeological Museum 5
Mosque of Djamissis 8
Naval Museum 1
Orthodox Cathedral 6

**ACCOMMODATIONS**
Amphitri Hotel 9
Casa Delfino 4
Hotel Palazzo 2
Hotel Porto Veneziano 13

**DINING**
Amphora Restaurant 3
Antigone Restaurant 12
Enomayirio 10
O Mathios 11
Remezzo Café 7
The Well of the Turk 14

Information
Post Office
OTE

Greece
Athens
Aegean Sea
Mediterranean Sea
CRETE
Chania

*Sea of Crete*

NEA HORA
SPLANTZIA
Municipal Market
Bus Terminal
Plateia 1866
Plateia 1821

Korai
Apokoronou
Tzanakaki
Konstantinou
Grigoriou E.
Stakianaki K.
Zimvrakidon
Konstantinoupoleos
Marigoniou
Xepapa G.
Kidonias
Skalidi
Hadzimikhali Giannari
El. Venizelou
Nikiforos Foka
Nikiforou Episkopou
Daskaloyiannis
A. Melidoni
Tsouderon
Skindlof
Halidon
Kriari
Manousogianakidon
Patriarhou Gerasimou
Patriarhou Nikiou
Metaxaki
Pireos
Kondilaki
Karaoli – Dimitriou
Zambeliou
Theotokopouli
Aiki Kountourioutou
Aposfolidon
Akti Kanari
Akti Enoseos
Ikarou
Kalergon
Sifaka
Vourdouba
Minoos
Arholeon
Akti Miaouli

100 m
100 y
0

N

Although **Khalki**, 75 Zambeliou, near the far end of the street (© 28210/75-379), is one of many little shops that sell ceramics along with other trinkets and souvenirs, it's worth seeking out. It carries the work of several local and Greek ceramists who draw on traditional motifs and colors. For a more sophisticated selection of Greek handicrafts, try **Mitos** at 44 Halidon (opposite the Orthodox Cathedral). For a varied selection by local amateur artisans, visit the **Local Artistic Handicrafts Association** (© 28210/41-885), located just where the new harbor turns the corner into the old harbor.

Finally, for a truly different souvenir or gift, try **Orphanos**, 24 Tsopuderon (by the stairs at the rear of the Public Market), with its unexpected collection of dolls and marionettes.

## WHERE TO STAY

### EXPENSIVE

**Casa Delfino** ★★    When did you last have the chance to stay in a 17th century Venetian mansion with fresh orange juice for breakfast? This mansion was converted into stylish independent suites and studios, whose tastefully decorated rooms are among the most elegant you will find on Crete. All units have modern bathrooms (and nine with Jacuzzi), and three have kitchenettes. One potential drawback, though: several rooms have beds on a second level—little more than sleeping lofts—and require you to go up and down stairs to the bathroom. If it doesn't appeal, do not book. Services of all kinds are provided, from airport transport to tour arrangements, although there's a casual air about the reception desk that might not appeal to everyone. You're only a block or so behind the harbor, but are far removed from its bustle and noise. This is an ideal way to combine a convenient location and comfortable amenities with old-world charm in a 17th-century neighborhood.

8 Theofanous 8, 73100 Chania, Crete. © 28210/87-400. Fax 28210/96-500. www.casadelfino.com. 21 units, each individually laid out. High season 185€–290€ double, low season 150€–230€. AE, MC, V. Free parking in nearby area. Open year-round (with central heating). **Amenities:** Courtyard breakfast area; small bar Jacuzzi; tour desk; car-rental desk; courtesy car or airport pickup arranged; conference facilities for 24; 24-hr. room service; babysitting; same-day laundry/dry cleaning services. *In room:* A/C, TV, kitchenette, minibar, hair dryer, safe.

**Creta Paradise Beach Resort Hotel** ★★ Kids    This already luxurious resort has recently been renovated and is perfect for those who want to sun on a beach or tour western Crete. In fact, it's a "full-service" resort and sometimes hosts large international conferences with its high-tech facilities. It also features weekly "theme nights," with Greek music and dancing. But you can partake of what appeals, and it should be especially appealing to families with young children as it has a small petting zoo as well as a very active children's program. A unique delight are the turtles that come onto the hotel's beach to lay their eggs from May to June; these hatch in late August. Guest rooms are a bit severe for Americans accustomed to upholstered luxury (don't expect overstuffed beds), but everything is tasteful and comfortable and bathrooms are up to date. Beautifully landscaped in the style of a Mediterranean villa, the resort lives up to its image.

Gerani Beach, (14km/9 miles west of Chania on coast road). P.O. Box 89, 73100 Hania © 28210/61-315. Fax 28210/61-134. www.cretaparadise.gr. 230 units. High season 195€–250€; low season 110€–150€ double. Rates include buffet breakfast. Considerably lower rates for tour groups include half-board plan (breakfast and dinner). AE, DC, MC, V. Ample parking. Taxi or bus to Chania. **Amenities:** Restaurant; poolside taverna; 2 bars; 2 pools, 2 children's pools; tennis court; fully equipped gym with sauna; aerobics; extensive watersports equipment rentals; children's program; game room (or video arcade); concierge; tour desk; car-rental desk; airport pickup arranged; secretarial services; shopping arcade; salon; 24-hr. room service; babysitting; same-day laundry/dry cleaning services; nonsmoking rooms; minigolf; volleyball; water polo; billiards; table tennis; shooting and archery lessons. *In room:* A/C, TV, minibar fridge on request, hair dryer, safe.

**Louis Creta Princess** ★ Even more family oriented than the Creta Paradise (see above), to which it is close in both its location and facilities (and in fact they belong to the same Louis Chain). In fact it's a bit like a Club Med, with its "animation team" of young people who conduct activities and diversions, from water polo to impromptu games, for both children and adults. The turtles (described under Creta Paradise, above) also come to this beach, which has been awarded a Blue Flag of the European Community for its fine condition. Guest rooms are neither spacious nor plush but are comfortable and modern; bathrooms are modern. There are conference facilities but not as ambitious as those at Creta Paradise. An in-house nightclub opens in high season, at which time there are also weekly "Cretan nights" with Greek music and dancing.

P.O. Box 9, 73014 Platanias, Crete (18km/12 miles west of Chania on coast road). ⓒ 28210/62-702. Fax 28210/62-406. www.louishotels.com. 420 units. High season 90€–140€; low season 40€–55€ double. Rates include buffet breakfast; half board supplement 18€. Reduced rates for 3rd person in room and for children. AE, DC, MC, V. Ample parking. Closed Oct–Mar. Taxis and free buses to Chania. **Amenities:** 2 restaurants; beach taverna; 4 bars; 2 pools; children's pool, all freshwater; 2 tennis courts; extensive watersports equipment rentals and scuba diving lessons; ambitious children's program; electronic games room; concierge; tour desk; car-rental desk; courtesy car or airport pickup arranged; business center; secretarial services; 24-hr. room service; babysitting; same-day laundry/dry cleaning services; minigolf; archery; basketball; volleyball; tabletennis; parts handicapped accessible. *In room:* A/C, TV, minibar, fridge, hair dryer, safe (for fee).

## MODERATE

**Doma** ★★ This has long been regarded as one of the most distinctive hotels on Crete, in part because it was one of the first in Greece to locate in a converted fine old building. (There is, however, an elevator for those who can't take stairs.) In this case, it's a neoclassical mansion from the turn of the century that was once, among other things, the British consulate; its public areas are decorated with authentic Cretan heirlooms and historical pictures. Bedrooms and bathrooms are not especially large, but are perfectly adequate. The four suites, however, are roomier. Front units have the great view of the sea but also the sound of passing traffic, although the hotel is far from the noise of the center of town. The third-story dining room offers fresh breezes and a superb view of Old Chania; breakfast here includes several homemade delights, while evening dinner brings Cretan specialties. Among its special features is a museum-quality display of headdresses from all over the world. The Doma is not for those seeking luxury, but should appeal to travelers who appreciate a discreetly old-world atmosphere.

24 Venizelou (3km/2 miles from town center along coastal road to airport), 73100 Chania, Crete. ⓒ 28210/51-772. Fax 28210/41-578. www.hotel-doma.gr. 25 units, all with private bathroom (22 with shower only). 110€ double; 180€–260€ suite. Rates include buffet breakfast. Special rates for more than 2 persons in suite; reduced rates for longer stays. AE, MC, V. Closed Nov–Mar. Free parking on nearby streets. Bus to Halepa or Chania center; can be reached by taxi or on foot. **Amenities:** Restaurant; bar; concierge; tours and car rentals arranged; airport pickup arranged; same-day laundry/dry cleaning services; nonsmoking room. *In room:* A/C, TV, hair dryer.

**Halepa Hotel** Like the better-known Doma, this hotel is in a converted neoclassical mansion. The Halepa is located in a quiet neighborhood, buffered from the street by its front garden. It's a restful oasis, with classical music often wafting through the air. Bedrooms are fair sized, bathrooms modern. The owners—Greek-Americans—can take care of your every need, from laundry to car rentals. Facilities include a sunroof that offers a spectacular view of Chania and the bay. *Tip:* Ask for a room in the main, or traditional, mansion—otherwise you must settle for a room (albeit quiet and comfortable) in the rather nondescript new wing.

164 Eleftherios Venizelou (on the street in Halepa just after the right turn to the airport), 73133 Chania, Crete. ⓒ 28210/28-440. Fax 28210/28-439. www.halepa.com. 49 units (some with tub only, some with shower

only). High season 110€ double; 130€–180€ suite for 2. Low season 85€ double, 155€ suite for 2. Rates include buffet breakfast. AE, DC, MC, V. Parking nearby. Open year-round with central heating. Frequent public buses to Chania (a 20-min. walk along the coast). **Amenities:** Breakfast room; bar; concierge; tours and car rentals arranged; airport pickup arranged; babysitting; same-day laundry/dry cleaning services. *In room:* A/C, TV, minibar, hair dryer.

**Hotel Porto Veneziano** ★ Thanks to the fact that the owner/manager is "on the scene," this hotel combines the best of old fashioned Greek hospitality and a modern service environment. As a member of the Best Western chain, it obviously has to maintain high standards. The tasteful bedrooms are relatively large, bathrooms are modern, and many rooms have a fine view of the harbor. (Be warned—that can also mean harbor noise early in the morning!) Six suites offer even more space. Located at the far end of the so-called Old Harbor (follow the walkway from the main harbor all the way around to the east, or right), this hotel offers proximity to the center with a sense that you're off in old Chania. No restaurant, but there are many within a few yards, and refreshments from the hotel's own Café Veneto may be enjoyed in the garden or in front overlooking the harbor. The desk personnel are genuinely hospitable and will make any arrangements.

Akti Enosseos 73100 Chania, Crete. ☏ 28210/27-100. Fax 28210/27-105. www.greekhotel.com. 57 units, all with private bathroom (51 with shower only). High season 130€ double; low season 115€. Rates include buffet breakfast. AE, DC, MC, V. Free parking nearby. Within walking distance of everything. **Amenities:** Breakfast room; cafe-bar; concierge; tour and car rentals arranged; airport pickup arranged; room service 7am–12pm; babysitting; same-day laundry/dry cleaning services. *In room:* A/C, TV, minibar, hair dryer.

## INEXPENSIVE

**Amphitri Hotel** This unpretentious hotel is an old favorite of regular visitors to Chania, who value the spectacular views over the harbor enjoyed by some rooms, the quiet street, the proximity to the very heart of Chania's action, and the comfortable rooms and homey atmosphere. Decidedly low-key; it should appeal to those who prize convenience above all. And you can enjoy your breakfast on a balcony with a view to die for. You don't get many amenities for your money but you do get location.

31 Lithinon, 73100 Chania, Crete. ☏ 28210/56-470. Fax 28210/52-980. 22 units. High season 105€ double. Low season 90€ double. Rates include continental breakfast. Parking on nearby streets.

**Hotel Palazzo** This Venetian town house, now a handsome little hotel, gives the feel of old Crete, but various amenities make it a comfortable hotel—a fridge in every room, a TV in the bar, a roof garden with a spectacular view of the mountains and sea. Nothing fancy about the rooms but they are good sized; those on the front have balconies. It's generally quiet, and if occasionally the still night air is broken by rowdy youths (true of all Greek cities), that seems a small price to pay for staying on Theotokopouli—the closest some will come to living on a Venetian canal. The owners speak English and will graciously help with all your needs—including laundry service, car rentals, and tours.

54 Theotokopouli (around the corner of the far leftwest arm of harbor), 73100 Chania, Crete. ☏ 28210/93-227. Fax 28210/93-229. 11 units, some with shower only, some with tub only. High season 75€ double; low season 55€ double. Rates include breakfast. MC, V. Ample parking 100m (328 ft.) away. Closed Nov–Mar (but will open for special groups). Within easy walking distance of all of Chania. **Amenities:** Bar; car rentals arranged; laundry service. *In room:* TV, fridge.

## WHERE TO DINE

### EXPENSIVE

**Nykterida** ★★ GREEK Many would nominate this as one of the finest restaurants in all Crete, especially for its setting, high on a point with spectacular nighttime views of Chania and Soudha Bay. The cuisine is traditional Cretan-Greek, but many of the dishes have an extra something. For an appetizer, try the *kalazounia* (cheese pies with specks of spinach) or the special *dolmades* (made with squash blossoms stuffed with spiced rice and served with yogurt). Any of the main courses will be well done, from the basic steak filet to the chicken with okra. Complimentary *tsoukoudia* (a potent Cretan liquor) is served at the end of the meal. On Monday, Thursday, and Friday evenings through the high season (until the end of Oct), traditional Cretan music is performed.

Korakies, Crete (about 6.4km/4 miles from town on road to airport, left turn opposite NAMFI Officers Club). © 28210/64-215. www.nykterida.gr. Reservations recommended for parties of 7 or more. Main courses 5€–15€. MC, V. Mon–Sat 6pm–1am. Parking on site. Open year-round. Taxi required if you don't have a car.

## MODERATE

**Amphora Restaurant** GREEK  This is a favorite when it comes to balancing price with quality, choice with taste, location with location. As with any Greek restaurant, if you order the lobster or steak, you'll pay a hefty price. But you can also assemble a delicious meal here at modest prices. To start, try the aubergine croquettes and the specialty of the house, a lemony fish soup. This restaurant belongs to the Amphora Hotel, a Category A, and although its tables and location suggest a basic harbor taverna, its food and friendly service make it first class.

49 Akti Koundouriotou 49 (near the far right/western curve of the harbor). © 28210/93-224. Fax 28210/93-226. Main courses 5€–14€; fixed-price meals 9€–21€. AE, MC, V. Daily 11:30am–midnight. Closed Oct–Apr.

**Antigone Restaurant** ★ GREEK/SEAFOOD  One of the many better-than-average restaurants located down along the new harbor. Start off here with an unusual appetizer such as a dip made of limpets and mussels, then move on to a specialty such as stuffed crab or whatever's the catch of the day, and you'll be eating fresh produce of the sea. Trust the staff to direct you to whatever is best that day. With its colorful interior, fresh flowers on the tables, and a view of the harbor, this can be a most pleasant dining experience.

Akti Enoseos (at farthest corner of new harbor). © 28210/45-236. Main courses 5€–14€. No credit cards. Daily 10am–2am. Parking at side of restaurant if you approach from behind; otherwise walk from the harbor.

**The Well of the Turk** ★ MIDDLE EASTERN/MEDITERRANEAN  This restaurant offers one of the more distinctive dining "experiences" in Crete through the combination of the menu and the setting. It is located in the heart of the old Turkish quarter (Splanzia), in a historic old building with an interior well. Diners may choose to sit outside in a quiet street-court. The chef brings to the cuisine imaginative touches that make it more than standard Middle Eastern. In addition to tasty kebabs, there are such specialties as meatballs with eggplant mixed in, and *laxma bi azeen*, a pita-style bread with a spicy topping. Middle Eastern musicians sometimes play here, and you can settle for a quiet drink at the bar.

1–3 Kalinikou Sarpaki (a small street off Daskaloyiannis). © 28210/54-547. Reservations recommended for parties of 7 or more. Main courses 6€–15€. No credit cards. Wed–Mon 7pm–midnight. No parking in immediate area; leave car and just walk into old quarter.

## INEXPENSIVE

**Enomayirio** SEAFOOD  Here's a special treat for those who can handle eating in a cramped, unstylish restaurant smack in the center of the great public market of Chania. The fish and other seafood come from stalls barely 4.5m (15 ft.) away. All the other ingredients also come straight from the nearby stands.

Food doesn't get any fresher nor a dining experience more "immediate." Sit here and watch the world go by.

In the Public Market, at the "arm" with the fish vendors. Main courses 5€–12€. A gigantic platter of mixed fish for 2 is 22€. No credit cards. Mon–Sat 9am–3:30pm.

**O Mathio** GREEK   At this traditional harborside taverna, you can enjoy a decent meal while watching the boats bobbing at the quay and the cats stalking beneath the tables. Long a favorite of the locals, but foreigners are welcomed and will enjoy its service (prompt no-nonsense) and food (as good as any in its class). Fish dishes are the specialty (and as elsewhere can cost considerably more than other choices). Even if you settle for the basic Greek dishes—tzatziki and Greek salad, moussaka, or stuffed tomatoes—you can't go wrong.

3 Akti Enoseos 3 (about midway along new harbor). © 28210/54-291. Main courses 4€–10€. No credit cards. Daily 11am–2:30am.

**Remezzo Cafe** INTERNATIONAL   Sooner or later, every tourist will say, "Enough of Greek salads!" and want to indulge in a club sandwich or tuna salad. Remezzo, at the very center of the action on the old harbor, is a great choice for breakfasts and light meals (omelets, salads, and so on), and also offers a full range of coffee, alcoholic drinks, and ice-cream desserts. Sitting in one of the heavily cushioned chairs as you sip your drink and observe the lively scene, you'll feel like you have the best seat in the house.

16A Venizelou (on corner of main square at old harbor). © 28210/52-001. Main courses 4€–10€. No credit cards. Daily 7am–2am.

## CHANIA AFTER DARK

Chania's nightlife need not be limited to heading for a club/bar/disco packed with young people or walking around the harbor and Old Town—the ritual known in Greece as the **volta.** Instead, wander into the back alleys and see both the old Venetian and Turkish remains and the modern tourist enterprises. Sit in a quayside cafe and enjoy a coffee or drink, or treat yourself to a ride in a horse-drawn carriage down at the harbor. Or at the other extreme, stroll through the new town and be surprised at the modernity and diversity (and prices) of the stores patronized by typical Chaniots.

**Clubs** come and go from year to year, of course, so there's no use getting excited over last year's "in" place. Some popular spots include **El Mondo** and **Nota Bene,** both on Kondilaki (the street leading away from the center of old harbor); **Idaeon Andron,** 26 Halidon; and **Ariadne,** on Akti Enoseos (around the corner where the old harbor becomes the new). On Angbelou (up from the Naval Museum) is **Fagotta,** a bar that sometimes offers jazz. **Meltemi,** at the far left (west) corner of the new harbor, is one of the more cosmopolitan cafes, attracting both locals and foreigners, some young, some old.

Two cafes stand out because of their special locations. One is the **Fortezza,** situated midway along the outer quay of the harbor; a little ferry carries you back and forth if you don't (or can't) walk here. Then there is **Pallas Roof Garden Cafe-Bar,** on Akti Tobazi (right at the corner where the new harbor meets the old harbor). You can sit high above the harbor, watch the blinking lights, listen to the murmur of the crowds below, and nurse a refreshing drink or ice cream. There has to be some drawback, and there is—you must climb 44 stairs to get here, but as the sign says, it's worth it.

A more unusual cafe is the **Tzamia-Krystalla,** at 35 Skalidi, the main street heading east out of the 1866 Square (© 28210/71-172; tza-ury@otenet.gr). A welcome addition to the usual tourist scene, it's a combination art gallery/cafe/performance space. The gallery hosts changing exhibits by Greek artists, as well as the award-winning ceramics of one of the owners. The cafe serves a standard selection of alcoholic and nonalcoholic drinks (no cover or minimum), and at times offers performances of live music. If you'd prefer to hear traditional Cretan music, try the **Café Lyriaka**, 22 Kalergon (behind the arsenali along the harbor).

There has long been a gay community in Chania; one hangout has been **Ta Padia Paizei**, on Archoleon, at the far (east) end of the new harbor. The club has no street address but is distinguished by the wheelbarrows with flowers at the door.

There are several **movie houses** around town, too—both outdoor and indoor. They usually show foreign movies in the original language. (The one in the Public Gardens is especially enjoyable.) Watching a movie on a warm summer night in an outdoor cinema in Greece is one of life's simpler pleasures.

In recent years, there's been an effort to provide a **summer cultural festival** of sorts—occasional performances of dramas, symphonic music, jazz, dance, and traditional music. These performances take place from July into September at several venues: the **Firka** fortress at the far left of the harbor; the **Venetian arsenals** along the old harbor; the **East Moat Theater** along Nikiforou Phokas; or in the **Peace and Friendship Park Theater** on Demokratias, just beyond the Public Gardens. For details, inquire at one of the tourist information offices as soon as you arrive in town.

## A SIDE TRIP FROM CHANIA: THE SAMARIA GORGE ★★

Everyone with an extra day on Crete—and steady legs and solid walking shoes—should consider the descent through the Gorge of Samaria. This first involves getting to the top of the gorge, a trip of some 42km (26 miles) from Chania. Second comes the descent by foot and passage through the gorge itself, some 18km (11 miles). Third, a boat takes you from the village of Ayia Roumeli, at the end of the gorge, to Khora Sfakion; from there, it's a bus ride of about 75km (46 miles) back to Chania. (Some boats go westward to Paleochora, approximately the same distance by road from Chania.)

Most visitors do it all in a long day, but there are modest hotels and rooms at Ayia Roumeli, Paleochora (to its west) Souya (to its east), Khora Sfakion, (main port to meet buses), and elsewhere along the south coast where you can put up for the night. We strongly advise most people to sign up with one of the many travel agencies in Chania that get people to and from the gorge. This way, you are assured of guaranteed seats on the bus and boat.

In recent years, the Gorge of Samaria has been so successfully promoted as one of the great natural splendors of Europe that on certain days, it seems that half of the continent is trekking through. It's only open from about mid-April through mid-October (depending on weather conditions), so your best chance for a bit of solitude is near those two extremes. On the most crowded days, you can find yourself walking single file with several thousand other people many of those 18km (11 miles). As a hike or trek, it's relatively taxing, and here and there you will scramble over some boulders. Bring your own water and snacks and wear those comfortable shoes.

After all this, is it worth it? (And by the way, it now charges 6€ admission.) Most everyone who makes the trip thinks so. The gorge offers enough opportunities to break away from the crowds in places. You'll be treated to the fun of crisscrossing the water, not to mention the sights of wildflowers and dramatic geological formations, the sheer height of the gorge's sides, and several chapels that you'll come across—it will all add up to a worthwhile experience, even a metaphor of your visit to Crete.

## 3 Rethymnon (Rethimno)

72km (45 miles) E of Chania; 78km (50 miles) W of Iraklion

Whether visited on a day trip from Chania or Iraklion or used as a base for a stay in western Crete, Rethymnon can be a most pleasant town—provided you pick the right Rethymnon.

The town's defining centuries came under the Venetians in the late Middle Ages and the Renaissance, then under the Turks from the late 17th century to the late 19th century. Its maze of streets and alleys are now lined with shops, its old beachfront is home to restaurants and bars, and its new beach-resort facilities (to the east of the old town) offer a prime (some might say appalling) example of how a small town's modest seacoast can be exploited. Assuming you have not come to see these "developments," however, we'll help you focus your time and attention on the old town—the side of Rethymnon that can still work its charm.

## ESSENTIALS

### GETTING THERE
Rethymnon lacks an airport but is only about 1 hour from Chania's and 1½ hours from Iraklion's.

**By Boat**  Rethymnon does have its own ship line, offering daily trips (about 10 hr.) direct to and from Piraeus.

**By Car**  Many people now approach Rethymnon by car, taking the highway from either Iraklion (some 79km/49 miles) or Chania (72km/45 miles). There is a public parking lot at Plateia Plastira, at the far (western) edge, just outside the old harbor; it is best approached via the coast road from the west.

**By Bus**  If you don't have your own vehicle, the bus offers frequent service to and from Iraklion and Chania—virtually every half-hour from early in the morning until mid-evening. (In high season, buses depart Rethymnon as late as 10pm.) The fare has been about 12€ roundtrip. The **KTEL** bus line (② 28310/22-212) that provides service to and from Chania and Iraklion is located at Akti Kefaloyianithon, at the west edge of the city (so allow an extra 10 min. to get there).

### VISITOR INFORMATION
The **National Tourism Office** (② 28310/29-148) is on Venizelou, near the center of the town beach. In high season it's open Monday through Friday from 8am to 2:30pm; off season its hours are unpredictable. Of the numerous private travel agencies in town, one of the oldest is **Creta Travel Bureau**, 3 Venizelou (② 28310/22-915), which can arrange trips to virtually anywhere on the island.

### GETTING AROUND
Rethymnon is a walker's town—bringing a car into the maze of streets and alleys is more trouble than it's worth. The sites you'll want to see are never more than a 20-minute walk from wherever you are. Taxis, meanwhile, are there for anyone who can't endure a short walk—especially in the heat of the day.

To see the countryside of this part of Crete, unless you have unlimited time to use the buses, you'll need to rent a car. Among the many agencies with offices in Rethymnon are **Motor Club** (② 28310/54-253), **Budget** (② 28310/56-910), **Europeo** (② 28310/51-940), and **Hertz** (② 28310/26-286).

**ATTRACTIONS**
Entrance to Venetian Fortezza 1
Historical & Folk Art Museum 8
Mosque of Nerantzes 9
Orthodox Church of the
Four Martyrs 11
Porta Guora 10
Rimondi Fountain 7

**ACCOMMODATIONS**
Kyma Beach Hotel 15
Hotel Fortezza 5
Hotel Ideon 4
Hotel Olympic 14

**DINING**
Mezedopolio Taverna 6
Famagusta 5
Fanari ("The Lantern") 2
Ovelistirion 11
Taverna Mourayiou Maria 6

Information *i*
Post Office ⊠
OTE ☏

Map labels:
Zabellou
Moatsou
Prevelaki
Hatzidaki
Daskalaki
Kazantzaki
Marouli
Hortatzi
Giaboudaki
Iroon
Plateia
Arkadiou
Kallergi
Afentouli
Venizelou
Dimitrakaki
Gerakari
Tobazi
Antistaseos
Kountouriori
Dimakropoulou
Platonos
Municipal
Gardens
Tim Vasou
Igoumenou Gavril
Bus
Station
Nik Foka
Patelarou
Navarinou
Grigoriou
Sofokleous
Vernadou
Souliou
Kormarou
Paleologou
Dikastiriou
Plateia
Georgiou
Athinon
Plateen
Smirnis
Melissinou
Kapsali
Katehaki
Archaeological
Museum
Plastira
Venetian Fortezza
Venetian Harbor
Sea of Crete

Inset map:
Sea of Crete
Mediterranean Sea
Aegean Sea
CRETE
Rethymnon
Athens
Greece

## Finds  For Wine Lovers

Rethymnon's annual wine festival takes place for about 10 days starting near the end of July. It's centered around the Public Gardens, with music and dancing to accompany the samplings of local wines. It's a modest affair, but we find it a welcome change from some of the more staged festivals.

**FAST FACTS**    Several **banks** in both the old town and new city have ATMs and currency-exchange machines. The **hospital** is at 7–9 Trantallidou in the new town (© 28310/27–491). For **Internet access,** try the Caribbean Bar Café (behind the Rimondi Fountain) or the Alana Taverna (on Salaminas near the Hotel Fortezza). The most convenient **laundry** is next to the Youth Hostel, 45 Tombazi; open Monday through Saturday from 8am to 8pm. The **tourist police** (© 28310/28-156) share the same building with the tourist office, along the beach. The **post office** is east of the Public Gardens at 37 Moatsu 37 (© 28310/22-571); open Monday through Friday from 8am to 8pm, Saturday from 8am to noon. The **telephone office (OTE)** is at 40 Kountourioti 40; open daily from 7:30am to midnight.

## WHAT TO SEE & DO ATTRACTIONS

**Historical and Folk Art Museum** ✦    Housed in a Venetian mansion, this small museum displays ceramics, textiles, jewelry, artifacts, implements, clothing, and other vivid reminders of the traditional way of life of most Cretans across the centuries.

30 Vernadou. © 28310/23-398. Admission 3€. Mon–Sat 9am–1pm.

**The Venetian Fortezza** ✦    Dominating the headland at the western edge of town, this massive fortress is the one site everyone should give at least an hour to visit. Built under the Venetians (but *by* Cretans) from about 1573 to 1580, its massive walls, some 1,130m (1,819 ft.) in perimeter, were designed to deflect the worst cannon fire of the day. In the end, of course, the Turks simply went around it and took the town by avoiding the fort. There's a partially restored mosque inside as well as a Greek Orthodox chapel. It's in this vast area, by the way, that most of the performances of the annual **Rethymnon Renaissance Festival** take place (see below).

Just outside the entrance to the Fortezza is the **Archaeological Museum** (© 28310/29-975). Its exhibits are not of much interest; we recommend instead the little Folk Art Museum (described above).

© 28310/28-101. Admission 5€. Daily 8:30am–7pm. On foot, climb Katehaki; a fairly steep road opposite the Hotel Fortezza on Melissinou; by car, ascend the adjacent Kheimara.

## A STROLL THROUGH THE OLD TOWN

Rethymnon's attractions are best appreciated by walking through the old town and focusing on whatever appeals to you. Start by getting a free map from the tourist office, located down along the beachfront.

If you have limited time, the first place you should visit is the **Venetian Fortezza** (see above). Then make your way back along Melissinou to the corner of Mesologiou, with the Catholic church at the corner. Proceeding down Salaminos, you'll come to Arkadiou; make a left here to the western edge of the **old harbor.** Curving right down to that harbor brings an unexpected sight: the wall of restaurants and bars that effectively obliterates the quaint harbor that drew them here in the first place. Making your way through that, you'll emerge at the southeast corner of this curved harbor and come to a square that faces the town's long beach, its broad boulevard lined with even more restaurants and cafes. Turn right up Perikhaki; and at the first crossroads you'll see the **Venetian Loggia** (ca. 1600)—for many years the town's museum and now a Ministry of Culture gallery that sells officially approved reproductions of ancient Greek works of art. Continue up past it on Paleologou to the next crossroads, where you'll come, on the right, to the **Rimondi Fountain** (1623).

Leaving the fountain at your back, head onto Antistaseos toward the 17th-century **Mosque of Nerantzes** with its minaret (open for climbing Mon–Fri 11am–7:30pm, Sat 11am–3pm; closed in Aug). If you follow Antistaseos to its end, you'll come to the **Porta Guora,** the only remnant of the Venetian city walls.

Emerging at that point onto the main east-west road, opposite and to the right are the **Municipal Gardens.** On your left is the **Orthodox Church of the Four Martyrs,** worth a peek in as you walk east along Gerakari, until you come to a large open square that serves as the crossroads between the old town and the new beachfront development.

Turning back into the old town on Arkadiou, you'll see on your left the **Mosque of Kara Pasha,** now restored and used as a botanical museum (open daily 9am–6pm). As you continue along Arkhadiou, in addition to the modern shops and their offerings, note the several remains of the Venetian era that survive—particularly the **facade of no. 154.** From this point on, you're on your own to explore the various narrow streets, to shop, or to simply head for the waterfront and enjoy some refreshment.

## OUTDOOR PURSUITS

If you're interested in horseback riding, try the **Riding Center,** located southeast of town at Platanias, 39 N. Fokas (© **28310/28-907**). Among the newer diversions offered in Rethymnon are the daily **excursion boats** that take people on a day trip for **swimming** on the beach either at **Bali** (to the east) or **Marathi** (on the Akrotiri to the west). The price, which has been about 25€ for adults, includes a midday meal at a local taverna as well as all the wine you care to drink. You can sign on at the far end of the harbor. **Nias Tours,** 4 Arkadiou (© **28310/ 23-840**), also offers an **evening cruise** that provides a view of Rethymnon glittering in the night.

## SHOPPING

Here, as in Chania and Iraklion, you may be overwhelmed by the sheer number of gift shops offering largely the same objects—mostly souvenirs. Those looking for something a bit different might try Nikolaos Papalasakis's **Palaiopoleiou,** 40

---

*Moments*  **The Rethymnon Renaissance Festival**

Rethymnon's cultural festival offers varied events—mostly musical and theatrical—from July to early September. Productions range from ancient Greek dramas to more contemporary artistic endeavors (and now include folk and rock concerts). Most performers are Greek; some are foreigners. The majority of performances are staged in the Fortezza itself—there's nothing quite like listening to 17th-century music or seeing a Renaissance drama in this setting. For details, inquire at the tourist information office.

Souliou, which is crammed with some genuine antiques, old textiles, jewelry, and curiosities such as the stringed instruments made by the proprietor. At **Olive Tree Wood,** 35 Arambatzoglou, the name says it all—the store carries various bowls, containers, and implements carved from olive wood.

For a nice selection of Cretan embroidery, see **Haroula Spridaki,** 36 Souliou. Those interested in modern ceramics should stop into **Omodamos,** 3 Souliou, where the original works reflect imaginative variations on traditional Greek pottery. And **Talisman,** 32 Arabatzoglou, offers an interesting selection of blown glass, ceramics, plaques, paintings, and other handmade articles.

## WHERE TO STAY

There is no shortage of accommodations in and around Rethymnon—but it has become increasingly harder to find a place in town that offers a convenient location, some authentic atmosphere, and a quiet night's sleep. Our choices try to satisfy the last-mentioned criterion first. Note that many places in Rethymnon shut down in winter.

### MODERATE

**Hotel Fortezza** ★    Fortezza is one of the more appealing hotels in Rethymnon, as its location isolates it from the noise of the inner town. This is especially true of its inside rooms, which overlook the modest but welcome pool. You're only a few blocks from the inner old town and then another couple of blocks to the town beach or the Venetian harbor. The Venetian Fortezza rises just across the street. All guest rooms are good sized with modern bathrooms, and most have balconies. Half of the rooms have air-conditioning and phones. This relatively new hotel has become so popular that we recommend making reservations for the high season.

16 Melisinou (at western edge of town, just below the Venetian Fortezza, which is approached by this road), 74100 Rethymnon. ✆ **28310/55-551.** Fax 28310/54-073. 54 units. High season 110€ double; low season 90€ double. Rates include buffet breakfast. Surcharge for 3rd person sharing room; babies stay free. AE, DC, MC, V. Parking nearby. Public bus service 100m (328 ft.). **Amenities:** Restaurant; bar; pool; TV room; card-playing room; concierge; tour and car rentals arranged; babysitting. *In room:* A/C.

**Hotel Ideon**    This old favorite now boasts a new pool and a sunbathing area as well as a conference room that can handle up to 50 persons. The friendly desk staff will arrange for everything from laundry service to car rentals. The guest rooms are the standard modern of Greek hotels. We like this place because it offers an increasingly rare combination in a Cretan hotel: It's near the active part of town and near the water (although it doesn't have a beach), yet it's relatively isolated from night noises. A solid choice for sheer convenience.

10 Plateia Plastira (on coast road just west of the Venetian harbor), 74100 Rethymnon. ✆ **28310/28-667.** Fax 28310/28-670. www.hotelideon.gr. 86 units, some with shower only, some with tub only. High season 62€ double; low season 52€ double. Rates include buffet breakfast. Reduced rates for 3rd person in room and children. AE, DC, MC, V. Parking on adjacent street. Closed Nov to mid-Mar. **Amenities:** 2 bars; pool; concierge; tours and car rentals arranged; babysitting. *In room:* A/C, fridge, safe.

**Kyma Beach Hotel**    What recommends this is that it is a modern hotel that is both close to the old town with its attractions and close to a beach. Its somewhat austere gray exterior might put off some people but in fact it's a relatively well-designed hotel. Although its rooms are hardly spacious, they are well furnished; some, however, have sleeping lofts, and if this doesn't appeal, speak up. Bathrooms are up to date. All rooms have balconies, but insist on a higher floor to escape street noise. The outdoor café is a popular watering hole for locals so you can feel you're part of the town and not in some foreigners' compound. This is a city hotel, not a resort hotel, designed for people who want to take in Rethymnon but retire to a beach at the end of the day.

**Platai Iroon** (at eastern edge of old town and its beach) 74111 Rethymnon © **2831/0/55-503**. Fax 2831/27-746. 35 units, some with tub, some with shower. High season 80€ double low season 63€ double. Rates include continental breakfast. AE, MC, V. Parking nearby. Public buses nearby. **Amenities:** 2 restaurants; 2 bars; Internet access; concierge; tours and car rentals arranged; babysitting; same day laundry and dry cleaning. *In room: A/C, TV, minibar, safe.*

**Mare Monte Beach Hotel** ★ Located on a beautiful beach, here's an alternative for those who want to focus their Cretan stay on Rethymnon and Chania and western Crete, yet prefer to be based well away from a noisy town. Everything about this place is first class, yet you'll feel like you're living on a remote beach with the sea before you and the mountains behind. The village of Georgioupolis is close enough for an evening stroll. Guest rooms are of moderate size but have fully modern bathrooms; although it lacks the luxury of the grand resorts to the east of Rethymnon, the Mare Monte is more than adequate.

Georgioupolis 73007 (25 min. west of Rethymnon, on the main road to Chania), Crete. © **28250/61-390.** http://travel.yahoo.com. 200 units. High season 85€ double; low season 65€. Rates include breakfast. DC, MC, V. Parking on site. Closed Nov–Mar. **Amenities:** 2 restaurants; 2 bars; pool; children's pool; 2 night-lit tennis courts; extensive watersports; children's playground; concierge; tours and car rentals arranged; secretarial services; 24-hr. room service; babysitting; laundry and dry cleaning arranged; minigolf; archery; horseback riding arranged; table tennis. *In room: A/C, TV, safe.*

## INEXPENSIVE

**Hotel Olympic** Not for everyone, but it offers fair value for budget travelers. It's about 300 yards removed from the town beach, yet it's removed from the main traffic of the center of town. Rooms are not especially large and bathrooms are just adequate; all have balconies if not special views—ask for an interior room if you want complete quiet.

Corner Moutsou and Demokratias (1 block up from Koundouriotou 74100 Rethymnon © **2831/27-761.** 65 units. High season 70€ double; low season 58€ double. Rates include continental breakfast. AE, MC, V. Parking nearby. Public buses nearby. **Amenities:** Breakfast room; bar; roof garden; tours and auto rentals arranged. *In room: A/C.*

## WHERE TO DINE

For standard but tasty Greek foods, you might consider the **Mezedopolio Taverna, Plateia Plastira** (© **2830/53-598**), behind the far western end of old harbor; or the **Ovelistirion,** Arambatzoglou, on the square overlooking the Church of the Annunciation.

## EXPENSIVE

**Cava d'Oro** ★ GREEK/SEAFOOD In recent years, this has emerged as the Venetian harbor restaurant with the reputation for the most pleasant ambience and with food at least as good as any other's. But part of that appeal is based on its air-conditioned dining room—not everyone's idea of being on a Cretan harbor—and its very reputation has made it crowded, especially when tour groups move in. Seafood is its specialty, naturally, and this means the high end of the menu prevails; you would hardly go here for the cheaper dishes. Save this for a special occasion—and go off-peak season and/or hours.

42 Nearchou Street (Venetian Harbor). © **2831/24-446.** Main courses 4.50€–15€. AE, DC, MC, V. Daily 11am–midnight. Closed Nov–Mar.

**Taverna Mourayiou Maria** GREEK/SEAFOOD Like all of the restaurants on the Venetian harbor, this one specializes in lobster and fish in season, but it also offers a choice of traditional Greek dishes at the lower end of the price scale.

The popularity of the area has somewhat overwhelmed the picturesque charm that originally attracted restaurants such as this one, but every visitor will want to try at least one meal on the harbor—and this is as good a choice as any.

45 Nearchou (Venetian harbor). ☎ 28310/26-475. Main courses 4.50€–15€. AE, MC, V. Daily 9am–midnight. Closed Nov–Mar.

## MODERATE

**Famagusta** GREEK/INTERNATIONAL   A well-tested restaurant in a location that is removed from the hustle of the harbor yet convenient to the center's attractions and enjoying a view of the sea. The menu offers several Cretan specialties such as breaded zucchini deep fried with yogurt lightly flavored with garlic, or *halumi*, a grilled cheese. Grilled fish and filets are the core of the main courses, but the adventurous chef also includes such dishes as Chinese style mandarin beef and that old basic, chili con carne. Eating here makes you feel like you're at an old-fashioned seaside restaurant, not some touristic confection.

6 Plastira Square (near Ideon Hotel, on coast road just to west of Venetian Harbor) Rethymnon. ☎ 28310/23-881. Main courses 3.50€–11€. AE, DC, MC, V. Daily 10am–midnight. Closed Christmas through New Year's. Parking lot nearby.

## INEXPENSIVE

**Fanari (The Lantern)** (Value) GREEK   We list this place not because its menu or cooking are so exceptional, but because its location is so pleasant, overlooking the sea and well removed from the bustle of the center of Rethymnon. It offers prompt and pleasant service as well. The old harbor and the old beach strip have now become so geared to tourism that an unpretentious taverna like this comes as a relief and a retreat. Take a table at the railing, order a cool drink, and enjoy your meal: You can't go wrong with the standard fare, and fish here can be as tasty as at most of the more expensive locales.

16 Kefaloyianithon (on coast road just west of Venetian harbor—past Ideon Hotel and Famagusta Restaurant). ☎ 28310/54-849. Main courses 3€–10€. Daily special combination plates about 3.50€–10€. No credit cards. Daily 11am–1:30am. Parking lot nearby.

## 4 Ayios Nikolaos

69km (43 miles) E of Iraklion

Ayios Nikolaos tends to inspire strong reactions, depending on what you're looking for. Until the 1970s, it was a lazy little coastal settlement, with no archaeological or historical structures of any interest. Then the town got "discovered," and the rest is the history of organized tourism in our time.

For about 5 months of the year, Ayios Nikolaos becomes one gigantic resort town, taken over by the package-tour groups who stay in beach hotels along the adjacent coast, but come into town to eat, shop, and stroll. During the day, Ayios Nikolaos vibrates with people. At night, it vibrates with music—the center down by the water is like one communal nightclub.

Yet somehow the town remains a pleasant place to visit, and serves as a fine base for excursions to the east of Crete. And if you're willing to stay outside the very center, you can take only as much of Ayios Nikolaos as you want—and then retreat to your beach or explore the east end of the island.

## ESSENTIALS

**GETTING THERE   By Plane**   Ayios Nikolaos does not have its own airport but can be reached in 1½ hours by taxi or bus from the Iraklion airport. During the high season **Olympic Airways** also offers several flights weekly to Sitia,

# Ayios Nikolaos

Sea of Crete

Quay

Archaeological Museum

Milatou

Akti Koundourou

Kortsas

Koraka

Prigipos Georgiou

Kantanoleontos

Katerlaki

Paleologou

D. Solonos

Ethniks Antistaseos

Theotokouloud

Kobnarouv

Plastira

Titou

Fileiinon

El. Venizelou

Tavla

Kozri

Akti Atlantidos

**Bus Station**

Plateia Venizelou

Koundourou

28 Octobriou

Omirou

25 Martiou

Polytechniou

Manousogianakis

K. Sfakianaki

Alexomanoli

M. Sfakianaki

Lasthenous

Koundourou

Pastias

Ariadnis

Ebans

Milou

Kondiaki

Lake Voulismeni

*Kitroplatia Beach*

0    100 m
0    100 y

N

## ACCOMMODATIONS

Hotel Hermes **2**
Minos Beach **1**

## DINING

Hollands Restaurant—
De Molen (The Mill) **4**
Itanos **6**
La Casa **5**
Pelagos **3**

Greece

Athens

Aegean Sea

Ayios Nikolaos

CRETE

Mediterranean Sea

325

the town to the east of Ayios Nikolaos, but the drive from there to Ayios Niko-laos is a solid 2 hours.

**By Boat**  There are several ships a week each way that link Ayios Nikolaos to Piraeus (about 11 hr.) There are also ships that link Ayios Nikolaos to Sitia (just east along the coast) and on, via the islands of Kassos, Karpathos, and Khalki, to Rhodes. In summer, there are several ships that link Ayios Nikolaos to San-torini (4 hr.), and then via several other Cycladic islands to Piraeus. Schedules and even ship lines vary so much from year to year that you may want to wait until you get to Greece to make specific plans.

**By Bus**  Bus service almost every half-hour of the day each way (in high sea-son) links Ayios Nikolaos to Iraklion; almost as many buses go to and from Sitia. The **KTEL** bus line (© **28410/22-234**) has its terminal at Akti Atlantidos by the marina, around the headland.

**VISITOR INFORMATION**  The **Municipal Information Office** (© **28410/22-357**) is one of the most helpful in all of Greece, perhaps because it's staffed by eager young seasonal employees. It's open April 15 through October, daily from 8am to 10pm. In addition to providing maps and brochures, it can help arrange accommodations and excursions. Among the scores of travel agencies, we recom-mend **Creta Travel Bureau,** at the corner of Paleologou and Katehaki, just oppo-site Lake Voulismeni (© **28410/28-496;** fax 28410/223-749).

**GETTING AROUND**  The town is so small that you can walk to all points, although there are taxis available. The KTEL buses (see above) service towns, hotels, and other points in eastern Crete. If you want to explore this end of the island on your own, it seems as though car and moped/motorcycle rentals are at every other doorway. We found some of the best rates at **Alfa Rent a Car,** 3 Kap. Nik. Fafouti, the small street between the lake and harbor road (© **28410/24-312;** fax 28410/25-639). Foris Aretakis is the man to deal with.

**FAST FACTS**  There are several **ATMs** and currency-exchange machines along the streets leading away from the harbor. The **hospital** (© **28410/22-369**) is on the west edge of town, at the junction of Lasithiou and Paleologou. For **Internet access,** head to Peripou, 25 28th Octobriou (© **28410/24-876;** peripou2@agn. forthnet.gr); open daily in high season from 9am to 9pm. The most convenient **laundry** is the Xionati Laundromat, 10 Chortatson (a small street leading up from Akti Nearchou, down by the bus terminal and beach); open Monday through Fri-day from 8am to 2pm and 5 to 8pm, Saturday from 8am to 4pm. **Luggage storage** is available at the main bus station, at Akti Atlantidos (by the marina). The **tourist police** (© **28410/26-900**) are at 34 Koundoyianni. The **post office** is at 9 28th Octobriou (© **28410/22-276**). In summer, it's open Mon-day through Saturday from 7:30am to 8pm; in winter, Monday through Saturday from 7:30am to 2pm. The **telephone office (OTE),** 10 Sfakinaki, at the corner of 25th Martiou (© **28410/131**), is open Monday through Saturday from 7am to midnight, Sunday from 7am to 10pm.

## WHAT TO SEE & DO

The focal point in town is the harbor and the small pool, formally called **Lake Voulismeni,** just inside the harbor—you can sit on the edge of it while enjoying a meal or drink. Inevitably, it has given rise to all sorts of tales: that it's bottom-less (it's known to be about 65m/213 ft. deep); that it's connected to Santorini, the island some 104km (65 miles) to the north; and that it was the "bath of Athena." Originally it was a freshwater pool, probably fed by some subterranean river draining water from the mountains inland. The channel was dug sometime early in the 20th century, so the freshwater now mixes with seawater.

**Archaeological Museum** ★   This is a fine example of one of the relatively new provincial museums that are appearing all over Greece—in an effort both to decentralize the country's rich holdings and also to allow local communities to profit from the finds in their regions. It contains a growing collection of Minoan artifacts and art that is being excavated in eastern Crete. Its prize piece is the eerily modern ceramic **Goddess of Myrtos**, a woman clutching a jug, found at a Minoan site of this name down on the southeastern coast. The museum is worth at least a brief visit.

74 Paleologou. ℂ **28410/24-943.** Admission 5€. Tues–Sun 8:30am–3pm (the museum may reduce hours in low season so call ahead).

## SHOPPING

Definitely make time to visit **Ceramica**, 28 Paleologou (ℂ **28410/234-075**); you will see many reproductions of ancient Greek vases and frescoes for sale throughout Greece, but seldom will you have a chance to visit the workshop of one of the masters of this art, Nikolaos Gabriel. His authentic and vivid vases range from 25€ to 200€ Across the street, at no. 1A, is **Xeiropoito**, which carries some handmade rugs.

**Marieli,** 33 28th Octobriou, leading away from the harbor (ℂ **28410/28-813**), carries some interesting ceramics, candlesticks, jewelry, and other crafts. **Pegasus,** 5 Sfakianakis, on the corner of Koundourou, the main street up from the harbor (ℂ **28410/24-347**), offers a selection of jewelry, knives, icons, and trinkets—some old, some not, and you'll have to trust the owner, Kostas Kounelakis, to tell you which is which.

For something truly Greek, what could be better than an icon, a religious painting on a wooden plaque? The tradition is kept alive in Elounda at the **Petrakis Workshop for Icons,** 22 A. Papendreou, on the left as you come down the incline from Ayios Nikolaos, just before the town square (ℂ **28410/41-669**). Here in their studio/store, Georgia and Ioannis Petrakis work seriously at maintaining this art. Their icons are in demand from Orthodox churches in North America as well as in Greece. Stop by and watch the artists at their painstaking work—you don't have to be Orthodox to admire or own one. They also have a selection of local artisans' jewelry, blown glass, and ceramics.

## WHERE TO STAY
### INSIDE TOWN

**Hotel Hermes**   This is perhaps the best you can do if you want to stay as close to the center of town as possible, yet be free from as much of the noise as possible. It's just far enough and around the corner from the inner harbor to escape the nightly din. This won't be in everyone's budget, but it's a compromise between the deluxe beach resorts and the cheaper in-town hotels. Guest rooms are done in the standard style, and most enjoy a view over the sea. There's a private terrace (not a beach) on the shore, just across the boulevard. On the roof is a pool, with plenty of space to sunbathe.

If the Hermes is booked, you might try the **Hotel Coral,** Akti Koundourou next door to the Hermes on the shore road (ℂ **28410/28-253**). It's under the same management, almost as classy, and slighty cheaper.

Akti Koundourou (on the shore road around from the inner harbor), 72100 Ayios Nikolaos, Crete. ℂ **28410/ 28-253.** www.hermes-hotels.gr. 206 units. High season 175€ double; low season 135€ double. **Note:** Rates include half-board plan (breakfast and dinner); special rate for longer stays. AE, DC, MC, V. Parking on opposite seawall (but beware of seaspray!). Closed Nov–Mar. **Amenities:** 2 restaurants; 2 bars; swimming pool; fitness center and sauna; video games; conference facilities; billiards. *In room:* A/C, TV, fridge, hair dryer.

**Minos Beach** ⭐⭐       We have to admit that we recommend this place out of a certain historical loyalty—to the first of the luxury beach-bungalow resorts in all of Greece. It remains a favorite among many loyal returnees, but it must also be admitted that the common areas are not as glitzy as at newer resorts and its grounds now look a bit overgrown with greenery. As with almost all Greek deluxe hotels, the mattresses seem a bit thin—to Americans, at least. But the hotel does have a civilized air, enhanced by the original works by world-famous modern sculptors located around the grounds. It's a great place to enjoy complete peace and quiet and yet not be that far from Ayios Nikolaos. Let's conclude by saying that it will appeal to those who like a touch of the "Old World" when they go abroad.

Amoudi (a 10-min. walk from center), 72100 Ayios Nikolaos. ℗ **28410/22-345.** Fax 28410/22-548. www.greekhotel.com/crete/agiosnikolaos. 12 units (in main building), 120 bungalows. High season 125€–195€ double/bungalow; low season 110€–155€. **Note:** All rates are per person and include buffet breakfast. Special rates for children. AE, DC, MC, V. Closed late Oct to late Apr. Frequent public buses to Ayios Nikolaos center or Elounda. **Amenities:** 5 restaurants; 2 bars; saltwater pool; night-lit tennis court; health club and sauna; Jacuzzi in some bungalows; watersports equipment rentals; TV room; bike rentals; concierge; tours and car rentals arranged; airport transport arranged; conference center; secretarial services; salon; room service 7:30am–9:30pm; babysitting; same-day laundry and dry-cleaning service; table tennis; safe-deposit at desk; newspaper delivery. *In room:* A/C, TV, minibar, hair dryer.

## OUTSIDE TOWN

### Elounda Beach ⭐⭐⭐       This is truly a world-class resort, consistently on all the lists of "best" and "top" and "great" hotels and resorts. But this also means that, like buying a yacht, if you have to ask the price, you can't afford it. It offers more extras than we can list, including a gala dinner every Sunday and open-air movies on Monday nights. There's not much more to say about such a place except that it's truly deluxe. From the prunes at the lavish breakfast buffet to the mini-TV at your bathroom mirror, the management has thought of everything. Rooms and bathrooms are appropriately luxuriously appointed. Its restaurants provide truly haute cuisine. And oh, in case you're concerned, the hotel does have its own heliport, so you can arrive that way if you please. Its clientele include the wealthy and well-known from all over the world but the fact is that if you are able to pay at least the minimal low-season rates, its rates are not all that extreme as expensive hotels now go. Definitely a once-in-a-lifetime experience.

72053 Elounda (8km/5 miles from center of Ayios Nikolaos), Crete. ℗ **28410/41-412.** Fax 28410/41-373. www.eloundabeach.gr. 243 units (including 21 suites and bungalows with private swimming pools). High season 225€–375€ double, 280€–750€ bungalow suite; low season 110€–195€ double, 140€–305€ bungalow suite. **Note:** Rates are per person per day and include breakfast (1 meal supplement costs 35€ extra). AE, DC, MC, V. Closed early Nov to early Apr. Public buses to Ayios Nikolaos or Elounda every hr.; Elounda is a 15-min. walk. **Amenities:** 4 restaurants; 4 bars; pool (and 25 suites with own pools); 5 night-lit tennis courts; health club, sauna; watersports including scuba diving and sailing; bike rentals; children's program; concierge; tours and car rentals arranged; transport from airport arranged (car or helicopter); business center; secretarial services; shopping arcade; salon; 24-hr. room service; massage; babysitting; same-day laundry and dry cleaning; volleyball; table tennis; billiards; newspaper delivery. *In room:* A/C, TV, fridge, hair dryer, safe, Jacuzzi.

**Istron Bay** ⭐⭐       Still another relatively new and beautiful (and quiet!) beach resort, this one is nestled against the slope on its own bay. It's the resort's location, plus its own beach and the sense of being in some tropical paradise, that makes this such a special place. Plus, it's family owned and thus maintains a touch of the traditional Cretan hospitality—inviting newcomers to a cocktail party to meet others, for instance. The comfortable guest rooms have modern bathrooms and spectacular views. If you can tear yourself away from here, you're well situated to take in all the sights of eastern Crete. The main dining room has a fabulous view to go with its award-winning cuisine; it takes special pride in offering choices based on the "Cretan diet," internationally recognized as especially healthy. This place also offers several different activities, including an authorize scuba diving school, nature walks in the spring and autumn, wine tastings, fishing trips, even Greek lessons.

72100 Istro (12km/7 miles east of Ayios Nikolaos), Crete. ✆ **28410/61-303.** Fax 28410/61-383. www.istronbay.com. 145 units (including 27 bungalows). High season 190€ double, 275€ suite or bungalow; low season 150€ double, 215€ suite or bungalow. Rates include buffet breakfast. Special rates for extra beds in room, for children, for June, and for half-board plan. AE, DC, MC, V. Closed Nov–Mar. Public buses every hour to Ayios Nikolaos or Sitia. **Amenities:** 3 restaurants; 2 bars; sea-water swimming pool and children's pool; night-lit tennis court; watersports equipment rentals; children's program; concierge; tours and car rentals arranged; airport transport arranged; conference facilities; salon; room service 7am–11pm; massage; babysitting; laundry and dry cleaning service; volleyball; table tennis; billiards.

## WHERE TO DINE

Ayios Nikolaos and nearby Elounda have so many restaurants that it's hard to know where to start or stop. When deciding, consider location and atmosphere; those factors have governed our recommendations below.

### MODERATE

**Hollands Restaurant—De Molen (The Mill)** DUTCH/INDONESIAN
Who would go to Crete to eat Indonesian cuisine? Someone looking for a change from the basic Greek menu. Aside from offering a new experience for your palate, this place commands the most dramatic nighttime view of Ayios Nikolaos. Specialties include pork filet in a cream sauce. Vegetarian? Try the crepe with eggplant, mushrooms, carrots, and cabbage, tied up with leeks. We tasted something even more exotic: one of the Indonesian dishes, Nasi Goreng—a heaping plate of rice with vegetables and pork, in a satay (peanut) sauce. Somehow it seemed to go with our perch overlooking exotic Ayios Nikolaos.

10 Dionysos Solomos (the road at the highest point above the lake). ✆ and fax **28410/25-582.** Main courses 4.50€–12€ combination plates offered. V. Daily 10am–11:30pm. Closed Nov–Mar. A taxi is your only choice if you can't make it up the hill.

**La Casa** GREEK/INTERNATIONAL With its lakeside location, tasty menu, and friendly Greek-American proprietress, this might be many travelers' first choice in Ayios Nikolaos. You'll enjoy any of the fine meals Marie Daskaloyiannis cooks up, including such specialties as fried rice with shrimp, lamb with artichokes, and rabbit stifado. Or try the "Greek sampling" plate—moussaka, dolmades, stuffed tomato, meatballs, and whatever other goodies Marie heaps on. There's always a slightly special twist to the food here.

31 28th Octobriou. ✆ **28410/26-362.** Main courses 4€–12€. AE, DC, DISC, MC, V. Daily 9am–midnight No parking in immediate area.

**Pelagos** ★ GREEK/SEAFOOD Looking for a change from the usual touristy seafront restaurant—something a bit more cosmopolitan? Try Pelagos, in a handsome old house a block up from the hustle and bustle of the harbor. As its name suggests, it specializes in seafood, and from squid to lobster (expensive, as always in Greece), it's all done with flair. You can sit indoors in a subdued atmosphere or out in the secluded garden; either way you'll be served with style. This restaurant lets you get away from the crowd and share a more intimate meal.

10 Ketahaki (at corner of Koraka) a block up from the waterfront). (C) **28410/25-737.** doxan45@hotmail.com. Reservations recommended in high season. Main courses 4€–15€. MC, V. Daily noon–1am. Closed Nov–Feb. Parking on adjacent streets—but all but impossible in high season.

**Vritomartes** GREEK/SEAFOOD   It takes a slight amount of effort to get to this taverna out in Elounda, but it's worth the effort to sit out on the water and contemplate the scene at Elounda. Besides, there are buses every hour as well as taxis for the 12km (8-miles) trip, and anyone who's come as far as Ayios Nikolaos should get out to Elounda at least once. You can't beat dining at this old favorite—there's been at least a lowly taverna here long before the beautiful people and group tours discovered the area. (They're the reason you should either come early or make a reservation.) The specialty, no surprise, is the seafood. (You may find the proprietor literally "out to sea," catching that night's fish dinners.) If you settle for the red mullet and a bottle of Cretan white Xerolithia, you can't go wrong. The dining area itself is pretty plain, but this is still one experience you won't forget.

Elounda (on the breakwater). (C) **28410/41-325.** Reservations recommended for dinner in high season. Main courses 4€–29€; fish platter special for two 46€. MC, V. Daily 10am–11pm. Closed Nov–Mar. Parking lot nearby.

## INEXPENSIVE

**Itanos** GREEK   A now familiar story on Crete: A simple local taverna where you go to experience "the authentic" gets taken up by the tourists, changing the scene somewhat. But the fact is, the food and prices haven't changed *that* much. It's still standard taverna oven dishes—no-nonsense chicken, lamb, and beef in tasty sauces with hearty vegetables—and grilled meats. The house wine comes out of barrels. During the day, you sit indoors, where you'll experience no-nonsense decor and service. But at night during the hot months, tables appear on the sidewalk, a roof garden opens up on the building across the narrow street, and your fellow travelers take over. Come here if you need a break from the harbor scene and want to feel you're in a place that still exists when all the visitors go home.

1 Kyprou (just off Plateia Venizelos, at top of Koundourou). (C) **28410/25-340.** Reservations not accepted, so come early in high season. Main courses 3.50€–11€. No credit cards. Daily 10am–midnight.

# The Cyclades

*by Sherry Marker*

When most people think of the "Isles of Greece," they're thinking of the Cyclades, the rugged (even barren) chain of Aegean islands whose villages of dazzling white houses look from a distance like so many sugar cubes. The Cyclades got their name from the ancient Greek word meaning "to circle," or "surround," because the island chain encircles Delos, the island long sacred to the god Apollo. Today, it's the visitors who circle these islands, taking advantage of the swift island boats and hydrofoils that link them.

If you were to come up with a few words to describe the best-known Cycladic islands (roughly from north to south), **Tinos** would probably be called the "Lourdes of Greece." Its famous church of the Panagia Evangelistria is Greece's most important pilgrimage destination, especially on the Feast of the Assumption (Aug 15). **Mykonos'** perfect Cycladic architecture and jetset attractions (you can get a margarita as easily as an ouzo) first made it popular in the '60s. Although many of the Beautiful People have moved on, Mykonos remains a favorite, although expensive, island—especially in the summer, when reservations are imperative. Some think of **Paros** as the poor man's Mykonos, with excellent windsurfing and a profusion of restaurants and nightspots less pricey than those on its better-known neighbor. **Naxos** is green, fertile, its hills dotted with dovecots and a profusion of small Byzantine chapels. The Venetians ruled here and

left behind a splendid kastro (castle) in Naxos town. The crescent of **Santorini (Thira)**, with its black sand beaches and blood-red cliffs, is all that remains of the island that was blown apart in antiquity by a volcano that still steams and hisses today. Santorini's exceptional physical beauty, dazzling relics, and elegant restaurants and boutiques give it its sophisticated image. Unfortunately, Santorini's charms draw so many daytrippers from cruise ships that the island almost sinks under the weight of tourists each summer. **Folegandros** is the perfect counterbalance to Santorini: as yet, this little island is not overwhelmed with visitors. Folegandros has good beaches and a capital—that many say is the most beautiful in all the Cyclades—largely built into the walls of a medieval kastro. **Sifnos**, long popular with Athenians, increasingly draws summer visitors to its handsome whitewashed villages, which many consider to have the finest architecture in all the Cyclades. In the spring this is one of the greenest and most fertile of the islands. As for **Siros**, this island is as "undiscovered" as it is possible for one of the larger Cycladic islands to be—and has a distinguished capital, crowned by the remains of Venetian city and kastro, with many handsome neoclassical 19th century buildings. That's a very few introductory words, indeed, on each of the islands we'll be visiting; if you wanted to describe the Cyclades in their entirety, you could do worse than to string together some perfectly deserved superlatives: wonderful! Magical! Spectacular!

**Tips** **Beware of Price Gouging During the Olympics**

Hotel prices were accurate at press time, but price increases of 20% and more are rumored as hoteliers throughout Greece gear up for the August 2004 Olympics in and around Athens. Horrific price hikes of between 50% and an unbelievable 300% are rumored for the period leading up to, during, and after the games.

The sea and sky really are bluer here than elsewhere, the islands on the horizon always tantalizing. In short, the Cyclades are very "more-ish:" once you've visited one, you'll want to see another, and then another, and then, yes, yet another.

A few practicalities: As you might expect, the Cyclades are crowded and expensive in the high season, roughly mid-June to mid-September—and the season seems to get longer every year. If this doesn't appeal to you, visit off season; the best times are in the autumn (mid-Sept to Oct) or in the spring (May to early June—Apr can still be very cold in these islands). While the restaurant you'd hoped to eat in may be closed, and some of the chic shops shuttered, you'll be able to enjoy the islands without feeling that you're surrounded by other visitors. Should you visit in winter or spring keep in mind that many island hotels have minimal heating; make sure that your hotel has genuine heat before you check in. Keep in mind that most hotels charge **a supplementary fee of 10%** for a stay of less than three nights.

On most of these islands, the capital town has the name of the island itself. It is also sometimes called "Hora," or

"Chora," a term meaning "the place" that's commonly used for the most important regional town. The capital of Paros, Parikia, is also called Hora, as is Apollonia, the capital of Sifnos.

**STRATEGIES FOR SEEING THE ISLANDS** Although the Cyclades are bound by unmistakable family resemblance, each island is rigorously independent and unique, making this archipelago an island-hopper's paradise. Ease of travel is facilitated by frequent ferry service—although changes in schedules can keep travelers on their toes (or waiting for unpredictable hours on the harborside). Hydrofoils, in particular, are notoriously irregular, and service is often canceled at the whim of the *meltemi* (severe summer winds). A new fleet of catamarans has greatly facilitated travel between Piraeus and the Cycladic islands of Siros, Paros, Naxos, Mykonos, and Santorini. Service to most islands is highly seasonal, with frequency dropping off significantly between October and April. Between May and September, you can go just about anywhere you want, whenever you want, although, as noted, winds will often upset the most carefully arranged plans.

## 1 Santorini (Thira)

233km (126 nautical miles) SE of Piraeus

Especially if you arrive by sea, you won't confuse Santorini with any of the other Cyclades—although you might be confused to learn that it's also known as Thira. While large ships to Santorini (pop. 7,000; 240km/130 nautical miles southeast of Piraeus) dock at the port of Athinios, many small ships arrive in Skala, a spectacular harbor that's part of the enormous caldera (crater) formed when a volcano blew out the island's center around 1450 B.C. To this day, some

# The Cyclades

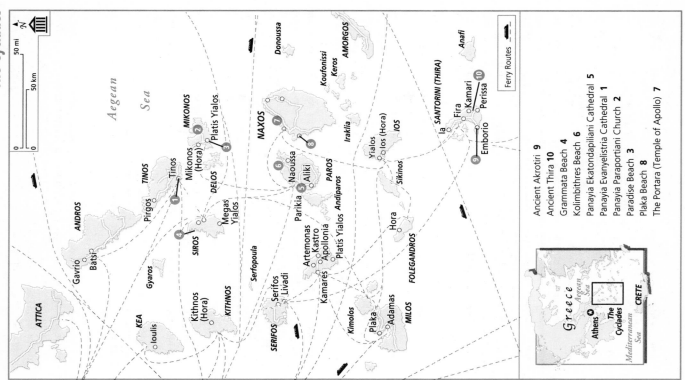

**Greece**
- Athens ⭑
- Aegean Sea
- The Cyclades
- Mediterranean Sea
- CRETE

Ferry Routes - - -

Ancient Akrotiri **9**
Ancient Thira **10**
Grammata Beach **4**
Kolimbithres Beach **6**
Panayia Ekatondapiliani Cathedral **5**
Panayia Evanyelistria Cathedral **1**
Panayia Paraportiani Church **2**
Paradise Beach **3**
Plaka Beach **8**
The Portara (Temple of Apollo) **7**

scholars speculate that the destruction gave birth to the myth of the lost continent of Atlantis. In short, this is physically one of the most spectacular islands in the world. Santorini's cliff-faced crescent isle graces tourist brochures and posters in Greek restaurants the world over. Many Greeks joke, somewhat grudgingly, that there are foreigners who know where Santorini is—but not where Greece is!

The real wonder is that Santorini itself meets and exceeds all glossy picture-postcard expectations. Like an enormous mandible, Santorini encloses the pure blue waters of its caldera, the core of an ancient volcano. Its two principal towns, **Fira** and **Ia,** perch at the summit of the caldera, their whitewashed houses resembling from an approaching ship a dusting of new snow on the mountaintop.

**Akrotiri** is Santorini's principal archaeological wonder: a town destroyed, but miraculously preserved under the layers of lava, when the volcano erupted here. If it weren't that Akrotiri steals its thunder, the site of **Ancient Thera** would be even more famous. Spectacularly situated atop a high promontory, overlooking a black lava beach, the remains of this Greek, Roman, and Byzantine city are extensive—and reached after a vertiginous hike or drive up, and up, and up to the acropolis itself.

Arid Santorini isn't known for the profusion of its harvests, but the rocky island soil has long produced a plentiful grape harvest, and the local wines are among the finest in Greece; be sure to visit one of the island **wineries** for a tasting. And keep an eye out for the tasty tiny unique Santorini tomatoes and white eggplants—and the unusually large and zesty capers. And, perhaps most importantly, be sure to allow time for at least one sunset over the caldera, perhaps at **Ia,** (best seen from the ramparts of the Kastro or the footpath between Fira and Ia).

The best advice we can offer is to visit some time other than July or August. Santorini experiences an even greater transformation during the peak season than other Cycladic isles. With visitors far in the excess of the island's small capacity, trash collects in the squares and crowds make movement through the streets of Fira and Ia next to impossible. Accommodation rates will also be as much as 50% lower if you can travel in May, June, or September.

## ESSENTIALS

**GETTING THERE    By Plane    Olympic Airways** (© 210/966-6666 or 210/936-9111; www.olympic-airways.gr) has daily flights between Athens and the Santorini airport at Monolithos (which also receives European charters). There is connection with Mykonos five times per week, service three or four times a week to and from Rhodes, and service two or three times a week with Iraklion, Crete. For information and reservations, check with the Olympic office in Fira on Ayiou Athanassiou (© 22860/22-493), just southeast of town on the road to Kamari, or in Athens at © 08210/44-444 or 210/998-8300 in Athens). **Aegean Airlines** (© 210/998-2888 or 210/998-500), also has several flights daily between Athens and Santorini. A bus to Fira (3€) meets most flights; the schedule is posted at the bus stop, beside the airport entrance. A taxi to Fira costs about 8€.

## Tips Remember

Many of the rural Greek National Tourist Offices (EOT) are being turned over to local authorities. In most cases, the office remains at the same address, with the same phone and work hours.

**By Boat** There is ferry service to and from Piraeus at least twice daily; the trip takes 9 to 10 hours by car ferry on the Piraeus-Paros-Naxos-Ios-Santorini route, or 4 hours by catamaran on the Piraeus-Paros-Santorini route. In July and August, ferries connect several times a day with **Ios** (1–2 hr.), **Naxos** (3 hr.), **Paros** (2½ hr. by hydrofoil, 4 hr. by car ferry), and **Mykonos** (4–6 hr.); almost daily with **Anafi** (2 hr.) and **Siros** (3 hr. by catamaran, 5–6 by hydrofoil or car ferry); five times a week with **Sikinos** (1 hr.) and **Folegandros** (1½ hr.); and twice weekly with **Sifnos** (3–4 hr.). Service to **Thessaloniki** (17–24 hr.) is four to five times per week. There is almost daily connection by excursion boat with **Iraklion** in Crete, but because this is an open sea route, the trip can be an ordeal in bad weather and is subject to frequent cancellation—better to fly. Confirm ferry schedules with the Athens **GNTO** (ⓒ **210/327-1300;** 210/331-0562), the **Port Authority in Piraeus** (ⓒ **210/459-3223;** 210/422-6000; phone seldom answered), or the **Port Authority in Santorini** (ⓒ **22860/22-239**). The Piraeus port authority (ⓒ 210/422-6000) has schedules (but seldom answers the phone).

Almost all ferries now dock at **Athinios,** where buses meet each boat, returning directly to the Fira station (the fare to Fira 2€); from the Fira station, buses depart for numerous other island destinations. Taxis are also available from Athinios, at nearly five times the bus fare. Ferry tickets can be purchased at most travel agencies on the island; although in the past any given travel agency would represent only a selection of the available ferries, a new system allowing any agency to sell tickets for all the boats is being implemented. The exposed port at

**Skala**, directly below Fira, is unsafe for the larger ferries, but is often used by small cruise ships, yachts, and excursion vessels; if your boat docks here, you can choose between the cable car (3€), a mule or donkey ride (3€), and a tough 45-minute uphill walk (be prepared to share the narrow path with the mules). We recommend a mule up and the cable car down.

**VISITOR INFORMATION** There's no official government tourist office, but there're a number of travel agencies. Several travelers have written of good experiences dealing with **Best of Cyclades Travel** (② 22860/22-622) in Fira; **Kamari Tours**, 2 blocks south of the main square on the right (② 22860/31-390; fax 22860/31-497; kamaritours@san.forthnet.gr). **Maria Tours** (② 22860/24-701; fax 22860/23-848) often seems to offer car rentals and island tours at an especially good price. Other agencies include **Joint Travel Service** (② 22860/24-900; fax 22860/24992; joint@otenet.gr), next to the Olympic Airways Office in Fira; **Nomikos Travel** (② 22860/23-660, 22860/23-666), with offices in Fira, Karterados, and Perissa; **Karvounis Tours** (② 22860/71-290; mkarvounis@otenet.gr) on the main street of Ia gets good reviews. Any of these agencies should be able to help you find accommodations, rent a car, get boat tickets, or book a tour. Expect to pay about 25€ to join a bus tour to Akrotiri or Ancient Thira, about the same for a daytrip boat excursion to the islands of the caldera.

**GETTING AROUND** **By Bus** Santorini has reliable bus service. The **central bus station** is just south of the main square in Fira. Schedules are posted here: Most routes are serviced every hour or half-hour from 7am to 11pm in high season. Fares, which range from 1€ to 3€, are collected by a conductor on board. Destinations include Akrotiri, Athinios (the ferry pier), Ia, Kamari, Monolithos (the airport), Perissa, Perivolas Beach, Vlihada, and Vourvoulos. Excursion buses travel to major attractions; ask a travel agent for details.

**By Car** Most travel agents can help you rent a car. You might find that a local company such as **Zeus** (② 22860/24-013) offers better prices than the big names, although the quality might be a bit lower. Of the better-known agencies, try **Budget Rent-A-Car**, a block below the bus stop square in Fira (② 22860/22-900; fax 22860/22-887), where a small car should cost about 50€ a day, with unlimited mileage. If you reserve in advance through Budget in the United States (② 800/527-0700), you should be able to beat that price.

If you park in town or in a no-parking area, the police will remove your license plates and you, not the car-rental office, will have to find the police station and pay a steep fine to get them back. There's free parking on the north side of the port.

**By Moped** The roads on the island are notoriously treacherous, narrow, and winding; add local drivers who take the roads at high speed and visiting drivers who aren't sure where they're going, and you'll understand the island's high accident rate. If you're determined to use two-wheeled transportation, expect to pay about 20€ per day (less off season).

**By Taxi** The taxi station is just south of the main square. In high season, you should book ahead by phone (② 22860/22-555 or 22860/23-951) if you want a taxi for an excursion; needless to say, be sure that you are in agreement about the price before you set out. For most point to point trips (Fira to Ia, for example), the prices are fixed. If you call for a taxi outside Fira, you'll be charged a pickup fee of at least 1.50€. If you call for a taxi outside Fira, you're required to pay the fare from there to your pickup point, although you can sometimes find one that has dropped off a passenger. All bus service usually shuts down at midnight, so it's a good idea to book a taxi in advance if you need it after midnight. If you find yourself walking home, keep in mind that lots of drivers on the roads are new-comers to the island and may not know every twist and turn.

**FAST FACTS** The **American Express** agent is X-Ray Kilo Travel Service (© 22860/22-624; fax 22860/23-600), at the head of the steps to the old port facing the caldera, above Franco's Bar; open daily from 8:30am to 9pm. The **National Bank** (open Mon–Fri 8am–2pm), with an ATM, is a block south from the main square on the right near the taxi station. The **health clinic** (© 22860/22-237) is on the southeast edge of town on Ayiou Athanassiou, immediately below the bus station and the new archaeological museum.

For **Internet access**, try **P.C. Club**, on the main square in Fira, in the office of Markozannes Tours (© 22860/25-551) or **Lava Internet** (© 22860/25-551), just off the main square. **Penguin Laundry** (© 22860/22-168) is at the edge of Fira on the road to Ia, 200m (656 ft.) north of the main square. The **police** (© 22860/22-649) are several blocks south of the main square, near the post office. For the **port police,** call (© 22860/22-239. The **post office** (© 22860/22-238), open Monday through Friday from 8am to 1pm, is south of the bus station. The **telephone office (OTE)** is off Ipapantis, up from the post office; open Monday through Saturday from 8am to 3pm.

## THE TOP ATTRACTIONS

If you're planning to visit both the important ancient sites and the two associated museums, get the economical 8€ multiple ticket for the Archaeological Museum, Museum of Prehistoric Thera, Akrotiri and Ancient Thera.

**Ancient Akrotiri** ★★★  Since the beginning of excavations in 1967, this site has provided the world with a fascinating look at urban life in the Minoan period. This city—sometimes nicknamed the "Minoan Pompeii"—whose elaborate architecture and vivid frescoes demonstrate the high level of culture, was frozen in time around 1450 B.C. by a cataclysmic eruption of the island's volcano. Most scholars think that this explosion was so powerful that it destroyed the flourishing Minoan world on Crete. Pots and tools are still where their owners left them before abandoning the town (the absence of human remains indicates that the residents had ample warning of the town's destruction). You enter the Akrotiri site along the ancient town's main street, and on either side are the stores or warehouses of the ancient commercial city: Numerous large earthen jars, or *pithoi,* were found here, some with traces of olive oil, fish, and onion inside. You can get the best sense of the scale and urban nature of this town in the triangular plaza, near the exit, where buildings rise to two stories and create a spacious gathering place. You can imagine yourself some 3,000 years ago leaning over a balcony and spying on the passing scene—presumably a better-dressed and more decorous one than at the height of today's tourist season! There are descriptive plaques in four languages at various points along your path through the town, but unfortunately only a few poor reproductions of the magnificent wall paintings, some of which are on view at the Museum of Prehistoric Thera in Fira. As you leave the site, you may notice a cluster of flowers beside one of the ancient walls. This marks the spot where Akrotiri's excavator, Professor S. Marinatos, who died in a fall at Akrotiri, is buried. Allow at least an hour here.

The impressive site of Akrotiri was found in 1860 when workers quarrying blocks of volcanic ash for use in building the Suez Canal hit the ancient site. Who knows what undiscovered treasures may have been walled into the canal before an alert workman noticed an ancient wall!

Akrotiri. © 22860/81-366. Admission 6€. Tues–Sun 8:30am–3pm.

## Insider Tip

Akrotiri is enclosed by a large metal shed that magnifies the afternoon heat. This, combined with the growing crowds, is a good argument for arriving as early in the day as possible.

**Ancient Thira** ★★ The two popular beaches of Kamari and Perissa are separated by a high rocky headland called Mesa Vouna, on which stand the ruins of Ancient Thira. It's an incredible site, with cliffs dropping precipitously to the sea on three sides and dramatic views of Santorini and neighboring islands. The hilltop was first inhabited by the Dorians in the 9th century B.C., though most buildings date from the Hellenistic era when the site was occupied by Ptolemaic forces; there are also extensive Roman and Byzantine remains. One main street (intersected by many side-streets) runs the length of the site, passing first through two agoras. The arc of the theater embraces the town of Kamari, Fira beyond, and the open Aegean. This is an extensive group of ruins, not easy to take in, because of the many different periods on view—Roman baths jostle for space beside the remains of Byzantine walls—and Hellenistic shops. You may not decipher everything, but do take in the view from the large Terrace of the Festivals. This is where naked lads danced naked to honor Apollo (inadvertently titillating, some of the graffiti suggests, a number of the spectators!). You can reach the site by taxi or, even better, on foot—passing on the way a cave that holds the only spring on the island (see "Walking" under "Outdoor Pursuits," below). Allow several hours here—at least 4, if you walk up and down.

Kamari. ℂ 22860/31-366. Admission 4€. Daily 8am–2:30pm. On a hilltop 3km (2 miles) south of Kamari by road.

**Boutari Winery** Boutari is the island's largest winery, and Greece's best known wine export. The admission cost includes a tasting of six wines, with *mezedes* or light snacks. There are three grape varieties grown on Santorini: Asirtiko, Aidani, and Athiri. From these are made the three whites for which the island is known: Nichteri, with its high alcohol content; Kalliste, a wine aged in smoked oak barrels; and Vin Santo, a sweet dessert wine traditionally used for communion in the local churches. Rounding out the tasting are reds and whites from Northern Greece.

Megalohori. ℂ 22860/81-011. Admission and tasting 6€. Daily 10am–sunset. Located 1½ km (1 mile) south of Akrotiri village. Just outside Megalohori, on the main road to Perissa.

**Museum of Prehistoric Thira** ★★ This new museum, which opened in 2000, has several frescoes from Ancient Akrotiri, along with many finds from Akrotiri and objects imported from Crete and the Northeastern Aegean Islands. Some of the pots—cups, jugs and *pithoi*—are delicately painted with motifs familiar from the wall paintings. We highly recommend visiting both the museum and the archaeological site at Ancient Akrotiri—in the same day, if possible. At present, the museum occupies only a small part of its building, and expansions are anticipated in the near future.

Fira. ℂ 22860/22-217. Free admission. Tues–Sun 8:30am–3pm. Across the street from the bus stop in Fira; the entrance is behind the Orthodox Cathedral.

**Thira Foundation: The Wall Paintings of Thira** ★ This exhibition presents copies of the wall paintings from ancient Akrotiri, created using a sophisticated technique of three-dimensional photographic reproduction that closely approximates the originals. Housed in a former wine storage cave, the exhibit presents some of the paintings in basic simulations of their original architectural context. The terrace in front of the foundation offers an astonishing view toward Fira and Imerovigli. For the moment, until the archaeological museum in Fira is expanded, this remains the only way to view all the extraordinary wall paintings of Akrotiri in a form approximating their original physical presence.

Petros Nomikos Conference Center, Fira. © **22860/23-016.** Admission 3€. Recorded tour 3€. On the caldera, 5 min. past the cable car on the way to Firostephani.

## EXPLORING THE ISLAND
### FIRA

Location, location, location: To put it mildly, Fira has a spectacular location on the edge of the caldera. Just as you think you've grown accustomed to the view down and out to sea and the off-shore islands, you'll catch a glimpse of the caldera from a slightly different angle—and hear yourself gasp, yet again. If you're staying overnight on Santorini, take advantage of the fact that almost all the day-trippers from cruise ships leave in the late afternoon. Try to explore Santorini's capital Fira in the early evening, between the departure of the day-trippers and the onslaught of the evening revelers. As you stroll, you may be surprised to discover that Fira has a Roman Catholic cathedral and convent in addition to the predictable Greek Orthodox cathedral, a legacy from the days when the Venetians controlled much of the Aegean. The name Santorini, in fact, is a Latinate corruption of the Greek for "Saint Irene." The **Megaron Gyzi Museum** (© **22860/22-244**) by the cathedral has church and local memorabilia, including some before and after photographs of the island at the time of the devastating earthquake of 1956. It is open from 10:30am to 1pm and 5pm to 8pm Monday to Saturday; 10:30am to 4:30pm Sunday; admission is 3€.

M. Nomikou street follows the edge of the caldera, and the evening **volta** (**stroll**) along this street is one of the most exquisite in the Cyclades—the chanted tones of evening prayer often resound from the Orthodox Cathedral. By contrast, the town supports a wild bar scene that continues throughout the night, banishing all thought or hope—despite fervent prayers—of sleep in high season.

Not surprisingly, Fira is Santorini's busiest and most commercial town. The abundance of **jewelry stores** is matched in the Cyclades only by Mykonos—as are the crowds in July and August. At the north end of Ipapantis (also known as "Gold Street" for its abundance of jewelry stores), you'll find the **cable-car station.** The Austrian-built system, the gift of wealthy shipowner Evangelos Nomikos, can zip you down to the port of Skala in 2 minutes. The cable car makes the trip every 15 minutes from 7:30am to 9pm for 3€, and it's worth every euro, especially on the way up.

Up and to the right from the cable-car station is the small **Archaeological Museum** (© **22860/22-217**), which has some early Cycladic figurines, vases from Ancient Thira, some interesting Dionysiac figures, and finds from Ancient Thira. It's open Tuesday through Sunday from 8:30am to 3pm. Admission is 2€.

There's a new way to explore Santorini: a 1-hour submarine under the surface of the caldera, sinks to 25m to 30m (82 ft.–98 ft.) below the surface and offers a glimpse into the submerged volcanic crater. The trip costs 50€; information is available at most travel agents and at © **22860/28-900.**

### IA

Ia gets most visitors's votes as the most beautiful village on the island. It was severely damaged by the 1956 earthquake, a virtual ghost town for several decades thereafter, and there aren't many buildings remaining from before the earthquake. A few notable exceptions are the fine **19th-century mansions** at the top of the town near the castle—examples of restored neoclassical houses from this period include the **Restaurant-Bar 1800** and the **Naval Museum**. Much of the reconstruction continues the ancient Santorini tradition of dwellings excavated from the cliff face, and the island's most beautiful cliff dwellings can be found here. There are basically only two streets, one with traffic and the much more pleasant inland pedestrian lane, Nikolaos Nomikou (the other end of the Nomikos street that began in Fira), paved with marble and lined with an increasing number of jewelry shops (as if there weren't enough in Fira), tavernas, and bars.

The battlements of the ruined **Kastro** (fortress) at the western end of town is the best place to catch the famous Ia sunset. Below the castle, a long flight of steps leads down to the pebble beach at **Ammoudi**, which is okay for swimming and sunning, and has some excellent fish tavernas (see "Dining" later in this chapter). To the west is the more spacious and sandy **Koloumbos Beach**. To the southeast below Ia is the fishing port of **Armeni**, where ferries sometimes dock and you can catch an excursion boat around the caldera.

The **Naval Museum** (☏ 22860/71-156) ★ is a great introduction to this town, where, until the advent of tourism, most young men found themselves working at sea—and sending money home to their families. The museum is housed in a restored neoclassical mansion; almost completely destroyed during the 1956 earthquake, the house was meticulously rebuilt using photographs of the original structure. The extensive collection includes ship models, figureheads, naval equipment, and some fascinating old photographs. The official hours are Wednesday through Monday from 12:30 to 4pm and 5 to 8:30pm, although these seem to vary considerably; admission is 2€.

## THE VILLAGES

It's easy to spend all your time in Fira and Ia, with excursions to the ancient sites and beaches and to neglect Santorini's villages. Easy, but a shame, as there are some very charming villages on the island. As you travel about, keep an eye out for the troglodytian cave houses hollowed into the solidified volcanic ash. At the south end of the island, on the road to Perissa, is the handsome old village of **Emborio**. The town was fortified in the 17th century, and you can still see the towers of this village, a graceful marble statue of the muse Polyhymnia in the cemetery, and modern-day homes built into the ruins of the citadel.

**Pirgos**, a village on a steep hill just above the island's port at Athinios, is a maze of narrow pathways, steps, chapels, and squares. Near the summit of the village is the crumbling Venetian Kastro, plus several public squares with excellent views of the surrounding countryside. There is a merciful absence of tourism, and the central square, just off the main road, has the only shops and cafes in town.

The Church of the Panagia at the hamlet of **Gonias Episkopi** ★ is an astonishingly well-preserved 11th- to 12th-century Byzantine church. As is often the case, the builders pillaged classical buildings and you will see the many fragments they appropriated incorporated into the walls—and two ancient marble altars supporting columns. There are also frescoes; keep an eye out for the figure of a dancing Salone.

As you explore the island and its villages, you may be confused to notice what look like large, brown, circles of intertwined sticks on the ground in many fields. These are the wreaths that Santorinians weave growing grape vines into. The grapes are gently placed inside the protective circle of the vines, so that they are not harmed by the island's fierce winds.

**ACCOMMODATIONS** ■

Hotel Aressana 11
Hotel Kavalari 6
Hotel Keti 8
Hotel Tataki 4
Loucas Hotel 5
Pension Blue Sky 3

**DINING** ◆

Barbara's Cafe-Brasserie 7
Crêperis House 2
Koukoumavlos 12
Selene 9
Sphinx Restaurant 10
Taverna Nikolas 1

Catholic Cathedral ✝
Archaeological Museum
Cable-Car Station
Nomikos
Ipapantis
Ayiou Ioannou

Walking Path to Imerovigli & Ia ↗
Walking Path to Skala Fira ↙
CLIFFS
CLIFFS
CLIFFS

5
6
Ipapantis
Orthodox Cathedral ✝
Mitropoleos
8
9
10
11
7
4
1

Main Square (Plateia Theotokopoulou)
Port Police
25 Martiou
Ayiou Athanassiou

New Archaeological Museum
Bus Station

✉

To Karterados, Kamari & Perissa ←
To Ia →
To Ia →

2
3 ↓

**Legend:**
✝ Church
+ Clinic
⌂ OTE
P Parking
✉ Post Office
▥ Steps

## THE CALDERA ISLETS

These tantalizing **islands** ✶ in the caldera are part of the glory of Santorini's seascape, reminders of the larger island that existed before the volcano left today's crescent in the sea. Fortunately, you can visit the islands, look back at Santorini, and try to imagine how large the island once was.

**Thirassia** is a small, inhabited island west across the caldera from Santorini; a clifftop village of the same name faces the caldera, and is still a quiet retreat from Santorini's summer crowds. The village is reached from the caldera side only by a long flight of steep steps, as Fira and Ia were originally. Full-day **boat excursions** departing daily from the port of Fira (accessible by cable car, donkey, or on foot) make a brief stop at Thirassia, just long enough to have a quick lunch in the village; the cost of the excursion (which also includes Nea Kameni, Palea Kameni, and Ia) is about 20€ per person. Another option is **local caïques** (skiffs), which make the trip in summer from Armeni, the port of Ia; ask for information at Karvounis Tours (see "Visitor Information," above). The local ferry is impractical, as it visits Thirassia only once a week.

The two smoldering dark islands in the middle of the caldera are **Palea Kameni** (Old Burnt), the smaller and more distant one, which appeared in A.D. 157; and **Nea Kameni** (New Burnt), which began its appearance sometime in the early 18th century. The day excursion to Thirassia (a far more exciting destination) happens to include these two, unfortunately often litter-strewn volcanic isles.

## OUTDOOR PURSUITS

**BEACHES** Santorini's beaches may not be the best in the Cyclades, but the black sand here (formed from the volcanic lava) is unique—and gets very hot, very fast, as you might expect of a substance created by a volcanic explosion! **Kamari**, a little over halfway down the east coast, has the largest beach on the island. It's also the most developed, and lined by hotels, restaurants, shops, and clubs. The natural setting is excellent, at the foot of cliffs rising precipitously toward Ancient Thira, but the black pebbled beach becomes unpleasantly crowded in July and August. Kamari also has the **Volcano Diving Center** (© **22860/33-177;** www. scubagreece.com), which offers guided snorkel swims for around 20€ and scuba lessons from around 50€. **Perissa**, to the south, is another crowded beach resort with little to recommend it.

There are small beaches all along the east coast of the island, the best of which are **Baxedes** and **Koloumbos**, near Ia at the north end of the island. Baxedes is accessible by bus from Ia, and offers clean water and several shade trees, while the kilometer of sand at Koloumbos is a 15-minute walk further down the road. Koloumbos has the benefit of remaining half in shade for most of the afternoon. **Monolithos**, near the end of the road to the airport, has a small, sheltered beach that tends not to get crowded and is popular with families; there are a couple of tavernas here. The **Red Beach**, or Paralia Kokkini, at the end of the road to Ancient Akrotiri, is composed of small red volcanic pebbles. There's a fine taverna just down from the parking for Ancient Akrotiri: **Melina's** (© **22860/82-764**), open from 9am to 11pm.

**BICYCLING** Cyclists should know that although Santorini's roads are in fairly good condition, it's the drivers you should be worried about: the combination of local drivers who know the roads with their eyes shut (and sometimes seem to drive that way) and visitors who have no idea where they are is a bad one. Unfortunately, all too many visitors attempt to emulate speed-demon local drivers, with the results you might expect—no fun for cyclists. That said, high-quality suspension mountain bikes with toe clips, helmet, pump, and repair kit can be rented from 10€ per day. Mountain bikes can also be rented at **Moto Chris** (© 22860/23-431) in Fira for 12€ a day, or at **Moto Piazza** (© 22860/71-055) on the main road in Ia for the same price, but at both places the bikes are in sorry shape and receive almost no maintenance.

**WALKING**   The path from **Fira to Ia** follows the edge of the caldera, passing several churches and climbing two substantial hills along the way. Beginning from Fira, follow the pedestrian path on the caldera rim, climbing past the Catholic Cathedral to the villages of Firostephani and Imerovigli. In Imerovigli, there are signs on the path pointing the way to Ia—you'll be okay so long as you continue north, eventually reaching a dirt path along the caldera rim which parallels the vehicular road. The trail leaves the vicinity of the road with each of the next two ascents, returning to the road in the valleys. The descent into Ia eventually leads you to the main pedestrian street in town. The distance is 10km (6 miles); allow yourself at least 2 hours. This walk is especially beautiful around sunset.

In **Imerovigli**, there's a rocky promontory jutting into the sea, known locally as **Skaros.** From medieval times until the early 1800s, this was the site of an elaborate building complex which housed all the administrative offices of the island. There is little to be seen of the Skaros castle now, and it is thought that it was all but eradicated by a 19th-century earthquake. Skaros now offers a fantastic view of the caldera (especially at sunset) and a tranquil haven from the crowds and bustle of the adjacent towns. The trail begins from the terrace of a church just below the Blue Note Taverna in Imerovigli; from here it descends steeply to the isthmus connecting Skaros with the mainland. The path wraps around the promontory, reaching after a mile a small chapel with a unique panoramic view of the caldera. On the way, note the cliffs of glassy black volcanic rock, beautifully reflective in the brilliant sun—this is one of the materials with which so many of the older buildings on Santorini were built and decorated.

The trail from Kamari to the site of **Ancient Thira** is steep but worth the trouble; happily, it passes the beautiful site of Santorini's only freshwater spring. To reach the trail from Kamari, follow the automobile road to Ancient Thira past the Kamari Beach parking, turning right into the driveway of a new hotel opposite the Hotel Annetta, just to the right of a minimarket. The trail begins just behind the hotel. Climbing quickly by means of sharp switchbacks, the trail soon reaches a small chapel with a terrace and olive trees at the mouth of a cave. You can walk back into the cave, which echoes with the purling water, a surprising and miraculous sound in this arid place. Continuing up, the trail rejoins the car road after a few more switchbacks, about 300m (984 ft.) from Ancient Thira. The full ascent from Kamari takes about an hour.

## SHOPPING

If you're interested in fine **jewelry,** keep in mind that many prices in Fira are higher than in Athens, but the selection is fantastic. **Porphyra** (© 22860/22-981), in the Fabrica Shopping Center near the cathedral, has some impressive work. Santorini's best-known jeweler is probably **Kostas Antoniou** (© 22860/22-633), on Ayiou Ioannou north of the cable-car station. And there are plenty of shops between the two. Generally the further north you go, the higher the prices and the less certain the quality.

In Firostephani, **Cava Sigalas Argiris** (© 22860/22-802) stocks all the local wines, including their own. Also for sale are locally grown and prepared foods, often served as *mezedes* (hors d'oeuvres or snacks); *fava*, a spread made with chickpeas; *tomatatha*, small pickled tomatoes; and *kapari*, or capers. The store is open from 8am to midnight.

The main street in Ia, facing the caldera, has many interesting stores in addition to the inevitable souvenir and post-office rates. Further south on the main street is **Nakis** (© 22860/71-813), which specializes in amber jewelry and has a collection of insects in amber.

## WHERE TO STAY

Santorini is packed in July and August: try to make a reservation with deposit at least 2 months in advance or be prepared to accept pot luck (at best—we hear travelers tales of people sitting miserably in cafes all night). Except in July and August, don't accept lodging offered at the port unless you're exhausted and don't care how meager the room and how remote the village you wake up in the next morning. In July and August, be very grateful for whatever you get if you show up without a reservation.

The barrel-vaulted **cave houses**, built for earthquake resistance and economy, may at first strike you as rather cramped, dark, and stuffy, but like most newcomers, you'll probably soon find them another aspect of the island's special charm. The best of them are designed with enough cross-ventilation that they always have fresh air, and since they are carved into the cliff face, these rooms have the welcome quality of remaining relatively cool throughout the summer.

Many apartments and villas have efficiency kitchens, but in many cases these are extremely minimal facilities. If you plan to do much cooking, check to see what's in the drawers and cupboards, or you may find yourself frustrated if you try to prepare anything more elaborate than a coffee.

## FIRA

In addition to the choices below, you might consider **Pension Blue Sky** (© 22860/24-351 or 22860/25-121; fax 22860/25-120), a humble but comfortable place on the edge of town, or **Hotel Tataki** (© 22860/22-389; fax 22860/23-311; hoteltataki@san.forthnet.gr), a simple hotel offering clean rooms, a central location, and air-conditioning, fridges, and TVs. **Note:** Due to the noise in Fira, you may want to consider one of the more remote villages, unless you are in the quieter hotels we suggest. Two youth hostels, near Thira's main square, the **Thira Youth Hostel** (© 22860/22-472), usually offer the island's cheapest accommodations, at around 15€ per person. You don't have to be young to stay at these hostels, but it helps to be young-at-heart and, as always with hostels, relaxed about shared facilities and noise.

**Hotel Aressana** ★★ This newer hotel compensates for its lack of a caldera view with a large swimming pool and lots of mod cons and is one of the island's many popular honeymoon destinations. The Aressana is tucked away behind the Orthodox Cathedral, in a relatively quiet location. Most rooms have balconies or terraces; many have the high barrel-vaulted ceilings typical of this island. The breakfast room opens onto the pool terrace, as do most of the bedrooms; the elaborate buffet breakfast includes numerous Santorinian specialties. The Aressana also maintains seven nearby apartments facing the caldera, starting at 220€, which includes use of the hotel pool.

Fira, 84700 Santorini. © **22860/23-900.** Fax 22860/23-902. www.aressana.gr. 55 units (1 with shower only). 200€ double; from 245€–380€ suites. Rates include full breakfast. AE, DC, MC, V. Closed mid-Nov to Feb. **Amenities:** Snack bar; bar; freshwater pool; room service 7am–12pm. *In room:* A/C, TV, minibar.

**Hotel Keti** *(Value)*    This tiny hotel is very plain, but does offer one of the best bargains on the caldera. All of the rooms have the traditional vaulted ceilings, and open onto shared terraces overlooking the caldera; bathrooms are at the back of the rooms, carved into the rock of the cliff face. The rooms are on the small side, the furnishings are plain. This place offers an experience more "authentic" than that of the slick hotels that surround it: Laundry hangs on the terrace, and local children play on the stairs.

Fira, 84700 Santorini. © **22860/22-324** or 22860/22-380. Fax 22860/25-171. 7 units. 70€ double. No credit cards. Closed mid-Oct to mid-April.

**Loucas Hotel** ★    This is one of the oldest and best hotels on the caldera—and has its own pool. Its terraces cascade down the side of the cliff, connected by a giddily steep flight of steps—definitely not for the acrophobic. The impeccably maintained bedrooms have barrel-vaulted ceilings; many of the bathrooms are carved into the rock of the cliff wall. Although many of the terraces overlooking the caldera are shared between rooms, thoughtful design provides a surprising degree of privacy. The Renaissance Bar is situated on a broad terrace above the rooms, and the unexceptional Aris Restaurant immediately below.

Fira, 84700 Santorini. © **22860/22-480** or 22860/22-680. Fax 22860/24-882. 16 units. 150€ double. MC, V. Closed mid-Oct to mid-April. **Amenities:** Restaurant; bar; pool. *In room:* A/C, TV.

## FIROSTEPHANI

This quieter and less-expensive neighborhood is just a 10-minute walk from Fira. The views of the caldera are just as good, if not better.

**Dana Villas**    These terrace villas cling to the cliff face, perched vertiginously over the sea. They stand out from most of the other caldera villas by virtue of their tasteful well-maintained furnishings and thoughtful design: Each villa has a small terrace, and more than a few villas have private terraces. The suites have two bedrooms and can sleep four adults comfortably; VIP suites are somewhat larger and come with added amenities like a king bed and Jacuzzi bath. The pool is quite large by local standards, and there's a poolside bar. Villas 20 and 22 are the studios to reserve well in advance, while 21 is the best apartment.

Firostephani, 84700 Santorini. © **22860/24-641** or 22860/24-643. Fax 22860/22-985. 30 units. 140€–200€ double/apartment. AE, DC, MC, V. Closed mid-Oct to mid-April. **Amenities:** Bar; pool. *In room:* A/C, TV.

**Tsitouras Collection** ★    This top-of-the line luxury hotel will either dazzle or dismay you: understatement is conspicuous by its absence here, where antiques and reproductions jostle for space in 5 separate themed villas (including the "House of Portraits" and the "House of Porcelain"). The villa you stay in is all yours, which ensures blissful privacy. The absence of televisions helps to ensure tranquility; the absence of a pool in such a deluxe hotel seems more than odd. We're eager to hear reader's reports on Tsitouras Collection: thus far, we've had almost as many thumbs down for the haphazard service as we have had raves for the serious luxury and quiet location just out of Thira itself.

Firostefani, 847 00 Santorini. © **22860/23-747.** fax 22860/23-918. tsitoura@otenet.gr. 5 villas (each villa can accommodate at least 4). 500€ for 2 sharing a villa; 150€ for each additional guest. MC, V. **Amenities:** Restaurant; cafe. *In room:* A/C, minibar, kitchenette.

## IMEROVIGLI

The next village north along the caldera rim is so named because it is the first place on the island from which one can see the rising sun: The name translates to "day vigil." By virtue of its height, Imerovigli also has the best views on this part of the caldera.

While everyone else is jostling for a place to see the sunset at Oia, head to Imerovigli and take the path over to the promontory of Skaros, with the picturesque remains of the medieval kastro. Amazingly, this deserted and isolated spot was the island's first capital. It's also a blissful place to watch the sunset in more-or-less (we seem to encounter Germans with telephoto camera lenses here) solitary splendor.

**Astra Apartments** ★★★     Perched on a cliff-side, with spectacular views, this is one of the nicest places to stay in all of Greece—in fact, friends who stayed here recently say that this was the highlight of their entire holiday! The Astra Apartments look like a tiny, whitewashed village (with an elegant pool) set in the village of Imerovigli, which is still much less crowded than Fira or Oia. Every detail here is perfect. Best of all, although each unit has its own kitchenette, breakfast is served on your private terrace or balcony, and you can order delicious salads and sandwiches from the bar day and night. Manager George Karayiannis is always at the ready to arrange car rentals, recommend a wonderful beach or restaurant—or even help you plan your wedding and honeymoon here. Our only problem when we stayed here: We didn't want to budge from our terrace, especially at sunset, when the view over the offshore islands is dazzling. You may want to go whole hog, as it were, and book one of the new apartments and or suites, two with private Jacuzzis, two with private pools.

Imerovigli, 847 00 Santorini. ☎ 22860/23-641. Fax 22860/24-765. www.astra.gr. 25 units. 220€–310€ standard double apartment; 370€–590€ suite. AE, MC, V. **Amenities:** Bar; pool. *In room:* A/C, TV, minibar, hair dryer, radio.

**Chromata** ★     A wonderful view, wonderful pool, lovely rooms and excellent service. If it weren't that its neighboring Astra is so special, Chromata would be the place to stay. If Astra is full, you'll be happy here.

Imerovigli, 84700 Santorini. ☎ 22860/24-850. 17 units. 150€–300€ double. AE, MC, V. **Amenities:** Bar; pool. *In room:* A/C, TV, minibar.

## KARTERADOS

About 2km (1¼ miles) southeast of Fira, this small village is proliferating with new hotels and rooms to let. Buses stop at the top of Karterados's main street on their way to Kamari, Perissa, and Akrotiri. Nevertheless, it's a somewhat inconvenient location, not especially close either to Fira or to the beach. Karterados beach is a 3km (2-mile) walk from the center of town, and the longer beach of Monolithos is accessible by continuing south along the water's edge an additional half mile. There's one budget-value place here worth staying at: the 20-unit **Pension George** ★ (www.pensiongeorge.com) with a small pool, simple, attractive, reasonably priced accommodations, and very helpful owners, George and Helen Halaris; doubles 50€ to 80€.

## OIA

Oia was virtually a ghost town until it was rebuilt after the 1956 earthquake and resettled. Now its chic shops (check out **The Art Gallery** and **Art Gallery Oia** on Oia's meandering main drag) and gorgeous sunsets make it an increasingly popular place to stay or to visit-especially with those who find Fira too frenetic. If you travel to either village (local buses run there from Fira, or you can take a taxi), keep a lookout for some of the island's cave dwellings (homes hollowed out of Santorini's soft volcanic stone).

**Canaves Ia Traditional Houses**   These houses are fashioned in traditional island style, with curved white walls carved into the cliffside; the two-bedroom apartments are especially spacious. All apartments have views of the caldera, and some also offer private terraces. In each a small bedroom (with double bed) opens onto a living room with barrel-vaulted ceiling. Bathrooms are extremely compact. There are two complexes within 200m (656 ft.) of each other, each with its own pool and bar; the newer of the two is somewhat more luxurious (and more expensive), with marble floors and counters.

Ia, 84702 Santorini. © **22860/71-453.** Fax 22860/71-195. canaves@otenet.gr. 32 units. 250€–350€ double. MC, V. Closed Nov–Apr. **Amenities:** Restaurant; 2 bars; 2 pools. *In room:* A/C, TV, minibar, kitchenette, hair dryer.

**Chelidonia**   Many thoughtful details add up to make these among the most appealing traditional apartments in Santorini. Most units are lovingly restored former homes—although one was a bakery! These were all traditional Santorini buildings, each with its own unique geometry, and some with skylights illuminating rooms from above. Most have truly private terraces, many with small gardens of flowering plants and herbs for cooking. The rooms are spacious, the bathrooms luxuriously large, and the interiors simple and highly elegant: Slabs of white marble combine with extensions of the walls to form tables and shelves. All units enjoy the famous Ia view across the caldera toward Imerovigli, Fira, and the southern end of the island. Although there is little luxury here—though there is daily maid service—there is clearly a great understanding of what makes guests feel at home.

Ia, 84702 Santorini. © **22860/71-287.** Fax 22860/71-649. www.chelidonia.com. 10 units. 130€–160€ double. Daily rates also available—call for information. No credit cards. Closed mid-Oct–mid-April. *In room:* A/C, kitchenette.

**Hotel Finikia**   *(Value)*   This small, appealing hotel offers tastefully furnished rooms, several with traditional domed ceilings. Most units have semiprivate balconies or terraces with views toward the sea—the hotel is on the east-sloping side of the island, so the view is gentle rather than spectacular. The pool is good sized and the restaurant/bar is open almost all day. Irene and Theodoris Andreadis are your very helpful and friendly hosts. They also have adjacent apartments for rent.

Finikia, 84702 Santorini. © **22860/71-373,** or 210/654-7944 in winter. Fax 22860/71-118. finikia@otenet.gr. 15 units. From 80€ double. Rates include breakfast. MC, V. Closed Nov–Mar. **Amenities:** Restaurant; bar; pool. *In room:* A/C, minibar.

**Katikies** ★★   If you find a more spectacular pool anywhere on the island, let us know: This one runs virtually to the side of the caldera, so that you can paddle around and enjoy an endless view. (There's also a smaller pool intended for the use of guests who have suites.) The hotel's island-style architecture incorporates twists and turns, secluded patios, beamed ceilings, and antiques. If the people in the next room like to sing in the shower, you might hear them—but most people who stay here treasure the tranquility. The top-of-the-line honeymoon suite has its own Jacuzzi, just in case you can't be bothered going to either outdoor pool. The new White Cave restaurant has only three tables, so be sure to book ahead!

Oia, 84702 Santorini. © **22860/71-401.** Fax 22860/71-129. www.katikies.com. 22 units. 160€–200€; 350€–500€ honeymoon double. Rates include breakfast. MC, V. **Amenities:** 2 restaurants; bar; 2 pools. *In room:* A/C, TV, minibar, hair dryer.

**Perivolas Traditional Settlement** ★★ You could be forgiven for thinking that this is a pool with a nice little hotel attached: the *Condé Nast Traveler* cover photo of Perivolas's pool meeting the edge of the sky and the lip of the caldera put this place on the jetsetters' map. The 17 houses that make up the hotel offer studios and junior and superior suites. Price differences reflect the varying sizes of the three categories; all units have kitchenettes and a terrace. The superior suites have a separate bedroom, whereas the other units are open plan. The architecture (wall niches, skylights, stonework) and some of the furnishings of these (greatly enhanced) cave dwellings are traditional—but everything is rather more elegant than in its original—including the in-house library and internet service! The hotel café is open until 9pm and the bar stays open most nights until midnight. The only downside here is that just a couple of the units have terraces with a significant degree of privacy—but that is true of virtually all Santorini hotels.

Ia, 84702 Santorini. ⓒ 22860/71-308. Fax 22860/71-309. www.perivolas.gr. 17 units. 420€–520€ double/suite. Rates include buffet breakfast. No credit cards. Closed mid-Oct to mid-April. **Amenities:** Café; bar; pool. *In room:* A/C, full kitchen.

**Youth Hostel Ia** ★ *Value* This exceptional facility occupies the grounds of a former convent, although the only older building remaining is a beautiful long room (now divided into two women's dorms) with a high vaulted ceiling. Most of the buildings surrounding the hostel's bright courtyard were built 10 years ago; the dorms are large and well ventilated, and the bathrooms reliably clean. Breakfast is served on a large terrace with fine sea views, or in the hostel café, where light meals are available throughout the day. Laundry service is available.

Ia (near the bus stop), 84702 Santorini. ⓒ and fax 22860/71-465. 7 units (4-, 6-, and 10-person dormitories). 15€–20€ per person. Rates include continental breakfast. No credit cards. Closed Nov–Apr. **Amenities:** Breakfast room.

## MEGALOHORI

**Villa Vedema Hotel** ★★ The sleepy village of Megalohori is not where you'd expect to find a luxury hotel, but Santorini is full of surprises. The hotel is a self-contained world, surrounded by a wall like a fortified town. A member of "Small Luxury Hotels of the World," the Vedema is justly proud of its attentive but unobtrusive service (as well it should be at these prices!). The residences are set around several irregular courtyards, much like those found in the village. Each apartment is unique, comfortable, and tastefully furnished, with a huge marble bathroom. The restaurant is excellent and there's a candle-lit wine bar—in a lovingly restored 300-year-old wine cellar. The principal disadvantage of a stay here is the location: Megalohori is not a particularly convenient base for exploring the island. But then, at these prices, and with this amount of luxury, perhaps you won't want to budge!

Megalohori, 84700 Santorini. ⓒ 22860/81-796 or 22860/81-797. www.vedema.gr. 42 units. 300€–900€ doubles/suites. Minimum 3-night stay. AE, DC, MC, V. Closed mid-Oct to mid-April. **Amenities:** Restaurant; bar; pool; concierge; airport pickup arranged; 24-hr. room service. *In room:* A/C, TV, minibar, hair dryer.

## KAMARI

Most of the hotels at Santorini's best and best-known beach resort are booked by tour groups in summer (we suggest one that usually is not). You might also try the 42-unit **Hotel Astro**, which has rooms with balconies, a fresh-water pool, and is just off the beach (and just away from most of the noise of the nightlife). Another option is the 27-unit **Matina Hotel** (ⓒ 22860/31-491; fax 22860/31-860), which has no views to speak of but is just a 2-minute walk from the beach; doubles at both hotels from 100€. If you can't find a room, try the local office of **Kamari Tours** (© 22860/31-390 or 22860/31-455), which manages many of the hotels in Kamari and may be able to find you a vacancy.

**Rooms Hesperides**    This neat, modern pension in the middle of the pistachio orchard (complete with excavated Byzantine ruins) is owned by Akis Giannakulias, a former ship's captain who also runs the Akis Hotel across the street; go to the Akis reception to book a room. Each of the simple guest rooms has a balcony with a view of the sea or of Mount Profitis Elias. If you prefer a slightly larger room with fridge and air-conditioning, try the Akis, located across the street: The 20 rooms in this older building are clean, comfortable, and reasonable, from 60€ for a double. Breakfast for guests at both hotels is served at the Akis on a sunny terrace.

Kamari, 84700 Santorini. © **22860/31-670.** Fax 22860/31-423. 20 units. 60€–100€ double Rates include continental breakfast. AE, MC, V. Closed mid-Oct to mid-April. Located 50m (164 ft.) from the beach, near the Kamari bus stop. **Amenities:** Breakfast room/bar. *In room:* Some rooms with A/C, fridge.

## WHERE TO DINE
### FIRA

As you might expect, there are both blah and beatific restaurants here. The bad ones have, understandably, chosen to stint on quality and service because they know that most tourists are here today and gone tomorrow. The good places cater to the Greek and foreign visitors who come back and back again—and to those who may come only once, but who come in part because they have heard of world-class restaurants like Selene.

If all you want is breakfast or a light, cheap meal, try **Créperis House,** Theotokopoulou Square (no phone), or **Barbara's Café-Brasserie,** in the Fabrica Shopping Center up from the bus station toward the cathedral (no phone). After 7pm, Barbara's becomes one of the least expensive bars in town.

**Note:** Many of the restaurants near the cable car fall into the forgettable category. In addition, some of these restaurants have been known to present menus without prices, and then charge exorbitantly for food and wine. If you are given a menu without prices, ask for one with prices.

**Koukoumavlos** ★★ GREEK    The terrace at Koukoumavlos enjoys the famous caldera view, but unlike most caldera restaurants where a spectacular view has to compensate for mediocre food, here the view is a distraction from the delights of the kitchen. The menu here changes often, as the chef tries out new dishes with ingredients not always used in Greece (a wide variety of mushrooms, for example). Many dishes offer creative variations on traditional Greek food, like the fava, which is served hot in olive oil with grilled zucchini, onions, tomato, olives, and toasted almonds, or shrimp poached in retsina. The monkfish with grilled vegetables, sun-dried tomatoes, black olives, thyme, and feta is wonderful. For dessert, try the yogurt pannacotta with pistachios, thyme honey, and sour cherry.

Below the Hotel Atlantis, facing the caldera. © **22860/23-807.** Reservations recommended for dinner. Main courses 15€–25€. AE, MC, V. Daily noon–3pm and 7:30pm–12:30am.

**Selene** ★★★ GREEK    The best restaurant on Santorini—and one of the best in all Greece—Selene uses local produce to highlight what owners Evelyn and George Hatziyiannakis call the "creative nature of Greek cuisine." The appetizers, including a delicious sea urchin salad on artichokes and fluffy fava balls with caper sauce, are deservedly famous. Entrees include a seafood stew (*brodero*) that will convert even the most dedicated red-meat eaters, sea bass grilled with pink peppers, rabbit, quail, and saddle of lamb with yogurt and mint sauce. If you eat only one meal on Santorini, eat it here, in a truly distinguished restaurant with distinctive local architecture—and be sure to try the enormous local capers. In short, everything—location, ambience, view, service—comes together to form the perfect setting for the delicious, inventive (but, unlike some trendy spots, never pretentious or coy) food. If you want to learn to make some of these dishes yourself, check out Selene's 1-day and 1-week cooking schools at www.selene.gr. Fira (in the passageway between the Atlantis and Aressana hotels). ℂ 22860/22-249. Fax 22860/24-395. Reservations recommended. Main courses 17€–25€. AE, MC, V. Apr–Oct Daily 7pm–midnight. Closed late Oct to early Apr.

**Sphinx Restaurant** INTERNATIONAL This restored old mansion has been decorated with antiques, sculpture, and ceramics by local artists; there's also a large outdoor terrace with views of the caldera and the port at Skala Fira. You may not decide that you've come to Santorini to eat ostrich, but the fresh pasta is tasty, as are the fish dishes.

Odos Mitropoleos, near the Atlantis Hotel. ℂ 22860/23-823. Reservations recommended. Main courses 10€–25€; fish priced by the kilo. AE, DC, MC, V. Daily 11am–3pm and 7pm–1am.

**Taverna Nikolas** (Value) GREEK This is one of the few restaurants in Fira where locals queue up alongside throngs of travelers for a table—high praise, for a place that has been here forever. There aren't any surprises here, just traditional Greek dishes (the lamb with greens in egg lemon sauce is delicious) prepared very well. The dining room is always busy, so arrive early or plan to wait.

Just up from the main square in Fira. No phone. Main courses 7€–15€. No credit cards. Daily noon–midnight.

## IA

The best place to eat in Ia is the port of **Ammoudi,** hundreds of feet below the village, huddled between the cliffs and the sea. Two of the fish tavernas in Ammoudi are excellent. **Katina's** (★) (ℂ 22860/71-280) and **Captain Dimitri's** (★) (ℂ 22860/82-210). Both have perfected the art of cooking fish on the charcoal grill, and at both restaurants the view is exceptional. Both are usually open from 10am to midnight; prices for fish, as always, vary and are by the kilo—so be sure to check the price before you order. That said, two should be able to eat sensibly here for 50€ (no credit cards). If you don't want to trek all the way down to the beach, stop along the way at **Kastro** (ℂ 22860/71-045), where you'll still have a fine view and can enjoy Greek dishes, or pasta, or fresh fish. To get here, follow the stepped path down from the vicinity of Lontza Castle, hire a donkey (4€ one-way), or call a taxi. We recommend the walk down (to build an appetite) and a taxi or donkey up.

**Restaurant-Bar 1800** ★ CONTINENTAL For many years recognized as the best place in Ia for a formal dinner, the 1800 has a devoted following among visitors and locals. The restaurant, housed in a splendidly restored neoclassical captain's mansion, has undeniable romantic charm (curtains billow at some windows and there's often candlelight). After you eat, you can decide whether the owner (an architect and chef) deserves more praise for his skill with the decor or the cuisine.

Odos Nikolaos Nomikos. ℂ 22860/71-485. Main courses 15€–30€. AE, DC, MC, V. Daily 6pm–midnight.

**Skala** (Value) GREEK Skala has perfectly fine taverna food, at prices that are less steep than many places here. All the staples of traditional Greek (if not local

Santorini) food are reliably good, and the management is helpful and friendly. The roasted meats are good here, as are the vegetable appetizers.

Odos Nikolaos Nomikos. ☏ 22860/71-362. Main courses 7€–15€. Daily 1pm–midnight. MC.

## KAMARI

**Camille Stephani** ★ GREEK/INTERNATIONAL    Even if you're not staying at Kamari, you might like to head out to the beach for a meal at this excellent seaside place. An old standard, the restaurant's kitchen continues to produce memorable fare (the house specialties are terrific *mezedes* and a tender beef filet with green pepper in Madeira sauce). The outside tables face the water, and a moonlight stroll along the beach is the perfect end to a fine meal.

North end of Kamari Beach, 500m from the bus stop. ☏ 22860/31-716. Reservations recommended July–Sept. Main courses 10€–25€. DC, MC, V. Daily noon–midnight (Fri–Sun in winter). Open year-round.

## SANTORINI AFTER DARK

The height of the tourist season is also the height of the music season in Santorini: If you are here in July, you may want to take in the annual Santorini Jazz Festival (www.jazzfestival.gr), which has been bringing several dozen international jazz bands and artists here every summer since 1997. Many performances are on Kamari Beach. In August and September, the 2-week **Santorini International Music Festival** (☏ 22860/23-166), with international singers and musicians, gives performances of classical music at the Nomikos Centre in Fira. Admission to most events is from 15€.

Fira has nightlife aplenty and in some variety. We suggest starting the evening with a drink on the caldera, taking in the spectacular sunset. **Franco's** (☏ 22860/22-881) is still the most famous and best place for this magic hour, but be prepared to pay about 10€ and up per drink. For more reasonable prices, a bit more seclusion, and the same fantastic view, continue through the Canava Café and below the Loucas Hotel to the **Renaissance Bar** (☏ 22860/22-880). Underneath the square, the **Kirathira Bar** plays jazz at a level that permits conversation, and the nearby **Art Café** usually has muted music so that you can enjoy your conversation, or your thoughts. Cross the main street and wander around the shopping area to find a number of smaller bars that come alive after 9pm. The **Town Club** appeals to clean-cut rockers, while the **Two Brothers** pulls in the biggest, chummiest, and most casual crowd on the island. A bit further north, the outdoor **Tropical Bar** attracts a louder, rowdier gang. For bouzouki, find **Bar 33. Ellenes** has loud Greek dancing music, starting no earlier than 11pm, usually. Discos come and go, and you only need to follow your ears to find them. The **Koo Club** is the biggest, while the **Enigma** is still popular with those interested in good music. **Tithora** is popular with a young, heavy-drinking crowd. There's usually no cover, but drinks start at most places at 10€.

In Ia, **Zorba's** is a popular cliffside pub. The fine restaurant/bar **1800** is a quiet and sophisticated place to stop in for a drink—and certainly for a meal. Kamari has its share of bars. The **Yellow Donkey Disco** (☏ 22860/31-462) is popular with younger partyers, and the more sophisticated usually seek the chic **Valentino's**, near the bus stop.

At **Messaria**, there is often a floor-show of Greek dancing (the dancers in traditional costumes) at the **Canava Roussos Winery** (☏ 22860/31-276); call first to see if there is a show and to make a reservation.

## 2 Folegandros

181km (98 nautical miles) SE of Piraeus

Say that you're off to Folegandros and you're likely to get one of two reactions: from many, a quizzical expression—but from those who know this island, an envious glance. Folegandros has one of the most perfect capital towns in the islands: **Hora**. In this town (almost more village than town) huddled at cliff's edge, one small shaded square spills into the next, with green and blue paving slates outlined in brilliant white. As you prowl the streets, you'll realize that much of Hora is built into the walls of a medieval castle (the kastro). Small houses with over-hanging wooden balconies freighted with pots of geraniums line the narrow lanes. There's one majestic church, the **Panayia**, dominating Hora from the highest point in town—and built on the foundations of the ancient Greek town here. The church's icon of the Virgin is paraded through Hora's streets with great ceremony and rejoicing each Easter Sunday. Blessedly, since the town is so compact, and so contained in those castle walls, new development has taken place outside the town, leaving its traditional character intact.

Many travelers who've only heard vaguely of Folegandros have seen it only when en route somewhere else. As boats pass the island's forbidding northern coast, precipitous cliffs rise to a height of 250m (820 ft.). As for the main port, Karavostasis, if you didn't know about Hora, and the beguiling landscape of the island's interior, you could almost be forgiven for keeping going to the next port of call and not getting off here. **Karavostasis** itself straggles along the harbor and has a grab-bag of small restaurants, a hotel or two, some shops—but, frankly, little appeal (although there is a nice little park). Perhaps the port's minimal appeal is why, thus far, relatively few have ventured up to experience the spare beauty of the island.

The rugged northern slopes of Folegandros offer a contrast to the austere civility of Hora's streets and squares. Here the hills are ribboned with the terraced fields that allow local farmers to grow barley on the island's steep slopes. Rocky coves shelter pristine pebble beaches, and many trails weave their way through the hills, some of them ancient paths paved with marble or carved from the bedrock. If you want to explore Folegandros, you can do a good deal by local bus, but you'll also want to walk—and, if you do, you'll find yourself enjoying some very beautiful terraced hillsides.

## ESSENTIALS

**GETTING THERE    By Boat**    Three ferries a week stop at Folegandros on the Santorini-Folegandros-Sikinos-Ios-Naxos-Paros-Piraeus route; travel times are about 2 to 3 hours to Naxos, 4 hours to Paros (or 1 hr. by hydrofoil), and 10 hours to Piraeus. The Piraeus port authority (© **210/422-6000**) has scheduled (but seldom answers the phone). Two ferries per week stop on the Folegandros–Milos-Sifnos-Paros-Mykonos-Tinos-Siros hydrofoil run; it's 2 hours to Sifnos, 3 to 5 hours to Mykonos, 5 to 6 hours to Tinos, and 6 hours to Siros. Off season, infrequent service and bad weather could easily keep you here longer than you'd intended. The port police are at (© **22860/41-273**) also has island boat information.

**VISITOR INFORMATION**    The **Maraki Travel Agency** (© **22860/41-273**), just around the southwest corner of the bus-stop square in Hora, exchanges money, helps with travel arrangements, sells maps of the island, and offers internet facilities. There's also a branch of Maraki Travel at the port (© **22860/41-198**), where

the ferries stop and has a contrast. The **Maraki Travel Agency** (© **22860/41-273**); **Maraki Travel Agency** (© **22860/41-249**); **Maraki Travel Agency** (© **22860/41-273**), you can buy ferry tickets. **Diaplous** (© **22860/41-158;** fax 22860/41-159; diaplous@x-treme.gr), opposite Polikandia Hotel off the bus-stop square in Hora, offers tickets for excursion boats, hotel reservations, money exchange, and luggage storage. **Sottovento Travel** (© **22860/41-444;** fax 22860/41-430) also serves as the local Italian consulate; it's located at the stop for the Angali and Ano Meria bus, at the opposite side of Hora from the bus stop to the port. Here you can book beach trips by caïque, arrange boat tours, book accommodations, and store luggage.

**GETTING AROUND   By Bus**   The bus to Hora meets all ferries in peak season, and most ferries during the rest of the year; it also makes eight or nine trips a day along the road which runs along the spine of the island between Hora and Ano Meria at the island's northern end. The fare is 1€.

**By Moped**   There are two moped-rental outfits on Folegandros: **Jimmy's Motorcycle** (© **22860/41-448**) in Karavostassis, and **Moto Rent** (© **22860/ 41-316**) in Hora, near Sottovento Travel.

**By Boat**   From mid-June through August, boat taxis or caïques provide transport to the island's southern beaches. From Karavostassis, boats depart for Katergo and Angali (6€ round-trip); another boat departs from Angali for Ayios Nikolaos, Livadaki, and Ambeli (8€ round-trip). There is also a 7-hour tour of the island's beaches that departs from Karavostassis at least three times weekly in summer, and makes stops at five beaches; the cost is 25€ per person, including lunch. Reservations can be made at Diaplous or Sottovento Travel (see above); note that tickets must be purchased a day in advance.

**FAST FACTS**   Folegandros has neither bank nor ATM, but you can exchange money at **Maraki Travel** (© **22860/41-273**), **Sottovento Travel** (© **22860/ 41-444**), or **Diaplous** (© **22860/41-158**). Note that commissions on money exchange are particularly high in Folegandros due to the absence of a local bank. The **post office** and **telephone office (OTE)** are right off the central square in Hora, open Monday through Friday from 8am to 3pm. The **police station** (© **22860/41-249**) is behind the post office and OTE. There's one **taxi** (© **22860/41-048**) on the island, but with the frequency of bus service and dearth of places to drive to, you're unlikely to need it.

## WHAT TO SEE & DO

Visitors arrive in the unimpressive port of **Karavostasis,** where there's a decent beach and a few hotels and rooms to let. Most will jump aboard the bus that's waiting to chug the 4km (2½ miles) up to Hora.

**Hora** ★ is one of the most beautiful capitals in the Cyclades. The town is centered around five closely connected squares, along and around which you'll find churches, restaurants, and shops. Even from the bus-stop square, you'll find of the cliff offers an awesome sight. On the right in the next square, you'll find the **Kastro:** two narrow pedestrian streets connected by tunnel-like walkways, squeezed between the town and the sea cliffs, with remnants of the medieval castle. Above, the Panayia Church tempts the energetic to climb the hillside for a closer look and incredible views.

Continue west from Hora by foot or bus to reach the village of **Ano Meria.** The small farms here are so widely dispersed that they're barely recognizable as a community, though Ano Meria is the island's second-largest town.

As you rush from island to island, checking in and checking out of hotels, it's not always easy to get a sense of the rhythm of island life. One great way to do just that is to visit Folegandros's small **Folk Museum,** in the village of Ano

Meria. The tools and household items give you a glimpse of life as it has been lived for generations, and still is lived here. The museum (no phone) is usually open 5pm to 8pm weekdays in July and August, and the local bus can drop you a pleasant stroll away. If the museum turns out to be closed, console yourself that this, too, is an insight into the rhythm of island life!

## BEACHES

Swimmers will want to get off the bus to Ano Meria at the first crossroad and walk down to **Angali**, the largest (and most crowded) fine-sand beach on the island. There are a few tavernas on the beach and rooms to let. **Ayios Nikolaos**, another popular beach where clothing is optional, is a couple of kilometers farther west—a well-used path follows the coast west from Angali, or you can take the boat (5€ one-way from Angali). West from Ayios Nikolaos is a series of beaches, the best of which are **Livadaki** and **Ambeli**—both can be reached by boat from Angali (5€ one-way) or on foot from the end of the road to Ano Meria (see "Walking," below). The best beach of the island, **Katergo** ★, is a stretch of fine pebbles at the base of a low cliff on the south side of the island, protected from the wind by rocky headlands. It is only accessible on foot (about 2km/1¼ miles from Livadi Beach, or 3km/2 miles from the port at Karavostassi) or by water: A boat departs from Karavostassi mid-June to August (6€ round-trip). At the far northwest end of the island is **Ayios Yeoryios**, a pristine pebble beach in a rocky cove, accessible only on foot (the excursion boats don't often stop here). It's a great walk (see "Walking," below), but the beach is usually too windy for swimming, although on a still day it can be a good option for avoiding the crowds. For information on boat taxis to the beaches, inquire at Sottovento Travel or Diaplous (see above).

## WALKING

The footpaths through the northern part of the island are for the most part well used and easy to follow. Numerous paths branch off to the southwest from the paved road through Ano Meria—the region of hills traversed by these trails, between the road and the sea, is particularly beautiful. One path that's easy to follow leads **from Ayios Andreas to the bay at Ayios Yeoryios**. Take the bus to the next-to-last stop, at the northern end of Ano Meria; it's next to the church of Ayios Andreas, and at the stop is a sign reading AG. GEORGIOS 1.5, and pointing to the right. Follow the sign, and continue along a road that quickly becomes a path and descends steeply toward the bay. Follow the main path at each of several intersections; you'll be able to see the bay for the last 20 minutes of the walk. The bay of Ayios Yeoryios holds a small pebble beach; there's no fresh water here, so be sure to bring plenty. Allow 2 hours round-trip.

The walk to **Livadaki Beach**, near the lighthouse of Aspropounta on Folegandros's sheltered southwestern coast, begins at the end of the paved portion of the road to Ano Meria. Take the bus to the last stop, in front of the Merovigli Taverna, and continue about 200m (656 ft.), on the wide dirt road to a sign indicating the trail to Livadaki on the left. From here it's about 40 minutes down to the beach through terraced fields, passing on the way the remote hilltop church of Ayii Anaryiri. The beach itself is well worth the trouble: a stretch of fine pebbles in a glorious rocky cove, protected from the wind and with a gradually sloping bottom. Also beginning from the end of the bus line, you can continue a few meters past the turnoff for Livadaki to the signposted trail to **Ambeli Beach**, also a 40-minute walk. Ambeli is a lovely, small, intimate beach with some trees offering shade. Be sure to bring plenty of water.

## WHERE TO STAY

We recommend that you stay in beautiful cliff-top Hora. Keep in mind that the island's limited facilities are fully booked in July and August, and advance reservations are essential. We suggest the two best places on the island; if you surf the web, you will find others—but, if possible, accept no substitutes!

**Anemomilos Apartments** ★★   This is a very congenial place—one that not surprisingly began to turn up on lists of the best island retreats soon after it opened 10 years ago. Anemomilos is spectacularly situated at the edge of a cliff overlooking the sea. You don't have to feel rueful being so far from the sea: there's a fine pool here. All but two of the very attractively furnished (nice wood furniture, nice weavings) units have terraces facing the sea. One apartment is wheelchair-accessible. Every unit has a well-stocked kitchenette—you can actually do some cooking here. If you don't want to bother with breakfast, Cornelia Patelis, who manages the hotel with her husband, Dimitris, makes a delicious sweet breakfast pie with local cheese. (Breakfast and snacks are served throughout the day on the pool terrace.) The hotel will arrange transport to and from the port for about 5€ per person one-way.

Hora (just up from the central bus stop), 84011 Folegandros. © 22860/41-309, or 210/682-7777 in Athens. Fax 22860/41-407, or 210/682-3962 in Athens. 17 units. 90€–150€ double. Compulsory continental breakfast 14€. V. Closed mid-Oct to Easter. **Amenities:** Breakfast room/bar; pool. *In room:* A/C, minifridge.

**Castro Hotel** ★★   The Castro is a Venetian castle built in 1212; it's the oldest part of Hora, wedged against the cliffs and facing the Aegean 250m (820 ft.) below. Guest rooms are small but comfortable, and seven are on the phenomenal cliff side of the hotel. The two most desirable units have balconies surveying the extraordinary view; these don't cost extra, and are a great bargain. (Try to reserve room 3, 4, 5, 13, 14, 15, or R1.) For those units without the view, a shared rooftop terrace offers the same magnificent prospect. The charming Despo Danassi, whose family has owned this house for five generations, will make you feel at home here—and her homemade fig jam is fabulous.

Hora, 84011 Folegandros. © 22860/41-230, or 210/778-1658 in Athens. Fax 22860/41-230, or 210/778-1658 in Athens. 12 units. 70€–100€ double. Continental breakfast 10€. AE, V. Closed Nov–April. **Amenities:** Breakfast room.

## WHERE TO DINE

Main courses for all the restaurants listed here are 5€ to 15€; hours are generally from 9am to 3pm and 6pm to midnight.

The local specialty is a dish called *matsata*, made with fresh pasta and rabbit or chicken. The best place to sample it is **Mimi's**, in Ano Meria (© 22860/41-377), where the pasta is made on the premises. Also in Ano Meria are **Sinandisi** (© 22860/41-208), also known as Maria's, which has good *matsata* and swordfish (take the bus to the Ayios Andreas stop); and **Barbakosta** (© 22860/41-436), a tiny room that serves triple duty as bar, taverna, and minimarket; you buy a drink or sample the dish of the day here. (The bus stop has no name, so ask the driver to let you know when to disembark.)

Hora has a number of tavernas, whose tables spill into and partially fill the central squares. On the bus-stop square, **Pounda** (© 22860/421-063) serves a delicious breakfast of crepes, omelets, yogurt, or coffee cakes; lunch and dinner, including a variety of vegetarian dishes, are also available. **Silk** (© 22860/41-515), on the Piatsa (third) Square, offers delicious variations on taverna fare, including numerous vegetarian options. **Piatsa** (© 22860/41-274), also on the third square, is a simple taverna operated by the friendly Yiannis Sideris and his wife, Kiriaki, **O Kritikos** (© **22860/41-219**) is another local favorite, known for its grilled chicken.

## 3 Sifnos

172km (93 nautical miles) SE of Piraeus

Everyone falls in love with at least one of the Cyclades; we fell in love with Sifnos. Some say that Naxos is the greenest of the Cyclades—if you've been to Sifnos, you can only assume that those who give Naxos pride of place have not. Perhaps it is because Sifnos keeps its riches concealed within a hilly interior—and has a rather desultory port. But once your are inland, you will see elegantly ornamented dovecotes above cool green hollows, while ancient fortified monasteries and watchtowers occupy the arid summits of the island's hills. The slate and marble paths across the island are a miracle of care, and beauty. The island is a hiker's—even a stroller's—delight. In addition, beaches along the southern coast offer long stretches of fine amber sand; several smaller rocky coves are also excellent for swimming.

The island is sufficiently small that any town can be used as a base for touring; the most beautiful are the **seven settlements** spread across the central hills (notably Apollonia and Artemonas) and **Kastro**, a small medieval fortified town atop a rocky pinnacle on the eastern shore. A combination of bus rides and some short walks will allow you to visit the top attractions: the ancient acropolis at **Ayios Andreas**, the town of Kastro and its tiny but excellent **archaeological museum,** the southern **beaches,** and, for the ambitious, the **walled monastery of Profitis Elias** on the summit of the island's highest mountain. While you're on the island, don't miss the **pottery workshops:** Sifnos is renowned for its ceramics, and some of the island's best practitioners are in Kamares and Platis Yialos. It's also famous for its olive oil and excellent cooking, both of which you can enjoy while here.

## ESSENTIALS

**GETTING THERE    By Boat** There's one ferry daily from (3 hr.); contact the GNTO in Athens (© **210/327-1300;** 210/331-0562) or the **Port Authority in Piraeus** (© **210/459-3223;** 210/422-6000; phone seldom answered) or the **Sifnos Port Authority** (© **22840/33-617**) for information. Ferries travel daily to nearby islands such as **Serifos** (30–60 min.), **Kimolos** (30–40 min.), **Milos** (45 min.), and **Kithnos** (1½ hr.). Hydrofoils travel two or three times a week on the route Santorini-Folegandros-Milos-Sifnos-Paros-Mykonos-Tinos-Siros (with variations); travel times are about 1 hour to Paros, 2 hours to Folegandros or Mykonos, 2½ hours to Tinos, and 3 hours to Santorini or Siros. *Note:* In the off season, ferry connections to Sifnos are particularly sparse.

**VISITOR INFORMATION** You can book a room, buy ferry tickets, rent a car or motorbike, arrange excursions, and usually leave your luggage at the **Aegean Thesaurus Travel and Tourism office** ★★ on the port (© **22840/32-152;** www.thesaurus.gr); Aegean Thesaurus handles tickets for all hydrofoils and ferries. Check to see if Aegean Thesaurus, which also has an office on the main square in Apollonia (© **22840-151;** fax 22840/332-190), still has its excellent information packet on Sifnos for 2€. Other useful travel agents include **Siphanto Travel** (© **22840/32-034;** fax 22840/31-024), or at **Katzoulakis Tourist Agency** (© **22840/32-362**) on the port. At press time, **Ventouris Ferries** (© **22840/31-700**) in Kamares handled hydrofoil (flying dolphin) tickets, while Aegean Thesaurus handled hydrofoil (flying dolphin) tickets.

**GETTING AROUND** **By Bus** Apollonia's central square, **Plateia Iroon,** is the main bus stop for the island. Buses run regularly to and from the port at Kamares, north to Artemonas, east to Kastro, and south to Faros, Platis Yialos, and Vathi. Pick up a schedule at Aegean Thesaurus Travel (see "Visitor Information," above).

**By Car & Moped** Many visitors come to Sifnos just for the wonderful hiking and mountain trails. A car or moped isn't really necessary, but cars can be rented at **Aegean Thesaurus** (© 22840/33-151) in Apollonia, or in Kamares at **Sifnos Car** (© 22840/31-793). Apollonia has a few moped dealers; try **Yanni's** (© 22840/31-155), on the main square, or **Easy Rider** (© 22840/31-001), on the road circling the village. As always, exercise caution if you do decide to rent a car or moped; many drivers, like you, will be unfamiliar with the island roads. The daily rate for an economy car with full insurance is about 50€; a moped rents for about 22€.

**By Taxi** Apollonia's main square is the island's primary taxi stand. There are about 10 taxis on the island, each privately owned, so you'll have to use the **mobile phone numbers** and hope someone's phone is turned on: Try © 0977/777-1742, 094/444-904, 094/761-210, or 094/493-6111.

**FAST FACTS** Visitor services are centered in Apollonia. The **National Bank** (© 22840/31-317), with ATM, just past the Hotel Anthousa on the road to Artemonas, is open Monday through Thursday from 8am to 2pm, Friday from 8am to 1:30pm. The **post office** (© 22840/31-329), on Plateia Iroon, the main square, is open in summer Monday through Friday from 8am to 3pm, Saturday and Sunday from 9am to 1:30pm. The **telephone office (OTE)**, just down the vehicle road, is open daily from 8am to 3pm, and in summer from 5 to 10pm as well. There's a rudimentary **laundry** service in the courtyard of the Hotel Anthousa in Apollonia; inquire at Yerontopoulos patisserie, on the ground floor of the hotel. The **police** (© 22840/31-210) are just east of the square, and a **first-aid station** is nearby; for **medical emergencies** call © 22840/31-315.

## WHAT TO SEE & DO

The capital town of the island, **Apollonia,** is one of the **seven settlements,** which have grown together on these lovely interior hills. It's 5km (3 miles) inland from Kamares; a local bus makes the trip hourly in summer. The town's central square, **Plateia Iroon (Heroes' Square),** is the transportation hub of the island: All the vehicle roads converge here, and this is where you'll find the bus stop and taxi stand. Winding pedestrian paths of flagstone and marble slope up from the square and lead through this beautiful village. **Lakis Kafenion,** an open-air cafe on the square, is the island's principal hangout. Also on Plateia Iroon is the small **Popular and Folk Art Museum;** it's open July 1 to September 15 from 10am to 1pm and 6 to 10pm (admission is 1.50€).

**Kastro** ★ is the finest medieval town on Sifnos, built on the dramatic site of an ancient acropolis. Until several decades ago, Kastro was almost entirely deserted; now it has cafes, restaurants, and shops. The 2km (1¼-mile) walk from Apollonia is easy, except under the midday sun: Start out on the footpath that passes under the main road in front of Hotel Anthousa, and continue through the tiny village of Kato Petali, finishing the walk into Kastro on a paved road. Whitewashed houses, some well preserved and others eroding, adjoin one another in a defensive ring abutting the sheer cliff. Venetian coats of arms are still visible above the doorways of the older houses. Within the maze of streets are a few tavernas, some beautiful rooms to let, and a gem of an **Archaeological Museum** (© 22840/31-022) housing pottery and sculpture found on the island;

open Tuesday through Saturday from 9am to 3pm, Sunday and holidays from 10am to 2pm (admission is free).

About 2km (1¼ miles) south of Apollonia on the road to Vathi is a trail leading to the hilltop church of **Ayios Andreas** and the excavations of an **ancient acropolis**. Broad stone steps begin a long climb to the summit; count on about 20 vigorous minutes to ascend and 15 minutes to come back down. The ruins of the acropolis are at the top of the hill on your left. These ruins are made up of the outer walls and a block of houses from a Mycenaean fortified town. Excavations haven't been completed and there's no interpretive information at the site, but the location is stirring—it's worth a visit if only for the view.

Well into the 1980s, there were many potteries on Sifnos. Now, there are only a handful. That means that the distinctive brown and blue glaze Sifnian pottery that is still being made has become something of a collector's item. If you fall for some, buy it—with more and more potteries closing down, you can't be sure of finding this distinctive ware forever.

## BEACHES

The central part of **Kamares** cove harbors a sandy beach lined with tamarisk trees and dune grass, but due to the traffic of ferries and other boats in the harbor, the water here is not so clean.

The southern end of the island shelters a trio of coves with fine-sand beaches. The most popular of these is **Platis Yialos**, where a slew of hotels, tavernas, and shops have grown up around the beach. More upscale than Kamares, this town attracts the yachting crowd in summer. From here, it's a half-hour walk east through the olive groves and intoxicating oregano and thyme patches over the hill to **Panayia Chrissopiyi**, a double-vaulted whitewashed church on a tiny island. There's good swimming at **Apokofto**, a cove with a long sand beach and several shade trees just beyond the monastery, where rocky headlands protect swimmers from rough water. Nude bathing is permitted at nearby **Fasolou**.

Until 1997, the beach at **Vathi** was accessible only by foot or by boat, but a new automobile road has opened and permits regular bus service. There are a few tavernas here (but not yet the dense development of Kamares and Platis Yialos), plus one of the best beaches on the island.

## WALKING

More and more asphalt roads are appearing on Sifnos, but you'll still be able to do most of your walking on the island's distinctive flagstone and marble paths. You'll probably see village women whitewashing the edges of the paving stones, transforming the monochrome paths into elaborate abstract patterns. Throughout the island, you'll see dovecotes, windmills, and small white chapels in amazingly remote spots.

Sadly, the continuity of these fine paths has been interrupted—even destroyed—in many places by the construction of new roads and houses.

Our favorite walk on the island leads **from Apollonia to Profitis Elias**, taking you through a valley of extraordinary beauty to the summit of the island's highest mountain, with a short detour to the church and ruined monastery at Skafis. From the center of Apollonia, walk south along the main pedestrian road, past Sifnos Taverna and the cathedral. About 1km (½ mile) from the center of Apollonia you'll reach the village of Katavati; look out for the small black arrow pointing to the right, painted with the words PR. ELIAS in Greek. From here the trail descends toward a paved road, makes a short jog to the right on the road, then turns left onto a footpath (with another PR. ELIAS arrow at the left turn).

After about 1km (½ mile) of walking along the base of a valley, the path to the summit branches to the right. From here it's another hour or so of easy climbing to the summit. The 12th-century walled monastery is a formidable citadel, its interior courtyard lined with the monks' cells. The lovely chapel has a fine marble iconostasis. If you continue straight from the point where the summit path branches right and walk straight through the next intersection, you'll soon reach the church of Skafis, situated within the ruins of an old monastery and overlooking a small valley shaded by olive trees. Look for the remains of paintings on the walls of the ruined monastery, in what must have been a tiny chapel. Allow about 3 hours for the round-trip to Profitis Elias, with an additional half-hour for the detour to Skafis.

## SHOPPING

Famed in antiquity for its riches, then for its ceramics, Sifnos now rests its artistic pride on its pottery. Sifnian ceramics are exported throughout Greece; they're in wide use because of their durability and charming folk designs. One of the most interesting shops is the ceramics workshop of **Antonis Kalogirou** (© 22840/31-651), on the main harborside lane in Kamares. Antonis sells folk paintings of island life and the typical pottery of Sifnos, which is manufactured in his showroom from the deep gray or red clay mined in the inland hill region. Another fine ceramics workshop is that of **Simos and John Apostolidis** (© 22840/71-258), on the main street in Platis Yialos.

In Apollonia, **Hersonissos** (© 22840/32-209) has a choice selection of contemporary jewelry and ceramics. There are several other contemporary ceramics galleries featuring the excellent work of Greek artisans in the town's winding back streets.

## WHERE TO STAY
### APOLLONIA

Many young Athenians vacation on Sifnos, particularly on summer weekends, when it can be virtually impossible to find a room. If you plan to be in Apollonia or Kamares during the high season, be sure to make reservations by May. If you're here off season, many of these hotels are closed, but several remain open year-round. With advance notice, the efficient **Aegean Thesaurus Travel Agency** (see "Visitor Information," above) can usually place you in a room in a private house with your own bathroom, in a studio with a kitchenette, or in other, more stylish accommodations.

The island's capital and one of its most beautiful villages, Apollonia is our recommendation as a base on Sifnos. Buses depart from the central square to most island towns, and stone-paved paths lead to neighboring villages.

Numerous rooms in private houses (most are adjacent to the owner's house) can be booked through **Aegean Thesaurus Travel** (see "Visitor Information," above). A double costs from 50€ in high season. We especially recommend the following two choices, both run by friendly proprietors (neither of whom speak English). Opposite Hotel Petali is the house of **Eirini Yeronti**. The view here is good, and the super-clean rooms open to a terrace shaded by a grape arbor. The rooms of **Margarita Kouki** are perched high above town, a 10-minute walk up from Plateia Iroon; the view is fantastic, but this isn't the place to go if you're traveling with heavy bags.

**Hotel Anthoussa** This hotel is above the excellent and popular Yerontopoulos cafe and patisserie, on the right past Heroes' Square. Although street-side rooms offer wonderful views over the hills, they overlook the late-night sweet-tooth crowd and can be recommended only to night owls. Back rooms are quieter and overlook a beautiful bower of bougainvillea.

Apollonia, 840 03 Sifnos. ⓒ 22840/31-431. 15 units. 60€ double. MC, V. **Amenities:** Breakfast room. *In room:* A/C, TV.

**Hotel Petali** ★★ This would be a nice place to spend a week, on a relatively quiet side street not far (but all of it uphill) from Apollonia's main square, Platia Iroon. There are lovely views over Ano Petali (a suburb of Apollonia) to the sea, a large terrace with handsome, comfortable chairs, rooms furnished in Cycladic style, good beds, modern bathrooms, and a small restaurant that serves delicious Sifnian specialties. You may want to check to see if the pool and Jacuzzi promised for 2003 have materialized. Although the Hotel Petali does not accept credit cards, its managing office, Aegean Thesaurus Travel Agency (ⓒ 22840/32-152; www.thesaurus.gr) accepts MasterCard and Visa.

Apollonia, 84003 Sifnos. ⓒ and fax 22840/33-024. petali@par.forthnet.gr. 11 units. 120€–140€ double. MC, V. **Amenities:** Restaurant; bar. *In room:* A/C, TV.

**Hotel Sifnos** ★★ Many consider this family-owned and operated hotel on a quiet pedestrianized street off the Plateia Iroon the most congenial in Apollonia—and one of the nicest small hotels in the Cyclades. The hospitable owners have tried hard to make it reflect island taste, using local pottery and weavings in the good-size, bright rooms. The hotel restaurant (see "Where to Dine," below) offers good basic meals beneath a broad arbor, and it's just as popular with locals as it is with travelers and hotel guests.

Apollonia, 840 03 Sifnos. ⓒ and fax 22840/31-624. 9 units. 80€ double. AE, MC, V. Usually open in winter. **Amenities:** Restaurant; bar. *In room:* A/C, TV.

## ARTEMONAS

A small village overlooking terraced fields and the distant sea, Artemonas is a pleasant base, especially good if you have your own transport or don't mind the 15-minute walk to Apollonia.

**Hotel Artemon** Built in 1968, this quiet, comfortable place is among the oldest hotels on Sifnos; the generic character of the building is offset by the friendly attentiveness of the owner, Voula Lembessis. Rooms on the ground floor have patios and views of the small hotel gardens; the units above have balconies and a view of wheat fields and olive groves sloping down to the sea. The Artemon has a large terrace shaded by a luxuriant grape arbor; breakfast is served here or in the adjoining dining room. The restaurant also serves lunch and dinner in July and August.

Artemonas, 84003 Sifnos. ⓒ 22840/31-303 or 22840/33-158. Fax 22840/32-385. 23 units. 70€ double. Continental breakfast 5€. AE, MC, V. Closed Oct–Mar. Located on the road to Apollonia, just beyond the central plateia of Artemonas (where the bus from Apollonia turns around). **Amenities:** Restaurant. *In room:* A/C.

## KASTRO

**Aris Rafeletos Apartments** These traditional rooms and apartments are distributed throughout the medieval town of Kastro. Most have exposed ceiling beams, stone ceilings and floors, and the long narrow rooms typical of this fortified village. The two small units are somewhat dark and musty, but the three apartments are spacious and charming. All apartments have kitchenettes and terraces; three have splendid sea views. The largest apartment is on two levels and can comfortably sleep four. If the antiquity and charm of this hilltop medieval village appeals to you, then these accommodations may be the perfect base for your explorations of the island.

Kastro. (© and fax **22840/31-161.** 6 units. 60€–180€ studio/suite. No credit cards. The rental office is at the north end of the village, about 50m (164 ft.) past the Archaeological Museum. **Amenities:** Breakfast room/bar. *In room:* Some units with kitchenette.

## KAMARES

The port of Kamares has the greatest concentration of hotels and pensions on the island, but unfortunately it has little of the beauty of Sifnos's traditional villages. Two moderately priced hotels that have been here a while are the 14-unit harborside **Hotel Stavros** and the 18-unit **Hotel Stavros,** a 10-minute walk from the beach and harbor. Information on both is available from Stavros Kalogirou (© **22840/333-83**).

**Hotel Boulis**   This newer hotel, capably managed by Lyn and Antonis Kalogirou (whom readers have praised for their helpfulness), is right on the port's beach. The large, carpeted rooms have balconies or patios, most with beach views; all have fridges and ceiling fans. The hotel has a spacious, cool, marble-floored reception area and a bright breakfast room.

Kamares, 84003 Sifnos. (© **22840/32-122.** Fax 22840/32-381. 45 units. 90€–120€ double. Rates include breakfast. AE. Closed Oct–Apr. Follow the main street 300m (984 ft.) from the ferry pier, turning left opposite the Boulis Taverna (operated by the same family). The hotel is on your left. **Amenities:** Breakfast room/bar. *In room:* Fridge.

## PLATIS YIALOS

A busy beach resort on the island's south coast, Platis Yialos is a convenient base for visiting the southern beaches. The town exists for tourism during high season.

**Hotel Philoxenia**   A step above the town's average beachfront lodgings, this simple hotel on the main street facing the bay offers spacious, clean rooms, all with balconies. All units have refrigerators, and most have a view toward the beach. Bathrooms are small but efficient.

Platis Yialos, 84003 Sifnos. (© **22840/71-221.** Fax 22840/71-222. philoxenia@infixnet.gr. 9 units. 80€–100€ double. Breakfast 5€. MC, V. Closed Nov–Mar.

**Hotel Platis Yialos** ★ *Kids*   The island's best hotel is ideally situated overlooking the beach on the west side of the cove, set apart from the rest of the town's densely populated beach strip. This is an ideal place to stay if you are traveling with young children; we speak from experience. Originally a government-owned Xenia hotel, its design is functional rather than beautiful. The ground-floor guest rooms, with patios facing the garden and water, are especially desirable; rooms on the upper stories have balconies. A new suite contains flagstone floors, beamed ceilings, beds for up to six people, and two bathrooms, one with Jacuzzi; it opens to a small terrace with views of the bay. Frescoes and small paintings by a local artist are displayed throughout the hotel. The Platis Yialos's flagstone sun deck extends from the beach to a dive platform at the end of the cove; a bar and restaurant share the same Aegean views.

Platis Yialos, 84003 Sifnos. (© **22840/31-324,** or 0831/22-626 in winter. Fax 22840/31-325, or 0831/55-042 in winter. 29 units. 150€–200€ double Rates include breakfast. No credit cards. Closed Oct–Mar. **Amenities:** Restaurant; bar. *In room:* A/C, minifridge.

## WHERE TO DINE

### APOLLONIA

**Apostoli's Koutouki Taverna** GREEK   There are several tavernas in Apollonia, but this one with outdoor tables along the main pedestrian street is the

## Moments A Special Feast

The **Prophet Elijah's feast day** (which usually falls between the 20th and 22nd of July) is one of the most important religious holidays on Sifnos, which has had a monastery dedicated to this saint for at least 800 years. The celebration begins with a mass outing to the monastery of Profitis Elias on the summit of the island's highest mountain, and continues through the night with dancing and feasting.

best for simple Greek food. The vegetable dishes, most made from locally grown produce, are delicious. The service is slow, even by taverna standards.

Along the main pedestrian street. ⓒ 22840/31-186. Main courses 5€–15€. No credit cards. Daily noon–midnight.

**Sifnos Cafe-Restaurant** ★ GREEK   You can start the day here with breakfast, including fresh fruit juice and your choice of a dozen coffees. Stop by later in the day for a snack, light meal, ouzo and mezedes, or dessert. This place (in the Hotel Sifnos, see above) often has delicious rivithia (chickpeas), a Sifnian specialty, on Sunday.

Apollonia. ⓒ 22840/31-624. Main courses 4€–15€. AE, MC, V. Daily 8am–midnight.

## ARTEMONAS

**To Liotrivi (Manganas)** ★★ GREEK   One of the island's favorite tavernas is in the pretty village of Artemona, just over a mile's walk from Apollonia. Taste for yourself why the Sifnians consider Yannis Yiorgoulis one of their best cooks. Try his delectable *kaparosalata* (minced caper leaves and onion salad), *psarokeftedes* (croquettes of ground chickpeas), or *ambelofasoula* (crisp local black-eyed peas in the pod). In short, there're lots of vegetarian delights here, but there's also a very tasty beef filet with potatoes baked in foil. This place usually has the excellent Sifnian specialty of chickpeas *rivithia* on Sundays.

Artemona. ⓒ 22840/31-246. Main courses 6€–18€. No credit cards. Daily noon–midnight. From Apollonia, follow the pedestrian street north from Plateia Iroon, past Mama Mia and the Hotel Petali; it's a pleasant 10- to 15-min walk.

## KAMARES

**Boulis Taverna** GREEK   With an unexceptional location at the top of the town's busy main street, this isn't the place to go for a romantic evening, but it does offer some of the best Greek food in town. Operated by Andonis Kalogirou of the Hotel Boulis, most of the vegetables, cheeses, and meats are raised on the organic family farm. The walls of the vast interior room are lined with wooden wine casks. Outside, lamb, chicken, and steaks cook on the grill.

At the top of the main street through town. ⓒ 22840/31-648. Main courses 5€–15€. No credit cards. Daily 11am–1am.

**Captain Andreas** SEAFOOD   Captain Andreas, a favorite place for seafood, has tables right on the town beach. Andreas, the proprietor and fisherman, serves the catch of the day. It's usually simply prepared and accompanied with terrific chips or a seasonal vegetable dish.

On the town beach. ⓒ 22840/32-356. Main courses 5€–12€, fish priced by the kilo. No credit cards. Daily 1–5pm and 7:30pm–12:30am.

**Pothotas Taverna O Simos** GREEK   This unobtrusive portside place has a basic Greek menu, and everything is done well. The bread brought to your table is sprinkled with sesame seeds, the *horiatiki* salad is made with local *mizithra* cheese, the fish is fresh and not expensive, and the individually baked pots of moussaka are delicious.

On the port. © 22840/31-697. Main courses 4€–10€. No credit cards. Daily 11am–midnight.

## PLATIS YIALOS

**Sofia Restaurant** GREEK   Platis Yialos's best restaurant for Greek taverna fare is popular for its outdoor terrace and large wine list. For many in Apollonia, the casual seaside ambience warrants an evening outing.

At the east end of the beach. © 22840/71-202. Main courses 5€–12€. No credit cards. Daily 9pm–1am.

## SIFNOS AFTER DARK

In Apollonia, the **Argo Bar** is one of the oldest establishments, and plays European and American pop music with some Greek tunes thrown in. **Botzi** and **Volto** on the main pedestrian street are good for the latest European and American pop music at very loud volumes. **Isadora** and **Doloma** also blast out jazz and rock music. In summer, the large **Dolphin Pub** becomes a lively and elegant nightspot; it closes for the season in mid-September.

In Kamares at sunset, you can seek relative tranquility near the beach at the picturesque **Old Captain's Bar.** Or join the yacht set drinking Sifnos Sunrises at the rival **Collage Club.** Later, the **Mobilize Dance Club** and the more elegant **Follie-Follie,** right on the beach, start cranking up the volume for dancing.

If this kind of music doesn't appeal to you, check to see whether the **Cultural Society of Sifnos** has scheduled any concerts in Artemonas (usually only in summer).

## 4 Paros

168km (91 nautical miles) SE of Piraeus

Paros is accurately known as the "transportation hub" of the Cyclades: almost all island boats stop here en route to someplace else. As a result, Paros, unjustly, suffers from the reputation of a place on the way to the place you are going. This overlooks the island's charms, which include a handsome capital, inland villages of great charm, and some excellent beaches. At present, Paros is cheaper than either Mykonos or Santorini—in fact, some call it the "poor man's Mykonos"—although rising prices here are rapidly making that nickname outdated. Comparisons aside, Paros's good beaches and nightlife have made it a very popular destination in its own right—and students of antiquity will be eager to see the island that supplied the Parian marble so famous in ancient Greece. The marble came from Mt. Profitis Elias, the massive peak that dominates the island.

Admittedly, if you come by ship, your first impression will be of the travel agents, cafes, and the not terribly enticing fast food joints lining the harborfront. Take a few steps inland, and you'll be struck by the charms of **Parikia,** the lively capital, with its energetic marketplace, the remains of a Venetian castle, and a fine Byzantine cathedral, which is one of the three largest (and oldest) churches in the Greek islands.

On the north coast, the fishing village of **Naoussa** has grown into a full-scale resort, and is almost as crowded as Parikia in July and August; the most popular

Paros beaches are within easy commuting distance of Naoussa's hotels. The west coast of the island has long stretches of fine sand, plus wind conditions that have made this the site of the World Cup windsurfing championship every year since 1993.

When you head inland, you'll find narrow, winding streets and lots of characteristic white sugar-cube Cycladic architecture. Charming **Lefkes**, set within the island's inland hills, has preserved many of its medieval buildings amidst a maze of steep narrow streets.

If possible, take a day or two to explore the island and visit its attractions. Paros is large enough that renting a car makes sense. Then, you can make an around-the-island tour that includes a morning visit to the Valley of the Butterflies (**Petaloudes**), a visit to Lefkes, a stop for a good lunch in Naoussa, a swim at your beach of choice, and a night back in Parikia, where you can shop and stroll the evening away.

## ESSENTIALS

**GETTING THERE   By Plane   Olympic Airways** (© **210/966-6666** or 210/936-9111; www.olympic-airways.gr) has at least two flights daily between Paros and Athens; in Parikia, call © **22840/21-900** for flight information.

**By Boat**   Paros has more connections with more ports than any other island in the Cyclades. The main port, Parikia, has connections at least once daily with Piraeus by ferry (5–6 hr.) and high-speed ferry (3–4 hr.). Confirm schedules with the Athens **GNTO** (© **210/327-1300**; 210/331-0562) or the **Port Authority in Piraeus** (© **210/459-3223** or 210/422-6000; phone seldom answered). Daily ferry and hydrofoil service links Parikia with Ios, Mykonos (1½ hr.), Naxos (30 min.), Santorini (2½ hr. by hydrofoil, 4 hr. by car ferry), and Tinos (1½–3 hr.). Several times a week, boats depart for Folegandros (2 hr. by hydrofoil, 4 hr. by car ferry), Sifnos (1 hr. by hydrofoil, 3 hr. by car ferry), and Siros (1–4 hr.). There are daily excursion tours from Parikia or Naoussa (the north coast port) to Mykonos. There's also overnight service to Ikaria and Samos (7–10 hr.) four times a week. (From Samos you can arrange a next-day excursion to Ephesus, Turkey.) In high season, there's hourly caïque service to Andiparos from Parikia and Pounda, a small port 6km (4 miles) south of Parikia, with regular connection by bus. The east coast port of Piso Livadi is the point of departure for travelers heading to the "Little Cyclades": Ferries depart four times weekly for Heraklia, Schinoussa, Koufonissi and Katapola.

For general ferry information, call **Santorineos Travel** in Parikia (© **22840/ 24-245**) or try the **port authority** (© **22840/21-240**). Ferry tickets are sold by

---

**Tips   Check Your Calendar**

The Feast of the Dormition of the Virgin (Aug 15) is one of the most important religious holidays in Greece—and the most important, after Easter, in Paros. Pilgrims come here from throughout the Cyclades to attend services at the Panayia Ekatondapilliani, which is dedicated to the Virgin. If you come here then, make reservations well in advance, or you will probably find yourself sleeping rough. And on the subject of dates: if you are coming to Paros to see its famous butterflies, remember that they usually only come here in May and June.

numerous agents around Mavroyenous Square and along the port; schedules are posted along the sidewalk.

**VISITOR INFORMATION**   There is a **visitor information office** on Mavroyenous Square, just behind and to the right of the windmill at the end of the pier. This office is often closed, but there are numerous travel agencies on the seafront, including the helpful **Santorineos Travel** (C **22840/24-245;** fax 22840/23-922; santorineos@travelling.gr). 100m (328 ft.) south of the pier (to the right as you get off the boat). Here you can store luggage, buy ferry and airline tickets, rent a car, and exchange money. The municipality information office in the Paraika town hall can be reached at C **22840/22-078.** The island has a helpful website, **www.parosweb.com.**

**GETTING AROUND   By Bus**   The **bus station** (C **22840/21-133**) in Parikia is on the waterfront, left from the windmill. There is hourly service between Parikia and Naoussa from 8am to midnight in high season. The other buses from Parikia run hourly from 8am to 9pm in two general directions: south to Aliki or Pounda, and southeast to the beaches at Piso Livadi, Chrissi Akti, and Drios, passing the Marathi Quarries and the town of Lefkes along the way. Schedules are posted at the stations.

**By Car & Moped**   Paros is large enough that renting a car makes sense; there are many agencies along the waterfront, and except in July and August you should be able to bargain. You can also try **Santorineos Travel** (C **22840/24-245**); Nikos Santorineos works with several agencies in town, and will call around to find the best price; expect to pay from 50€ per day. Most of the town's moped dealers (including the efficient **Iria Cars & Bikes,** C **22840/21-232**) can be found along the waterfront, left from the windmill. Depending on size, mopeds cost around 20€ per day.

**By Taxi**   Taxis can be booked (C **22840/21-500**) or hailed at the windmill taxi stand. Taxi fare to Naoussa with luggage should be around 10€.

**FAST FACTS**   The **American Express** agent is Santorineos Travel, on the seafront 100m (328 ft.) south of the pier (C **22840/24-245;** fax 22840/23-922; santorineos@travelling.gr). There are five **banks** in Parikia on Mavroyenous Square, and one in Naoussa; open Monday through Thursday from 8am to 2pm, Friday from 8am to 1:30pm. The private **Medical Center of Paros** (C **22840/ 24-410**) is to the left (north) of the pier, across from the post office; the public **Parikia Health Clinic** (C **22840/22-500**) is on the central square, down the road from the Ekatondapiliani Cathedral. **Internet access** is available on the Wired Network (www.parosweb.com) at eight locations around the island; you can buy a "smart card" that stores your personal settings and provides access at any of these locations; about 6€ an hour. The main office is in Parikia at the Wired Cafe on Market Street (C **22840/22-003**).

The **Laundry House** is on the paralia near the post office (C **22840/24-898**). For the **police,** call (C **22840/100** or 22840/23-333. In Marpissa, call (C **22840/ 41-202;** in Naoussa, C **22840/51-202.** The **post office** in Parikia (C **22840/ 21-236**) is left from the windmill on the waterfront road, open Monday through Friday from 7:30am to 2pm, with extended hours in July and August. The **telephone office (OTE)** in Parikia (C **22840/22-135**) is just to the right from the windmill; open from 7:30am to 2pm. (If the front door is closed, go around to the back, as wind direction determines which door is open.) There's a branch in Naoussa with similar hours.

# WHAT TO SEE & DO

## THE TOP ATTRACTIONS

### Archaeological Museum

The museum's most valued holding is a fragment of the famous Parian Chronicle, an ancient chronology. The Ashmolean Museum at Oxford University has a larger portion of the chronicle, which is carved on (Parian, of course!) marble tablets. Why is this document so important? Because it lists dates from Cecrops, the legendary first king of Athens, to 263 or 264 B.C. Just to confuse and irritate historians, the chronicle gives information about artists, poets, and playwrights—but doesn't bother to mention many important political leaders or battles. The museum also contains a Winged Victory from the 5th century B.C.; some objects found at the local temple of Apollo; and part of a marble monument with a frieze of Archilochus, the important 7th-century B.C. lyric poet known as the inventor of iambic meter and for his ironic detachment—"What breaks me, young friend, is tasteless desire, lifeless verse, boring dinners."

Parikia. ☎ 22840/21-231. Admission 2€. Tues–Sun 8:30am–2:30pm. Behind the cathedral, opposite the playing fields of the local school.

### Panayia Ekatondapiliani Cathedral ★★

The town's most famous sight is the Byzantine cathedral of Panayia Ekatondapiliani (Our Lady of a Hundred Doors). The large square by the cathedral was expanded in 1996 for the church's 1,700th birthday! According to tradition, the church was founded by Saint Helen, the mother of Constantine the Great, the emperor whose conversion to Christianity led to its becoming the official religion of the Roman Empire. Saint Helen is said to have stopped here en route for the Holy Land, where the faithful believe that she found the True Cross. Her son fulfilled her vow to found a church here and successive emperors and rulers expanded it—which may in part explain the church's confusing layout, an inevitable result of centuries of renovations and expansions.

The cathedral is surrounded by a high white wall built as protection from pirates; in the thickness of the wall are rows of monk's cells, now housing a small shop and ecclesiastical museum. After you step through the outer gate, the noise of the town vanishes, and you enter a garden with lemon trees and flowering shrubs. The cathedral contains several icons dating back as far as the 15th century, and a fine cruciform baptismal font from the 4th century. The museum contains many 16th- to 19th-century icons, religious vestments, and beautiful objects used to celebrate the varied ceremonies of the Orthodox Church; although the museum is small, it's well worth the entrance fee.

Parikia. Museum. ☎ 22840/21-243. Admission 2€. Daily 8am–1pm and 4–9pm. On the central square of Parikia, opposite and north of the ferry pier.

### Marathi Marble Quarries

The inland road to Lefkes and Marpissa will take you up the side of a mountain to the marble quarries at Marathi, source of the famous Parian marble. This marble was prized for its translucency and fine, soft texture, and was used by ancient sculptors for their best work, including the *Hermes* of Praxiteles and the *Venus de Milo*. The turnoff to the quarries is signposted, and a path paved with marble leads up the valley toward a group of deserted buildings. These once belonged to a French mining company, the last to operate here, which in 1844 quarried the marble for Napoleon's tomb. There isn't much to see now unless you're a spelunker at heart, in which case you'll find it irresistible to explore the deep caverns opened by the miners high above the valley (bring a flashlight).

Marathi. Open site.

## The Valley of Petaloudes and Convent of Christou stou Dhassous ★

Another name for this oasis of plum, pear, fig, and pomegranate trees is *Psychopiani* (soul softs). The butterflies, actually tiger moths (*Panaxia quadripunctaria poda*), look like black-and-white–striped arrowheads until they fly up to reveal their bright red underwings. They have been coming here for at least 300 years because of the freshwater spring, flowering trees, dense foliage, and cool shade, and are usually most numerous in the early mornings, or evenings, in June. Donkey or mule rides from Parikia to the site along a back road cost about 10€. You can take the Pounda and Aliki bus, which drops you off at the turnoff to the nunnery; you'll have to walk the remaining 2.5km (1½ miles) in to Petaloudes. Be sure to scowl at the inevitable visitors who clap and shout to alarm the butterflies and make them fly about. There's a small snack bar here with refreshments, where men can wait, while women visit the nearby Convent of Christou stou Dhassous, which does not welcome male visitors (although they can cool their heels in the courtyard and dream of getting their revenge when they visit Mount Athos, forbidden to women visitors).

Petaloudes. Admission 3€. Daily 9am–1pm and 4–8pm. Closed Oct–May. Head 4km (2½ miles) south of Parikia on the coast road, turn left at the sign for the nunnery of Christou sto Dassos, and continue another 2½km (1½ miles).

## BEACHES

The beaches of Paros are small and overcrowded in comparison with those of nearby Naxos, but there is an abundance of sea sand and a few truly exceptional beaches. One of the island's best and most famous, picturesque **Kolimbithres** (fonts), is an hour's walk or a 10-minute moped ride west from Naoussa. It has smooth giant rocks, some reminiscent of baptismal fonts, that divide the gold-sand beach into several tiny coves. There are a few tavernas nearby; we recommend the **Dolphin Taverna**, to the south, open from 7am to 2am, for traditional Greek food. North of the beach at Kolimbithres, by the Ayios Ioannis Church, is **Monasteri Beach**, with some nude sunning, and the **Monasteri Club**, a bar/restaurant with music and beach service.

About 2.5km (1½ miles) north of Naoussa on an unimproved road is the popular **Langeri Beach**. A 10-minute walk further north will bring you to the nudist beach, with a gay and straight crowd. Before you reach Langeri, the road forks to the right and leads to **Santa Maria Beach ★**, one of the most beautiful on the island. It has particularly clear water and shallow dunes (rare in Greece) of fine sand along the irregular coastline. It also offers some of the best windsurfing on Paros. The nearby **Santa Maria Surf Club** (✆ **22840/52-490**) provides windsurfing gear and lessons for about 20€ per hour. There's bus service to Santa Maria beach from Naoussa twice a day; caïque day trips from Naoussa are 10€ round-trip.

Southeast of Naoussa, connected by public bus, is the fishing village of **Ambelas**, which has a good beach and some inexpensive tavernas. About a half-hour's hike south of Ambelas along the east coast brings you to **Glyfades** and, just beyond it, **Tsoukalia**, which attract radical windsurfers. Both beaches have a few studios to rent and a restaurant. The main north-south road is almost 1km (½ mile) inland at this point.

The better beaches on the east coast can be reached by bus from Parikia and Naoussa. Unfortunately, the road is inland and you can't scope out the beaches from the bus window. Ask around about crowd conditions on the several beaches; once you've reached a beach, it's several miles to the next one.

**Molos,** at the tip of a small peninsula, is beautiful and convenient to the attractive inland villages of Marmara and Marpissa, where there are rooms to let, so it can sometimes get crowded.

The next major beach, **Chrissi Akti (Golden Beach)** ✦, a kilometer of fine golden sand, is generally considered the best beach on the island. It's also the windiest, although the wind is usually offshore. As a result, this has become the primary windsurfing center on the island and has hosted the World Cup championship every year since 1993. Many overnight visitors head south to nearby **Drios,** a pretty village that is fast becoming a resort town, with hotels, luxury villas, and waterside tavernas. Buses run from Drios to Parikia five times daily, hourly in summer. The **Aegean Diving School** (✆ 22840/92-071; www.eurodivers.gr) offers scuba instruction and guided dives here.

Just south of Aliki, on the south shore of the island, is beautiful, sheltered **Faranga Beach,** a short walk in from the main road.

The next beach south of Drios, **Loleantonis,** is about 200m (656 ft.) long and protected from the *meltemi* winds by a rocky headland. The beach is usually uncrowded, and has a small taverna and a snack shop. If you take the bus, you'll have to walk in 1.5km (1 mile) along a gravel road, signposted from the Drios-Parikia road.

## TOWNS & VILLAGES

Until recently, **Naoussa** was a fishing village with simple white houses in a labyrinth of narrow streets, but it's now a growing resort center with good restaurants, trendy bars, and sophisticated boutiques. Most of the new building has been concentrated along the nearby beaches, so the town itself still retains much charm—but for how long? Colorful fishing boats fill the harbor and fishermen calmly go about their work on the docks, all in the shadow of a half-submerged ruined Venetian fortress. There are a number of good beaches within walking distance of town, or you can catch a caïque to the more distant ones.

The ruins of the Venetian fortress on the east end are most impressive when lighted at night. The most colorful local **festival** is held on August 23, when the battle against the pirate Barbarossa is reenacted by torch-lit boats converging on the harbor; this is followed by feasting and dancing.

The ever helpful **Nissiotissa Tours** (✆ 22840/51-480 or 22840/52-094; fax 22840/51-189) is off the left side of the main square near the bus station, across the lane from the Naoussa Sweet Shop. Cathy and Kostas Gavalas, Greek Americans who are experts on this area of the island, can help you find accommodations, change money, rent a car, book flights or ferries, and arrange excursion tickets, island tours, and outdoor activities.

Buses to Parikia leave the main square in Naoussa on the half-hour from 8:30am to 8:30pm, more frequently in July and August. Service to other villages on narrow dirt roads is infrequent (check the schedule at the station). There are daily excursion tours from Naoussa to Mykonos; inquire with Nissiotissa Tours or any other local travel agent.

Hilltop **Lefkes** ✦ is the medieval capital of the island. Its whitewashed houses with red-tile roofs form a maze around the central square. Lefkes was built in such an inaccessible location and with an intentionally confusing pattern of streets to thwart pirates. Test your own powers of navigation by finding the **Ayia Triada** (Holy Trinity) **Church,** whose carved marble towers are visible above the town. The Lefkes Village Hotel here is one of the nicest places on the island to stay (see "Where to Stay," later in this chapter).

##  The Cave of Andiparos

To get away from all the crowds in Parikia, plan a visit to **Andiparos** (Opposite Paros). This islet, about a kilometer (½ mile) off the western coast of Paros, was once connected to it by a natural causeway. In recent years, Andiparos has begun to attract its own crowds—but even though you may not be able to completely escape civilization, this smaller, quieter island still has much to offer, including a huge cave full of fantastic stalactites. It was discovered on Andiparos during the time of Alexander the Great, and has been a compelling reason to visit ever since.

Excursion caïques leave the port of Parikia regularly (every 30 min. in summer) beginning at 9:45am for the 45-minute ride to the busy little port of Andiparos (2€ one-way). There is also a shuttle barge, for vehicles as well as passengers, that crosses the channel between the southern port of Pounda and Andiparos continuously from 9am; the fare is 1€, 5€ with a car, and you can take along your bicycle for free. There are also caïque excursions that include a visit to the cave for about 12€ departing from Parikia or Naoussa.

The impressive **cave** is a half-hour walk up from the boat landing or a 2-hour hike from the port of Andiparos; buses travel regularly between Andiparos and the cave (4€ round-trip). From the church of Ayios Ioannis, you'll have an excellent view of Folegandros (farthest west), Sikinos, Ios, and part of Paros. Tourists once entered the cave by rope, but a concrete staircase now offers more convenient—if less adventuresome—access. The cave is about 90m (300 ft.) deep, but the farthest reaches are now closed to visitors. Through the centuries, visitors have broken off parts of stalactites as souvenirs and left graffiti to commemorate their visit, but the cool, mysterious cavern is still worth exploring. An hour spent in the dark, echo-filled chamber trying to decipher some of the inscriptions offers a unique contrast to all your hours devoted to lying on a sun-drenched beach. You'll also be in the company of such distinguished guests as Lord Byron and King Otho of Greece, who each left behind evidence of his visit. The Marquis de Nointel celebrated Christmas mass here in 1673 with 500 paid attendants, plus explosions to add drama.

**Andiparos town,** with a permanent population of about 700, has several travel agents, a bank with limited hours, a post office, a telephone office (OTE), and an ATM. You'll find a plentiful selection of shops and tavernas along the harborfront, and inland a fine **Kastro,** the remains of the medieval fortified town.

If you decide to spend the night, there are plenty of places offering "Rent Rooms"—but remember that here, as on Paros itself, rooms are hard to come by in high season. The **Hotel Anaghyros** (*C* 22840/61-206) and the **Hotel Mantalena** (*C* 22840/61-206; mantalenahotel@par.forth net.gr) both offer doubles from 80€ and have rooms with views of the sea and port.

## OUTDOOR PURSUITS

**WALKING** Paros has numerous old stone-paved roads connecting the interior towns, many of which are still in good condition and perfect for walking. One of the best known trails is the **Byzantine Road** between Lefkes and Prodromos, a narrow path paved along much of its 4km (2½-mile) length with marble slabs. Begin in Lefkes, since from here the way is mostly downhill. There isn't an easy way to find the beginning of the Byzantine Road among the labyrinthine streets of Lefkes; we suggest starting at the church square, from which point you can see the flagstone-paved road in a valley at the edge of the town, to the west. Having fixed your bearings, plunge into the maze of streets and spiral your way down and to the right. After a 2-minute descent, you emerge into a ravine, with open fields beyond, and a sign indicates the beginning of the Byzantine Road. It's easy going through terraced fields, a leisurely hour's walk to the Marpissa Road, from which point you can catch the bus back to Parikia (check the schedule and exact pick-up point beforehand). This also makes a challenging mountain-bike outing.

**WINDSURFING** The continuous winds on Paros's east coast have made it a favorite destination for windsurfers, and the **World Cup** has been held on Golden Beach for the past 7 years. The best months are July and August, but serious windsurfers may want to visit earlier or later in the season to avoid the crowds. The free *Paros Windsurfing Guide* is available at most tourist offices in Parikia or Naoussa. On Golden Beach, **Sunwind Surf Center** ★ (℮ **22840/42-900**, fax 22840/42-901; www.sunwind.gr) charges about 15€ for 1-hour rental of a board, sail, harness, and wet suit; instruction is an additional 6€ per hour. Reasonable rates for daily or weekly rental are also available; Sunwind can assist in booking complete holiday packages as well. In Naoussa, you can rent equipment from **Club Mistral** (℮ **22840/52-010**, fax 22840/51-720), at the Porto Paros Hotel near Kolimbithres Beach.

## SHOPPING

**Market Street** in Parikia is the shopping hub of the island, with many interesting alternatives to the ubiquitous souvenir stores. At **Geteki** (℮ **22840/21-855**), you'll find paintings and sculpture by French artist Jacques Fleureaux, now a full-time resident of Paros. He makes use of local materials (clay, driftwood) and motifs (Cycladic figurines) in his work. Also for sale here are Afghani rugs and local ceramics by other artists. Yvonne von der Decken's shop **Palaio Poleio** ★ (℮ **22840/21-909**), opposite the Apollon Restaurant in the agora, has a fine selection of antique vernacular furniture from the islands and the Greek mainland. There are also many smaller items, such as finely decorated mirror frames, water jugs hollowed from solid wood, and handmade household utensils. **Enosis** ★ (run by the Agricultural Collective; ℮ **22840/22-181**) sells local cheeses, honey, and wine in its shop on Manto Mavroyennis Square.

In Naoussa's old town, be sure to visit the **Metaxas Gallery** (℮ **22840/52-667**), which has exhibitions of paintings by local artists (sometimes for sale) and locally crafted jewelry. Also in Naoussa is the gallery **Ira**, opposite Nissiotissa Tours, just down the lane from the Naoussa Sweet Shop (℮ **22840/53-566**). It offers local pottery, jewelry, carpets from Greece and Turkey, and fine-arts books of local interest. Owner Hera Papamihail is a talented photographer, and her prints are also available for purchase.

Perched above the village of Kostos, on the road between Parikia and Lefkes, you'll find **Studio Yria** (℮ **22840/29-007**), where Stelio and Monika Ghikis produce functional earthenware that incorporates indigenous designs, including an abstract octopus motif. They also sell weavings and objects of cast bronze, forged iron, and Parian marble. In Lefkes, **Anemi** (© 22840/41-182) has hand-loomed fabrics. In addition, nuns in several of the convents often sell handicraft.

## WHERE TO STAY
### PARIKIA

The port town has three basic hotel zones: the **agora,** the **harbor,** and the **beach.** The agora is the heart of Parikia, and can get noisy; accommodations in the quiet back streets are most enticing. The harborside near the windmill is a convenient and lively place, but it's often too loud for a good night's rest. The strip of hotels along Livadi beach—north of the windmill, left coming from the ferry—have three common features: bland decor, proximity to the crowded town beach, and sea views.

We recommend ignoring the room hawkers at the port unless you're absolutely desperate—the rooms offered are usually a considerable distance from town, and many don't meet basic standards of comfort and cleanliness.

In addition to the choices below, you might also consider the small, simple, and inexpensive **Hotel Captain Manolis,** in the center of the agora (© **22840/21-244**).

**Hotel Argonauta** ★  This charming and comfortable hotel is refreshingly quiet. The marble-floored bedrooms are reached through a flower-filled courtyard. All units have balconies overlooking the street, but double-paned window glass assures that you won't be disturbed by late-night revelry. One of the first hotels in Parikia, this place has been under the same ownership since 1977—Soula and Dimitri Ghikas make their spacious and attractive lobby feel like home.

Agora, Parikia, 84400 Paros. © **22840/21-440.** Fax 22840/23-442. 15 units. 75€ double. MC, V. Closed mid-Oct to Easter. At the far end of Mavroyenous Square, opposite the Ethniki (National) Bank. **Amenities:** Break-fast room/bar. *In room:* A/C.

**Hotel Dina** ★ (Value  More pension than hotel, these cozy rooms are reached through a narrow, plant-filled courtyard off one of the finest small plazas in Parikia. Dina Patelis has been the friendly proprietor for nearly 3 decades, and she offers a personal touch that keeps guests coming back year after year. Three bedrooms open to the square; room 2, with a private balcony, is especially desirable. The rest of the units face a small garden courtyard, and room 8 has the additional benefit of a view toward the hills and a private terrace.

Market St., Parikia, 84400 Paros. © **22840/21-325** or 22840/21-345. Fax 22840/23-525. 8 units. 50€–65€ double. No credit cards. The entrance is just off Market St., next to the Apollon Restaurant and across from the Pirate Bar. *In room:* A/C.

**Pandrossos Hotel** ★★  As so often is the case, the good news and the bad news are the same: this hotel is on a hill above town, where you will be more quiet than in town—but not in the heart of the action, if that is your desire. Rooms have balconies with sea views (the sea is only 100m/328 ft. away). The terrace restaurant is more than good enough to keep you from feeling that you should head out at night—and has glorious views at sunset. Best of all, there's a pool.

Parikia, 84400 Paros. © **22840/22-903,** 210/923-4897 (Athens). 46 units. 80€–100€ double. No credit cards. **Amenities:** Restaurant; bar; freshwater pool. *In room:* A/C, TV, minibar.

### SOUTH OF PARIKIA

**Hotel Iria** ★ (Kids  This new bungalow resort complex (completely renovated in 2003) is just too good to be ignored—and just the place to head for if you are traveling with young children, for whom there's a playground and pool—and a beach about 150m (492 ft.) away. The architecture is traditional with a village-like plan, and while not all units have a sea view, the grounds are so beautifully landscaped that you may not feel deprived if your room faces inward (room price depends on view). The staff has been praised as helpful.

Parasporos, 84400 Paros. (C) 22840/24-154. Fax 22840/21-167. info@yriahotel.gr. 68 units. 180–250 double. Rates include full buffet breakfast. Lunch or dinner 20€. AE, DC, MC, V. Closed mid-Nov to Apr. Located 2½ km (1½ miles) south of the port. Amenities: Restaurant; bar; freshwater pool; tennis; concierge; car rental; laundry. In room: A/C, TV, minibar, hair dryer.

## NAOUSSA

If you're unable to find a room, try **Nissiotissa Tours** (C) 22840/51-480), just off the east (the left) side of the main square. In addition to the following choices, you might try the moderately priced **Captain Dounas Apartments** (C) 22840/ 52-525 or 22840/52-585; in winter 210/894-4047; fax 22840/52-586; dounas@par.forthnet.gr), which stand on a rocky promontory between Naoussa and Ayii Anaryiri Beach.

**Astir of Paros** ★★  The most extravagant hotel on the island is built like a self-contained Cycladic village within a luxurious garden—and its own private beach, a 3-hole golf course, a good pool, a tennis court, and a gym—and a staff praised as efficient. Double rooms are unexceptional, but the suites are spacious and elegantly furnished. Four units offer handicapped access. Produce for the two hotel restaurants is grown on a nearby farm, and meals are particularly sumptuous—the breakfast buffet (not included in the room rates) includes more than 70 items.

Kolimbithres Beach (west of Naoussa, off the south end of the beach), 84401 Paros. (C) 22840/51-976 or 22840/51-707. Fax 22840/51-985. Astir@otenet.gr. 61 units. 180€–230€ double. 190€–430€ suite. Rates include continental breakfast. AE, DC, MC, V. Closed Oct 20 to Easter. Amenities: Restaurant; bar; freshwater pool; 3-hole golf course; tennis; health club; concierge; partially handicapped accessible. In room: A/C, TV, minibar, hairdryer.

**Hotel Petres** ★  Clea and Sotiris Hatzinikolakis have decorated their charming reception area with antiques, and the guest rooms with loving care. The beds have handsome woven covers, the walls are hung with prints from the Benaki Museum. The "honeymoon suite" contains Kuria Hatzinikolakis's grandmother's marriage bed. The buffet breakfast-brunch served from 9am to 11:30am is extensive and tasty, and dinner is available on request; most Saturdays in summer there's a barbecue at the poolside grill. The location outside Naoussa is very quiet; if you want to get to town, the hotel offers a frequent mini-bus shuttle. One wonderful extra here—and an unusual one at that: the hotel offers Massage Siatsou, Reiki, and Aromatherapy services.

Naoussa (1km/½ miles from town), 84401 Paros. (C) 22840/52-467. Fax 22840/52-759. www.petres.gr. 16 units. 100€ double. Rates include breakfast. No credit cards. Closed Nov–Mar. Amenities: Breakfast room/bar; freshwater pool; tennis; airport/port pickup. In room: A/C, TV, minibar, hair dryer.

**Papadakis Hotel** ★  The new Papadakis offers the best views in town—enjoyed from every room as well as from the new pool with Jacuzzi. The large guest rooms were renovated in 1998, with new wardrobes, beds, and desks in dark walnut; several units also have sofa beds. The excellent breakfast includes home-made baked goods prepared by owner Argyro Barbarigou, who happens to be an incredible chef—be sure to visit her new venture, the Papadakis fish taverna (see "Where to Dine," below)

Naoussa (a 5-min. walk uphill from the main square), 84401 Paros. © **22840/51-269.** Fax 22840/51-269. 19 units. 75€ double. Breakfast 10€ extra. No credit cards. **Amenities:** Restaurant, bar; freshwater pool; Jacuzzi. *In room:* A/C, TV, minibar.

## LEFKES

**Hotel Fotilia**   Climb to the top of the steps at the end of town, and to the left of the hilltop church you'll see a restored windmill and pool terrace behind a stone archway. If he knows that you're coming, the companionable Michel Leondaris will probably meet you with a cup of coffee or glass of wine. The hotel bedrooms are spacious and furnished in an elegant country style, with crisp blue-and-white curtains that open to balconies overlooking the old harbor and bay. Studio apartments with kitchenettes are available for the same price as a room.

Naoussa, 84401 Paros. © **22840/52-581** or 22840/52-582. Fax 22840/52-583. 14 units. 100€ double. Breakfast 6€ extra. No credit cards. *In room:* A/C.

**Lefkes Village Hotel** ★★★   This handsome new hotel 10km (6 miles) from Parikia is designed to look like a small island village (admittedly, one with a pool and some rather imposing buildings!) and is situated in Lefkes, probably the most charming inland village on the island. There are spectacular views over the countryside to the sea (and a pool so that you don't mind not being on the sea). Rooms are light and bright, with good bathrooms; some have balconies. In addition to all the things you'd expect in a classy hotel, there's even a small Museum of Popular Aegean Culture and a winery.

P.O. Box 71, Lefkes Village 844 00 Paros. © **0284/41-827** and 210/251-6497. Fax 0284/41-827. www.lefkes village.gr. 25 units. 100€–140€ double. Rates include buffet breakfast. **Amenities:** Restaurant; bar; freshwater pool; Jacuzzi. *In room:* A/C, TV, minibar.

## WHERE TO DINE
### PARIKIA

Walk along the bed of the dry river that cuts through Mavroyenous Square's north side to **Symposium** ★ (© **22840/24-147**), an elegant coffeehouse perched on a bridge. Enjoy a slow cup of coffee or tea here, or try the dependable continental breakfast or crepes. You may find when you look at your watch that you've spent several pleasant hours here.

**Bountaraki** GREEK   Many small details set this taverna apart from its neighbors: fresh brown bread that's refreshingly flavorful and simple main courses that aren't overwhelmed by olive oil. There's a small porch in front, facing the quieter southern end of the paralia. As with all the local tavernas, don't bother with the desserts, which are clearly an afterthought.

Paralia. © **22840/22-297.** Main courses 5€–15€. No credit cards. Daily 1–5pm and 7pm–midnight. At the southern extremity of the paralia, just over the bridge.

**Happy Green Cows** VEGETARIAN   Four tables huddle in the tiny dining room of the Happy Green Cows, a funky place with simple vegetarian dishes thoughtfully prepared. Traditional Greek dishes are available, if you can call "souvlaki soya" traditional, and are joined by tacos, falafel, burritos, and curries; all the above are also available at the restaurant's take-out window, the only option if you feel like eating outside.

Agora. © **22840/22-691.** Main courses 4€–12€. No credit cards. Daily noon–3pm and 6pm–2am.

**Levantis** ★ GREEK/INTERNATIONAL   This place gets high praise for its off-beat dishes that combine local produce with international ingredients—

where else on the island will you find Thai dishes along side stuffed eggplant? Owner-chef George Mavridis likes to cook and likes to talk food, so this is a place where you can enjoy what you eat and often learn about what's happening in the kitchen. We've had reports that this is one place where the desserts are well-worth saving room for, especially if you're a chocoholic. If you're too full for dessert, you can just relax and enjoy the pleasant garden.

Paralia (on the market street). © 22840/23-613. Main courses 5€–15€. AE, V. Daily 7pm–midnight.

**Porphyra** ★ GREEK/FISH The small Porphyra serves the best fish in town. The nondescript, utilitarian service and decor are typical of your average taverna; the difference here is that the owner cultivates the shellfish himself, resulting in an exceptional Mussels Saganaki (mussels cooked with tomato, feta, and wine). The *tzatziki* and other traditional cold appetizers are also very good. The fish is predictably fresh, and offerings vary with the season.

Paralia. © 22840/22-693. Main courses 5€–18€; fish priced by the kilo. AE, V. Daily 6:30pm–midnight. Closed Jan–Feb. Between the pier and the post office, just back from the waterfront.

**Tamarisco** ★ GREEK/VEGETARIAN If you're looking for traditional Greek food that's full of surprises and refreshingly contemporary, this is the place. Eleni, who runs the restaurant with her husband, Stavros, is a native of Paros and uses many local recipes. The menu features subtle and delightful use of fresh herbs, innovative vegetable dishes, fresh pasta, and a variety of fish. Although most summer diners will sit outside in the garden courtyard, the indoor dining room here is particularly pleasant: Exposed ceiling beams, a flagstone floor, simple furniture, and tapestried walls combine to create a space of unusual comfort and warmth.

Agora. © 22840/24-689. Reservations recommended July–Aug. Main courses 6€–15€. AE, V. Daily 7pm–midnight. Closed Jan–Feb. Follow the signs from Market St. to this quiet back plaza of busy Parikia.

## NAOUSSA

Naoussa's main square has plenty of casual eateries. The **Naoussa Pâtisserie,** on the east side of the square, has delicious cheese pies, pastries, and espresso. The village's **bread bakery** is past the church near Christo's Taverna. The beautiful **Kavarnis Bar,** Archilochus, around the corner from the post office (© 22840/51-038), takes you back to Paris in the 1920s, serving up elaborate cocktails and delectable crepes.

**Barbarossa Ouzeri** GREEK This authentic ouzeri is right on the port. Old, wind-burned fishermen sit for hours nursing their milky ouzo in water and their miniportions of grilled octopus and olives. If you haven't partaken of this experience yet, this is the place to try it.

Naoussa waterfront © 22840/51-391. Appetizers 2€–8€. No credit cards. Daily 1pm–1am.

**Christo's Taverna** ★ EURO-GREEK Christo's has been here 25 years and is increasingly known for its eclectic menu and Euro-Greek style. Dinner is served in a beautiful garden filled with red and pink geraniums. The color of the dark purple grape clusters dripping through the trellised roof in late summer is unforgettable. Classical music soothes as you dine on elegantly prepared veal, lamb, or steak dishes.

Archilochus. © 22840/51-442. Reservations recommended July–Aug. Main courses 6€–15€. No credit cards. Daily 7:30–11:30pm.

**Papadakis** ★★ INNOVATIVE GREEK Papadakis is on our short list of terrific restaurants in the Cyclades, a place where every item on the menu seems to have benefited from the same high level of thoughtfulness and culinary invention.

Fresh fish grilled to perfection by Manolis Barbarigou is one of the specialties here, but be sure not to rush to the main course—the appetizers are meant to be savored slowly. Argyro Barbarigou is a truly imaginative chef, and her talent for invention is clear in the many subtle variations on traditional dishes. The *tzatziki* with dill is delicious and refreshingly different, the traditionally prepared *melitzanosalata* is redolent of wood-smoked eggplant, and fresh stuffed pies (fillings vary with the season) are delightful. Save room for one of the incredible desserts—we had the *kataifi ekmek*, a confection conjured from honey, walnuts, cinnamon, custard, and cream.

Naoussa waterfront. © 22840/51-047. Reservations recommended. Main courses 8€–30€. AE, V. Daily 7:30pm–midnight.

**Pervolaria** GREEK   There's something for everyone in this restaurant is set in a lush garden with geraniums and grapevines behind a white stucco house decorated with local ceramics. There's pasta and pizza, and schnitzel a la chef (veal in cream sauce with tomatoes and basil). If you want to eat Greek, order the souvlaki and varied appetizers special.

About 100m (328 ft.) back from the port. © 22840/51-598. Main courses 6€–15€. AE, V. Daily 7pm–midnight.

## PAROS AFTER DARK

Just behind the windmill in Parikia is a local landmark, the **Port Cafe**, a basic kafenio lit by bare incandescent bulbs and filled day and night with tourists waiting for a ferry, bus, taxi, or fellow traveler. The cafe serves coffee, pastry, and drinks; it's a good place for casual conversation.

The **Pebbles Bar** ★ on the paralia plays classical music at sunset; it's a highly congenial place, as popular with locals as it is with visitors. Continue south from Parikia along the coast road, turn left at the bridge, and about 100m (328 ft.) later you should have no difficulty finding **Dubliner** (© 22840/22-759), a complex with several bars and a disco; the crowd here is very young.

If you're not in the mood to party, Parikia offers several more-elegant alternatives. The **Pirate Bar** ★ (© 22840/21-114), a few doors from the Hotel Dina in the agora, is a tastefully decorated nightspot with a stone interior and dark wooden beams; it plays mellow jazz, blues, and classical music. Back on the paralia, **Evinos Bar** has a great view of the harbor—it's above the retaining wall south of the OTE, high enough above the crowd that you can hear the music and enjoy the scenery; **Simple** is another roof-top place. **Alexandros** (© 22840/23-133), in a restored windmill by the harbor usually plays music that you can actually hear, rather than simply feel. The outdoor **Ciné Rex** (© 22840/21-676) in Parikia shows two features, often in English.

There seems to be little traditional Greek entertainment on Paros, but if you're interested, ask about the possibility of seeing a performance by the local community dance group in Naoussa—there are usually performances once in a

---

### Tips   Beware the *Bomba*

Several places on the strip in Parikia offer very cheap drinks or "buy one, get one free"—this is usually locally brewed alcohol that the locals call *bomba*. This speakeasy brew is made privately (and often illegally)—and our sources agree that it makes one intoxicated quickly—and very sick for a long time afterward!

fortnight. You can get information and purchase tickets at **Nissiotissa Tours** in Naoussa (© **22840/51-480**).

Bars in Naoussa tend to be more sophisticated and considerably less raucous than in Parikia. Try **Agnosto** (no phone) for an after-dinner drink. There's also an outdoor movie theater in Naoussa, **Makis Cinema** (© **22840/22-221**), with nightly features usually at 10pm and midnight; these are often action films in English. **Music-Dance Naousa** (© **22840/52-284**) often gives performances of Greek dances; the group wears costumes and is very good. Performances are usually advertised by posters that you will see on the island.

## 5 Naxos

191km (103 nautical miles) SE of Piraeus

Green, fertile, largely self-sufficient Naxos has not needed to go all out to attract tourists. This wealthy agricultural island exports an abundant harvest of olives, grapes, and potatoes throughout the Aegean, and only recently has begun to import tourists. A new airport and speedier inter-island travel has made it easier for visitors to get here. There are new hotels in the port, and clusters of hotels on island beaches.

Thankfully, the character of the island still isn't completely dominated by the recent development. The inland mountain villages, huddled on the lower slopes of imperious Mount Zas, the highest mountain in all the Cyclades, still preserve the rhythms of agrarian life. In Apiranthos, you can taste bread redolent with the smoky aroma of a wood oven, and in Filoti sample local wines under the arms of a venerable plane tree. The locals still have an attitude of friendly indifference (which could be misconstrued as surliness) to the visitors who pass through.

The architecture of Naxos is distinct from that of any other Cycladic isle. The Venetians ruled this island from 1207 until the island fell to the Turks in 1566. Some descendants of the Venetians still live here and the influence of Venetian architecture is obvious in the Kastro in Hora and the fortified Venetian towers, or *pirgi*, punctuating the hillsides. Also specific to Naxos is the remarkable abundance of small **Byzantine chapels,** many of which contain exceptional frescoes dating from the 9th to the 13th centuries.

Naxos is very well connected to other islands by ferry, so you shouldn't have any trouble getting here at most times of year. It's possible to catch a bus to a village that interests you, then explore it leisurely on foot; keep in mind that island buses are reliable but infrequent. A bike may be all the transport you need to the island's beaches, which happen to be among the best in the Cyclades.

### ESSENTIALS
**GETTING THERE By Plane Olympic Airways** (© **210/966-6666** or 210/936-9111; www.olympic-airways.gr) has at least one flight daily between Naxos and Athens. For information and reservations on Naxos, call Olympic or visit **Naxos Tours,** toward the south end of the paralia (© **22850/23-043;** naxos-tours@naxos-island.com), the local representative for Olympic.

**By Boat** From Piraeus, there is at least one daily ferry (6 hr.) and one daily high-speed ferry (4 hr.); schedules can be checked with the Athens **GNTO** (© **210/327-1300** or 210/331-0562), the **Port Authority in Piraeus** (© **210/459-3223** or 210/422-6000; phone seldom answered), or the **Naxos Port Authority** (© **22850/22-300**). There is at least once-daily ferry connection with Ios, Mykonos (1–2 hr.), Paros (30–60 min.), and Santorini (2–4 hr.). There is ferry connection several times weekly with Síros (1½–2½ hr. by high-speed ferry or hydrofoil), Tínos (2–4 hr.), and Sámos (7 hr. to Vathí); and somewhat less frequently with Sífnos (1½ hr. by hydrofoil), and Folégandros (3 hr.). For ferry tickets, try **Zas Travel** (② 22850/23-330), on the paralia opposite the ferry pier.

**VISITOR INFORMATION** The privately operated **Naxos Tourist Information Center** (② 22850/25-201; fax 22850/25-200), across the plaza from the ferry pier (not to be confused with the small office on the pier itself, which is often closed), is the most reliable source of information. This office provides ferry information, books charter flights between various European airports and Athens, books accommodations, arranges excursions, sells maps, exchanges money, holds luggage, assists with phone calls, provides 2-hour laundry service, and offers a **24-hour emergency number** (② 22850/24-525) for travelers on Naxos who need immediate assistance.

Naxos has an excellent website, **www.naxosnet.com**, with maps, bus schedules, hotel listings, and a photo tour of the island.

You will want to find a good map as soon as possible, as Hora (Naxos town) is old, large (with a permanent population of more than 3,000), and complex. The free *Summer Naxos* magazine has the best map of the city. The *Harms-Verlag Naxos* is the best map of the island, but somewhat pricey at 7€.

**GETTING AROUND    By Bus** The bus station is right in the middle of the port plaza at the north end of the harbor. Ask at the nearby KTEL office, across the plaza to the left, for specific schedules. There's regular service throughout most of the island two or three times a day, more frequently to major destinations. In summer, there's service every 30 minutes to the nearby south coast beaches at Ayios Prokopios and Ayia Anna. A popular day trip is to Apollonas, near the northern tip. In summer, the competition for seats on this route can be fierce, so get to the station well ahead of time. In addition to the public buses, there are various excursion buses that can be booked through travel agents.

**By Bicycle & Moped    Moto Naxos** (② 22850/23-420), on Protodikiou Square south of the paralia, has the best mountain bikes as well as mopeds for rent. A basic bike is about 6€ a day; aluminum-frame mountain bikes range from 7€–12€ a day. For a moped, expect to pay 20€ a day. Naxos has some major inclines that require a strong motor and good brakes, so a larger bike (80cc or greater) is recommended.

**By Car** This is the ideal mode of transport on Naxos, and most travel agents rent them. A basic four-door car is about 40€–50€ per day at **AutoTour** (② 22850/25-480), off the north end of the port, up from the bus station across from the elementary school or at **Auto Naxos** (② 22850/23-420), on Protodikiou Square.

**By Taxi** The taxi station (② 22850/22-444) is on the port. A taxi trip within Naxos town shouldn't cost more than 4€; the fare to Ayia Anna is about 7€, and to Apiranthos, 16€.

**FAST FACTS** The **Commercial Bank**, on the paralia, has an ATM. It and other banks are open Monday through Thursday from 8am to 2pm, Friday from 8am to 1:30pm. Naxos has a good 24-hour **health center** (② 22850/23-333) just outside Hora on the left of Papavasiliou, the main street off the port. **Holiday Laundry**, on Perifeirakos Road, Grotta area (② 22850/23-988), offers drop-off service—you can leave your laundry with most hotels and some tourist offices. The **police** (② 22850/22-100) are beyond Protodikiou Square, by the Galaxy Hotel. To find the **post office**, continue south on the paralia past the

OTE to the basketball court; it's opposite the court on the left, on the second floor (open 8am–2pm). The **telephone office (OTE)** is at the south end of the port; summer hours are daily from 7:30am to 2pm.

## WHAT TO SEE & DO
## THE TOP ATTRACTIONS

**Kastro/Archaeological Museum/Venetian Museum** ✪✪ The archaeological museum is located in the heart of the exquisite Venetian Kastro, the medieval citadel that dominates the town. The Kastro (Castle) is Horá's greatest treasure, and you should allow yourself several hours to explore it. Built in the 13th century by Marco Sanudo, nephew of the doge of Venice, it was the domain of the Catholic aristocracy. By walking up from the seafront in Horá you'll soon reach the outer wall of the castle, which has three entryways. The most remarkable of these is the north entry, known as the **Trani Porta** or Strong Gate, a narrow marble arched threshold marking the transition to the Kastro's medieval world. Look for the incision on the right column of the arch, which marks the length of a Venetian yard, and was used to measure the cloth brought here for the ladies of the Venetian court. At the center of the Kastro is the 16th-century **Catholic cathedral,** with its brilliant marble facade; it contains an icon of the Virgin which is thought to be older than the cathedral itself. To the right behind the cathedral is the French School of Commerce and the former **Ursuline Convent and School,** where young ladies of the Venetian aristocracy were educated.

The French School has housed schools run by several religious orders, and among its more famous students was the Cretan writer Nikos Kazantzakis, who studied here in 1896. It now houses the **Archaeological Museum** ✪. There have been many archaeological finds on Naxos, and this museum has a great diversity of objects from several different periods. Among the highlights are the early Cycladic figurines in white marble, the earliest example of sculpture in Greece. The other prize of this museum is its collection of late Mycenaean period (1400–1100 B.C.) artifacts found near Grotta, including vessels with the octopus motif that still appears in local art. The museum occupies long vaulted chambers in the walls of the Kastro, with a great view from its terrace and balconies to the hills of Naxos. There is little in the way of interpretive information, and almost all of it is in Greek; serious museum-goers will appreciate the descriptive booklet available at the ticket desk for 5€.

The **Venetian Museum,** located at the north entry to the Kastro, is a typical Kastro house, home of the Della-Rocca family, recently opened to the public. The 40-minute tours, offered in English and Greek, is a wonderful chance to get an inside look at a survival of one of the great Venetian homes and to learn about the island's Catholic aristocracy and the Kastro. You'll probably want to spend half a day exploring these three sights.

Be sure to find out whether any concerts are being given in the garden of the Venetian Museum while you are on Naxos. You can ask at the museum, or at the Naxos Tourist Information Center, or keep an eye out for posters. If there is a concert, you may get to spend a pleasant evening listening to Greek music, a string quartet, or some jazz. Whatever you hear, the setting could not be nicer. Horá. Archaeological Museum. ℂ **22850/22-387.** Admission 6€. Daily 10am–3pm. Venetian Museum. ℂ **22850/22-725.** Admission 2€. Tues–Sun 8am–2:30pm. Venetian Museum. ℂ **22850/22-387.** Admission 6€. Tues–Sun 8am–2:30pm.

**Mitropolis Site Museum** This innovative new museum, located in the square facing Naxos town's Mitropolis Cathedral, preserves the open space of the square while providing access to the excavated archaeological site below. Excavations undertaken from 1982 to 1985 revealed a history of continuous occupation from Mycenaean times to the present, with significant remains of a classical shrine to the founders of the city buried beneath the remains of the Roman city. The museum, a single subterranean room circled by a suspended walkway, is sited inconspicuously beneath the surface of the square. You'll probably want to spend no more than half an hour.

Hora. © 22850/24-151. Free admission. Tues–Sun 8am–2:30pm. Turn in from the paralia at Zas Travel, and continue about 100m (328 ft.) until you see the Mitropolis Cathedral Square on your right.

**The Portara**  Naxos harbor is dominated by the picturesque silhouette of the Portara (Great Door) on the islet of Palatia, accessible by a causeway off the northern tip of the harbor. The massive door is all that remains of an obviously enormous Temple of Apollo. In fact, this 6th century B.C. temple was intended to be so huge that it was never finished. The temple was once thought to honor Dionysos, the island's patron, and is associated in the popular imagination with his rescue of Ariadne after she was abandoned on Naxos by the ungrateful Theseus. Most scholars think that the temple was in fact dedicated to Apollo, in part because of a brief reference in the Delian Hymns and in part because it directly faces Delos, Apollo's birthplace. Over the centuries, most of the temple was carted away to build other monuments and buildings, including Naxos's Venetian Kastro. Fortunately the massive posts and lintel of the Portara were too heavy—each of the four surviving blocks in the gates weighs about 20 tons—for the Venetians to handle.

When the midday sun is blazing, the causeway by the Portara, is not a place to linger. But at sunset, **Palatia**, the small café/ouzeri at the end of the causeway, below the Portara, is a superb spot to watch the sunset.

Hora. Open site.

**Sangri and the Temple of Demeter**  Until recently, the temple, built in the 6th century B.C., was in a state of complete ruin; it had been partially dismantled in the 6th century A.D. to build a chapel on the site, and what was left was plundered repeatedly over the years. A few years ago, it was discovered that virtually all the pieces of the original temple were on the site, either buried or integrated into the chapel. Then began a long process of reconstruction, which continues at present. Most of the work has been completed, and it's possible to see the basic form of the temple—one of the few known temples to be square in plan. Although work continues, the site is open to the public and free.

Temple of Demeter at Ano Sangri. Depart from Hora on the road to Filoti, and turn off after about 10km (6 miles) on the signposted road to Ano Sangri and the Temple of Demeter. From here it's another 3.5km (2 miles) to the temple, primarily on dirt roads (all the major turnings are signposted).

## BYZANTINE CHURCHES

There is a remarkable number of small Byzantine chapels on Naxos, most dating from the 9th to the 15th centuries, many in or near some of the island's loveliest villages (see Villages, below). The prosperity of Naxos during this period of Byzantine and Venetian rule meant that sponsorship existed for elaborate frescoes, many of which can still be seen on the interior walls of the chapels. Restoration has revealed multiple layers of frescoes, and whenever possible the more recent ones have been removed intact during the process of revealing the initial paintings. Several frescoes removed in this way from the churches of Naxos can be seen at the Byzantine Museum in Athens. Anyone with a particular interest in these churches (of which we mention only a few) would enjoy Paul Hetherington's *The Greek Islands: Guide to the Byzantine and Medieval Buildings and their Art.*

Just south of Moni, near the middle of the island, is the important 6th-century monastery of **Panayia Drossiani** (★) (Our Lady of Refreshment), which contains some of the finest (and oldest, dating from the 7th century) frescoes on Naxos. The icon of the Virgin is credited with ending a severe drought on the island shortly after the frescoes were painted. The church is all that survives of what we are told was an extensive monastery—what an appealing place to have led a contemplative life! Visits are allowed at all hours during the day; when the door is locked, ring the church bell to summon the caretaker (remember to dress appropriately). To get here, drive about 1km (½ mile) south from Moni and look for the low, gray rounded form of the church on your left.

About 8km (5 miles) from Hora along the road to Sangri, you'll see a sign on the left for the 8th-century Byzantine cathedral of **Ayios Mamas**, which fell into disrepair during the Venetian occupation but has recently been partly restored. The **view** alone from this charming church *vaut le voyage.* Sangri (the Greek contraction of Sainte Croix) today is made up of three villages, and has the ruins of a medieval castle. The church of Ayios Nikolaos, which dates to the 13th century, has well-preserved frescoes, with a lovely figure of the personified River Jordan. To see them, ask around to see what villager has the keys.

About 1km (½ mile) west of Sangri on the road to Halki is the **Kaloritsa Chapel** (★), a cave inside the hilltop ruins of a Byzantine chapel. The earliest of the frescoes seen here date from the 10th century. The chapel is accessible only on foot; for directions, see "Walking," below.

You could cheerfully spend a week seeing the Byzantine churches of Naxos; you can see a handful in a day. Getting to each one involves at least some walking, and some time in finding the caretaker to see the interiors. Alas, these churches are kept locked, due to increasing problems with theft, although the caretaker often makes an early morning or early evening visit.

## THE VILLAGES

There are many small villages within the folds of Naxos's hills and many of the nicest are in the lush **Tragaea Valley** (★) in the center of the island. Each is unique, and you could easily spend several days exploring them. The bus between Hora and Apollonas makes stops at each of the villages mentioned below, but you'll have considerably more freedom if you rent a car.

**Halki,** 16km (10 miles) from Hora, has a lovely central square shaded by a magnificent plane tree. The 19th-century neoclassical homes of this town lend the streets a certain grandeur. The fine 11th-century white church with the red-tiled roof, **Panayia Protothronos** (Our Lady Before the Throne), is sometimes open in the morning. Turn right to reach the Frankopoulos (or Grazia) tower. The name says it's Frankish, but it was originally Byzantine; a marble crest gives the year of 1742, when it was renovated by the Venetians. Climb the steps for an excellent view of Filoti, one of the island's largest inland villages.

The brilliant white houses of **Filoti,** 2km (1¼ miles) up the road from Halki, are draped elegantly along the lower slopes of **Mount Zas,** the highest peak in the Cyclades. The center of town life is the main square, shaded by a massive plane tree; the kafenion at the center of the square and two tavernas within 50m (164 ft.) are all authentic and welcoming. In the center of town is the church of **Kimisis tis Theotokou** (Assumption of the Mother of God), with a lovely marble iconostasis and a Venetian tower.

**Apiranthos** (★), 10km (6 miles) beyond Filoti, the most enchanting of the mountain villages, is remarkable in that its buildings, streets, and even domestic

---

**Tips** **Remember the Repellent**

Note that both Ayios Prokopios and Ayia Anna have a mosquito problem in the summer due to several stagnant ponds behind the beach that serve as breeding grounds.

---

walls are built of the brilliant white Naxos marble. The people of Apiranthos were originally from Crete, and fled their home during a time of Turkish oppression. Be sure to visit **Taverna Lefteris,** the excellent café/restaurant just off the main square (see "Where to Dine," below).

**Apollonas,** at the northern tip of the island, is a small fishing village on the verge of becoming a rather depressing resort. It has a sand cove, a pebbled beach, plenty of places to eat, rooms to let, and a few hotels. From the town, you can drive or take the path that leads about 1km (½ mile) south to the famous **kouros** (a monumental statue of a nude young man). The kouros, some 10m (33 ft.) tall, was begun in the 7th century B.C. and abandoned probably because of the fissures that time and the elements have exacerbated. Some archaeologists believe it was meant for the nearby temple of Apollo, but the beard suggests that it's probably the island's patron deity, Dionysos. When you visit the National Museum in Athens, you can see a number of statues of successfully completed kouroi.

## BEACHES

Naxos has the longest and some of the best beaches in the Cyclades, although you wouldn't know it looking at the crowded **Ayios Yioryios** beach just south of Hora. The next beach south is **Ayios Prokopios,** around the headland of Stel-lida. This fine-sand beach is less crowded at its northern end. **Ayia Anna,** the next cove south, is much smaller, with a small port for the colorful caiques that transport beachgoers from the main port. Both Ayios Prokopios and Ayia Anna are accessible by public bus in the summer.

South of Ayia Anna you'll find **Plaka Beach** ✦, the best on the island, a 5km (3-mile) stretch of almost uninhabited shoreline; you can reach it by walking south from Ayia Anna. Further south, 16km (10 miles) from Hora, are **Micri Vigla,** known for its windsurfing center, and **Kastraki Beach,** with waters rated the cleanest in the Aegean several years ago and a 7km (4½-mile) stretch of beach; both remain relatively uncrowded, even in peak season. Further still, 21km (13 miles) from Hora, **Pyrgaki,** the last stop on the coastal bus route, offers excellent swimming in the large protected bay. The 150m (492 ft.) of sand and cobble beach in the sheltered cove of **Abrami,** about 6km (4 miles) past the beach resort of **Apollonas** at the north end of the island, is secluded and uncrowded. It's 500m (1,640 ft.) in from the main road on a rough one-lane dirt track.

## WALKING

If you're going to spend some time on the island, we recommend buying a copy of Christian Ucke's excellent guide *Walking Tours on Naxos.* Most of the start and finish points for the walks can be reached by island bus. It's available for 15€ at **Naxos Tourist Information Center** on the paralia. As with all the Cyclades, you should also go equipped with a map and a good sense of direction (and, to be on the safe side, a compass).

One fascinating Naxos site that can only be reached on foot is **Kaloritsa Chapel** ✦, near the town of Ano Sangri. Inside the ruins of this Byzantine Church is a cave containing an iconostasis and some fine 13th-century frescoes—it's best seen in the late afternoon, when the low sun illuminates the cave's interior. You can take the bus to Ano Sangri and walk from there, or you can drive—200m (656 ft.) past Ano Sangri on the road to Filoti, there's a fork to the right at a JetOil station, signposted for Kaloritsa. Another 200m (656 ft.) brings you to the striking **Pirgos Timios Stavros**, park just past this medieval tower, where another sign for Kaloritsa points up the side of the hill. Look up the hill in the direction of the sign, and you'll see the ruined remains of the Kaloritsa Chapel about halfway up. There isn't a trail, but there are some goat paths that make the going easier. Make your way to a low stone wall that climbs in the direction of the chapel—there's a path along its base that goes most of the way. The cave itself is blocked off, but you can get a good view of the interior from above; binoculars are helpful for making out the details of the icons and frescoes inside.

## SHOPPING

Hora is a fine place for shopping, both for value and variety. **Zoom** (© 22850/23-675) on the waterfront is the place to head for books and magazines; there's a good selection of books on the island itself. To the right and up from the entrance to the Old Market is **Techni** ★ (© 22850/24-767), which has two shops within 20m (66 ft.) of each other. The first shop contains a good array of silver jewelry at fair prices; above it the second and more interesting of the two has textiles, many handwoven, and some by local women. Many are from earlier in the century, when the traditions of weaving and embroidery were still flourishing. There are also hand-painted copies of icons made at Mount Athos.

On the paralia next to Grotta Tours is tiny **Galini** (© 22850/24-785), with a collection of local ceramics. Continue south along the paralia to the OTE, turn left on the main inland street, Papavasiliou, and continue up the left side of the street until your nose leads you into the **Tirokomika Proionda Naxou** (© 22850/22-230). This delightful old store is filled with excellent local cheeses (*kephalotiri*, a superb sharp one, and milder *graviera*), barrels of olives, local wines, honey, spices, and other dried comestibles. It's also a good place to pick up a bottle of *kitron*, the island's famous sweet citron liqueur.

In the Kastro itself, **Antico Veneziano** ★ (© 22850/26-206) has just that, antiques from the island's Venetian period—and glassware, wood carvings, and old weavings from throughout Greece. This is a lovely place to browse in, as it occupies one of the handsome Venetian-period houses.

In the interior of Naxos, on the stretch of road between Sangri and Halki, you'll see a sign pointing toward the **Damalas Pottery Workshop** (© 22850/32-890); 200m (656 ft.) along this one-lane road brings you to the small workshop, operated by a father-and-son team. The father learned his trade on Sifnos, an island renowned for its pottery, and now father and son produce a variety of forms, some of them specific to Naxos.

In Apiranthos, some local weaving and needlework is sold by the village women. **Stiasto** (© 22850/61-392) has a good selection of popular art, including good ceramics.

## WHERE TO STAY

Hora's broad paralia is too busy for quiet accommodations, so we recommend hotels in nearby areas, all within a 10-minute walk of the Kastro: Bourgo, the old section of town just above the harbor below the Kastro; Grotta, a development of newer houses left (north) and up from the port; behind the town; and Ayios Yioryios, a beach resort just south (right from the harbor) of town.

## BOURGO

**Apollon** What more appropriate spot to stay, on an island famous for its marble, than in a former marble workshop—one that has a quiet location, and has been nicely converted into a small hotel. The rooms have balconies (always a big plus) and are simply, but tastefully, furnished. Although there is no garden to speak of, there are lots of plants everywhere. In short, a welcome and welcoming spot to stay in Naxos town—just behind the imposing Orthodox Cathedral.

Fontana, Hora, 84300 Naxos. © 22850/22-468. 12 units. 80€–100€ double. Rates include breakfast. No credit cards. Closed Nov–Mar. **Amenities:** Breakfast room/bar. *In room:* A/C.

**Chateau Zevgoli** ★ This small hotel, easily the most attractive in Naxos, is located at the foot of the Kastro walls. The lobby/dining area has been charmingly decorated with antiques and family heirlooms by the gracious owner, Despina Kitini. All guest rooms open onto a central atrium with a lush garden. The units are small but distinctively furnished; room 8 features a canopy bed and a private terrace, and several units have views of the harbor. For those interested in an experience of medieval grandeur, Despina Kitini also has four apartments in a 12th-century house in the Kastro, just 100m (328 ft.) from the hotel. These share a magisterial sitting room, stone walls and floors, and appropriately antiquated and austere furnishings. The bedrooms here are simple and unremarkable, with the exception of the honeymoon suite, which has a balcony overlooking the town and the sea.

Bourgo, Hora, Naxos. © 22850/22-993 or 22850/26-123. Fax 22850/25-200. www.greekhotel.net/cyclades/naxos/chora/zevgoli. 14 units. 80€–100€ double. Hotel rates include breakfast. AE, MC, V. Closed Nov–Mar. **Amenities:** Breakfast room/bar. *In room:* A/C.

**Hotel Anixis** This simple hotel near the Kastro's Venetian tower offers comfortable accommodations in a desirable old neighborhood of Hora. Located on a narrow pedestrian street, the entrance leads through a small walled garden to a terrace overlooking town and sea. The friendly manager, Dimitris Sideris, knows the island well, so be sure to ask him about excursions to uncrowded beaches, Byzantine chapels, and ancient sites. The rooms on the top floor have the best view of the sea, and six of them have their own small balcony. The breakfast terrace enjoys a splendid sea view. If you make advance arrangements, Dimitris will meet you at the port and drive you to the base of the hill—you'll still have to walk the last 100m (328 ft.) up to the hotel!

Bourgo, Hora, 84300 Naxos. © 22850/22-932 or 22850/22-782 in winter. Fax 22850/22-112. 19 units. 70€ double. Continental breakfast 5€ extra. V. Closed Oct–Mar. From the bus station, take the nearest major street (with traffic) off the port and turn right through the lancet archway into the Old Market area; follow the stenciled blue arrows to the hotel. **Amenities:** Breakfast room/bar. *In room:* A/C.

## AYIOS YIORYIOS

If the following choices are booked, you can try the unexciting but reliable **Galaxy Hotel**, 75m (246 ft.) from the beach at Ayios Yioryios (© **22850/22-422** or 22850/22-423; fax 22850/22-889); some rooms have balconies or terraces facing the water.

**Hotels Galini and Sofia** ★ The hotels Galini and Sofia share the same building, the same friendly management, and the same sea views. In fact, they represent the curious phenomenon of one hotel with two names. There are some differences: The Sofia's bedrooms are decorated in bright pastels, while those in the Galini are a more conservative white. All but two unfortunate units on the interior courtyard have balconies with excellent sea views; the view from rooms 11 and 14 is especially good. The hotels are both run by the charming Sofia and her amiable son George. Guests are free to send and receive e-mail (in moderation) from the hotel computer. Transportation is provided to and from the port if you make arrangements in advance. There's a small playground for children.

Ayios Yioryios, Hora, 84300 Naxos. © 22850/22-516 or 22850/22-114. Fax 22850/22-677. www.naxos-island.com/hotels/galini. 30 units. 80€ double. Breakfast 4.30€ extra. AE, V. Closed Nov–Mar. **Amenities:** Breakfast room/bar; pool. *In room:* A/C, TV.

## OUT ON THE ISLAND

The charms of Hora are such that there's no place, or places, away from Hora that we'd recommend over the places in and just out of Hora itself. If you do want to head out on the island, check out **Orkos Village Hotel** ✯ (© 22850/75-321; www.orkos-naxos.com) a 28-unit apartment complex (most in bungalows) constructed to suggest a small Cycladic village. Many units have sleeping lofts; all have fully equipped kitchenettes and balconies. Run by a Hellenophile Norwegian, the hotel has its own excellent restaurant—and a small library—and is only 100m (328 ft.) from the beach. No wonder that many guests return here year after year. Doubles from 80€.

## WHERE TO DINE
### HORA

**The Bakery,** on the paralia (© 22850/22-613), has baked goods at fair prices. Further north, across from the bus station, **Bikini** (© 22850/24-701) is a good place for breakfast and crepes. **Meltemi** (© 22850/22-654) and **Apolafsis** (© 22850/22-178) on the waterfront both offer all the Greek staples; Apolafsis also has live music many nights in summer.

**Nikos** GREEK   This is one of the most popular restaurants in town. The owner, Nikos Katsayannis, is himself a fisherman, and the range of seafood available will amaze you. It's all pretty good, and those not in the mood for fish can try the *eksohiko*, fresh lamb and vegetables with fragrant spices wrapped in crisp filo (pastry leaves). The wine list is quite long, with lots of local and Cyclades choices. The ice-cream desserts are also delightful.

Paralia, above the Commercial Bank. © 22850/23-153. Main courses 6€–14€; fish by the kilo. MC, V. Daily 8am–1am.

**The Old Inn** ✯   INTERNATIONAL   Dieter Ranizewski, who operated for many years the popular Faros Restaurant on the paralia, now runs this place. The courtyard offers a green haven from the noise and crowds of the paralia. The restaurant inhabits several buildings around the courtyard, once a small monastery, and the wine cellar is situated in a former chapel. Another vaulted room houses an eclectic collection of old objects from the island and from Dieter's native Berlin. The Germanic menu (this is one of relatively few places in the Cyclades where you can get jellied or smoked pork) offers an alternative to standard taverna fare, and the food is simple, hearty, and abundant.

100m (328 ft.) in from the port. © 22850/26-093. Main courses 5€–15€. AE, DC, MC, V. Daily 6pm–2am.

**Taverna To Kastro** GREEK   Just outside the Kastro's south gate you'll find the small Braduna Square, which is packed with tables on summer evenings. There's an excellent view toward the bay and St. George's beach, and at dusk a pacifying calm pervades the place. The specialty here is rabbit stewed in red wine with onions, spiced with pepper and a suggestion of cinnamon. The local wines are light and delicious.

Braduna Sq. © 22850/22-005. Main courses 5€–12€. No credit cards. Daily 7pm–2am.

## APIRANTHOS

**Taverna Lefteris ★ GREEK**   Find your way to Apiranthos, perhaps the most beautiful town in Naxos, where you'll find one of the island's best restaurants. The small menu features the staples of Greek cooking, prepared in a way that reminds you how good this food can be. The dishes highlight the freshest of vegetables and meats, prepared with admirable subtlety; the hearty homemade bread is delicious. A cozy marble-floored room faces the street, and in back is a flagstone terrace shaded by two massive trees. The homemade sweets are an exception to the rule that you should avoid dessert in tavernas—it's worth making the trip for the sweets alone.

Apiranthos. © 22850/61-333. Main courses 4.30€–9€. No credit cards. Daily 11am–11pm.

## NAXOS AFTER DARK

Naxos certainly doesn't compare to Mykonos or Santorini for wild nightlife, but it has a lively and varied scene. **Portara**, just below its namesake at the far end of the harbor, is an excellent place to enjoy the sunset. Next, you can join the evening **volta** (stroll) along the paralia. **Fragile** (© **22850/25-336**), through the arch in the entrance to the Old Town, is one of the older bars in town and worth a stop. Up in the Kastro, **Notos** offers a sedate evening with mellow jazz.

**Day and Night**, opposite the OTE, has a good blend of music which becomes more purely Greek in the early morning. At the end of the waterfront past the National Bank, you'll find **Vengera** (© **22850/23-567**), which doesn't open until 9pm and doesn't get warmed up until much later; it plays mostly '70s and '80s rock. Its neighbor, **Cream** (who thinks up these names??) (no phone) tries to break existing island records for high decibel levels. **Naxos By Night**, on the way to the beach from Protodikiou Square, has bouzouki music and dancing.

177km (96 nautical miles) SE of Piraeus

If you haven't been to Mykonos (pop. 15,000) for a number of years, you'll probably wander around muttering "ruined" when you arrive. Then you'll realize that once you're away from the shops, bars, and restaurants along the harbor, you're pleasantly surprised at how familiar many of the twisting back streets seem. You might even admit that it's not half bad to have such a wide choice of restaurants, shops, and bars. If this is your first visit, you'll find lots to enjoy—especially if you avoid July and August, when it seems that every one of the island's 800,000 annual visitors is here.

What makes this small (about 16km/10 miles long), arid island so popular? At least initially, it was the exceptionally handsome Cycladic architecture–and the fact that many on the poor island were more than eager to rent their houses to visitors. First came the jet-setters, artists, and expatriates (including many sophisticated gay visitors), as well as the mainland Greeks who opened many of the chic shops and restaurants–all followed by a curious mixture of jet-set wannabes and backpackers. Now, with cruise ships lined up in the harbor all summer and as many as 10 flights each day from Athens, it's easier to say who doesn't come to Mykonos than who does. During high season (July and Aug), the overcrowding is truly overwhelming. The best way to avoid the crowds is to get up early, visit the beaches before noon, and explore the streets of Hora in the late afternoon, when almost everyone in town wakes up and heads for the beach. (Mykonos is one of the only islands in the Aegean where scuba diving is permitted, and there are several dive centers that rent equipment and offer instruction.)

It's **very** important not to arrive here without reservations in the high season, unless you enjoy sleeping outdoors–and don't mind being moved from your sleeping spot by the police, who are not always charmed to find foreigners alfresco.

If you come here in September or October, you'll find a quieter Mykonos, with a pleasant buzz of activity, but less clogged streets and restaurants. Unlike many of the islands, Mykonos remains active year-round, and in winter hosts numerous cultural events, including a small film festival. Many who are scared off by the summer crowds find a different, tranquil Mykonos during this off season, drawn by the deserved reputation of Hora as one of the most beautiful towns in the Cyclades.

## ESSENTIALS

**GETTING THERE   By Plane**   Olympic Airways (© 210/966-6666 or 210/936-9111; www.olympic-airways.gr) has several flights daily (once daily in off season) between Mykonos and Athens, and one flight daily from Mykonos to Iraklion (Crete) and Santorini. Book flights in advance and reconfirm with Olympic in Athens or on Mykonos (© 22890/22-490 or 22890/22-237). The Mykonos office is near the south bus station; open Monday through Friday from 8am to 3:30pm. There are also several travel agencies on the port that sell Olympic tickets. **Aegean Airlines** (© 210/998-8300 or 210/998-2888; www.aegeanair.com) has initiated service to Myconos, daily in summer.

**By Boat**   From Piraeus, **Ventouris Lines** (© 210/482-5815; 210/482-8001) has departures at least once daily, usually at 8am, with a second on summer afternoons. From Rafina, **Strintzis Lines** has daily ferry service; schedules can be checked with the Port Police (© 22890/22-218). There's daily ferry connections between Mykonos and Andros, Paros, Syros, and Tinos; five to seven trips a week to Ios; four a week to Iraklio, Crete; several a week to Kos and Rhodes; and two a week to Ikaria, Samos, Skiathos, Skyros, and Thessaloniki. **Hellas Flying Dolphins** offers service from **Piraeus** (© 210/419-9100; 210/419-9000; booking@nfd.gr) in summer.

On Mykonos, your best bet for getting boat information is to check at individual agents, or to see if either the **port authority** (© 22890/22-218) (by National Bank), **tourist police** (© 22890/22-482) at the north end of the harbor, or the **tourist office** (© 22890/23-990; fax 22890/22-229), also on the harbor, has an up-to-date list of sailings.

Hydrofoil service to Crete, Ios, Paros, and Santorini is often irregular. For information, check at the **Port Authority** in Piraeus (© 210/451-1311 or 210/422-6000; phone seldom answered), Rafina (© 22940/23-300), or Mykonos (© 22890/22-218).

*Warning:* Check each travel agent's current schedule because most ferry tickets are not interchangeable. Reputable agents on the main square in Mykonos (Hora) town include: **Delia Travel** (© 22890/22-490; fax 22890/24-440), **Sea & Sky Travel** (© 22890/22-853; fax 22890/24-753), and the **Veronis Agency** (© 22890/22-687; fax 22890/23-763).

**VISITOR INFORMATION**   The **Mykonos Accommodations Center,** at the corner of Enoplon Dhinameon and Malamatenias (© 22890/23-160; mac@mac.myk.forthnet.gr), as its name implies, helps visitors find accommodations. It also functions as a tourist information center. **Windmills Travel** (© 22890/23-877; www.windmills-travel.com) has an office at Fabrica Square where you can get general information, book accommodations, arrange excursions, and rent a car or

Aylou Stefanou

North Bus Station

Archaeological Museum

Polikandhioti

Beach

Harbor

Island Ferries

Boats to Delos

Tourist Police

Folklore Museum

Panayia Paraportiani Church

LITTLE VENICE

Aegean Sea

Al Mavroyenous

Drakopoulou

Ayion Anaryiron

Beach

Windmills

Ayion Ioannou

To Ano Mera

Taxi Square (Plateia Mantos Mavroyenous)

Delia Travel (American Express)

Matoyianni

Mikonos Accommodations Center

Maritime Museum

Kaloyera

Enoplon Dinameon

Cathedral (Mitropolis)

Mitropoleos

Rohari

Plateia Tria Pigadia

Plateia Laka

Olympic Airways

South Bus Station

Ipirou

Xenias

Ayiou Ioannou

To Ornos

Greece

Aegean Sea

Mykonos Town

The Cyclades

Athens

Mediterranean Sea

387

OTE

Post Office

Rest Rooms

moped. Look for the free *Mykonos Summertime* magazine, available in cafes, shops, and hotels throughout the island.

**GETTING AROUND**　One of the best things to happen to Mykonos was the government decree that made Hora an architectural landmark and prohibited motorized traffic from its streets. You will see a few small delivery vehicles, but the only way to get around town is to walk. There is a busy peripheral road along which many of the town's large hotels are found, and much of the rest of the island is served by a good transportation system.

**By Bus**　Mykonos has one of the best bus systems in the Greek islands; the buses run frequently and on schedule. Depending on your destination, a ticket costs about .50€ to 3.50€ There're two bus stations in Hora: one near the archaeological museum and one near the Olympic Airways office (follow the helpful blue signs). Check at the tourist office to see which station the bus you want leaves from or look for one of the schedules sometimes available in hotels. Bus information in English is sometimes available from the **KTEL** office (© **22890/23-360**).

**By Boat**　Caïques to Super Paradise, Agrari, and Elia depart from Platis Yialos every morning, weather permitting; there is also service from Ornos in high season (July and Aug) only. Caïque service is highly seasonal, with almost continuous service in high season and no caïques from October through May. Excursion boats to Delos depart Tuesday through Sunday between 8:30am and 1pm, from the west side of the harbor near the tourist office. (For more information, see a travel agent; guided tours are available.)

**By Car & Moped**　Rental cars are available from about 60€ per day, including insurance, in high season; most agencies are near one of the two bus stops in town. One reliable shop is **Apollon** (© **22890/24-136**), with offices at the south bus station, the airport, and at Ornos Beach. The largest concentration of moped shops is just beyond the south bus station. Expect to pay about 15€ to 30€ a day, depending on engine size. Take great care when driving: The roads on the island can be treacherous.

*Warning* If you park in town or in a no-parking area, the police will remove your license plates, and you—not the rental office—will have to find the police station and pay a steep fine to get them back.

**By Taxi**　There are two types of taxis in Mykonos: standard **car taxis** for destinations outside town, and tiny **scooters with a car in tow** that buzz through the narrow streets of Hora. The latter are seen primarily at the port, where they wait to bring new arrivals to their lodgings in town—a good idea, since most in-town hotels are a challenge to find. Getting a car taxi in Hora is easy: Walk to Taxi (Mavro) Square, near the statue, and join the line. A notice board gives rates for various destinations. You can also call © **22890/22-400.** For late hours and out-of-town service, call © **22890/23-700.**

**FAST FACTS**　The **Commercial Bank** and **National Bank of Greece** are on the harbor a couple blocks west of Taxi Square; both open Monday through Friday from 8am to 2pm. ATMs are available throughout town. The **Mykonos Health Center** (© **22890/23-994** or 22890/23-996) handles routine medical complaints; serious cases are usually airlifted to the mainland. The **tourist police** (© **22890/22-482**) are on the west side of the port near the ferries to Delos; the local **police** (© **22890/22-235**) are behind the grammar school, near Platia Laka. The **post office** (© **22890/22-238**) is next to the police station; open Monday through Friday from 7:30am to 2pm. The **telephone office (OTE)** is on the north side of the harbor beyond the Hotel Leto (© 22890/22-499), open Monday through Friday 7:30am to 3pm. **Ace Laundry** (© 22890/28-389) is on Ayios Efthimiou, 100m (328 ft.) toward the port from the south bus station. **Internet** access is expensive here: The **Mykonos Cyber Café**, 26 M. Axioti, on the road between the south bus station and the windmills (© 22890/27-684), is usually open daily 9am to 10pm and charges 15€ per hour or 4€ for 15 minutes. **Angelo's Internet Café**, on the same road, (© 22890/24-106) may have lower rates.

## WHAT TO SEE & DO
## BEACHES

The beaches on the **south shore** of the island have the best sand, views, and wind protection, but these days are so popular that you'll have to negotiate a forest of beach umbrellas to find your square meter of sand. A few (**Paradise, Super Paradise**) are known as party beaches, and guarantee throbbing music and loud revelry until late at night. Others (**Platis Yialos, Psarou, Ornos**) are quieter and more popular with families. With all the south coast beaches, keep in mind that most people begin to arrive in the early afternoon, and you can avoid the worst of the crowds by going in the morning. The **north coast beaches** are less developed but just as beautiful. Since the buses and caïques don't yet make the trip, you'll have to rent a car or scooter; you'll be more than compensated for the trouble by the quiet and lack of commercial development.

**Megali Ammos** (Big Sand), about a 10-minute walk south—it's very crowded and not particularly scenic. The nearest to the north is 2km (1¼ miles) away at **Tourlos**, where a new cruise-ship pier was recently completed. **Ornos**, about 2.5km (1½ miles) south of town, has a fine-sand beach in a sheltered bay with extensive hotel development along the shore; buses run hourly from the south station between 8am and 11pm. This beach is popular with families.

**Platis Yialos** is the best first stop: Although the beach is unexceptional and likely to be extremely crowded, from here you can catch a caïque to the more distant beaches of Paradise, Super Paradise, Agrari, and Elia. The bus runs every 15 minutes from 8am to 8pm, then every 30 minutes until midnight. Nearby **Psarou** is less overwhelmed by resort hotels and has a lovely pale-sand beach that remains reasonably uncrowded except in high season. Its watersports facilities include the **Diving Center Psarou**, waterskiing, and windsurfing. **Paranga**, further east, can be reached easily on foot via an inland path from Platis Yialos; this small cove is popular with nudists, and usually isn't too crowded.

### Beach Notes

Activity on the beaches is highly seasonal, and all the information offered here pertains only to the months of June through September. The prevailing winds on Mykonos (and throughout the Cyclades) blow from the north, which is why the southern beaches are the most protected and calm. The exception to this rule is a weather pattern with southern winds that occurs periodically during the summer months, making the northern beaches more desirable for sunning and swimming. In Mykonos town, this southern wind is heralded by particularly hot temperatures and perfect calm in the harbor. On such days, those in the know will avoid Paradise, Super Paradise, and Elia, heading instead to the northern beaches of Ayios Sostis and Panormos.

**Paradise** ★, the island's most famous beach, is accessible by footpath from Platis Yialos (about 2km/1¼ miles), by bus, or by caïque. This was the original nude beach of the island, and still attracts many nudists. A stand of small trees provides some shade, and it's well protected from the predominant north winds. Several bars line the waterfront and pump out loud music throughout the day and night.

**Super Paradise** (Plindri) is in a rocky cove just around the headland from Paradise; it's somewhat less developed than its neighbor, but no less crowded. The beach is accessible on foot, by bus, and by caïque; if you go by car or moped, be very careful on the extremely steep and narrow access road. The left side of the beach is a nonstop party in summer, with loud music and dancing, while the right side is mostly nude and gay, with the exclusive Coco Club providing a relaxed ambience for its chic clientele. Further east across the little peninsula is **Agrari**, a lovely cove sheltered by lush foliage, with all states of dress common and a good little taverna.

**Elia**, a 45-minute caïque ride from Platis Yialos and the last regular stop, is a sand-and-pebble beach with crowds nearly as overwhelming as at Paradise and minimal shade. Nevertheless, this is a beautiful beach, and one of the longest on the island. It's also accessible by bus. The next major beach is **Kalo Livadi** (Good Pasture). In a farming valley, this long, beautiful beach is accessible by a scramble over the peninsula east from Elia and by bus from the north station. There's a taverna and a few villas and hotels in the hills adjacent to the beach.

The last resort area on the southern coast accessible by bus from the north station is at **Kalafatis** ★. This fishing village was once the port of the ancient citadel of Mykonos, which dominated the little peninsula to the west. A line of trees separates the beach from the rows of buildings which have grown up along the road. This is one of the longest beaches on Mykonos, and less crowded than its neighbors to the west. Adjacent to Kalafatis in a tiny cove is lovely **Ayia Anna**, a short stretch of sand with a score of umbrellas. Several kilometers further east, accessible by a fairly good road from Kalafatis, is **Lia**, which has fine sand, clear water, bamboo wind breaks, and a small taverna.

Most of the north coast beaches are too windy to be of interest to anyone other than windsurfers—the long fine-sand beach at **Ftelia** would be one of the best on the island if it didn't receive the unbroken force of the north wind. There are, however, two well-sheltered northern beaches, and because you can only reach them by car or moped, they're much less crowded than the southern beaches. Head east from Mykonos town on the road to Ano Mera, turning left after 1.5km (1 mile) on the road to Ayios Sostis and Panormos. At **Panormos**, you'll find a cove with 100m (328 ft.) of fine sand backed by low dunes. Another 1km (¾ mile) down the road is **Ayios Sostis** ★, a lovely small beach just below a village. There isn't any parking, so it's best to leave your vehicle along the main road and walk 200m (656 ft.) down through the village. There's an excellent small taverna just up from the beach that operates without electricity, so it's open only during daylight hours. Both Panormos and Ayios Sostis have few amenities—no beach umbrellas, bars, or snack shops—but they do offer a break from the crowds.

Beaches to avoid on Mykonos because of pollution, noise, and crowds, include **Tourlos** and **Korfos Bay.**

With so many sun-worshippers on Myconos, local merchants have figured out that they can charge pretty steep prices for suntan lotions and sunscreens. You might want to bring some with you. If you want to try a Greek brand, the oddly-named Carrot Milk is excellent.

## DIVING

Mykonos is known throughout the Aegean as a place for diving—it's one of the few islands where this sport hasn't been forbidden to protect undersea archaeological treasures from plunder. The best month is September, when the water temperature is typically 24°C (75°F) and visibility is 30m (98 ft.). Certified divers can rent equipment and participate in guided dives; first-time divers can rent snorkeling gear or take an introductory beach dive. The best established dive center on the island is **Mykonos Diving Centre**, at Psarou Beach (€ and fax **22890/24-808;** prodive@otenet.gr), which offers 5 day PADI certification courses in English for about 500€ (including equipment). Certified divers can join guided dives for 50€ per dive; beginners can take a 2-hour class and beach dive for 60€. There's a nearby wreck at a depth of 20m to 35m (66 miles–98 miles), and wreck dives are offered for 60€. Other diving centers offering lessons and equipment rental include **Dive Adventures**, on Paradise Beach (€ and fax **22890/26-539**) and **Psarou Diving Center** in Mykonos town (€ **22890/ 24-808**). As always, before you sign up for lessons, be sure that all instructors are PADI certified.

## ATTRACTIONS

Getting lost in the labyrinthine alleys of Hora is an essential element of every Mykonian holiday. Searching for the right bar, a good place to eat, or your hotel is sure to be twice as difficult as you'd expect and twice as enjoyable. Despite its intense commercialism and seething crowds in high season, Hora is still the quintessential Cycladic town, and is worth a visit to the island in itself.

The best way to see the town is to simply venture inland from the port and wander. Just keep in mind that the town is bounded on two sides by the bay, and on the other two by the busy vehicular District Road, and that all paths funnel eventually into one of the few main squares: **Plateia Mantos Mavroyenous,** on the port (called **Taxi Square** because it's the main taxi stand); **Plateia Tria Pigadia;** and **Plateia Laka,** near the south bus station.

Hora also has the remains of a small **Venetian Kastro** (fortress) and the island's most famous church, the **Panagia Paraportiani** (Our Lady of the Postern Gate), a thickly whitewashed asymmetrical edifice made up of four small chapels. Beyond the Panagia Paraportiani is the **Alefkandra** quarter, better known as Little Venice ★★, for its cluster of homes built overhanging the sea. Many buildings here have been converted into fashionable bars prized for their sunset views; you can sip a margarita and listen to Mozart most nights at the Montparnasse or Kastro bar (see "Mykonos After Dark," later in this chapter).

Another nearby watering spot is at the famous **Tria Pigadia (Three Wells) ★★**. Local legend says that if a virgin drinks from all three she is sure to find a husband, but it's probably not a good idea to test this hypothesis by drinking the brackish well water. After you visit the Tria Pigadia, you may want to take in the famous **windmills** of **Kato Myli** and enjoy the views back toward Little Venice.

You may not have come here for the museums, but save some time to visit the island's clutch of pleasant little museums. **The Archaeological Museum** (© **22890/22-325**), near the harbor, has finds from Delos; it's open Monday and Wednesday to Saturday 9am to 3:30pm, Sunday and holidays 10am to 3pm. Admission is 3€; free on Sunday. The **Nautical Museum of the Aegean** (© **22890/22-700**), across from the park on Enoplon Dinameon Street, has just what you'd expect, including some handsome ship models. It's open daily 10:30am to 1pm and 7 to 9pm; admission is 1€. The **Museum of Folklore**

(☎ 22890/25-591), in a 19th-century sea captain's mansion near the quay, has examples of local crafts and furnishings and a re-created 19th-century island kitchen. It's usually open Monday to Saturday 4 to 8pm; admission is free.

When you've spent some time in Hora, you may want to visit **Ano Mera, 7km** (4 miles) east of Hora near the center of the island, a quick bus ride from the north station. Ano Mera is the island's only other real town and we especially recommend this trip to those interested in religious sites—the **Monastery of Panayia Tourliani** southeast of town dates from the 18th century and has a marble bell tower with intricate folk carvings. Inside the church are a huge Italian baroque iconostasis (altar screen) with icons of the Cretan school, an 18th-century marble baptismal font, and a small museum containing liturgical vestments, needlework, and wood carvings. One kilometer (½ mile) southeast is the 12th-century **Monastery of Paleokastro,** in one of the greenest spots on the island. Ano Mera also has the most traditional atmosphere on the island, with a fresh-produce market on the main square selling excellent local cheeses, and it's the island's place of choice for Sunday brunch.

## SHOPPING

Mykonos has a lot of shops, many selling overpriced souvenirs, clothing, and jewelry to cruise ship day-trippers. That said, there are also a number of serious shops here, selling serious wares—at serious prices. The finest jewelry shop is **Lalaounis** ★, 14 Polykandrioti (☎ 22890/22-444), associated with the famous Lalaounis museum and shops in Athens. It has superb reproductions of ancient and Byzantine jewelry as well as original designs. (When you leave Lalaounis, have a look at **Yiannis Galantis** [☎ 22890/22-255), which sells clothing designed by the owner.) If you can't afford Lalaounis, you might have a look at one of the island's oldest jewelry shops, the **Gold Store,** right on the waterfront (☎ 22890/22-397), or **Delos Dolphins,** Matoyanni at Enoplon Dinameon (☎ 22890/22-765), which specializes in copies of museum pieces, or **Vildiridis,** 12 Matoyanni (☎ 22890/23-245), which also has designs based on ancient jewelry.

Mykonos has lots of art galleries, including some based in Athens that move here for the summer season. The **Scala Gallery** ★, Matoyanni 48 (☎ 22890/23-407; fax 22890/26-993; www.scalagallery.gr), is one of the best galleries in town. All the artists represented are from Greece, many of them quite well known. There is a selection of jewelry, plus an interesting collection of recent works by Yorgos Kypris, an Athenian sculptor and ceramic artist. Nearby on Panahrandou is **Scala II Gallery** (☎ 22890/26-993), where the overflow from the Scala Gallery is sold at reduced prices.

At **Apocalypse** ★ (☎ 22890/24-267), on Ayios Vlasis, just in from the port, you'll find the icon workshop of Maria Adama and Mercourios Dimopoulos.

---

**Tips** **Finding an Address**

Although some shops hand out a map of Mykonos town, you'll probably do better finding restaurants, hotels, and attractions by asking people to point you in the right direction. Many streets do not have their names posted, and the map leaves off lots of small, twisting, streets—and Mykonos has almost nothing but small, twisting, streets! The map published by **Stamatis Bozinakis** is sold at most kiosks for 2€ and is quite decent; the excellent **Mykonos Sky Map** is free at some kiosks and shops.

Their materials and techniques are drawn from the ancient tradition of icon painting. Much of their exquisite work is done on commission for churches and individuals. **Orama Art Gallery** (© 22890/26-339; fax 22890/24-016) features the work of local painters Luis Orozco and Dorlies Schapitz. Many of the paintings depict local scenes, but this is not tourist art.

There was a time when Mykonos was world-famous for its vegetable-dyed hand-loomed weavings, especially those of the legendary Kuria Vienoula. Today, **Nikoletta** (© 22890/27-503) is one of the few shops where you can still see Myconos's traditional loomed goods. Eleni Kontiza's tiny shop **Hand Made** (© 22890/27-512), on a lane between Plateia Tria Pigadia and Plateia Laka, has a good selection of handwoven scarves, rugs, and tablecloths from around Greece.

The best bookstore on Mykonos is **To Vivlio** ★ (© 22890/27-737), on Zouganeli, one street over from Matoyianni. It carries a good selection of books in English, including many works of Greek writers in translation, plus some art and architecture books and a few travel guides.

Works of culinary art can be found at **Skaropoulos** (© 22890/24-983), 1.5km (1 mile) out of Hora on the road to Ano Mera, featuring the Mykonian specialties of Nikos and Frantzeska Koukas (Nikos's grandfather started making confections here in 1921, winning prizes and earning a personal commendation from Winston Churchill). Try their famed *amygdalota* (an almond sweet) or the almond biscuits (Churchill's favorite). You can also find Skaropoulos sweets at **Pantopoleion**, Kaloyerou 24 (© 22890/22-078), along with Greek organic foods and natural cosmetics. The shop is in a beautifully restored 300-year-old Mykonian house.

When you finish your shopping, treat yourself to an almond biscuit (or two, or three) from Skaropoulos or **Efthemios**, 4 Florou Zouganeli (© 22890/22-281), off the harborfront.

If you're on Mykonos, probably one reason is the travel posters and postcards you've seen of sun setting behind funky whitewashed buildings with wooden balconies overhanging the sea. That's the district called Little Venice and almost every other building is now a bar where you can watch the sunset—or, you can sit by the three windmills and get a spectacular view of Little Venice itself at sunset. Either way, if you're in luck, you'll be able to combine listening to Mozart, with sipping the drink of your choice (how about a margarita?), as the sun turns the sea rose red.

## WHERE TO STAY

In summer, if you arrive by ferry, you're met by a throng of people hawking rooms, some in small hotels, others in private homes. If you don't have a hotel reservation, one of these rooms may be very welcome. If you're pretty sure that won't suit your needs, be sure you have reserved a room 1 to 3 months in advance of your visit. Many hotels are fully booked all summer by tour groups or regular patrons. Keep in mind that Mykonos is an easier, more pleasant place to visit in the late spring or early fall-and off-season hotel rates are sometimes half the quoted high-season rate. Also keep in mind that many small hotels (and restaurants and shops) close in winter, especially if business is slow.

**Mykonos Accommodations Center** (Mac), Enoplon Dinameon 10 (© 22890/ 23-160 or 22890/23-408; fax 22890/24-137; http://mykonos-accommodation. com), will correspond, talk by phone, or meet with you to determine the best accommodation for your budget. The service is free when booking hotel stays of 3 nights or longer; check for the current price for booking a shorter stay or budget accommodations (expect to pay around 20€).

## IN HORA

In addition to the options listed below, **Dimitris Roussounelos** (© and fax **22890/26-993;** scala@otenet.gr) of the Scala Gallery manages a number of simple studios and apartments in Hora. All have TVs and kitchen facilities; most are equipped with phones and air-conditioning. The largest apartment (Fratzeska's) has two bedrooms, two bathrooms, and a shaded terrace with views across the bay to Delos. Nightly rates are from 125€ for most studios to 200€ for "Fratzeska's apartment."

**Belvedere Hotel** ★   The spiffy Belvedere, in part occupying a handsome and handsomely restored 1850s town house on the main road into town, has stunning views over the town and harbor, a few minutes' walk away. Rooms are nicely, if not distinctively, furnished. This is the place to stay if you want many of the creature comforts of Mykonos's beach resorts, but prefer to be within walking distance of Hora. The in-house **Remvi** restaurant, has a cellar with 5,000 bottles of wine, and is excellent (and pricey); there's also a sushi bar. In season, there is often massage, hairdresser, and barber service. Off season, there are often excellent specials, including a free jeep for a day if you stay 4 nights or a 5th night free after a 4-night stay.

Hora, School of Fine Arts District. 846 00 Mykonos. © **22890/25-122.** Fax 22890/25-126. belvedere@mykonos-accommodation.com. 48 units. 125€–250€ double. Rates include American buffet breakfast. Considerable off-season reductions usually available. AE, MC, V. **Amenities:** 2 restaurants; bar; pool; fitness center; Jacuzzi; sauna. *In room:* A/C, TV, dataport in 10 units, minibar, hair dryer.

**Cavo Tagoo** ★★   This elegant hotel set into a cliff with spectacular views over Mykonos town is hard to resist—and consistently makes it onto *Odyssey* magazine's list of ten best Greek hotels. Cavo Tagoo's island-style architecture has won awards, and its gleaming marble floors, nicely crafted wooden furniture, queen- and king-size beds, and local-style weavings are a genuine pleasure. It's only a 15-minute walk to Hora's harbor, although you may find it hard to budge: A (saltwater) pool and a good restaurant are right here.

Hora, 846 00 Mykonos. © **22890/23-692,** 22890/23-693, or 22890/23-694. Fax 22890/24-923. cavotagoo@ mykonos-accommodation.com. 72 units. 180€–320€ double. Rates include buffet breakfast. AE, MC, V. Closed Nov–Mar. **Amenities:** Restaurant; bar saltwater pool. *In room:* A/C, TV, minibar, hair dryer.

**Matina Hotel** ★   This small hotel set in a large garden is surprisingly quiet, given its central location. If you want to avoid the large, isolated hotels and enjoy the comings and goings in a Hora neighborhood, this may be the place for you. Rooms are a bit on the small side, but modern and comfortable, and the owner has been described by several readers as "very helpful." We agree.

3 Fournakion, Hora, 846 00 Mykonos. © **22890/22-387.** Fax 22890/24-501. 19 units. 90€ double. AE, MC, V. Closed Nov–Mar. **Amenities:** Breakfast room; garden.

**Philippi Hotel**   Each room in this homey little hotel in the heart of Mykonos town is different, so you might want to have a look at several before choosing yours. The owner tends a lush garden that often provides flowers for her son's restaurant, the elegant Philippi (see "Where to Dine," below), which can be reached through the garden.

25 Kaloyera, Hora, 846 00 Mykonos. © **22890/22-294.** Fax 22890/24-680. 13 units. 60€ double. No credit cards. **Amenities:** Restaurant; breakfast room.

## OUT ON THE ISLAND

Although most visitors prefer to stay in Hora and commute to the beaches, there are hotels on or near many of the more popular island beaches.

There are private studios and simple pensions at Paradise and Super Paradise beaches, but rooms are almost impossible to get, and prices more than double in July and August. Contact the **Mykonos Accommodations Center** (© **22890/23-160**)—or, for Super Paradise, **GATS Travel** (© **22890/22-404**)—for information on the properties they represent. The tavernas at each beach may also have suggestions.

**AT KALAFATI**    The sprawling **Aphrodite Hotel** (© **22890/71-367**) has a large pool, two restaurants, and 150 rooms. It's a good value in May, June, and October, when a double costs about 100€. This place is popular with tour groups and Greek families.

**AT ORNOS BAY ★★**    The elegant **Kivotos Club Hotel ★★**, Ornos Bay, 846 00 Mykonos (© **22890/25-795**; fax 22890/22-844; www.kivotosclubhotel.gr) is a small luxury hotel most of whose 45 distinctively decorated units overlook the Bay of Ornos. If you don't want to walk that far for a swim, head for the saltwater or freshwater pool, or the Jacuzzi and sauna. Kivotos Clubhouse is small enough to be intimate and tranquil; the service (including frozen towels to cool pool-side guests on hot days) here gets raves from guests. If you ever want to leave (there are several restaurants), the hotel minibus will whisk you into town. In short, it's no surprise that this popular honeymoon destination has appeared on *Odyssey* magazine's annual list of the best hotels in Greece. Doubles from 350€ to 515€; suites priced from 620€ to 1000€. The enormous **Santa Marina**, also at Ornos Bay (© **22890/23-200**; fax 22890/23-412; info@santa-marina.gr) has 90 suites and villas in 20 landscaped acres overlooking the bay. If you don't want to swim in the sea, two pools and spa facilities are available at the hotel (which has its own restaurant). Suites with private pool are available from 1500€. If you wish, you can arrive here by helicopter and land on the hotel pad. Doubles from 365€ to 450€; suites and villas from 525€ to 2400€. The more modest 25-unit **Bestwestern Dionysos Hotel** (© **22890/23-313;** www.dionysoshotel.com), is steps from the beach and has a pool, restaurant, bar, air conditioned rooms with fridges and TV; doubles from 190€. The yet more modest 42-unit **Hotel Yiannaki** (© **22890/23-393; 22890/23-443**) is about 200m (656 ft.) away from the beach, has its own pool and restaurant, and has doubles from 125€. The nicest have seaviews and balconies.

Families traveling with children will find staying at one of the Ornos Bay hotels especially appealing. The beach is excellent and slopes into shallow, usually calm, water. Furthermore, this is not one of Mykonos's all-night party beaches. If you hotel does not have watersports facilities, several of the local tavernas have surfboards and pedalboats to rent, as well as umbrellas. *One minus:* the beach is quite close to the airport, so you will hear planes come and go.

**AT PLATI YIALOS**    The 82 units at the **Hotel Petassos Bay**, Plati Yialos, 846 00 Mykonos (© **22890/23-737;** fax 22890/24-101), all have air-conditioning and minibars, and are large and comfortable. Doubles rent for about 150€. Each has a balcony overlooking the (relatively secluded) beach, which is less than 36m (132 ft.) away. The hotel has a good-size pool and sun deck, Jacuzzi, gym, and sauna, and offers free round-trip transportation from the harbor or airport, safety boxes, and laundry service. The new seaside restaurant has a great view and serves a big buffet breakfast. (a continental, but not the buffet breakfast, is included in-room rate).

**AT AYIOS STEPHANOS**    This popular resort, about 4km (2½ miles) north of Hora, has a number of hotels; the 38-unit **Princess of Mykonos**, Ayios

Stephanos beach, 846 00 Mykonos (© 22890/23-806; fax 22890/23031), is the most elegant. The Princess has bungalows, a gym, a pool, and an excellent beach; doubles cost from 180€. The **Hotel Artemis**, Ayios Stephanos, 846 00 Mykonos (© 22890/22-345), near the beach and bus stop, offers 23 units with bathroom from 115€, breakfast included. The small **Hotel Mina**, Ayios Stephanos, 846 00 Mykonos (© 22890/23-024), uphill behind the Artemis, has 15 doubles with bathroom that go for 70€. All these hotels are usually closed November to March.

**AT PSARROU BEACH  Grecotel Mykonos Blu ★★**, Psarrou Beach, 846 00 Mykonos (© 22890/27-9000; fax 22890/27-783; www.grecotel.gr) is another of the island's serious luxury hotels with award-winning Cyclades-inspired architecture. Like Cavo Tagoo and Kivotos, this place is popular with wealthy Greeks, honeymooners, and jet-setters. The private beach, large pool, and in-house "Poets of the Aegean" restaurant allow guests here to be just as lazy as they wish (although there is a fitness club and spa for the energetic) when deciding whether to head out on the island. Doubles 250€ to 400€.

## WHERE TO DINE

**Camares Cafe** (© 22890/28-570) on Mavroyenous (Taxi) Square has light meals and a fine view of the harbor from its terrace; its big plus: it's open 24 hours and, for Mykonos, very reasonably priced. As usual on the islands, most of the harborside tavernas are expensive and mediocre, although **Kounelas ★** on the harbor (no phone; no credit cards) is still a good value for fresh fish—as the presence of locals dining here attests.

You'll find plenty of fish on the menu at most Mykonos restaurants; not all of it is local, still less fresh. But, if you eat squid from the far east or shrimp from Africa in the Aegean, perhaps you can think of this as simply proving that the world has indeed become a global village.

Restaurants come and go here, so if possible, check with other travelers or locals as to what's just opened and getting good reviews—and let us know if you find something you like!

**Antonini's** GREEK  Antonini's is one of the oldest of Mykonos's restaurants, and it serves consistently decent stews, chops, and mezedes. Locals still eat here, although in summer, they tend to leave the place to tourists.

Plateia Manto, Hora. © 22890/22-319. Main courses 8€–15€ No credit cards. Daily noon–3pm and 7pm–1am in summer. Usually closed Nov–Mar.

**Edem Restaurant ★** GREEK/CONTINENTAL  This is one of the oldest restaurants in Hora, with a reputation for good food built over 30 years. Tables are clustered around a courtyard pool—diners have been known to make a splash upon arrival with a pre-prandial swim—and the sunny courtyard is a pleasant place to enjoy a leisurely dinner even if you aren't dressed for the water. Edem is known especially for its variety of lamb dishes and fresh fish—but the eclectic menu also includes steaks, pasta, and a variety of traditional Greek and continental dishes. The service is good, and the produce as fresh as you'll see on Mykonos.

Above Panachra church, Hora. © 22890/23-355. Reservations recommended July–Aug. Main courses 8€–30€; fish priced by the kilo. AE, DC, MC, V. Daily 6pm–1am. In off season, sometimes open for lunch. Walk up Matoyianni, turn left on Kaloyera, and follow the signs up and to the left.

**El Greco/Yorgos** GREEK/CONTINENTAL  Put aside your suspicions of a place called El Greco and prepare to enjoy traditional recipes collected from various regions of Greece. The eclectic menu includes traditional dishes like the *bourdeto* from Kerkira, a monkfish-and-shellfish stew in tomato and wine sauce, and many concoctions featuring local produce, like the mushrooms with Mykonian cheese. This place is doing something right: it's been here since the 1960s.

Plateia Tria Pigadia, Hora. © **22890/22-074.** Main courses 8€–30€; fish priced by the kilo. AE, DC, MC, V. Daily 7pm–1am.

**La Maison de Catherine** ★ GREEK/FRENCH    This is a very pleasant place to spend the evening, enjoying a seafood soufflé or a seafood pasta—or grilled or roast lamb. The candlelit dining room is so elegant that you won't mind being indoors. In addition to a wide variety of entrees, there is a range of excellent desserts.

Ayíos Gerasimos, Hora. © **22890/22-169.** Reservations recommended July–August. Main courses 12€–25€. AE, DC, MC, V. Daily 7pm–1am.

**Maria's Garden** ★ GREEK    This is another long-time favorite, with a lovely garden and, often, live music and outbursts of dancing. The vegetable dishes are always fresh and tasty, the lamb succulent, and the seafood enticing. In short, a place where the ambience and the cuisine come together to create a very successful restaurant. There's also a good-value set menu, for around 25€.

30 Kaloyera, Hora. © **22890/27-565.** Reservations recommended July–August. Main courses 15€–30€. V. Daily 7pm–1am.

**Philippi** ★ GREEK/CONTINENTAL    One of the island's most romantic dining experiences, Philippi is in a quiet garden. Old Greek favorites share space on the menu with French dishes and a more than usually impressive wine list. What this restaurant provides in abundance is *atmosphere*, and that's what has made it a perennial favorite.

Just off Matoyianni and Kaloyera behind the eponymous Hotel, Hora. © **22890/22-294.** Reservations recommended July–August. Main courses 10€–25€. AE, MC, V. Daily 7pm–1am.

**Sea Satin Market** ★ GREEK/SEAFOOD    Below the windmills, beyond the small beach adjacent to Little Venice, the paralia ends in a rocky headland facing the open sea—this is the remarkable location for one of Hora's most charming new restaurants. Set apart from the clamor of the town, it's one of the quietest spots in town, and on a still summer night just after sunset, the atmosphere is all you could hope for on a Greek island. In the front of the restaurant, the activities of the kitchen are on display along with the day's catch sizzling on the grill. You can make a modest meal on *mezedes* here, or let it rip, with grilled bon filet.

Near the Mitropolis Cathedral, Hora. © **22890/24-676.** Main courses 8€–35€. AE, V. Daily 6:30pm–12:30am.

**Sesame Kitchen** GREEK/CONTINENTAL    This small, health-conscious taverna, which serves some vegetarian specialties, is next to the Naval Museum. Fresh spinach, vegetable, cheese, and chicken pies are baked daily. There's a large variety of salads, brown rice, and soy dishes, including a vegetable moussaka, stir-fried veggies, and lightly grilled and seasoned meat dishes.

Plateia Tria Pigadia, Hora. © **22890/24-710.** Main courses 6€–18€. AE, V. Daily 7pm–12:30am.

## MYKONOS AFTER DARK

Mykonos has the liveliest, most abundant, and most varied nightlife in the Aegean. It's a barhopper's paradise, and you'll enjoy wandering through the maze of streets looking for the right spot—and looking at everyone else looking. We're trying to suggest a few durable favorites and some new places that were popular last year. We've given phone numbers where available; if you dial one of these places and get no reply, don't assume it is closed; when business is brisk, phones are often not answered.

*Be warned:* Drinks in Mykonos often cost more than they do in London or New York.

Watching the sunset is a popular sport at the sophisticated bars in Little Venice. The **Kastro** (☎ 22890/23-072), near the Paraportiani Church, is famous for classical music and frozen daiquiris. This is a great spot to watch (or join in with) handsome young men flirting with each other. If you find it too crowded or tame, sashay along to **Le Caprice**, which also has a seaside perch, or **Porta** (☎ 22890/27-807), a popular gay cruising spot. The **Montparnasse** (☎ 22890/23-719), on the same lane, is cozier, with classical music and Toulouse-Lautrec posters. The **Veranda** (☎ 22890/23-290), in an old mansion overlooking the water with a good view of the windmills, is as relaxing as its name implies. **Galeraki** (☎ 22890/27-118) has a wide variety of exotic cocktails (and customers) and the in-house art gallery that gives this popular spot its name (little gallery).

The decibel level is considerably higher along the harbor, where **Piero's** (☎ 22890/22-177), popular with gay visitors, rocks all night long to American and European music; the adjacent **Icarus** is best known for its drag shows. The **Anchor** plays blues, jazz, and classic rock for its 30-something clients, as does **Argo. Stavros Irish Bar** and the **Scandanavian Bar-Disco** draw customers from Ireland, Scandinavia, and, quite possibly, as far away as Antarctica. If you'd like to sample some Greek music and dancing, try **Thalami** (☎ 22890/23-291), a small club underneath the town hall, and if you'd like to relax at a movie, head for **Cinemanto** (☎ 22890/27-190), which shows films nightly around 9pm. Many films are American; most Greek films have English subtitles.

How much are you going to spend going out on the town for a drink or two in Mykonos? As little as 10€—and after that, the sky really is the limit here!

If you're visiting between July and September, you may want to find out what's happening at the **Anemo Theatre** (☎ 22890/23-944), an outdoor venue for the performing arts in a garden in Rohari, just above town. There's usually a wide variety of concerts, performances, and talks here.

## 7 Delos

The small island of **Delos** ★★★ just 3km (2 miles) offshore from Mykonos, was considered by the ancient Greeks to be the holiest of sanctuaries, the sacred center around which the other Cyclades circled. Delos is known locally as the "brightest" island in the Cyclades, a tradition that seems to indicate both its continued significance as a sacred place and the simple fact that this is one place where you'll want to have sunglasses. It is unquestionably one of the most remarkable archaeological preserves in the world, displaying ample evidence of its former grandeur. Always a place set apart, with different rules than those of neighboring islands, in ancient times people were not allowed to die or be born on this sacred island. Today, they are not allowed to spend the night, and the site can be visited only between the hours of 8:30am and 3pm.

We recommend visiting Delos as early as possible in the day, especially in summer, when the crowds and heat become overwhelming by early afternoon. Sturdy shoes and water are necessary; a hat or cap and food are also advised. (There is a cafe near the museum, but the prices are high, the quality poor, and the service even worse.)

**Delos**

_Stadium_

_Gymnasium_

_Greece_

_Aegean Sea_

_Athens_ ✪

_Delos_

_The Cyclades_

_CRETE_

_Mediterranean Sea_

Sanctuary of the Syrian Gods

Terrace of the Foreign Gods

Shrine of the Egyptian Gods

Heraion

Grotto of Hercules

▲ _Mt. Kinthos_

Tourist Pavilion

Museum

Sanctuary of Dionysos

House of Hermes

House of the Trident

House of the Dolphins

Lake House

Palestra by the Lake

Roman Wall

_Sacred Lake_

Agora of the Italians

House of Dionysos

Theater

House of the Masks

**LION DISTRICT**

House of the Diadumenos

**SANCTUARY OF APOLLO**

Apollo Temples

**THEATER DISTRICT**

Cistern

Institution of the Poseidoniasts

Terrace of the Lions

House of the Naxians

Sacred Way

**MARITIME QUARTER**

House of Cleopatra

Agora of the Competialists

_Sacred Harbor_

■ Boats

_Commercial Harbor_

Warehouses

0 ___ 100 m
0 ___ 100 y

N ▲

## ESSENTIALS

**GETTING THERE**  If you want to go to Delos, head there at the first opportunity: the island can be visited only by sea—and many days the sea is too rough for boats to put in here. The site is usually open from 8:30am to 3pm and is always closed on Monday. Most people visit on excursion boats from nearby Mykonos, although there are excursions from other neighboring islands, and Delos is a prominent stop for cruise ships and yachts. Spending the night is not allowed. From Mykonos, organized guided and unguided excursions leave about 4 times a day from Tuesday to Sunday from the west end of the harbor; the trip takes about 40 minutes and costs about 10€ round-trip for transportation alone (departure from Mykonos around 8:30am; return to Mykonos around 3pm). **Yiannakis Tours** (© **22890/22-089**) offers guided tours for about 30€ that depart at 9 or 10am and return at 12:30 or 2pm.

High seas can prevent boats going to Delos at any time of the year, so if you want to go here, don't put it off when you visit, as the weather can change unexpectedly.

When you go, try to leave as early as possible in the morning, especially in the summer, when both the afternoon heat and the crowds are intense. Be sure to wear sturdy shoes, sunscreen, and a hat, and bring water and a snack. (There's a café near the museum, but the prices are high and the quality is poor.)

## EXPLORING THE SITE

Entrance to the site costs 6€, unless this was included in the price of your excursion; it's open Tuesday through Sunday from 8:30am to 3pm, and is closed on Mondays. At the ticket kiosk, you'll see a number of site plans and picture guides for sale; we recommend *Delos & Mykonos: A Guide to the History and Archaeology*, by Konstantinos Tsakos (Hesperos Editions), a reliable guide to the site and the museum. Because the excavations at Delos have been conducted by the French School, many signs are in French, and a thorough English map and guide are especially useful.

To the left (north) of the new jetty where your boat will dock is the **Sacred Harbor,** now too silted for use, where pilgrims, merchants, and sailors from throughout the Mediterranean used to land. The commercial importance of the island in ancient times was due to the protection its harbor offered in the shelter of surrounding islands, the best anywhere between mainland Greece and its colonies and trading partners in Asia Minor.

If you're not on a tour and have the energy, you should definitely head up to **Mount Kinthos ★,** the highest point on the island. It offers an overview of the site and a fine view of most of the Cyclades: the neighboring island of Rinia with Siros beyond it to the west, Tinos to the north, Mykonos to the northeast, Naxos and Paros to the south. From the summit, with the islands of the Cyclades sprawled on all sides, close up and low to the horizon, you get the sense that this is indeed the center of the archipelago. On your way down, don't miss the remarkable **Grotto of Hercules,** a small temple built into a natural crevice in the mountainside—the roof is formed of massive granite slabs held up by their own enormous weight. The grotto commands a fine view of the harbor and much of the archaeological site.

Just south (to the right) from the Sacred Harbor is the fascinating **Maritime Quarter,** a residential area with the remains of houses from the Hellenistic and Roman era, when the island reached its peak in wealth and prestige. Reminiscent of Pompeii, the outlines of the ancient city are remarkably preserved. Several houses contain brilliant **mosaics ★,** and in most houses the cistern and sewer systems can be seen. Among the numerous small dwellings are several palaces, built around a central court and connected to the street by a narrow passage. The mosaics in the courtyards of the palaces are particularly dazzling, and include such famous images as Dionysos riding a panther in the **House of the Masks,** and a similar depiction in the **House of Dionysos.** Further to the south is the massive **Theater,** which seated 5,500 people and was the site of choral competitions during the Delian Festivals, an event held every 4 years and comprising athletic competitions in addition to musical contests. Behind the theater is a fine arched **cistern,** which was the water supply for the city.

Adjacent to the Sacred Harbor is the **Agora of the Competialists,** built in the 2nd century B.C., when the island was a bustling free port under Rome. Roman citizens, mostly former slaves, worshipped the *lares competales,* who were minor "crossroad" deities associated with the Greek god Hermes, patron of travelers and commerce. From the far left corner of the Agora of the Competialists, the **Sacred Way**—once lined with statues and votive monuments—leads north toward the Sanctuary of Apollo. By retracing the steps of ancient pilgrims along it, you will pass the scant remains of several temples (most of the stone from the site was taken away for buildings on neighboring islands, especially Mykonos and Tinos). At the far end of the Sacred Way was the **Propylaea**, a monumental marble gateway that led into the sanctuary. In ancient times, the sanctuary was crowded with temples, altars, statues, and votive offerings.

The **museum** contains finds from the various excavations on the island. It displays some fine statuary, reliefs, masks, and jewelry, and is well worth a visit. Admission to the museum is included in the entrance fee to the site.

North of the Tourist Pavilion on the left is the **Sacred Lake**, where the oracular swans once swam. The lake is now little more than a dusty indentation most of the year, surrounded by a low wall. Beyond it is the famous **Avenue of the Lions** ★, made of Naxian marble and erected in the 7th century B.C. (There were originally at least nine. One was taken away to Venice in the 17th century and now stands before the Arsenal there. The whereabouts of the others lost in antiquity remains a mystery—although some of the five survivors have been taken off to the museum for restoration and preservation. Reproduction replacements are planned.) Beyond the lake to the northeast is the large square courtyard of the Gymnasium and the long narrow Stadium, where the athletic competitions of the Delian Games were held.

## 8 Tinos

161km (87 nautical miles) SE of Piraeus

Tinos, sometimes called the "Lourdes of Greece," is one of the most important places of religious pilgrimage in all Greece, yet it remains one of the least commercialized islands of the Cyclades—and a joy to visit for that reason. **Panayia Evanyelistria** (Our Lady of Good Tidings), the "Lourdes of Greece," draws thousands of pilgrims seeking the healing and comforting assistance of the miraculous icon enshrined there. Almost any day of the year you can see people, particularly elderly women, crawling from the port on hands and knees up the long, steep street leading to the hilltop cathedral. (Do keep in mind that this *is* a religious shrine: it is considered very disrespectful to be in the precincts of the church in shorts, short skirts, halters, or sleeveless shirts.) The market street of Tinos town is lined with stalls selling holy water vials, incense, candles (up to 2m/7 ft. long), and mass-produced icons. Don't even think about arriving without a reservation around **August 15** (Feast of the Assumption), when thousands of pilgrims travel here to celebrate the Feast of the Assumption of the Virgin. **March 25** (Feast of the Annunciation) is the other important feast day here, but draws fewer pilgrims because it is less easy to travel on the sea in March.

The inland villages of Tinos are some of the most beautiful in the Cyclades. Many of the most picturesque are nestled into the slopes of **Exobourgo**, the rocky pinnacle visible from the port, connected by a network of walking paths that make this island a hiker's paradise. In these villages and dotting the countryside, you'll see the ornately decorated medieval dovecotes for which the island is famous, and above the doors of village houses elaborately carved marble lintels. According to one tradition (popular on virtually every one of the Cyclades), there are 365 churches scattered across the island, one for every day of the year; others boast that the island has 1,000 churches. The island's beaches aren't worthy of superlatives, but they are plentiful and uncrowded throughout the summer. All this may change if an airport is built here—all the more reason to visit Tinos now.

Tinos is famous for its **dovecotes**, stout stone towers elaborately ornamented with slabs of the local shale. The first dovecotes were built here by the Venetians. Some scholars speculate that they brought their love of doves, and dovecots, with them from Italy, along with the dovecot's distinctive miniature tower-architecture. The doves were an important part of the local diet, and their droppings were used as fertilizer. The towns of **Tarambados** and **Smardakito** have some of the most elaborate dovecotes, but you hardly have to make an effort to see these elaborate birdhouses, as there are said to be 2,000 of them on the island.

## ESSENTIALS

### GETTING THERE
There are several ferries to Tinos daily from Piraeus (5 hr.) and at least one catamaran daily from Rafina (1½ hr.); schedules should be confirmed with the Athens **GNTO** (© **210/331-0562**), the **Port Authority in Piraeus** (© **210/459-3223** or 210/422-6000; phone seldom answered), or the **Rafina Port Authority** (© **22940/22-300**). Several times a day, boats connect Tinos with nearby Mykonos (15–40 min.), Boats to Siros (20–50 min.), and hydrofoils to Santorini (4–6 hr.), Paros (1½ hr.), and Naxos (2 hr.) are regular in summer and somewhat less frequent during the winter months (though Tinos has more winter connections than most Cycladic isles due to its religious tourism, which continues year-round). In summer, a day excursion to Delos and Mykonos usually departs from Tinos at 10am Tuesday through Sunday, returning to Tinos at 7pm; the fare is 25€ for adults and 9€ for children under 11.

There are three piers in Tinos harbor. Be sure to find out from which pier your ship will depart; most ferries still dock at the old pier in the town center. It can happen that due to weather conditions, ferries will use a different pier than expected, in which case there will be an announcement by loudspeaker at the intended pier as little as 10 minutes prior to arrival—at this point you'll see a convoy of hotel buses and travelers mobilize themselves to get promptly to the other port. The **Tinos Port Authority** (not guaranteed to be helpful) can be reached at © **22830/22-348.**

### VISITOR INFORMATION
For information on accommodations, car rentals, island tours, and Tinos in general, head to **Windmills Travel** (© **22830/23-398**; fax 22830/23-398; windmills-@travelling.gr), near the new port, opposite the children's park. Sharon Turner is the friendly and outgoing manager.

### GETTING AROUND By Bus
The **bus station** (© **22830/22-440**) is on the harbor, opposite the National Bank of Greece. Schedules are usually posted or available here (you can also ask about bus times at Windmills Travel). There are frequent daily buses to most island villages.

### By Car & Moped
Again, inquire at Windmills Travel, or try the most reliable rental company in town, **Vidalis** (© **22830/23-400**), just off the harbor at 16 Alavanou and **Dimitris Rental** (© **22830/23-585**) next door; both have car rentals from 25€ and mopeds from 12€.

### By Taxi
The principal taxi stand (© **22830/22-470**) is on the harbor, by the south (old) pier.

### FAST FACTS
There are several **banks** on the harbor, open Monday through Thursday from 8am to 2pm and Friday from 8am to 1:30pm; all have ATMs. The **first-aid center** can be reached at © **22830/22-210.** There's a drop-off **laundry** service (© **22830/32-765**) opposite the Vidalis car-rental agency—but be forewarned that it can be slow, up to 3 days in peak season. For **luggage storage,** try

Windmills Travel (© 22830/23-398), near the new port. The **police** (© 22830/22-348) are just after the new pier, past the children's park and the Asteria Hotel. The **post office** (© 22830/22-247), open Monday through Friday from 7:30am to 2pm, is at the south end of the harbor next to the Tinion Hotel. The **telephone office (OTE)**, open Monday through Friday from 7:30am to 12:30pm, is on the main street leading to the church of Panayia Evanyelistria, about halfway up on the right (© 22830/22-399).

## WHAT TO SEE & DO

Panayia Evanyelistria Cathedral and Museums ★★ Each year, the **Church of Panagia Evangelistria (Our Lady of Good Tidings)** draws thousands of pilgrims seeking the aid of the church's miraculous icon. according to local lore, one night in 1822, a nun named Pelagia dreamed that a miraculous icon was buried nearby. Pelagia led her neighbors to the place she had seen in her dream, and when they began to dig, they discovered the remains of a Byzantine church with the icon. As is the case with many of the most holy icons, the Panagia Evangelistria is believed to be the work of Saint Luke. The massive church—made of marble from the islands of Paros and Tinos, with a distinctive bell tower—was built in 1824 to house the icon.

A broad flight of marble stairs flanked by lovely pebble mosaics leads to the church; inside, hundreds of gold and silver hanging lamps illuminate the holy icon of the Virgin and the gifts—many in gold, silver, and precious jewels—dedicated by the faithful. Even those who do not make a lavish gift customarily light one of the many candles burning inside the church. The pilgrims' devotion is manifest in these gifts—and in the piety of those who crawl on their knees to the church from the dock.

To enter the church, men must wear long pants and shirts with sleeves, and women must wear dresses or skirts and blouses with sleeves. If there is a church service while you are here, you will hear the beautiful, resonant chanting that typifies a Greek Orthodox service—but remember that it's not appropriate to explore the church during a service.

Beneath the church is the crypt where the icon was found, surrounded by smaller chapels; the crypt is often crowded with Greek parents and children in white, waiting to be baptized with water from the font. Particularly interesting are the hundreds of objects in silver and gold hanging from the roof—sometimes a hand or foot, a child's crib, a house, a car, and, to the right of the entrance, a gold lemon tree. Each one has a story to tell, a tale of thanks for a prayer answered.

Within the high walls that surround the church are various museums and galleries, most of which are interesting primarily as curiosities. The gallery of 19th-century religious art is to the left as you pass through the main gateway; another gallery houses Byzantine icons, and to the left of the foundation offices is a fascinating display of gifts offered to the cathedral. The sculpture museum, to the right and up a flight of stairs, is one of the best galleries; it contains gifts from sculptors, many quite renowned, who studied with the help of the cathedral charitable foundation. Just below the cathedral precinct on Leoforos Megaloharis is a small **Archaeological Museum,** open Tuesday through Sunday from 8:30am to 3pm; admission is 2€. The collection includes finds from the ancient sanctuary of Thesmophorion near Exomvourgo, plus a sundial from the 2nd century A.D. found at the Sanctuary of Poseidon and Amphitrite at Kionia.

Hora, Tinos. Free admission. Cathedral daily 8am–8pm (off season daily noon–6pm). Galleries Sat–Sun (some weekdays during July and Aug) 8am–8pm (off season noon–6pm).

## EXPLORING THE ISLAND

If it's a clear day, one of your first sights of the island of Tinos from the ferry will be the pinnacle of rock towering over Hora (Tinos town): **Exobourgo** ✪, the mountain eminence crowned by a Venetian *kastro* (castle) some 15km (9 miles) outside of Hora. The fortress is surrounded by sheer rock walls on three sides; the only path to the summit stairs behind a Catholic church at the base of the rock, on the road between Mesi and Koumaros. As you make the 15-minute ascent, you'll pass several lines of fortification—the whole hill is riddled with walls and hollow with chambers. As you might expect, the view over the Cyclades is superb from the summit (565m/1,853 ft.). The fortress itself has long been in ruins— and was never as imposing as, for example, the massive Venetian fortress at Nafplion in the Peloponnese. The Turks defeated the Venetians here in 1714 and drove them from the island.

The towns circling Exobourgo are some of the most picturesque on the island, and can be visited by car or on foot (see "Walking," below). **Dio Horia** and **Monastiri** have beautiful village houses and Dio Horia has a spring in the main square, where some villagers still wash their clothes by hand. There's a town bus to the nearby **Convent of Kerovouniou,** one of the largest in Greece—almost a town in its own right—and dating to the 10th century. This was the home of Pelagia, the nun whose vision revealed the location of the island's famed icon; you can visit her cell and see a small museum of 18th- and 19th-century icons.

**Loutra** ✪ is an especially attractive village with a 17th-century Jesuit monastery that contains an excellent museum of village life—implements for making olive oil and wine are on display alongside old manuscripts and maps; it's open mid-June to mid-September daily from 10:30am to 3:30pm. **Volax** is situated in a remote valley known for a bizarre lunar landscape of rotund granite boulders—the villagers have recently constructed a stone amphitheater for theatrical productions, so be sure to ask at **Windmills Travel** (✆ and fax **22830/23-398**) for a schedule of performances (most occur in Aug). Volax is also known for its local basket weavers, whose baskets are remarkably durable and attractive; ask for directions to their workshops. Be sure to visit the town spring, down a short flight of steps at the bottom of the village: Channels direct the water to the fields, and the basket weavers' reeds soak in multiple stone basins.

**Koumaros** is a beautiful small village on the road between Volax and Mesi with many *stegasti,* streets occupying tunnels beneath the projecting second-floor rooms of village houses. At the tiny **self-service cafe,** visitors are invited to take what they want from an assortment of drinks, snacks, and ice creams, leaving payment in a box on the counter. You'll also find postcards, board games, and information about Koumaros. This small place in the center of town is open throughout the day.

**Pirgos,** at the western end of the island, is one of Tinos's most beautiful villages. Renowned for its school of fine arts, the town is a center for marble sculpting, and many of the finest sculptors of Greece have trained here. The **Dellatos Marble Sculpture School** (✆ **22830/23-164**) offers 1 and 2 week workshops for would-be marble workers. A small **museum** houses mostly sculpture by local artists; it's open Tuesday through Sunday from 11am to 1:30pm and 5:30 to 6:30pm, and is located near the bus station, on the main lane leading toward the village. You'll see workshops of local sculptors offering their works for sale.

## BEACHES

There's a decent fine-sand beach 3km (2 miles) west of Tinos town at **Kionia,** and another 2km (1¼ miles) east of town at busy **Ayios Fokas.** From Tinos, there's bus service on the south beach road (usually four times a day) to the resort of **Porto**, 8km (5 miles) to the east. Porto offers several long stretches of uncrowded sand, a few hotel complexes, and numerous tavernas, several at or near the beach. The beach at Ayios Ioannis facing the town of Porto is okay, but you'd be better off walking west across the small headland to a longer, less populous beach, extending from this headland to the church or Ayios Sostis at its western extremity; you can also get here by driving or taking the bus to Ayios Sostis. There are two beaches at **Kolimbithres** on the north side of the island, easily accessed by car, although protection from the meltemi winds can be a problem—the second is the best, with fine sand in a small rocky cove and two tavernas. There are more beaches around the headland from here—longer, less populous, and more exposed to the wind; you can reach these by a short drive on a poor dirt road beyond the beach mentioned above. The pebble cove at **Livada** is accessible only by a long, rough dirt road, and the north-facing beach receives the worst of the meltemi winds. Several beaches on the southwest coast (**Ayios Romanos, Ayios Petros,** and **Isternion**) are accessible by paved road.

## WALKING

Tinos is a walker's paradise, with a good network of paths and remote interior regions waiting to be explored. Some of the best walks are in the vicinity of **Exobourgo**—paths connect the cluster of villages circling this craggy fortress, offering great views and many places to stop for refreshment along the way. There isn't currently an English-language guide to walks in Tinos, but you can ask for information at **Windmills Travel** (© and fax **22830/23-398**) in Tinos town; the office is planning to arrange walking tours in the future, and may be able to offer information about organized walks or about routes for you to explore on your own.

## SHOPPING

In Hora, the **flea market** on Odos Evanyelistria is a pleasant place for a ramble; Evanyelistria parallels Leoforos Megaloharis, the main street from the harbor up to the cathedral. The colorful stalls lining the street sell icons, incense, candles, medallions, and *tamata* (tin, silver, and gold votives). You'll also find local embroidery, weavings, and the delicious local nougat, as well as *loukoumia* (Turkish delight) from Siros. There's also a **fish** and a **farmer's market** weekdays in the square by the docks.

**Harris Prassas Ostria-Tinos,** Evanyelistria 20 (© **22830/23-893**; fax 22830/24-568), is particularly recommended for his fine collection of jewelry in contemporary, Byzantine, and classical styles; silver work; and beautiful religious objects, including reproductions of the miraculous icon. Harris is friendly, informative, and famous for the quality of his work. Near the top of the street on the left is the small **O Evangelismos Weaving School** (© **22830/22-894**) and a store selling reasonably priced tablecloths, bedcovers, and other woven items produced at the school.

Those interested in authentic hand-painted icons should find the small shop of **Maria Vryoni,** the first left from the port off Leoforos Megaloharis, the second shop on the left. Maria spends at least a week on each of her works of art; they start at around 200€.

## WHERE TO STAY

Unless you have reservations, avoid Tinos during important religious holidays, especially **March 25** (Feast of the Annunciation) and **August 15** (Feast of the

Assumption). It is also advisable to have reservations for summer weekends, when Greeks travel here by the hundreds to make a short pilgrimage to the Panayia Evanyelistria.

For those planning to stay a week or longer, contact **Windmills Travel** (see "Visitor Information," above), which has houses for rent in several villages—a great way to see more of the island and get a taste for village life. The weekly cost is from 1000€ for a one-bedroom house, including car rental.

**Akti Aegeou Apartments**    The Akti Aegeou is built right on the sand of Porto Beach, one of the island's finest, and maintains an atmosphere of friendly informality. There are 5 rooms and 6 apartments; each roomy apartment has a kitchenette and a balcony facing the beach and all the units are decorated with island rugs and weavings. The place was constructed with many traditional details, such as pebble designs on the terraces, flagstone floors, and beamed ceilings. Meals are served in a small restaurant on the pool terrace.

Ayios Panteleimon Beach, 84200 Tinos (5km east of Tinos town on the road to Porto). ☎ 22830/24-248 or 22830/25-523. Fax 22830/23-523. 11 units. 100€ double. No credit cards. Closed Nov–Mar. **Amenities:** Restaurant; bar; pool. *In room:* A/C, TV, fridge.

**Avra Hotel** ★    A wooden spiral staircase leads to high-ceilinged rooms in this charming old hotel on the harbor, one of the first in Tinos when it was built in 1921. The hotel received a new look when its neo-classical facade was renovated in 1999; the interior was renovated in 2002. Several bedrooms have a view of the harbor, and three have balconies; unfortunately these front rooms also get the harbor noise. Other units face a rear courtyard and share a sunny terrace filled with palms and ferns.

Hora, 84200 Tinos. ☎ 22830/22-242. Fax 22830/22-176. 17 units. 70€ double. No credit cards. **Amenities:** Breakfast room/bar. *In room:* A/C.

**Porto Tango**    At present, this is the island's only resort hotel, with all the frills (sauna, and so on) that one expects at a resort hotel. The decor is a bit ponderous and gloomy and unfortunately when we visited in 2003, the hotel was under renovations.

Porto, 84200 Tinos. ☎ 22830/24-411. Fax 22830/24-416. www.portango.gr. 61 units. 120€–150€ double; 250€ suite. AE, MC, V. **Amenities:** 2 restaurants; bar; pool; health club and spa. *In room:* A/C, TV, minibar, hair dryer.

**Tinion Hotel** ★    This venerable hotel retains an old-world charm with marble floors, dark polished wood, and lace curtains. The guest rooms have high ceilings, tile floors, and handsome brass or carved walnut beds. The front rooms all have balconies with harbor views. Tinion is on a small square, just far enough from the harbor and its late-night activity to provide a quiet night's sleep.

1 Alavanou, Hora, 84200 Tinos. ☎ 22830/22-261. Fax 22830/24-754. kchatzi@ath.forthnet.gr. 20 units. 80€ double. MC, V. Closed Nov–Mar. From the old harbor, walk south (right) along the paralia; the hotel is just past the supermarket on the left. **Amenities:** Breakfast room/bar. *In room:* A/C, TV.

**Tinos Beach Hotel** ★ (Kids    Despite a somewhat impersonal character and fading 1960s elegance, this is the best choice in a beachfront hotel near Hora. The spacious rooms all have balconies, most with views of sea and pool (the view affects the room price). The suites are especially pleasant—large sitting rooms open onto poolside balconies. Rooms located in a cluster of bungalows built to resemble a Cycladic village are similar in size and furnishings; all have shaded terraces, and most offer a view toward the sea. The pool is the longest on the island, and there's a separate children's pool as well. There are umbrellas on the stretch of sand and cobble beach fronting the hotel; paddleboats and canoes are available for rent.

Kionia (4km/2½ miles west of Tinos town on the coast road), 84200 Tinos. © **22830/22-626** or 22830/22-627. Fax 22830/23-153. www.tinosbeach.gr. 180 units. 120€–150€ double. Rates include breakfast. Children 7 and under stay free in parents' room. AE, DC, MC, V. Closed Nov–Mar.

## WHERE TO DINE

As usual, avoid most harborfront joints, where food is generally inferior and service can be rushed. In addition to the places listed below, you'll find decent, simple fare at the following establishments: **Lefteris** (© **22830/23-013**), a fish taverna on the harborfront, has a large and varied menu. There's plenty of room for dancing, and the waiters often demonstrate and urge diners to join in. **Palea Pallada** (© **22830/23-516**), a venerable and popular place, is just in from the dolphin fountain on the harborfront, near the Seajet pier. **Peristerionas** (© **22830/23-425**) is a friendly place where the food is filling and plentiful; to get here, turn in from the harborfront on Leoforos Megalohoris and take the first left.

**Caffe Italia TRATTORIA**  Dora Coluccio and her husband, Yorgos Marazlis, are the owners of this cozy spot near the new harbor. The stone-walled dining room decorated with old photos of Rome is a great place to linger over a cappuccino or a plate of pasta topped with one of Dora's delectable sauces—the *putanesca* is our favorite. The menu changes often, making use of seasonal local produce as well as cheese and wine imported from Italy. If you enjoy satisfying, simple fare and good company, you're likely to join the many locals and travelers who come back night after night.

New port, Hora. © **22830/25-756.** Main courses 5€–15€. No credit cards. Daily 10am–3pm and 6pm–12:30am. Behind the children's park and just down the street from Windmills Travel.

**Taverna Drosia GREEK**  This taverna, perched at the head of a steep valley overlooking the sea, seems a world away from the crowds and traffic of the harbor. From the shaded flagstone terrace, you can watch ships slowly approaching; Siros sits across the water, and in the valley are terraced fields, dovecotes, and an old windmill. The food is basic taverna fare, though considerably better than average—bread arrives at the table in thick wholesome slabs, salads are sprinkled with succulent capers, and everything is very fresh.

Ktikades, 5km (3 miles) from Tinos town. © **22830/41-387.** Main courses 5€–12€. Daily 11am–midnight.

**To Koutouki tis Eleni GREEK**  There's usually no menu at this excellent small taverna, known in town simply as Koutouki. Basic ingredients are cooked up into simple meals that remind you how delightful Greek food can be. Local cheese and wine, fresh fish and meats, delicious vegetables—these are the staples that come together so well in this taverna, which demonstrates that you don't have to pay a fortune to experience good *paradisiako* (traditional) home cooking.

Paralia, Hora. © **22830/24-857.** Main courses 5€–15€. No credit cards. Daily noon–midnight. From the harbor turn onto Evangelistria, the market street; take the 1st right up a narrow lane with 3 tavernas; Koutouki is the 1st on the left.

**Xynari** ⭐⭐ **GREEK**  Now, this is a restaurant worth seeking out! Once you eat here, you may eat nowhere else. First, the surroundings are lovely: several rooms in a distinguished 19th century house. In good weather, tables are also set up on the balcony. Most important, the food is delicious: The grills make you realize how poorly many places do meat; the eggplant dishes are perky and piquant; even that old international stand-by, the stuffed baked potato, is delicious.

13 Evangelista, Hora. ☎ 22830/23-665. Main courses 6€–25€. AE, MC, V. Daily 7pm–midnight.

## 9 Siros (Syros)

144km (78 nautical miles) SE of Piraeus

Siros offers a rare opportunity to vacation as the Greeks do. Excellent food, a long tradition of the popular music known as *rembetika*, glorious little-known beaches, and the most energetic island capital in the Cyclades are among its pleasures.

The island's capital, **Ermoupolis** is also the administrative capital of the Cyclades. In the 19th century, this was the busiest port in Greece—far busier than Piraeus—and a center of ship-building. You'll see several surviving shipyards along the harbor. Signs of the island's former affluence are concentrated in the vicinity of the harbor, where neoclassical mansions abut the rocky waterfront and grandiose public buildings line spacious squares. Although Ermoupolis saw a considerable period of design in the 20th century, recent restoration efforts have brought back much of the glory of the city's heyday; several of the most elaborate mansions have been restored as homes and others have been converted to hotels and guesthouses. Other signs of urban revival are a busy calendar of lively public events and some of the best food in the Cyclades.

The north end of the island is a starkly beautiful region of widely dispersed farms, terraced fields, and plentiful walking paths. The best beaches of the island are here, accessible only on foot or by boat, and the spectacularly situated Cycladic site at Kastri can be reached by trail. The San Mihali and kopanisti cheeses are made here, as well as a delicious thyme honey; all of these can be found in the Ermoupolis open-air market.

The best months to visit Siros are May, June, and September; the worst month is August, when vacationing Greeks fill every hotel room on the island. Getting around this small island by bus is so easy and convenient that you may not need to rent a car or moped.

## ESSENTIALS
### GETTING THERE    **By Plane**    In summer, there's at least one flight daily from Athens. Contact the **Olympic Airways** in Athens (☎ **210/966-6666** or 210/936-9111; www.olympic-airways.gr) or at their office in Ermoupolis, 100m (328 ft.) from the port in the direction of Hotel Hermes (☎ **22810/88-018** or 22810/82-634).

**By Boat**    Ferries connect Siros at least once daily with Piraeus (2½ hr. by high-speed ferry, 4½ hr. by ferry), Naxos (1½ hr. by high-speed ferry or hydrofoil, 2½ hr. by ferry), Mykonos (30 min. by high-speed ferry, 1½ hr. by ferry), Paros (45 min. by high-speed ferry, 1½ hr. by ferry), Tinos (1 hr.), and Santorini (4–7 hr.); and once or twice weekly with Folegandros (5–6 hr.), Sifnos (3 hr.), Iraklion (5–10 hr.), Samos (7–9 hr. to Vathi), and Thessaloniki (12–15 hr.). There are also daily catamarans from Rafina (2 hr.). You'll find numerous ferry-ticket offices at the pier. **Alpha Syros** (☎ **22810/81-185**), opposite the ferry pier, and its sister company, **Teamwork Holidays** (☎ **22810/83-400;** teamwork@otenet.gr), sell tickets for all the ferries. Ferry information can be verified with the local **Port Authority** (☎ **22810/88-888** or 22810/82-690); Piraeus ferry schedules can be confirmed with the **GNTO** in Athens (① **210/327-1300; 210/331-0562**) or the **Port Authority in Piraeus** (① **210/459-3223** or 210/422-6000; phone seldom answered); for Rafina schedules, call the **Port Authority in Rafina** (① **22940/28-888**).

**VISITOR INFORMATION** The **Hoteliers Association of Siros** operates an information booth at the pier in summer; it's open daily from 9am to 10pm. Note that the list of hotels they offer is not complete. At press time there were rumors that the former GNTO, now under local management, was closing. If it remains open, you may find it at 10 Dodekanisou, a side street just to the left of the pier (① **22810/86-725**; fax 22810/82-375), open Monday through Friday from 7:30am to 2:30pm. If it is closed, **Teamwork Holidays** (① **22810/83-400**; fax 22810/83-508) and **Enjoy Your Holidays** (① **22810/87-070**; enjoy-holidays.gr) on the harbor can book rooms; change money; sell airline tickets; sell ferry tickets; and arrange rental cars. In the summer, these agencies also offer around-the-island full-day beach tours by yacht (30€) and a full-day beach tours by yacht (30€); a full-day excursion to Mykonos and Delos is 50€.

**GETTING AROUND By Bus** The **bus stop** in Ermoupolis is at the pier; the schedule is posted here. Buses circle the southern half of Siros hourly in summer between 8am and midnight. There are no buses to the northern part of the island. The off-season schedule is irregular due to the fact that the buses also bring children to and from school.

**By Car & Moped** Of the several car-rental places along the harbor in the vicinity of the pier, a reliable choice is **Siros Rent A Car** (① **22810/80-409**), next to the GNTO office on Dodekanisou, a side street just to the left of the pier. A small car will cost from 55€ per day, including insurance. A 50cc scooter rents from 25€ a day.

**By Taxi** The taxi stand is on the main square, Plateia Miaoulis (① **22810/86-222**).

**FAST FACTS** Several **banks** on the harbor have ATMs. The Ermoupolis **hospital** (① **22810/86-666**) is the largest in the Cyclades; it's just outside town to the west near Plateia Iroon. There's a friendly drop-off **laundry/dry-cleaning** service opposite the post office on Protopapadaki. For free **luggage storage**, ask at Teamwork Holidays (① **22810/83-400**). The **police** (① **22810/82-610**) are on the south side of Miaoulis Square. The **port authority** (① **22810/88-888** or 22810/82-690) is on the long pier at the far end of the harbor, beyond Hotel Hermes. The **post office** (① **22810/82-596**) is between Miaoulis Square and the harbor on Protopapadaki; open Monday through Friday from 7:30am to 2pm. The **telephone office (OTE)** is on the east side of Miaoulis Square (① **22810/87-399**), open Monday through Saturday from 7:30am to 3pm.

## WHAT TO SEE & DO
## MUSEUMS

**Ermoupolis Industrial Museum** Behind the copious cranes and warehouses of the Neorion Shipyard at the southern end of the port, you'll find the new Industrial Museum of Ermoupolis, which opened in 2000. It's just outside town to the west near Plateia Iroon. It's worth the 20-minute walk from the ferry pier to check out this extensive collection of artifacts from the town's industrial past: weaving machines, metalworking tools, and, of course, a collection relating to the town's famed shipyards. Also check out the fine collection of original drawings by the architects of Ermoupolis's neoclassical heyday, the interesting photographs and engravings depicting various aspects of island life, and the old maps of Siros and the Cyclades.

Just off Plateia Iroon and opposite the hospital, Ermoupolis. ✆ **22810/86-900.** Admission 3€ students; free on Wed. Tues–Sun 10am–2pm and 6–9pm.

**Archaeological Museum** The highlight of this museum's small collection is a room containing finds from the excavations at Halandriani, a prehistoric cemetery in the northern hills of Siros, including several fine Cycladic figurines. (You can visit the Bronze Age fortified settlement at Kastri, near Halandriani, where many of the museum's artifacts were found—see "Hiking in Northern Siros," below.) Since Ermoupolis is the capital of the Cyclades, the archaeological museum has holdings from many of the smaller Cycladic island, including two beautiful miniature Hellenistic marble heads, a Roman-era sculpture from Amorgos, and a black granite statue from Egypt which dates back to 730 B.C.

On the west side of the town hall below the clock tower, Ermoupolis. ✆ **22810/86-900.** Admission 2€. Tues–Sun 8:30am–3pm.

## EXPLORING ERMOUPOLIS

Ermoupolis is a flourishing city, a city with a life of its own that clearly doesn't rely on tourism. If you arrive on Siros by boat, you'll immediately be aware of the lay of the land of the capital: two hills loom over the waterfront. Originally, the term **Ano Siros** (which simply means the area above Siros) was used to describe the peaks of both hills. This is where islanders retreated when threatened by pirate raids. Today, the term Ano Siros describes the taller hill seen to the left of Ermoupolis as you enter the harbor. This was (and is) the Catholic quarter of the town, founded by the Venetians in the 13th century. Much of the intricate maze of streets from that period remains today. Several Roman Catholic churches stand here; the most important is the **Church of Ayios Yioryios** (mass usually celebrated Sundays at 11am). The large buff-colored building on the hilltop is the medieval **Monastery of the Capuchins.** Remnants of castle walls, stone archways, and narrow lanes make this area a delight to explore. (Onirou, one of the streets that run uphill, is probably your best bet for an assault on Ano Siro.)

The other hill, **Vrondado,** with its blue-domed Greek Orthodox Church of the Resurrection, was built up as the town grew when Greeks from other islands, especially Chios, moved here at the time of the Greek War of Independence in the 1820s. Its narrow streets, marble-paved squares, and dignified mansions lend a certain old-world charm to the busting inner city. There's a great view of Ermoupolis and the neighboring islands from the terrace outside the **Church of the Resurrection.** This also where the island's two main cemeteries are, the Catholic one with the more imposing marble monuments, reflecting the long-standing prosperity of that community.

The sophisticated neoclassical architecture of Ermoupolis's 19th century glory days dominates the low-lying areas of the city in the vicinity of the harbor. The central square, **Plateia Miaoulis,** and the elaborately elegant neo-classical **Town Hall** (designed by Ernst Ziller, who designed the Grande Bretagne and Parliament House in Athens) are conspicuous reminders of Ermoupolis's heyday. (To reach Plateia Miaoulis from the port, turn inland on Venizelou, near the bus station.) Plateia this grand are unknown on other Cycladic islands. Ringed by high palm trees and facing the Town Hall, Plateia Miaoulis is the center of civic life in Ermoupolis. Outdoor theatrical and musical events are often put on here, and every night the square is filled with promenading Ermoupolites.

A couple of blocks northeast of the Town Hall is the 19th-century **Apollon Theater** ★, a smaller version of Milan's La Scala. It's being restored, thanks to funding from the European Union, and there may be performances here by the time that you visit. (Contact the **GNTO** at © **22810/86-725** for information and tickets.) Northeast behind it is the imposing Greek Orthodox church of **Ayios Nikolaos**, with a green marble iconostasis carved by Vitalis, a famed 19th-century marble carver from Tinos. (Vitalis also sculpted the monument to an unknown soldier in the garden near the entrance.) A short stroll beyond the church will bring you to the neighborhood called **Vaporia**, named after the steamships that brought it great prosperity.

## BEACHES

Beaches are not the island's strong suit, but there are a number of perfectly adequate places to swim and sun. **Megas Yialos**, as its name states, is the largest beach on the island and the prettiest on the south coast. Its sandy beach is shaded by tamarisk trees and is especially good for families because it's gently shelved. There are a number of small tavernas. **Agathopes**, a 10-minute walk south of Possidonia in the island's southwest corner, has a sandy beach and a little offshore islet; the beach here is not yet overdeveloped.

A few kilometers to the north, **Galissas** has one of the best beaches on the island, a crescent of sand bordered by tamarisks; it's popular weekends with locals and in high season with tourists. Camp sites, small restaurants, and bars are growing up here. **Armeos beach**, a short walk south of town, is less crowded and often nude.

**Kini** is a small fishing village on the west coast with two beaches on sheltered Delfini Bay, valued for its sunsets and a local family of bouzouki musicians that sometimes plays. The best of the two beaches at Kini is the primarily nudist **Delfini beach**, 2km (1¼ miles) north of town over the headland; there's a small taverna here that operates in summer. The bus from Ermoupolis makes the trip to Kini hourly in summer.

**Lia** and **Grammata**, two of the finest beaches on the island, can be reached only by boat or on foot. There is no regular boat taxi service to these beaches, although there are numerous boat owners who may be willing to take you there. For information, contact **Teamwork Holidays** (© **22810/83-400**). To get here on foot, see "Hiking in Northern Siros," below.

## HIKING IN NORTHERN SIROS

The northern part of Siros is hilly and wild, with poor roads, no bus service, and widely dispersed houses. It's a beautiful part of the island to explore on foot, and has several marked hiking trails. The region is home to dairies that produce the popular San Mihali cheese, milk, and butter that visiting Greeks love to take home.

**Kastri** ★, north of Halandriani, is thought to be one of the oldest archaeological sites in the Cyclades, and its remote cliff-rimmed perch high above the Aegean makes a great destination for a hike. It's a long walk from Ermoupolis, about 7km (4 miles) each way, but you can shorten the hike considerably by taking a taxi to the tiny village of Halandriani, about 4.5km (3 miles) north of Ermoupolis, off the Kampos road. The marked trail to Kastri is signposted from the village—follow the signs and painted arrows through terraced fields to the bottom of a dry streambed near a remote beach. From here, the trail climbs steeply to the top of a long, narrow ridge with the remains of the settlement at its summit, surrounded by craggy slopes on three sides. There isn't much to see—the ruins of a defensive outer wall and the outlines of the individual houses—but the view is spectacular and the setting satisfyingly remote. A great way to end the day is with dinner at Mitakas (see "Where to Dine," below), one of the island's best tavernas, located about 3km (2 miles) from Ermoupolis on the main northern (Kampos) road.

The best **beaches** on Siros are at the north end of the island, and all are accessible only on foot or by boat. Sheltered in sandy coves, these quiet and idyllic beaches are shaded by tamarisk and palm trees. There isn't reliable fresh water, so be sure to bring your own. The beach trails begin at Kastri, about 8km (5 miles) north of Ermoupolis; the best way to get there is by rental car or moped, since the public buses don't travel this far north and there are no public phones you can use to call a return taxi. Just before the road turns to dirt, you'll see a sign for **Lia**, the longest of the northern beaches; the walk is about an hour round-trip. **Grammata ★**, the most beautiful small beach on the island, is situated in a palm oasis at the outlet of a natural spring. The walk in from Kampos is 2 hours round-trip; there's no shade on the trail, so try to avoid walking during the hottest midafternoon hours.

## WHERE TO STAY

The kiosk of the **Hoteliers Association of Siros**, right as you come off the ferry in Ermoupolis, provides a list of island hotels. Note that hotels pay to become members of this association, so not all of the island's best lodgings are represented. In August, when vacationing Greeks pack the island, don't even think of arriving without a reservation.

**Hotel Apollonos**    This mansion on the water in Vaporia has been meticulously restored and decorated; it's one of the best of the town's period hotels. Those looking for a fully authentic restoration might be disappointed—the furnishings and lighting are contemporary in style—but the overall effect is one of complete harmony between new and old, creating an atmosphere of understated elegance. The best bedrooms are the two facing the water at the back of the house: Both are quite spacious, and one has a loft sleeping area with sitting room below. Bathrooms are large, with tile and wood floors. A large common sitting room faces the bay, while a breakfast room faces the street.

8 Apollonos, Ermoupolis, 84100 Siros. **☎ 22810/81-387** or 22810/80-842. Fax 22810/81-681. 3 units. 175€ double. Rates include breakfast. No credit cards. **Amenities:** Breakfast room/bar. *In room:* A/C.

**Hotel Hermes**    The Hermes presents a bright, modern facade to busy Plateia Kanari at the east end of the harbor; what you can't see from the street is that many of the rooms face directly onto a quiet stretch of rocky coast at the back of the building. The functional, rather dull standard rooms have shower-only bathrooms and views of the street or a back garden. The deluxe rooms in the new wing are worth the extra money for their size, furnishings, and balconies (which allow early risers to see the sunrise). The hotel restaurant serves three meals a day and offers quality Greek food at reasonable prices.

Plateia Kanari, Ermoupolis, 84100 Siros. **☎ 22810/83-011** or 22810/83-012. Fax 22810/87-412. 51 units. 75€–90€ double. Continental breakfast 5€. AE, DC, MC, V. **Amenities:** Restaurant, bar. *In room:* A/C, TV.

**Hotel Omiros ★**    In 1988, when the work of restoration was begun, this building was in a state of near ruin; now the transformation is complete, and the Omiros has become one of the most appealing of the neoclassical mansion hotels in Ermoupolis. Rooms are furnished with simple antiques; some details from the original building have been retained, such as marble hand basins and massive fireplaces. The architectural highlight of the building is the spiral stair that climbs through a shaft of light to the glass roof. Breakfast, drinks, and light meals are served in a small walled garden. The hotel is on a hill above Miaoulis Square—it's a steep climb from the port, so it's best to take a taxi. There is parking, although the route from the port is complex and difficult to follow; call ahead for directions.

43 Omirou, Ermoupolis, 84100 Siros. © 22810/84-910 or 22810/88-756. Fax 22810/86-266. 13 units. 100€ double. Continental breakfast 10€ extra. MC, V.

**Hotel Vourlis** ★  On a hill overlooking the fashionable Vaporia district, the elegant Hotel Vourlis occupies one of the finest of the city's mansions. Built in 1888, the house has retained all its grandeur and charm. The fine details which have sadly been lost in many other restored mansions are here in all their glory: The plaster ceilings in the front rooms are especially resplendent. Most furniture also dates to the 19th century, creating a period setting which incorporates all the comforts you expect from a fine hotel. Bathrooms are spacious, and all have tubs. The two front rooms on the second floor have great sea views. Winter guests will be glad to know that the house is centrally heated. The adjacent 5-unit **Ipatia Guesthouse** (© 22810/83-575; ipatiaguest@yahoo.com) also occupies a nicely restored town house.

5 Mavrokordatou, Ermoupolis, 84100 Siros. © and fax 22810/88-440 or 22810/81-682. 8 units. 100€–150€ double. Continental breakfast 9€. MC, V. Open year-round. **Amenities:** Breakfast room/bar. *In room:* A/C, TV.

## WHERE TO DINE

There are numerous excellent tavernas in and around Ermoupolis. The **Boubas Ouzeri** and the **Yacht Club of Siros** are both excellent for ouzo and mezedes. In addition to the tavernas mentioned below, try the excellent **Petrino Taverna** (© 22810/84-427), around the corner from To Arhontariki; and **Fragosiriani** (© 22810/84-888), with a great view from its high terrace in Ano Siros (just down the street from Taverna Lilis).

**Taverna Lilis** ★  GREEK/SEAFOOD  Lilis is one of the best of the tavernas in Ano Siros, the quarter cresting the high conical hill behind Ermoupolis. From the outdoor terrace, there's a stellar view of Ermoupolis, the bay, distant Tinos, and, even farther out, the shores of Mykonos. It's highly calming to sit here as the sun sets and watch the ships moving silently into port. The food is better-than-average taverna fare—meats and fish are grilled on a wood fire, and the ingredients are reliably fresh.

Ano Siros. © 22810/88-087. Reservations recommended in July/Aug. Main courses 6€–15€. No credit cards. Daily 7pm–midnight. Follow Omirou from the center of Ermoupolis, past the Hotel Omiros, and continue straight up the long flight of steps that leads to Lilis's brightly lit terrace. If all those steps don't appeal, call a taxi.

**Taverna Mitakas** GREEK  You will have go out of your way to find this small taverna in the hills north of Ermoupolis, but this is one detour you won't regret. Much of the farming in Siros takes place on the slopes of these northern hills, so the food on your plate is mostly local and consistently fresh. The cheeses from nearby San Mihali are especially delicious, and the lamb is from local farms. The *melitzanosalata* is near perfection—redolent of wood smoke and lemon and just the right amount of garlic. The view from the terrace is great, but if the wind is blowing at all you'll want to a table indoors or behind the sheltering hedgerow.

Mitakas (☎ 22810/82-752. Main courses 4€–15€. No credit cards. Daily 11am–midnight. About 3km (2 miles) from Ermoupolis on the Kampos road.

**To Arhontariki** GREEK This small place fills the narrow street with tables precariously perched on the cobblestones and is probably the best of the tavernas in Ermoupolis center. It's easy to find—just plunge into the maze of streets at the corner of Miaoulis Square between Pyramid Pizzeria and Loukas Restaurant, and weave your way left—it's 2 blocks or so in, between Miaoulis and the harbor. The menu is largely composed of specials that change daily. It always includes a few vegetable main courses, which are subtly spiced and delicious.

Ermoupolis. (☎ 22810/81-744. Main courses 4€–15€. No credit cards. Daily noon–midnight.

**To Koutouki Tou Liberi** ★★ GREEK This place has become legendary in Siros. You'll have to hire a taxi to get here—it's not easy to find, and your driver may have some difficulty if he hasn't been here before. It may seem like a lot of trouble, but this place is definitely worth it. There is no menu—the night's offerings are brought out to you on a massive tray, and each dish is explained in turn. The food is often innovative, making slight but significant departures from traditional recipes. The spicing is subtle, and the dishes make use of the best of what's in season. The owner is also renowned locally for his bouzouki playing—late at night, after the last diners have finished their meals, there are sometimes impromptu traditional music sessions. And did we mention the view? It's exquisite.

Kaminia (2km/1¼ miles from Ermoupolis center). (☎ 22810/85-580. Reservations recommended several days in advance in high season. Main courses 5€–18€. No credit cards. Fri–Sat 9pm–1am.

## SIROS AFTER DARK

In Ermoupolis, the waterfront is the best place to be at sunset. **Kimbara** (☎ 22810/80-878) maintains a calm mood with soft rock, while the music at **Highway** is loud and gets louder as the evening continues. You can also join in the evening **volta** (stroll) around Plateia Miaoulis, or take a seat to watch it. There's also the outdoor **Pallas Cinema**, east of the main square, which has one nightly showing, often in English.

Be sure to pick up a list of events scheduled as part of **Ermoupoleia**, a summer-long arts festival featuring prominent visiting artists; all events are free. The principal venues include the Apollon Theater, Miaoulis Square, and Pallas Cinema, with several theatrical, musical, or cinematic events each week. Programs are available at the GNTO office, most hotels, and travel agencies throughout town.

Ermoupolis has the only **Casino** (☎ 22810/84-400) in the Cyclades, and it's quite an elegant establishment, worth a look even if you aren't interested in gambling. The main entrance is directly opposite the bus station and ferry pier; there's another entrance on the street immediately behind the harbor. The management is British, and most of the staff speak perfect English. The entrance fee is 20€; the minimum bet is 5€. There are also slot machines that take euro coins. There's no cover charge for the restaurant and bar, on the back street. The casino is open daily from 8pm to 6am in summer; slot machines are open from 2pm.

Siros was among the most fertile grounds for *rembetika* (the famous rembetika star Markos Vamvakaris was born here) and you will find this special music played more authentically in several venues outside town, such as **Rahanos** and **Lilis** (☎ 22810/28-087) in Ano Siros, which sometimes have late-night performances on the weekends; reservations are a must.

# The Dodecanese

*by John S. Bowman*

The first thing to notice about this far-eastern Greek archipelago is that the Dodecanese—"the 12"—is in fact comprised of 32 islands: 14 inhabited and 18 uninhabited. They have been known collectively as "the Dodecanese" since 1908, when 12 of them joined forces to resist the recent revocation of the special status that they had long enjoyed under the sultans.

The Dodecanese are far-flung from the Greek mainland and mostly hug the coast of Asia Minor. As frontier or borderline territories, their struggles to remain free and Greek have been intense and prolonged. Although they have been recognizably Greek for millennia, only in 1948 were the Dodecanese reunited with the Greek nation.

Long accustomed to watching the seas for invaders, these islands now spend their time awaiting tourists—who, like migrating birds, show up each spring and stay until October. The coming of the tourist season awakens a pattern of activity largely created and contrived for the sake of drawing and entertaining outsiders. Such is the reality of island life today. As in the past, however, the islanders proudly retain their own character even as they accommodate the onslaught of foreigners.

The islands we feature represent a considered selection from "the 12." In high season, you can travel easily from one to the other. The principal islands, south to north, are **Rhodes, Kos,** and **Patmos.** North of Rhodes lies the lesser yet exquisite island of **Simi.** Patmos and Simi are quite barren in summer, while the interiors of Rhodes and Kos remain fertile and forested. The spectacular historical sights, from ancient ruins to medieval fortresses, are concentrated on Patmos, Kos, and Rhodes; so are the tourists. Simi is the not-quite-secret getaway you will not soon forget.

**STRATEGIES FOR SEEING THE ISLANDS** In planning your excursion to the Dodecanese, keep in mind that the longest tourist season is on Rhodes. So, if you're pushing the season in April, begin in Rhodes, or, if you're stretching the season into October, end up in Rhodes. In general, avoid the Dodecanese from late July through August, when they are so glutted with tourists that they nearly sink.

The three islands most worth visiting—both for their own sake and as bases to explore other nearby islands—are **Rhodes, Kos,** and **Patmos.** From the mainland, all are best reached by air. Rhodes and Kos have airports; Patmos is a short jaunt by hydrofoil from Samos, which also has an airport. From Kos and Rhodes, you can get just about anywhere in the eastern Aegean, including nearby **Turkey,** which is worth at least a day's excursion. **Simi** can be reached by ferry from Piraeus but most people will approach it by boat as an excursion from Rhodes.

## 1 Rhodes (Rodos)

250km (155 miles) E of Piraeus

Selecting a divine patron was serious business for an ancient city. Most Greek cities played it safe and chose a mainline god or goddess, a ranking Olympian, someone like Athena or Apollo or Artemis or Zeus himself. It's revealing that the people of Rhodes, even then, chose **Helios**, the Sun, as their signature god. Indeed, millennia later, the cult of the Sun is alive and well on Rhodes, and, in return for its solar piety, the island receives on average more than 300 days of sunshine a year. What's more, Rhodes is a place of pilgrimage for sun-worshipers from colder, darker, wetter lands around the globe.

But Rhodes has more to offer its visitors than a tan. Rhodes's unique location at the intersection of east and west ensured that it would be in the thick of commerce and conflicts. The scars left by its rich and turbulent history have become its treasures. Knights, Turks, Italians—all the island's invaders—left behind objects of great beauty in the trail of devastation. Through it all, Rhodes remains beautiful. Its beaches are among the cleanest in the Aegean, and its interior is still home to unspoiled mountain villages, rich fertile plains—and butterflies.

Several days in Rhodes will allow you to gaze at its marvels as well as to bake a bit, adding, perhaps, a day trip to the idyllic island of Simi or to the luring shoreline of Turkey. If Rhodes is your last port of call, it will make a grand finale; if it is your point of departure, you can launch out happily from here to just about anywhere in the Aegean or Mediterranean.

## ESSENTIALS

**GETTING THERE   By Plane   Olympic Airways** offers domestic service between Rhodes and the following Greek airports: Athens, Crete (Iraklion), Karpathos (Kasos), Kastellorizo, Mykonos, Santorini, and Thessaloniki. The local Olympic office is at 9 Ierou Lohou (① **22410/83-214**) is 13km (8 miles) southwest of the city and is served from 6am to 10:30pm by bus. The bus to the city center (Platia Rimini) is 2€. A taxi costs 14€. By the way—some taxi drivers will resist taking passengers who have hotels in the Old City; take their number and be prepared to report them and they will usually relent.

**By Boat**   Rhodes is a major port with sea links not only to Athens, Crete, and the islands of the Aegean, but also to Cyprus, Turkey, and Israel. Service and schedules are always changing; check with the tourist office or a travel agency for the latest information.

In late spring and summer, there's daily hydrofoil or catamaran service from Mandraki Harbor to Kos, Tilos, Nissiros and Simi, and less predictable service to many destinations, including Kalimnos, Leros, Patmos, Kastellorizo, and Samos. The advantage of hydrofoils and catamarans is that they make the voyage in half the time. But when the wind blows up the waves, the sailings are canceled. Air quality is also poor, especially compared to the air on larger open-deck excursion boats or ferries.

Flights fill quickly, so reserve in advance. **Aegean Air** (① **22410/24-571** or 22410/24-555). Tickets for any flight in or out of Rhodes can be purchased directly from **Triton Holidays**, near Mandraki Harbor, 9 Plastira, Rhodes city (① **22410/21-690**; fax 22410/31-625; www. tritondmc.gr). Triton will either send your tickets to you or have them waiting for you at the airport.

The Rhodes **Paradissi Airport** (① 22410/83-214) now has some flights to Athens and Iraklion, Crete. Tickets for any flight in or out of Rhodes can be purchased directly from **Triton Holidays**, near Mandraki Harbor, 9 Plastira, Rhodes city (① **22410/21-690**; fax 22410/31-625; www. tritondmc.gr). Triton will either send your tickets to you or have them waiting for you at the airport.

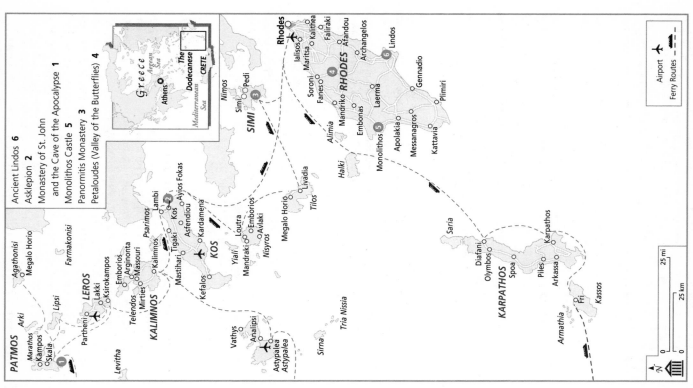

# The Dodecanese

Ancient Lindos **6**
Asklepion **2**
Monastery of St. John
and the Cave of the Apocalypse **1**
Monolithos Castle **5**
Panormitis Monastery **3**
Petaloudes (Valley of the Butterflies) **4**

Greece
Aegean Sea
Athens
The Dodecanese
Mediterranean Sea
CRETE

Airport ✈
Ferry Routes

**PATMOS**
Arki
Marathos
Kampos
Skala
Agathonisi
Megalo Horio
Farmakonisi
Lipsi
Levitha

**LEROS**
Partheni
Lakki
Ksirokampos

**KALIMNOS**
Telendos
Mirties
Emborios
Arginonta
Massouri
Kalimnos
Kefalos
Psarimos

Vathys
Analipsi
**Astypalea**
Astypalea
Sirna
Tria Nissia

Mastihari
Tigaki
Asfendiou
Kardamena
Lambi
Kos
Ayios Fokas
**KOS**
Yiali
Mandraki
Nisyros
Avlaki
Emborios
Loutra
Megalo Horio
Tilos
Livadia

Nimos
Pedi
Simi
**SIMI**
Rhodes ✈
Ialisos
Maritsa
Kalithea
Soroni
Fanes
Faliraki
Afandou
Archangelos
Lindos
Mandriko
**RHODES**
Embonas
Laerma
Gennadio
Alimia
Apolakia
Messanagros
Plimiri
Halki
Monolithos
Kattavia

Saria
Diafani
Olymbos
Spoa
Karpathos
**KARPATHOS**
Piles
Arkassa
Fri
Armathia
Kassos

N
25 mi
25 km
0
0

Wherever it is you want to go, whether by ferry, hydrofoil, catamaran, or excursion boat, schedules and tickets are available from **Triton Holidays**, 25 Plastira (© 22410/21-690; fax 22410/31-625; www.tritondmc.gr). Although travel agents throughout Rhodes city and island can issue air and sea tickets, we recommend Triton Holidays because the staff focuses on catering to independent travelers.

**VISITOR INFORMATION**   The staff at the **South Aegean Tourist Office**, at the intersection of Makariou and Papagou (© 22410/20-245), can provide advice and help about all the Dodecanese islands as well as Rhodes. Hours are Monday through Friday from 8am to 3pm. There's also a helpful **Rhodes Municipal Tourist Office** down the hill at Plateia Rimini near the port taxi stand (© 22410/35-945). It has information and advice on local excursions, buses, ferries, and accommodations, and offers currency exchange as well. It's open June to mid-July, Monday through Saturday from 8am to 9pm and Sunday from 8am to 2pm; and mid-July through October, Monday through Saturday from 9am to 10pm and Sunday from 8am to 2pm. The oft-recommended **Triton Holidays** (see above), whose office is a stone's throw from the Mandraki Harbor, is also ready, willing, and able to answer any traveler's question, free of obligation. Triton Holidays is sometimes open when the tourist offices are closed.

**GETTING AROUND**   Rhodes is not an island you can exhaust on foot. You need wheels of some sort: public buses, group-shared taxis, a rental car, or an organized bus tour for around-the-island excursions. The city is a different story. Walking is the best and most pleasurable mode of transport; you'll need a taxi only if you're going to treat yourself to a meal at one of the farther-out restaurants or if you're decked out for the casino and don't want to walk. Note that wheeled vehicles, except those driven by permanent Old Town residents, are not allowed within the walls. This goes for all taxis, unless you have luggage.

**By Bus**   There's a good public bus system throughout the island; the tourist office publishes a schedule of routes and times. Buses to points **west** (except for the eastern coastal road as far as Faliraki) leave from the East Side Bus Station on Plateia Rimini, while buses to points **west**, including the airport, leave from the nearby West Side Bus Station on Averof. Buses for the eastern coastal road as far as Faliraki also leave from the West Side Bus Station. Island fares range from .8€ within the city to 5€ for the most remote destinations. The city bus system also offers six different tours, details of which are available from the tourist office.

**By Bicycle, Moped & Motorcycle**   Petitions have been filed to reserve a strip of the newly widened major island roadways for bicycles, but until that is approved, cyclists are up against very uneven odds. Remember that you need a proper license to rent anything motorized. The **Bicycle Center**, 39 Griva (© 22410/28-315), rents bikes, mopeds, and motorcycles. The best-looking mountain bikes we've seen are at **Moto Pilot**, 12 Kritis (© 22410/32-285). Starting prices per day are roughly 6€ for a 21-speed; 10€ for an aluminum mountain bike; from 12€ for a moped; and 25€ to 35€ for a motorcycle.

## Rhodes Attractions

Acropolis of Rhodes **8**
Archeological Museum
of Rhodes **2**
Church of Our Lady
of the Castle **4**
Clock Tower **5**
Hospice of St. Catherine **9**
Mosque of Suleiman **6**
Municipal Art Gallery **3**
Municipal Baths **7**
Square of the Jewish
Martyrs **10**
Street of the Knights **1**

**By Taxi**  In Rhodes city, the largest of many taxi stands is in front of the Old Town, on the harborfront in Plateía Rimíni (© **22410/27-666**). There, posted for all to see and agree upon, are the set fares for sightseeing throughout the island. Since many of the cab drivers speak sightseer English, a few friends can be chauffeured and lectured at a very reasonable cost. Taxis are metered, but fares should not exceed the minimum on short round-the-city jaunts. For longer trips, negotiate directly with the drivers. Or better yet, **Triton Holidays**, at no extra charge, can arrange for a private full- or half-day taxi with a driver who will not only speak English fluently but will also respect your wishes regarding smoking or nonsmoking en route. For **radio taxis**, call (© **22410/64-712**. There is a slight additional pickup charge when you call for a taxi.

**By Car**  Apart from the array of international companies—among them **Alamo/National** (© **2410/73-570**), **Avis** (© **2410/82-896**), **Europcar** (© **22410/21-958**), and **Hertz** (© **22410/21-819**)—there are a large number of local companies. The latter often offer the lowest rates, but the concern here is whether, with possibly only a handful of cars, they have the resources to back you up in the event of an accident. Be very certain that you are fully covered before signing anything. An established Greek company with roughly 200 cars—reputedly the newest fleet on Rhodes—is **DRIVE Rent-a-Car** (© **22410/68-243**), with an excellent reputation for personal service, as well as low prices (from about 50€ per day).

**By Organized Tour & Cruise** Several operators feature nature, archaeology, shopping, and beach tours. In Rhodes city, **Triton Holidays** (see above) is one of the largest and most reliable agencies and the only one offering excursions designed for the independent client. Triton offers day and evening cruises, hiking tours, and excursions in Rhodes, as well as to the other Dodecanese islands and to Mamaris in Turkey. We recommend the full-day guided tours, either the tour to Lindos (28€) or the "Island Tour" (30€), which takes you to small villages, churches, and monasteries, including lunch in the village of **Embonas,** known for its local wines and fresh-grilled meat. There is also a fascinating half-day guided tour to the Filerimos Monastery, the Valley of the Butterflies, and to the ancient city of Kamiros (28€). Along Mandraki Harbor, you can find excursion boats that leave for **Lindos** at 9am and return around 6pm (18€); and daily excursions to **Simi** also for (20€). For an in-depth island experience, Triton Holidays also offers a combination package of car rental and hotel accommodation in four small villages around the island (Kalavarda, Monolithos, Prassonisi, and Asklepion), ranging from 4 to 10 nights.

**CITY LAYOUT** Rhodes is not the worst offender in the Dodecanese, but it does share the widespread aversion to street signs. This means that you need a map with every lane on it, so that you can count your way from one place to another. We recommend the two maps drawn and published by Mario Camerini in 1995, of which the mini-atlas entitled *Map of Rhodes Town* is the best. You'll wind up buying it eventually, so you might as well start out with it.

Rhodes city (pop. 42,400) is divided into two sections, the Old Town, dating from medieval days, and the New Town. Overlooking the harbor, the **Old Town** ✪ is surrounded by massive walls—4km (2½ miles) around and in certain places nearly 12m (40 ft.) thick—built by the Knights of St. John. The **New Town** embraces the old one and extends south to meet the **Rhodian Riviera,** a strip of luxury resort hotels. At its north tip is the city beach, in the area called 100 Palms, and famed **Mandraki Harbor,** now used as a mooring for private yachts and tour boats.

Walking away from Mandraki Harbor on Plastira, you'll come to **Cyprus Square,** where many of the New Town hotels are clustered. Veer left and continue to the park where the mighty fortress begins. Down the slope is Plateia Rimini and the Municipal Tourist Office (see "Visitor Information," above).

**FAST FACTS** The local **American Express** agent is Rhodes Tours, Ammochostou 29 (☎ 22410/21-010), in the New Town; open Monday through Saturday from 8:30am to 1:30pm and 5 to 8:30pm. The **National Bank of Greece,** on Cyprus Square, exchanges currency Monday through Thursday from 8am to 2pm, Friday from 8am to 1:30pm, Saturday from 9am to 1pm. There are other currency-exchange offices throughout the Old Town and New Town, often with rates better than those of the banks. For emergency care, call the **hospital** (☎ 22410/80-000) or, if necessary, an **ambulance** (☎ **166**).

For **Internet access,** the **Cosmonet Internet Cafe** has two sites: in the Old Town at 45B Evreon Martyron Square, and in the New Town at 17E G. Papanikolao (opposite the Rhodes Casino); usually open daily from 10am to midnight. **Express Laundry,** 5 Kosti Palama 5, behind Plateia Rimini (☎ 22410/22-514), is open daily from 8am to 11pm. The **Wash-O-Matic** on 33 Platonos (leading off Sokratous) keeps the same hours. The **International Pharmacy,** 22 A. Kiakou (☎ 22410/75-331), is near the Thermai Hotel. There are **public toilets** at 2 Papagou and across from 10 Papagou; there is also one just outside the wall at the

Tips   From the Outside Looking In

Of all the inns on the Street of the Knights, only the **Inn of France** is open to the public (Mon–Fri from 8am–noon). The ground floor houses the Institut Français, but you can see its garden and an occasional art show held in the second-floor gallery. The other inns are now offices or private residences and are closed to the public.

Marine Gate by the Old Harbor. The **police** (© 22410/23-849) in the Old Town are available from 10am to midnight to handle any complaints of overcharging, theft, or other price-related problems. The **tourist police** (© 22410/27-423), on the edge of the Old Town near the port, address tourists' queries, concerns, and grievances. The main **post office** on Mandraki Harbor is open Monday through Friday from 7am to 8pm. A smaller office is on Orfeon in the Old Town, open daily with shorter hours.

## WHAT TO SEE & DO IN RHODES CITY

Rhodes is awash in first-rate sights and entertainment. As an international playground and a museum of both antiquity and the medieval era, Rhodes has no serious competitors in the Dodecanese and few peers in the eastern Mediterranean. Consequently, in singling out its highlights, we necessarily pass over sights that on lesser islands would be main attractions.

### EXPLORING THE OLD TOWN

Best to know one thing from the start about Old Town: It's not laid out on a grid—not even close. There are roughly 200 streets or lanes that simply have no name. Getting lost here is not a defeat; it's an opportunity. Whenever you feel the need to find your bearings, you can ask for **Sokratous,** which is the closest Old Town comes to having a main street.

When you approach the walls of Old Town, you are about to enter the oldest inhabited medieval town in Europe. It's a thrill to behold. Although there are many gates, we suggest that you first enter through **Eleftheria (Liberty) Gate,** identified by the votive offerings found here, which may date from the 3rd century B.C. The remains of the temple are next to a parking lot (driving is restricted in the Old Town), which rather diminishes the impact of the few stones and columns still standing. Nevertheless, the ruins are a reminder that a great Hellenistic city once stood here and encompassed the entire area now occupied by the city, including the old and new towns. The population of the Hellenistic city of Rhodes is thought to have equaled the current population of the whole island (roughly 100,000).

Plateia Simi is also home to the **Municipal Art Gallery of Rhodes,** above the Museum Reproduction Shop (hours vary but are generally Monday through Saturday from 8am to 2pm; admission is 2€), whose impressive collection is comprised mostly of works by eminent modern Greek artists. The gallery now has a second beautifully restored venue in the Old Town (across from the Mosque of Suleiman) to house its collection of antique and rare maps and engravings (open Mon–Fri 8am–2pm); and, within the next several years, it will expand into a new and third site located in the New Town. One block farther on is the **Museum of Decorative Arts,** which contains finely made objects and crafts from Rhodes and other islands, most notably Simi (open Tues–Sun 8:30am–3pm; admission is 2€). Continue through the gate until you reach Ippoton, also known as the Street of the Knights. **Note:** If you are ready for serious sightseeing, there is a ticket for 10€ that gains admission to the Museum of Decorative Arts, the Archaeological Museum, the Church of our Lady of the Castle, and the Palace of the Knights.

The **Street of the Knights** (Ippoton on maps) ★★ is one of the best preserved and most delightful medieval relics in the world. The 600m (1,968-ft.) long, cobble-paved street was constructed over an ancient pathway that led in a straight line from the Acropolis of Rhodes to the port. In the early 16th century, it became the address for most of the inns of each nation, which housed Knights who belonged to the Order of St. John. The inns were used as eating clubs and temporary residences for visiting dignitaries, and their facades reflect the various architectural details of their respective countries.

Begin at the lowest point on the hill at the **Spanish House,** now used by a bank. Next door is the **Inn of the Order of the Tongue of Italy,** built in 1519 (as can be seen on the shield of the order above the door.) Then comes the **Palace of the Villiers of the Isle of Adam,** built in 1521, housing the Archaeological Service of the Dodecanese. The **Inn of France** now hosts the French Language Institute, constructed in 1492. It's one of the most ornate of the inns, with the shield of three lilies (fleur-de-lis), royal crown, and that of the Magister d'Aubusson (the cardinal's hat above four crosses) off center, over the middle door. Typical of the late Gothic period, the architectural and decorative elements are all somewhat asymmetrical, lending grace to the squat building. Opposite these inns is the side of the **Hospital of the Knights,** now the **Archaeological Museum,** whose entrance is on Museum Square. It's a grand and fascinating structure and well worth a visit. Like so many public buildings in Rhodes, its hours are subject to change without much notice, but in summer it's generally open Tuesday through Friday from 8am to 7pm and Saturday and Sunday from 8:30am to 3pm. Admission is 3€. Across from the Archaeological Museum is the **Byzantine Museum,** housed in the **Church of Our Lady of the Castle** ★, the Cathedral of the Knights, and often hosting superior rotating exhibits of Christian art. Its hours vary but are generally Tuesday through Sunday from 8am to 7pm or later; admission is 3€.

The church farther on the right is **Ayia Triada** (open when it's open), next to the Italian consulate. Above its door are three coats-of-arms: those of France, England, and the pope. Past the arch that spans the street, still on the right, is the **Inn of the Tongue of Provence,** which was partially destroyed in 1856 and is now shorter than it once was. Opposite it on the left is the traditionally Gothic **Inn of the Tongue of Spain,** with vertical columns elongating its facade and a lovely garden in the back.

The culmination of this impressive procession should be the **Palace of the Knights** ★★★ (also known as the Palace of the Grand Masters), but it was destroyed in a catastrophic accidental explosion in 1856. What you see before you now is a grandiose palace built in the 1930s to accommodate Mussolini's visits and fantasies. Its scale and grandeur are more reflective of a future that failed to materialize than of a past that has disappeared. Today it houses mosaics stolen from Kos by the Italian military as well as a collection of antique furniture. Hours vary, but in summer are Monday from 12:30 to 7pm, Tuesday through Sunday from 8am to 7pm. Admission is 5€.

The **Mosque of Suleiman** and the public baths are two reminders of the Turkish presence in Old Rhodes. Follow Sokratous west away from the harbor or walk a couple of blocks south from the Palace of the Knights, and you can't miss the mosque with its slender, though incomplete, minaret and pink-striped Venetian exterior.

The **Municipal Baths** (what the Greeks call the "Turkish baths") are housed in a 7th-century Byzantine structure. They merit a visit by anyone interested in the vestiges of Turkish culture that still remain in the Old Town, and are a better deal than the charge for showers in most pensions. The *hamam* (most locals use the Turkish word for "bath") is in Plateia Arionos, between a large old mosque and the Folk Dance Theater. Throughout the day, men and women go in via their separate entrances and disrobe in the private shuttered cubicles. A walk across the cool marble floors leads you to the bath area—many domed, round chambers sunlit by tiny glass panes in the roof. Through the steam you'll see people seated around large marble basins, chatting while ladling bowls of water over their heads. It's open Tuesday through Saturday from 11am to 7pm; the baths cost 2€ on Tuesday, Thursday, and Friday, but only 1€ on Wednesday and Saturday. Note that Saturday is extremely crowded with locals. In the summer of 2000, the baths were closed for restoration, so they are likely to emerge quite enhanced.

The Old Town was also home to the Jewish community, whose origins go back to the days of the ancient Greeks. Little survives in the northeast or Jewish Quarter of the Old Town other than a few homes with Hebrew inscriptions, the Jewish cemetery, and the **Square of the Jewish Martyrs** (Plateia ton Martiron Evreon, also known as Seahorse Square because of the seahorse fountain). There is a lovely **synagogue**, where services are held on Friday night; a small black sign in the square shows the way. The synagogue is on Dosiadou, off the square, and is usually open daily from 10am to 1pm. (and there's a small museum attached). This square is dedicated to the 1,604 Jews who were rounded up here and sent to their deaths at Auschwitz. If you walk around the residential streets, you'll still see abandoned homes and burned buildings.

While you are at the Square of the Jewish Martyrs, be sure to visit the **Hospice of St. Catherine** ★ (open Mon–Fri from 8am to 2pm; free admission), a prizewinner in 1997 for its restoration and interpretive presentation. Built in the late 14th century by the Order of the Knights of St. John (the Knights Hospitaller) to house and entertain esteemed guests, it apparently lived up to its mission; one such guest, Niccole de Martoni, described it in the 1390s as "beautiful and splendid, with many handsome rooms, containing many and good beds." The description, in fact, still fits, though only one "good bed" can be seen today. The restored Hospice has exceptionally beautiful sea-pebble and mosaic floors, carved and intricately painted wooden ceilings, a grand hall and lavish bedchamber, and engaging exhibits. There's a lot here to excite the eyes and the imagination.

After touring the sites of the Old Town, you might want to walk around the **walls.** (The museum operates a 1-hr. tour on Tues and Sat at 3pm, beginning at the Palace of the Knights.) The fortification has a series of magnificent gates and towers, and is remarkable as an example of a fully intact medieval structure. Much of the structure can be viewed from just walking around the outside but to walk the walls requires an admission fee of 4€ for adults, 2€ for students.

## EXPLORING THE NEW TOWN

The New Town is best explored after dark, since it houses most of the bars, discos, and nightclubs, as well as innumerable tavernas. In the heat of the day, its beaches—**Elli Beach** and the **municipal beach**—are also popular. What few people make a point of seeking out but also can't miss are landmarks such as **Mandraki Harbor** and the wannabe imperial architecture (culminating in the Nomarhia or Prefecture) along the harbor, all of which date from the Italian occupation. Other draws are the lovely park and ancient burial site at **Rodini** (2km/1¼ miles south of the city) and the impressive ancient **Acropolis of Rhodes** on Mount Smith.

**The Acropolis of Rhodes**   High atop the north end of the island above the modern city, with the sea visible on two sides, stand the remains of the ancient Rhodian acropolis. This is a pleasant site to explore leisurely and enjoy a picnic, with plenty of shade available. The restored stadium and small theater are particularly impressive, as are the remains of the Temple of Pythian Apollo. Even though only several pillars and a portion of the architrave stand in place, they are provocative and pleasing, giving loft to the imagination.

Open site.

## SHOPPING

In Rhodes city, it's the Old Town that is of special interest to shoppers. (*But be warned:* Most of these shops close between end of Nov and don't open until Mar.) Here you'll find classic and contemporary **gold and silver jewelry** almost everywhere. The top-of-the-line Greek designer **Ilias LaLaounis** has a boutique on Plateia Alexandrou. **Alexandra Gold,** at 18 Sokratous next to the Alexis Restaurant, offers stylish European work, elegant gold and platinum link bracelets, and beautifully set precious gems. For a dazzling collection of authentic antique and reproduction jewelry, as well as ceramics, silver, glass, and everything you'd expect to find in a bazaar, drop into **Royal Silver,** 15 Apellou 15 (off Sokratous).

For imported **leather goods** and **furs** (the former often from nearby Turkey and the latter from northern Greece), stroll the length of Sokratous. Antiquity buffs should drop into the **Ministry of Culture Museum Reproduction Shop,** on Plateia Simi, which sells excellent reproductions of ancient sculptures, friezes, and tiles. True **antiques**—furniture, carpets, porcelain, and paintings—can be found at **Kalogirou Art,** 30 Panetiou, in a wonderful old building with a pebble-mosaic floor and an exotic banana-tree garden opposite the entrance to the Knights Palace.

Although most of what you find on Rhodes can be found throughout Greece, several products bear a special Rhodian mark. **Rhodian wine** has a fine reputation, and on weekdays you can visit two distinguished island wineries: **C.A.I.R.,** at its new factory 2km (1¼ miles) outside of Rhodes city on the way to Lindos; and **Emery,** in the village of Embonas. Another distinctive product of Rhodes is a rare form of **honey** made from bees committed to Thimati (very like oregano). To get this you may have to drive to the villages of Siana or Vati and ask who has some extra. It's mostly sold out of private homes, as locals are in no hurry to give it up. **Olive oil** is also a local art, and the best is sold out of private homes, meaning that you simply have to make discreet inquiries regarding the best current sources.

Rhodes is also famed for handmade **carpets** and **kilims,** an enduring legacy from centuries of Ottoman occupation. There are currently some 40 women around the island who make carpets in their homes; some monasteries are also in on the act. There's a local carpet factory known as **Kleopatra** at Ayios Anthonias, on the main road to Lindos near Afandou; and, in the Old Town, these and other Rhodian handmade carpet and kilims are sold at **Royal Carpet** at 45 Aristotelos and 15 Apellou. At **Pazari** at 1 Aristoteous and Dimokritou you can watch carpets being made. Finally, there is "Rhodian" **lace** and **embroidery,** much of which comes from Hong Kong. Ask for help to learn the difference between what's local and what's imported.

## SPORTS & OUTDOOR PURSUITS

Most outdoor activities on Rhodes are beach- and sea-related. For everything from **parasailing** to **jet skis** to **canoes,** you'll find what you need at **Faliraki,** if you can tolerate everything and everyone else that you'll have to wade through to get to it.

No license is required for **fishing,** with the best grounds reputed to be off Kamiros Skala, Kalithea, and Lindos. Try hitching a ride with the fishing boats that moor opposite Ayia Katerina's Gate. For sailing and yachting information, call the **R Yacht Club** (© 22410/23-287) or the **Yacht Agency Rhodes** (© 22410/22-927;** fax 22410/23-393), which is the center for all yachting needs.

If you've always wanted to try scuba diving, both **Waterhoppers Diving Schools** (© and fax 22410/38-146) and **Dive Med** (© 22410/61-115; fax 22410/66-584; www.rodos.com/dive-med/index.html) offer 1-day introductory dives for beginners, diving expeditions for experienced divers, and 4- to 5-day courses leading to various certifications.

Other sports are available at the **Rhodes Tennis Club** (© 22410/25-705) in the resort of Elli, or the **Rhodes-Afandu Golf Club** (© 22410/51-225), 19km (12 miles) south of the port. A centrally located, fully equipped fitness center can be found at the **Fitness Factory** (© 22410/37-667), at 17 Akti Kanari.

If you want to get some culture as you get in shape, information on taking traditional **Greek folk-dance lessons** can be obtained from the **Old Town Theater** (© 22410/29-085), where Nelly Dimoglou and her entertaining troupe perform, or by contacting the **Traditional Dance Center,** 87 Dekelias 87, Athens (© 210/25-1080). Classes run from June to early August, 30 hours per week; each week, dances from a different region are studied. There are also shorter courses available.

## WHERE TO STAY IN RHODES CITY IN THE OLD TOWN

Accommodations in the Old Town have the aura of ages past, but character does not always equal charm. There are few really attractive options here, and they are in considerable demand, with all of the attending complications. One is that some hosts, regardless of the ethics and legalities involved, will hold you to the letter of your intent—so if you need or wish to cancel a day or more of your stay, they will do their best to extract the last drachma. And there is some hedging of bets, which means that the exact room agreed upon may at the end of the day be "unavailable." You should also try to be explicit and keep a paper trail.

### Expensive

**S. Nikolis Hotel** ★★  This hotel is one of a kind and, within the old city walls, it is the only hotel with real finesse and class. Don't confuse this with five-star luxury: What you pay for and get here is neither grand nor sumptuous, but it is unique, and in its own way exquisite. Host Sotiris Nikolis is a true artisan with a fine eye. Here, on the site of an ancient Hellenistic agora, he has restored several medieval structures using the original stones and remaining as faithful as possible to the original style. The result is immensely pleasing (though not plush); also, some rooms have sleeping lofts—be sure to inquire if that concerns you. Many of the furnishings are true antiques. Some suites have a kitchenette and a Jacuzzi. In the hotel's enclosed garden are a small fitness center and computer nook with Internet access. If you are resolved to stay within the walls of the Old Town—an unforgettable experience—and if you are willing and able to pay a premium for aesthetic taste, this is the place. (Note that smoking is not permitted here.) Be sure to check out the adjacent **Ancient Agora Bar and Restaurant,** where, in 1990, a 10-ton marble pediment dating from the 2nd century was found beneath the medieval foundations. Plans are underway for a deluxe business suite complete with fax and computer. Also, Nikolis has 8 cheaper units at a nearby building and by 2004 should have opened still another hotel in the old Turkish baths.

16 Ippodamou, 85100 Rhodes. ☎ 22410/34-561. Fax 22410/32-034. www.greekhotel.com. 12 units. 95€–150€ double; 250€ suite. Rates include breakfast. AE, MC, V. Parking within reasonable distance. Open year-round (but call ahead to confirm from Nov–Mar). **Amenities:** Restaurant; bar; Jacuzzi in some suites; concierge; tours and car rentals arranged; concierge; tours and car rentals arranged; nonsmoking rooms; Internet access. *In room:* A/C, TV, fridge, hair dryer.

## Moderate

**Marco Polo Mansion** ⭐    Featured in several glossy fashion and travel magazines, the Marco Polo Mansion has captured attention with its timeless style and good taste. As if squeezed from tubes of ancient pigments and weathered in the bleaching sun, the color palate here is all deep blues, mustard, wine, and pitch, the colors of boats as much as temples. Each guest room is unique, steeped in a history of its own and furnished with antiques and folk art. One was a harem, another a *hamam* (Turkish bath). The "Imperial Room" has six windows, while the "Antika 2" room, lined with kilims, has a view of minarets. The smaller garden rooms, nestled in fragrant greenery, reflect the house's Italian period. Ceiling fans and cross breezes stand between you and the heat of the day. If you want a history lesson as well as a room, plus a bit of exotic fantasy with your morning coffee, you'll find it and more here.

42 A. Fanouriou, 85100 Rhodes. ☎ and fax 22410/25-562. www.marcopolomansion.web.com. 7 units. 65€–115€ double with bathroom. Rates include breakfast. V. No parking in the immediate area. Closed Nov–Mar.

## Inexpensive

**Andreas Pension**    This exceptionally well-run pension offers relief from the cardboard walls and linoleum floors that haunt many of the town's budget choices. Housed in a restored 400-year-old Turkish sultan's house, it also offers attractive rooms, some of which have panoramic views of the town. Other units have wooden lofts, which can comfortably sleep a family of four. The bedrooms (with commendably firm beds) were once occupied by the sultan's harem, while the sultan held forth in room 11, a spacious corner unit with three windows and extra privacy, perfect for a guy for whom every day was a honeymoon! Hosts Dmitri and Josette serve breakfast on a shaded terrace that boasts gorgeous vistas of the town and the harbor, the best views in Old Town. A full bar with wide-screen TV is also at hand, patrolled by a pet tortoise. Laundry service is provided. Rooms 10 and 11 have the best views; rooms 8 and 9 have private terraces.

28D Omirou (located between Omirou 23 and 20, *not* just before 29), 85100 Rhodes. ☎ 22410/34-156. Fax 22410/74-285. andreaschi@otenet.gr. 12 units, 6 with private bathroom. 30€–45€ double with bathroom. Breakfast 8€ per person extra. AE, V. No parking in immediate area. Closed Nov–Feb.

**Hotel La Luna** ⭐    This small, delightful hotel is a block in from the taverna-lined, touristy Orfeos, nestled between two churches in a calm residential neighborhood. It features a large, shaded garden with bar and breakfast tables.

# Rhodes Accommodations & Dining

**ACCOMMODATIONS** ■
Andreas Pension **20**
Esperia **5**
Hilton Resort Hotel **4**
Hotel La Luna **10**
Hotel Mediterranean **2**
Ibiscus **1**
Marco Polo Mansion **16**
Maria's Rooms **11**
Rodos Palace **3**
Rodos Park **9**
S. Nikolis Hotel **19**
Spot Hotel **21**

**DINING** ◆
Alexis Taverna **13**
Diafani Garden Restaurant **18**
Goniako Palati **7**
Hatzikelis **22**
Iannis Taverna **17**
Kafenio Turkiko **12**
Kioupia **24**
Kon Tiki Floating Restaurant **8**
Manolis Dinoris Fish Taverna **14**
Memories **6**
Palia Historia **23**
Romeo **17**

Looking at the clean, modest rooms, all without toilet or bathtub, you may wonder why this is a prime spot in Old Town, sought after by diplomats, barons, and movie stars like Ben Kingsley and Helen Mirren. The answer is charm, which the ancient Greek poets knew to be capricious and inscrutable. It also has a lot to do with the private 300-year-old Turkish bath, which more than makes up for the one you don't have in your room. This is a place for visitors who want and respect quiet; blast your radio or make a ruckus, and you'll be asked to leave. Our favorite double is room 2 (Ben stayed in room 1). Currently, just beyond the encircling walls of La Luna, there is a fascinating archaeological project underway, involving two ancient churches, a traditional Turkish residence and garden, a Byzantine monastery, and much more, making this an even more intriguing corner of Old Town in which to ensconce yourself.

21 Ierokleus 21, 85100 Rhodes. ℂ and fax **22410/25-856.** www.helios.gr/exr. 7 units, none with bathroom. 50€ double. Rates include breakfast. No credit cards. No parking in immediate area. Closed Nov–Mar. Turn off Orfeos between the 2 halves of the Don Kichotis taverna.

**Maria's Rooms** This pristine little pension near the Archontiko Restaurant merits very high marks for both price and quality. The accommodations are sparkling white and squeaky clean, and Maria is a warm and welcoming hostess. Even without air-conditioning, the rooms are cool and enjoy enough seclusion from the bustle of the Old Town to be surprisingly quiet.

**Spot Hotel** Spotless would be a more suitable name for this small hotel. By Old Town standards, this building is an infant, only 30 years old, but the proprietors have gradually been adding architectural enhancements that give Spot more of an island and medieval atmosphere in keeping with its location. The garden and terrace sitting areas have also been enlarged. The rooms are simple and tasteful if not especially bathed in light. Guests enjoy a large communal fridge, access to a phone for free local calls, free limited use of a PC for e-mail, and free luggage storage. Spot is located near the harbor right off Plateia Martiron Hevreon.

21 Perikleous, 85100 Rhodes. ② 2410/34-737. www.islandsinblue.gr. 9 units. 40€–50€ double. No credit cards. No parking in immediate area. *In room:* A/C in some units.

## IN THE NEW TOWN & ENVIRONS

Unlike the Old Town, the New Town doesn't prohibit new construction. You'll find a wild array of options, from boardinghouses to package-tour hotels to luxury resorts. Most are dull and some are dazzling, but the vast majority are so undistinguished that you may forget which one you're in. Cleanliness, a little comfort, and proximity to beaches and bars are what most travelers expect, so this is what you'll find.

### Very Expensive

**Hilton Rhodes Resort Hotel** ✦ Long familiar as the Rodos Imperial until Hilton took over in 2001, this luxurious Aegean-style hotel, across the road from the beach, offers relative proximity to the town of Rhodes along with extensive private resort facilities. Its guest rooms are spacious and comfortable, each with a large balcony—but on their own they don't have much over a top-of-the-line Holiday Inn. The high season offers everything from live entertainment to fish festivals, from paragliding to Greek dance lessons. The Imperial's amenities are almost too numerous to list; its restaurants remind one of being on a luxury cruise ship.

Leoforos Ialisou, Iksia (4 km/2½ miles out of the New Town), 85100 Rhodes. ② 2410/75-000. Fax 2410/76-690. 404 units. 285€ double with sea view. Rates include buffet breakfast. AE, DC, MC, V. Free parking. Closed Nov–Mar. Frequent public buses. **Amenities:** 3 restaurants; 3 bars; 2 pools; children's pool; 2 night-lit tennis courts; health club and spa, with sauna; aerobics classes; extensive watersports equipment rentals; bike rental; children's program; game room (or video arcade); concierge; tours and car-rental arrangements; airport pickup arranged; secretarial services; shopping arcade; salon; 24-hr. room service; massage; babysitting; same-day laundry/dry cleaning services; squash court. *In room:* A/C, TV, minibar, fridge, hair dryer, safe.

**Rodos Palace** ✦✦ "Palace" is indeed the word for Greece's largest five-star hotel (as opposed to beach resort), set amid 30 acres of gardens and facing the sea just outside Rhodes city. It was decorated by the famed designer Maurice Bailey, who cut his teeth designing the sets for *Quo Vadis* and *Ben-Hur*. This has been the uncontested king of the mountain on Rhodes for the past 30 years. It has never rested on its laurels, but is always adding to and improving what it offers, and in 2001 it completed major renovations of all the public and many of the private rooms. Beyond the usual children's center, this hotel offers what is a family center, a resort within a resort designed to provide the ultimate holiday for families with children. The largest of the several pools lies beneath a massive dome constructed by Boeing—and while you're swimming, you can have a suit custom cut for you, from the finest English wool, by the hotel tailor. It is all but impossible to recount the full array of dining options, entertainment, shopping, and so on offered within this world-class resort.

147-2 Menekleous, 85100 Rhodes. ② 2410/22-169. vasilpyrgos@hotmail.com. 8 units, 3 with bathroom. 30€–40€ double with private bathroom. No credit cards. No parking in immediate area. Open Easter–Oct.

## Expensive

**Rodos Park** ⭐ This superb New Town luxury hotel, with gleaming marble and polished wood interiors, enjoys a uniquely convenient yet secluded location just outside the Old Town. This is not a beach resort—it's a fine city hotel. But if you want a Jacuzzi in your room, opt for a suite, preferably one with a superb view of the Old Town walls. If you need to work off surplus calories from the 24-hour room service or the in-house gourmet restaurant, head down to the fitness center, then pamper yourself with a Swedish massage, sauna, or steam bath. A dip in the outdoor pool will offer the perfect finish to your regime. But the biggest fringe benefit of all is the Park's location on the perimeter of the old walls, placing its guests within a short stroll to all of the city's attractions—only a few minutes from the Old Town and Mandraki Harbor, yet convenient to the New Town shopping and dining areas.

12 Riga Fereou, 85100 Rhodes. © **800/525-4800** in the U.S., or 22410/89-700. Fax 22410/24-613 www.rodospark.gr. 60 units. High season 310€ double; 460€ suite; low season 225€ double, 325€ suite. Rates include breakfast. AE, MC, V. Parking nearby. Open year-round. **Amenities:** 3 restaurants; 2 bars; pool; health club; Jacuzzi in suites; concierge; tours and car rentals arrangement; conference facilities; fax and computer facilities; 24-hr. room service; babysitting; same-day laundry/dry cleaning services. *In room:* A/C, TV, minibar, hair dryer.

Leoforos Trianton, Ixia, 85100 Rhodes. © **22410/25-222.** Fax 22410/25-350. www.rodos-palace.com. 785 units, including 20 bungalows, 6 suites, 2 presidential villas. High season 265€–310€ double; 420€ and up for suites. Closed Dec–Mar. Frequent public buses. **Amenities:** 6 restaurants; 4 bars; 3 pools; children's pool; golf course nearby; health club and spa, with Jacuzzi and aerobics classes; extensive watersports equipment rentals including scuba classes; bike rental; children's program; game room; concierge; tours and car rentals arranged; airport pickup arranged; conference center; business center; secretarial services; shopping arcade; salon; 24-hr. room service; massage; babysitting; same-day laundry/dry cleaning services; horseback riding school; water polo. *In room:* A/C, TV, minibar, fridge, hair dryer, safe.

## Moderate

**Hotel Mediterranean** ⭐ Since its major renovation in 1999, this hotel has undergone a transformation so dramatic and successful that its former self drops from memory. Directly across from Kos Beach and next to the new Playboy Casino, its location speaks for itself. The Aquarium is also nearby. The interior of the hotel, from the common to the private rooms, is grand and elegant. The Mediterranean calls itself "Rhodes's newest boutique hotel," which suggests stylish sophistication, and rightfully so. The double rooms have adjoining twin beds, pull-out sofas, and spacious tiled baths. Of the three views offered, the spectacular sea view far outshines the garden (pool and veranda) or side (city) view. (Rates vary according to the view.) The suites all have sea views, sitting areas, and king-size beds. All units have balconies. Handicapped-accessible rooms are available upon request.

35 Kos Beach, 85100 Rhodes. © **22410/22-410.** Fax 22410/22-828. www.mediterranean.gr. 241 units. 75€–140€ double; 105€–145€ suite. Rates include breakfast. AE, DC, MC, V. Free parking. Open year-round. Frequent public buses. **Amenities:** 2 restaurants; bar; outdoor freshwater pool; night-lit tennis court nearby; watersports equipment rentals; concierge; tours and car rentals arranged; airport pickup arranged; conference facilities; 24-hr. room service babysitting; same-day laundry/dry cleaning services. *In room:* A/C, TV, minibar, hair dryer.

**Ibiscus** ⭐ The Ibiscus was already an attractive and well-situated beachfront hotel before it underwent a makeover in 2000. But "makeover" doesn't really suffice—this qualifies as major metamorphosis, taking the Ibiscus from attractive to striking. The spacious marble entrance hall opens into a stylish cafe bar, from which you can take your drinks out front to face the beach or back into the garden veranda, poolside. The tasteful, spacious, and fully carpeted double rooms have king-size orthopedic beds, large wardrobes, ample desk areas, tile and marble baths, and hair dryers. The suites are especially appealing, with rich wood paneling, parquet floors, and two bedrooms (one with a king bed and one with twin beds). Every unit has a balcony, many of which face the sea.

Kos Beach, 85100 Rhodes. ☎ 22410/24-421. Fax 22410/27-283. 205 units. 75€–110€ double; 105€–130€ suite. Rates include breakfast. AE, DC, MC, V. Free parking. Closed Nov–Mar. Frequent public buses. **Amenities:** Restaurant; bar; dipping pool; concierge; tours and car rentals arranged; shops. *In room:* A/C, TV, minibar, hair dryer.

## Inexpensive

**Esperia** *Value* This hotel is a class above its cost. It is rare in Rhodes to find this kind of quality at such reasonable rates. Newly renovated by 2000, the guest rooms are tasteful and exceptionally clean, each with a large balcony with pleasant views. New double-glazed sliding balcony doors effectively seal the rooms off from most of the town's noise. TVs are available on request at a small additional cost. The bar, lounge, and breakfast room are inviting, and the walled outdoor pool and poolside bar are well above average for a modest hotel. The hotel is located near the restaurant district and only a short walk from the beach. It also has 19 apartments for rent, but only in the winter.

7 Griva, 85100 Rhodes. ☎ 22410/23-941. Fax 22410/77-501. 171 units. 45€–80€ double. Rates include breakfast. AE, DC, MC, V. Open year-round. **Amenities:** Breakfast room; bar; pool. *In room:* A/C, fridge, hair dryer.

## WHERE TO DINE IN RHODES CITY

### IN THE OLD TOWN

The Old Town is thick with tavernas, restaurants, and fast-food nooks, all doing their best to lure you into their lair, which in some cases is just where you want to be. The more brazen their overtures, the bolder you must be in holding to your course. Don't imagine, however, that all Old Town restaurants are tourist traps. Many Rhodians consider this area to have some of the best food on the island, particularly for fish. And by the way, don't even think of trying to drive to these places; drive or taxi to an entrance to the Old City and walk in.

### Expensive

**Alexis Taverna** ★ GREEK/SEAFOOD For more than 40 years, this fine restaurant has been the one to beat in Old Town, setting the standard by which all the other seafood restaurants are measured. Two brothers, Iannis and Constantine, today preserve the tradition established by their grandfather Alexis. The list of appreciative diners over the years includes Winston Churchill, Jackie Kennedy, presidents, royalty, and innumerable tourists in the know. This is one place, if you can afford it, to abandon restraint and invite Iannis to conceive a seafood feast for you, selecting a perfect wine from his cellar (which represents vineyards all over Greece). Iannis goes down to the harbor himself each day and chooses the best of the catch. Insisting on quality and freshness, he and Constantine have built their own greenhouse on the outskirts of town to cultivate organic vegetables. Start with a bounteous seafood platter, with delicately flavored sea urchins, fresh clams, and a tender octopus carpaccio. Try the sargos, a sea-bream-type fish, charcoal-grilled to perfection. The creamy Greek yogurt with homemade green-walnut jam is a perfect ending for a superb culinary experience. Every meal here begins with a chef's consultation and should end with applause.

18 Sokratous 18. ☎ 22410/29-347. Reservations recommended. Individually designed dinners without wine average 50€. AE, V. Mon–Sat 10am–4pm and 7pm–1pm.

**Manolis Dinoris Fish Taverna** ★ GREEK/SEAFOOD This restaurant, housed in the former stables of the 13th-century Knights of St. John's Inn, provides a unique setting to enjoy delicious and fresh seafood delights. Either choose a la carte or the set menu, which includes coquille St. Jacques, Greek salad, grilled prawns, swordfish, baklava, coffee, and brandy. In warm weather, the quiet side garden is delightful; in winter, a fire roars in the old stone hearth indoors.

14A Museum Sq. ⓒ **22410/25-824.** Main courses 25€–45€. AE, MC, V. Year-round daily noon–midnight.

## Moderate

**Hatzikelis** ★ GREEK/SEAFOOD    This delightful fish taverna enjoys a peaceful and pleasant setting, in the midst of a small neighborhood park just behind the Church of Our Lady of the Burgh in the Square of the Jewish Martyrs. Although there is an extensive a la carte menu, the various special dinners for two are all but irresistible, even if you must loosen your belt and consume it all on your own. The Fisherman's Plate offers lobster, shrimp, mussels, octopus, squid, and a liter of wine, while the plates of traditional Rhodian dishes include such specialties as pumpkin balls and shrimp saganaki. The portions are challenging, but the quality of the cuisine and the fact that you have until 2am to do your duty practically ensure congenial closure to your meal. To find Hatzikelis easily without winding your way through the Old Town, just enter the walls at the Pili Panagias (St. Mary's Gate).

9 Alhadeff ⓒ **22410/27-215.** Main courses 7€–14€. No credit cards. Year-round daily 11am–2am.

**Romeo** ★ GREEK/SEAFOOD    Though under siege from tourists, many locals gladly frequent the Romeo, as there is a good deal that's authentic within its walls. For one thing, there are the walls themselves, roughly 500 years old. More important, besides the predictable taverna fare, are the number of local dishes on offer. The gracious and helpful waiters will happily explain and discuss the menu with you and accommodate special preferences whenever possible—including special vegetarian meals. Two of the specialties of the house are the mixed fish grill and the stuffed souvlaki. The fish grill is comprised of whatever you select from a generous array of fresh deep-sea options. The tender grilled octopus is an especially gripping surprise. The finely cut grilled souvlaki stuffed with melted cheese and tomatoes, a regional specialty from the north end of the island, is also a sit-up-and-take-notice selection. With each, the very reasonably priced dry house wines are quite suitable. Set back in a quiet enclave, just off and out of the crush of Sokratous, Romeo offers both courtyard and roof garden seating, as well as tasteful live traditional Greek music and song. If you're keen on a smoke-free environment, the roof garden is usually quite breezy and the air particularly fresh.

7–9 Menekleous (off Sokratous). ⓒ **22410/25-186.** Main courses 6€–18€. AE, MC, V. Mid-Mar to mid-Nov daily 10am–1am.

## Inexpensive

**Diafani Garden Restaurant** (Value) GREEK    Several locals recommended this family-operated taverna, which cooks up fine traditional Greek fare at bargain prices. Sitting under the spreading walnut tree in the vine-shaded courtyard, we enjoyed the potpourri of the Greek plate and the splendid *papoutsaki*, braised eggplant slices layered with chopped meat and a thick, cheesy béchamel sauce, delicately flavored with nutmeg and coriander. You won't find better authentic Greek home cooking than this anywhere in Rhodes, especially at lunch.

3 Plateia Arionos (opposite the Turkish bath). ⓒ **22410/26-053.** Main courses 4€–12€. No credit cards. Open year-round daily noon–midnight.

**Iannis Taverna** ★ GREEK    For a budget Greek meal, visit chef Iannis's small place on a quiet back lane. The moussaka, stuffed vegetables, and meat dishes are flavorful and well prepared by a man who spent 14 years as a chef in the Greek diners of New York. His Greek plate is the best we found in Rhodes, with an unbelievably large variety of tasty foods. Portions are hearty and cheap, and the friendly service is a welcome relief from nearby establishments. The breakfast omelets are a great deal, too.

41 Platonos ✆ 22410/36-535. Main courses 3€–10€. No credit cards. Open year-round daily 9am–midnight.

**Kafenio Turkiko** SNACKS   Located in a Crusader structure, this is the only authentic place left on touristy Sokratous, otherwise replete with Swatch, the Body Shop, Van Cleef, and a multitude of souvenir shops. Each rickety wooden table comes with a backgammon board for idling away the hours while you sip on Greek coffee or juice. The old pictures, mirrors, and bric-a-brac on the walls enhanced our feeling of bygone times. Somewhat restored in 2001, Kafenio Turkiko emerged only mildly different and ready for a new millennium.

76 Sokratous. No phone. Drinks/snacks 1€–4€. No credit cards. Year-round daily 11am–midnight.

## IN THE NEW TOWN & ENVIRONS

### Expensive

**Kioupia** ★★ GREEK   Rated by the *London Guardian* as one of the world's 10 best restaurants, this unique place offers an exquisite gourmet experience that you will long treasure. Kioupia was founded in 1972 by the creative and artistic Michael Koumbiadis, called by Athenian society "the Colossus of Rhodes," who has discovered the true harmony in the taste of Greek traditional cuisine, using the best of local ingredients and village recipes. In this elegantly decorated, rustic old house, the meal begins with a rinsing of hands in rosewater, and then perhaps a choice from three soups, including the unusual *trahanas*, a Greek wheat-and-cheese soup. And then, another difficult choice from an amazing array of appetizers: sautéed wild mushrooms, pumpkin *beignee* (dumplings), savory braised red peppers in olive oil, accompanied by home-baked carrot bread and pastrami bread. The main dishes are equally superb—broiled veal stuffed with cheese and sprinkled with pistachio nuts with yogurt sauce, or delectable pork souvlaki with yogurt and paprika sauce on the side. For dessert, go all the way with light crepes filled with sour cherries and covered with chocolate sauce and vanilla crème. Many of the foods are prepared in a traditional wood-burning oven in clay pots, the faint smell of wood permeating the restaurant. The grand fixed-price meal, like the Orthodox liturgy, requires fasting, devotion, and time (roughly 3 hr.), and involves no small share of mystery.

Tris Village, 7 miles south of Rhodes Town. ✆ 22410/91-824. Reservations required. Fixed-price meals 25€ and 45€ per person, wines and service extra. A la carte also available. MC, V. Year-round Mon–Sat 8pm–midnight. Sun lunch.

### Moderate

**Goniako Palati (Corner Palace)** GREEK   The new Goniako Palati may not be a palace, but it is on the corner—a busy corner, something you overlook once the food arrives. Great canvas awnings spread out to cover the seating area, raised well above street level. The extensive taverna menu is basic Greek, fresh and skillfully prepared in a slightly upscale environment at reasonable prices. This is one place local New Towners go for reliable, and then some, taverna fare. The grilled swordfish souvlaki, served with a medley of steamed vegetables, is quite tasty. The saganaki here is a performance art, and delicious to boot.

110 Griva 110 (corner of Griva and 28 Oktobriou). ✆ 22410/33-167. Main courses 6€–20€. AE, MC, V. Year-round daily 9am–midnight.

**Kon Tiki Floating Restaurant** ★ GREEK/INTERNATIONAL    Still floating after 40 years of serving good food, this was one of Rhodes's first decent restaurants, and it's still a great place to watch the yachts bobbing alongside while enjoying well-prepared, creative dishes, such as the sole *valevska* (filet of sole with shrimps, crabs, and mushrooms gratinéed in a béchamel sauce). The *saganaki* shrimp are exceptionally tasty, served with feta cheese, local herbs, and tomato sauce. The new owner is implementing tasteful incremental enhancements in the decor and unleashing the chef's imagination, with immediate and enticing results like the Royal Greenland shrimps. The restaurant is also open for breakfast and for coffee or a drink at the bar, if that's all you want.

Mandraki Harbor. ℂ **22410/22-477.** Main courses 6€–20€. AE, MC, V. Year-round daily 8am–midnight.

**Palia Historia (The Old Story)** ★ GREEK    Actually, this restaurant is not an old story, as it is only about 15 years old—but it is well on its way to becoming a legend. It's worth a taxi ride from wherever you're staying. Most of the clientele is Greek, drawn by the subtle cuisine and lack of tourists. If you've maxed out on run-of-the-mill Greek taverna fare, this is one place to come. The marinated salmon and capers are worthy of the finest Dublin restaurant, and the broccoli with oil, mustard, and roasted almonds is inspired. As a main course, the shrimps saganaki leave nothing to the imagination. With fish, the dry white Spiropoulos from Mantinia is perfect. For a great finish, go for the banana flambé.

108 Mitropoleos (south in new town, below modern stadium). ℂ **22410/32-421.** Reservations recommended. Main courses 10€–20€. AE, MC, V. Year-round daily 7pm–midnight.

# RHODES CITY AFTER DARK

Rhodes by night is brimming with energy. Outside of Athens, Rhodes claims one of the most active nighttime scenes in Greece. Granted, some of that energy is grounded in the resort complexes north of the city, but there is enough to go around.

Your own good sense is as good a guide as any in this ever-changing scene. In a city as compact as Rhodes, it's best to follow the lights and noise, not worrying about getting a little lost. When you decide to call it quits, shout down a taxi to bring you back, if you can remember where you're staying.

As a rule of thumb, the **New Town** is more lively than the Old Town. In the New Town, several **cafe scenes** are on the harbor, behind Academy Square, or on Galias, near New Market. The **bar scene** tends to line up along Diakonou. There are at least 100 **nightclubs** on Rhodes, so you're sure to find one to your liking. Complicating matters is a recent announcement that the police, after countless complaints of noise and mayhem until all hours, have decided to designate one area of the city for discos and bars, enabling them to stay open until whenever. When this area will be designated and where it will be is anyone's guess.

**Gambling** is a popular nighttime activity in Greece. Rhodes has had for many years one of only three legal casinos in Greece, a government-operated roulette and blackjack house adjoining the Grand Hotel. In January 1999, however, this was replaced by a much more extensive casino and hotel operated by Playboy International. The home of this new complex is the once-grand **Hotel Rodon** facing Elli Beach.

The **Sound-and-Light** (*Son et Lumière*) presentation dramatizes the life of a youth admitted into the monastery in 1522, the year before Rhodes fell to invading Turks. In contrast to Athens's Acropolis show, the dialogue here is more illuminating, though the lighting is unimaginative. Nevertheless, sitting in the lush gardens below the palace on a warm evening can be pleasant, and we heartily recommend it to those smitten by the medieval Old Town. Check the posted schedule for English-language performances; they take place at Papagou, south of Plateia Rimini (© 22410/21-922). Admission is 8€ for adults, 4€ for youths, and free for children under 11.

We thoroughly recommend the **Traditional Folk Dance Theater**, presented by the Nelly Dimoglou Dance Company, Adronikou, off Plateia Arionos, Old Town (© 22410/20-157). It is always lively, filled with color, and totally entertaining. Twenty spirited men and women perform dances from many areas of Greece in colorful, often embroidered, flouncy costumes. The five-man band plays an inspired and varied repertoire. Performances take place from May through early October, Monday, Wednesday, and Friday at 9:15pm. Admission is 12€ for adults.

## EXPLORING THE ISLAND

Sun, sand, and the rest is history. That's nowhere more true than on Rhodes. Ruins and beaches—that nearly sums up what lures visitors out of Rhodes city. First things first: For the best **beaches**, head to the east coast of the island. Visitors also flock to archaeological sites identical to the three original Dorian city-states, all nearly 3,000 years old: **Lindos, Kamiros,** and **Ialisos**. Of these, Lindos was and is preeminent; it is by far the top tourist destination outside of Old Town. So we begin here with Lindos, and then explore the island counterclockwise.

### LINDOS

Lindos is without question the most picturesque town on the island of Rhodes. Since Lindos has been designated a historic settlement, the Archaeological Society has control over all development in the village (God bless 'em!), and the traditional white stucco homes, shops, and restaurants form the most unified, classically Greek expression in the Dodecanese. Be warned, however, that Lindos is often deluged with tourists, and your first visit may be unforgettable for the wrong reasons. Avoid the crush of mid-July to August, if at all possible. The frequent public buses leave Plateia Rimini and cost 4€; a taxi would cost 30€ one-way.

There are two entrances to the town. The first and northernmost leads down a steep hill to the bus stop and taxi stand, then veers downhill to the beach. If you're driving, park above the town in the lot. At this square you'll find the friendly, extremely informative **Tourist Information Kiosk** (© 22440/31-900; fax 22410/31-288), where Michalis will help you from April through October, daily from 9am to 10pm. Here, too, is the commercial heart of the village with the Acropolis above. The rural **medical clinic** (© 22410/31-224), **post office,** and **telephone office (OTE)** are nearby. The second road leads beyond the town and into the upper village, blessedly removed from the hordes. This is the better route for people more aesthetically minded. Just follow signs to the Acropolis. For 4€ you can ride a donkey (also known as a Lindian taxi) all the way to the top; you'll pass their stand.

All along the way, your path will be strewn with embroidery and lace, which may or may not be the handiwork of local women. Embroidery from Rhodes was highly coveted in the ancient world. In fact, it is claimed that Alexander the Great wore a grand Rhodian robe into battle at Gangemila, and in Renaissance Europe, the French ladies used to yearn for a bit of Lindos lace. Much of what is for sale in Lindos today, however, is from Hong Kong.

Before you start the final ascent to the acropolis, be sure to inspect the **relief carving of a trireme** ✦, or three-banked ship, dating from the 2nd century B.C.

At the top, from the fortress ramparts, there are glorious views of medieval Lindos below, where most homes date from the 15th century. To the south you can see the lovely beach at St. Paul's Bay—named from the tradition that St. Paul put ashore here—along with Rhodes's less-developed eastern coastline. Across to the southwest rises Mount Krana, where caves, dug out to serve as ancient tombs, are thought to have been cult places to Athena well into the Christian period.

The **Acropolis** ★ (ⓒ **22410/27-674**) is open Tuesday through Sunday from 8am to 7pm, Monday from 12:30 to 7pm. Admission is 6€ for adults and 4€ for students and children. This is one of three original Dorian acropolises in Rhodes. Ensconced within the much later medieval walls stand the impressive remains of the Sanctuary of Athena Lindos, with its large Doric portico from the 4th century B.C. St. John's Knights refortified the Acropolis with monumental turreted walls and built a small church to St. John inside. Today, stones and columns are strewn everywhere as the site undergoes extensive restoration.

On your descent, as you explore the labyrinthine lanes of medieval Lindos, you will come to the exquisite late 14th- or early 15th-century **Byzantine Church of the Panayia** ★, still the local parish church (Admission 1.50€). More than 200 iconic frescoes (dating from the 18th century) cover every inch of the walls and arched ceilings. Quite recently, all of the frescoes were painstakingly restored at great expense and with stunning results. Be sure to spend time with these icons, many of them sequentially narrative, depicting the Creation, the Nativity, the Christian Passover, and the Last Judgment. And after you've given yourself a stiff neck looking up, be sure to look down at the extraordinary floor, made of sea pebbles.

Adjoining the Church of the Panayia is the **Church Museum** (ⓒ **22440/ 32-020**), open April through October daily from 9am to 3pm; admission 1.50€. The historical and architectural exhibits and collected ecclesiastical items, including frescoes, icons, texts, chalices, and liturgical embroidery, comprise a surprisingly significant collection. A visit here will prove helpful in guiding you through the medieval town.

Then, of course, there's the inviting **beach** below, lined with cafes and tavernas.

## Where to Stay & Dine in Lindos & Environs

In high season, Lindos marks the spot where up to 10,000 day-trippers from Rhodes city converge with 4,000 resident tourists. Since no hotel construction is permitted, almost all of the old homes have been converted into pensions (called "villas" in the brochures) by English charter companies. **Triton Holidays** (ⓒ **22410/21-690;** fax 22410/31-625; www.tritondmc.gr) books six-person villas, including kitchen facilities (reservations are often made a year in advance). In peak season, the local **Tourist Information Kiosk** (ⓒ **22440/31-900;** fax 22440/31-288) has a list of homes that rent rooms. Plan to pay 30€ for a double and 38€ to 55€ for a studio apartment.

Just opening in Spring 2004 should be the new **Melenos Hotel,** in an authentically Lindian-style villa, with hand-painted tiles, local antiques, handcrafted lamps—in short, traditional splendor combined with every contemporary comfort and convenience. To contact the owner Michalis Melenos, send a fax to **22440/32-060** or e-mail mime@astronet.gr.

You'll have a paralyzing array of restaurants and tavernas to choose from in tiny Lindos. On the beach, the expansive **Triton Restaurant** gets a nod because you can easily change into your swimsuit in its bathroom, essential for nonresidents who want to splash in the gorgeous water across the way. It's also not as pricey as all the others.

**Argo Fish Taverna** ★ GREEK/SEAFOOD Haraki Bay is a quiet fishing hamlet with a gorgeous, crescent-shaped pebbly beach and this excellent seafood taverna. Consider stopping here for a swim and lunch on a day trip to Lindos. We appreciated the freshness of the food, as well as the creative variation on a Greek salad: an addition of mint and dandelion leaves with fresh herbs, served with whole-wheat bread. The lightly battered fried calamari was tasty and a welcome relief from the standard over-battered fare. The mussels, baked with fresh tomatoes and feta cheese, were also right on.

Haraki Beach (10km/6 miles north of Lindos). © 22440/51-410. Reservations recommended. Main courses 13€–50€. AE, MC, V. Daily noon–1am Easter–Oct.

**Atrium Palace** ★ Located just over 6.4km (4 miles) out of Lindos on the long beach of crystal-clear Kalathos Bay, this luxurious resort hotel features an eclectic architectural design—a neo-Greek, Roman, Crusader, and Italian pastel extravaganza. The inner atrium is an exotic, tropical garden of pools and waterfalls. The beautifully landscaped outside pool complex is a nice alternative to the nearby beach, and the indoor pool, sauna, and fitness club will keep you busy. To keep the whole family fully entertained on the rainy days that never occur, there are game rooms, a mini-club for young children, and an arcade of shops. Despite its five-star status, the atmosphere here is relaxed, without pretense, and quite friendly, all perhaps due to the Atrium Palace's excellent staff.

Kalathos Beach, 85100 Rhodes. © 22440/31-601. Fax 22440/31-600. 256 units. 88€–150€ double; 102€–325€ suite for 2. Rates include breakfast. AE, DC, MC, V. Closed Nov–Mar. In room: A/C, TV, minibar.

**Ladiko Bungalows Hotel** Anthony Quinn obtained permission to build a retirement home for actors on this pretty little bay on the road to Lindos, 3km (2 miles) south of the swinging beach resort of Faliraki; he never realized his plans, but the bay retains his name. We especially enjoyed the quiet and the convenient location of this friendly family-operated lodge, with nature-lover activities such as swimming, fishing, and hiking to nearby ruins and less-frequented beaches, and its proximity (a 20-min. walk) to noisy and bustling Faliraki. The new (in 2000) outside terrace bar and dining area with a splendid view of the Ladiko Bay provides a lovely tranquil spot for a drink or a meal. The guest rooms are not exceptional, but are quite comfortable and have new mattresses. Fourteen rooms come with fridges.

Faliraki, P.O. Box 236, 85100 Rhodes. © 22410/85-560. Fax 22410/80-241. 42 units. 50€–75€ double. Rates include breakfast. MC, V. Closed Nov–Mar. In room: A/C.

**Lindos Mare** ★ This relatively small and classy cliffside resort hotel is a prime site to drop anchor on the east shore. The rooms are a grade up from most of the otherwise comparable luxury hotels on the coast, and the views of the bay below are heart-stopping. A tram descends from the upper lobby, restaurant, and pool area to the lower levels of attractive Aegean-style bungalows, and continues onward down to the beach area, where there are umbrellas and watersports. It's only a 2km (1¼ miles) walk or ride into Lindos, although you just might want to stay put in the evenings to enjoy the in-house social activities, such as barbecue, folklore evenings, or dancing.

Lindos Bay, 85100 Rhodes. © 22440/31-130. Fax 22440/31-131. lindmare@otenet.gr. 138 units. 90€–160€ junior suite for 2 with half-board plan (breakfast and dinner). AE, DC, MC, V. Closed Nov–Mar. In room: TV.

**Mavrikos** ★ GREEK/FRENCH Brothers Michalis and Dimitri continue a family tradition of fine Greek and French cuisine, such as their oven-baked lamb and fine beef filets, or the perfectly grilled and seasoned fresh red snapper. The venerable restaurant and expansive shaded terrace have retained their special rustic charm—David Gilmore of Pink Floyd fame was so furious when they brought in new, modern chairs that Michalis quickly restored and returned the originals. Other notable fans have included Nelson Rockefeller and Jackie Kennedy. More recently, in July 2000, King Abdullah of Jordan, when visiting Rhodes, had his private yacht sail to Lindos just to eat his supper here at Mavrikos. Clearly, this is not just our first choice for a memorable meal in Lindos or, for that matter, on Rhodes.

The Mavrikos also run a great ice-cream parlor, **Geloblu,** serving homemade frozen concoctions and cakes. It's located within the labyrinth of the old town near the church.

Main Sq., Lindos. © **22440/31-232.** Reservations recommended. Main courses 5€–11€. V. Year-round daily noon–midnight.

## SIGHTS & BEACHES ELSEWHERE ON THE ISLAND

An around-the-island tour provides a chance to view some of the wonderful variations of Rhode's scenery. The sights described below, with the exception of Ialisos and Kamiros, are not of significant historical or cultural importance, but if you get bored with relaxing, these places provide a pleasant diversion. The route traces the island counterclockwise from Rhodes city, with a number of suggested sorties into the interior. Even a cursory glance at a map of Rhodes will explain the many zigs and zags in this itinerary. Keep in mind that not all roads are equal and that all-terrain vehicles are required for some of the detours suggested below. Rhodian rental-car companies usually stipulate that their standard vehicles be driven only on fully paved roads.

**Ialisos** was the staging ground for the four major powers that were to control the island. The ancient ruins and monastery on Mount Filerimos reflect the presence of two of these groups. The Dorians ousted the Phoenicians from Rhodes in the 10th century B.C. (An oracle had predicted that white ravens and fish swimming in wine would be the final signs before the Phoenicians were annihilated. The Dorians, quick to spot opportunity, painted enough birds and threw enough fish into wine jugs so that the Phoenicians left without raising their arms.) Most of the Dorians left Ialisos for other parts of the island; many settled in the new city of Rhodes. During the 3rd to 2nd centuries B.C., the Dorians constructed a temple to Athena and Zeus Polios, whose ruins are still visible, below the monastery. Walking south of the site will lead you to a well-preserved 4th-century B.C. fountain.

When the Knights of St. John invaded the island, they too started from Ialisos, a minor town in Byzantine times. They built a small, subterranean chapel decorated with frescoes of Jesus and heroic knights. Their little white-washed church is built right into the hillside above the Doric temple. Over it, the Italians constructed the **Monastery of Filerimos,** which remains a lovely spot to visit. Finally, Süleyman the Magnificent moved into Ialisos (1522) with his army of 100,000 and used it as a base for his eventual takeover of the island.

The site of Ialisos is open in summer, Monday through Saturday from 8am to 7pm; the rest of the year, irregular hours. Proper dress is required. Admission is 3€. Ancient Ialisos is 6km (3½ miles) inland from Trianda on the island's northwest coast; buses leave from Rhodes frequently for the 14km (8½-mile) ride.

**Petaloudes** is a popular attraction because of the millions of black-and-white-striped **"butterflies"** (actually a species of moth) that overtake this verdant valley in July and August. When resting quietly on plants or leaves, the moths are well camouflaged. Only the wailing of infants and the Greek rock blaring from portable radios disturbs them. Then the sky is filled with a flurry of red, their underbellies exposed as they try to hide from the summer crush. The setting, with its many ponds, bamboo bridges, and rock displays, is admittedly a bit too precious; Petaloudes is 25km (15½ miles) south of Rhodes and inland; it can be reached by bus, but is most easily seen on a guided tour. It's open daily from 8:30am to 6:30pm; admission is 3€ from mid-June to late September and 1€ the rest of the year.

The ruins at **Kamiros** are much more extensive than those at Ialisos, perhaps because this city remained an important outpost after the new Rhodes was completed in 408 B.C. The site is divided into two segments: the upper porch and the lower valley. The porch served as a place of religious practice and provided the height needed for the city's water supply. Climb up to the top and you'll see two aqueducts, which assured the Dorians a year-round supply of water. The small valley contains ruins of homes and streets, as well as the foundations of a large temple. The site is in a good enough state of preservation to imagine what life in this ancient Doric city was like more than 2,000 years ago. (Think about wearing a swimsuit under your clothes: There's a good stretch of **beach** across from the site, where there are some rooms to let, a few tavernas, and the bus stop.) The site is open Tuesday through Sunday from 8:30am to 3pm. Admission is 3€. Kamiros is 34km (21 miles) southwest of Rhodes city, with regular bus service.

Driving south along the western coast from Kamiros, you'll come to the late 15th-century Knights castle of **Kastellos** (Kritinias Castle), dominating the sea below. From here, heading south and then cutting up to the northeast, make your way inland to **Embonas**, the wine capital of the island and home to several tavernas famed for their fresh meat barbecues. This village is on the tour-group circuit, and numerous tavernas offer feasts accompanied by live music and folklore performances. If you then circle around the island's highest mountain, **Ataviros** 1,196m (3,986 ft.), you come to the village of **Ayios Issidoros,** where devoted trekkers can ask directions to the summit. (It's a 5-hr., round-trip hike from Ayios Issidoros to the top of Mount Ataviros.) Otherwise, proceed to the picturesque village of **Siana,** nestled on the mountainside. From here, head to **Monolithos,** with its spectacularly sited crusader castle perched on the pinnacle of a coastal mountain.

If, to reach the eastern coast, you now decide to retrace your path back through Siana and Ayios Issidoros, you will eventually reach **Laerma,** where you might consider taking a 5km (3-mile) seasonal road to the **Thami Monastery,** the oldest functioning monastery on the island, with beautiful though weather-damaged frescoes. From Laerma, it's another 10km (6 miles) to Lardos and the eastern coastal road, where you can either head straight to **Lindos** (see above) or take another detour to **Asklipio,** with its ruined castle and impressive Byzantine church. The church has a mosaic-pebbled floor and gorgeous cartoon-style frescoes, which depict the 7 days of Creation (check out the octopus) and the life of Jesus.

The **beaches** south of Lindos, from Lardos Bay to Plimmiri (26km/16 miles in all), are among the best on Rhodes, especially the short stretch between Lahania and Plimmiri. At the southernmost tip of the island, for those who seek off-the-beaten-track places, is **Prasonisi** (Green Island), connected to the main island by a narrow sandy isthmus, with waves and world-class windsurfing on one side and calm waters on the other.

From Lindos to Faliraki, there are a number of sandy, sheltered beaches with relatively little development. **Faliraki Beach** is the island's most developed beach resort, offering every possible vacation distraction imaginable—from bungee jumping to laser clay shooting. The southern end of the beach is less crowded and frequented by nude bathers.

North of Faliraki, the once-healing thermal waters of **Kalithea**, praised for their therapeutic qualities by Hippokrates, have long since dried up—but this small bay, only 10km (6 miles) from Rhodes city, is still a great place to swim and snorkel. Mussolini built a fabulous Art-Deco spa here; its derelict abandonment retains an odd grandeur evoking an era thankfully long gone.

## 2 Simi

11km (7 miles) N of Rhodes

Tiny, rugged Simi is often called "the jewel of the Dodecanese." Arriving by boat affords a view of pastel-colored neoclassical mansions climbing the steep hills above the broad, horseshoe-shaped harbor. Yialos is Simi's port, and Horio its old capital. The welcome absence of nontraditional buildings is due to an archaeological decree that severely regulates the style and methods of construction and restoration for all old and new buildings. Simi's long and prosperous tradition of shipbuilding, trading, and sponge diving is evident in its gracious mansions and richly ornamented churches. Islanders proudly boast that there are so many churches and monasteries that one could worship in a different sanctuary every day of the year.

During the first half of this century, Simi's economy gradually deteriorated as the shipbuilding industry declined, the maritime business soured, and somebody went and invented a synthetic sponge. Simiots fled their homes to find work on nearby Rhodes or in North America and Australia, though they have also had a startling 70% return rate later in life. Today, the island's picture-perfect traditional-style houses have become a magnet for moneyed Athenians in search of real-estate investments, and Simi is a highly touted "off-the-beaten-path" resort for European tour groups trying to avoid other tour groups. The onslaught of tourists for the most part arrives at 10:30am and departs by 4pm.

In recent years, the **Simi Festival**, running from June through September, has put Simi on the cultural map as a serious seasonal contender, offering an exciting menu of international music, theater, and cinema. In July, August, and September, there's something happening virtually every night.

By the way, there is no natural source of water on Simi—all their water has to be transported by boat from nearby islands. Day visitors will hardly be aware of this but everyone is asked to be careful about any water they have occasion to use.

## ESSENTIALS

**GETTING THERE**   Many if not most visitors to Simi approach it by boat on an excursion from Rhodes. Several **excursion boats** arrive daily from Rhodes; two of them (the *Simi I* and *Simi II*) are owned cooperatively and are booked locally in Rhodes through **Triton Holidays** (© **22410/21-690**). Round-trip tickets are 24€. The schedules and itineraries for the boats vary, but all leave from Mandraki Harbor and stop at the main port of Simi, Yialos, with an additional stop at Panormitis Monastery or the beach at Pedi, before returning to Rhodes. Currently, there are daily **car ferries** from Piraeus, and two **local ferries** weekly via Tilos, Nissiros, Kos, and Kalimnos. From late spring to summer, **hydrofoils**

and a **catamaran** skim daily from Rhodes to Simi, usually making both morning and afternoon runs.

**VISITOR INFORMATION**    Check out the wonderfully helpful website launched by Simi's delightful and informative independent monthly, *The Symi Visitor:* **www.symi-island.com.** Through the site's e-mail option, you can request information on accommodations, buses, weather, and more. Webmaster Wendy Wilcox says you can ordinarily expect a response within an hour. Or you can address your queries to *The Symi Visitor,* P.O. Box 64, Simi, 85600 Dodecanese. Don't ask them, however, to recommend one hotel over another; just say exactly what you're looking for and they'll provide suggestions. *The Symi Visitor* can also be reached at ✆ and fax **22410/72-755** or via its own website, **www.symivisitor.com.** Once you're on Simi, you'll find free copies of the latest *Symi Visitor* at tourist spots.

The resourceful George Kalodoukas of **Kalodoukas Holidays** (✆ **22410/71-077;** fax 22410/71-491), just off the harbor up the steps from the Café Helena, can help with everything from booking accommodations (often at reduced rates) to chartering a boat. Once you've arrived on Simi, drop into the office, open Monday through Saturday from 9am to 1pm and 5 to 9pm. In summer, George plans a special outing for every day of the week, from cruises to explorations of the island. Most outings involve a swim and a healthy meal, and sometimes champagne.

A **tourist information kiosk** is on the harbor, but its hours remain an enduring mystery. Information and a free pamphlet may also be obtained at the **Town Hall,** located on the Town Square behind the bridge.

**GETTING AROUND**    Ferries and excursion boats dock first at hilly **Yialos** on the barren, rocky northern half of the island. Yialos is the liveliest village on the island and the venue for most overnighters. The clock tower, on the right as you enter the port, is used as a landmark when negotiating the maze of car-free lanes and stairs. Another landmark used in giving directions is the bridge in the center of the harbor.

Simi's main road leads to **Pedi,** a developing beach resort one cove east of Yialos, and a new road rises up to **Horio,** the old capital. The island's 4,000 daily visitors most often take an excursion boat that stops at the Panormitis Monastery or at the beach at Pedi. **Buses** leave every hour from 8am until 11pm to Pedi via Horio (.70€). There are a grand total of four **taxis** on the island—leaving from the taxi stand at the center of the harbor and charging a set fee of 2.50€ to Horio and 3€ to Pedi. **Mopeds** are also available, but due to the limited network of roads, you'd do better on public transportation and your own two feet. **Caïques** shuttle people to various beaches: Nimborios, Ayia Marina, Ayios Nikolaos, and Nanou; prices range from 6€ to 9€ depending on distance.

**FAST FACTS**    For a **doctor,** call ✆ **22410/71-316;** for a dentist, ✆ **22410/71-272,** for the **police,** ✆ **22410/71-11.** The **post office** (✆ **22410/71-315**) and **telephone office** (OTE) (✆ **22410/71-212**) are located about 100m (328 ft.) behind the waterfront; both open Monday through Friday from 7:30am to 3pm. For **Internet access,** try the Vapori Bar (vapori@otenet.gr), just in from the harbor at the taxi stand and next to the Bella Napoli Restaurant, open most evenings.

# WHAT TO SEE & DO

Simi's southwestern portion is hilly and green. Located here is the medieval **Panormitis Monastery,** dedicated to St. Michael, the patron saint of seafaring

Greeks. The monastery is popular with Greeks as a place of pilgrimage and of refuge from modern life; young Athenian businessmen speak lovingly of the monk cells and small apartments that can be rented for rest and renewal. There is also an "alms house" that provides a home for the elderly. Call the **guest office** (© 22410/72-414) to book accommodations, ranging from 15€ to 40€ for an apartment or house. All units are self-contained, with their own stove and fridge. The least expensive units have shared outdoor toilets. Most sleep at least four people.

The whitewashed compound has a verdant, shaded setting and a 16th-century gem of a church inside. The **Taxiarchis Mishail of Panormitis** boast icons of St. Michael and St. Gabriel adorned in silver and jewels. The combined folk and ecclesiastical museums are well worth the 2€ entrance fee, which all goes to support the "alms house" mentioned above.

The town of **Panormitis Mihailis** is most lively and interesting during its annual festival on November 8, but can be explored year-round via local boats or bus tours from Yialos. The hardy can hike here—it's 10km (6 miles), about 3 hours from town—and then enjoy a refreshing dip in the sheltered harbor and a meal in the taverna.

In Yialos, by all means hike the gnarled, chipped stone steps of the **Kali Strate** (the good steps). This wide stairway ascends to Horio, a picturesque community filled with images of a Greece in many ways long departed. Old women sweep the whitewashed stone paths outside their homes, and occasionally a young boy or very old man can be seen retouching the neon-blue trim over doorways and shutters. Nestled between the immaculately kept homes, dating back to the 18th century, are abandoned villas, their faded trim and flaking paint lending a wistful air to the village. Renovated villas are now rented to an increasing number of tourists. And where tourists roam, tavernas, souvenir shops, and bouzouki bars soon follow. Commercialization has hit once-pristine Simi, but it remains at a bearable level despite constant pressure to transform the island for the worse.

## A Pair of Local Crafts

One local craft still practiced on Simi is **shipbuilding.** If you walk along the water toward Nos beach, you'll probably see boats under construction or repair. It's a treat to watch the men fashion planed boards into a graceful boat. Simi was a boat-building center in the days of the Peloponnesian War, when spirited sea battles were waged off its shores.

**Sponge fishing** is almost a dead industry in Greece. Only a generation ago, 2,000 divers worked waters around the island; today only a handful undertake this dangerous work, and most do so in the waters around Italy and Africa. Working at depths of 50m to 60m (164 ft.–197 ft.) (in the old days often without any apparatus), many divers were crippled or killed by the turbulent sea and too-rapid depressurization. The few sponges that are still harvested around Simi—and many more imported from Asia or Florida—are sold at shops along the port. Even if they're not from Simi's waters, they make inexpensive and lightweight gifts. For guaranteed-quality merchandise and an informative explanation and demonstration of sponge treatment, we recommend the **Aegean Sponge Center** (© 22410/71-620), operated by Kyprios and his British wife, Leslie.

There's an excellent small **Archaeological Museum** in Horio, housing archaeological and folklore artifacts that the islanders consider important enough for public exhibition. You can't miss the blue arrows that point the way; it's open Tuesday through Saturday from 9am to 2pm. Admission is 2€. The **Maritime Museum** in the port also costs 2€ and is open daily from 11am to 2:30pm.

Crowning Horio is the **Church of the Panavia.** The church is surrounded by a fortified wall and is therefore called the *kastro* (castle). It's adorned with the most glorious frescoes on the island, which can be viewed only when services are held (Mon–Fri 7–8am, all morning Sun).

Simi is blessed with many, but not wide or sandy, beaches. Close to Yialos are two beaches: **Nos,** a 15m (50-ft.) long rocky stretch, and **Nimborios,** a pebble beach.

A bus to **Pedi** followed by a short walk takes you to either **St. Nikolaos beach,** with shady trees and a good taverna, or **St. Marina,** a small beach with little shade but stunning turquoise waters and views of the islet St. Marina and its cute church.

The summertime cornucopia of outings provided by Kalodoukas Holidays has already been mentioned; but if you want to set out on your own, be sure to pick up a copy of *Walking on Symi: A Pocket Guide,* a private publication of (guess who?) George Kalodoukas (7€). It outlines 25 walks to help you discover and enjoy Simi's historic sites, interior forests, and mountain vistas.

## WHERE TO STAY

Many travelers bypass hotels for private apartments or houses. Between April and October, rooms for two with shower and kitchen access go for 30€ to 50€. More luxurious villa-style houses with daily maid service rent for 65€ to 110€. To explore this alternative, contact Kalodoukas Holidays or the Simi website (see "Visitor Information," above).

**Aliki Hotel** ✦ This grand Italianate sea captain's mansion, dating from 1895, is the most elegant and exclusive tourist address on Simi. Restored and redecorated with fine Italian taste in 2000, it has the atmosphere of a boutique guesthouse, intimate and charming. It offers tastefully styled accommodations furnished with Italian antiques. Four rooms have balconies. Several units enjoy dramatic waterfront views, and the roof garden provides a spectacular 360-degree vista of the sea, town, and mountains. The Aliki has become a chic overnight getaway from bustling Rhodes; reservations are absolutely required.

Akti Gennimata, Yialos, 85600 Simi. ⓒ **22410/71-665.** Fax 22410/71-655. 15 units. 95€–115€ standard double; 115€–125€ suite. Rates include breakfast. MC, V. Closed mid-Nov to Mar. *In room:* A/C.

**Dorian Studios** Located in a beautiful part of town, only 10m (33 ft.) from the sea, this rustically furnished hotel offers comfortable lodging (orthopedic beds!) and a kitchenette in every room. Some of the studios have bedrooms with vaulted beamed ceilings as well as balconies or terraces overlooking the harbor, where you can enjoy your morning coffee or evening ouzo.

Yialos, 85600 Simi. ⓒ **22410/71-181.** 10 units. 40€–55€ double. MC, V. Just up from the Akti Gennimata at the Aliki Hotel. Closed Nov to mid-Apr. *In room:* A/C in 5 units.

**Hotel Nireus** ✦ This beautifully maintained, new (in 1994) hotel right on the waterfront has become a popular venue for vacationing Greeks. The traditional Simiot-style facade has been preserved, while the spacious guest rooms are contemporary and comfortable. All have fridges, and the beds are perhaps the best we've found in Greece. Ask for one of the 18 units that face the sea and offer stunning views; if you're fortunate, you might get one with a balcony. All four suites face the sea. This is a most gracious and inviting hotel, with its own shaded seafront cafe and restaurant, sunning dock, and swimming area. For its location, amenities and price, this is our personal favorite on Simi.

Akti Gennimata, Yialos, 85600 Simi. © **22410/72-400.** Fax 22410/72-404. 37 units. 62€–80€ double; 70€–80€ suite. Rates include breakfast buffet. MC, V. Open Easter–Oct. *In room:* A/C, TV.

**Hotel Nirides**  If you crave tranquil seclusion, this small cluster of studio apartments, on a rise overlooking Nimborios Bay and only minutes on foot from the one-taverna-town of Nimborios, may be exactly what you're looking for. It's about 35 minutes from Yialos on foot and appreciably less by land or sea taxi. Each attractive and spotless apartment sleeps four (two in beds and two on couches) and has a bedroom, bathroom, salon, and kitchenette. Seven apartments have balconies, three have terraces, and all face the sea. The Nirides has its own small bar and rents bicycles for excursions to town or beyond. There's a small beach with pristine water just several minutes down the hill.

Nimborios Bay, 85600 Simi. © and fax **22410/71-784.** 11 units. 55€–75€ double. Rates include breakfast. MC, V. Closed Nov–Mar. *In room:* A/C.

## WHERE TO DINE

For traditional home cooking and a respite from the crowds, you might try the tiny **Family Taverna Meraklis,** hidden on a back lane behind the Alpha Credit Bank and the National Bank (© **22410/71-003).**

**Hellenikon (The Wine Restaurant of Simi)** ⊛ GREEK/MEDITER-RANEAN  If you have the impression that the Greek culinary imagination spins on a predictable wheel, you need a night at the Hellenikon. In addition to spectacular fare, this diminutive open-air restaurant on the Yialos town square often provides, by virtue of its location, free evening concerts, compliments of the Simi Festival. The menu is a real page-turner. The chef's fish soup, which starts with the head of a grouper and finishes with saffron and yogurt, is spectacular, as are the grilled vegetables. In additional to a stimulating array of other entrees, you can select one of seven homemade pastas and combine it with any of 19 sauces. The black pasta with shrimp, tomatoes, saffron, and feta is magnificent. Meanwhile, host Nikos Psarros is a wine master who has over 140 Greek wines in his cellar, all organic and all from small independent wineries. Every meal here begins with a personal consultation with Nikos in his cellar, where he will help you select an exquisite wine for your meal.

Yialos. © **22410/72-455.** psarrosn@otenet.gr. Main courses 9€–14€. MC, V. May–Oct daily 8pm–midnight.

**Milo Petra (The Mill Stone)** ⊛ MEDITERRANEAN  Owners Eva and Hans converted this 200-year-old flour mill into an exquisite setting for a gourmet dining experience. Their collection of antique Greek furniture and fabrics graces this most unusual space in simple yet elegant style. (Note the 2,000-year-old grave visible through a glass window in the floor; it's made of pebble mosaic and rose marble.) Find an excuse to ascend to the toilet on the upper veranda to get an overall view of the wonderful interior. Guests dine outdoors on the patio or inside by the open kitchen, enjoying a different menu every day. We were especially impressed by the lamb and fish dishes, using wonderful Simiot hill spices, and the homemade pastas, such as ravioli Larissa, filled with potatoes and homemade cheese and served in sage butter.

Yialos. © **22410/72-333.** Fax 22410/72-194. Main courses 14€–30€. V. May–Oct daily 7pm–midnight.

**Muragio Restaurant** ★ GREEK/SEAFOOD This restaurant, which opened in 1995, has become a big hit among locals, who praise the generous main courses and the quality of the food. Try the *bourekakia*, skinned eggplant stuffed with a special cheese sauce and then fried in a batter of eggs and bread crumbs. We were told to try the extremely popular lemon lamb, but instead we chose the saganaki shrimp in tomato sauce and feta cheese, and were delighted.

Yialos. ☎ 22410/72-133. Main courses 5.50€–24€. V. Year-round daily 11am–midnight.

**Nireus Restaurant** ★ GREEK Michalis, the chef of this superior restaurant located in the Nireus Hotel on the waterfront has gained quite a reputation in recent years. Kudos goes to his *frito misto*, a mixed seafood plate with tiny, naturally sweet Simi shrimp and other local delicacies. We also recommend the savory filet of beef served with a Madeira sauce. They say you can't eat the scenery, but the view from here is delicious all the same.

Yialos. ☎ 22410/71-841. Main courses 3.50€–15€. No credit cards. Open year-round daily 11am–midnight.

**Taverna Neraida** (Value) SEAFOOD Proving the rule that fish is cheaper far from the port, this homey taverna on the town square has among the best fresh-fish prices on the island, as well as a wonderful range of *mezedes*. Try the black-eyed-pea salad and *skordalia* (garlic sauce). The grilled daily fish is delicious, while the very typical ambience is a treat.

Yialos. ☎ 22410/72-400. Main courses 5€–15€. MC, V. Daily 11am–11pm Easter–Oct.

## 3 Kos

370km (230 miles) E of Piraeus

Kos has been inhabited for roughly 10,000 years, and has for a significant portion of that time been both an important center of commerce and a line of defense. Its population in ancient times may have reached 100,000, but today is less than a third of that number. Across the millennia, the unchallenged favorite son of the island has been Hippokrates, the father of Western medicine, who has left his mark not only on Kos but also on the world.

Today, Kos is identified with and at times nearly consumed by tourism, in which perhaps three-quarters of the island's working people are directly engaged. The scale of demand tells you something about Kos's beauty and attractions, which some visitors have done their best to diminish. But the island and its people have endured greater threats, and so will you, with a little determination and good advice.

The principal attractions of Kos are its **antiquities**—most notably the Asklepion—and its **beaches.** You can guess which are more swamped in summer. But the taste of most tour groups is thankfully predictable and limited. The congestion can be eluded, if that's your preference.

You'll get the most out of Kos by learning to follow the locals. If you're in a village and see no schools or churches, and no old people, chances are you're not in a village at all, but in a resort. Kos has many, especially along its coasts. In Kos town, the same is true of neighborhoods and, by extension, restaurants. Greek food is what Greeks eat, not necessarily what they sell.

Kos town is still quite vital. Since the island is small, you can base yourself in Kos Town, in an authentic neighborhood if possible, and venture out from there.

**GETTING THERE  By Plane**  The only scheduled flights into and out of Kos airport are via **Olympic Airways,** whose Kos town office is at 22 Vas. Pavlou

(© 22420/28-331). Although Olympic has experimented with expanded service and may do so again, at present the only direct flights to Kos are from Athens and Rhodes. Currently, there are three flights daily from Athens, and several each week from Rhodes. From **Hippokrates Airport** (© 22420/51-229), a bus will take you the 26km (16 miles) to the town center for 3.50€, or you can take a taxi for 14€. If you're flying out of Kos, Olympic will provide bus service to the airport, provided you arrive at its town center office 2 hours prior to departure.

**By Boat** As the transportation hub of the Dodecanese, Kos offers, weather permitting, a full menu of options: car ferries, passenger ferries, hydrofoils (Flying Dolphins), excursion boats, and caiques (converted fishing boats). Though most schedules and routes are always in flux, the good news is that you can, with more or less patience, make your way to Kos from virtually anywhere in the Aegean. Currently, the only ports linked to Kos with year-round nonstop and at least daily ferry service are Piraeus, Rhodes, Kalimnos, and Bodrum. Leros and Patmos enjoy the same frequency but with a stop or two along the way. The Kos harbor is strewn with travel agents who can assist you, or check current schedules with the Municipal Tourism Office (see below).

**VISITOR INFORMATION** The **Municipal Tourism Office** (© 22420/24-460; fax 22420/21-111; dotkos@hol.gr), on Vas. Yioryiou, facing the harbor near the hydrofoil pier, is your one-stop source of information in Kos. It's open May through October, Monday to Friday from 8am to 8:30pm and Saturday and Sunday from 8am to 3pm; and November through April, Monday to Friday from 8am to 3pm. Hotel and pension owners keep the office informed of what rooms are available in the town and environs; you must, however, book your room directly with the hotel. Be sure to pick up a free map of Kos. For a more extensive and detailed guide to Kos—beaches, archaeological sites, birds, wildflowers, tavernas, and much more—pick up a copy of *Where and How in Kos*, available at most news kiosks for 3.75€.

**GETTING AROUND** **By Bus** The **Kos town (DEAS) buses** offer service within roughly 6.4km (4 miles) of the town center, while the **Kos island (KTEL) buses** will get you nearly everywhere else. For the latest schedules, consult the **town bus office**, on the harbor at Akti Kountourioti 7 (© 22420/26-276), or the **island bus station**, at 7 Kleopatras (© 22420/22-292), around the corner from the Olympic Airways office. The majority of DEAS town buses leave from the central bus stop on the south side of the harbor.

**By Bicycle** This is a congenial island for cyclists. Most of Kos is quite flat, and the one main road from Kos town to Kefalos has all but emptied the older competing routes of traffic. Since bike trails are provided until well beyond Kos town, you can also avoid the congested east-end beach roads. But don't expect to pedal one-way and then hoist your bike onto a bus, because that won't work here. Rentals are available throughout Kos town and can be arranged through your hotel. Prices range from 4€ to 12€ per day.

**By Moped & Motorcycle** It's easy to rent a moped through your hotel or a travel agent, or, as with bicycles, to walk toward the harbor and look for an agency. Rentals range from 16€ to 22€. Or call **Motoway**, 9 Vas. Yioryiou 9 (© 22420/20-031), for mopeds and motorcycles.

**By Car** It's unlikely that you'd need to rent a car for more than a day or two on Kos, even if you wanted to see all its sights and never lift a foot. Numerous companies, including **Avis** (© 22420/24-272), **Europcar** (© 22420/24-070), and

## Moments While You're Here

From the Kos Museum, you might want to walk directly across to the **Municipal Fruit Market**, then have a picnic at the foot of the oldest tree in Europe, only a short walk toward the harbor at the entrance bridge to the castle. Standing with extensive support, this is said to be the **Tree of Hippokrates** ★, where he once instructed his students in the arts of empirical medicine and its attending moral responsibilities.

**Hertz** (② 22420/28-002), rent cars and all-terrain vehicles. Expect to pay at least 95€ per day including insurance and fuel. Gas stations are open Monday through Saturday from 7am to 7pm; there are also several stations open (in rotation) in Kos town on Sunday; ask your hotelier or the tourist office for directions.

**By Taxi**  For a taxi, drop by or call the **harbor taxi stand** beneath the minaret and across from the castle (② 22420/23-333 or 22420/27-777). All Kos drivers are required to know English, but then again you were once required to know trigonometry.

**ORIENTATION**  Kos town is built around the harbor from which the town fans out. In the center is an **ancient city** (*polis*) consisting of ruins, an old city limited mostly to pedestrians, and the new city with wide, tree-lined streets. Most of the town's hotels are near the water, either on the road north to Lambi or on the road south and east to Psalidi. If you stand facing the harbor, with the castle on your right, **Lambi** is to your left and **Psalidi** on your right. In general, the neighborhoods to your right are less overrun with and defined by tourists. This area, although quite central, is overall more residential and pleasant. The relatively uncontrolled area to your left (except for the occasional calm oasis, like that occupied by the Pension Alexis) has been largely given over to tourism. Knowing this will help you find most of the tourist-oriented services by day and action by night, as well as where to find a bit of calm when you want to call it quits. Most recommended places to stay lie to your left, east of the castle.

**FAST FACTS**  Of the three banks offering currency exchange, the **Ionian Bank of Greece**, El Venizelou, has the most extensive hours: Monday through Friday from 8am to 2pm and 6 to 8pm. The **hospital** is at Hippokratous 32 (② 22420/22-300). The **Del Mare Internet Cafe**, 4a Megalo Alexandrou (② 22420/24-244; www.cybercafe.gr) is open daily from 9am to 2am. **Happy Wash**, 20 Mitropoleos, across from Ayios Nikolaos (② 22420/23-424), is open May through October, daily from 8am to 9pm, and November through April, daily from 9am to 1:30pm and 4 to 9pm. The **post office** on Vas. Pavlou (at El. Venizelou) is open Monday through Friday from 7:30am to 2:30pm. Across from the castle, the **tourist police** (② 22420/22-444) are available 24 hours to address any outstanding need or emergency, even roomlessness.

## WHAT TO SEE & DO
## ATTRACTIONS IN KOS TOWN

Dominating the harbor, the **Castle of the Knights** stands in and atop a long line of fortresses defending Kos since ancient times. What you see today was constructed by the Knights of St. John in the 15th century and fell to the Turks in 1522. Satisfying your curiosity is perhaps the only compelling reason to pay the minimal admission of 3€. The castle is a hollow shell, with nothing of interest inside that you can't imagine from the outside, except when it serves as a venue for concerts. Best to stand back and admire from a distance this massive reminder of the vigilance that has been a part of life in Kos from prehistory to the present.

At the intersection of Vas. Pavlou and E. Grigoriou stands the **Casa Romana** (✆ 22420/23-234), a restored 3rd-century Roman villa that straddles what appears to have been an earlier Hellenistic residence. It's open Tuesday through Sunday from 8:30am to 3pm and costs 2€ for adults. If you have no fire in your belly for ruins, this won't ignite one. Nearby, however, to the east and west of the Casa Romana, are a number of interesting open sites, comprising what is in effect a small archaeological park. To the east lie the remains of a **Hellenistic temple** and the **Altar of Dionysos,** and to the west and south a number of impressive excavations and remains, the jewel of which is the **Roman Odeon,** with 18 intact levels of seats. The other extensive area of ruins is in the agora of the **ancient town** just in from Akti Miaouli. Kos town is strewn with archaeological sites opening like fissures and interrupting the flow of pedestrian traffic. Rarely is anything identified for passersby, so they seem like mere barriers or building sites, which is precisely what they were. The rich architectural tradition of Kos did not cease with the eclipse of antiquity—Kos is adorned with a surprising number of striking and significant structures, sacred and secular, enfolded unselfconsciously into the modern town.

And while you're strolling about town, you might take note of the sculptures by Alexandros Alwyn in the Garden of Hippokrates opposite the Dolphins Square down along the Old Harbor. A painter and sculptor with something of an international reputation, Alwyn long maintained a studio in the village of Evangelistra.

**Asklepion** ✦ Unless you have only beaches on the brain, this is reason enough to come to Kos. On an elevated site with grand views of Kos town, the sea, and the Turkish coastline, this is the Mecca of modern Western medicine, where Hippokrates—said to have lived to the age of 104—founded the first medical school in the late 5th century B.C. For nearly a thousand years after his death, this was a place of healing where physicians were consulted and gods invoked in equal measure. The ruins date from the 4th century B.C. to the 2nd century A.D. Systematic excavation of the site was not begun until 1902. Truth to tell, this is one of those archaeological sites that work best for those who bring something to them—namely some associations, some knowledge, some respect for the history behind the ruins. In this case, a sense of the role of Hippokrates in our own lives.

Located 4km (2½ miles) southwest of Kos town. ✆ 22420/28-763. Admission 3€ adults, 2€ seniors and students, free for children under 17. Oct to mid-June Tues–Sun 8:30am–3pm; mid-June to Sept Tues–Fri 8:30am–7pm and Sat 8:30am–3pm.

**Kos Museum** For a town the size of Kos, this is an impressive archaeological museum, built by the Italians in the 1930s to display mostly Hellenistic and Roman sculptures and mosaics uncovered on the collection. Although there is nothing startling or enduringly memorable in the collection, a visit reminds visitors of the former greatness of this now quite modest port town. Look in the museum's atrium for the lovely 3rd-century mosaic showing how Hippokrates and Pan once welcomed Asklepios, the god of healing, to this, the birthplace of Western medicine.

Platia Eleftherias (across from the Municipal Market). ✆ 22420/28-326. Admission 3€ adults, 2€ seniors and students, free for children under 17. Year-round Tues–Sun 8:30am–3pm.

## SHOPPING

Kos town is compact and the central shopping area all but fits in the palm of your hand, so you can explore every lane and see what strikes you. If you've grown attached to the traditional music you've been hearing since your arrival in Greece and want some help in making the right selection, stop by either of the **Ti Amo Music Stores,** 11 El. Venizelou and 4 Ipsilandou, where Giorgos Hatzidimitris will help you find the traditional or modern Greek music that suits you best. At either shop you may sit and listen before making a purchase.

If you're unwilling to pack another thing, you won't notice the weight of the unique handmade gold medallions at the jewelry shop of **N. Reissi,** opposite the museum at 1 Plateia Kazouli (© **22420/28-229**). Especially striking are the Kos medallions designed and crafted by Ms. Reissi's father (60€–110€). Handcrafted rings, charms, and earrings are also on display. For some unusual ceramic pieces, visit the shop of **Lambis Pittas** at 6 Kanari (leading away from the inner harbor) or his factory at G. Papendreou (on the coast leaving town for the southeast).

Another sort of treasure to bring home is a hand-painted Greek icon. **Panajiotis Katapodis** has been painting icons for over 40 years, both for churches and for individuals. His studio and home are on a lovely hillside little more than a mile west of Kos center at Ayios Nektarios, and visitors are welcome from April through October, Monday through Saturday from 9am to 1pm and 4 to 9pm. The way is signposted from just east of the Casa Romana.

## BEACHES & OUTDOOR PURSUITS

The beaches of Kos are no secret. Every foot of the 290km (180 miles) of mostly sandy coastline has been discovered. Even so, for some reason, people pack themselves together in tight spaces. You can spot the package-tour sites from afar by their umbrellas, dividing the beach into plots measured in centimeters. **Tingaki** and **Kardamena** epitomize this avoidable phenomenon. Following are a few guidelines to help you in your quest for uncolonized sand.

The beaches just 3km to 5km (2 miles–3 miles) east of Kos town are among the least congested on the island, probably because they're pebbled rather than sandy. Even so, the view is splendid and the nearby hot springs worth a good soak. In summer, the water on the northern coast of the island is warmer and shallower than that on the south, though less clear due to stronger winds. If you walk down from the resorts and umbrellas, you'll find some relatively open stretches between **Tingaki** and **Mastihari.** The north side of the island is also best for **windsurfing;** try Tingaki and Marmara, where everything you need can be rented on the beach. A perfect day exploring the northwestern tip of the island would consist of a swim at **Limnionas Bay** followed by grilled red mullets at Taverna Miltos.

Opposite, on the southern coast, **Kamel Beach** and **Magic Beach** are less congested than **Paradise Beach,** which lies between them. Either can be reached on foot from Paradise Beach, a stop for the Kefalos bus. The southwestern waters are cooler yet calmer than those along the northern shore; and, apart from Kardamena and Kefalos Bay, the beaches on this side of the island are less dominated by package tourists. Note that practically every sort of water sport, including jet-skiing, can be found at **Kardamena.** Finally, for **surfing,** the extreme southwestern tip of the island, on the **Kefalos peninsula** near Ayios Theologos, offers an ideal stretch of remote shoreline. You can end the day watching the sunset at **Sunset Wave Beach,** where you can also enjoy a not-soon-forgotten family-cooked feast at the **Agios Theologos Restaurant,** which rents molded plastic surfboards as well.

For yachting and sailing, call the **Yachting Club of Kos** (© 22420/20-055) or **Istion Sailing Holidays** (© 22420/22-195; fax 22420/26-777). For diving, contact the **Kos Diving Centre**, Plateia Koritsas 5 (© **22420/20-269** or 22420/22-782), **Dolphin Divers** (© **2940/548-149**), or **Waterhoppers** (© **22420/27-815**; mobile 69440/130533).

As already outlined (see "Getting Around," above), the island is especially good for **bicycling**, and rentals are widely available. Guided horseback excursions are also available through the **Marmari Riding Centre** (© **22420/41-783**), which offers 1-hour beach rides and 4-hour mountain trail rides. For **bird-watchers**, there are at least two unique offerings: Wild peacocks inhabit the forests at Skala, and migrating flamingos frequent the salt-lake preserve just west of Tingaki.

## EXPLORING THE HINTERLANDS

The most remote and authentic region of the island is comprised of the forests and mountains stretching roughly from just beyond Platani all the way to Plaka in the south. The highest point is Mount Dikeos, reaching nearly 900m (3,000 ft.). The mountain villages of this region were once the true center of the island. Only in the last 30 years or so have they been all but abandoned for the lure of more level, fertile land and, since the 1970s, the cash crop of tourism.

There are many ways to explore this region, which begins little more than a mile beyond the center of Kos town. Trekkers will not find this daunting, by car or motorbike it's a cinch, but by mountain bike the ups and downs may be a challenge. Regardless of which way you go, the point is to take your time. You could take a bus from Kos to Zia and walk from Zia to Pili, returning then from Pili to Kos town by bus. The 5km (3-mile) walk from Zia to Pili will take you through a number of traditional island villages. Sights along the way include the ruins of **old Pili**, a mountaintop castle growing so organically out of the rock that you might miss it; and, as your reward at day's end, a **dinner in Zia** at the **Sunset Taverna,** where at dusk the view of Kos island and the sea is magnificent. Zia also has a ceramics shop and a Greek art shop to occupy you as you wait for your taxi. For those looking to get away from the crowds, an hour's drive from Kos town all the way to the southwest coast leads to **Sunset Wave Beach** below Ayios Theologos; there the Vavithis family, including some repatriated from North America, maintain a restaurant that makes for a most enjoyable setting and meal.

## VENTURING OFFSHORE

Two very nearby explorations offer unique opportunities. Hop one of the daily ferries from Kardamena and Kefalos to the small island of **Nissiros.** Nissiros is not quite attractive, but has at its center an active volcano, which blew the top off the island in 600 B.C. and last erupted in 1873. There are also daily ferries from Kos harbor to **Bodrum, Turkey** (ancient Halikarnassos). Note that you must bring your passport to the boat an hour before sailing so that the captain can draw up the necessary documents for the Turkish port police.

## WHERE TO STAY

Kos is not a safe drop-in location in either high season, and most places are booked solid in summer and closed tight in winter. Plan ahead and make a reservation well in advance.

### EXPENSIVE

**Hotel Kipriotis Village**  If you wish to spend part of your vacation amid loads of fun-seeking Europeans with all the possible holiday facilities, try this luxurious new resort, only 4km (2½ miles) from Kos and right on the beach.

Constructed as a village of sorts, the two-story bungalows and apartments surround an attractively designed activity area. There's a full day of supervised activities for children. You would never have to leave the premises if you're here just to soak up the sun, but there is public transportation every 15 minutes into Kos town. It tends to be booked by groups, so don't expect a cozy atmosphere, but it is a classy place.

P.O. Box 206, Psalidi Beach, 85200 Kos (3 miles south of Kos Town). © 22420/27-640. Fax 22420/23-590. 512 units. 150€ double; 175€ bungalow for 2 (including breakfast). AE, MC, V. Closed mid-Oct to mid-Apr. Parking on premises. **Amenities:** 3 restaurants; 4 bars; 3 pools (1 indoors and heated); tennis; health center with sauna and hydromassage; watersports equipment; children's program; tours and car rentals arranged; babysitting; salon; same day laundry and dry cleaning; minigolf; volleyball; basketball; billiards; table tennis; Turkish bath; solarium. *In room:* A/C (July–Aug only), TV, fridge, hair dryer.

## MODERATE

**Hotel Astron** ★    This is the most attractive hotel directly on the harbor (and some 360m/1,181 ft. from a swimming beach). The entrance and lobby—a mélange of glass, marble, and Minoan columns—are quite striking and suggest an elegance that does not in fact extend to the rooms and suites. All units are tasteful and very clean, with firm beds and balconies. The pricier units include extras such as harbor views and Jacuzzis. In the larger and more expensive suites, the extra space is designed to accommodate a third person and is wasted if you intend to use it as a sitting area. The only extra worth the money, in our opinion, is a harbor view, but remember that by night you are facing the action—Kos is no retirement community. In summer, about 65% of the rooms here are allotted to package tours. The 14m (46 ft.) pool, and patio behind the hotel are pleasant, although diminished by the adjoining vacant lot.

31 Akti Kountourioti 85300 Kos. © 22420/23-703. Fax 22420/22-814. 80 units. 75€–90€ double; 85€–110€ suite. Rates include breakfast. AE, MC, V. Open year-round. **Amenities:** Restaurant; bar; swimming pool; children's pool; Jacuzzi; tours and car rentals arranged. *In room:* A/C, TV, fridge.

## INEXPENSIVE

**Hotel Afendoulis** *Value*    Nowhere in Kos do you receive so much for so little. Nestled in a gracious residential neighborhood a few hundred yards from the water and less than 10 minutes on foot from the very center of Kos, Afendoulis offers the magical combination of convenience and calm. The rooms are clean and altogether welcoming, with firm beds. Nearly all units have private balconies, and most have views of the sea. Whatever room you have, you can't go wrong here. This is a long-established family place, and the Zikas family—Alexis, Hippokrates, Dionisia and Kiriaki—spare nothing to create a very special holiday community in which guests enjoy and respect one another. If you are coming to Kos to raise hell, do it elsewhere. Note that the hotel has an elevator.

Although this is likely to be many people's nonnegotiable first choice in Kos, don't despair if you haven't made a reservation. Alexis Zikas holds several extra rooms, including a two-room apartment, open and unreserved in order to accommodate such emergencies. He also owns a pension several blocks away and can usually accommodate anyone who just shows up.

1 Evrepiou, 85300 Kos. © 22420/25-321. Fax 22420/25-797. 17 units. 35€–48€. No credit cards. Closed mid-Oct to mid-Apr.

**Hotel Yiorgos**    This is an inviting, family-run hotel a block from the sea and no more than a 15-minute walk from the center of Kos town. Although the immediate neighborhood is not residential, the hotel enjoys a relatively quiet location. Guest rooms are modest and very clean. All units have balconies, most with pleasant but not spectacular views of either sea or mountains. Each room contains a fridge, radio, and coffeemaker—and individually controlled central heating makes this an exceptionally cozy small hotel at the chilly edges of the tourist season. Convenience, hospitality, and affordability have made this a place to which guests happily return.

9 Harmilou, 85300 Kos. © 2240/23-297. Fax 2240/27-710. yiorgos@kos.fortnet.gr. 35 units. 25€–38€ double. Rates include breakfast. No credit cards. Open year-round. *In room:* Fridge, coffeemaker.

**Pension Alexis**  Ensconced in a quiet residential neighborhood only a stone's throw from the harbor, Pension Alexis feels like a home because it is one, or was until it opened as a guesthouse. The expansive rooms have high ceilings and open onto shared balconies. Most have sweeping views of the harbor and the Castle of the Knights. This is a gracious dwelling, with parquet floors and many tasteful architectural touches. Individual rooms are separated off from the halls by sliding doors, and share three large bathrooms. Room 4 is a truly grand corner space with knock-out views. What was a great location is now even better with the new Hippokrates Gardens located just across from the pension, closing the one street to cars. In summer, the heart of the pension is the covered veranda facing private gardens, where guests can enjoy breakfast and share their stories late into the night.

9 Irodotou, 85300 Kos. © 2240/28-798 or 2240/25-594. Fax 2240/25-797. 14 units. 23€–30€ double. No credit cards. Closed mid-Oct to mid-Apr.

## WHERE TO DINE

In Kos, as anywhere else, there's a lot of fast food, fast consumed and fast forgotten. But there's no need to make eating on Kos a Greek tragedy; the key is to follow the locals, who know where not to be disappointed. Along with your meals, you may want to try some of the local wines: the dry **Glafkos**, the red **Appelis**, or the crisp **Theokritos** retsina.

### EXPENSIVE

**Petrino ★ GREEK**  When royalty come to Kos, this is where they dine—so why not live the fantasy yourself? Housed in an exquisitely restored, century-old, two-story stone (*petrino*) private residence, this is hands-down the most elegant taverna in Kos, with cuisine to match. In summer, sit outside on the spacious three-level terrace looking out over the ancient agora; but be sure to take a look inside (especially upstairs), because this is an architectural glory.

Although the menu focuses on Greek specialties, it is vast enough to include lobster, filet mignon, and other Western staples. But don't waste this opportunity to experience Greek traditional cuisine at its best. The stuffed peppers, grilled octopus, and *beki meze* (marinated pork) are perfection. More than 50 carefully selected wines, all Greek, line the cellar—this is your chance to learn why Greece was once synonymous with wine. The dry red kalliga from Kefalonia is exceptional.

1 Plateia Theologou (abutting the east extremity of the ancient agora). © 2420/27-251. Reservations recommended. Main courses 7.50€–42€. AE, DC, MC, V. Mid-Dec to Nov daily 5pm–midnight.

### MODERATE

**Platanos Restaurant ★ GREEK/INTERNATIONAL**  Situated in the best location in Kos overlooking the Hippokrates Tree, this restaurant is in a gorgeous building that was a former Italian officers' club, replete with arches and the original tile floor. Try reserving a place on the upstairs balcony with its impressive vista. The creatively prepared appetizers include chicken stuffed with dates in a spicy sauce; for a change try the mixed vegetable salad with its larger selection than the usual Greek salad. For a main course, try the souvlaki that is a combination of chicken, lamb, and beef; or the duck Dijonnaise, duck in a tasty sauce with a tasty selection of vegetable in season. A generous selection of choice wines, live music, and gracious service make for a splendid evening.

Plateia Platanos. ℡ 22420/28-991. Main courses 13€–24€. AE, MC, V. Apr–Oct daily noon–11:30pm.

**Taverna Mavromatis ★ GREEK** One of the best choices in town is this 30-year-old vine- and geranium-covered beachside taverna run by the Mavromati brothers. Their food is what you came to Greece for: melt-in-your-mouth saganaki, mint- and garlic-spiced sousoutakia, tender grilled lamb chops, moist beef souvlaki, and perfectly grilled fresh fish. In summer, the taverna spills out along the beach; you'll find yourself sitting only feet from the water watching the sunset and gazing at the nearby Turkish coast. A dinner here can be quite magical, something locals know very well; so arrive early to ensure a spot by the water.

Psalidi Beach. ℡ 22420/22-433. Main courses 4€–13€. AE, MC, V. Year-round Wed–Sun 11am–11pm. A 20-min. walk southeast of the ferry port, or accessible by the local Psalidi Beach bus.

## INEXPENSIVE

**Arap (Platanio) Taverna GREEK/TURKISH** Like the population of Platinos, the food here is a splendid mix of Greek and Turkish. The pride and spirit of this unpretentious family restaurant are contagious. The menu is extensive, and we know no way of going wrong no matter which direction you take. Although there are many meat dishes, vegetarians will have a feast. The roasted red peppers stuffed with feta and the zucchini flowers stuffed with rice are splendid, as are the bourekakia (a kind of fried pastry roll stuffed with cheese). If you want to be sure to experience the "best of show," just put yourself in the hands of the Menis brothers and let them design your meal. Afterwards, you can walk across the street for the best homemade ice cream on Kos, an island legend since 1955. This combination is well worth the walk or taxi ride.

Platinos-Kermetes. ℡ 22420/28-442. Main courses 4.50€–10€. No credit cards. Apr–Oct daily 10am–midnight. Located 2km (1¼ miles) south of town on the road to the Asklepion.

**Olimpiada Value GREEK** Located around the corner from the Olympic Airways office, this is one of the best values for simple Greek fare. The food is fresh, flavorful, and inexpensive, and the staff is remarkably courteous and friendly. The okra in tomato sauce and the several vegetable dishes are a treat.

2 Kleopatras. ℡ 22420/23-031. Main courses 3.80€–9€. MC, V. Year-round daily 11am–11pm.

**Taverna Ampavris ★ GREEK** This is undoubtedly one of the best tavernas on Kos. It's outside the bustling town center on the way to the Asklepion, down a quiet village lane. In the courtyard of this 130-year-old house, you can feast on local dishes from Kos island. The salamura from Kefalos is mouth-watering pork stewed with onions and coriander; the lahano dolmades (stuffed cabbage with rice, minced meat, and herbs) is delicate, light, and not at all oily. The fasikbab (veal stew on rice) is tender and lean, while the vegetable dishes, such as the broad string beans cooked and served cold in garlic and olive-oil dressing, are out of this world. Hats off to Emanuel Scoumbourdis and his family, who operate this fine place.

Ampavris, Ampavris. ℡ 22420/25-696. Main courses 3€–9€. No credit cards. Apr–Oct daily 5:30pm–1am.

**Taverna Ampeli ★ GREEK** This may be as close as you can come in Kos to authentic Greek home cooking, due in no small part to the fact that Mom is in the kitchen here. Facing the sea and ensconced in its own vineyard, Ampeli is delightful even before you taste the food. The interior is unusually tasteful, with high beamed ceilings, and the outside setting is even better. The dolmades are the best we've had in Greece. Other excellent specialties are the *pliogouri* (gruel), *giouvetsi* (casserole), and *revithokefteves* (meatballs); if you're less venturesome, the fried potatoes set a new standard. The house retsina is unusually sweet, almost like a sherry. The house white wine, made from the grapes before your eyes, is dry and light and quite pleasing, while Ampeli's own red is less memorable. If you're here on Saturday or midday on Sunday, the Easter-style goat, baked overnight in a low oven, is not to be missed.

Tzizifies, Zipari.Village (5 miles from Kos Town). ☏ 22420/69-682. Main courses 3.50€–11€. MC, V. Apr–Oct daily 10am–midnight; Nov–Mar daily 6–11pm. Closed Easter week and 10 days in early Nov. Just off the beach road 1km (½ mile) east of Tingaki. Take a bus to Tingaki and walk, or take a taxi.

**Taverna Nikolas** *Value* GREEK/SEAFOOD  Known on the street as Nick the Fisherman's, this is one taverna in Kos that wasn't created for tourists. Year-round, it's a favorite haunt for locals, with whom you'll have to compete for one of its eight tables—until summer, when seating spills freely out onto the street. Although you can ask for and get everything from filet mignon to goulash, the point of coming here is seafood. If the Aegean has it, you'll find it here: grilled octopus, shrimp in vinegar and lemon, calamari stuffed with cheese, and mussels souvlaki, for a start. The menu is extensive, so come with an appetite.

21 G. Averof. ☏ 22420/23-098. Main courses 3.50€–9€; fixed-price dinners 7€–11€, with a seafood dinner for two 24€. No credit cards. Year-round daily noon–midnight.

## KOS AFTER DARK

Kos nightlife is no more difficult to find than your own nose. Just go down to the harbor and follow the noise. The **port-side cafes** opposite the daily excursion boats to Kalimnos are best in the early morning. **Platanos,** across from the Hippokrates Tree, has live music, often jazz; and just across from Platanos is the beginning of **Bar Street,** which needs no further introduction. The lively **Fashion Club,** Kanari 2 Dolphins Square, has the most impressive light-and-laser show. On Zouroudi there are two popular discos, **Heaven** and **Calua,** with its swimming pool. If you want to hit the bar scene, try the **Hamam** on Akti Kountourioti, **Beach Boys** at 57 Kanari, or **The Blues Brothers** on Dolphins Square. Another option is an old-fashioned outdoor movie, Kos style, at the **Open Cine Orfeas,** 10 Vasileos Yioryiou, showing relatively recent films, often in English, and costing 6€.

## 4 Patmos ★

302km (187 miles) E of Piraeus

Architects sometimes speak of "charged sites," places where something so powerful happened that its memory must always be preserved. Patmos is one such place. It is where **St. John the Divine** ★, traditionally identified with the Apostle John, spent several years in exile, dwelling in a cave and composing the Apocalypse, or the Book of Revelation. From that time on, the island has been regarded as hallowed ground, re-consecrated through the centuries by the erection of more than 300 churches, one for every nine residents.

This is not to say that either the people of Patmos or their visitors are expected to spend their days in prayer, but it does show that the Patmians expect and deserve a heavy dose of respect for their traditions. Some guidebooks highlight the island's prohibitions on nude bathing and how to get around them—but if this is a priority for you, then you've stumbled on the wrong island. Go to Patmos and enjoy your stay, by all means, but don't go there looking for raucous nightlife.

Rather, if we were to compose and dedicate a piece to Patmos, it might be a suite for rooster, moped, and bells (church and goat), for these are the sounds that fill the air. But just because Patmos is wonderfully unspoiled, don't imagine that it's "primitive." In fact, in recent years it has begun to develop quite sophisticated tourist facilities—and following. So when we say it is a place for those looking for a "retreat," we do not mean to suggest some religious calling, only that it offers a more subdued, civilized alternative to some of the major touristic destinations.

## ESSENTIALS

### GETTING THERE

**By Plane**  Patmos has no airport, but it is quite convenient (especially by hydrofoil and catamaran in spring and summer) to three islands that do: Samos, Kos, and Leros. Rather than endure an all but interminable ferry ride from Piraeus, fly from Athens to one of these, then hop a boat or hydrofoil the rest of the way to Patmos. Samos is your best bet: with the right schedule, you can get from the Athens airport to Patmos in 3 hours via Samos.

**By Boat**  Patmos, the northernmost of the Dodecanese Islands, is on the daily ferry line from Piraeus to Rhodes—confirm schedules with the **Piraeus Port Authority** (© 210/417-2657 or 210/451-1310) or the **Rhodes Port Authority** (© 22410/23-693 or 22410/27-695). It has numerous sea links with the larger islands of the Dodecanese, as well as with the islands of the northeast Aegean. Options are limited from late fall to early spring, but from Easter through September, sea connections with most of the islands of the eastern Aegean are numerous and convenient. With the new high speed ferries of the **Blue Star Line,** (www.bluestarferries.com) travel time from Piraeus is cut down to about 6 hours.

### VISITOR INFORMATION

The **tourism office** (© 22470/31-666) in the port town of Skala is directly in front of you as you disembark from your ship; it's open June through August daily from 9am to 10pm. It shares the Italianate "municipal palace" with the post office and the **tourist police** (© 22470/31-303), who take over when the tourism office is closed. The **port police** (© 22470/31-231), in the first building on your left on the main ferry pier, are very helpful for boat schedules and whatever else ails or concerns you; it's open year-round, 24 hours a day. There is also a host of helpful information about Patmos at **www.travelpoint.gr.**

**Apollon Tourist and Shipping Agency,** on the harbor near the central square (© 22470/31-724; fax 22470/31-819), can book excursion boats and hydrofoils and arrange lodging in hotels, rental houses, and apartments throughout the island. It's open year-round from 8am to noon and 4 to 6pm, with extended summer hours. **Astoria Tourist and Shipping Agency** (© 22470/31-205; fax 22470/31-975) is also helpful. For the "do-it-yourselfer" in you, pick up a free copy of *Patmos Summertime*. It should be noted, however, that the map of the island provided in that publication is grossly inaccurate, as are many other tourist maps of Patmos. Figure that out!

### GETTING AROUND

**By Bus**  The entire island has only one bus, whose current schedule is available at the tourist office and is posted at various locations on the island. Needless to say, it provides very limited service—to Skala, Hora, Grikos, and Kambos—so it's probably best to think of other ways to get around.

**By Moped & Bicycle**  Mopeds are definitely the vehicle of choice on the island, provided you have a proper license. At the shops that line the harbor,

1-day rentals start around 10€ and go up to 30€. Michael Michalis at **Australis Motor Rent** (© 22470/32-284), in Skala's new port, operates a first-rate shop and is quite conscientious. Unlike at most dealers, you can rent for less than a full day at a discounted rate. You can also contact **Billis** (© 22470/32-218) or **Theo & Georgio's** (© 22470/32-066), both on the harbor in Skala. Bicycles are hard to come by on the island, but Theo & Georgio's has 18-speed mountain bikes for 6€ per day.

**By Car**   Two convenient car-rental offices, both in Skala, are **Patmos Rent-a-Car,** just behind the police station (© 22470/32-203); and **Avis,** on the new port (© 22470/33-095). Daily rentals in high season start at 30€. The island has only two gas stations, the **Argo** station at the east side of the harbor in Skala, and the **Elin** station just out of Scala on the road to Kambos.

**By Taxi**   The island's main taxi stand is on the pier in Skala Harbor, right before your eyes as you get off the boat. From anywhere on the island, you can request a taxi by calling © 22470/31-225. As the island is quite small, it's much cheaper to hire a taxi than to rent a car.

**ORIENTATION**   Patmos lies along a north-south axis; were it not for a narrow central isthmus, it would be two islands, north and south. **Skala,** the island's only town of any size, is situated near that isthmus joining the north island to the south. Above Skala looms the hilltop capital of **Hora,** comprising a mazelike medieval village and the fortified monastery of St. John the Divine. There are really only two other towns on Patmos: **Kambos** to the north and **Grikou** to the south. While Kambos is a real village of roughly 500 inhabitants, Grikou is mostly a resort, a creation of the tourist industry.

Most independent visitors to Patmos, especially first-timers, will choose to stay in Skala (Hora has no hotels) and explore the north and south from there. Patmos is genuinely infectious, an island to which visitors, Greek and foreign, return year after year. Consequently, on your first visit to Patmos, it makes sense to be centrally located. From then on, when you return, you will have no need for our advice.

**FAST FACTS**   The **Commercial Bank of Greece** on the harbor and the **National Bank of Greece** on the central square offer exchange services and ATMs. Both are open Monday through Thursday from 8am to 2pm and Friday from 8am to 1:30pm. You will also find an ATM where ferries and cruises dock at the main pier. For **dental or medical emergencies,** call © 22470/31-211; for special **pharmaceutical needs,** call © 22470/31-500. The **hospital** (© 22470/31-211) is on the road to Hora. The **post office** on the harbor is open Monday through Friday from 8am to 1:30pm. The **tourist police** (© 22470/31-303) are directly across from the port.

For **Internet access,** the Internet Cafe at Blue Bay (Blue Bay Hotel) is open April through October, daily from 8am to 8pm, and the Millennium Internet Cafe (on the lane to Horio, near the OTE office) is open year-round, daily from 9am to 10pm. A short walk down toward the new port will bring you to **Just Like Home** (© 22470/33-170), where a load of laundry costs 15€. It's open

---

## Tips  For Your Health

One essential you need to know about Patmos from the outset is that tap water is not for drinking. *Drink only bottled water.*

daily until 9pm year-round, and until 10pm in July and August. Cold-water wash and rinse are available, as are hand washing and dry cleaning.

## WHAT TO SEE & DO
### THE TOP ATTRACTIONS

What Patmos lacks in quantity it makes up in quality. Apart from its natural beauty and its 300-plus churches, to which we can't possibly provide a detailed guide here, there are several extraordinary sights: the **Monastery of St. John**, the **Cave of the Apocalypse**, and the medieval town of **Hora** ✦. The latter is simply there to be explored, a labyrinthine maze of whitewashed stone homes, shops, and churches, in which getting lost is the whole point.

Off season, the days and times of opening for the **cave** and the **monastery** are unpredictable, as they are designed to accommodate groups of pilgrims and cruise-ship tours rather than individual visitors. Neither is a public place. The cave is enclosed within a convent, and the monastery is just that. It's best to consult the tourist office or one of the travel agents listed above for the open hours on the day of your visit (the times given below are for the peak season from May–August). To visit both places, appropriate attire is required, which means that women must wear long skirts or dresses, and men must wear long pants.

The road to Hora is well marked from Skala; but if you're walking, take the narrow lane to the left just past the central square. Once outside the town, you can mostly avoid the main road by following the uneven stone-paved donkey path, which is the traditional pilgrims' route to the sanctuaries above.

### Cave of the Apocalypse ✦

Exiled to Patmos by the Roman Emperor Domitian in A.D. 95, St. John the Divine is said to have made his home in this cave, though Patmians insist quite reasonably that he walked every inch of the small island, talking with its people. The cave is said to be the epicenter of his earthshaking revelation, which he dictated to his disciple and which has come down as the Book of the Apocalypse, or Revelation, the last book of the Christian Bible. The cave is now encased within a sanctuary, which is in turn encircled by a convent. A stirring brochure written by Archimandrite Koutsanellos, Superior of the Cave, provides an excellent description of the religious significance of each niche in the rocks, as well as the many icons in the cave. Other guides are also available in local tourist shops. The best preparation, of course, is to bone up on the Book of Revelation.

On the road to Hora. ✆ **22470/31-234.** Free admission. May–Aug Sun 8am–1pm and 2–6pm, Mon 8am–1:30pm, Tues–Wed 8am–1:30pm and 2–6pm, Thurs–Sat 8am–1:30pm. Otherwise, hours vary (as described above).

### Monastery of St. John ✦

Towering over Skala and, for that matter, over the south island, is the medieval Monastery of St. John, which looks far more like a fortress than a house of prayer. Built to withstand pirates, it is certainly up to the task of deterring runaway tourism. The monastery virtually controls the south island, where the mayor wears a hat but the monastic authority wears a miter. In 1088, with a hand-signed document from the Byzantine Emperor Alexis I Comnenus ceding the entire island to the future monastery, Blessed Christodoulos arrived on Patmos to establish here what was to become an independent monastic state. The monastery chapel is stunning, as is the adjoining **Chapel of the Theotokos**, whose frescoes date from the 12th century. On display in the treasury are but a fraction of the monastery's exquisite Byzantine treasures, second only to those of the monastic state of Mount Athos.

Hora. © 22470/31-234. Free admission to monastery; 4€ to treasury. May–Aug Sun 8am–1pm and 2–6pm, Mon 8am–1:30pm, Tues–Wed 8am–1:30pm and 2–6pm, Thurs–Sat 8am–1:30pm. Otherwise, hours vary (as described above).

## OUTDOOR PURSUITS

The principal outdoor activities on Patmos are walking and swimming. The best **beaches** are highlighted below (see "Exploring the Island") and the best **walking trails** are the unmarked donkey paths, which crisscross the island. You won't find jet-skis or surfboards on Patmos, although limited **watersports** are available. Paddleboats and canoes can be rented and water-skiing arranged on Agriolivada Beach at Hellen's Place, as well as on the beach at Grikos. Also at Grikos is a **summer club** where you can join in a volleyball game or play tennis (rackets and balls provided). For **snorkeling** and **skin diving,** accompanied if you wish by your own underwater photographer and cameraman, call © 22470/33-059.

## SHOPPING

Patmians are quick to lament and apologize for the fact that just about everything, from gas to toothpaste, is a bit more expensive here. Patmos doesn't even have its own drinking water, and import costs inevitably get passed along to the customer. That said, the price differences are much more evident to the locals than to tourists.

There are several excellent jewelry shops, like **Iphigenia** (© 22470/31-814) and **Midas** (© 22470/31-800) on the harbor, though **Filoxenia** (© 22470/31-667) and the **Art Spot** (© 22470/32-243), both just behind the main square in the direction of Hora, have more interesting contemporary designs, often influenced by ancient motifs. The Art Spot also sells ceramics and small sculptures, and is well worth seeking out. Farther down the same lane is **Parousia** (© 22470/32-549), the best single stop for hand-painted icons and a wide range of books on Byzantine subjects. The proprietor, Mr. A. Alafakis, is quite learned in the history and craft of icon painting and can tell you a great deal about the icons in his shop and the diverse traditions they represent.

The most fascinating shop on Patmos may be **Selene** (© 22470/31-742), directly across from the Port Authority office. The highly selective array of Greek handmade art and crafts here is extraordinary, from ceramics to hand-painted Russian and Greek icons to marionettes, some as tall as 1m (4 ft.). And be sure to notice Selene's structure, also a work of art. Built in 1835, it was once a storage space for sails and later a boat-building workshop. Look down at the shop's extraordinary floor made of handmade stamped and scored bricks, quite unique and traditional to Patmos.

## WHERE TO STAY IN SKALA

There are no hotels or pensions in Hora, although Skala makes up for it. Unless you're planning to visit Patmos during Greek or Christian Easter or from late July through August, you should not have difficulty finding a room upon arrival, though it's always safer to book ahead. You will probably be met at the harbor by residents offering private accommodations. If you're interested in renting a kitchenette apartment or villa, contact the **Apollon Agency** (© 22470/31-724; fax 22470/31-819).

### EXPENSIVE

**Porto Scoutari ★** High on a bluff overlooking Meloï Bay, this new luxury hotel is seductively gracious, with the largest rooms and the largest pool on the island. Ground-level suites are designed with families in mind, while upper-level suites, with four-poster beds and bathtubs, have honeymoon written all over them. The decor, a blend of reproduction antiques and contemporary design, offers elegance and comfort. Each bungalow-style studio has a kitchenette, year-round climate control, and private balcony. The common areas—breakfast room, lounge, piano bar, and pool—are simultaneously informal and refined. This is the most ambitious "full-service" hotel on the island and probably won't appeal to those who are on Patmos for a brief visit.

Scoutari, 85500 Patmos. (ⓒ 22470/33-123. Fax 22470/33-175. www.portoscoutari.com. 30 units. 105€–160€ double; 115€–250€ studio or suite. Rates include full breakfast buffet. MC, V. Open Easter–Oct. Note that this hotel overlooks, but is not in, Meloi Bay—so follow the signs to Kambos, not to Meloi Bay. It's less than 2 miles from the center of Skala. **Amenities:** Restaurant; pool; Internet and fax facilities; room service; transfers arranged; laundry and dry cleaning arranged. *In room:* A/C, TV, minibar, coffeemaker, hair dryer, safe.

## MODERATE

**Romeos Hotel** Of all Skala's newer lodgings, this one, run by a Greek-American family from Virginia, is especially commodious, with its large pool and quiet garden. The simply decorated, spotless rooms come with countryside-view balconies, and are built like semi-attached bungalows on a series of tiers, with views across to Mount Kastelli. Large honeymoon suites, with double beds, full bathtubs, and a small lounge, are also available. One slight downside is the undeveloped lot in front of the property, though it's hardly a factor once you're inside the hotel compound.

Skala (in the back streets behind the OTE), 85500 Patmos. (ⓒ 22470/31-962. Fax 22470/31-070. romeosh@ 12net.gr. 60 units. 88€ double; 115€ suite. Rates include breakfast. MC, V. Closed Nov–Mar. *In room:* A/C, minibar.

**Skala Hotel** Tranquilly but conveniently situated well off the main harbor road behind a lush garden overflowing with arresting pink bougainvillea, this comfortable hotel has aged like a fine wine to become an established Skala favorite. Attractive features include the beautifully landscaped garden, a large pool with an inviting sun deck and bar, the large breakfast buffet, and personalized service. The three views to choose from are the sea, the western mountains, and the Monastery of St. John—and all are striking. At Easter or in late July and August, you're likely to be out of luck without an advance reservation, but at other times, you'll probably be able to find a room here.

Skala, 85500 Patmos. (ⓒ 22470/31-343. Fax 22470/31-747. skalaht@12net.gr. 78 units. 70€–110€ double. Rates include breakfast. MC, V. Closed Nov–Mar. **Amenities:** Restaurant; 2 bars; pool; conference facilities. *In room:* A/C, TV, minibar.

## INEXPENSIVE

**Australis Hotel and Apartments** ✦ On approach, you may have misgivings regarding the location of this hotel, down a less than charming lane off the new port area. But all your doubts will vanish when you enter the startlingly lovely hotel compound, a veritable blooming hillside oasis. Once featured in *Garden Design* magazine, the grounds are covered with bougainvillea, fuchsias, dahlias, and roses. The pleasant communal porch, where breakfast is served, offers delightful views of the open harbor. The guest rooms are bright, tasteful, and impeccably clean, with some of the best (firmest) beds we've found in Greece. Within the same compound and enjoying the same floral and sea vistas, Fokas Michellis's four new luxury apartments offer spacious homes away from home for families or groups of four to six people. They are fully equipped with kitchenettes, TVs, and heat for the winter months. In addition to these apartments,

Fokas's oldest son, Michael Michellis, has three handsome new studios over his house on the old road to Hora. Each has a well-stocked kitchen and goes for 37€ to 55€ per day.

Skala (a 5-min. walk from the center), 85500 Patmos. © 22470/31-576. Fax 22470/32-284. 29 units. 40€–55€ double; 67€–155€ apt, depending on size and season. Room rates include breakfast. No credit cards. Closed Nov–Mar. *In room:* TV in some, fridge in some.

**Blue Bay Hotel** ★    Two unique features distinguish this hotel: First, its stellar location on the southwest side of the harbor offers a rare fusion of convenience and quiet. Second, guests are requested not to smoke anywhere in the hotel except on their private balconies. The bedrooms are spacious, immaculate, and comfortable. Rooms 114 and 115 share a terrace the size of a tennis court overlooking the sea. There is a special emphasis here on service and gracious hospitality. In addition to the breakfast room, there is a private bar and the new Blue Bay Internet Café, offering Internet access for 2€ per 20 minutes.

Skala, 85500 Patmos. © 22470/31-165. Fax 22470/32-303. bluebayhotel@yahoo.com. 26 units. 45€–60€ double; 55€–75€ suite. Breakfast buffet 6€ extra. MC, V. Closed Nov–Mar. *In room:* A/C.

**Castelli Hotel**    Guests are accommodated here in two white-stucco blocks framed with brown shutters. The rooms, with white walls and beige tile floors, are large and spotless and have their own fridges and covered balconies, while the common lounge and lobby areas are filled with photographs, flower-print sofas, seashells, fresh-cut flowers from the surrounding gardens, and other knickknacks of seaside life. The hotel's striking sea vista can be enjoyed from cushioned wrought-iron chairs on each room's balcony or from a pleasant covered guests' terrace/bar. The price you pay for the view is a mildly challenging 5-minute climb from the harbor.

Skala, 85500 Patmos. © 22470/31-361. Fax 22470/31-656. 45 units. 50€–62€ double. Rates include breakfast. No credit cards. Open year-round. *In room:* A/C.

**Villa Knossos**    This small white villa just off the new port is set within an abundant garden of palms, purple and pink bougainvillea, potted geraniums, and hibiscus. The tasteful bedrooms are spacious with high ceilings (making them cool even in the summer's heat), and all but one have private balconies. The two units facing the back garden are the most quiet, while room 7 in front has its own private veranda. There's a comfortable guests' sitting room, and all rooms have their own fridge.

Skala, 85500 Patmos. © 22470/32-189. Fax 22470/32-284. 7 units. 35€–50€ double. No credit cards. Closed Nov–Mar.

## WHERE TO DINE IN SKALA & HORA

The culinary scene in Skala and Hora is at present surprisingly unpredictable. There are no true standout restaurants in Skala and Hora, though there are many that will not disappoint. In Hora, on the path to the Monastery of St. John, you'll find the **Pirgos;** the **Balcony View** facing Skala Harbor; the **Patmian House;** and (following signs from the monastery) **Vagelis** in Plateia Theofakosta (Central Square). Vagelis enjoys lovely views of the south island. In Skala, you will want to browse for yourself, though we suggest below our favorite local haunts. Your alternative is to venture out to the north and south islands, which offer some of Patmos's most enticing dining opportunities, in particular the restaurant at the Petra Apartments Hotel (see "Exploring the Island," below).

**Grigoris Grill** GREEK    One of Skala's better-known eateries, this place was formerly the center of Patmian chic. We recommend any of the grilled fish or meat dishes, particularly in the off season, when more care and attention are paid to preparation. Well-cooked veal cutlets, tender lamb chops, and the swordfish souvlaki are favorites. Grigoris also offers several vegetarian specials. Both curbside seating and a more removed and quiet roof garden are available.

Opposite Skala car ferry pier; ☏ 22470/31-515. Main courses 4.60€–9€. No credit cards. Easter–June and Sept–Oct 6pm–midnight; July–Aug 11am–midnight.

**Pantelis Restaurant** GREEK　Pantelis is a proven local favorite for no-frills Greek home cooking. The food here is consistently fresh and wholesome—the basics prepared so well that they surprise you. Daily specials augment the standard menu. Portions are generous, so pace yourself, and if you're not yet a convert to the Greek cult of olive oil, speak up or order something grilled. The lightly fried calamari, chickpea soup, swordfish kebab, and roasted lamb were all up to expectation. In winter, the spacious dining hall with very high ceilings makes this a relatively benign environment for nonsmokers.

Skala (1 lane back from the port). ☏ 22470/31-922. Main courses 3.50€–12€. No credit cards. Year-round daily 11am–11pm.

## PATMOS AFTER DARK

Going to Patmos for nightlife is a little like going to Indiana to ski. The scene here, while not ecclesiastical, doesn't swing. Clubs tend to open for a few weeks in season, then close, like flowers. In Hora at Plateia Agia Lesvias, there's **Kafe 1673**, locally known as **Astivi**, where you can dance to whatever the DJ offers. In Scala, a sturdy standby—never fully "in" and never fully "out"—that survives each year's fads is the **Consolato Music Club**, to the left of the quay. At press time, Skala also has the **Kalhua Club**, at the far end of the new port, and **Sui Generis**, behind the police station. Although their posters abound and their T-shirts are worn with pride, these newcomers may not survive the test of time. In a lesser but more reliable key, both Hora and Skala have a number of **bars**, which you can't miss; and, on a more traditional note, the **Aloni Restaurant** in Hora offers Greek music and dance performances in traditional costume a few nights each week in summer.

## EXPLORING THE ISLAND

Apart from the seductive contours of the Patmian landscape, the myriad seascapes, and the seemingly countless churches, it's the **beaches** of Patmos that draw most visitors beyond the island's core. Don't be tempted to think of the strand between the old and new ports in Skala as a beach. Better and safer to take a shower in your room. Most beaches have tavernas on or very near the beach, as well as rooms to rent by the day or week. They're too numerous and similar to list here.

### THE NORTH ISLAND

The most desirable beaches in the north lie along the northeastern coastline from Lambi Bay to Meloï Bay. The northwestern coastline from Merika Bay to Lambi is too rocky, inaccessible, and exposed to warrant recommendation. The most desirable northern beaches are located in the following bays (proceeding up the coast from south to north): **Meloï, Agriolivada,** and **Lambi.** Meloï offers some shade and good snorkeling. **Kambos Bay** is particularly suitable for children and families, offering calm, shallow waters, rental umbrellas, and some tree cover, as well as a lively seaside scene with opportunities for windsurfing, paragliding, sailing, and canoeing. Its waterside taverna also happens to serve the best lobster on the island. East of Kambos Bay at Livada, it's possible to swim or sometimes to walk across to **Ayíou Yíoryíou Isle;** be sure to bring shoes or sandals, or the rocks will do a number on your feet. The stretch of shoreline from **Thermia to Lambi** is gorgeous, with crystalline waters and some rocks from which you can safely dive. The drawback here is that access is only by caïque from Skala. Also, avoid the north coast when the *meltemi* (severe north summer winds) are blowing.

## Where to Stay & Dine

**Aspri** GREEK    Poised on a north island headland just minutes by taxi from Skala, this dramatically situated restaurant enjoys splendid views of Meloï Bay, Aspris Bay, and Skala and Hora from its multiple terraces. While you're feasting your eyes, it can be easy to neglect the feast on your plate, which would be a serious mistake. Apart from the standard taverna fare offered throughout the islands, which Aspris prepares with great skill, there are some more unusual and enticing items on this menu, such as cuttlefish with Patmian rice. The portions are very generous (something for which you will be glad!) and extra attention is paid to presentation in this quite stylish and widely recommended spot.

Geranos Cape. ℂ **22470/32-240.** Main courses 4.50€–15€. MC, V. June–Sept 7pm–midnight.

**Patmos Paradise**    Perched high above Kambos Bay, this is one of several upscale hotels on the island. The rooms are spacious and inviting, with private balconies that enjoy spectacular sea vistas, in some cases broken by a power line. Amenities include a large terrace pool, sauna, and outdoor tennis and indoor squash courts. This place is exceptionally pleasant and quite chic, while avoiding any major pretense. Down below, in Kambos Bay, there's a modest strand, a handful of shops and tavernas, and the opportunity to rent windsurfing boards, paddleboats, and canoes. A hotel minibus will bring you to and from Skala Harbor when you arrive and depart Patmos.

Kambos Bay, 85500 Patmos. ℂ **22470/32-590.** Fax 22470/32-740. 37 units. 65€–135€ double. Rates include breakfast. MC, V. Open Easter–Oct. *In room: A/C, minibar.*

**Taverna Leonida** ★ GREEK    Ancient Leonidas died defending his land from the invading Persians. Today's more benign invaders are tourists, and Leonidas of Lambi is winning his eternal fame preparing for them "the best saganaki in the world" according to at least one Patmian in the know. A taxi driver once added his two cents, saying "number-one taverna" as he dropped off his passengers on Leonida's pebble beach. The drama of this restaurant begins with its location, only several yards in high tide from the pounding waters of Lambi Bay, and continues with the arrival of your flaming saganaki (grilled cheese). Next comes a visit to the day's catch, soon to appear on your plate. The rest is history. Icons of the chef are available in shops around the island.

Lambi Bay. ℂ **22470/31-490.** Main courses 5€–7.50€. No credit cards. Daily noon–11pm Easter–Oct.

**Taverna Panagos** GREEK    Just above Kambos Bay sits the sleepy village of Kambos; and squarely on its pulse, directly across from the village church, sits the Cafe-estiatorion-taverna (covering every base) Panagos. There are no sea vistas, only myriad glimpses into Patmian village life as it touches base here in what is clearly the local hangout for everyone from children and cats to timeless, bent figures in black. The food is what the village eats at home, only here they don't have to cook it for themselves. The menu is eclipsed by the recital of the day's specials, whose origins are visible on the nearby hillsides. Capons in wine, kid in tomato sauce, lamb in lemon sauce, Patmian goat cheese—all are succulent. It's the total experience you want and receive here, and you can take it with you.

Kambos. ℂ **22470/31-570.** Main courses 5€–23€. No credit cards. Year-round daily noon–midnight.

## THE SOUTH ISLAND

There are two principal beaches in the south of the island, one at **Grikou Bay** and the other at **Psili Ammos.** Grikou Bay, only 4km (2½ miles) from Skala, is the most developed resort on Patmos and home to most of the package-tour groups on the island. Psili Ammos is another story, an extraordinary isolated fine-sand cove bordered by cliffs. Most people arrive by one of the caïques leaving Skala Harbor at 10am, and on arrival (at 10:45am) proceed to do battle for the very limited shade offered by some obliging tamarisks. The only way to ensure yourself of a place in the shade is to arrive before 10:30am; the best way to do that is to take a taxi to Diakofti for 10€ and ask the driver to point the way to Psili Ammos, which is from here about a 30-minute trek on goat paths (wear real shoes). The caïques returning to Skala leave Psili Ammos around 5pm. At any given time, there are a range of caïques providing this service; the shapeliest of these is appropriately named the *Afroditi* and charges 10€ round-trip and 6€ one-way.

Another reason for heading south is to dine at Benetos (only a short taxi ride from Skala), currently touted as the finest restaurant on the island.

## Where to Stay & Dine

**Benetos Restaurant** ★ MEDITERRANEAN  A Tuscan villa at sea's edge, light jazz filling the air, a fresh arugula salad with shaved Parmesan, shrimp baked in filo, filet mignon, a finale of Bailey's chocolate-chip cheesecake, all accompanied by an exclusively Greek wine list—where could this all be happening? The only answer is Benetos, named by the Greek *Alpha Guide* in 2000 as the best restaurant on Patmos and, one of the 30 finest restaurants in Greece. Benetos and Susan Matthaiou have made it their goal to give Greeks and their visitors "a night out" from what they will find anywhere else on these islands. Their winning recipe begins with the freshest and finest local ingredients, mostly from their own organic garden and from nearby waters, and adds to them an element of surprise. The regular menu is quite focused—striking primarily Greek notes with its appetizers and a more Italian theme with its entrees—while offering a handful of daily specials inspired by the day's best crop or catch. For fashionable and fine dining on Patmos, without pretense, this is currently the place; and, with only 12 tables on offer, you would do well to reserve yours several days in advance.

Sapsila. ② **22470/33-089.** Reservations necessary in high season. Main courses 5€–16€. No credit cards. June–Sept Tues–Sun 7:30pm–1am.

**Joanna Hotel-Apartments**  These comfortable, relatively spacious and fully equipped apartments are situated only a few minutes on foot from the beach. Each has a fridge, kitchenette, balcony, and fan. (Rooms with air-conditioning cost an extra 4€ per day.) The layout and feel of the one-bedroom apartments is better than that of the two-bedroom apartments, in which the kitchen area is very limited. Room 15 has a large private deck enjoying a sea view, but is usually reserved for friends, clients, and guests staying 2 to 3 weeks—still, there's no harm in asking. A special feature is the attractive air-conditioned lounge with satellite TV and a bar.

Grikos, 85500 Patmos. ② **22470/31-031.** Fax 22470/32-031, or 210/981-2246 in Athens. 17 units. 50€–60€ apt for 2 persons. Full hot breakfast 5€ extra. V. Open Easter to mid-Oct. *In room:* A/C (4€ extra).

**Petra Hotel and Apartments** ★  Petra Hotel, true to its name, has long been a rock-solid sure thing, and since its renovations completed in 2002 it has been added to the prestigious "Golden List" of the best hotels in all of Greece.

This recognizes the care lavished by the Stergiou family on these stylish, spacious apartments—either one- or two-bedroom—with handsome bathrooms and (except for one) balconies that enjoy splendorous views of Grikos Bay. Each is simply and handsomely decorated, with the necessities of home plus some local touches. It's a perfect family place, just a 2-minute walk from the beach, but also ideal for couples who wish to enjoy a special moment sipping a drink at Petra's elegant, romantic main veranda. Room service and Internet connections are also among its offerings. In 2002, too, the Stergious introduced an evening prix fixe 4-course meal (30€), offering both choices each night and a daily change of menu; with such delicious appetizers as seafood crepes and main courses as salmon topped with salmon roe and cream, the hotel now offers a special dining experience. All these attractions make the Petra popular, especially in August, so advance reservations are advised.

Grikos, 85500 Patmos. © **22470/31-035.** Fax 22470/34-020. Off season © and fax in Athens 210/806-2697. www.petrahotel.gr. 14 units. 110€–185€ apt for 2 persons. Breakfast 8€ extra. MC. Closed Oct–May. *In room:* A/C, TV, kitchenette, fridge, Internet connection.

**Stamatis Restaurant** GREEK   Stamatis, offering consistently reliable taverna fare since 1965, is a landmark by now in Grikou. On its covered terrace practically at water's edge, diners enjoy drinks and consume prodigious amounts of fresh mullet while watching yachts and windsurfers. This is a very pleasant spot to let the evening unravel while enjoying delicious island dishes.

Grikos Beach. © **22470/31-302.** Main courses 3€–11€. No credit cards. Daily 10am–11pm Easter–Oct.

In Hora at Plateia Agia Lesvias, within earshot of the monastery, there's **Kafe 1673,** locally known as **Astivi,** where you can dance to whatever the DJ offers.

# 12

# Central Greece

*by Sherry Marker*

Central Greece (Sterea Ellada) is the least well-defined area of the country. Unlike, for example, the Peloponnese, which is clearly set off from the rest of Greece by the Corinth Canal, or Macedonia, which has a distinct identity, Central Greece is harder to define. In fact, the name Central Greece dates only from 1821, when it was used as a shorthand term for the area of mainland Greece that had been liberated from the Turks. Today, most Greeks would agree that Central Greece stretches from Boeotia and Phocis in the south to as far north as Thessaly. Some Greeks hold that Mount Olympus is the southernmost point in Northern Greece, while others consider Olympus to be the northernmost point in Central Greece.

Central Greece has one of Greece's most varied landscapes. There's the shore that runs along the Gulf of Corinth and the heights of Mount Parnassus. This is where Greece's most famous ancient oracle and most beautiful ancient site, Delphi, is located. There's the city of Thebes, famed for its magnificence in Mycenaean days, today an undistinguished modern town. There's the dusty plain of Thessaly and the extraordinary cliffs and promontories of the monasteries of the Meteora. As if that weren't enough, there are famous ancient battle sites—Thermopylae and Chaironeia—and one of the legendary beauty spots of Greece, the Vale of Tempe.

**STRATEGIES FOR SEEING THE REGION**  If you're setting out from Athens, head via Thebes to Osios Loukas and Delphi and try to spend 2 nights in Delphi. Then head up to the Meteora for another night or two.

## 1 Delphi

178km (110 miles) NW of Athens

Delphi is the big enchilada of Greek sites. More than even Olympia, this place has everything: a long and glorious history, spectacular ancient remains, a superb museum, and a heartbreakingly beautiful location on the slopes of Mount Parnassus. Look up and you see the cliffs and crags of Parnassus; look down and you see Greece's most beautiful plain of olive trees stretching as far as the eye can see toward the town of Itea on the Gulf of Corinth.

*Tips*  **Beware of Price Gouging During the Olympics**

Hotel prices were accurate at press time, but price increases of 20% and more are rumored as hoteliers throughout Greece gear up for the August 2004 Olympics in and around Athens. Horrific price hikes of between 50% and an unbelievable 300% are rumored for the period leading up to, during, and after the Olympics.

**Central Greece**

Mountain

Ferry Routes

The Vale of Tempe **2**

Osios Loukas **4**

Monastery of
Roussanou,
Ayiou Stefanou,
The Great Meteoron,
Anapaphsas,
Ayios Nikolaos
Ayia Triada,
Monasteries of
The Meteora **1**

Site and Museum **3**
Delphi,

Athens

CENTRAL
GREECE

Mediterranean
Sea

Aegean
Sea

Greece

Ionian Sea

Corinthian Gulf

Athens

Megara

Eleusina

Ayia Marina

Thebes

Distomo

Livadia

Osios
Loukas

Arachova

Delphi

**Mt. Parnassus**

Orchomenos

Amfissa

Ayios
Konstandinos

Kamena Vourla

Thermopylae

Lamia

Stilida

Glifa

Almiros

Farsala

Palamas

Makrinitsa

Volos

Larissa

Ayia

Tirnavos

Elassona

Platamonas

Leptokaria

Litochoro

**Mt. Olympus**

**Mt.
Pelion**

Pelion
Peninsula

Aegean Sea

Pagasitic
Gulf

SKIATHOS

SKOPELOS

ALONISSOS

Gulf of Evvia

EVVIA

Patras

Messolongi

Agrinio

Karpenisi

Kardítsa

Trikkala

Meteora
(Kalambaka)

Metsovo

Ioannina

ZAGORI

Lake Pamvotis

Paras

25 mi
25 km

N

20

15

6

6

3

9

1

5

20

48

8a

8a

1

3

44

1

27

27

1

5

1

**Tips Remember**

Many of the rural Greek National Tourist Offices (EOT) are being turned over to local authorities. In most cases, the office remains at the same address, with the same phone and work hours.

Delphi is especially magical in the spring, when there's both snow and wildflowers on Parnassus—and relatively few tourists tramping around the site. But whenever you visit, you'll understand why the ancient Greeks believed that Delphi was the center of the world, the spot Apollo chose as the home of his most famous oracle.

## A LOOK AT THE PAST

Pilgrims came to Delphi from all of the Greek world and much of the non-Greek world to ask Apollo's advice on affairs of state as well as small, personal matters. Unfortunately, the god's words were famously hard to interpret. "Invade and you will destroy a great empire," the oracle told Lydian King Croesus when he asked whether he should go to war with his Persian neighbors. Croesus invaded and destroyed a great empire: his own.

Delphi was also the site of the Pythian Games, the most famous festival in Greece after the Olympics. The games commemorated Apollo's triumph over his oracular predecessor here, the snaky Python. Because Apollo was the god of music, the Pythian games had more artistic contests than the Olympic Games. When you sit in the theater here, you can imagine the flute and lyre contests and the dances and plays staged every 4 years throughout antiquity to honor Apollo.

Like so many ancient sites, Apollo's sanctuary at Delphi was first neglected, then virtually forgotten, during the Christian era. Kings and generals looted Delphi of its treasures; later, locals hacked up the buildings to build their houses. The modern village of Delphi sat atop the ancient site until the 19th century, when it was relocated just down the road so that archaeologists could help Delphi reclaim its past.

## ESSENTIALS

**GETTING THERE** **By Bus** There are five daily buses to Delphi from the Athens bus station at 260 Liossion (Athens © **210/831-7096;** Delphi © **22650/82-317**).

**By Car** Take the Athens–Corinth National Highway about 74km (46 miles) west of Athens to the Thebes turnoff. Continue west to Levadia. If you wish to stop at the monastery of Osios Loukas, take the Distomo turnoff and continue 9km (5½ miles) to Osios Loukas (be prepared to meet tour buses thundering along this road). Return to Distomo and continue via Arachova 26km (16 miles) or the seaside town of Itea 65km (40 miles) to Delphi. The beautiful approach from Itea, on a road that winds and climbs higher and higher until it reaches Delphi, is well worth the time, if you are not in a hurry—and are not troubled by switchback turns.

**By Organized Tour** Athens-based companies such as **GO,** 31–33 Voulis (© 210/322-5951), and **CHAT,** 4 Stadiou (© 210/322-3137), offer 1- and 2-day trips to Delphi. If possible, take the 2-day trip, which lets you enjoy a less frantic visit. Most tours leave Athens by 8am and arrive at Delphi by 3pm after a stop at Osios Loukas. On the 2nd day, you leave Delphi around 3pm, arriving back in Athens about 7pm. The price (including transportation, site and museum admissions, guide, hotel, and most meals) is about 150€ for one person in a

# Ancient Delphi

1 Roman Agora ( Marketplace)
2 Votive offering of Corfu ("Bull")
3 Votive offering of Athens ("Victory at Marathon")
4 Votive offering of Lacedaemonians
5 Votive offering of Argos
6 Votive offering of Argos ("Seven Against Thebes")
7 Votive offering of Argos ("Descendants")
8 Votive offering of Taras ("The King of Argos")
9 Treasure House of Sikyon
10 Treasure House of Siphnos
11 Treasure House of Megara
12 Treasure House of Thebes
13 Treasure House of Boeotia
14 Treasure House of Potidaea
15 Treasure House of Athens
16 Bouleuterion (Council House)
17 Treasure House of Cnidus (Knidos)
18 Rock of Sibylla
19 Naxian Column
20 Asklepion
21 Portico of the Athenians
22 Treasure House of Corinth
23 Prytaneion (Magistrates' Building)
24 Treasure House of Cyrene
25 Supporting Polygonal Wall
26 Tripod of Plataee
27 Votive offering of Rhodes
28 Grand Altar
29 Spring
30 Temple of Apollo
31 Votive Tripods
32 Treasure House of Acanthus
33 Portico of Attalus
34 Shrine of Neoptolemos
35 Votive offering of Daochos
36 Club of the Cnidians
37 Kassotis Spring
38 Ischegaon–Supporting Wall
39 Votive offering of Krateros
40 Theater
41 Western Portico

private room. An exceptionally well-traveled friend who was leery of a group tour had nothing but praise for her 2-day excursion in May 2000.

**VISITOR INFORMATION** Most services, such as the post office and banks, are located in the village of Delphi (pop. 2,500) on the obvious main street, which is named after King Paul and Queen Frederika, although no one seems to use the name. The **tourist office** (© 22650/82-900), in the town hall on the main street, is open Monday through Friday from 8am to 2:30pm and sometimes reopens from 6 to 8pm in summer. If you are here in June or July, check at the tourist office for information on the Delphi festival of ancient Greek drama. In 2002, performances were held not at the ancient theater (which was undergoing restoration work), but in the European Cultural Center of Delphi. It is hoped to resume performances in the ancient theater once the work there is finished. The ancient site (signposted) is about 1km (½ mile) out of town, on the Arachova Road.

**GETTING AROUND** If you can, you should walk everywhere in Delphi. Parking spots are at a premium both in the village and at the site. If you have to drive to the site rather than making the 5- to 10-minute walk from town, be sure to set off early to get one of the few parking places. Whether you walk or drive, keep an eye out for the enormous tour buses that barrel down the center of the road—and for the not terribly well marked one-way streets in the village.

Delphi taxi driver **Elias Karatzoglas** (© 22650/82-741; mobile 093/202-3659) speaks English, drives an air-conditioned taxi, and will whisk you off to see Osios Loukas, Arachova, Mount Parnassos, or just about anywhere you want to go at competitive prices. If he is not available, ask at the tourist office for the name of another English speaking taxi driver.

**FAST FACTS** There are several banks on the main street where you can exchange currency or use the ATM; the **National Bank of Greece**, in addition to normal weekday hours, is sometimes open from 6 to 7pm in summer. The **police** (© 22650/82-222) are in the town hall (© 22650/82-310) on the main street. For **first aid**, call (© 22650/82-307). Both the **post office** and the **telephone office (OTE)** are on the main street. In addition to normal weekday hours (Mon–Fri 8am–2pm), the post office and OTE are sometimes open Sunday from 9am to 1pm.

## WHAT TO SEE & DO

As at Olympia, the most important thing is to begin your visit as early as possible. If you are visiting both the site and the museum, be sure to hold onto your 9€ ticket, good for both. It's hard to resist heading immediately for the site, but beginning your visit with the museum has certain benefits. Perhaps most importantly, seeing the collection will help you to put flesh on the bones of the archaeological remains, as you will have fresh in your mind images of the sculptures and works of art that adorned the sanctuary. *Tip:* Both the site and museum are sometimes relatively uncrowded during the hour before closing time or during the mid-day lunch break that most tour groups take.

**The Angelos and Eva Sikelianos Museum** The road that leads steeply uphill through the village of Delphi ends at the handsome stone-and-brick Sikelianos home, now a museum commemorating the work of the Greek poet Sikelianos and his American wife, Eva Palmer. An artist, writer, and, ultimately, costume designer, Eva helped her husband stage Greek tragedies in Delphi's theater in the 1920s and 1930s. The couple's attempts to revive the Pythian games was not long-lived, but their desire to make use of Greece's ancient theaters had lasting effects, as all who have seen plays performed here or at the theater at Epidaurus know. This museum is a pleasant place to spend an hour and see Sikelianos's manuscripts and the beautiful costumes Eva designed. Few tourists visit this elegant home, which has spectacular views from most windows, cozy fireplaces, and the best bathroom in town. A pleasant place to spend an hour.

© 2650/82-173. Fax 2650/82-722. epkdelfi@otenet.gr. Admission 1.50€. Wed–Mon 8:30am–3pm.

## The Delphi Museum ★★★

*Note:* In June 2003, it was announced that the Delphi Museum would be closed until the Olympics in August 2004, reopen for the Olympics (Aug 13–29), and then close indefinitely thereafter. Be sure to call ahead to make sure the museum is open. Almost everyone who was anyone in the ancient world sent gifts to Delphi. Since much of what you are seeing here is what remains of those gifts and of the architectural sculpture that adorned the splendid buildings here, you are seeing some of the finest works that survive from classical antiquity. Even works that may not immediately strike you as magnificent are important, such as the 4th-century B.C. **marble egg,** a copy of the yet older egg (or *omphalos*) that symbolized Delphi's unique position as the center (or navel) of the world. According to legend, when Zeus wanted to determine the earth's center, he released two eagles from Olympus. When the eagles met over Delphi, Zeus had his answer. You may still see eagles in the sky above Delphi, but more often than not, the large birds overhead are the less distinguished Egyptian vultures.

The star of the museum, with a room to himself, is the famous 5th-century B.C. **Charioteer of Delphi,** a larger-than-life bronze figure (part of a group that originally included a four-horse chariot). The wealthy Sicilian city of Gela dedicated this near monumental work to honor its tyrant Polyzalos's chariot victory here. It's an irresistible statue: Don't miss the handsome youth's delicate eyelashes shading wide enamel-and-stone eyes, or the realistic veins that stand out in his hands and feet.

Although the Charioteer is the star of the collection, he's in good company here. Like Olympia, Delphi was chockablock with superb works of art donated by wealthy patrons, such as King Croesus of Lydia, who gave the massive **silver bull** on display here. And keep an eye out in the display of bronzes for the tiny **bronze ornament** showing Ulysses clinging to the belly of a ram. When Ulysses and his men were trapped in the cave of the ferocious (but nearsighted) one-eyed monster Cyclops, they tied themselves to the bellies of the Cyclops's sheep. When the sheep went out of the cave to pasture, they carried the Greek heroes with them to safety. You could spend hours here, but allow at least 1 hour.

Delphi: © 2650/82-312. Admission 9€ (includes admission to site); museum only 6€. Summer Mon 11am–7pm; Tues–Fri 8am–7pm; Sat–Sun and holidays 8am–3pm. Winter Mon 11am–5:30pm; Tues–Fri 8am–5:30pm; Sat–Sun and holidays 8am–5pm. (Be sure to check these hours when you arrive in Delphi, as they can change without warning.)

## The Sanctuary of Apollo ★★★

The Sanctuary of Apollo is immediately beyond and just above the museum. The less well-known Sanctuary of Athena on the lower slopes of Parnassus is a 10-minute walk past the museum. The Castalian Spring is between the two sanctuaries. If you can't visit everything here, spend your time at the Sanctuary of Apollo, stroll to the Castalian Spring, and then cross the Delphi-Arachova Road to take a peek down at the Sanctuary of Athena. You may want to buy a site map when you get your ticket to help you orient yourself at this sprawling site, many of whose monuments are unlabeled.

As you enter the Sanctuary of Apollo, you'll be on the marble **Sacred Way,** the road that visitors here have walked for thousands of years. The road runs uphill past the remains of **Roman stoas** and a number of **Greek treasuries** (including the Sifnian and Athenian treasuries, whose sculpture is in the museum). Cities built these small templelike buildings at Delphi for several reasons: to impress their neighbors and to store riches and works of art dedicated to Apollo. Take a close look at the **treasury walls.** You'll see not only beautiful dry-wall masonry but also countless inscriptions. The Greeks were never shy about using the walls of their buildings as bulletin boards.

Alas, so many recent visitors were bent on adding their names to the ancient inscriptions that the Greek archaeological service no longer allows visitors inside the massive 4th-century B.C. **Temple of Apollo,** which was built after the 7th- and 6th-centuries B.C. temples were destroyed. In antiquity, one of the three Pythian priestesses on duty gave voice to Apollo's oracles from a room deep within the temple. That much is known, although the details of what precisely happened here are obscure. Did the priestess sit on a tripod balanced over a chasm, breathing in hallucinatory fumes? Did she chew various herbs, including the laurel leaf sacred to Apollo, until she spoke in tongues, while priests interpreted her sayings? Perhaps wisely, the oracle has kept its secrets.

From the temple, it's a fairly steep uphill climb to the remarkably well-preserved 4th-century B.C. **theater** and the **stadium,** which was extensively remodeled by the Romans. Events in the Pythian festival took place in both the stadium and the theater. In 1927, the Greek poet and eccentric Angelos Sikelianos and his equally eccentric wife attempted to revive the ancient contests here (see the Sikelianos Museum, above). Today, the theater and stadium are used most summers for the **Festival of Delphi,** which, on occasion, has featured exceptionally unclassical pop music.

Keep your ticket as you leave the Sanctuary of Apollo and head along the Arakova-Delphi Road toward the Sanctuary of Athena (also called the Marmaria, which simply refers to all the marble found here). En route, you'll pass the famous **Castalian Spring,** where Apollo planted a laurel he brought here from the Vale of Tempe. Drinking from the spring inspired legions of poets in antiquity; now, poets have to find their inspiration elsewhere, as the spring is off-limits, purportedly to allow repairs to the Roman fountain facade. (Once an antiquity is closed in Greece, it often stays closed quite a while.) Above are the rose-colored cliffs known as the **Phaedriades** (the Bright Ones), famous for the way that they reflect the sun's rays.

North of the Castalian Spring, a path descends from the main road to the **Sanctuary of Athena,** the goddess of wisdom who shared the honors at Delphi with Apollo. As the remains here are quite fragmentary, except for the 4th-century B.C. **gymnasium,** you can simply wander about and enjoy the site without trying too hard to figure out what's what. The round 4th-century **tholos** with its three graceful Doric columns is easy to spot, though no one knows why this building was built, why it was so lavishly decorated, or what went on inside. Again, the oracle keeps its secrets. You could easily spend all day here, but allow at least 3 hours for a quick visit.

## WHERE TO STAY

There's no shortage of hotels in Delphi; you can usually find lodging even in July or August. When tourists are few, you may be able to improve on these rates. When you are offered a room, and told the price, simply ask if there is a cheaper or August. When you are offered a room, and told the price, simply ask if there is a cheaper

Sanctuary of Apollo, Castalian Spring and Sanctuary of Athena Pronaia ⓒ 2650/82-313. Admission 9€ (includes admission to site); site only 6€. Summer Mon 11am–7pm; Tues–Fri 8am–7pm; Sat–Sun and holidays 8am–3pm. (Be sure to check these times as soon as you arrive at Delphi, as they can change without warning.)

room available. Still, if you want to be sure that you get a room in a specific price category (or with a view, or a pool), it's best to make a reservation. Finally, consider staying in nearby Arachova, where the hotels are usually less crowded in summer and the restaurants are better (see "Side Trips from Delphi," below).

In addition to the following options, we've also had good reports of the **Pan Hotel**, 53 Vasileos Pavlou and Frederikis (© **22650/82-294**), the adjacent **Olympic Hotel**, 53a Vasileos Pavlou and Frederikis (© **22650/82-793;** fax 22650/82-780), and the **Hermes Hotel**, 29 Vasileos Pavlou and Frederikis (© **22650/82-318;** fax 22650/82-639). The last two are both owned by the Droseros family.

**Amalia Hotel** ★ *Kids* Like most of the chain of Amalia hotels, the Delphi Amalia has all the creature comforts and is located outside town (above the Delphi-Itea road) in a quiet location. You probably won't want to stay here unless you have a car—but, if you are traveling with children, you may find the Amalia's pool irresistible. Many of the bedrooms face each other across a generous garden; when several tour groups are in residence, you'll be aware that you are not alone here.

Signposted on the Delphi-Itea Rd., 33054 Delphi. © **22650/82-101**. Fax 22650/82-290.hotamal@hellasnet.gr. 185 units. 150€ double. Rates include breakfast. AE, MC, V. **Amenities:** Restaurant; bar; pool; room service 7am–12pm. *In room: A/C, TV,* minibar, hair dryer.

**Hotel Varonos** ★ This small, family-owned hotel has very clean, spare bedrooms with fine views out over the olive plain. If you can, take in the rooftop view. This is a very welcoming place: We once arrived with an ailing gardenia plant, and the entire family pitched in to make sure it was well taken care of during our stay. The breakfast room is pleasant; if you plan to have an early breakfast, tell the desk the night before. Be sure to check out the owners' shop next door, with local produce and crafts.

25 Vasileos Pavlou and Frederikis, 33054 Delphi. © and fax **22650/82-345**. 11 units (10 shower, 1 with shower/tub). 70€–80€ Rates include breakfast (although room without breakfast. sometimes possible). Inquire about the Frommer's 20% discount sometimes available. MC, V. **Amenities:** Breakfast room; lounge with fireplace. *In room: A/C, TV.*

**Hotel Vouzas** ★ If you don't mind sacrificing the swimming pool at the Amalia, this is the place to stay—cozy fireplace in the lobby, spectacular views, and a short walk to everything you've come to see. That said, perhaps you could persuade the owners that running a wide band at eye level through the dining-room picture window is not very clever. The bedrooms and bathrooms here are quite comfortable (and were partly renovated in 1999); balconies have not only a table and chairs, but also, in season, a welcoming pot of basil.

1 Frederikis (at Vasileos Pavlou), 33054 Delphi. © **22650/82-232**. Fax 22650/82-033. 59 units. 120€–150€ double. AE, DC, MC, V. **Amenities:** Restaurant; bar. *In room: A/C, TV.*

## The Festival of Delphi

Each summer (usually in June), the European Cultural Center of Delphi sponsors a festival featuring ancient Greek drama and works inspired by ancient drama. Tickets and schedules are usually available at the center's Athens office at 9 Frynihou, Plaka (© **210/331-2798**), and at the center's Delphi office (© **22650/82-733**), just out of town on the Itea road (set back from the road in a grove of trees).

**Kastalia Hotel** The Kastalia, on Delphi's main street, has been here since 1938, but was completely remodeled in 1986, and has been redecorated regularly since then. Actually, it looks more "traditional" now than it did originally, with attractive projecting balconies, a white stucco facade, and some nice touches (embroideries, hand-loomed rugs) in the guest rooms. The back bedrooms have fine views over the olive plain. If the Kastalia is full, the Maniatis family may suggest that you try their other hotel, the Frederikis, at 38 Pavlou and Frederikis.

13 Vasileos Pavlou and Frederikis sts, 33054 Delphi. ✆ **22650/82-205**. Fax 22650/82-208. 26 units. 85€–89€ double. Rates include breakfast. AE, DC, V. Usually closed weekdays Jan–Feb. **Amenities:** Restaurant. *In room:* A/C in 12 units, TV.

## WHERE TO DINE

Frankly, we have never been bowled over by a meal in Delphi—and we've had meals here over a number of decades. The problem: restaurateurs know that they probably will never see you again—which never inspires good service or loving food preparation. We suggest that you consider eating in Arachova, 10km (6 miles) east of Delphi, where the restaurants cater to a more local crowd—or to the Athenians who come here to ski and who know their Greek food!

**Taverna Skala** ★ GREEK We've had some good meals here in winter and noticed locals eating here in summer. The menu is typical Greek taverna fare (grills, stews), but there's usually a wide variety of *mezedes*, and the wood-paneled room (just about everything that can be wood-paneled in Delphi is!) is cozy.

Vasileos Pavlou and Frederikis. ✆ **22650/82-762**. Main courses 6€–10€. No credit cards. Daily noon–around midnight.

**Taverna Vakchos** ★ Value GREEK This small taverna gets many of its customers from the youth hostel next door. This means that the prices are very reasonable, the clientele casual, and the food basic. The back room has good views over Delphi, the plain of olives, and to the Corinthian Gulf.

31 Apollonos. ✆ **22650/82-448**. Main courses 5€–10€. No credit cards. Daily noon–around midnight.

**Topiki Gefsi** GREEK This large restaurant on the main street has a nice view and reasonably good food. Unfortunately, as with most establishments here, the staff is pretty sure that they'll never see you again and the service is consequently haphazard. That said, the stuffed vine leaves and stews are usually reliable, and there's sometimes live music in the evening.

19 Pavlou and Frederikis. ✆ **22650/82-480**. Main courses 8€–15€. AE, DC, MC, V. Daily noon–around midnight.

## SIDE TRIPS FROM DELPHI
### ARACHOVA

Arachova's main feast day is April 23, the festival of St. George, the patron saint of shepherds, celebrated with the consumption of roasted lambs and, often, folk dancing and music until the wee hours (unless Apr 23 falls during Lent, in which case the feast day is usually celebrated on the Tuesday after Easter). If you are going to be here then, be sure you have a reservation. Also be sure to wish anyone named George "Chronia Polla (many more years)."

The mountain village of **Arachova**, 10km (6 miles) east of Delphi, clings to Mount Parnassus some 950m (3,116 ft.) above sea level. Arachova is famous for its hand-loomed rugs, including fluffy flokati, tagari bags, and blankets. When several tour buses stop here during the daytime, this tiny village can be seriously crowded. Don't despair: Try to come back in the evening, when the shops are still open and the cafes and restaurants give you a chance to escape from the tourist world of Delphi to the village world of Greece. There's usually an energetic evening **volta** (stroll) on Delphon, the main street, and if you climb the steep stairs to the upper town, you'll find yourself on quiet neighborhood streets, where children play and families sit out in front of their homes.

On the main street, there are a number of shops with crafts. Sometimes a shop will close, reopen under new management—and have very similar goods. You might see if there are weavings on display in Georgia Charitou's shop **Anemi** (© 22670/31-701), which also has some nice reproductions of antiques. **Katina Panagakou** (© 22670/31-743) has examples of local crafts as well, as do several other shops strung out along the long main street.

For lunch or dinner here, try the simple family fare at the **Taverna Karathanassi**, by the coffee shops in the main street square with the lovely freshwater springs. The nearby **Taverna Dasargyri**, which specializes in delicious *kokoretsi* (stuffed entrails), *loukanika* (sausages), and grills, often has an almost entirely local crowd. If you don't want to sit on the main street, head uphill on the stepped street and then ask for directions to Plateia Tropeou and the **Kaplanis** restaurant. This place has splendid views over the town and countryside and, usually, a variety of stews, grills, and *mezedes* Expect to pay about 15€ for dinner (perhaps as much as 20€ at Kaplanis).

If you want to stay in Arachova, the **Xenia Hotel** (© **22670/31-230;** fax 22670/32-175), with 44 rooms, each with a balcony (but charmless decor), has doubles at 80€). The very pleasant **Anemolia** (© **22670/31-640;** fax 22670/31-642), with 52 rooms, on a hill just outside Arachova above the Delphi road, was originally a member of the Best Western chain and its rooms are large and comfortable. Tentative prices for 2003 are 85€ for a double (prices sometimes are much as 20€–50€ higher on the weekend); the dining room is unexceptional. The **Arachova Inn**, with 42 rooms and a cozy fireplace in the lobby, is just outside town; it charges 80€, except on winter weekends, when the price rises to 100€ and higher for a double. All these hotels are usually full on winter weekends, when Greeks flock here to ski Parnassus.

## PARNASSUS (PARNASSOS)

**Parnassus ★★★** is an odd mountain: It's difficult to see its peaks from either Delphi or Arachova, although if you approach from the north, you'll have fine views of the twin summits.

The good news is that you can drive the 27km (17 miles) from Arachova to the **ski resort at Fterolaki**, 2,253m (7,390 ft.) up Mount Parnassus, in about an hour. The bad news is that the road and several incipient hamlets of ski lodges (the Alexander Resort, 7km/4¼ miles outside Arachova is one of the more tasteful developments) are spoiling the mountain's isolation and much of its beauty. If you drive to Fterolaki in summer, don't expect to find any of the shops, cafes and restaurants (still less the dozen ski runs!) open. If you do come in winter, you can rent ski equipment either in Arachova or at the ski resort at Fterolaki. Keep in mind that fog and high winds often sweep in here suddenly. When this happens, the ski lifts close down, the road down the mountain is often also closed, standing day-trippers until it reopens. In fact, fog can close this road at almost any time, even in summer—something to keep in mind if you decide to drive up for a look around. We were very glad to have a bottle of water and some cookies in the car when this happened to us one May afternoon.

If you want to hike Parnassus, there are two possibilities. (As always in the mountains, it's not a good idea to make such an excursion alone.) You can head uphill in Delphi past the Sikelianos house and keep going. Four hours will bring you to the upland meadows known as the **Plateau of Livadi**, where shepherds traditionally pasture their flocks. If you plan to continue on past the meadows to the **Corycrian Cave** (known locally as Sarantavli, or "Forty Rooms"), where Pan and the Nymphs once were thought to live, or to the summits, you should check on conditions locally or with the **Hellenic Mountaineering Club** in Athens (© 210/323-4555). It's also possible to begin your ascent from Arachova, where you can get directions locally. The excellent Road Edition map of Parnassos (No. 42 in the series of mountain maps) is an excellent investment (6€), as is Tim Salmon's *The Mountains of Greece* (Cicerone Press), but nothing substitutes for a companion, especially one who knows the terrain.

## THE MONASTERY OF OSIOS LOUKAS

You'll probably want to see Osios Loukas en route to or from Delphi, although you could do the 96km (60-mile) round-trip via Arachova as a day excursion. If you go to Osios Loukas via Levadia, pause at **Schisste (Triodos)**, where three roads cross. This is the spot where the ancients believed that Oedipus unknowingly slew his father. Things got worse. Still unknowingly, he married his mother and brought tragedy on himself and his descendants.

**Osios Loukas** (the Monastery of Saint Luke) ★★ is a spectacular church and monastery founded in the 10th century, with much of what you see dating from at least the 11th century. This is not just a tourist destination: Devout Greek Orthodox visitors consider it a holy spot, something to keep in mind during your visit. This is not the place for sleeveless shirts, shorts, or a casual attitude toward the icons or the tomb of Saint Luke.

Osios Loukas is a lavishly decorated complex—not just brick but a wide variety of different jewel-like polychrome marbles were used in the buildings. Along with the mosaics at Daphne, outside Athens, and the splendid churches of Thessaloniki, Osios Loukas's **mosaics** are among the finest in Greece. If you are lucky enough to be here when the **Katholikon (Main Church)** isn't too crowded, let yourself enjoy the changing light and shadow they play on the marbles and mosaics. You may see visitors handing their family icons to a monk, who takes it into the church for a special blessing. Then head over to the smaller **church of the Theotokos (Mother of God)**, with its lovely mosaic floor. If you have time, visit the crypt, with its frescoes, and then sit in the courtyard and imagine what Osios Loukas would have been like when hundreds, not today's handful, of monks lived and worshipped here.

Admission to Osios Loukas costs 3€. Hours are daily from 8am to 2pm and 4 to 7pm from early May to mid-September, 8am to 5pm the rest of the year. (Note that these are the posted times; they are not always observed.) There's a small cafe on the grounds, where you can get soft drinks, coffee, snacks and local delicacies. Allow at least an hour for your visit.

## 2 Thebes

87km (53 miles) W of Athens off the Athens-Corinth National Hwy.

Thebes was one of the most important Mycenaean settlements in Greece. The Athenian dramatist Agamemnon commemorated Thebes in his play *Seven Against Thebes*, and the poet Pindar was born here. When Alexander the Great captured Thebes in 336 B.C., he leveled the town, sparing only Pindar's birthplace.

Unfortunately, several 20th-century earthquakes have also leveled a good deal of Thebes, and the new city, though energetic, is not charming. If you're pressed for time, you might give Thebes a miss altogether, unless you're heading for the

Archaeological Museum (see below). There's no really good hotel here—and several really down-at-the-heels ones—so we don't recommend spending the night. As for food, you won't starve, but if you find a superior restaurant, please let us know. We haven't, despite many attempts.

If you're driving, the turnoff for Thebes, just after Eleusis, is signposted on the National Highway. Allow 2 hours from Athens. Frequent buses depart from the Athens station, 260 Liossion (© **210/831-7096**), arriving at the Thebes bus station (© **22620/275-11**) in the center of town.

**The Archaeological Museum**    There's only one thing to detain you in Thebes: the Archaeological Museum, which has a handy easy-to-spot Frankish tower in its garden. Although the collection includes a wide range of pottery, inscriptions, and sculpture, the Mycenaean objects are the highlight. There are several painted Mycenaean sarcophagi, some fine gold jewelry, and handsome body armor. The scant remains of ancient Thebes—the unexcavated ancient city lies under the modern one—are signposted at the museum. Allow an hour for your visit.

Pindarou. © **22620/27-913.** Admission 2€. Mon and Wed–Sat 8:30am–3pm; Sun 9am–2pm. Pindarou is Thebes's main street. There is parking on side streets nearby.

## 3  Two Famous Battlefields: Thermopylae & Chaironeia

### THERMOPYLAE
194km (120 miles) N of Athens on the Athens-Thessaloniki National Hwy.

If you find yourself on the Athens-Thessaloniki Highway, keep an eye out for the larger-than-life-size **statue of the Spartan king Leonidas,** about halfway through the 6.4km (4-mile) long Pass of Thermopylae that snakes between the mountains and the sea. One of the most famous battles in history was fought here in 480 B.C. during the Persian King Xerxes's attempt to conquer Greece. To this day, historians speculate on just how different the world might have been if Xerxes had succeeded, and Greece had become part of the Persian Empire.

When Xerxes invaded Greece in 480 B.C. with perhaps 100,000 men, soldiers from almost every city-state in south and central Greece rushed to Thermopylae to try to stop the Persian king's advance. The Greeks might have succeeded in holding the narrow pass of Thermopylae had not a traitor told the Persians of a secret mountain path that allowed them to turn the pass. As Leonidas and his 300-man royal guard stood and fought at Thermopylae, the main Greek force retreated south to regroup and fight another day. When the fighting at Thermopylae was over, Leonidas and his men lay dead, but the Spartan king had earned immortal fame for his heroism.

The name Thermopylae (Hot Gates) refers to the warm springs that bubbled here in antiquity, when the pass was considerably narrower than it is now that centuries of silt have built up the seashore. Many of Thermopylae's springs have been partly diverted to spas, such as Kamena Vourla, but unfortunately, overdevelopment has seriously undercut the former charm of the seaside towns nearby. If you want to take a fast look at some of the springs, keep an eye out for plumes of smoke when you park near the statue of Leonidas. If you don't see the plumes, follow your nose: The smell of sulfur is strong.

### CHAIRONEIA
132km (81 miles) NW of Athens on the Athens-Levadhia-Lamia Hwy.

Just north of Levadhia, the Athens-Lamia Highway passes an enormous **stone lion** that marks the site of the common grave of the Theban Sacred Band of warriors, who died here in the Battle of Chaironeia in 338 B.C. It was at Chaironeia that Philip of Macedon, with some 30,000 soldiers, defeated the combined forces of Athens and Thebes and became the most powerful leader in Greece. It was also at Chaironeia that Philip's 18-year-old son Alexander first distinguished himself on the battlefield, when he led the attack against the superbly trained Theban Sacred Band, which fought to the last man. Philip's admiration for the Thebans' courage was such that he allowed them to be buried where they fell on the battlefield.

The lion itself, sitting on its haunches with a surprisingly benign expression on its face, was probably erected by Thebes sometime after the battle. With the passing of time, the winds blew soil from the plain almost entirely over the lion. In 1818, two English antiquarians stumbled upon the lion's head; excavations in 1904 and 1905 led to the lion's restoration and re-erection here on the dusty plain of Chaironeia.

## 4 The Vale of Tempe & Ambelakia

326km (202 miles) N of Athens; 27km (16 miles) N of Larissa

**The Vale of Tempe** ★, a steep-sided 8km (5-mile) gorge between Mounts Olympus and Ossa has been famous since antiquity as a beauty spot. According to legend, this is where Apollo caught a glimpse of the lovely maiden Daphne, bathing in the Peneios River. When Apollo pursued Daphne, she cried out to the gods on nearby Olympus to save her—which they did, by turning her into a laurel tree (*daphne* in Greek). Apollo, who didn't give up easily, then plucked a branch from the tree and planted it at his shrine at Delphi. Thereafter, messengers came to Tempe from Delphi every 9 years to collect laurel for Apollo's temple.

To this day, there are laurel, chestnut, and plane trees growing in the Vale of Tempe. Unfortunately, since virtually all north-south traffic in Greece now passes through the Vale, this is no longer the sylvan spot that was once the haunt of nightingales. Still, if you're lucky enough to be here off-season, the sound of the gurgling river may be louder than that of tourists' footsteps on the suspension bridge over the gorge. The car toll is 1.50€. If you park and walk through the Vale, allow at least an hour for your visit.

Keep an eye out for the remains of the **Kastro tis Oreas** (Castle of the Beautiful Maiden) on the cliffs above Tempe and the little chapel deep in the gorge. Unfortunately, you won't have any trouble spotting the souvenir stands throughout the Vale, or the signs advertising a "Love Boat" cruise on the river.

If you can, take an hour or two to visit the mountaintop village of **Ambelakia** ★, some 6km (4 miles) southeast of the Vale of Tempe, with spectacular views of Mount Olympus. The village is one of six in Greece to have formed the **National Network of Tradition, Culture, and Community Life** to attempt to preserve their traditions and base economic development on local crafts.

Ambelakia, whose name means "vineyards" in Greek, is perched amidst old oak trees on Mount Kissavos. Astonishingly, this tiny village was an important center of cotton and silk production in the 17th century, with offices in far-off London. Today, little remains of Ambelakia's earlier wealth, but what does remain is well worth a visit: the handsome late 18th-century **Schwarz House** ★. (It's open somewhat unpredictably, but is usually closed Mon and open Tues–Sun 9am–2pm; admission 3€; no phone) The Schwarz brothers were two of Ambelakia's wealthiest merchants, who lived and worked in Austria, hence the name "Schwarz," a translation of their Greek name "Mavros." Their handsome wooden house, with its overhanging balconies and elaborately frescoed interiors, is an absolute delight—and it is a delight to see it so carefully restored and cared for. Allow an hour for the guided tour of the house.

If you want to stay here, it's a good idea to call ahead to the charming little **Nine Muses Hotel** (© **24950/93-405** or 2410/550-774), which has 12 rooms at 40€ to 50€ double, but is not always open. If the Nine Muses is full, ask for help finding a room in one of the local "rent rooms" bed-and-breakfasts. There are several small restaurants on the main square serving simple grills and salads. If you want a break from tourist Greece, spend a night or two here, and experience village Greece—and spectacular views of Mount Olympus.

## 5 Mount Olympus

390km (241 miles) N of Athens; 70km (43 miles) N of Larissa

Greece's most famous mountain range, home of the Olympian gods, towers 2,919m (9,751 ft.) above the plains of Thessaly and Macedonia. From a distance, it's almost impossible to pick out Olympus's summit, Mytikas—nicknamed the "needle," or **Stafani**, and called the "throne of Zeus"—although the massive, gnarled, snowcapped range is often visible from Thessaloniki (albeit less and less so, given the area's increasing pollution).

The first recorded successful ascent of the summit was in 1913, when two Swiss mountaineers with a local guide made it to the top. For such an imposing mountain, Olympus is surprisingly easy to climb, in large part because so many people since 1913 have climbed it. Consequently, there are a number of well-marked paths to the summit as well as shelters at Stavros (944m/3,096ft.) and Spilios Agapitos (2,100m/6,888 ft.), where climbers can rest or even spend the night. In summer, these paths can be very heavily trafficked, with some elegant Greek women making the ascent in high heels.

Still, Olympus is a serious mountain, and no one should attempt it alone. As always in the mountains, weather conditions can change for the worse without warning. Well into May, severe snowstorms are not uncommon on the heights of Olympus—which helps to explain why the area has been developed in recent years as a ski resort. The main town on the slopes, and the base camp, as it were, for climbers, is Litochoro.

## ESSENTIALS

**GETTING THERE    By Bus**    Four buses that stop at the Litochoro station (© 23520/81-271) run daily from Athens to Katerini; seven buses per day run from Athens to Larissa, from which there is frequent service to Litochoro. All buses leave Athens from the station at 260 Liossion (© **210/831-7059**). There are at least eight buses a day from Thessaloniki to Litochoro.

**By Train**    There are frequent daily trains from Athens to Larissa, and from Thessaloniki to Larissa; from Larissa, you can continue to Litochoro by bus. You can also take a train from Athens or Thessaloniki to the Litochoro station (© **23520/22-522**)—but the station is on the coast 9km (5½ miles) from town, and you'll have to continue on by bus or taxi. Only train lovers will want to come here this way.

**By Car**    Take the Litochoro exit on the Athens-Salonika Highway.

**VISITOR INFORMATION**    The **tourist office** (© **23520/83-100**) faces the bus stop. The **Hellenic Mountaineering Club** (EOS) (© **210/323-4555**) can be reached at © **210/323-4555** in Athens, 231/278-288 in Thessaloniki; or 23520/81-944 in Litochoro. The HMC can give you information on conditions on

Olympus, which is usually climbable from June 1 to October 1, and will let you know whether you can just show up at, or need a misthi reservation for, one of its overnight shelters. The **Spilios Agapitos** refuge can be reached at C 23520/81-800; rates are rather flexible, but usually less than 15€.

**FAST FACTS** The **National Bank of Greece,** on Plateia Kentriki, offers currency exchange and has an ATM. The **clinic** (C 23520/22-222), 5km (3 miles) outside Litochoro, is signposted; in the event of a nonemergency try to get to Thessaloniki for medical care. The **police station** (C 23520/81-110-1) is signposted just off the central square (Plateia Kentriki) on the road up Olympus to Priona. The **post office** is on Plateia Kentriki. The **telephone office (OTE)** is just off Plateia Kentriki on the road up Olympus to Priona.

## CLIMBING MOUNT OLYMPUS

If you plan to climb Olympus ✰✰✰, you will want to check with the EOS (see above) and probably get a copy of Marc Dubin's *Trekking in Greece* and the excellent Road Edition map of Olympus (no. 31; 6€). You should not attempt the climb alone; weather here can change in an instant from pleasant to life-threatening. In July and August of 1998, high winds whipped the flames of a serious fire that burnt portions of Olympus's magnificent forests.

Purists will want to begin the ascent at the rapidly developing **ski resort of Litochoro,** while others may prefer to drive from Litochoro as far as **Prionia** (18km/11 miles) and begin the climb there. On foot, it takes about 4 hours from Litochoro to Prionia; by car, it's about an hour, but seems longer on the twisting road. Fortunately, there's a small **café** at Prionia, where you can reward yourself with a decent meal, or even a stiff drink.

From Priona, it's at least a 3-hour climb, much of it over slippery schist slopes and knobby limestone outcroppings, to the **shelter at Spilios Agapitos.** If you don't mind communal quarters, this is the place to spend the night, especially since both bedding and meals are available. Most climbers begin the final 3-hour ascent at dawn and then do the entire descent, arriving back in Litochoro before dusk. The **Monastery of Ayios Dionysos,** not far from Spilios Agapitos, is a good place to break your downward trek and enjoy the views. The monastery was destroyed by the Germans during World War II, but is now being rebuilt. In short, your climb will take at least a day and you will probably want to overnight at one of the shelters.

## WHERE TO STAY & DINE

You can get information on the **refuges** on Mount Olympus from the EOS (see "Visitor Information," above). As far as the dining scene is concerned, one has to conclude that climbers are not foodies. There are a number of small restaurants in Litochoro, none is top-notch, although we've heard tantalizing travelers' tales of roast boar at the **Olympos Taverna** (C 23520/084-28).

**Dion Palace Resort Hotel** ✰ *Kids* This enormous beachfront resort has a main hotel building, its own disco, lots of cabanas, and some small "villas." The guest rooms are large and comfortable if, as is almost always the case in Greece, bland. In summer, this is a popular family destination, and anyone with children will see why. If you stay here, let us know what the Dion means when it advertises "live music and spectacle (some days)."

Litochoro Beach, Pierias, 60200 Macedonia. C 23520/22-731. Fax 23520/22-735. 182 units. 100€–150€ double. AE, MC, V. Sometimes closed in winter. **Amenities:** 2 restaurants; bar; health club; tennis. *In room:* A/C, TV, minibar, hair dryer.

**Markissia Hotel** We're had good reports of this hotel in the center of Litochoro. All units have minifridges, some have kitchenettes, and the rooms are light, bright, and more cheerful than at most Greek hotels in this price range. Litochoro, Pierias, 60200 Macedonia. © 23520/81-831. Fax 23520/61-862. 19 units. 60€. MC, V. **Amenities:** Bar/breakfast room. In room: A/C, TV.

**Mirto Hotel** Like many of the newer hotels in Litochoro, the Mirto is built in a sort of pseudo–Swiss chalet style, with lots of wood. The guest rooms have nice balconies, firm beds, and adequate bathrooms. Litochoro, Pierias, 60200 Macedonia. © 23520/81-398. Fax 23520/82-298. 20 units. 70€. No credit cards. **Amenities:** Bar/breakfast room. In room: TV.

**Villa Drossos** ★ *Kids* The big plus here (which makes reservations in summer a necessity) is the swimming pool in the garden (which makes the hotel popular with families traveling with children). The guest rooms have balconies, and many are furnished in bright pastels and floral prints. Litochoro, 60200 Macedonia. © 23520/84-561. Fax 23520/84-563. 13 units. 80€. MC, V. **Amenities:** Bar/breakfast room; pool. In room: A/C, TV.

## 6 The Meteora

Kalambaka is 356km (220 miles) NW of Athens; the circuit of the Meteora monasteries is approximately 25km (15 miles)

As you drive across the plain of Thessaly, which can seem endless on a hot summer's day, you'll suddenly see a cluster of gnarled black rocks. Some travelers have compared these crags to the mountains of the moon, but the fact is that the rock formations of the **Meteora** (the word means "in midair") ★★★ are unique. Many geographers speculate that some 30 million years ago, all Thessaly was a vast inland sea; when the sea receded, sweeping the topsoil along, only rock formations were left behind. Over the millennia, the Peneios River and the wind carved the rock into the weird, twisted shapes that now rise some 300m (984 ft.) above the plain. The Meteora is especially stunning in winter, when the Pindos range is capped with snow and mists swirl around the monasteries.

When you get closer to the Meteora and see that these sheer, slippery, seemingly unscalable rocks are topped with large monasteries, you'll probably find yourself asking two questions: Why did monks settle here, and how did they build anything larger than a hut on the rocks? Small wonder that many monks believe that St. Athanasios, founder of the first monastery here, the Great Meteoron (Monastery of the Transfiguration), did not scale the rock, but was carried there by an eagle.

The first monks who came here were probably 10th-century ascetics who scaled the rocks, lived as hermits in caves, and spent their days in prayer and meditation. In fact, the word monk comes from the Greek for "alone." Over the centuries, more and more hermits and monks seeking to lead the solitary life made their way to the Meteora until, by the 14th century, there were enough monks here for St. Athanasios to found the Great Meteoron. While some monks continued to live alone and pursue the solitary religious life called idiorrhythmic, others chose to live together and follow the cenobitic, or communal, life.

By 1500, there were 24 monasteries here, of which six—the Great Meteoron, Varlaam, Rousanou, Ayia Triada, Ayios Nikolaos Anapaphsas, and Ayiou Stefanou—are still inhabited and welcome visitors.

Visiting the Meteora is not recommended for those suffering from acrophobia, or any who might find it difficult to climb steep flights of stairs cut in the rock face. Still, even these vertiginous stepped paths are an improvement over what earlier travelers had to endure. When the English traveler Leake visited here in the 19th century, he was ferried up to the Great Meteoron in a net attached by a slender rope to a winch. Leake later wrote, "Visitors' morale was not helped by persistent rumors that the monks only replaced the homemade ropes which held the nets when they broke—usually in midair."

## ESSENTIALS

**GETTING THERE** **By Train** There are usually about five daily trains from Athens's Larissa station (✆ 210/821-3882) to Larissa and thence to the Kalambaka station (✆ 24320/22-451). Allow at least 8 hours for the Athens-Kalambaka trip.

**By Bus** There are seven daily buses to Trikkala from the Athens terminal at 260 Liossion (✆ 210/831-1434). Allow at least 8 hours for the Athens-Kalambaka trip. There are frequent buses from Trikkala (✆ 24310/73-130) to Kalambaka (✆ 24320/22-432). Several buses a day connect Kalambaka and the Meteora monasteries.

**By Car** From Athens, take the Athens-Thessaloniki National Highway north to Lamia; from Lamia, take the highway northwest to Kalambaka. From Delphi, take the Lamia-Karditsa-Trikkala-Kalambaka Highway north. Allow at least 6 hours for the Athens-Kalambaka trip.

**GETTING AROUND** If you don't have a car, you may want to hire a taxi to visit the Meteora monasteries. Expect to pay between 30€ and 100€ to visit the six monasteries usually open to the public. Your fee will vary depending on whether you simply want a drive-by tour with a stop at one or two monasteries or a more thorough visit with stops at each. Be sure you are in agreement as to how long you will have at each monastery; most drivers are content to wait 30 minutes at each one, while some drivers will accompany you into the monastery and act as guide.

**FAST FACTS** The **National Bank** and the **Ionian Bank** on Plateia Riga Fereou, the main square, exchange currency and have ATMs. The **clinic** in Kalambaka (✆ 24320/24-111), the **police** (✆ 24320/22-109), and the **tourist police** (✆ 24320/76-100) are about 1km (½ mile) outside town on the road to Ioannina. The **post office** and **telephone office (OTE)** are signposted off Plateia Riga Fereou. For **Internet access,** try the Café Hollywood, Trikalon 67 (✆ 24320/24-964; hollynet@hotmail.com) or the All Time Internet Café in Kastraki, just outside Kamambaka en route to the Meteora. Despite its name, this cafe often closes in mid-afternoon.

## WHAT TO SEE & DO
## THE METEORA MONASTERIES

The road from Kalambaka through the Meteora takes you past Ayios Nikolaos, Roussanou, the Great Meteoron, Varlaam, Ayia Triada, and Ayios Stephanos. What is perhaps most impressive about the Meteora—the three star attraction, so to speak—is the bizarre and stunning visual melding of the rocks and the monasteries. This is certainly a case when the sum is greater than its parts. That said, each monastery is well worth visiting. Still, if you only have time to visit one monastery, it should be the **Great Meteoron.** Try to allow time for a leisurely visit, so that you can chat with the monks and enjoy the stunning views through the forest of rocks from monastery to monastery. You'll find souvenir

## Tips Important Reminders

Although many of the monasteries are officially open from 9am to 6pm, many close from about 1 to 3pm, and others keep abbreviated hours. It's best to start your visit as early in the day as possible, so that you're not left cooling your heels while the monks and nuns have their afternoon siestas. Try to allow at least a full day here—the last thing you want to do is to rush experiencing the contemplative life! That said, if you are on a tight schedule, you can visit several, and drive (slowly, please!) past the others, in about 4 hours. Don't forget modest attire: long-sleeved shirts and skirts for women, slacks and shirts for men. If you come in winter, dress warmly, as many of the monasteries have little or no heat. Also note that in winter, many small restaurants and hotels in the area may be closed. In compensation, you might get to see the Meteora at its most beautiful: covered in snow and shrouded in mists.

stands and places to buy bottled water or soft drinks (but usually no food) outside each monastery.

We've listed the individual phone number for each monastery below, but don't be surprised if no one answers: Telephones and the monastic life are not really compatible. There's also a central number for the monasteries (© **24320/22-649**). And don't be surprised if you find one or more of the monasteries closed—usually the one you've just climbed up a long series of rock-cut steps to reach.

**Ayios Nikolaos Anapaphsas**    This little 14th-century monastery, approached by a relatively gentle path, has splendid **frescoes** by the 16th-century Cretan painter Theophanes the Monk. Don't miss the delightful fresco of the garden of Eden, with elephants, fantastic beasts, and all manner of fruits and flowers. There's also a nice painting of the death of St. Ephraim the Syrian, which shows scenes from the saint's life, including the pillar that he lived atop for many years in the Syrian desert.

At the time of our visit, there were no monks in residence at Ayios Nikolaos, and because tour buses often rush past to get to the Great Meteoron, you may find that you have this spot all to yourself.

© **24320/22-375.** Admission 2€. Daily 9am–6pm. Often closed in winter.

**Ayiou Stefanou**    Founded in the 14th century, Ayiou Stefanou, now a nunnery, is almost on the outskirts of Kalambaka. A bridge from the main road makes it easy to get here, and the nuns usually make you feel glad that you've come. The nuns sometimes sell very reasonably priced embroideries.

Ayiou Stefanou was badly damaged in both World War II and the Civil War that followed. Many priceless frescoes were defaced and others were totally destroyed, but the monastery's most famous relic was saved: the **head of St. Charalambos,** whose powers include warding off illness. There's also a small **museum** here, with ecclesiastical robes and paraphernalia. Recently, the nuns have been attempting to restore sections of the monastery that had been allowed to decline. Donations are welcomed.

No phone. Admission 2€. Usually open Tues–Sun 9am–1pm and 3:20–6pm.

**Ayia Triada**    It's not easy to say which of the monasteries has the most spectacular position, but Ayia Triada would be near the top of most lists. Perched on a slender pinnacle, reached only by laboring up 140 steps, Ayía Triáda really does seem to belong to another world. The one monk who lives here is usually glad to see visitors and show them around the **church, refectory,** and **courtyard.** Don't miss the **winch,** for years used to bring up supplies and visitors. If this monastery looks more familiar to you than the others, perhaps you remember it from the James Bond movie *For Your Eyes Only,* which was filmed here.

243/202-2220. Admission 2€. Daily 8am–1pm and 3–6pm.

**The Great Meteoron** ✶✶    Although the Great Meteoron was founded in the 14th century, most of what you see here was built in the 16th century by monks from the Holy Mountain of Mount Athos. The **church** here is especially splendid, in the form of a Greek cross inscribed on a square, topped by a **12-sided dome.** Once your eyes get accustomed to the darkness, you'll be able to enjoy the elaborate **frescoes.** If you look up to the dome, you'll see Christ, with the four evangelists, apostles, and prophets ranged below, the church fathers by the altar, and the liturgical feasts of the church year along the walls of the nave. There's also a rather bloodcurdling *Last Judgment* and *Punishment of the Damned* in the narthex. After visiting the church, you may wish to sit awhile in the shady courtyard before visiting the small **museum,** which has a collection of icons and illustrated religious texts. Don't miss the **wine cellar,** whose enormous wooden barrels suggest that monastic life is not all prayer and meditation.

24320/22-278. Admission 2€. Wed–Mon 9am–1pm and 3:20–6pm.

**Roussánou**    Roussánou is relatively accessible, thanks to its new bridge. This 13th-century monastery is now a nunnery, whose inhabitants are usually much more jolly than the monks. If the nuns offer you sweets while you sit in the courtyard between the refectory and the octagonal-domed church, be sure to leave a contribution in the church collection box.

No phone. Admission 2€. Daily 9am–1pm and 3–6pm.

**Varlaám**    A narrow bridge from the main road runs to this 16th-century monastery, which was named for a hermit who lived here in the 14th century and built a tiny chapel on this promontory. The **chapel,** considerably enlarged and decorated with **frescoes,** is now a side chapel of the main church. Varlaám's founders were two brothers from Ioánnina, who found the monastery and gentle lakeside scenery there too sybaritic for their tastes. Presumably the brothers found the Meteóra's harsh landscape more to their liking: According to legend, they had to drive away the monster who lived in a cave on the summit before they could settle here. The nicest thing about Varlaám is its **garden,** and the monk who sometimes sits here and is willing to chat with visitors.

24320/22-277. Admission 2€. Sat–Thurs 9am–1pm and 3:30–6pm.

## THE CATHEDRAL OF THE DORMITION OF THE VIRGIN & THE CENTER OF CONTEMPORARY ART

After visiting the monasteries of the Meteóra, you may find it a relief to know that there's only one church to see back in Kalambáka: the 12th-century Cathedral of the Dormition of the Virgin, which is often locked. If it's open, take a look at the frescoes, which date from the 12th to the 16th centuries. You might also keep an eye out for the ancient marble blocks and column drums that the builders of this church pilfered from the earlier Temple of Apollo that once stood here.

Then, for a complete change of subject and mood, head to the new Center of Contemporary Art, 38 Patriarchou Dimitriou (24320/22-346), which

Houses the extensive private collection of Leonidas Beltsios. At present, the museum is open 9am to 3pm and 5 to 9pm daily.

## SHOPPING

There are a lot of tourist shops in Kalambaka (most of which close for the winter) that sell the usual carved wooden canes and spoons, rugs, ceramics, and more rugs. One shop that opened a couple years ago is worth a look: **Kava Nikos**, on the main drag, 114 Trikalon (© and fax **24320/77-881**). This small wine-and-liquor shop has a good selection of wines both in the bottle and from the barrel, and also stocks local Macedonian and Thessalian *tsipouro*, a firewater that makes ouzo seem like a delicate aperitif. If you're lucky enough to be in Kalambaka on a Friday, you can't help but notice the **farmers' market** that spills out into the streets off Kondyli.

## WHERE TO STAY

For now, we're only suggesting hotels in Kalambaka, and not in the hamlet of Kastraki, just outside Kalambaka. This village has become very noisy, due to the coaches that rumble to and from the Meteora, the proliferating campgrounds, and the discos. Let us know if you find a place you like in Kastraki.

**Amalia** ★★  This rather handsome, large new hotel—with two restaurants, a souvenir shop, and a pool—looks almost like a small village from the road. Like most other Amalia hotels, this one is located just too far out of town to make walking there appealing. The large bedrooms (most with balconies) are tastefully decorated, and bathrooms have actual shower stalls. This is a very comfortable place to stay, although you may find yourself feeling like the odd man out if all the other rooms are occupied by tour groups. On the other hand, this is a popular spot for local wedding receptions and baptisms, so you may get to spy on Kalambaka society.

Outside Kalambaka on the Meteora Rd., 42200 Kalambaka. © **24320/72-216.** Fax 24320/72-457. Hotamal@ hellasnet.gr. 173 units. 150€ double. Rates include breakfast buffet. Often significantly cheaper off-season. AE, DC, MC, V. **Amenities:** Restaurant; bar; pool; concierge; shop; room service 7am–12pm. *In room: A/C, TV, mini-bar, hair dryer.

**Divani Motel** ★★  Like the Amalia, the slightly cheaper and less fancy Divani has a pool—although it doesn't hold a candle to the Amalia's. One thing that may sway you toward the Divani: Rooms at the back have very nice balconies and especially fine views toward the Meteora. The restaurant is perfectly decent but bland—as you'd expect, since it turns out masses of meals for tour groups, many of which are Greek in the summer, Japanese in the winter

Outside Kalambaka on the Meteora Rd., 42200 Kalambaka. © **24320/23-330.** Fax 24320/23-638. 165 units. 120€ double. Often significantly cheaper off-season. AE, DC, MC, V. **Amenities:** Restaurant; bar; pool. *In room: A/C, TV, minibar, hair dryer.

**Edelweiss** ★  The Edelweiss is low-key and attractive, and—two real pluses—has a small swimming pool for summer months and is open all winter. Some guest rooms have views of the Meteora.

3 El. Venizelou, 42200 Kalambaka. © **24320/23-884.** Fax 24320/24-733. 48 units. 70€ double. Rates include breakfast. MC, V.

**Hotel Meteora** ★ (Value)  The price is right, some of the rooms have balconies with Meteora views, and there's Internet access for about 4€ per hour. All that and the very helpful manager, Costa Gekas, make this an excellent budget choice.

14 Ploutarchou, 42200 Kalambaka. © 24320/22-367. Fax 24320/75-550. gekask@otenet.gr. 20 units. 60€. Rates include breakfast. No credit cards.

## WHERE TO DINE

We have to admit that we've never had a drop-dead wonderful meal in Meteora—maybe the influence of the monks inhibits tendencies to explore haute cuisine. The places we suggest are perfectly fine, but do let us know if you find something out of the ordinary.

**Gertzos** ★ GREEK This simple taverna has been in Kalambaka for more than 50 years, serving up the standard Greek fare but also offering a number of dishes reflecting the owners' Greek heritage in Asia Minor. Unless it's so hot—as it can be in the summer here—that you feel you must order a cold drink, try one of the local wines.

4 Economou. © 24320/22-316. Main courses 6€–12€. No credit cards. Usually closed Nov–Easter. In season, daily 12pm–11pm.

**Panellino** GREEK When we were here on one chilly, but beautiful, February visit to the Meteora, the Panellino was resolutely open when many other places were closed. The menu consisted of the usual chops and stews, as well as some tasty vegetable dishes.

Plateia Riga Fereou. © 24320/24-735. Main courses 4€–12. No credit cards. Daily 12pm–11pm.

**Skaros Taverna** GREEK This small place serves up truck-driver sized portions of grills and roasts, which you may chose to wash down with the local white wine. Nothing fancy, but most things (including a good eggplant salad in summer) are tasty.

Trikalon. © 24320/24-252. Main courses 5€–12€, many roast meats priced by the kilo. No credit cards. Daily 12pm–11pm.

**Vachos** GREEK If you want to eat outdoors, head for Vachos's small garden with views toward Meteora. As at Gertzos, the food here is so well prepared that even standard dishes like zucchini and eggplant stuffed with rice and ground meat taste new and different. One plus here: There are usually several tasty sweets on the menu, so you don't have to finish your meal and then search out a *zacheroplastirion* (sweet shop) for dessert.

Plateia Riga Fereou. © 24320/24-678. Main courses 6€–12€. No credit cards. Usually closed Nov–Feb. In season, daily 12pm–11pm.

# 13

# The Sporades

*by John S. Bowman*

Looking to experience some Greek islands that no one else in your crowd knows about? Try the Sporades ("Scattered" Islands), verdant islands with fragrant pine trees growing down to the edge of golden sand beaches. The Sporades would seem to have always been natural magnets for tourists, but lacking major archaeological remains and historical associations, for a long time did not compete with other parts of Greece.

The Sporades are no longer quite the natural retreats they once were. Skiathos and Skopelos are the most popular islands, with excellent beaches, fine restaurants, fancy hotels, and an international (heavily British) following. **Skiathos** is among the most expensive islands in Greece and becomes horrendously crowded in high season, but in spring and fall remains a lovely and pleasant place. It's still worth a visit, especially by those interested in a beach vacation, good food, and active nightlife. **Skopelos** is nearly as expensive as Skiathos in the high season, but isn't quite as sophisticated. Its beaches are fewer and less impressive, but Skopelos town is among the most beautiful

ports in Greece, and the island offers some pleasant excursions. More remote **Skyros** seems hardly a part of the group, especially as its landscape and architecture are more Cycladic. But it has a few excellent beaches, as well as a colorful local culture, and it remains a good destination for those who want to get away from the crowds. Although space limits do not allow us to describe the fourth of these islands, Alonissos might also be attractive to those seeking an even less frequented island.

**STRATEGIES FOR SEEING THE ISLANDS** If you have only 1 to 3 days, you had better settle on just one of the Sporades. If you have a bit more time, you will be able to get a ship directly (from various ports, identified below for each island) to any of them—and a plane in the case of Skiathos and Skyros; if time is a factor, we strongly advise flying to Skiathos or Skyros. If you have more time, you can continue around the islands via hydrofoils (known as "Flying Dolphins") or ferryboats. (Note, however, that the frequency of all connections is cut back considerably from Sept–May.)

## 1 Skiathos

108km (58 nautical miles) from Ayios Konstandinos, which is 166km (103 miles) from Athens

Skiathos remained isolated and agrarian until the early 1970s. Today it's one of the most cosmopolitan and attractive islands in Greece, and this rapid change has created a few disturbing ripples. Although the island's inhabitants are eager to please, in high season they can be overextended, inevitably relying on imported help, many from Athens, who often don't care much about providing any local flavor. Meanwhile, the sheer numbers of foreigners means that some show little concern for the island's indigenous character. This is a "package tour" island, and Skiathos town at high season can have the atmosphere of a shopping mall. Yet Skiathos town, sometimes called Hora, does have attractive elements, and at its best seems fairly sophisticated, with the handsome Bourtzi fortress on its harbor, elegant shops, excellent restaurants, and a flashy nightlife. And if you want a break from all this, take one of the horse-drawn carriages around town.

The rest of the island retains much of its natural allure. For most visitors, in fact, the main attractions are the purity of its natural allure. For most visitors, in beaches. The island boasts more than 60 beaches, the most famous of which, **Koukounaries**, is considered one of the very best in Greece. If you relish sun, sand, sea, and crowds, you'll love it.

If possible, visit Skiathos before or after July 10 to September 10, when the tourist crush is at its worst and the island's population of under 5,000 swells to over 50,000. If you must visit during high season, reserve a room well ahead of time and be prepared for the crush.

## ESSENTIALS

### GETTING THERE　By Plane　**Olympic Airways** has service daily (twice daily in Apr and May; five times daily June–Sept) from Athens; contact the Athens office (© **210/966-6666**) for information and reservations. At this time, Olympic does not maintain an office in Skiathos town, but can be reached at the nearby airport (© **24270/22-049**). Public bus service to and from the airport is so infrequent that everyone takes a taxi; expect to pay about 3€ depending on your destination.

**By Boat**　Skiathos can be reached by either ferryboat (3 hr.) or hydrofoil (1½ hr.) from Volos or Ayios Konstandinos. (Ayios Konstandinos is a 3-hr. bus ride from Athens.) From Kimi on Evvia, there is also hydrofoil service (50 min.) and ferryboat service (4 hr.). In high season, there are frequent hydrofoils daily from Volos and from Ayios Konstandinos, as well as service from Thessaloniki (3 hr.). There are also the hydrofoils linking Skiathos to Skopelos (30–45 min.), Alonissos (60–75 min.), and Skyros (2⅓ hr.).

In Athens, **Alkyon Travel**, 97 Akademias, near Kanigos Square (© **210/383-2545**; fax 210/383-3948), can arrange bus transportation from Athens to Ayios Konstandinos as well as hydrofoil or ferry tickets. Alkyon will not accept phone reservations—you must appear in person. The 3-hour bus ride costs about 15€ one-way.

For hydrofoil schedules and information, contact the **Flying Dolphins** in Athens (© **210/428-0001**; fax 210/428-0001; sales@mfd.gr). For ferryboat information, contact the **G.A. Ferries** line in Piraeus (© **210/458-2640**; fax 210/451-0777) or at their Athens office, 32 Leoforos Amalias (© **210/321-0061**; fax 210/321-8178) Ferry tickets can be purchased at travel agents in Athens or on the islands. During high season, we recommend that you try to purchase your boat tickets in advance through the boat lines. While you may purchase ferry tickets at Alkyon in person, they will not reserve ferryboat or hydrofoil tickets for you in advance, and these often sell out.

**VISITOR INFORMATION**　The town maintains an **information booth** at the western corner of the harbor; in summer at least, it's open daily from about 9am to 8pm. Meanwhile, private travel agencies abound and can help with most all of your requests. We highly recommend **Mare Nostrum Holidays**, 21 Papadiamandis (© **24270/21-463**; fax 24270/21-793). It books villas, hotels, and

The Sporades

Ferry Routes
Airport

487

Mediterranean Sea

Greece
Aegean Sea
Athens
THE SPORADES

EVVIA

Sarakiniko
Kimassi
Angali
Paralia Kostikias
Vassilikia

To Kimi

Skyros
Kalamitsa
Linaria
Acherounes
Aspous
Perkos
Ayios Fokas
Skyros
Mayazia
Atsitsa
Kira Panayia

Skandzoura

Aegean Sea

Skopelos
Agnondas
Skopelos
Panormos
Elios
Loutraki
Glossa

Patitiri
Peristera
Old Alonissos
Steni Vala

Koukounaries
Skiathos
Skiathos
Lalaria

Alonissos
Kira Panayia

Piperi

Gioura

N

0        20 mi
0        20 km

rooms; sells tickets to many around-the-island, hydrofoil, and beach caïque (skiff) trips; books Olympic flights; exchanges currency; and changes traveler's checks without commission. Katerina Michail-Craig, the managing director, and her staff speak excellent English, are exceedingly well informed, and have lots of tips on everything from beaches to restaurants. The office is open daily from 8am to 10pm.

**GETTING AROUND** **By Bus** Skiathos has public bus service along the south coast of the island from the bus station on the harbor to Koukounaries 1.50€ with stops at the beaches in between. A conductor will ask for your destination and assess the fare after the bus is in progress. Buses run at least six times daily April through November; every hour from 9am to 9pm May through October; every half-hour from 8:30am to 10pm June through September; and every 20 minutes from 8:30am to 2:30pm and 3:30pm to midnight July through August.

**By Car & Moped** Reliable car and moped agencies, all located on the paralia, include **Avis** (© **24270/21-458;** fax 24270/23-289; avis.skiathos@skiathoinfo. com), run by the friendly Yannis Theofanidis; **Aivalioti's Rent-A-Car** (© **24270/21-246**); and **Creator** (© **24270/22-385**). In high season, expect to pay 65 to 85€ for a car. Mopeds start at about 20€ per day.

**By Boat** The north coast beaches, adjacent islands, and historic Kastro are most easily reached by caïque; these smaller vessels, which post their beach and island tour schedules on signs, sail frequently from the fishing harbor west of the Bourtzi fortress. An around-the-island tour that includes stops at Lalaria Beach and Kastro will cost about 20€.

The Flying Dolphins agent, **Skiathos Holidays,** on the paralia, is open from 7am to 9:30pm; in high season there are as many as eight high-speed hydrofoils daily to Skopelos and Alonissos. There are also daily excursions to Skyros in high season. Call © **24270/22-018** for up-to-date schedules. Note that even if you have a ticket, you must appear at the agent's ticket office at least 30 minutes before the scheduled sailing to get your ticket confirmed and seat assigned. **Vasilis Nikolaou** (© **24270/22-209**), the travel agent at the corner of the paralia and Papadiamandis, sells tickets for the ferryboats to the other islands.

**FAST FACTS** The official **American Express** agent is Mare Nostrum Holidays, 21 Papadiamandis (© **24270/21-463;** fax 24270/21-793); open daily from 8am to 10pm. There are many banks in town, such as the **National Bank of Greece,** Papadiamandis, open Monday through Friday from 8am to 2pm and 7 to 9pm, Sunday from 9am to noon. The **hospital** (© **24270/22-040**) is on the coast road at the far west edge of town. For **Internet access,** try Internet Zone Café, 28 Evangelistrias (zonecafe@hotmail.com), or Internet Center, 13 Miauli (off Evangelistrias.) Hopefully, at least one will still be in operation at the time of your visit.

A self-service **laundry** is at 14 Georgios Panora, 85m (279 ft.) up Papadiamandis, opposite the National Bank (© **24270/22-341**); or you can drop off a load at the Snow White Laundry one street up from the paralia, behind the Credit Bank (© **24270/24-256**); both are open daily from about 8am to 2pm and 5 to 11pm. The **police station** (© **24270/21-111**) is about 250m (820 ft.) from the harbor on Papadiamandis, on the left. The **tourist police** booth is about 15m (49 ft.) further along on the right. The **post office** (© **24270/22-011**) is on Papadiamandis, away from the harbor about 160m (525 ft.) and on the right; open Monday through Friday from 7:30am to 2pm. The **telephone**

**office (OTE)** is on Papadiamandis, on the right, some 30m (98 ft.) beyond the post office; open Monday through Friday from 7:30am to 10pm, Saturday and Sunday from 9am to 2pm and 5 to 10pm (© **24270/22-135**).

## WHAT TO SEE & DO

Skiathos is a relatively modern town, built in 1930 on two low-lying hills, then reconstructed after heavy German bombardment during World War II. The handsome **Bourtzi fortress** (originally from the 13th century, but greatly rebuilt across the centuries) jutting out into the middle of the harbor is on an islet connected by a broad causeway. Ferries and hydrofoils stop at the port on the right (east) of the fortress, while fishing boats and excursion caïques dock on the left (west). Whitewashed villas with red-tile roofs line both sides of the harbor, with the small church of **Ayios Nikolaos** dominating the hill on the east side and the larger church of **Trion Ierarchon** (Three Archbishops) on the west side.

The main street that leads away from the harbor and up through town is named **Papadiamandis**, after the island's best-known son (see description of the Papadiamandis House, below). Here you'll find numerous restaurants, cafes, and stores, plus services such as Mare Nostrum Holidays, post office, telephone office, and tourist police.

On the west flank of the harbor (the left side as you disembark from the ferry) are numerous outdoor cafes and restaurants, excursion caïques (for the north coast beaches, adjacent islands, and around-the-island tours), and, at the far corner, the stepped ramp (above the Oasis Café) leading up to the town's next level. Mounting these broad steps will lead you to **Plateia Trion Ierarchon**, a stone-paved square around the town's most important church. The eastern flank, technically the New Paralia, is home to many tourist services as well as a few recommended hotels and many restaurants; at the far end the harborfront road branches right along the yacht harbor, an important nightlife area in summer, and left toward the airport and points of interest inland.

**The Papadiamandis House**   Alexandros Papadiamandis (1851–1911) was born on Skiathos, and after his adult career as a journalist in Athens, returned in 1908 and died in this very house. His nearly 200 short stories and novellas, mostly about Greek island life, assured him a major reputation in Greece, but his rather idiosyncratic style and vernacular language made his work difficult to translate into foreign languages. His house is more of a shrine than a museum, with his personal possessions and tools of his writing trade. (A statue of Papadiamandis stands in front of the Bourtzi fortress on the promontory at the corner of the harbor.)

An alley at right of Papadiamandis (main street), 50m (164 ft.) up from harbor. © **24270/23-843**. Admission 2€. Tues–Sun 9:30am–1pm and 5–8pm.

## BEACHES

Skiathos is famous for its beaches, and we'll cover the most important ones briefly, proceeding clockwise from the port. The most popular beaches are west of town along 12km (8 miles) of coastal highway. At most of them, you can rent an umbrella and two chairs for about 15€ per day. The first, **Megali Ammos,** is the sandy strip below the popular package-tour community of Frelia; so close to town and packed with the groups, it probably won't appeal to most. **Vassilias** and **Achladias** are also crowded and developed; **Tzanerias** and **Nostos** are slight improvements. Further out on the Kalamaki peninsula, south of the highway, **Kanapitsa** begins to excite some interest, especially among those fond of water sports; **Kanapitsa Water-Sport Center** (© 24270/21-298) has water and jet skis, windsurfing, air chairs, sailing, and speedboat hire. Scuba divers will want to stop at the **Dolphin Diving Center** (© 24270/22-520) at the big Nostos Hotel.

Across the peninsula, **Vromolimnos** (Dirty Lake) is fairly attractive and usually relatively uncrowded, perhaps because of its unsavory name and the cloudy (but not polluted) water from which it comes; it offers water-skiing and windsurfing. **Koulos** and **Ayia Paraskevi** are fairly well regarded. **Platanias**, the next major beach, is usually uncrowded, perhaps because the big resort hotels here have their own pools and sundecks. Past the next headland, **Troulos** is one of the prettiest because of its relative isolation, crescent shape, and the islets that guard the small bay. Nearby, too, is the **Victoria Leisure Center** (© 24270/49-467), which has rooms to rent, a pool, shops, and two tennis courts.

The last bus stop is at the much ballyhooed **Koukounaries** ★ 16km (10 miles) from Skiathos town. The bus chugs uphill past the Pallas Hotel luxury resort, then descends and winds alongside the inland waterway, Lake Strofilias, stopping at the edge of a fragrant pine forest. *Koukounaries* means "pine cones" in Greek, and behind this grove of trees is a half-mile-long stretch of fine gold sand in a half-moon–shaped cove. Tucked into the evergreen fold are some changing rooms, a small snack bar, and the concessionaires for beach chairs, umbrellas, and windsurfers. The beach can be extremely crowded but with an easy mix of families, singles, and topless sunbathers. On the far west side of the cove is the Xenia Hotel; renovated and reopened in 2003 after a long abandonment, we do not yet know enough about it to recommend it. (There are many lodgings in the area, but because of the intense mosquito activity and ticky-tacky construction, we prefer to stay back in town or along the coast road.)

**Ayia Eleni**, a short but scenic walk from the Koukounaries bus stop (the end of the line) west across the tip of the island, is a broad cove popular for windsurfing, as the wind is a bit rougher than at the south coast beaches but not nearly as gusty as at the north. Across the peninsula behind the former Xenia Hotel, 15 to 20 minutes of fairly steep grade from the Koukounaries bus stop, is **Banana Beach** (sometimes called Krassa). It's slightly less crowded than Koukounaries, but with the same sand and pine trees. There's a snack bar or two, plus chairs, umbrellas, windsurfers, and jet skis for rent. One stretch of Banana Beach is the island's most fashionable nude beach.

**Limonki Xerxes**, also called Mandraki, north across the tip of the island, a 20-minute walk up the path opposite the Lake Strofilias bus stop, is a cove where Xerxes brought in 10 *triremes* (galleys) to conquer the Hellenic fleet moored at Skiathos during the Persian Wars. It's a pristine and relatively secluded beach for those who crave a quiet spot. **Elia**, east across the little peninsula, is also quite nice. Both beaches have small refreshment kiosks.

Proceeding along the northeast coast from Mandraki, you arrive at **Megalos Aselinos**, a windy beach where free camping has taken root. It is linked to the southern coastal highway via the road that leads to the Kounistria monastery (see below); you must continue north when the main road forks off to the right toward the monastery. There's also an official campsite and a fairly good taverna. **Mikros Aselinos**, further east, is smaller and quieter, and you can reach it via a dirt road that leads off to the left just before the monastery.

Skiathos's north coast is much more rugged and scenically pure, with steep cliffs, pine forests, rocky hills, and caves. Most of these beaches are accessible only by boat, but one definitely rewards those willing to make the trip: **Lalaria** ★, on the island's northern tip, is regarded as one of the most picturesque beaches in Greece. One of its unique qualities is the **Tripia Petra,** perforated rock cliffs that jut out into the sea on both sides of the cove. These have been worn through by the wind and the waves to form perfect archways. You can lie on the gleaming white pebbles and admire the neon-blue Aegean and cloudless sky through their rounded openings. The water at Lalaria is an especially vivid shade of aquamarine because of the highly reflective white pebbles and marble and limestone slabs, which coat the sea bottom. The swimming here is excellent, but the undertow can be quite strong; inexperienced swimmers should not venture very far. There are several naturally carved caves in the cliff wall that lines the beach, providing privacy or shade for those who have had too much sun exposure. Lalaria is reached by caïque excursions from the port; the fare is about 20€ for an around-the-island trip, which usually includes a stop for lunch (not included in the fare) at one of the other beaches along the northwest coast.

Three of the island's most spectacular grottoes—**Skotini, Glazia,** and **Halkini**—are just east of Lalaria. Spilia Skotini is particularly impressive, a fantastic 6m (20-ft.) tall sea cave reached through a narrow crevice, just wide enough for caïques to squeeze through, in the cliff wall. Seagulls drift above you in the cave's cool darkness, while below, fish swim down in the 9m (30-ft.) subsurface portion. Erosion has created spectacular scenery and many sandy coves along the north and east coasts, though none are as beautiful or well sheltered from the meltemi as Lalaria beach.

## THE KASTRO & THE MONASTERIES

For those preferring other pursuits, there is at least one excursion that should appeal: the **Kastro,** the old fortress capital, located on the northernmost point of the island, east of Lalaria beach. Kastro was built in a remote and spectacular site in the 16th century, when the island was overrun by the Turks. It was abandoned shortly after the War of Independence, when such fortifications were no longer necessary. Once joined to firm ground by a drawbridge, it can now be reached by cement stairs. The remains of more than 300 houses and 22 churches have mostly fallen to the sea, but three of the churches, with porcelain plates imbedded in their worn stucco facades, still stand, and the original frescoes of one are still visible. From this citadel prospect there are excellent views to the **Kastronisia** islet below and the sparkling Aegean. Kastro can be reached by excursion caïque, by mule or donkey tour (available through most travel agencies), or by car via the road that leads northeast out of town, passing the turnoff to the Moni Evangelistrias (see below), and continuing on to the end near the church of Panayia Kardasi; from here it is a mildly demanding 2km (1¼-miles) walk.

The **Moni Evangelistrias** ★ is the more rewarding of the two monasteries that draw many visitors. There are occasional public buses, but with your own vehicle it can be easily visited in not much more than an hour from Skiathos town; this will also allow you to stop and admire the views. Take the road out of the northeast end and pass by the turnoff to the airport; after less than a kilometer take the sharp right turnoff (signed) and climb about 3km (2 miles) to the monastery. Dating from the late 18th century, it has been completely (but authentically) restored; its architecture, icons, and woodcarvings reward even those who do not know of its intimate involvement with the history of the island.

The other monastery, **Panayia Kounistria,** is approached from the coastal highway along the beaches (described above); just before Troulos Beach, take the right branch of the road (signed ASELINOS) and climb about 4km (2½ miles) to the monastery; a pretty 17th-century structure containing some fine icons (although its most important icon is now displayed in the Tris Ierarches Church in Skiathos town). Nothing spectacular, but a satisfying excursion. Horseback enthusiasts should note that the **Pinewood Horse Riding Club** is also located on the road to this monastery.

## SHOPPING

Skiathos town has no shortage of shops, many offering the standard wares but some offering distinctive items. The highlight for Greek crafts and folk art is **Archipelago** (© 24270/22-163), adjacent to the Papadiamandis House; it offers a world-class assemblage of exquisite objects of art and folklore, both old and new, including textiles, jewelry, and sculpture. **Galerie Varsakis** (© 24270/22-255), on Trion Ierarchon Square above the fishing port, also has a virtually museum-quality collection of folk antiques, embroidered bags and linens, rugs from around the world, and other collectibles. Less stylish but full of curiosities is the **Gallery Seraina** (© 24270/22-0390), at the first junction of Papadiamandis (opposite the alleyway to the Papadiamandis House); it has a goodly selection of ceramic plates, jewelry, some textiles, and unusual glass lampshades.

## WHERE TO STAY

Between July 1 and September 15, it can be literally impossible to find accommodations. Try calling ahead from Athens to book a room or, better still, book your accommodations before you leave home. Note that most of the "luxury" hotels were thrown up quickly some years ago, and some have since been managed and maintained poorly—so if you plan an extended stay at a beach resort, we recommend you first check into one of the hotels in town and then look over the possibilities before you commit to an extended rental.

If you crave the restaurant/shopping/nightlife scene, or you've arrived without reservations at one of the resort communities, try setting up base in **Skiathos town**. From here, you can take public buses to the beaches on the south coast or go on caïque excursions to the spectacular north coast or other islands. Then again, many families prefer to stay in two- to four-bedroom villas outside of town or at hotels overlooking a beach, with only an occasional foray into town.

One of the most pleasant parts of Skiathos town is the quiet neighborhood on the hill above the bay at the western end of the port. Numerous **private rooms** to let can be found on and above the winding stairs/street. Take a walk and look for the signs, or ask a passerby or neighborhood merchant. All over the hillside above the eastern harbor are several unlicensed "hotels," basically rooms to rent. Ask passersby, and you'll be surprised at which buildings turn out to be lodgings.

By the way, the in-town hotels (Alkyon excepted) cannot provide adjacent parking, but there are possibilities at the far eastern edge of the harbor.

## IN & AROUND SKIATHOS TOWN

In addition to the following options, consider the moderately priced **Hotel Athos,** on the "ring road" that skirts above Skiathos town (© and fax 24270/22-477), which offers ready access to town without the bustle; and the **Hotel Meltemi,** on the paralia (© 24270/22-493), a comfortable, modern place on the east side of the harbor (but avoid the front units, which can be noisy). An inexpensive choice is the 30-unit **Hotel Bourtzi,** 8 Moraïtou (© 24270/21-304; fax 24270/23-243), where doubles go for 70€. Ask for a unit that faces the back garden.

**Hotel Alkyon** ✶    This is probably the favored place for those who want it all—to be near the harbor of Skiathos town, to enjoy some quiet seclusion, and to return to a hotel with some creature comforts. It's not glitzy or luxurious, but modern and subdued; its rooms are of medium size (and offer taped music) and bathrooms are modern. On site is a small swimming pool with an adjacent bar. Best of all, it's a great place for those who look forward to a shady retreat after time in the sun or at the town's activities.

At far eastern end of paralia, 37002 Skiathos. © **24270/22-981**. Fax 24270/21-643. 89 units. 95€ double. Rates include buffet breakfast. AE, MC, V. Parking in adjacent area. *In room:* A/C, minibar.

**Hotel Australia**   If you've come to Skiathos expecting some style, this plain, clean, quiet hotel is not for you. Run by a couple who lived in Australia and speak English quite well, the rooms are sparsely furnished but comfortable, with small balconies; bathrooms are small but functional, and guests can share a fridge in the hallway. Definitely for budget travelers—no phones in the room, for example.

Parados Evangelistrias, 37002 Skiathos. © **24270/22-488**. 18 units. 45€ double; 60€ studio with kitchen. No credit cards. Turn right off Papadiamandis at the post office, then take the first left.

**Hotel Morfo**   Looking for a slightly "atmospheric" offbeat hotel? Turn right off the main street opposite the National Bank, then left at the plane tree (signed), and find this attractive hotel on your left on a quiet back street in the center of town. You enter through a small garden into a festively decorated lobby. The rooms are comfortable and tastefully decorated.

23 Anainiou, 37002 Skiathos. © **24270/21-737**. Fax 24270/23-222. 17 units. 70€ double. No credit cards. *In room:* A/C, fridge.

**Hotel Orsa ★**   One of the most charming small hotels in town is on the western promontory beyond the fishing harbor. To get here, walk down the port west all the way past the fish stalls, proceed up two flights of steps, and watch for a recessed courtyard on the left, with handsome wrought-iron details. Rooms are standard in size but tastefully decorated; most have windows or balconies overlooking the harbor and the islands beyond. A lovely garden terrace is a perfect place for a tranquil breakfast. Contact Heliotropio Travel on the east end of the harbor (© **24270/22-430**; fax 24270/21-952; helio@n-skiathos.gr) for booking.

Plakes, 37002 Skiathos. © **24270/22-430**. Fax 24270/21-952. helio@n-skiathos.gr. 17 units. 90€ double. Rates include breakfast. No credit cards.

## ON THE BEACH

**Atrium Hotel**   This is probably the class act of Skiathos when it comes to hotels. Its location (on a pine-clad slope overlooking the sea) plus its various amenities make it a most pleasant place to vacation. A sandy beach is some 100m (328 ft.) below; a beautiful pool sits on a plaza high above the Aegean. The rooms are fair-size, but compensate with balconies or terraces that offer views over the sea; bathrooms are fully appointed. The hotel has a bar and restaurant popular with guests. If you like, you can enjoy your meal outdoors on the veranda. We have always found the desk personnel and staff most courteous and helpful, and yes, both they and their guests observe a certain level of style in dress and conduct.

Platanias (some 8km/5 miles along the coast road southeast of Skiathos town), 37002 Skiathos. © **24270/49-345**. Fax 24270/49-444; www.atriumhotel.gr. 75 units. 140€ double, 185€ for family of four. Rates include buffet breakfast. MC, V. Parking on grounds. **Amenities:** Restaurant; bar; fitness room; watersports gear; car rentals and tours arranged; gift shop; billiards; ping-pong. *In room:* A/C, TV, fridge, hair dryer.

**Troulos Bay Hotel** *Value*   Though it's not exactly luxurious, this is our first choice among beach hotels. It's set on handsomely landscaped grounds on one of the south coast's prettiest little beaches. Like most of Skiathos's hotels, it's used mostly by groups, but individual rooms are often available. The restaurant serves good food at reasonable prices, and the staff is refreshingly attentive and truly helpful. The bedrooms are large, attractive, and comfortably furnished; most have a balcony overlooking the beach with the lovely wooded islets beyond.

Troulos (9km/6 miles along the coast road southeast of Skiathos, down from the Alpha Supermarket), 37002 Skiathos. © 24270/49-390. Fax 24270/49-218. troulosbay@skt.forthnet.gr. 43 units. 100€ double. Rates include breakfast. MC, V. Parking on grounds.

## WHERE TO DINE

As is the case with most of Greece's overdeveloped tourist resorts, there's a plethora of cafes, fast-food stands, and overpriced restaurants, but there are also plenty of good and even excellent eateries in Skiathos town. Some of the more well-regarded restaurants are above the west end of the harbor, approaching and beyond Trion Ierarchon church.

## EXPENSIVE

**Asprolithos** ★ GREEK/INTERNATIONAL An elegant ambience and friendly, attentive service combined with superb meals of light, updated taverna fare make this one of our favorites on Skiathos. You can get a classic moussaka here if you want to play it safe, or try specialties like artichokes and prawns smothered in cheese. The excellent snapper baked in wine with wild greens is served with thick french fries that have obviously never seen a freezer. The main dining room is dominated by a handsome stone fireplace, and there are also tables outside where you can catch the breeze.

Mavroyiali and Korai (up Papadiamandis a block past the high school, then turn right). © 24270/21-016. Reservations recommended. Main courses 6€–18€. MC, V. Daily 6pm–midnight. Closed late Oct to mid-Mar.

**Le Bistrot** CONTINENTAL/CHINESE This intimate restaurant and its twin (which functions as a bar), across the street, are lovely spaces overlooking the water. The full-course meals are beautifully prepared from their own stocks and sauces and should be savored slowly, so as to leave room for the delicious desserts. And at least during the year 2002, Le Bistrot also offered a Chinese menu prepared by a special Asian chef.

Martinou (high above western end of harbor). © 24270/21-627. Reservations recommended. Main courses 7€–15€. MC, V. Daily 7pm–1am.

**The Windmill Restaurant** ★★ INTERNATIONAL The town's most special dining experience is at what is literally an old windmill, visible from the parttalia. (There are several ways to approach it, but the signed one begins on the street between the back of the Akti and the San Remo hotels at the eastern end of the harbor.) It is quite a climb, but well worth it. You couldn't ask for a more romantic setting than one of the terraces, where you can enjoy the sunset with your meal. From year to year the menu changes, but many of the main courses are distinctive, even exotic. The desserts, too, are unusual, and there are nearly two dozen wines to choose from, including the best from Greece.

Located on peak east of Ayios Nikolaos church. © 24270/24-550. www.skiathosinfo.com. Reservations strongly recommended. 8€–20€. MC, V. Daily 7–11pm.

## MODERATE

**Carnayio Taverna** TAVERNA/SEAFOOD One of the better waterfront tavernas is next to the Hotel Alkyon. Favorites over the years have been the fish soup, lamb *youvetsi*, and grilled fish. The garden setting is still special, and if you're here late enough, you might be lucky to see a real round of dancing waiters and diners.

Paralia. © **24270/22-868.** Main courses 4€–12€. AE, V. Daily 8pm–1am.

**Taverna Limanakia** TAVERNA/SEAFOOD  In the style of its next-door neighbor Carnayio, the Limanakia serves some of the best taverna and seafood dishes on the waterfront. We vacillate about which of the two we prefer, but we've always come away feeling satisfied after a meal at this reliable eatery.

Paralia (at far eastern end, past Hotel Alkyon). © **24270/22-835.** Main courses 5€–14€. MC. Daily 6pm–midnight.

**Taverna Mesoyia** TAVERNA  You'll have to exert yourself a bit to find some of the best authentic traditional food in town, as this little taverna is in the midst of the town's most labyrinthine neighborhood, above the western end of the harbor, but there are signs once you approach it. Try an appetizer such as the fried zucchini balls, enjoy the evening specials, or go for fresh fish in season. (As all Greek restaurants are supposed to, this one discloses when something is frozen—as some fish must be at certain times of the year, when it's illegal to catch.) You'll feel like you're at an old-fashioned neighborhood bistro, not a large tourist attraction.

Grigoriou (follow the signs behind Trion Ierarchon, high above western end of the harbor). © **24270/21-440.** Main courses 5€–11€. No credit cards. Daily 7pm–midnight.

### INEXPENSIVE

**Kabourelia Ouzeri** GREEK  Although it bills itself as an ouzeri—for drinks and snacks—this is really your standard taverna, and one of the most authentic eateries in town. You can have the ouzo and octopus (which you can see drying on the front line!) combo for 5.50€ or even make a meal of the rich supply of cheese pies, fried feta, olives, and other piquant mezedes.

Paralia (on western stretch of harbor). © **24270/21-112.** Main courses 3€–10€. AE, MC, V. Daily 10am–1am.

## SKIATHOS AFTER DARK

The **Aegean Festival** presents nightly performances of ancient Greek tragedies and comedies, traditional music and dance, modern dance and theater, and visiting international troupes. Festival events take place from late June to early October in the outdoor theater at the **Bourtzi Cultural Center,** on the promontory on the harbor. (The center itself, open daily from 10am to 2pm and 5:30 to 10pm, hosts art exhibits in its interior.) Performances begin at 9:30pm and usually cost 15€; call © **24270/23-717** for information.

Skiathos town has a lively nightlife scene, more concentrated on each end of the port, but many prefer to pass the evening with a **volta** (stroll) along the harbor or around and above the Plateia Trion Ierarchon. In fact, we feel the best-kept secret of Skiathos town is the **little outdoor cafe** at the tip of the promontory with the Bourtzi fortress, a 3-minute stroll from the harbor. Removed from the glitter of the town, you can sit and enjoy a (cheap) drink in the cool of the evening and watch the ships come and go—this is the Aegean lifestyle at its best.

The main concentration of **nightclubs** is in the warren of streets west of Papadiamandis (left as you come up from the harbor). On the street opposite the post office is the **Blue Chips Club.** Further along Papadiamandis, another turn to the left leads to the **Borzoi,** which claims to be the oldest club on the island; you may want to check it out several times during the evening, as it generally gets livelier toward midnight. Continue past it to find the **Banana Bar**, for "surprising dance music," on the right; then the **Admiral Benbow Club**, which offers something more soulful. Across from the Benbow Club is the flashy **Spartacus**. At the next intersection south you'll find **Kiriki**, which offers jazz and blues.

Back across Papadiamandis, just before the post office, along Parados Evangelistrias you can find **Adagio**, a gay establishment that plays classical music and Greek ballads at volumes low enough for conversation. Wander back down the main street to find **Kentavros Bar**, on the left beyond the Papadiamandis House, which plays classic rock and jazz.

On the far west end of the harbor, if you want videos with your drinks, try the **Oasis Cafe**, where the draft beer is only 2€; if there's a game of any sort going on, it'll be on the tube. Meanwhile, at the far eastern end of the harbor are three clubs popular with the younger set—the **Kavos**, **Remezzo**, and **B.B.C.** Movie fans might enjoy the **Cinema Paradiso**, up along the "ring road," which shows recent films in English nightly at 8:30 and 11pm; tickets are 5€.

## 2 Skopelos

121km (65 nautical miles) from Ayios Konstandinos, which is 166km (103 miles) from Athens

It was inevitable that handsomely rugged Skopelos would follow Skiathos in its development, but it has done so a bit more wisely and at a slower pace. Its beaches are not so numerous or as pretty, but Skopelos town is one of the most beautiful ports in Greece, and the island is richer in vegetation, with windswept pines growing down to secluded coves, wide beaches, and terraced cliffs of angled rock slabs. The interior is densely planted with fruit and nut orchards. The famous plums and almonds from Skopelos are liberally used in the island's unique cuisine. The coastline, like that of Skiathos, is punctuated by impressive grottoes and bays, and you'll find frequent need for a camera. Skopelos is also known for keeping alive the rembetika music, the Greek version of American "blues," to be heard in several tavernas late in the evening.

## ESSENTIALS

**GETTING THERE**  **By Plane**  Skopelos cannot be reached directly by plane, but you can fly to nearby Skiathos and take a hydrofoil or ferry to the northern port of Loutraki (below Glossa) or the more popular Skopelos town.

**By Boat**  If you're in Athens, take a boat or hydrofoil from Ayios Konstandinos to Skopelos (75 min). **Alkyon Travel**, 97 Akademias, near Kanigos Square (© 210/383-2545), can arrange the 3-hour bus ride from Athens to Ayios Konstandinos (about 15€ for hydrofoil or ferry tickets). Coming from Central or Northern Greece, depart for Skopelos from Volos (about 2 hr.). For ferryboat information, contact the **G.A. Ferries** line in Piraeus (© 210/458-2640); fax 210/451-0777) or at their Athens office, 32 Leaforos Amalias (© 210/321-0061; fax 210/321-8178).

From Skiathos, the ferry to Skopelos takes 90 minutes if you call at Skopelos town, or 45 minutes if you get off at Glossa/Loutraki; the one-way fare to both is about 6€. Ferry tickets can be purchased at **Vasilis Nikolaou** (© 24270/22-209), the travel agent at the corner of the Paralia and Papadiamandis. The Flying Dolphin hydrofoil takes 15 minutes to Glossa/Loutraki (4–5 times daily; 9€), and 45 minutes to Skopelos (6–8 times daily, 10€). From Skiathos, you can also take one of the many daily excursion boats to Skopelos.

It's possible to catch a regular ferry or hydrofoil from Alonissos to Skopelos (seven times daily; 9€) or ride on one of the excursion boats. Expect to pay a little more on the excursion boats—but if they're not full, you can sometimes negotiate the price.

There are infrequent ferryboat connections from Kimi (on Evria) to Skopelos. Check with the **Skopelos Port Authority** (℡ **24240/22-180**) for current schedules, as they change frequently. We think hydrofoils are worth the extra expense for hopping around the Sporades.

In the port of Skopelos town, hydrofoil tickets can be purchased at the Flying Dolphin agent, **Madro Travel,** immediately opposite the dock (℡ **24240/22-300**); it's open all year, also operates as the local Olympic Airways representative, and can generally make any arrangements you need.

**VISITOR INFORMATION**   The **Municipal Tourist Office** of Skopelos is on the waterfront, to the left of the pier as you disembark (℡ **24240/323-231**); open daily from 9:30am to 10pm in high season. It offers information, changes money, and reserves rooms. If you want to call ahead to book a room, the **Association of Owners of Rental Accommodation** maintains a small office on the harbor (℡ **24240/24-567**).

At the travel agency **Skopelorama Holidays,** about 100m (328 ft.) beyond the Hotel Eleni on the left (east) end of the port (℡ **24240/23-040;** fax 24240/23-243), the friendly staff can help you find a room, exchange money, rent a car, or take an excursion; they know the island inside-out and can provide information on just about anything. It's open daily from 8am to 10pm.

**GETTING AROUND   By Bus**   Skopelos is reasonably well served by public bus; the bus stop in Skopelos town is on the east end of the port. There are four routes. Buses run the main route every half-hour in the high season beginning in Skopelos and making stops at Stafilos, Agnondas, Panormos, the Adrina Beach Hotel, Milia, Elios, Klima, Glossa, and Loutraki. The fare from Skopelos to Glossa is 2€.

**By Car & Moped**   The most convenient way to see the island is to rent a car or moped at one of the many shops on the port. A four-wheel-drive vehicle at **Motor Tours** (℡ **24240/22-986;** fax 24240/22-602) runs around 90€, including insurance; expect to pay a few thousand drachmas less for a Fiat Panda. A moped should cost about 20€ per day.

**By Taxi**   The taxi stand is at the far end of the waterfront, and taxis will provide service to almost any place on the island. Taxis are not metered—negotiate the fare before accepting a ride. A typical fare, from Skopelos to Glossa, runs 25€.

**By Boat**   To visit the more isolated beaches, take one of the large excursion boats; these cost about 50€ including lunch, and should be booked a day in advance in high season. Excursion boats to Glisteri, Gliphoneri, and Sares beaches operate only in peak season (about 10€). From the port of Agnondas, on the south coast, there are fishing boats to Limnonari, one of the island's better beaches.

**FAST FACTS**   There are several **ATMs** at banks around the harbor. The **health center** is on the road leading out of the east end of town (℡ **24240/22-222**). Plynthria, a self-service **laundry,** is located (in a basement) just past the Adonis Hotel on the upper road at the east end of the harbor (℡ **24240/22-123**); open Monday through Saturday from 9:30am to 1:30pm and 6 to 8pm. The **police station** (℡ **24240/22-235**) is up the narrow road (Parados 1) to the right of the National Bank, along the harbor. For **Internet access,** try Click & Surf (ermis777@hotmail.com), just up from the police station. The **post office,** on the far east end of the port (take the stepped road leading away from the last kiosk, opposite the bus/taxi station), is open Monday through Friday from 8am to 2:30pm. The **telephone office (OTE)** is at the top of a narrow road leading away from the center of the harbor; open Monday through Saturday from 8am to 5pm.

## WHAT TO SEE & DO

The ferries from Alonissos, Skyros, and Kimi and most of the hydrofoils and other boats from Skiathos dock at both Glossa/Loutraki and Skopelos town. Most boats stop first at **Loutraki,** a homely little port near the northern end of the west coast, with the more attractive town of **Glossa** ✦ high above it. We suggest you stay onboard for the trip around the northern tip of the island and along the east coast—getting a better sense of why the island's name means "cliff" in Greek—to the island's main harbor, especially if this is your first visit. You'll understand why when your boat pulls around the last headland into that huge and nearly perfect C-shaped harbor, and you get your first glimpse of Skopelos town rising like a steep amphitheater around the port.

**Skopelos town** (also called Hora) is one of Greece's most treasured towns, on a par with Hydra and Simi. It scales the steep, low hills around the harbor and has the same winding, narrow paths that characterize the more famous Cycladic islands to the south. Scattered on the slopes of the town are just a few of the island's 123 churches, which must be something of a record for such a small locale. The oldest of these is **Ayios Michali,** up past the police station. The waterfront is lined with banks, cafes, travel agencies, and the like. Interspersed among these prosaic offerings are some truly regal-looking shade trees. Many of the shops and services are up the main street leading away from the center of the paralia. The back streets are amazingly convoluted (and unnamed); the best plan is to wander around and get to know a few familiar landmarks.

The **Venetian Kastro,** which overlooks the town from a rise on the western corner, has been whitewashed and looks too new to have been built over an archaic temple of Athena, and too serene to have been deemed too formidable for attack by the Turks during the War of Independence in the early 19th century.

At the far eastern end of town is the **Photographic Center of Skopelos** (© 24240/24-121), which during the high season sponsors quite classy photography exhibitions in several locales around town.

## SHOPPING

Skopelos has a variety of shops selling Greek and local ceramics, weavings, and jewelry. One of the most stylish is **Armoloi,** in the center of the shops along the harbor (© 24240/22-707). It sells only Greek jewelry, ceramics, weavings, and silver; some of the objects are old, and most of the handsome ceramics are made by the owners. Another special store is **Ploumisti,** (at a corner of an alley about

---

*Finds*

## National Marine Park

One of the more unusual attractions of a stay on Skopelos could be a day's excursion to the National Marine Park off the adjacent island of Alonissos where you are guaranteed to see some of the many dolphins that frequent this protected area. The trip also includes a stop at the islet of Psathoura, with a chance to dive into a sunken city, and a visit into the Blue Grotto of Alonissos. Any travel agency in Skopelos will be able to arrange for such an excursion on one of several licensed ships.

midway along the Paralia) (© 24240/22-059; kalaph-skp@skt.forthnet.gr); it sells beautiful Greek rugs, blankets, jewelry, pottery and crafts, and its friendly proprietors, Voula and Kostas Kalafatis, are full of helpful information for visitors, especially about the rembetiko music scene. **Nick Rodios (© 24240/22-924)**, whose gallery is located between the Hotel Eleni and the Skopelorama Holidays agency, is from a Skopelos family who have made ceramics for three generations. His elegant black vessels, at once both classical and modern, are a change from the usual pottery found around Greece.

## EXPLORING THE ISLAND

The whole island is sprinkled with monasteries and churches, but five **monasteries** south of town can be visited by following a pleasant path that continues south from the beach hotels. The first, **Evangelistria**, was founded by monks from Mount Athos, but it now serves as a nunnery, and the weavings of its present occupants can be bought at a small shop; it's open daily from 8am to 1pm and 4 to 7pm. The fortified monastery of **Ayia Barbara**, now abandoned, contains 15th-century frescoes. **Metamorphosis**, very nearly abandoned, is very much alive on the 6th of August, when the feast of the Metamorphosis is celebrated here. **Ayios Prodromos** is a 30-minute hike further, but it's the handsomest and contains a particularly beautiful iconostasis. **Taxiarchon**, abandoned and overgrown, is at the summit of Mount Polouki to the southeast, a hike recommended only to the hardiest and most dedicated.

There is basically only one highway on the island, with short spurs at each significant settlement. It runs south from Skopelos town, then cuts north and skirts the west coast northwest, eventually coming to Glossa, then down to Loutraki. The first spur leads off to the left to **Stafilos**, a popular family beach recommended by locals for a good seafood dinner, which you must order in the morning. About half a kilometer across the headland is **Velanio**, where nude bathing is common.

The next settlement west is **Agnondas**, named for a local athlete who brought home the gold from the 569 B.C. Olympics. This small fishing village has become a tourist resort thanks to nearby beaches. **Limnonari**, a 15-minute walk further west and accessible by caïque in summer, has a good fine-sand beach in a rather homely and shadeless setting.

The road then turns inland again, through a pine forest, coming out at the coast at **Panormos.** With its sheltered pebble beach, this has become the island's best resort with a number of taverns, hotels, and rooms to let, as well as watersports facilities. The road then climbs again toward **Milia ★**, which is considered **the island's best beach.** You will have to walk down about half a kilometer from the bus stop, but you'll find a lovely light-gray sand-and-pebble beach with the island of Dassia opposite and watersports facilities at the **Beach Boys Club** (© 24240/23-995).

The next stop, **Elios,** is a town that was thrown up to shelter the people displaced by the 1965 earthquake. It's become the home of many of the locals who operate the resort facilities on the west coast, as well as something of a resort itself.

The main road proceeds on to **Glossa ★** which means "tongue," and that's what the hill on which the town was built looks like from the sea. It was mostly spared during the earthquake, and remains one of the most Greek and charming towns in the Sporades. Those who are tempted to stay overnight will find a number of rooms for rent, a good hotel, and a very good taverna. Most of the coastline here is craggy, with just a few hard-to-reach beaches. Among the best places to catch some rays and do a bit of swimming is the small beach below the picturesque monastery of **Ayios Ioannis,** on the coast east from town, which reminds many of Meteora. (Bring food and water.) As for the port of **Loutraki,** it's a winding 3km (2 miles) down; we don't recommend a stay there.

That ends the road tour of Skopelos. Along the east coast north of Skopelos is **Glisteri,** a small pebbled beach with a nearby olive grove offering some respite from the sun. It's a good bet when the other beaches are overrun in summer. You can also go by caïque to the grotto at **Tripiti,** for the island's best fishing, or to the little island of **Ayios Yioryios,** which has an abandoned monastery.

The whole of Skopelos's 95 sq. km (38 sq. miles) is prime for **biking,** and the interior is still waiting to be explored. There's also **horseback riding, sailing** (ask at the Skopelos travel agencies), and a number of interesting **excursions** to be taken from and around the island. Skopelorama Holidays (see "Visitor Information," above) operates a fine series of excursions, such as monasteries by coach, a walking tour of the town, and several cruises. One boat excursion that might appeal to some is to the waters around Skopelos that are part of the **National Marine Park;** if you're lucky, you will see some of the Mediterranean monk seals, an endangered species that is protected within the park.

## WHERE TO STAY

In high season, Skopelos is nearly as popular as Skiathos. If you need advice, talk to the Skopelorama Holidays agency (see "Visitor Information," above) or the officials at the town hall. Be sure to look at a room and agree on a price before accepting anything, or you may be unpleasantly surprised. To make matters confusing, there are few street names in the main, older section of Skopelos town, so you'll have to ask for directions in order to find your lodging.

## IN SKOPELOS TOWN

The handsome, traditional-style **Hotel Amalia,** along the coast, 500m (1,640 ft.) from the center of the port (© **24240/22-688;** fax 24240/23-217), is largely occupied by groups, but should have some spare rooms in spring and fall.

**Hotel Denise** One of the best hotels in Skopelos thanks to its premier location, clean facilities, and pool, the Hotel Denise stands atop the hill overlooking the town and commands spectacular vistas of the harbor and Aegean. Each of the hotel's four stories is ringed by a wide balcony. The guest rooms have hardwood floors and furniture, and most boast a view that is among the best in town. The Denise is popular and open only in high season; before hiking up the steep road, call for a pickup and to check for room availability—or better yet, reserve in advance.

Skopelos Town 37003. © **24240/22-678.** Fax 24240/22-769. www.denise.gr. 25 units, 85€ double. Rates include continental breakfast. Credit cards accepted for deposit only. *In room:* A/C, minibar.

**Hotel Drossia** *Value* This small hotel next to the Hotel Denise (see above), atop the hill overlooking the town, is for bargain-hunters. The Drossia is of the same vintage as the Denise, with exceptional views but slightly less expensive and less well-equipped rooms. All in all, it represents good value.

Skopelos Town 37003. © **24240/22-490.** 10 units, 50€ double. No credit cards. Open June–Sept only.

**Hotel Eleni** The Hotel Eleni is a modern hotel, set back from the coast and 300m (984 ft.) to the left from the center of the harbor. After many years spent operating several pizzerias in New York, Charlie Hatzidrosos returned from the Bronx to build this establishment. His daughter now operates the hotel and provides gracious service. All guest rooms have balconies.

Skopelos Town 37003 © **0424/22-393.** Fax 0424/22-936. 37 units. 58€ double. AE, MC, V. *In room:* TV, fridge.

**Hotel Prince Stafilos** ★ Although it charges considerably more than other Skopelos hotels, this one is well worth it. The most handsome and traditional hotel on the island is about a half mile south of town. (It provides rides from the ferry dock.) The friendly owner, Pelopidas Tsitsirgos, is also the architect responsible for the establishment's special charm. The lobby is spacious and attractively decorated with local artifacts. This is a hotel for those who can afford to spend a civilized vacation on Skopelos. The hotel provides transportation to and from the town center.

About 1 mile from center of Skopelos Town 37003. © **24240/22-775.** Fax 24240/22-825. 65 units. 190€ double. Rates include large buffet breakfast. AE, MC, V. **Amenities:** Restaurant; 2 bars; pool. *In room:* A/C.

**Skopelos Village** This is for visitors intending to settle in for a while so that they can take advantage of this mini-resort's various amenities. The buildings are tastefully constructed as "traditional island houses." Each bungalow is equipped with kitchen, private bathroom, and one or two bedrooms, and can sleep from two to six persons. Facilities include a breakfast room and snack bar. In the evening, the restaurant offers Greek meals accompanied by Greek music and dance. The hotel provides free transport to various beaches.

About a ½ mile southeast of town center, Skopelos 37003. © **24240/22-517.** Fax 24240/22-958. 36 units. Bungalow for 2 persons, with a kitchen, high season 175€, mid-season 135€. MC, V. **Amenities:** 2 restaurants; pool; tennis nearby; children's playground; 24-hr. room service. *In room:* A/C, TV, minibar.

## IN PANORMOS

This pleasant little resort is on a horseshoe-shaped cove along the west coast, about halfway between Skopelos town and Glossa. Here you'll find several cafeteria-style snack bars and minimarkets. We recommend it as a base, especially since one of the best hotels on the island—the Adrina Beach Hotel—is just above it. As for restaurants, a particularly lively taverna, the **Dihta,** is right along the beachfront.

The **Panormos Travel Office** (© **24240/23-380;** fax 24240/23-748) has some decent rooms to let, offers phone and fax services, exchanges money, arranges tours (including night squid fishing), and rents cars, motorbikes, and speedboats.

**Adrina Beach Hotel** ★ This traditional-style hotel, 500m (1,640 ft.) on the beach beyond Panormos, rates as one of the better ones on the island. The guest rooms are large and tastefully furnished in pastels, each with its own balcony or veranda. In addition to the main building's rooms, eight handsome "maisonettes" are ranked down the steep slope toward the hotel's private beach. The complex has a big saltwater pool with its own bar, a restaurant, a bar, a buffet room, spacious sitting areas indoors and out, a playground, and a minimarket.

If you can't get a room at the Adrina, try the 38-unit **Afroditi Hotel** (© **24240/23-150;** fax 24240/23-152), a more modern choice about 100m (328 ft.) across the road from the beach at Panormos.

Panormos, 37003 Skopelos. © **24240/23-373,** or 210/682-6886 in Athens. Fax 24240/23-372. 55 units. 130€ double. Rates include breakfast. AE, DC, MC, V. **Amenities:** 2 restaurants; bar; pool; children's playground; minimarket. *In room:* A/C.

## IN GLOSSA

There are approximately 100 rooms to rent in the small town of Glossa. Expect to pay about 40€ for single or double occupancy. The best way to find a room is to visit one of the tavernas or shops and inquire about a vacancy. You can ask George Antoniou at the **Pythari Souvenir Shop** (© 24240/33-077) for advice. If you can't find a room in Glossa, you can always take a bus or taxi down to Loutraki and check into a pension by the water or head back to Panormos.

## WHERE TO DINE
## IN SKOPELOS TOWN

**Anatoli Ouzeri** GREEK   It's quite a climb (or else take a taxi) to reach this diminutive ouzeri high above town, but many feel the whole experience justifies the effort. A usual meal features several delicious mezedes, including lightly fried green peppers and an exceptional octopus salad. Specialties include *bourekakia* (fried eggplant) and fried cheese pie. *Note:* No wine is served—only *tsipouro*, a strong ouzo-like drink. If you're in luck, Yiorgios Xindaris, the rail-thin proprietor/chef, will play his bouzouki and sing classic remberika songs, sometimes with accompanists. If you come early or late in the season, bring a sweater.

On a hill south of town. © **24240/22-851.** Main courses 4€–8€. No credit cards. Summer daily 8:30pm–1am. Closed in winter.

**Finikas Taverna and Ouzeri** ★ GREEK   Tucked away in the upper backstreets of Skopelos is a picturesque garden taverna/ouzeri dominated by a broadleaf palm. The Finikas offers what might be Skopelos's most romantic setting, thanks to its isolated and lovely garden seating. Among the many fine courses are an excellent ratatouille and pork cooked with prunes and apples, a traditional island specialty.

Upper backstreet of Skopelos town. © **24240/23-247.** Main courses 4€–7€. No credit cards. Daily 7pm–2am.

**The Garden Restaurant** GREEK   Some locals claim this is the best restaurant in town, at least for a complete dining experience. Two young brothers operate what most people call simply "The Garden," with a garden-like setting and a casual atmosphere. The food is tasty and often a bit different; appetizers such as mushrooms with garlic, and main courses such as kalamares with cheese.

At far eastern end of harbor, first left at corner of Amalia Hotel. © **24240/22-349.** Reservations recommended in high season. Main courses 4€–14€. MC, V. Daily 11am–midnight. Closed Oct to mid-June.

**Platanos Jazz Bar** SNACK/BAR FOOD   For everything from breakfast to a late-night drink, try this pub. Breakfast in the summer starts as early as 5 or 6am for ferry passengers, who can enjoy coffee, fruit salad with nuts and yogurt, and fresh-squeezed orange juice, all for about 8€. Platanos is equally pleasant for evening and late-night drinks. Accompanying your meal will be music from the proprietors' phenomenal collection of jazz records.

Beneath the enormous plane tree just to the left of the ferry dock. © **24240/23-661.** Main courses 3€–7€. No credit cards. Daily 5am–3am.

## IN GLOSSA

**Taverna T'agnanti** ★ TRADITIONAL SKOPELITIAN   This is the place to meet, greet, and eat in Glossa. The food is inexpensive, the staff friendly, and the view spectacular. The menu is standard taverna style, but the proprietors make a point of using the finest fresh products and wines. Specialties include herb fritters, fish stifado with prunes, pork with prunes, and almond pie.

There's occasionally traditional music. The Stamataki and Antoniou families run this and the nearby souvenir shop Pythari.

Glossa. © 2420/33-076. agnanti@hotmail.com. Main courses 3€–11€. No credit cards. Daily 11am–midnight. About 200m (656 ft.) up from the bus stop.

## SKOPELOS AFTER DARK

The nightlife scene on Skopelos isn't nearly as active as on neighboring Skiathos, but there are still plenty of bars, late-night cafes, and discos. Most of the coolest bars are on the far (east) side of town, but you can wander around checking out the scene around Platanos Square, beyond and along the paralia. Above the Hotel Amalia is the indoor **Cocos Club**; continue on along the beachfront to find the outdoor **Karyatis**. The best place for bouzouki music is the **Metro**. And don't forget the possibility of live music at the **Anatoli Ouzeri**, above the town and offering a spectacular view.

## 3 Skyros (Skiros)

47km (25 nautical miles) from Kimi, which is 182km (113 miles) from Athens

Skyros is an island with good beaches, attractive whitewashed pillbox architecture, picturesque surroundings, low prices—and relatively few tourists. Why? First, it's difficult to get to. In summer, there are occasional ferries and hydrofoils linking Skyros to the other Sporades as well as to ports on the mainland, but these links are either fairly infrequent or involve land transportation to ports that are not on most tourists' itineraries. Second, most visitors to the Sporades seem to prefer the other, more thickly forested (and thickly touristed) islands. Some of us find that Skyros's more meager tourist facilities and the stark contrast between sea, sky, and rugged terrain make it all the more inviting.

Also, many Skyriots themselves are ambivalent, at best, about developing this very traditional island for tourism. Until about 1990, there were only a handful of hotels on the entire island. Since then, Skyros has seen a miniboom in the tourist business, and with the completion of a giant marina, it's setting itself up to become yet another tourist Mecca. Don't let this deter you, however; at least for now, Skyros remains an ideal place for a getaway vacation.

## ESSENTIALS

**GETTING THERE  By Plane**  In summer, **Olympic Airways** has about two flights a week between Athens and Skyros. Call the Olympic office in Athens (© 210/966-6666) for information and reservations; the local Olympic representative is **Skyros Travel and Tourism** (© 22220/91-123). A bus meets most flights and goes to Skyros town, Magazia, and sometimes Molos; the fare is 2€. A taxi from the airport is about 6€, but expect to share a cab.

**By Boat**  The **Skyros Shipping Company** offers the only ferry service to Skyros; it's operated by a company whose stockholders are all citizens of the island. In summer, it runs twice daily (usually early afternoon and early evening) from Kimi (on the east coast of Evvia) to Skyros and twice daily (usually early morning and mid-afternoon) from Skyros to Kimi; the trip takes a little over 2 hours. Off season, there's one ferry each way, leaving Skyros early in the morning and Kimi in late afternoon. The fare is 10€. For information, call the company's office either in Kimi (© 2220/22-020) or Skyros (© 2220/91-789). The Skyros Shipping Co.'s offices also sell connecting bus tickets to Athens; the fare for the 3½-hour ride is about 13€. In Athens, **Alkyon Travel**, 97 Akademia, near

Kanigos Square (© 210/383-2545), also arranges bus transportation to Kimi and sells hydrofoil and ferry tickets to the Sporades.

In summer, Skyros can also be reached from several ports by the hydrofoils known as Flying Dolphins; this is the most convenient way to go, though a little more expensive than the ferry. (For example, the hydrofoil between Kimi and Skyros costs about 5.50€.) Hydrofoil schedules both ways are: about once a week from and to Kimi; about twice a week from and to Ayios Konstandinos; about once a week from and to Volos (4½ hr.); and about twice a week from and to Thessaloniki (a 6-hr. ride, or 5 hr. if you get on at Moudiana, south of Thessaloniki). From other Sporades, in summer there are several trips per week between Skyros and Skiathos, Skopelos, and Alonissos (about five times a week, starting in mid-May, daily in July and Aug.). For hydrofoil information, contact the **Hellas Flying Dolphins Line** in Piraeus (© 210/419-9100; www.dolphins.gr).

If you're trying to "do" the Sporades and want to make connections at Kimi, the tricky part can be the connection with ferries or hydrofoils from the other Sporades islands. When they don't hold to schedule, it's not uncommon to see the Skyros ferry disappearing on the horizon as your ship pulls into Kimi. You might have to make the best of the 24-hour layover and get a room in Paralia Kimi. (We recommend the **Hotel Kimi,** at © **22220/22-287.**)

From Athens, buses to Kimi and Ayios Konstandinos leave the Terminal B 260 Lission) six times a day, though you should depart no later than 1:30pm; the fare for the 3½-hour trip is about 15€. From Kimi, you must take a local bus to Paralia Kimi. Ask the bus driver if you're uncertain of the connection.

On Skyros, the ferries and hydrofoils dock at **Linaria,** on the opposite side of the island from Skyros town. The island's only public bus will meet the boat and take you over winding, curvy roads to Skyros town for 1€. On request, the bus will also stop at Magazia beach, immediately north below the town, next to the Xenia Hotel.

**VISITOR INFORMATION**    The largest tourist office is **Skyros Travel and Tourism** (© **22220/91-123;** fax 22220/92-123), next to Skyros Pizza Restaurant in the main market. It's open daily from 8am to 2:30pm and 6:30 to 10:30pm. English-speaking Lefteris Trakos offers assistance with accommodations, currency exchange, Olympic Airways flights (he's the local ticket agent), phone calls, some interesting bus and boat tours, and Hellas Flying Dolphin tickets.

**GETTING AROUND    By Bus**    The only scheduled service is the Skyros-Linaria shuttle that runs four to five times daily and costs 1€. Skyros Travel (see above) offers a twice-daily beach-excursion bus in high season. It now also offers day-long excursions around the island in a small bus with an English-speaking guide (35€); for many this may be the best way to get an overview of the island.

**By Car & Moped**    A small car rents for about 70€ per day, including insurance. Mopeds and motorcycles are available near the police station or the taxi station for about 25€ per day. The island has a relatively well-developed network of roads.

**By Taxi**    Taxis can be hired to go about any place on the island at the standard Greek rates, but discuss the price before setting off; service between Linaria and Skyros costs about 13€.

**On Foot**   Skyros is a fine place to hike. The island map, published by Skyros Travel and Tourism, will show you a number of good routes, and it seems to be pretty accurate.

**FAST FACTS**   As of this writing, there is only one ATM on Skyros, at the **National Bank of Greece** in the main square of Skyros town. Because of its limited hours (Mon–Fri 8am–2pm), and in case its ATM is out of service, we recommend bringing cash and/or traveler's checks. The **clinic** is near the main square (© **22220/92-222**). The **police station** (© **22220/91-274**) is on the street behind the Skyros Travel Center. The **post office** is near the bus square in Skyros town; open Monday through Friday from 8am to 2pm. The **telephone office (OTE)** is opposite the police station. It's open Friday only, from 7:30am to 3pm, but there are card phones in town.

## WHAT TO SEE & DO

**The Faltaits Historical and Folklore Museum**   Located in a large, old house of the Faltaits family, this is the private collection of Manos Faltaits, and it's one of the best island folk-art museums in Greece. It contains a large and varied collection of plates, embroidery, weaving, woodworking, and clothing, as well as many rare books and photographs, including some of the local men in traditional costumes for Carnival. Attached to the museum is a workshop where young artisans make lovely objects using traditional patterns and materials. The proceeds from the sale of workshop items go to the upkeep of the museum. The museum also has a shop, **Argo**, on the main street of town (© **22220/92-158**), open daily from 10am to 1pm and 6:30 to 11pm.

Plateia Rupert Brooke. © 22220/91-232. 2€. Summer daily 10am–1pm and 6–9pm; in off season, ring the bell and someone will let you in.

## EXPLORING THE ISLAND

All boats dock at **Linaria,** a plain, mostly modern fishing village on the west coast, pleasant enough but not recommended for a stay. Catch the bus waiting on the quay to take you across the narrow middle of the island to the west coast capital, Skyros town, which is built on a rocky bluff overlooking the sea. (The airport is near the northern tip of the island.) **Skyros town,** which is known on the island as Horio or Hora, looks much like a typical Cycladic hill town, with whitewashed houses built on top of one another. The winding streets and paths are too narrow for cars and mopeds, so most of the traffic is by foot and hoof. As you alight from the bus at the bus stop square, continue on up toward the center of town and the main bus tourist services.

Near the market, signs point up to the town's **Kastro.** It's a 15-minute climb, but worth it for the view, and on the way you'll pass the church of **Ayia Triada,** which contains some interesting frescoes, and the monastery of **Ayios Yioryios Skyrianos.** The monastery was founded in 962 and contains a famous black-faced icon of St. George that was brought from Constantinople during the Iconoclastic controversy. From one side of the citadel, the view is over the rooftops of the town, and from the other the cliff drops precipitously to the sea. According to one myth, King Lykomides pushed Theseus to his death from here.

The terrace at the far (northern) end of the island is **Plateia Rupert Brooke,** where the English poet, who is buried on the southern tip of the island, is honored by a nude statue, "Immortal Poetry." (Brooke died on a hospital ship off Skyros in 1915 while en route to the Dardanelles as an army officer.) The statue is said to have greatly offended the local people when it was installed; you're more likely to be amused when you see how pranksters have chosen to deface the hapless bronze figure. (The Faltaits Folklore Museum, described above, is located near this site, as is the not especially distinguished archaeological museum.)

Local customs and dress are currently better preserved on Skyros than in all but a few locales in Greece. Older men can still be seen in baggy blue pants, black caps, and leather sandals constructed with numerous straps, and older women still wear long head scarves. The **embroidery** you will often see women busily working at is famous for its vibrant colors and interesting motifs—such as people dancing hand-in-hand with flowers twining around their limbs and hoopoes with fanciful crests.

Peek into the doorway of any Skyrian home and you're likely to see what looks like a room from a dollhouse with a miniature table and chairs, and **colorful plates**—loads of plates hanging on the wall. The story behind these displays is said to have begun during the Byzantine era, when the head clerics from Epirus sent 10 families to Skyros to serve as governors. They were given control of all the land not owned by Mount Athos and the Monastery of St. George. For hundreds of years, these 10 families dominated the affairs of Skyros. With Kalamitsa as a safe harbor, the island prospered, and consulates opened from countries near and far. The merchant ships were soon followed by pirates, and the ruling families went into business with them; the families knew what boats were expected and what they were carrying, and the pirates had the ships and bravado to steal the cargo. The pirates, of course, soon took to plundering the islanders as well, but the aristocrats managed to hold on to much of their wealth.

Greek independence reduced the influence of these ruling families, and during the hard times brought by World War I, they were reduced to trading their possessions to the peasant farmers for food. Chief among these bartered items were sets of dinnerware. Plates from China, Italy, Turkey, Egypt, and other exotic places became a sign of wealth, and Skyrian families made elaborate displays of their newly acquired trophies. Whole walls were covered, and by the 1920s local Skyrian craftsmen began making their own plates for the poorer families who couldn't afford the originals. This, at least, is the story they tell.

Skyros is also the home of a unique breed of **wild pygmy ponies**, often compared to the horses depicted on the frieze of the Parthenon and thought to be at least similar to Shetland ponies. Most of these rare animals have been moved to the nearby island of Skyropoula, though tame ones can still be seen grazing near town. Ask around and you might be able to find a local who will let you ride one.

Every July 15, the ponies of Skyros are assembled and rated as to their characteristics and then young boys race some of the ponies around a small track.

## BEACHES & OUTDOOR PURSUITS

To get to the beach at **Magazia,** continue down from Platcia Rupert Brooke. (If your load is heavy, take a taxi to Magazia, as it is a hike.) From Magazia, once the site of the town's storehouses (magazines), it's about a half mile to **Molos,** a fishing village, though the two villages are quickly becoming indistinguishable because of development. There's windsurfing along this beach, and there are some fair isolated beaches beyond Molos, with some nudist activity.

South of town, the beaches are less enticing until you reach **Aspous,** which has a couple of tavernas and some rooms to let. **Ahili,** a bit further south, is where you'll find the big new **marina,** so it's no longer much of a place for swimming. Further south, the coast gets increasingly rugged and there is no roadway.

*Moments*  **The Famous Carnival of Skyros**

The 21-day Carnival celebration is highlighted by a 4-day period leading up to Lent and the day known throughout Greece as *Kathari Deftera* (Clean Monday). On this day, Skyros residents don traditional costumes and perform dances on the town square. Unleavened bread (*lagana*) is served with *taramosalata* and other meatless specialties. (Traditionally, vegetarian food is eaten for 40 days leading up to Easter.) Much of this is traditional throughout Greece, but Skyros adds its own distinctive element. Culminating on midafternoon of the Sunday before Clean Monday are a series of ritual dances and events performed by a group of weirdly costumed men. Some dress as old shepherds in animal skins with a belt of sheep bells and a mask made of goatskin. Other men dress as women and flirt outrageously. (Skyros seems to have an age-old association with cross-dressing: It was here that Achilles successfully beat the draft during the Trojan war by dressing as a woman, until shrewd Odysseus tricked him into revealing his true gender.) Other celebrants caricature Europeans, and all behave outlandishly, reciting ribald poetry and poking fun at bystanders. This ritual is generally thought to be pagan in origin and causes some people to reflect on the antics of ancient Greek comedy and even tragedy (goat song), with men playing all the roles, and catharsis as the goal.

If you head back across the narrow waist of the island to **Kalamitsa**, the old safe harbor, 3km (2 miles) south of Linaria, you'll find a good clean beach. It's served by buses in summer.

The island is divided almost evenly by its narrow waist; the northern half is fertile and covered with pine forest, while the southern half is barren and quite rugged. Both halves have their attractions, though the most scenic area of the island is probably to the south toward **Tris Boukes,** where Rupert Brooke is buried. The better beaches, however, are in the north.

North of Linaria, **Acherounes** is a very pretty beach. Beyond it, **Pefkos,** where marble was once quarried, is better sheltered and has a taverna that's open in summer. The next beach north, **Ayios Fokas,** is probably the best on the island, with a lovely white pebble beach and a taverna open in summer. Locals call it paradise, and like all such places it's very difficult to reach. Most Skyrians will suggest walking, but it's a long hilly hike. To get here from Skyros town, take the bus back to Linaria, tell the driver where you're going, get off at the crossroads with Pefkos, and begin your hike west from there.

North of Ayios Fokas is **Atsitsa,** another beach with pine trees along it, but it's a bit too rocky. It can be reached by road across the Olympos mountains in the center of the island, and it has a few rooms to let. It is also the location of a **holistic health-and-fitness holiday community;** for information on its activities, contact Skyros Holistic Vacations, 92 Prince of Wales Rd., London NW5 3NE (© **0207/284-3065** in England; www.skyros.com). (This same British outfit runs the **Skyros Centre** at the edge of Skyros Town; it differs from the one at Atsitsa in that it offers courses and a somewhat more conventional touristic experience.) There's a sandy beach a 15-minute walk further north at **Kira Panayia** that's a bit better.

The northwest of the island is covered in dense pine forests, spreading down to the Aegean. The rocky shore opens onto gentle bays and coves. This area provides wonderful **hiking** for the fit. Take a taxi (20€) to **Atsitsa**, and arrange for it to return in 5 or 6 hours. Explore the ruins of the ancient mining operation at Atsitsa, then head south for about 7km (4½ miles) to **Ayios Fokas**, a small bay with a tiny taverna perched right on the water. Kali Orfanou, the gracious hostess, will provide you with the meal of your trip: fresh fish caught that morning in the waters before you, vegetables plucked from the garden for your salad, and her own feta cheese and wine. Relax, swim in the bay, and then hike back to your taxi. The ambitious may continue south for 11km or 12 km (7 miles or 8 miles) to the main road and catch the bus or hail a taxi. Note that this part of the road is mainly uphill. In case you tire or can't pry yourself away from the secluded paradise of Ayios Fokas, Kali offers two extremely primitive rooms with the view of your dreams, but without electricity or toilets.

## SHOPPING

Skyros is a good place for buying local crafts, especially embroidery and ceramics. **Ergastiri,** on the main street, has interesting ceramics, Greek shadow puppets, and a great selection of postcards. Popular for his handmade plates is **Yiannis Nicholau,** whose studio is next to the Xenia Hotel. You can find good hand-carved wooden chests and chairs made from beech (in the old days it was blackberry wood) from **Lefteris Avgoklouris,** former student of the recently departed master, Baboussis, in Skyros town; his studio is on Konthili, around the corner from the post office (✆ **22220/91-106**). Another fine carver is **Manolios,** in the main market.

## WHERE TO STAY

The whole island has only a few hotels, so most visitors to Skyros take private rooms. The best are in the upper part of Skyros town, away from the bus stop, where women in black dresses accost you with cries of "Room! Room!" A more efficient procedure is to stop in at Skyros Travel and Tourism (see "Visitor Information," above). The island of Skyros is somewhat more primitive in its facilities than the other Sporades, so before agreeing to anything, check out the room to ensure that it's what you want.

### IN SKYROS TOWN

**Hotel Nefeli** One of the best in-town options is built in the modern Skyrian style. The bedrooms and bathrooms are decent sized and well appointed; many units have fine views, and the large, downstairs lobby is a welcoming space. As the Nefeli is one of the favorite choices on Skyros, you'd do well to reserve in advance.

Skyros town center, 34007 Skyros. ✆ **22220/91-964.** Fax 22220/92-061. 16 units. 75€ double. Breakfast 5€ extra. AE, MC, V.

### IN MAGAZIA BEACH & MOLOS

**Hotel Angela** (Value) This is among the most attractive and well-kept abodes in the Molos/Magazia beach area, located near the sprawling Paradise Hotel complex. All rooms are clean and tidy with balconies, but because the hotel is set back about 100 yards from the beach, there are only partial sea views. Nevertheless, the facilities and hospitality of the young couple who run the Angela make up for its just-off-the-beach location, and it's the best bet for the money.

**Paradise Hotel** This pleasant lodging is at the north end of Magazia beach, in the town of Molos. The older part of the hotel has 40 rooms; these more basic units run about 50% less. We recommend one of the newer section's 20 rooms, which are better kept and have much better light. The hotel is somewhat removed from the main town, but there is a taverna on the premises and another down the street.

Molos, 34007 Skyros. © **22220/91-764.** Fax 2222/92-030. anghotel@otenet.gr. 14 units. 75€ double. No credit cards.

**Pension Galeni** The small but delightful Pension Galeni offers modest rooms, all with private bathroom. We like the front, sea-facing rooms on the top floor for their (currently) unobstructed views. The Galeni overlooks one of the cleanest parts of Magazia beach.

Magazia Beach, 34007 Skyros. © **22220/91-220.** Fax 22220/91-443. 60 units. 65€ double in the new building. Breakfast 4€ extra. No credit cards.

**Xenia** With the best location on the beach at Magazia, the Xenia offers some of the best (if not cheapest) accommodations on Skyros. The guest rooms have handsome 1950s-style furniture and big bathrooms with tubs, as well as wonderful balconies and sea views. You can get all your meals here if you so desire. Perhaps the hotel's greatest drawback is the unsightly concrete breakwater that's supposed to protect the beach from erosion.

Magazia Beach, 34007 Skyros. © **22220/92-063.** Fax 22220/92-062. 22 units. 98€ double. Rates include buffet breakfast. V.

## IN ACHEROUNES BEACH

**Pegasus Apartments** These fully equipped studios and apartments were built by the resourceful Lefteris Trakos (owner of Skyros Travel). They are located at Acherounes, the beach just south of the port of Linaria, on the east coast. One of the pluses of staying here is the chance to see (and ride, if you're under 15) Katerina, a Skyriot pony.

Acherounes Beach, 34007 Skyros. © **22220/91-552.** 8 units. 45€ studio for 2 persons; 95€ apt for 3–5 persons. MC, V. *In room:* minibar.

## IN YIRISMATA

**Skyros Palace Hotel** ★ This out-of-the-way resort—about a mile north of Molos, thus 3km (2 miles) north of Skyros town—offers the most luxurious accommodations on the island. The guest rooms are plainly furnished but comfortable, with large balconies. The beach across the road is an especially windy, rocky stretch of coastline, with somewhat treacherous water. Facilities include a lovely (seawater) pool and adjacent bar, some air-conditioned rooms, and a well-planted garden—not to mention a soundproofed disco, the most sophisticated on the island. A minibus heads into town twice a day. If you want to get away from it all and enjoy some upscale amenities to boot, this might be the place for you.

Yirismata, 34007 Skyros. © **22220/91-994.** Fax 22220/92-070. 80 units. 90€ double. Rates include breakfast. AE, DC, MC, V. **Amenities:** 2 restaurants; bar; pool. *In room:* TV.

## WHERE TO DINE

The food in Skyros town is generally pretty good and reasonably priced. **Anemos,** on the main drag (© **22220/92-155**), is a good place for breakfast, with filtered coffee, omelets, and freshly squeezed juice. The nearby **Skyros Pizza Restaurant** (© **22220/91-684**) serves tasty pies as well as other Greek specialties. For dessert, there's the **Zacharoplasteio,** the Greek name for sweet shop/bakery, in the center of town.

In Linaria, there are three decent tavernas to choose from—**Almyra, Filippeos,** and **Psariotos.**

**Kristina's/Pegasus Restaurant** (★ INTERNATIONAL   Kristina's has been an institution in Skyros town for some years, but in 2000 it moved to the locale of the former Pegasus Restaurant, a neoclassical building (ca. 1890) in the center of town. The Australian proprietor/chef, Kristina, brings a light touch to everything she cooks. Her fricasseed chicken is excellent, her herb bread is tasty, and her desserts, such as cheesecake, are exceptional. Definitely the place if you need a break from standard Greek fare.

Skyros town. © **22220/91-123.** Reservations recommended in summer. Main courses 6€–13€. No credit cards. Mon–Sat 7am–4pm and 7pm–1am.

**Maryetes Grill**   GRILL   One of the oldest and best places in town, the Maryetes is a second-generation-run grill that's equally popular with locals and travelers. The dining room is as simple as simple gets, so what you go for is the food. We recommend the grilled chicken and meat. There's a small sampling of salads as well.

Skyros town. © **22220/91-311.** Main courses 4.50€–8€. No credit cards. Daily 1–3pm and 6pm–midnight.

**Restaurant Kabanero** (*Value* GREEK   One of the best dining values in town, this perpetually busy eatery serves the usual Greek menu: moussaka, stuffed peppers and tomatoes, fava, various stewed vegetables, and several kinds of meat. The dishes are tasty and prices somewhat lower than at most other places in town.

Skyros town. © **22220/91-240.** Main courses 3.50€–6€. No credit cards. Daily 1–3pm and 6pm–midnight.

## SKYROS AFTER DARK

If you've gotta dance, try the **Kastro Club,** in Linaria, or **Stone,** on the road to Magazia. Linaria's **O Kavos** is another popular hangout. Aside from these, there are few evening diversions other than barhopping on the main street of Skyros town. **Apocalypsis** draws a younger crowd. **Kalypso** attracts a more refined set of drinkers who appreciate its better-made but pricier cocktails. **Renaissance** is loud and lively. **Rodon** is best for actually listening to music, while **Kata Lathos** ("By Mistake") has also gained a following.

# 14

# Highlights of Western Greece: Epirus & Ioannina

*by John S. Bowman*

**E**vergreen slopes, deep-set rivers and lush valleys, villages of timbered houses with slate or tile roofs—this can't be Greece. But it is. It's the northwestern corner the Greeks know as **Epirus.** Plentiful rainfall, the rugged Pindos mountains, and a generally more temperate climate seem to remove this region from familiar Mediterranean Greece—at times, it almost seems Alpine. It's one of the few places in Greece where you'll spend time away from the sea.

Epirus and its capital city, **Ioannina,** seem immune to the throngs who crowd the beaches and restaurants, the ferries and ancient sites, of so many parts of Greece these days. It isn't the travel-poster Greece many have come to expect, and it certainly hasn't organized itself around tourism and foreigners. Although there are plenty of hotels and restaurants, the pace of life in Ioannina and other cities, not to mention in the villages, is governed by local customs. During the off season, for instance, places such as the post office and information offices may be closed all weekend. Museum hours are cut back, as are the hours of gift shops and many restaurants. And except for some staff in the hotels, better restaurants, and visitor information and car-rental offices, few people speak English, although they may speak Italian, French, or German. You may find yourself sharing a hotel with Greek commercial travelers, and it will

probably be harder to find your English-language newspaper or fresh-squeezed orange juice. In other words, it's for those who enjoy traveling in an authentic foreign land.

**A STRATEGY FOR SEEING THE REGION** Visitors to this corner of Greece will come by ship from Italy or Corfu (via Igoumenitsa), by plane from Athens or Thessaloniki, or by car or bus from other parts of Greece. We recommend basing yourself in Ioannina, a city that offers a fine mix of natural attractions, historical associations, and modern amenities. It's easy to fill the better part of 2 days by walking around Ioannina, and you could visit Epirus's other main destination, **Metsovo,** by bus. But you really should rent a car to see most of the other attractions of Epirus—**Dodona** and the cave at **Perama. We** recommend a minimum of 4 days for Epirus—2 days for Ioannina and Dodona, 1 day for Metsovo, and 1 day for Perama Cave.

**A LOOK AT THE PAST** In its history, Western Greece and Epirus in particular have often gone in different directions from the rest of the country. It was settled by Greek-speaking peoples about the same time as other parts of Greece (ca. 2000 B.C.), and over the centuries they worshipped many of the same gods and carried on much the same culture. But there were many non-Greek peoples in this area, and

**Tips Travel Tip**

Epirus is one part of Greece best visited between early June and late September, unless you don't mind cooler weather. In the winter, you can come up here to ski.

this plus a natural remoteness meant that the region did not participate in the grand classical civilization. Social organization remained more tribal, led by small-time kings. The greatest of the Epirote kings, **Pyrrhus** (318–272 B.C.), was constantly making war, and his victories over the Romans outside Rome have given us the term Pyrrhic victory—because won at great cost, they came to nothing. Epirus itself was reduced to a Roman province after 168 B.C.

During the **Middle Ages,** Greece's whole western region was constantly prey to invaders, and with the conquest of Constantinople by the Crusaders in 1204, some Greeks decided to set up a new state with Ioannina as the capital, the so-called Despotate of Epirus. It never amounted to much and soon fell under outside control. Finally it was taken over by the Turks in 1431, and soon they controlled virtually all of Greece, although the Venetians and various other Western Europeans would gain possession of parts of Western Greece.

It was near the end of this long phase that Epirus experienced its most dramatic moment in the spotlight of history, under the "Lion of Ioannina,"

**Ali Pasha** (1741–1822). He was born in Albania and rose to prominence fighting on behalf of the Ottoman Sultan in Constantinople. But in 1788, Ali Pasha decided to set up a virtually independent domain with his capital in Ioannina. An international celebrity in his day, visited by Byron among others, he was a cruel despot who boasted of killing 30,000 people, often in the most brutal fashion. The Ottomans tolerated Ali Pasha as long as they could, but in 1822 sent a large force to capture him; he hid in a monastery on the islet off Ioannina but was tracked down, killed, and beheaded.

When the Greeks rose up against the Turks in the 1820s, the southern part of Western Greece, centered around Messolonghi, took on an active role, but the bulk of Epirus did not join in. The southwestern district of Arta was freed from Turkish rule in 1881, but Epirus was not formally joined to Greece until after the Second Balkan War of 1913.

Epirus became a battleground twice more, against the invading Italians and Germans in World War II, and then in the Greek civil war. Since then it has enjoyed peace and quiet prosperity.

## 1 Getting to & Around Epirus

### GETTING THERE

**By Plane** Olympic Airways (© **210/966-6666;** www.olympic-airways.gr) offers flights to Ioannina from Athens—usually two a day. At least once a day there are Olympic flights between Ioannina and Thessaloniki. **Aegean Cronus Airlines** (© **280/112-0000)** offers daily flights between Athens and Ioannina; call ahead or contact a travel agent. Olympic also flies about once a day from Athens to Aktion, just outside Preveza on the southernmost coast of Epirus; from here you can get a bus to Igoumenitsou and Ioannina or even to the island of Lefkada, which is connected by a viaduct to the mainland.

**By Boat** **Igoumenitsou,** on the coast opposite Corfu, is the point of entry to northwestern Greece for many people. In summer, ferries connect hourly to Corfu (a trip varying from 1–2 hr., depending on the ship) and less frequently to Kefalonia, Ithaka, and Paxi. There is also hydrofoil service, twice daily at least during high season, between Corfu and Igoumenitsou (a trip of about half an hour). Numerous ferries and ships that put into Igoumenitsou go to and from ports in Italy—Ancona, Bari, Brindisi, Venice; some of these connect to Patras or Piraeus in Greece or even more distant ports such as Iraklion in Crete, or Cesme in Turkey.

In high season, there is also a ferry connecting **Astakos**—on the Ionian coast south of Preveza and north of Messolonghi—and the offshore islands of Ithaka and Kefalonia.

There are so many changes in scheduling of all these ships that it's useless to provide specific details, but if you want information in advance, contact **Thalassa Travel** in Igoumenitsou, located at 20 Ethniki Antistaseos (© **26650/ 22-001;** fax 26650/22-506).

**By Bus** The **KTEL** line (© **210/512-5954** in Athens; **26510/26-211** in Ioannina) enters northwestern Greece from distant points such as Athens (7½ hr.) or Thessaloniki (8 hr.).

**By Car** There are several approaches to Western Greece from distant points. **From Athens,** there are two main routes. One is the inland route north via Livadia, Lamia, Karditsa, Trikkala, Kalambaka, and Ioannina. The second is via Corinth and then along the southern coast of the Gulf of Corinth to Rion; by 2004 the brand new bridge should be opened, but if it is not take the ferry to Antirion, and then via Messolonghi, Agrinio, Arta, and Ioannina. Alternatively, you can head to the Ionian coast after Messolonghi, and go up to Igoumenitsou via Astakos, Preveza, and Parga.

The preferred route **from Thessaloniki** is via Veria west to Kozani and Konitsa and then south to Ioannina. If the former Yugoslavia has settled down enough to allow for transit, it might be possible to take the once well-traveled route from western Europe via Skopje (now capital of the Former Yugoslavia Republic of Macedonia) down into Northern Greece at Florina, and from there south to Kastoria and Ioannina.

## GETTING AROUND

**By Bus** With enough time, you can see most of Western Greece by bus, but as always, you'll need extra hours for the little side trips. But given the many mountainous roads and curves, you might prefer to let others do the driving. **KTEL** provides bus links between virtually all points in Western Greece. Points to **Athens** and the **north, northwest,** and **northeast** (Igoumenitsou, Metsovo, Konitsa, Kastoria, and Thessaloniki) are serviced from Ioannina's **main bus terminal** at 4 Zosimadon 4 (© 26510/26-211). Points to the **south** (Parga, Arta, Preveza, Astakos, Messolonghi, and Patras) are serviced from a smaller **bus terminal** in Ioannina at 19 Vizaniou (© **26510/25-014**).

**By Car** Having a car is probably the best way to experience the full variety of Western Greece. Distances are not all that great, although trips do take much longer than a map might suggest due to the many mountainous and curving roads. (Mopeds or motorcycles are not advised except for the most experienced.) Western Greece doesn't offer the choice in car rentals as in more touristy parts of Greece. We think **Budget Rent-A-Car** in Ioannina, at 109 Dodonis 109

(✆ 26510/43-901; fax 26510/45-382), is the best to deal with; it's a family affair, run by owner Angela Tsamatos, her son Stelios, and the genial manager, Paul Angelis. But don't expect to haggle during high season—there are a limited number of vehicles for the influx of tourists.

**By Taxi** There are so many switchbacks and hairpin roads here that you might prefer to take a taxi. Agree on a fee before you set out. Each hour's drive into the countryside should cost about 20€; each hour's waiting, about 7€ so that a full day's excursion would run to about 100€. Try to get a driver who speaks at least basic English, or a foreign language you understand—and you'll get a guide in the bargain. He in turn should get a generous tip.

106km (65 miles) E of Igoumenitsou, 452km (277 miles) N of Athens

Ioannina had long been a sleepy medieval town when Greeks fleeing Constantinople after its capture by the Crusaders in 1204 arrived to make it the capital of the Despotate of Epirus. The first Despot, Michael 1, started building the walls that over the next centuries would be enlarged and strengthened by various conquerors—Greeks, Italians, Serbs, and Turks—to become the quite magnificent walled old town that still exists.

## ESSENTIALS

**GETTING THERE Ioannina** is a good 7 hours from Athens by car. **Olympic Airlines** flies to Ioannina from Athens, usually twice a day. At least once a day there are Olympic flights between Ioannina and Thessaloniki. **Aegean Cronus Airlines** (✆ 280/112-0000) also has been offering daily flights from and to Athens.

**Olympic's office** in downtown Ioannina is in a building at the far side of the triangle of greenery at the top of the Central Square (✆ 26510/26-518 or 26510/23-120). Hours are Monday through Friday from 8am to 3pm; outside of those hours, try the airport office at (✆ 26510/39-131. Aegean Airlines office is at 11 Pirsinella (off Central Square). The **airport** is about 4km (2½ miles) from the center of town; it's well serviced by public buses (nos. 2 and 7) from the main square, but you will probably find it more convenient to take a taxi.

**VISITOR INFORMATION** Ioannina's **Epirus Tourism Directorate** office is located at 39 Leoforos Dodonis, up past the Xenia Hotel (✆ 26510/41-868; fax 26510/49-139). Summer hours are Monday through Friday from 7:30am to 2:30pm and 5:30 to 8:30pm, Saturday from 9am to 1pm; winter hours are Monday through Friday from 7:30am to 2:30pm.

In summer, the city also maintains an information booth down on the lake, to the left of the fortress and by the quay where you get the boats to the islet Nissi; it's open Monday through Saturday from 10am to 8pm.

Also helpful are the many travel agencies, in particular **Daskalopoulos Yiannis Tour World**, 13 28th Octobriou (✆ 26510/29-667; fax 26510/21-222).

**FAST FACTS** There are numerous **ATMs** in the center of Ioannina (and also a couple in Metsovo): branches of the big national **banks** can handle all money exchanges. There is an internationally known medical school and **hospital** at Dourouti, some 7km (4 miles) south of Ioannina. There is another hospital at Hatzikosta (2km/1¼ miles). For **Internet access,** try the **Webcafé** (✆ 26510/83-215), well back on the left in the Sarka Stoa, opposite 16 Pirsinella (leading off the main square); it's open daily from 11am to 3am.

# Ioannina

**Lake of Ioannina (Pamvotis)**

Citadel

Karamanlis

Plateia Mavili

Ethn. Antistaseos

Mitropolis

Archaeological Museum

Metsovu

Ioann Metaxa

Pamvotidos

Ay. Marinis

Ayia Marini

Bizaniou

Town Hall

Aviron

Papagou

Patriarchu Athenagoru

Stratarchu Alexandru Papagu

Main Bus Station

Police Station

Plateia Pirrou

Secondary Bus Station

Marku Botsari

Koran Tsirigoti

28 Octobriou

Ch. Trikupi

Michael Angelou

Plateia Salongu

Stadium

Elef. Venizelou

Dodonis

Napoleontos Serva

0    200 m
0    200 y

N

**Greece**

Aegean Sea

Athens

Peloponnese

Mediterranean Sea

Ioannina

## ACCOMMODATIONS ■
Hotel du Lac **14**
Hotel Olympic **10**
Hotel Palladion **9**
Xenia Hotel **13**

## ATTRACTIONS ●
Boats to Island **2**
Byzantine Museum **4**
Folk Art Museum **8**
Kastro **12**
Municipal Popular Art Museum **3**
Old Bazaar **7**
Synagogue **5**

## DINING ◆
La Fontantina **11**
The Pharos **1**
To Mantelo **6**

Information
OTE
Post Office

The **Self Service Laundry**, 3 Tsirigoti, around the corner from the KTEL bus station (☎ 26510/25-542), is open Monday through Saturday from 8am to 2pm, and also Tuesday, Thursday, and Friday from 5 to 8:30pm. The **tourist police** are located at **Police Headquarters**, 11 28th Octobriou 11 (☎ 26510/25-673); open daily from 7am to 2am. The main **post office** is on 3 28th Octobriou (☎ 26510/26-437). It's open Monday through Saturday from 7:30am to 8pm; in the off season, it's closed on Saturdays. The **telephone office (OTE)** is at the rear (right) on 4 28th Octobriou; open daily from 7am to 10pm.

## WHAT TO SEE & DO

**Ioannina Museum** ★ Housed in a modern building, this fine little provincial museum has just enough to engage anyone who has come this far. Most displays are from graves and burial sites in Epirus, but the range of items extends from Paleolithic implements (including one of the oldest stone tools in all Greece) through the Bronze Age to Roman times. Various bronze works are especially interesting, as is the superb Attic-style sarcophagus dating from the 2nd to 3rd centuries A.D., with carved scenes from the *Iliad*.

But undoubtedly, the display case that will entrance most people holds some of the little lead tablets found at the **Oracle of Dodona**. People from all stations of life came to Dodona and had some desire or query inscribed on a strip of lead that was then submitted to the oracle. Today we can read these actual pleas. Some are quite practical: "Should I buy a certain property?" "Should I engage in shipping?" Others have a religious tinge: "To which god should we pray or sacrifice to get certain results?" But the most intriguing are the personals: "Is it better to marry?" "Shall I take another wife?" "Am I the father of her children?" These tablets speak to us as do few remains from the ancient world.

Plateia 25 Martiou (behind clock tower and the Greek Army base on Central Sq.). ☎ 26510/25-490. Fax 26510/22-595. Admission 3€ adults, 1.50€ for EU seniors over 65. Tues–Sun 8:30–3pm.

## A STROLL AROUND THE *FROURIO*: THE WALLED OLD TOWN & CITADEL ★

For many of the centuries that Ioannina fell under the occupation of foreign conquerors, city walls enclosed all the most important structures. There's virtually nothing of historic or architectural importance outside the citadel except on the isler of Nissi. Originally the fortress was separated from the mainland by a moat, which was crossed by three bridges. The moat has since been filled in. An esplanade now circles the lakeside below the walls, and there are several openings in the wall, but most people will enter the walls from the **Plateia Yioryio**, which is lined by tavernas and gift shops.

A left turn inside the Plateia Giorgio gate onto Ioustinianou leads (in about 2 blocks) to the **Synagogue.** Dating from 1790, this white-walled synagogue, with a Hebrew inscription above its locked door, will be interesting to those willing to track down someone who can let you in—try asking at the shop of Mrs. Allegra Matsa, 18 Anexartisias (☎ 26510/27-008). The Jewish community of Ioannina traces its origins to Jews who came here at least by the 13th century. The Germans removed all 5,000 or so in 1941 and took them to labor and extermination camps. After the war, about 150 survivors came back, but today only some 100 Jews still live in Ioannina. A small **Holocaust Memorial** is just outside the citadel, on the corner of Karamanlis and Soutsou.

If you continue on around the inside perimeter of the walls, you will come to a large clearing. From here, ascend a cobblestoned slope to the **Aslan Pasha Cami,** a 17th-century school with cells for Islamic scholars. Its **mosque** now houses the **Municipal Popular Art Museum.** In summer, it's open daily from 8am to 8pm; in winter, Monday through Friday from 8am to 3pm, Saturday and Sunday from 9am to 3pm. Admission is 3€. The mosque was erected in 1618 on the site of an Orthodox church, razed by Aslan Pasha to punish the Christian Greeks for a failed revolt. Entering the mosque, observe in the vestibule the recesses for shoes. The exhibits, which include traditional costumes, jewelry, weapons, documents, and household wares, are grouped around the three major religious-ethnic communities of Ioannina: the Orthodox Greeks, the Muslims, and the Jews. There's an adjacent minaret, and when it and the mosque are illuminated each night, the scene from the lake is captivating.

In the opposite and far corner of the walled town is the innermost citadel, known by its Turkish name, **Irz Kale.** Within it are the Victory Mosque (**Fethiye Cami**); the base of a circular tower; the remains of the palace of Ali Pasha, the cruel Albanian who dominated Epirus from 1788 until 1822; and the alleged **tombs** of Ali Pasha and his wife. The Greek army long occupied this part of the citadel, but its structures have now been restored and there is an interesting **Byzantine Museum** here, located in two buildings, the virtually rebuilt **palace** and the **harem.** The former houses the icons and other church-related objects, the latter concentrates on silver work. Hours are daily from 9am to 3pm; admission is 3€.

## A STROLL AROUND IOANNINA

Ioannina has become a busy commercial center for all of northwestern Greece (its population is some 100,000), and its streets can be filled with vehicles of all kinds generating noise and fumes, but there are some interesting retreats from all this. One is the old **Turkish Bazaar,** down near the walled town and just off the main street, Averoff. Although gradually vanishing, in its tiny shops you will still see a few men practicing the old crafts—metal smiths, jewelry makers, cobblers, tailors, and the like. Proceeding up Averoff, you come to the edge of the Central Square with the **clock tower** (on the left). Up behind this is the city's **archaeological museum** (see above). When you leave the museum, stroll across the broad terraced gardens built over the site of what was once the **walled Kastro,** where the Christians lived during the Turkish era. There was a cafe/restaurant on the far corner, but as of our last visit it was closed; hopefully new owners will revive it, as the location's outdoor tables provide a fine view of the lake and distant mountains. Returning to the main street, you are now on the **Central Square** (officially Plateia Pyrros), also with its share of cafes and restaurants.

## A BOAT TRIP TO THE ISLET OF NISSI (NISSAKI) ✦

If you have only a day in Ioannina, try to spend at least 2 to 3 hours (including an hour for a meal) on a visit to **Nissi,** the islet in Lake Panvotis. Small boats leave from the quay below the fortress every half-hour in summer, from 6:30am to 11pm. In the off season, service is every hour—but note that the last boat leaves the island around 10pm. The fare is .80€. The lake has unfortunately become overgrown with algae and is so polluted that local restaurants do not serve the fish taken from it (or so we've been assured).

The boat ride is barely 10 minutes and, day and night, provides a fine view of Ioannina. You get off in what is virtually the lobby of three restaurants—each displaying a tank filled with seafood. Resist all until you are truly ready to eat. The specialties of these restaurants include eel, frogs' legs, carp, crayfish, trout, and other imported fish.

The small village here is said to have been founded only in the 16th century by refugees from the Mani region of the Peloponnese, but its five monasteries predate this, and they are your destination. Take the narrow passage between the two restaurants; signs are posted to your left and right. Following the signs to the left (east), you will come to the **Monastery of Panteleimon.** Although founded in the 16th century, it has been so heavily restored that little of the original remains.

The monastery houses a **small museum** devoted to the infamous **Ali Pasha,** with numerous pictures and personal items including his clothing and water pipe. It's open daily, and an attendant will come if it's closed. Admission is .80€. Pasha took refuge here in 1820 and was eventually killed here in 1822 by Turks. You may even be shown holes in the floor where it is alleged he was shot from below.

Directly beside this monastery is the **Monastery of the Prodromos (St. John the Baptist),** but most people will want to move on to the western edge of the islet, following the signs to the **Moni Filanthropinon** (also known as the **Monastery of Ayios Nikolaos Spanos**). It's sometimes referred to as the "Secret School" because of claims that Orthodox priests maintained a secret school here during the Turkish occupation. Founded in the 13th century, it was rebuilt in the 16th century, when magnificent frescoes were painted on its walls. (There's no admission, but it's customary to leave a gratuity with the caretaker.) Seldom does the public get to view such an ensemble of Byzantine frescoes so close up. Although the dim light can be a problem (bring a flashlight), you should be able to recognize such subjects as the life of Christ on the walls of the central dome, and the many saints. Most unexpected, however, are the portrayals of ancient Greek sages on the wall of the narthex as you enter—Apollonius, Aristotle, Cheilon, Plato, Plutarch, Solon, and Thucydides.

About 100m (328 ft.) farther along the trail is **Ayios Nikolaos Dilios** (or **Moni Stratgopoulou**), the oldest monastery (dating from the 11th century) on Nissi. Its 16th-century frescoes are also of some interest but are in poor condition. (A small tip to the caretaker is also called for.) The fifth monastery, **Ayios Eleouses**, is closed to the public.

By now you have earned your meal on Nissi. Choose one of the restaurants (see "Where to Dine," below). And as you sip your wine, you can contemplate what such a locale means while enjoying the view.

## SHOPPING

If you get the impression that every third store in old Ioannina sells jewelry, silverware, hammered copper, and embossed brass work, you're right—these are the traditional crafts here. Many of the jewelry stores really sell nothing but modern work in gold and silver and/or precious and semiprecious jewels. Prices are probably lower than in more cosmopolitan cities, but be wary of "antiques" that may be offered in some shops—they may not be all that old, and if they are older than 1830, you need an export license!

There's a cluster of jewelry and gift shops opposite the walled citadel. Typical selections of metal work (and also water pipes) may be found at **Politis Douvflis**, 12 Plateia Yioryio, or at **Nikos Gogonis**, 13 Karamanlis. At two shops on 56 and 65 Averoff, **George Minos Moschos** offers a somewhat more unusual selection of silver, jewelry, and older secondhand objects (antiques). Here and there you may see embroidered clothing or woven socks, but this is not a region known for delicate needlework.

## WHERE TO STAY

Ioannina and its immediate environs don't offer luxury resorts, but that's not why travelers come here. There are, however, several quite special hotels and plenty of more-than-adequate accommodations.

In addition to the following options, the **Hotel Galaxy**, Plateia Pyrros (Central Square), 45221 Ioannina (© **26510/25-432**; fax 26510/30-724), offers convenient, clean, and cheap rooms.

**Hotel du Lac** (★    This hotel opened in the summer of 1998 and immediately became Ioannina's prime showplace. With its marble and woodwork and carpets, it exudes luxury; more important, its service lives up to its image. The rooms are a bit larger than in many Greek hotels and most enjoy a view across to the lake; bathrooms are state-of-the-art. The buffet breakfast is almost excessive; the regular meals are what you'd expect from a fine hotel. Some might find its distance from the center (a 15-min. walk) a downside, but in return you get a quiet lakeside locale. Perhaps the only negative might be that a large conference is in session and you could feel you were out of your element.

Leoforos Andrea Miaouli and Ikkou (along the lake, half a mile right of walled citadel), 45221 Ioannina. © **26510/59-100.** Fax 26510/59-200. 139 units. All year 135€ double. Rates include buffet breakfast. AE, DC, MC, V. Open year-round. Parking on grounds. Taxis can be ordered from desk. **Amenities:** 2 restaurants; 2 bars; pool; children's pool; children's playground; concierge; tours and car rentals arranged; 24-hr. room service; babysitting; same-day laundry and dry cleaning; conference center; secretarial service. *In room:* A/C, TV, minibar, hair dryer, safe, data and computer lines.

**Hotel Olympic**   For those who like to be at the center of the action, such as it is in Ioannina, the Olympic is the hotel. It has long attracted members of the foreign diplomatic corps, government dignitaries, and such. All that means nothing, of course, if you aren't made to feel welcome and comfortable, and you can be assured of both. The lobby is modest, but the desk service and 24-hour room service are what count. All the corridors, bedrooms, and bathrooms have recently been renovated. Ask for an upper-story front room that enjoys a view of the distant lake.

2 Melanidi (1 block off Central Sq.), 45220 Ioannina. © **26510/25-888.** Fax 26510/22-041. www.hotel olymp.gr. 54 units. High season 78€ double; low season 65€ double. No credit cards. Open year-round. Parking in lot across from hotel. *In room:* A/C, TV, fridge, safe.

**Hotel Palladion**   We like this place for its combination of features: convenient yet quiet, a professional and helpful desk staff, no frills but good value. Rooms are of decent size and decor; windows insulate from most street noise; bathrooms are standard issue; everything works. (And when we asked to move from one because of lingering cigarette odor, this happened instantly and with no further questions. Since then, the hotel has set aside floors for non-smokers.) The Palladion often hosts small groups, but this should not interfere with your stay. A final advantage: The hotel has its own parking lot.

1 Botsari (off 28 Octobriou), 45444 Ioannina. © **26510/25-856.** Fax 26510/74-034. 128 units. High season 75€ double; low season 60€ double. Rates include buffet breakfast. AE, DC, MC, V. Open year-round. Private parking lot. **Amenities:** 2 restaurants; bar; tours and car rentals arranged; conference facilities; business center; airport transfer arranged; babysitting; same-day laundry and dry cleaning. *In room:* A/C, TV, hair dryer, safe.

**Xenia Hotel**   This was long Ioannina's finest, and although the rooms are not exceptional (but certainly tasteful and comfortable), what you get for your money is a sense of seclusion in a park at the very heart of town. The hotel is set well back from the street, and the bedrooms at the rear enjoy fine views. There's an outdoor cafe that allows you to relax in a garden atmosphere; the indoor restaurant is highly regarded and certainly convenient if you don't care to explore Ioannina's many others. The front desk will see to basic needs and room service is available. For those who prefer a slightly subdued, genteel atmosphere.

33 Dodonis (up past the Central Sq.), 45221 Ioannina. © **26510/47-301.** Fax 26510/47-189. 60 units. 96€ double. Rates include buffet breakfast. AE, DC, MC, V. Open year-round. Parking on grounds. An easy walk from the Central Sq., or take one of the many public buses that pass by. **Amenities:** 2 restaurants; bar; concierge; tours and car rentals arranged; conference rooms; 24-hr. room service; same-day laundry and dry cleaning. *In room:* A/C, TV, fridge, minibar.

# WHERE TO DINE
## MODERATE

**The Gastra Restaurant** ★ GREEK REGIONAL   This is a must for all those willing to try a special type of regional cooking that involves heaping red-hot embers over a *gastra*—the conical cast-iron lid that's lowered onto the baking dish holding the food (lamb, goat, pork, or chicken), which then roasts slowly to appear on your table as an especially succulent meal. It's delicious. The restaurant also has other specialties; for an appetizer, try the *skordalia karithia* (walnut-garlic dip), and for dessert, the special crème caramel.

In pleasant weather, you can eat out front in the shaded garden and watch your meal cooking in the open fireplace. On cooler evenings, you can sit inside the handsome restaurant. When the spirit moves, diners are encouraged to dance to the music. Come here for a leisurely experience, not just for the food. (And if it's too crowded and you need your gastra, proceed less than a mile after taking the left turn signed to Igoumenitsou to another such restaurant, the **Diogenes**.)

Eleousa, along the Airport–Igoumenitsou Hwy. (7km/4 miles outside Ioannina; 3km/2 miles past the airport, just before turnoff to Igoumenitsou). © 26510/61-530. Reservations recommended in high season on weekend evenings; on Sun, you are advised to leave it to the citizens of Ioannina. Main courses 5€–14€. No credit cards. Tues–Sun 1–5pm and 8pm–1am. Open year-round. Public bus 2.

**La Fontantina** GREEK/ITALIAN  This is the house restaurant of the Olympic Hotel and has become a favorite gathering spot for foreigners and Greeks who like to feel they're at Ioannina's crossroads. The decor is hotel stuffy, service is a bit casual, and the menu ranges from Greek to Italian standards. But go for a change from the usual Greek foods, to enjoy the risotto or spaghetti carbonara or a steak filet with one of the fine red wines from Northern Greece—a Naoussa, an Amyntaion, or a Carras. Florence it's not, but La Fontantina offers a taste of upscale Ioannina.

2 Melanidi (on ground floor of Olympic Hotel, 1 block off Central Sq.). © 26510/25-147. Fax 26510/22-041. Reservations recommended on holidays and weekends in high season. Main courses 5€–15€. No credit cards. Daily 10am–midnight.

## INEXPENSIVE

**Pamvotis** GREEK/SEAFOOD  If you have only one meal to eat in Ioannina, it has to be at one of the restaurants on the islet out in the lake. And if you ask around as to which is the best, you'll get a different answer from everyone. In fact, they're all about the same quality, so choose one with a location that appeals. We like this one—located near the dock where the little ferries put in, so you get a lively scene along with the local specialties. (If you prefer a more natural setting, go to the **Propodes Restaurant** at the side of the Ayios Panteleimon Monastery, which you'll want to visit. See "A Boat Trip to the Islet of Nissi [Nisaki]," above.) You can pick your lobster, *karavides* (a cross between crayfish and shrimp), trout, or other fish of the day right out of holding tanks. If you're game, try one of the two local specialties: frogs' legs or eel. The white Zitsa Primus, a slightly sparkling white wine from the region, is a perfect accompaniment.

Nissi Ioannina (the offshore islet). © 26510/81-081. Fax 26510/81-631. Main courses 4€–12€. MC, V. High season daily 11am–midnight; low season daily 11am–10pm. Ferry from Ioannina's lakefront.

**The Pharos** GREEK  One of several restaurants set back from the lakefront, the Pharos should appeal to those who just want a good meal in a pleasant setting. In warm weather, you can sit under the awning in the square opposite. The menu is traditional but with some variants. For an appetizer, try the fried peppers in a garlic sauce. For your main course, order whatever's being grilled that day, and get the pilaf instead of potatoes. If you're feeling flush, try the crab or trout; if you're just there for the location, try the fresh fruit salad plate.

13 Plateia Mavili (down along lakefront). © 26510/26-506. Main courses 4.50€–12€. No credit cards. Daily 9am–10pm. Closed mid-Oct to Mar. Bus from Central Sq. or a 10-min. walk.

**To Mantelo** *Value* GREEK TAVERNA    Here's one for those who prefer their Greek tavernas to look traditional and to attract Greeks. It's a no-frills place that gives you a front-row seat on the square outside the old walled town, where all kinds of characters congregate. For an appetizer, try one of the fried-marinated dishes—peppers, squash, or eggplant. Go for any of the grilled dishes—veal, chicken, lamb—or the calves' liver. In all cases, ask for the pilaf. The taverna can feel cramped when it's crowded, but that's what makes it Greek.

Plateia Georgio 15 (opposite the main entrance to citadel). © 2651O/25-452. Main courses 3€–6.50€. No credit cards. Daily 10am–2am.

## 3 Side Trips from Ioannina

### DODONA (DODONI)

Even if you aren't the kind who chases after every classical ruin, this one offers a real reward: a spectacular theater at one of the major oracles of the ancient world. In August there are performances of the classical Greek dramas; ask at travel agencies if you wish to plan your visit around them.

**Dodona** ★ is located only 22km (14 miles) from Ioannina, so it can easily be visited in about 2 hours if you have a car. The bus service is inconvenient—basically only one bus very early in the morning, and then you're stuck here for many hours; it's better to spring for a **taxi**—about 35€ for the round-trip, including an hour's wait. The first 7km (4 miles) are on a main highway due south (signed to Arta); the turn to the left becomes (after an additional 3km/2 miles) an ascending and curving road. You'll arrive on a plateau ringed by mountains. The trip becomes part of the experience—you get the sense that you're on a pilgrimage to a remote shrine. Admission to the sacred precincts is 2€. In high season, it's open daily from 8am to 8pm; off season, Monday through Saturday from 10am to 3pm.

The **Oracle of Zeus** at Dodona traces its roots back to the early Hellenistic peoples who had arrived in northwestern Greece by about 2000 B.C. They themselves probably worshipped Zeus, but it now appears that at Dodona there was already some cult of the earth goddess, possibly with an oracle that based its interpretations on the flights of pigeons. In any case, by about 1400 B.C., it appears that the Zeus-worshipping Greeks had imposed their god on the site and turned the goddess into his consort, Dione.

By this time, too, the priests were linking Zeus's presence to the rustling leaves of an oak tree at Dodona and were interpreting these sounds as oracular messages. The Greeks set up a shrine around this tree, at first nothing more than a protective fence. Over the centuries they built more and more elaborate structures on the site, but the first temple to Zeus was not erected here until the 4th century B.C.

Eventually the oracle spoke through the bronze statue of a youth with a whip that was stirred by the wind to strike adjacent metal cauldrons, and the reverberating sound was interpreted. Many ambitious structures, both religious and secular, were erected at Dodona, but the oracle effectively ceased functioning in the 4th century A.D.—about the time when, it is claimed by some, the original oak died. The oak now on the site of the shrine is, of course, a recent planting.

Only traces of walls are left of other structures, but the magnificent **theater** survives, albeit thanks to what was virtually a reassembling in the 19th century. The first theater was built in the 3rd century B.C. and was said to have seated 17,000. It was destroyed, but another as large replaced it in the 2nd century B.C.

Later, the Romans converted it into an arena for gladiatorial contests. The theater was one of the largest on the Greek mainland and has almost the same marvelous acoustics as the famous (but smaller) one at Epidaurus. Even if you do not explore the other remains, just to sit in this theater for a while is an evocative experience.

## PERAMA CAVE ★

Only some 5km (3 miles) north of Ioannina (the turnoff is past the airport), this cave—actually more a series of caverns—was discovered in 1941, during World War II, when people were seeking hiding places. It has since been thoroughly developed, with electric lights, steps, and handrails that allow for a perfectly safe walk through. In high season, it's open daily from 8am to 8pm; in winter, from 9am to sunset (© 26510/81-521). Guided tours set out about every 15 minutes from the well-signed entrance in Perama village; the fee is 4€. The guides often don't speak much more English than to repeat the names assigned to unusually shaped stalagmites or stalactites, and they have an annoying habit of making everyone rush through—but you can in fact linger behind and join the next group!

Whether or not Perama lives up to its boast as one of the most spectacular caves in the world, it's worth a visit if you haven't been in many such caves. *Warning:* At the very end, you must climb what seems like an endless number of steps to come out of the cave—but at least you finish at a cafe!

## METSOVO ⊙★

This is a traditional mountain village that has become so popular that at times the original appeal is in danger of being overwhelmed by tourism at its worst. Still, most visitors find it satisfying—some even find it magical. It's about a 1½-hour bus ride east of Ioannina. Although there are a couple of buses to Metsovo in the morning, there's really only one back from Metsovo in the late afternoon that allows for a day in the village—so either pay close attention to the always-changing bus schedule or, better still, rent a car. (It can also be approached by buses coming from Athens or Thessaloniki.)

The village sits at about 1,000m (3,300 ft.) above sea level, nestled among peaks of the Pindos mountains, so in addition to attracting day-trippers, it draws serious nature lovers and hikers from all over Greece and Europe. Overnight accommodations are often strained, especially during Greek holidays. And because there are ski slopes nearby, Metsovo is a popular destination even during the winter.

Assuming that you'll come here on a day's excursion, what you will experience is a village that has maintained a certain style of architecture; traditional customs such as clothing and dances; crafts such as weaving, embroidery, and woodwork; and several food specialties. The buildings, of course, can be seen at all times just by strolling around. They're what most of us think of as Alpine style—stone, with wooden balconies and slate roofs. A declining few of the older people wear traditional clothing all the time, but the fancier costumes are worn only on Sundays and holidays.

If you want to see the **dances,** July 26 is the village's feast day, but also one of its most overcrowded days. **Crafts** are always on display and for sale in dozens of shops up and down the main street. Some is touristy kitsch, but some is authentically local and handsome. The best of the latter is at the **Metsovo Folk Art Cooperative,** about 50m (164 ft.) from the Egnatia Hotel on the slope above it. The traditional **Epirote foods** can be sampled in several restaurants (see "Where to Dine," below). Disneyland it ain't, but don't go to Metsovo thinking you're discovering a quaint native village. There's even a fairly ambitious conference center in town.

There remains yet another reason to go to Metsovo. It's the center (in Greece, at least) of the **Vlach people,** who claim descent from Latin-speaking Wallachians of what is now Romania. The Vlachs were originally shepherds who followed their flocks, and some still do just that; but over the centuries, many other Vlachs settled down in northern Greece and prospered in crafts, commerce, and trade. Some of the wealthier Vlachs have made their money from dealing in wool and other products from the flocks, and now many in Metsovo prosper from the tourist trade. Because the Vlachs wrote little of their distinctive Latin-based language down and because it's not taught in the schools, it's in danger of being lost as the new generation marry and move out of their relatively small circles. You'll find the Vlachs of Metsovo extremely congenial—and patient as foreigners constantly ask them to "say something in Vlach." (Don't expect your Latin to help much!)

In addition to walking about the village, there are several special attractions that may appeal. The **Museum of Folk Art** is in the Arhondiko Tositsa, a 17th-century mansion that's been completely restored by Baron Michalis Tositsa, a wealthy Vlach living in Switzerland. With its paneled rooms, furniture, rugs, clothing, crafts, and domestic furnishings of all kinds, it's a superb example of how a prosperous family might once have lived in Epirus. The museum, located on a road above the main street, is open in summer, Monday through Wednesday and Friday through Saturday from 8:30am to 1pm and 4 to 6pm; in winter, it's open the same days but from 3 to 5pm only. Admission is 2€.

Much more typical of Metsovo is the little **church of Ayia Paraskevi** on the main square, with its carved-wood altar screen, silver chandeliers, and copies of Ravenna mosaics.

And if you can handle the half-hour walk down and an hour walk (including frequent stops for air!) back up, you can visit the restored 14th-century **Moni Ayios Nikolaos.** A signed trail for this monastery leads off from the main square; take the second left, head for the clock tower, then follow the signs. You can drive closer to it by taking the road out of the town square (signed Ioannina) at about 1km (½ mile) turn left onto the asphalt road where it is signed Anilio, and wind downward for another 3.5km (2 miles); the monastery sits up on the slope and you have to scramble up through the vineyard. The resident caretaker (a lovely lady who has some of her own handsome weavings for sale) will allow entry during all reasonable hours (until 7:30pm in high season). The church has some quite spectacular 18th-century frescoes (long lost until the 1950s), a fine iconostasis, and several icons.

## WHERE TO STAY

If you want to overnight in Metsovo, there are about a dozen hotels to choose from, all quite acceptable and all to some degree decorated in the traditional style of the region.

**Galaxias** ⭐   If you want to be at the center of things, then this should be your choice—but it's for travelers who appreciate staying in a country inn. It's by no means a fancy hotel—the rooms are modest in size and decor, the bathrooms just adequate. Ask for a room in the front with a view of the distant mountains.

The homey atmosphere emanates from the Barbayanni family, who run this hotel and the restaurant reviewed below.

On a terrace above the main square. ✆ **26560/41-202.** Fax 26560/41-124. 10 units, some with shower, some with tub. High season 78€ double; low season 55€ double. Rates include continental breakfast. MC, V. *In room:* TV.

**Hotel Victoria** (★   If you want a more natural setting and a bit more luxury, try the Victoria, out on the edge of town. As you approach the hotel down a steep road, the traditional Epirote style of architecture will remind you somewhat of an Alpine inn. The interior, with its generous use of natural materials and large fireplaces (functioning in winter), plus its hearty furnishings, confirm this impression. The rooms are not especially large, but feel quite cozy; all have balconies and/or views. And because the Victoria is relatively new (from the late 1980s), its bathrooms are modern. The hotel maintains its own fine restaurant, but what you really come here for is the isolation and the views. In winter, it becomes a ski lodge, but it's highly popular year-round with Greeks and Europeans, so reservations are advised. By the way—the proprietors are Vlach—here's your chance to learn a few words!

About 1km (½ mile) from the main square. ✆ **26560/41-771.** Fax 26560/41-454. 37 units, some with shower, some with tub. Regular season 78€ double; Christmas and Easter seasons 95€. Rates include continental breakfast. MC, V. *In room:* TV.

**Kassaros Hotel**   For a location away from the square, but not as far as the Victoria, and as a favor to your budget, try the Kassaros Hotel. This is the perfect place for those who intend an extended or active stay in Metsovo—the proprietor also runs a travel agency, Kassaros Travel, which has ski equipment and a snowmobile for rent as well as its own buses for excursions throughout Epirus.

About 90m (300 ft.) along road leading from main square back to Ioannina. ✆ **26560/41-800.** Fax 26560/41-262. 31 units, some with shower, some with tub. High season 68€ double; low season 55€ double. Rates include continental breakfast. AE, DC, MC, V. *In room:* TV.

## WHERE TO DINE

Even if you spend only a few hours in Metsovo, you should try a meal at a restaurant that offers traditional Epirote fare. There are a couple decent ones along the main street, Tositsa—**Taverna Panormiko, Restaurant Toxotis,** and **Cafe Chroni Roof Garden**—but the following is far and away our favorite.

**Galaxias** (★  GREEK/REGIONAL   In warm weather, you can sit outdoors; in cooler weather, eat in the handsome dining room warmed by a cheerful fire. Begin a meal of the local specialties with the bean soup (*trachana*) or a cheese pie with leek. Move on to the spicy sausage or beef patties with leeks and celery baked in a pot. For dessert, try the baklava or yogurt, but be sure to save room for one of the local cheeses, of the smoked variety (*metsovonay*), or the mild *vlachotiri*. To accompany your meal, ask for the local red wine, Katoyi, or if that's in short supply, just the house wine.

In the Galaxias Hotel, just above the main square. ✆ **26560/41-202.** Main courses 3.50€–12€. MC, V. Daily noon–11pm.

# 15

# The Ionian Islands

*by John S. Bowman*

"The isles of Greece, the isles of Greece"—when Lord Byron tossed his bouquet, he was not under the spell of today's popular Cycladic islands but of the Ionian Islands. Located off Greece's northwest coast, the Ionians offer some of the loveliest natural settings (and beaches) in the country, a fine selection of hotels and restaurants, a distinctive history and lore, and some unusual architectural and archaeological sites.

The Ionians are rainier, greener, and more temperate than other Greek islands, with a high season lasting from late June to early September. The roads are generally in good condition, even if unavoidably steep and twisting. Accommodations range from luxury resorts to quiet little rooms on remote beaches. The local cuisine and wines offer numerous special treats. Among the best are *sofrito*, a spicy veal dish; *bourdetto*, a spicy fish dish; and the Theotaki and Liapaditiko wines.

The Ionian Islands include **Corfu** (Kerkira), **Paxos** (Paxoi), **Levkas** (Lefkas, Lefkada), **Ithaka** (Ithaki), **Kefalonia** (Kefallinia, Cephalonia), and **Zakinthos** (Zakynthos, Zante); the seventh, **Kithira** (Cythera, Cerigo), is linked only as a government administrative unit. There are many more islands in the archipelago along Greece's northwest coast, including several that are inhabited.

**STRATEGIES FOR SEEING THE ISLANDS** In this chapter, we single out **Corfu** and **Kefalonia**, with a side trip to **Ithaka**. With a couple of weeks to spare, you can take a ship or plane to either Corfu at the north or Zakinthos in the south and then make your way by ship to several of the others (although outside high season, you will have to do some backtracking). If you have only a week, you should fly to one and then use ships to get to a couple of the others. In either case, rent a car to get around the larger islands. If it comes down to visiting only one, Corfu is a prime candidate, but if you want to get off the beaten track, consider Kefalonia or Ithaka. All the Ionians—especially Corfu—are overrun in July and August; aim for June or September.

**A LOOK AT THE PAST** In the fabric of their history, the Ionian Islands can trace certain threads that both tie and distinguish them from the rest of Greece. During the late Bronze Age (1500–1200 B.C.), there was a Mycenaean culture on at least several of these islands. Although certain names of islands and cities were the same as those used today—Ithaka, for instance—scholars have never been able to agree on exactly which were the sites described in the *Odyssey*.

The islands were recolonized by people from the city-states on the Greek mainland, starting in the 8th century B.C. The Peloponnesian War, in fact, can be traced back to a quarrel between Corinth and its colony at Corcyra (Corfu) that led to Athens's interference and eventually the full-scale war. The islands later fell under the rule of the Romans, then the

**Tips** **Kerkira=Corfu**

Kerkira is the modern Greek name for Corfu. Look for it in many schedules, maps, and so on.

Byzantine empire, and remained prey to warring powers and pirates in this part of the Mediterranean for centuries. By the end of the 14th century, Corfu fell under Venice's control, and the Italian language and culture—including the Roman Catholic church—came to predominate.

With the fall of Venice to Napoleon's France in 1797, the French took over and held sway until 1815. The Ionian Islands then became a protectorate of the British; although the islands did experience peace and prosperity, they were in fact a colony. When parts of Greece gained true

independence from the Turks by 1830—due in part to leadership from Ionians such as Ioannis Capodistrias—many Ionians became restless under the British. Attempts at gaining union with Greece culminated with Prime Minister Gladstone's granting this in 1864.

During World War II, the islands were at first occupied by the Italians, but when the Germans took over from them, the islands, especially Corfu, suffered greatly. Since 1945, the Ionian Islands have enjoyed considerable prosperity, due mainly to the waves of tourists.

## 1 Corfu (Kerkira)

32km (20 nautical miles) W of mainland; another 558km (342 miles) NW of Athens

There's Corfu the coast, Corfu the town, and Corfu the island, and they don't necessarily appeal to the same vacationers. Corfu the coast lures those who want to escape civilization and head for the water—whether an undeveloped little beach, with a simple taverna and some rooms to rent, or a spectacular resort. Then there's the more cosmopolitan **Corfu town**, with its distinctive layers of Greek, Italian, French, and British elements. Finally, there's a third and little-known Corfu, the interior with its lush vegetation and gentle slopes, modest villages and farms, and countless olive and fruit trees. (It should also be admitted that there's now a fourth Corfu—rather tacky beach resorts crowded with "package tourists" from Western Europe who sometimes can be a bit raucous. We prefer to think that our readers will know enough to avoid this Corfu.)

Whichever Corfu you choose, it should prove pleasing. It was, after all, this island's ancient inhabitants, the Phaeacians, who made Odysseus so comfortable. Visitors today will find Corfu similarly hospitable.

## ESSENTIALS

**GETTING THERE** **By Plane** **Olympic Airways** provides at least three flights daily from and to Athens and three flights weekly from and to Thessaloniki. One-way fare for each route is about 135€. The Olympic Airways office in Corfu town (© 26610/38-694) is at 11 Polila, down from the Ionian Islands Tourism Office, but many agents all over town sell tickets. **Aegean Airlines** also offers occasional but slightly cheaper flights; in Athens, call © 210/998-8422; in Corfu, call © 26610/27-070.

**Corfu Airport** is about 4km (2½ miles) south of the center of Corfu town. Fortunately, the flight patterns of most planes do not bring them over the city,

## Western Greece & the Ionian Islands

**527**

Ferry Routes
Mountain

ALBANIA

Paleokastritsa
Corfu Town
Benitses
Kavos
CORFU (KERKIRA)

Lakka
PAXOS
ANTIPAXOS

Filiates
Igoumenitsou
Margariti
Parga

ZAGORI
Perama
Metsovo
Trikkala
Islet of Nissi
Lake Pamvotis
Ioannina
Dodona
6
5
E15
EPIRUS

Paramythia
Nikopolis
Preveza
Action (Actium)
Lefkas
LEFKADA
Vassiliki
Nydri

Zalongo
Arta
Ambracian Gulf
Vonitsa
5
Amfilohia
Aetos
Agrinio
Mitikas
E19
Messolongi

Antirrio
Rio
Gulf of Patras
Patras
9
PELOPONNESE
74
Amalias
Pirgos

Astakos
Frikes
Vathy
ITHAKA
Sami
Poros
Skala

Fiskardo
KEFALONIA
Lixouri
Argostoli
Metaxata

Kyllini
Zakinthos
Vassilikos
Laganas
ZAKINTHOS

Ionian Sea

To Ancona, Bari & Brindisi

25 mi
25 km

N

Greece
Athens
Aegean Sea
WESTERN GREECE & THE IONIAN ISLANDS
Mediterranean Sea

Everyone takes taxis into town; a standard fare should be about 8€ but may fluctuate with the destination, amount of luggage, and time of day.

**By Boat** There are many lines and ships linking Corfu to both Greek and foreign ports. There are ferries almost hourly between Igoumenitsou, directly across on the mainland (1–2 hr.), and several weekly to and from Patras (about 7 hr.). At least during high season, there is now a twice-daily hydrofoil express (about 30 min.) between Corfu and Igoumenitsou. Also in high season are daily ships linking Corfu to one or another ports in Italy—Ancona, Bari, Brindisi, Trieste, Venice—or to Piraeus and/or Patras. The schedules and fares vary so much from year to year that it would be misleading to provide details here; deal with a travel agent in your homeland or Greece (or Italy). The ship lines involved are **Adriatica** (© 210/429-0487 in Piraeus), **ANEK Lines** (© 210/323-3481 in Athens), **Fragline** (© 210/821-4171 in Athens), **Hellenic Mediterranean Line (HML)** (© 210/422-5341 in Piraeus), **Minoan Lines** (© 210/408-0006 in Piraeus), **Strintzis Lines** (© 210/422-5015 in Piraeus), and **Ventouris Line** (© 210/988-9280 in Piraeus). In high season, the typical one-way cost from Brindisi or Ancona to Corfu is about 176€ to 200€ for two people in a double cabin and with a (standard-size) vehicle.

Corfu town is also one of Greece's official entry/exit harbors, with customs and health authorities as well as passport control. This is of special concern to those arriving from foreign lands on yachts.

**By Bus** KTEL offers service all the way from Athens or Thessaloniki, with a ferry carrying you between Corfu and Igoumenitsou on the mainland opposite. This mode of transportation also allows you to get on or off at main points along the way, such as Ioannina. The buses are comfortable enough, but be prepared for many hours of winding roads. The **KTEL office** (© **26610/39-627**) is located along Leoforos Avramiou, up from the New Port.

**VISITOR INFORMATION** The **Ionian Islands Tourism Directorate** office (© **26610/37-520**; fax 26610/30-298) is on the second floor of a modern building (unnumbered) on the corner of Rizospaston and Polila in the new town, a block across from the post office. It's open Monday through Friday from 8:30am to 1:00pm; in July and August, also open on Saturdays. You can only hope that they will have a supply of brochures with maps of the town and island.

**GETTING AROUND By Bus** The dark-blue public buses service Corfu town, its suburbs, and nearby destinations. The semiprivate green-and-cream KTEL buses offer frequent service to points all over the island—Paleokastritsa, Glifada, Sidari, and more. For the KTEL station, see "Getting There," above.

**By Taxi** In and around Corfu town, a taxi is probably your best bet—sometimes the only way around, such as to and from the harbor and the airport. Although taxi drivers are supposed to use their meters, many don't, so you should agree on the fare before setting out. You may also decide to use a taxi to visit some of the sites outside Corfu town; again, be sure to agree on the fare beforehand.

**By Car** There are myriad car-rental agencies all over Corfu; even so, in high season it can be very difficult to get a vehicle at the spur of the moment. If you're sure of your plans on Corfu, make arrangements with an established international agency before departing home. Otherwise, try **Greek Skies Travel Agency**, in Corfu town at 20A Kapodistriou (© **26610/33-410**; fax 26610/36-161), or **Avanti Rent A Car**, 12A Ethnikis Antistasseos, along the new port (© **26610/42-028**).

**Corfu Town** map

- Information ⓘ
- 0 300 m / 0 300 y

**NEW PORT**

**OLD PORT**

**NEW FORTRESS (NEO FROURIO)**

**OLD VENETIAN QUARTER**

**OLD FORTRESS, (PALEO FROURIO)**

Mandraki Harbor

Garitsa Bay

Avrami Hill

San Rocco Square Local Bus Station

Bus Station

Streets: Xenofondos Stratigou, Donzelot, Arseniou, N. Theotoki, Zavitsianou, Solomou, Velissariou, G. Markora, I. Theotoki, Polichroni Konstanda, Avramiou, Mitropolis Methodou, G. Theotoki, Paleologo, Pandova, Dessila, N. Zambell, Voulgareos, Guilford, Kapodistriou, Eleftherias, Plateia, Esplanade, Espalande, Vraila, Alexandros, Rizospaston Voulefton, Dimokratias

Inset map: **WESTERN GREECE & THE IONIAN ISLANDS**, Greece, Athens, Aegean Sea, Ionian Sea, Mediterranean Sea, Corfu Town

Archaeological Museum **7**
Ayios Spyridon Cathedral **4**
Byzantine Museum **2**
Ionian Academy **6**
Museum of Asian Art **3**
Palace of St. Michael & St. George **3**
Synagogue **1**
Town Hall **5**

**By Moped**   It's easy to rent all kinds of mopeds and motorcycles, but the roads are so curvy, narrow, and steep that you should be very experienced before taking on such a vehicle. And insist on a helmet.

**CITY LAYOUT**   The **new town** of Corfu town is relatively modern and even a bit cosmopolitan. You probably won't be spending much time in this new town, except for visits to the post office or the GNTO office.

It's easy to spend several days wandering through the **old town**, with its *cantouni*, Greece's largest complex of picturesque streets and buildings, effectively unchanged for many centuries. The crown jewel of the old town is the **Liston,** the arcaded row of cafes where you can spend a lazy afternoon watching a cricket match on the great green of the adjacent Esplanade (Spianada).

**FAST FACTS**   The official **American Express** agent for Corfu is Greek Skies Travel Agency, 20A Kapodistriou (© 26610/33-410; fax 26610/36-161). There are numerous **banks** in both the Old Town and New Town; you'll find ATMs on most of their exteriors. The **British Consul** is at 1 Menekrates (© 26610/30-055), at the south end of the town, near the Menekrates monument; it will take care of all British Commonwealth citizens. There is no U.S. consulate in Corfu. The **hospital** is on Julius Andreatti, and is signed from around town.

There are two convenient **Internet cafes:** the Online Cafe, 28 Kapodistriou, along the Esplanade (cafe_online1@yahoo.com), and the Netoikos, on 14 Kalochairetou, behind Ayios Spiridon Church; both are open daily from late morning to late evening. You can count on quick, careful, and fair-priced **laundry** or **dry cleaning** at the Peristeri, 42 Ioannis Theotikos (leading from San Rocco Square on the way to the KTEL Bus Terminal). It's open Monday through Saturday from 8am to 2pm, with additional hours on Tuesday, Thursday, and Friday from 6 to 8pm. The **police station** (© **26610/39-575**) is at 19 Leoforos Alexandros (near the post office). The **post office** (© **26610/25-544**) is at 26 Leoforos Alexandros. It's open Monday through Friday from 7:30am to 8pm; in July and August, it's usually open for a few hours on Saturday. The main **telephone office** (OTE) is at 9 Mantzarou; it's open Monday through Friday from 7:00am to midnight, to 10pm on Saturdays and holidays.

## WHAT TO SEE & DO
### THE TOP ATTRACTIONS

**Archaeological Museum** (★)    Even if you're not a devotee of ancient history or museums, you should take an hour to visit this small museum. On your way to see its masterwork, as you turn left off the upstairs vestibule, you'll pass the **stone lion** dating from around 575 B.C. (found in the nearby Menekrates tomb, along the waterfront just down from the museum). Go around and behind it to the large room with arguably the finest example of Archaic temple sculpture extant, the **pediment from the Temple of Artemis.** (The temple itself is located just south of Corfu town and dates from about 590 B.C. The remains are not of interest to most people.) The pediment features the **Gorgon Medusa,** attended by two pantherlike animals. You don't need to be an art historian to note how this predates the great classical works such as the Elgin marbles—not only in the naiveté of its sculpture but also in the emphasis on the monstrous, with the humans so much smaller.

Interesting for comparison is the fragment from another Archaic pediment found at Figare, Corfu. Displayed in an adjoining room, it shows Dionysos and a youth reclining on a couch. In this work, only a century younger than the Gorgon pediment, the humans have reduced the animal in size and placed it under the couch.

1 P. Armeni-Vraila. (on the corner of Demokratias, the boulevard along the waterfront) © **26610/30-680.** Admission 4€; free on Sun. Tues–Sun 8:30am–2:30pm. Wheelchair accessible.

**The Kalypso Star** (*Kids*)    The *Kalypso Star* is a glass-bottomed boat that takes small groups on trips offshore and provides a fascinating view of the marine life and undersea formations.

Old Port. Corfu town. © **26610/46-525.** Fax 26710/23-506. Fee 10€ adults, 5€ children. In high season, trips leave daily, hourly from 10am–6pm, plus a 10pm night trip; off season, call for schedule.

**Museum of Asian Art**    The museum's building itself is an impressive example of neoclassical architecture. It was constructed between 1819 and 1824 to serve as the residence of the Lord High Commissioner, the British ruler of the Ionian islands; to house the headquarters of the Order of St. Michael and St. George; and to provide the assembly room for the Ionian senate. When the British turned the Ionians over to Greece, this building was given to the king of Greece. As the king seldom spent much time here, it fell into disrepair, until after World War II when it was restored and turned into a museum.

The centerpiece of the museum is the collection of Chinese porcelains, bronzes, and other works from the Shang Dynasty (1500 B.C.) to the Ching Dynasty (19th c.). There are also strong holdings of Japanese works—woodblock prints, ceramics, sculpture, watercolors, and *netsuke* (carved sash fasteners). You may not have come to Greece to appreciate Asian art, but this is one of several unexpected delights in Corfu.

The Palace of St. Michael and St. George, north end of Esplanade. © 26610/38-124. protocol@hepka. culture.gr. Admission 4€. Tues–Sun 8am–2:30pm.

**Old Fort (Paleo Frourio)**  Originally a promontory attached to the mainland, its two peaks—*koryphi* in Greek—gave the modern name to the town and island; the promontory itself was for a long time the main town (and appears as such in many old engravings). The Venetians dug the moat in the 16th century, enabling them to hold off several attempts by the Turks to conquer this outpost of Christianity; the apparent Greek temple at the south side is in fact a British church (1830). Each peak is crowned by a castle; you can get fine views of Albania to the east and Corfu, town and island, to the west.

In summer, a **Sound-and-Light** show is held several nights a week (in different foreign languages, so be sure to check the schedule).

The Esplanade (opposite the Liston). Admission 4€ adults, 2€ students and seniors over 60. Tues–Fri 8am–8pm; Sat–Sun and holidays 8:30am–3pm.

**The Petrakis Line**  During high season, this line offers several 1-day excursions a week to destinations including Albania, Kefalonia, and Paxoi. On Kefalonia, you visit the Melissani Grotto and the Drogarati Cave (see later in this chapter) but not Argostoli. The excursion to Albania has become fairly popular these days, but be aware that you do not get to the capital, Tirana; the fare for a day trip—including lunch—now costs about 60€ but there are several other fees for visas, additional meals, and such.

9 Venizelou, New Port, Corfu town. © 266/103-1649. Fax 26610/38-787. petrakis@hol.gr.

## A STROLL AROUND CORFU TOWN

This is definitely a browser's town, where as you're strolling around in search of a snack or souvenir, you'll serendipitously discover an old church or monument. To orient yourself, start with the **Esplanade area** bounded by the Old Fort (see above) and the sea on one side; the small haven below and to the north of the Old Fort is known as **Mandraki Harbor**, while the shore to the south is home port to the **Corfu Yacht Club.**

The Esplanade is bisected by Dousmani; at the far side is the circular monument in the center of the Ionian Islands with Greece in 1864. The north part has the field known as the **Plateia,** where cricket games are played on lazy afternoons. At the far north side of the Esplanade is the Palace of St. Michael and St. George, now housing the **Museum of Asian Art** (see above). If you proceed along the left (northwest) corner of the palace, you'll come out above the coast and can make your way around Arseniou above the medieval sea walls (known as the *mouragia*).

On your way you will pass (on the left, up a flight of stairs) the **Byzantine Museum** in the **Church of Antivouniotissa.** Even those who have never been especially taken by Byzantine art should enjoy its small but elegant selection of icons from around Corfu; of particular interest are works by Cretan artists who came to Corfu, some of whom went on to Venice. It's open Monday from 12:30 to 7pm, Tuesday through Saturday from 8am to 7pm, and Sunday and holidays from 8:30am to 3pm. Admission is 3€.

Proceed along the coast road and come down to the square at the Old Port; above its far side rises the **New Fortress,** and beyond this is the New Port. Off to the left of the square is a large gateway, what remains of the 16th-century Porta Spilia; proceeding through this leads you into the Plateia Solomou.

If you go left from Plateia Solomou along Velissariou, you'll see on the right (with the green doors) the 300-year-old **Synagogue,** with its collection of torah crowns. It's open on Saturday from 9am until early evening. To gain entry during the week, call the Jewish Community Center at ☏ **26610/38-802.**

This is now a good way to continue into the section of Old Corfu known as **Campiello,** with its stepped streets and narrow alleys. You may often feel lost in a labyrinth—and you will be—but sooner or later you'll emerge onto one or another busy commercial street that will bring you down to the Esplanade.

Heading south on the Esplanade, you'll see a bandstand and at its far end the **Maitland Rotunda,** commemorating Sir Thomas Maitland, the first British lord high commissioner of the Ionian Islands. Past this is the statue of Count Ioannis Kapodistrias (1776–1836), the first president of independent Greece. On the edge of the south end of the Esplanade is a newly renovated building that once housed the Ionian Academy and is now used by the Ionian University.

If you head south along the shore road from this end of the Esplanade, you'll pass the Corfu Palace Hotel (see below) on your right; then the **Archaeological Museum** (see above), up Vraila on the right. After two more blocks, off to the right on the corner of Marasli, you'll see the **Tomb of Menekrates,** a circular tomb of a notable who drowned about 600 B.C. Proceeding to the right here onto Leoforos Alexandros will bring you into the heart of new Corfu town.

Back at the Esplanade, the western side of the north half is lined by a wide tree-shaded strip filled with cafe tables and chairs, then a street reserved for pedestrians, and then arcaded buildings patterned after Paris's Rue de Rivoli. These arcaded buildings, known as the **Liston,** were begun by the French and finished by the British. Sit here with a cup of coffee (or a glass of ginger beer) and enjoy the passing scene.

At the back of the Liston is **Kapadistrion,** and perpendicular from this extend several streets that lead into the heart of Old Corfu—a mélange of fine shops, old churches, souvenir stands, and other stores in a maze of streets, alleys, and squares that seem like Venice without the water. The broadest and most stylish is **Nikiforio Theotoki.** At the northern end of Kapadistrion, you turn left onto Ayios Spiridon and come to the corner of Filellinon and the **Ayios Spiridon Cathedral,** dedicated to Spiridon, the patron saint of Corfu. A 4th-century bishop of Cyprus, Spiridon is credited with saving Corfu from famine, plagues, and a Turkish siege. The church hosts the saint's embalmed body in a silver casket, as well as precious gold and silver votive offerings and many fine old icons. Four times a year the faithful parade the remains of St. Spiridon through the streets of old Corfu: on Palm Sunday, Holy Saturday, August 1, and the first Sunday in November.

Proceeding up Voulgareos behind the southern end of the Liston, you'll come up along the back of the **Town Hall,** built in 1663 as a Venetian loggia; it later served as a theater. Turn into the square it faces and enter into what seems like a Roman piazza, with steps and terraces, the Roman Catholic cathedral on the left, and, reigning over the top, the restored Catholic archbishop's residence (now housing the Bank of Greece).

From here, finish your walk by wandering up and down and in and out the streets of old Corfu.

## SHOPPING

Corfu town has so many shops selling jewelry, leather goods, olive wood objects, and handmade needlework that it is impossible to single out one or another. All we can advise is to look around—especially along Filarmonikis (off N. Teotoki), if needlework's your thing—and select something that pleases; prices are generally fair and uniform.

One would never recommend a trip to Corfu JUST for the kumquat liqueur, but this Chinese fruit has been cultivated on the island since the late 1800s and the liqueur makes a unique treat—or gift if it doesn't appeal to you!

Standing out from the many standard souvenir-gift shops, **Antica,** 25 Ayios Spiridon, leading away from the north end of Liston (© 26610/32-401), offers unusual older jewelry, plates, textiles, brass, and icons. **Gravures,** 64 Ev. Voulgareos, where the street emerges from the old town to join the new town (© 26610/41-721), has a fine selection of engravings and prints of scenes from Corfu, all nicely matted. Originals (taken from old books or magazines) can cost 150€, reproductions as little as 10€. The elegant **Terracotta,** 2 Filarmonikis, just off N. Theotoki, the main shopping street (© and fax 26610/45-260), sells only contemporary Greek work: jewelry, one-of-a-kind pieces, ceramics, and small sculptures, some by well-known Greek artists and artisans. Nothing is cheap, but everything is classy.

There is no end of ceramics to be found in Corfu, but we like the **Pottery Workshop,** 15km (10 miles) north of Corfu on the right of the road to Paleokastritsa (© 26610/90-704), where you get to observe Sofoklis Ikonomides and Sissy Moskidou making and decorating all the pottery on sale here. Whether decorative or functional, something here will certainly appeal to your taste. Two kilometers (1¼ mile) further along the road, on the left, is the **Wood's Nest,** offering a large selection of olive wood objects just slightly cheaper than in town.

## WHERE TO STAY

The island of Corfu has an apparently inexhaustible choice of accommodations, but in high season (July and Aug) many will be taken by package groups from Europe. Reservations are recommended if you have specific preferences for that period, especially for Corfu town.

## IN TOWN
### Very Expensive

**Corfu Palace Hotel** ✹✹    This is a grand hotel with every creature comfort, modern business and conference services, and elegant service that lives up to its decor. It combines the most up-to-date features of a Swiss enterprise (which it is) with Greek hospitality. The landscaping creates a tropical ambience; the lobby and public areas bespeak luxury. Bedrooms are not exceptionally large, but they are highly comfortable and well appointed. (For those who want something grander, there are executive and VIP suites.) Bathrooms are large and marbled! All units enjoy balconies and views of the sea. Aside from the splendid surroundings, superb service, and grand meals, the main appeal of this hotel is probably its combination of restful isolation above the bay with its proximity to the city center. The hotel's two restaurants, the Scheria (a grill room on the poolside terrace) and the Panorama (with a view of the bay), serve both Greek and international menus; both vie to claim the finest cuisine on Corfu. Guests can use the facilities of the nearby Corfu Tennis Club and Yacht Club and the Corfu Golf Club, 14km (9 miles) away.

2 Leoforos Demokratias (along Garitsa Bay, just south of center), 49100 Corfu. © 26610/39-485 to 487. Fax 26610/31-749. www.corfupalace.com. 115 units. High season 200€–300€ double; low season 150€–225€ double. Children up to age 12 stay free in parents' room (without meals). Rates include buffet

breakfast; half-board available. AE, DC, MC, V. Free parking. A 5-min. walk from Esplanade. **Amenities:** 2 restaurants; 3 bars; 3 pools (1 for children); night-lit tennis courts nearby; game room; concierge; tours and car rentals arranged; conference facilities; bicycle rentals; salon; 24-hr. room service; babysitting; 1-day laundry and dry-cleaning; newspaper delivery. *In room:* A/C, TV, minibar, safe, hair dryer.

## Moderate

If you prefer old-fashioned period hotels to shiny new accommodations, consider the **Astron Hotel,** 15 Donzelot (waterfront road down to old harbor), 49100 Corfu (✆ **26610/39-505;** fax 26610/33-708). Renovated in 2001, it offers up-to-date bathrooms and other facilities while retaining touches of its original charm.

**Arcadion Hotel** (★) This hotel's total renovation—in fact, more like a total reconstruction—completed in late 2000, now makes it as pleasurable as it is convenient. The new rooms now have furniture and fabrics in a traditional Corfiot style; bathrooms are up to the highest standards for this class. If you like to be at the center of a city, you can't get much closer than this: When you step out the door, the Esplanade and the Liston are 15m (50 ft.) away (while a beach is only about 900m/270 ft. away). Admittedly, this also means that on pleasant evenings there will be crowds in front of the hotel, but just ask for a room off the front. (All windows are double-glazed for sound control.) Hard to beat for location and comfort. And in the evenings, you can sit on their new roof garden and enjoy cool drink with a fabulous view.

44 Kapodistriou 44 (catercorner from south end of Liston, facing the Esplanade), 49100 Corfu. ✆ **26610/30-104.** Fax 26610/45-087. 33 units. High season 130€ double; low season 110€ double. Rates include buffet breakfast. AE, MC, V. Open year-round. Public parking lot (fee) nearby. **Amenities:** Restaurant; bar; health club; concierge; tours and car rentals arranged; 24-hr. room service; 1-day laundry and dry cleaning; salon. *In room:* A/C, TV, minibar, hair dryer, safe, computer dataport.

**Bella Venezia** (Value) Like the gold-medal winner of the decathlon, this hotel may not win in any single category, but its combined virtues make it the first choice of many. The building is a restored neoclassical mansion, with character if not major distinction. The location is just a bit off center and lacks fine views, but it's quiet and close enough to any place you'd want to walk to; a decent beach is 300 yards away. The common areas are not especially stylish, but do have a certain atmosphere. Although not luxurious or large, the guest rooms have some old-world touches; the showers, however, are undeniably cramped. There is no restaurant, but there's a colorful patio-garden for breakfast and an enclosed kiosk for light snacks. Finally, its rates are below what similar hotels charge.

4 N. Zambeli (approached from far south end of Esplanade), 49100 Corfu. ✆ **26610/46-500.** Fax 26610/20-708. belvenit@hol.gr. 32 units. High season 90€ double; low season 70€ double. Rates include buffet breakfast. AE, DC, MC, V. Open year-round. Parking on adjacent streets. Within walking distance of old and new town. *In room:* A/C, TV.

**Cavalieri** (★) If you like your hotels in the discreet old European style, this place is for you; those who prefer glitz should look elsewhere. The Cavalieri is in an old building with a small elevator. The main lounge is Italian-velvet, its restaurant is nothing special, service is low-key, rooms are spare, and bathrooms standard. But the hotel must be doing something right, as advance reservations are usually required. Location answers for much of the appeal: Ask for one of the front rooms on the upper floors, which boast great views of the Old Fort. Another draw is the rooftop garden, which after 6:30pm offers drinks, sweets, and light meals along with a spectacular view; even if you don't stay here, it's a grand place to pass an hour in the evening.

4 Kapodistriou (at far south end of Esplanade), 49100 Corfu. © **26610/39-041.** Fax 26610/39-283. 50 units. High season 100€; low season 75€. Rates include buffet breakfast. AE, DC, MC, V. Open year-round. Parking on adjacent streets. Within easy walking distance of old and new town. **Amenities:** Bar; concierge; tours and car rentals arranged; room service 7am–midnight; 1-day laundry and dry cleaning. *In room:* A/C, TV, minibar, hair dryer.

## OUTSIDE TOWN
### Expensive

**Corfu Holiday Palace (formerly Hilton)** ★ This is a grand hotel in the contemporary manner—more like a resort in the range of its facilities and amenities. Its lobby sets the tone—spacious and relaxed—while the staff is professional yet friendly. Rooms are standard Greek-hotel-size, with comfortable beds and state-of-the art bathrooms. The grounds create a semitropical ambience. In addition to the pools, there's a lovely private beach down below. The famous locale known as Kanoni is a couple hundred yards from the hotel. The island's airport is off in the middle distance—not a major problem unless your windows are open, but we suggest you ask for a room facing the sea and not the airport. Patrons get a 50% discount at Corfu Golf Club (18km/12 miles away) and—perhaps the biggest surprise of all—there's a casino on the premises.

P.O. Box 124, Nausicaa, Kanoni (some 5km/3 miles south of Corfu town), 49100 Corfu. © **26610/36-540.** Fax 26610/36-551. 266 units. High season 125€–150€ double; low season 85€–100€ double. Rates include buffet breakfast. Half board includes a fixed price menu. Special packages for extended stays. AE, DC, MC, V. Open year-round. Free parking on grounds. Hotel offers a shuttle bus; public bus no. 2 stops 200m (656 ft.) away; a taxi is easily summoned. **Amenities:** 2 restaurants; 2 bars; 2 pools; night-lit tennis courts; watersports equipment; health club; concierge; tours and car rentals arranged; conference facilities; boutiques; salon; babysitting; 1-day laundry and dry cleaning; jogging track; bowling, billiards, table tennis. *In room:* A/C, TV, minibar, hair dryer.

### Inexpensive

**Hotel Royal** (Value This might be considered an alternative to the nearby Corfu Holiday Palace if your desire is to stay outside Corfu town but you can't afford the Palace. It's a kind of funky place: The architecture is neo-baroque, the interior decor is folksy, and the lobby is filled with traditional works of art. The rooms and bathrooms are standard but there is no air-conditioning or TV. The most spectacular features are the three tiered pools—it's a great place to come back to (in high season only) with the kids after a day spent sightseeing. As with the Palace, the airport is off in the middle distance, but the noise problem exists only during a relatively small portion of the day. It's a big hotel with a family atmosphere, and you can't beat the rates.

110 Figareto, Kanoni (3km/2 miles from Corfu center, a few hundred yards before Corfu Holiday Palace, above), 49100 Corfu. © **26610/37-512.** Fax 26610/38-786. 125 units. High season 55€ double; low season 45€ double. Rates include continental breakfast. No credit cards. Closed Nov–Mar. Parking on grounds. Public bus no. 2 stops 100m away, but a taxi may be easier. **Amenities:** 3 pools; concierge; tours and car rentals arranged.

## WHERE TO DINE
### IN TOWN
### Expensive

If you're in a celebratory mood, you might also consider **Chambor**, 71 Guilford (© **26610/39-031**); certainly a cut above your average Greek restaurant but much of what you pay goes for the elaborate settings and presentation.

**Venetian Well** ★ MIDDLE EASTERN/INTERNATIONAL/GREEK This remains our top pick in Corfu town. Diners sit at a candlelit table in a rather austere little square with a Venetian wellhead (1699) and a church opposite. (When the weather changes, guests sit in a stately room with a mural.) The atmosphere is as discreet as the food is inventive. There is no printed menu—you learn what's available from a chalkboard or from your waiter—and there's no predicting what the kitchen will offer on any given evening. Since the chef uses seasonal vegetables, salads vary from month to month. Main courses may range from standard Greek dishes such as beef *giouvetsi* (cooked in a pot) to chicken prepared with exotic ingredients. The wine list is more extensive than in most Greek restaurants. Plateia Kremasti (small square up from Old Harbor, behind Greek Orthodox cathedral). © 26610/44-761. Reservations recommended in high season. Main courses 10€–20€. No credit cards. Open year-round Mon–Sat noon–midnight.

## Moderate

If you want to dine along the coast, consider **Antranik,** 19 Arseniou (© 26610/22-301), located under the awnings on the seaside of the road leading from north of the Esplanade down to the New Port. **Faliraki,** at the corner of Kapodistrias and Arseniou, below the wall (© 26610/30-392), also has a wonderful location, right on the water (although the food is standard Greek fare).

**Aegli Garden Restaurant** GREEK/CONTINENTAL   The tasty and varied menu of this old favorite attracts both residents and transients to its several dining areas—indoors, under the arcade, along the pedestrian mall of Kapodistriou, or under awnings across from the arcade. Try the selection of *orektika* with some of the wine or beer on tap. The staff takes special pride in their Corfiote specialties, several of which are traditional Greek foods with rather spicy sauces: filet of fish, octopus, *pastitsada* (baked veal), *baccala* (salted cod fish), and *sofrito* (veal). If spiciness isn't your thing, try the swordfish or prawns. Everything is done with great care, including a delicious fresh-fruit salad that you can order by itself. 23 Kapodistriou (within Liston). © 26610/31-949. Fax 26610/45-488. Main courses 5€–12€. AE, DC, MC, V. Open year-round daily 9am–1am.

**Bellissimo** GREEK/INTERNTIONAL   This restaurant has lived up to its promise of being a welcome addition to the Corfu scene—unpretentious but tasty. Located on a central and lovely town square, it's run by the hospitable Stergiou family, Corfiots who returned from Canada. They offer a standard Greek menu with some "exotics," including hamburgers and chicken curry. Especially welcome is their modestly priced "Greek sampling plate"—tzatziki, tomatoes-and-cucumber salad, *keftedes* (meatballs), fried potatoes, grilled lamb, and pork souvlaki.
Plateia Lemonia (just off N. Theotoki). © 26610/41-112. Main courses 4€–13€. No credit cards. Daily 10:30am–11pm.

**Gloglas Taverna** GREEK   You want authenticity? This is it, right on a corner in the heart of the old town, a block back from the Esplanade. You sit under a grape arbor among your fellow diners, a mixture of locals and tourists, united in their desire for a no-nonsense taverna meal. The specialties of the house tend to be off the spit or grill. Winners include souvlaki (kebab), chicken, pork, and kokoretsia (lambs' intestines roasted on the spit). The cooked vegetables—green beans, eggplant, and whatever is in season—are also tasty. Add a glass of the house red and you'll wonder why anyone would want to go to a fancier place.
16 Guilford. © 26610/37-147. Main courses 4€–10€. No credit cards. Daily 11:30am–midnight.

## CORFU TOWN AFTER DARK

Corfu town definitely has a nightlife scene, though many people are content to linger over dinner and then, after a promenade, repair to one of the cafes at the

Liston, such as the **Capri, Liston, Europa,** or **Aegli**—all of which have a similar selection of light refreshments and drinks. (Treat yourself to the fresh-fruit salad at the Aegli!) Others are drawn to the cafes at the north end of the Esplanade, just outside the Liston—**Café Bar 92,** the **Magnet,** or **Cool Down.** For a special treat, ascend to the rooftop cafe/bar at the **Cavalieri** hotel (see "Where to Stay," above). Another change of scene is the **Lindos Café,** overlooking the beach and facilities of the Nautical Club of Corfu; it is approached by a flight of steps leading off Leoforos Demokratias, just south and outside the Esplanade. And one of the best-kept secrets of Corfu town is the little **Art Café,** to the right and behind the Palace that now houses the Museum of Asian Art; its garden provides a wonderful cool and quiet retreat from the hustle and bustle of the rest of the town.

If you enjoy a bit more action, there are several nightspots along the coast to the north, between Corfu town and the beach resort of Gouvia; they include **Ekati,** a typical Greek nightclub; **Esperides,** featuring Greek music; and **Corfu by Night,** definitely touristy. Be prepared to drop some money at these places.

As for the younger crowd, there are any number of places that go in and out of favor (and business) from year to year. Among the more enduring up around the Esplanade are the relatively sedate **Aktaion,** just to the right of the Old Fort, and the **Café Classico,** in an old mansion at 10 Kapodistriou, featuring the latest music. Young people seeking more excitement go down past the New Port to a strip of flashy discos—**Apokalypsis, Hippodrome,** and **DNA.** Be aware that these clubs charge a cover (usually about 10€, including one drink).

In summer, there are frequent **concerts** by the town's orchestras and bands, mostly free, on the Esplanade. Corfu town boasts the oldest band in Greece. The **Sound-and-Light** performances are described in the listing for the Old Fort (see "What to See & Do," earlier in this chapter). September brings the **Corfu Festival,** with concerts, ballet, opera, and theater performances by a mix of Greek and international companies. **Carnival** is celebrated on the last Sunday before Lent with a parade and a burning of an effigy representing the spirit of Carnival.

For those who like to gamble, there's a well-known **casino** at the **Corfu Holiday Palace** (see "Where to Stay," above), a few miles outside of town. Bets are a 4€ minimum and a 750€ maximum. Open nightly, it may not have the glamour of Monte Carlo, but it attracts quite an international set during the high season.

# SIDE TRIPS FROM CORFU TOWN
## KANONI, PONDIKONISI & ACHILLEION

Although these sites and destinations are not literally next door to one another and have little in common, they are grouped here because they do, in fact, all lie south of Corfu town and can easily be visited in half a day's outing. And they are all places that everyone who comes to Corfu town will want to visit, even if they go nowhere else on the island. History buffs will revel in their many associations, and even beach people cannot help but be moved by their scenic charms.

**Kanoni** is approached south of Corfu town via the village Analepsis; it's well signed. Ascending most of the way, you come at about 4km (2½ miles) to the circular terrace (on the right), the locale known as Kanoni (after the cannon once sited here). Make your way to the edge and enjoy a wonderful view. Directly below in the inlet are two islets. If you want to visit one or both, you can take a 10-minute walk down a not-that-difficult path from Kanoni; with a vehicle you must retrace the road back from Kanoni a few hundred yards to a signed turnoff (on the left coming back).

One islet is linked to the land by a causeway; here you'll find the **Monastery of Vlakherna.** To get to the other islet, **Pondikonisi (Mouse Island),** you must be ferried by a small boat, which is always available (2€). Legend has it that this rocky islet is a Phaecian ship that was turned to stone after taking Odysseus back to Ithaka. The chapel here dates from the 13th century, and its setting among the cypress trees makes it most picturesque. Many Corfiotes make a pilgrimage here in small boats on August 6. It's also the inspiration for the Swiss painter Arnold Boecklin's well-known work *Isle of the Dead,* which in turn inspired Rachmaninoff's music of the same name.

There is a causeway across the little inlet to Perama over on the main body of the island (the Kanoni road is on a peninsula), but it is only for pedestrians. So to continue on to your next destination, the villa known as the **Achilleion,** you must drive back to the edge of Corfu town and then take another road about 8km (5 miles) to the south, signed to Gastouri and the villa of Achilleion. It's open daily from 9am to 4pm. Admission is 4€. Bus no. 10, from Platia San Rocco, runs directly to the Achilleion several times daily.

This villa was built between 1890 and 1891 by Empress Elizabeth of Austria, whose beloved son Rudolf and his lover died mysteriously (most likely a double suicide) at Mayerling in 1889. The empress identified him with Achilles, and so the villa is really a memorial to Rudolf (and her grief)—thus the many statues and motifs associated with Achilles (including the dolphins, for Achilles' mother was the water nymph Thetis). As you approach the villa from the entrance gate, you will see a slightly Teutonic version of a neoclassical summer palace. Take a walk through at least some of the eclectic rooms. Among the curiosities is the small saddle-seat that Kaiser Wilhelm II of Germany sat on while performing his imperial chores. (He bought the villa in 1907, after Elizabeth was assassinated in 1898.)

The terraced gardens that surround the villa are now lush and tropical. Be sure to go all the way around and out to the back terraces. Here you will see the most famous of the statues Elizabeth commissioned, *The Dying Achilles,* by the German sculptor Herter; also you cannot miss the 4.5m (15-ft.) tall Achilles that the Kaiser had inscribed, "To the greatest Greek from the greatest German," a sentiment removed after World War II. But for a truly impressive sight, step to the edge of the terrace and enjoy a spectacular view of Corfu town and much of the eastern coast to the south.

If you have your own car, you can continue on past the Achilleion and descend to the coast between **Benises** and **Perama;** the first, to the south, has become a popular beach resort. Proceeding north along the coast from Benises, you come to Perama (another popular beach resort), where a turnoff onto a promontory brings you to the pedestrian causeway opposite Pondikonisi (see above). The main road brings you back to the edge of Corfu town.

## PALEOKASTRITSA

If you can make only one excursion on the island, this is certainly a top competitor with Kanoni and the Achilleion. Go to those places for their fascinating histories, to Paleokastritsa for its natural beauty.

The drive here is northwest out of Corfu town via well-marked roads. Follow the coast for about 8km (5½ miles) to Gouvia, then turn inland. (It is on this next stretch that you pass the **Pottery Workshop** and the **Wood's Nest;** see "Shopping," earlier in this chapter.) The road eventually narrows but is asphalt all the way as you gradually descend to the west coast and **Paleokastritsa** (25km/16 miles). There's no missing it: It's been taken over by hotels and restaurants,

### Taking a Dive

All of the bays and coves that make up Paleokastritsa boast sparkling-clear turquoise waters. There is a professional diving school here, run by a German, called **Korfu Diving**. If you're interested in its weeklong courses for beginners or day excursions for advanced divers, call or fax ☎ **26630/41-604** for details.

although some of the bays and coves that make up Paleokastritsa are less developed than others. Tradition claims it as the site of **Scheria**, the capital of the Phaeacians—and thus one of these beaches is where Nausicaa found Odysseus, though no remains have been found to substantiate this.

You can continue on past the beaches and climb a narrow winding road to the **Monastery of the Panayia** at the edge of a promontory (it's about a mile from the beach, and many prefer to go by foot as parking is next to impossible once you get there). Although founded in the 13th century, nothing that old has survived, but having come this far, it's worth a brief visit, especially at sunset. It's open April through October, daily from 7am to 1pm and 3 to 8pm.

More interesting in some ways, and certainly more challenging, is a visit to the **Angelokastro**, the medieval castle that sits high on a pinnacle overlooking all of Paleokastritsa. Only the most hardy will choose to walk all the way up from the shore, a taxing hour at least. The rest of us will drive back out of Paleokastritsa (about 2.5km/1½ miles) to a turnoff to the left, signed LAKONES. There commences an endless winding and ascending road that eventually levels out and provides spectacular views of the coast as it passes through the villages of Lakones and Krini. (*A word of warning:* Don't attempt to drive this road unless you are comfortable pulling over to the very edge of narrow roads—with sheer drops—to let trucks and buses by, something you will have to do on your way down.) Keep going until the road takes a sharp turn to the right and down, and you'll come to the end of the line and a little parking area. From here you walk up to the castle, only 200m (656 ft.) away but seemingly further because of the condition of the trail. What you are rewarded with, though, is one of the most spectacularly sited medieval castles you'll ever visit, some 300m (1,000 ft.) above sea level.

If you've come this far, reward yourself with a meal and the spectacular view at one of the restaurant/cafes on the road outside Lakones—the **Bella Vista, Colombo,** or **Casteltron. Be forewarned:** At mealtimes in high season, these places are taken over by busloads of tour groups. If you have your own transport, try to eat a bit earlier or later.

On your way back to Corfu town from Paleokastritsa, you can vary your route by heading south through the **Ropa Valley,** the agricultural heartland of Corfu. Follow the signs indicating Liapades and Tembloni (but don't bother going into either of these towns). If you have time for a beach stop, consider going over to **Ermones Beach** (the island's only golf club is located above it) or **Glifada Beach.**

**WHERE TO STAY & DINE**   If you want to spend some time at Paleokastritsa, it's good to get away from the main beach. We like the 70-unit **Hotel Odysseus** (☎ **26630/41-209;** fax 26630-41342), high above the largely undeveloped cove before the main beach. A double in high season goes for 65€, in low season 50€; both rates include buffet breakfast. It's open May to mid-October, and there's a pool.

On its own peninsula and both fancier and pricier is the 127-unit **Akrotiri Beach Hotel** (© 26630/41-237), where an air-conditioned double in high season goes for 120€, in low season 75€, including buffet breakfast. All rooms have balconies and sea views. In addition to the adjacent natural beaches, there are two pools. It's open May through October.

The restaurants on the main beach in Paleokastritsa strike us as over-touristy. However, if you like to eat where the action is, the best value and most fun at the main beach can be had at the **Apollon Restaurant** in the Hotel Apollon-Ermis (© 26630/41-211). Main courses are 4€ to 12€. It's open mid-April to late October, daily from 11am to 3pm and 7 to 11pm.

We prefer someplace a bit removed, such as the **Belvedere Restaurant** (© 26630/41-583), just below the Hotel Odysseus and serving solid Greek dishes at reasonable prices. Main courses range from 3€ to 11€. It's open mid-April to late October from 9am to midnight.

## 2 Kefalonia (Cephalonia)

Don't come to Kefalonia for glamour. Come to spend time in a relaxing environment, to enjoy handsome vistas and a lovely countryside. This is a Greek island the way they used to be—it pretty much goes its own way while you travel around and through it. It does boast several natural wonders, a few historical buildings and archaeological sites, and many fine beaches. Kefalonia also has a full-service tourist industry, with some fine hotels, restaurants, travel agencies, car-rental agencies, the whole show. Since Kefalonia was virtually demolished by the earthquake of 1953, most structures on this island are fairly new. It has long been one of the more prosperous and cosmopolitan parts of Greece, thanks to its islanders' tradition of sailing and trading in the world at large.

### ESSENTIALS

**GETTING THERE  By Plane**  From Athens, there are at least three flights daily on **Olympic Airways** (with some flights via Zakinthos). The Argostoli office is at 1 Rokkou Vergoti, the street between the harbor and the square of the Archaeological Museum (© 26710/28-808). The **Kefalonia airport** is 8km (5 miles) outside Argostoli. As there is no public bus, everyone takes a taxi, which costs about 10€ to Argostoli.

**By Boat**  As with most Greek islands, it's easier to get to Kefalonia in summer than in the off-season, when weather and reduced tourism eliminate the smaller boats. Throughout the year there is one car-passenger ferry that leaves daily from Patras to Sami (about 2½ hr.); for details, call the **Patras Port Authority** (© 2610/341-002) or **Sami Port Authority** (© 26740/22-031). There is also at least one car-passenger ferry daily (1½ hr.) from Killini (out on the northwest tip of the Peloponnese) to Argostoli and Poros (on the southeastern coast of Kefalonia) via the **Strintzis Line** (© 210/823-6011 in Athens); if you haven't made arrangements with a travel agent, you can buy tickets dockside.

Beyond these more or less dependable services, during the high-season months of July and August there are usually other possibilities—ships to and from Corfu, Ithaka, Levkas, or other islands and ports—but they do not necessarily hold to the same schedules every year.

**VISITOR INFORMATION**  The **Argostoli Tourism Office** information office in Argostoli is at the Port Authority Building on Ioannis Metaxa along the harbor (© **26710/22-248**). It's open in high season, daily from 7:30am to 2:30pm and 5 to 10pm; low season, Monday through Friday from 8am to 3pm.

**GETTING AROUND  By Bus**  You can get to almost any point on Kefalonia—even remote beaches, villages, and monasteries—by **KTEL bus** (© **26710/22-276** in Argostoli). Schedules, however, are restrictive and may cut deeply into your preferred arrival at any given destination. KTEL also operates special tours to several of the major destinations around the island. The new **KTEL station** is on Leoforos A. Tritsi, at the far end of the harbor road, 200m (656 ft.) past the Trapano Bridge.

**By Taxi**  For those who don't enjoy driving twisting mountain roads, taxis are the best alternative. If you're based in Argostoli, go up to Central (Vallianou) Square and work out an acceptable fare. A trip to Fiskardo, with the driver waiting a couple of hours, might run to 125€—with several passengers splitting the fare, this isn't unreasonable. Aside from such ambitious excursions, taxis are used by everyone on Kefalonia. Although drivers are supposed to use their meters, many don't, so agree on the fare before you set off.

**By Car**  There are literally dozens of car-rental firms, from the well-known international companies to hole-in-the-wall outfits. In Argostoli, we found both **Auto Europe,** 3 Lassis (© **26710/24-078**), and **Euro Dollar,** 3A R. Vergoti (© **26710/23-613**), to be reliable. In high season, you'll find rental cars scarce, so don't expect to haggle. A compact will come to at least 60€ a day (gas extra); better rates are usually offered for rentals of 3 or more days.

**By Moped & Motorcycle** The roads on Kefalonia are asphalt and in decent condition, but are often very narrow, lack shoulders, and twist around mountain ravines or wind along the edges of sheer drops to the sea. That said, many choose to get around Kefalonia this way. Every city and town has places that will rent mopeds and motorcycles for about 20€ to 30€ per day for a two-seater.

**FAST FACTS** There are several **banks** in the center of Argostoli with ATMs. The **hospital** (© 26710/22-434) is on Souidias (the upper road, above the Trapano Bridge). **Internet access** is available at Excelixis Computers, 3 Minoos (© 26710/25-530; xilixis@otenet.gr). **Express Laundry,** 46B Lassi, the upper road that leads to the airport, is open Monday through Saturday from 9:30am to 9pm. A load costs 3€. Argostoli's **tourist police** (© 26710/22-200) are on Ioannis Metaxa, on the waterfront across from the Port Authority. The **post office** is in Argostoli on Lithostrato, opposite no. 18 (© 26710/22-124); open Monday through Saturday from 7:30am to 2pm. The main **telephone office (OTE)** is at 8 G. Vergoti. It's open daily, April through September from 7am to midnight and October through March from 7am to 10pm.

## WHAT TO SEE & DO

Kefalonia's capital and largest city, **Argostoli** has far and away its most diverse offering of hotels and restaurants. Staying here allows you to go off on daily excursions to the beaches and mountains, yet return to the comforts of a city. For those who find that Argostoli doesn't offer enough in the way of old-world charm or diversions, we point out some of the other "getaway" possibilities on Kefalonia.

Argostoli's appeal does not depend on any archaeological, historical, architectural, or artistic particulars. It's a city for those who enjoy strolling or sitting in a foreign land and observing the passing scene—ships coming and going along the waterfront, locals shopping in the market, children playing in the squares. There are plenty of cafes on the **Central (Vallianou) Square** and along the **waterfront** where you can nurse a coffee or ice cream. The **Premier Cafe** on the former and the **Hotel Olga** on the latter are as nice as any.

If you do nothing else, though, walk down along the waterfront and check out the **Trapano Bridge,** a shortcut from Argostoli (which is actually on its own little peninsula) to the main part of the island.

There are a couple of fine **beaches** just south of the city in the locale known as **Lassi,** which now has the numerous hotels, pensions, cafes, and restaurants that package groups love.

**Historical and Folklore Museum of the Corgialenos Library** ★ Many so-called folklore museums, little more than typical rooms, have sprung up in Greece in recent years, but this is one of the most authentic and satisfying. Meticulously maintained and well-labeled displays showcase traditional clothing, tools, handicrafts, and objects used in daily life across the centuries. Somewhat unexpected are the various displays revealing a stylish upper-middle-class life. Most engaging is a large collection of photographs of pre- and post-1953 earthquake Kefalonia. The gift shop has an especially fine selection of items, including handmade lace.

Ilia Zervou (2 blocks up the hill behind the public theater and the square with Archaeological Museum). © 26710/28-835. Admission 2€. Apr–Oct Mon–Sat 9am–2pm; off season, by arrangement.

## SHOPPING

Interesting ceramics are for sale at **Hephaestus,** on the waterfront at 21 May; **Alexander's,** on the corner of Plateia Museio (the square one block back from the waterfront); and **The Mistral**, 6 Vironis, up the hill opposite the post office, offering the work of the potter/owner.

For a taste of the local cuisine, consider Kefalonia's prized Golden Honey, tart quince preserve, or almond pralines. Another possibility is a bottle of one of Kefalonia's wines. You can visit the **Calliga Vineyard** (selling white Robola and red Calliga Cava) or the **Gentilini Vineyard** (with more expensive wines), both near Argostoli, or the **Metaxas Wine Estate**, well south of Argostoli. The tourist office (see "Visitor Information," above) on the waterfront will tell you how to arrange a tour.

## WHERE TO STAY

Accommodations on Kefalonia range from luxury hotels to basic rooms. During peak times, we recommend making reservations; **Filoxenos Travel** (© 26710/23-055; fax 26710/28-114) can help.

## EXPENSIVE

**White Rocks Hotel & Bungalows ★**   The White Rocks is the kind of low-key place where people catch up on the reading they've meant to do all year. Although not the most elaborate, it is probably the most elegant hotel on Kefalonia, located a couple of miles south of Argostoli just above two beaches, one small and for hotel guests, the other larger and public. On arriving, you descend a few steps from the main road to enter an almost tropical setting. The lobby is subdued and stylish, a decor that extends to the hotel's guest rooms, which are modest in size but have first-rate bathrooms.

Platys Yialos (the beach at Lassi, outside Argostoli), 28100 Argostoli. © 26710/28-332 or 26710/28-335. Fax 26710/28-755. 102 units, 60 bungalows. High season 135€ double; low season 100€ double. Rates are for either rooms or bungalows and include breakfast and dinner. AE, DC, V. Open May–Oct. Private parking. Occasional public buses go from the center of town to and from Yialos, but most people take taxis. **Amenities:** Restaurant; bar; pool; concierge; tours and car rentals arranged; conference facilities; room service 7am to midnight; 1-day laundry and dry cleaning. *In room:* A/C.

## MODERATE

In addition to the following options, you might consider the 60-unit **Hotel Miramare**, I. Metaxa 2, at the far end of the paralia (© 26710/25-511; fax 26710/25-512); it's slightly removed from the town's hustle yet within walking distance of any place you'd want to go.

**Cephalonia Star**   A location along the bay and balconied front rooms with fine views earn this Class C hotel more appeal than many. Rooms are standard size, bathrooms standard issue, but all are clean and well serviced. There's a cafeteria-restaurant on the premises, but except for breakfast, you'll probably want to patronize Argostoli's many fine eateries, all within a few minutes' walk. In August, a mobile amusement park has been known to set up on the quay just opposite, but then August all over Greece is a carnival. Definitely for those who enjoy being on a waterfront.

50 I. Metaxa (along waterfront, across from the Port Authority), 28100 Argostoli. © 26710/23-180. 40 units, some with shower, some with tub. High season 55€ double; low season 40€ double. Rates include breakfast. MC, V. Open year-round. Street parking. *In room:* A/C, TV.

**Hotel Ionian Plaza ★**   Although it isn't quite a grand hotel, this is the class act of "downtown" Argostoli and a fine deal. The lobby, public areas, and rooms share a tasteful, comfortable, and natural tone. Bedrooms are larger than most, while bathrooms are modern if not mammoth. Breakfast takes place under the awning, the evening meal at the hotel's own **Il Palazzino** restaurant, indoors and outdoors; the menu has a strong Italian flavor and prices are surprisingly modest. Stay here if you like to be in the heart of a city; the front rooms look out over the Central Square, but as no vehicles are allowed there, it's not especially noisy.

Vallianou Sq. (the Central Sq.), 28100 Argostoli. ☎ 26710/25-581. Fax 26710/25-585. 43 units. High season 75€ double; low season 50€ double. Rates include buffet breakfast. AE, MC, V. Open year-round. Street parking. *In room:* A/C, TV.

**Mouikis Hotel** This is your basic Class C hotel, popular with groups but usually with a few rooms available for individual travelers. Although its rooms don't provide air-conditioning or TVs, its common areas do. The desk has safe boxes. Bathroom facilities are standard for the class. Definitely for those on a limited budget.

3 Vironis, 28100 Argostoli. ☎ 26710/23-281. Fax 26710/28-010. www.mouikis.com. 39 units. High season 85€ double; low season 50€ double. Rates include buffet breakfast. AE, MC, V. Open year-round. Street parking.

## WHERE TO DINE

Try to taste at least one of the two local specialties: *kreatopita* (meat pie with rice and a tomato sauce under a crust) and *crasato* (pork cooked in wine). The island's prized white wines include the modest Robola and the somewhat over-priced Gentilini.

### EXPENSIVE

**Captain's Table** GREEK/INTERNATIONAL This slightly upscale choice offers specialties such as the Captain's Soup (fish, lobster, mussels, shrimp, and vegetables), filets of beef, delicate squid, and fried *courgette* (small eggplants). You could get our cheap by ordering the low end of the menu, but then why eat here? Most guests dress up a bit, and there's definitely a touch of celebration to meals here. It can also get crowded in high season. Go early, order a bottle of wine, and enjoy!

Leoforos Rizopaston (just around corner from Central Sq.; identifiable by its boat-model display case). ☎ 26710/23-896. Main courses 4€–15€. MC, V. Daily 6pm–midnight.

### MODERATE

Also consider the **Old Plaka Taverna**, 1 I. Metaxa 1, at the far end of the water-front (☎ 26710/24-849), for modest prices and tasty Greek dishes.

**La Gondola** GREEK/ITALIAN Everyone will want to eat at least one meal on the main square to experience the sense of attending a "dinner theater," with Argostoli's citizens providing the action. Frankly, all of the restaurants on the square are about the same in quality and menu, but we've enjoyed some special treats at this one. It offers a house wine literally made by the house, and serves a special pizza-dough garlic bread, a zesty chicken with lemon sauce, and a cannelloni that stands out with its rich texture and distinctive flavor. Both the staff and your fellow diners always seem to be enjoying themselves, so we think you will, too.

Central Sq. ☎ 26710/23-658. Main courses 3€–10€. AE, MC, V. Daily 6pm–2am.

**Patsouras** ★ GREEK Patsouras continues to live up to its reputation as the favorite for those seeking authentic Greek taverna food and ambience. Dine under the awnings on the terrace across from the waterfront, and try either of the local specialties, *kreatopita* (meat pie) or *crasto* (pork in wine). We found a special zest to even such standards as the tzatziki and moussaka. Greeks love these unpretentious tavernas, and you'll see why if you eat at Patsouras.

32 I. Metaxa (along waterfront). (C) 26710/22-779. Main courses 3€–12€. V. Daily noon–midnight. A 5-min. walk from Central Sq.

## INEXPENSIVE

**Portside Restaurant**  GREEK  This unpretentious taverna is what the Greeks call a *phisteria*, a restaurant specializing in meats and fish cooked on the grill or spit. Run by a native of Argostoli and his Greek-American wife, it offers hearty breakfasts, regular plates with side portions of salads and potatoes, and a full selection of Greek favorites. On special nights outside the high season, the restaurant roasts a suckling pig. It's popular with Greeks as well as foreigners, and you've got a front-row seat for the harborside activities.

58 I. Metaxa (along the waterfront, opposite Port Authority). (C) 26710/24-130. Main courses 3€–10€. MC, V. Apr–Oct daily 10am–midnight.

## ARGOSTOLI AFTER DARK

**Free outdoor concerts** are occasionally given in the Central Square. At the end of August, there's a **Choral Music Festival**, with choirs from all over Greece and Europe participating. There's a quite new and grand **public theater** where plays are performed, almost always in Greek and seldom in high season. Popular cafes include **Mythos** and **Politiko**. Young people looking for a bit more action can find a number of cafes, bars, and discos in the streets leading away from the Central Square; they change names from year to year, but **Da Capo, Polo, Antico**, and **Metropolis** have been fairly steady. At the beach resort of Lassi, the **So Simple Bar** has become popular. If your style runs more to British-style pub-crawling, try the **Pub Old House**, I. Metaxas 57, on a corner of tiny streets between the Central Square and the waterfront.

## SIDE TRIPS FROM ARGOSTOLI
## FISKARDO, ASSOS & MYRTOS BEACH

This is probably the preferred excursion for those who have only 1 day for a trip outside Argostoli. The end destination is **Fiskardo**, a picturesque port-village, which owes its appeal to the fact that it's the only locale on Kefalonia to have survived the 1953 earthquake. Its charm comes from its many surviving 18th-century structures and its intimate harbor.

You can make a round-trip from Argostoli to Fiskardo in 1 day on **KTEL** bus line (6€). But with a rental car, you can also detour to the even more pictur-esque port-village of **Assos** (another 10km/7 miles up the upper coast road) and then reward yourself with a stop at **Myrtos Beach**, a strong candidate for one of the great beaches of Greece.

There are plenty of restaurants around Fiskardo's harbor. We recommend **Tas-sia's, Vassos, Nicholas Taverna**, and the **Panormos**. The latter two offer rooms as well. For advance arrangements, contact **Fiskardo Travel** ((C) **26740/41-315**; fax 26710/41-026) or **Aquarius Travel** ((C) and fax **26740/41-306**). Britons may prefer to deal with the **Greek Islands Club**, which specializes in waterfront apartments and houses; its main office is at 66 High St., Walton-on-Thames, Surrey KT12 1BBU ((C) **1932/20-477**; fax 1932/229-346).

## SAMI, MELISSANI GROTTO & DROGARATI CAVE

Many who come to Kefalonia arrive at Sami, the town on the east coast. The island's principal point of entry before tourism put Argostoli in the lead, Sami is still a busy port. Sami itself is nothing special, although its harbor is framed by unusual white cliffs. Of more interest to travelers are the **two caves** to the north of Sami, both of which can easily be visited on a half-day excursion from Argostoli.

The first is **Spili Melissani**, about 5km (3 miles) north of Sami and well signed. Proceeding through the entryway, you get into a small boat and are rowed around a relatively small, partially exposed, partially enclosed lake, whose most spectacular feature is due to the sun's rays striking the water and creating a kaleidoscope of colors. It's open daily from 9am to 6pm. Admission is 4€. It was once believed that this water flowed underground westward to a locale outside Argostoli, Karavothres; it's now known that the flow is from Karavothres into Melissani.

On the road that leads away from the east coast and west to Argostoli (4km/2 miles from Sami), there's a well-signed turnoff to the **Drogarai Cave**. Known for its unusual stalagmites, its large chamber has been used for concerts (once by Maria Callas). You walk through it on your own; it's well illuminated but can be slippery. It's open daily from 9am to 6pm, with an admission of 3€.

## ITHAKA

Because of its association with Odysseus, Ithaka might seem to rate the treatment of a major destination. But it is small, not easily approached, and does not in fact offer that many touristy or historical attractions. Given its "sites" linked to the Homeric epic, however, it will appeal to certain travelers, and its rugged terrain and laid-back villages reward those who enjoy driving through the unspoiled Greek countryside.

We strongly recommend that you rent a car in Argostoli first. The boat connecting to Ithaka sails not from Argostoli but from Sami, the port on the east coast of Kefalonia; to make a bus connection with that boat, and then to take a taxi from the tiny isolated port where you disembark on Ithaka, takes far too much time. Rather, in your rented car, drive in 40 minutes from Argostoli to Sami; the boat fare for the car is 10€, for each individual 2€. Once on Ithaka, you can drive to **Vathy**, the main town, in about 10 minutes, and you'll have wheels to explore Ithaka and return to Argostoli, all within 1 day.

Vathy itself is a little port, a mini version of bigger Greek ports with their bustling tourist-oriented facilities. For help in making any arrangements, try **Polycror Tours** on the main square (© **26740/33-120**). You might enjoy a cold drink or coffee and admire the bay stretching before you, but otherwise there's not much to do or see here. Instead, drive 16km (10 miles) north to **Moni Katheron;** the 17th-century monastery itself is nothing special, but the bell tower offers a spectacular view over much of Ithaka. For a more ambitious drive, head north via the village of **Anogi**, stopping in its town square to view the little church with centuries-old frescoes and the Venetian bell tower opposite it; proceed on via Stavros and then down to the northeast coast to **Frikes**, a small fishing village; then take a winding road along the coast to **Kioni**, arranged like an amphitheater around its harbor.

As for the sites associated with the *Odyssey*, what little is to be seen is questioned by many scholars, but that should not stop you; after all, it's your imagination that makes the Homeric world come alive. There are four principal sites (all signed from the outskirts of Vathy). Three kilometers (1½ miles) northwest of Vathy is the so-called **Cave of the Nymphs**, where Odysseus is said to have hidden the Phaeacians' gifts after he had been brought back (supposedly to the little **Bay of Dexia**, north of the cave); known locally as Marmarospilia, the small cave is about a half-hour's climb up a slope.

The **Fountain of Arethusa,** where Eumaios is said to have watered his swine, is some 7km (4 miles) south of Vathy; it is known today as the spring of Perapigadi. The **Bay of Ayios Andreas,** below, is claimed as the spot where Odysseus landed in order to evade the suitors of Penelope. To get to the fountain, drive the first 3km (2 miles) by following the sign-posted road to south of Vathy as far as it goes; then continue on foot another 3km (2 miles) along the path.

About 8km (5 miles) west of Vathy is the site of **Alalkomenai,** claimed by Schliemann among others as the site of Odysseus's capital; in fact, the remains date from several centuries later than the accepted time of the Trojan War. And finally, a road out of Stavros leads down to the **Bay of Polis,** again claimed by some as the port of Odysseus's capital; in the nearby cave of Louizou was found an ancient pottery shard inscribed "my vow to Odysseus," but its age suggests only that this was the site of some hero-cult.

For lunch, we recommend **Gregory's Taverna,** on the far northeast corner of Vathy's bay (keep driving, with the bay on your left, even after you think the road may be giving out). Ideally you will find a table right on the water, where you can look back at Vathy while you enjoy your fresh fish dinner (not cheap, but then fresh fish never is in Greece).

Most visitors will be able to see what they want of Ithaka in a day before setting off back to the little port, where the last ferryboat to Kefalonia leaves, usually at 5pm—but ask!

# 16

# Highlights of Northern Greece: Thessaloniki, Mount Athos & the Philip & Alexander Sites

*by Sherry Marker*

Northern Greece, with its lofty mountain ranges, deep rivers, wide plains, and profusion of little-known archaeological and historic monuments, is rapidly losing its status as one of Greece's few remaining "undiscovered" regions. Although the monasteries of the Holy Mountain of Mount Athos are still off-limits to women, improved roads mean that Athos is no longer a difficult trek from Northern Greece's largest city, Thessaloniki (Salonika). In addition, the formerly difficult-to-reach sites connected with the mighty warrior Philip II of Macedon and his famous son, Alexander the Great, are now linked

by good, new roads. Furthermore, the National Road from Athens to Thessaloniki makes it possible to drive between Greece's two most important cities in 6 to 8 hours. Thessaloniki is the best place to begin your explorations of Northern Greece—and you'll find plenty to explore both in and around Greece's "Second City." In 1997, Thessaloniki was the European City of Culture, and much of the waterfront and many monuments were repaired and restored. One very pleasant legacy is the Ladadika District, many of whose old warehouses were smartened up and turned into cafes, restaurants, and galleries.

## 1 Thessaloniki (Salonika)

516km (320 miles) N of Athens

When a Greek tells you he's from Athens, he always sounds a bit apologetic, or regretful; Greeks from Thessaloniki, on the other hand, sound, if not smug, very pleased to be from Greece's "Second City." Thessaloniki may be second to Athens in political importance and population, but in popular songs, Thessaloniki is celebrated as "the mother of Macedonia," "the most blessed of cities," and "the city whose praises are sung."

You, too, may be tempted to sing this city's praises when you take in its wonderful situation along the broad expanse of the Thermaic Gulf. You're never far from the sea here; when you least expect it, you'll catch a glimpse of waves and boats in the distance. Alas, especially in the summer, you'll almost certainly get less pleasant whiffs of the harbor's ripe, polluted odor. If you're very lucky, you'll see Mount Olympus while you're here: Pollution has increasingly obscured even that imposing landmark.

**Map legend:**
- ✠ Church
- Ferry Routes

Greeks are fond of reminding foreigners that when their ancestors were painting themselves blue, or living in rude huts, Greeks were sitting in the shade of the Parthenon, reading the plays of Sophocles. Similarly, Thessalonians are like to remind Athenians that when Athens languished in the long twilight

## Macedonian Wine

One of the many pleasures of Macedonia is its wine. The reds and whites of the Boutsaris winery in Naoussa are famous throughout Greece—and, increasingly, abroad. Check out www.wineroads.gr.htm for information on the vineyards and wineries of Macedonia. www.greekwineguide.gr and www.greekwine.gr are also very helpful, as is Miles Lambert's paperback *The Wines of Greece*. You may decide to plan your visits to the Philip and Alexander sites around your visits to local vineyards!

## Tips Beware of Price Gouging During the Olympics

Hotel prices were accurate at press time, but price increases of 20% and more are rumored as hoteliers throughout Greece gear up for the August 2004 Olympics in and around Athens. Horrific price hikes of between 50% and an unbelievable 300% are rumored for the period leading up to, during, and after the Olympics.

of its occupation by the Romans and Ottomans, Thessaloniki flourished. It's true: Thessaloniki's strategic location on the main land route from Europe into Asia made it a powerful city during the Roman Empire—you'll see many monuments built here by the 4th-century A.D. emperor Galerius.

During the Byzantine Empire (the 4th–15th centuries A.D.), Thessaloniki boasted that it was second only to the capital, Constantinople. That's when Thessaloniki's greatest pride, its superb and endearing churches, were built. After the Turks conquered the Byzantine Empire, Thessaloniki continued to flourish as an important commercial center and port. In the 18th and early 19th centuries, the city's Jewish community was so strong and so prosperous that some called Thessaloniki the "second Jerusalem."

Then, in August 1917, a devastating fire destroyed 80% of the city. Phoenix-like, Thessaloniki rose from the ashes. Unfortunately, only part of the city was rebuilt according to the grand plan of the French architect Ernest Hébrard—in part because of the 130,000 Greek refugees from Asia Minor who flooded into Thessaloniki between 1922 and 1923, almost doubling the city's population and leading to enormous unregulated development. Still, Thessaloniki has the broad tree-lined boulevards and parks that Athens so sadly lacks.

After World War II, and again in the 1960s, two more growth spurts left much of the city's outskirts crowded and ugly—and all too much of the city center lined with bland apartment buildings. You'll notice, however, that Thessaloniki has none of the horizon-blocking skyscrapers that have proliferated in Athens—earthquake regulations forbid this. The last major earthquake was in 1978.

Glimpses of the sea, tree-lined streets, magnificent Byzantine churches—all these make visiting Thessaloniki delightful. And there's something else here that's quite wonderful: the food. In part, this is because of the long tradition of Macedonian cuisine; in part, because the refugees who came here from Turkey in 1922 brought with them the zesty cuisine of the Pontus (the area around the Black Sea where most of the refugees had lived). In addition, this is still a city whose establishments are supported by local customers. There are no restaurants here—as yet—that make their living off tourists.

If you're a visitor to Thessaloniki, you'll appreciate all this. You'll also enjoy the fact that Thessaloniki's location in the virtual center of Macedonia makes it the perfect place from which to set off to the sites associated with **Philip II of Macedon** and his son **Alexander the Great.**

## Tips High Season

The busiest time of the year in Thessaloniki is not summer, but fall, when the International Trade Fair and Festival of Greek Songs take place in September, followed by the Demitria celebrations of the city's patron saints in October and November. There is also a Film Festival here in November. If you come between September and November, be sure to book a hotel in advance—and be prepared to pay top money for your room (price hikes of 25% are common).

If you are a man, you can also take in the monasteries of **Mount Athos**, the Holy Mountain. If you are a woman, you'll have that much more time to enjoy Thessaloniki—or to sit patiently in the little port of Ouranopolis, the jumping-off point for Mount Athos, and envy those lucky enough to travel on to the Holy Mountain.

**STRATEGIES FOR SEEING THESSALONIKI**   Our suggestions on exploring Thessaloniki (see "Suggested Itineraries," later in this chapter) are really just that: suggestions. Unlike Athens, which few visitors would be bold enough to visit without seeing the Acropolis, Thessaloniki has no one "must-see" monument. Some might argue that the splendid **Archaeological Museum** or the **Museum of Byzantine Culture** fit the bill, but others would plead the case of the **Upper City (Ano Poli),** the old Turkish Quarter. Still others would recommend a loop through both the Upper City and the **city center** to take in as many Byzantine churches and Roman monuments as possible. In short, you're here to enjoy the city itself: a city filled with Byzantine churches and chapels, a city with squares built around Roman palaces, whose markets pulse with life, and whose harborside cafes and promenade refresh the weary.

## ESSENTIALS

**GETTING THERE   By Plane**   Thessaloniki is served from Athens by **Olympic Airways** (© 210/966-6666 or 210/936-9111; 2310/368-311 [in Thessaloniki]; www.olympic-airways.gr); **Aegean Air** (© 210/998-8300; www. aegeanair) has flights from Athens. In addition, **EasyJet** (© 210/967-0000; www.easyjet.com) is planning to add service to Thessaloniki from London and Athens. From the U.S., there are no direct flights to Thessaloniki. Connections can be made at a number of European cities, including London, Amsterdam, Brussels, Frankfort, Stuttgart, Munich, Zurich, and Vienna. From London, there are direct flights on **Olympic.** Thessaloniki's airport (© **2310/411-997** or 2310/473-212; http://users.otenet.gr/~cpnchris/skg.html) is 17km (11 miles) southeast of the city at Mikras, a 30-minute drive from the city center. Bus no. 78 runs into the city (usually stopping in Aristotelous Square and at the train station) from about 6am to 11pm and costs 1€. A taxi ride is about 8€.

**By Train**   Five daily express trains officially make the trip from Athens to Thessaloniki in about 6 hours, but most are extremely crowded, without air-conditioning, and subject to various unexplained delays. If you must take a train, then let it be the overnight sleeper, which has first-class compartments for four to six passengers and sleeper compartments for four to six passengers. Nothing, however, can be done about the noisy and sometimes bumpy ride on antiquated tracks. Reservations for sleeping compartments should be made many days in advance at the Larissa train station in Athens (© **210/323-6747**). In Thessaloniki, you can purchase tickets at the OSE (train) office in Aristotle Square (© **2310/517-517**). Coach tickets Athens–Thessaloniki from 35€; express train service from 45€; sleeper service from 60€.

In Thessaloniki, the **train station** (© **2310/517-517**) is on Monastiriou, which is the extension of Egnatia west of Vardari Square, site of numerous shady bars. A taxi ride to Aristotelous Square takes about 10 minutes and costs about 5€. To avoid the trek to the train station to get information and buy tickets, use the OSE (train) office at 18 Aristotelous Square 18 (© **2310/518-113**), 9am to 9pm, Monday to Friday; 9am to 3pm Saturday; closed Sunday.

**By Bus**   Ten daily buses from Athens make the trip to Thessaloniki in about 7 hours, including a 20-minute stop at a roadside restaurant with toilet facilities. Buses are air-conditioned and usually arrive on time. Reservations should be made in advance at the Athens bus terminal, 100 Kifissou (© **201/512-9233**)

A one-way fare costs 30€. The buses arrive in Thessaloniki at the station at 65 Monastiriou (② **2310/510-834** or 2310/512-122) opposite the train station, where there are taxis.

**By Car   From Athens,** take the 516km (320-mile) National Road, a four-lane highway that's the best in Greece, although stretches are always being repaired or widened, which leads to frequent slow-downs. The trip from Athens takes 6 to 8 hours. Much of the drive is extremely scenic. Although there are gas stations at frequent intervals along the National Road, you often must exit to reach them.

If you're coming from other parts of **Europe,** you must take the ferry from the Italian ports of Bari, Ancona, or Brindisi to Igoumenitsou on the northwest coast of Greece, and then drive across the Pindus Mountains to Thessaloniki. The trip takes 7 to 8 hours and is scenically spectacular. The southern route via Ioannina and Kalambaka to Larissa and the National Road is much less treacherous than the northern alternative through Kozani—particularly in winter—and is thus recommended (although snow can close both routes). The southern route also will give you the opportunity to stop at Kalambaka and visit the monasteries perched on the awesome pinnacles of the Meteora (see chapter 12). Again, you will almost certainly encounter road work as work continues on the National Highway (called the Via Egnatia, after its Roman predecessor) designed to link Patras (in the Peloponnese) with Central Greece and Central Greece with Macedonia.

**VISITOR INFORMATION** The main office of the **Greek National Tourism Organization (EOT)** is at 8 Aristotelous Square (© **2310/271-888** or 2310/222-935); open Monday through Friday from 8am to 8pm and Saturday from 8:30am to 2pm. There's also a branch at the airport (© **2310/985-215** or 2310/473-212, ext. 215). A useful magazine to buy a virtually any newspaper kiosk is the quarterly *Pilotos*, which lists in Greek all of the cultural and entertainment goings-on in the city. *Pilotos* has an English-language "Blue Pages" section with all the important addresses and phone numbers you could want, from the police and radio taxis to consulates, banks, bars, and cinemas.

**CITY LAYOUT** Thessaloniki rests on the northern coast of the Thermaic Gulf like a somewhat lopsided turban tilted slightly to the northwest. In its center sits the city's most famous landmark, the **White Tower,** the best-known remnant of the walls that once encircled the city. The great walls—begun in antiquity and extended and expanded by the Byzantines, Venetians, and Turks—came down as the population grew and the city expanded in the late 19th and early 20th centuries. To the east sprawl the ever-expanding residential districts, while to the west, situated in the area once defined by its fortresslike Byzantine walls, is the **commercial heart** of the city.

In this latter area, bounded on the south by the harbor and on the north by the rising heights of what is called the **Ano Poli** or the **Upper City,** are Thessaloniki's most important shops, banks, hotels, restaurants, archaeological remains, and churches. On its western edge are the train station, most bus terminals, many shipping docks, the customs building, and streets lined with warehouses—many now converted into the chic restaurants and galleries of the **Ladadika district.** Ladadika blurs into **Ksiladika,** the woodworkers district, which increasingly has chic restaurants and shops, as well as the carpenter's workshops which originally gave the district its character. On the city center's eastern side, just north of the White Tower and outside of what was once the eastern gate, are the grounds of Aristotle University, the International Trade Fair, and the **Archaeological** and **Byzantine museums.** Between the latter and the White Tower are the **Municipal Park** and the **State Theater of Northern Greece.**

The commercial area of the city is traversed by four main streets running on an oblique angle from the southwest to the northeast. The largest, **Egnatia,** runs across the northern side of the commercial district. On its western end at **Vardari (Dimokratias) Square,** it connects with roads to the west, north, and east; on its eastern end (under the name of New Egnatia), it connects with highways to the airport and to the peninsulas of Halkidiki. Along its route in the heart of the city are discount shops, cheap hotels, and affordable restaurants. The city's second most important commercial route is **Tsimiski,** which parallels Egnatia 2 blocks to the south and runs one-way from east to west. Along its tree-shaded length are the city's most prestigious shops and department stores. One block south of Tsimiski and running one-way from west to east is **Mitropoleos,** so named because the Metropolitan Cathedral is situated near its center. Like Tsimiski, it has a number of fine shops and boutiques. Finally, another block to the south and running along the seaside promenade is **Leoforos Nikis.** Also one-way from west to east, it begins at the shipping docks and ends at the White Tower. Along its length is a virtually uninterrupted line of outdoor cafes and bars.

The heart of downtown Thessaloniki is the spacious expanse of **Aristotelous Square,** which borders the sea. Ringed with outdoor cafes and restaurants, it's also the site of the city's major political rallies. Running north and south and connecting Aristotelous with the city's other major square, Dikasterion, is **Aristotelous.** Along its arcaded sidewalks are a number of book and record stores. **Dikasterion Square** overlooks the partially excavated Roman marketplace and has welcome trees, the lovely Byzantine church called Our Lady of the Copper Smiths (the Panayia Chalkeon), and a restored Turkish bathhouse. Increasingly, Greek and other refugees from eastern Europe hold an informal market here. This is also where most local buses begin and end their runs to and from the heart of the city.

To the south of Dikasterion Square, across Egnatia and on either side of Aristotelous, are the city's main **market areas,** where you can find flowers, fish, sandals, and just about anything else you can think of. To the east of Aristotelous is the city's second main north-south route, **Ayias Sofias.** In its center, between Egnatia and Tsimiski, is the major Byzantine church of St. Sofia. Along Ayias Sofias are a number of excellent clothing stores. **Pavlou Mela** runs diagonally southeast from the rear of the church to the White Tower and has a number of fine bars and cafes; leading directly south to Tsimiski from virtually the same point are the tree-lined pedestrian walkways of **Iktinou** and **Zevksidos,** site of several outdoor cafes and restaurants. Two blocks east of the rear of Ayias Sofias Square is Thessaloniki's major pedestrian walkway, **Dimitriou Gounari.** Its shop-lined length covers a major Roman thoroughfare leading down from the arch to the imperial palace. The area containing the palace is now partially excavated and opens into the tree-shaded park of **Navarino Square,** crowded with outdoor cafés, bars, and tavernas, and second only to Aristotelous as the city's major gathering place—although many of the artists and intellectuals who gather here would place it first.

Another 2 blocks east is **Ethnikis Aminis.** While it runs one-way south from Egnatia down to the State Theater and the White Tower, it becomes a two-way street above Egnatia at **Sintrivaniou (Fountain) Square** (the former eastern gate of the city) and leads into winding roadways that run outside the ancient walls to the Upper City.

On the hillside leading down to Thessaloniki proper from the Upper City is the old **Turkish Quarter**—called, variously, **Ano Poli** (the **Upper City**), Eptapirgou (the Seven Gates), and **To Kastro** (Fortress)—where some of the finest Byzantine churches are located. This is easily the most pleasant part of Thessaloniki to explore, especially the winding streets around Kalitheas Square, such as Irodotou, and in pleasant squares such as Romfei Square, in the district known as Koule Kafe, and Tsinari Square, at the juncture of Kleious and Alexandras Papadopoulou. The Seih Sou, the pine forest on the upper hills, was a very pleasant place to wander or rest until severe fires in 1997 and 1998 greatly damaged the pines of Seih Sou. A reforestation project has begun, but it will be years before new growth brings back Thessaloniki's "green lungs."

Just to the north of the Upper City is the **Ring Road,** which goes around Thessaloniki from the southwest to the southeast and connects the National

Road from Athens with highways to Thrace and Halkidiki and the airport at Mikras along the sea to the east.

**FINDING AN ADDRESS**   Because of the orderly east-west, north-south arrangement of streets, finding an address in the city center is not difficult. Numbers begin at the eastern and southern ends of streets and go upwards, with even numbers on the right and odd numbers on the left. However, most Thessalonians think of addresses in terms of the cross streets or various well-known structures near them, and buildings seldom have visible numbers; ask for what you want by name, not number.

Outside of the city center, particularly north of Egnatia, finding what you want is difficult, as the streets begin to meander. Even with a good map, you'll probably have trouble, but take it, as the Greeks say, *"Siga, Siga"* ("Slowly, Slowly"), and you'll find your way.

**MAPS**   The GNTO office on Aristotelous Square often has maps and the free booklet *Thessaloniki and Halkidiki*. Two excellent guides to the city are *The Thessaloniki Handbook* (with section-by-section maps), by Christos Zafiris, and *Monuments of Thessaloniki* (with an excellent city-center map), by Apostolos Papagiannopoulos. Both are usually available at **Molho's Bookstore,** 10 Tsimiski, as is an anonymous Mohlo Editions volume also titled *Monuments of Thessaloniki*. The most detailed map, but very cumbersome, is the one published by **Welcome Tourist Guides,** available at most bookstores.

**GETTING AROUND**   In the city center, most of the attractions, restaurants, and shops are easily reachable on foot in no more than 20 minutes. Otherwise, taxis are your best bet, unless you're going to the Upper City, which is a steep uphill walk, but served by bus nos. 22 and 23, which leave from Eleftherias Square. Taxis are reluctant to take this trip because there is little guarantee of a return fare down, and they may—unlawfully—refuse. But if you're in the cab before you state your destination, there's little the driver can do but take you there.

**By Bus**   Buses with double cars are boarded in the rear, where there is a conductor to make change and give you a ticket. Single-car buses are boarded in the front. On these, exact fare is required, so try to have a variety of change with you. Deposit the fare in a ticket-issuing machine situated behind the driver's seat. You should keep your ticket in case a conductor boards the bus to check. Fares vary according to the distance traveled; at press time, an average journey within Thessaloniki cost about .50€.

---

*Tips*

## Driving to Thessaloniki

If you drive to Thessaloniki from Athens, you'll soon realize that driving here is as vexing as in Athens (the system of one-way streets is not indicated accurately on maps). Officially, there is one car for every 3 Thessalonians—although it often seems that the ratio is closer to one per inhabitant! If your hotel does not have parking facilities, your best bet will be to leave your car in the large parking garage in Eleftherias Square, as on-street parking is very difficult. When Thessaloniki gets its long-promised Metro, congestion here, as in Athens, should be greatly alleviated. Until then, find a secure place to leave your car and walk, or take buses or taxis.

**By Taxi**  This is your best bet except, as noted, when you want to go to the Upper City. Take along a map or have someone write out your destination in Greek, so that you can show the driver where you want to go. Rates are moderate when compared to those in the U.S.; tips are not expected—rounding up the fare as a modest tip is appreciated. Make sure, however, that the driver turns on his meter and that, within the city limits, the rate that it uses is number 1. Rate number 2 is for outside the city limits. There's an extra 2€ charge for trips from the airport. After midnight, all fares on the meter are doubled.

**By Car**  There is little reason to use a car within Thessaloniki. Traffic is terrible and legal parking spots are almost impossible to find. But having a car for excursions into Northern Greece will allow you to see and enjoy a lot more than you would either with a bus or on a guided tour. Keep in mind that if you take a day trip, you'll spend at least an hour getting out, and another hour getting back into the city. It makes much better sense to see what you want to see outside of town on your way in, or out, of Thessaloniki.

**Budget Rent-a-Car** has offices at the airport (② **2310/471-491**) and in the city at 15 Angelaki (② **2310/274-272** or 2310/229-519), opposite the International Fairgrounds. Other options are **Avis**, 3 Leoforos Nikis (② **2310/227-126** or 2310/683-300), at the western end of the harbor, opposite the docks; **Europcar**, 5 Papandreou (② **2310/836-333**); and **Hertz**, 4 El. Venizelou on Eleftherias Square (② **2310/224-906**). Booking in advance (especially from abroad) usually gets you a cheaper rate. A car with unlimited mileage costs around 60€ per day in high season. (*Reminder:* High season is not summer, but the time of the Sept–Oct trade and other festivals.) Be sure to ask if the price quoted includes all taxes and insurance—and be sure to take full insurance if your credit card does not provide it.

If you need to park within Thessaloniki, and the centrally located pay garage in Plateia Eleftherias is full, you might try the free **Municipal Parking Lot** just south of the Museum of Byzantine Culture at the eastern end of Vas. Olgas. It's about a 20-minute walk from the city center, but very near the White Tower and Archaeological Museum. Unfortunately, late at night this is not a very savory spot.

**By Boat**  It's possible to take ferries and boats from Thessaloniki to a number of Aegean islands, including Crete, Santorini, Mykonos, and to the Sporades (Skiathos, Skopelos, and Alonissos). There are lots of travel agents around Plateia Eleftherias and Aristotelous Square, many of which sell ferry tickets. Centrally located agencies include: **Polaris Travel**, 25 Paleon Patron Germanou (② **2310/232-078** or 2310/278-613); and **Zorpidis Travel**, 76 Egnatia, at Aristotelous (② **2310/244-400;** zorpidis@zorpidis.gr). The harbor police can be reached at (② **2310/531-504-7**).

 **FAST FACTS: Thessaloniki**

*American Express*  The office is at 19 Tsimiski (② **2310/239-797**); open Monday through Thursday from 8am to 2pm and Friday from 8am to 1:30pm.

*Currency Exchange/ATMs*  All banks exchange currency, as do most hotels and the central post office. The major banks along Tsimiski and Aristoteleos Square have ATMs.

**Doctors & Dentists** The **U.S. Consulate** (© 2310/266-121 or 2310/260-716) has a continually updated list of recommended doctors. In addition, most of the better hotels can reach an English-speaking doctor or dentist.

**Drugstores** See "Pharmacies," below.

**Embassies/Consulates** The **U.S. Consulate** (© 2310/242-905 or 2310/260-716) is at 43 Tsimiski. It offers a bare minimum of services. The **UK/Commonwealth Honorary Consul** is at 8 Venizelou (© 2310/278-006 or 2310/269-984), by appointment only.

**Emergencies** The **police hot line** is © **100**; for non-urgent help, call © 2310/863-393. For **first aid**, call © **166**. For **car breakdowns**, call © **104** (the Greek Automobile Touring Club, or ELPA). Also try the **tourist police**, 4 Dodekanisou, near the eastern end of Tsimiski (© 2310/554-870 or 2310/554-871).

**Hospitals/Clinics** The main hospital is the **Ippokration** (© 2310/892-2000 or 2310/837-921) at 50 Papanastasiou; doctors who speak some English are usually available here. Two private clinics, **Ahepa Hospital**, 1 Kiriaki (© 2310/993-111), and **Ayios Loukas** (St. Luke's), on the road to Panorama village northeast of the city (© 2310/342-102 to 2310/342-104), both have English-speaking doctors.

**Internet Access** Thessaloniki has lots of Internet cafes, including Link, 50 Dimitriou (© 2310/207-953); **Globus Internet Cafe**, 12 Aminta (© 2310/232-901); **Ground Floor**, 82 Pavlo Melas (© 2310/282-450); and **Indigo Internet Cafe**, 53 Meg. Alexandrou (© 2310/851-581).

**Lost Property** Call the tourist police at © 2310/554-870 or 2310/554-871.

**Newspapers & Magazines** English-language publications are available at several kiosks in Aristotelous Square, along Tsimiski, and at the excellent **Molhos Bookstore**, 10 Tsimiski, at the corner of El. Venizelou.

**Pharmacies** Pharmacies alternate late-night hours. Lists and addresses of the ones open on a particular night can be found in the local newspapers and the windows of all pharmacies.

**Police** The 24-hour emergency number is © **100**. The tourist police number is © 2310/554-870 or 2310/554-871.

**Post Office** The main post office is at 45 Tsimiski, just east of Aristotelous (© 2310/278-924). Hours are Monday through Friday from 7:30am to 8pm, Saturday from 7:30am to 2pm, and Sunday from 9am to 1:30pm.

**Restrooms** All but the smallest eateries and bars have rest rooms that you can request to use without embarrassment. As always when traveling, carrying some tissues is a good idea.

**Safety** Thessaloniki is still an extremely safe city, although the influx of a rough element in recent years means that anyone walking around alone late at night should exercise caution. The only area absolutely to avoid is around Vardaris (Dimokratias) Square, which attracts some shady characters.

**Taxis** Radio taxis in the city center can be called at © 2310/517-417. See also "Getting Around," above.

*Fun Fact* **Catching a Local Festival**

If you are in Salonika in September, check with the GNTO for details on the weeklong wine festival usually held for a week in Anhialos, a village 15km (9 miles) northwest of Thessaloniki. Information on the festival is usually available at www.wineroads.gr/engindex.htm. If you are there around May 21, ask at the GNTO for information on the celebrations in the village of Langadas, 12km (7 miles) northeast of Thessaloniki. This is one of a handful of places in Greece and Bulgaria where the devout walk on fire (coals, actually). No one is really sure why the firewalkers (*anastenarides*) do this: theories include the survival of a pagan custom, or the commemoration of an occasion when the devout saved icons from a church conflagration without suffering any burns.

## SUGGESTED ITINERARIES

If you've already been to Athens, you probably arrived there with a pretty clear idea of what you wanted to see first: The Acropolis, the National Archaeological Museum, and Plaka head most lists. Thessaloniki also has its top attractions—the **Archaeological and Byzantine museums** and its superb **Byzantine churches**—but one of the great delights of visiting here is getting to know the city itself. Thessaloniki—rather than any monument or museum—is its own greatest attraction. There are lots of pleasant squares here, often near the churches and monuments you want to see, often with the shady trees that make this city so much more pleasant to visit than Athens.

Be sure to give yourself time to stroll along the waterfront (especially if the oft-delayed harbor cleanup has reduced the ripe summer smell of the polluted water), time to sit in cafes across from the marvelous Byzantine churches, and time to wander the streets high above the city in the old Turkish quarter, the **Upper City (Ano Poli)**, also known as **To Kastro** (the Castle). You may find that you agree with those who think that whereas Athens is a great place to visit, but not live, Thessaloniki is both a wonderful place to visit and an appealing spot to live.

### If You Have 1 Day

The city's two major museums—the **Archaeological Museum** and the **Museum of Byzantine Culture**—are handily located side by side near the fairgrounds. Decide whether you'd rather see the gold from the tomb of Philip of Macedon or images of life in Byzantine Thessaloniki, and be the first one through the door at the museum you choose. Then, head next door to the other museum, perhaps treating yourself en route to a coffee at a nearby cafe. After visiting the museums, stroll back along the harbor past the White Tower to the center of town for lunch. If you feel more energetic, hop a bus or taxi up to the **Upper City (Ano Poli)**, have lunch and stroll downhill—but remember: Most of the churches you want to see here are closed in midafternoon.

After a nap, you might visit the churches of **Ayia Sofia** and **Ayios Dimitrios** in the city center and see some of the Roman monuments, keeping in mind that there are cafes handily located near most of what you'll want to see. When you're ready for dinner, head to one of the restaurants in the restored warehouse district, **Ladadika,** or the always lively **Thanasis,** in the Modiano Market.

*Note:* This makes for a very full day, and you'll certainly enjoy Thessaloniki a lot more if you have more than a day here. Byzantine churches take time to find, to see, and to enjoy. Many of the frescoes and mosaics are high up on walls, or faded by time (be sure to bring a strong flashlight). If you possibly can, see some one day, some another day.

## If You Have 2 Days

Abbreviate your first day, so that you are not trying to wipe out the city in one fell swoop. You might begin your second day with the **Upper City** and work your way downhill. Start at the **Vlatadon Monastery** and then stroll downhill, stopping at the enchanting little churches of **Osios David, Nikolaos Orphanos,** and **Profitias Elias.** Even if church architecture, mosaics, and frescoes are not your passion, you'll be walking through the narrow streets of very charming old neighborhoods. If you didn't see them on your first day, take in the churches of Ayia Sofia and Ayios Dimitirios when you get back down to the city center.

Then, for a change of pace, take in the **Modiano Market,** the **Outdoor Market,** and the **Flea Market.** If you visit all three, you can buy anything from a copper bucket—to milk a sheep into—to the sheep itself. Along the way, you can nibble souvlaki, pastry, or whatever seasonal fruit catches your fancy. In the cool of evening, you may want to have a look at the **arch of Galerius,** the **Rotunda,** and the **Roman agora** while relaxing at a nearby café.

## If You Have 3 Days or More

Thessaloniki is a very lively town; it's pleasant to spend a day here simply wandering and browsing through the shops and galleries along **Tsimiski, Aristotelous, Ayias Sofias,** and pedestrianized **Dimitriou Gounari.** Like all Greeks, the Salonikans are serious shoe-shoppers—don't miss the enormous neon high heel at Karidas Shoe Store on the Via Egnatia across from the ruined Turkish bath. Even if you think you can't face one more museum, stop in at the wonderful **Museum of Musical Instruments** and enjoy the reproductions of classical and Byzantine wind and string instruments.

Or you may want to head out of Thessaloniki to see some of the sites associated with Philip and Alexander, such as **Vergina, Dion,** or **Pella.** The easiest way to do this is to sign up for one of the efficient day trips that take in these sites (see "Organized Tours, later in this chapter). If you plan to do this by car, try exploring on your way out of town rather than as a day trip to avoid fighting your way in and out of city traffic.

## THE TOP ATTRACTIONS

**The Arch of Galerius**   If you need directions here, try asking for *ee kamara* (the arch), which is what Thessalonians call this hefty monument that Galerius built around A.D. 305 to celebrate a victory over the Persians a few years earlier. Originally, the arch was even larger. Almost half—another entire arch—is missing. You'll see the Persians, some in the peaked caps and trousers that the Greeks and Romans found so effeminate and absurd, in the carved panels that tell the story of Galerius's battles. Until 1953, the tram line ran right under this arch, which still sits in the middle of the traffic whose fumes are steadily eroding many sculptural details. You can take this in with a glance, or spend a pleasant half-hour admiring the sculptural and architectural detail.

Just below the Rotunda on Egnatia and Dimitriou Gounari.

**The Archaeological Museum** ★★★    The stars of the museum are the finds displayed in Room 9 from the tombs at Derveni and the Royal Tombs at Vergina. Most Greek (and fewer non-Greek) archaeologists think that the gold *larnax* (box) with the 16-pointed star held the bones of Philip II of Macedon, the father of Alexander the Great, that the small ivory head is his portrait, and that the bronze greaves were part of his armor. The spoilsport foreign scholars think these finds belonged to another royal Macedonian—but just try telling that to any Greek, especially since the Former Yugoslav Republic of Macedonia began to lay claim to a Macedonian heritage, and tried to put the 16-point star on its flag. The 4th-century bronze crater from Derveni, with wild scenes of a Dionysiac revel, is less controversial, and absolutely superb. Once you've seen it, you'll know that the Hellenistic Greeks did not go in for understatement. While you're at the museum, check to see if the 3rd-century B.C. Derveni papyrus. The papyrus, found in one of the Derveni tombs, seems to be a philosophical tract, and is the only substantial papyrus found in Greece. Virtually all known ancient papyrus manuscripts have been found in Egypt, whose dry climate preserved them for posterity.

Don't let these treasures, however famous and wonderful, keep you from the rest of the museum, whose exhibits are nicely displayed to suggest the history of Thessaloniki from prehistoric days through the Roman period. These rooms are usually uncrowded, and the delicate Hellenistic glass—how could these paper-thin vessels have survived?—and Roman mosaics from private houses are quite wonderful. There's also a portrait bust of the 4th-century A.D. Emperor Galerius, whose arch is one of Thessaloniki's landmarks. Galerius looks like what he was: a brawler who entered the army as a recruit and ended as emperor.

This severe, low museum was built in 1962, and is considered to be the best example of "architectural modernism" in Thessaloniki—a sad commentary on that genre. The museum shop has postcards, guidebooks, and a number of souvenirs with the 16-point star of Macedon. The museum toilet facilities are good. Allow several hours here.

## *Tips* An Important Warning

Strikes that close museums and archaeological sites can occur without warning. Decide what you most want to see in Thessaloniki and go there as soon as possible after your arrival. The fact that something is open today says nothing about tomorrow. One thing to check as soon as you arrive: In January 2000, plans were announced to keep all major attractions open in summer until 7pm. If you're here off season, check with the **Greek National Tourism Organization** (© **2310/271-888** or 2310/222-935) for the abbreviated winter hours of sites and museums. Keep in mind that the opening hours posted at sites and listed at the tourist office often vary considerably. Alas, no information is utterly reliable.

6 Manoli Andronikou (opposite the south side of the International Fairgrounds). ☎ 2310/830-538. Fax 2310/861-306. Admission 6€; combined admission to both the Archaeological and Byzantine museums 9€. Mon noon–7pm; Tues–Sun 8am–7pm. Hours subject to unannounced changes. Bus no. 58 from Dikasterion Sq. or bus no. 11 heading east from anywhere on Egnatia.

**The Greek Agora and Roman Forum**  In the 1960s, workmen digging to lay the foundations of new law courts for Thessaloniki came across the remains of the city's ancient Greek agora, later the Roman forum. Archaeologists took over and excavated the large complex you see today, bounded by one of the city bus terminals; excavations have resumed in the last few years. As in Athens, this agora/forum was the heart of the ancient city: its commercial, governmental, social, and artistic center.

When the Romans came here, they inevitably expanded the Greek agora, creating a forum that was on two levels. You can see the arched remains of the **cryptoporticus,** a retaining wall that supported part of the upper forum. The best-preserved remain here is the large **Odeum,** or Odeon, a theater where Romans enjoyed watching both musical performances and fights to the death between gladiators and wild beasts. The Odeum is sometimes used today for summer concerts.

In modern times, the most famous monument here was the stoa with a series of statues facing the Via Egnatia, known as the *Colonnade of the Enchanted Idols,* or *Incantadas,* the name given them by Thessaloniki's then-flourishing community of Sephardic Jews. By the 19th century, much of the colonnade was lost, but a segment remained, incorporated into the courtyard of a Jewish home. When the French scholar Emmanuel Miller saw the colonnade, he knew he had to have it—and got permission to cart the remaining "incantadas" off to the Louvre, where they are to this day. If you browse in book and print shops in Thessaloniki, you'll probably see reproductions of a charming engraving of the colonnade by the 18th-century English antiquarians Stuart and Revert. Allow an hour here.

Dikasterion Sq., bounded by Filipou, Agnostou Stratiotou, Olimbou, and Makedonikis Amnis sts.

**The Hippodrome**  We know that the ancient hippodrome, where chariot races took place, lies under the square of the same name, because of finds made when today's apartment blocks were built here. There's virtually nothing above ground to see of this ancient racetrack where, in A.D. 390, the Emperor Theodosius the Great ordered the slaughter of some 7,000 spectators. The reason: Theodosius's favorite charioteer had been lynched by a mob that supported one of his opponents. After that terrible day, the Hippodrome was abandoned and gradually covered by layers of buildings from successive eras; some say that they can still make out the oval shape of the Hippodrome in the shape of today's square.

Ippodromou Square is generally a place of evil associations: In 1566, St. Cyril was executed here by the Turks for not converting to Islam. The charming little church of St. Anthony here was, during the Turkish Occupation, a lunatic asylum. You can still see some of the manacles with which "patients" were imprisoned on view in the church. Allow half an hour here.

Ippodromou Sq.

**Museum of Byzantine Culture ★★★**  At present, this is the only museum in the world entirely devoted to Byzantine art and civilization. When all the exhibits here are in place, the museum will cover the 1,100-year development of Byzantine culture from its early beginnings in the Roman world through the fall of Constantinople in 1453; it will also explore the lasting influence of Byzantine culture on Greek art. At present, exhibits on three topics have been installed: Early Christian Churches, the Early Christian City and Private Homes, and Burials and Cemeteries in the Early Christian World. As at the Archaeological Museum, the exhibits here attempt to tell the story of Thessaloniki and look at its social history through art and artifacts.

The most impressive exhibits are the 4th- to 6th-century barrel-vaulted tombs found in Thessaloniki, with frescoes showing Old and New Testament scenes as well as scenes in Paradise. You'll see Daniel in the Lions' Den, Christ as the Fisher of Men, and blissful scenes in Paradise, where fruit, fowl, and wine are shown in abundance. The text accompanying the exhibit looks at the transition from the ancient image of the Afterworld as the Elysian Fields to the Christian images of Paradise. There are also some bright mosaics and elaborately carved marble panels salvaged from the church of Ayios Dimitrios after the great fire of 1917.

This museum took as long to build as some of Thessaloniki's Byzantine monuments—work began in 1989 and was finished in 1993, and the museum opened in 1997. The bricks in the severe facade are meant to remind visitors of the Byzantine use of bricks—and do, although the comparison works to the detriment of this bland building. The museum shop usually has a range of books on Byzantine culture (sometimes including the superb catalogue of the Treasures of Mount Athos exhibit), as well as museum reproductions and postcards. The toilet facilities are good. Allow several hours here.

2 Leoforos Stratou (just west of the Archaeological Museum). © 2310/868-570. Fax 2310/838-597. Admission 6€; combined admission to both the Byzantine and Archaeological museums 9€. Mon noon–7pm; Tues–Sun 8am–7pm. Hours subject to unannounced changes. Bus no. 58 from Dikasterion Sq. or bus no. 11 heading east from anywhere on Egnatia.

**The Palace**    Of course, Galerius built himself a palace in Thessaloniki. After all, his co-emperor Diocletian was building himself a perfectly splendid palace at Split, on the Dalmatian coast. Little remains of Galerius's palace, but even these low remains give an idea of how large this two-story palace with a large, central courtyard must have been—fit, in short, for an emperor. The best-preserved part of the complex is the **Octagon**, the mysterious building that some archaeologists think may have been Galerius's throne room. Why do they think this? First, the Octagon was exceptionally richly decorated with a multicolored marble floor and interior recesses, of which one is a good deal larger than the others—the ideal place for a throne. That said, it should be noted that a very similar structure built by Diocletian in Spoleto, Italy, was not a throne room, but a mausoleum. Allow half an hour here.

Navarino Sq.

**The Rotunda (also known as Ayios Yioryos, after the adjacent church)** ★★    Some say that Galerius built this massive brick-and-stone structure as his modest mausoleum, while others think that he intended it to be a temple, perhaps of Zeus. Later in the 4th century, the Byzantine emperor Theodosius the Great converted the rotunda into a church of St. George, and began the ornamentation of its 6m (20-ft.) thick walls with mosaics. When the Turks conquered Thessaloniki in the 15th century, they converted it into a mosque (you'll see the one minaret left from this period), and destroyed many of the exquisite mosaics.

The Rotunda reopened in 1999 after more than a decade of restoration to repair the damage done in the horrific earthquake of 1978. Artisans and archaeologists worked with literally millions of tesserae to restore these dazzling

## History 101: The Galerian Monuments

In the 4th century, the Roman empire was briefly ruled by a complicated system of two primary emperors, each of whom had an assistant—an emperor in training, as it were. The idea was that this system (known as the tetrarchy) would make it easier to administer the vast Roman empire. In the early 4th century A.D., Galerius, one of the tetrarchs, moved his capital from Asia Minor to Thessaloniki. Then he did what no Roman, emperor or not, could ever resist—he began to build. As a good Roman, he built on a nice, neat, north-south axis flanking the Via Egnatia. The **Rotunda**, the **Arch of Galerius**, the **Palace** at Navarino Square, the **Hippodrome**, and the **Greek Agora** and **Roman Forum** are some of what survive from his ambitious building program.

mosaics. Now you can see (especially if you bring binoculars) the indigo peacocks, garlands of flowers and fruit, and blond, curly-haired saints and martyrs (and martyred saints) in the mosaics that cover the walls. If possible, try to visit on a Wednesday, when the neighborhood street market stretches for blocks around the Rotunda—and keep an eye out for notices of special exhibits or concerts here. Allow an hour here.

Ayios Yioryos Sq. at Filipou (1 block north of the juncture of Egnatia and Dimitriou Gounari, just above the Arch of Galerius). ⓒ 2310/213-627. Free admission except for special events. Daily 8:30am–3pm. Bus nos. 10 or 11 heading east from anywhere on Egnatia.

**The White Tower** ★  What Big Ben is to London, or the Eiffel Tower to Paris, the 16th-century White Tower is to Thessaloniki: the city's most famous landmark—although the tower is no longer white, having had its whitewash removed when it was restored in 1985 as part of the celebrations of the 2,300th anniversary of Thessaloniki's foundation. The tower was built as part of the city's defense walls, and then used as an Ottoman prison and place of execution (when it was known as the Bloody Tower). Today, several floors of the former prison house the Museum of the History and Art of Thessaloniki, whose artifacts give an idea of life here through the centuries.

Although the museum is charming, the most fun here is the building itself, with its steep winding staircase that goes up six floors and offers terrific views of the city and harbor. Each floor has a round room with alcoves, some of which were once prison cells. At the very end, a rooftop café rewards you for the climb. If you're here in winter, you'll get an idea of just how dank and forbidding a prison this thick-walled stone tower must have been. Allow an hour here.

Nikis and Pavlou Mela on the seaside promenade just south of the Archaeological Museum. ⓒ 2310/267-832. Free admission. Tues–Fri 8am–7pm; Sat–Sun 8:30am–3pm. Bus no. 58 from Dikasterion Sq. or bus no. 11 heading east from anywhere on Egnatia.

## CHURCHES

Thessaloniki's **churches** ★★★ are a clear case of the whole being greater than the sum of its parts. Although Ayia Sofia and Ayios Dimitrios are the two best-known churches, your greatest pleasure may come from seeing the smaller churches. As you visit, try to identify those that were built in the **basilica form** (usually a rectangular church with side aisles) and those in the **cross-in-square form**, which is just what its name says.

Keep in mind that many of these churches keep irregular hours, often closing from about 1 to 5pm. In short, the best way to see them is probably on one or more morning excursions. At present, admission to all churches is free; it is appreciated if you leave a small donation in the alms box, usually found near the door, or where votive candles are sold.

You could easily spend a week visiting these churches. You can also see the better-known ones in a day. Keep in mind that simply getting from church to church takes up a certain amount of time.

## IN DOWNTOWN THESSALONIKI

**Ayios Panteleimon**    This church, dedicated to one of the physician saints, is a popular place to light a candle and say a prayer for good health. The church, all that remains of a large monastery on this spot, is usually closed, but its elaborate brick and stone work makes it a delight even to glimpse from the street. If you do get inside, note how the central dome is supported by four barrel vaults, a distinctive characteristic of Macedonian churches.

Corner of Egnatia and Iassonidou.

**Church of Ayia Sofia** ★    It's a pity that Thessaloniki's two most important churches—Ayia Sofia (Holy Wisdom) and Ayios Dimitrios (St. Demetrios)—are both heavily restored. Still, each is worth visiting for its importance in the city's history and for its fine mosaics, although both lack the pleasantly dusty ambience and odor of sanctity of Thessaloniki's less heavily restored churches.

Thessaloniki's 7th-century Ayia Sofia was inspired by the emperor Justinian's famous 6th-century church of Ayia Sofia in Constantinople—although there may have been an earlier, more modest, church here. Like the majestic Ayia Sofia in Constantinople (today's Istanbul), Salonika's namesake has an impressively large dome—in fact, this was an astonishingly large—and technically astonishing—dome when it was built here. The ornately carved marble columns supporting the dome were, as so often in antiquity and throughout the Byzantine era, pillaged from earlier monuments.

Fortunately, some of Ayia Sofia's original mosaics have survived. The Ascension, with an oddly foreshortened Christ (supported by young angels), and the Virgin Mary with the infant Jesus are especially fine. If you look carefully at the mosaics, you'll notice that some show only crosses and stars and have no human representations. These date from the 8th-century Iconoclastic period, when there was a ban on showing the human figure in religious art. The iconoclasts destroyed many earlier works of art, including many sacred icons—and left us with the word "iconoclast" to describe someone who destroys the past or challenges tradition.

**Ayia Sofia Square** is one of Thessaloniki's nicest, and most important, squares—this is where the service of Thanksgiving was held when the city was liberated from the Germans on November 2, 1944. Today, much of Thessaloniki heads here for Easter and other important services. Keep an eye out for the "red house," at 36 Ayias Sofias, built in 1925 for a wealthy industrialist, and one of

## Tips Dress Appropriately & Keep an Eye on the Time!

All these churches are places of worship where casual attire (short skirts for women, shorts or sleeveless shirts for men or women) is considered highly disrespectful. Remember to wear clothing that covers your arms and legs. And also remember that most churches are closed from about 1pm to 5pm.

few fine old houses here to have survived the fire of 1917 that gutted Thessaloniki—and, of course, severely damaged Ayia Sofia church. Across the way at 33 Ayias Sofias, now with the Terkenlis and Byzantium pastry shop on the ground floor, is another handsome mansion built in the 1920s. The pastry shop is an excellent spot to rest and refresh after seeing the church.

Ayia Sofia Sq., between Tsiniski and Egnatia. (2) **2310/270-253.** Daily 8am–9pm (but often closed about 1–5pm).

## Church and Crypt of Ayios Dimitrios (sometimes given as Ayios Demetrios) ★

Like Ayia Sofia, Ayios Dimitrios was heavily restored—in fact, almost entirely rebuilt—after the fire of 1917. Consequently, this is a church with an imposing history, some fine mosaics, but very little soul. That's a shame, because the story of Dimitrios is quite stirring: In the 4th century A.D., this site was occupied by a Roman bath, a corner of which was used as a makeshift jail. In 303 A.D., one of the prisoners was young Dimitrios, who had gotten into trouble by preaching the Gospel in Salonika. Dimitrios not only refused to renounce his faith, but seems to have converted another prisoner, a gladiator who fought and killed the emperor Galerius's favorite gladiator. Galerius was furious and had Dimitrios executed at once. Soon, there was a shrine here to commemorate the martyred Dimitrios; then a small church was built, and in the 7th century A.D., the church was considerably enlarged into its present five-aisled basilical form. After the 1917 fire, the church was rebuilt on and off from 1926 to 1949, and you can still see scorch marks from the 1917 conflagration on some of the interior walls.

Almost all the mosaics here are restorations of what was lost in 1917, but a cluster of mosaics survive from the 5th to 7th centuries A.D. Keep an eye out for the lovely original portrait of the boyish saint with two young children and the representation of Demetrios with the church founders. (You can see other mosaics salvaged after the fire on display in the Museum of Byzantine Culture.) The crypt, which you enter down a narrow, twisting staircase, is pleasantly mysterious, with several small anterooms and remains of the Roman baths. There are sometimes exhibits here. Particularly venerated are the spot where Dimitrios is believed to have been martyred (where a vial of blood, believed to be the saint's was found) and the spot with a holy water font. For centuries, the faithful noted a sweet scent here, and believed that a myrrh, or perfumed fluid, from the saint himself flowed from the font.

As you leave the church, have a look at the delightful chapel of St. Euthymius, built into the wall of Ayios Dimitrios. The 14th-century frescoes in the little chapel have all the verve that the heavily restored mosaics in Ayios Dimitrios lack.

Corner of Ayiou Dimitriou and Ayiou Nikolaou, 1 block north of the Roman market, at the base of the Upper City. (2) **032/0213-627.** Church and crypt usually open Mon 12:30–7pm; Tues–Sat 8am–8pm; Sun 10:30am–8pm. Bus nos. 22 or 23, which leave about every 10 min. from the southeast side of Eleftherias Sq., stop near the church.

## The Panayia Acheiropoietos (The Church of the Virgin Made Without Hands) ★

This charming 5th-century basilica is the only church from Thessaloniki's early Christian days to have survived virtually intact, without the restorations and renovations that have changed the character of Ayia Sofia and Ayios Dimitrios. The marble columns, with their elaborate "perforated" acanthus leaf decorations, give you a good idea of the Byzantine love of the elaborate—which was achieved here by vigorous drill work. What a contrast to the mosaics, with the simple gold cross and the delicate floral and vine motifs interspersed with birds. The 13th-century frescoes showing some of the 40 Martyrs are equally appealing; those that are missing were destroyed when this church was converted to a mosque. Due to the inexorable rise in the street level over the centuries, the church now sits below the level of today's streets and roads.

Ayias Sofia, north of Egnatia. No phone.

**The Panayia Chalkeon (The Virgin of the Copper Workers)** ★  This tiny church with its three domes looks as if it would fit nicely into a miniature village. It has some fine frescoes, but its real glory is its facade, with windows piled above windows, domes above domes. Like the Panayia Acheiropoietos, the 11th-century Panayia Chalkeon now sits considerably below Thessaloniki's modern street level. Several nearby streets still have the copper workers' shops from which, centuries ago, this church took its name. Locals call this the "red church" for its rosy bricks.

Dikasterion Sq. No phone.

## IN THE UPPER CITY (ANO POLI)

One of the great pleasures of visiting these churches is exploring the narrow streets of the **Upper City** ★★★, with the considerable remains of the massive Byzantine Eptapirigion Walls (Seven-Gated Walls). The Upper City is a maze of cobbled streets, wooden houses with the second floor overhanging the first, street-side fountains, corner groceries, and cafes. In the 1960s, this area was practically falling down; now, as young Thessalonians reclaim the old quarter, an address here is considered very chic. When you come here, be prepared to get lost at least once—and probably to find a wonderful little church, or courtyard, or schoolyard, while you try to find your way back to your original destination. **Remember:** All these churches are closed from about 1 to 5pm.

It's very pleasant to ride up to the Upper City on bus nos. 22 or 23 from Eleftherias Square, then walk back downhill. When you get out of the bus in the Upper City, have a look at the Byzantine walls around the Acropolis and the Byzantine defense tower called the Tower of Trigoniou.

You will probably want to spend at least half a day here.

**Ayia Katerini**  This is another of Thessaloniki's fine 14th-century churches, built with a central dome flanked by four cupolas, and elegant brick and stone work. Now surrounded by new apartment buildings and old homes, it is a dignified reminder of one of the city's finest artistic periods. If you get inside, look for the wall painting showing the healing of the blind.

Corner of Sachini and Tsamadou, near the Byzantine walls.

**Ayios Nikolaos Orfanos** ★★  Like Osios David, this seemingly unprepossessing brick-and-stone church holds an astonishing treasure: well-preserved frescoes from the 14th century, the zenith of Thessaloniki's artistic excellence. You can pick out St. Nikolaos himself, with his halo, standing at the helm of the little boat that he's guiding across stormy waters. The other frescoes, as usual in such cycles, show scenes from the Old and New Testaments, as well as depicting saints and prophets. Next to the church, part of its once-flourishing monastery, with an attractive veranda, has just been restored, and makes the traveler envy those lucky enough to live here. You may acquire a retinue of curious neighborhood children here; most drift away in time, but some have hopes of sweets or even money and can be unpleasantly persistent.

Apostolou Pavlou.

**Osios David (The Latomou Monastery)** ★★ We manage to get lost almost every time we come here, but always eventually find this absolutely charming 5th- or 6th-century church, with its pleasant shaded courtyard. Indeed, what a tempting fantasy to think of taking over the caretaker's job, sitting with a book in the little shelter in the courtyard, tending the flowers, and unlocking the church for visitors—who are bound to be impressed, because nothing about Osios David's simple exterior can prepare you for the glorious mosaic of the vision of Ezekiel inside. The vision shows Christ surrounded by the symbols of the four apostles (the angel, eagle, lion, and bull). If there's a finer mosaic in the city, we can't imagine what it could be. According to local lore, the mosaic spent several centuries hidden beneath a calf's skin, which prevented the Turks from finding and destroying it. If you wish, ask the caretaker to turn on the lights—and slip him something for his troubles.

Timotheou, off Ayias Sofia.

**Profitias Elias** ★ This substantial 14th-century church, whose elaborate brick exterior has recently been restored, is nice in and of itself, and is a fine vantage point to look out over the city. Women, who cannot visit Mount Athos, will get an idea from Profitias Elias of the cross-in-square with central dome style of many of the churches on Mount Athos.

Olympiados.

**Vlatodon Monastery (also known as Vlatades)** As you toil uphill, you'll keep seeing the overhanging walls of the substantial Vlatodon Monastery, founded in the 14th century. In the last few years, it has been substantially renovated and expanded, and has lost its "old" feeling. Still, the inner courtyard is still charming—and a cool spot to rest for a moment or two. If the main church is locked, don't feel too bad: the frescoes were badly damaged by the Turks, and have not been restored. By tradition, the little chapel of saints Peter and Paul was built on the spot where St. Paul preached when he visited Thessaloniki in A.D. 50.

By the Gate to the Acropolis.

## MARKETS

You could easily spend a day exploring Thessaloniki's **markets** ★★ or get a sense of them in an hour or two. Try to allow time for at least one meal here.

**The Bezesteni** ★ It would be wonderful to have a bird's-eye view of the Bezesteni's six domes and four entrances, one on each side. This covered market, today specializing in textiles and jewelry, was built in the late 15th century by Sultan Bayezid II, and is one of the best preserved Turkish monuments in Thessaloniki. It's also a terrific place to browse and feel transported into an Oriental bazaar.

Venizelou and Solomou. Usually Mon–Sat 9am–7pm.

**The Flea Market** ★ Just what its name implies, this market, which sprawls along Tositsa, sells everything from genuine junk to genuine antiques (much more of the former than the latter). Of late, many Eastern Europeans sell their wares here, usually leather jackets, fake Leica cameras and designer watches, and an odd assortment of alarm clocks, mirrors, and socks.

Tositsa. Usually Mon–Sat 8am–7pm.

**The Kapani (Vlali) Market** ★ This market sells foods, dry goods, fabrics, and just about everything else you can think of, in a hodgepodge of ramshackle shops crowded one next to the other for as far as the eye can see. There's been a market here at least since Turkish times, and probably long before that.

Bounded by Kominon, Egnatia, Aristotelous, and Menexe sts. Mon–Sat about 8am–5pm.

**The Modiano Market** ★★   It's been a while since we've seen gypsies with dancing bears in the Modiano Market, although there are still gypsies aplenty, as well as other street musicians, here most days. You could easily spend a morning in the glass-roofed market that covers an entire square block, happily wandering from stall to stall and eyeing the fish, meat, fruit, vegetables, flowers, spices, and baked goods on sale. Whenever you get hungry, sit down in any one of a number of cafes or ouzo joints (including the delicious **Thanasis**).

The roofed market was built in 1922 by the wealthy Jewish merchant Eli Modiano, whose handsome family mansion at 68 Vas. Sophias is now the home of the **Folklore and Ethnography Museum of Macedonia.** If you wish, take a bus or walk along both Megalou Alexandrou and Vas. Olgas & Sophias and have a look at Thessaloniki's surviving ornate 19th-century mansions. Vas. Olgas, particularly, was once known as the "Boulevard of the Chateaux" for its imposing town houses.

The block bounded by Aristotelous, Ermou, Vasileos Irakleiou, and Komninon sts. Mon–Sat about 7am–5pm.

## MORE ATTRACTIONS

**The Alatza Imaret** *⊘*   Along with the Bezesteni, the Alatza Imaret, a former 15th-century mosque with a poorhouse, or almshouse, is one of the best-preserved Turkish buildings in Thessaloniki. "Alatza" means "many-colored," and refers to the tiles and stones that covered the mosque in its days of glory. If you're lucky, it may be open when you visit, as exhibitions are sometimes held here. Allow half an hour if the Imaret is open.

Dimitrion Sq., just off Ayiou Nikolaou, half a block north of Kassandrou, 1½ blocks north of the church of Ayios Dimitrios. *©* **2310/278-587.** Free admission. Open intermittently for exhibitions.

**Atatürk's Birthplace**   Just behind the consulate, this modest wood-framed house was the birthplace in 1881 of Mustafa Kemal (Atatürk), the man who created the modern Turkish state and was its first president. Given to Turkey as a present by the Greek government in 1933, the house has been restored and furnished to reflect the way it must have been at Atatürk's birth. It contains numerous photos of the man, young and old; various letters and papers; and cases containing the clothes and uniforms he wore. There is an excellent English-language booklet available with all the relevant information as well as photos. This is also the Turkish consulate and you usually get a guided tour by an official. Allow an hour here for the tour.

17 Apostolou Pavlou (8 short blocks east of the church of Ayios Dimitrios). *©* **2310/248-452.** Free admission. Daily 10am–5pm. Bus no. 22 or 23 from Eleftherias Sq. or stops along El. Venizelou north to Ayiou Dimitriou. Entrance through the front gate of the Turkish consulate, passport or identity card necessary.

**Folk and Ethnological Museum** *⊘★*   Be sure to call before you visit this museum, which hopes to reopen in 2003—but has had similar aspirations for years. That said, if it is open, the collection of costumes and items of Macedonian daily life is superb. The elegant 19th-century town house that houses the museum once belonged to the prominent Greek-Jewish Modiano family, after whom the Modiano Market takes its name. Allow several hours here.

68 Vas. Olgas 68. *©* **2310/830-591.** Hours and admission not available.

**International Fairgrounds**   If you're in Thessaloniki during the September Trade Fair, you may want to take in some of the exhibits here. Usually any special exhibitions or events taking place are posted conspicuously throughout Thessaloniki. This is also the home of the **Macedonian Museum of Contemporary Art** (① **2310/240-002**), open Tuesday through Sunday from 9am to 5pm, June through September, and Tuesday through Sunday from 10am to 2pm and 5 to 9pm, October through May. Admission is 2€. Allow several hours here.

Entrances at the corners of Angelaki and Tsimiski, and Angelaki and Egnatia. Free admission except during special exhibitions. Open irregular hours.

**Jewish History Museum (also known as the Museum of the Jewish Presence in Thessaloniki)** ★   This small museum in the heart of the Modiano Market uses photographs and artifacts to portray Jewish life in Thessaloniki. Thessaloniki Jews established the city's first printing press in the early 1500s, and founded the city's first newspaper, *El Lunar*, in 1865. The community thrived under the Ottoman Empire, and in 1900, 80,000 of Thessaloniki's 173,000 inhabitants were Jews. Just before World War II, there were 60,000 Jews here; 2,000 survived the death camps. Today there are perhaps 1,000 living here.

(To visit or attend services at one of Thessaloniki's remaining synagogues, or to see the Holocaust Monument, phone the **Jewish Community Office,** 24 Tsimiski (① **2310/272-840.** If you're interested in learning more about the Jewish community in Greece, ask at the GNTO office for the excellent pamphlet *Jewish Heritage in Greece* and keep an eye out for the locally published *Jewish Community of Thessaloniki* and Niko Stavroloulakis's books *The Jews of Greece* and *Jewish Sites and Synagogues of Greece.*) Allow at least an hour for your visit to the museum.

13 Agios Mina. ① **2310/250-406.** Fax 2310/275-701. jct@compulink.gr. Free admission. Mon–Fri and Sun 11am–2pm; Wed and Thurs usually also open 5pm–8pm.

**Lambrakis Monument**   On May 22, 1963, a leftist member of the parliament, Grigoris Lambrakis, who had been speaking at a peace meeting, was run down and killed on this spot. Vassilis Vassilikos based his novel *Z* on Lambrakis's death; the novel was later adapted for a film by Costas-Gavras and starred Yves Montand. Lambrakis's assassination by right-wing forces and the protests that followed were part of a long series of events culminating in the dictatorship of the colonels in the late 1960s. The monument shows a bronze figure, arms upraised in supplication, flanked by a dove of peace.

Intersection of Venizelou, Ermou, and Spandoni.

**The Museum of Ancient Greek, Byzantine, and Post Byzantine Musical Instruments**★★   What is it about music museums? The one in Athens is one of that city's finest small museums, and Thessaloniki has its own appealing music museum. The three floors here house beautifully displayed reproductions of stringed and wind instruments, along with marvelous photographs of depictions of the instruments from ancient vase paintings or Byzantine manuscripts. Purists may object to the predominance of reproductions here, but the reproductions do their best to give viewers a sense of what the actual instruments looked like. Music sometimes softly plays in the background, and there's a café that is sometimes open. If you're lucky, there will be a concert here during your time in Salonika. Allow several hours here.

12–14 Katouni, Ladadika. ① **2310/238-391.** www.fhr.org/culture97/tour/museums/22.html. Admission 5€. Tues–Sun 9am–3pm and 5–10pm.

## *Tips* Hitting the Beach

Any beaches within the bay of Thessaloniki are too polluted to be safe, although people do swim here. Those in the communities of Perea and Ayia Triada, 16km to 24km (10–15 miles) along the bay east of the city, are considered reasonably safe. Just past Ayia Triada, on the headland of the bay, is the Greek National Tourism Organization facility of **Akti Thermaikou,** which also has a children's playground, changing cabins, snack bars, and tennis courts.

**Museum of the Macedonian Struggle** As its name suggests, this museum (in a handsome neoclassical building) contains artifacts, uniforms, and weapons from the struggle that raged on and off from 1870 to 1919 to liberate Macedonia. The exhibits are stirring, and several new English-language brochures help explain this long and bloody conflict. Allow at least an hour here.

23 Proxenou Koromila. (© 2310/229-778. Fax 2310/233-108. Free admission. Tues, Thurs, and Fri 9am–2pm; Wed 9am–2pm and 6–8pm; Sat–Sun 11am–2:30pm.

## ART GALLERIES

Thessaloniki has a number of excellent galleries that often have exhibitions well worth taking in. You can find out about them from posters in town, from the Greek National Tourism Organization office in Aristotelous Square, and from the listings usually published on Tuesdays in *Kathimerini,* the English-language supplement to the *International Herald Tribune.* You'll also see galleries as you explore the city; feel free to step inside and have a look. Galleries worth checking out include **Apothiki,** on Nikis by the waterfront (© **2310/240-877**); **Foka,** 17 Foka (© **2310/240-362**); and **Metamorfosis,** 128 Tsimiski (© **2310/285-071**).

In addition to these, several museums and galleries emphasize the art and life of Thessaloniki and Macedonia, with particular reference to the lively pre– and post–World War II art scene here. These include the **Gallery of Fine Arts,** 1 Nicephoros. Germanou, inside the National Theater Building (© **2310/238-601**); the **Municipal Gallery,** 162 Vas. Olgas (© **2310/425-531**); the **Macedonian Museum of Contemporary Art,** in the International Fairgrounds (© **2310/240-002**); the **National Museum of Contemporary Art in Thessaloniki,** 21 Kolokotroni, in the Lazariston Monastery (© **2310/589-140**); and the **National Bank Cultural Foundation,** 108 Vas. Olgas (© **2310/295-170**). Most of these places keep irregular hours; we advise checking with the GNTO office in Aristotelous Square for information.

## ORGANIZED TOURS

Reputable companies offering tours of Thessaloniki and of the Philip and Alexander sites include **Zorpidis Travel,** 76 Egnatia, at Aristotelous (© **2310/244-400;** zorpidis@zorpidis.gr) and **Kinissi Tour Agency,** 43 Tsimiski, (© **2310/237-000;** fax 2310/264-569). Try the respected British agency **Filoxenia,** fourth floor (© **2310/280-560;** fax 2310/285-170; www.filoxenia.co.uk), for "green" ecological tours to the countryside as well as mountaineering excursions.

## SPECTATOR SPORTS

Like most Greeks, Thessalonians are keen soccer and basketball fans, rooting for the home teams (confusingly, the Aris and PAOK stadiums are home to both basketball *and* soccer teams). Your best bet if you don't speak or read Greek and want to catch a game is to check with the concierge at your hotel, or at the GNTO tourist office in Aristotelous Square (don't attempt this by phone). In general, soccer games are in the spring and fall, basketball year-round. The **Aris stadium** is in the suburb of Harilaou (© **2310/305-402**), while the much-easier-to-reach **PAOK stadium** is on Ayios Dimirios, 2 blocks northeast of the International Fairgrounds (© **2310/238-550**).

## SHOPPING

As you'd expect from Greece's second-largest city, Thessaloniki has a wide variety of shops, and since the city center is quite compact, it's easy to explore the major shopping districts. As in Athens—indeed, throughout Greece—most chic boutiques stock imported goods from Europe and the States, usually with a hefty import duty that is passed on to the customer. If you shop the winter (Jan) and summer (late July and Aug) sales, you may find some bargains.

If you want to see where Thessalonians shop, take a stroll along **Tsimiski, Mitropoleos,** and **Proxenou Koromila** streets between **Pavlou Mela** (the diagonal street connecting the church of Ayia Sofia with the White Tower) and the north-south vertical of **Venizelou.** In this area are the city's few department stores, many boutiques selling the latest in expensive haute couture, shops selling jeans and casual clothing, *lots* of shoe stores, jewelry and antiques stores, record shops selling both Greek and foreign items, the best English- and French-language book and magazine store in town, and a number of confectioneries. There are also several Hondos Center mini-malls.

Thessaloniki also still has a number of shops selling the handiwork of local craftspeople, such as coppersmiths and jewelers. This is where you're likely to find something tempting, sometimes at what constitutes a bargain price for a foreigner. Not surprisingly, most of the shops are near the church of the Panayia Chalkeon (The Virgin of the Copper Makers) in **Dikasterion Square.**

What you won't find in Thessaloniki is anything remotely equivalent to the streets of shops packed with souvenirs—many made in the Far East—that have proliferated in Athens and on many islands. If you get a souvenir here, it's likely to be just that: something you find that will remind you of your visit, rather than a mass-produced memento.

## ANTIQUES

**Relics,** 3 Yioryio Lassani (© **2310/226-506**), offers high-quality antiques, from silver- and glassware to jewelry, ceramics, prints, Art-Nouveau lamps, and Victorian-era dolls. This is a serious shop with serious prices. It's located a block east of the Mitropoleos Cathedral off Mitropoleos; closed Sundays.

---

*Tips* **Details, Details**

In Thessaloniki, old-style, pre-European Community **shopping hours,** unfathomable to foreigners, still predominate. Stores open at about 9am and close around 1:30 or 2pm for the afternoon siesta. Stores open on Tuesday, Thursday, and Friday evenings, some (but not all) reopen from about 5:30 to 8:30pm. In July, however, virtually all shops are closed in the evening. The safest course is to shop in the morning. Note that many of these stores will take major credit cards, but almost all, especially the smaller ones, prefer not to.

## ART

One of the best galleries in Thessaloniki for paintings, engravings, and sculpture, **Terracotta**, 13 Chrys. Smirnis and 76 Mitropoleos (℡ **2310/235-689; fax 2310/220-191; www.terracotta.gr),** features works from all of the most famous contemporary Greek artists, such as Fasianos, as well as those of the emerging generation. It's located 1½ blocks north of the U.S. Consulate between Leoforos Nikis and Mitropoleos; closed August. You can also try **Art Forum,** 29 Nikiforo Foka (℡ **2310/224-060),** a gallery focusing on contemporary Greek art. It's off Tsimiski, a block east of Navarino Square. Hours are Monday, Tuesday, Thursday, and Friday from 10am to 2:30pm and 6 to 9pm; closed July through August.

## BOOKS, NEWSPAPERS & MAGAZINES

**Apostolic Diakonta Bookstore** ★  Although this handsome bookstore specializes in books on religious matters, it also carries a wide selection (in English and French, as well as in Greek) on Greece. This is a wonderful place to browse, and even if you can't afford one of the superb books of photos of Greece, you can find wonderful cards, as well as nice reproductions of icons. 9A Ethnikis Aminis, near the Archaeological and Byzantine museums. ℡ **2310/275-126.**

**Molhos** ★★  Molhos has the best selection of foreign-language books, magazines, and newspapers in the city, and this wonderful family-run, multiple-level bookstore is a Thessaloniki institution. These people love books, and the staff can assist you in English, French, and German—and probably a great many other languages. Many of the most tempting books (including some dazzling books on Greece) are on the second floor. If you don't find what you want here, try some of the bookshops around the corner on Aristotleos, such as **Ianos** and **Mariaris.** 10 Tsimiski (between El.Venizelou and Dragoumi). ℡ **2310/275-271. Fax 2310/229-738. molho@imagine.gr.**

**Rentzis**  This small bookstore in an arcade between Mitropoleos and Tsimiski has a helpful staff and a good selection of English-language books on Thessaloniki and Greece. 24 Tsimiski. ℡ **2310/236-175. Fax 2310/271-477.**

## COPPER

At the family-run **Adelphi Kazanzidi**, 12 Klissouras off the western side of Dikasterion Square, a block north of Egnatia (℡ **2310/262-741),** the copperworking skills have been passed down from generation to generation. It sells numerous finely crafted copperware items such as wine carafes, skillets, water heaters, and trays, all handmade on the premises.

## CRAFTS

**Skitso,** 11 Grigori Palama (℡ **2310/269-822),** sells a delightful variety of handmade objects, mostly in wood, including puppets, ships, crosses, and children's toys. It's a block west of the intersection of Pavlou Mela and Tsimiski. **Ergasterio Kouklis,** 2 Mitropolitou Gennadiou (℡ **2310/236-890)** has wonderful dolls—for collectors, as well as for children.

## DEPARTMENT STORES

**Fokas,** with three centrally located branches at 48–50 Tsimiski (℡ **2310/241-954),** 64 Tsimiski (℡ **2310/268-031),** and 14 Ermou (℡ **2310/279-876),** has got it all, including men and women's clothing and shoes. If you want to check out the offerings before you visit, go to www.fokas.gr. Meanwhile, **Lambropoulos,** 18 Tsimiski (℡ **2310/269-971),** is the best in the city with five floors

## Tips Pack 'n' Send

Office supplies may sound like just what you *don't* want to think about on vacation, but if you need stationery, packing tape, scissors, or large envelopes to mail purchases home, **Spondilides,** 24 Tsimiski, in the stoa (© **2310/269-825**), is your place. Remember, don't seal up your packages until you get to the post office. All parcels must be inspected before they are shipped.

full of everything and anything you might want, from cosmetics to basketballs. It's located a block west of Aristotelous, at the corner of Komninon.

### FASHION

For both men's and women's fashions, try the department stores such as **Lambropoulos** (see above) or the chic—and expensive—boutiques on pedestrian **Dimitriou Gounari.** One centrally located men's shop (with staff speaking some English) is the long-established **Oxford Company,** 4 Palaion Patron Germanou (© **2310/273-087**), with nice photos on the walls of the family's old cotton mills in Volos.

### GIFTS & SOUVENIRS

At **Tanagrea,** on Vogatsikou (a block east of the Metropolitan Cathedral between Mitropoleos and Proxenou Koromila), you'll find a wide selection of handcrafted items by a stable of artisans employed by this well-known chain of stores, which also has outlets in Athens, Crete, and Spetsai. Offerings include ceramics, pewter, silver, leather goods, paintings, glassware, and jewelry.

Pronounced *zeeta mee,* **ZM,** 1 Proxenou Koromila, a block east of Aristotelous Square (© **2310/240-591**), offers three floors of expensive but well-crafted Greek souvenir items such as worry beads, pottery, folk art, rugs, toys, handcrafted caïques, prints, and a few antique silver place settings and jewelry. An extremely tempting place to browse.

### JEWELRY

Specializing in gold, but not exclusively, the eponymous owner of **Marina,** 62 Mitropoleos, a block east of the Metropolitan Cathedral (© **2310/238-361**), offers her own designs as well as copies of the works of famous Greek jewelers such as Lalaounis, with whom she apprenticed.

### LEATHER

The best of several leather-goods shops in the area is **Falli,** 11 Askitou (© **2310/229-197**). Located on the southwest corner of the outdoor market, near Ermou and El Venizelou, Falli makes and sells shoulder bags, backpacks, attaché cases, and sandals. Some of these items are of very high quality and very reasonably priced. You should try to bargain by looking downcast and disappointed when you hear the price. Often, if you thank the clerk at that point and head for the door, the price may come down. Or, simply say you can not spend that much and ask for something less expensive. (If you want good quality leather, you should also resist the price.)

### MARKETS

See "Markets" (p. 568 and 569) for the Modiano, Kapani, Bezesteni, and Flea markets.

## MUSIC

Both **Blow Up: The Music Stores,** 8 Aristotelous, on the east side of the street a block north of Tsimiski (© **2310/233-255;** fax 2310/237-101; www.blowup.gr; and **Patsis,** 39 Tsimiski, at the corner of Aristotelous (© **2310/231-805),** have excellent selections of Greek music well displayed in their windows and on their shelves. **En Chordes,** 3 Ipodromiou (© **2310/282-248),** has a wide selection of musical instruments and CDs, including Byzantine music.

## PERFUME

The little shop **Aroma,** 62 Mitropoleos, a block east of the Mitropoleos Cathedral (© **2310/286-010),** with its enticing rows of colored perfume jars, offers a multitude of scents, copying famous perfumes or mixing ones of your own choosing at extremely reasonable prices. If you don't find what you want here, most Greek pharmacies have a wide range of scents.

## SHOES

**Pak,** 3 Ayias Sofias Square, opposite the north side of the church (© **2310/274-863),** carries a wide selection of high-quality Greek shoes—from hiking boots to high heels—at very acceptable prices. It also carries foreign brands, but these are much more expensive.

## SWEETS

In a city where sweetness is next to godliness, the venerable **Agapitos,** 53 Tsimiski, (© **2310/279-107),** is heaven's best. There are a wide variety of items to choose from, all made with great, mouthwatering, high-caloric care. Another excellent sweet shop, **Terkenlis,** is at 30 Tsimiski, so you can easily compare and contrast. Both closed Sundays.

## WHERE TO STAY

Because of Thessaloniki's long history as a center for national and international trade, its large hotels have traditionally focused on serving the needs of commercial rather than leisure travelers. Most are blandly functional, and the few that aspire to elegance are almost entirely lacking in charm—the one notable exception being the Mediterranean Palace Hotel (see below). In recent years, Thessaloniki has gained several "boutique" hotels, notably the Andromeda and the Capsis Bristol Hotel.

Reserve in advance during both summer and winter to avoid difficulties during the numerous trade fairs and associated cultural events. Bookings peak in September and October, when the International Trade Fair is quickly followed by the monthlong Demetria cultural festival (not to mention the Festival of Greek Songs and Film Festival!). During the Demetria, there is often a hefty surcharge (as much as 25%) on the regular rates.

### VERY EXPENSIVE

**Andromeda** ★★    The very elegant and appealing Athens Andromeda , the city's first boutique hotel, has a loyal following. Now they, and others, have a place to stay in Thessaloniki. The rooms in this lovingly (and lavishly) restored 1920s town house just off central Aristotle Square (and 30m/98 ft. from the harborfront) are both elegant and inviting, with nothing of the impersonal hotel about them. As with the Athens Andromeda, this is a blissful refuge.

5 Komminion, 54640 Thessaloniki (near the Texaco Station). © **2310/373-700.** www.andromeda thessaloniki.gr. 44 units. 270€–350€ double. AE, DC, MC, V. **Amenities:** Restaurant; bar; concierge; airport pickup arranged; business center; 24-hr. room service; nonsmoking rooms. *In room:* A/C, TV, minibar, hair dryer.

**Capsis Bristol Hotel** ★ This very small, very elegant boutique hotel in the Ladadika district is the place to stay if you want to be in Ladadika and the Mediterranean Palace hotel is too big and impersonal for your tastes. Rooms here are individually, and lovingly, decorated with antiques and paintings—and named after famous Macedonian heroes (you might choose the Alexander room!)

2 Oplopiou & Katouni, 54626 Thessaloniki. ⓒ **2310/506-500.** www.capsisbristol.gr. 16 units, 200€–250€ double. AE, DC, V. **Amenities:** Breakfast room/bar; concierge. *In room:* A/C, TV, minibar, hair dryer.

**Makedonia Palace** ★ Kids The Macedonia Palace is now managed by the Grecotel Group, and seems to be back on track as a five-star luxury resort hotel, drawing both business travelers and Greek families on holiday—not to mention high-stepping gamblers (Europe's largest casino is next door). All the large rooms have been redone, but only in the usual Greek hotel decor, which seems to concentrate the glitz in the lobby and leave the bedrooms rather bland. All units have balconies, but if you stay here, insist on a seaside room. (Why pay all that money and not have the view?) By the way, there's an old-fashioned boardwalk along the sea, the perfect spot for sunset strolls. If you don't want to head back into town, the roof-top Porfyra restaurant has splendid views over the city and Gulf (and good "international" cuisine.)

2 Leoforos Megalou Alexandrou (on the seafront promenade half a mile east of the White Tower), 54640 Thessaloniki. ⓒ **231/089-7197.** Fax 231/089-7211. 284 units. 250€–425€. Parking 12€ a day. AE, DC, MC, V. **Amenities:** 3 restaurants; 2 bars; 2 pools (both outdoors, 1 salt, 1 fresh); tennis courts; health club and spa; concierge; airport pickup arranged; shopping arcade; 24-hr. room service. *In room:* A/C, TV, dataport (some units), minibar, hair dryer, safe (some units).

**Mediterranean Palace Hotel** ★★ The Mediterranean Palace opened in the Ladadika district, with its tempting restaurants and cafes, in 1997, and its location, comforts, and service make it Thessaloniki's best hotel. Front rooms have balconies overlooking the harbor, and virtually every unit in the house is large and furnished with comfortable beds, spiffy wall-to-wall carpeting, and cozy chairs, including some relaxing leather recliners. Many of the guest rooms have especially nice touches, such as decorative moldings and large walk-in closets—and if you want to make a phone call from your bathroom, this is the place to do it. As for the suites, with their large living rooms, kitchenettes, and bedrooms, we could happily live in one for months. Small wonder that this consistently appears in *Odyssey* magazine's lists of the best hotels in Greece. Everyone we know who has stayed here agrees that this is *the* place to stay in Thessaloniki.

3 Salaminos & Karatassou, 54626 Thessaloniki. ⓒ **2310/552-554.** Fax 2310/552-622. www.mediterranean-palace.gr. 120 units. 150€–300€ double. American-style buffet breakfast 12€. AE, DC, MC, V. **Amenities:** 2 Restaurants; 2 bars; concierge; business center; shopping arcade; 24-hr. room service; same-day laundry/dry cleaning services; nonsmoking rooms. *In room:* A/C, TV, dataport, kitchenette (suites), minibar, hair dryer, safe.

## EXPENSIVE

**Capsis Hotel** The best feature of this large 17-year-old hotel on busy Monastiriou, which becomes Egnatia as it gets closer to the center of town (at least 15 min. by foot), is its rooftop pool. The Capsis does a lot of convention business, so you can't expect much in the way of a personal touch, but you will get the comforts (including free parking, in-house laundry service, and a hairdresser) of a hotel that caters to business travelers. The guest rooms (recently renovated thoroughly) are furnished in pale pastels and have decent reading lights, small desks, large (king-size) beds and good-size bathrooms. The in-house restaurant is nothing special; the breakfast buffet is good (and should be at 10€!)

## A Note About Rates

The rates given in this section are for high season in summer—they should be lower in winter, and higher during trade fairs and the Demetria. As always, ask about discounts if you plan a long-term or off-season visit. Note that many hotels require that you pay for an expensive breakfast.

18 Monastiriou, 54629 Thessaloniki. © **2310/521-321.** Fax 2310/510-555. Capsishotel@capsishotel.gr. 422 units. 180€–200€ double. Compulsory breakfast 10€. AE, DC, MC, V. **Amenities:** Restaurant; 2 bar; outdoor pool; concierge; 24-hr. room service. *In room:* A/C, TV, dataport (some units), minibar, hair dryer.

**Electra Palace Hotel**  Overlooking Thessaloniki's main square, the Electra Palace, with its handsome, curved, arcaded facade, has the nicest location in town—except when there are noisy demonstrations in Aristotle Square. It has recently reopened as a Five Star Hotel after a long-overdue renovation, which we hope will return it to its former excellence. Perhaps the most important change here: the new roof-top pool and restaurant. If you stay here, insist on one of the fourth- or fifth-floor rooms with balcony overlooking the square; some of the interior rooms are quite small.

9A Aristotelous Sq., 54624 Thessaloniki. © **2310/232-221** to 229. Fax 2310/235-947. electrapalace@the. forthnet.gr. 70 units. 180€–300€. Rates include American-style buffet breakfast. AE, DC, MC, V. **Amenities:** 2 restaurants; 2 bars; outdoor roof-top pool; health club and spa; concierge; business center; 24-hr. room service; nonsmoking rooms. *In room:* A/C, TV, minibar, hair dryer.

**Hotel Astoria** ★  The Astoria, recently renovated, is still one of the best hotels in town, although the Mediterranean Palace, just around the corner, aces it for luxury, and the Electra on Aristotelous Square has a better location—although the staff here is generally more helpful than the Electra's. The Astoria offers all the creature comforts of a business traveler's hotel: bedrooms (admittedly, with resolutely anonymous decor) with balconies, decent bathrooms, soundproofed windows, and an in-house restaurant and bar (which sometimes has a "Happy Hour"). The location just off the harbor in the Ladadika district, with its restaurants, cafes, and galleries, is only a 10-minute walk from the center of town.

9 Salaminos (at the corner of Tsimiski), 54626 Thessaloniki. © **2310/500-910** or 2310/500-914. Fax 2310/531-564. astoria@napcorp.gr. 90 units, 30 with shower only. 160€ double. AE, MC, V. **Amenities:** Restaurant; bar. *In room:* A/C, TV, minibar, hair dryer.

**Hotel Olympia**  Like most hotels in Thessaloniki, the Olympia caters to businesspeople, but Greek families also stay here. The bathrooms are somewhat archaic and the bedrooms are rather bland, with carpets and chairs that have seen better days (the last overhaul here was in 1980). In short, your heart won't leap up at the sight of your room here, but the Olympia's location, at the northern end of the Roman market, is convenient for visiting the city, and traffic here is less thunderous than on some of the top floors tend to be quieter than those closer to the street—and, in this case, the flea market.

65 Olympou, 54631 Thessaloniki. © **2310/235-421.** Fax 2310/276-133. 111 units. 140€. Compulsory breakfast 10€. AE, DC, MC, V. **Amenities:** Restaurant; bar. *In room:* A/C, TV, minibar.

## MODERATE

**Hotel ABC**  The ABC juts out into busy Sindrivaniou Square, across from the International Fairgrounds and a short walk from Aristotle University and the

Archaeological Museum. Staff members claim that the windows are sound-proofed, but we'd say that you'll still be well aware of traffic noises from the lower floors of this eight-story hotel. The bedrooms, many decorated in bland browns and beiges, are perfectly functional and perfectly charmless, despite recent renovations. Why stay here? The price isn't bad, and you're very close to the Archaeological Museum and the inexpensive restaurants that cater to the area's university students. The hotel's own restaurant is not worth trying for lunch or dinner.

41 Angelaki, 54621 Thessaloniki. **☎ 2310/265-421.** Fax 2310/276-542. hotelabc@spark.netgr. 102 units. 140€. Compulsory breakfast 10€. AE, MC, V. **Amenities:** Restaurant; bar. *In room:* A/C, TV, minibar.

**Hotel Queen Olga** ★ Most of the Olga's good-size rooms have balconies and fully modern bathrooms. The decor is the usual pastel walls and pine beds—standard hotel stuff—but the balconies are a very nice feature. One of the pleasures of staying here is walking along the street that Thessalonians call the "Avenue of the Mansions" and looking at the elegant 19th-century buildings. This hotel is in the eastern part of town, but buses run frequently along Vas. Olgas into the center (about a 20-min. walk).

44 Vas. Olgas, 54641 Thessaloniki. **☎ 2310/824-621.** Fax 2310/868-581. 148 units. 135€–180€ double. DC, MC, V. **Amenities:** Restaurant; bar. *In room:* A/C, TV, minibar.

**Hotel Tourist** A friend of ours has stayed here every time she has visited Thessaloniki in the last 30 years. What she likes is that the hotel has changed imperceptibly over that time—although a recent renovation has spruced things up a bit. True, there are now TVs in the rooms, but many guests prefer to gather and watch television in the communal sitting rooms, with their ornate hanging chandeliers and amazingly uncomfortable chairs. When we stayed here, we loved our old-fashioned, high-ceilinged bedroom and tolerated the archaic bathroom (a little closet shoehorned into the room). We were less fond of the constant noise of traffic and the middle-of-the-night comings and goings to the rooms of some young, female Russian guests who described themselves as "entertainers."

21 Mitropoleos, 54624 Thessaloniki. **☎ 2310/270-501.** Fax 2310/226-865. 37 units. 100€ double. Inquire about reduced rates. No credit cards. *In room:* A/C, TV.

**Palace (Pallas) Hotel** We're including the Palace (also known as the Pallas) because several readers mentioned liking its central location and good-size rooms. A renovation in 1998 freshened things up considerably, while maintaining the gold and gilt "palatial" style—of the public rooms. The bedrooms are bland. When we visited, we found the desk staff curt and the rooms in need of another round of freshening up. Let us know what you think.

12 Tsimiski, 54624 Thessaloniki. **☎ 2310/257-400.** Fax 2310/256-589. 58 units. 120€ double. MC, V. **Amenities:** Bar. *In room:* A/C, TV.

## INEXPENSIVE

**Hotel Orestias Castorias** We were seriously tempted to stay at this small, very cheap, modest hotel across from the Roman Forum. Room 27, overlooking a quiet garden, was especially tempting. What made us hesitate was that almost every guest here seemed to be part of a large group of eastern Europeans, and we had the feeling that we might be crashing a quite lively private party. We'd be eager to have an update on this hotel, whose manager assured us that we would be "comfortable and safe" at his establishment.

14 Agnostou Stratiotou, 54631 Thessaloniki. **☎ 2310/536-280.** Fax 2310/276-572. 28 units. 50€. No credit cards.

## JUST OUTSIDE THESSALONIKI

We're assuming that you want to spend your time in Thessaloniki, rather than staying outside the city and going back and forth. But, just in case you want to stay out of town, here are some suggestions.

For those who cannot abide staying in any city in the summer, but still want to spend some time in one, the **Philippion,** (© **2310/203-321**) (in the forest of Sheih-Sou to the north of the Upper City), a sprawling, modern four-story hotel complex, renovated in 1998, is a good choice. Unfortunately, the fires of 1998, 1999, and 2000 harmed the lovely surrounding forests. The Philippion overlooks Thessaloniki from a hilltop and is a 10-minute drive from the city center (hotel shuttle buses go into town frequently). The guest rooms are large and sunny, the best being on the third floor to the rear, with a view of the city.

Facilities include a pool, children's playground, and good restaurant, with local specialties such as mussels in hot pepper sauce; there's sometimes live entertainment in the evening. The clientele are mostly vacationing Greek families, who can be rather boisterous. The hotel's proximity to the Ring Road makes it extremely easy to reach the airport (15 min. away) and the main highways to Athens, Halkidiki, and Thrace.

If the Philippion is full, and you want a place out of town, try the **Panorama** (© **2310/341-266**), 26 Analipsos, Panorama, a lovely, wooded suburb of Thessaloniki. This hotel does not have the facilities for children that the Philippion has and is usually very quiet, with fine views toward Thessaloniki and Mount Olympus. The restaurant is well-thought-of.

Finally, if you are just passing through and changing planes at the Thessaloniki airport, try the **Hyatt Regency Thessaloniki** (© **2310/401-234;** www. thessaloniki.hyatt.com). It's near the airport, some 13km (8 miles) from Thessaloniki itself, and has pools, tennis, spas, restaurants—everything, in short, to pass the time between flights.

The Panorama's double rooms begin at 120€; the Philippion's doubles begin at 150€; the Hyatt Regency's doubles begin at 200€.

## WHERE TO DINE

The cuisine of Thessaloniki has long been renowned throughout Greece for its delicate, aromatic character (a heritage of its historically close contact with the Levant) and the splendid variety of its game and hors d'oeuvres (*mezedes* or *mezedakia*). Recently, due to the efforts of a number of enterprising young Thessalonians, it has now become better than ever before, perhaps the finest in all of Greece.

Even in the most expensive establishments, the dress code is very casual for men, with ties and jackets rarely worn. Women, on the other hand, are usually resolutely chic, in little black dresses or more conservative trouser suits. Reservations can be made, but the only guarantee that a table will be available when you arrive is if you get there before most Greeks come out to dine. If you don't want to risk waiting, try to arrive for lunch before 1pm and dinner no later than 8:30pm.

Restaurants and tavernas offer cuisine of a distinctly Thessalonian character, including game, while ouzeries specialize almost exclusively in mezedes. The former may usually have an excellent selection of mezedes as well (you may be tempted to make a meal of starters alone), while the ouzeries may also offer more-substantial main courses. Sadly, the increased pollution in the bay has reached a point that we no longer recommend that visitors head off to one of the fish tavernas on the outskirts of town.

***Note:*** Most Thessaloniki restaurants do not accept credit cards.

## The Food of Thessaloniki

Without examining the vexed question of the extent to which Thessaloniki's cuisine has been heavily influenced by Turkish cuisine, let us just observe that the use of spices, the delicate hand with fish, the wide variety of vegetable dishes, and the extravagantly rich pastries so popular in Thessaloniki are not unknown in Turkey. As any Greek will tell you, this is because the Turks, during their long occupation of Greece, absorbed—stole, actually—the secrets of Greek cuisine. Some might argue that when the Turks withdrew from Greece, they took many of those secrets with them. Others would simply say that in some parts of Greece—such as Thessaloniki—a love of cuisine and a devotion to spices lives on.

In fact, it's the spices that set Thessaloniki's cuisine apart from that of the rest of Greece. Take the peppers. The most famous Macedonian peppers are the red *florines*, originally grown in the town of Florina, but now raised throughout Macedonia. These can be sweet, or so hot that they lift off the top of your head. We like both varieties, but we'd be a lot more relaxed when taking that first bite if we knew whether any individual *florina* were going to be sweet or pyrotechnic.

In addition to the florines, there are some *really* hot peppers traditionally grown in the Macedonian town of Piperia (pepper). These peppers are dried, then flaked, and the result, called *boukovo*, is sprinkled liberally into just about anything you'd care to cook. In some Thessaloniki restaurants, in addition to the salt and black pepper on your table, you'll find another shaker, of red pepper. Treat it with respect.

## RESTAURANTS & TAVERNAS

### Expensive

**Aigli** GREEK/CONTINENTAL Established in 1992 in an exquisitely restored Turkish hamam (bathhouse), this is certainly the most beautiful restaurant in Thessaloniki. Indoors, one dines beneath the high double domes of the former bathhouse; outdoors, in the gardened grounds of an old, open-air cinema that sometimes shows films in summer at 9 and 11pm. The Aigli used to boast the best haute cuisine in Thessaloniki, but the management has recently decided to shift its emphasis from cooking to entertainment and to booking the entire establishment for private parties. That said, the food is still very good; specialties include chicken kebab, Turkish dolmades, and grilled filet of chicken breast. There's often live music in the evening.

Kassandrou and Ayiou Nikolaou (near the church of Ayios Dimitrios) © 2310/270-715. Reservations seldom taken. Main courses 12€–22€. Surcharge of 15€ when there is entertainment. No credit cards. Thurs–Sun 10pm–2:30am. Mon–Wed usually open only for private parties.

### Moderate

**Draft** GREEK/INTERNATIONAL Draft is yet another newish Ladadika spot capitalizing on the seemingly endless local love of beer and *mezedes*. After all, what could be more pleasant than to sit in Draft's garden nibbling on salmon rolls with caviar, a selection of vegetable dips and fritters, and some shrimp in hot sauce? That may be why we've never managed to order an entree here, but chosen instead to make a very tasty meal out of the mezedes. Non-beer loving friends report that there's also a wide variety of ouzo and wine available.

3 Lycourgous, Ladadika. © 2310/555-518. www.draft.gr. Main courses 10€–15€ ($7–$12). DC, V. Mon–Sat 9pm–1am.

**Kioupia ★ GREEK** There are more than 65 items on the menu at this taverna with brick walls and a wood floor in the old warehouse district. There's excellent *stifada* (stews), *keftadakia* (meat balls), and spicy *gardoubitsa* (liver and garlic). A number of dishes including eggplant, zucchini, lamb and cheese, and minced beef and cheese are wrapped in crisp layers of filo (pastry). Dessert brings a range of Greek and Turkish sweets, the house retsina is excellent, and there's an extensive wine list. The same management runs the nearby **Amorgos,** 4 Panaiou and Doxis, Ladadika (© **2310/557-161**), which specializes in fresh fish.

3–5 Morihovou Sq., Ladadika. © **2310/553-239.** Fax 2310/553-579. www.kioupia.gr. Reservations recommended after 9pm. Main courses 10€–15€. AE, MC, V. Mon–Sat 1pm–1am.

**Krikelas ★★ GREEK** In 1999, Krikelas, a Thessaloniki institution since the 1940s, opened a branch in the Ladadika district, just across from the Mediterranean Palace Hotel. For visitors to Thessaloniki, the new Krikelas is very conveniently located, and all the reports are that the food here is just as good as ever. The specialties are the mouthwatering variety of *mezedes* and whatever game is in season (including quail, pheasant, rabbit, boar, and partridge). For starters, try the special feta cheese, creamed with butter and hot green peppers, or the smoked Gruyère from Metsovo. An interesting regional specialty is *spetzofai,* a mixture of seasonal vegetables and pungent country sausage. For dessert, try the homemade halva with almonds. The wine list at both branches is serious, although you can get a perfectly fine bottle for less than 12€.

32 Eth. Antistaseos © **2310/451-690,** and 6 Salaminos, Ladadika © and fax 2310/501-600). Reservations usually not accepted. Main courses 12€–20€. No credit cards. Mon–Sat 11:30am–2am. Usually closed July–Aug (but the Ladadika branch is possibly open then).

**Le Café GREEK/CONTINENTAL** You can get a salad, spaghetti, a sandwich, or just a coffee at this cafe, which has a curved balcony and large windows on the ground floor. Some people seem to show up to read their morning paper and are still here by midafternoon. This is a nice spot to sit and read, people-watch, and eavesdrop on cellphone conversations.

12 Tsimiski (corner of Tsimiski and Venizelou). © **2310/275-625.** Fax 2310/221-270. Main courses 6€–12€. No credit cards. Mon–Sat about 9am–1am.

**Tiffany's ★ GREEK/CONTINENTAL** This popular place, with wood paneling and pictures of old Salonika on the walls, seats about 100 and attracts an interesting mix of people—those who seem to drop in every night for a quick bite, and then the gaggles of 20-somethings who sit in the window tables and wait to be watched. We're in the distinct minority in that we find the two house specialties, *bifteki* Tiffany's (stuffed with cheese and tomatoes) and *hanoym borek* (casserole of roasted chicken, ham, veal, and cheese) both rather bland. On the other hand, we've had fun trying to figure out the principle behind the music here, which sometimes alternates Harry Belafonte and Greek golden oldies.

3 Iktinou (on the walkway between Tsimiski and the church of Ayia Sofia). © **2310/274-022.** Reservations recommended after 10pm. Main courses 8€–20€. No credit cards. Daily 11:30am–2am.

**Wolves GREEK** This warm, dark-wood, old-fashioned restaurant, established in 1977, has a cook reputed among locals to be one of the best in Thessaloniki when it comes to making a delicacy out of such basic Greek fare as pastitsio and moussaka. Try the roasted red peppers from Florina as one of your starters. For the main course, sample the moussaka Wolves, the oregano-flavored stewed pork or lamb, or the batter-fried codfish in garlic sauce—or take a look in the display counter in the kitchen at whatever specialty might be available that particular day.

6 Vas. Olgas (1 block in and 2 blocks east of the Macedonia Palace Hotel). ℰ 2310/812-855. Main courses 8€–15€. No credit cards. Mon–Sat 12:30pm–1am; Sun 12:30–5pm. Usually closed Dec 12–March 1 and Aug 5–15.

Zythos ★ GREEK/CONTINENTAL   This was one of the first restaurants to open in the restored warehouse district, and it's still very popular with ladies who lunch, young lovers, harried businessmen, and groups of golden youths. The decor is lots of wood and brick, as you'd expect in a former warehouse—although the slim young waiters in their chic black slacks or skirts hardly suggest warehouse workers. We can vouch for the croquettes of vegetables, *saganaki* (fried cheese), and veggie pasta. There are usually two daily specials, including one vegetarian choice, on the menu.

5 Katouni, Ladadika. ℰ 2310/540-284. Main courses 8€–15€. No credit cards. Daily 11am–1am.

### Inexpensive

If you're around Aristotelous Square, **Lokanda**, at the corner of Mitropoleos and Venizelou (ℰ **2310/288-432**), is a good spot for a coffee, stuffed croissant, or sandwich—at prices much lower than similar places in the square. **Tsarouhas,** 78 Olymbou, near Dikastirion Square, seems to be open all hours (although it closes in July and Aug), and serves up *patsatzidhika:* the tripe soup that's supposed to cure all that ails you. In the Upper City, head to **To Yedi,** 13 Ioanni Papareska, outside the gates of the Eptapirgiou prison (ℰ **2310/246-695**), to sit under the trees, relax, and try the keftedes and other mezedes.

**Corner** PIZZA   Locals and visiting pizza fans agree that this place serves the best pizza in town, perhaps because a wood-burning oven is used. Not surprisingly, it's a popular hangout for young Salonikans. There's another branch at 28 Ayias Sofias 28.

12 Ayias Sofias and 6 Ethnikis Aminis, a block north of the White Tower, behind the State Theater. ℰ 2310/426-531. Main courses 6€–15€. No credit cards. Daily about 11am–1am.

**Kentrike Stoa** ★ GREEK/CONTINENTAL   This snacks-and-drinks place in the Central Market is up a winding metal staircase from the market itself. The ceiling is covered with parachute cloth, jazz contends with the shouts from the market below, and the languid 20-something crowd tolerates outsiders gracefully—and are fun to spy on as they vie to impress one another.

32 Vas. Irakleiou 32. ℰ 2310/278-242. Snacks 3€–10€. No credit cards. Mon–Sat noon–1am.

**Loutros** ★★ GREEK   For years, Loutros occupied part of an old Turkish bath; now it's in new quarters, but still serves up fried minnows (which you eat whole) and delicious mussels, as well as tasty *horta* (greens) and *florines* (spicy red peppers). The music here is usually very Levantine-sounding—which, in Greece, is a polite way of saying that it sounds absolutely Turkish.

5 M. Kountoura (opposite the Bezesten). ℰ 2310/228-895. Main courses 7€–12€. No credit cards. Mon–Sat 11am–midnight.

**Thanasis (Mypobolos Smyrnh)** ★★★ GREEK   For 47 years, Thessalonians have been beating a path to this small taverna that serves home-style cooking—including stuffed squid and mussels, both fried and steamed—with zest. In fact, the first customer through the door here in the new millennium was Greek Prime Minister Simitis. The sign over the door reads H MYPOBOLOS SMYRNH (ee-me-*ro*-volos *smear*-ni) and translates as "Miraculous Smyrna," but everyone knows it equally well by the name of its marvelously genial owner, Thanasis. He, his wife, and relatives labor incessantly during market hours to satisfy the cravings of a seemingly endless number of workers, businesspeople, artists, prostitutes, actors, and various other characters from the high and low walks of Thessaloniki. The potato salad, cheese croquettes, spicy peppers with cheese, squid stuffed with cheese and rice, grilled fish and meats, and excellent battered cod (*bakaliaro*) are all wonderful, as is the mood in this tiny restaurant with photos and old prints on the walls. The music is usually very loud here, but if we could eat at only one place in Thessaloniki, this would be it.

Emou and 32 Komninon (just inside the Modiano Market). © 2310/274-170. Fax 2310/347-062. Reservations necessary after 10pm. Main courses 6€–12€. No credit cards. Mon–Sat about 8am–3am.

**To Makedoniko** GREEK   You couldn't get more basically Greek than this. Rugged, rudimentary, and full of local color, To Makedoniko is a watering hole and eatery equally popular among the neighborhood working class and the downtown intellectuals, artists, and university students. If you have the constitution to handle it, you must drink the local schnapps—*tsipouro*, a delicately perfumed but powerful variety of ouzo—with your *mezedes*. While the limited menu can vary from day (or even from hour to hour), the pork *riganato* and mussels in a hot-pepper broth (*midia saganaki*) are usually available.

32 Yioryiou Papadopoulou (in the Upper City, inside the arch at the western end of the walls). © 2310/627-438. Main courses 5€–12€. No credit cards. Mon–Sat 9am–2am. Sometimes closed in Jan. Bus no. 23.

## OUZERIES

As can be gathered from the name, ouzeries are places specializing in ouzo and the *mezedes* that go with them. One need not, however, drink ouzo—or any kind of alcoholic beverage—to enjoy the marvelous variety of foods they offer: octopus, meatballs, shrimp, squid, taramosalata (fish roe puréed with oil and bread), tzatziki (cucumber, yogurt, and garlic), melitzanosalata (eggplant purée), cheeses, and potato, beet, and bean salads. Go with your waiter to look at the offerings and point out what you want.

**Aproopto Light** GREEK   Highly popular with professionals of the nearby State Theatre and other artistic types, this place serves excellent *mezedes* as well as some main-course dishes. Its relatively small, well-decorated sidewalk and interior dining areas are usually packed and rife with conviviality. Try the mussels with spinach and the leeks a la Parisienne as well as the *taganaki*, a cheese-and-potato dish.

6 Zevksidos (a pedestrian walkway off the eastern end of the church of Ayia Sofia). © 2310/241-141. Main courses 6€–15€. No credit cards. Daily noon–1:30am.

**Aristotelous** ★★★ GREEK   In just about everyone's opinion, the best ouzo place in Salonika. Highly popular with writers, artists, and everyone else in the know, Aristotelous is constantly packed during the peak lunch and dinner hours, so you should come either early or late, or you'll end up waiting at least 20 minutes. Indoor and outdoor seating areas in between high-rise office buildings contribute to the crush and somehow the charm. You can and should linger for hours, which is why it's often so hard to get a table. The variety of *mezedes* is sumptuous. Try the fried zucchini and eggplant; the feta cheese mashed with hot peppers and olive oil (*ktipití*); and, for something more substantial, the stuffed cuttlefish (*soupiá*). Also delicious is the homemade halva for dessert.

© 2310/230-762. Reservations not accepted. 12€–30€ for a variety of mezedes. No credit cards. Mon–Sat 10am–2am; Sun 11am–6pm.

**Totti's** GREEK Facing the broad east-to-west expanse of Thessaloniki harbor, Totti's is a place to linger, particularly in the evenings when the sun sets into the sea in front of you—and especially since the service here is very slow. The food is typical ouzeri fare, but the tableware and other accoutrements exhibit considerably more elegance, which is reflected in the price. This is also a great place for breakfast. There are a number of Totti's in Thessaloniki; you'll bump into others in your explorations.

3 Aristotelous Sq (southwest corner fronting the sea). © 2310/237-715. Main courses 10€–15€. No credit cards. Daily 7am–2am.

## THESSALONIKI AFTER DARK

Thessaloniki does not really awaken until after dark, and when it does, it seems at times as if the entire populace has come out to amuse itself. In addition to the cultural festivals held in the fall, numerous theatrical events and pop and classical concerts take place year-round. Meanwhile, the city seems festooned with enough bars and clubs to serve a population twice its size, yet all of them are crowded to the bursting point—and more open every year.

While there are a number of publications listing the various events, and posters splattered everywhere announcing them, they will all be Greek to you, so the best thing to do is ask for information at your hotel or stop by the office of the **Greek National Tourism Organization (EOT)**, Aristotelous Square 8 (© 2310/271-888 or 2310/222-935).

## ONLY IN THESSALONIKI

Taking what the Greeks call a *volta* (stroll) along the seaside promenade, particularly at sunset or under a full moon, is one of the great pleasures of being in Thessaloniki. Start at **Aristotelous Square,** perhaps with a coffee, a drink, or sweets at one of its many cafes, and walk east past the White Tower and toward the bright lights of the city's amusement park at the other end of the promenade, about 3km (2 miles) distant. Along **Leoforos Nikis,** which borders the promenade in the city center, are a number of cafes and bars. At the **White Tower,** there are usually peanut vendors and, occasionally, the city's only horse-drawn carriage for rent.

You might also decide to take an hour (or longer) **cruise** around the harbor on the various small boats that dock just east of the tower. You'll see signs posted advertising cruises of different lengths and prices.

## THE PERFORMING ARTS

The **State Theatre of Northern Greece (Kratiko Theatro)** has two venues. In winter, it stages plays in the **Royal State Theatre,** which is next to the White Tower (© 2310/860-966); in summer, at the **Forest Theatre (Theatro Dasous),** an open-air amphitheater located in the forested hilltop area east of the Upper City (© 2310/245-307). The company presents both ancient and modern Greek plays, as well as Greek translations of old and new foreign plays, including those by such well-known playwrights as Christopher Marlowe and Arthur Miller.

## Late-Night Bites

Virtually all cafes and many restaurants stay open almost all night in summer, but in case you're in town in winter, when things tend to close down much earlier, try one of the two branches of **Corner,** 28 Ayias Sofias, between the church of Ayia Sofia and Egnatia (☎ **2310/273-310),** and 6 Ethnikis Aminis, a block north of the White Tower, behind the State Theater (☎ **2310/426-531).** They serve alcoholic drinks, the best pizza in town, and other delicacies until 1am (see also "Where to Dine," above). Another option is **Xatzi,** 50 Eleftheriou Venizelou, just north of Egnatia (☎ **2310/ 279-058;** www.chatzis.gr) established in 1908 and now run by the fourth generation of the same family. It's the perfect place to go for a midnight sweet—or breakfast coffee, since it opens before 7am. There's a superb selection of Levantine pastries and desserts whose recipes have not changed an iota since its opening. Xatzi also now has a shop at Them. Sofouli and Argonafton streets (☎ **2310/415-474),** where you can get the same rich treats to eat in or take away.

In summer, the Forest Theatre, which has a marvelous view of the city, also hosts lively, well-attended concerts by popular Greek singers and composers, as well as performances by visiting ballet companies.

Thessaloniki's new **Concert Hall** (Megaron Mousikis), 25 Martiou & Paralia (☎ **2310/895-800)** opened in 2000. Check at the Concert Hall or at the GNTO for a concert schedule. There are also concerts at the **Aristotle University concert hall** on Nea Egnatia, opposite the northern entrance of the International Trade Fairgrounds, from September through May (☎ **2310/283-343).**

## FESTIVALS

**THE DEMETRIA FESTIVAL**    In honor of the patron saint of Thessaloniki, St. Dimitrios, whose nameday is October 26, this prestigious cultural festival runs every October and includes the Greek Film Festival as well as many theatrical and musical events, all of them performed by major and minor artists from all over the country.

**THE FEAST OF SAINTS CONSTANTINE & ELENI (MAY 21)**    On or around the feast of the first Christian emperor and his mother, villagers in the village of **Ayia Eleni** (80km/50 miles northeast of Thessaloniki) and at **Langadas** (12km/7 miles northeast of Thessaloniki) engage in *pirovasia* (fire dancing). Crowds come from all over Macedonia to see the faithful dance over a bed of hot coals. When they're done, they feast on the roasted black bull that has been sacrificed earlier in the day. Just in case you're wondering—yes, much of what's done here preserves pre-Christian rites.

**THE INTERNATIONAL TRADE FAIR FESTIVAL**    This takes place every year during the first 2 weeks in September and draws businesspeople from around the world. There are lots of exhibits at the international fairgrounds—and hotel rooms are very hard to find.

## THE BAR, CLUB & MUSIC SCENE

In the summer, virtually all of Thessaloniki's best bars and clubs shut down. Some immediately reopen branches along a section of the road leading east along the coast, about a mile before the airport. This, plus the fact that new or newly decorated and renamed venues are constantly opening, while others go out of fashion and close, makes it virtually impossible to recommend any with certainty.

There is one place, however, that we can recommend without hesitation. Not only is it a permanent fixture of Thessaloniki nightlife year-round, but it also incorporates by far the best of the bar, music, and club scenes in the city.

**Milos** ✸✸ Within the grounds of an old, wonderfully restored flour-mill complex, the Milos (*mee-los*) complex contains a club for blues, folk, jazz, and pop groups; a nightclub featuring Greek singers and comedians; a bar/disco; an outdoor concert stage and movie theater; several exhibition rooms and art galleries; a cafe; and an ouzeri serving more than 30 kinds of *mezedes*. Almost as soon as it opened in 1990, Milos became one of the top musical venues in the country. Each summer, performers from literally around the world (and from throughout Greece) appear here. If you want to be sure of a seat, it's a good idea to arrive before the clubs open at 10pm. The ouzeri, cafe, and galleries open from about 11am on. 56 Andreadou Vioryiou. ✆ 2310/551-838 or 2310/525-968. Cover varies depending on entertainment, usually no more than 30€; drinks around 10€. Go west on Tsimiski to its end and turn left onto 28 Octobriou. At the first traffic light, turn right onto Andreadou Vioryiou and continue to the end of the street. This is quite a hike from the center, and you may want to take a cab.

## 2 In the Footsteps of Philip of Macedon & Alexander the Great

Every year, more people head north to Macedonia to see the cluster of ancient sites associated with **Philip II of Macedon** (382–336 B.C.) and his famous son, **Alexander the Great** (356–323 B.C.); these include **Pella, Vergina,** and **Dion.** Many of those visiting Northern Greece these days are Greeks, whose interest in things Macedonian was enormously intensified a few years ago when, just across the border, the former Yugoslavian district of Macedonia proclaimed itself a republic. How dare these non-Greeks take the name of Macedonia, Greeks asked—forgetting that their own ancestors had not considered Philip of Macedon a Greek! Most of all, Greeks were furious that Philip's best-known royal symbol—a star with 16 rays—appeared on the new Macedonia's flag. Throughout Greece, debates raged over whether the new self-styled Macedonia had imperialistic aims. For once, Greece's longstanding enmity with Turkey was virtually ignored, as Greeks painted MACEDONIA IS GREECE on virtually every road and wall in the country. Things have calmed down now that the new Republic of Macedonia has changed its flag, but Greeks are still rediscovering their ancestral links with Philip, the northern king who conquered Greece in 338 B.C.

The renewed interest in Philip, Alexander, and Macedonia itself has led the Greek Archaeological Service to redouble its efforts to excavate the Macedonian royal sites and build site museums. And that, of course, means that there's much more to see above ground than there was even a few years ago.

## ESSENTIALS

**GETTING THERE** The only enjoyable and efficient way to see the places where Philip of Macedon and Alexander the Great lived and reigned is by car or with a tour. **Budget Rent-A-Car** has offices at the airport (✆ 2310/471-491) and in the city at Angelaki 15 (✆ 2310/274-272 or 2310/229-519), opposite the International Fairgrounds. Other rental offices are **Avis,** Leoforos Nikis 3 (✆ 2310/227-126 or 2310/683-300), at the western end of the harbor, opposite the docks; **Europcar,** Papandreou 5 (✆ 2310/836-333); and **Hertz,** El.

Venizelou 4 (© **2310/224-906**), on Eleftherias Square. (See "Getting Around" in the Thessaloniki section, p. 557, for more car-rental information.)

Several Athens-based companies, such as **CHAT** and **American Express,** offer tours of Central and Northern Greece that take in the most important Macedonian sites. Reputable Thessaloniki companies offering tours of the Philip and Alexander sites include **Zorpidis Travel,** 76 Egnatia, at Aristotelous (© **2310/244-400;** zorpidis@zorpidis.gr) and **Kinissi Tour Agency,** 43 Tsimiski, (© **2310/237-000;** fax 2310/264-569). A day trip to Pella, Edessa, Veria, and Vergina or to Philippa, Kavala, and Amphipolis costs from 100€. It is vital to make an advance reservation. If possible, avoid visiting on a summer weekend, when crowds of Greeks flock to these sites.

**By Bus**  If you try to visit these sites by local bus, you may feel that it is taking you longer to see them than it took Alexander to conquer the world. Still, if you have lots of time and love buses, you can visit the following sites by bus from Thessaloniki. For **Pella,** there are sometimes direct buses; failing that, take a bus to Edessa and ask to be let off at Pella. For **Vergina,** take a bus to Veria, and then a local bus to the site of Vergina. If you wish to go to Pella and continue to Vergina, you can do so by taking the Thessaloniki bus from Pella to the town of Halkidona, where you can get a bus to Veria. This may involve a substantial wait. For **Dion,** take a bus to Katerini and then a local bus to Dion. For up-to-date information on bus schedules and departure points, check with the **Greek National Tourism Organization** in Thessaloniki (© **2310/271-888**); the bus information line (© **2310/512-122**) is unlikely to have English speakers answering the phone. If you read Greek, the Thessaloniki daily newspaper *Macedonia* also lists bus schedules.

**VISITOR INFORMATION**  If you're stopping in Athens or Thessaloniki before visiting these sites, drop by the **Greek National Tourism Organization (EOT)** in Athens at Tsoha 7 St., (© **210/870-7000**), or in Thessaloniki at Aristotelous Square (© **2310/271-888**), and get a copy of the brochure *Greece/Macedonia* and any other brochures available for individual sites. At each site, ask whether there is a free Culture Ministry brochure available.

## PELLA

Pella, once the capital of the Macedonian kingdom and the birthplace of Philip II of Macedon in 382 B.C. and his famous son, Alexander the Great, in 356 B.C., is easy to spot: The **archaeological site and museum** (© **23820/31-160**) are right beside the highway (a 40km/24-mile drive west of Thessaloniki on the E86 highway to Edessa). Museum admission is 3€; site admission is 3€. Hours are Monday from noon to 7pm, Tuesday through Friday from 8am to 7pm, and Saturday, Sunday, and holidays from 8:30am to 3pm. Allow at least 2 hours to visit the site and museum.

In antiquity, Pella's situation was more appealing—a navigable inlet connected it to the broad Thermaic Gulf that borders Thessaloniki. Over the centuries, the inlet silted up, leaving Pella landlocked, but in Philip and Alexander's day, ships would have sailed here and docked at what is now a dusty plain. The city itself is thought to have covered at least 13 sq. km (5 sq. miles), of which only a fraction has been excavated.

Nonetheless, there's more than enough of Pella above ground to give you an idea of this stylish city, with its large, square agora (market and civic center) bordered by colonnaded stoas and flanked by streets lined with shrines, sanctuaries, temples, and private homes. The lovely frescoes that once adorned the house

## Philip & Alexander

When Philip was born in 382 B.C., most Greeks thought of Macedonians—if they thought of them at all—as one of the rude northern tribes of barbarians who lived in the back of beyond. Macedonians, after all, were not even allowed to participate in the Panhellenic Games at Delphi. Clearly, this irritated Philip. By 346 B.C., after conquering a number of Athenian colonies and allied cities, Philip had won a place on Delphi's governing board. A few years later, in 338 B.C., despite Demosthenes's best oratorical efforts to alert the Athenians to Philip's intentions, the Macedonian king had conquered all of Greece. Two years later, Philip was dead, cut down as he strolled to see a performance in the theater at his capital city of Vergina. Some said that his young son Alexander was behind the assassination, while others wondered how the unproven youth could rule Macedonia, let alone Greece.

No one, except perhaps Alexander himself, could have imagined that by the time he died at 33, he would have conquered much of the known world as far east as India. Alexander's early death makes it impossible to know what he would have done with the rest of his life, once he had no new worlds to conquer. Some scholars think that Alexander was a visionary bent not just on conquering, but also uniting the world into a "brotherhood of man." This, they suggest, is why Alexander contracted so many foreign marriages and accepted conquered princes into his retinue. Other scholars, more cynical, think that both Alexander's marriages and his use of former enemies were simply shrewd political moves. The truth probably lies somewhere in between the two theories.

In any event, after Alexander's death, his former comrades turned on one another and destroyed his empire. Within a few generations, Macedon was once more a northern kingdom in the back of beyond, living on memories of its brief period of international importance.

walls are gone, but a number of the handsome **pebble mosaic floors** remain, both on the site and in the museum. These houses must have been exceptionally pleasant, with their gaily painted walls, handsome mosaic floors, and sheltered inner courtyards. There families could have passed an evening, perhaps discussing the Athenian playwright Euripides's *The Bacchae*, which had its premiere around 408 B.C. in the as yet undiscovered theater here.

Unfortunately, the dwelling you'd probably most like to see—the **palace** where both Philip and his son Alexander were born—is not yet open to the public. Not to worry: You can drive or walk to the hilltop north of the site, peer over the wire fence, and get an idea of how large this royal home was. In fact, the palace covered 60,000 sq. m—only 10,000 less than the agora itself? Somewhere in this vast complex, Aristotle tutored the young Alexander. The view from the hill is still tremendous, but must have been truly breathtaking in antiquity, when the palace overlooked both the plain and the channel down which ships sailed, bringing supplies here from around the Mediterranean.

Pella's small **museum** is superb, especially its glorious pebble mosaics found in some of the 4th-century B.C. homes excavated here. The two best-known mosaics show a lion hunt and the god of wine, Dionysos, riding a leopard. The lion hunt is worth looking at not only for its powerful depiction of two youths and a lion, but also because this mosaic may show Alexander himself. Some scholars have suggested that the mosaic records the incident when the young Alexander was saved by a friend from a lunging lion. Others suspect that it's too good to be true that the mosaic actually shows that famous incident and suggest that this is simply a genre scene of a hunt. You can compare the marble bust of Alexander in the museum with the youth under attack in the lion hunt and decide for yourself.

## WHERE TO STAY & DINE

After you visit the site, you may want to take in **Edessa,** 45km (27 miles) west of Pella, a scenic clifftop town with bubbling waterfalls and several pleasant small cafes and restaurants beside them. We've eaten at several, and can't say that we find one better than another—the real point of dining here is enjoying the rushing waterfall. Note that this is not the best place to visit on summer weekends, when many Thessalonians come here to escape the summer heat.

If it's the weekend, or if you're rushed after visiting Pella, you can grab a bite at one of the small roadside restaurants by the fountain beside the (signposted) remains of "Baths of Alexander," a Hellenistic fountain incorporated into a Roman bath about a kilometer from Pella on the Edessa road.

As far as overnighting here, keep in mind that Edessa is a very popular year-round destination for Thessalonians, that it has only about 125 hotel rooms, and that you may have trouble finding a vacancy if you simply appear on the weekend. That said, we suggest the 44-unit **Katarraktes,** 18 Karanou, Edessa (© **2381O/22-3OO;** fax O38/1O2-7237), which has a nice location near a waterfall. Its guest rooms, which go for 70€ double, are furnished in the usual bland Greek-hotel style: pine beds, pale walls—acceptable, but in no way memorable. If the Katarraktes is full, you might try the modest 36-room **Alfa,** 36 Egnatia (© **2381O/22-221;** fax 2381O/24-777); friends of ours found it just fine for a night.

## VERGINA & ENVIRONS: THE TOMBS AT LEUKADIA, THE TOWN OF VERIA & NEARBY VINEYARDS

Vergina is 20km (12 miles) south of Pella, and 62km (38 miles) west of Thessaloniki; located just outside the hamlet of Palatitsa, it's very well signposted. If you only have time to visit either the site or the museum, there's no choice here—head for the museum. If you have time for both, here's what you'll see at the **Vergina site** and **Royal Tombs Museum** (© **2331O/92-347).** Museum admission is 3€; site admission is 3€. Summer hours for both are Monday from noon to 7pm and Tuesday through Sunday from 8:30am to 7pm; the site and museum close at 5pm in the off season. Allow at least 3 hours to visit the site and museum.

**Vergina** (anciently known as Aigai) was where Philip lived when not at Pella and where he died in 336 B.C., and is the most important of the royal Macedonian sites. Preliminary excavations suggest that the palace was enormous, with an inner courtyard some 147 feet square. Around the courtyard ran a Doric colonnade; the bases of some of the 60 columns of the colonnade are still in place and give a sense of the courtyard's size. The palace also had a long airy colonnaded veranda running the length of its north side, overlooking the theater. It's quite possible that the royal family watched some spectacles in the theater from the comfort of the palace veranda.

Unfortunately for Philip, that's not what he did on the fatal day in 336 B.C. when he was assassinated en route from the palace to take in a performance at the theater. Some said Alexander himself was behind the assassination, others simply said that the young prince was not notably grief-stricken by the death of his father. You can sit in the **theater**—the only really impressive remains—and contemplate the moment when Philip realized that he was about to be struck down.

As you drive from the site to the Royal Tombs Museum, you'll notice hundreds of low mounds on the gentle hills of the Macedonian plain. These are some of the more than 300 **burial mounds** found here, some dating from as long ago as the Iron Age, but many from the time of Philip himself. Virtually all of these graves were robbed in antiquity, but fortunately—and almost miraculously—the tomb identified as that of Philip himself was undisturbed for almost 2,000 years. How it was found is one of the great stories of archaeology, deserving a place beside accounts of how Schliemann found Troy and excavated the "Tomb of Agamemnon" at Mycenae.

Vergina's first excavator, the French archaeologist Leon Heuzey, prophesied in 1876 that when Vergina was fully excavated, "the importance of its ruins for Macedonia will be comparable to Pompeii." The Greek Archaeological Service began to work here in the 1930s, and uncovered several tombs that looked like small temples. For years, the excavators nibbled away at the largest burial mound of all, the **Great Tumulus**, measuring 110m (361 ft.) across and 12m (39 ft.) high, containing a number of burials. One tomb they found was almost totally destroyed, another well preserved but robbed. Still, head excavator Manolis Andronikos remained convinced that he was excavating ancient Aigai, Philip's capital city, and might yet find Philip's own tomb.

Finally, in 1977—on the last day of the excavation season—Andronikos and his workers opened the massive marble gates of the last remaining tomb. As Andronikos later wrote in *Vergina: The Royal Tombs:*

*We saw a sight which it was not possible for me to have imagined, because until then such an ossuary [container for bones] had never been found... all-gold... with an impressive relief star on its lid. We lifted it from the sarcophagus, placed it on the floor, and opened it. Our eyes nearly popped out of our sockets and our breathing stopped; there unmistakably were charred bones placed in a carefully formed pile and still retaining the colour of the purple cloth in which they had once been wrapped... If those were royal remains... then... had I held the bones of Philip in my hands?*

Andronikos—and virtually all of Greece—answered his question with a resounding "Yes," in large part because of the other objects found in the tomb. The gold wreaths, Andronikos felt, were too fine to belong to anyone but a king. And surely the little ivory portrait heads were the spitting images of Philip and Alexander themselves. And, most persuasive of all, what about the bronze greaves (shin guards) found in the tomb? Were they not of unequal length? And was not Philip known to have legs of different length, due to an early injury?

It is difficult to overestimate the Philip-fever that swept through Greece when Andronikos announced that he had found Philip's tomb and identified Vergina as Ancient Aigai, Philip's capital city. Although some scholars have questioned whether this is, in fact, Philip's tomb, those scholars are not Greek. Greeks regard with horror any suggestion that this splendid tomb may have belonged to Arrhidaeos, the son of Philip known only for his lack of distinction.

The arched roof of the **Royal Tombs Museum** re-creates a sense of the Great Tumulus itself, as does the passageway leading into the tomb area. Each of the five tombs is protected by a glass wall, but seeing the tombs this way is the next-best thing to being able to stand inside them. Give your eyes time to get accustomed to the darkness, then enjoy the lovely decorative paintings on the facades of the templelike tombs. And, of course, be sure to see the treasures from these tombs now on display in the Archaeological Museum in Thessaloniki.

## A DETOUR TO LEUKADIA

If Vergina has whetted your appetite for royal tombs, you might consider heading north to Leukadia, 20km (12 miles) south of Edessa in the beautiful foothills of Mount Vermion. *Be forewarned:* This is one of those excursions based on suggestions such as "ask for directions in the village" and "ask if the custodian will accompany you and open the tombs." If you're lucky and find the custodian and the tombs (ask in cafes and the main square in Leukadia), you'll get to see three spectacular tombs. The 3rd-century B.C. **Great Tomb** is decorated with paintings of battles of Lapiths and Centaurs and Greeks and Persians. The **Kinch Tomb** (named after its discoverer) and the **Tomb of Lyson and Kallikles** are decorated with paintings of funeral swags of pomegranates and snakes, a symbol both of the underworld (since snakes often live underground) and rebirth (because snakes shed old skins for new ones). The claustrophobic may find the descent down a dank shaft into the Tomb of Lyson and Kallikles unappealing. If the custodian does take you to see these tombs, you should slip him perhaps 5€, along with your thanks. Allow at least 3 hours to find the caretaker and visit the tombs.

## VERIA (VEROIA) & ITS TURKISH REMAINS

If an excursion to Leukadia seems too much like work, try the nearby hill town of Veria (Veroia), 15km (9 miles) northwest of Vergina. The Municipal Culture Office at the corner of Pavlou Mela and Bizantiou (© **23110/27-914**) in the center of town has several helpful maps and brochures. Veria is in the throes of development, but still has a number of old streets, wood houses with overhanging bay windows, more than 50 small Byzantine churches (usually locked), a 15th-century cathedral, and a good number of buildings from the Ottoman period, including a former mosque and *hamam* (bath). At the corner of Anixeos and Pasteur, the handsome 1930s Vlachoyiannis town house has the collection of the Museum of Modern History and Art. There's a cluster of other 20th-century "eclectic" style houses nearby and you can get a sense of how people lived here then in the restored rooms of the museum, which has a cafe. Nearby, the new **Byzantine Museum** is in the restored Markos mill (© **23310/29-737**). Only the truly devoted will wish to visit the small **Archaeological Museum,** 47 Anoixeos (© **23310/24-972**), with finds from local sites (admission is 2€; open Tues–Sun from 8:30am–3pm). Don't feel bad if it's closed; you'll have much more fun just wandering the streets of this old town, with its considerable Turkish remains and old Jewish quarter. You can stop here for a quick coffee and get a sense of the town—or spend a pleasant day here.

## THE NAOUSSA VINEYARDS

About halfway between Veria and Edessa, on the slopes of Mount Vermion, several vineyards are open to the public; you'll see their roadside signs. At Naoussa, a region famous for its wine, the **Stenimachos Winery,** run by the well-known Boutari vintners, is open to the public. Tours of the winery are given most workdays and are sometimes offered in English. For information, call ⓣ 23320/41-666, or check with the GNTO in Thessaloniki (ⓣ 2310/271-888).

## WHERE TO STAY & DINE

The 37-unit **Hotel Makedonia,** 50 Kontogeorgaki, Veria (ⓣ and fax 23310/66-902 or 23310/66-946), is the best hotel in town, with a quiet location. It basically has the bland ambience of a businessman's, rather than a traveler's, hotel; rooms come with air-conditioning and TVs. The new **Veria,** kilometer 6.5 on the Veria-Naousa Highway (ⓣ 23310/93-112; fax 23310/93-556), gets a fair amount of tour business. Although staying here makes exploring Veria itself a mini-excursion, you may find the pool so welcoming that you never leave. The rooms are standard Greek-hotel quality, but most have pleasant balconies as well as air-conditioning and TVs; the hotel is set back from the highway just enough to make the traffic noise manageable.

Near the Vergina site, there are a number of small cafes and restaurants, including the pleasant **Filippion,** as well as several overnight possibilities at "rented rooms" establishments. Veria's restaurants serve food that is almost guaranteed to be better than that dished out around the site of Vergina. You should eat well at either **Saroglou** or **Kostalar,** both on Afroditis, on a tree-shaded square.

## DION

The **Dion archaeological site** and **museum** (ⓣ 23510/53-206) are outside the village of Dion, about 8km (5 miles) west of the Dion sign on the E75, the main Athens-Thessaloniki highway (and 78km/48 miles south of Thessaloniki). **Warning:** This is a dangerous turn off the highway; reentry is also difficult. Admission to site is 3€; museum admission is 3€. Hours are Monday from 10:30am to 7pm and Tuesday through Sunday from 8:30am to 7pm; the site and museum close at 3pm in the off season. Allow at least 2 hours for your visit.

If you haven't been to Dion in a few years, you may want to know that there's good news and bad news. The good news is that excavations are continuing, unearthing more of ancient Dion. New pathways have been constructed to help visitors tour the site, and helpful signs have gone up. In mid-August, the **Olympos Festival** (ⓣ 23510/76-401) presents concerts at the ancient site.

The bad news is that this site, until recently one of the few left in Greece that you could wander around at will, imagining that you had just stumbled upon an ancient city, has been fenced in and tidied up with a vengeance.

Nonetheless, Dion still has a beautiful location, just outside the Vale of Tempe, in the foothills of Mount Olympus. This is an unusually green spot, with pine groves and farm fields watered by springs fed by the melting snow that clings to Olympus's peaks year-round. If you can, bring a picnic; after you visit the excavations and museum, you can linger a while at the picnic tables at the site.

Dion was founded as a religious sanctuary, and for some time was Macedonia's most important sanctuary, something of a sacred city. Later, its constant water supply led both Philip and Alexander to establish military training camps here. Philip bivouacked here before he marched south to conquer Greece, while Alexander drilled his men here before heading east to conquer Asia.

According to a story preserved by the 2nd-century A.D. biographer Plutarch, it was at Dion that Alexander, then only 8 years old, first saw Bucephalos, the handsome black stallion soon to be his favorite mount. Philip himself had bought the horse, but found that neither he nor any of his men could ride it.

Alexander asked his father if he could have a go at taming the creature. Muttering that if *he* could not tame the horse, an 8-year-old hardly could, Philip nonetheless agreed to give Alexander a chance. Immediately, Alexander turned Bucephalos so that he could not see his shadow, leapt up, and galloped away. When the young prince returned from his ride, Philip said, "My son, look for a kingdom equal to you. Macedonia is too small."

Although Dion—which sits by a narrow pass between Thessaly and Macedonia—was an important military camp for first the Macedonians and then the Romans, it was not merely the Fort Bragg of antiquity. The Romans adorned Dion with a **theater** (bigger and better than the Hellenistic one, as was the Roman habit), and built **sanctuaries** to the healing god Asclepius, the nurturing goddess Demeter, and the popular Egyptian goddess Isis. In addition, of course, the Romans built **baths**—and baths being the large structures that they are, a good deal remains for you to explore. Copies of some of the statues found in the sanctuaries have been erected at the site, while the originals are tucked away safely in the museum.

There's a great deal to see at Dion, but we have to confess that some of our happiest visits here have been spent in the shade of the trees with a picnic. From here, you can make excursions onto the site, following the course of a stoa, admiring the statue of Isis seemingly admiring her reflection in a pool, and imagining the day that Alexander, all of 22 years old, mounted Bucephalos and set off to conquer the world.

The Dion **museum** is a heartening example of what a provincial museum can be when it is well funded and well cared for. An English-language video and the English-language museum labels help foreign visitors understand the importance of what they are seeing, while models of the ancient site make the Dion of Philip and Alexander easy to visualize. Exhibits include statues of the children of Asclepius (lined up as though posing for a family photo), grave monuments, votive offerings, mosaics, and, best of all, a wonderful copper water organ, probably made in the 2nd century A.D., that would be the hit of any music hall today.

## WHERE TO STAY & DINE

There are several cafes and restaurants in the village of Dion near the Hotel Dion and also along the road that bisects the site and museum; an archaeologist friend reports eating well at the **Dionysos**, which serves good roast goat, *loukanika* (sausages), and the usual chops and salads. Expect to pay about 8€ for lunch or dinner unless you go overboard on the roast goat, which is priced by the kilo and may bring your tab to 10€ to 12€.

**Dion Palace Resort Hotel** ★ *Kids*   This is an enormous beachfront resort, with rooms available in the hotel itself, and in cabana/villas, with the villas being more expensive than the in-hotel accommodations. It is very popular with Greek and German families—and anyone with children will see why. Others may prefer the little Hotel Dion, near the site, described below.

Litochoro Beach, Gritsa, 60200 Macedonia. © 03520/61-431. 182 units. 100€–200€ double. Compulsory breakfast 10€. AE, MC, V. Sometimes closed in winter. **Amenities:** Restaurant; 2 bars; 2 pools (fresh and salt water); tennis; concierge. *In room:* A/C, TV, minibar, hair dryer.

**Hotel Dion** ★   The rooms here are good sized, economically furnished, and pleasant; most have balconies. When we stayed here, the town was deliciously quiet all night—except for a few late-night motorcycles and some early-morning roosters. One problem: The owners are not always around, so if you stop here without a reservation, it may take a bit of time to find them.

Dion, 60200 Macedonia. © 23510/53-336, 20 units, 60€ double. Rates include breakfast. MC, V. Considerable reductions often possible off season. **Amenities:** Breakfast room/bar. *In room:* TV.

## 3  Mount Athos (The Holy Mountain)

130km (80 miles) SE of Thessaloniki

The most important thing to know about Mount Athos is that you can't just come here. And if you're a woman, you can't come here at all (see "Permits," below). Recently, there have been mutterings that antidiscrimination regulations of the European Common Market may force Athos to open its doors to women; to avoid any potential complications, Mount Athos has refused any Common Market funds for restoration of monasteries. It is highly unlikely that the bureaucrats of the Common Market will prove a match for the monks of Athos and their centuries of tradition.

Many destinations are hyped as being a "step back in time" or a "glimpse of an unknown world," but both statements really are true of Mount Athos. Most monasteries here still follow the Julian calendar, which puts Athos 13 days behind the Gregorian calendar. The day is divided not into 24 equal hours, but organized according to an elaborate Byzantine scheme based on the times of sunset and sunrise; midnight, in this system, is at sunset. The flag that flies outside most monasteries is the double-headed eagle of Byzantium—symbol of the empire that fell in 1453.

Athos is very much a place of prayer and contemplation, and while some monks welcome visitors, most simply tolerate them, unless a visitor has a sincere interest in the Greek Orthodox faith and the monastic life. The monks' life focuses on prayer—usually 8 hours a day—and meditation. A local saying sums up the monks' life: "Write, read, sing, sigh, pray, keep silent."

No one is sure when monks and hermits first began to live on this rugged promontory. Some say that the place became holy when a storm blew the Virgin Mary's ship ashore here, as she was traveling from Jerusalem to Cyprus. As she stepped ashore, all the pagan idols crashed to the ground and were destroyed, a sure sign that this was a holy place.

Certainly, there were enough men of God here by A.D. 885 for the Byzantine Emperor Basil I to formally declare all Athos a "place of Quietism." The first, and still most important monastery, the **Great Lavra** or **Meyistis Lavras** ("Lavra" simply means a community of monks), was founded around 960, and others quickly followed. In 1060, an imperial decree barred "every woman, every child, eunuch, smooth faced person, and female animal" from Athos, which suggests that there had been incidents of inventive nonchastity over the years. In recent years, hens have been allowed onto Athos to produce eggs, and cats to catch vermin.

### What to Pack for Mount Athos

Bring sturdy shoes, long-sleeved shirts and long slacks (the monks are offended by short-sleeved shirts and shorts), a hat, insect repellent, a flashlight, reading material, any prescription or nonprescription medication you might need, a map, and the best lightweight (you will have to carry it everywhere) guide you can find. If you own the archaeologically oriented *Blue Guide* to Greece, you can photocopy the excellent section on Athos to bring along. One book you may enjoy reading is Robert Byron's *The Station*, an account of his visit here in 1931.

Until the fall of Constantinople in 1453, successive Byzantine emperors gave the monasteries rich donations of icons and manuscripts. After the fall of Byzantium, and during the Turkish occupation of Greece, the monasteries struggled to survive; many treasures were neglected, some sold. When the traveler Robert Curzon visited Athos in 1849, he inquired about purchasing a manuscript. To his horror, Curzon later recorded in his *Visits to the Monasteries of the Levant,* a monk pulled out his knife and "cut out an inch thickness of the leaves before I could stop him."

In 1917, the execution of the Russian royal family put an end to Athos's last major source of royal patronage. In 1926, Athos was declared a Theocratic Republic. Although it is part of Greece, it is self-governing—hence, the need for an entry permit. Today, there are 20 active monasteries, with at least that many again having closed over the centuries. There are still solitary hermits on Athos, but most monks follow a communal (cenobitic) rather than an isolated (idiorhythmic) life. In fact, of late, monastic life has had something of a revival; Father Gabriel, gardener at the Iviron Monastery, was quoted in the July 28, 1988, Athenian newspaper *Kathimerini* as saying that, "More are interested in becoming monks than we are ready to accept." According to the same story, Father Gabriel has added to his gardening duties the preparation of a computer catalog of manuscripts and icons. When asked if this would not take a very long time, he replied, "We've got all eternity."

## ESSENTIALS

**PERMITS** Unless you have proof that you are a Greek national or Greek Orthodox, you must be at least 21 and male, as well as have an entry permit (25€), to visit Mount Athos. To get a permit, it's a good idea to check for up-to-date information at www.medialab.ntua.gr/athos. In brief, at press time, you needed your **passport** and a **letter of recommendation** from your embassy or consulate in Athens or Thessaloniki. The United States does not charge for this; the United Kingdom and most other embassies charge about 15€. Getting the letter of recommendation is usually pro forma, but it's a good idea to have yourself described as a student or scholar.

Once you have the letter, take it to the **Ministry of Foreign Affairs,** in Athens at 3 Akadamias, fifth floor (open Mon, Wed, and Fri 11am–1pm), or to the **Pilgrims' Office for Mount Athos** (*Grafeo Pfoskyniton Ayiou Oros*), in Thessaloniki at 14 Konstantinou Karamanli (© **2310/861-611;** fax 2310/861-811), open Monday through Friday from 8:30am to 1:30pm and Monday, Tuesday, Thursday, and Friday from 6 to 8pm. It may help expedite matters if you fax all your documents in advance to the latter office, telling them when you will arrive. After a wait, which may be minutes or even days, you will be issued a permit for a 4-day visit to Mount Athos.

When you reach Ouranopolis, the jumping-off point for Athos, you must take your permit to the **Grafio Proskyniton** (Visitors Bureau), open daily from 8:30am to 2pm, and pay 30€ for a *diamonitirion*—your passport, as it were, to Mount Athos. *Important note:* The names and phone numbers of the monasteries are posted in this office; it is advisable to phone ahead to make a reservation at the monasteries where you want to stay the night. Increasingly, monasteries are requiring visitors to make reservations in advance.

When you reach Mount Athos, you must present your diamonitirion at the monastery/hamlet of Khilandariou, where you will be registered. Thereafter, you may be asked for your diamonitirion from time to time as you visit the monasteries.

## Tips Visiting Athos

On Mount Athos, you will be walking almost everywhere you go, and staying and eating at the monasteries you have come to visit, which certainly simplifies things. "Simple" is a key word here—both your accommodations and food (Athos is a vegetarian's paradise) will be very basic. Look out for some of the wine made on Athos and sold throughout Greece; the Tsantali white (not all of which is made here, despite its labels) is particularly refreshing, while the Metochi Mylopotamou made at the Great Lavra Monastery is well regarded. Keep in mind that although most monasteries will not accept cash offered in direct payment for food and lodgings, you can always make a donation in the church.

As always when walking in Greece, keep the danger of fires in mind, and be sure to dispose of any matches or cigarettes with care.

Finally, remember that many monasteries close (and lock) their gates during the midday siesta, and virtually all close (and lock) their gates at sunset.

**GETTING THERE By Car** If you drive to Mount Athos from Thessaloniki, check with the **Greek National Tourism Organization** in Aristotelous Square to see if there is road work on any of the major roads you might take, as this may help you plan the best route. You can take the E90 across the top of Chalkidiki east as far as Stavros, and then head south along the coast to Ouranopolis, or you can head south from Thessaloniki along the airport road and then continue across the southern coast of Chalkidiki to Ouranopolis. Allow 4 to 8 hours, depending on how many stops you want to make en route.

**By Bus** From Thessaloniki, take the bus to Ouranopolis from the Halkidiki terminal at Karakassi 68. Allow 6 hours.

**By Boat** However you reach Ouranopolis, you will continue from there to Mount Athos by boat. There is almost always at least one boat a day at 9:45am from Ouranopolis to Mount Athos. In summer, there are usually additional departures scheduled, as well as excursion boats that circle Mount Athos, so that those who do not wish—or are not allowed—to go ashore can see Mount Athos.

**GETTING AROUND** Be prepared to do a lot of walking on Mount Athos. Feet are the preferred method of transportation. There are many footpaths on the island, and you would do well to get as good a map as you can find either in Thessaloniki or in Ouranopolis (compare maps and dates to see which is most detailed and up-to-date).

**FAST FACTS Ouranopolis**, the jumping-off point for Mount Athos, has a **post office** and **telephone office (OTE)**; it may have a bank or ATM by the time that you visit, but don't count on it. **Karyes**, the main town on Athos, also has both a **telephone office (OTE)** and **post office**. It, too, is awaiting the opening of a bank—but do not count on this having happened before you visit. At present, a **mobile bank van** appears on an irregular schedule in Ouranopolis, so be sure to take adequate funds with you.

## WHAT TO SEE & DO

**Ouranopolis** is the jumping-off point for Mount Athos, but unfortunately, it has become a nasty little town filled with tacky souvenir shops in recent years. However, the handsome tower immortalized in Joyce Nankivell Loch's *A Fringe* *of Blue* still stands (and is rumored to open someday as a museum of Byzantine art). Joyce Loch and her husband, Sydney, both Quakers, lived in Ouranopolis on and off from the 1920s to the 1960s and worked with villagers and refugees from Asia Minor. For some years, the tower was both the Lochs's home and a weaving school.

If you can't go to Athos itself, try to take one of the **excursion boats** from Ouranopolis that cruises around the peninsula (when Prince Charles visited Athos in 1999, his companion, Camilla Parker-Bowles, circled the Holy Mount on the Royal Yacht). The views of the rugged, pine-clad mountain promontory are superb, and you'll be able to see a number of the monasteries. Most look like little villages from the outside, perched on astonishingly high and sturdy stone foundations and surrounded by massive walls. Virtually all of the monasteries are built according to a similar plan, in which a **central church** (the katholikon) fronts an arcaded courtyard, often with a bell tower. Around the courtyard are the monastic buildings, including the dining quarters (refectory or trapeza), kitchens, laundry rooms, and bedrooms (the cells).

If you do take a boat trip around Athos, and encounter rough seas, you'll understand why the Persian King Xerxes tried to cut a channel through Athos at just about the point where Ouranopolis sits today. He wanted to spare his fleet the rough seas here as he sailed north to attack Athens in 480 B.C. For centuries, scholars thought that Herodotus's story of Xerxes's canal was one of the historian's flights of fancy. The technology, the scholars said, simply didn't exist so long ago for such a massive project. In 1998, archaeologists and geologists announced that they had discovered at Ouranopolis—just where Herodotus placed it—signs of Xerxes's canal. Soundings revealed a massive channel some 20m (65 ft.) wide at its base, 34m (114 ft.) broad at the top, hidden beneath the 6.5m (22 ft.) of earth that slowly filled in the canal over the centuries.

At present, there are 20 functioning monasteries on Mount Athos. Given the rough terrain, there's no way you can visit them all during a 4-day visit—thus we mention here just the five most important monasteries. Keep in mind that if you can't visit Athos, you can see most of these monasteries from the sea. Almost all were built close enough to the water to be able to get supplies ashore with ease.

**THE GREAT LAVRA**    The first (about A.D. 960) monastery founded on Athos and hence the foremost, the Great Lavra has the red-painted *katholikon* characteristic of Athos's monasteries. Its 15th-century frescoes, especially those showing exuberant singers and dancers in the Chapel of Koukouzelissa, are delightful. Try © 23370/23-758 to make a reservation to spend the night here.

**THE MONASTERY OF CHELANDARIOU**    This monastery was founded in the 12th century by St. Sabbas of Serbia. Fortunately, Sabbas's father was the King of Serbia, which guaranteed a handsome endowment. Some scholars think that the lovely frescoes in the church here were done by the same painter who decorated the walls of Ayios Nikolaos Orfanos in Thessaloniki (p. 567). You can try to make a reservation here by calling © 23370/23-797.

**THE MONASTERY OF DIONYSIOU**    This 14th-century monastery seems to grow right out of a rock above the sea, and has dizzily overhanging balconies, braced by rather precarious-looking wood supports. Favored by the emperor Alexios III Komnenos, Dionysiou has a superb collection of manuscripts, as well as an icon said to be the oldest on Athos. You can try to make a reservation here by calling © 23370/23-687 or faxing 23370/23-686.

**THE MONASTERY OF IVERON** Iveron, founded in the 10th century, looks from the sea like a medieval hilltown—only the hill is actually the monastery's solid foundation. Try © **23370/23-643** for overnight reservations.

**THE MONASTERY OF VATOPEDI** Founded only a decade after the Great Lavra, Vatopedi's long outline with red-and-white tile-roofed buildings is clearly visible from the sea. Try © **23370/23-219** for overnight reservations.

## WHERE TO STAY IN OURANOPOLIS

**Xenia** This sprawling beachside resort hotel with two-story stone-and-concrete bungalowlike units by the sea is less than 5 minutes outside Ouranopolis. The large, tile-floored rooms have balconies (ask for a room facing the sea), most have desks and good reading lamps, and all have excellent bathroom facilities. The Xenia offers all the creature comforts you may have missed visiting Athos, including several restaurants and fresh- and saltwater pools.

Ouranopolis, 63075 Macedonia. © **23770/71-412.** Fax 23770/71-362. Xenia@papcorp.gr. 120 units. 150€ double. Compulsory breakfast 10€. AE, DC, MC, V. **Amenities:** Restaurant; bar; 2 pools (1 fresh, 1 saltwater); tennis. *In room:* A/C, TV, minibar, hair dryer.

# 17

# The Northeastern Aegean Islands

*by John S. Bowman*

The four islands covered in this chapter—Samos, Hios, Lesvos (Mitilin), and Limnos—are dispersed along the coast of Turkey, and far removed from the mainland and the other Aegean islands. Their remoteness is definitely a benefit. Unlike other areas of Greece, parts of these islands remain relatively undiscovered. The crowds here tend to be concentrated in a few resorts, leaving the vast interior (and much of the coast) open to exploration. Along the coastline you'll find some of the finest beaches in the Aegean, and within the interior richly forested valleys, precipitous mountain slopes, and exquisite mountain villages. Since these are agricultural islands, olives, grapes, and honey are produced in abundance, providing the basis for excellent food and wine.

The influence of Asia Minor is not as evident as you might expect, given the proximity of the **Turkish coast.** What you may notice is the sizable Greek military presence—large areas of each island are occupied by the military and are strictly off-limits (an annoyance to hikers and mountain bikers). Even though this military presence is a sore point with the Turks, who frequently demand the demilitarization of Limnos in particular and stage regular flyovers in defiance of Greek airspace, travel between Greece and Turkey remains unrestricted and relations between Greeks and Turks on a personal level

seem to be mostly amicable. Many travelers use the Northeastern Aegean islands as jumping-off points to Turkey: **Samos** is the closest island (only 3km/2 miles at the closest point) with easy access to Ephesus; **Lesvos** is the closest to Ancient Troy; and **Limnos** to Istanbul.

**STRATEGIES FOR SEEING THE ISLANDS** Since the distances between islands are substantial, island-hopping by boat can be costly and time-consuming. Add the fact that each island is quite large, and it becomes clear that you're best off choosing one or two islands to explore in depth rather than attempting a grand tour. **Olympic Airlines'** flights between the islands are inexpensive, frequent, and fast; **Aegean Cronus Airlines** offers daily flights between Lesvos (Mitilini in their literature) and Athens; and several other smaller airlines may be initiating service to these islands in the near future. If you travel by **ferry,** you'll find that departure times are more reasonable for travel from north to south, whereas traveling in the opposite direction usually involves departures in the middle of the night. The islands are too large and the roads too rough for mopeds to be a safe option; since the bus routes and schedules are highly restricting, you'll find that if you want to get around it's necessary to rent a car.

## 1 Samos

322km (174 nautical miles) NE of Piraeus

The most mountainous and densely forested of the Northeastern Aegean isles, Samos appears wild and mysterious as you approach its north coast by plane or ferry. The abrupt slopes of hills plunging to the sea are jagged with cypresses, and craggy peaks hide among the clouds. Samos experienced a series of wildfires during the summer of 2000, which briefly brought the island to the attention of the international press—the signs of these recent events are still visible and it will be some time before the interior forests fully recover.

In recent years, Samos has played host to a highly impersonal form of mass tourism involving "package" groups from Europe. This is mostly confined to the eastern coastal resorts—Vathi, Pithagorio, and Kokkari—which have all developed a generic waterfront of cafes, souvenir shops, and big hotels. The most interesting and beautiful villages are found in the rugged splendor of the island's interior. Difficult terrain and a remote location made these villages an apt refuge from pirates in medieval times; in this age, the same qualities have spared them from tourism's worst excesses.

Although Samos has several fine archaeological sites, the island is most notable for its excellent beaches and abundant opportunities for hiking, cycling, and windsurfing. Also, Samos is the best crossover point for those who want to visit **Ephesus**, one of the most important archaeological sites in Asia Minor.

### GETTING THERE

**By Plane** **Olympic Airways** has three flights daily (five daily in summer) between Athens and Samos. The **Olympic office** (✆ 22730/27-237) in Vathi is at the corner of Kanari and Smirnis, 1 block from the bus station. Contact Olympic Airways in Athens at ✆ **210/926-9111** or check out **www.olympic-airways.gr**. The Samos airport is 3km (2 miles) from Pithagorio, on the road to Ireon; from the airport you can take a taxi to Vathi (14€) or Pithagorio (8€).

**By Boat** The principal port of Samos is at **Vathi**, also called Samos; the other two ports are **Karlovassi** and **Pithagorio.** Ferries from the Cyclades usually stop at both Vathi and Karlovassi; Take care not to get off at the wrong port! There are daily boats (sometimes two) from Piraeus to Karlovassi (11–14 hr.) and Vathi (8–14 hr.); in the opposite direction ferries travel daily or nearly daily from Samos to Mykonos (5½ hr.). Boats to Hios from Vathi via Karlovassi (5 hr.) travel three times per week; there is also a once-weekly Rhodes-Vathi-Lesvos-Alexandroupoli run. Boats (mostly hydrofoils) to the Dodecanese islands depart regularly from Vathi and Pithagorio. If you want to travel one-way to Turkey, there are daily Turkish ferries (Apr 1–Oct 31; less regular off season); a visa is required for all American, British, and Irish citizens who intend to stay for more than 1 day—be sure to inquire in advance about current visa regulations with a local travel agency. For more information on visas, see "A Side Trip to Turkey: Kusadasi & Ephesus," later in this chapter. Contact **I.T.S.A. Travel** (✆ **22730/23-605;** fax 22730/27-955; www.itsatravel.com for current schedules, or visit **www.gtp.gr.** Otherwise, try the **port authority** in Piraeus (✆ **210/459-3223),** Vathi (✆ 22730/27-318), Pithagorio (✆ 22730/61-225), or Karlovassi (✆ 22730/30-888).

## VATHI, KARLOVASSI & THE NORTHERN COAST

Vathi (sometimes referred to as "Samos Town") on the northeast coast and Karlovassi to the northwest are the two principal ports of Samos, and the island's

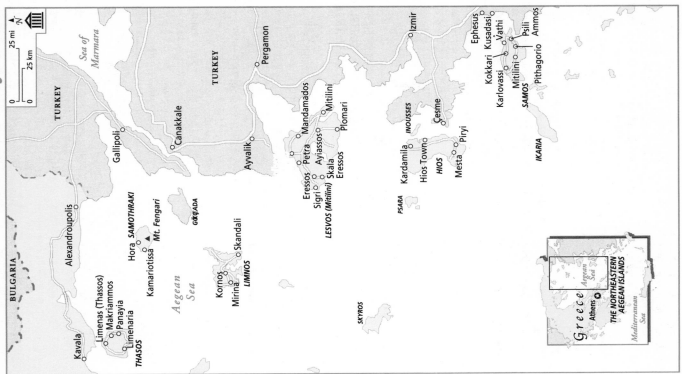

# The Northeastern Aegean Islands

largest towns. Neither is particularly exciting, and we recommend both as convenient bases rather than as destinations in themselves.

Vathi is a tired resort town, beautifully situated in a fine natural harbor. An extensive development project in Pithagora Square and along the paralia, completed in 2001, resulted in a widened pedestrian walkway along the water and a large bandstand for open-air concerts. The old town, **Ano Vathi**, rises to the hilltops in steep narrow streets that hide a few small tavernas and cafes. Karlovassi is somewhat less interesting as a town—although it's adjacent to several of the best beaches on the island, the town is spread out and offers fewer amenities than Vathi. Most tourist facilities are clustered along the water at the west end of town, forming a tiny beach resort with several hotels, restaurants, grocery stores, and souvenir shops. The old town hovers above the lower town near the seafront, and the lovely small chapel of **Ayia Triada** at the summit of the rock. Along the seafront to the east is the former industrial quarter, with rows of abandoned stone warehouses once used by a flourishing leather industry.

The **north coast** of the island is wild and steep, with mountains rising abruptly from the water's edge. One of the most interesting areas to explore is the **Platanakia** region, known for its rushing streams, lush valleys, and picturesque mountain villages. There is also a sequence of excellent **beaches** between Kokkari and Karlovassi, with the two finest beaches on the island—**Micro Seitani ⭐** and **Megalo Seitani ⭐**—a short boat excursion or somewhat long hike to the west of Karlovassi.

## ESSENTIALS

### VISITOR INFORMATION   The Greek National Tourism Organization (EOT) no longer maintains a presence on Samos, so visitors must rely on private travel agencies for help. Over the years we have found **I.T.S.A. Travel** (© **22730/23-605;** fax 22730/27-955; itsa@otenet.gr), the agency nearest the port in Vathi, one of the best and friendliest; here you can make travel arrangements (including excursions to Turkey, Patmos, and Fourni, as well as tours of Samos), find accommodations, change money at good rates, and store your luggage for free. The Diavlos website (www.diavlos.gr) has information on ferries, attractions, and accommodations.

### GETTING AROUND   **By Bus**   There's good public bus service on Samos throughout the year, with significantly expanded summer schedules. The **Vathi bus terminal** (© 22730/27-262) is a block inland from the south end of the port on Kanari. The bus makes the 20-minute trip between Vathi and Pithagorio frequently. Buses also travel to Kokkari, the inland village of Mitilini, Pirgos, Marathokambos, Votsalakia beach, and Karlovassi. Schedules are posted in English at the bus terminal.

**By Boat**   From Karlovassi there are daily excursion boats to **Megalo Seitani,** the best fine-sand beach on the island. A once-weekly around-the-island tour aboard the *Samos Star* is a great way to see the island's remarkable coastline, much of it inaccessible by car. The excursion boat departs from Pithagorio at 8:30am (a bus from Vathi departs at 7:30am), currently on Tuesdays, and returns to Pithagorio at 5:30pm; the fare is 42€. Most excursions depart from Pithagorio, although many offer bus service from Vathi an hour prior to departure; for descriptions see "Pithagorio & the Southern Coast," later in this chapter.

**By Car & Moped**   **Aramis Rent a Motorbike-Car** at the pier in Vathi (© 22730/23-253) offers the best prices and selection. The least expensive car is

Map labels: Mikalis, To Ano Vathi, Olympic Airways, Kanari, Tourist Police, Bus Station, Smirnis, Mikras Assias, Alex. Pashali, Sahtouri, Archaeological Museum, Kaperan Katevani, Stamati, Tompazi, Plateia Pithagora, St. Nicholas Square, Logotheti, N. Smyrnis, Sofouli, Market, Kalomiri, Stamatiadou, Likourgou, Koundourioti, Sokratous, Asklipiadou, 28 Oktobriou, 9 Augusto, Grigoriou, Kondou, Ippokratous, 12 Matou, Kleanti, Iras, Lykoppli, Stadium, Gagou Beach, Ferry Pier, Vathi Bay

Inset map: Greece, Aegean Sea, Vathi, Athens, Mediterranean Sea

Scale: 100 m / 100 y

### Legend
- First Aid
- Information
- OTE
- Post Office

## ACCOMMODATIONS ■
Hotel Paradise **6**
Ionia Maris **1**
Pension Avli **3**
Pythagoras Hotel **2**
Samos Hotel **7**

## DINING ◆
Christos Taverna **4**
Ta Kotopoula **5**

---

about 42€, including insurance and 100 free kilometers. Mopeds go for 12€ to 22€ a day. There are plenty of other agencies, so shop around.

**By Taxi** The principal taxi stand in Vathi is on Plateia Pithagora, facing the paralia. The fare from Vathi to Pithagorio is 12€. To book by phone, call *(* 22730/ 28-404* in Vathi; 22730/33-300 in Karlovassi.

**FAST FACTS** The **banks** in Vathi are on the paralia in the vicinity of Plateia Pithagora, and are open Monday through Thursday from 8am to 2pm, Friday from 8am to 1:30pm; most have ATMs. Most travel agents change money, sometimes at bank rates, and they're open later. The island's **hospital** (*(* 22730/27-407* or 22730/27-426) is in Vathi. **Internet access** is available at Diavlos (www.diavlos.gr) on the paralia next to the police station, just around the corner from the bus stop. Diavlos is open daily from 9:30am to 11pm, and it's a bargain at 2€ for 30 minutes. There's a **self-service laundry** (*(* 22730/28-833*) behind the Aeolis Hotel on the town's market street, open daily from 8am to 11pm. The **post office** (*(* 22730/27-304*) is on the same street as the Olympic Airways office, 1 block further in from the paralia and 2 blocks from the bus station. The **telephone office (OTE)** is just down the street from the Olympic Airways office in the direction of the archaeological museum (*(* 22730/ 28-499*). The **tourist police** (*(* 22730/81-000*) are on the paralia, by the turn in to the bus station.

## ATTRACTIONS

**Archaeological Museum** ✦    This fine museum is comprised of two buildings at the south end of the harbor, near the post office. The newest building houses sculpture—much in demand, the island's best sculptors traveled all over the Hellenistic world to create their art. The most remarkable work is a massive *kouros* (statue of a boy), which stands 5m (16 ft.) tall. The large and varied collection of bronze votives found at the Heraion is also impressive.

Kapetan Yimnasiarhou Kateveni (near park and behind Town Hall) ✆ 22730/27-469. Admission 3€, 2€ seniors, Tues–Sun 8:30am–3pm.

**Moni Vronta**    The 15th-century fortified monastery of Moni Vronta is on a high mountain overlooking the sea and the lovely hilltop village of Vourliotes. *Vrontiani* means "thunder on Mount Lazarus," a name resonant with the majesty of this mountain setting. There is only one monk left in the monastery, and 10 soldiers who operate a nearby surveillance post. If the gate is locked when you arrive, try knocking and one of the soldiers may be around to let you in. Ask to see the *speleo*, or cave, an old chapel in the thickness of the outer wall containing a collection of ancient objects, some from the time of the monastery's founding. To get there, continue driving uphill about 2km (1¼ miles) past the village of Vourliotes.

Vourliotes (14 miles west of Vathi). No phone. Free admission. Daily 8am–5pm. 23km (14½ miles) west of Vathi.

## THREE HILL TOWNS ON THE RUGGED NORTH COAST

Amidst the densely wooded valleys, cascading streams, and terraced slopes of Samos's *Platanakia* Region, many hidden villages were settled as an attempt to evade the pirates who repeatedly ravaged all settlements visible from the sea. Three of the most picturesque of the surviving hill towns in this region are Manolates; Vourliotes, about 20km (12½ miles) west of Vathi; and Stavrinides (not far from Manolates).

**Manolates** is a 4km (2½-mile) drive uphill from the coast road. The village was until recently inaccessible by car, but once the paved road was built, many more visitors have come here to explore the steep, narrow cobblestone streets. There are several tavernas, numerous shops, and two katenions (where the locals go).

**Vourliotes** was settled largely by repatriated Greeks from the town of Vourla in Turkey. It's the largest producer of wine in the region, and the local wine is among the best on the island. Walk from the parking lot at the Moni Vronta turnoff to the charming central square. Try **Manolis Taverna** (✆ 22730/93-290), on the left as you enter the square, which has good *renidokeftedes*, a delicious local dish made with chickpea flour and cheese. The proprietress, Elena Glavara, is originally from Mexico and makes a fine chili con carne. Also on the square, across from Manolis, is a small market whose displays seem not to have changed in the past 50 years. Be sure to visit the monastery of **Moni Vronta** (also known as Vrontiani), just 2km (1¼ miles) above the town (see "Attractions," above).

**Stavrinides,** perched on the mountainside high above Ayios Konstandinos, is the least touristic of the Platanakia villages. Here the tavernas and the few shops cater primarily to the villagers. **Taverna Irida** in the first square of the village offers good simple food. A walking path between Stavrinides and Manolates makes an exceptional outing; the route out from Stavrinides is signposted.

The easiest way to visit these towns is by car; the island buses are also an option if you don't mind the steep 4km to 6km (2½-mile–3¾-mile) walk from the coast road to the villages. There are abundant footpaths connecting these villages—ask locally for particular routes. **Ambelos Tours** (✆ 22730/94-136; fax 22730/ 94-114; ambelos@sam.forthnet.gr) in Ayios Konstandinos, operated by the friendly and extremely knowledgeable Mihailis Folas, is a useful resource. Also ask Mihailis about traditional houses for rent in the hilltop village of Ano Ayios Konstandinos: Each apartment sleeps three, and costs about 28€ per night.

## A SIDE TRIP TO TURKEY: KUSADASI & EPHESUS

In high season there are two boats a day between Vathi and Kusadasi, Turkey, a popular, well-developed resort 20 minutes from the magnificent archaeological site at Ephesus; there's one excursion each week from Pithagorio to Turkey, currently on Thursdays. A round-trip ticket to Kusadasi runs 40€; the guided tour with entrance fee and transport from the port is an additional 25€. If you're not returning the same day, you'll need to investigate visa requirements. Visas are granted without difficulty, and cost $50 for Americans, £10 for Irish citizens, £10 for U.K. citizens, C$50 for Canadians, and A$25 for Australians; New Zealanders don't need a visa. A helpful and knowledgeable agency for making all arrangements is **I.T.S.A. Travel** (© **22730/23-605**), operator of the *Samos Star*, a boat traveling between Vathi and Kusadasi.

## BEACHES

The closest decent beach to Vathi is **Gagou,** 2km (1¼ miles) north of the pier. But the best beaches on Samos are found along the north coast, the most beautiful and rugged part of the island. The busy seaside resort of **Kokkari,** 10km (6 miles) west of Vathi, has several beaches in rock coves as well as the crowded stretch of sand running parallel to the town's main road; to find the smaller cove beaches, head seaward from the main square. Just west of Kokkari is **Tsamadou,** a short walk down from the coast road, which offers sufficient seclusion for nudism at one end. Continue west past Karlovassi to find **Potami,** an excellent long pebble-and-sand beach with road access.

The two best beaches on the island, **Micro Seitani** ✦ and **Megalo Seitani** ✦, are accessible only on foot or by boat; boat excursions depart daily from the pier in Karlovassi. To get here on foot, continue past the parking lot for the beach at Potami on a dirt road; the walking time to the first beach is 45 minutes. After about 5 minutes of uphill walking, the road splits—turn right, continuing to follow the coast. After another 5 minutes of walking, there are three obvious paths turning off to the right in close succession. Take the third, marked by a cairn, and follow the well-worn path another half-hour to Micro Seitani, a glorious pebble-and-cobble beach in a rocky cove. On the far side of the beach a ladder scales the cliff, leading to the continuation of the trail which will take you after an additional 30 minutes of walking to Megalo Seitani, as incredible a stretch of sea sand as any in the Aegean. At the far end of Megalo Seitani are a few houses and a taverna; the near end, at the outlet of a magnificent cliff-walled gorge, is completely undeveloped.

## OUTDOOR PURSUITS

**BICYCLING** Samos has many dirt roads and trails that are perfect for mountain biking. The only obstacles are the size of the island, which limits the number of routes available for day trips, and the fact that much of the backcountry is off-limits due to Greek military operations. Bike rentals, information about trails, and guided mountain-bike tours are available at **Bike** (© **22730/24-404**), managed by the friendly and knowledgeable Yiannis Sofoulis. The shop is open daily from 8:30am to 2pm and 5 to 9pm; it's behind the old church opposite the port, on the market street. The bikes are very high quality—aluminum frames with front or full suspension and good components—and the rental includes helmet, pump, and repair kit; clipless pedals and shoes are also available for an extra charge. The basic aluminum-frame bike is 8€ per day; the full-suspension bike is 15€.

**WALKING**    Some of the best walking on the island is in and around the Platanakia region of Samos's north coast, where well-marked trails connect several lovely hilltop villages—Manolates and Vourliotes (see above) are among the villages on this network of trails. There is also a trail from Manolates to the summit of Mount Ambelos, the second-highest peak on Samos at 1,153m (3,780 ft.); the round-trip time for this demanding walk is about 5 hours. For information on walking in the Platanakia region, contact Mihalis Folas of **Ambelos Tours** (② 22730/94-136; fax 22730/94-114; ambelos@sam.forthnet.gr) in Ayios Konstandinos. Those seeking a more "professional" exploration of the truly natural Samos might be interested in the British outfit, **Nature Trek** (www.naturetrek.co.uk), which provides trained botanists and ornithologists to lead 8-day trips (starting from London) that track the island's flora and fauna.

## WHERE TO STAY
### Vathi

**Hotel Paradise**    Despite a central location just off the paralia and a block away from the bus station, the walled garden and pool terrace here seem a world away from the traffic and dust of Vathi. Drinks and simple Greek food are served all day at the poolside bar—the pool invites lingering, with lounge chairs and umbrellas for sunning and shaded tables for a meal or drinks. All guest rooms have balconies, although the views aren't great; bathrooms are small, but they do have full tubs. You should note that although there is air-conditioning in every room, it isn't turned on until sometime in July (unlike the majority of hotels, which will turn on the A/C in June if it's needed—and it usually is).

21 Kanari, Vathi, 83100 Samos. ② 22730/23-911. Fax 22730/28-754. 51 units, 68€ double. Rates include continental breakfast. MC, V. Closed Nov–Mar. **Amenities:** Restaurant; bar; pool; tours and car rentals arranged; 24-hr. room service. *In room:* A/C, TV, minibar, hair dryer.

**Ionia Maris**    The Ionia Maris is the best beachfront hotel in Vathi. It has a good location and facilities but somewhat plain rooms. Gagou is a pleasant pebble beach 2km (1¼ miles) north of Vathi, with a small taverna; the hotel is 50m (164 ft.) back from the water. There is a large pool terrace with two pools (one for children), a snack bar, and abundant umbrellas. A buffet breakfast and dinner are served daily, and full-board rates are available. The rooms are moderate in size, with tile floors and small balconies—units on the pool side of the hotel have an oblique view toward the sea. Two rooms are wheelchair accessible.

Gagou Beach, Vathi, 83100 Samos. ② 22730/28-428 or 22730/28-429. Fax 22730/23-108. 56 units, from 80€ double. Rates include breakfast. MC. Closed Nov–Mar. *In room:* A/C, TV.

**Pension Avli** (Value    Although you won't find any luxuries here, you will discover the most charming and romantic pension on the island. Abundant bougainvillea fills the arcaded courtyard of this former 18th-century convent. Most rooms have been renovated within the last few years. The rooms are spartan, with minimal furnishings and bare walls; bathrooms are tiny and encased completely in a shell of bright orange plastic, making a shower a surreal experience.

2 Areos, Vathi, 83100 Samos. ② 22730/22-939. 20 units 30€ double. No credit cards. Turn in from the paralia at the Agrotiki Trapeza (just down from the Aeolis Hotel), turn left on the town's market street, and you'll see the Avli's unassuming sign directly ahead. *In room:* No phone.

**Pythagoras Hotel**    This plain but comfortable family hotel on a hill overlooking Vathi Bay offers the best views in town from its nine seaside units and from the restaurant terrace. Guest rooms on the side of the road can be very noisy—book ahead to ensure a seaside unit. Rooms and bathrooms are small, clean, and minimally furnished. The neighborhood cafe downstairs serves a good, inexpensive breakfast, light meals, and snacks from 6:45am to midnight. Stelios Michalakis, the friendly manager, will meet you at the port at any time, a generous offer given the frequency of early-morning ferry arrivals.

Kalami, Vathi, 83100 Samos. © 22730/28-422. Fax 22730/28-893. smicha@otenet.gr. 19 units. From 32€ double. MC, V. On the coast road, 600m (1,968 ft.) north of the pier. In room: No phone.

**Samos Hotel**  For those who need a modern hotel with all (well, most all) of the amenities and also like to be on an island's harbor, this is THE place in Vathy. Located right along the paralia, or waterfront promenade; of course this also means you are subject to a certain amount of harbor noise. But the hotel is air conditioned, which means that it is somewhat insulated from that same noise, and it was quite thoroughly renovated in 2001. Rooms—which have ceiling fans in place of A/C units—are nothing special in size or decor but beds and bathrooms are comfortable; most have balconies overlooking the harbor. It's only about a 20-minute walk from Gagou Beach. This is a functional hotel, not for those seeking atmosphere.

11 Themistokli Sofouli, 83100 Vathi. © 22730/28-377. Fax 22730/28-842. 105 units. High season 68€ double; low season 58€. Rates include continental breakfast. MC, V. Amenities: 2 restaurants; 2 bars; pool; Jacuzzi; game room; concierge; tours and car rentals arranged; conference facilities; 24-hr. room service; roof garden. In room: TV, fridge, hair dryer, safe, ceiling fan.

## Ayios Konstandinos

This coastal town in the heart of the Platanakia region is a great base for touring the north coast of Samos. Ask Mihailis Folas of **Ambelos Tours** © 22730/94-136; fax 22730/94-114; ambelos@sam.forthnet.gr) about several traditional houses for rent: Each apartment sleeps three, and costs only 28€ per night.

**Daphne Hotel ★**  The Daphne is the finest small hotel on the island. Artfully incised into the steep hillside in a series of terraces, the hotel commands a fine view of the stream valley leading to Manolates and a wide sweep of sea. The dining room has a large picture window and an outdoor terrace that steps down to the pool and an exquisite view. All rooms are moderate in size and have balconies with the same great view; bathrooms have both shower and tub. This is a good location for walkers, with many trails nearby to Manolates and other hill towns. Make your reservations well in advance, as this hotel is filled through much of the summer by European tour groups. There is free transportation to and from the airport or the port; due to the somewhat remote location, you'll probably want a car during your stay here.

Ayios Konstandinos, 83200 Samos. © 22730/94-003 or 22730/94-493. Fax 22730/94-594. www.daphne-hotel.gr. 35 units. 48€ double. Rates include breakfast. V. Take the 1st right after turning onto the Manolates road, 19km (12 miles) from Vathi. Closed Nov–Apr. In room: A/C.

## WHERE TO DINE

### Vathi

The food along the paralia in Vathi is mostly tourist-quality and mediocre; the best restaurants are to be found in the small towns. The local wines on Samos have long had the reputation for their excellence. (As Byron exclaimed, "Fill high the bowl with Samian wine!") A preferred wine is the dry white called Samaina. There's also a delicious relatively dry rose called Fokianos. The Greeks here also like sweet wines, with names like Nectar, Dux, and Anthemis. Almost any restaurant on the island will serve one or all of these wines.

**Christos Taverna** GREEK   This simple little taverna, under a covered alleyway decorated with odd antiques, is left off Plateia Pithagora as you come up from the port. The food is simply prepared and presented; it comes in generous portions and is remarkably good. Try the *revidokeftedes*, a Samian specialty made with cheese fried in a chickpea batter.

Plateia Ayiou Nikolaou. (© 22730/24-792. Main courses 4€–8€. No credit cards. Daily 11am–11pm.

**Ta Kotopoula** GREEK   Ta Kotopoula is on the outskirts of Vathi, somewhat hard to find but worth the trouble. From the south end of the harbor, walk inland past the Olympic Airways office and the post office, bearing right with the road as it climbs toward Ano Vathi. Where the road splits around a large tree, about 700m (2,296 ft.) from the harbor, you'll see the vine-sheltered terrace of this taverna on the left. The food is basic Greek fare, but the ingredients are exceptionally fresh—chicken being the specialty as the name suggests. Local wine is available by the carafe.

Vathi. (© 22730/28-415. Main courses 3.50€–9€. No credit cards. Daily 11am–11pm.

## Ayios Nikolaos

**Psarades** ★ GREEK/SEAFOOD   This restaurant is on the water, and the outside terrace overlooks tide pools and a long stretch of coast to the west—it's a highly romantic setting, and a fabulous place to watch the sunset. The fish, simply prepared and cooked on a wood fire, is consistently excellent. The tastes are strong and straightforward, like the *tzatziki* pungent with garlic, or the *melitzanosalata* redolent with the smoky aroma of roasted eggplant.

Ayios Nikolaos. (© 22730/32-489. Main courses 3.50€–14€. No credit cards. Daily 8am–midnight. Drive 6km (3¾ miles) east from Karlovassi, turning left at the sign for Ayios Nikolaos, and descend the treacherously narrow road to the sea.

## Ayios Konstandinos

**Platanakia Paradisos** GREEK   Paradisos is a large garden taverna located at the Manolates turnoff from the coast highway; it has been in the Folas family for nearly 30 years, and has been operating as a taverna for more than 100. Mr. Folas, the owner, makes his own wine from the excellent Samian grapes. Mrs. Folas's *tiropita* (freshly baked after 7pm) is made from local goat cheese and butter; it's wrapped in a flaky pastry. Live traditional music is performed Wednesday and Saturday nights in the summer.

Ayios Konstandinos. (© 22730/94-208. Main courses 3.50€–12€. No credit cards. Daily 3–11pm.

## VATHI AFTER DARK

The hottest disco in Vathi is **Metropolis**, behind the Paradise Hotel. For bouzouki, there's **Zorba's**, out of town on the road to Mitilini. There are several bars of various kinds on the lanes just off the port. **Number Nine**, at 9 Kephalopoulou, beyond the jetty on the right, is one of the oldest and best known.

## PITHAGORIO & THE SOUTHERN COAST

Pithagorio, south across the island from Vathi, is a charming but overcrowded seaside resort built on the site of an ancient village and harbor. Although this is a convenient base for touring the southern half of Samos, the town exists primarily for the tour groups that pack its streets in the summer. We recommend staying here for a day or two to explore the nearby historic sites, then moving on to the more interesting and authentic villages of the north coast.

## ESSENTIALS

**GETTING THERE** **By Plane** The Samos airport is 3km (2 miles) from Pithagorio; from the airport, you can take a taxi into town for 7€.

**By Boat** Ferries from the Cyclades typically don't stop at Pithagorio, so you'll need to take a taxi or bus from Vathi. There is near-daily hydrofoil service between Pithagorio and Patmos (60–90 min.), Lipsi (1½–3 hr.), Leros (1½–3 hr.), Kalymnos (3–6 hr.) and Kos (3–4 hr.); there are also excursion boats to Patmos four times weekly. Check the most current ferry schedules at the **Pithagorio Municipal Tourist Office** (✆ **22730/61-389** or 22730/61-022), **www.gtp.gr**, or the **Pithagorio Port Authority** (✆ **22730/61-225**).

**By Bus** The trip between Vathi and Pithagorio takes 20 minutes, and buses depart frequently. Contact the **Vathi bus terminal** (✆ **22730/27-262**) for current schedules.

**VISITOR INFORMATION** The **Pithagorio Municipal Tourist Office** (✆ **22730/61-389** or 22730/61-022) is on the main street, Likourgou Logotheti, 1 block up from the paralia; open daily from 8am to 10pm. Here you can get information on ferries, buses, island excursions, accommodations, car rental, and just about anything else. Pick up the handy *Map of Pithagorion*, which lists accommodations, attractions, and other helpful information.

**GETTING AROUND** **By Bus** The Pithagorio **bus terminal** is in the center of town, at the corner of Polykrates (the road to Vathi) and Likourgou Logotheti. The bus makes the 20-minute trip between Vathi and Pithagorio frequently. There are also four buses daily from Pithagorio to Ireon (near the Heraion archaeological site).

**By Boat** Summertime **excursion boats** from the Pithagorio harbor go to **Psili Ammos beach** (on the east end of the island) daily, and to the island of **Ikaria** three times weekly. There is a popular day cruise to **Samiopoula**, a small island with a single taverna and a long sandy beach; boats leave daily at 9:15am and return to Pithagorio at 5pm; the fare of 20€ includes lunch. Four times each week the *Samos Star* sails to **Patmos**, departing from Pithagorio at 8am and returning the same day at 4pm; travel time to Patmos is 2 hours, and the fare is 30€. A Sunday excursion to the tiny isle of **Fourni**, also aboard the *Samos Star*, leaves you with 6 hours to check out the beaches and sample the island's renowned fish tavernas; the boat leaves Pithagorio at 8:30am and the cost is 25€ per person. A once-weekly **around-the-island tour** aboard the *Samos Star* offers a great way to see this island's remarkable coastline, much of it inaccessible by road. The excursion boat departs from Pithagorio at 8:30am (a bus from Vathi departs at 7:30am), currently on Tuesdays, and returns to Pithagorio at 5:30pm; the fare is 40€.

**By Car & Moped** **Aramis Rent a Motorbike-Car** has a branch near the bus station in Pithagorio (✆ **22730/62-267**); it often has the best prices, but shop around.

**By Taxi** The taxi stand is on the main street, Likourgou Logotheti, where it meets the harbor. The fare from Vathi to Pithagorio is 12€. To book by phone, call ✆ **22730/61-450**.

**FAST FACTS** The **National Bank** (✆ **22730/61-234**), opposite the bus stop, has an ATM. A small **clinic** is on Plateia Irinis, next to the town hall, 1 block in from the beach near the port police (© 22730/61-111). There's **Internet access** at **Nefeli** (© 22730/61-719), a café on the north side of the paralia (left if you're facing the harbor), open from 11am to 2am daily. There are currently two computers, and the rate is 5€ per hour. Alex Stavrides runs a self-service **laundry** off the main street on the road to the old basilica, Metamorphosis Sotiros; open daily from 9am to 9pm, in summer until 11pm. The **post office** is several blocks up from the paralia on the main street, past the bus stop. The **telephone office** (OTE) is on the paralia near the pier (© 22730/61-399). The **police** (© 22730/61-100) are a short distance up Polikrates, the main road to Vathi.

## ATTRACTIONS

**Epfalinion Tunnel** ✦ One of the most impressive engineering accomplishments of the ancient world, this 1,000m (3,280 ft.) tunnel through the mountain above Pithagorio was excavated to transport water from mountain streams to ancient Vathi. The great architect Efpalinos directed two teams of workers digging from each side, and after nearly 15 years they met within a few meters of each other. If you can muster the courage to squeeze through the first 20m (66 ft.)—the tunnel is a mere sliver in the rock for this distance—you'll see that it soon widens considerably, and you can comfortably walk another 100m (328 ft.) into the mountain. Even though there is a generator that supposedly starts up in the event of a power outage, you might be more comfortable carrying a flashlight. Pithagorio. © 22730/61-400. Admission 2€ adults, 1€ students and seniors, free for youths under 18. Tues–Sun 8:45am–2:45pm. Located 3km (2 miles) northwest of Pithagorio, sign posted off the main road to Vathi.

**Heraion** All that survives of the largest of all Greek temples is its massive foundation, a lone reconstructed column, and some copies of the original statuary. The temple was originally surrounded by a forest of columns, one of its most distinctive and original features. In fact, rival Ionian cities were so impressed that they rebuilt many of their ancient temples in similar style. The Temple of Artemis in nearby Ephesus is a direct imitation of the great Samian Structure. The Heraion was rebuilt and greatly expanded under Polycrates; it was damaged during numerous invasions and finally destroyed by a series of earthquakes. Ireon. © 22730/95-277 or 22730/27-469 (the Archaeological Museum in Vathi). Admission 3€ adults, 1.50€ students and seniors, free for youths under 18. Tues–Sun 8am–2:30pm. Located 9km (5½ miles) southwest of Pithagorio, signposted off the road to Ireon.

## BEACHES

In Pithagorio, the local beach stretches from Logotheti Castle at the west side of town several kilometers to Potokaki and the airport. Expect this beach to be packed throughout the summer. Excursion boats depart daily in the summer for **Psili Ammos**, 5km (3 miles) to the east. Boat excursions leave daily from Pithagorio for **Samiopoula**, an island off the south coast with two good beaches.

On the south coast of the island, the most popular beaches are on Marathokambos Bay. The once-tiny village of **Ormos Marathokambos** has several tavernas and a growing number of hotels and pensions; its rock-and-pebble beach is long and narrow, with windsurfing an option. A couple of kilometers further west of Ormos Marathokambos is **Votsalakia**, a somewhat nicer beach.

## WHERE TO STAY

Rooms in Pithagorio are quickly filled by tour groups, so don't count on finding a place here if you haven't booked well in advance.

**George Sandalis Hotel** Above Pithagorio, this homey establishment has a front garden bursting with colorful blossoms. The tastefully decorated rooms all have balconies with French doors. In back, the rooms face quiet hills and another flower garden, while the front units face a busy street and can be noisy. The friendly Sandalises are gracious hosts; they spent many years in Chicago and speak perfect English.

Pithagorio, 83103 Samos. (○ **22730/61-691.** Fax 22730/61-251. 13 units. 48€ double. No credit cards. Head north on Polykrates (the road to Vathi), and you'll see the hotel on your left, about 100m (328 ft.) from the bus station. *In room:* No phone.

**Hotel Zorba** *Value*   This homely place is more pension than hotel, but the rooms are comfortable; seven units have great views of Pithagorio Harbor. The atmosphere is decidedly casual and friendly—the hotel lobby doubles as the Mathios family's living room. The hotel is on a steep hill on the north side of town, a steep climb up from the paralia at the port police station. Rooms facing the sea all have spacious balconies with a view over the rooftops to fishing boats docked in the harbor, while street-side rooms are a bit noisier and have no view. Breakfast is served on a terrace facing the sea.

Damos, Pithagorio, 83103 Samos. (○ **22730/61-009.** Fax 22730/61-012. 12 units. 45€ double. Breakfast 5€. No credit cards.

## WHERE TO DINE

**Esperides Restaurant** INTERNATIONAL   This pleasant restaurant with a walled garden is a few blocks inland from the port, and west of the main street. There are uniformed waiters and a dressier crowd here. The continental and Greek dishes are well presented and will appeal to a wide variety of palates. You run the risk of frozen french fries served with the tasty baked chicken, but the meats and vegetables are fresh.

Pithagorio. (○ **22730/61-767.** Reservations recommended in summer. Main courses 5€–14€. No credit cards. Daily 6pm–midnight.

**Varka** ★ GREEK/SEAFOOD   This ouzeri/taverna is in a stand of salt pines at the south end of the port. Delicious fresh fish, grilled meats, and a surprising variety of *mezedes* (appetizers) are produced in the small kitchen. The grilled octopus, strung up on a line to dry, and the pink *barbounia* or clear gray mullet, all cooked to perfection over a charcoal grill, are the true standouts of a meal here. The new cafe pavilion by the water is a cool, breezy location for a drink or dessert.

Paralia, Pithagorio. (○ **22730/61-088.** Main courses 7€–17€. MC. V. Daily noon–midnight. Closed Nov–Apr.

## 2 Hios (Chios)

### 283km (153 nautical miles) NE of Piraeus

"Craggy Hios," as Homer dubbed it, remains very much unspoiled—and that's why we recommend it. The black-pebble beaches on the southeast coast of the island are famous and not neglected, but there are white-sand beaches on the west coast that see only a few hundred people in a year. The majestic mountain setting of **Nea Moni**, an 11th-century Byzantine monastery in the center of the island, and the extraordinary mosaics of its chapel make for a unforgettable visit. The mastic villages in the south of the island are among the finest medieval towns in Greece, and the crop for which they are named (a tree resin used in chewing gum, paints, and perfumes) is grown nowhere else in the world.

The paralia of **Hios town** is likely to be your first glimpse of the island, and it isn't a pretty sight—unappealing modern buildings and generic cafes have taken over what must once have been a fine harbor. Thankfully, there are a few pockets of the original town further inland that have survived earthquakes, wars, and neglect. The Kastro, the mosque on the main square, the mansions of Kampos, and the occasional grand gateway (often leading nowhere) are among the only signs of a more prosperous and architecturally harmonious past.

## ESSENTIALS

### GETTING THERE

**By Plane** **Olympic Airways** (© 28010/44-444 or 210/966-6666; www.olympic-airways.gr) has flights four times a day between Athens and Hios. There is a connection once or twice a week with Lesvos (Mitilini) and Thessaloniki. The **Olympic office** in Hios town is in the middle of the harborfront (© 22710/24-515). To contact the **airport,** call © 22710/23-998. If you arrive by plane, count on taking a cab into town at about 10€ for the 7km (4¼-mile) ride.

**By Boat** From Piraeus, one car ferry leaves daily bound for Hios (8–9 hr.); there's also daily connection with Lesvos (3 hr.). There are three ferries weekly to Limnos (9 hr.) and Thessaloniki (16–19 hr.), two ferries weekly to Samos (5 hr.), and one weekly to Siros (5 hr.). Check with the **Hios Port Authority** (© 22710/44-434) or **www.gtp.gr** for current schedules.

**VISITOR INFORMATION** The **Tourist Information Office** on Kanari 18 (© 22710/44-389) stocks a remarkable amount of useful free brochures, including many maps; it's located on the second street from the north end of the harbor, between the harbor and the Central (Plastira) Square. It's open Monday to Friday from 7am to 2:30pm and 7 to 10pm, Saturday from 10am to 1pm, and Sunday from 7 to 10pm.

Another mine of information is **Hios Tours** (© 22710/29-444; fax 22710/21-333), at the southern end of the paralia. The office is open Monday through Saturday from 8:30am to 1:30pm and 5:30 to 8:30pm; the staff will assist you with a room search, often at a discount. Hios Tours or the tourist office will change money after the port-side banks' normal hours. The free *Hios Summertime* magazine has a lot of useful information, as well as maps. The site **www.chios.com** is also helpful.

### GETTING AROUND

**By Bus** All buses depart from one of the two bus stations in Hios town. The **blue buses** (© 22710/22-079), which leave from the blue bus station on the north side of the public garden by Plateia Plastira, serve local destinations like Karfas to the south and Daskalopetra to the north. The **green long-distance KTEL buses** (© 22710/27-507) leave from the green bus station, a block south of the park near the main taxi stand. There are six buses a day to Mesta, eight a day to Piryi, five to Kardamila, and four to Emborio, but only two buses a week to Volissos and to Nea Moni. Fares are .60€ to 4€.

**By Car** Hios is a large island and fun to explore, so a car is highly recommended. We suggest **John Vassilakis Rent-A-Car** (© and fax **22710/29-300**), at Evgenias Handri 3 (the same street as the Hotel Kyma) in Hios, or at the branch office in **Megas Limionas** (© 22710/31-728), about 10km (6 miles) south of Hios town. There's no extra charge for airport pickup.

**By Taxi** Taxis are easily found at the port, though the taxi station is beyond the OTE, on the northeast corner of the central square. You can call © **22710/41-111** or 22710/26-379 for a cab. Fares from Hios town run about 16€ to Piryi, 20€ to Mesta, and 22€ round-trip to Nea Moni.

**By Moped** Hios is too large, and the hills too big, for mopeds—if you don't have the license to rent a genuine motorbike, you would be better off with a car.

**Tips** **An Important Note on Car Rentals**

Currently, anyone who is not carrying a driver's license from a country in the European Union will need an international driver's license to rent a car anywhere on Hios. If you expect to rent a car during your stay on Hios, plan to acquire an international driver's license before leaving your home country.

**FAST FACTS** The **Commercial Bank** (Emboriki Trapeza) and **Ergo Bank,** both at the north end of the harbor near the corner of Kanari, have ATMs; both are open Monday through Thursday from 8am to 2pm, Friday from 8am to 1:30pm. The English-speaking **dentist** Dr. Freeke (© 22710/27-266) is highly recommended. The **hospital** is 7km (4¼ miles) from the center of Hios town (© 22710/44-301). **Internet access** is available at **Enter Internet Café** (© 22710/41-058), on the south end of the paralia next to the Metropolis Café. It's open daily from 9am to midnight; 1 hour online costs 4€. There's a full-service **laundry** just around the corner from the post office on Psichari (© 22710/44-801); one load costs 12€, and the turnaround time is about 24 hours. The **post office** is at the corner of Omirou and Rodokanaki (© 22710/44-350). The **telephone office** (OTE) is across the street from the tourist office on Kanari (© 131). The **tourist police** are headquartered at the northernmost tip of the harbor, at Neorion 35 (© 22710/44-427).

## ATTRACTIONS

**Argenti Museum and Korai Library ★** Philip Argenti is the great historian of Hios, a local aristocrat who devoted his life and savings to the recording of island history, customs, customs, and architecture. The museum consists largely of his personal collection of folk art, costumes, and implements, supplemented with a gallery of family portraits and copies of Eugene Delacroix's *Massacre of Hios,* a masterpiece depicting the Turkish massacre of the local population in 1822. The entrance lobby has numerous old maps of the island on display. The library is excellent, with much of its collection in English and French. Those who have any interest in local architecture and village life should ask to see the collection of drawings made by Dimitris Pikionis (a renowned 20th-century Greek architect) of the Kampos mansions and village houses—the drawings are beautiful, and have yet to be published.

Korai, Hios town. © 22710/44-246. Museum admission 2€; free admission to library. Both open Mon–Thurs 8am–2pm; Fri 8am–2pm and 5–7:30pm; Sat 8am–12:30pm.

**Nea Moni ★** The 11th-century monastery of Nea Moni is one of the great architectural and artistic treasures of Greece. The monastery is in a spectacular setting high in the mountains overlooking Hios town. Its grounds are extensive—this monastery was once home to 1,000 monks—but the present population has dwindled to two monks and a single elderly nun (the monks often give tours of the monastery in Greek or French). The focus of the rambling complex is the katholikon, or principal church, whose nave is square in plan with eight niches supporting the dome. Within these niches are a sequence of extraordinary mosaics, among the finest examples of Byzantine art—sadly, a seemingly interminable process of restoration continues to conceal the most beautiful of these behind scaffolding. You can still see the portrayals of the saints in the narthex, and a representation of Christ washing the disciples' feet. The museum contains a collection of gifts to the monastery, including several fine 17th-century icons. Also of interest is the cistern, a cavernous vaulted room with columns (bring a flashlight), and the small Chapel of the Holy Cross at the entrance to the monastery, dedicated to the martyrs of the 1822 massacre by the Turks (the skulls and bones displayed are those of the victims themselves). The long barrel-vaulted refectory is currently being restored—it's a beautiful space, and its curved apse dates from the 11th century.

The bus to Nea Moni is part of an island excursion operated by KTEL, departing from the Hios town bus station Tuesday and Friday at 9am and returning at 4:30pm. The route is Hios town to Nea Moni to Anavatos to Lithi beach to Armolia and back to Hios town; it costs 16€ per person. A taxi will cost about 22€ round-trip from Hios town, including a half-hour at the monastery.

Nea Moni. No phone Free admission to monastery grounds and katholikon; museum admission 2€ adults, 1€ students and seniors. Monastery grounds and katholikon daily 8am–1pm and 4–8pm; museum, Tues–Sun 8am–1pm. Located 17km (10½ miles) west of Hios town.

## A DAY TRIP TO THE MASTIC VILLAGES: PIRYI, MESTA & OLIMBI ★

The most interesting day trip on Hios is the excursion to the mastic villages in the southern part of the island, which offer one of the best examples of medieval town architecture in all of Greece. Mastic is a gum derived from the resin of the mastic tree, used in candies, paints, perfumes, and medicines. It was a source of great wealth for these towns in the Middle Ages, and is still produced in small quantities. All the towns were originally fortified, with an outer wall formed by an unbroken line of houses with no doors and few windows facing out. You can still see this distinctive plan at all three towns, although in Piryi and Olimbi the original medieval village has been engulfed by more recent construction.

**Piryi** is known for a rare technique of geometric decoration, known as *Kísti*. In the main square this technique reaches a level of extraordinary virtuosity. The beautiful **Ayioi Apostoli** church and every available surface of every building are covered with horizontal banded decorations in a remarkable variety of motifs. At the town center is the tower for which the village was named, now mostly in ruins. It was originally the heart of the city's defenses, and a place of last refuge in time of siege.

**Mesta** is the best preserved medieval village in Hios, a maze of narrow streets and dark covered passages. The town has two fine churches, each unique on the island. **Megas Taxiarchis**, built in the 19th century, is one of the largest churches in Greece, and it was clearly built to impress. The arcaded porch with its fine pebble terrace and bell tower create a solemn and harmonious transition to the cathedral precinct. The other church in town, **Paleos Taxiarchis**, is located a few blocks below the main square. As the name suggests, this is the older of the two, built in the 14th century. The most notable feature here is the carved wooden iconostasis, whose surface is incised with miniature designs of unbelievable intricacy. If either church is closed, you can ask for the gatekeeper in the central square; Despina Flores of the **Messaionas Taverna** (© 22710/76-050) will probably know where he can be found.

**Olimbi** is the least well known of the three, not so spectacular as Piryi nor as intact as Mesta, but many of its medieval buildings still exist. There is a central tower similar to that of Piryi, and stone vaults connecting the houses.

Piryi is the closest of the three villages to Hios town, at 26km (16 miles); Olimbi and Mesta are both within 10km (6 miles) of Piryi. The easiest way to see all three villages is by car. Taxis from Hios to Piryi cost about 16€. KTEL buses travel from Hios to Piryi eight times a day, and to Mesta five times a day. The bus to Piryi is 3.20€, and to Mesta 4.50€.

## BEACHES

There's no question that Hios has the best beaches in the Northeastern Aegean. They're cleaner, less crowded, and more plentiful than those of Samos or Lesvos, and would be the envy of any Cycladic isle.

The fine-sand beach of **Karfas**, 7km (4¼ miles) south of Hios town, is the closest decent beach to the town center; it can be reached by a local (blue) bus. The rapid development of tourism in this town assures, however, that the beach will be crowded.

The most popular beach on the south coast is **Mavra Volia** (black pebbles) in the town of Emborio. Continue over the rocks to the right from the man-made town beach to find the main beach. Walking on the smooth black rocks feels and sounds like marching through a room filled with marbles. The panorama of the beach, slightly curving coastline, and distant headland is a memorable sight. There are regular buses from Hios town or from Piryi (8km/5 miles away) to Emborio. A short distance south is the best beach of the south coast, **Vroulidia** ★, a 5km (3-mile) drive in from the Emborio road. This white-pebble-and-sand beach in a rocky cove offers great views of the craggy coastline.

The west coast of the island has a number of stunning beaches. **Elinda Cove** shelters a long cobble beach, a 600m (1,968-ft.) drive in from the main road between Lithi and Volissos. Another excellent beach on this road is **Tigani-Makria Ammos,** about 4km (2½ miles) north of Elinda; turn at a sign for the beach and drive in 1½km (1 mile) to this long white-pebble beach (there's also a small cove-sheltered cobble beach about 300m (984 ft.) before you reach the main beach). There are three beaches below Volissos, the best of which is Lefkathia, just north of the harbor of Volissos (Limnia).

South of Elinda, the long safe beach at **Lithi Bay** is popular with families. There are several tavernas, of which **Ta Tria Adelphia,** The Three Brothers (© 22710/73-208), is recommended—it's the last taverna you come to as you're walking along the beach.

The beaches of the north coast are less remarkable. **Nagos** (4km/2½ miles north of Kardamila) is a charming town in a small spring-fed oasis, with a cobble beach and two tavernas on the water. This beach can get very crowded—the secret is to hike to the two small beaches a little to the east. To find them, take the small road behind the white house near the windmill.

## WHERE TO STAY
### HIOS TOWN

**Chios Chandris Hotel**    For those who prefer a modern hotel with several resort-type facilities yet within walking distance to the town's attractions, this is the place to be. Completely renovated in 2000, it offers several of the amenities associated with beach resorts. Rooms are of standard size and decor, but there are suites and studios for those who want something a bit roomier; almost all units have views overlooking the port of Chios Town. During the summer you can take your meals or drinks at the poolside cafe.

There's no need to oversell this hotel—what recommends it is the fact that after a day of enjoying other locales in town or around the island, you can stroll back from town in about 10 minutes and be in the pool.

Port, 82100 Hios. © 22710/44-401. Fax 22710/25-768. www.chandris.gr. 139 units. 125€–145€ double. 155€–210€ suite or studio. DC, MC, V. Rates include breakfast. Parking adjacent to hotel. **Amenities:** Restaurant; 2 bars; pool; tennis courts nearby; concierge; tours and car rentals arranged; salon; 24-hr. room service; same-day laundry and dry cleaning service. *In room:* A/C, TV, minibar, hair dryer, computer and fax outlets.

**Hotel Kyma** ★ Our favorite in-town lodging was built in 1917 as a private villa for John Livanos. (You'll notice the portraits of the lovely Mrs. Livanos on the ceiling in the ground-floor breakfast room.) Though the hotel is of historic interest (the treaty with Turkey was signed in the Kyma in 1922), most of the original architectural details are gone, and the rooms have been renovated in a modern style. Many units have views of the sea, and a few have big whirlpool baths.

1 Evgenias Handri, 82100 Hios. © 22710/44-500. Fax 22710/44-600. kyma@chi.forthnet.gr. 59 units, 75€ double. Rates include breakfast. No credit cards. *In room:* A/C, TV.

## KARFAS

Karfas, 7km (4½ miles) south of Hios town around Cape Ayia Eleni, is an exploding tourist resort with a fine-sand beach lined with resort hotels. The area is packed with tour groups throughout the summer months.

**Hotel Erytha** Built in 1990, the Erytha currently offers the most luxurious accommodations in the vicinity of Hios town. The spacious double rooms of this sprawling resort are distributed among five beachfront buildings connected by plant-filled terraces. The outdoor breakfast area steps down to the pool terrace, which is just above a tiny cove and private beach. Guest rooms are simply furnished: All have balconies and most face the sea, although a few open onto the terraces between buildings. Bathrooms are moderate in size, and include a bathtub with shower. There are 21 studios and apartments in a separate building, but these aren't as well maintained as the main hotel, and the kitchen facilities are very minimal: You're better off avoiding them entirely. The air-conditioning operates only in July and August.

Karfas, 82100 Hios. © 22710/32-060 or 22710/32-064. Fax 22710/32-182. erytha@compulink.gr. 102 units. 110€ double. Rates include breakfast. AE, DC, MC, V. *In room:* A/C, TV, minibar.

## KARDAMILA

Kardamila, on the northeastern coast, is our choice among the resort towns because it's prosperous, self-sufficient, and not at all touristy.

**Hotel Kardamila** ★ This modern resort hotel was built for the guests and business associates of the town's ship owners and officers, and it has its own small cobble beach. The guest rooms are large and plain, with modern bathrooms and balconies overlooking the beach. The gracious Theo Spordilis, formerly with the Hotel Kyma, has taken over its management, so you can be sure the service will be good.

Kardamila, 82300 Hios. © 22720/23-353. Fax 22710/23-354. (Contact Hotel Kyma for reservations.) 32 units. 90€ double. Rates include breakfast. No credit cards. *In room:* A/C.

## VOLISSOS

This small hilltop village is one of the most beautiful on the island. A fine Byzantine castle overlooks the steep streets of the town, which contains numerous cafes and tavernas. It's too far north to be a convenient base for touring the whole island, but if you want to get to know a small part of the island, you couldn't choose a better focus for your explorations.

**Volissos Traditional Houses** ★ The care with which these village houses have been restored is unique on this island, if not in the whole Northeastern Aegean. Stella Tsakiri is a trained visual artist, and the influence of her discerning eye is evident in every detail of the reconstruction. The beamed ceilings, often supported by a forked tree limb—a method of construction described in the *Odyssey*—are finely crafted and quite beautiful. Built into the stone walls are niches, fireplaces, cupboards, and couches. This spirit of inventiveness is also seen in imaginative recycling: A cattle yoke serves as a beam, while salvaged doors and shutters from the village become a mirror or piece of furniture. The houses and apartments are distributed throughout the village of Volissos, so your neighbors are likely to be locals rather than fellow tourists. All apartments and houses have a small kitchen, a spacious bathroom, and one or two bedrooms; the largest places (on two floors of a house) have two bedrooms, a sitting room, a kitchen, and a large terrace.

Volissos, Hios. © 22740/21-421 or 22740/21-413. Fax 22740/21-521. volissos@otenet.gr. 16 units. 45€–82€ per night. No credit cards. *In room:* No phone.

## MESTA

The best-preserved medieval fortified village on Hios, Mesta is a good base for touring the mastic villages (see above) and the island's south coast.

**Pipidis Traditional Houses** ★    These four homes, built more than 500 years ago, have been restored and opened by the Greek National Tourism Organization as part of its traditional settlements program. The apartments have a medieval character, with vaulted ceilings and irregularly sculpted stone walls (covered in plaster and whitewash). One unfortunate aspect of these authentic dwellings is the dearth of natural light: If a room has any windows at all, they're usually small and placed high in the wall. Each house comes equipped with a kitchen, bathroom, and enough sleeping space for two to six people. They're managed by the admirable Pipidis family.

Mesta, Hios. © 22710/76-029. 4 units. 45€ double; 55€ for 4 persons. No credit cards. *In room:* No phone.

## WHERE TO DINE
### HIOS TOWN

**Hios Marine Club** GREEK    This good, simple taverna serves the usual Greek dishes, pasta, grilled meats, and fish. Don't be put off by the ugly yellow-and-white concrete facade—the sign in front reads simply RESTAURANT-FRESCA PSARIA. It's on the bay at the edge of town, just south of the port, 50m (164 ft.) beyond the Hotel Chandris.

1 Nenitousi. © 22710/23-184. Main courses 3.50€–13€. MC, V. Daily noon–2am.

**Hotzas Taverna** GREEK    Hotzas is a small taverna that offers simple, well-prepared food. It's the best option in a town not known for its restaurants. The summer dining area is a luxuriant garden with lemon trees and abundant flowers. There's no menu, just a few unsurprising but delicious offerings each night. You won't find much fish, as most of the dishes are meat-based. This place isn't easy to find—take Kountouriotou in from the harbor, and look for the first right turn after a major road merges at an oblique angle from the right; after this it's another 50m (164 ft.) before the taverna appears on your left.

3 Yronjou Kondili. © 22710/23-117. Main courses 3.50€–13€. No credit cards. Mon–Sat 6–11pm.

**Theodosiou Ouzeri** ★ GREEK    In the evening, many residents pull up a streetside chair at a cafe along the waterfront and eat *mezedes* with *ouzo*. Of the many ouzeries on the paralia, we like Theodosiou, located on the far right (north) side of the port, for both the scene and its menu.

Paralia, Hios. No phone. Appetizers 2.50€–12€. No credit cards. Daily 7pm–midnight.

## LANGADA

**Yiorgo Passa's Taverna** ★ GREEK/SEAFOOD   Langada is a fishing village with a strip of five or six outdoor fish taverns lining the harbor. Our favorite of these is Yiorgo Passa's Taverna, the first on the left as you approach the waterfront. Prices are low—fish is traditionally priced per kilo—portions are generous, and the ambience is warm and friendly. *Note:* There are evening dinner cruises to Langada from Hios; check with Hios Tours (see "Visitor Information," earlier in this chapter) for details.

Langada. ⓒ 22710/74-218. Fish from 38€ per kilo. No credit cards. Daily 11am–2am. Located 20km (12 miles) north of Hios town on the Kardamila road.

## MESTA

**Messaiones Taverna** GREEK   You'll find Despina Sirimi's taverna on the main square in Mesta. The menu features a great variety of *mezedes*, many with interesting variations on traditional dishes. The stuffed tomatoes with pine nuts and raisins are delicious, as are the fried dishes like *domatokeftedes* (fried tomatoes with herbs) or *tiropitakia* (fried cheese balls). Despina knows the village well, and can direct you to its most distinctive features, like Paleos Taxiarchis church and its remarkable carved wooden iconostasis.

Mesta. ⓒ 22710/76-050. Main courses 3.80€–9€. No credit cards. Daily 11am–midnight.

348km (188 nautical miles) NE of Piraeus

Roughly triangular Lesvos—now called Mitilini in many Greek publications—is the third-largest island in Greece, with a population of nearly 120,000. At the tips of the triangle are the three principal towns: **Mitilini, Molivos,** and **Eressos.** Due to its remote location, Eressos is a good destination for a day trip, but not a recommended base for touring the island.

Mitilini and Molivos are about as different as two towns on the same island could possibly be. Loud and obnoxious, Mitilini is a tough cousin to Thessaloniki, a port town low on sophistication or pretense, with little organized tourism and lots of local character. Molivos is a picture-postcard seaside village, a truly beautiful place, but in the summer existing only for tourism.

Not to be missed are the Archaeological and Theophilos museums in Mitilini; the town of **Mandamados** and its celebrated icon (the east coast road, between Mandamados and Mitilini, is the most scenic on the island); the remarkable, mile-long beach of Eressos; and the labyrinthine streets of Molivos's castle-crowned hill.

Getting around on Lesvos is greatly complicated by the presence of two huge tear-shaped bays in the south coast, which divide the island down its center. East-west distances are great, and since bus service is infrequent, this is one island where you'll definitely need a car.

**GETTING THERE   By Plane**   The **airport** ⓒ 22510/61-490 or 22510/61-590) is 3km (2 miles) south of Mitilini; there's no bus to the town, and a taxi will cost about 5€. **Olympic Airways** (ⓒ 28010/44-444 or 210/966-6666; www.olympic-airways.gr) has several flights daily to Mitilini from Athens. There are connections with Thessaloniki daily; with Limnos three times weekly; and with Hios twice weekly. The **Olympic office** in Mitilini (ⓒ 22510/28-660) is at Kavetsou 44, about 200m (656 ft.) south of Ayia Irinis park. To find it, walk 300m (984 ft.) south from the harbor; turn right at a large park, just before the World War II monument (a statue of a woman with sword); take the first right;

and the office will be immediately on your left. **Aegean Cronus Airlines** (C 210/ **998-2888** in Athens), with an office at the Mitilini airport (C **22510/61-120**), also has three flights daily between Athens and Mitilini, and one or two flights daily between Thessaloniki and Mitilini.

**By Boat**    The principal port of Lesvos is Mitilini, and almost all the ferries arrive and depart from here, although there is some ferry traffic through the west coast port of Sigri. There's one ferry daily to Mitilini from Piraeus, stopping at Hios (10–12 hr.); there are also several ferries weekly from Rafina to Sigri (9 hr.). There are daily boats in both directions between Mitilini and Hios (3 hr.), and four ferries weekly from Mitilini to Limnos (6–7 hr.); there are also two ferries weekly between Sigri and Limnos (4½ hr.). Two boats call weekly to Mitilini from Kavala (10 hr.) and Thessaloniki (10–13 hr.), stopping at Limnos on the way; there's also one ferry a week from Siros (9 hr.). Check schedules with a local travel agent, **www.gtp.gr**, the **Mitilini Port Authority** (C **22510/28-827**), or the **Sigri Port Authority** (C **22530/54-433**).

Once you get to Lesvos double-check the boat schedule for your departure, as the harbor is extremely busy in the summer and service is often inexplicably irregular.

## MITILINI & SOUTHEAST LESVOS

With a big-city ambience more like a mainland city than an island capital, Mitilini isn't to everyone's taste. Your first impression is likely to be one of noise, car exhaust, and crazy taxi drivers. Sadly, recent development has resulted in a generic paralia; the only signs of a more auspicious past are the cathedral dome and the considerable remains of a hilltop castle. Still, once you leave the paralia there's little or nothing in the way of amenities for tourists, a quality that can be remarkably refreshing. In the vicinity of Ermou (the market street), Mitilini's crumbling ochre alleys contain a mix of traditional coffeehouses, the studios of artisans, ouzeries, stylish jewelry shops, and stores selling antiques and clothing. Although good restaurants are notably absent in the town center, there are a few authentic tavernas on the outskirts of town.

## ESSENTIALS

**VISITOR INFORMATION**    The Greek National Tourism Organization (EOT) has turned its functions over to the North Aegean Islands Tourism Directorate; its office is at 6 J. Aristarchou, 81100 Mitilini (C **22510/42-511**; fax 22510/42-512), 20m (66 ft.) back from the building housing the Customs office and the tourist police, to the left (east) from the ferry quay, in what may appear at first to be a private house. This is primarily an administrative center, and the office is not very well equipped. It's open daily from 8am to 2:30pm, with extended hours in the high season. The **tourist police** (C **22510/22-276**) may also be helpful.

**GETTING AROUND    By Bus**    There are two bus stations in Mitilini, one for local and the other for round-the-island routes. The **local bus station** (C **22510/28-725**) is near the north end of the harbor, by the (closed) Folklife Museum and across from the Commercial Bank (Emporiki Trapeza). Local buses on Lesvos are frequent, running every hour from 6am to 9pm most of the year. The destinations covered are all within 12km (7½ miles) of Mitilini, and include Thermi, Moria, and Pamfilla to the north and Varia, Ayia Marina, and Loutra to the south. The most expensive local fare is 2€. The posted schedule is hard to read, but there's usually someone selling tickets who can decipher it. You can catch the

**round-the-island KTEL buses** (© 22510/28-873) in Mitilini at the south end of the port behind the Argo Hotel. There's daily service in summer to Kaloni and Molivos (four times), Mandamados (once), Plomari (four times), and to Eressos and Sigri (once).

**By Car**   Rental prices in Mitilini tend to be high, so be sure to shop around. A good place to start is **Payless Car Rental** (automoto@otenet.gr), with offices at the airport (© **22510/61-665**) and on the port in Mitilini (© **22510/43-555**), near the local (north) bus station. Summer daily rates start at around 55€ with 100 free kilometers; each kilometer over 100 is an additional .65€. Assuming an average day's drive is 150km (94 miles), count on paying about 90€ a day.

**By Taxi**   Lesvos is a big island. The one-way taxi fare from Mitilini to Molivos is about 35€; from Mitilini to Eressos or Sigri, about 55€. The main taxi stand in Mitilini is on Plateia Kyprion Patrioton, a long block inland from the southern end of the port; there's a smaller taxi stand at the north end of the port, near the local bus station and the (closed) Folklife Museum.

**FAST FACTS**   The **area code** for Mitilini is 0251, for Molivos (Mithimna) and Eressos 0253, and for Plomari 0252. There are **ATMs** at several banks on the port, including the Ioniki Trapeza and Agrotiki Trapeza (both south of the local bus station). The **Vostani Hospital** (© **22510/43-777**) on P. Vostani, just southeast of town, will take care of emergencies. **Glaros Laundry** (© **22510/27-065**), opposite the tourist police near the ferry pier, is open from 9am to 2pm and 6 to 8pm; the turnaround time is usually 24 hours. The **post office** and the **telephone office (OTE)** are on Plateia Kyprion Patrioton, 1 block inland from the town hall at the south end of the port. The principal **taxi stand** is also on Plateia Kyprion Patrioton. The **tourist police** (© **22510/22-776**) are located just east (left) from the ferry quay.

## ATTRACTIONS

### Archaeological Museums of Mitilini

The excellent Mitilini Archaeological Museum was augmented recently by the construction of a large new museum a short distance up the hill toward the Kastro. The museums have the same hours, and the price of admission includes both locations. The new museum presents extensive Roman antiquities of Lesvos and some finds from the early Christian basilica of Ayios Andreas in Eressos. The highlight of its collection is a reconstructed Roman house from the 3rd century B.C., whose elaborate mosaic floors depict scenes from comedies of the poet Menander and from Classical mythology. All the exhibits are thoughtfully presented, with plentiful explanatory notes in English. Entering the yard of the original archaeological museum, you're greeted by massive marble lions rearing menacingly on their hind legs, perhaps representing the bronze lion sculpted by Hephaestus, which is said to roam the island of Lesvos and serve as its guardian. A rear building houses more marble sculpture and inscribed tablets, while the main museum contains figurines, pottery, gold jewelry, and other finds from Thermi, the Mitilini Kastro, and other ancient sites of Lesvos.

7 Eftaliou, Myrina. © 22510/28-032. Admission 2€ adults, 1€ students and seniors. Tues–Sun 8:30am–3pm. A block north of the tourist police station, just inland from the ferry pier.

### Kastro

Perched on a steep hill just north of the city, the extensive ruins of Mitilini's castle are fun to explore and offer fine views of city and sea from the ramparts. The Kastro was founded by Justinian in the 6th century A.D., and was restored and enlarged in 1737 by the Genoese; the Turks also renovated and built extensively during their occupation of the castle. In several places you can see fragments of marble columns embedded in the castle walls—these are blocks taken from a 7th-century B.C. temple of Apollo by the Genoese during their rebuilding of the walls. Look for the underground cistern at the north end of the castle precinct: This echoing chamber is a beautiful place, with domed vaults reflected in the pool below. In summer, the castle is sometimes used as a performing-arts center.

8th Noemvriou, Mitilini. © **2510/27-297.** Admission 2€ adults; 1€ students and seniors. Tues–Sun 8am–2:30pm. Just past the new Archaeological Museum, turn right on the path to the Kastro.

**Theophilos Museum** ✿  One of the most interesting sights near Mitilini is this small museum in the former house of folk artist Hatzimichalis Theophilos (1868–1934). Most of Theophilos's works adorned the walls of tavernas and ouzeries, often painted in exchange for food. Theophilos died in poverty, and none of his work would have survived if it weren't for the efforts of art critic Theriade (see below), who commissioned the paintings on display here during the last years of the painter's life. These primitive watercolors depicting ordinary people, daily life, and local landscapes are now widely celebrated, and are also exhibited at the Museum of Folk Art in Athens. Be sure to take in the curious photographs showing the artist dressed as Alexander the Great.

Varia. © **2510/41-644.** Admission 2€ Tues–Sun 9am–1pm and 4:30–8pm. Located 3km (2 miles) south of Mitilini, on the road to the airport, next to the Theriade Museum.

**Theriade Library and Museum of Modern Art**  The Theriade Library and Museum of Modern Art is in the home of Stratis Eleftheriadis, a native of Lesvos who emigrated to Paris and became a prominent art critic and publisher (Theriade is the Gallicized version of his surname). On display are copies of his published works, including the *Minotaure* and *Verve* magazines, as well as his personal collection of works by Picasso, Matisse, Miro, Chagall, and other modern artists.

Varia. © **2510/23-372.** Admission 2€. Tues–Sun 9am–1pm and 5–8pm. Located 3km (2 miles) south of Mitilini, on the road to the airport, next to the Theophilos Museum.

## A SIDE TRIP TO TURKEY: AYVALIK, PERGAMUM & ANCIENT TROY

From Mitilini, there's a direct connection to Turkey via its port of Ayvalik; about 3,000 tourists make the crossing annually. Ayvalik, a densely wooded fishing village, makes a refreshing base camp from which to tour Pergamum or ancient Troy. The acropolis of Pergamum is sited on a dramatic hilltop, with substantial remains of the town on the surrounding slopes. The complex dates back to at

*Moments*  **Excursion to a Mountain Village**

An enjoyable destination for a day trip is the rural hamlet of **Ayiassos,** 23km (14 miles) west of Mitilini. The town, built up on the foothills of Mount Olymbos, consists of traditional gray stone houses (with their wooden "Turkish" balconies, often covered in flowering vines), narrow cobblestone lanes, and fine small churches. Here local craftsmen still turn out their ceramic wares by hand. There are excursion buses from Mitilini, or you can share a taxi (about 40€ for the ride and a reasonably brief wait).

least the 4th century B.C., and there are significant remains from this period through to Roman and Byzantine times. It is one of Turkey's most important archaeological sites. All-inclusive tours to Pergamum with lunch, bus, and round-trip boat fare are available; inquire at Mitilini travel agencies. Ships to Turkey sail Wednesday, Friday, and Saturday. Tickets for the Turkish boats are sold by **Aeolic Cruises Travel Agency** (© **22510/23-960**), on the port in Mitilini. The round-trip excursion fare (returning the same day) is about 75€ and a visa is not required; the fare on the Turkish boat is 55€ round-trip, with an additional visa fee upon arrival in Turkey ($50 for Americans, £5 or Irish citizens, £10 for U.K. citizens, C$50 for Canadians, and A$25 for Australians; New Zealanders don't currently need a visa).

## WHERE TO STAY

**Hotel Erato**     On a busy street just south of the port, this hotel offers convenience, cleanliness, a friendly and helpful staff, and a noise level marginally below that experienced in the many portside hotels. Most of the small bright rooms have balconies facing the street, with a view over the traffic to Mitilini Bay. The four-story hotel was converted from a medical clinic, and does retain an atmosphere of institutional anonymity; on the positive side, it's very well maintained, and the high-pressure showers and fluffy towels are a bonus. *An important note: Although credit cards are accepted, the hotel staff doesn't seem accustomed to dealing with them, and there can be long delays. If you intend to pay by credit card, do so well in advance of your planned departure.

P. Vostani, Mitilini, 81000 Lesvos. © 22510/41-160. Fax 22510/47-656. 22 units. 58€ double. MC, V. Open year-round. *In room:* A/C, TV.

**Hotel Sappho**     The Sappho is one of the better hotels on the port, offering simple accommodations in a recently renovated building. Nine rooms have balconies facing the port; the rest have no balcony and face a sunny rear courtyard. All units have wall-to-wall carpets, white walls, minimal furnishings, and tiny bathrooms with showers. A breakfast room on the second floor has an outdoor terrace with a fine port view.

Kountourioti, Mitilini, 81000 Lesvos. © 22510/22-888. Fax 22510/24-522. 29 units. 55€ double. Continental breakfast 5€. AE, V. *In room:* A/C, TV.

**Villa 1900**     The Villa 1900 is a somewhat upscale pension in a fine old house on the edge of town, about 700m (2,296 ft.) south of the Mitilini port. The best rooms (nos. 3 and 7) are quite spacious, with ornate painted ceilings. However, the smaller ones (nos. 6, 8, and 9) are claustrophobic and overpriced. The remaining two units are plain but adequate, and offer reasonable value for your money. The house is buffered from the noise of the street by a small garden in front; a larger garden with abundant fruit trees begins at the back terrace and offers a pleasant shaded retreat. The amiable owners speak no English, but there is usually someone on hand to translate.

24 P. Vostani, Mitilini, 81000 Lesvos. © 22510/23-448. Fax 22510/28-034. 7 units. 37€–50€ double. No credit cards. Located 150m (492 ft.) south of the Olympic Airways office, opposite the stadium. *In room:* A/C, fridge, no phone.

## WHERE TO DINE

Mitilini has more portside cafes than your average bustling harbor town. A cluster of chairs around the small lighthouse at the point heralds the most scenic (as well as the windiest) of the many small ouzeries, specializing in grilled octopus, squid, shrimp, and local fish. We found the best restaurants to be a short taxi ride outside the city.

**Averof 1841 Grill** GREEK   This taverna, located midport near the Sappho Hotel, is one of the better grills around, and one of the only restaurants in Mitilini center worth trying. It has particularly good beef dishes. Try any of the tender souvlaki dishes or the lamb with potatoes.

Port, Mitilini. © **22510/22-180.** Main courses 3.90€–12€. No credit cards. Daily 7am–5pm and 7–11pm.

**O Rembetis** GREEK   Kato Halikas is a hilltop village on the outskirts of Mitilini, and although this simple taverna might be hard to find, it's well worth the effort. At the south end of the terrace you can sit beneath the branches of a high sycamore and enjoy a panoramic view of the port. The food isn't sophisticated or surprising, but it's very Greek, and the clientele is primarily local. There's no menu, so listen to the waiter's descriptions or take a look in the kitchen—there's usually some fresh fish in addition to the taverna standards. The wind can be brisk on this hilly site, so bring a jacket if the night is cool. The best way to get here is by taxi; the fare is about 3€ each way.

Kato Halikas, Mitilini. © **22510/27-150.** Main courses 3.70€–12€. No credit cards. Daily 8pm–12am.

**Salavos** GREEK   Despite its location on the busy airport road, this small taverna is one of the best in Mitilini. A garden terrace in back offers partial shelter from the road noise. The seafood is fresh and delicious; try the kalamari stuffed with feta, vegetables, and herbs. The restaurant is very popular with locals, who fill the place on summer nights. Traveling south from Mitilini toward the airport, it's about 3km (2 miles) south of town on the right. Taxi fare is about 3€ each way.

Mitilini. © **22510/22-237.** Main courses 3.90€–12€. No credit cards. Daily noon–1am.

## MITILINI AFTER DARK

In Mitilini, there's plenty of nightlife action on both ends of the harbor. The east side tends to be younger, cheaper, and more informal—the **Hott Spot** (63 Koundouriotou) being one such. The more sophisticated places are off the south end of the harbor. There's also the outdoor **Park Cinema,** on the road immediately below the stadium, or the **Pallas,** on Vounazo (by the Post Office), both open May through September. There are also occasional entertainment events at the Kastro during the summer.

## MOLIVOS & NORTHEAST LESVOS

Molivos, also known by the more specifically Hellenic name "Mithimna," is at the northern tip of the island's triangle. It's a highly picturesque castle-crowned village with stone and pink-pastel stucco mansions capped by red-tile roofs, balconies, and windowsills decorated with geraniums and roses.

The town has long been popular with package-tour groups, especially during the summer months. Souvenir shops, car-rental agencies, and travel agents outnumber local merchants, and the restaurants are geared toward tourists. Despite this, it is a beautiful place to visit and a convenient base for touring the island.

## ESSENTIALS

**GETTING THERE   By Bus   KTEL buses** (© **22510/28-873**) connect Molivos with Mitilini four times daily in the high season. The Molivos bus stop is just past the Municipal Tourist Office on the road to Mitilini.

**By Taxi**   The one-way taxi fare from Mitilini to Molivos is about 35€.

**VISITOR INFORMATION** The **Municipal Tourist Office** (℃ 22530/71-347), housed in a tiny building next to the National Bank on the Mitilini Road, is open Monday through Friday. **Tsalis Tours,** on the road heading down to the sea from the National Bank (℃ 22530/71-389; fax 22530/71-345; tsalis@otenet.gr), can book car rentals, accommodations, and excursions; open daily in summer from 8:30am to 9:30pm.

**GETTING AROUND　By Car** There are numerous rental agencies in Molivos, and rates are comparable to those in Mitilini.

**By Boat** Boat taxis to neighboring beaches can be arranged at the port or in a travel agency (see Tsalis Tours, above).

**By Bus** Tickets for day excursions by bus can be bought in any of the local travel agencies. The destinations include Thermi/Ayiasos (35€), Mitilini Town (15€), Sigri/Eressos (35€), and Plomari (38€); the excursions are offered once or twice each week in the summer.

**FAST FACTS** There's an ATM at the **National Bank,** next to the Municipal Tourist Office on the Mitilini Road. There's **Internet access** at Communication and Travel (℃ 22530/71-900) on the main road to the port. The **police** (℃ 22530/71-222) are up from the port, on the road to the town cemetery; the **port police** (℃ 22530/71-307) are (predictably) on the port. The **post office** (℃ 22530/71-246) is on the path circling up to the castle—turn right (up) just past the National Bank.

## ATTRACTIONS

**Kastro** The hilltop Genoese castle is in a better state of preservation than that of Mitilini Town but it's much less extensive and not as interesting to explore. There is, however, a great view from the walls, worth the price of admission in itself. There's a stage in the southwest corner of the courtyard, often used for theatrical performances in the summer. To get here by car, turn uphill at the bus stop and follow signs to the castle parking lot; on foot, the castle is most easily approached from the town, a steep climb no matter which of the many labyrinthine streets you choose.

Molivos. No phone. Admission 2€ adults, 1€ students and seniors. Tues–Sun 8:30am–3pm.

**Mandamados Monastery** ★ Mandamados is a lovely village on a high inland plateau, renowned primarily for the remarkable icon of the Archangel Michael housed in the local monastery. A powerful story is associated with the creation of the icon: It is said that during a certain pirate raid (these raids were tragically common during the later middle ages), all but one of the monks were slaughtered. This one survivor, emerging from hiding to find the bloody corpses of his dead companions, responded to the horror of the moment with an extraordinary act. Gathering the blood-soaked earth, he fashioned in it the face of man, an icon in relief of the Archangel Michael. This simple icon, its lips worn away by the kisses of pilgrims, can be found at the center of the iconostasis at the back of the main chapel.

Mandamados. Free admission. Daily 6am–10pm. Located 24km (15 miles) east of Molivos, 36km (22½ miles) northwest of Mitilini.

## BEACHES

The long, narrow town beach in Molivos is rocky and crowded near the town, but becomes sandier and less populous as you continue south. The beach in **Petra,**

6km (3¾ miles) south of Molivos, is considerably more pleasant. The beach at **Tsonia**, 30km (19 miles) east of Molivos, is only accessible via a difficult rutted road, and isn't particularly attractive. The best beach on the island is 70km (44 miles) west of Molivos at **Skala Eressos** (see "An Excursion to Western Lesvos," below).

## SHOPPING

Molivos is unfortunately dominated by tacky souvenir shops. To find more authentic local wares you'll have to explore neighboring towns. **Mandamados** is known as a center for pottery, and there are numerous ceramics studios here. **Eleni Lioliou** (② 22530/61-170), on the road to the monastery, has brightly painted bowls, plates, and mugs. **Anna Fonti** (② 22530/61-433), on a pedestrian street in the village, produces plates with intricate designs in brilliant turquoise and blue. Also in Mandamados is the diminutive studio of icon painter **Dimitris Hatzanagnostou** (② 22530/61-318), who produces large-scale icons for churches and portable icons for purchase.

## WHERE TO STAY

**Hotel-Bungalows Delphinia** ★ The best thing about this white-stucco and gray-stone resort is its panoramic setting above the Aegean. A path leads 200m (656 ft.) from the hotel to a fine-sand beach and a recreation complex with saltwater swimming pool, snack bar, and tennis courts (the latter illuminated for night games). The hotel rooms are simple, with small shower-only bathrooms. The 57 bungalows are more spacious: The living room has a couch that pulls out to provide an extra bed, most bathrooms include a bathtub, and all units have a large terrace or balcony. Breakfast at the hotel is served in a large dining room, while the bungalows include free room service for breakfast only. The second-floor rooms in the bungalows are the most spacious, have the best views, and cost a bit more.

Molivos, 81108 Lesvos. (1 mile from town center). ② 22530/71-315 or 22530/71-580. Fax 22530/71-524. http://users.otenet.gr/d/delphinia. 125 units. 68€–85€ double; 98€–116€ 2-person bungalow. Rates include buffet breakfast. AE, DC, V. Parking adjacent. **Amenities:** Restaurant; bar; pool; 3 night-lit tennis courts; children's playground; tours and car rentals arranged; 24-hr. room service; babysitting; same-day laundry and dry cleaning; fax and photocopying arranged; basketball; volleyball; table tennis. *In room:* A/C, TV, minibar.

**Hotel Olive Press** The most charming hotel in town is built down on the water in the traditional style. The rooms are on the small side, but they're quiet and very comfortable, with terrazzo floors, handsome furnishings, and bathtubs. Some of the units have windows opening onto great sea views, with waves lapping just beneath. There is a nice inner courtyard with several gardens. The staff is gracious and friendly. There's neither air-conditioning nor TV in the rooms, so this is a place for those who prefer old fashioned atmosphere.

Molivos, 81108 Lesvos. ② 22530/71-205 or 22530/71-646. Fax 22530/71-647. 50 units. 82€ double (includes breakfast); 118€ studio. AE, DC, V.

**Sea Horse Pension (Thalassio Alogo)** A cluster of recently built Class C hotels is set below the old town, near the beach—among them is this smaller, homier pension. The friendly manager, Stergios, keeps the rooms (which have good views) tidy. All rooms come with a balcony facing the sea; four also have minimal kitchen facilities. On site are a restaurant and an in-house travel agency.

Molivos, 81108 Lesvos. ② 22530/71-630 or 22530/71-320. Fax 22530/71-374. 16 units. 50€ double. Continental breakfast 7€. No credit cards. *In room:* A/C, TV, fridge, hair dryer.

## WHERE TO DINE

**Captain's Table** ★ SEAFOOD/VEGETARIAN   Overlooking the harbor at Molivos, this would be nominated as the island's favorite by many visitors to Lesvos. It's run by Melinda, an Australian, and her Greek husband, Theo. Although the emphasis is now on fresh fish, the menu still offers some of the excellent vegetable dishes that were the trademark of her former establishment—try the Imam Bayeldi, a dish made with eggplant, onions, tomato, and garlic. Then there's the smoked and grilled mackerel—or the fresh mussels with the house white if that's to your taste. There's live bouzouki music 3 nights a week. Needless to say, it's crowded in high season.

The Harbor, Molivos. ⓒ 22530/71-241. Main courses 3.50€–14€. V. Daily 11am–1am.

**Octopus** SEAFOOD   One of the oldest restaurants on the harbor of Molivos, it has to be tasty to survive the tides of fashion that have changed the texture of life on Lesvos in recent years. It specializes in grilled fish and meats but offers a selection of other dishes—peppers stuffed with spicy cheese being one that has found favor. Yannis the waiter can not only help you assemble your meal but advise you about the attractions of the island.

The Harbor, Molivos. ⓒ 22530/71-869. Snacks/desserts 2€–11€. No credit cards. Daily 8am–1am.

**Tropicana** ★ CAFE FARE   Stroll up into the old town to sip a cappuccino or have a dish of ice cream at this outdoor café, which offers soothing classical music and a relaxed ambience. The owner, Hari Procoplou, learned the secrets of ice creamery in Los Angeles.

Molivos. ⓒ 2330/71-332. Main courses 3.50€–14€ No credit cards. Daily 11am–1am.

## MOLIVOS AFTER DARK

**Vangelis Bouzouki** (no phone) is Molivos's top acoustic bouzouki club. It's located west from Molivos on the road to Efthalou, past the Sappho Tours office. After about a 10-minute walk outside of town, you'll see a sign that points to an olive grove. Follow it for another 500m (1,640 ft.) through the orchard until you reach a clearing with gnarled olive trees and a few stray sheep. When you see the circular cement dance floor, surrounded by clumps of café tables, you've found it. Have some ouzo and late-night *mezedes*, and sit back to enjoy the show. Inquire at the tourist offices about summer theatrical performances in the Kastro.

## AN EXCURSION TO WESTERN LESVOS: ERESSOS & SKALA

Western Lesvos is hilly and barren, with many fine-sand beaches concealed among rocky promontories. Admirers of Sappho's poems (this was her birthplace) and avid beachgoers should be sure to travel the steep and winding 65km (41 miles) between Molivos and Eressos, on the island's westernmost shore. Excursion buses (30€) make this trip daily from Mitilini; inquire at **Samiotis Tours,** Kountourioti 43 (ⓒ 22510/42-574).

**Eressos** is an attractive small village overlooking the coastal plain. Its port, Skala Eressou, 4km (2½ miles) to the south, has become a full-blown resort popular with Greek families as well as with gay women. This isn't surprising, since the beach here is the best in Lesvos, a wide, dark sandy stretch over a mile long and lined with tamarisks; a stretch of sandy beaches and coves extends from here to Sigri, the next town to the north. Skala Eressou has a small **archaeological museum** (ⓒ 22530/53-332), near the 5th-century basilica of Ayios Andreas, with local finds from the Archaic, Classical, and Roman periods. It's open Tuesday through Sunday from 7:30am to 3:30pm; admission is free.

## 4 Limnos (Lemnos)

344km (186 nautical miles) NE of Piraeus

Limnos is decidedly tame in comparison with its Northeastern Aegean neighbors. Here low hills break up the cultivated plains, circled by a rocky but gently sloping coastline. The towns are more functional than beautiful, and the beaches pleasant but not spectacular. This absence of superlatives, combined with a remote location at the edge of Asia Minor, explains the small scale of local tourism and the refreshing simplicity of village life in the principal port of Mirina.

Low on picture-postcard sights but full of small-town charm, **Mirina** is the best base for exploring the island. Several of the town's restaurants and hotels cluster around a small square at the port, in the shadow of the fine Ottoman castle on its lofty promontory. Connecting port and beach is the market street, P. Kida, where you can find preserves made from the local black plums, Limnian honey (a favorite of the gods), and the famous Limnian wines—Kalavaki, a dry white (Aristotle's favorite), and the sweet Moschato. The two town **beaches**—Romeikos Yialos and Riha Nera—are slivers of sand extending north as far as the renowned Akti Marina luxury resort, now a private club. Don't miss the excellent **archaeological museum** on Romeikos Yialos; it's a good introduction to the rest of the island's archaeological sites.

Due to its remote location, Limnos is one island you'll want to reach by plane—ferry journeys can be painfully long. Once on the island, you'll find that public bus schedules are scarce, and that a rented car or moped is the best option.

## ESSENTIALS

**GETTING THERE**   **By Plane**   **Olympic Airways** (© 28010/44-444 or 210/966-6666; www.olympic-airways.gr) has three flights daily between Limnos and Athens; one connection daily with Thessaloniki, Lesvos and Rhodes; and about two flights a week to and from Chios. The office (© 22540/22-214) is on Garoufalidou, in Mirina. You are now forced to take a taxi into town at a fee of about 10€.

**By Boat**   The principal port of Mirina has frequent connections with Northeast Aegean destinations: Ferries depart four times weekly for the port of Kavala in Macedonia (4–5 hr.), and five times weekly for Mitilini in Lesvos (5–6 hr.). There is twice-weekly service to and from Hios (11 hr.) and Samothrace (1½ hr.). There is also a connection three or four times weekly with Rafina (10–15 hr.) and Thessaloniki (8 hr.). We recommend avoiding the 21-hour journey from Mirina to Piraeus via Lesvos and Hios—instead, catch a ferry on the Mirina-Ayios Efstratios-Piraeus route (10 hr.), or opt to fly (1 hr.). For current ferry information, contact **Vayiakos Travel** (© 22540/22-460) on the port in Mirina, **www.gtp.gr**, or the **Mirina Port Authority** (© 22540/22-225).

**VISITOR INFORMATION**   The Greek National Tourist Organization (EOT) no longer maintains an office in Mirina, so visitors are dependent on private travel agencies. Fortunately there are several helpful ones: **Petrides Travel** 116 Karatsa (© 22540/22-998; fax 22540/22-219; mapet@lim.forthnet.gr), 50m (164 ft.) beyond the main square on the town's market street (P. Kida), offers car rentals, accommodations booking, luggage storage, and island excursions. **Pravlis Travel** (© and fax 22540/22-471), on the port square, specializes in air tickets and will also book accommodations.

**GETTING AROUND**   **By Bus**   In Mirina, the **central bus station** (© 22540/22-464) is 3 blocks up from the main (taxi) square on the right. A schedule is posted, but you're not likely to find much on it. Except for Moudros and Kondias, most places on the island get service only once a day, usually in the afternoon. Excursion bus tours can be booked through Petrides Travel, and include various combinations of island villages and archaeological sites. The frequency depends upon demand; tours depart at least weekly in the summer. The cost is 9€ for the half-day and 16€ for the full-day tour.

**By Boat** There are caïques on the north side of the harbor in Mirina; they offer service to the island's beaches and the grottos at Skala. You can buy tickets at most of the town's travel agencies.

**By Car** Car-rental prices on Limnos tend to be high compared with its Northeastern Aegean neighbors. We recommend **Myrina Rent a Car** (☎ 22540/24-476), where a basic car costs about 60€ in the peak season, with insurance.

**FAST FACTS** Both the **National Bank** and the **Agrotiki Trapeza,** 100m (328 ft.) past the square in the direction of Romeïkos Yialos, have **ATMs.** There's a drop-off **laundry** (☎ 22540/24-392) on Garoufalidou across from the Olympic Airline office, next to the Hotel Astro; if it's closed, ask for help at the hotel. Continue a couple of blocks past the laundry and turn left to find the **hospital** (☎ 22540/22-222). The **post office** is on Garoufalidou, 1 block toward Romeïkos Yialos from the square and to the right, just down the street from the Olympic Airlines office. The **taxi station** (☎ 22540/23-033 or 22540/22-348) marks what might conveniently be called a main square, midway along the market street. The **telephone office (OTE)** is on this square, as is the National Bank. The **tourist police** (☎ 22540/22-200) are on the port, just down from the port police.

## ATTRACTIONS

### Archaeological Museum ★

This unassuming building, originally a Turkish Commandery during the Ottoman occupation, was thoroughly renovated and now houses one of the better archaeological museums in the Aegean islands. The artifacts are very well presented, and the descriptive plaques offer fascinating insights concerning the exhibits. If your appetite for exploration is whetted by the exhibits, it is possible to visit three of the island's archaeological sites by bus excursion: Poliochni, the Ifestia (sanctuary of Hephaestus), and the sanctuary of the Kaviri (see "Getting Around," above).

Mirina. ☎ 22540/22-990. Admission 2€ adults, 1€ students and seniors. Tues–Sun 8am–2:30pm. On Romeïkos Yialos Beach/Esplanade, next to the Castro Hotel.

## EXPLORING THE ARCHAEOLOGICAL SITES

There isn't much to see at the archaeological sites on Limnos's northern and eastern shores, but they do offer a great follow-up to the fascinating exhibits of

### Kastro

The Ottoman fortress that dominates Mirina from its craggy perch is easily accessible from the town, and the extensive ruins are a delight to explore. The climb from the port is long and exposed, so go in the early morning or wait for the relative cool of late afternoon. The foundations of the walls date to Byzantine times, and rock-carved inscriptions indicate that the site was once occupied by a temple to Artemis. There are numerous subterranean vaults and caves within the castle walls, so bring a flashlight. The shores of the castle's rocky promontory offer several secluded coves for bathing.

Mirina. Open site. The best access path is reached via a steeply climbing road from the port, between the port police and the police station.

Mirina's archaeological museum. **Kavirio**, dramatically situated on a rocky coastal promontory 10km (6 miles) north of the Hephaïstia, is the most spectacularly placed of the three sites; only the floor plan remains of the once extensive temple. The **Hephaïstia** on the island's northern shore, about 40km (25 miles) from Mirina, is the ruins of an ancient city dedicated to Hephaestus, the god of metal-lurgy who is said to have inhabited a volcano. Born ugly, Hephaestus was rejected by his father, Zeus, and as Milton wrote, "Dropt from the zenith like a falling star, on Limnos, the Aegean isle." At the site is a Greek theater, a temple of Hephaestus, and the excavation site of a pre-Hellenic necropolis which provided many of the items now housed in the archaeological museum in Mirina. Of less interest is **Poliochni**, about 5km (3 miles) east of Moudros, which is still being excavated and offers little for the imagination. All three sites are open from 9:30am to 3:30pm, and admission is free. Some travel agencies include one or two of these sites as part of a **bus tour** of Limnos (see "Getting Around," above); the only alter-native is to rent a car.

## WHERE TO STAY

**Castro Hotel**    The Castro is the best seafront hotel in Mirina, its neoclassical facade facing the water and the narrow strip of sand called Romeïkos Yialos. The marble reception room is built on a large scale and offers a suggestion of elegance, which is, unfortunately, not continued in the rest of the hotel. The rooms are plain, with wall-to-wall carpeting and more amenities than any of the neighbor-ing hotels along the paralia. All units have balconies, although only a few actually face the sea—so it might be worth paying the bit extra for one of these.

Romeïkos Yialos, Mirina, 81400 Limnos. © **22540/22-772** or 22540/22-748. Fax 22540/22-784. 76 units. 68€–78€ double. Rates include breakfast. AE, MC, V. Located 1km (½ mile) north of the port. *In room:* A/C, TV, minibar.

**Hotel Ifestos**    The Ifestos is in a quiet neighborhood of Mirina, surrounded by greenery. Built in 1991, the hotel facade imitates the wide arcaded porches of the town's older houses. The rooms are plain and clean; all have a small balcony or terrace and views over the neighboring gardens. The beach is a 2-minute walk, and the port a leisurely 15-minute walk.

Riha Nera, Mirina, 81400 Limnos. © **22540/24-960.** Fax 22540/23-623. 41 units. 70€ double. Rates include breakfast. MC, V. Located 2km (1¼ miles) north of the port.

**Hotel Lemnos**    This hotel on the harbor is attractive, clean, comfortable, and quiet. Less than 100m (328 ft.) from the ferry pier, it's the most convenient option if you're arriving by boat. The owners, Harry Geanopoulos and Bill Stamboulis, spent many years in New Jersey and speak excellent English. They've also pat-terned their hotel on an American standard: a good night's sleep at a fair price. Breakfast (not included in the room rate) is available a la carte in the hotel cafe.

Avrantaki, Mirina, 81400 Limnos. © **22540/22-153.** Fax 22540/22-329. 29 units. 55€. No credit cards. *In room:* TV.

## WHERE TO DINE

Mirina is not known for its restaurants. A host of fast-food places inhabit the paralia along Romeïkos Yialos Beach, but the most attractive options are on the market street or at the port. Fish is about the only specialty of the island, so take advantage of it.

**Taverna Avra**  GREEK    Sheltered from the bustle of the port by a luxuriant grape arbor, the Avra is a good basic taverna with fair prices. There isn't a menu, so go inside and choose from the dishes displayed on the steam table. There's nothing surprising about the offerings, except perhaps the scarcity of fish in a taverna meters from the sea.

Mirina. ⓒ **22540/22-523.** Main courses 3.50€–9€. No credit cards. Daily 11:30am–12:30am. Next to the Port Authority, near the pier.

**Taverna O Platanos** GREEK   O Platanos is a good, reliable taverna. The "platanos" in question is a handsome mammoth of a planetree arching above this small square on Mirina's market street, offering abundant shade in the afternoon. The limited menu changes daily; and the standard taverna fare is complemented by a variety of vegetables.

Mirina. ⓒ **22540/22-070.** Main courses 3.50€–11€. No credit cards. Daily 11am–11pm. On the market street, 100m (328 ft.) from the central square toward Romeïkos Yialos.

# Appendix A:
# The Greek Language

## 1 Making Your Way in Greek

There are many different kinds of Greek—the Greek of conversation in the street, the Greek used at a fashionable dinner party, the Greek used in newspapers, the Greek of a government notice, the Greek used by a novelist or a poet, and more—and they can differ from one another in grammar and in vocabulary much more than the English of, for example, a conversation at the water cooler and that of an editorial in the *New York Times*. Why that should be so is a long—and we mean *long*—story. (Much of the difficulty has arisen because Greek, like English, has a long written history in which it has been molded by influential works of literature, works that continue to be read and studied for centuries—in Greek even for millennia—so that, as in English, older words and styles of expression remain available for use even while the spoken language goes on happily evolving on its own. Also like English, Greek has kept the spelling of its words largely unchanged even though their pronunciation has changed in fundamental ways; in English this spelling lag has extended for some 5 centuries, but in Greek it is 25 centuries old. This makes it easier for us to read Shakespeare and for Greeks to read Herodotus than it would otherwise be, but it also means that Greek children, like English speakers, have a long, long row to hoe in school as they learn to spell the words they already know how to speak and to use.)

Our dilemma is further complicated by the fact that many Greek words and names have entered our language not directly but by way of Latin or French, and so have become familiar to English speakers in forms that owe something to those languages. When these words are directly transliterated from modern Greek (and that means from Greek in its modern pronunciation, not the ancient one that Romans heard as they borrowed them into Latin), they almost always appear in a form other than the one you may have read about in school. "Perikles" for Pericles or "Delfi" for Delphi are relatively innocent examples; "Thivi" for Thebes or "Omiros" for Homer can give you an idea of the traps often in store for the innocent traveler. The bottom line is that the names of towns, streets, hotels, items on menus, historical figures, archaeological sites—you name it—are likely to have more than one spelling as you come across them in books, on maps, or before your very eyes.

Sometimes the name of a place has simply changed over the centuries. If you think you've just arrived in Santorini but you see a sign welcoming you to Thira, smile, remember you're in Greece, and take heart. (Santorini is the name the Venetians used, and it became common in Europe for that reason; Thira is the original Greek name.) You're where you wanted to be. Besides, you will acquire more compassion for first-time visitors to the United States who land at JFK and find themselves welcomed to "The Big Apple."

What we offer here are a few aids to making your way in Greek. First: remember that literacy is virtually universal in Greece. The table below will help you move from Greek signs or directions to a sense of how they should sound. This scheme for transliterating modern Greek is the one we have used throughout this book, except when referring to names which have become household words in English, like Athens, Socrates, Olympus, and so on. The good news here is that you won't be confused as long as you have your nose in your book; the bad news is that some confusion is probably inevitable as soon as your eyes leave the page. But all you have to do is to say what you are looking for, as closely as you can to the way it should sound, raising your voice at the end of the word to let your listener know it's a question, and bingo!—you'll find you're right on the mark. Just remember that *óhi*, although it can sound a bit like "okay," in fact means "no," and that *ne*, which can sound like a twangy "nay," means "yes." To complicate matters, some everyday gestures will be different from what you are used to: Greeks nod their heads upward to express an unspoken *óhi* and downward (or downward and to one side) for an unspoken *ne*. When a Greek turns his or her head from side to side at you—and you will sometimes, despite your best efforts, have this happen—it is a polite way of signaling "I can't make out what you're saying." And remember: Almost any Greek 40 can read Greek and most people under 30 can also make out some English. If you find that your attempts at speaking fall on deaf ears, show someone the word for what you want and if you stumble over "efharisto" (the Greek for thank you) you can always simply say "merci" (French for thanks), or place your hand over your heart and bow your head slightly.

## ALPHABET

| ALPHABET | | TRANSLITERATED AS | PRONOUNCED AS IN |
|---|---|---|---|
| A α | alfa | a | father |
| B β | víta | v | viper |
| Γ γ | gámma | g before α, o, ω, and consonants | get |
| | | y before αι, ε, ει, ι, οι, υ | yes |
| | | ng before κ, γ | singer |
| Δ δ | thélta | th | *the* (not as the *th-* in "thin") |
| E ε | épsilon | e | set |
| Z ζ | zíta | z | lazy |
| H η | íta | i | magazine |
| Θ θ | thíta | th | *thin* (not as the *th-* in "the") |
| I ι | ióta | i | magazine |
| | | y before a, o | yard, yore |
| K κ | káppa | k | keep |
| Λ λ | lámtha | l | leap |
| M μ | mi | m | marry |
| N ν | ni | n | never |
| Ξ ξ | ksi | ks | taxi |
| O o | ómicron | o | bought |
| Π π | pi | p | pet |
| P ρ | ro | r | round |
| Σ σ/ς | sígma | s before vowels or θ, κ, π, τ, φ, χ, ψ | say |
| | | z before β, γ, δ, ζ, λ, μ, ν, ρ | lazy |

| ALPHABET | TRANSLITERATED AS | PRONOUNCED AS IN |
|---|---|---|
| Τ τ | taf | t | take |
| Υ υ ipsilon | i | magazine |
| Φ φ fi | f | fee |
| Χ χ chi | h | hero (before e and i sounds; like the ch- in Scottish "loch" otherwise) |
| Ψ ψ psi | ps | collapse |
| Ω ω ómega | o | bought |

| COMBINATIONS | TRANSLITERATED AS | PRONOUNCED AS IN |
|---|---|---|
| αι | e | get |
| αϊ | ai | aisle |
| αυ before vowels or β, γ, δ, ζ, λ, μ, ν, ρ | av | Ave Maria |
| αυ before θ, κ, ξ, π, σ, τ, φ, χ, ψ | af | pilaf |
| ει | i | magazine |
| ευ before vowels or β, γ, δ, ζ, λ, μ, ν, ρ | ev | ever |
| ευ before θ, κ, ξ, π, σ, τ, φ, χ, ψ | ef | left |
| μπ at beginning of word | b | bane |
| μπ in middle of word | mb | lumber |
| ντ at beginning of word | d | dumb |
| ντ in middle of word | nd | slender |
| οι | i | magazine |
| οϊ | oi | oil |
| ου | ou | soup |
| τζ | dz | roads |
| τσ | ts | gets |
| υι | i | magazine |

## 2 Useful Words & Phrases

When you're asking for or about something and have to rely on single words or short phrases, it's an excellent idea to use "sas parakaló" to introduce or conclude almost anything you say.

| | |
|---|---|
| Airport | Aerothrómio |
| Automobile | Aftokínito |
| Avenue | Leofóros |
| Bad | Kakós, -kí, -kó* |
| Bank | Trápeza |
| The bill, please. | Tón logaryazmó(n), parakaló. |

| English | Greek |
| --- | --- |
| Breakfast | Proinó |
| Bus | Leoforío |
| Can you tell me? | Boríte ná moú píte? |
| Car | Amáxi |
| Cheap | Ft(h)inó |
| Church | Ekklissía |
| Closed | Klistós, stí, stó* |
| Coast | Aktí |
| Coffeehouse | Kafenío |
| Cold | Kríos, -a, -o* |
| Dinner | Vrathinó |
| Do you speak English? | Miláte Angliká? |
| Excuse me. | Signómi(n). |
| Expensive | Akrivós, -í, -ó* |
| Farewell! | Stó ka-ló! (to person leaving) |
| Glad to meet you. | Chéro polí.** |
| Good | Kalós, lí, ló* |
| Goodbye. | Adío or chérete.** |
| Good health (cheers)! | Stín (i)yá sas or Yá-mas! |
| Good morning or Good day. | Kaliméra. |
| Good evening. | Kalispéra. |
| Good night. | Kaliníchta.** |
| Hello! | Yássas or chérete!** |
| Here | Ethó |
| Hot | Zestós, -stí, stó* |
| Hotel | Xenothochío** |
| How are you? | Ti kánete or Pós íst(h)e? |
| How far? | Pósso makriá? |
| How long? | Póssi óra or Pósso(n) keró? |
| How much does it cost? | Póso káni? |
| I am a vegetarian. | íme horophágos. |
| I am from New York. | íme apó tí(n) Néa(n) Iórki. |
| I am lost or I have lost the way. | Écho chathí or Écho chási tón drómo(n).** |
| I'm sorry. | Singnómi. |
| I'm sorry, but I don't speak Greek (well). | Lipoúme, allá thén miláo elliniká (kalá). |
| I don't understand. | Thén katalavéno. |
| I don't understand, please repeat it. | Thén katalavéno, péste to páli, sás parakaló. |
| I want to go to the airport. | Thélo ná páo stó aerothrómio. |
| I want a glass of beer. | Thélo éna potíri bíra. |
| I would like a room. | Tha théla ena thomátio. |
| It's (not) all right. | (Dén) íne en dáxi. |
| Left (direction) | Aristerá |
| Ladies' room | Ghinekón |
| Lunch | Messimerianó |
| Map | Chártis** |
| Market (place) | Agorá |
| Men's room | Andrón |
| Mr. | Kírios |

| | |
|---|---|
| Mrs. | Kiría |
| Miss | Despinís |
| My name is . . . | Onomázome. . . |
| New | Kenoúryos, -ya, -yo* |
| No | Óchi** |
| Old | Paleós, -leá, -leó* (*pronounce* palyós, -lyá, -lyó) |
| Open | Anichtós, -chtí, -chtó* |
| Pâtisserie | Zacharoplastío** |
| Pharmacy | Pharmakío |
| Please *or* You're welcome. | Parakaló. |
| Please call a taxi (for me). | Parakaló, fonáxte éna taxi (yá ména). |
| Point out to me, please. . . | Thíkste mou, sas parakaló, . . . |
| Post office | Tachidromío** |
| Restaurant | Estiatório |
| Rest room | Tó méros *or* I toualétta |
| Right (direction) | Dexiá |
| Saint | Áyios, ayía, (*plural*) áyi-i (*abbreviated* ay.) |
| Shore | Paralía |
| Square | Plateía |
| Street | Odós |
| Show me on the map. | Díxte mou stó(n) chárti.** |
| Station (bus, train) | Stathmos (leoforíou, trénou) |
| Stop (bus) | Stási(s) (leoforíou) |
| Telephone | Tiléfono |
| Temple (of Athena, Zeus) | Naós (Athinás, Diós) |
| Thank you (very much). | Efcharistó (polí).** |
| Today | Símera |
| Tomorrow | Ávrio |
| Very nice | Polí oréos, -a, -o* |
| Very well | Polí kalá *or* En dáxi |
| What? | Tí? |
| What time is it? | Tí óra íne? |
| What's your name? | Pós onomázest(h)e? |
| Where is. . .? | Poú íne. . .? |
| Where am I? | Pou íme? |
| Why? | Yatí? |

\* Masculine ending -os, feminine ending -a or -i, neuter ending -o.

\*\* Remember, *ch* should be pronounced as in Scottish *loch* or German *ich*, not as in the word *church*.

## NUMBERS

| | | | | | |
|---|---|---|---|---|---|
| 0 | Midén | 7 | Eftá | 14 | Dekatéssera |
| 1 | Éna | 8 | Októ | 15 | Dekapénde |
| 2 | Dío | 9 | Enyá | 16 | Dekaéxi |
| 3 | Tría | 10 | Déka | 17 | Dekaeftá |
| 4 | Téssera | 11 | Éndeka | 18 | Dekaoktó |
| 5 | Pénde | 12 | Dódeka | 19 | Dekaenyá |
| 6 | Éxi | 13 | Dekatría | 20 | Íkossi |

| | |
|---|---|
| 21 | Íkossi éna |
| 22 | Íkossi dío |
| 30 | Triánda |
| 40 | Saránda |
| 50 | Peninda |
| 60 | Exinda |
| 70 | Evdominda |
| 80 | Ogdónda |
| 90 | Eneninda |
| 100 | Ekató(n) |
| 101 | Ekatón éna |
| 102 | Ekatón dío |
| 150 | Ekatón peninda |
| 151 | Ekatón |
| 152 | Ekatón peninda dío |
| | Ekatón peninda éna |
| 200 | Diakóssya |
| 300 | Triakóssya |
| 400 | Tetrakóssya |
| 500 | Pendakóssya |
| 600 | Exakóssya |
| 700 | Eftakóssya |
| 800 | Oktakóssya |
| 900 | Enyakóssya |
| 1,000 | Chílya* |
| 2,000 | Dío chilyádes* |
| 3,000 | Tris chilyádes* |
| 4,000 | Tésseris chilyádes* |
| 5,000 | Pénde chilyádes* |

## DAYS OF THE WEEK

| | |
|---|---|
| Monday | Deftéra |
| Tuesday | Tríti |
| Wednesday | Tetárti |
| Thursday | Pémpti |
| Friday | Paraskeví |
| Saturday | Sávato |
| Sunday | Kiriakí |

## THE CALENDAR

| | |
|---|---|
| January | Ianouários |
| February | Fevrouários |
| March | Mártios |
| April | Aprílios |
| May | Máios |
| June | Ioúnios |
| July | Ioúlios |
| August | Ávgoustos |
| September | Septémvrios |
| October | Októvrios |
| November | Noémvrios |
| December | Dekémvrios |

## MENU TERMS

| | |
|---|---|
| **arní avgolémono** | lamb with lemon sauce |
| **arní soúvlas** | spit-roasted lamb |
| **arní yiouvétsi** | baked lamb with orzo |
| **astakós (ladolémono)** | lobster (with oil-and-lemon sauce) |
| **bakaliáro (skordaliá)** | cod (with garlic) |
| **barboúnia (skáras)** | red mullet (grilled) |
| **briám** | vegetable stew |
| **brizóla chiriní** | pork steak or chop |
| **brizóla moscharísia** | beef or veal steak |
| **choriátiki saláta** | "village" salad ("Greek" salad to Americans) |
| **chórta** | dandelion salad |
| **dolmádes** | stuffed vine leaves |
| **domátes yemistés mé rízi** | tomatoes stuffed with rice |
| **eksóhiko** | lamb and vegetables wrapped in filo |
| **garídes** | shrimp |
| **glóssa (tiganití)** | sole (fried) |

**kalamarákia (tiganitá)** squid (fried)

**kalamarákia (yemistá)** squid (stuffed)

**kaparosaláta** salad of minced caper leaves and onion

**karavídes** crayfish

**keftédes** fried meatballs

**kokorétsia** grilled entrails

**kotópoulo soúvlas** spit-roasted chicken

**kotópoulo yemistó** stuffed chicken

**kouloúri** pretzel-like roll covered with sesame seeds

**loukánika** spiced sausages

**loukoumádes** round donut center—like pastries that are deep-fried, then drenched with honey and topped with powdered sugar and cinnamon

**melitzanosaláta** eggplant salad

**moussaká** meat-and-eggplant casserole

**oktapódi** octopus

**païdákia** lamb chops

**paradisiakó** traditional Greek cooking

**pastítsio** baked pasta with meat

**piláfi rízi** rice pilaf

**piperiá yemistá** stuffed green peppers

**revídia** chickpeas

**revidokeftédes** croquettes of ground chickpeas

**saganáki** grilled cheese

**skordaliá** hot-garlic-and-beet dip

**soupiés yemistés** stuffed cuttlefish

**souvláki** lamb (sometimes veal) on the skewer

**spanokópita** spinach pie

**stifádo** stew, often of rabbit or veal

**taramosaláta** fish roe with mayonnaise

**tirópita** cheese pie

**tsípoura** dorado

**tzatzíki** yogurt-cucumber-garlic dip

**youvarlákia** boiled meatballs with rice

* Remember, ch should be pronounced as in Scottish *loch* or German *ich*, not as in the word *church*.

# Appendix B:
# Useful Toll-Free Numbers & Websites

## AIRLINES

**Aer Lingus**
✆ 800/474-7424 in the U.S.
✆ 01/886-8888 in Ireland
www.aerlingus.com

**Air Canada**
✆ 888/247-2262
www.aircanada.ca

**Air France**
✆ 800/237-2747 in U.S.
✆ 0820-820-820 in France
www.airfrance.com

**Air Malta**
✆ 800/756-2582 in U.S.
✆ 356/2169-0890 in Malta
www.airmalta.com

**Air New Zealand**
✆ 800/262-1234 or -2468 in the U.S.
✆ 800/663-5494 in Canada
✆ 0800/737-767 in New Zealand
www.airnewzealand.com

**Airtran Airlines**
✆ 800/247-8726
www.airtran.com

**Alitalia**
✆ 800/223-5730 in U.S.
✆ 8488-65641 in Italy
www.alitalia.it

**American Airlines**
✆ 800/433-7300
www.aa.com

**American Trans Air**
✆ 800/225-2995
www.ata.com

**Austrian Airlines**
✆ 800/843-0002 in U.S.
✆ 43/(0)5-1789 in Austria
www.aua.com

**BMI**
No U.S. number
www.flybmi.com

**British Airways**
✆ 800/247-9297
✆ 0345/222-111 or 0845/77-333-77
in Britain
www.british-airways.com

**Continental Airlines**
✆ 800/525-0280
www.continental.com

**Delta Air Lines**
✆ 800/221-1212
www.delta.com

**Easyjet**
No U.S. number
www.easyjet.com

**Iberia**
✆ 800/772-4642 in U.S.
✆ 902/400-500 in Spain
www.iberia.com

**Icelandair**
✆ 800/223-5500 in U.S.
✆ 354/50-50-100 in Iceland
www.icelandair.is

**Jet Blue Airlines**
✆ 800/538-2583
www.jetblue.com

## KLM
- ✆ 800/374-7747 in U.S.
- ✆ 020/4-747-747 in Netherlands

www.klm.nl

## Lufthansa
- ✆ 800/645-3880 in U.S.
- ✆ 49/(0)-180-5-8384267 in Germany

www.lufthansa.com

## Northwest Airlines
- ✆ 800/225-2525

www.nwa.com

## Olympic Airways
- ✆ 800/223-1226 in U.S.
- ✆ 80/111-44444 in Greece

www.olympic-airways.gr

## Qantas
- ✆ 800/227-4500 in the U.S.
- ✆ 612/9691-3636 in Australia

www.qantas.com

## Scandinavian Airlines
- ✆ 800/221-2350 in U.S.
- ✆ 0070/727-727 in Sweden
- ✆ 70/10-20-00 in Denmark
- ✆ 358/(0)20-386-000 in Finland
- ✆ 815/200-400 in Norway

www.scandinavian.net

## Singapore Airlines
- ✆ 800/742-3333 in U.S.
- ✆ 65/6223-8888 in Singapore

www.singaporeair.com

## Song
- ✆ 800/359-7664

www.flysong.com

## Swiss International Airlines
- ✆ 877/359-7947 in U.S.
- ✆ 0848/85-2000 in Switzerland

www.swiss.com

## TAP Air Portugal
- ✆ 800/221-7330 in U.S.
- ✆ 351/21-841-66-00 in Portugal

www.tap-airportugal.com

## Tarom Romanian
- ✆ 212/560-0840 in U.S.
- ✆ 4021/2041000 in Romania

www.tarom.ro

## Thai Airways International
- ✆ 800/426-5204 in U.S.
- ✆ (66-2)-535-2081-2 in Thailand

www.thaiair.com

## Turkish Airlines
- ✆ 800/874-8875 in U.S.; 212/339-9650 in NY, NJ, CT
- ✆ 90-212-663-63-00 in Turkey

www.flyturkish.com

## United Airlines
- ✆ 800/241-6522

www.united.com

## US Airways
- ✆ 800/428-4322

www.usairways.com

## Virgin Atlantic Airways
- ✆ 800/862-8621 in Continental U.S.
- ✆ 0293/747-747 in Britain

www.virgin-atlantic.com

# CAR-RENTAL AGENCIES

## Advantage
- ✆ 800/777-5500

www.advantagerentacar.com

## Alamo
- ✆ 800/327-9633

www.goalamo.com

## Auto Europe
- ✆ 800/223-5555

www.autoeurope.com

## Avis
- ✆ 800/331-1212 in Continental U.S.
- ✆ 800/TRY-AVIS in Canada

www.avis.com

## Budget
- ✆ 800/527-0700

www.budget.com

## Dollar
- ✆ 800/800-4000

www.dollar.com

**Enterprise**

☏ 800/325-8007

www.enterprise.com

**Hertz**

☏ 800/654-3131

www.hertz.com

**Kenwel Holiday Auto (KHA)**

☏ 800/678-0678

www.kenwel.com

**National**

☏ 800/CAR-RENT

www.nationalcar.com

**Payless**

☏ 800/PAYLESS

www.paylesscarrental.com

**Rent-A-Wreck**

☏ 800/535-1391

www.rentawreck.com

**Thrifty**

☏ 800/367-2277

www.thrifty.com

# Frommer's
# Portable Guides

## Complete Guides for the Short-Term Traveler

Portable Acapulco, Ixtapa & Zihuatanejo
Portable Amsterdam
Portable Aruba
Portable Australia's Great Barrier Reef
Portable Bahamas
Portable Berlin
Portable Big Island of Hawaii
Portable Boston
Portable California Wine Country
Portable Cancún
Portable Charleston & Savannah
Portable Chicago
Portable Disneyland®
Portable Dublin
Portable Florence
Portable Frankfurt
Portable Hong Kong
Portable Houston
Portable Las Vegas
Portable London
Portable Los Angeles
Portable Los Cabos & Baja

Portable Maine Coast
Portable Maui
Portable Miami
Portable New Orleans
Portable New York City
Portable Paris
Portable Phoenix & Scottsdale
Portable Portland
Portable Puerto Rico
Portable Puerto Vallarta, Manzanillo & Guadalajara
Portable Rio de Janeiro
Portable San Diego
Portable San Francisco
Portable Seattle
Portable Sydney
Portable Tampa & St. Petersburg
Portable Vancouver
Portable Venice
Portable Virgin Islands
Portable Washington, D.C.

**Available at bookstores everywhere.**

# HIT THE ROAD WITH
# FROMMER'S DRIVING TOURS!

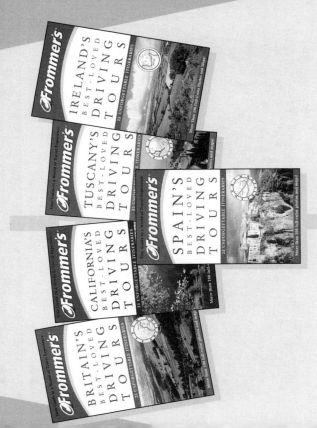

Frommer's Britain's Best-Loved Driving Tours
Frommer's California's Best-Loved Driving Tours
Frommer's Florida's Best-Loved Driving Tours
Frommer's France's Best-Loved Driving Tours
Frommer's Germany's Best-Loved Driving Tours
Frommer's Ireland's Best-Loved Driving Tours
Frommer's Italy's Best-Loved Driving Tours
Frommer's New England's Best-Loved Driving Tours
Frommer's Northern Italy's Best-Loved Driving Tours
Frommer's Scotland's Best-Loved Driving Tours
Frommer's Spain's Best-Loved Driving Tours
Frommer's Tuscany & Umbria's Best-Loved Driving Tours

Available at bookstores everywhere.

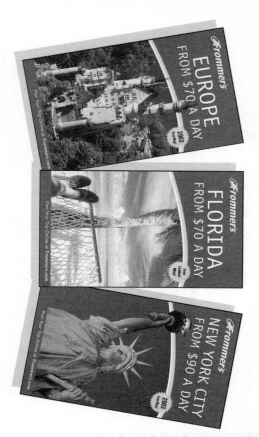

## FROMMER'S® MEMORABLE WALKS

Chicago
London

New York
Paris

San Francisco

## FROMMER'S® WITH KIDS GUIDES

Chicago
Las Vegas
New York City

Ottawa
San Francisco
Toronto

Vancouver
Washington, D.C.

## SUZY GERSHMAN'S BORN TO SHOP GUIDES

Born to Shop: France
Born to Shop: Hong Kong,
Shanghai & Beijing

Born to Shop: Italy
Born to Shop: London

Born to Shop: New York
Born to Shop: Paris

## FROMMER'S® IRREVERENT GUIDES

Amsterdam
Boston
Chicago
Las Vegas
London

Los Angeles
Manhattan
New Orleans
Paris
Rome

San Francisco
Seattle & Portland
Vancouver
Walt Disney World®
Washington, D.C.

## FROMMER'S® BEST-LOVED DRIVING TOURS

Britain
California
Florida
France

Germany
Ireland
Italy
New England

Northern Italy
Scotland
Spain
Tuscany & Umbria

## HANGING OUT™ GUIDES

Hanging Out in England
Hanging Out in Europe

Hanging Out in France
Hanging Out in Ireland

Hanging Out in Italy
Hanging Out in Spain

## THE UNOFFICIAL GUIDES®

Bed & Breakfasts and Country
Inns in:
  California
  Great Lakes States
  Mid-Atlantic
  New England
  Northwest
  Rockies
  Southeast
  Southwest
Best RV & Tent Campgrounds in:
  California & the West
  Florida & the Southeast
  Great Lakes States
  Northeast
  Mid-Atlantic
  Northwest & Central Plains

Southwest & South Central
  Plains
  U.S.A.
Beyond Disney
Branson, Missouri
California with Kids
Central Italy
Chicago
Cruises
Disneyland®
Florida with Kids
Golf Vacations in the Eastern U.S.
Great Smoky & Blue Ridge Region
Inside Disney
Hawaii
Las Vegas
London
Maui

Mexico's Best Beach Resorts
Mid-Atlantic with Kids
Mini Las Vegas
Mini-Mickey
New England & New York with
  Kids
New Orleans
New York City
Paris
San Francisco
Skiing & Snowboarding in the West
Southeast with Kids
Walt Disney World®
Walt Disney World® for
  Grown-ups
Walt Disney World® with Kids
Washington, D.C.
World's Best Diving Vacations

## SPECIAL-INTEREST TITLES

Frommer's Adventure Guide to Australia &
  New Zealand
Frommer's Adventure Guide to Central America
Frommer's Adventure Guide to India & Pakistan
Frommer's Adventure Guide to South America
Frommer's Adventure Guide to Southeast Asia
Frommer's Adventure Guide to Southern Africa
Frommer's Britain's Best Bed & Breakfasts and
  Country Inns
Frommer's Caribbean Hideaways
Frommer's Exploring America by RV
Frommer's Fly Safe, Fly Smart

Frommer's France's Best Bed & Breakfasts and
  Country Inns
Frommer's Gay & Lesbian Europe
Frommer's Italy's Best Bed & Breakfasts and
  Country Inns
Frommer's Road Atlas Britain
Frommer's Road Atlas Europe
Frommer's Road Atlas France
The New York Times' Guide to Unforgettable
  Weekends
Places Rated Almanac
Retirement Places Rated
Rome Past & Present

# Fly.
# Sleep.
# Save.

Now you can book your flights and hotels together, so you can get even better deals than if you booked them separately.

**Travelocity**

**Visit www.travelocity.com
or call 1-888-TRAVELOCITY**

AOL Keyword: Trav